A
Who's Who
of
Sports
Champions

Books by Ralph Hickok

A Who's Who of Sports Champions

Who Was Who in American Sports

The New Encyclopedia of Sports

The Encyclopedia of
North American Sports History

A
Who's Who
of
Sports
Champions

★

Their Stories and Records

Ralph Hickok

Houghton Mifflin Company

BOSTON • NEW YORK

1995

Copyright ©1995 by Ralph Hickok

All rights reserved
For information about permission to reproduce
selections from this book, write to
Permissions, Houghton Mifflin Company,
215 Park Avenue South, New York,
New York 10003.

Library of Congress Cataloging-in-Publication Data
Hickok, Ralph.
A who's who of sports champions: their stories
and records / Ralph Hickok.
p.   cm.
Includes bibliographical references and index.
ISBN 0-395-68195-2 (cloth) : $29.95
ISBN 0-395-73312-X (paper) : $19.95
1. Athletes — United States — Biography —
Dictionaries.   2. Athletes — North America —
Biography — Dictionaries.   I. Title
GV697.A1H53 1995
796'.092'2 — dc20   94-49144
[B]   CIP

Printed in the United States of America

VB 10 9 8 7 6 5 4 3 2 1

Symbols created by Troy Patterson,
Brandy Hinkle, Shannon Kosicki,
and Paul Saikia

Book design: Robert Overholtzer

To Mary

A TRUE CHAMPION
IN HER OWN WAY,
AND IN MORE WAYS
THAN I CAN SAY

Acknowledgments

This book would be a great deal smaller and poorer without the considerable contributions of Joan Bisbee, a researcher *par excellence* who delights in digging out obscure facts; that is, facts that are obscure until she brings them to light. Quite apart from her splendid qualities as a researcher, Joan is a very good friend whose support was very important to me while I was working on this project.

Many others contributed by responding to query letters or, in a few cases, phone calls. They are, in alphabetical order:

Gary Abbott, Director of Communications, USA Wrestling; Thomas Bates, Sports Information Director, U.S. Naval Academy; Marty Bauman, Director of Public Relations, U.S. Equestrian Team; Larry Baumann, Sports Information Director, New York University; Craig Brand, Executive Director, U.S. Squash Racquets Association; Bob Brendel, Sports Information Director, University of Missouri

Alan Cannon, Sports Information Director, Texas A & M University; Bob Cornell, Sports Information Director, Colgate University; Jim Daves, Sports Information Director, University of Washington; Jim DeLorenzo, Sports Information Director, Villanova University; Larry Eldridge, Sports Information Director, University of Pittsburgh

Mike Finn, Sports Information Director, Georgia Tech University; Steve Fleming, Director of Communications, Professional Rodeo Cowboys Association; Bud Ford, Sports Information Director, University of Tennessee; William Guilfoyle, Vice President, National Baseball Hall of Fame and Museum

Phil Haddy, Sports Information Director, University of Iowa; Jim Hadley, Executive Director, U.S. Badminton Association; Peter Hammel, Executive Director, National Museum of Racing and Hall of Fame; Mike Houck, Sports Information Office, University of Wisconsin; Christopher Humm, Sports Information Director, Brown University

Kurt Kiehl, Sports Information Director, Princeton University; Nellie King, Sports Information Director, Duquesne University; Bob Kinney, Sports Information Director, U.S. Military Academy; Peter Kowalski, Sports Information Director, Rutgers University; Laura LaMarca, Membership & Communications, U.S. Sychronized Swimming, Inc.; Preston Levi, Director of Research Services, The Henning Library; Bill Little, Sports Information Director, University of Texas

Bruce Madej, Sports Information Director, University of Michigan; Kristin Matta, Communications Director, U.S. Figure Skating Association; Christine McCartney, Executive Director, National Archery Association; Jimmy McClure, Olympic Chairman, U.S. Table Tennis Association; Maureen Merhoff, Director of Public Relations, U.S. Rowing Association; Gary Migdol, Sports Information Director, Stanford University; Cheri Morden, Director of Public Relations, U.S. Handball Association; Rich Murray, Sports Information Director, University of Virginia

Tony Neely, Sports Information Director, Vanderbilt University; Reid Oslin, Sports Information Director, Boston College; John Pawlak, Publicity Department, U.S. Trotting Association; Steve Penny, Public Relations Director, U.S. Cycling Federation; Luan Peszek, Director of Public Relations, U.S.A. Gymnastics; David Plati, Sports Information Director, University of Colorado; Susan Polakoff-Shaw, Media Contact, U.S. International Speedskating Union; Keith Prince, Sports Information Director, Louisiana Tech University; Mike Prusinsky, Sports Information Director, University of Oklahoma

Kae Rader, Executive Director, U.S. Table Tennis Association; Marc Ryan, Sports Information Director, University of Minnesota; Rick Schaeffer, Sports Information Director, University of Arkansas; Donald Smith, Vice President-Public Relations, Pro Football Hall of Fame; Steve Snapp, Sports Information Director, Ohio State University; Gary Squires, U.S. Squash Tennis Association; Gail Stasvili, Co-Sports Information Director, University of Pennsylvania; William C. Steinman, Sports Information Director, Columbia University; Debbie Sterling, Assistant to the Director of Athletics, Yale University

Tim Tessalone, Sports Information Director, University of Southern California; Budd Thalman, Sports Information Director, Penn State University; Gloria Urbin, Executive Administrator, American Powerboating Association; Doug Vance, Sports Information Director, University of Kansas; John Veneziano, Sports Information Director, Harvard University; Herb Vincent, Sports Information Director, Louisiana State University; Colleen Walker-Mar, Media Relations Director, U.S. Fencing Association; Rich Wanninger, Media Relations, U.S. Volleyball Federation; Dave Wohlhueter, Sports Information Director, Cornell University; Tim Yount, Media Contact, Triathlon Federation USA.

Contents

Preface

A Who's Who of Sports Champions was planned and written to fill a serious gap in sports biography. It is the first single-volume work in more than sixty years to include biographies encompassing the entire spectrum of North American sports, from air racing to yachting.

Although the book is meant to be a handy reference work, I hope *A Who's Who of Sports Champions* is also an enjoyable browsing book for the sports fan — in large part, perhaps, because I like such books myself. The browser should be able to find pleasure in some unexpected discoveries: an interesting anecdote here, an illuminating quotation there.

And the reader looking for a specific bit of information can easily become a browser, lured farther into the book by similar discoveries. For example, someone who picks up *A Who's Who of Sports Champions* to check out Henry Aaron's career batting average will find, immediately afterward, Ruth Hughes Aarons, perhaps the best American woman table tennis player in history.

To that end, I've included a number of lesser-known sports figures. My thinking is that in virtually any sport there are one or two athletes who deserve to be better known than they are. Judy Devlin and David G. Freeman, for example, dominated their sport for long periods, and it seems to me unfair to ignore their remarkable records merely because they happened to be badminton players.

I've also included a number of people simply because they seem interesting to me; among them are George Eyser, a gymnastics champion who had a wooden leg, and Margaret Abbott, who was the first woman to win an Olympic gold medal and never even knew it.

The only other book I know of with similar scope is *Who's Who in American Sports*, which was published in 1928 by the American Biographical Society. This 964-page work was the first major attempt to collect biographical data about sports figures. It was also the only such attempt for more than forty years.

During the early 1970s, Arlington House published a series of *Who's Who* books devoted to various sports, including professional baseball, basketball, boxing, football, golf, hockey, and track and field, and my own *Who Was Who in American Sports* was brought out by Hawthorn Books. That book was obviously somewhat limited in scope since the 1,500 or so persons included were all dead; the living were not admitted.

Since then, biographical information of various sorts has proliferated, as a glance at the bibliography to this book will reveal. Some sources are basically anecdotal while others, such as the annual guides to major professional sports and the several large reference books on baseball, contain birth and death dates and places along with year-by-year statistics but little in the way of human interest or anecdote.

The most ambitious and broadest-ranging of the many sources is *The Biographical Dictionary of American Sports*, originally a four-volume set to which a fifth, supplementary volume has been added. At a total cost of nearly $400, this work is found primarily in library reference rooms and is not usually circulated, and so is out of the reach of most sports fans who are interested in biographical information.

A Who's Who of Sports Champions offers brief biographies, ranging from 60 to nearly 1,000 words, of 2,233 sports figures. Entries are arranged alphabetically, from Aaron, Henry, to Zuppke, Bob. My editor, Liz Kubik, and I briefly considered organizing the entries by sport, but we quickly realized that system would raise questions with a number of athletes. Where, for example, does Babe Didrikson Zaharias belong under such an arrangement? Or Bo Jackson? Faced with such dilemmas, we agreed on the alphabetical approach, with an index by sport.

With that out of the way, the next problem was selecting the people who should be included. The starting point for such a project has to be the many Halls of Fame that honor sports figures. However, it's impossible to include all members of all Halls of Fame. Doing so would create a definite imbalance, since the Halls of Fame for some of the "minor" sports have more members than those for some of the major sports. Also, many Halls of Fame are overloaded with "contributors."

My emphasis is on participants; that is, athletes, coaches, and baseball managers, and I have included only a few nonparticipants, those who seem to me most important in the history of American sports — Walter Camp, Bill France, Kenesaw Mountain Landis, and James Naismith, for example.

Among the major team sports, all players and coaches in the Basketball and Pro Football Halls of Fame are included, as are all players and managers in the Baseball Hall of Fame. Most, but not all, members of the College Football and Hockey Halls of Fame are included. Both of those Halls have so many members that including all of them would have inflated this book beyond its planned length.

I have also included all winners of major awards, such as player of the year, most valuable player, the Cy Young Award, the Heisman Trophy, the Ross Trophy, and the Hart Trophy. Most winners of the Outland Trophy are included, too. (The problem a writer often faces with a football lineman is that there simply isn't much to say; backs and wide receivers have most of the statistics and receive most of the glory. Even an exhaustive search of *New York Times* microfilm and query letters to colleges and universities failed to elicit any significant or interesting information about some of the Outland winners.)

A Who's Who of Sports Champions contains biographies of professional athletes who have led a league in a major statistical category more than once and who are high on the all-time list in career statistics in important categories, as well as a few who have accomplished unique feats.

Most members of the PGA, LPGA, World Golf, and International Tennis Halls of Fame are included. There are a few exceptions. Since this book focuses on American champions, I've omitted some of the non-Americans. The basic criterion is whether the athlete had a significant impact or influence on the course or history of sport in America.

Fans who follow golf or tennis in the media certainly know, and are probably interested in, figures such as Seve Ballesteros, Steffi Graf, Ivan Lendl, and Greg Norman. Those who go back somewhat farther (as I do) undoubtedly remember and are interested in Margaret Court Smith, Rod Laver, and Gary Player. They are included, along with a number of other foreign athletes.

All members of the U.S. Olympic Hall of Fame are included along with many other Olympians. In general, I've written biographies of every athlete from the U.S. or Canada who won two or more individual gold medals. Many who won just one gold medal are also included, especially athletes from sports where American gold medalists are rare.

A few words about names: an athlete is listed, alphabetically, under the name by which he or she best known. If the first name happens to be a nickname, the full first name and middle initial follow in parentheses. For example, Whitey Ford is listed as *Ford, Whitey (Edward C.)* However, in cases where the nickname is a simple shortening of the first name, I haven't bothered to list it. Thus Vince Lombardi can be found under *Lombardi, Vincent T.*

When a person is known by his or her middle name, or an abbreviation of the middle name, it is shown in parentheses, along with the first name. For example, Eddie Arcaro is list as *Arcaro, Eddie (George Edward)*.

A married woman athlete presents a bit of problem, especially if she was known by her maiden name for part of her career and by her married name or names during her later career. In such a case, I've listed her under the name that is probably best known, with a cross-reference. Babe Didrikson Zaharias, for example, is listed as *Zaharias, Babe (Mildred E. Didrikson)*, and Helen Wills Moody is listed as *Wills, Helen (Mrs. Moody)*. Helen Wills Moody, by the way, later became Mrs. Roark, but there's no cross-reference under that name because she never used it as a tennis player.

One other special case arises most often among boxers: the pseudonym, or *nom de sport*, if you will. In such a case, the athlete is listed under the pseudonym, with the real name in brackets. Thus Jersey Joe Walcott, whose real name was Arnold R. Cream, is listed as *Walcott, Jersey Joe [Arnold R. Cream]*. There's no cross-reference simply because I don't think anyone would look for Arnold R. Cream when seeking information about Joe Walcott.

Each entry has a heading with the person's name on the first line, the sport or sports on the next line, and his or her birth date and birthplace on the third line, with the date of death, if applicable and available, on a fourth line. Beyond that point, there is no standard format. I approached each biography as an individual writing project.

The *Biographical Dictionary of American Sports* usually includes information on family background, marriages, and children. I haven't done that unless such information seemed relevant or interesting in some way. For example, I do think it's interesting that the father of Karch Kiraly, America's greatest volleyball player, was a member of the Hungarian national team who escaped from that country during the 1956 revolution. And that swimmer Eleanor Holm first married bandleader Ned Jarrett and became a singer with his band, and later married showman Billy Rose, founder of the Aquacade.

Similarly, I haven't usually included information on a person's life after sports. Again, there are some exceptions. It would be silly, I think, to write a biography of Byron R. "Whizzer" White without mentioning that he is now an associate justice of the Supreme Court. And I believe there's some interest in the fact that pole vaulter Don Bragg became one of the many movie Tarzans (although with little success or acclaim).

In many of the biographies, the final paragraph contains selected statistical data. If the person belongs to one or more major sports Hall of Fame, that information is on the final line.

I've assumed that anyone interested in a book such as *A Who's Who of Sports Champions* brings to it a certain amount of knowledge about sports and would know, for example, that "NFL" stands for "National Football League" and that "ERA" stands for "Earned Run Average" and not for "Equal Rights Amendment" in this context. I've tried, however, to avoid overuse of abbreviations. A conference name, for example, is usually spelled out at first mention in an entry, with the abbreviation in parentheses if I use it later in that entry. I also spell out the full name of a college or university in its first use within an entry and apply the shortened form subsequently. A list of commonly used abbreviations begins on the following page.

Abbreviations

AAU Amateur Athletic Union
ABA American Basketball Association
ABC American Broadcasting Company or American Bowling Congress
AFC American Football Conference
AFL American Football League
AIAW Association of Intercollegiate Athletics for Women
AL American League (baseball)
AP Associated Press
CBS Columbia Broadcasting System
ERA Earned Run Average
ESPN Entertainment and Sports Programming Network
IBF International Boxing Federation
IC4A Inter-Collegiate Association of Amateur Athletes of America
LPBT Ladies' Professional Bowlers Tour
LPGA Ladies' Professional Golf Association
NABF North American Boxing Federation
NAIA National Association for Intercollegiate Athletics
NBA National Basketball Association or National Boxing Association
NBC National Broadcasting Company
NCAA National Collegiate Athletic Association
NFC National Football Conference
NFL National Football League
NHL National Hockey League
NL National League (baseball)
PBA Professional Bowling Association
PGA Professional Golf Association
RBI Run(s) Batted In
TAC The Athletics Congress
UPI United Press International
WBA World Boxing Association
WBC World Boxing Council
WHA World Hockey Association
WIBC Women's International Bowling Congress

A
Who's Who
of
Sports
Champions

★ ★ A ★ ★

Aaron, Henry L. (Hank)

BASEBALL

b. Feb. 5, 1934, Mobile, Ala.

Aaron began his professional baseball career as an 18-year-old shortstop for the Indianapolis Clowns of the Negro American League. A right-handed hitter, he batted cross-handed, with his right hand below his left hand. Still, he showed enough promise as a hitter that the Boston Braves bought his contract and changed his grip. After two years in the minor leagues, Aaron became the starting left fielder for the Braves in 1954, the team's second season in Milwaukee. He replaced the veteran Bobby Thomson, who had broken his ankle.

No one could have imagined that the slender, 160-pound rookie would eventually break Babe Ruth's career home run record, although he hit a respectable .280 with 13 home runs before breaking an ankle in September. In 1955, Aaron became the Braves' starting right fielder, and he won the NL batting title in 1956 with a .328 average and 26 home runs. By 1957, Aaron was a solid 180-pounder, a feared power hitter and a genuine superstar. He was the league's most valuable player that season, leading in home runs with 44, runs batted in with 132, and runs scored with 118. The Braves won the pennant and beat the New York Yankees in a seven-game World Series, led by Aaron's .393 average, 3 home runs, and 7 RBI.

His all-time career mark of 755 home runs was built on a remarkable 20-season stretch from 1955 through 1974. He hit 40 or more home runs in 8 of those seasons, 30 or more in 15, and 20 or more in all 20. He also batted over .300 14 times. His top batting average was .355 in 1959; his best home run season was 1971, when he had 47. Interestingly, he hit 44 home runs — his uniform number — in three different seasons, 1957, 1963, and 1965.

Entering the 1974 season, Aaron had 713 home runs, one shy of Ruth's record. The Braves, who had moved to Atlanta in 1966, announced that he would be held out of the opening series in Cincinnati so he would have a chance to break the record before his home fans. However, Baseball Commissioner Bowie Kuhn ordered the team to use Aaron in Cincinnati, and he tied the record in his first trip to the plate.

In his first home game, on April 8, Aaron hit his 715th home run to break Ruth's record. The pitcher was Al Downing of the Los Angeles Dodgers; the ball went into the Braves' bullpen in left field, where it was caught by relief pitcher Tommy House.

After the 1974 season, Aaron returned to Milwaukee, which had a new AL team, the Brewers. He spent two years there as a designated hitter. When he retired, he held all-time major league records for extra base hits, 1,477; total bases, 6,856; and runs batted in, 2,297.

Aaron then returned to Atlanta to work in the Braves' front office, where he became one of the first blacks in upper-level management as vice president of player development.

★ Baseball Hall of Fame

Aarons, Ruth Hughes

TABLE TENNIS
b. 1910, Stamford, Conn.
d. 1980

The only American to win a world table tennis championship, Ruth Aarons never lost a match in tournament play during her four-year career in top competition.

She won the U.S. national singles championship four years in a row, from 1934 through 1937, and she also won the mixed doubles title each year, with four different partners: Sam Silberman, Sidney Heitner, Victor Barna, and Robert Blattner. In 1936, when she won the world singles title, Aarons teamed with Anne Sigman to win the national women's doubles championship.

Aarons was a member of the U.S. squad that won the 1937 Corbillon Cup, emblematic of the world women's team championship.

Abbott, Jim (James A.)

BASEBALL
b. Sept. 19, 1967, Flint, Mich.

Abbott was the first baseball player to win the Sullivan Award as the nation's outstanding amateur athlete, in 1987. Born without a right hand, Abbott spent hours as a youngster bouncing a ball off a wall to practice fielding as well as throwing. He was the starting quarterback on his high school football team, which went to the finals of the Michigan state championship, and he showed enough promise as a pitcher to be drafted by the Toronto Blue Jays shortly after graduation.

However, Abbott went to the University of Michigan on a baseball scholarship. He had a career record of 26 wins and 8 losses at the school. As a member of Team USA in 1987, he became the first American pitcher in 25 years to beat a Cuban team on Cuban soil. The team won a silver medal at the Pan-American Games, and Abbott won the U.S. Baseball Federation's Golden Spikes award as the best amateur player in the country.

In the 1988 Olympics, Abbott was the winning pitcher in a 5–3 victory over Japan that brought the U.S. its first gold medal in baseball. Chosen by the California Angels in the first round of the 1988 amateur draft, he went directly to the major leagues and had a 12–12 record, with a 3.92 earned run average, in 1989. In 1991, his best season to date, he won 18 and lost 11. Despite an ERA of 2.77, Abbott was only 7–15 in 1992, when the Angels scored an average of only 2.54 runs in games that he started.

He was traded to the New York Yankees after the season and had an 11–14 record with them in 1993. Among his victories was a no-hitter against the Cleveland Indians on September 4.

Through the 1994 season, Abbott had a 65–74 record with 5 shutouts and a 3.66 ERA. He had struck out 693 hitters and walked 424 in 1,221⅓ innings.

Abbott, Margaret I.

GOLF
b. June 15, 1878, Calcutta, India
d. June 10, 1955

The little-known Abbott was the first American woman to win an Olympic gold medal, and she didn't even know it. It happened during the poorly organized Paris Games of 1900, the second modern Olympics, when even some of the track & field medalists thought they were competing in just another track meet.

Abbott, who was the daughter of novelist Mary Ives Abbott, had gone to Paris with her mother in 1899 to study art. The following year, she was one of ten women who entered a 9-hole golf tournament. The other women, she lightheartedly told relatives, "apparently misunderstood the nature of the game scheduled for the day and turned up to play in high heels and tight skirts." Abbott, more sensibly attired, won the tournament with a 47.

In 1902 she married political satirist Finley Peter Dunne, creator of "Mr. Dooley." She never knew she'd won an Olympic event; only recent research has established that the tournament was on the 1900 Olympic program.

Abdul-Jabbar, Kareem [Lewis Ferdinand Alcindor, Jr.]

BASKETBALL
b. April 16, 1947, New York, N.Y.

When he was 13, Lew Alcindor was 6-foot-8, and college scouts were already eyeing him. At Power Memorial Academy, he scored 2,067 points and had 2,002 rebounds as he led the team to 53 consecutive victories.

Alcindor was recruited by more than 200 colleges. He chose UCLA, where he played for the legendary John Wooden. With Alcindor starting at center, UCLA won three consecutive NCAA championships, 1967 through 1969, and Alcindor was named the tournament's most valuable player, as well as an All-American, all three years. He scored a total of 2,325 points, averaging 26.4 a game, at UCLA.

There had never been a basketball player like him. At 7-foot-2 and 235 pounds in his prime, he could score, rebound, pass, play defense, and block shots. Bob Cousy said that he "pretty much combines what Bill Russell and Wilt Chamberlain have individually specialized in."

The Milwaukee Bucks of the National Basketball Association and New Jersey Nets of the American Basketball Association both drafted him. To avoid a major bidding war, Alcindor asked them each to submit a sealed bid, and Milwaukee won with a contract offer of more than $1 million.

Alcindor won the NBA rookie of the year award in 1969–70, when he scored 2,361 points and had 1,190 rebounds, and he won the first of his six most valuable player awards in 1970–71, when he was the league's top scorer with 31.7 points per game. He teamed with Oscar Robertson that season to lead the Bucks to their first NBA championship.

A Muslim since 1968, Alcindor formally changed his name to Kareem Abdul-Jabbar after that season. Many fans and sportswriters were shocked; Kareem, always rather moody and aloof, became virtually unapproachable because of the adverse publicity. But it didn't affect his play. He again led the NBA in scoring and was its MVP in 1971–72.

Kareem was traded to the Los Angeles Lakers in 1975 and spent 14 seasons there, during which the Lakers won five NBA championships. As time went on, his unsurpassed skills and growing cordiality won the fans and writers back. Boston Celtic fans gave him a ten-minute standing ovation when he broke Wilt Chamberlain's career scoring record in 1984, and fans everywhere rewarded him with ovations and gifts when he made his farewell tour in the spring of 1989, after announcing his retirement.

He holds NBA records for most seasons, 20; most games, 1,560; most minutes played, 57,448; most points, 38,387; most field goals, 15,837; and most blocked shots, 3,189. He was the NBA's regular season MVP in 1971, 1972, 1974, 1976, 1977, and 1980, and the playoff MVP in 1971 and 1985. Kareem was first-team all-star center in 1971, 1972, 1973, 1974, 1976, 1977, 1980, 1981, 1984, and 1986, and second-team in 1970, 1978, 1979, 1983, and 1985.

Abel, Sidney G.

HOCKEY
b. Feb. 22, 1918, Melville, Sask.

Abel began his National Hockey League career in 1938 and became best known as the play-making center on the Detroit Red Wings' "Production Line," with Gordie Howe at right wing and Ted Lindsay at left wing. Coach Jack Adams, who put the line together for the 1947–48 season, said of the trio, "They could score goals in their sleep. They always seem to know where the play will develop."

Abel's best season was 1948–49, when he won the Hart Trophy as the league's most valuable player and was a first-team all-star. Against Montreal in the 1949 Stanley Cup semifinals, Abel's line scored 12 of Detroit's 17 goals in a seven-game victory, but Detroit lost to Toronto in the finals.

In 1949–50, Lindsay won the league scoring title with 78 points, Abel was second with 69, and Howe was right behind him with 68. Abel was again named all-star center. The Red Wings were down three games to two to the New York Rangers and losing 4–3 in the third period of the sixth game in the Stanley Cup finals that season. Abel assisted on Lindsay's tying goal, then scored the winner, and the Red Wings went on to win the seventh game and the Stanley Cup.

The Chicago Black Hawks traded for Abel before the 1952–53 season and installed him as player-coach. He led Chicago to a third-place tie and its first playoff berth in seven years. He retired from playing after that season and was fired as coach when the team slumped in 1953–54. In 1957, he took over as Detroit's coach and also became general manager in 1962. Abel left Detroit in a management squabble in January 1971, served briefly as St. Louis Blues coach and general manager that year, and ended his long career in hockey as coach of the Kansas City Kings for just three games in the 1975–76 season.

In 610 regular season games, Abel scored 189 goals and 283 assists; he added 28 goals and 30 assists in 97 playoff games. As a coach, he had a 382–426–155 record.
★ Hockey Hall of Fame

Abel, Taffy (Clarence J.)
HOCKEY
b. May 28, 1900, Sault Ste. Marie, Mich.
d. Aug. 1, 1964
Abel was the first American to carry the flag in the opening ceremonies of the Winter Olympics and the first American Olympic hockey player to be on a Stanley Cup champion.

A defenseman, he spent most of his amateur career with the St. Paul, MN, Athletic Club, and he was on the U.S. team that won the silver medal in 1924. Two years later, he joined the New York Rangers as one of the first U.S.-born players in the National Hockey League, and he was with the Rangers when they won their first Stanley Cup in 1928.

After one more season with the Rangers, Abel went to the Chicago Black Hawks and spent five seasons there be-

fore retiring. In his eight NHL seasons, he had 18 goals and 18 assists in regular-season play, with 1 goal and 1 assist in the playoffs.
★ U.S. Hockey Hall of Fame

Adamek, Donna
BOWLING
b. Feb. 1, 1957, Duarte, Calif.
"Mighty Mite" dominated women's professional bowling from 1978 through 1981. She was Woman Bowler of the Year each year, and in that four-year period, she won the Women's Open in 1978 and 1981, the WIBC Queens in 1979 and 1980, and the WPBA National Championship in 1980. Adamek led the WPBA tour in winnings for three consecutive years, 1978 through 1980.

Adamek teamed with Nikki Gianulias to win the WIBC doubles title in 1980. The following year, she and Pat Costello tied with the team of Shirley Hintz and Lisa Wagner for the title. During the 1981–82 season, Adamek rolled three perfect 300 games, a record she shares with four other women.

Adams, Jack (John James)
HOCKEY
b. June 14, 1895, Ft. William, Ont.
d. May 1, 1968
Adams was a pretty good hockey player, but he's in the Hall of Fame because, as a coach and manager, he built Detroit Red Wing teams that won 12 regular-season National Hockey League championships and went to 15 Stanley Cup finals, winning 7 of them, during a 35-year period.

His professional career began with the Toronto Arenas in the 1917–18 season. The following year he went to Vancouver and won the Pacific Coast League scoring title. Adams returned to Toronto with the St. Pats in 1922, played there through the 1925–26 season, then spent one year with Ottawa. He was ninth in scoring in 1923–24 with 16 points, seventh in 1925–26 with 26 points. During his seven NHL seasons, he had 82 goals and 29 assists, with 11 goals and 1 assist in Stanley Cup play.

Adams retired as a player in 1927 to

become Detroit coach and manager. The team was then known as the Cougars; it became the Falcons in 1930, the Red Wings in 1933. In Adams's first eight seasons, Detroit got into the playoffs only four times, losing in the Stanley Cup finals in 1934. But they finished first in the NHL's American Division and won the Stanley Cup in 1936 and 1937.

During the next ten seasons, Detroit reached the Stanley Cup finals four times, winning in 1943 and losing in 1941, 1942, and 1945. After the 1946–47 season, Adams left coaching but remained as the team's general manager for another 15 seasons. The Red Wings won seven consecutive regular season championships, from 1949 through 1955, and another in 1957. They won the Stanley Cup in 1950, 1952, 1954, and 1955.

Although he was known as "Jovial Jawn," Adams liked big, tough players and physical play. After a 15-minute brawl marred the last game of the 1940 Stanley Cup semifinals between Detroit and Toronto, Maple Leaf management called the Red Wings "a bunch of hoodlums." Adams responded, "We're just sorry we can't play the Leafs seven nights in a row."

Adams became president of the new Central Professional Hockey League in 1963. The Jack Adams Award, presented since 1974 to "the NHL coach adjudged to have contributed the most to his team's success," is named for him. As a coach, Adams had 413 wins, 390 losses, and 161 ties. In Stanley Cup play, his teams won 52, lost 52, and tied 1.
★ Hockey Hall of Fame

Adams, John
HORSE RACING
b. Sept. 1, 1915, Iola, Kans.
Adams led the nation's jockeys in winning mounts in 1937, 1942, and 1943. He got his first ride at a county fair, where his father was delivering feed for the horses and other livestock, but his parents didn't want him to become a jockey. They refused to sign the necessary papers for an apprenticeship, so

Adams lied about his age and became a journeyman immediately.

After a slow start, in part because he wasn't given the apprentice's weight allowance, Adams became a leading jockey beginning in the mid-1930s, with 43 percent of his mounts finishing in the top three over a 24-year period ending in 1958, when he retired because of a back injury.

Adams rode a total of 20,159 mounts, with 3,270 wins, 2,704 second-place finishes, and 2,635 third-place finishes, earning purses of $9,743,109.
★ National Horse Racing Hall of Fame

Adderley, Herbert A.
FOOTBALL
b. June 8, 1939, Philadelphia, Pa.
As a rookie running back in the Green Bay Packers training camp in 1962, Adderley wasn't playing as well as expected. The coaching staff eventually found out that he wanted to play defense instead of offense.

The 6-foot, 200-pound Adderley had been an offensive star at the University of Michigan, the team's leading rusher in 1959, its leading receiver in 1959 and 1960. He was the Packers' first pick in the 1961 National Football League.

Moved to defensive back, Adderley quickly became one of the best ever. He led the NFL in yards on interception returns in 1965 and 1969 and in touchdowns on interception returns in 1962 and 1965. With the Packers from 1961 through 1969, he played on five NFL championship teams, in 1961 and 1962 and from 1965 through 1967. The team won the first two Super Bowls, and Adderley's 60-yard touchdown run on an interception return against Oakland in Super Bowl II was the first in Super Bowl history.

Traded to Dallas in 1970, Adderley played on two National Football Conference champions and another Super Bowl winner before retiring after the 1972 season. All told, he started in four of the first six Super Bowls and was on the winning team three times.

In his 12 seasons, Adderley returned 48 interceptions for 1,046 yards, a 21.8

average, and had 7 touchdowns. He also returned 120 kickoffs for 3,080 yards, a 25.7 average.

★ Pro Football Hall of Fame

Agase, Alexander A.

FOOTBALL
b. March 27, 1922, Evanston, Ill.

A 5-foot-10, 205-pound guard, Agase is the only player ever to be named an All-American at two different schools. He played at Illinois in 1942. As a Marine Corps trainee, he was sent to Purdue the following season, when he made All-American for the first time. After serving in the Pacific during World War II, he returned to Illinois in 1946 and was again an All-American.

Agase played professional football with the Los Angeles Dons and Chicago Rockets of the AAFC in 1947, the Cleveland Browns from 1948 through 1951, and the Baltimore Colts in 1953.

In 1964, Agase was named head coach at Northwestern University in his native Evanston. When the school placed second in the Big Ten in 1970, its highest finish in 22 years, Agase was voted coach of the year by the Football Writers Association of America. He left Northwestern in 1973 to take over at Purdue for four seasons. His overall coaching record was 50 wins, 83 losses, and 2 ties.

★ College Football Hall of Fame

Agassi, Andre

TENNIS
b. April 29, 1970, Las Vegas, Nev.

Although his talent and athletic ability were obvious, many tennis writers and fans wondered for a time if Agassi was more style than substance. With his long blond hair and his fluorescent outfits, he was famous, or notorious, for several years before he won a major title. Some people, including Agassi, wondered if he would ever win one of the grand slam events until he finally broke through at Wimbledon in 1992. He won his second grand slam title, the U.S. Open, in 1994.

Agassi turned professional in 1987, shortly after his seventeenth birthday,

and he won the last tournament of that year and the first tournament of 1988. He advanced from 25th to 4th in the computer rankings by winning six championships in 1988. Twice he went to the semifinals of a grand slam event, losing both times, to Mats Wilander in an exciting five-set match at the French Open and to Ivan Lendl in four sets at the U.S. Open.

However, he didn't win a single tournament in 1989, and reached the finals only once, in the Italian Open. Agassi beat Germany's Boris Becker in the semifinals of the 1990 U.S. Open but lost to Pete Sampras in the final match, and he was beaten by little-known Andres Gomez in the French Open final.

His frustrations reached a peak in 1991, when he lost to Jim Courier in the semifinals of the U.S. Open. Until then, Agassi had been the most successful graduate of the Bollettieri Tennis Academy in Florida, but he was now ranked behind his classmate Courier.

After losing in the first round in 1987, Agassi drew criticism for passing up Wimbledon three years in a row. The reason he gave was that he wasn't allowed to wear his colorful outfits there, but many critics felt he was simply afraid of repeated failure.

He returned to Wimbledon in 1991 and was seeded only twelfth in 1992. Agassi upset Boris Becker in the quarterfinal and John McEnroe in the semifinal, then met Goran Ivanisevic of Croatia, the eighth seed. Ivanisevic was favored in part because his serve and volley style is better suited to the grass at Wimbledon than Agassi's baseline bashing style.

Despite 37 aces by Ivanisevic, Agassi won a dramatic five-set match and sounded remarkably humble after his victory. "To do it here is more than I could ask for," he said. "If my career was over tomorrow, I had a lot more than I deserved."

Aguirre, Mark A.

BASKETBALL
b. Dec. 10, 1959, Chicago, Ill.

In three years as a starter at DePaul

University, Aguirre scored 2,182 points, averaging 24.5 a game. A two-time All-American, he was named to the 1980 U.S. Olympic team that didn't play because of the country's boycott of the Moscow Games. As a junior in 1981, he was a consensus college player of the year.

The 6-foot-6, 232-pound Aguirre entered the NBA's college draft before his senior year and was the first player chosen, by the Dallas Mavericks. Strong and clever around the basket, Aguirre is also a good outside shooter for a big man, but he developed a reputation for moodiness and not always playing at his best which sometimes hampered him as a professional.

Injuries limited him to just 51 games and an 18.7-point average in his rookie year. He had his finest professional season in 1983–84, when he led the NBA in field goals with 925, averaging 29.5 points per game.

Late in the 1988–89 season, Dallas traded him to the Detroit Pistons, where he became a part-time player, brought off the bench for his scoring ability. He played on two NBA championship teams with the Pistons, in 1989 and 1990.

Aguirre retired after playing part of the 1993–94 season with the Los Angeles Clippers. He scored 18,458 points in 923 NBA games, an average of 20.0 per game.

Ahearn, Daniel F.

TRACK AND FIELD
b. April 2, 1888, County Limerick, Ireland
d. Jan. 10, 1949

Ahearn was the only American to hold the world record in the triple jump — known as the hop, step, and jump in his era — until Willie Banks came along in 1985. Ahearn set the record at 50 feet, 11 inches on May 5, 1911, during the AAU national championships. He broke a record set by his older brother Timothy, who competed for Ireland in the 1908 Olympics.

The younger Ahearn was AAU national champion in the event seven times, in 1910 and 1911 and from 1913 through 1918.

In 1920, Ahearn led a revolt of American athletes at the Antwerp Olympics. The athletes had crossed the Atlantic on a crowded ship and were being quartered in an abandoned schoolhouse. Ahearn found a better room at an inn. When he didn't show up at the official barracks, he was suspended for insubordination.

Ahearn gave an angry speech, stirring up the U.S. team, who petitioned for better living conditions, and Ahearn's reinstatement was presented to team officials. The threat was a boycott. Judge Barrow S. Weeks, chairman of the American Olympic Committee, responded by saying, "You must carry on. The committee must carry on. What would you do if the committee quit?"

The athletes had an answer for that: "Get a better one!"

The upshot was that Ahearn was reinstated. However, living conditions didn't change, and none of the athletes refused to compete.

Aikman, Troy K.

FOOTBALL
b. Nov. 21, 1966, W. Covina, Calif.

Aikman played at the University of Oklahoma in 1984 and 1985, then transferred to UCLA. After sitting out a year to regain his eligibility, he was a starter in 1987 and 1988, when he was named a consensus All-American and winner of the Davey O'Brien Award as the best college quarterback of the year. In his college career, Aikman completed 401 of 637 pass attempts for 5,436 yards and 40 touchdowns.

Chosen by the Dallas Cowboys as the first pick in the 1988 NFL draft, Aikman became a starter during his rookie year. The 6-foot-4, 222-pounder has helped lead Dallas to two consecutive Super Bowl championships, after the 1992 and 1993 seasons, with a combination of accurate throwing and the ability to read defenses.

In Super Bowl XXVII, he completed 22 of 30 passes for 273 yards and 4 touchdowns. He completed 19 of 27 for 207 yards in Super Bowl XXVIII. Aikman had completed 1,424 passes in 2,281 attempts for 16,303 yards and 82 touchdowns in regular season play through 1994.

Ainge, Danny (Daniel R.)
BASKETBALL
b. March 17, 1959, Eugene, Oreg.

An All-American and winner of the Wooden Award as college basketball player of the year in 1981, Ainge also played professional baseball while attending Brigham Young University. In parts of three seasons with the AL's Toronto Blue Jays, he batted only .220, playing primarily at second base.

Because he seemed intent on baseball as a career, Ainge wasn't chosen until the second round of the 1981 NBA draft, by the Boston Celtics. The Celtics bought out his Toronto contract, and he joined the team for the 1981–82 season.

At 6-foot-5 and 185 pounds, Ainge started for two NBA championship teams with Boston, in 1984 and 1986. A good outside shooter, Ainge is known for hustling, aggressive play that has involved him in a number of on-court fights.

Boston traded him to the Sacramento Kings late in the 1988–89 season, and he went to the Portland Trail Blazers in 1990. After two seasons with Portland, Ainge became a free agent and signed with the Phoenix Suns in 1992.

Through the 1992–93 season, he had scored 11,393 points in 968 NBA games, an average of 11.8, and he also had 3,989 assists and 2,659 rebounds.

Albert, Frank C.
FOOTBALL
b. Jan. 27, 1920, Chicago, Ill.

The first modern T-formation quarterback, Albert was Stanford's starting single-wing tailback in 1939. When Clark Shaughnessy became the school's coach in 1940, he installed the T-formation and moved Albert to quarterback.

The new formation called for skilled ball-handling and faking as well as accurate passing, and Albert was very good at all three, as well as kicking. He had a 79-yard punt against Oregon State in 1940. Stanford was undefeated that season, and Albert kicked all three extra points in a 21–13 win over Nebraska in the Rose Bowl. He was named All-American quarterback and finished third in Heisman Trophy voting.

Albert was an All-American again in 1941, when Stanford won six of nine games. After serving in the Navy in World War II, he signed with the San Francisco 49ers of the new All-America Football Conference. During the AAFC's four years, the 49ers were always just behind the Cleveland Browns, and Albert was usually overshadowed by Otto Graham, the Browns' great quarterback.

However, in 1948 he led the AAFC with 29 touchdown passes and shared the Most Valuable Player award with Graham. He was also named Pro Football Player of the Year by *Sport* magazine. The following season, he threw five touchdown passes in a 56–28 win over Cleveland, had an 82-yard punt against Buffalo, and led the AAFC with a 48.2-yard punting average. He had to be named to the All-AAFC team, and he was — as a halfback, a position he hadn't played since his sophomore year at Stanford. Graham was again the All-AAFC quarterback.

The AAFC was absorbed into the National Football League in 1950, and the 49ers were one of three teams, with the Browns and the Baltimore Colts, to enter the NFL. Albert played in the first Pro Bowl that season. The next two years, he shared the quarterback position with Y. A. Tittle, and in 1953 he closed out his professional career with the Calgary Stampeders of the Canadian Football League.

Albert returned to the 49ers as head coach in 1956 and had a 19–16–1 record in three seasons. In his professional career, he completed 935 of 1,789 passes for 12,363 yards and 127 touchdowns, punted 347 times for a 42.6 average, and ran for 29 touchdowns.

★ College Football Hall of Fame

Albright, Tenley E.

FIGURE SKATING
b. July 18, 1935, Newton Centre, Mass.

In her early teens, Tenley Albright had two ambitions: to become a surgeon, like her father, and to win a gold medal in figure skating. She achieved both in a remarkably short time.

Albright began taking skating lessons when she was nine years old. Nonparalytic polio kept her inactive for several months, but she then returned to the sport, partly to strengthen the back muscles that had been weakened by inactivity.

She won the Eastern regional championship for juveniles under 12, then the national novice title, then the national junior championship. In 1952, at the age of 16, she won the first of five consecutive U.S. women's singles titles, and followed that with a silver medal at the Winter Olympics in Oslo.

Albright in 1953 became the first American woman to win the world championship in figure skating. She also won the U.S. and North American titles that year to become the first triple crown winner ever.

A few months later, she entered Radcliffe College as a pre-med major. Her practice sessions were scheduled from four to six a.m. Then she had her college classes, study, and homework as well as ballet lessons. Early in 1955, she took a leave of absence from college to win her second world championship.

Less than two weeks before the 1956 Winter Olympics in Cortina, Italy, Albright fell after hitting a rut in the ice while practicing. Her left skate cut so deeply into her right ankle that it slashed a vein and scraped bone. Her father flew to Italy and did some emergency repair work. Skating beautifully despite the pain, Albright became the first American woman to win the figure skating gold medal, getting first-place votes from 10 of the 11 judges.

Two weeks later, still bothered by the ankle injury, she finished second to another American, Carol Heiss, in the world championships.

Despite her grueling schedule, she graduated from Radcliffe at 21, after just three years of undergraduate work, and began her studies at Harvard Medical School, one of only six women in a class of 130 students.

★ International Women's Sports Hall of Fame; Olympic Hall of Fame

Albritton, David D.

TRACK AND FIELD
b. April 13, 1913, Danville, Ala.
d. May 14, 1994

Albritton had a remarkably long career for a high jumper. A sophomore at Ohio State, he won the NCAA championship in 1936. At the Olympic trials that year, he and Cornelius Johnson both jumped 6 feet, 9¾ inches, together becoming the first blacks to hold the world record in the event. They had also tied at 6 feet, 8 inches, in the AAU championships. Johnson won the gold medal in Berlin, and Albritton was second.

However, Albritton won two more NCAA titles, in 1937 and 1938, was AAU outdoor champion in 1937, 1946, and 1947, and tied for the title in 1938, 1945, and 1950. He tied for the AAU indoor title in 1944.

★ National Track & Field Hall of Fame

Alcott, Amy S.

GOLF
b. Feb. 22, 1956, Kansas City, Mo.

Joining the LPGA tour shortly after her nineteenth birthday, Alcott won the third tournament she entered, the 1975 Orange Blossom Classic, setting a record for the fastest career win. She was named the tour's rookie of the year.

Her first major victory was in the 1979 Peter Jackson (now du Maurier) Classic. The following year she won the U.S. Women's Open and averaged 71.51 strokes per round to claim the Vare Trophy. Alcott's third major tournament win came in the Nabisco Dinah Shore in 1983. She won that event again in 1988 and 1991.

Alcott set a tournament record of 65 for one round in winning the 1984 Lady Keystone Open, and she tied JoAnne Carner's tour record by winning at least one tournament in 12 straight years. In 1988, she became the third woman golfer to pass $2 million in career earnings.

Through 1994, Alcott had 29 career wins, tied for thirteenth on the all-time list.

Aldrich, Ki (Charles C.)
FOOTBALL
b. June 1, 1916, Temple, Tex.
d. March 12, 1983

Aldrich cried a lot as an infant, and his not-much-older brother called him "Ki Baby." Part of the nickname stuck, even after he had grown to be a 5-foot-11, 215-pound football star.

At Texas Christian University, Aldrich was the All-Southwest Conference (SWC) center from 1936 through 1938 and a consensus All-American in 1938, when he captained the team to an 11–0–0 record, the national championship, and a 15–6 win over Carnegie Tech in the Sugar Bowl.

The first SWC lineman chosen in the first round of the National Football League draft, Aldrich played for the Chicago Cardinals in 1939 and 1940 and the Washington Redskins in 1941 and 1942. After serving in the Navy during World War II, Aldrich played three more seasons with the Redskins, from 1945 through 1947, before retiring.
★ College Football Hall of Fame

Alexander, Bill (William A.)
FOOTBALL
b. June 6, 1889, Mud River, Ky.
d. April 23, 1950

The first coach to take a team to all four major bowl games, Alexander was associated with Georgia Tech for more than 40 years. He played football and track at the school, graduating in 1912, was an assistant to John W. Heisman for seven years, and became head football coach in 1920, when Heisman left for the University of Pennsylvania.

From 1920 through 1928 Alexander's teams won 58 games, lost 17, and tied 7. The 1928 team won all ten of its games, was voted national champion, and beat California, 8–7, in the Rose Bowl. How-

ever, Alexander came under fire for losing too many games during the next decade: From 1929 through 1938, Georgia Tech won only 36 of 99.

But Alexander took teams to three more bowl games in the next five years. Georgia Tech beat Missouri, 21–17, in the 1940 Orange Bowl, lost to Texas, 14–7, in the 1943 Cotton Bowl, and beat Tulsa, 20–10, in the 1944 Sugar Bowl. The 1942 team had a 9–1–0 record, winning Alexander the Coach of the Year award.

He retired from coaching after the 1944 season and served as athletic director until his death. Alexander had an overall record of 133–95–8.
★ College Football Hall of Fame

Alexander, Grover Cleveland
BASEBALL
b. Feb. 16, 1887, St. Paul, Nebr.
d. Nov. 4, 1950

A master of the curveball, "Old Pete" started his professional career in 1909 and arrived in the major leagues with the NL's Philadelphia Phillies in 1911, when he led the league with 31 complete games, 367 innings, 7 shutouts, and 28 victories against 13 losses.

After going 19–7 in 1912 and 22–8 in 1913, when he had a league-leading 9 shutouts, Alexander led the NL in victories four years in a row, with 27 in 1914, 31 in 1915, 33 in 1916, and 30 in 1917. He also led in complete games all four years, in shutouts with 12 in 1915, 16 in 1916, and 8 in 1917, and in ERA with 1.22 in 1915 and 1.55 in 1917.

Traded to the Cubs, Alexander spent most of the 1918 season in the Army. He lost the hearing in one ear because of shelling, and he also developed epilepsy. When he returned after World War I, he began drinking heavily.

However, he led the league in ERA the next two years with 1.72 in 1919, when he was 16–11, and 1.91 in 1920, when he also led in victories with 27 against 14 losses.

Alexander's skills suddenly declined in 1921, probably because of his alcoholism, although he remained an above-average pitcher. He did have a 22–12 record for Chicago in 1923, but after the 1925 season he entered a sanatorium, and in 1926 he was suspended by the Cubs and then waived to St. Louis.

The Cardinals won the pennant that season, and Alexander became a World Series hero. He beat the New York Yankees, 6–2, in the second game and 10–2 in the sixth. Dozing in the bullpen during the seventh inning of the final game, Alexander was awakened and told to warm up. He entered the game with St. Louis leading 3–2, the bases loaded, and two outs. He struck out the dangerous Tony Lazzeri on four pitches and pitched two more scoreless innings to get a save.

Alexander had one more fine year, going 21–10 in 1927, but he won just 25 games while losing 17 over the next two seasons and was 0–3 with the Phillies in 1930 before being released.

He spent four years with the barnstorming House of David team and for a time appeared in a Times Square side show. Epilepsy and alcohol continued to trouble him, and he lost an ear to cancer shortly before his death.

Alexander won 373 games, tying him with Christy Mathewson for the NL career record, and lost 208. He holds league records for most complete games with 437 and shutouts with 90. He struck out 2,198 hitters while walking only 951 in 5,189 innings.

★ Baseball Hall of Fame

Alexander, Joseph

FOOTBALL
b. April 1, 1898, Silver Creek, N.Y.
d. Sept. 12, 1975

For a man who chose a healing profession, Alexander was evidently a very rough football player. He was with the New York Giants when they faced the barnstorming Chicago Bears and halfback Red Grange at the Polo Grounds on Dec. 6, 1925. The *Chicago Tribune* reported, "Joe Alexander, the Giants' center, stopped a line play and squatted on the ground with Grange in his lap, trying to twist his head off to see what kind of sawdust he's stuffed with. The officials told Alexander he oughtn't to do that but didn't charge him anything for it."

Alexander played five varsity seasons at Syracuse University and was an All-American guard in 1918 and 1919. Walter Camp cited Alexander and Swede Youngstrom of Dartmouth as "the greatest pair of defensive guards that have ever been seen on the gridiron."

After receiving his medical degree from Syracuse in 1921, Alexander played two seasons of pro football, with the Rochester Jeffersons and Milwaukee Badgers, then began practicing medicine in New York City. He was the first player to sign with the Giants when the team was organized in 1925. He was player-coach in 1926, when the Giants had an 8–4–0 record, and he was a starter on the 1927 team that won all 11 of its games and the National Football League championship.

After that season, Alexander returned to medical practice and later helped found one of New York City's first tuberculosis clinics.

★ College Football Hall of Fame

Ali, Muhammad [Cassius M. Clay]

BOXING
b. Jan. 18, 1942, Louisville, Ky.

The colorful and controversial Ali began taking boxing lessons when he was 12 years old at the urging of a Louisville policeman he talked to after his bike was stolen. As a high school student, he won the national Golden Gloves middleweight championship in 1959 and 1960 and the AAU national light heavyweight title in 1960, then went on to a gold medal in the Olympic light heavyweight division.

Under his given name, Cassius Clay, he had his first professional fight on October 29, 1960. Before his sixth professional bout, against Lamar Clark on April 19, 1961, Clay predicted a 2nd-round knockout, and he was right. He continued his predictions, often in rhyme, making them come true until March 13, 1963. On that date, he won a questionable 10-round decision over Doug Jones after predicting a 4th-round knockout.

Clay was a heavy underdog when he met Sonny Liston for the heavyweight championship on February 25, 1964, at

Miami Beach, Florida. But he won the fight when Liston failed to come out for the 8th round, claiming a shoulder injury. In a rematch on May 25, 1965, Clay knocked Liston out with a "phantom punch" that few observers saw in the 1st round at Lewiston, Maine.

Shortly after becoming champion, Clay announced that he had become a Black Muslim and changed his name to Muhammad Ali. He defended the title eight times in the next 20 months. In the meantime, he had refused induction into the Army. As a result, his license was revoked by the New York State Boxing Commission, his title was stripped, and he was sentenced to five years in prison for draft evasion.

While the conviction was being appealed, Ali was inactive for more than two years and announced his retirement early in 1970. He returned to the ring shortly afterward, knocking out Jerry Quarry in the 3rd round on October 26, 1970, at Atlanta. After a court ordered New York to restore his license, he fought the new champion, Joe Frazier, at Madison Square Garden on March 8, 1971. Frazier won a brutal 15-round fight on a unanimous decision.

The U.S. Supreme Court overturned his conviction on June 29, 1971, and Ali won the North American Boxing Federation's championship by knocking out Jimmy Ellis in the 12th round less than a month later. He lost it on a 12-round decision to Ken Norton, regained it by outpointing Norton in 12 rounds, and then beat Frazier on a 12-round decision to gain a world title fight against George Foreman, who had also beaten Frazier.

Ali knocked Foreman out in the 8th round on October 30, 1974, at Kinshasa, Zaire, in the first heavyweight championship fight ever held in Africa. He was named fighter of the year by *Ring* magazine. He and Frazier shared the 1975 award after their celebrated "Thrilla in Manila" fight on October 1, when Ali won with a 14th-round knockout.

After ten defenses, Ali lost the title to Leon Spinks on a 12-round decision February 15, 1978, but regained it for a third time with a 15-round decision on September 15. He then announced his retirement.

He came out of retirement for another championship fight, against Larry Holmes on October 2, 1980. Holmes knocked him out in the 11th round. Ali retired for good after losing a 1981 decision to Trevor Berbick.

"Float like a butterfly, sting like a bee," a phrase coined by corner man Drew "Bundini" Brown, aptly described Ali's remarkable combination of speed and power during his prime, when he fought at about 210 pounds. Ali won 56 of his 61 professional fights, 37 by knockout; he lost 5, 1 by knockout.
★ International Boxing Hall of Fame; Olympic Hall of Fame

Allen, Dick (Richard A.)
BASEBALL
b. March 8, 1942, Wampum, Pa.

Proud, outspoken, and independent, Allen was one of the first black professional athletes who was willing to be controversial. Partly as a result of that attitude, he was traded five times during his 15-year major league career.

Called "Richie" by sportswriters when he joined the Philadelphia Phillies at the end of the 1963 season, Allen soon insisted on being known as "Dick," and he won his point. He led the NL in triples with 13 and runs scored with 125 in 1964, his first full season in the majors.

The right-handed, 5-foot-11, 190-pound Allen was a fine hitter with power. His best year with the Phillies was 1966, when he batted .317 with 40 home runs, 110 RBI, and 112 runs scored, leading the league in slugging percentage at .632.

Late in the 1967 season, Allen began a campaign to get the Phillies to trade him by creating disciplinary problems. The front office wanted him to stay with the team and wouldn't allow managers to discipline him. As a result, manager Gene Mauch was fired, and his successor, Bob Skinner, resigned.

Allen failed to show up for a doubleheader in June 1969. He was suspended without pay for 26 days and then returned with the agreement that the Phillies would release him when the season was over.

He signed with the St. Louis Cardinals in 1970, then spent a season with the Los Angeles Dodgers before going to the AL with the Chicago White Sox in 1972. He was named the league's most valuable player after hitting .308 and leading the league in home runs with 37, in RBI with 113, and in slugging percentage with .603.

Allen was rewarded with a $225,000 contract in 1973, making him baseball's highest-paid player. Injuries limited him to just 72 games that season, but in 1974 he again led the AL in home runs with 32 and in slugging percentage with .563.

He returned to the Phillies in 1975 and was a part-time player on the team that won the NL Eastern Division in 1976. Allen finished his career by playing in 54 games with the 1977 Oakland Athletics.

In 15 major league seasons, Allen batted .292 with 1,848 hits, including 320 doubles, 79 triples, and 351 home runs. He scored 1,099 runs and drove in 1,119.

Allen, Forrest C. ("Phog")

BASKETBALL
b. Nov. 18, 1885, Jamesport, Mo.
d. Sept. 16, 1974

The first true basketball coach, Allen learned the sport at the University of Kansas, where James Naismith was coach. Naismith, who had invented basketball in 1891, felt that the sport was too spontaneous to be coached. "Well," Allen replied, "you can coach them to pass at angles and run in curves."

In his senior year, 1908–09, Allen coached the team. He also coached at two nearby schools, Baker University and Haskell Indian Institute. Kansas was 25–3 that season, Baker, 22–2, and Haskell, 27–5, for a combined record of 74 wins and 10 losses.

Allen went on to the Kansas College of Osteopathy. Although he never set up practice, he did treat a number of well-known athletes. He coached at Warrensburg Teachers College (now Central Missouri State) from 1912–13 through 1918–19 and at Kansas from 1919–20 through 1955–56, compiling an overall record of 770 wins and 223 losses.

Kansas won the 1952 NCAA tournament; the 1923 and 1924 teams were chosen national champions by the Helms Athletic Foundation. Under Allen, Kansas won or shared 30 championships in the Missouri Valley, Big Seven, and Big Eight conferences. Among his pupils were Adolph Rupp, Dutch Lonborg, and John Bunn, all members of the Basketball Hall of Fame.

Allen was a founder of the National Association of Basketball Coaches in 1927 and served as its first president. He led the drive to have basketball made an Olympic sport in 1936, and he was also instrumental in having the NCAA tournament established in 1939. The University of Kansas's 17,500-seat arena, Allen Field House, is named for him.
★ Basketball Hall of Fame

Allen, Marcus

FOOTBALL
b. March 26, 1960, San Diego, Calif.

After starring as a quarterback and defensive back in high school, the heavily recruited Allen went to the University of Southern California. A tailback as a freshman, he moved to fullback in his sophomore year and was used mostly as a blocker for Charles White, who won the Heisman Trophy in 1979.

Allen returned to tailback in 1980 and led the nation in all-purpose yards with an average of 179.4 per game. As a senior, he set NCAA records for rushing yards with 2,432; most 200-yard games with eight; highest average rushing yards per game, 212.9; and most all-purpose yards, 2,550. He was a consensus All-American and won both the Heisman and Maxwell trophies as the outstanding college player of the year.

The first draft choice of the NFL's Los Angeles Raiders, Allen was *The Sporting News* rookie of the year in 1982, when he rushed for 697 yards and led the league in touchdowns with 14. He gained more than 1,000 yards each of the next three seasons, with a high of 1,759 yards in 1985, when he led the NFL. He set a record with 2,314 total yards rushing and receiving and was named the league's player of the year.

Allen's production fell off for the next three seasons, when he averaged less than four yards a carry, and he missed much of the 1989 season with a knee injury. Relegated to part-time play from 1990 through 1992, he was signed by the Kansas City Chiefs in 1993 as an unrestricted free agent. Given more playing time, he had a fine season, rushing for 764 yards and leading the AFC with 15 touchdowns.

A consensus All-Pro in 1982 and 1985, Allen was named most valuable player when the Raiders beat the Washington Redskins, 38–9, in Super Bowl XVIII to win the 1983 NFL championship. He carried 20 times for 191 yards and scored two touchdowns in the game. From October 28, 1985, through September 14, 1986, Allen rushed for more than 100 yards in 11 consecutive games, breaking Walter Payton's record.

Through 1994, the 6-foot-2, 210-pound Allen had appeared in 176 NFL games, rushing 2,485 times for 10,018 yards, a 4.1 average, and 88 touchdowns. He caught 520 passes for 4,847 yards, a 9.3 average, and 21 touchdowns.

Allison, Bobby (Robert A.)

AUTO RACING
b. Dec. 3, 1937, Miami, Fla.

Before he had a driver's license, Bobby Allison was practicing spins in an empty field. He entered his first race during his senior year in high school, finishing tenth, but after a couple of accidents, his father ordered him to quit.

Allison then tested engines for a time, became a NASCAR mechanic, and began racing in the sportsman class. He won his first national championship in 1962 in the modified special division, won it again in 1963, and won the national modified title in 1964.

He moved gradually into Grand National (GN) racing in 1965. The following year, he spent a reported $8,000 and 384 hours of work converting a Chevelle into a GN racing machine, and he won 3 of 34 starts. By 1970, he had finished

among the top five in more than 35 percent of the GN races he'd entered; that year he had his first major victory, beating Cale Yarborough by 50 feet in the Atlanta 500 and setting a new race record for average speed with 139.650 miles per hour.

He replaced David Pearson as driver for the Holman-Moody racing operation in 1971 and had a tremendous year. After a narrow loss to his younger brother Donnie in the Winston 500 at Talladega, Allison won the World 600, the Dover 500, the Motor State 500, and the Riverside 500. He lost another close race, to Richard Petty, in the Dixie 500 and then closed out the year with wins in the Michigan 500, Talladega 500, Southern 500, and National 500. His eight victories in races of 500 miles or more is still the NASCAR record.

Throughout his career, Allison had remarkable success in superspeedway races. He won the Mason-Dixon 500 and the Budweiser 500 five times each; the Southern 500 four times; and the Coca-Cola 500, Atlanta Journal 500, World 600, and Carolina 500 three times each. After going 55 straight starts without a victory, he won his fifth Winston 500 at Talladega in 1986, and in 1988 he won the Daytona 500 for the third time, just edging out his son Davey. That was Allison's 84th GN win, third on the all-time list behind Richard Petty and David Pearson. He's fifth on the NASCAR career money list, with more than $7 million in earnings.

Despite all his GN victories, the Winston Cup championship eluded Allison until 1983, when he finally won it at the age of 46. His last race was the Miller High Life 500 at Pocono, Pennsylvania, on June 19, 1988, when he was involved in a nearly fatal crash on the first lap. But he survived and received a standing ovation at the NASCAR annual banquet that year, when he and his wife, Judy, received the association's Award of Excellence.

The Pocono crash ended Allison's career, but sons Davey and Clifford carried on. Davey, 31, won the Daytona 500 in 1992 and was congratulated by his proud father. Less than six months later, 27-year-old Clifford died of injuries suffered while practicing for a NASCAR race at Michigan International Speedway. Davey was killed in August 1993 in the crash of a helicopter he was piloting.

Allison, Wilmer L.

TENNIS
b. Dec. 8, 1904, San Antonio, Tex.
d. April 20, 1977

Allison didn't begin playing tennis seriously until he was 20 years old, but less than three years later he won the intercollegiate singles championship, representing the University of Texas.

During the late 1920s and early 1930, Allison and John Van Ryn formed probably the best doubles team in the world, winning Wimbledon in 1929 and 1930, the U.S. Nationals in 1931 and 1935, and teaming for a 14–2 record in Davis Cup play.

But Allison's chief goal, the national singles title, eluded him for a long time. He reached the finals six times in seven years, losing to Fritz Mercur in 1929, Frank Shields in 1930, Berkeley Bell in 1931, Henri Cochet in 1932, and Fred Perry in 1934, when the final match went five sets, Perry winning 8–6 in the fifth.

In 1935 Allison finally broke through, beating Perry in the semifinals and Sidney Wood in the championship. He then cut back on serious competition. Allison also reached the Wimbledon finals in 1930, losing to Bill Tilden. He had a 17–10 record in Davis Cup singles.

From 1956 through 1972, Allison served as unpaid tennis coach at the University of Texas. The school won four Southwestern Conference championships during his tenure.
★ International Tennis Hall of Fame

Alomar, Roberto V.

BASEBALL
b. Feb. 5, 1968, Ponce, P.R.

The son of former major league player Sandy Alomar Sr. and brother of major league catcher Sandy Jr., Roberto signed with the NL's San Diego Padres in 1985 and played both shortstop and sec-ond base in the minor leagues until early in the 1988 season, when he became San Diego's starting second baseman.

The Padres traded him to the AL's Toronto Blue Jays in 1991. Always a good hitter, Alomar improved dramatically as a fielder in a very short time. He led the NL at his position with 17 errors in 1990, but in 1992 he tied an AL record with just five errors in 152 games.

Alomar's best offensive season was 1993, when he batted .326 with 17 home runs, 93 RBI, and 55 stolen bases. The 6-foot, 185-pounder was named most valuable player in the 1992 AL championship series, when he batted .423 with 4 runs scored, 4 RBI, and 5 stolen bases in Toronto's six-game victory over the Atlanta Braves.

He won three consecutive Golden Gloves, from 1991 through 1993, and was named to *The Sporting News* AL all-star team in 1992. Alomar is a switch-hitter. Through the 1993 season, he had a .310 career average with 1,174 hits, including 206 doubles, 41 triples, and 64 home runs. He had stolen 266 bases, scored 626 runs, and driven in 433.

Alston, Walter E. ("Smokey")

BASEBALL
b. Dec. 1, 1911, Venice, Ohio
d. Oct. 1, 1984

The consummate professional baseball manager, Alston had one major league at-bat, a strikeout in 1936. He later became a minor league manager. When Charlie Dressen asked the Brooklyn Dodgers for a three-year contract in 1954 after winning two consecutive pennants, the Dodgers declined and hired Alston.

The low-key Alston was virtually unknown. One New York sportswriter commented, "The Dodgers do not need a manager. That's why they got Alston." After the team finished in second place, many thought he would be gone. But Alston signed another one-year contract — one of 23 he signed with the Dodgers before retiring — and guided them to a pennant and their first World Series victory in 1955.

Alston was the Dodgers' manager when they moved from Brooklyn to Los Angeles in 1958, and he took the Los Angeles Dodgers to the pennant and a World Series championship in 1959. Under Alston, the Dodgers won a total of seven NL pennants and four World Series. His last World Series victory came in 1965, and he won just two pennants after that, but he almost always had his team in the running.

He announced his retirement and was replaced with four games left and the Dodgers ten games out of first place during the 1976 season. Alston had a won-lost record of 2,040–1,613 for a .558 winning percentage.

The teams Alston managed in Brooklyn were built around power. When the Dodgers moved to Los Angeles, pitching and speed were emphasized. That Alston was able to win consistently with both types of teams is a measure of his ability.

★ Baseball Hall of Fame

Alworth, Lance D.

FOOTBALL
b. Aug. 3, 1940, Houston, Tex.

The first American Football League player elected to the Pro Football Hall of Fame, Alworth was a running back at the University of Arkansas. He led the nation in punt return yardage in 1960 and 1961.

The San Diego Chargers drafted Alworth in the second round in 1962 and moved him to wide receiver. Nicknamed "Bambi" because of his slender build, speed, and grace, the 6-foot, 180-pound Alworth played with the Chargers for nine seasons and was an all-AFL selection seven consecutive times, from 1963 through 1969.

He finished his career with the Dallas Cowboys of the NFL in 1970 and 1971. When Alworth retired, he held records for the most consecutive games with a reception, 96, and the most games with 200 or more yards on receptions, 5. Both records have since been broken, but Alworth is still the only receiver to average more than 100 yards a game in three consecutive seasons, 1964 through 1966.

During his 11 professional seasons, Alworth caught 542 passes for 10,266 yards and 85 touchdowns. His average of 18.9 yards per reception is sixth best among receivers who caught 20 or more passes.

★ College Football Hall of Fame; Pro Football Hall of Fame

Ambers, Lou [Luigi d'Ambrosio]

BOXING
b. Nov. 8, 1913, Herkimer, N.Y.

Ambers was a tough fighter who made up for lack of boxing skill with gutsiness. The "Herkimer Hurricane" had lost only once in more than three years as a professional when he met lightweight champion Tony Canzoneri on May 10, 1935. He lost a 15-round decision, then won his next 15 fights and won the lightweight championship by decisioning Canzoneri in 15 rounds on Sept. 3, 1956.

He lost the title in what might have been his greatest fight. Matched against Henry Armstrong on Aug. 17, 1938, Ambers was knocked down twice, in the 5th and 6th rounds, and appeared to be badly beaten, but he came back strongly and lost a controversial split decision.

He regained the title with a 15-round decision over Armstrong on Aug. 22, 1939, then was knocked out in the 3rd round by Lew Jenkins on May 10, 1940. In his last fight, a rematch, he was knocked out by Jenkins in the 7th round on Feb. 28, 1941.

In 102 fights, Ambers won 88, 29 on knockouts; lost 8, 2 by knockouts; and had 6 draws.

★ International Boxing Hall of Fame

Ameche, Alan D.

FOOTBALL
b. June 1, 1933, Kenosha, Wis.
d. Aug. 8, 1980

Pro football's first sudden death game was the NFL championship contest between the Baltimore Colts and the New York Giants on December 28, 1958. The Colts had driven 79 yards to the Giants' 1-yard line. A field goal seemed the obvious decision, but instead Baltimore quarterback Johnny Unitas handed the ball to Alan "The Horse" Ameche, who scored the winning touchdown in a 23–17 victory.

Ameche was an All-American at the University of Wisconsin, where he played linebacker as well as fullback in those single-platoon days. In four years, he gained 3,212 yards, then the NCAA record, scored 25 touchdowns, and averaged 4.8 yards a carry. He won the Heisman Trophy in 1954.

He joined the Colts in 1955, when he was named Rookie of the Year and All-Pro fullback. The 6-foot, 215-pound Ameche was not only a strong, durable runner, he was also an excellent blocker who helped protect the valuable Unitas from blitzing linebackers.

In his 6 professional seasons, Ameche carried the ball 964 times for 4,045 yards, a 4.2 average, and scored 44 touchdowns. He also caught 101 passes.
★ College Football Hall of Fame

Ames, Knowlton L. ("Snake")
FOOTBALL
b. 1868
d. Dec. 23, 1931

In an era of mass plays and bone-breaking football, Ames was a fast, shifty runner, the first of the type. As a senior in 1889, he had runs of 89 and 65 yards in Princeton's 41–15 victory over Harvard. He was named tõ the first All-American team after that season.

Known as "Snake" because of his slithering runs, he was also an excellent kicker. He is sometimes credited with inventing the spiral punt.

Ames was co-coach of Purdue with "Sport" Donnelly in 1891 and 1892. Purdue won all 12 of its games during those two seasons.
★ College Football Hall of Fame

Amling, Warren
FOOTBALL
b. Dec. 29, 1924, Pana, Ill.

Amling entered Ohio State University in 1942 and enlisted in the Army after his freshman year. Assigned to Ohio State by the Army in 1944, Amling continued his studies and played football. A 6-foot, 197-pound lineman, he

was named All-American as a guard in 1945 and as a tackle in 1946. Amling captained the 1946 team.

After graduating in 1947, Amling turned down a chance to play for the NFL's New York Giants in order to practice veterinary medicine.
★ College Football Hall of Fame

Amyot, Frank
CANOEING
b. Sept. 14, 1904, Toronto, Ont.
d. Nov. 21, 1962

The only Canadian to win a gold medal at the 1936 Olympic Games, Amyot had to pay his own way to get to Berlin for the games because the Canadian Olympic Committee refused to sponsor him.

In the 1,000-meter canoe singles, it looked as if Amyot would lose after Bohuslav Karlik of Czechoslovakia passed him at the 750-meter mark. But Amyot put on a brilliant sprint to retake the lead just 50 meters from the finish line, and he held on to win.

The winner of six national canoe titles and one kayak championship, Amyot also coached and managed the Canadian Olympic canoeing team.
★ Canadian Sports Hall of Fame

Anders, Beth (Elizabeth)
FIELD HOCKEY
b. Nov. 13, 1951, Norristown, Pa.

A brilliant scorer on penalty corner shots, Anders became a member of the U.S. national field hockey team in 1969 and played through the 1984 season. She also played on every U.S. World Cup team from 1971 through 1983, and led the U.S. in scoring in each tournament.

Anders scored six penalty corner goals in seven matches during the 1983 World Cup tournament. When the U.S. won the Four-Nations cup that year, she scored four penalty corner goals in just three matches. She captained the 1984 Olympic team that won a bronze medal, the highest finish ever for the U.S.

As field hockey coach since 1980 at Old Dominion University, Anders has guided her team to seven NCAA Division I championships, from 1982 through 1984, in 1988, and from 1990 through 1992. Her teams have won 28 of 33 games in 12 years of tournament competition.

Andersen, Morten
FOOTBALL
b. Aug. 19, 1980, Struer, Denmark

Andersen went to high school in Indianapolis and played football at Michigan State University. The place-kicker on *The Sporting News* All-American team in 1981, Andersen was chosen by the New Orleans Saints in the fourth round of the 1982 NFL draft.

The 6-foot-2, 221-pounder led the NFL with 28 field goals in 36 attempts in 1987. He holds the league's career record with 21 field goals of 50 yards or more and tied a single-game record by kicking 2 field goals of 50 or more yards on December 11, 1983.

Through the 1994 season, Andersen had scored 1,318 points with 302 field goals in 389 attempts and 412 extra points in 418 attempts. His career field goal percentage of .776 is an NFL record.

Anderson, Andy (Harold J.)
BASKETBALL
b. Sept. 11, 1902, Akron, Ohio
d. June 13, 1967

A graduate of Otterbein, Anderson coached high school basketball in Toledo and Akron before becoming head coach at the University of Toledo in 1935. He was there through the 1941–42 season, then went to Bowling Green from 1942–43 through 1962–63. He had a 142–41 record at Toledo and a 362–185 record at Bowling Green for an overall mark of 504 wins and 226 losses.

Six of Anderson's teams went to the National Invitation Tournament, and one played in the NCAA tournament. He coached two other members of the Hall of Fame, Al Bianchi and Nate Thurmond.
★ Basketball Hall of Fame

Anderson, Dick (Richard P.)
FOOTBALL
b. Feb. 10, 1946, Midland, Mich.

A fullback in high school, Anderson became a defensive back at the University of Colorado and was named an All-American in 1967, his senior season. Anderson had 14 career interceptions, and he ran back 2 punts for touchdowns in the post-season Blue-Gray all-star game.

The 6-foot-2, 200-pounder was chosen by the AFL's Miami Dolphins in the 1968 AFL-NFL draft and was named the league's defensive rookie of the year. He was an All-Pro safety from 1972 through 1974 as one of the leaders of Miami's "no-name" defense.

After the AFL merged into the NFL in 1970, the Dolphins won three straight AFC titles, from 1971 through 1973, and were Super Bowl champions after the 1972 and 1973 seasons.

Because of a knee injury, Anderson missed much of the 1975 season and all of the 1976 season. He made a comeback in 1977 and then retired. During his professional career, he returned 34 interceptions for 792 yards, a 23.3 average, and 3 touchdowns. He also ran back 40 punts for 272 yards and returned 7 kickoffs 114 yards.

The president of the NFL Players Association from 1975 to 1977, Anderson served as a Florida state senator for one term. He became a very successful businessman after leaving football.
★ College Football Hall of Fame

Anderson, Eddie (Edward N.)
FOOTBALL
b. Nov. 13, 1900, Oskaloosa, Iowa
d. April 26, 1976

Anderson started at end for Notre Dame from 1918 through 1921 and captained the team in his senior year. Though he was 5-foot-10 and weighed only 150 pounds, Anderson was never knocked off his feet, according to Coach Knute Rockne.

After graduating in 1922, he became coach at Columbia (now Loras) College in Iowa, where his teams won 16 games, lost 6, and tied 2 in three seasons. Anderson went to DePaul University, Chicago, in 1925 and compiled a 21–22–4 record in seven seasons.

During his early years as a coach, he also played five seasons of professional football with the Rochester Jeffersons, Chicago Cardinals, Chicago Bears, and Chicago Bulls, and studied for a degree at Rush Medical College. He received the degree in 1929 and practiced medicine throughout the rest of his long coaching career.

Holy Cross hired Anderson in 1933. He produced two unbeaten teams, in 1935 and 1937, and had a 47–7–4 record in six seasons there. In 1939, he signed a three-year contract with the University of Iowa, which had won just 22 games in nine seasons. His first team won 6, including a 7–6 upset of Notre Dame, while losing 1 and tying 1.

During the next three seasons, his teams went 13–13. Anderson served in the U.S. Army Medical Corps from 1943 through 1945, then returned to Iowa and had a 16–19–1 record in four more years there.

Holy Cross rehired him in 1950, after Iowa refused to give him tenure, and he remained there until his retirement after the 1964 season. In this stint, he won 82 games, lost 60, and tied 4. His 1951 and 1952 teams both won 8 of 10 games.

Overall, Anderson coached 201 victories against 128 losses and 15 ties, a .606 percentage. He was the sixth coach to win more than 200 games.

★ College Football Hall of Fame

Anderson, Gary L.
SHOOTING
b. Oct. 8, 1939, Holdredge, Nebr.

Anderson won gold medals in three-position free rifle shooting at the 1964 and 1968 Olympics. His record score of 1,153 in 1964 stood until 1972, when Lones Wigger broke it.

Ironically, Anderson helped Wigger win two medals in 1964. Wigger, taking part in his first major international competition, was unnerved by the size of the crowd. Anderson advised him to become part of the crowd instead of being intimidated. Aided by that advice, Wigger relaxed and won a gold medal in the small-bore rifle, three position, and a silver in the small-bore rifle, prone.

Anderson won 11 national championships and 6 world titles in both small-

bore and free rifle competition. A graduate of Hastings College in Nebraska, he attended a seminary in California and became a Presbyterian minister in 1972. He later served as a Nebraska state senator and as executive director of the National Rifle Association.

Anderson, Jodi
TRACK AND FIELD
b. Nov. 10, 1957, Chicago, Ill.

Representing California State-Northridge, the 5-foot-6, 125-pound Anderson won the AIAW long jump in 1977 and 1979 and was the pentathlon champion in 1979. She was also the national outdoor long jump champion in 1977, 1978, 1980, and 1981.

Anderson finished first in the long jump and pentathlon at the 1980 Olympic trials, but the U.S. boycotted the Moscow Games that year. After missing most of the 1983 season with a knee injury, she was second in the pentathlon at the 1984 trials. However, the knee injury recurred at the Olympics, and she was forced to withdraw.

Anderson played "Pooch" in the 1982 movie *Personal Best.*

Anderson, Kenneth A.
FOOTBALL
b. Feb. 15, 1949, Batavia, Ill.

Anderson starred in both basketball and football at little Augustana, IL, College, graduating in 1971. He was chosen by the Cincinnati Bengals in the third round of the NFL draft and became the team's starting quarterback during his second season, 1972.

A very accurate short-range passer, the 6-foot-3, 212-pounder was named All-Pro quarterback and was a consensus player of the year in 1981, when he led the Bengals to the AFC championship and Super Bowl XVI, where Cincinnati lost, 26–21, to the San Francisco 49ers.

Anderson led the AFC in passing efficiency from 1973 through 1975 and from 1981 through 1982. He set an NFL record for completion percentage with 70.6 in 1982, when he completed 20 consecutive passes in a game, a record at the time.

Anderson retired after the 1984 season. He completed 2,654 of his 4,475 passes for 32,838 yards and 197 touchdowns, with only 160 interceptions. His 59.3 completion percentage is sixth best all-time. He also ran 399 times for 2,220 yards, a 5.6-yard average, and 20 touchdowns.

Anderson, Miller A.

DIVING
b. Dec. 17, 1922, Columbus, Ohio
d. Oct. 29, 1965

Anderson won his first national diving championship in 1942, in the 3-meter springboard. A flyer during World War II, he was forced to parachute from his plane on his 112th mission, and his left leg was severely injured. A silver plate was inserted into his knee, and he had to learn to dive all over again after the war.

Representing Ohio State, Anderson won the NCAA 3-meter championship, the national 1-meter championship, and the national 3-meter championship in 1946, 1947, and 1948. He also won silver medals in the Olympic springboard event in 1948 and 1952. Anderson was the first to perform a forward one-and-a-half somersault with two twists and a backward one-and-a-half with one twist.

Anderson, O. J. (Ottis J.)

FOOTBALL
b. Feb. 19, 1957, W. Palm Beach, Fla.

A 6-foot-2, 225-pound running back with speed and power, Anderson was named to some All-American teams in 1978, his senior year at the University of Miami. He was the first draft choice of the NFL's St. Louis Cardinals. In his first professional game, against the Dallas Cowboys, he rushed for 193 yards.

Anderson gained 1,605 yards that season, a rookie record at the time, and he was named rookie of the year, player of the year, and All-Pro. After rushing for more than 1,000 yards each of the next two seasons, he had 587 yards in just eight games in 1982 because of the NFL

Players' Association strike and then went over 1,000 yards again in 1983 and 1984.

A foot injury limited him to part-time duty in only nine games in 1985. After four games with the Cardinals in 1986, he was traded to the New York Giants for two draft choices. Anderson saw little action with the Giants until 1989, when he again became a starter and gained 1,023 yards, scoring 14 touchdowns.

After rushing for 784 yards and scoring 11 touchdowns in 1989, Anderson was named the most valuable player in Super Bowl XXV, gaining 102 yards on 21 carries in the Giants' 20–19 victory over the Buffalo Bills.

Anderson retired after carrying the ball only 63 times in 23 games during the 1991 and 1992 seasons. He appeared in 182 NFL games, gaining 10,273 yards on 2,562 carries, a 4.0 average, and rushing for 81 touchdowns. He also caught 376 passes for 3,062 yards, an 8.1 average, and 5 touchdowns.

Anderson, Paul E.

WEIGHTLIFTING
b. Oct. 17, 1932, Toccoa, Ga.
d. Aug. 15, 1994

Although his competitive career was very brief, Anderson may have been the best American weightlifter ever. He won the U.S. heavyweight championship in 1955 and 1956. After winning the world championship by a record margin of 82 pounds, he was strongly favored for the 1956 Olympic gold medal. He had a surprisingly hard time winning it.

Needing 187.5 kilograms in his third lift to match Humberto Selvetti of Argentina, Anderson failed twice but made the lift on his third and final try. He won the medal because he weighed 13 pounds less than Selvetti.

Anderson went on to set many records as a professional powerlifter, including a bench press of 627 pounds, a squat of 1,200, and a dead lift of 820. On June 12, 1957, he lifted the greatest weight ever, 6,270 pounds in a back lift off trestles.

Anderson, Sparky (George L.)

BASEBALL
b. Feb. 22, 1934, Bridgewater, S.Dak.

Like many successful major league managers, Anderson was not particularly successful as a player. He batted just .218 with the Philadelphia Phillies in 1959, his only season in the major leagues, and spent five years as a minor league manager before taking over the Cincinnati Reds in 1970.

A virtual unknown when he arrived, Anderson guided the "Big Red Machine" to four pennants in seven seasons, including consecutive World Series victories in 1975 and 1976. With Cincinnati, he was nicknamed "Captain Hook" because he was so quick to replace pitchers.

Fired in 1979 after two consecutive second-place finishes, Anderson took over the Detroit Tigers. He was named the AL manager of the year by the Baseball Writers' Association of America in 1984, when the Tigers won the Eastern Division with a 104–58 record and went on to win the World Series, taking seven of eight post-season games in the process.

The Tigers won another division title and Anderson was consensus manager of the year in 1987. However, Detroit lost in the American League championship series.

Through 1994, Anderson had a record of 2,134 wins and 1,750 losses, a .533 winning percentage, in 24 seasons.

Anderson, Willie

GOLF
b. May 1880, North Berwick, Scotland
d. Oct. 25, 1910

America's first great golfer, Anderson was the son of a Scottish greenskeeper. He came to the U.S. in 1895 and two years later, at 17, he finished second in the U.S. Open. He won the title in 1901 by beating Alex Smith in a playoff at the Myopia Hunt Club in South Hamilton, Massachusetts. After finishing fifth in 1902, he won three Opens in a row, 1903, 1904, and 1905. He is the only golfer to accomplish that, and one of only four

to win the title four times. (The others are Ben Hogan, Bobby Jones, and Jack Nicklaus.)

Anderson was also a four-time winner of the Western Open, which was then the second most important U.S. tournament. He won that event in 1902, 1904, 1908, and 1909. His 1909 score of 288 was a record for 72 holes on a full-length course.

Anderson was known as a serious, even grim, competitor. He certainly took the Open very seriously: In both 1906 and 1910 he took jobs at the club that was to host the next tournament. Off the course he was friendly and convivial among friends and fellow golfers. His sudden death at the age of 30 is generally attributed to arteriosclerosis, but some have speculated that it was caused by heavy drinking.

★ World Golf Hall of Fame

Andretti, Mario

AUTO RACING
b. Feb. 28, 1940, Montana, Italy

Mario Andretti and his twin brother, Aldo, began in Formula Junior Racing, Italy's answer to Little League Baseball, when they were 13. Two years later the Andretti family came to the United States and settled in Nazareth, Pennsylvania. The twins worked in an uncle's garage and began racing a modified 1948 Hudson, taking turns behind the wheel. In their first four races, each of them won twice.

Aldo crashed, fracturing his skull, in the fifth start. That didn't stop the twins from racing, but their father refused to speak to them for a time. Aldo married and got out of racing while Mario climbed through the ranks, getting his first IndyCar ride in 1964. He qualified fourth fastest in the 1965 Indianapolis 500, finished third in the race, and went on to win the IndyCar championship, finishing in the top four in 10 of his 17 starts.

Andretti was champion again in 1966, then began to try other kinds of racing. He won NASCAR's Daytona 500 in 1967, and in 1968 he got his first Formula One ride in the U.S. Grand Prix at

Watkins Glen, where he qualified first but was forced out early by clutch trouble. After finishing second in the IndyCar championship in 1967 and 1968, he won the title again in 1969, when he had nine victories, including his first in the Indy 500.

For several years, Andretti tried juggling IndyCar, Formula One, and Can-Am racing, but with little success. He began to concentrate on Formula One in 1977, winning four events, and in 1978 he won six races and became the second American to win the World Driving Championship. (The first was Phil Hill.) He is the only driver ever to win an IndyCar championship and the WDC.

Andretti returned to IndyCar racing full-time in 1982, and two years later he won his fourth championship. However, he never managed to win the Indy 500 for a second time, although it seemed he had for a time in 1981. Bobby Unser beat him by eight seconds in that race, but the following day Unser was penalized a lap for passing cars under a yellow caution flag, and Andretti was declared the winner. Four months later an appeal panel reversed the ruling and fined Unser $40,000, while returning the victory. Andretti also finished second in the 1985 Indy 500, and he won his fourth IndyCar championship in 1987.

Only A. J. Foyt can come close to Andretti for longevity and versatility. Andretti won the USAC dirt track title in 1974, when he also fell just eight points shy of the Formula 5000 championship. Andretti is the only person to be named Driver of the Year in three different decades, 1967, 1978, and 1984. He is one of only three drivers to win races on paved ovals, road courses, and dirt tracks in a single season, and he accomplished that four times. Andretti is second to Foyt in all-time IndyCar victories, with 52, is the career leader in pole positions with 67, and is fifth in earnings with $10,887,392 — and that doesn't include more than $1 million won in other types of racing.

In 1991, Andretti was seventh in the IndyCar point standings. His son Michael won the championship that year,

and in 1992 Mario, Michael, and another son, John, all finished in the top ten. Mario retired during the 1994 season.
★ Indianapolis 500 Hall of Fame

Anson, Cap (Adrian C.)

BASEBALL
b. April 17, 1851, Marshalltown, Iowa
d. April 14, 1922

Anson not only batted over .300 in 24 of his record 27 major league seasons, he managed the Chicago NL team to five pennants. Although he was once considered the first player to collect 3,000 hits, recent research has lowered his total to 2,995. However, Anson was the first baseball player to write his autobiography.

After attending Notre Dame for a year, Anson joined the Rockford team in the National Association in 1871, the first year of its existence, then spent the next four seasons with the association's Philadelphia Athletics.

When the National League was formed in 1876, Anson joined its Chicago team. Originally used primarily as a catcher and outfielder, he moved to first base in 1879 and stayed at that position for the rest of his career. He also became the team's captain, the equivalent of playing manager, in 1879, earning the nickname "Cap." As he continued playing well into his forties, he became known as "Pop."

A poor fielder with little mobility, Anson was an outstanding hitter and an innovative manager. He led the NL in hitting with a .399 average in 1881 and a .344 average in 1888, and was the RBI leader from 1880 through 1882, 1884 through 1886, and in 1888 and 1891.

He is often credited with inventing the hit and run play; he certainly used it frequently. In 1885, Anson became one of the first managers to take a team south for spring training, and he was a tough disciplinarian who fined players for being overweight, for drinking, and for missing curfews at a time when players weren't often disciplined.

While Anson is sometimes blamed for the banning of black players from organized baseball, it is unlikely that he was that powerful. He *was* a bigot who protested vehemently when the Newark Little Giants wanted to start a black pitcher, Harry Stovey, in an 1887 exhibition game against Chicago; as a result, Stovey was held out of the game. Given the temper of the times, however, blacks probably would have been banned even without Anson's outburst. A short time before, the minor International League had formally voted to prohibit black players.

Anson guided Chicago to pennants from 1880 through 1882 and in 1885 and 1886. He was fired by a new owner after the 1897 season, then went to New York to manage the Giants, but he lasted less than a season there.

In 22 seasons as a major league player, Anson batted .329 with 2,995 hits, including 528 doubles, 124 triples, and 97 home runs. He scored 1,719 runs and drove in 1,879. As a manager, he had a 1,296–947 record for a .578 winning percentage.
★ Baseball Hall of Fame

Anthony, Earl R.

BOWLING
b. April 27, 1938, Kent, Wash.

Nicknamed "Square Earl" by his fellow bowlers because of his crewcut and glasses, Anthony had aspirations of playing major league baseball as a left-handed pitcher, but an ankle injury destroyed his hopes. He then took up bowling and joined the pro tour for seven tournaments in 1963, but didn't win any money and went home to Washington.

He tried again in 1970, and within a short time Anthony was the best bowler on the tour. He earned $107,585 in 1975, becoming the first to win more than $100,000 in a season. Anthony was named bowler of the year from 1974 through 1976 and from 1981 through 1983. He led the PBA tour in scoring from 1973 through 1975, in 1980, and in 1983.

Anthony retired temporarily in 1984 with records of $1,216,421 in career winnings and 41 tour victories. He won the ABC Masters tournament in 1977 and 1984, the PBA national from 1973 through 1975 and from 1981 through 1983, and the Firestone Tournament of Champions in 1974 and 1978.

After bowling in just one tournament a year for three years, Anthony entered 12 tournaments in 1987 but won only $8,850. He then joined the new PBA senior tour in 1988 and won four tournaments before retiring permanently in 1991.

Although his 41 wins is still the record, he now ranks fourth in career earnings because prize money has increased so much since his peak years.
★ ABC Hall of Fame; PBA Hall of Fame

Aparicio, Luis E., Jr.

BASEBALL
b. April 29, 1934, Maracaibo, Venezuela

He had a lifetime batting average of only .262, but Aparacio's great defensive skill and base-stealing ability got him into the Hall of Fame.

Aparicio's father was considered Venezuela's greatest shortstop, though he never got a chance to play in the major leagues. "Little Luis" joined the AL's Chicago White Sox in 1955 and immediately replaced another Venezuelan, Chico Carrasquel, at shortstop. He batted only .266 but led the league in stolen bases with 21 and was named rookie of the year.

The 5-foot-9, 160-pound Aparicio was the AL's leading base stealer the next eight years in a row, with highs of 64 in 1957, 61 in 1953, 60 in 1951, and 56 in 1959. He led the league's shortstops in fielding percentage eight consecutive seasons, from 1959 through 1966, and won nine Gold Gloves.

The White Sox won the pennant in 1959, when Aparicio finished second to his double-play partner, second baseman Nellie Fox, in the most valuable player voting. He was traded in 1963 to the Baltimore Orioles, where he played on another pennant winner in 1966.

Aparicio returned to the White Sox from 1968 through 1970 and finished his career with the Boston Red Sox from

1971 through 1972. In his 18 major league seasons, he batted .262 in 2,599 games, with 506 stolen bases in 642 attempts.

★ Baseball Hall of Fame

Appling, Luke (Lucius B. Jr.)

BASEBALL
b. April 2, 1907, High Point, N.C.
d. Jan. 3, 1991

Early in his major league career, Appling was known as "Fumblefoot" and "Kid Boots" because of his poor fielding. He eventually became an adequate shortstop, but he was much better known for his hitting.

Appling arrived in the majors late in the 1930 season with the Chicago White Sox. In 1933, he batted .300 for the first time; he was to do it 15 times in all, including a league-leading .388 average in 1936, the best ever by a twentieth-century shortstop.

The gangly 5-foot-10, 180-pounder was a hypochondriac who acquired yet another nickname, "Old Aches and Pains." He once told his manager that he couldn't play because he was "dying," and the manager replied, "You might as well die out there at shortstop instead of cluttering up the clubhouse."

Ironically, Appling suffered a chronic ankle injury that he never complained about. His healthiest season was 1942, when he hit just .262. A year later, he won his second batting title with a .328 average despite an eye infection, a badly spiked knee, bouts with indigestion and the flu, and several muscle pulls.

After spending most of two seasons in the Army, Appling returned to the White Sox late in 1945 and played five more seasons. He retired after batting only .234 in 50 games in 1950. Appling was later a minor league manager and major league coach. He managed the Kansas City Athletics to a 10–30 record for part of the 1967 season.

In 2,422 games, Appling batted .310 and had 2,749 hits, including 440 doubles, 102 triples, and 45 home runs. He scored 1,319 runs, drove in 1,116, and stole 179 bases.

★ Baseball Hall of Fame

Arbanas, Frederick V.

FOOTBALL
b. Jan. 14, 1939, Detroit, Mich.

Named the tight end on the all-time All-AFL team, Arbanas joined the Dallas Texans in 1961 after playing at Michigan State University. He missed all of his rookie season because of a back injury but took over as a starter in 1962. The Texans became the Kansas City Chiefs the following year.

The 6-foot-3, 240-pound Arbanas was used primarily as a blocker in the Dallas / Kansas City offense. His best seasons as a receiver were 1963 and 1964, with 34 catches each of those years. Arbanas was mugged during the 1964 season, and the attack damaged the vision in his left eye. However, he played through 1970, the year the AFL merged into the NFL.

Arbanas was named All-AFL in 1963, 1964, and 1966. During his nine seasons, he caught 218 passes for 3,107 yards, a 14.2 average, and scored 34 touchdowns.

Arbour, Alan

HOCKEY
b. Nov. 1, 1932, Sudbury, Ont.

Twice an all-star defenseman, Arbour played for three Stanley Cup champions, with the Chicago Black Hawks in 1961 and with the Toronto Maple Leafs in 1963 and 1964. He began his NHL playing career with the Detroit Red Wings in 1953 and also played for the St. Louis Blues before retiring after the 1970–71 season.

Arbour also coached St. Louis in his final season as a player. He was fired early in the 1972–73 season. The following year, he took over the New York Islanders. He guided the team to five first-place finishes in the Patrick Division and four consecutive Stanley Cups, from 1980 through 1983.

After the 1985–86 season, Arbour left coaching to become New York's vice president of player development. However, he ended up coaching again during the 1988–89 season.

As a player, Arbour scored 70 points on 12 goals and 58 assists in 626 regular season games. He added 1 goal and 8 assists for 9 points in 86 playoff games. As a coach, he had a 745–541–236 regular season record for a .567 winning percentage through the 1992–93 season, and he was 123–82 in the playoffs.

Arcaro, Eddie (George Edward)

HORSE RACING

b. Feb. 19, 1916, Cincinnati, Ohio

One of only two jockeys to win the Kentucky Derby five times, Arcaro won the Preakness a record six times and is tied with Jimmy McLaughlin for most wins in the Belmont with six. Arcaro left school to become an exercise boy in 1930, when he was 14. He began jockeying the following year but didn't get his first victory until January 1932, at Caliente Park in Mexico.

Arcaro was the leading apprentice jockey at New Orleans in 1933, but missed three months with a fractured skull and punctured lung after a fall at Chicago in June. He began riding for Calumet Farm in 1934, and during the next several years he established himself as one of the top jockeys in the country.

In 1938, Arcaro won his first Kentucky Derby aboard Lawring, and he won the triple crown with Whirlaway in 1941. He had a chance to make it three Kentucky Derby victories in five years when Greentree Stables in 1942 let him choose between Shut Out and Devil Diver. He finished sixth on Devil Diver, while Shut Out won the race. Later that year, though, he rode Shut Out to victory in the Belmont.

The top money winner in 1940, Arcaro repeated in 1942, even though he was suspended for the last four months because he tried to ride another jockey into the rail.

He won his third Kentucky Derby aboard Hoop Jr. and his third Belmont aboard Pavot in 1945, then began riding for Calumet Farm again in 1948. He rode Coaltown early in the year, but after Citation's jockey, Albert Snider, disappeared during a hunting expedition, Arcaro was given another choice: Coaltown or Citation. He choose Citation and won his second triple crown, the only jockey ever to accomplish that. After Citation beat Coaltown in the Kentucky Derby, Arcaro gave half of his winnings to Snider's widow.

Arcaro set a record with $1,686,230 in winnings that year. He was the leader again with $1,410,160 in 1950, when he won the Preakness on Hill Prince. He won the Preakness once more in 1951 with Bold Ruler, and in 1952 he took his fifth Kentucky Derby aboard Hill Gail and his fifth Belmont aboard One-Count, breaking his own record with $1,859,591 in winnings.

After winning the Preakness with Hasty Road in 1955, Arcaro rode Nashua to second behind Swaps in the Kentucky Derby, then won the Preakness and Belmont, neither of which Swaps entered. That set up a $100,000, winner-take-all match race, and Arcaro rode Nashua to an easy victory. He led in winnings for the fifth and final time with $1,864,796 that year.

Arcaro had his last victory in a triple crown race with Fabius, a son of Citation, in the 1956 Preakness. He retired early in 1962 because of bursitis in his right arm. He later served as a television commentator and as a public relations person for the Golden Nugget Casinos.

In 24,092 races, Arcaro had 4,779 wins, 3,807 seconds, and 3,302 third-place finishes, with $30,039,543 in purses. His record of 554 stakes victories was broken by Willie Shoemaker in 1972.

★ National Horse Racing Hall of Fame

Archibald, Nate (Nathaniel)

BASKETBALL

b. Sept. 2, 1948, New York, N.Y.

Nicknamed "Tiny" early in his career, the 6-foot-1, 160-pound Archibald later preferred to be called "Nate." He spent a season at Arizona Western, a junior college, averaging 29.5 points a game, then transferred to the University of Texas–El Paso, where he averaged an even 20 points from 1967–68 through 1969–70.

Drafted in the second round by the NBA's Cincinnati Royals in 1970, Archibald was a backup for two seasons and moved into the starting lineup as a point guard after the team became the

Kansas City / Omaha Kings in 1972–73. He led the NBA in scoring with a 34.0 average and in assists with 11.4 per game, becoming the only player ever to lead in both those categories in the same season.

Archibald was traded to the New York Nets in 1976 but appeared in only 34 games because of injuries. He then went to the Buffalo Braves. After he missed the entire 1978–79 season with a torn Achilles tendon, Archibald was traded to the Boston Celtics. He played as a backup in his first season with Boston but became a starter again in 1979–80.

The Celtics released him after the 1982–83 season, and Archibald finished his career with the Milwaukee Bucks in 1983–84. In 876 regular season games, he scored 16,481 points, an average of 18.8, with 6,476 assists. He added 667 points and 306 assists in 47 playoff games.

Arfons, Arthur E.

AUTO RACING
b. Feb. 3, 1926, Akron, Ohio

Arfons began the pursuit of the land speed record by accident — almost literally. An avid pilot, he drove to the Akron airport one Sunday to discover that the road was blocked and lined with people. He thought there had been a plane crash, but it turned out to be a drag race on the runway. He was instantly converted to the sport.

He and his older brother Walter put together a dragster called the Green Monster because they had painted it with leftover green tractor paint. It could do only 85 mph. But the brothers kept working at it, building one Green Monster after another, culminating in a jet dragster that Art drove 342 mph at the Bonneville, Utah, Salt Flats in the fall of 1960. That was still more than 50 mph short of the 1947 record set by John Cobb.

The brothers broke apart for unexplained reasons, and Walter prepared a car for Tom Green, who raised the land speed record to 413.2 mph on October 2, 1964. Three days later Art did 434 mph in the latest Green Monster. Craig Breed-

love raised the mark to 526.28 mph on October 16, and Art regained the record with 536.71 mph on October 27.

Breedlove came back a little more than a year later, averaging 555.127 mph on November 3, 1965. Art was ready to retake the record four days later, but a right tire exploded on his second run, when he was averaging more than 577 mph. He survived, and made his last try on November 17, 1966. By then, Breedlove's record was 600.6 mph. Arfons was doing more than 600 mph when a wheel came off his car. Again he survived without serious injury, but he never made another run at the land speed record. He did occasionally do drag racing exhibitions, but after his car went out of control and killed three spectators in 1971, he quit entirely.

Arguello, Alexis

BOXING
b. April 19, 1952, Managua, Nicaragua

Tall and slender at 5-foot-10 and 130 pounds, Arguello was a great tactical boxer with a surprisingly powerful punch. He began fighting in his native Nicaragua when he was 16. After winning 35 of 37 bouts, Arguello took the World Boxing Association featherweight championship by knocking out Ruben Olivares in the 13th round on November 23, 1974, at Inglewood, California.

Arguello won the vacant world featherweight title with a 2nd round knockout of Rigoberto Riasco on May 31, 1975, in Granada. He relinquished the championship after two defenses to move into the junior lightweight division in 1977.

On January 28, 1978, Arguello faced Alfredo Escalera, and knocked him out in the 13th round to win the World Boxing Council championship. He defended the title eight times, winning all by knockout, and then moved up to the lightweight division.

Arguello won a 15-round decision over Scotland's Jim Watt in London on June 20, 1981, to become lightweight champion. He knocked out four challengers in the next year and then attempted to win a world title in a fourth division, the light welterweight. However, champion Aaron Pryor knocked out Arguello in the 14th round on November 22, 1982. After being knocked out again by Pryor the following year, Arguello retired.

He won 77 of his 83 professional fights, 59 by knockout, and lost 6, 3 by knockout.

★ International Boxing Hall of Fame

Arie, Mark P.

SHOOTING
b. March 27, 1882, Thomasboro, Ill.
d. Nov. 19, 1958

Arie competed in trap shooting's Grand American Handicap for more than 30 years. He won the first GAH doubles championship in 1912 and won it for the second time 22 years later, at the age of 52.

In 1917, he tied for the singles title but lost the shoot-off. In the GAH, contestants shoot from varying distances based on their averages. Arie in 1923 became the first ever to win the championship from the maximum distance of 23 yards, and he did it again in 1928. He was a member of the All-American trap shooting team six times, including the first four years the team was selected, 1927 through 1930.

Arie won the trap shooting gold medal at the 1920 Olympics and was also on the gold medal U.S. team.

Arizin, Paul

BASKETBALL
b. April 9, 1928, Philadelphia, Pa.

Arizin couldn't make his high school basketball team, but he practiced constantly at night during his senior year in high school and his freshman year at Villanova University, and made the Villanova varsity as a sophomore.

He had developed a quick, accurate jump shot that made him a prolific scorer. Arizin later explained that the shot came to him by accident. Practicing and playing on a gym floor that had been waxed for dances, he lost his footing when he tried a hook shot, so he went to the jump shot instead.

As a junior, he once scored 85 points in a game, and he led the nation in scoring with 25.3 points a game as a senior in 1949–50, when he was a consensus All-American. The first draft choice of the Philadelphia Warriors in the NBA, he led the league in scoring his second year, 1951–52, with 25.4 points a game.

After serving in the Marine Corps for two years during the Korean conflict, Arizin returned to the Warriors and led the league for a second time with a 25.6 average in 1956–57. In ten seasons, all with Philadelphia, he averaged 22.8 points. He was the fifth player in NBA history to score more than 10,000 points, finishing his career with 16,266 points and 6,546 rebounds.

At 6-foot-4 and 210 pounds, Arizin was small for a forward, but his quick leap enabled him to get the shot off over bigger defenders. An asthma sufferer with sinus problems, he seemed constantly out of breath on the court, but he said the condition never bothered his endurance.

Arizin was named to the NBA Silver Anniversary team in 1971.

★ Basketball Hall of Fame

Armitage, Norman C. [Norman C. Cohn]

FENCING
b. Jan. 1, 1907, Albany, N.Y.
d. March 14, 1972

Armitage took part in six Olympics, the first in 1928, the last in 1956. He was a member of the three-man color guard that carried the U.S. flag in the 1948 opening ceremonies, and he was the lone flag bearer in 1952 and in 1956. But because fencing is barely publicized in America, he is virtually unknown.

He didn't take up the sport until he was a student at Columbia. In less than three years he won the Intercollegiate Fencing Association sabre championship in 1928. Armitage fenced in the national championships 25 times, finished among the top 3 in sabre 22 times, and won 10 championships, in 1930, from

1934 through 36, from 1939 through 1943, and in 1945.

A chemical engineer and later a patent attorney, Armitage suffered third-degree chemical burns on his right hand and arm in a 1936 accident, and doctors said he would never fence again. Yet he made the Olympic team that year, and he was on the bronze medal sabre team in 1948.

Armour, Tommy (Thomas D.)

GOLF
b. Sept. 24, 1895, Edinburgh, Scotland
d. Sept. 11, 1968

During World War I, Armour was blinded by a head wound but regained the sight in his right eye after a six-month convalescence. He had been a good golfer in his youth, and while recuperating, he decided to try to make a career in the sport.

After winning the French Amateur in 1920, he boarded a ship for the United States and met Walter Hagen, who was returning from the British Open. Hagen got Armour a job as secretary of the Westchester-Biltmore Club.

He became a professional golfer in 1924 and soon had a fine reputation as a teacher. Bobby Jones came to Armour for help with his swing in 1926 and went on to win both the U.S. and British Opens that year.

In 1927, Armour won the U.S. Open, his first major victory. He shot two under par on the last six holes to tie Henry Cooper and then beat Cooper in a playoff, 76 to 79. He also won the Canadian Open and four other tournaments. He won four more tournaments in 1928, and he made a 72-hole record of 273 in winning the 1929 Western Open.

Armour reached the finals of the PGA tournament twice, beating Gene Sarazen at Sarazen's home course in 1930 but losing to Johnny Revolta in 1935. He completed his sweep of the three most important tournaments open to professionals at the time by winning the 1931 British Open.

After 1935, Armour retired from major competition but continued teaching.

Among his pupils were Lawson Little and Babe Didrikson Zaharias. He charged $50 a lesson, sitting under a beach umbrella at the Boca Raton Club in Florida and sipping a drink while he watched his pupil hit 20 balls. After Armour delivered an often caustic analysis of the swing, the pupil would hit another 20 balls and listen to another analysis.

Armour played exhibitions for the Red Cross, the USO, and other causes during World War II. In 1952, he and Herb Graffis wrote *How to Play Your Best Golf All the Time,* which became the best-selling golf instruction book in history.

★ PGA Hall of Fame; World Golf Hall of Fame

Armstrong, Debbie (Deborah)

SKIING
b. Dec. 6, 1963, Salem, Oreg.

The bouncy, effervescent Armstrong was a surprise winner in the women's giant slalom at the 1984 Winter Olympics. A fine athlete, she began skiing at the age of three and starred in basketball and soccer in high school. After graduating in 1980, she concentrated on ski racing.

She was named to the U.S. downhill team to take part in international competition, but a broken leg in training ended her season. Armstrong was relatively little known going into the Olympics, although she finished second in the U.S. national combined in 1983. Her best World Cup finish was a third place in a supergiant slalom early in 1984.

At the Olympics, Armstrong had the second fastest time in the first run, .1 second behind teammate Christin Cooper. As the second and final run approached, Cooper recalled, Armstrong "was so hyped up, it was really funny. She kept coming up to me and bouncing all over and telling me to have a good time. She would say, 'I'm just going to have fun out there, just have fun, have fun!'"

Armstrong had only the fourth best time in the second run, but Cooper's run was fifth best, allowing Armstrong to win the gold. Asked by a sportswriter what she'd had to sacrifice to become a champion, she replied, "Nothing. Skiing is my life. That's what I love to do. It's fun."

The national giant slalom champion in 1987, Armstrong was also a member of the 1988 Olympic ski team.

Armstrong, Henry [Henry Jackson, Jr.]

BOXING
b. Dec. 12, 1912, Columbus, Miss. d. Oct. 22, 1988

As an amateur, originally fighting under the name Melody Jackson, Armstrong won 58 of 62 bouts. His professional career got off to a bad start on July 27, 1931, when he was knocked out by Al Iovino in the 3rd round at Braddock, Pennsylvania. However, he went on to become the first fighter to hold three world championships simultaneously.

An unrelenting attacker, Armstrong was known variously as "Perpetual Motion," "Homicide Hank," the "Human Buzzsaw," and "Hurricane Henry." He won the world featherweight title by knocking out Petey Sarron in the 6th round on October 29, 1937. Then he stepped all the way up to the welterweight division and won that championship with a 15-round decision over Barney Ross on May 31, 1938.

Less than three months later, Armstrong dropped down to win the lightweight championship with a hard-fought, controversial 15-round decision over Lou Ambers on August 17.

Armstrong never defended the featherweight championship, and surrendered it late in 1938 because he couldn't make the weight. He lost the lightweight title to Ambers on a 15-round decision on August 22, 1939. Armstrong went for a fourth championship, in the middleweight class, against Ceferino Garcia on March 1, 1940, but Garcia retained his title in a 10-round draw.

After 20 successful defenses, Armstrong lost the welterweight championship to Fritzie Zivic on a 15-round decision on October 4, 1940. Their rematch at Madison Square Garden on January 17, 1941, drew 23,190 fans, the largest crowd ever to watch an indoor sporting event at the time. Zivic knocked out Armstrong in the 12th round.

Armstrong continued fighting into early 1945 before retiring. He later became a Baptist minister and worked with young men in Los Angeles and St. Louis.

In 174 professional fights, Armstrong had 145 victories, 98 by knockout. He lost 20, 2 by knockout, and had 8 draws and 1 no-decision.

★ International Boxing Hall of Fame

Ashburn, Richie (Don Richie)

BASEBALL
b. March 19, 1927, Tilden, Nebr.

When Ashburn joined the NL's Philadelphia Phillies in 1948, Harry "The Hat" Walker, who had won the 1947 batting championship, was the starting center fielder. But Ashburn took over the job and held it for 12 years.

The speedy Ashburn batted .333, led the league in stolen bases with 32, and was named rookie of the year. An outstanding leadoff man, Ashburn lacked power, but he had an extremely good batting eye, enabling him to earn a lot of walks, and he beat out many infield hits, leading one sportswriter to comment, "He's no .300 hitter. He hits .100 and runs .200."

Ashburn hit over .300 in 9 of his 15 major league seasons and led the league with .338 in 1955 and .350 in 1958. He was also the league leader in hits with 221 in 1951, 205 in 1953, and 215 in 1958; in triples with 14 in 1950 and 13 in 1958; and in walks with 125 in 1954, 94 in 1957, 97 in 1958, and 116 in 1960. An outstanding defensive center fielder, Ashburn had more than 500 putouts in four different seasons, and he tied Max Carey's record by leading in putouts and total chances nine times.

Ashburn was traded to the Chicago Cubs after the 1959 season, and in 1962 he became one of the original members of the New York Mets. He batted .308 and was selected to play in the all-star game for the fifth time. He might have had a few years left, but he retired after that season, in part because of frustration with his inept teammates.

In 2,189 games, Ashburn had 2,574 hits, 1,322 runs scored, 234 stolen bases, and a .308 batting average.

Ashe, Arthur R., Jr.

TENNIS
b. July 10, 1942, Richmond, Va.
d. Feb. 6, 1993

Ashe began playing tennis seriously when he was ten, under the tutelage of Dr. R. Walter Johnson, a Charlottesville physician who had helped make Althea Gibson the first black tennis champion.

After his junior year in high school, he moved to St. Louis, where he could face stiffer competition. Ashe won four straight American Tennis Association championships, from 1960 through 1963, and in 1965 he was the NCAA tennis champion, representing UCLA.

While serving in the Army in 1968, Ashe became the first black male to win a national title, taking both the first U.S. Open and the U.S. amateur championship. He turned professional after leaving the Army in 1969 and won the 1970 Australian Open. As the culmination of his career, he won the Wimbledon singles title in 1975, the first black male to do so.

Slender, at 6-foot-1 and only 158 pounds, Ashe was a graceful yet powerful player who hit hard top-spin ground strokes and had an excellent first serve. He was ranked among the top ten players in the U.S. 15 times, and 11 times he was in the top 3. In 304 singles tournaments, Ashe had 52 victories and was the runner-up 42 times.

A heart attack forced his retirement in 1980. "It's very hard for an athlete to leave center stage," he said. "What do you replace it with?"

Ashe found a great deal to replace it with. Criticized early in his career for not speaking out strongly on racial issues, he became a champion of human rights and spent a great deal of time warning young blacks that education, not sports, should be paramount. He also wrote a newspaper column for the *Washington Post*, and in 1988 he published a three-volume history of blacks in sports, *A Hard Road to Glory*.

In 1988, he learned that he had contracted the HIV virus from a transfusion during heart bypass surgery in 1983. The news became public in 1992. After his initial anger at the disclosure, Ashe became involved in the anti-AIDS cause, establishing the Arthur Ashe Foundation for the Defeat of AIDS and making many appearances on its behalf.

He died of pneumonia, a complication of AIDS. His last newspaper column, which appeared the day after his death, urged civil rights leaders to work for change in college and professional sports.

★ International Tennis Hall of Fame

Ashenfelter, Horace III ("Nip")

TRACK AND FIELD
b. Jan. 23, 1923, Collegeville, Pa.

Ashenfelter was one of America's premier distance runners during the 1950s, winning 17 national championships at a variety of distances. But his most remarkable achievement was winning the gold medal in the 1952 Olympic 3,000-meter steeplechase.

An FBI agent, Ashenfelter trained for the Olympics at night, using park benches for hurdles. In his first heat at the U.S. trials, he ran an American record 9:06.4, and he lowered that by more than 15 seconds, to 8:51.0, in the finals.

Vladimir Kazantsev of the Soviet Union was favored to win the Olympic event, and Ashenfelter wasn't given much of a chance for any kind of medal. However, he and Kazantsev took the lead on the third lap and broke away from the field. Rounding the last turn, the Russian edged ahead, but he stumbled slightly on the last water jump. Ashenfelter took it cleanly and pulled away to win by nearly 30 yards.

Ashenfelter was the first American since James Lightbody in 1904 to win the Olympic steeplechase. His time was another American record, 8:45.4. In less than a month, Ashenfelter had improved his personal best by more than 30 seconds. He won the 1952 Sullivan Award as the nation's outstanding amateur athlete.

An all-around athlete in high school, Ashenfelter served in World War II and then attended Penn State. He won the NCAA 2-mile run in 1949, the IC4A outdoor 2-mile in 1948 and 1949, and the IC4A indoor 2-mile in 1948. He was also AAU national champion in cross-country, 1951, 1955, and 1956; the steeplechase, 1951, 1953, and 1956; the 3-mile run, 1954 and 1955; the 6-mile, 1950; and the indoor 3-mile, 1952 through 1956.

★ National Track & Field Hall of Fame

Ashford, Evelyn (Mrs. Washington)
TRACK AND FIELD
b. April 15, 1957, Shreveport, La.

Despite injuries and Olympic disappointments, Ashford had one of the longest and most successful careers of any sprinter in history. A member of five U.S. Olympic teams, she won a total of nine medals, including four golds, three of them as a member of sprint relay teams.

Ashford was the only girl on the boys' high school track team in Roseville, California, and she co-captained the team in her senior year. One of the first women to receive an athletic scholarship from UCLA, she finished fifth in the 100-meter dash at the 1976 Olympics the summer after her freshman year.

She won AIAW championships in the 100-meter and 200-meter dashes and the 800-meter relay in 1977, repeated in the 200-meter and finished second in the 100-meter in 1978, then left school to train full-time for the 1980 Olympics.

Ashford won both short sprints in the 1979 World Cup championships, beating two East German world record holders, Marlies Gohr in the 100-meter and Marita Koch in the 200-meter. But like many American athletes, she was bitterly disappointed by the U.S. boycott of the 1980 Moscow Olympics.

So she set her sights on the 1984 Olympics. She repeated her double sprint victories in the 1981 World Cup championships. However, after winning two previous heats in the 100-meter

dash at the 1983 world championships, Ashford pulled her right hamstring muscle and fell in the finals.

The hamstring continued to bother her in 1984, as she went into the Olympics. She withdrew from the 200-meter in order to protect her injured leg and concentrate on the 100, where she edged Heike Drechsler of East Germany to win the gold medal she had sought for so long.

Ashford was known as being reserved and unemotional, but she was in tears through her victory lap and during the medal ceremony. She said afterward, "When I caught my first glimpse of the gold medal while I waited on the victory stand, I was emotionally overcome. I couldn't believe it was over. I couldn't stop crying."

That was the culmination of her career, but not nearly the end. Ashford was also on the gold medal 4 x 100-meter relay team, and two weeks later, she ran a world record 10.76 in the 100-meter in Zurich.

Married to Herbert Washington, Ashford took 1985 off to have a daughter, Raina. She came back to win the 100-meter at the Goodwill Games.

The troublesome hamstring kept Ashford out for much of the 1987 season. But she was on the U.S. Olympic team once again in 1988, winning a silver medal in the 100-meter and running on the gold medal relay team. And in 1992, considered "the grand old lady of track" at the age of 35, she won her fourth gold medal, again as a runner on the 4 x 100-meter relay team.

Ashworth, Jeanne C.
SPEED SKATING
b. July 1, 1938, Burlington, Vt.

One of the first world-class speed skaters from the United States after World War II, Ashworth won a bronze medal in the 500-meter event at the 1960 Winter Olympics, when she was a physical therapy student at Tufts University. She also finished eighth in both the 1,000- and 3,000-meter races that year, and in 1964 she finished fourth in the 500-meter.

Ashworth was the national outdoor champion in 1961, 1963, and 1967, the indoor champion in 1957, 1959, and 1963. She won the open outdoor title in 1966 and 1967, the open indoor in 1966, and was North American outdoor champion in 1961.

Atkins, Douglas L.

FOOTBALL
b. May 8, 1930, Humboldt, Tenn.

Atkins went to the University of Tennessee on a basketball scholarship and was talked into going out for football by Coach Bob Neyland He was named to some All-American teams as a tackle in 1952.

Drafted in the first round by the NFL's Cleveland Browns in 1953, the 6-foot-8, 275-pound Atkins was moved to defensive end. His combination of size, speed, and agility made him a premier pass rusher. Atkins could overpower blockers who tried to take him on high, and he often leaped over blockers who tried to cut him down. Quarterback Fran Tarkenton once said of him, "If he gets to you, the whole world suddenly starts spinning."

After two seasons with the Browns, Atkins was traded to the Chicago Bears in 1955. He spent eight seasons there, was an All-Pro in 1960 and 1963, and played in eight Pro Bowls. After the 1966 season, Atkins demanded a trade and was sent to the New Orleans Saints, where he finished his career in 1969.
★ College Football Hall of Fame;
  Pro Football Hall of Fame

Atkinson, Juliette P.

TENNIS
b. April 15, 1873, Rahway, N.J.
d. Jan. 12, 1944

Atkinson and her younger sister, Kathleen, taught themselves how to play tennis. Probably the first woman to come to the net and volley, she won her first national championships in 1894, teaming with Helen Hellwig in the women's doubles and with Edwin P. Fischer in the mixed doubles.

In 1895, Atkinson won her first national singles title and also took both

doubles titles again, with the same partners. Bothered by an ankle sprain suffered during a riding accident, she lost to Elisabeth Moore in the 1896 challenge round, but teamed with Moore to win the women's doubles and with Fischer to win a third consecutive mixed doubles title.

Until 1902, women played the best-of-five format in the final round, and Atkinson never lost a five-set match, beating Moore in five sets in 1897 and Marion Jones in 1898. Her 6–3, 5–7, 6–4, 2–6, 7–5 win over Jones is still the longest match ever played in the women's national singles. The Atkinson sisters won the women's doubles in 1897 and 1898.

Atkinson didn't play in the nationals again until 1901, when she lost in the singles finals but won the women's doubles championship with Myrtle McAteer. In 1902, in her final appearance, she lost in the singles finals once more but won the women's doubles with Jones.
★ International Tennis Hall of Fame

Atkinson, Ted (Theodore F.)

HORSE RACING
b. Sept. 18, 1911, Toronto, Ont.

Atkinson was known both as a tough, competitive jockey and as an intelligent, articulate person with a lot of class. Fellow jockeys called him "the Professor." Sportswriter Joe Palmer wrote of him, "While he cannot come in ahead of the horse, he can be depended upon to get as much out of his mounts as heredity and the trainer have put in."

He grew up in upstate New York and began racing at 21, a rather late age. Atkinson's best years were 1944 and 1946. He led in wins and purses both years, with 287 victories and $899,101 in 1944, 233 victories and $1,036,825 in 1946, when he became the first jockey to surpass $1 million in a year.

In 1949, Atkinson rode Capot to a Preakness win in a record time of 1:56.0, and he also won the Belmont with Capot.

A back injury forced him to retire in 1959. He ranks 24th in races won with

3,795 in 23,661 starts. His horses earned $17,449,360.

★ National Horse Racing Hall of Fame

Attell, Abe (Abraham W.) [Albert Knoehr]

BOXING
b. Feb. 22, 1884, San Francisco, Calif.
d. Feb. 6, 1970

Like many boxers of his time, Attell learned to fight on the streets. In his case, he was protecting himself from Irish-American kids who didn't like having the son of Jewish immigrants living in the neighborhood. And like many such fighters, he learned to punch first — but then he learned to box from experts such as George Dixon.

At 5-foot-4, Attell was a natural featherweight, but he fought and beat many of the best lightweights around as well as several welterweights who outweighed him by 25 pounds or more.

His first professional fight was in 1900. He claimed the vacant featherweight championship after beating former champion George Dixon in a 15-round decision on October 28, 1901. Tommy Sullivan knocked Attell out in five rounds on October 13, 1904, and claimed the title, but his claim wasn't recognized because he was over the weight limit.

Three of Attell's title defenses were classic fights against English boxers, none of which resulted in a decision. He fought a 25-round draw and a 23-round draw against Owen Moran in 1908, and on February 19, 1909, he and English lightweight champion Jem Driscoll fought a 10-round no-decision contest that Nat Fleischer of *Ring* magazine called "one of the best exhibitions of ring science ever seen in New York."

Attell lost the title on a 20-round decision to Johnny Kilbane on February 22, 1912. He continued fighting into 1915. An attempted comeback ended abruptly when he was knocked out by Phil Virgets in the 4th round on January 8, 1917. Two years later, Attell became involved in baseball's "Black Sox Scandal" as the representative of gambler Arnold

Rothstein. It was Attell who gave $10,000 to several Chicago White Sox players who had agreed to throw the World Series with Cincinnati. When the scandal broke in 1920, Attell went to Canada for a year to avoid being subpoenaed.

Attell won 91 of his 168 fights, 47 by knockout. He lost 10, 3 by knockout, and also had 17 draws and 50 no-decisions.

★ International Boxing Hall of Fame

Auerbach, Red (Arnold)

BASKETBALL
b. Sept. 20, 1917, Brooklyn, N.Y.

A self-described "dictator with compassion," Auerbach once said about coaching, "Strategy is something anyone can learn, but not all coaches take the time to understand a man's personality."

Small but fiercely competitive, Auerbach played basketball at George Washington College and led the team in scoring his senior year with 10.6 points a game. After three years as a high school coach, he served at the Norfolk, Virginia, Naval Air Station during World War II, then became coach of the Washington Capitols of the newly organized Basketball Association of America in 1946.

Auerbach won 123 games and lost 62 in three seasons at Washington, then went to the Tri-Cities Blackhawks for one season. Despite a 29–35 record there, he was offered $10,000 a year to coach the Boston Celtics beginning with the 1950–51 season.

Auerbach believed in a running game. He had turned the Celtics into winners, but he needed someone to get the rebounds to make the running game. The Celtics were unsuccessful in the playoffs until the 1956–57 season, when Bill Russell came along. Auerbach took a bold step by trading two proven veterans, "Easy Ed" Macauley and Cliff Hagan, to the St. Louis Hawks for the rights to Russell, a rookie who had led the University of San Francisco to two straight NCAA championships.

Russell was the final ingredient. Not

only could he get the rebounds to start the fast break, but his shot-blocking ability turned the high-scoring Celtics into a strong defensive team. They won 11 NBA championships in the next 13 seasons. Auerbach coached them to the first nine, including eight in a row, from 1959 through 1966. Then he was replaced by Russell but remained as the team's general manager.

A strong believer in the team concept as opposed to individual stardom, Auerbach was a master at finding veteran players who could fit into that concept. Among those role players who helped the Celtics to championships at one time or another were Paul Silas, Don Nelson, Clyde Lovellette, Willie Naulls, Bailey Howell, and M. L. Carr.

Auerbach retired as general manager in 1984 and became president of the team, still wielding considerable power as an adviser. During his 34 years as general manager, the Celtics won 16 NBA titles. As a coach, he had a record 1,037 victories against 548 losses.
★ Basketball Hall of Fame

Aulby, Mike (Michael)

BOWLING
b. March 25, 1960, Indianapolis, Ind.

Named bowler of the decade for the 1980s, Aulby won three major tournaments during the period, the PBA National in 1985 and the BPAA U.S. Open and ABC Masters tournaments in 1989. He had previously won the PBA National in 1979.

Aulby was bowler of the year and top money winner in 1985 and 1989, when he set a record with $298,237 in earnings. Through 1994, he had won 22 tour titles and earned $1,404,710, fourth on the all-time list.

Austin, Tracy

TENNIS
b. Dec. 12, 1962, Rolling Hills, Calif.

The winner of a record 25 national junior titles, Austin was a prodigy whose career ended prematurely, prob-ably because she undertook a grueling schedule at an early age.

At 14, she won the first professional event she entered, an Avon Futures tournament in Portland, Oregon. That year, 1977, she became the youngest player ever to enter Wimbledon and the U.S. Open and the youngest to be ranked among the top ten U.S. players.

In 1978, she was ranked among the top ten in the world, and she became the youngest woman ever to represent the U.S. in Wightman and Federation Cup play. Austin was named female athlete of the year by the Associated Press in 1979, when she won the U.S. Open at 16 years and 9 months, another "youngest" record. She had earlier won the Italian Open, breaking Chris Evert's string of 125 consecutive victories on clay courts.

The following year, Austin and her brother John became the only siblings to win the Wimbledon mixed doubles title. But her physical problems began that year with back pain caused by sciatic nerve damage. She couldn't play for eight months, yet she returned to beat Martina Navratilova in the final of the 1981 U.S. Open. After losing the first set 6–1, she won 7–6 tie-breakers in the next two sets and was again named Associated Press female athlete of the year.

Her back began to bother her again late in 1982, and she then suffered a shoulder injury. The accumulating injuries forced her to announce her retirement in June 1983.
★ International Tennis Hall of Fame

Averill, Earl (Howard Earl)

BASEBALL
b. May 21, 1902, Snohomish, Wash.
d. Aug. 16, 1983

Averill became a major league player rather late in life, and his career lasted less than 13 seasons, yet he made the Hall of Fame with a live bat and a good glove.

He played semipro baseball until he was 24, then joined the San Francisco team in the Pacific Coast League. After three good seasons there, the Cleveland Indians bought his contract for $50,000, and he became their starting center fielder in 1929. Averill hit a home run in his first major league at-bat.

A right-handed thrower but left-handed hitter, Averill batted .332 as a rookie and had 388 putouts to lead AL outfielders. On September 17, 1930, he hit four home runs in five times at bat during a doubleheader.

The 5-foot-9½ 172-pound Averill had his most productive seasons in 1931 and 1932. He hit 32 home runs each year, with 140 runs scored and 143 RBI in 1931, 116 scored and 124 RBI in 1932.

After being troubled by a series of injuries in 1935, Averill led the AL in hits with 232 and triples with 15 in 1936, when he batted .378. In eight major league seasons, he had batted over .300 seven times, scored more than 100 runs seven times, and driven in more than 100 runs five times.

Midway through the 1937 season, Averill suffered a brief paralysis of his legs, caused by a congenital spinal problem. He played the entire season, hitting .299 with 21 home runs, and in 1938 he batted .330 but had only 14 home runs. Cleveland traded him to Detroit early in the 1939 season, and he became a part-time player. He finished his major league career by playing eight games with the Boston Braves in 1941.

In 1,668 games, Averill had 2,019 hits for a .318 average, with 401 doubles, 128 triples, and 238 home runs. He scored 1,224 runs and drove in 1,164.

★ Baseball Hall of Fame

★ ★ B ★ ★

Babashoff, Shirley

SWIMMING
b. Jan. 31, 1957, Whittier, Calif.

Because she never won an individual gold medal, Babashoff was considered a failure by some. But she won a total of eight medals at two Olympics and two world championships, captured 27 national championships, set six world records, and was a member of five world record relay teams.

Babashoff entered the 1972 Olympics holding the world record of 2:05.21 in the 200-meter freestyle. She lowered that by nearly a second, swimming 2:04.33 in the final, but Australia's Shane Gould won in 2:03.56. However, Babashoff won a gold on the U.S. 4 x 100-meter relay team and also won a silver medal in the 100-meter freestyle. She beat Gould in that race, which was won by teammate Sandra Neilson.

Her 1976 Olympic experience was similar. She held the world record of 8:39.63 in the 800-meter freestyle, lowered it by more than two seconds to 8:37.59, but lost to Petra Thumer of East Germany, who swam 8:37.14. Babashoff again won a gold for the relay and added silver medals in the 200- and 400-meter freestyles and the 400-meter individual medley.

Babashoff's world championships came in 1975, in the 200- and 400-meter freestyle.

★ Olympic Hall of Fame

Bacallao, Pedro A.

SQUASH TENNIS
b. 1937, Havana, Cuba

The short, pudgy Bacallao looked little like an athlete, yet for years he dominated the U.S. championship in one of the world's fastest sports, squash tennis.

He learned to play in his native Cuba, where the squash court has three walls rather than four, and he won the Cuban national championship in 1955. Born into a wealthy family, he received a doctorate of law at the University of Havana.

Shortly after Fidel Castro took control of Cuba in 1959, Bacallao came to the U.S. He didn't play squash again until 1965, and then it took him some time to master the four-walled court. Once he did, though, he was virtually unbeatable. Bacallao won the national squash tennis championship nine years in a row, from 1969 through 1977.

He also served as president of the U.S. Squash Tennis Association from 1969 through 1982.

Badger, Sherwin C.

FIGURE SKATING
b. Aug. 29, 1901, Boston, Mass.
d. April 8, 1972

After a successful stint as a singles skater, winning five consecutive U.S. championships from 1920 through 1924, Badger retired for a time and then returned as a pairs skater, teaming with Beatrix Loughran to win national titles from 1930 through 1932. They won the silver medal at the 1932 Winter Olympics.

A banking writer for the *Wall Street Journal* and *Barron's*, Badger was president of the U.S. Figure Skating Association for several years during the 1930s.

Badgro, Red (Morris H.)

FOOTBALL
b. Dec. 1, 1902, Orillia, Wash.

At 78, Badgro was the oldest person ever inducted into the Pro Football Hall of Fame and the man who waited longest for induction after his retirement, 45 years. Red Grange once said of him, "Playing offense and defense equally well, he was one of the best half-dozen ends I ever saw."

Badgro won a total of 12 letters in baseball, basketball, and football at the University of Southern California and was all-conference in both basketball and football in his senior year. After leaving school in 1927, he signed contracts with baseball's St. Louis Browns and the NFL's New York Yankees.

He left football in 1928 to concentrate on baseball and was a part-time outfielder with the Browns in 1929 and 1930. Badgro then returned to football with the New York Giants. He started for them from 1930 through 1935 and finished his career in 1936 with the NFL's Brooklyn Dodgers. He then returned to USC to get the credits he needed to graduate.

An All-Pro in 1931, 1933, and 1934, Badgro tied for the league lead with 16 receptions in 1934. He was the first player to score a touchdown in an NFL championship game, catching a 29-yard pass to give the Giants a 7–6 lead over the Chicago Bears in 1933. However, the Bears went on to win, 23–21.
★ Pro Football Hall of Fame

Baeza, Braulio

HORSE RACING
b. 1940, Panama

Taller than most jockeys at 5-foot-4½, Baeza was dignified and elegant as a person and as a jockey, with a knack for getting the most out of horses without seeming to try. "The horses seem to want to run for him," Eddie Arcaro once said.

Baeza in 1967 became the first jockey to go over $3 million in purses in a year, with $3,088,888 on 256 wins in 1,064 starts. He was also the leading money winner in 1965 with $2,582,701; in 1966 with $2,951,022; in 1968 with $2,835,108; and in 1975 with $3,674,498.

The Eclipse Award winner as the year's outstanding jockey in 1972 and 1975, Baeza won four triple crown races. He rode Sherluck to victory in the 1961 Belmont, won the Kentucky Derby and Belmont on Chateaugay in 1963, and took a third Belmont victory aboard Arts and Letters in 1969.
★ National Horse Racing Hall of Fame

Bailey, Ace (Irvine W.)

HOCKEY
b. July 3, 1903, Bracebridge, Ont.
d. April 1, 1989

An outstanding stick-handler, Bailey scored 193 points in 313 games at left wing for the Toronto Maple Leafs beginning in 1926, and he was the National Hockey League's leading scorer in 1928–29 with 32 points on 22 goals and 10 assists.

On December 12, 1933, Toronto was playing at Boston Garden when Bruins' defenseman Eddie Shore was checked hard. Shore mistakenly thought Bailey had been the culprit, and he retaliated by hitting Bailey from behind, flipping him into the air. Bailey came down on his head. He underwent brain surgery twice for his injury.

To raise money for Bailey and his family, the Maple Leafs played an exhibition game against a team of NHL all-stars on February 12, 1934. Shore was one of the all-stars. He and Bailey met at center ice before the game, shook hands, and then embraced. The game was the forerunner of the annual NHL all-star game.
★ Hockey Hall of Fame

Baker, Cannonball (Erwin G.)

AUTO RACING
b. March 12, 1882, near Lawrenceburg, Ind.
d. May 10, 1960

Baker is the only famous auto racer who never won a major race. His specialty was driving cross-country, usually for a manufacturer who wanted to demonstrate the speed and durability of a new vehicle.

He began as a motorcycle racer for the Indian factory team and won the 10-mile national championship at the new Indianapolis Speedway in 1909. After a 1912 promotional tour through Central America and the Caribbean, he rode an Indian motorcycle across the country, his first such trip.

"Cannonball" became his nickname after he drove a Stutz Bearcat from San Diego to New York in 11 days, 7 hours, and 15 minutes in 1915. He lowered that to 7 days, 11 hours, and 52 minutes in a Cadillac a year later and began promoting his services to manufacturers with the slogan, "No record, no pay."

In addition to cross-country trips, Baker set records on a number of shorter runs: from Detroit to Indianapolis, from Chicago to Indianapolis, and from New York to Chicago. One of his most grueling transcontinental trips was made in 1924, when he became the first person to drive cross-country during the winter. It took 110 hours and 15 minutes through snow, slush, mud, and fog.

When Eddie Rickenbacker started manufacturing cars in the 1920s, he hired Baker as chief test driver. Baker broke his own winter cross-country record with a 71½-hour trip (driving time only). He also drove a Rickenbacker on a "three flag" journey from Vancouver, British Columbia, to Tijuana, Mexico, in 40 hours and 57 minutes.

Baker's fastest official cross-country time was 60 hours, 31 minutes in a Stutz Versaille, though he later did an unofficial 53½-hour drive in a 1933 Graham. His most publicized feat was a race from New York to Chicago in a Franklin Airman Speedster against the famous 20th Century Limited passenger train in 1928. Baker won, averaging 46 mph in a car with a top speed of only 70.

In 1948 Baker set his last record, climbing Mt. Washington, New Hampshire, in 15 minutes, 12.75 seconds in a Nash. That year he was named the first commissioner of NASCAR, mainly for publicity.

Baker, Frank (John Franklin)

BASEBALL
b. March 13, 1886, Trappe, Md.
d. June 28, 1963

Although he hit fewer home runs in his 13 major league seasons than Babe Ruth hit in 1926 and 1927, Baker was one of the premier power hitters during baseball's dead-ball era.

He joined the AL's Philadelphia Athletics in the 1908 season and became the team's starting third baseman the following year, when he hit .308 and led the league with 19 triples.

The left-handed-hitting Baker won the first of his four home run titles in 1911, with 11. He won the nickname "Home Run Baker" by hitting 2 homers in the World Series that year. His .375 average helped lead the As to a six-game victory over the New York Giants.

In 1912, Baker hit .347, again led the league in home runs with 10, and was also the RBI leader with 130. He led the AL in home runs once more with 12 and in RBI with 117 in 1913, when he batted .450 in Philadelphia's five-game World Series victory over the Giants.

Baker and Sam Crawford tied for the home run title with 9 in 1914. When he failed to get a raise, Baker sat out the 1915 season and was then sold to the New York Yankees. After his wife's death, Baker missed the 1920 season and finished his career with the Yankees in 1921 and 1922.

In 1,575 major league games, Baker had a .305 average, with 315 doubles, 103 triples, 96 home runs, and 987 RBI.
★ Baseball Hall of Fame

Baker, Hobey (Hobart A. H.)

HOCKEY
b. Jan. 1892, Wissahickon, Pa.
d. Dec. 21, 1918

Baker was a rover, the seventh player in the days of seven-man hockey. He also took part in football, golf, swimming, and track at Princeton, captaining the football team in 1913, when he was named a third-team All-American halfback by Walter Camp. He had an 85-yard punt return for a touchdown that year and kicked a 44-yard field goal to give Princeton a 3–3 tie against Yale.

But hockey was easily his best sport. The Princeton team was known as "Baker and six other players" during his tenure. After graduating in 1914, he played for the St. Nicholas Arena amateur team in New York. In 1915 St. Nicholas was chosen to play against defending champion Montreal for the Ross Cup, a rare honor for an American team. Baker had 3 goals and 2 assists in the first game, a 6–2 victory. The teams tied at 2–2 in the second game, and Montreal retained the cup by winning the third game, 2–1.

A Montreal sportswriter wrote after the series, "A few minutes of Baker on the ice convinced the most skeptical. He could catch a place, and a star's place, on any of our professional teams."

Baker was one of the first pilots sent overseas when the United States entered World War I. After the war ended, he tested a plane that was having carburetor trouble. It crashed, and he died in an ambulance en route to the hospital.

★ Hockey Hall of Fame; U.S. Hockey Hall of Fame

Baker, Terry W.

BASKETBALL, FOOTBALL
b. May 5, 1941, Pine River, Minn.

The only Heisman Trophy winner ever to play in the NCAA basketball tournament, Baker starred as a football quarterback and basketball guard at Oregon State after having been a high school All-American in both sports. He went to the school on a basketball scholarship and also became a starter in football during his sophomore season.

As a senior in 1962, Baker led the nation in total offense with 2,276 yards, was a consensus All-American, and won both the Heisman and Maxwell Trophies as the season's outstanding college player. He averaged more than 10 points a game in the 1961–62 and 1962–63 basketball seasons, helping to lead Oregon State into the NCAA tournament both years.

The first player chosen in the 1963

NFL draft, Baker played with the Los Angeles Rams for three seasons but never became a starter. He retired after the 1965 season to earn a law degree.

★ College Football Hall of Fame

Baldwin, Ralph N.

HARNESS RACING
b. Feb. 25, 1916, Lloydminster, Sask.
d. Sept. 26, 1982

A long-time trainer and driver for Castleton Farms, Baldwin was best known for his success with Speedy Scot, Harness Horse of the Year in 1963. Speedy Scot not only took the trotting triple crown with victories in the Hambletonian, Kentucky Futurity, and Yonkers Futurity, he also won the Dexter Cup.

Speedy Scot won 13 of 15 heats that year. One loss came when he threw a shoe and broke stride. The other was in the first heat of the Hambletonian, and it took a world record 1:57⅗ by Florlis to do it. But Baldwin drove Speedy Scot to victories in the next two heats, and later that year they also broke Florlis's record with a 1:56⅘ at Lexington.

Baldwin was convinced that horses know when race day has arrived. On the morning of a race, he had his horses walked to calm them down, and sometimes even jogged them to make them think it was an ordinary day of training.

Ballard, Del, Jr.

BOWLING
b. July 1, 1963, Richardson, Tex.

Ballard made his debut on the PBA tour in 1982, when he was only 19, but he didn't get his first victory until 1987. It was a big one, the $100,000 U.S. Open championship. Later that year he won the Brunswick Memorial World Open.

In 1988 Ballard won his second major title, the ABC Masters. He drew media attention when he admitted, early in 1989, that he had suffered from a drinking problem that hurt his play during his early years on the tour, and was ostracized by some older players for the admission, though others applauded him for it.

Ballard won the Firestone Tournament of Champions in 1989 and took the U.S. Open for a second time in 1993. Through the 1994 PBA season, he had 12 career victories and nearly $1 million in earnings.

Ballesteros, Severino

GOLF
b. April 9, 1957, Pedreña, Spain

As a young caddie in Spain, Ballesteros taught himself to play golf, using a single iron that had been given to him. Because caddies weren't supposed to use the course, he had to sneak in his practice time, often after dusk.

He began playing professionally in 1974 and came to prominence in 1976, when he tied Jack Nicklaus for second place in the British Open. After a stint in the Spanish Air Force, Ballesteros became the top money winner on the European tour in 1978, collecting more than $800,000.

Ballesteros attracted such a following in a few U.S. tournaments that he was offered a free card to play on the PGA tour, but he declined because he wanted to maintain his home base in Spain, and felt the rigors of frequent air travel would hurt his game.

In 1979, Ballesteros won the British Open, becoming the youngest winner since Tom Morris, Jr., in 1868. He won the tournament again in 1984 and 1988, tying him with seven other golfers, including Bobby Jones, Jack Nicklaus, and Gary Player, for fourth on the all-time victory list in that event.

Ballesteros made his mark on American television in 1980, when he won his first Masters championship. He had a 9-stroke lead after shooting 66, 69, and 68 on the first three rounds and a 33 on the front nine in the final round. His lead suddenly shrank to 4 shots with five holes to play after he double-bogeyed the 12th hole and bogeyed the 13th, but he pulled himself together and finished strongly to claim the title.

At the 1983 Masters, Ballesteros trailed by a stroke after the first three rounds. He then took the lead with a brilliant stretch of golf, going birdie, eagle, par, and birdie on the first four holes of the final round and finishing solidly once again for another four-shot victory.

Through 1993, Ballesteros had won 68 tournaments on five continents. He led the European tour in money won from 1976 through 1978, and in 1986, 1988, and 1991.

The 6-foot, 180-pound Ballesteros can hit the ball a long way, but his drives are often erratic. He makes up for that with an aggressive style of play out of bunkers and rough and, as *Sports Illustrated* described it, "a magical short game to conjure his way out of trouble."

Banach, Lou (Ludwig)

WRESTLING
b. Feb. 6, 1960, Newton, N.J.

At the University of Iowa, Banach had a 92–14–3 record as a heavyweight wrestler, winning NCAA championships in 1981 and 1983. He won the gold medal in the light-heavyweight class at the 1984 Olympics, and his twin brother, Ed, won the 198-pound division.

Banach trained for the Olympics while serving in the Army and as assistant wrestling coach at the U.S. Military Academy. He later conducted wrestling clinics and studied for a master's degree at Penn State University, where he was a graduate assistant coach.

Bancroft, David E.

BASEBALL
b. April 20, 1892, Sioux City, Iowa
d. Oct. 9, 1972

One of baseball's first switch hitters, Bancroft won the nickname "Beauty" during his minor league days because of his habit of saying "Beauty" if a pitch went past him for a called third strike.

He arrived in the major leagues as the starting shortstop for the NL's Philadelphia Phillies in 1915. Though not exceptionally fast, Bancroft was very quick and had great lateral range. He often led the league in both chances and errors.

During the 1920 season, Bancroft was traded to the New York Giants, where he became a favorite of manager John

McGraw because he was both crafty and fiery. McGraw appointed Bancroft team captain and batted him second.

His highest average with Philadelphia had been .273, but Bancroft hit .318, .321, and .304 in his three full seasons in New York, and in 1922 he set a record with 984 chances in the field. The Giants won pennants all three of those years.

In 1924, Bancroft became playing manager of the Boston Braves. An appendectomy limited him to just 79 games that season. He batted .319 in 1925 and .311 in 1926, then slumped to .243 and was released.

After two seasons as a player and unofficial assistant manager of the Brooklyn NL team, Bancroft returned to the Giants as a player-coach in 1930. He appeared in only 10 games that season before retiring as a player. Bancroft coached with the Giants for two more years and later was a minor league manager.

In 1,913 games, Bancroft batted .279 and scored 1,048 runs. He led NL shortstops in fielding percentage in 1920 and 1925.

★ Baseball Hall of Fame

Banks, Ernie (Ernest)

BASEBALL
b. Jan. 31, 1931, Dallas, Tex.

Banks was spotted by major league scouts while playing for the Kansas City Monarchs in the Negro American League in 1950. After spending two years in the Army, he was sold to the Chicago Cubs for $10,000, and he joined the team at the end of the 1953 season without ever playing in the minor leagues.

The 6-foot-1, 180-pound Banks set a record by playing in 424 consecutive games from the start of his career with the Cubs. After batting .275 with 19 home runs in 1954, his first full season, he hit 44 home runs in 1955, a record for shortstops. He broke that with a league-leading 47 home runs in 1958, when he also led the league with 129 RBI and a .614 slugging percentage.

Banks was named the NL's most valuable player in 1958 and in 1959, when he batted .304 with 45 home runs and 143 RBI. He also excelled at shortstop, leading the league in fielding percentage three times in eight seasons, including a record .985 in 1959.

He led the league in home runs for the second time with 41 in 1960. The following season, the Cubs moved Banks to left field and then to first base, where he spent the rest of his career. After initial problems making the transition, he became a good fielder at that position.

His offensive numbers were not as spectacular from 1961 on, though he hit more than 30 home runs twice and drove in more than 100 three times in the next ten seasons. Banks became a part-time player in 1970 and retired after appearing in just 39 games in 1971.

The smiling, enthusiastic Banks was nicknamed "Mr. Cub," and in 1969 he was voted the team's best player ever by Chicago fans. An 11-time All-Star, he was fond of saying, "It's a great day for baseball. Let's play two today."

In 2,528 games, Banks had 2,583 hits, including 407 doubles, 90 triples, and 512 home runs. He drove in 1,636 runs and scored 1,305.

★ Baseball Hall of Fame

Banks, Willie (William A. III)

TRACK AND FIELD
b. March 11, 1956, Travis AFB, Calif.

As a triple jumper at UCLA, Banks failed to capture a major title, though he finished second in the NCAA outdoor championships in 1977 and 1978. He suffered severe muscle spasms in his lower back during the 1978 AAU national championships and decided to retire.

Within a short time, Banks realized he missed the sport and began training again while attending law school. He won the national outdoor championship in his event in 1980, 1981, 1983, and 1985. Banks set a U.S. record of 57 feet, 7½ inches at the 1981 meet and a world record of 58 feet, 11½ inches in 1985, when he also won the World Cup championship and was named athlete of the year by *Track and Field News.*

Barkley, Charles W.

BASKETBALL
b. Feb. 20, 1963, Leeds, Ala.

Controversy has often obscured Barkley's formidable basketball skills, but he finally won the NBA's most valuable player award for his performance during the 1992–93 season.

At Auburn University, Barkley often ballooned to over 300 pounds, and he was nicknamed the "Round Mound of Rebound." The 6-foot-6 Barkley was not an overpowering scorer in college, averaging 14.1 points and nearly 10 rebounds a game in three seasons as a starter.

He entered the NBA draft in 1984, after his junior season, and was chosen by the Philadelphia 76ers in the first round as the fifth pick overall. Barkley made the league's all-rookie team, averaging 14.0 points a game.

Often criticized by teammates during his early years because of inconsistent play and temper tantrums, Barkley came into his own during the 1987–88 season, when he kept his weight consistently at 252 pounds, averaged 28.3 points a game, and was named to the All-NBA team for the first of four consecutive years.

In 1991–92, Barkley increasingly criticized teammates and Philadelphia ownership, and he had his poorest season since 1986–87, though he still averaged 23.1 points a game and made second-team All-NBA.

After playing for the U.S. "Dream Team" that won the 1992 Olympic gold medal, Barkley was sent to the Phoenix Suns for three players. With a contending team, he returned to his previous form, averaging 25.6 points a game and winning the MVP award as the Suns went to the NBA finals, only to lose to the Chicago Bulls.

A talker who enjoys interacting with fans, whether friends or foes, Barkley was intensely criticized in March 1991, when he apparently spat at a child sitting at courtside. He explained afterward that he'd meant to hit a fan who was taunting him with racial epithets.

Barkley's play and outspokenness made him one of the most visible athletes of the early 1990s, second perhaps only to Michael Jordan, and won him many commercial endorsements. Even one of his commercials sparked controversy: in a 1993 Nike television spot, he solemnly warned the audience, "I am not a role model. . . parents should be role models."

During a preseason drill in October 1993, Barkley collapsed when his legs went numb, stirring fears because of the death earlier that year of Boston's Reggie Lewis. Tests revealed a back injury that didn't appear to be serious, but Barkley announced a few days later that he would retire after the 1993–94 season.

Through 1993–94, Barkley had scored 17,530 points in 751 games, a 23.3 average. He also had 8,753 rebounds, 2,957 assists, 1,227 steals, and 717 blocked shots. He returned to Phoenix for the 1994-95 season.

Barlow, Babe (Thomas B.)

BASKETBALL
b. July 9, 1896, Trenton, N.J.
d. Sept. 26, 1983

When Barlow's team was scheduled to play in Madison Square Garden during the late 1920s, Tex Rickard, the Garden owner, put up a huge photo of him with the headline CAVEMAN BARLOW HERE TONIGHT! Barlow complained, and Rickard gave him $75 for the use of his photo.

At 6-foot-1 and 200 pounds, Barlow was a big man for his era, and he was a tough, aggressive player who often got involved in fights. He began his professional career in 1912 with the Trenton Tigers and, like most pro stars at the time, also played for several other teams in various leagues until 1921, when he signed with Eddie Gottlieb's SPHAs, who later became the Philadelphia Warriors. Barlow remained with the Warriors through 1927, then returned to the Tigers. He retired in 1932.

★ Basketball Hall of Fame

Barnes, Long Jim (James M.)

GOLF
b. 1887, Lelant, Cornwall, England
d. May 24, 1966

Barnes came to the United States to seek his golfing fortune in 1906, after working as a caddie and clubmaker in England. His first victory didn't come until 1913, in the Pacific-Northwest Open. He also tied for fourth in the U.S. Open that year.

The first PGA championship was held October 10–16, 1916, in Bronxville, New York. It was a match-play tournament with 31 entrants. Barnes won the $500 prize by beating Jock Hutchison, Sr., one-up in the final match. Because of World War I, the second PGA wasn't held until 1919, when Barnes won again, beating Fred McLeod.

He won the U.S. Open in 1921, shooting a 289 to beat Walter Hagen and Fred McLeod by nine strokes. In 1925, he won the British Open, becoming the first golfer to win the three major professional championships of the era. Barnes was also runner-up in the PGA championship in 1921 and 1924. His last victory was in the 1937 Long Island Open, when he was 50 years old.

★ PGA Hall of Fame; World Golf Hall of Fame

Barney, Lemuel J., Jr.

FOOTBALL
b. Sept. 8, 1945, Gulfport, Miss.

Barney had 26 interceptions in three seasons at Jackson State University and also did the team's punting. He joined the Detroit Lions in 1967 and quickly became one of the NFL's top defensive backs. The 6-foot-2, 190-pound Barney had sprinter speed and was a threat to score whenever he touched the ball.

In his first season, he ran back 3 of his league-leading 10 interceptions for touchdowns and was selected the NFL's defensive rookie of the year. Barney was named to the All-Pro team in 1968, 1969, and 1972 and played in 10 Pro Bowls.

He retired after the 1977 season. During his career, Barney intercepted 56 passes and returned them for 1,077 yards, an average of 19.2, and scored 8 touchdowns; he returned 143 punts for 1,312 yards, a 9.2 average, and 2 touchdowns; and he had 50 kickoff returns for 1,274 yards, a 25.5 average, and 1 touchdown. Barney also punted 113 times for a 35.5-yard average.

★ Pro Football Hall of Fame

Barone, Marian E. (Twining)

GYMNASTICS, TRACK AND FIELD
b. March 18, 1924, Philadelphia, Pa.

One of a very few athletes to win a national title in more than one sport, Marian Twining won the basketball throw at the national indoor track and field championship in 1941. The meet wasn't held for the next two years because of World War II, but she won the event at the next two championships, in 1945 and 1946. In 1951, as Mrs. Barone, she won the basketball throw for the fourth time.

She also won national gymnastic championships in the uneven parallel bars in 1945 and 1951 and in the vault in 1950. She tied with Clara M. Schroth for the vault championship in 1945, and she was a member of the U.S. women's Olympic gymnastics team that won a bronze medal in 1948.

Barrasso, Tom (Thomas)

HOCKEY
b. March 31, 1965, Boston, Mass.

Barrasso joined the NHL's Buffalo Sabres as a first-round draft choice in 1983. He won the Vezina Trophy as the league's best goaltender with a 2.84 goals-against average and was also the Calder Trophy winner as the league's rookie of the year. He was the third player in history to win both awards in the same year.

Although he was sent to the minors for five games after a slow start in the 1984–85 season, Barrasso led the league with a 2.66 average and 5 shutouts.

After three mediocre seasons, Barrasso was traded to the Pittsburgh Penguins early in the 1988–89 season. He has played on two Stanley Cup champions, in 1991 and 1992, and he tied the

NHL record for playoff wins with 16 in 1991.

Through the 1993–94 season, Barrasso had played in 546 NHL games, giving up 1,794 goals, a 3.42 average, and he had 21 career shutouts. He had a 3.10 goals-against average and 4 shutouts in 82 playoff games.

Barrett, Charles

FOOTBALL
b. Nov 3, 1893, Bellevue, Pa.
d. May 21, 1924

An All-American quarterback at Cornell in 1915, when he captained an unbeaten team, Barrett was a triple threat as a runner, passer, and kicker. As late as 1954, he was on Grantland Rice's all-time All-American team. Rice wrote of him, "He was a brilliant, hard-running back who put everything he had into every play."

Barrett died at 31 as an aftermath of wounds received during World War I. Former University of Pennsylvania players who had competed against him erected a tablet in his memory at Franklin Field.

★ College Football Hall of Fame

Barrow, Edward G.

BASEBALL
b. May 10, 1868, near Springfield, Ill.
d. Dec. 15, 1953

Baseball's first real general manager, Barrow was the man behind the New York Yankee dynasties of the 1920s and 1930s. He became involved with organized baseball in 1894 as the partner of Harry Stevens, who operated the concessions for the Pittsburgh team in the National League.

Barrow then served as a minor league manager, owner, and executive, while also promoting boxing matches, before becoming manager of the Detroit Tigers in 1903. He left that job midway through the 1904 season and became a minor league manager once more, then spent three years in the hotel business.

In 1910, Barrow returned to baseball as a manager in Montreal, and he was named president of the Eastern League in 1912. The Boston Red Sox hired him as manager in 1918, and Barrow guided them to the world championship that year, aided by a young left-handed pitcher named Babe Ruth.

The Red Sox slipped to sixth place in 1919 and finished fifth in 1920, when Ruth was sold to the Yankees. After that season, Barrow became the Yankees' business manager, but he was given control of all baseball operations, which included the job of signing and trading players. Within a short time his title was general manager.

In Barrow's first eight years with the Yankees, they won six pennants. Barrow established a network of scouts to seek out talent all over the country, and in 1932 he began to put together an extensive system of minor league farm teams. The Yankees won four more pennants during the 1930s, and Barrow was named team president in 1939. After four more pennants, the Yankees came under new ownership in 1945. Barrow resigned two years later after clashes with the new owners, but they honored him with an "Ed Barrow Day" on May 13, 1950.

★ Baseball Hall of Fame

Barry, Rick (Richard F. III)

BASKETBALL
b. March 28, 1944, Elizabeth, N.J.

A unanimous choice as an All-American forward at the University of Miami in 1965, Barry led the nation in scoring with an average of 37.4 points per game, and then married the daughter of his college coach, Bruce Hale.

The 6-foot-7, 215-pound Barry joined the NBA's San Francisco Warriors and was named 1966 rookie of the year after averaging 25.7 points per game. The following season, he led the league in scoring with 35.6 points per game.

In 1967, Barry signed a five-year contract with the Oakland Oaks of the new American Basketball Association. His father-in-law had become general manager of the Oakland team. Barry still had a year left on his contract with San Francisco, and a lawsuit by that team kept him out of basketball for a season.

Barry joined Oakland in 1968, but a knee injury limited him to only 35 games. However, he averaged 34.0 points to lead the league. When the Oaks became the Washington Capitals for the 1968–69 season, Barry signed once more with the San Francisco Warriors. Another lawsuit forced him to remain with Washington.

He led the Capitals into the ABA playoffs by averaging 27.7 points a game, leading the league with an .864 free throw percentage. When the team moved to Virginia in 1970, Barry refused to go and was sent to the New York Nets for $200,000 and a first-round draft choice.

After two seasons with the Nets, Barry's ABA contract had expired and a federal court ruled that he would now have to honor the contract he'd signed with the San Francisco Warriors four years before. Barry was happy to do so; in fact, he signed a new six-year contract with San Francisco, and he was named most valuable player in the 1975 playoffs, when the Warriors won the NBA championship.

Barry signed as a free agent with the NBA's Houston Rockets in 1978 and finished his career there in 1979–80. Although best known for his shooting ability, he was also an outstanding passer and a fine defender who led the NBA in steals with 228 in 1974–75. The last player to shoot free throws underhand, he led the ABA in free throw percentage three times and was the best in the NBA four times.

In 1,020 regular season games, Barry scored 25,279 points, a 27.8 average. He also had 5,168 rebounds, 4,017 assists, and 1,104 steals.
★ Basketball Hall of Fame

Barry, Sam (Justin M.)

BASKETBALL
b. Dec. 17, 1892, Aberdeen, S.Dak. d. Sept. 23, 1950

Barry was a very successful college coach, but his biggest contribution to basketball may have been the present rule that allows the team that has been scored against to take possession of the ball at the baseline under its own basket.

Until 1937, a center jump was held at mid-court after each score. Teams often had one tall player whose sole purpose was to win the tip and regain possession. Barry began campaigning for a new rule in 1928. Other coaches joined the campaign, but many of them, including Nat Holman, felt the team that had scored should be rewarded with possession of the ball, and some wanted the ball to be put in play from out of bounds at mid-court. When the National Basketball Committee finally eliminated the center jump in 1937, Barry's view prevailed.

After graduating from the University of Wisconsin, Barry coached high school basketball, then went to Knox College in Illinois and to the University of Iowa. He had his greatest success at the University of Southern California, from 1930 through 1941 and 1946 through 1950. Three of his players, Alex Hannum, Bill Sharman, and Tex Winter, became outstanding coaches. Barry's college teams won 365 games, losing 217.

Barry also coached the USC baseball team, winning the NCAA championship in 1948, and was an assistant football coach. He died of a heart attack shortly before a football game that he was going to scout.
★ Basketball Hall of Fame

Bartholomew, Kenneth E.

SPEED SKATING
b. Feb. 10, 1920

His long career was interrupted by World War II, but Bartholomew nevertheless won more speed skating championships than any other American. He won the U.S. outdoor championship for the first time in 1939, when he was 19, and for the last time in 1960, when he was 40 years old. He also won the title in 1941, 1942, 1947, from 1950 through 1956, and in 1959, and he tied for the championship in 1957.

Bartholomew was North American outdoor champion in 1941, 1942, and 1956. He and U.S. teammate Bobby Fitzgerald tied for the silver medal in the 500-meter race with a time of 43.2 seconds at the 1948 Winter Olympics.

Basilio, Carmen

BOXING
b. April 2, 1927, Canastota, N.Y.

After working as an onion picker for a time, Basilio served in the Marine Corps from 1945 to 1947. He won 11 of 14 amateur bouts after his discharge and became a professional boxer in 1948, knocking out his first three opponents. That began a long climb to the top for Basilio.

He won the New York State welterweight championship with a 12-round decision over Billy Graham on June 6, 1953, and defended it successfully in a 12-round draw with Graham on July 25. However, world champion Kid Gavilan beat Basilio on a 15-round decision in a title fight on September 18.

Basilio finally won the world championship by knocking out Tony DeMarco in the 12th round on June 10, 1955. He lost it less than a year later, on March 14, 1956, to Johnny Saxton in a 15-round decision, then knocked Saxton out in the 9th round on September 12 to regain the title.

In his only defense, he knocked Saxton out in the 2nd round on February 22, 1957. Basilio then moved up in weight to win the middleweight championship with a 15-round decision over Sugar Ray Robinson on September 23, after which he resigned the welterweight title.

Robinson won a 15-round decision in their rematch on March 25, 1958. Basilio had three more middleweight championship fights. He was knocked out twice by Gene Fullmer, in 1958 and 1959, and he lost a 15-round decision to Paul Pender on April 22, 1961. Basilio announced his retirement three days later.

He won 56 of his 79 professional fights, 27 by knockout, and lost 16, 2 by knockout. Basilio also fought 7 draws.
★ International Boxing Hall of Fame

Baston, Bert (Albert P.)

FOOTBALL
b. Dec. 3, 1894, St. Louis Park, Minn.
d. Nov. 16, 1979

An All-American end at Minnesota in both 1915 and 1916, Baston teamed with "Pudge" Wyman to form one of the Midwest's first outstanding passing combinations. Although upset by Illinois, 14–9, the 1916 team scored 348 points in only 7 games, an average of nearly 50 a game. In a 54–0 win over Wisconsin, Baston made a leaping catch for a touchdown, taking the ball off a defender's fingers after it had apparently been intercepted.

Baston became an automobile dealer after graduating, but he also worked as an assistant coach at Minnesota from 1932 to 1950. ·
★ College Football Hall of Fame

Bathgate, Andy (Andrew J.)

HOCKEY
b. Aug. 28, 1932, Winnipeg, Man.

After captaining his Guelph team to the Memorial Cup in 1952, Bathgate joined the New York Rangers for 18 games in the 1952–53 season. He was the team's leading scorer over the next ten seasons and won the Hart Trophy as the league's most valuable player in 1959. He tied Bobby Hull for the scoring championship with 84 points in 1961–62 and set an NHL record by scoring goals in ten straight games the following season.

Bathgate and Don McKenney were traded to the Toronto Maple Leafs midway through the 1963–64 season for five players. Bathgate's 58 assists that season tied Jean Beliveau's record; it was broken by Stan Mikita in 1964–65.

McKenney and Bathgate combined for 9 goals and 12 assists during the 1964 playoffs, leading Toronto to a Stanley Cup. However, the team slipped the following season, and Bathgate criticized coach Punch Imlach for working his players too hard in practice. Imlach promptly traded him to Detroit. The Pittsburgh Penguins chose Bathgate in the 1967 expansion draft, and he played with them until retiring after the 1970–71 season.

In 1,069 regular-season games, Bathgate had 349 goals and 624 assists. He scored 21 goals and 14 assists in 54 playoff games.
★ Hockey Hall of Fame

Battles, Clifford F.

FOOTBALL
b. May 1, 1910, Akron, Ohio
d. April 28, 1981

Battles was a Phi Beta Kappa student at little West Virginia Wesleyan College, where he played baseball, basketball, and track as well as football. He didn't receive any All-America mentions, but Navy players named him as a halfback on their all-opponent team in 1930.

The 6-foot-1, 200-pounder was a versatile runner who could plunge between tackles like a fullback or turn the ends and run in the open field like a halfback. In 1930, he had 6 touchdown runs of 70 or more yards, and in his senior season, 1931, he scored 15 touchdowns in 10 games, including 4 runs of more than 50 yards.

Battles played for the NFL's Boston Braves in 1931. In 1932, the team became known as the Redskins, and Battles was named an All-Pro after leading the league in rushing with 737 yards on 146 carries, a 5.0 average. He was the first NFL runner to gain more than 200 yards in a game, with 215 yards on only 16 attempts against the New York Giants.

He was an All-Pro again in 1936, when the Redskins won the Eastern Division championship. Because of poor attendance in Boston, they played the NFL championship game in the Polo Grounds, losing to the Green Bay Packers.

The Redskins moved to Washington, D.C., in 1937. That was Battles's best season and, ironically, his last. He led the league in rushing again with 874 yards on 216 carries, a 4.0 average, and was named an All-Pro for the third time.

In the last game of the season against the New York Giants, the Eastern Division title was on the line. Battles scored three touchdowns on runs from scrimmage of 4 and 73 yards and a 76-yard interception return in a 49–14 victory. A week later, in the championship game against the Chicago Bears, Battles had a 43-yard run on the first play from scrimmage, and he scored Washington's first touchdown on a 7-yard run. The Redskins won the championship, 28–21.

That was the first season for the great Sammy Baugh, who earned much more than the $3,000 Battles received. When Washington owner George Marshall refused to give him a raise, Battles retired to accept a $4,000 job as an assistant coach at Columbia University.

★ College Football Hall of Fame; Pro Football Hall of Fame

Bauer, Hank (Henry A.)

BASEBALL
b. July 31, 1922, E. St. Louis, Ill.

Service in the Marine Corps during World War II delayed Bauer's professional baseball career, and he didn't arrive in the major leagues until late in the 1948 season, when he was 26. The following year, he became the starting right fielder for the AL's New York Yankees.

Bauer was a solid, dependable, if unspectacular player with the Yankees for 11 seasons, a three-time All-Star and a member of nine pennant-winning teams. He led the league with 9 triples in 1957.

The Yankees traded Bauer to the Kansas City Athletics in 1960, and he became the team's manager early in the 1961 season, his last as a player. He was fired after a ninth-place finish in 1962.

The Baltimore Orioles hired him in 1964, and he guided the team to its first pennant in history in 1966. Baltimore beat the favored Los Angeles Dodgers in four straight World Series games.

Bauer was replaced midway through the 1968 season. He ended his managerial career with the Oakland A's in 1969. As a manager, Bauer had a 594–544 record for a .522 winning percentage. As a player, he had a career average of .277 with 1,424 hits, including 229 doubles, 57 triples, and 164 home runs.

Bauer, Marlene (Mrs. Hagge)

GOLF
b. Feb. 16, 1934, Eureka, S.Dak.

Bauer began playing golf when she was three. Twelve years later, in 1949, she won the U.S. girl's junior championship and was named teenager of the year, golfer of the year, and the Associated Press female athlete of the year. She joined the LPGA tour at 16, the youngest member ever; 40 years later, she was its oldest active member.

Her finest year was 1956, when she beat Patty Berg in a sudden death playoff to win the second LPGA championship. She was the tour's top money winner that year with $20,235. In 1971, she set a 9-hole record of 29 that stood until 1984.

Bauer, Sybil

SWIMMING
b. Sept. 18, 1903, Chicago, Ill.
d. Jan. 31, 1927

Bauer won an Olympic gold medal and 11 national championships, and she undoubtedly would have won more if there had been more backstroke events for women when she was swimming competitively.

Going into the 1924 Olympics, she held world records at every backstroke distance. In fact, at an informal meet in Bermuda in 1922, she had done the 440-yard backstroke in 6:24.8, four seconds better than the men's world record. Unfortunately, that time was never recognized because the meet was unsanctioned.

Bauer easily won the only Olympic backstroke event, the 100-meter. Her time of 1:23.2 was more than four seconds faster than the silver medalist's 1:27.4.

Her national championships came in the outdoor 100-yard backstroke in 1922, the 150-meter in 1923, the 220-yard in 1924 and 1925, and the indoor 100-yard backstroke from 1921 through 1926. In six years of swimming competitively, she set 23 world records.

As a student at Northwestern University, Bauer also competed in basketball and field hockey. She was engaged to marry Ed Sullivan, then a Chicago sportswriter and later a New York Broadway columnist and long-time host of the television variety show, when she was stricken by cancer.

★ International Swimming Hall of Fame

Baugh, Sammy (Samuel A.)

FOOTBALL
b. March 17, 1914, near Temple, Tex.

During much of his professional career, Baugh was a T-formation quarterback known for his passing, but he was also a great all-around athlete. A three-sport star in high school, he was recruited by Texas Christian University baseball coach Leo "Dutch" Meyer in 1933.

Meyer became head football coach in 1934 and made Baugh his starting tailback in 1935. He was not only a great passer but an outstanding punter and defensive back and a good, intelligent runner. TCU beat Louisiana State in the 1936 Sugar Bowl, 3–2, on a rainy day when passing was inadvisable. Baugh had a 45-yard run, intercepted two passes, and punted 14 times for an average of 48 yards a kick.

He was named to some All-American teams after that season and was a consensus choice in 1936, when he completed 109 of 219 passes for 1,890 yards and two touchdowns. TCU lost only once that year, a game that Baugh missed because of a leg injury, and beat Marquette 16–6 in the Cotton Bowl.

Baugh signed as a third baseman with the St. Louis Cardinals after graduating, but he was sent to the minor leagues, and decided to give professional football a try. He had only a week of practice with the Washington Redskins before the 1937 season opened and wasn't supposed to start. However, tailback Cliff Battles couldn't play because of an infected knee, and Baugh completed 11 of 16 passes for 116 yards as the Redskins beat the New York Giants, 13–3.

Washington beat the Chicago Bears for the NFL championship in his rookie season. Baugh threw a 42-yard pass to Battles, now playing fullback, to set up the first touchdown, but the Redskins were behind, 14–7, at halftime. In the second half, Baugh had touchdown passes of 55, 78, and 33 yards to lead the team to a 28–21 victory.

The Redskins and Bears played for the title three more times in the next six years. After a humiliating 73–0 defeat in 1940, Baugh threw a 23-yard touchdown pass, and his punting kept the Bears out of scoring range in a 14–6 win in 1942. He threw two early touchdowns passes in the 1943 game but had to leave because of a concussion, and the Bears ended up winning, 41–21.

The Redskins got into the championship once more during Baugh's tenure, in 1946, and once again he was hurt during the game. He continued playing despite two separated ribs but was not effective, and the Cleveland Rams beat Washington, 15–14.

Baugh, who had switched from single-wing tailback to T-formation quarterback in 1944, played six more seasons with mediocre teams. One of his greatest games was on Sammy Baugh Day in 1947. He passed for 365 yards and 6 touchdowns in a 45–21 victory over the Chicago Cardinals, who went on to win the NFL championship.

Perhaps his greatest season was 1943, when he became the only player ever to lead the NFL in passing, punting, and interceptions. Baugh was an All-Pro in 1937, 1940, 1943, 1945, 1947, and 1948. When he retired after the 1952 season, he held most of the NFL's passing records. His punting average of 51.4 yards a kick in 1940 and his passing completion mark of 70.3 percent in 1945 are still records.

During his 16-year career, Baugh completed 1,693 of 2,995 passes for 21,886 yards and 186 touchdowns. He punted 338 times for a 44.9-yard average.

Baugh coached Hardin-Simmons University for five years, beginning in 1955, winning 23 games while losing 28. He then became coach of the New York Titans (now the Jets) in the American Football League for two seasons, 1960–61, and had a 7–7 record each season.

★ College Football Hall of Fame; Pro Football Hall of Fame

Baughan, Maxie C., Jr.

FOOTBALL
b. Aug. 3, 1947, Forkland, Ala.

An All-American center/linebacker at Georgia Tech in 1959, Baughan joined the NFL's Philadelphia Eagles as a second-round draft choice in 1960. He became a starter at right linebacker immediately and was named to the 1964 all-pro team.

The 6-foot-1, 227-pound Baughan was traded to the Los Angeles Rams for three players before the 1966 season and made all-pro again in 1967. The captain of the Los Angeles defensive unit, Baughan was responsible for coordinating George Allen's very complex defense that gave up just 186 points. The Rams won the Coastal Division championship that season.

Ankle surgery in 1968 and knee surgery in 1969 slowed Baughan, but he played through pain for two more seasons. When Allen took over the Washington Redskins in 1971, he again traded for Baughan. However, the injuries forced his retirement before the season began. Baughan had 18 career interceptions and scored 1 touchdown.

★ College Football Hall of Fame

Baumann, Alexander

SWIMMING
b. April 21, 1964, Prague, Czechoslovakia

Baumann's family was visiting New Zealand in 1968, when Russian tanks went into Czechoslovakia to quell a short-lived revolution. Rather than returning, they went to Canada and settled in Sudbury, Ontario.

An outstanding all-around swimmer, Baumann held 38 Canadian records at various strokes by the time he was 17. On the international level, he excelled at the individual medley, winning gold medals in both the 200- and 400-meter events in the 1982 Commonwealth Games and the 400-meter championship in the 1983 World University Games.

At the 1984 Olympics, Baumann won the 400-meter individual medley in a world record time of 4:17.41, bringing Canada its first swimming gold medal since 1912. He took another gold in the 200-meter event, setting another world record of 2:01.42, and was named Canada's male athlete of the year for his accomplishment.

★ Canadian Sports Hall of Fame

Bausch, James A. B.

FOOTBALL, TRACK AND FIELD
b. March 29, 1906, Marion, S.Dak.
d. July 9, 1974

One of the very few athletes in the halls of fame for two different sports, Bausch competed in basketball, football, and track at Wichita University before transferring to Kansas University. A full-back, he set a Kansas scoring record in 1930.

He also threw the discus, javelin, and shot on the track team, but he wasn't quite good enough to win a national championship, so he became a multi-event competitor, winning the national pentathlon in 1931 and the national de-cathlon in 1932. At the 1932 Olympics in Los Angeles, he set a new world re-cord of 8,462 points in the decathlon with great scores in the field events. His best performance was a pole vault of 13 feet, 1½ inches, which would have been good for fifth place in the Olympic vault competition. Bausch won the 1932 Sul-livan award as the nation's top amateur athlete.

As a direct result of his Olympic vic-tory, the decathlon scoring tables were revised to give more weight to track events.

★ College Football Hall of Fame;
National Track & Field Hall of Fame

Baxter, Irving K.

TRACK AND FIELD
b. March 25, 1876, Utica, N.Y.
d. June 13, 1957

The only man ever to win the Olym-pic high jump and pole vault, Baxter did it in 1900, when he also won silver med-als in the standing high jump, standing long jump, and standing triple jump.

His pole vault victory was something of a fluke. Baxter had just won the high jump when the pole vault competition began. Two of the entrants, Charles Dvorak and Bascom Johnson, had left the field because the competition had supposedly been postponed. A third, Daniel Horton, refused to compete be-cause it was Sunday. So Baxter entered on the spur of the moment and won.

Baxter tied for the 1901 British pole vault championship in an even stranger way. On the way to Paris for the 1900 Olympics, the U.S. team stopped in Eng-land, and Baxter won the high jump at the British national meet. He returned in 1901 and won the high jump again. Only one competitor had entered the pole vault, so Baxter decided to try it. He hadn't brought his pole, and the other competitor refused to let Baxter use his, so Baxter pulled a flagpole out of the ground and matched the other man's vault.

He was the U.S. national pole vault champion in 1899, but Baxter went on to much greater success in the high jump, winning the national championship in the event from 1907 through 1910 and in 1912. Representing the University of Pennsylvania, Baxter was also the IC4A high jump champion in 1899.

Baylor, Don E.

BASEBALL
b. June 28, 1949, Austin, Tex.

An aggressive hitter who became known as a team leader, Baylor was named the AL's most valuable player with the California Angels in 1979, when he led the league with 139 RBI and 120 runs scored. He hit .296 with 36 home runs to lead the Angels to the Western Division championship that season.

Baylor entered the major leagues with the Baltimore Orioles in 1970, but appeared in just 9 games in his first two seasons. He became a starter in the outfield and at first base in 1972. Begin-ning in 1973, he was primarily an out-fielder and designated hitter.

The Orioles traded him to the Angels in 1976, and he went to the New York Yankees as a free agent in 1983. After three seasons with New York, Baylor joined the Boston Red Sox for the 1986 season. Traded by the Red Sox to Minne-sota late in the 1987 season, Baylor finished his career with the Oakland Athletics in 1988.

In 2,292 games, he had a .260 batting average on 2,135 hits, including 366 doubles, 28 triples, and .338 home runs. He drove in 1,276 runs and scored 1,236.

Baylor became manager of the expansion Colorado Rockies in 1993. He had a 120-159 record in his first two seasons.

Baylor, Elgin

BASKETBALL
b. Sept. 16, 1934, Washington, D.C.

Baylor played both football and basketball for a year at the tiny College of Idaho, then transferred to the University of Seattle. After sitting out a year to establish his eligibility, he led the nation in rebounding and was third in scoring as a junior in 1956–57. As a senior, he was a consensus All-American forward, second in the nation in scoring with 31.5 points a game and third in rebounding.

The financially troubled Minneapolis Lakers signed Baylor to an NBA contract in 1958, and season ticket sales immediately surged. According to owner Bob Short, Baylor's signing probably saved the franchise from bankruptcy.

The 6-foot-5, 225-pound Baylor, a remarkable combination of strength and grace, could power to the basket and perform acrobatic moves to score once he got close. He was also an excellent passer and rebounder.

The Lakers moved to Los Angeles in 1960, when they signed guard Jerry West. Baylor averaged more than 30 points a game in each of his first three seasons in Los Angeles, teaming with West to form the NBA's most potent two-player scoring combination. He scored 71 points against the New York Knicks in 1960, a league record broken by Wilt Chamberlain in 1962.

Baylor broke a kneecap in a 1965 playoff game and came back slowly the following season. He was never quite the same player after that, though he averaged more than 26 points a game in 1966–67 and 1967–68 and more than 24 points in 1968–69 and 1969–70, his last full season.

After missing almost the entire 1970–71 season because of a torn Achilles tendon, Baylor attempted to come back in the fall of 1971 but retired after just nine games. In his 14 NBA seasons,

he scored 23,149 points, an average of 27.4 per game. Baylor also had 11,463 rebounds and 3,650 assists.

★ Basketball Hall of Fame

Beagle, Ronald

FOOTBALL
b. Feb. 7, 1934, Hartford, Conn.

Beagle played high school football in Cincinnati and entered the U.S. Naval Academy in 1952. The 6-foot-1, 185-pound end was an All-American in 1954 and 1955, and he won the 1954 Maxwell Trophy as the nation's outstanding college football player, becoming one of the few linemen and only a handful of underclassmen to be given the award.

A broken hand hampered him somewhat in his senior season, but he finished his college career with 64 pass receptions for 840 yards and 8 touchdowns.

After four years in the Navy, where he suffered a knee injury playing football, Beagle tried out with the Oakland Raiders of the American Football League in 1960 but failed to make the squad.

★ College Football Hall of Fame

Beamon, Bob (Robert)

TRACK AND FIELD
b. Aug. 29, 1946, Jamaica, N.Y.

After Beamon's famous long jump at the 1968 Olympics, Soviet competitor Igor Ter-Ovanesyan said, "Compared to this jump, we are as children." English jumper Lynn Davies said to Beamon angrily, "You have destroyed this event!"

Beamon had not only become the first man to jump more than 28 feet — he had gone beyond 29 feet. The length was officially announced as 8.90 meters, which converts to 29 feet, 2½ inches. That shattered the world record of 27 feet, 4¾ inches set by Ralph Boston in 1965. Beamon's record was finally broken 24 years later by Mike Powell in the 1992 world championships.

Although Beamon had won 22 out of 23 meets he'd entered in 1968, he wasn't generally considered the Olympic favorite. That honor was shared by Ter-Ovanesyan and Boston. Beamon had a history of inconsistency and was prone to fouling. He had also been suspended from the University of Texas–El Paso track team four months before because he'd refused to compete in a meet against Brigham Young University, as a protest against Mormon racial policies.

The suspension left Beamon without a coach. Ironically, Boston had been coaching him unofficially. When Beamon fouled on his first two qualifying jumps at the Olympics, Boston pointed out that he could take off well before the board and still qualify. On his final jump, Beamon took off from a foot behind the board and easily made the qualifying distance, then went on to make history in the finals.

Beamon won only one national long jump championship, also in 1968. However, he set a national high school record for the triple jump in 1965.

★ National Track & Field Hall of Fame; Olympic Hall of Fame

Beatty, Jim (James T.)

TRACK AND FIELD
b. Oct. 28, 1934, New York, N.Y.

Beatty's best time in the mile while running for the University of North Carolina was just 4:06. Within three years of his graduation in 1957, he was one of the best distance runners in the world as a member of the Los Angeles Track Club.

In 1960, Beatty set U.S. records of 3:58.0 in the mile and 13.51.7 in the 5,000-meter. A strained foot ligament hampered his running at the Olympics, and he failed to reach the final of the 5,000-meter event.

Beatty won the Sullivan Award as the nation's outstanding athlete of the year in 1962 for a series of brilliant performances. He became the first person to run an indoor mile in less than 4 minutes, with a 3:58.9 time on February 10. Later, he ran a world record 8:29.8 in the 2-mile and set U.S. records of 3:39.4 for 1,500 meters, 7:54.2 for 3,000 meters, 13:45 for 5,000 meters, 3:56.3 for 1 mile, and 13:19.2 for 3 miles.

The AAU national champion in the outdoor mile in 1962, Beatty was the indoor champion from 1961 through

1963. He retired after a foot injury forced him to drop out of a 5,000-meter heat in the 1964 Olympics.

★ National Track & Field Hall of Fame

Beban, Gary J.

FOOTBALL
b. Aug. 5, 1946, San Francisco, Calif.

The 6-foot, 190-pound Beban was UCLA's starting quarterback for three seasons, from 1965 through 1967. During that period, the school won 25 games, lost 4, and tied 1. The only loss in his sophomore season came against unbeaten Michigan State, but UCLA came back to beat Michigan State, 14–12, in the post-season Rose Bowl.

Beban was one of the first players to win the Heisman Trophy largely because of television exposure. He played brilliantly in a nationally televised 21–20 loss to the University of Southern California and O. J. Simpson in 1967, and his performance undoubtedly won him many votes for the award.

He was chosen by the Los Angeles Rams in the first round of the 1968 NFL college draft, but the Rams refused to pay him as much as he wanted and traded his rights to the Washington Redskins. Beban never made it as a quarterback with the Redskins, but he was used occasionally both at running back and wide receiver. He retired after the 1970 season.

★ College Football Hall of Fame

Becker, Boris

TENNIS
b. Nov. 22, 1967, Leimen, Germany

Becker exploded onto the tennis scene in 1985, when he became the youngest male, at 17, ever to win the Wimbledon singles championship. His victory was considered a fluke by some because none of the top seeds reached the final that year; Becker won a four-set over unheralded Kevin Curren to take the title.

However, Becker proved it was no fluke by winning the championship again in 1986, this time beating Ivan Lendl. Then he reached the finals four years in a row, from 1988 through 1991, though he won the title just once, in 1989.

Becker also won the U.S. Open in 1989 and the Australian Open in 1991. Through 1994, Becker had 38 tournament wins, tenth all-time, and was third in career earnings with $13,436,281.

Becker, Elizabeth A. (Mrs. Pinkston)

DIVING
b. March 6, 1903, Philadelphia, Pa. d. April 6, 1988

On her doctor's advice, Becker began swimming as a child to strengthen her body and then became a diver. The U.S. indoor 3-meter champion in 1922 and 1923 and the 1-meter champion in 1924, Becker won a gold medal in the springboard diving event at the 1924 Olympics and took a silver in the platform.

At the Olympics, she met Clarence Pinkston, the winner of two bronze medals. They were married a year later, and she gave birth to twins in 1926. Pinkston retired from competition after 1924 and became Becker's coach. She won the national indoor 3-meter title in 1926 and a second Olympic gold medal, in the platform event, on August 11, 1928, the day the twins turned two years old.

She and Pat McCormick are the only women ever to win gold medals in both springboard and platform diving.

Beckley, Jacob P.

BASEBALL
b. Aug. 4, 1867, Hannibal, Mo. d. June 25, 1918

The 5-foot-10, 200-pound Beckley, who sported a splendid handlebar moustache, batted over .300 in 13 of his 22 major league seasons, played a record 2,368 games at first base, and had a record 23,696 putouts. A left-handed hitter and thrower, he was nicknamed "Eagle Eye" because of his hitting ability.

The NL's Pittsburgh Pirates paid his minor league team $4,000 for his contract early in the 1888 season, when he hit .343, just one point behind the league leader. After batting .301 in 1889, Beck-

ley jumped to the Pittsburgh team in the new Players' League.

That league folded after just one season, and Beckley rejoined the Pirates in 1891. He had his best season there in 1894, when he hit .345. The Pirates traded him to the New York Giants during the 1896 season, and it seemed as if his career was over when the Giants released him early the following year.

But Beckley had another decade of baseball left. He joined Cincinnati for the rest of the 1897 season and ended with a .325 average. On September 26, he hit three home runs in a game. No other player did that until 1922.

After hitting .333 in 1899 and .343 in 1900, Beckley became a utility player with the Reds. He finished his major league career with St. Louis from 1904 through 1907.

A fine fielder who often pulled the hidden ball trick on runners, Beckley had a terrible throwing arm. He once threw the ball over the pitcher's head and into right field after a bunt. When Beckley retrieved the ball, the runner was nearly at third base. Rather than risk another throw, he raced the runner to home and just barely beat him to make the tag.

Beckley was a minor league player-manager for several years after leaving the majors. He hit .282 in 1911, his last season as a player, when he was 44.

In 2,386 games, Beckley had 2,930 hits and a .308 average, with 473 doubles, 243 triples, and 86 home runs. He scored 1,600 runs and drove in 1,575.
★ Baseball Hall of Fame

Beckman, John

BASKETBALL
b. Oct. 22, 1895, New York, N.Y. d. June 22, 1968

Beckman learned to play basketball in high school and became one of the first professional stars. It is believed that he was the highest-paid member of the Original Celtics, although a couple of the other players, Nat Holman and Joe Lapchick, are probably better known than he.

He became a professional at 19 with

a Kingston, New York, team. In 1921 he joined the Original Celtics, then in their second season. When the Celtics played the New York Whirlwinds in a two-game series that year, Beckman scored 25 points, 23 of them on free throws, in a 40–27 loss in the first game, and he scored 17 of their points, 11 on free throws, in a 26–24 victory.

Beckman was among the finest free throw shooters in the game, which made him very valuable because at that time one player could shoot his team's free throws, no matter who had been fouled. One of his teammates, Dutch Dehnert, called Beckman "the smartest man who ever played basketball."

In 1926, he became player-coach with the Baltimore Orioles of the American Basketball League and later played with Rochester and Cleveland before returning to the Celtics for the 1929–30 season. He remained with them until the team disbanded in 1941. He later became athletic director at a center for retarded children.

★ Basketball Hall of Fame

Beckner, John G.
GYMNASTICS
b. June 9, 1930, Los Angeles, Calif.

Competing for the University of Southern California, Beckner won the NCAA parallel bars championship in 1951 and both the parallel bars and the all-around title in 1952. After graduating, he became the school's unpaid gymnastics coach while continuing to compete for the Los Angeles Turners.

Beckner won four straight national all-around championships, from 1956 through 1959; he was the national horizontal bars champion in 1958 and 1960, and the pommel horse champion in 1959. A member of three Olympic teams, in 1952, 1956, and 1960, Beckner barely failed to make the 1964 team.

He retired from competition in 1967 and could then officially become a salaried member of the USC athletic staff. He coached the team through 1982, and was also the coach of the 1968 U.S. Olympic team. USC won the 1968 NCAA team championship.

Bednarik, Chuck (Charles P.)
FOOTBALL
b. May 1, 1925, Bethlehem, Pa.

The last of pro football's full-time two-way players, Bednarik served in the Air Force during World War II and then starred as a center and linebacker at the University of Pennsylvania. He was a consensus All-American in 1947 and 1948, and he won the 1948 Maxwell Award as the outstanding college player of the year.

He sat out the first two games of his professional career with the Philadelphia Eagles because of injury and then missed only one more game in his 14 seasons. After playing offensive center in 1949 and 1950, when he was named to the Associated Press All-Pro team, Bednarik was moved to linebacker and was an All-Pro at that position 6 consecutive years, from 1951 through 1956.

When the Eagles were depleted by injuries in 1960, Bednarik played on offense and defense for most of the season. He was rewarded with a $250 bonus and another All-Pro selection as a linebacker. Philadelphia beat the Green Bay Packers, 17–13, in the NFL championship game when Bednarik made a touchdown-saving tackle on Green Bay fullback Jimmy Taylor with time running out.

His most famous tackle, though, came earlier in the season against the New York Giants. With the Eagles leading 17–10 in a game that effectively decided the Eastern Division championship, New York halfback Frank Gifford caught a pass in Philadelphia territory and was trying to get out of bounds to stop the clock when Don Burroughs tackled him low and Bednarik hit him high.

The Eagles recovered the resulting fumble and Bednarik did a victory dance while Gifford lay motionless with a severe concussion. New York fans booed, but Bednarik later explained that he hadn't realized Gifford had been hurt and that he was celebrating only because of the fumble recovery. Gifford spent a year in retirement because of the play.

Bednarik retired after the 1962 sea-

son. In his 14 seasons, all with the Eagles, he intercepted 20 passes, returning them for 268 yards and 1 touchdown.
★ College Football Hall of Fame; Pro Football Hall of Fame

Bedrosian, Stephen W.

BASEBALL
b. Dec. 6, 1957, Methuen, Mass.

Nicknamed "Bedrock," the right-handed Bedrosian won the NL Cy Young Award in 1987, when he appeared in 65 games for the Philadelphia Phillies, compiling a 5–3 record with 40 saves and a 2.83 ERA.

After a brief appearance with the Atlanta Braves in 1981, Bedrosian became the team's chief reliever the following season and was named the NL's rookie pitcher of the year by *The Sporting News* for picking up 11 saves to go with an 8–6 record and a 2.42 ERA.

Bedrosian developed arm trouble late in the 1984 season and was ineffective in 1985, spurring a trade to the Phillies. After his Cy Young performance, he missed the early part of the 1988 season. Philadelphia traded him to San Francisco during the 1989 season, and in 1991 he went to the Minnesota Twins.

He became a free agent in 1992 but wasn't signed, and his career seemed to be over. However, he joined the Braves again in 1993 and was a middle-inning relief pitcher on their Western Division championship team.

Through 1994, Bedrosian had a 75–72 record and 184 saves in 703 games. He had pitched 1,162⅔ innings, with 899 strikeouts and 506 walks.

Bedwell, Guy (Harvey Guy)

HORSE RACING
b. June 22, 1874, Roseburg, Oreg. d. Jan. 1, 1952

Bedwell worked as a cowboy and operated a small stable for some years, then moved to Maryland in 1908 to begin training thoroughbred horses for major races. He led the nation's trainers in victories in 1909 and from 1912 through 1917. Sir Barton, who became the first triple crown winner in 1919, was trained by Bedwell.

In 1921, Bedwell argued with the Jockey Club, which had suspended Carroll Schilling, one of his top jockeys. His New York license was revoked, so Bedwell's horses raced primarily in Maryland for nearly 20 years before he was restored to favor in New York.

After Sir Barton, Bedwell never trained a winner of another triple crown race, but he saddled more than 2,100 winners and earned more than $2.5 million during his career. He was still active as a trainer when he died of a heart attack in 1952.
★ National Horse Racing Hall of Fame

Bee, Clair F.

BASKETBALL
b. March 2, 1900, Grafton, W.Va. d. May 20, 1983

After graduating from high school in 1917, Bee served in World War I, played some semipro football, and then attended Waynesburg, Pennsylvania, College, where he played baseball, basketball, and football. He became basketball and football coach at Rider College in New Jersey in 1928. In three seasons there, his basketball teams won 55 games while losing only 7, and his football teams were 17–7–1.

Bee moved on to Long Island University as basketball coach for the 1931–32 season and soon made the Bluebirds one of the top teams in the country. They were undefeated in 1935–36 and 1938–39, in one stretch winning 43 consecutive games. The streak was broken in one of basketball's most significant games, when Hank Luisetti of Stanford introduced the one-hand shot to the East, leading his team to a 45–31 victory at Madison Square Garden in December 1936.

Bee's LIU teams won the National Invitation Tournament in 1939 and 1941. He missed two years while serving in World War II but returned in 1946. Some of his players were involved in the point-shaving scandal that was revealed in 1951, and Bee promptly resigned. He coached the NBA's Baltimore Bullets for three seasons, from 1951–52 through

1953–54, then left coaching to direct basketball camps and clinics.

Bee is considered the inventor of the 1-3-1 defense. He was a leading advocate of the 3-second rule, and he helped the NBA develop its 24-second clock, which probably saved professional basketball from extinction. He was also a prolific writer, producing 21 nonfiction books and 23 books in the "Chip Hilton" juvenile sports fiction series.

Bee had a record of 357 wins and 79 losses at LIU for an overall mark of 412–86 and a winning percentage of .827, the best in history.

★ Basketball Hall of Fame

Belfour, Edward
HOCKEY
b. April 21, 1965, Carmen, Man.

After a season in the Manitoba Junior Hockey League, Belfour entered the University of North Dakota in 1986 and was named goalie on the NCAA all-tournament team after the school won the 1987 Division I championship.

The Chicago Blackhawks signed Belfour as a free agent in 1987. He spent nearly two seasons in the minor leagues before being called up to Chicago in 1988–89, and he spent the following season with the Canadian national team.

Belfour became Chicago's starting goalie in 1990–91, when he won the Vezina Trophy as the NHL's best goaltender with a 2.47 goals-against average. He was also voted winner of the Calder Trophy as the league's rookie of the year. Belfour won the Vezina again in 1993 after compiling a 2.59 goals-against average in 71 games.

Through the 1993–94 season, he had played in 290 regular season games, allowing 731 goals, a 2.76 average, and recording 23 shutouts.

Beliveau, Jean
HOCKEY
b. Aug. 31, 1932, Three Rivers, P.Q.

Beliveau was a political issue for a couple of years. The Montreal Canadiens coveted him when he was playing in the Quebec Senior League, supposedly as an amateur, earning $20,000 a year, but Quebec legislators allegedly threatened to take away the Montreal Forum's liquor license if the team signed him. Finally, the Canadiens bought the entire league in 1950 just to acquire Beliveau.

He was remarkably big for a hockey player, at 6-foot-3 and 210 pounds. Bill Ezinicki, one of the best checkers in the game, recalled hitting Beliveau for the first time: "It was like running into the side of a big oak tree. I bounced right off the guy and landed on the seat of my pants."

Beliveau had deceptive speed because of his long skating strides. During his first couple of seasons with the Canadiens, he was often criticized for being too passive, but in 1952–53 he began hitting people and was among the league's leaders both in scoring and in penalty minutes.

He spent 19 seasons with Montreal, 10 as captain, and scored 25 or more goals in 13 of them. He appeared in the NHL playoffs 16 consecutive years, a record. Beliveau won the Hart Trophy as the league's most valuable player in 1956 and 1964 and was a first-team all-star ten times.

In 1,055 regular season games, he scored 482 goals and 661 assists, adding 73 goals and 81 assists in 142 playoff games.

★ Hockey Hall of Fame

Bell, Bobby (Robert L.)
FOOTBALL
b. June 17, 1940, Shelby, N.C.

The remarkably versatile Bell played quarterback, linebacker, offensive center, and defensive tackle at the University of Minnesota. He was a consensus All-American tackle in 1962, when he won the Outland Trophy as college football's outstanding lineman.

The 6-foot-4, 225-pound Bell had gigantic shoulders and a large chest, a 32-inch waist, and halfback speed. He joined the Kansas City Chiefs in 1963 and was listed as a defensive end during his first two seasons, but he often dropped back into a linebacker position in passing situations.

An All-AFL selection in 1964, Bell

moved to linebacker the following season and was an All-AFL/AFC choice at the position eight consecutive years. He played in six straight AFL All-Star games and the first four AFC/NFC Pro Bowl games.

Bell helped lead the Chiefs to AFL championships in 1966 and 1969 and to a 23–7 victory over the Minnesota Vikings in Super Bowl IV. He retired after the 1974 season. In 12 years with the Chiefs, he intercepted 26 passes and returned them 479 yards, scoring 6 touchdowns. He also scored one touchdown on a fumble recovery and one on a kickoff return.

★ Pro Football Hall of Fame

Bell, Cool Papa (James T.)

BASEBALL
b. May 17, 1903, Starkville, Miss.

Quite possibly the fastest player in baseball history, Bell never got a chance to prove it in the major leagues because he was black. But in an exhibition game against the Cleveland Indians in 1948, when he was nearly 45, Bell astounded the Indians and the crowd by scoring from first base on a bunt.

A switch-hitting center fielder, Bell began his professional career with the St. Louis Stars of the Negro National League in 1922. His manager there called him "a real cool papa," and the nickname stuck.

Bell played with St. Louis through 1931, and like many black stars, he also played winter ball in Cuba and Mexico virtually every year. He went to the Detroit Wolves in 1932 and joined the Homestead Grays later that year.

In 1933, Bell moved on to the Pittsburgh Crawfords. He reportedly stole 175 bases in about 200 games that season. He remained with the Crawfords through 1936, then spent one season playing in the Dominican Republic and four in Mexico.

Because of World War II, Bell returned to the U.S. to play for the Chicago American Giants in 1942 and with the Homestead Grays from 1943 through 1946. He was playing manager of the independent Detroit Senators in

1947 and of the Kansas City Stars from 1948 through 1950.

After retiring as a player, Bell spent four years as a freelance scout for the AL's St. Louis Browns.

Sometimes known as the "black Ty Cobb," Bell reportedly batted over .400 a number of times, including a .437 average in 1940, when he was playing in Mexico. Because of his great speed, he could play a very shallow center field, which sometimes allowed him to sneak in behind a runner for a pickoff at second base.

★ Baseball Hall of Fame

Bell, George A. M.

BASEBALL
b. Oct. 21, 1959, San Pedro de Macoris, Dominican Republic

For a four-year period from 1984 through 1987, Bell was one of the most feared power hitters in baseball. He had a sensational season in 1987, batting .308 with 47 home runs and a league-leading 134 RBI to win the AL's most valuable player award.

Bell played with the Toronto Blue Jays for part of the 1981 season but missed most of the following season with an injury. He became a starting outfielder with Toronto in 1984. Over the next four years, he hit 132 home runs and had 424 RBI.

The right-handed Bell, who led AL outfielders in errors three times, continually resisted attempts by Toronto management to make him a designated hitter. His batting average and home run totals declined during the next three seasons, though he had 104 RBI in 1989.

The NL's Chicago Cubs signed him as a free agent in 1991, and he went to the White Sox in 1992, when he had 25 home runs and 112 RBI, though his batting average was only .255. Injuries limited his playing time in 1993, when he batted .217 with just 13 home runs and 64 RBI.

Through 1993, Bell had a .278 average with 1,702 hits in 1,587 games, including 308 doubles, 34 triples, 265 home runs, and 1,002 RBI. He played in Japan during the 1994 season.

Bell, Gregory C.

TRACK AND FIELD
b. Nov. 7, 1930, Terre Haute, Ind.

Bell had a long jump of 26 feet, 6½ inches in 1956. It was the second longest jump in history, the closest anyone had ever come to breaking the world record of 26-8¼, set by Jesse Owens 21 years before. Bell jumped 26-7 twice, in 1957 and 1959, but Owens's record stood up until Ralph Boston broke it in 1960.

Bell won the Olympic high jump in 1956 with a leap of 25 feet, 8¼ inches. Representing Indiana, he was the NCAA champion in 1956 and 1957; he won the national outdoor championship in 1955 and 1959, the national indoor title in 1958.

★ National Track & Field Hall of Fame

Bell, Matty (Madison A.)

FOOTBALL
b. Feb. 22, 1899, Ft. Worth, Tex.
d. June 30, 1983

One of the greatest coaches in Southwest Conference history, Bell coached five schools to winning records during his 26-year career. He played end at Centre College in Kentucky from 1916 through 1919. During that period, the team won 25 games while losing only 2 and tying 3.

Bell took up coaching at Haskell Institute in Kansas in 1920, planning to save money so he could go to law school. After two seasons there and one at Carroll College, he became head coach at Texas Christian in 1923. His teams won 33 games, lost 17, and tied 5 in six seasons.

Texas A & M hired him away in 1929. He was fired after the 1933 season, mainly because he failed to beat Southern Methodist, managing only a tie and four losses in five games. Commenting on the lack of material to work with, Bell said, "Any expert diamond cutter, laboriously, painstakingly, and with delicate craftsmanship, can trim the uneven stone which nature gave him, and polish the facets to gleaming brilliance, but I never heard of anyone doing it with a hunk of coal."

Ironically, he took over at Southern Methodist in 1935 after a year out of football, and he had his greatest success there. His first team won all 12 of its regular season games before losing to Stanford, 7–0, in the Rose Bowl.

After serving in the Navy from 1942 through 1944, Bell returned to SMU in 1945. Led by Doak Walker, the school won 9 games and tied 1 in 1947 and had an 8-1-1 record in 1948. In two Cotton Bowl appearances, SMU tied Penn State, 13–13, and beat Oregon, 21–13.

Bell retired from coaching after the 1949 season and served as SMU's athletic director until 1964. His overall coaching record was 154–87–17, including an 88–39–7 mark at SMU.

★ College Football Hall of Fame

Bellamy, Walter J.

BASKETBALL
b. July 24, 1939, New Bern, N.C.

The 6-foot-11, 245-pound Bellamy averaged 20.6 points a game in three years as the starting center at the University of Indiana and was chosen by the Chicago Packers in the first round of the 1961 NBA draft. He averaged 31.6 points a game, his career high, and was named the league's rookie of the year.

The team was renamed the Zephyrs in 1962, then moved to Baltimore and became known as the Bullets for the 1963–64 season. Baltimore traded Bellamy to the New York Knicks during the 1965–66 season. He went to the Detroit Pistons in December 1968 and then to the Atlanta Hawks in February 1970. Bellamy was selected by the New Orleans Jazz in the 1974 expansion draft but was released after playing just one game, and he announced his retirement.

In 1,043 regular season games, Bellamy scored 20,941 points, a 20.1 average, and pulled down 14,241 rebounds. His career .632 field goal percentage is second only to Wilt Chamberlain's in NBA history. Bellamy added 850 points in 46 playoff games, an 18.5 average, and had 680 rebounds.

★ Basketball Hall of Fame

Bellino, Joseph M.

FOOTBALL
b. March 13, 1938, Winchester, Mass.

A starting halfback for three years at the U.S. Naval Academy, the 5-foot-9, 180-pound Bellino won the Heisman Trophy as the nation's outstanding college football player after a brilliant 1960 season. He rushed 168 times for 834 yards, caught 17 passes for 280 yards and 3 touchdowns, and also threw 2 touchdown passes on the halfback option. Bellino not only returned kicks, he did Navy's punting.

Bellino spent his mandatory four years in service after graduating and then joined the AFL's Boston Patriots in 1965. In his three seasons with the Patriots, he was used mainly as a kick returner. He ran back 43 kickoffs for 905 yards, a 21.0 average, and 19 punts for 148 yards, a 7.8 average. Bellino also rushed 30 times for 64 yards and caught 11 passes for 153 yards and 1 touchdown.
★ College Football Hall of Fame

Belote, Melissa

SWIMMING
b. Oct. 10, 1956, Washington, D.C.

Belote loved swimming but hated getting chlorine in her eyes, so she specialized in the backstroke. And she specialized well enough to win three gold medals at the 1972 Olympics.

The 15-year-old wasn't at all well known going into the U.S. Olympic trials, where she beat American record holder Susie Atwood in the 100-meter backstroke and set a world record of 2:20.64 in the 200-meter. She won both events at the Olympics, setting another world record of 2:19.19 in the 200-meter backstroke, and she also swam on the gold medal 4 x 100-meter medley relay team.

Belote won the AAU outdoor 100-meter backstroke in 1973, the outdoor 200-meter backstroke in 1973 and 1975, and the indoor 200-yard backstroke in 1973. As a student at Arizona State University, she also won four AIAW championships.

Benbrook, Albert

FOOTBALL
b. Aug. 24, 1887, Dallas, Tex.
d. Aug. 16, 1943

An All-American guard in 1909 and 1910, Benbrook captained the 1910 Michigan team that was undefeated in 6 games, winning 3 and tying 3, including a scoreless tie against a Pennsylvania squad that won 9 of 11 games and lost only 1 that year. He was named to Bob Zuppke's all-time All-American team in 1951.

Benbrook starred in Michigan's 6–0 victory over Minnesota in 1910. After blocking a field goal attempt, he made the key block on Michigan's game-winning touchdown, the only one scored against Minnesota that season.
★ College Football Hall of Fame

Bench, Johnny L.

BASEBALL
b. Dec. 7, 1947, Oklahoma City, Okla.

Considered by many the greatest catcher in history because of his combination of defensive skill, offensive power, and durability, Bench was one of the leaders of Cincinnati's "Big Red Machine" that won six Eastern Division titles, four NL pennants, and two world championships during the 1970s.

The 6-foot-1, 208-pound Bench joined the Reds late in the 1967 season and became a starter in 1968, when he set records for a catcher by playing in 154 games and hitting 40 doubles. He was named the league's rookie of the year.

He won his first most valuable player award in 1972. Bench's league-leading 45 home runs and 148 RBI helped the Reds to the division title. He came close to duplicating those numbers in 1974, again leading the league with 40 home runs and 125 RBI to win another MVP award as the Reds won another division title. They won the pennant both seasons but lost twice to the Oakland Athletics in the World Series.

In 1974, Bench led the league in RBI for the third time, with 129. The Reds finally won the World Series in 1975, and they repeated the following year. Bench's offensive numbers weren't nearly as spectacular in those seasons, but he was still clearly the best catcher in the league. In 1977, he was named the All-Star starter for the tenth consecutive year.

Knee problems began to bother Bench in 1978, and he was limited to just 52 games in 1981, when he played primarily at first base. He was also used at third base and in the outfield at times during his last two years. He retired after the 1983 season and became a radio broadcaster.

Bench, who won ten Gold Glove Awards, pioneered the one-handed style of catching, keeping his left hand behind his back to protect it from foul tips and using a very flexible glove to snare the ball, a technique now used by virtually all major league catchers.

In 2,158 games, all with Cincinnati, Bench batted .267, with 2,048 hits, including 381 doubles, 24 triples, and 389 home runs. He drove in 1,376 runs and scored 1,091.

★ Baseball Hall of Fame

Bender, Chief (Charles A.)
BASEBALL
b. May 5, 1884, Brainerd, Minn.
d. May 22, 1954

The son of a German-American father and a Chippewa Indian mother, Bender played baseball and football at Carlisle Indian Institute in Pennsylvania and entered semipro baseball after graduating in 1902.

The Philadelphia Athletics signed Bender in 1903, and he won his first game in relief without ever playing in the minor leagues. He had a 17–15 record as a rookie.

Because of illness, Bender slipped to 10–11 in 1904. Despite missing five weeks of the 1905 season, he had an 18–11 record, and he shut out the New York Giants for Philadelphia's only World Series victory.

During the next four seasons, Bender won 57 games while losing 35. His finest year was 1910, when he led the league with an .821 winning percentage on a 23–5 record. Bender beat the Chicago Cubs, 4–1, in the first game of the World Series but lost the fourth, 4–3, in 10 innings. Philadelphia won the series four games to one.

Bender again had the AL's best winning percentage, .773, in 1911, when his record was 17–5. After losing the opener of the World Series, 2–1, to the New York Giants on 2 unearned runs, he won the fourth and sixth games as the As beat the Giants again, four games to two.

After a 13–8 record in 1912, Bender won 21 games and lost 10 in 1913, then beat the Giants twice in the World Series, becoming the first pitcher to win 6 Series games. He had a 17–3 record, including 7 shutouts and 14 victories in a row, in 1914, when his .850 winning percentage was best in the league for the third time.

Bender jumped to the Federal League in 1915. The league folded after that season, and he won 15 games while losing 9 for the Philadelphia Phillies in 1916 and 1917.

After his major league playing career, Bender was a minor league player, college coach, and major league coach until his retirement in 1954. In 459 major league games, he had a 212–127 record and a 2.46 ERA with 40 shutouts. Bender struck out 1,711 hitters and walked 712 in 3,017 innings.

★ Baseball Hall of Fame

Benedict, Benny (Clinton)
HOCKEY
b. 1894, Ottawa, Ont.
d. Nov. 13, 1976

Though he played during a high-scoring era, Benedict still holds the record for most career playoff shutouts with 15 and the most in a single Stanley Cup playoff season, 4 in 1928.

Benedict entered the NHL with the Ottawa Senators in 1917. He led all goaltenders in 1919–20 with a 2.7 goals-against average and 5 shutouts in just 24 games; they were the league's only shutouts that season. He led again in 1920–21 with a 3.1 average and 2 shutouts.

Benedict went to the Montreal Maroons in 1924 and played there until his retirement in 1930. In the 1926 Stanley Cup finals, Benedict had 3 shutouts in 4 games against Victoria.

His nose was broken by a Howie Morenz shot during the 1929–30 season, and Benedict began wearing a mask for protection, probably the first goalie to do so, but he gave it up after a few games because he said it obscured is vision.

In 364 regular-season games, Benedict gave up just 864 goals, a 2.37 average, and had 57 shutouts. His 15 playoff shutouts came in 49 playoff games, in which he gave up 87 goals for a 1.78 average.

★ Hockey Hall of Fame

Benner, Joe (Huelet L.)

SHOOTING
b. Nov. 1, 1917, Jonesboro, Ark.

During practice a week before the 1948 Olympics, Benner was having equipment problems. The manager of the U.S. shooting team, Karl Frederick, loaned him a pistol. It happened to be the same pistol that Frederick had shot with to win an Olympic gold medal in 1920.

It didn't work that way for Benner. He finished fourth in 1948, but he returned to the Olympics with his own weapon and won a gold medal in the 50-meter free pistol event in 1952.

Benner won six national pistol championships, in 1947, 1949, 1951, 1955, 1956, and 1959, and he was the world champion in 1949, 1952, and 1954. He also won three individual championships and three team championships in the Pan-American Games in 1951 and 1955.

Bennett, Cornelius O.

FOOTBALL
b. Aug. 25, 1966, Birmingham, Ala.

As a linebacker at the University of Alabama, Bennett was named to the *Sporting News* All-American team three consecutive years, 1984 through 1986. In his senior season, he was a consensus All-American, and he won the Lombardi Award as the outstanding college lineman of the year.

The 6-foot-2, 238-pound Bennett was the first draft pick of the Indianapolis Colts, the second choice overall, but he refused to sign a contract, and the Colts traded his rights to the Buffalo Bills in a complex three-team deal that brought running back Eric Dickerson to Indianapolis from the Los Angeles Rams.

Bennett immediately became a star in the NFL. An All-Pro in 1988, he played in the Pro Bowl that year and from 1990 through 1993 and helped lead the Bills to four consecutive AFC championships, also from 1990 through 1993. However, they lost all four Super Bowls.

Through the 1993 season, Bennett had 40½ quarterback sacks and 4 interceptions, which he returned for 35 yards. He also recovered 12 fumbles, 1 for a touchdown, and scored a touchdown on an 80-yard return of a blocked field goal.

Bennett, Curt A.

HOCKEY
b. March 27, 1948, Regina, Sask.

Though born in Canada, Bennett grew up in Rhode Island, where his family moved when he was an infant. He starred as a defenseman at Brown University and signed with the NHL's St. Louis Blues after graduating in 1970.

As a professional, the 6-foot-3, 200-pound Bennett played center. St. Louis traded him to the New York Rangers before the 1972–73 season, and he went to the Atlanta Flames shortly afterward. Bennett had his best scoring season with Atlanta in 1975–76, with 65 points on 34 goals and 31 assists.

Bennett was traded back to St. Louis in 1977 and spent a final season, 1979–80, with Atlanta before retiring. In 580 regular season games, he scored 152 goals and had 182 assists for 334 points. He added 2 points on 1 goal and 1 assist in 21 playoff games.

Benoit, Joan (Mrs. Samuelson)

TRACK AND FIELD
b. May 16, 1957, Cape Elizabeth, Maine

After breaking a leg skiing as a youngster, Benoit began running to get back into shape and discovered that she liked it. While a senior at Bowdoin College in Maine, she entered the 1979 Boston Marathon as a virtual unknown and set an American women's record of 2:35:15.

Benoit underwent surgery on both Achilles tendons in 1981 but returned to top form in 1983, when she again won the Boston Marathon, setting a world record of 2:22:43. She also set American records that year in the 10-kilometer, half-marathon, 10-mile, and 25-kilometer runs.

Grete Waitz of Norway, who had won all seven marathons she'd entered and had beaten Benoit in 10 of 11 races, was favored to win the gold medal in the first Olympic women's marathon in 1984. However, Benoit took the lead just 3 miles into the race and never gave it up. She led Waitz by nearly a minute at the 15-kilometer mark and by nearly two minutes at the 25-kilometer mark.

She recalled, "When I came into the stadium and saw all the colors and everything, I told myself, 'Listen, just look straight ahead, because if you don't you're probably going to faint.'"

Benoit was named winner of the Sullivan Award as the outstanding U.S. amateur athlete of 1985, when she set an American record of 2:21:21 in the Chicago Marathon. She also won major 12-kilometer and 7-mile races that year.

Since then, she's been seriously hampered by injuries and has struggled to finish in the top ten in most of the races she's entered.

Bentley, Douglas W.
HOCKEY
b. Sept. 3, 1916, Delisle, Sask.
d. Nov. 24, 1972

For much of his 13-season NHL career, Bentley was the left wing on the Chicago Black Hawks' "Pony Line," with his brother Max at center and Bill Mosienko at right wing. He joined the Black Hawks for the 1939–40 season and played with them through 1952–53, missing one season while serving in World War II. He spent his final season, 1953–54, with the New York Rangers.

He was the league's leading scorer in 1942–43 with 73 points, edging Bill

Cowley of Boston, who had 72, and his brother Max, who had 70. The following season, he scored 77 points but finished second. He was among the top ten scorers four other times and was a first-team all-star three times.

Bentley had 219 goals and 324 assists in 566 regular season games during his career, and he added 9 goals and 8 assists in 23 playoff games.
★ Hockey Hall of Fame

Bentley, Maxwell H. L.
HOCKEY
b. March 1, 1920, Delisle, Sask.

The 145-pound Bentley was rejected by the Boston Bruins because he wasn't big enough, and the Montreal Canadiens turned him down because a team doctor said he had a heart problem. In 1940, he joined the Chicago Black Hawks and played 12 seasons in the NHL, missing two because of service in World War II. One of the finest stick-handlers of his era, he was also a clever, sharp-shooting scorer.

Bentley won the Lady Byng Trophy for combining sportsmanship with a high standard of play in 1943, and he won the Art Ross Trophy as the league's leading scorer with 61 points in 1945. The following year, he scored 72 points to win both the Ross Trophy and the Hart Trophy as the league's most valuable player.

He played on the "Pony Line" with his brother Doug until 1947–48, when he was traded to the Toronto Maple Leafs for six players, and in 1953–54 he and Doug were united for one final season with the New York Rangers.

In 646 regular season games, Bentley scored 245 goals and 299 assists. He added 18 goals and 27 assists in 52 playoff games.
★ Hockey Hall of Fame

Benvenuti, Nino (Giovanni)
BOXING
b. April 26, 1938, Trieste, Italy

After winning the 1960 gold medal in the welterweight class, Benvenuti turned professional in early 1961. He won the Italian middleweight championship in 1963 and became world junior welterweight champion and European middleweight champion in 1965. Benvenuti was undefeated until he lost the junior welterweight title on a 15-round decision to Ki-Soo Kim of Korea on June 25, 1966.

On April 17, 1967, Benvenuti became world middleweight champion by decisioning Emile Griffith in 15 rounds in New York City. He lost the title in a rematch, also a 15-round decision, on September 28, but regained it in yet another 15-round decision on March 4, 1968.

After four successful defenses, Benvenuti lost the title when he was knocked out by Carlos Monzon of Argentina in the 12th round of a fight in Rome on November 7, 1970. He retired after Monzon knocked him out again, this time in the 3rd round, on May 8, 1971.

In 90 professional bouts, Benvenuti had 82 victories, 35 by knockout. He lost 7, 3 by knockout, and fought 1 draw.

★ International Boxing Hall of Fame

Berenson, Senda (Mrs. Abbott)

BASKETBALL
b. March 19, 1868, Vilna, Lithuania
d. Feb. 16, 1954

Her family emigrated from Lithuania to Boston when she was seven years old, and the family name was changed from Valvrojenski to Berenson. After training at the Boston Normal School of Gymnastics, Berenson became the first director of physical education at Smith College in January of 1892, just a month after basketball had been invented by James Naismith at the International YMCA Training School in nearby Springfield.

She read about the sport and visited Naismith to learn more about it. On March 21, 1893, Berenson organized the first women's collegiate basketball game at Smith. Influenced by the thinking of her time about women's physical limitations, she soon adapted the rules to avoid the roughness of the men's game.

The major change she made was dividing the court into three areas. There were six players at the time, and two players were assigned permanently to each of the three areas. Attempting to steal the ball was forbidden. Because of that rule, dribbling was limited to three bounces, and a player was allowed to hold the ball for only three seconds.

Berenson's rules were first published in 1899. Two years later, she became editor of A. G. Spalding's first *Women's Basketball Guide,* which further spread her version of basketball for women.

After marrying in 1911, she left Smith. The sister of Bernard Berenson, a major authority on Italian Renaissance art, she later studied art in Europe. She and Margaret Wade were the first two women elected to the Basketball Hall of Fame.

★ Basketball Hall of Fame

Berg, Patty (Patricia J.)

GOLF
b. Feb. 13, 1918, Minneapolis, Minn.

"I'm very happy I gave up football, or I wouldn't be here tonight," Patty Berg said when she was inducted into the LPGA Hall of Fame. In her early teens she quarterbacked an otherwise all-boys' neighborhood football team, the 50th Street Tigers. Her parents, deciding she was too old to be playing such games with boys, steered her into golf when she was 14.

A year later, she won the Minneapolis city championship, and two years after that she was the state amateur champion. Berg won 29 titles in seven years, including the 1938 U.S. Amateur, and was easily the most famous woman golfer in the country. She turned professional in 1940 and worked for Wilson Sporting Goods, which began to manufacture Patty Berg clubs. There was no women's professional tour at that time, just three or four tournaments a year, so she earned her money by giving clinics and exhibitions.

A serious auto accident late in 1941 sidelined her for 18 months. After winning the 1943 Western Open and All-American at Tam O'Shanter, she joined the Marines. Returning to golf after the war, she won the 1946 U.S. Women's Open. More important for the future of women's golf, she became a founder and the first president of the Ladies' Professional Golf Association in 1948.

In the next 11 years, Berg won 39 LPGA tournaments. She was the leading money winner in 1954, 1955, and 1957, and she won the Vare Trophy for the lowest average round in 1953, 1955, and 1956. The Associated Press named her woman athlete of the year in 1955 for the third time; the other awards came in 1938 and 1943.

Berg was a tireless goodwill ambassador for golf, giving thousands of exhibitions and clinics and training young professionals who signed contracts with Wilson. She was also active in charity work. She was given the 1976 Humanitarian Sports Award by the United Cerebral Palsy Foundation, the first woman so honored, and in 1979 the LPGA established the Patty Berg Award for outstanding contributions to women's golf.

★ LPGA Hall of Fame; International Women's Sports Hall of Fame; World Golf Hall of Fame

Berger, Isaac

WEIGHTLIFTING
b. Nov. 16, 1936, Jerusalem, Israel

The longest weightlifting competition in Olympic history was the 1960 featherweight championship battle between Berger, the defending champion, and Yevgeny Minayev of the Soviet Union. It lasted ten hours, finally ending at 4 A.M., when Berger failed to lift 152.5 kilograms in the jerk. He had beaten Minayev six times in a row entering the Olympics, but this time he had to settle for second.

Berger came to the United States and become a naturalized citizen as a teenager. He won the U.S. featherweight championship seven times, from 1955 through 1961 and in 1964. He was world champion in 1958 and 1961, finishing second in 1957, 1959, and 1963. He set a world record of 352.5 kilograms for three lifts when he won an Olympic gold medal in 1956. Berger added the 1964 silver medal to the one he'd claimed in

1960, and he was also the Pan-American Games featherweight champion in 1959 and 1963.

Berlenbach, Paul

BOXING, WRESTLING
b. Feb. 18, 1901, New York, N.Y.

Stricken with scarlet fever when he was four years old, Berlenbach lost his hearing and could speak little. About seven years later, he climbed a telegraph pole, touched a live wire, and fell to the ground. His hearing returned as a result of the accident, and he soon learned to talk.

Berlenbach began wrestling at a YMCA and later became a member of the New York Athletic Club. He won the national 175-pound championship in 1922 and 1923. In the meantime he had also taken up boxing. Although left-handed, he was taught to fight right-handed. A devastating left hook, his best punch, earned him his nickname, the "Astoria Assassin."

He turned professional in October 1923 and won his first 10 fights, all by knockout, before being knocked out by Jack Delaney in March 1924. On May 30, 1925, he won the world light heavyweight championship with a 15-round decision over Mike McTigue. After three defenses, he lost the title to Delaney on a 15-round decision, June 16, 1926.

Berlenbach was knocked out twice in 1927, by McTigue and Delaney, and the New York State Athletic Commission ruled him physically unfit to keep boxing, but he was awarded a wrestling license in 1929. After that career didn't work out, he returned to boxing briefly, winning two fights by knockout in 1931. He didn't fight in 1932 and retired for good after losing his only 1933 fight.

In 49 professional fights, Berlenbach had 37 victories, 30 by knockout; 7 losses, 3 by knockout; 3 draws, 1 no-decision, and 1 no-contest.

Berning, Susie (Susan Maxwell)

GOLF
b. July 22, 1941, Pasadena, Calif.

After playing on the men's golf team

at Oklahoma City University, Berning joined the LPGA tour in 1964, when she was named rookie of the year. She has won only 11 LPGA tournaments, but three of her victories were in the U.S. Women's Open, in 1968, 1972, and 1973. Only three other players have won the Women's Open more than twice.

Berning's first tour victory was the Muskogee Civitan in 1965, when she also won the Western Open. Her playing schedule has been limited since 1968, when she married Dale Maxwell and played in only nine tournaments. Berning now plays in about 15 tournaments a year and her oldest daughter, Robin, often caddies for her.

Berra, Yogi (Lawrence P.)

BASEBALL
b. May 12, 1925, St. Louis, Ill.

After playing in the minor leagues in 1943, Berra joined the U.S. Navy. He returned to professional baseball in 1946. Called up by the New York Yankees for the last weeks of the season, he hit a home run in his first major league game.

In 1947 and 1948, Berra was a part-time catcher for the Yankees and was also often used in right field because of his hitting and strong arm. When Casey Stengel became the Yankee manager in 1949, he made Berra the starting catcher and hired former Yankee great Bill Dickey as a coach to help polish his defense.

Like Stengel, Berra was known for his malapropisms — he once said of Dickey, "He's learning me his experience" — but he was widely respected by people in the game for knowledge of baseball. Stengel called him "my assistant manager."

A left-handed hitter with power, Berra liked to swing at bad pitches, but it worked for him. He batted over .300 three times, hit 20 or more home runs nine times, and had 30 or more home runs twice.

A fine clutch hitter, he had the first pinch-hit home run in World Series history, in 1947, and he hit a grand slam home run in the 1956 series. Five times he drove in more than 100 runs.

Berra also became an outstanding defensive catcher. He once went a record 148 consecutive games without an error. His offensive and defensive skills combined to make him a three-time most valuable player, in 1951, 1954, and 1955.

During his 18 seasons with the Yankees, Berra played in a record 14 World Series, setting records for games played, 75; times at bat, 259; and hits, 71.

Immediately after retiring as a player, Berra became manager of the Yankees in 1964. He took them to a pennant that season, but was replaced after they lost the World Series to the St. Louis Cardinals. He joined the New York Mets as a coach in 1965 and became manager in 1972. The following year the Mets won the NL pennant, making Berra only the third manager in history to win pennants in both leagues.

Because of a dispute with the front office, Berra was fired during the 1975 season. He later coached with the Yankees and the Houston Astros. His son, Dale, was a major league infielder for 11 seasons.

In 2,120 games, Berra had a .285 batting average with 321 doubles, 49 triples, and 358 home runs. He drove in 1.430 runs and scored 1,175.

★ Baseball Hall of Fame

Berry, Raymond E.

FOOTBALL
b. Feb. 27, 1933, Corpus Christi, Tex.

Hard work finally made Berry a star, but not until his third season of professional football. As an end at Southern Methodist University, he caught only 33 passes and scored 1 touchdown in three seasons. When he joined the Baltimore Colts in 1955, he was given little chance to make the team. However, coach "Weeb" Ewbank was impressed with Berry's practice habits and his good hands and kept him as a part-time player.

In 1957, Berry became a starting end and led the NFL in reception yardage with 800 on 47 catches, scoring 6 touchdowns. When the Colts won the league's championship in 1958, Berry led in receptions with 56 and in touchdown receptions with 9, gaining 794 yards. He had an additional 12 catches for 194 yards and 1 touchdown in the Colts' celebrated 23–17 overtime victory over the New York Giants in the NFL title game.

Berry led the league in 1959 with 74 receptions, 959 yards, and 14 touchdowns, and led in receptions with 74 and yards with 1,298 the following season before undergoing knee surgery. Because of the operation, he was used primarily as a possession receiver for the rest of his career. In 1961, he caught 75 passes, his career high, but gained only 873 yards and didn't score.

Berry retired after catching only 11 passes in 1967. He held NFL records, since broken, with 631 receptions and 9,275 yards. He caught 68 touchdown passes.

The slender, 6-foot-2, 187-pound Berry lacked speed, but he developed a variety of moves to get free from defenders, and he virtually never dropped a pass he could get his hands on. He constantly worked on catching the ball before and after formal practice, even recruiting sportswriters, groundskeepers, and equipment managers to throw to him.

Berry took over as head coach of the New England Patriots in 1984. The Patriots got into the playoffs as a wildcard team in 1985 and won three games on the road to reach the Super Bowl, where they were demolished, 46–10, by the Chicago Bears. They won the AFC Eastern Division title in 1986 but lost to the Denver Broncos in the first round of the playoffs. Berry resigned during the 1989 season with a 51–41 record.
★ Pro Football Hall of Fame

Bertelli, Angelo B.

FOOTBALL
b. June 18, 1921, W. Springfield, Mass.

Known as the "Springfield Rifle" because of his strong, accurate arm, Bertelli was also a clever ball-handling quarterback and Notre Dame's punter for most of three seasons. In 1941, his sophomore year, he played tailback in the Notre Dame box formation and completed 70 of 123 passes for 1,027 yards.

The following season, Coach Frank Leahy switched to the T formation, in part to take full advantage of Bertelli's skills, and the junior quarterback responded by completing 74 of 165 passes for 931 yards.

In 1943, Notre Dame relied much more on the run. Bertelli completed 25 of only 36 passes for 512 yards and 10 touchdowns in 6 games before being drafted into the service. Despite his abbreviated season, he was named an All-American and won the Heisman Trophy as the outstanding college player of the year.

His successor at Notre Dame, Johnny Lujack, called him "the finest short passer that I've seen in the collegiate ranks," and sportswriter Grantland Rice said he was the finest ball-handler he'd ever seen.

After World War II, Bertelli played with the Los Angeles Dons of the All-America Football Conference in 1946 and with the AAFC's Chicago Rockets in 1946 and 1947. He completed 76 of 166 passes for 972 yards and 8 touchdowns as a professional.
★ College Football Hall of Fame

Berwanger, Jay (John J.)

FOOTBALL
b. March 19, 1914, Dubuque, Iowa

An All-American quarterback at the University of Chicago in 1935, Berwanger won the first Heisman Trophy that year. The 6-foot-1, 190-pound Berwanger could do the 100-yard dash in just over 10 seconds, and he was a very dangerous runner. In three years as a starter, he gained more than 5,000 yards.

He scored on runs of 65 yards against Dartmouth in 1933, 97 yards against Iowa in 1934, and 85 yards against Ohio State in 1935. Berwanger was also a fine kicker, a good passer — in 1934 his touchdown passes won three games — and an excellent defensive player. Sportswriter Christy Walsh called him "a defensive backfield all by himself."

Berwanger wore a face protector after

he suffered a broken nose as a freshman, and was sometimes called the "man in the iron mask." He was the first 1936 draft choice of the NFL's Philadelphia Eagles, who traded his rights to the Chicago Bears, but Berwanger elected not to play pro football.

★ College Football Hall of Fame

Bettenhausen, Tony (Melvin E.)
AUTO RACING
b. Sept. 12, 1916, Tinley Park, Ill.
d. May 12, 1961

His dream of winning an Indianapolis 500 kept Bettenhausen racing beyond his prime and ultimately led to his death. A combative youngster, he was such a good fighter that he was nicknamed "Tunney," after heavyweight champion Gene Tunney, and that eventually turned into "Tony." Bettenhausen began racing midget cars in the late 1930s and acquired a new nickname, "Flip," because he did it so often.

After service in World War II, Bettenhausen entered the Indy 500 for the first time in 1946 and was forced out by mechanical problems after 47 laps. That kept happening; he didn't finish a race at the "Brickyard" until 1958. But he did well on the USAC championship trail. In 1951 he scored a record 2,256 points, winning 8 of 14 starts and finishing second twice in Murrell Belanger's famous No. 99.

Bettenhausen announced his retirement from everything but the Indy 500 after that great year. But in 1953 he went back on the circuit with No. 99, winning two races. A 1954 accident put him in the hospital with head injuries, and in 1956 he broke a shoulder blade hitting the wall at Indianapolis. The following year, he placed 15th at Indy, again without finishing, skipped several races, and had little success when he returned to the circuit.

But in 1958 he made a remarkable comeback, finally finishing at Indy, in fourth place, and winning his second national championship. He was second to Rodger Ward for the title in 1959, again placing fourth in the Indy 500, and in 1960 he was fifth in the point standings, although he didn't win any races.

Shortly before the 1961 Indianapolis race, his friend Paul Russo asked Bettenhausen to test drive his car and suggest ways to improve its handling. The car crashed and Bettenhausen was killed.

★ Indianapolis Speedway Hall of Fame

Betz, Pauline (Mrs. Addie)
TENNIS
b. Aug. 6, 1919, Dayton, Ohio

An acrobatic tomboy as a child, Betz enjoyed walking on her hands to the corner to meet her father when he came home from work. Her mother, a high school physical education teacher, introduced her to tennis, thinking it was more ladylike.

Betz didn't take formal lessons until she was 15, but she won a tennis scholarship to Rollins College in 1939. While a student at Rollins, she became the U.S. women's champion in 1942, defended the title successfully in 1943 and 1944, and won for a fourth time in 1946, when she also swept to the Wimbledon championship without losing a set.

A fierce competitor, Betz was known for being able to retrieve seemingly impossible shots, and she had an excellent backhand. In 1947, the U.S. Lawn Tennis Association discovered that she and her husband were looking into the possibility of establishing a women's professional tour, and she was suspended from amateur competition.

She and Sarah Palfrey Cooke toured the country as professionals in 1947, playing exhibitions every day and earning about $10,000. Betz later toured with Jack Kramer, Pancho Segura, and "Gussy" Moran. After retiring from competition, she conducted tennis clinics for underprivileged children and wrote about the sport for newspapers and magazines.

★ International Tennis Hall of Fame

Bezdek, Hugo F.
BASEBALL, FOOTBALL
b. April 1, 1884, Prague, Czechoslovakia
d. Sept. 19, 1952

Strange but true: the only man ever to serve as a major league manager and a head coach in the NFL was a native of Czechoslovakia. Bezdek's family came to the U.S. when he was five years old and settled in Chicago. He played fullback under Amos Alonzo Stagg at the University of Chicago, graduating in 1906.

He became head coach at the University of Oregon, compiling a 5–0–1 record in his one season there. After a year out of football, he took over at the University of Arkansas in 1908. In five seasons there, his teams won 29, lost 13, and tied 1. The 1909 team won all 7 of its games.

Bezdek returned to Oregon in 1913 for six more seasons, during which he had a 30–10–4 record. The 1916 team had a 6–0–1 record and beat Pennsylvania, 14–6, in the Rose Bowl. He also worked as West Coast scout for the Pittsburgh Pirates of the National League. In the middle of the 1917 season, the last-place Pirates hired him as manager.

He guided them to fourth place finishes in 1918 and 1919, then left both the Pirates and Oregon to become head football coach and athletic director at Penn State University. He coached there from 1918 through 1929, winning 65 games while losing 30 and tying 11, including a 29-game undefeated streak from 1919 into 1922. His 1920 and 1921 teams were both undefeated, though each had two ties, and the 1922 team lost, 14–3, to Southern California in the Rose Bowl.

Bezdek remained as athletic director until 1937, when the NFL's Cleveland Rams hired him. He had a 1–10 record that season and was fired after the Rams lost their first three games in 1938. His overall college record was 124–54–16, and he won 166 games while losing 187 as Pittsburgh's manager.

A hard driving coach whose players looked forward to games because they were much easier than his practices, Bezdek pioneered in the use of a passing attack from the spread formation, and he's also credited with inventing the single wing's spinner play.

★ College Football Hall of Fame

Bible, Dana X.

FOOTBALL
b. Oct. 8, 1891, Jefferson City, Tenn.
d. Jan 19, 1980

After playing baseball, basketball, and football at Carson-Newman College and the University of North Carolina, Bible coached football for a year at Brandon Preparatory School in Tennessee, then took over at Mississippi College, where he had a 12–7–2 record from 1913 through 1915.

He was freshman coach at Texas A & M in 1916 when Louisiana State University lost its coach with three games to play in the season. Bible was loaned to LSU, which won one and tied two while he was there. He returned to Texas A & M as head coach and athletic director in 1917.

His first Aggie team won all eight of its games. He spent 1918 as a pilot in World War I, then coached Texas A & M to a 10–0–0 record in 1919. His 1927 team was also unbeaten, winning 8 games and tying 1. In 11 seasons, he had a 72–19–9 record and won five Southwest Conference championships.

Bible went to the University of Nebraska in 1929 and won six Big Six titles in eight seasons, compiling a 50–15–7 record. The University of Texas beckoned in 1937, offering an unheard-of 20-year contract for $15,000 a year, the first ten years as coach and athletic director, the second ten as athletic director only. There was an outcry in Texas, since Bible would be paid more than the college president, and the contract was held up until the Texas Legislature gave the president a raise.

At Texas, Bible divided the state into districts and put alumni in charge of recruiting the best football players for their alma mater. The "Bible plan," as it became known, was soon adopted by other state universities. It took some time to produce results, but from 1940 through 1946, Texas had 53 victories with only 13 losses and 1 tie, winning three SWC championships.

Three of Bible's Texas teams went to the Cotton Bowl. The 1942 team beat

Georgia Tech, 14–7; the 1943 team tied Randolph Field, a service team, 7–7; and the 1945 team beat Missouri, 40–25.

Bible retired after the 1946 season. His overall record in 33 seasons was 192 wins, 71 losses, and 23 ties, a .712 winning percentage.

His success was due, in part, to his use of psychology to motivate players. At halftime of the Texas / Texas A & M game in 1922, with the score tied, 7–7, Bible dragged his foot across the floor of the A & M locker room and said, "Those who want to go out and be known as members of an A & M team that defeated Texas in Austin, step over the line." Players rushed to cross the line, then went out to beat Texas, 14–7.

★ College Football Hall of Fame

Bierman, Bernie (Bernard W.)

FOOTBALL
b. March 11, 1894, Springfield, Minn.
d. March 8, 1977

Bierman had to use crutches as a child because of osteomyelitis, but an operation cured the problem and he became a three-sport star in high school and at the University of Minnesota, where he captained the 1915 football team as a senior.

He coached high school football for a year, served in the Marine Corps for two years, then went to Montana State University for three seasons, winning 9, losing 9, and tying 3. Bierman married in 1921 and became a bonds salesman, but his wife talked him into getting back into coaching because she didn't like staying home alone while he was on the road.

After assisting at Tulane, Bierman became head coach at Mississippi A & M (now Mississippi State) in 1925 and had an 8–8–1 record there in two seasons. At Tulane from 1927 through 1931, Bierman won 36 games, lost 10, and tied 3. His 1931 team won all 11 of its games, then lost 21–12 to Southern California in the Rose Bowl.

Bierman returned to Minnesota in 1932. In his first ten seasons, he produced five undefeated teams, won six

Big Ten championships, and had four national champions, in 1934, 1936, 1940, and 1941. After three years as a Marine colonel in World War II, he resumed coaching in 1945. He produced some good teams, but resigned after his 1950 team won only 1 game.

Quiet and cold, Bierman hated to talk to the press and was sometimes criticized by players for being uncommunicative. He believed in a conservative, run-oriented offense backed by solid defense. His failure to adapt to two-platoon football and the T-formation after World War II led to his downfall after compiling a 146–62–13 record in 25 seasons.

★ College Football Hall of Fame

Biletnikoff, Frederick

FOOTBALL
b. Feb. 23, 1943, Erie, Pa.

Although he was an All-American end at Florida State in 1964, many professional scouts doubted that he would make it in the NFL because he lacked speed. But, like Raymond Berry, Biletnikoff parlayed hard work, precise pass routes, and great hands into a Hall of Fame career with the Oakland Raiders. Coach John Madden called him "one of the most dedicated athletes I have ever seen."

A part-time player in 1965 and 1966, the 6-foot-1, 190-pound Biletnikoff became a starter in 1967, when he caught 40 passes. He caught 42 or more in each of the next nine seasons, with career highs of 61 in 1968 and 1971, when he led the NFL.

In Super Bowl XI, Biletnikoff was named most valuable player after catching 4 passes for 79 yards, setting up 3 touchdowns, in Oakland's 32–14 win over the Minnesota Vikings.

Biletnikoff retired after the 1978 season. He had 589 career receptions for 8,974 yards, a 15.2 average, and 76 touchdowns.

The high-strung Biletnikoff suffered from an ulcer through most of his professional career and threw up before every game because of his nerves. His trademark was large gobs of a gooey sub-

stance known as "stickum" which he smeared on his socks so he could apply some to his fingers before each play.
★ Pro Football Hall of Fame

Bing, Dave (David)

BASKETBALL
b. Nov. 19, 1943, Washington, D.C.

An outstanding shooter and play-maker, Bing starred at Syracuse for three seasons, 1963–64 through 1965–66. The 6-foot-3, 185-pound guard was a consensus All-American as a senior, when he finished fifth in the nation in scoring. He set school records for points in a season with 794, points per game with 28.4, and career points with 1,883. Remarkably, he also set a one-game rebounding record with 25.

Bing joined the Detroit Pistons of the NBA in 1966 and was the league's rookie of the year. After five seasons, he held all of the team's important scoring and assist records. The first guard ever to lead the league in scoring, with 27.1 points per game in 1968, he was a first-team all-star that year and in 1971.

A detached retina suffered in a 1972 pre-season game forced him to miss two months of the season, but he played all 82 games in 1973–74, averaging 22.3 points a game. The Pistons traded him to the Washington Bullets in 1975. After two seasons there, he finished his career with the Boston Celtics in 1977–78, scoring 1,088 points.

In his nine NBA seasons, Bing scored 18,327 points in 901 games, a 20.3 average, and had 5,397 assists.
★ Basketball Hall of Fame

Bionda, Jack A.

HOCKEY, LACROSSE
b. Sept. 18, 1933, Huntsville, Ontario

In the early part of the century, many hockey stars were also fine lacrosse players. Bionda was the last of this breed, but his lacrosse career was much more distinguished than his hockey career.

He began playing lacrosse in his native Ontario, then moved to British Columbia. Between 1955 and 1962 he played on five teams that won the Mann Cup, awarded to Canada's best amateur team. Bionda was twice most valuable player in the Mann Cup tournament, and he scored three or more goals in nine games, a career record.

Bionda also played four seasons in the National Hockey League with the Toronto Maple Leafs and the Boston Bruins, scoring 3 goals and 9 assists in 93 regular-season games between 1955–56 and 1958–59.
★ Canadian Sports Hall of Fame

Biondi, Matthew N.

SWIMMING
b. Oct. 8, 1965, Moraga, Calif.

Swimming in his third Olympics in 1992, Biondi won three medals for a total of 11, tying him with shooter Carl Osburn and swimmer Mark Spitz for most medals won by an American athlete.

Biondi won his first medal, a gold, as a little-known 18-year-old member of the 4 x 100-meter relay team in 1984. As a student at the University of California, Berkeley, he won the NCAA 100- and 200-yard freestyle championships in 1987.

Six weeks before the 1988 Olympics, he swam a 48.42 in the 100-meter freestyle to set a world record that still stands. At 6-foot-6 and 200 pounds, Biondi was unusually big for a swimmer, but he had a flawless stroke that powered him through the water with seemingly little effort, and he boasted great stamina that led one competitor to comment that if Biondi was leading halfway through a race, he was sure to win.

Biondi was one of the biggest stars of the Seoul Games in September 1988, winning seven medals, including five gold. He won individual golds in the 50- and 100-meter freestyle events, and was also a member of the 400- and 800-meter freestyle relay teams and the 400-meter medley relay team. He took a silver in the 100-meter butterfly and a bronze in the 200-meter freestyle.

He retired from competition after the 1992 Olympics, when he won a silver in the 50-meter freestyle and was a member of the gold medal 4 x 100 freestyle and 4 x 100 medley relay teams.

Bird, Larry J.

BASKETBALL
b. Dec. 7, 1956, French Lick, Ind.

Only 6 feet tall as a high school sophomore, Bird played guard for two years, then grew to 6-foot-4 and became a forward as a senior, averaging more than 30 points per game. He won a basketball scholarship to Indiana University in 1974 but left school after a month, went to a junior college for two months, then dropped out and returned home.

In 1975, he was given a scholarship at Indiana State, but had to sit out a year to become eligible. After averaging more than 30 points a game for two years, he was drafted by the NBA's Boston Celtics in the first round of the 1978 draft because his original class had graduated.

Bird opted to finish college. Now fully grown to 6-foot-9 and 220 pounds, he averaged 28.6 points and 14.9 rebounds a game to lead Indiana State to an undefeated regular season and the NCAA tournament finals, where Michigan State, led by Earvin "Magic" Johnson, won the title. Bird was a consensus All-American and college player of the year.

He then signed a five-year contract with the Celtics, reportedly for more than $3 million. Some critics doubted that he would be a professional star because he lacked foot speed and jumping ability. However, with Bird averaging 21.3 points and 10.4 rebounds a game, Boston had the greatest turnaround in NBA history, going from a 29–53 record to 61–21 in 1979–80. Bird was named the league's rookie of the year.

He led the Celtics to NBA championships in 1981, 1984, and 1986 and was the most valuable player in the playoffs in 1984 and 1986 and the league's most valuable player three years in a row, from 1984 through 1986. He was also named the Associated Press male athlete of the year and the *Sports Illustrated* sportsman of the year in 1986.

Heel problems began to bother him during the 1986–87 season, and he played in only six games in 1988–89 before having operations on both heels. He returned to play 75 games in 1989–90, but appeared in just 60 games in 1990–91 and 45 in 1991–92 before retiring.

Perhaps the most versatile player in basketball history, Bird could rebound and score from inside and was an outstanding outside shooter. He led the NBA in free throw percentage four times. And he may well have been the greatest passing forward ever. Although not a strong defender one on one, his anticipation and court sense made him a good team defender who often came up with important steals, especially on inbound passes.

An all-NBA forward nine consecutive seasons, from 1980 through 1988, Bird was named second-team all-NBA in 1990, and he was named to the all-defensive second team from 1982 through 1984. In 897 regular season games, he scored 21,791 points, a 24.3 average, and had 8,974 rebounds, 5,695 assists, 1,556 steals, and 755 blocked shots. He averaged 23.8 points in 164 playoff games.

Bjurstedt, Molla (Anna M.; Mrs. Mallory)

TENNIS
b. 1893?, Oslo, Norway
d. Nov. 21, 1959

After winning eight Norwegian national championships, Bjurstedt visited the U.S. in 1914 and liked it so much that she decided to stay. She went on to win a record eight national singles championships here as well.

An unusually hard hitter for a woman player in her era, Bjurstedt once said, "I believe in always hitting the ball with all my might." She attacked constantly. When she beat Hazel Wightman for her first U.S. championship in 1915, one sportswriter described her as "a panther stalking her prey." She also won titles from 1916 through 1918, from 1920 through 1922, and in 1926.

She was indoor singles champion in 1915, 1916, 1918, 1921, and 1922. She won women's outdoor doubles championships with Eleanora Sears in 1916 and

1917 and teamed with Marie Wagner to win the indoor doubles title in 1916. Bjurstedt and Bill Tilden won indoor mixed doubles championships in 1921 and 1922 and the outdoors doubles titles in 1922 and 1923. She also won the 1917 outdoor mixed doubles title with Irving C. Wright.

The highlight of her career was probably a famous match against French champion Suzanne Lenglen in the 1921 national tournament. Bjurstedt won the first set, 6–2. Lenglen walked off the court, pleading illness, after losing the first three points of the second set on her own serve.

Bjurstedt, who married Franklin Mallory, a wealthy stockbroker, retired from serious competition after losing to young Helen Wills in the 1923 national finals.

★ International Tennis Hall of Fame

Blaik, Red (Earl H.)

FOOTBALL
b. Feb. 15, 1897, Detroit, Mich.
d. May 6, 1988

Blaik was the first of many outstanding coaches to play football at Miami of Ohio, where he was on an undefeated team in 1916. He then won an appointment to the U.S. Military Academy, graduating in 1920.

He left the Army in 1922 and went to work for his father, but also worked as an assistant coach at the University of Wisconsin and at West Point. Blaik took his first head coaching job at Dartmouth in 1934, when he was 37 years old. In seven seasons at Dartmouth, Blaik had a 45–15–4 record, and his 1937 team was undefeated, with 2 ties in 9 games.

One of the victories during Blaik's last season at Dartmouth, 1940, came in a game that Dartmouth had apparently lost, 7–3, when Cornell scored a touchdown on the final play. However, Cornell had been given five downs on which to score and graciously relinquished the victory. The game went down in the record books as a 3–0 Dartmouth win.

Blaik returned to Army as head coach in 1941. The school had won just 4 games in the previous two seasons; Blaik

won 5 in his first year and also had a scoreless tie against a powerful Notre Dame team that won its other 8 games.

When World War II began, most other colleges were drained of players, while Army and Navy were able to build powerful teams. Led by "Doc" Blanchard and Glenn Davis, Army went undefeated from 1944 through 1946, winning 27 games and tying 1 — another scoreless tie against Notre Dame.

After the war, Blaik continued to turn out fine teams. In 1948, Army won 8 and tied 1; the Cadets won all 9 of their games the following season and had an 8–1–0 record in 1950.

In the spring of 1951, scandal hit West Point. More than 50 cadets, including 37 football players, were expelled for cheating on exams. Bob Blaik, the coach's son and starting quarterback, was among them. Blaik wanted to resign but was persuaded to stay on and rebuild the team.

It took two years, but Army was a power again in 1953, and Blaik finished his career with six consecutive winning seasons. His last team, in 1958, won 8 and tied 1 without a loss. That team used the "Lonesome End" formation, in which one end was split very wide and never entered the Cadet huddle. He was given the plays through hand signals from the quarterback.

Blaik's overall record was 166 wins, 48 losses, and 14 ties. He was named coach of the year in 1946. Nineteen of his players and assistant coaches went on to become head coaches in college or professional football.

★ College Football Hall of Fame

Blair, Bonnie

SPEED SKATING
b. March 18, 1964, Cornwall, N.Y.

Blair began in short-track speed skating, which has a whole pack of skaters racing around a track. When she was 16, she began Olympic-style racing, in which only two skaters are on the track, racing against time rather than against one another.

In 1982, Blair was advised to compete in Europe to sharpen her skills, but had difficulty raising money for the trip. The police department of Champaign, Illinois, where she was living, held a series of raffles and bake sales on her behalf, and Jack Sikma of the NBA's Milwaukee Bucks donated $1,500 to the cause. Blair gained much-needed experience in Olympic-style speed skating during her European tour.

Blair won the U.S. indoor title in 1983, 1984, and 1986, and was the North American indoor champion in 1985. She became a definite Olympic contender by setting a world record of 39.43 seconds in the 500-meter event at the 1987 worlds. At the 1988 Olympics, Blair set another world record to win a gold medal in the 500-meter event.

After winning the world over-all sprint title in 1989, she finished second in 1990 and third in 1991 and entered the 1992 Olympics as a favorite in the 500-meter and a strong contender in the 1,000-meter. She won both, becoming the first skater ever to win two consecutive gold medals in the 500-meter sprint, and she received the Sullivan Award as the nation's outstanding amateur athlete.

The 5-foot-4, 130-pound Blair, described as "disarmingly ebullient" by one sportswriter, became a favorite with media and fans. Almost always smiling, she once described herself as a person "who is never really unhappy."

She climaxed her career by winning the world sprint championship and gold medals in the Olympic 500- and 1,000-meter races in 1994.

Blake, Toe (Hector)

HOCKEY
b. Aug. 21, 1912, Victoria Mines, Ont.

Known as the "Old Lamplighter" for his scoring ability, Blake played 12 seasons with the Montreal Canadiens, winning 2 Stanley Cups, then coached them for 13 seasons and won 8 more Stanley Cups, including a record 5 in a row.

Blake played just three games for the Montreal Maroons in 1934 before going back down to the minor leagues. He joined the Canadiens in February 1936 and played with them until he broke his leg in January 1948, forcing his retirement. The bilingual Blake often played with English-speaking Elmer Lach and French-speaking Rocket Richard on the "Punch Line." In the 1946 Stanley Cup playoffs, he and Richard scored 7 goals each and Lach had 5 as the Canadiens eliminated the Chicago Black Hawks in four games, then beat the Boston Bruins in five games in the finals.

Blake was the NHL's leading scorer in 1939, and he won the Byng Trophy in 1946. He set a Stanley Cup record, since tied, with 5 assists in one game against Toronto in 1944. He had 235 goals and 292 assists in regular season play, with 25 goals and 37 assists in 57 playoff games.

After retiring as a player, Blake coached in the minor leagues, then took over to the Canadiens in 1955. He retired after the 1967–68 season, having coached Montreal to Stanley Cups from 1956 through 1960 and in 1965, 1966, and 1968.

Blake coached 914 regular season games, winning an even 500 against 255 losses and 159 ties. In Stanley Cup play, he had an 82–37 record, winning 18 series and losing only 5.

★ Hockey Hall of Fame

Blalock, Jane

GOLF
b. Sept. 19, 1945, Portsmouth, N.H.

Blalock began playing golf when she was 13. After graduating from Rollins College in Florida, she won the New England Amateur championship and then joined the LPGA tour. Her first professional victory came in the 1970 Lady Carling tournament.

From the time she joined the tour until 1980, Blalock made the cut in 299 consecutive tournaments, and she won 29 of them, leaving her just one short of automatic induction into the LPGA Hall of Fame. Her one major victory was in the 1972 Colgate / Dinah Shore tournament.

Since 1986, Blalock has worked as a full-time stockbroker and has played on the tour only occasionally.

Blanchard, Doc (Felix A.)

FOOTBALL

b. Dec. 11, 1924, Bishopville, S.C.

Notre Dame coach Ed McKeever sent a telegram after his 1944 team was devastated, 59–0, by Army: "Have just seen Superman in the flesh. He wears No. 35 on his Army jersey. His name is Felix 'Doc' Blanchard."

The son of a doctor who had played football at Tulane and Wake Forest, Blanchard was nicknamed "Little Doc" as a boy. After starring at St. Stanislaus College, actually a prep school in Mississippi, he entered the University of North Carolina in 1942.

Blanchard joined the Army after his freshman year and was appointed to the U.S. Military Academy in 1944. A fullback, he teamed with halfback Glenn Davis to help lead Army to three undefeated seasons. The only game Army didn't win during that period was a scoreless tie against Notre Dame in 1946.

Although Davis was known as "Mr. Outside" and the 6-foot, 208-pound Blanchard was "Mr. Inside," he was almost as fast as Davis. In 1945, he ran the 100-yard dash in 10 seconds flat in a dual meet against Cornell. He also won the IC4A shotput championship that year.

Blanchard scored three touchdowns, one on a 52-yard interception return, in Army's 32–13 win over Navy in 1945, when he won the Heisman Trophy as the nation's best college football player and the Sullivan Award as the outstanding amateur athlete of the year. He was the first football player to win the Sullivan.

An outstanding place-kicker and punter, Blanchard was also a fine pass receiver. He missed the first two games of the 1946 season with torn knee ligaments but returned to action against a strong Michigan team. Blanchard made a leaping catch of a pass from Davis to score a 41-yard touchdown, and he ran for another in Army's 20–13 victory. He returned a kickoff 92 yards for a touchdown against Columbia, and in a 21–18 victory over Navy, he scored on a 53-yard run and caught a 27-yard touchdown pass from Davis.

After graduating from West Point, Blanchard entered the Air Force and became a jet pilot. While he was stationed in England in 1959, his plane caught fire near London. Rather than abandoning the aircraft in a heavily populated area, he brought it down safely at an airfield and was cited for bravery.

★ College Football Hall of Fame

Blanchard, Theresa (Weld)

FIGURE SKATING

b. Aug. 21, 1893, Brookline, Mass.
d. March 12, 1978

Her father, A. Windsor Weld, was a charter member of the Skating Club of Boston, which championed the free, graceful international style of figure skating as opposed to the formal, stiff English technique. Known as "Tee," she began driving her pony cart to the club to take lessons when she was 12.

Although some judges lowered her marks because her athletic jumps and loops were considered unladylike, Blanchard was the U.S. singles champion six times, in 1914 and from 1920 through 1924. She also teamed with Nathaniel W. Niles to win nine national pairs titles, in 1918 and from 1920 through 1927.

In 1920, she won the first U.S. medal in the Winter Olympics, a bronze. She was also on the 1924 and 1928 Olympic teams. Married to Charles Blanchard in 1920, she kept competing until 1934, when she was a member of the U.S. champion fours team.

Blanchard and Niles in 1923 founded *Skating* magazine, which is now the official publication of the U.S. Figure Skating Association. After retiring from competition, she became a world judge and served on the USFSA executive board for 13 years.

★ International Women's Sports Hall of Fame

Blanda, George F.

FOOTBALL

b. Sept. 17, 1927, Youngwood, Pa.

After quarterbacking the University of Kentucky for three seasons, Blanda joined the NFL's Chicago Bears and had a fairly undistinguished ten-year career with them. He became Chicago's starting quarterback in 1953 and led the NFL in pass attempts with 362 and completions with 169, but his 46.7 completion percentage and 23 interceptions against 14 touchdowns left something to be desired.

An injury sidelined him for about half the 1954 season, and he became a backup quarterback and place-kicker for the rest of his time with the Bears. He retired in 1959 because the Bears wanted to use him only as a kicker.

When the Houston Oilers joined the new American Football League in 1960, Blanda came out of retirement to become the starting quarterback on a pass-happy team. He led the AFL in passing yardage with 3,330 and touchdown passes with 36 in 1961; in completions with 224 and yardage with 3,003 in 1963; completions with 262 in 1964 and 186 in 1965. The Oilers won the first two AFC championships, and Blanda was named the league's player of the year in 1961.

Though he wasn't a starter for all of 1966, he did Houston's kicking and led the league with 116 points. Then he was traded to the Oakland Raiders, where he was primarily a kicker. Blanda became a legend, especially among over-40 fans, with an incredible five weeks in 1970, when he was 43 years old.

It began on October 25, when he replaced an injured Daryle Lamonica and threw touchdown passes of 19, 43, and 44 yards in a 31–14 victory over Pittsburgh. The following week, he kicked a 48-yard field goal with three seconds left to give Oakland a 17–17 tie with Kansas City.

On November 8, he replaced Lamonica in the fourth quarter with Oakland trailing by a touchdown. Blanda threw a 14-yard touchdown pass to tie the game with 1:14 remaining, then won it with a 52-yard field goal with three seconds to play. Against Denver on November 15, Blanda came in with 4 minutes left and Oakland losing, 19–17. He led an 80-yard drive, culminating in a 20-yard touchdown pass to Fred Biletnikoff for another

victory. And on November 22, his 16-yard field goal with four seconds remaining gave Oakland a 20–17 win over San Diego.

Thanks to those heroics, Oakland won the AFC Western Division championship and Blanda was named the AFC player of the year and the Associated Press male athlete of the year.

He announced his retirement before the 1975 season, shortly before his forty-ninth birthday. During his incredible 26-year career, the longest in pro football history, Blanda completed 1,911 of 4,007 passes for 26,920 yards and 236 touchdowns, with 277 interceptions. He scored 9 touchdowns, kicked 943 extra points, and had 335 field goals for a record 2,002 points.

★ Pro Football Hall of Fame

Blatnick, Jeffery C.

WRESTLING
b. July 26, 1957, Schenectady, N.Y.

Competing for Springfield, Massachusetts, College, Blatnick won NCAA Division II heavyweight wrestling championships in 1978 and 1979. He then switched from freestyle to Greco-Roman wrestling and qualified for the 1980 Olympic team but didn't compete because the U.S. boycotted the Moscow Games that year.

The 1980 and 1981 AAU super heavyweight champion, Blatnick discovered a lump in his neck early in 1982 and was diagnosed with Hodgkin's disease, cancer of the lymphatic system. His spleen and appendix were removed, and he underwent radiation therapy.

The disease went into remission, and Blatnick made the 1984 Olympic team. In the final match, the 240-Blatnick faced 275-pound Thomas Johansson of Sweden. "The Swede is big," his father told him, "but you've come too far to let anything stop you now." Blatnick took a 2–0 victory, becoming only the second U.S. Greco-Roman wrestler in history to win a gold medal.

After a second bout with cancer, requiring 28 sessions of chemotherapy in 1985 and 1986, Blatnick retired from competition, but he served as a television commentator during the 1988 Olympics.

Blazejowski, Carol A. ("Blaze")
BASKETBALL
b. Sept. 29, 1956, Elizabeth, N.J.

Using a jump shot patterned after what she saw in televised professional games, Blazejowski became one of the greatest scorers in the history of women's basketball, although she didn't begin serious competition until her senior year in high school.

At Montclair, New Jersey, State College, the 5-foot-10 forward was a three-time All-American, from 1976 through 1978, and won the first Wade Trophy as the nation's finest collegiate woman player in 1978. She led the nation in scoring with 33.5 points a game in 1976–77 and with 38.6 per game in 1977–78. Blazejowski scored 40 or more points in each of her last three games, and she set a Madison Square Garden record for either sex with 52 points in a 1978 game against Queens College.

Only an alternate on the 1976 Olympic team, she led the 1977 World University Games team in scoring and had 38 points in a losing effort against the Soviet Union.

After finishing her college career with a record 3,199 points, she played two seasons of AAU basketball with the Allentown, Pennsylvania, Crestettes. The leading scorer on the national team that won the 1979 world championship, she was chosen for the 1980 Olympic team, but her hopes for a gold medal were crushed by the U.S. boycott of the Moscow Games.

In 1980, Blazejowski became the highest-paid player in the Women's Basketball League, signing a three-year contract for a reported $150,000 with the New Jersey Gems. However, the league folded after just one season, effectively ending her career.
★ Basketball Hall of Fame

Bleibtrey, Ethelda
SWIMMING
b. Feb. 27, 1902, Waterford, N.Y.
d. May 6, 1978

Bleibtrey held the world record in the 100-yard backstroke when women's swimming was added to the Olympic program in 1920. But the only three events were the 100-meter and 300-meter freestyles and the 4 by 100-meter freestyle relay. So she entered all three and won three gold medals.

Antwerp, Belgium, hosted those Olympics, less than two years after the end of World War I. There were no suitable pools, indoors or outdoors, so the swimming competition was held in a tidal estuary. Bleibtrey said afterward it was like swimming in mud. Nevertheless, she set a world record of 1:14.4 in the third heat of the 100-meter freestyle, and she lowered that to 1:13.6 in the final.

Bleibtrey won every race she swam in from 1920 through 1922. She was U.S. outdoor national champion in the 100-yard freestyle in 1920 and 1921; the 440-yard freestyle in 1919 and 1921; the 880-yard freestyle from 1919 through 1921; the 1-mile freestyle in 1920, and the long-distance (3-mile) race in 1921. She won indoor championships in the 100-yard freestyle in 1920 and 1922, and in the 100-yard backstroke in 1920.

In 1919, Bleibtrey broke a rule at Manhattan Beach by taking her stockings off; she was given a summons for "nude swimming." The resultant publicity brought an end to that rule. Nine years later, as part of a campaign for more public swimming facilities in New York City, she was jailed for swimming in the Central Park Reservoir. Not long afterward, the city opened its first large public pool.
★ International Swimming Hall of Fame

Blood, Ernest A.
BASKETBALL
b. Oct. 4, 1872, Manchester, N.H.
d. Feb. 5, 1955

Although Blood is best known as the coach of the Passaic, New Jersey, High School "Wonder Teams" of 1915–24, he coached for a total of 51 years at YMCAs, high schools, and colleges, compiling an incredible record of 1,268 wins and only 165 losses.

At Passaic, his teams won 200 of 201 games, including a 143-game winning streak. His only loss came in the finals of New Jersey's first state tournament in 1919. The streak was still intact when he left after the 1923–24 season; it reached 159 games before Passaic lost to Hackensack on February 6, 1925.

Blood believed in a fast-paced offense, and he was one of the first coaches to put his players through a total conditioning program so they could keep running throughout the game. His 1921–22 team scored 2,293 points in 33 games, an average of nearly 70 a game at a time when 30 or 40 points was usually enough to win.

He began his coaching career in 1895 at the Nashua, NH, YMCA and coached at other YMCAs until 1906, when he went to Potsdam, New York, State Normal (now Potsdam State University). While at Potsdam, he also coached Clarkson University for a time. After a 72–2 record at Potsdam and a 40–5 record at Clarkson, he moved on to Passaic.

Blood coached at the U.S. Military Academy in 1924–25 and 1925–26, then went to St. Benedict's Prep in Newark, where he spent the rest of his career, retiring in 1949. His St. Benedict's teams won five state championships.
★ Basketball Hall of Fame

Blouin, Jimmy (James)
BOWLING
b. Dec. 21, 1886, Trois Rivieres, P.Q.
d. April 6, 1947

One of the great match-game bowlers in the era before professional tournaments, Blouin was often challenged but rarely defeated. He won the match-game title at the 1922 World Open and defended it five times against some of the best bowlers of the day before retiring in 1926.

Blouin won the ABC all-events title in 1909 with an 1885 total for nine games and took the 1911 singles championship with a 681 score for six games.

In 19 ABC tournaments, he averaged 194 pins per game.
★ ABC Hall of Fame

Blount, Melvin
FOOTBALL
b. April 10, 1948, Vidalia, Ga.

After playing defensive back at Southern University, Blount (pronounced *blunt*) joined the NFL's Pittsburgh Steelers in 1970. He became a major part of the "Steel Curtain" defense that led the Steelers to Super Bowl victories that brought them the league's 1974, 1975, 1978, and 1979 championships.

Though he didn't have great speed, the 6-foot-3, 205-pound Blount was an expert at analyzing pass patterns and a very aggressive defender who moved to the ball quickly, either to make an interception or to hit the receiver as soon as the pass arrived.

Blount led the NFL in interceptions with 11 in 1975. During his 14-year career, he played in 5 Pro Bowls and was an all-conference choice at defensive back 3 consecutive years, from 1975 through 1977.

Blount had 57 career interceptions and returned them for 736 yards, a 12.9 average, scoring 3 touchdowns. He also returned 36 kickoffs for 911 yards, a 25.3 average.

Blount retired after the 1983 season. Shortly afterward, he became the NFL's director of player relations.
★ Pro Football Hall of Fame

Blozis, Albert C.
FOOTBALL, TRACK & FIELD
b. Jan. 5, 1919, Garfield, N.J.
d. Jan. 31, 1945, France

The 6-foot-6, 240-pound Blozis played football and was a weight thrower on the track team at Georgetown University, graduating in 1942. He won the NCAA, IC4A, and AAU shotput championships indoors and outdoors three years in a row, 1940–42, and was also the IC4A discus champion all three years.

Blozis was a tackle with the NFL's New York Giants from 1942 through 1944 and then entered the Army as a lieutenant. He was reported missing and later presumed dead after failing to return from a search for two enlisted men who were lost in the snow in France.

Blubaugh, Douglas M.

WRESTLING
b. Dec. 13, 1934, Ponca City, Okla.

At Oklahoma State University, Blubaugh won the NCAA and AAU national 157-pound championships in 1957. After graduating, he repeated as AAU champion in 1958 and 1959 and won gold medals at the 1959 Pan-American Games and the 1960 Olympics.

Blubaugh was named the world's outstanding wrestler after his Olympic championship. He later served as an assistant coach at several colleges before becoming head wrestling coach at Indiana University in 1972.

Blue, Vida R.

BASEBALL
b. July 28, 1949, Mansfield, La.

After appearing in just 18 games during brief stints with the Oakland Athletics in 1969 and 1970, Blue suddenly became the ace of the team's pitching staff in 1971, compiling a 24–8 record and leading the AL with 8 shutouts and a 1.82 ERA. He won the Cy Young Award and was named the league's most valuable player for that performance.

Blue earned only $13,000 that year, and he held out the following season for $90,000. He finally settled for less money and wasn't nearly as good a pitcher when he came back in 1972, winning 6 games against 10 losses.

He never duplicated his 1971 numbers, though he was 20–9 in 1973 and 22–11 in 1975, and *The Sporting News* named him the NL's outstanding pitcher in 1978, when he had an 18–10 record for the San Francisco Giants.

The left-handed Blue had a live fastball, a good curve, and exceptional control in his best years. After players were granted free agency in the 1976 Basic Agreement, controversial Oakland owner Charles O. Finley attempted to sell three of his best players for a total of $3.5 million. Blue was to go to the New York Yankees, but Commissioner Bowie Kuhn voided the sale on the grounds that it would be bad for baseball.

Blue was traded to San Francisco in 1977. He spent the 1982 and 1983 seasons with the Kansas City Royals, missed all of 1984 with an injury, then returned to San Francisco for two final seasons.

He had a 209–161 record in 17 seasons, with 37 shutouts and a 3.28 ERA. Blue struck out 2,175 hitters and walked 1,185 in 3,343 innings.

Blyleven, Bert (Rik Aalbert)

BASEBALL
b. April 6, 1951, Zeist, Holland

Blyleven grew up in California and began his professional baseball career in 1969. A right-hander, he joined the AL's Minnesota Twins during the 1970 season and was named the league's rookie pitcher of the year by *The Sporting News*, going 10–9 with a 3.18 ERA.

His best season was 1973, when he went 20–17 and led the league with 9 shutouts, 40 starts, and 25 complete games. Minnesota traded him to the Texas Rangers during the 1976 season, and on September 22, 1977, he pitched a 6–0 no-hitter against the California Angels.

The following season, he pitched for the Pittsburgh Pirates. After struggling to an 8–13 record in 1980, he went to the Cleveland Indians. Because of arm trouble, Blyleven missed much of the 1982 season and had only 24 starts in 1983, but he bounced back with a 19–7 record and a 2.87 ERA in 1984.

Blyleven returned to Minnesota during the 1985 season, and the Twins traded him to California after he had a 10–17 record in 1988. He was named the AL's comeback player of the year for his 17–5 record and 2.73 ERA in 1989, and the 300-victory milestone seemed within his reach.

However, he missed the entire 1991 season with a sore arm and ended his career with an 8–12 record for California in 1992. He had a 287–250 record with 60 shutouts and a 3.31 ERA. Blyleven struck out 3,701 hitters and walked 1,322 in 4,970⅓ innings.

Boddicker, Mike (Michael J.)

BASEBALL
b. Aug. 23, 1957, Cedar Rapids, Iowa

A right-handed pitcher who tantalized hitters with a change-up and slow curve, Boddicker spent parts of the 1980, 1981, and 1982 seasons with the AL's Baltimore Orioles before joining the team early in the 1983 season, when he had a 16–8 record with a 2.77 ERA and a league-leading 5 shutouts to win *The Sporting News* rookie pitcher of the year award.

In 1984, Boddicker led the league with 20 victories and a 2.79 ERA. He slumped for the next three years and was traded to the Boston Red Sox during the 1988 season. After going 15–11 in 1989 and 17–8 in 1990, Boddicker was signed by the Kansas City Royals as a free agent.

Boddicker was 12–12 with the Royals in 1991 and then developed arm trouble. He retired after having a 3–5 record for the Milwaukee Brewers in 1993.

During his 14 major league seasons, Boddicker had a 134–116 record with 16 shutouts and a 3.80 ERA. He struck out 1,330 hitters and walked 721 in 2,123⅓ innings. In his only World Series appearance, with Baltimore in 1983, Boddicker pitched a 3-hit shutout.

Boeheim, Jim (James A. Jr.)

BASKETBALL
b. Nov. 17, 1944, Lyons, N.Y.

After playing basketball at Syracuse University, graduating in 1966, Boeheim became the school's golf coach and a graduate assistant in basketball. He was named a full-time assistant basketball coach in 1972 and took over as head coach four years later.

Boeheim had a 26–4 record in 1976–77, the fifth best ever for a coach in his first year. Boeheim, a believer in the fast break, has consistently produced high-scoring, crowd-pleasing teams. The success of Syracuse's basketball program under his leadership led to the construction of the school's 33,000-seat Carrier Dome in 1984. Since then, Syracuse has led colleges in basketball attendance every year.

In 18 seasons through 1993–94, Boeheim had a 434–140 record. His .756 winning percentage is eleventh best all-time and his 17 seasons with 20 or more wins is twelfth best. Syracuse has a 21–15 record under Boeheim in 15 NCAA tournaments. Syracuse lost 74–73 to Indiana University in the 1987 championship game.

Boggs, Philip G.

DIVING
b. Dec. 29, 1949, Akron, Ohio

The only diver before Greg Louganis to win a world title in the same event three times, Boggs was the springboard champion in 1973, 1975, and 1978.

The strong, stylish Boggs won the 1971 NCAA 3-meter springboard title, representing Florida State. He then entered the U.S. Air Force. Boggs had risen to the rank of captain when he won a gold medal in the springboard event at the 1976 Olympics. Shortly after the Olympics, he left the service to study law at the University of Michigan.

The national 3-meter outdoor champion four years in a row, from 1972 through 1975, Boggs also won the indoor title in 1973 and 1975.

Boggs, Wade A.

BASEBALL
b. June 15, 1958, Omaha, Nebr.

Baseball's best hitter of the 1980s, Boggs won five AL batting titles in a six-year period, from 1983 through 1988, and set a major league record by collecting more than 200 hits in seven consecutive seasons.

The left-handed-hitting Boggs joined the Boston Red Sox during the 1982 season, when he was used in the outfield, at first base and third base, and as a designated hitter. He batted .349 in 104 games.

The following year, he became the team's starting third baseman and won his first batting title with a .361 average. After slipping to .325 in 1984, he won four titles in a row with averages of .368, .357, .363, and .366.

Boggs hit .300 each of the next four years, dropped all the way to .259 in 1992, then went to the New York Yankees as a free agent. He rebounded somewhat to hit .302 in 1993.

Blessed with an excellent eye, Boggs rarely strikes out and draws a lot of walks. He led the league in walks with 105 in 1986 and 1265 in 1988, in runs scored with 128 in 1988 and 113 in 1989, and in doubles with 45 in 1988 and 51 in 1989. He was also the league leader in on-base percentage in 1983, 1985, 1986, 1987, 1988, and 1989.

Though not a particularly good fielder in his early years, Boggs turned himself into a fine defensive third baseman through hard work. He was named to *The Sporting News* AL All-Star team at the position in 1983, from 1985 through 1988, and in 1991.

Boggs, who is married, got some unwelcome publicity in 1988 when a California woman, Margo Adams, filed a $6 million breach of promise suit against him, alleging that they had had a four-year affair. Boggs admitted the affair, but said it had lasted for only two years. The suit was dismissed in 1989.

Through 1994, Boggs had a .335 average with 2,392 hits, including 467 doubles, 49 triples, and 98 home runs. He had walked 1,139 times, struck out 548 times, scored 1,211 runs, and driven in 746.

Boitano, Brian

FIGURE SKATING
b. Oct. 22, 1963, Mountain View, Calif.

Early in his career, Boitano was a nearly flawless technical skater with incredible jumping ability whose scores often suffered because of his lack of artistic expression. He was the first skater ever to land a triple axel, at the 1982 U.S. championships, where he finished fourth.

After finishing second to Scott Hamilton in the 1983 and 1984 national championships, Boitano won the first of four consecutive U.S. titles in 1985 and he won the world title in 1986, making perfect landings on five triple jumps.

Boitano was second behind Canada's Brian Orser in the 1987 world championships, when he fell trying a quadruple loop. He then began working with a choreographer to improve his artistry, and he dropped the quadruple jump from his program. In 1988, he swept the U.S., Olympic, and world championships, edging Orser in both international events.

After five years of professional skating, Boitano went back into training for the 1994 Winter Olympics, when professionals were allowed to compete. He finished a disappointing sixth.

Bomar, Buddy (Herbert B.)

BOWLING
b. Sept. 27, 1916, Ardmore, Okla.

A high school basketball star despite the fact that his left hand had been badly mangled in a childhood accident, Bomar decided to concentrate on bowling after graduation. He won the prestigious All-Star tournament in 1944 and was the All-Star doubles champion in 1944 with Bill Flesch and in 1950 with Ned Day.

He was a member of ABC tournament team champions from 1947 through 1949. The bowler of the year in 1945 and 1947, Bomar was named to the *National Bowlers Journal* All-American team from 1943 through 1945 and from 1949 through 1950.
★ ABC Hall of Fame

Bomar, Lynn (Robert Lynn)

FOOTBALL
b. 1901

An All-American end at Vanderbilt in 1923, Bomar was an excellent pass receiver. In 1922, he caught touchdown passes of 40, 43, and 52 yards. The 6-foot-2, 215-pounder was often used as a blocking back on important running plays and as a linebacker on defense.

One of the first All-Americans from a southern school, Bomar also starred in baseball and basketball. He played for the NFL's New York Giants in 1925 and 1926.
★ College Football Hall of Fame

Bonds, Barry L.

BASEBALL
b. July 24, 1964, Riverside, Calif.

After being an All-American outfielder at Arizona State University, Bonds was chosen in the first round of the 1985 free-agent draft by the NL's Pittsburgh Pirates. He played just 115 games in the minor leagues before being called up during the 1986 season.

Within a short time, Bonds was being touted as the next great superstar, with a rare combination of hitting ability, power, speed, and defensive skill. The 6-foot-1, 190-pound Bonds, who is left-handed, batted only .223 as a rookie but hit 16 home runs and stole 36 bases in just 113 games.

He was named the league's most valuable player in 1990, when he hit .301 with 33 home runs, 104 runs scored, 114 RBI, and 52 stolen bases. He also led the league's outfielders with 14 assists. Bonds won the award again in 1992. He had a .311 average that season, led the league in runs scored with 109 and in walks with 127, hit 34 home runs and 103 RBI, and stole 39 bases.

Bonds went to the San Francisco Giants as a free agent in 1993 and had his best season to date, batting .336 with 46 home runs, 129 runs scored, 123 RBI, and 29 stolen bases, winning his third MVP award in four years.

The one blemish in his career so far is his post-season play, where he has batted only .191 in three league championship series with the Pirates.

Through 1994, he has a .283 average on 1,287 hits, including 276 doubles, 41 triples, and 259 home runs. He has stolen 309 bases, scored 890 runs, and driven in 760.

Bonds, Bobby L.

BASEBALL
b. March 15, 1946, Riverside, Calif.

In 1969, Bonds hit 32 home runs and stole 45 bases, becoming the third player in history to have more than 30 home runs and 30 stolen bases in a single season. The first two were Willie Mays and Henry Aaron. He narrowly missed becoming the first member of the "40–40

Club" in 1973, when he stole 43 bases and hit 39 home runs.

A right-handed outfielder, Bonds joined the NL's San Francisco Giants during the 1968 season. His best offensive year was 1970, when he batted .302 with 26 home runs, 48 stolen bases, and 134 runs scored.

He spent the 1975 season with the New York Yankees and then went to the California Angels. After two seasons there, Bonds was with the Chicago White Sox and Texas Rangers in 1978. He played for the Cleveland Indians in 1979, the St. Louis Cardinals in 1980, and the Chicago Cubs in 1981, his final season as a player.

His son, Barry, has been the NL's most valuable player three times since 1990. In his 14 major league seasons, Bonds batted .268 with 1,886 hits, including 302 doubles, 66 triples, and 332 home runs. He stole 461 bases, scored 1,258 runs, and had 1,024 RBI.

Bonthron, Bill (William R.)

TRACK AND FIELD
b. Nov. 1, 1912, Detroit, Mich.

Not many runners beat Glenn Cunningham during his best years. Bonthron beat him in two championship races in one year, 1934, and went on to win the Sullivan award as America's outstanding amateur athlete.

Running for Princeton, Bonthron showed a great finishing sprint to edge Cunningham in the 1934 NCAA mile run. At the AAU national championships in Milwaukee on June 30, 1934, Bonthron did it again, this time in the 1,500-meter run, and he set a world record of 3:34.8 in the process. He also won the IC4A outdoor 880-yard run and mile run in both 1933 and 1934 and the IC4A indoor mile in 1934.

Bonthron was involved in a historic mile run in 1933, when he ran a 4:08.7 for the mile, under the world record of 4:09.2. Unfortunately, he finished second to Jack Lovelock of New Zealand, whose 4:07.6 became the new world record.

Booth, Albie (Albert J. Jr.)

FOOTBALL
b. Feb. 1, 1908, New Haven, Conn.
d. March 1, 1959

When Army was leading Yale, 13–0, in the second quarter of their game on October 26, 1929, a 5-foot-6, 144-pound sophomore halfback came off the bench. He scored 14 points to give Yale the lead and then returned a punt 70 yards, running through the entire Army team, for another touchdown and a 21–13 victory. His name was Albie Booth, but the newspapers called him "Little Boy Blue" after that effort.

For someone his size Booth didn't have great speed, but he was a remarkably shifty runner who could change directions quickly, stop on a dime and then get started just as fast, and change speeds to deceive tacklers. He was also an excellent punter and drop-kicker and a good passer.

The captain of the team in 1931, his senior year, Booth returned a kickoff 96 yards against Dartmouth, had a 53-yard run from scrimmage for another touchdown, and scored a third on a pass reception. His field goal with seconds to play gave Yale a 3–0 win over Harvard.

Booth also captained the basketball team as a senior and played baseball as well. In the last game he played in any sport for Yale, he hit a grand-slam home run to beat Harvard, 4–3.

★ College Football Hall of Fame

Borg, Bjorn

TENNIS
b. June 6, 1956, Soldertaljie, Sweden

Borg's brilliant baseline play and the athletic ability that often enabled him to retrieve seemingly impossible shots made him the dominant male player in international tennis during the late 1970s and into the 1980s.

Even though he never played in the Australian Open and never won the U.S. Open, Borg won 11 singles championships in grand slam events, second only to Roy Emerson's 12. He won the Wimbledon title five years in a row, 1976 through 1980, and reached the finals again in 1981 but lost to John McEnroe.

Borg also won the French Open a record 6 times, in 1974 and 1975 and from 1978 through 1981. He lost in the U.S. Open finals four times.

Borg was an unusual champion in that he never followed the entire worldwide tour. He insisted on taking a four-month vacation, which embroiled him in a dispute with the men's tennis council in 1982. Borg was told he would have to enter the qualifying round for every major event that year because he refused to commit himself to playing the required number of tournaments. As a result, he took the year off and then announced his retirement in 1983, when he was only 27.

A major celebrity in Europe, Borg married Rumanian tennis pro Mariana Simionescu in Bucharest on July 24, 1980. It was the major social event of the year; a company paid about $200,000 for the right to photograph the ceremony and reception. That was just a fraction of Borg's non-tennis income, which reached about $4 million a year in commercial endorsements.

When he retired, he had a choice of homes: a penthouse in Monte Carlo, not far from his successful pro shop, and a small island off the Swedish coast. Borg attempted a comeback in 1991, still using his old wooden racket, but because of his long layoff and the fact that other players had begun using high-tension graphite rackets, he had little success and retired for good.

★ International Tennis Hall of Fame

Borgmann, Benny (Bernhard)

BASKETBALL
b. Nov. 1, 1899, Haledon, N.J.
d. Nov. 11, 1978

Borgmann began playing professional basketball as soon as he graduated from Clifton, New Jersey, High School in 1917. The 5-foot-8 forward eventually played an estimated 3,000 games for a variety of teams before retiring from the sport in 1937. He was one of the top scorers of his time, usually averaging in double figures when 50 points was a big total for both teams in a game.

After playing part of a season with

the Original Celtics, Borgmann joined the Ft. Wayne Hoosiers of the American Basketball League in 1926–27. He led the league in scoring average with 11.2 points per game, and he was also the league's top scorer in 1928–29 and 1929–30. After the ABL disbanded in 1930, Borgmann played for George Halas's Chicago Bruins. In his final season as a player, 1936–37, he was with New Britain, Connecticut, in a new ABL, and he also led that league in scoring.

Borgmann coached at St. Michael's College, Vermont, from 1945–46 through 1946–47 and at Muhlenberg College in Pennsylvania from 1950–51 through 1955–56.

★ Basketball Hall of Fame

Boros, Julius N.

GOLF
b. March 3, 1920, Fairfield, Conn.
d. May 28, 1994

An accountant, Boros decided to take a fling at the PGA tour shortly before his thirtieth birthday, and he became one of the tour's most consistent players. During the next 11 years, he finished in the top 5 at the U.S. Open 6 times, and from 1950 through 1963 in was in the top 10 in 9 Opens, a record second only to Ben Hogan's since World War II.

Boros won the Open by 4 strokes in 1952 and surprised almost everyone, including himself, with another victory in 1963. He finished with a 293 and was emptying his locker, getting ready to go home, when the other final scores began to come in. High winds at The Country Club in Brookline, Massachusetts, were driving scores up, and Boros learned he was in a three-way tie for the lead with Jackie Cupit and Arnold Palmer.

In the 18-hole playoff the following day, Boros shot a 33 on the front nine and won easily with a final 70 to Cupit's 73 and Palmer's 76. He became the oldest player ever to win a major tournament in 1968, when he took the PGA championship.

Gifted with a smooth, perfectly rhythmic swing, Boros didn't hit the ball far, but he was remarkably accurate. He rarely missed a fairway, and his ability

with iron shots made up for his lack of power. He never agonized over a shot or club selection; his style was to hit a shot, walk to the ball, pull a club from his bag, and hit his next shot.

★ PGA Hall of Fame; World Golf Hall of Fame

Borries, Buzz (Fred Jr.)

FOOTBALL
b. Dec. 31, 1911, Louisville, Ky.
d. Jan. 3, 1969

Borries was an All-American halfback at Navy in 1934, and two opposing coaches explained why. Columbia's Lou Little said, "Borries beat my Columbia team single-handed, and that was the only game we lost in 1934." Pittsburgh's Jock Sutherland described him as "the best football player we met all year."

His nickname was short for "Buzzsaw," because that was the way he ran, driving determinedly at the defense until he burst through. He was also a good passer and an outstanding defensive player.

★ College Football Hall of Fame

Bossy, Mike (Michael)

HOCKEY
b. Jan. 22, 1957, Montreal, P.Q.

Bossy was the key offensive player on the New York Islander teams that won four straight Stanley Cups from 1980 through 1983. He won the Conn Smythe Trophy as the most valuable player in the 1982 Stanley Cup series, when he tied a record by scoring 7 goals in a four-game sweep of the Vancouver Canucks in the final series.

He joined the Islanders in the 1977–78 season and spent his entire 10-year NHL career with the team, retiring after the 1986–87 season. In 752 games, Bossy scored 1,126 points on 573 goals and 553 assists. He had 85 goals and 75 assists for 160 points in 129 playoff games.

★ Hockey Hall of Fame

Boston, Ralph H.

TRACK AND FIELD
b. May 9, 1939, Laurel, Miss.

As a student at Tennessee A & I University (now Tennessee State), Boston improved dramatically as a long jumper in 1960, his senior season, when he concentrated on the event in order to make the Olympic team. In previous seasons, he had also competed in the high jump, sprints, and high hurdles, and he ranked only fourth in the country as a high jumper in 1959.

Boston set a world record of 26 feet, 11¼ inches in the long jump on August 12, 1960, breaking the mark set by Jesse Owens 25 years before. It was the first of five world records Boston established in the event.

Less than a month later, Boston broke Owens's 24-year-old Olympic record by jumping 26 feet, 7¾ inches to win the gold medal at the games in Rome. It was the first time four jumpers surpassed 26 feet at a single meet.

In May 1961, Boston broke his own record with a jump of 27 feet, ½ inch, becoming the first to leap more than 27 feet. He extended the record to 27-2 later that year.

Igor Ter-Ovanesyan of the Soviet Union set a new record of 27 feet, 3½ inches in June 1962. Boston tied that mark in August 1964 and broke it with a jump of 27-4¾ in September. He set his last world record, 27 feet, 5 inches, in May 1965.

Boston won the NCAA championship in 1960, the AAU outdoor championship from 1961 through 1966, and the AAU indoor championship in 1961. He won a silver medal at the 1964 Olympics and a bronze in 1968. He was also the AAU outdoor high hurdles champion in 1965, and he had the country's longest triple jump in 1963.

After retiring early in 1969, Boston provided commentary on televised track meets and served as an administrator at the University of Tennessee.

★ National Track & Field Hall of Fame; Olympic Hall of Fame

Bottomley, Jim (James L.)
BASEBALL
b. April 23, 1900, Ogleby, Ill.
d. Dec. 11, 1959

Known as "Sunny Jim" because of his cheerful disposition, Bottomley was one of the outstanding run producers of his era. A left-handed first baseman, he joined the NL's St. Louis Cardinals late in the 1922 season and became a starter in 1923, when he batted .371 to finished second in the league. Though he was a power hitter, the 6-foot, 175-pound Bottomley choked up about two inches on the bat and used a quick, compact swing to drive the ball.

On September 16, 1924, Bottomley drove in 12 runs, a record for a 9-inning game, with 6 hits in 6 times at bat. He hit .316 that season, with 14 home runs and 111 RBI.

Bottomley batted .367 in 1925, led the league in hits with 227 and doubles with 44, and had 21 home runs and 128 RBI. The following season, he helped the Cardinals win a pennant with 120 RBI, best in the league, and a .345 average.

After a .303 average, 19 homers, and 124 RBI in 1927, Bottomley was named the NL's most valuable player in 1928, when the Cardinals won another pennant. He led the league in RBI with 136 and in triples with 20, and he tied Hack Wilson of Chicago for the home run lead with 31.

Bottomley hit .314 and had 29 home runs and 137 RBI in 1929, yet faced a challenge for his job from Rip Collins the following season. He started for most of the season, however, batting .304 and driving in 97 runs.

Injuries sidelined him frequently early in the 1931 season, and he temporarily lost the starting job. Then Collins was also injured; Bottomley took over and was involved in the closest batting race in history. Chick Hafey won with a .3489 average, Bill Terry was second at .3486, and Bottomley finished third at .3482.

After a .296 performance in 1932, the Cardinals traded him to Cincinnati, where he spent three indifferent seasons. He returned to St. Louis with the AL's Browns in 1936 and became playing manager during the 1937 season, his last in the major leagues.

Bottomley both managed and played briefly in the minor leagues in 1938, then retired from baseball. He signed to manage another minor league team in

1957, but suffered a heart attack on opening day and was replaced. He died of a second heart attack less than three years later.

★ Baseball Hall of Fame

Boucher, Frank

HOCKEY
b. Oct. 7, 1901, Ottawa, Ont.

A very clever center who became an innovative coach, Boucher joined the Northwest Mounted Police at 17, then paid $50 to buy his way out so he could play professional hockey. He began his career with Ottawa in 1921. After one season there, he played for the Vancouver Millionaires in the Pacific Coast Hockey League from 1922–23 through 1926–27, then joined the New York Rangers of the NHL.

He was nicknamed "Raffles" after the gentleman thief in E. W. Hornung's stories because of his puck-stealing ability and his consistently clean play. Boucher won the Lady Byng Trophy, for combining sportsmanship with a high level of play, seven times in eight years, so the NHL finally gave it to him to keep in 1935 and had a new one made.

For much of his time with the Rangers, he centered Bill Cook at right wing and Bill's brother Bun at left wing. Boucher led the NHL's American Division with 35 points in 1927–28 and was among the top ten scorers six other times. He retired after the 1937–38 season and became the Rangers' coach in 1939.

Boucher was the first coach to pull his goaltender for an extra skater late in the game, and he developed the box defense for killing penalties. He also taught his teams to attack when shorthanded; in 1939–40, when the Rangers won the Stanley Cup, they scored almost twice as many goals on opponents' power plays as the opposition did.

In 1942, Boucher proposed adding the red line to the ice to speed up play. He later explained, "My thought was that hockey had become a see-saw affair. Defending teams were jammed in their own end for minutes because they couldn't pass their way out against the new five-man attack." At that time, teams weren't allowed to pass the puck out of the defensive zone; when the red line was added for the 1943–44 season, the rule was changed to allow passing from behind the blue line up to the red line.

Boucher made a brief comeback as a player in 1944 but gave it up after 15 games. He was replaced as the Rangers' coach during the 1948–49 season, returned to the job in 1953, and retired for good before the season was over.

In 557 regular season games, Boucher scored 161 goals and had 262 assists. He had 18 goals and 18 assists in 67 playoff games.

★ Hockey Hall of Fame

Boucher, Gaetan

SPEED SKATING
b. May 10, 1958, Charlesbourg, P.Q.

Something of a late bloomer, Boucher was a 35-year-old doing graduate work in marketing in 1984, when he won gold medals in the 1,000- and 1,500-meter events at the Olympics. He was the first Canadian ever to win two golds at the same Olympic Games.

Boucher also won a bronze in the 500-meter. He had won a silver medal in the 1,000-meter race in 1980.

★ Canadian Sports Hall of Fame

Boudreau, Louis, Jr.

BASEBALL
b. July 17, 1917, Harvey, Ill.

As a sophomore at the University of Illinois, Boudreau was named captain of the basketball team for the 1936–37 season, but early in 1938 he signed a professional baseball contract, forfeiting his college eligibility.

Boudreau played minor league baseball while continuing to attend college, graduating in 1939. He played one game with the Cleveland Indians in 1938 and was called up permanently during the 1939 season.

In 1940, his first full season with Cleveland, he batted .295, drove in 101 runs, and led AL shortstops in fielding percentage. He was also the league's top fielding shortstop in 1941, 1942, 1943,

1944, 1946, 1947, and 1948, and he held the career record for the position, .973, when he retired.

Boudreau led the league with 45 doubles in 1941. The following season he was named the Indians' manager, becoming the youngest, at 24, ever to manage a team from the beginning of the season. Boudreau was the AL's top hitter with a .327 average in 1944, but Cleveland had only indifferent success through his first seven seasons as manager.

New owner Bill Veeck wanted to replace him in 1948, but Cleveland fans protested vehemently, and Boudreau was kept on. He responded by guiding the Indians to their first pennant since 1920, hitting .355 with 18 home runs and 106 RBI to win the league's most valuable player award. He was also named male athlete of the year by the Associated Press.

The Indians and Red Sox tied for first and met at Fenway Park in the first AL playoff game ever. Boudreau got 4 hits, including 2 home runs, in an 8–3 win. Cleveland then beat the Boston Braves in a six-game World Series.

Cleveland fell to third place in 1949, to fourth in 1950, and Boudreau was released. He spent 1951 as a backup infielder with the Red Sox and became Boston's manager in 1952, his last season as a player.

Boudreau managed the Red Sox through 1954 and became the first manager of the Kansas City Athletics in 1955. He was fired by Kansas City after the 1957 season.

In 1960, Boudreau was working as a broadcaster for the Chicago Cubs when the team decided, early in the season, to have him switch jobs with manager Charlie Grimm. After a 54–83 record, Boudreau returned to broadcasting.

Chunky, at 5-foot-11 and 185 pounds, Boudreau lacked speed but made up for it with lateral quickness and a knowledge of where to play hitters. In 1,646 games, Boudreau batted .295 with 385 doubles, 66 triples, and 68 home runs. He scored 861 runs and drove in 789.

★ Baseball Hall of Fame

Bourque, Raymond J.
HOCKEY
b. Dec. 28, 1960, Montreal, P.Q.

After three seasons in the Quebec Major Junior Hockey League, Bourque was a first-round draft choice of the NHL's Boston Bruins in 1979, and he became a starting defenseman immediately.

Bourque won the 1980 Calder Trophy as the league's rookie of the year and was named Norris Trophy winner as the league's outstanding defenseman in 1987, 1988, 1990, and 1991.

The 5-foot-11, 210-pound Bourque is a very intelligent defenseman, almost subtle in his approach. While many other defensemen focus on checking as hard as possible, Bourque usually checks an opponent just hard enough to separate him from the puck, which he then takes control of.

Bourque excels on the power play because of his strong left-handed slap shot. Through the 1993–94 season, Bourque had played in 1,100 regular season NHL games and had scored 311 goals and 876 assists for a total of 1,187 points. He had 136 points on 33 goals and 103 assists in 152 playoff games.

Bowden, Bobby (Robert)
FOOTBALL
b. Nov. 8, 1929, Birmingham, Ala.

After playing freshman football at the University of Alabama, Bowden went to Howard College, where he was a Little All-American quarterback in 1953. He then became a graduate assistant coach at Peabody College, and after earning a master's degree, he returned to his alma mater as an assistant coach.

In 1959, Bowden became head coach at the school, which had been renamed Samford University. He had a 31–6 record there in four seasons, spent three seasons as an assistant at Florida State, and then became offensive coordinator at the University of West Virginia in 1966.

He became head coach in 1970 and posted a 42–26 record in six seasons. Bowden then returned to Florida State as head coach and installed a wide open offense featuring a passing attack and a variety of trick plays. He had a 5–6–0 record in his first season, 1976, but was 10–2–0 the following year and has never had a losing record since.

When Bowden's son Terry became head coach at Auburn University in 1993, it set up one of the year's most interesting sports stories. Florida State and Auburn were both undefeated after eight games of the season. However, Florida State lost to Notre Dame in its ninth game; Auburn went on to an 11–0–0 record but wasn't recognized in polls and wasn't allowed to play in a post-season bowl because the program was on NCAA probation.

Florida State has had ten top ten finishes during Bowden's tenure and has been in the top four in seven consecutive seasons through 1993. His teams were ranked second in 1987 and 1992. Through 1994, Bowden had a 174–43–4 record at Florida State and a 247–80–4 record overall. He ranks fourth all-time in NCAA Division I victories.

Bower, Johnny (John W.)

HOCKEY

b. Nov. 8, 1924, Prince Albert, Sask.

He didn't make it to the NHL until he was nearly 29 years old, yet Bower played in the league for 17 seasons, most of them with the Toronto Maple Leafs. A goalie, he was nicknamed "the Great Wall of China." Bower won the Vezina Trophy as the league's best goalie in 1961. Four years later, he and Terry Sawchuk alternated in goal for the Maple Leafs and became the first teammates to share the award.

Bower entered the league with the New York Rangers in 1953. He went to Toronto in 1958 and stayed with the Maple Leafs through the 1969–70 season. In 534 regular season games, he had 37 shutouts and a goals-against average of 2.53. He had 5 shutouts and an average of 2.58 goals-against in 72 playoff games.
★ Hockey Hall of Fame

Bowerman, Bill (William J.)

TRACK AND FIELD

b. Feb. 19, 1911, Portland, Oreg.

Bowerman played basketball and football for four years at the University of Oregon but took part in track, as a 440-yard runner, only during his last two years at the school. After graduating in 1934, he coached high school sports in Portland and Medford, OR, where he had gone to high school.

In 1948, Bowerman returned to the University of Oregon to replace his former track coach, Bill Hayward, who had died. He soon became known for developing excellent distance runners, but he also produced outstanding overall teams. Under his guidance, Oregon won NCAA outdoor championships in 1962, 1964, 1965, and 1970. His 440-yard and 4-mile relays teams both set world records in 1962.

Bowerman coached ten runners who broke the 4-minute mark in the mile, including Dyrol Burleson, Bill Dellinger, Jim Grelle, and Steve Prefontaine. He retired in 1972 after coaching the U.S. Olympic team that won six gold medals.

His influence extended far beyond his coaching. Bowerman co-authored *Jogging* with heart specialist Waldo Harris in 1967. Translated into six languages, the book sold more than a million copies and helped to make jogging a popular recreation. The waffle-soled running shoe he designed led to the establishment of the Nike Shoe Company, for which Bowerman served as director of research and development.
★ National Track & Field Hall of Fame

Bowman, Scotty (William Scott)

HOCKEY

b. Sept. 18, 1933, Montreal, P.Q.

The winningest coach in NHL history, Bowman took over the expansion St. Louis Blues during their first season, 1967–68, and won Western Division titles there in 1969 and 1970. He went to the Montreal Canadiens after the 1970–71 season.

In eight seasons with Montreal, he guided the team to five Stanley Cups, including four in a row from 1976 through 1979. After Montreal lost to the New York Islanders in the 1980 finals,

Bowman became general manager and coach of the Buffalo Sabres.

Bowman stepped down as coach after one season, but took over again late in the 1981–82 season. He left coaching once more in 1985. Impatient with the team's progress, Bowman coached the Sabres at the end of the 1985–86 and 1986–87 seasons.

After retiring from hockey for three years, Bowman was named director of player development for the Pittsburgh Penguins in 1990. When coach Bob Johnson developed a brain tumor in 1991, Bowman once again became a coach, taking the Penguins to the 1992 Stanley Cup championship.

In 22 years of coaching, Bowman has an 880–410–234 mark in the regular season, and he's 140–86 in the playoffs. He holds NHL records for wins, 880; winning percentage, .654; playoff games coached, 226; and playoff wins, 140. He won the Jack Adams Award as coach of the year in 1977 and was named NHL executive of the year in 1980.

★ Hockey Hall of Fame

Boyer, Kenton L.

BASEBALL
b. May 20, 1931, Liberty, Mo.
d. Sept. 7, 1982

A hard-hitting third baseman with power, Boyer was also a fine defensive player who led the NL in fielding average at the position in 1957 and 1964. He joined the St. Louis Cardinals in 1955 and hit 20 or more home runs eight times in his first ten seasons, with a high of 32 in 1960.

Boyer was named the league's most valuable player in 1964, when he batted .295 with 24 home runs and a league-leading 119 RBI to help lead the Cardinals into the World Series, where they defeated the New York Yankees in seven games. Boyer batted only .222 in the Series, but he hit a grand slam home run to beat the Yankees, 4–3, in the fourth game and added another home run in a 7–5 victory in the final game.

He was traded to the New York Mets in 1966, and the Mets sent him to the AL's Chicago White Sox during the 1967

season. Early in the 1968 season, the Los Angeles Dodgers acquired Boyer. He retired after appearing in 25 games with the Dodgers in 1969.

In 2,034 games, Boyer had a .287 career average on 2,143 hits, including 318 doubles, 68 triples, and 282 home runs. He scored 1,104 runs and drove in 1,141.

Boynton, Ben Lee

FOOTBALL
b. Dec. 6, 1898, Waco, Tex.
d. Jan. 23, 1963

If Boynton had played at a larger school, he would probably have been a first team All-American. As a quarterback at Williams College, he was named to Walter Camp's third All-American team in 1919 and 1920.

A fast, elusive runner, he tied a national collegiate record with a 110-yard punt return in 1920. During his three-year career at Williams, he had five other runs of more than 50 yards, and the school won 18 games while losing only 5 and tying 1.

Boynton played professional football with the Rochester Jeffersons in 1921 and 1922 and the Buffalo Bisons in 1924.

★ College Football Hall of Fame

Bradds, Gary ("Tex")

BASKETBALL
b. July 26, 1942, Jamestown, Ohio

Bradds originally enrolled at the University of Kentucky but spent only two days there before returning to his home state to attend Ohio State University. After serving as backup center to Jerry Lucas in 1961–62, the 6-foot-8, 210-pound Bradds became a starter as a junior, averaging 28.0 points per game.

He was named a consensus All-American and player of the year after averaging 30.6 points a game in 1963–64. Bradds joined the NBA's Baltimore Bullets but missed much of his rookie year and virtually all of his second year with injuries.

After sitting out the entire 1966–67 season, Bradds joined the Oakland team in the new American Basketball Association in 1967. He was with the ABA's Washington team in 1969–70 and ended his professional career with the Carolina and Dallas teams in 1970–71.

In 254 professional games, Bradds scored 3,106 points, an average of 12.3. He averaged 17.1 points in 22 playoff games.

Bradley, Bill (William W.)

BASKETBALL
b. July 28, 1943, Crystal City, Mo.

One of the most publicized college athletes of his era, Bradley starred at Princeton University for three seasons, scoring 2,503 points for an average of 30.1 per game. A 6-foot-5, 205-pound forward, he was named to some All-American teams in 1963 and was a consensus All-American in 1964 and 1965, when he was unanimously named the college player of the year.

Bradley, who captained the 1964 gold medal Olympic team, won the 1965 Sullivan Award as the outstanding amateur athlete of the year. He was the first basketball player to receive the award.

Before he had even graduated, Bradley was the subject of a book, John McPhee's *A Sense of Where You Are*, originally a series of articles in the *New Yorker*. The title referred to Bradley's court sense. Small for his position and lacking speed, Bradley used intelligence, quickness, and hours of practice on his own to become an outstanding passer and shooter.

He carried Princeton to three Ivy League titles. Bradley's value to the team was underlined in the 1964 Holiday Festival Tournament, when he scored 41 points against the University of Michigan to give Princeton a 75–63 lead before fouling out with about 4½ minutes to play. With Bradley on the bench, Michigan outscored Princeton, 17–3, to win, 80–78.

After scoring 58 points in his final game, an NCAA tournament loss to Wichita State, Bradley was drafted by the NBA's New York Knicks, but he accepted a Rhodes Scholarship to attend Oxford University in England, then served in the Air Force Reserve.

Bradley joined the Knicks in 1967 and was a key member of NBA championship teams in 1970 and 1973, fitting perfectly into a squad that emphasized team defense and unselfishness on offense. He retired after the 1976–77 season. Since 1979, Bradley has been a Democratic U.S. senator from New Jersey.

In his ten NBA seasons, Bradley scored 9,217 points in 742 games, an average of 12.4 per game. He also had 2,354 rebounds and 2,535 assists. He added 1,222 points, 333 rebounds, and 263 assists in 85 playoff games.
★ Basketball Hall of Fame

Bradley, Pat (Patricia E.)

GOLF
b. March 24, 1951, Westford, Mass.

The only golfer to win all four major women's tournaments, Bradley was a competitive skier and ski instructor before attending Florida International University, where she was an All-American golfer in 1970.

She joined the LPGA tour in 1974 and scored her first victory in the 1976 Girl Talk Classic. Bradley won her first major tournament, the Peter Jackson Classic, in 1980; the following year she won the U.S. Women's Open. Her third major victory was in the 1985 du Maurier Classic (formerly the Peter Jackson).

Bradley had an incredible 1986 season, winning three major championships, the Nabisco Dinah Shore, the LPGA championship, and the Du Maurier, to give her a total of six. She set a single season record by winning $492,021, was named player of the year, and won the Vare Trophy for the lowest average strokes per round. She also became the first woman golfer to surpass $2 million in career earnings.

Treatment for hyperthyroidism limited her playing time in 1988, but she did host the inaugural Planters Pat Bradley International in High Point, North Carolina, that year. She came back the following season, surpassed the $3 million career winning mark in 1990, and went over $4 million in 1991, when she also won her thirtieth tournament.

A great long iron player, Bradley holds the LPGA record for the lowest

54-hole score, 197, and shares the record for the lowest 9-hole score, 28.

★ LPGA Hall of Fame

Bradshaw, Terry P.

FOOTBALL
b. Sept. 2, 1948, Shreveport, La.

The only quarterback ever to take a team to four Super Bowl victories, Bradshaw played at Louisiana Tech and was the first player chosen in the 1970 NFL draft, by the Pittsburgh Steelers. The 6-foot-3, 215-pound Bradshaw became a starter in 1971.

The Steelers featured the "Steel Curtain" defense and a powerful running attack led by Franco Harris, but Bradshaw's strong arm gave them the threat of the deep pass, helping to loosen opposing defenses.

A tough competitor, Bradshaw excelled in big games. During his career he passed for more than 300 yards only seven times, but three of those performances came in post-season play, two of them in the Super Bowl.

Although he temporarily lost the starting job to Joe Gilliam in 1974, Bradshaw took over again during the season and helped take the Steelers to their first Super Bowl victory, a 16–7 win over the Minnesota Vikings, in which he completed 9 of 14 passes.

The following year, Bradshaw threw a 64-yard touchdown pass to Lynn Swann with a little more than 3 minutes remaining to beat the Dallas Cowboys, 21–17, in Super Bowl X.

Bradshaw had his finest season in 1978, when he won the Bert Bell Trophy as the NFL player of the year. He completed 207 of 368 passes for 2,915 yards and a league-leading 28 touchdowns. He was also most valuable player in the Super Bowl, completing 17 of 30 passes for 318 yards and 4 touchdowns in a 35–31 victory over Dallas.

He won his second consecutive most valuable player award in Super Bowl XIV, following the 1979 season. The Steelers beat the Los Angeles Rams, 31–16, with Bradshaw passing for 309 yards and 2 touchdowns on 14 completions in 21 attempts.

Bradshaw retired after the 1983 season. In his 14 NFL seasons, he completed 2,105 of 3,901 passes for 27,989 yards and 212 touchdowns. He also ran 444 times for 2,257 yards, a 5.1 average, and 32 touchdowns. Bradshaw holds NFL post-season records for passing attempts, 417; completions, 233; yards, 3,508; and touchdown passes, 58.

★ Pro Football Hall of Fame

Bragg, Donald G. ("Tarzan")

TRACK AND FIELD
b. May 15, 1935, Penns Grove, N.J.

Bragg's childhood ambition was to play Tarzan in the movies, and he chose sports as a path toward that goal. As a student at Villanova University, the 6-foot-3, 215-pound Bragg won the NCAA pole vault championship in 1955 and was the IC4A champion, both indoors and outdoors, from 1955 through 1957. He tied for the 1956 AAU indoor championship.

After graduating in 1957, Bragg entered the Army and continued to compete. He again tied for the AAU indoor championship in 1958, then won the event from 1959 through 1961. He was also the AAU outdoor champion in 1959.

At the 1960 Olympic trials, Bragg set a world record of 15 feet, 9¼ inches. That's still the best vault ever for an athlete using a metal pole; soon afterward most vaulters began using fiberglass poles. Bragg went on to win the Olympic gold medal, startling the crowd in Rome when he gave his Tarzan yell from the victory podium.

Bragg retired from competition after the Olympics. He did play Tarzan in a low-budget film, but it was never released because of copyright problems. He later became athletic director at a small New Jersey college and the owner of a summer camp.

Brand, Glen

WRESTLING
b. Nov. 3, 1923, Clarion, Iowa

After serving in the Marine Corps during World War II, Brand enrolled at Iowa State University and won 54 of 57 matches, including 35 in a row. He was the NCAA champion in the 175-pound division in 1948.

Brand won the gold medal in the 174-pound class at the 1948 Olympics. He then returned to college, but an injury ended his competitive career after seven more victories. He later served as a volunteer wrestling coach at the Omaha YMCA.

Breedlove, Craig (Norman Craig)
AUTO RACING
b. March 23, 1938, Los Angeles, Calif.

At 12, he was turning a $75 jalopy into a hot rod. At 16, he drove a dragster 154 mph at the Bonneville, UT, Salt Flats. At 22, he paid $500 for a surplus jet fighter engine. Three years later, with sponsorship from Shell Oil and Goodyear, he was back at Bonneville with a three-wheeled, jet-powered car called Spirit of America. He didn't come close to the sought-after land speed record.

He was back the following year, 1963, and Spirit of America now had a giant stabilizing tail designed by Breedlove. On August 5, he averaged 407.45 mph, well above John Cobb's 16-year-old record. But there was doubt about whether it would be accepted by the Federation Internationale de l'Automobile (FIA). Two questions were raised: Was Breedlove's three-wheeled vehicle an automobile or a motorcycle? Was a jet-powered vehicle, with no transmission and essentially no engine, an automobile at all, whether it had three or four wheels?

Eventually the FIA established two categories. John Campbell's speed of 403.164 mph, set in 1964, was recognized as the record for axle-driven vehicles, and Breedlove's was recognized as the jet-powered record. But Breedlove's speed was surpassed twice in 1964, by Tom Green and Art Arfons. On October 15, Breedlove reclaimed the record with an average of 526.61 mph. He was clocked at 539.89 mph on the second of the required two runs, which ended in a terrible crash when Breedlove couldn't

stop the vehicle. Basically uninjured, he announced, "For my next trick, I will set myself afire."

In 1965, Breedlove returned to Bonneville with a new $250,000 car, Sonic I, with a more powerful jet engine. After some fine tuning, he averaged 555.127 mph. Five days later, Arfons raised the mark to 576.553 mph. And eight days after that, on November 15, Breedlove averaged 600.601 mph. In two years, he had raised the land speed record by more than 200 mph and, in the process, had become the first person to travel more than 400 mph, more than 500 mph, and more than 600 mph on land.

Brennan, Joseph R.
BASKETBALL
b. Nov. 15, 1900, Brooklyn, N.Y.

Though he is little-known today, Brennan finished second to Johnny Beckman as the greatest player of his era in a poll of old-time players taken in 1950. He spent much of his career playing for various editions of the Brooklyn Visitation team, which he originally joined in 1919 after graduating from high school.

The 5-foot-10 Brennan was not only a fine scorer, he was usually the team captain at a time when the captain was virtually the coach. In addition to the Visitation team, Brennan played at one time or another for the New York Whirlwinds, the Troy Trojans, the Brooklyn Jewels, and teams in Holyoke, Massachusetts, Wilkes-Barre, and Philadelphia.

Brennan scored the winning basket when Brooklyn upset the Original Celtics in a 1925 game in Madison Square Garden. He captained the Visitations when they won American Basketball League championships in 1930 and 1931. The league disbanded for two years but was revived in 1933; he led Brooklyn to another championship in 1935, a year before retiring as a player.

While working full-time at a bank, as he had throughout his career, Brennan coached St. Francis College from 1941–

42 through 1947–48, winning 96 games and losing 46.

★ Basketball Hall of Fame

Bresnahan, Roger P.

BASEBALL
b. June 11, 1879, Toledo, Ohio
d. Dec. 4, 1944

Bresnahan had a rather brief major league career, but he was the outstanding catcher of his era, and his invention of shinguards earned him a place in baseball history.

Nicknamed the "Duke of Tralee" because he claimed to be a native of Tralee, Ireland, Bresnahan joined the NL's Washington Senators as a pitcher late in the 1897 season and had a 4–0 record. But the Senators wouldn't pay him what he wanted in 1898, so he returned to minor league baseball in the Midwest and made his debut as a catcher in 1899.

After playing one game with the Chicago Cubs in 1900, Bresnahan went to the Baltimore Orioles of the new American League the following season. Although primarily a catcher, he was also used at third base and in the outfield at times.

In the middle of the 1902 season, Bresnahan went to the NL's New York Giants with manager John McGraw and several other players. A leadoff hitter, he batted .350 and stole 34 bases in 1903. He became a full-time catcher in 1905, when he hit .302 during the regular season and .313 in the Giants' five-game World Series victory over the Philadelphia Athletics.

Catchers early in the century usually wore shin protection, often rolled-up newspapers, under their uniforms. In 1907, Bresnahan began wearing fiber shinguards over his uniform pants, an idea borrowed from cricket. He was derided by some and criticized by others who thought they were dangerous to runners sliding into the plate, but the league officially approved their use, and shinguards soon became standard equipment for catchers.

Bresnahan went to the St. Louis Cardinals as playing manager in 1909 and remained there through the 1912 season, then joined the Chicago Cubs. He managed the Cubs in 1915, after which he left baseball for a time. In 1923, Bresnahan bought the Toledo minor league franchise and managed the team. He later coached with the Giants and the Detroit Tigers.

In 1,446 games, Bresnahan batted .279, with 218 doubles, 71 triples, and 26 home runs. He scored 682 runs and drove in 530.

★ Baseball Hall of Fame

Brett, George H.

BASEBALL
b. May 15, 1953, Glendale, W.Va.

One of the biggest stories of the 1980 baseball season was Brett's drive to become the first player to bat .400 since Ted Williams in 1941. He was over the mark going into September, but a thumb injury hampered his swing, and he fell 5 hits short, ending with a .390 average, still the best for a major league hitter since Williams's feat. Brett won the AL's most valuable player award that season, when he also had 24 home runs and 118 RBI.

A left-handed hitter, Brett joined the Kansas City Royals briefly in 1973 and took over the third base job the following season. In 1975, he led the league with 195 hits and 13 triples. The following year, he won his first batting title with a .333 average and again led with 215 hits and 14 triples.

Brett hit 45 doubles in 1978 to lead the league. In 1979, he was the league leader in hits and triples for a third time, with 212 and 20, respectively.

After his great 1980 season, a leg injury limited him to 89 games in 1981. Although not known for his speed, Brett stole 103 bases from 1975 through 1980, but the injury slowed him and cut down his defensive range. From 1986 on, he was used primarily at first base and as a designated hitter.

In 1990, Brett won his third and last batting title with a .329 average and also led the league with 45 doubles. He collected his 3,000th career hit late in the 1992 season and retired after hitting .266 in 1993.

Brett was named to the AL All-Star team 11 years in a row, from 1976 through 1986, and again in 1988. An excellent situation hitter who could go to the opposite field when a single was needed, pull the ball when a home run was needed, and drive the ball into the air when a sacrifice fly was needed, Brett starred in post-season play.

In 6 league championship series encompassing 27 games, he had a .340 average on 35 hits, including 9 home runs, with 22 runs scored and 19 RBI. He batted .373 in 13 World Series games, in 1980 and 1985, collecting 19 hits, with 1 home run, 8 runs scored, and 4 RBI.

Brett had a career .305 batting average with 3,154 hits, including 665 doubles, 137 triples, and 317 home runs. He scored 1,583 runs and had 1,595 RBI.

Brewer, Charles

FOOTBALL
b. March 8, 1873, Honolulu, Hawaii
d. June 13, 1958

Brewer might well have been a four-time All-American, but he missed most of the 1894 season with an injury. He was on Walter Camp's All-American teams in 1892, 1893, and 1895. A halfback, Brewer was the ball carrier when Harvard introduced the famous "flying wedge" play against Yale in 1892. The result was a 30-yard run.

The play was outlawed before the 1894 season. However, Brewer ran 95 yards for a touchdown in a 26–6 victory over Brown in 1895 and also had a 40-yard touchdown run in a 17–14 loss to Pennsylvania that year. During his three All-American seasons, Harvard won 30 games, lost 4, and tied 1.
★ College Football Hall of Fame

Brickley, Charles E.

FOOTBALL
b. Nov. 24, 1891, Boston, Mass.
d. Dec. 28, 1949

The greatest drop-kicker of his time, Brickley brought Harvard the "Big Three" championship in 1913 by scoring all the school's points on field goals in a 15–0 win over Yale and a 3–0 win over Princeton. He had 13 field goals that sea-

son and a total of 34 for his three-year career, both records for drop-kicking.

An All-American halfback in 1912 and 1913, Brickley coached Boston College to a 12–4–0 record during the 1916 and 1917 seasons.
★ College Football Hall of Fame

Brimsek, Frankie (Francis C.)

HOCKEY
b. Sept. 26, 1915, Eveleth, Minn.

The Boston Bruins shocked their fans and many of their players when they sold star goaltender, Tiny Thompson, for $15,000 and replaced him with Brimsek early in the 1938–39 season. It didn't take Brimsek long to justify the move. After a 2–0 loss to Montreal in his first game, he recorded three consecutive shutouts and 231 minutes, 54 seconds of scoreless goaltending, a record at the time.

After that string was broken, Brimsek started another, going 220 minutes, 24 seconds without being scored upon, including three more shutouts. By then, he was known as "Mr. Zero." The Bruins won the Stanley Cup that season and Brimsek won the Calder Trophy as the league's outstanding rookie and the Vezina Trophy as its best goaltender. He had 10 shutouts and a 1.60 goals-against average in 43 games. In the Stanley Cup finals against Toronto, he had another shutout and gave up only six goals as the Bruins won in five games.

Brimsek joined the Coast Guard in 1943 and returned to the Bruins after World War II ended in 1945. He was traded to the Chicago Black Hawks in 1949 and retired after just one season Chicago.

Brimsek had 40 career shutouts and a 2.94 goals-against average in 478 regular-season games. He added 2 shutouts and a 2.74 average in 68 playoff games.
★ Hockey Hall of Fame; U.S. Hockey Hall of Fame

Brisco-Hooks, Valerie A.

TRACK AND FIELD
b. July 6, 1960, Greenwood, Miss.

Brisco won the 1979 AIAW 200-meter championship as a student at California State–Northridge and she was on the 4 x 100-meter relay team that won a gold medal at the Pan-American Games. She married former college track teammate Alvin Hooks, then a wide receiver with the Philadelphia Eagles, in 1981, and they had a son the following year.

She was 40 pounds overweight and didn't plan to return to running, but her husband talked her into it, and she went through a rigorous training period to get back into shape. Brisco-Hooks was rewarded for her effort with three gold medals at the 1984 Olympics, in the 200-meter, 400-meter, and 4 x 100-meter relay. She's the only athlete ever to win both the 200 and the 400 at a single Olympics.

Brisco-Hooks also won the national indoor 200 and outdoor 400 titles in 1984. She ran the 400 in 49.83 seconds, becoming the first American woman to break 50 seconds in the event. In 1985, she set a world indoor record of 52.99 seconds in the 400-yard run, and she was the national champion in the outdoor 400-meter again in 1986.

Britton, Jack [William J. Breslin]
BOXING
b. Oct. 14, 1885, Clinton, N.Y.
d. March 27, 1962

A very clever boxer, Britton practically made a career of fighting Ted "Kid" Lewis. They met in 20 bouts and fought for a total of 224 rounds. Most of their fights were no-decisions, but the welterweight title changed hands in four of them.

Britton's first recorded fight was a 6-round decision over Johnny Earle in 1905. After being knocked out by Steve Kinney later that year, Britton went undefeated in 48 fights until he lost on a foul to Kid Farmer in 1909. Later that year, he knocked Farmer out in the 7th round.

On June 22, 1915, Britton won the vacant welterweight championship by beating Mike Glover in a 12-round decision in Boston. But he lost his next fight, to Lewis, on August 31, giving up the title. After another loss to Lewis on September 27, Britton regained the title

with a 20-round decision over Lewis in New Orleans on April 24, 1916.

The two fought seven more times in the next 18 months. The first six were nontitle bouts, but on June 25, 1917, Lewis won back the championship with a 20-round decision in Dayton, Ohio. Britton won the title once more by knocking Lewis out in the 9th round on March 17, 1919, in Canton, Ohio. He held the championship until losing a 15-round decision to Mickey Walker on November 15, 1922, in New York City.

Britton continued fighting for eight more years but never had another title fight. He retired after winning an 8-round match over Young Bobby Buffalo on May 8, 1930. Britton was later a boxing instructor and manager.

He won 99 fights, 21 by knockout; lost 28, 1 by knockout, and fought 20 draws, 177 no-decisions, and 1 no-contest.
★ International Boxing Hall of Fame

Broadbent, Punch (Harry L.)
HOCKEY
b. 1892, Ottawa, Ont.
d. March 6, 1971

Broadbent's nickname had a double meaning: he had undoubted scoring punch, and he was also one of the best fighters in the NHL. In the 1921–22 season, he performed the rare feat of leading the league in scoring and penalty minutes. He set a record that season with at least one goal in each of 16 consecutive games.

His professional career began in 1908 with Ottawa of the National Hockey Association. After serving in World War I, he returned to the Ottawa team in 1919; the NHA had become the NHL in the meantime. Broadbent went to the Montreal Maroons in 1924, returned to Ottawa in 1927, then played one season with the New York Americans in 1928–29 before retiring to join the Royal Canadian Air Force.

He scored 122 goals and had 45 assists in his 11 NHL seasons, adding 10 goals and 3 assists in 10 playoff series.
★ Hockey Hall of Fame

Brock, Louis C.

BASEBALL

b. June 18, 1939, El Dorado, Ark.

The Chicago Cubs made one of the worst trades in baseball history when they sent Brock to the St. Louis Cardinals for three players during the 1964 season. None of the three players they received did much for the Cubs, while Brock led the NL in stolen bases 8 times, helped St. Louis get into 3 World Series in 5 years, and ended up in the Baseball Hall of Fame.

A left-handed outfielder, the 5-foot-11, 175-pounder joined the Cubs briefly in 1961 and became a starting outfielder in 1962. He was batting .251 for the Cubs when the trade was made. After joining the Cardinals, he hit .348 for the rest of the season, finishing with a .315 average, 43 stolen bases, and 111 runs scored.

Although he didn't steal a base in the Cardinals' seven-game World Series victory over the New York Yankees, Brock batted .300 and had 5 RBI.

Brock won four consecutive stolen base titles, with 74 in 1966, 52 in 1967, 62 in 1968, and 53 in 1969. Although known mainly for his speed, he could also hit for power. In 1967, he led the Cardinals in extra-base hits with 32 doubles, 12 triples, and 21 home runs, and he drove in 76 runs from the leadoff spot while leading the league in runs scored with 113.

The top hitter in the 1967 World Series with a .414 average, Brock stole 7 bases, scored 8 runs, and drove in 3 as St. Louis beat the Boston Red Sox in seven games. He led the league in 1968 with 46 doubles and 14 triples, then batted .464 with 7 stolen bases and 6 runs scored in the World Series. However, the Cardinals were defeated by the Detroit Tigers in seven games.

In 1971, Brock led the league in steals once more with 64 and in runs scored with 126. He was the league leader in stolen bases the next three seasons, culminating in a remarkable performance in 1974: at the age of 35, he had a record-breaking 118 steals.

That was his last stolen base title,

although he still had good numbers until an injury slowed him in 1978. Brock retired after the 1979 season.

In 19 seasons and 2,616 games, Brock had a .293 average on 3,023 hits, including 486 doubles, 141 triples, and 149 home runs, with 1,610 runs scored and 900 RBI. His 938 stolen bases was a major league record until 1991, when Rickey Henderson broke it.

★ Baseball Hall of Fame

Broda, Turk (Walter)

HOCKEY

b. May 15, 1914, Brandon, Man.

d. Oct. 17, 1972

Because he was chubby and not able to skate well, Broda was put in goal when his elementary school organized a hockey team. Weight remained a problem for him, but he became one of the best goalies in hockey history, so calm and unflappable that Coach Jack Adams once said of him, "He could play in a tornado and never blink an eye."

Broda played with the minor league Detroit Olympias in 1934–35, then was sold to the Toronto Maple Leafs for $8,000. He joined the NHL team in 1936 and remained there through the 1951–52 season, except for two years he spent in the service during World War II. The Maple Leafs won five Stanley Cups while he was in goal; Broda won the Vezina Trophy as the NHL's best goaltender in 1941 and 1948 and shared the trophy with Al Rollins in 1951.

On several occasions, Maple Leaf management threatened to bench or trade Broda if he didn't lose weight. He was suspended for one game in 1949 while he lost ten pounds to get down to his recommended playing weight of 190.

Broda had 62 shutouts and a 2.56 goals-against average in 628 regular season games. He was even better in Stanley Cup play, appearing in 101 games, a record for a goalie, with 13 shutouts and a 1.99 average, also a record. In the 1949 Stanley Cup finals, he held the powerful Detroit Red Wings to just 4 goals in a four-game Toronto sweep, and in

1951 he gave up just 9 goals in 8 playoff games.

★ Hockey Hall of Fame

Brodie, John R.

FOOTBALL
b. Aug. 14, 1935, San Francisco, Calif.

In three seasons as a quarterback at Stanford University, Brodie completed 296 of 536 passes for 3,594 yards and 19 touchdowns. He was a consensus All-American in 1956, his senior season, when he led the nation in passing.

Brodie joined the NFL's San Francisco 49ers in 1957 but didn't become the starting quarterback until his fifth season. He led the league in completion percentage in 1958 with 59.9, in 1965 with 61.9, and in 1968 with 57.9.

When the American Football League launched an all-out financial attack on the established NFL by trying to sign some of its best players, especially quarterbacks, Brodie became the highest-paid player of the time in 1967 by signing a 4-year, $827,000 contract with San Francisco.

His finest season came in 1970, when he led all NFL quarterbacks with 223 completions in 378 attempts for 2,941 yards and 24 touchdowns, with only 10 interceptions. He was named the league's player of the year, but the 49ers lost to the Dallas Cowboys in the NFC championship game.

Brodie retired after the 1973 season and worked as a commentator on network broadcasts of pro football and golf. A fine golfer, Brodie shot a 67 in the second round of the 1960 Yorba Linda Open to move into second place. However, he finished in a tie for 24th with an even par 288. He later played in PGA senior tour events.

During his NFL career, Brodie completed 2,469 of 4,491 passes for 31,548 yards and 214 touchdowns. He had 224 passes intercepted.

★ College Football Hall of Fame

Brooks, Bud (William)

FOOTBALL
b. 1933, Wynne, Ark.

The Outland Trophy winner as the nation's outstanding collegiate lineman in 1954, Brooks played offensive guard and defensive tackle at the University of Arkansas. His coach, Bowden Wyatt, said of him, "Bud played offensive right guard so that he could lead all the ball-carriers as an interferer, and played defensive left tackle better than most we have ever had. He had as much speed as linemen ever have and an amazing ability to go to the ball."

Although Arkansas lost, 14–6, to Georgia Tech in the Cotton Bowl, Brooks was voted the game's outstanding lineman, and he was also the outstanding lineman in the Senior Bowl all-star game. He never played professional football.

Brooks, Herbert P.

HOCKEY
b. Aug. 5, 1937, St. Paul, Minn.

Brooks played hockey at the University of Minnesota, graduating in 1959, and tried out for the 1960 U.S. Olympic team but was the last player cut from the squad. However, he played for the 1964 and 1968 Olympic teams and was also a member of the 1961, 1962, 1965, 1967, and 1970 national teams.

In 1972, Brooks became hockey coach at his alma mater. He guided Minnesota to NCAA Division I championships in 1974, 1976, and 1979 and then became coach of the U.S. national team.

A tough disciplinarian, Brooks was also an excellent organizer and motivator. Entering the 1980 Olympic hockey tournament, Brooks told his team, "You're meant to be here. This moment is yours. You're meant to be here at this time." The team upset the Soviet Union, 4–3, and beat Finland, 4–2, in its final game to take the gold medal.

Brooks turned down several NHL offers and coached a Swiss team in 1980–81, then returned to the U.S. to take over the New York Rangers of the NHL. He was named coach of the year by *The Sporting News* after the Rangers had a 39–27–14 record in his first season, but he was fired in January 1985.

He coached St. Cloud State College

in 1986–87 and was then named coach of the NHL's Minnesota North Stars. The team won only 19 games, and he was replaced after the season. Brooks coached the New Jersey Devils to a 40–37–7 record in 1992–93, then resigned because of a dispute with management. In five and a half NHL seasons, he had a record of 190 wins, 198 losses, and 61 ties.

★ U.S. Hockey Hall of Fame

Brooks, Steve

HORSE RACING
b. Aug. 12, 1921, McCook, Nebr.
d. Sept. 23, 1979

Known as "Cowboy Steve," Brooks grew up breaking and riding horses and became a professional jockey in 1938. He was the top money winner with $1,316,817 in 1949, when he rode Ponder to victory in the Kentucky Derby. Shortly afterward, he rode eight mounts at Churchill Downs, winning six races, placing second once, and placing third in the eighth race.

As a jockey for Calumet Farms, Brooks won the prestigious Hollywood Gold Cup aboard Citation in 1951 and was also the rider in Citation's final race, when the horse became the first in history to win more than $1 million.

He retired in 1970 but continued working with horses and made a brief comeback as a jockey in 1975. He died of injuries suffered when he was thrown by a horse he was exercising. In his 32-year career, Brooks won more than 4,000 races, and his mounts had $18,214,947 in winnings.

★ National Horse Racing Hall of Fame

Brough, Louise (Althea Louise)

TENNIS
b. March 11, 1923, Oklahoma City, Okla.

When she was four years old, Brough moved with her mother to California, where she learned to play tennis on public courts. She began to take lessons at 13. Within four years she was playing in the national junior championships in Philadelphia and the national women's championships in New York at the same time, driving back and forth with her aunt between matches.

Brough was much more successful in singles at Wimbledon than in the U.S. nationals. She won the U.S. singles title just once, in 1947, though she reached the finals five times. She was the Wimbledon singles champion three years in a row, from 1948 through 1950, and she won a fourth championship in 1955. Her fourth title was a major upset over Beverly Baker Fleitz. Brough trailed 5–4 in both sets but won 7–5 and 8–6.

Brough, with Margaret Osborne duPont, formed one of the greatest doubles combinations in history. They won the U.S. national title from 1942 through 1950 and from 1955 through 1957; the Wimbledon doubles in 1946, from 1948 through 1950, and in 1954; and the French doubles in 1946, 1947, and 1949.

Playing with four different male partners, Brough also won the U.S. mixed doubles in 1942 and from 1947 through 1949, and the Wimbledon mixed doubles from 1946 through 1948 and in 1950. She was perfect in Wightman Cup play, winning all 22 of her matches from 1946 through 1957.

She retired from competition in 1958 after marrying, but spent another 20 years teaching tennis to young players.

★ International Tennis Hall of Fame

Brouthers, Dan (Dennis J.)

BASEBALL
b. May 8, 1858, Sylvan Lake, N.Y.
d. Aug. 2, 1932

Brouthers played for 11 different major league teams, including a record nine NL teams, because he was a star during a turbulent era in baseball.

He began his career with a brief 1880 stint with the Troy, New York, team in the NL, then joined the NL's Buffalo team in 1881. In four-plus seasons with Buffalo, Brouthers combined with Hardie Richardson, Jack Rowe, and Deacon White to form the "Big Four," the era's equivalent of the New York Yankees' "Murderers' Row" of the 1920s and 1930s.

The 6-foot-2, 200-pound Brouthers, a left-handed-hitting first baseman, led the league in home runs with 8 in 1881 and in hitting with a .368 average in 1882 and a .371 average in 1883.

Because of financial problems, Buffalo sold all four stars to Detroit late in the 1885 season. Brouthers was credited with a .419 batting average, second in the league, in 1887, when walks counted as hits. His average without walks was actually .338.

Also in 1887, Brouthers became one of the leaders of the Brotherhood of Professional Baseball Players, the first association of professional athletes. The movement culminated three years later in the establishment of the Players' League.

The Detroit franchise folded after the 1888 season, and Brouthers went to Boston. He led the league in hitting at .373, then joined a Boston team in the Players' League in 1890, when he batted .345.

The league lasted just one season, but Brouthers remained in Boston, this time with a team in the American Association, then a major league. He won his fourth batting title with a .349 average. Brouthers moved to the Brooklyn NL team in 1892. He led the league in doubles with 33 and triples with 20, hitting .335 to tie for the batting title.

After one more year in Brooklyn, he was traded to Baltimore, where he spent the 1894 season. Early in 1895, Brouthers was sold to the Louisville NL team, and he spent his final major league season, 1896, with Philadelphia.

Brouthers continued to play in the minor leagues for several years, winning two more batting championships at that level. He played two games with the New York Giants in 1904 to close out his career. He later worked as a scout for the Giants and was press box attendant and night watchman at the Polo Grounds.

In 1,673 games, Brouthers batted .342 with 460 doubles, 205 triples, and 106 home runs. He scored 1,523 runs and drove in 1,296.

★ Baseball Hall of Fame

Brown, Bob (Robert S.)

FOOTBALL
b. Dec. 8, 1941, Cleveland, Ohio

One of the first of the gigantic offensive lineman, the 6-foot-4, 280-pound Brown had the speed to be a pulling guard as well as a tackle. A devastating blocker, he was an All-American guard at the University of Nebraska in 1963.

He joined the NFL's Philadelphia Eagles in 1964 and was named an All-NFL tackle in his rookie year. He also made the All-NFL team in 1965. The Eagles traded him to the Los Angeles Rams in 1968, when he was All-NFL for a third time.

Brown went to the Oakland Raiders in 1971. He was named to the All-AFC team in each of his three seasons there. He retired after the 1973 season.

★ College Football Hall of Fame

Brown, Earlene D.

TRACK AND FIELD
b. July 11, 1935, Laxeto, Tex.

The 5-foot-7, 225-pound Brown is the only American woman to win an Olympic medal in the shot put, a bronze in 1960. She didn't begin throwing weights until 1956, but she won the AAU shot put championship that year with a U.S. record of 45 feet, and she broke that with a put of 46-9½ at the Olympic trials.

Although she finished only sixth in the shot put and fourth in the discus at the Olympics, Brown set American records in both events. In 1958, she became the first American woman to break the 50-foot barrier in the shot put.

Brown won the AAU outdoor shot put championship eight times, from 1956 through 1962 and in 1964, and she was the discus champion in 1958, 1959, and 1961. She also won the basketball throw (since dropped from the program) in 1958, and she was the gold medalist in both the shot put and the discus at the 1959 Pan-American Games.

After placing twelfth in the shot put at the 1964 Olympics, Brown retired from track and field competition. She later became a star in the Roller Derby.

Brown, Gordon F., Jr. ("Skim")
FOOTBALL
b. Sept. 6, 1879, New York, N.Y.
d. May 10, 1911

One of only three players to be named an All-American four years in a row, the 6-foot-4, 200-pound Brown was a guard on Walter Camp's team from 1897 through 1900. He captained the 1900 Yale squad, known as the "Team of the Century," which won all 12 of its games and outscored the opposition 336 to 10. During his four-year career, Yale had a 37–4–3 record.

Camp wrote of his performance as a sophomore in 1898, "In defensive work, and in opening holes in the opposing line, under legal restrictions, he was at the top of his class."

Brown died of complications from diabetes.

★ College Football Hall of Fame

Brown, Jim (James N.)
FOOTBALL
b. Feb. 17, 1936, St. Simon Island, Ga.

Considered by many the greatest running back in history, Brown was also an exceptional all-around athlete. As a teenager, he turned down an offer to play baseball in the New York Yankee organization, and after graduating from Syracuse University, he turned down $150,000 to become a professional fighter. While in high school, he once jogged over from a pre-game lacrosse practice to win the high jump in a track meet.

In his senior year in high school in Manhasset, New York, he averaged 38 points a game in basketball and 14.9 yards per carry as a football player. He was an All-American in both lacrosse and football, and he also started at center in basketball for three years at Syracuse. In his last regular season football game, he scored 43 points against Colgate, and he had 21 in Syracuse's 28–27 loss to Texas Christian in the 1957 Cotton Bowl.

Brown joined the NFL's Cleveland Browns in 1957 and was named rookie of the year after gaining 942 yards on 202 carries. He set a single-game record of 237 yards against the Los Angeles Rams, scoring 4 touchdowns, that season.

During the next eight seasons, Brown rushed for more than 1,000 yards seven times, falling short by only 4 yards in 1962. He led the league in rushing every season he played except 1962, when he was edged out by Jim Taylor of the Green Bay Packers. Brown also led in rushing touchdowns from 1957 through 1959, in 1963, and in 1965.

The 6-foot-2, 228-pounder had sprinter speed and elusive moves. While he rarely ran over an opponent, he had the power to break through off-balance tackles set up by his cutting ability. An All-Pro from 1957 through 1961 and from 1963 through 1965, Brown was named the UPI player of the year in 1958, 1963, and 1965.

While making a movie during the summer of 1966, Brown made the surprising announcement that he was retiring from football to concentrate on acting. He was just 30 years old. In his eight seasons, he rushed 2,359 times for 12,312 yards, a 5.2 average, and 106 touchdowns. He also caught 262 passes for 2,499 yards and 20 touchdowns and returned 29 kickoffs for 648 yards, a 22.3 average.

★ Pro Football Hall of Fame

Brown, Larry (Lawrence H.)
BASKETBALL
b. Sept. 14, 1940, Brooklyn, N.Y.

The 5-foot-9, 160-pound Brown captained the University of North Carolina basketball team as a senior in 1962–63 and played for the U.S. team that won an Olympic gold medal in 1964. He then joined the Akron Goodyears AAU team for two seasons.

After serving as an assistant coach at North Carolina for two years, Brown joined the New Orleans Bucs of the new American Basketball League in 1967. He went to the Oakland Oaks in 1968 and helped bring them to the 1968–69 championship, leading the league in assists.

Brown also played for the ABA's Washington Capitals, Virginia Squires, and Denver Rockets. He retired as a player in 1972 to become head coach of the league's Carolina Cougars and was named ABA coach of the year in 1973.

After one more season with Carolina, Brown took over the Denver Rockets and won two more coach of the year awards there, in 1975 and 1976. The Rockets moved into the NBA and became known as the Nuggets in 1976–77. Brown guided them to Midwest division titles in 1977 and 1978 but resigned late in the 1978–79 season.

Brown was named head coach at UCLA in the fall of 1979. Despite a 42–17 record in two seasons, the team finished no better than third in the Pacific 10 Conference, and Brown returned to the NBA with the New Jersey Nets in 1981. He left that job late in the 1982–83 season and became head coach at the University of Kansas.

Kansas was the surprise winner of the 1988 NCAA championship, beating Oklahoma, 83–79, in the title game after having gone only 21–11 during the regular season. Brown won the Naismith Award as college coach of the year.

Shortly after the tournament victory, Brown was named head coach of the NBA's San Antonio Spurs. He was replaced during the 1991–92 season and took over the Los Angeles Clippers just a few days later.

Through the 1992–93 season, Brown had a record of 434–342 as an NBA head coach and was 177–61 on the college level.

Brown, Larry (Lawrence Jr.)
FOOTBALL
b. Sept. 19, 1947, Clairton, Pa.

A remarkable success story, Brown played for two seasons at Dodge City Junior College in Kansas and entered Kansas State University, where he was used primarily as a blocking back. He joined the NFL's Washington Redskins in 1969 as an eighth-round draft choice.

Redskin coach Vince Lombardi noticed that Brown sometimes didn't seem to know what play had been called. It was discovered that he was deaf in his right ear and Brown was fitted with a hearing aid. He responded by gaining 888 yards rushing as a rookie. In 1970, he led the league in rushing with 1,125 yards on 237 carries, a 4.4 average.

Two years later, Brown was again the NFL's leading rusher, gaining 1,216 yards on 285 attempts, a 4.3 average, and was named the league's player of the year. An All-NFC running back in both 1970 and 1972, Brown retired after the 1976 season.

In his eight professional seasons, Brown gained 5,875 yards in 1,530 attempts, a 3.8 average, and scored 35 touchdowns. He caught 238 passes for 2,485 yards, a 10.4 average, and 20 touchdowns.

Brown, Panama Al (Alphonse T.)
BOXING
b. July 5, 1902, Panama City, Panama
d. April 11, 1951

Both a clever boxer and a powerful puncher, Brown began fighting as an amateur about 1919 in Panama and turned professional in 1922. He came to the United States the following year and was undefeated until he lost a 10-round decision to Johnny Russo on January 3, 1925.

Unusually tall for a bantamweight, at 5-foot-11, Brown had a very long reach. He won the vacated world title in an elimination tournament, beating Vidal Gregorio on a 15-round decision in the final bout on June 18, 1929, in New York City.

From late 1930 on, Brown did most of his boxing in Europe. He lost his title to Baltazar Sangchili of Spain on a 15-round decision on June 18, 1935, in Valencia. He retired from fighting late in 1942.

Brown won 120 fights, 57 by knockout; lost 19, 1 by knockout; and fought 11 draws and 2 no-decisions.
★ International Boxing Hall of Fame

Brown, Paul E.
FOOTBALL
b. Sept. 7, 1908, Norwalk, Ohio
d. Aug. 5, 1991

A quarterback at Miami University (Ohio), Brown became a successful coach with Severn Prep and Massillon,

Ohio, High School for 12 years, then moved to Ohio State in 1941. After a 6–1–1 record in his first season, the team won 9 of 10 games in 1942. The only loss was at Wisconsin after a dozen players got sick during the trip.

Depleted by the World War II draft, the 1943 squad went only 3–6–0. Brown then entered the service and coached the powerful Great Lakes Naval Training Station team.

In the meantime, plans were being made for a new professional league, the All-America Football Conference, when the war ended. Mickey McBride, owner of the AAFC's Cleveland team, offered Brown an unprecedented $20,000 a year and 15 percent of the team's profits to coach a team named for him.

The AAFC began operating in 1946, and the Browns won all four of its championships, winning 47 games while losing only 4 and tying 3. Partly because of Cleveland's success, the league folded, but the Browns were among four AAFC teams that were absorbed into the NFL.

Many experts felt that the Browns would have trouble winning in the NFL, but they hardly missed a beat. After defeating the defending champion Philadelphia Eagles, 35–10, in their very first game, the Browns went on to win the NFL title in 1950. They won division championships in their first six years and reclaimed the league championship in 1954 and 1955.

Brown basically used a "pass and trap" offense during those seasons, relying on the passing of Otto Graham to set up draw plays for fullback Marion Motley and, later, Fred "Curly" Morrison. The passing attack used carefully planned pass patterns that were designed to get at least one receiver into the open against virtually any defense.

More important, Brown genuinely revolutionized the whole coaching approach. He hired the first full-time, year-round staff, used films to grade players on every assignment in every game, developed playbooks and meticulous game plans based on scouting reports, and held intensive classroom sessions for his team. No detail was left to

chance. Brown's teams practiced recovering fumbles, catching tipped passes, and forming a blocking wall after an interception.

Despite a 167–53–8 record and only 1 losing season in 17, Brown was fired after the 1962 season. A year after he was inducted into the Hall of Fame, he became coach and general manager of the Cincinnati Bengals, an expansion team in the American Football League, which merged into the NFL in 1970. Brown coached the team through 1975 and had a 55–56–1 record. The Bengals won division titles in 1970 and 1973.

After retiring as a coach, Brown continued to work for the Bengals as general manager and then as a consultant until shortly before his death.

★ Pro Football Hall of Fame

Brown, Rosie (Roosevelt Jr.)

FOOTBALL
b. Oct. 20, 1932, Charlottesville, Va.

One of the first players from a predominantly black college to make it in the NFL, and the first to join the Hall of Fame, Brown was a Little All-American tackle at Morgan State College in 1952. He joined the New York Giants the following season. Still only 20 years old, he knew nothing about professional football except what he had learned from listening to a championship game on the radio.

But he was 6-foot-3 and 255 pounds, and he was fast enough to pull out of the line to lead interference like a guard. He became a starter at offensive tackle in his first season and remained there for the rest of his career. In his 13 seasons with the Giants, he was an All-Pro eight years in a row, from 1956 through 1963, and he played in ten Pro Bowls. Brown was named outstanding lineman when the Giants beat the Chicago Bears, 47–7, for the 1956 NFL title.

Because of phlebitis, Brown retired after the 1965 season.

★ Pro Football Hall of Fame

Brown, Three-Finger (Mordecai P. C.)
BASEBALL
b. Oct. 18, 1876, Nyesville, Ind.
d. Feb. 14, 1948

At seven years old, Brown lost most of his index finger and had two other fingers and his thumb badly mangled when he stuck his right hand into a corn chopper.

The injury helped make him a great pitcher because it gave his curve ball an unusually deceptive break. Ty Cobb called it "the most devastating pitch I ever faced."

Brown began his professional career as a switch-hitting third baseman, but he soon became a pitcher. He entered the major leagues with the St. Louis Cardinals in 1903. The following year, he went to the Chicago Cubs, where he became famous with some great teams.

After winning a total of 33 games in his first two seasons with the Cubs, Brown went 26–6 with 9 shutouts in 1906. He was 1–2 in Chicago's six-game World Series loss to the Chicago White Sox.

In 1907, Brown won 20 and lost 6, but didn't appear in the World Series until the fifth game, when he beat the Detroit Tigers, 2–0, to win the championship for the Cubs.

In 1908, Brown became the first pitcher to record 4 consecutive shutouts. He had a 29–9 record that year. His most important victory came in the last game of the season against the New York Giants. The teams were tied for first place and had to replay a game that had ended in a tie. Brown came on in relief in the second inning with New York ahead, 1–0, and he went on to win, 4–2. The Cubs beat Detroit in a four-game series, with Brown winning the first game in relief and the fourth game as a starter.

After a 27–9 record in 1909, when the Cubs finished second, Brown was 25–14 in 1910, but lost 2 of 3 decisions in a five-game World Series loss to Philadelphia. He had his sixth and last 20-win season with a 21–11 record in 1911.

A knee injury limited him to a 5–6 record in 1912, and he was traded to Cin-

cinnati. Brown became player-manager of the St. Louis Federal League team in 1914, but was replaced as manager and then traded to Brooklyn. He went to the Chicago Federal League team in 1915, then returned to the Cubs for a final major league season.

Brown played and managed in the minor leagues through 1920, and he later managed a semipro team in Illinois.

In 481 games, Brown had a 239–130 record and a 2.06 ERA. He struck out 1,375 hitters and walked 673 in 3,172 innings.
★ Baseball Hall of Fame

Brown, Timothy D.
FOOTBALL
b. June 22, 1966, Dallas, Tex.

The fast, elusive, 6-foot-1, 195-pound Brown starred as a kick returner, wide receiver, and occasional running back at Notre Dame. He was named to most All-American teams in 1986 and 1987, and he won the 1987 Heisman Trophy as the outstanding college player of the year.

Brown totaled 5,024 yards at Notre Dame, averaging 116.8 per game, and scored 22 touchdowns. He was chosen in the first round, the sixth choice overall, by the Los Angeles Raiders in the 1988 NFL college draft.

As a rookie, Brown led the league in kickoff returns with 41 for 1,098 yards, a 26.8 average, and 1 touchdown. He also caught 43 passes for 725 yards, a 16.9 average, and 5 touchdowns; returned 49 punts for 444 yards, a 9.1 average; and rushed 14 times for 50 yards and 1 touchdown. His total of 2,317 yards was a rookie record.

Brown played only one game in 1989 because of a knee injury, and he came back slowly in 1990. However, he became a starter again in 1991 and had two more good seasons, though they weren't as spectacular as his rookie year.

Through 1993, Brown had caught 227 passes for 3,425 yards, a 15.1 average, and 27 touchdowns; returned 193 punts for 1,960 yards, a 10.2 average, and 2 touchdowns; and run back 47 kickoffs for 1,204 yards, a 25.6 average, and 1 touchdown.

Brown, Willie (William F.)

FOOTBALL
b. Dec. 2, 1940, Yazoo City, Miss.

Brown may not have invented the "bump and run" style of pass defense, but he certainly perfected it. Bumping the receiver near the line of scrimmage to knock him off stride and delay his route, then running with him as he tries to complete the route, requires strength and speed. The 6-foot-1, 210-pound Brown had both.

Virtually unknown coming out of Grambling College in 1963, he tried out with the AFL's Houston Oilers, was cut, and went to the Denver Broncos. He had four good seasons in Denver but became a superstar only after being traded to the Oakland Raiders before the 1967 season.

During his 12 seasons with Oakland, the team won 125 games while losing 35 and tying 7. The Raiders went to two Super Bowls during that time. When they beat the Minnesota Vikings, 32–14, for the 1976 NFL championship in Super Bowl XI, Brown set a championship game record with a 75-yard interception return for a touchdown.

Brown was an AFL/AFC all-star 10 consecutive years, 1964 through 1973. He retired after the 1978 season with 54 interceptions, which he returned for 472 yards and 2 touchdowns. He also ran back 3 punts for 29 yards and 3 kickoffs for 70 yards.

★ Pro Football Hall of Fame

Browne, Mary K.

TENNIS
b. June 1891, Ventura County, Calif.
d. Aug. 19, 1971

Little known today, Browne was the first American woman to play professional tennis. She was also one of only four women to win the U.S. triple crown — singles, doubles, and mixed doubles — three years in a row.

She accomplished that from 1912 through 1914. Her partners in the women's doubles were Dorothy Green in 1912 and Louise Riddell Williams in 1913 and 1914. She teamed with then little known Bill Tilden for her mixed doubles championships.

Browne began playing golf after World War I. Her most exceptional accomplishment was probably reaching the semifinals of the national tennis championships and the final round of the national women's amateur golf championships in 1924.

When C. C. Pyle put together the first professional tennis tour in 1926, Browne signed for a reported $30,000 to play against France's Suzanne Lenglen.

★ International Tennis Hall of Fame

Browner, Ross

FOOTBALL
b. March 22, 1954, Warren, Ohio

An All-American defensive end at Notre Dame in 1976 and 1977, Browner won the Outland Trophy as the nation's outstanding interior lineman in 1976 and the Lombardi Award as the outstanding college lineman of the year in 1977.

The 6-foot-3, 260-pounder was a first-round draft choice of the NFL's Cincinnati Bengals in 1978, the eighth player selected overall. He was a starter for the Bengals until 1985, when he was suspended for three months because of drug use.

Browner played briefly for the Houston Gamblers of the U.S. Football League in 1985, then returned to the Bengals for part of the season. He finished his career with the Green Bay Packers in 1987.

Browning, Skippy (David G. Jr.)

DIVING
b. June 5, 1931
d. March 14, 1956

Browning won his first national diving championship, the AAU outdoor 3-meter springboard competition, in 1949. As a student at Ohio State, he dominated springboard diving in 1951 and 1952, winning the NCAA 1-meter and 3-meter as well as the AAU indoor 1-meter and 3-meter championships in both years.

He was also the AAU outdoor 3-meter and platform champion and the indoor 1-meter and 3-meter champion, in 1954. Browning turned in an outstanding performance at the 1952 Olympics, winning a gold medal in the springboard competition without having a single score lower than 7.0 and averaging better than 8.0 on nine of his 12 dives.

Browning was an officer in the Navy when he died in the crash of a jet plane shortly before he was to begin training for the 1956 Olympics.

Broyles, Frank (John Franklin)
FOOTBALL
b. Dec. 26, 1924, Decatur, Ga.

Broyles was a quarterback at Georgia Tech from 1944 through 1946 and also lettered in baseball and basketball. He worked as an assistant coach at several colleges before becoming head coach at the University of Missouri in 1957.

He had a 5–4–1 record in his one season at Missouri and then went on to the University of Arkansas, where he rebuilt a struggling program. His 1964 team won all 11 of its regular season games, was voted national champion by the Football Writers Association of America, and beat Nebraska, 10–7, in the Cotton Bowl. Broyles shared the American Football Coaches Association coach of the year award with Ara Parseghian of Notre Dame that year.

In 19 seasons at Arkansas, Broyles won 144 games, lost 58, and tied 5. His teams won 7 Southwest Conference championships and played in 10 bowl games. He retired from coaching after the 1976 season but remained at Arkansas as athletic director.

★ College Football Hall of Fame

Brundage, Avery
TRACK AND FIELD
b. Sept. 28, 1887, Detroit, Mich.
d. May 8, 1975

A long-time spokesman for pure amateurism in the Olympics, Brundage graduated in 1909 from the University of Illinois, where he was on the track team. He continued his athletic career after graduation, finishing sixth in the 1912 Olympic decathlon and winning the national AAU championship in the all-around, an event similar to the decathlon, in 1914, 1916, 1918.

One of the original members of the American Olympic Association (AOA) in 1921, he became president of the organization in 1928, and he also served as president of the AAU from 1928 through 1932.

An idealist who believed that the Olympics should be above politics, Brundage had his first taste of major controversy in 1935, when there was a move to boycott the 1936 Berlin Olympics because of Nazi anti-Semitism. In a widely publicized statement, he blamed the move on "radicals and Communists," and the AAU decided to accept the Olympic invitation by a narrow vote.

In 1937, Brundage became a member of the International Olympic Committee's executive board. He came up with the idea for the Pan-American Games the same year. After a number of meetings with Latin-American leaders, the games were scheduled for 1942, but World War II forced their cancellation. Brundage revived the idea when the war was over and the first Pan-American Games were held in 1951 in Buenos Aires.

Brundage became president of the IOC in 1952. During the next 20 years, he fought to keep the Olympics free of any taint of professionalism. His stance was at first popular but, as time went on, it became less popular; by the time he resigned from the IOC after the 1972 Olympics, he was perceived as something of a dinosaur even by others in the Olympic movement.

In his last major act as IOC president, Brundage decreed that the 1972 Munich Games should go on after a day of mourning for 11 Israeli athletes who were murdered by Arab terrorists.

★ National Track and Field Hall of Fame; Olympic Hall of Fame

Bruton, Billy (William H.)
BASEBALL
b. Dec. 22, 1925, Panola, Ala.

Bruton joined the NL's Milwaukee Braves in 1953 and led the league in stolen bases his first three seasons with totals of 26 in 1953, 34 in 954, and 25 in 1955. He also led the NL with 15 triples in 1956 and 13 triples in 1960, when he was tops in runs scored with 112.

A left-handed-hitting, right-handed-throwing center fielder, Bruton was with pennant-winning teams in 1957 and 1958. He missed the 1957 World Series with a broken leg and batted .412 in 1958, when the Braves lost to the New York Yankees in seven games.

Bruton was traded to the AL's Detroit Tigers in 1961, and he finished has career with them in 1964. He had a career .273 average with 1,651 hits, including 241 doubles, 102 triples, and 94 home runs. He stole 207 bases, scored 937 runs, and had 545 RBI.

Bryan, Jimmy (James E.)
AUTO RACING
b. Jan. 28, 1927, Phoenix, Ariz.
d. June 19, 1960

An Air Force cadet during World War II, Bryan began racing hot rods after the war, moved into midget cars in 1947, and joined the USAC Championship Trail in 1953. He drove Indy cars for less than seven years but won 19 races, three national championships, and an Indianapolis 500 in that brief time.

His big break came in 1954 when mechanic Clint Brawner gave him a chance to drive the new Dean Van Lines car. He finished second at Indianapolis despite a broken spring, a broken shock absorber, and spray from a broken oil line that burned his left leg. He won the last four races of the season to win his first driving championship.

Bryan won the championship again in 1956 and 1957, and he won at Indianapolis in 1958, narrowly avoiding a terrible crash that killed Pat O'Connor and knocked 17 of the 33 starting cars out of the race. Afterward, Bryan announced he wouldn't defend his championship in 1959. He did finish second in the Monza Race of Two Worlds in Italy, which he had won in 1957, and he won one of the three stock car races he entered.

His 1960 Indy ride lasted 152 laps before motor problems forced him out.

Then Bryan agreed to return to dirt track racing as a favor to two old friends, the owners of the Langhorne, Pennsylvania, track. His car flipped on the first lap, and he died immediately.

★ Indianapolis Speedway Hall of Fame

Bryant, Bear (Paul W.)
FOOTBALL
b. Sept. 11, 1913, Fordyce, Ark.
d. Jan. 26, 1983

Bryant started at end for the University of Alabama from 1933 through 1935, then served as an assistant coach at Alabama and Vanderbilt University. After rising to the rank of lieutenant commander in the Navy during World War II, he became head coach at the University of Maryland in 1945 and had a 6–2–1 record.

In 1946, Bryant went to the University of Kentucky. He had a 60–23–5 record in eight seasons there, then took over at Texas A & M in 1954. His first team won only 1 of 10 games, but Bryant had a 24–4–2 record over the next three seasons. His 1957 team lost to Tennessee, 3–0, in the Gator Bowl.

Bryant returned to Alabama as head coach in 1958 and became the winningest coach in NCAA Division I history in 1981, breaking A. A. Stagg's record of 314 victories. He spent 25 seasons at Alabama, winning 232 games while losing 46 and tying 9. Bryant's teams won or shared 13 Southeastern Conference championships and were named national champions in 1964, 1965, 1973, 1978, and 1979.

He retired after the 1982 season with an overall record of 323–85–17. He holds the record for most major bowl games, 29, most bowl game wins, 15, and most losses, 12.

As a teenager, Bryant once wrestled a bear in a traveling show for a dollar a minute. He later said he never got paid, but he did get a nickname for the feat.

A tough disciplinarian, Bryant left Maryland after one season because he had suspended a player for breaking training rules, and the college president reinstated him without consulting Bryant. He also suspended star quarterback

Joe Namath in 1963, and Namath missed the 1964 Sugar Bowl game. Alabama beat Mississippi, 12–7, without him. Lee Roy Jordan, an All-American linebacker at Alabama in 1962, said of Bryant, "His feeling for people — whether one needs stroking or another needs chewing out — is uncanny. You loved him, yet you respected and feared him."

Though he had a reputation for running a conservative, ball control offense, Bryant could also coach a passing team when he had the right quarterback. With Vito "Babe" Parilli at quarterback in 1950, Kentucky set a record for touchdown passes with 27, and Bryant also had fine passing teams with Namath and Ken "Snake" Stabler at Alabama.

★ College Football Hall of Fame

Bryant, Phil (George Philip)

ARCHERY
b. Feb. 22, 1878, Melrose, Mass.
d. April 18, 1938

A graduate of Harvard College and Harvard Law School, Bryant was a Boston attorney whose hobby was archery. He won two gold medals at the 1904 Olympics, in the double York round and double American round, and he was also a member of the Boston Archers, who won a bronze medal in the team round.

Bryant was the national archery champion in 1905, 1909, 1911, and 1912.

Buchanan, Buck (Junious)

FOOTBALL
b. Sept. 10, 1940, Gainesville, Ala.
d. July 16, 1992

A Little All-American tackle in 1962, Buchanan played both offense and defense at Grambling State University. He also played basketball and ran the 440-yard dash in track.

The first player chosen in the American Football League draft, by the Dallas Texans, Buchanan was a first-round draft pick of the NFL's New York Giants. He chose to sign with the Dallas team, which moved to Kansas City and became known as the Chiefs before the 1963 season.

The 6-foot-8 Buchanan played at any-

where between 250 and 270 pounds while in college, but his weight often reached 300 pounds during his professional career. He had the strength to push offensive linemen right into the backfield, along with the speed and agility to spin around blockers to get to the passer.

Buchanan was also very durable: he played in 181 of a possible 182 regular season games during his 13-season professional career.

Named to the All-AFL team from 1966 through 1970, Buchanan played in six consecutive AFL All-Star games, from 1964 through 1969, and in two Pro Bowls after the AFL and NFL merged in 1970. He was a defensive star on the Kansas City teams that appeared in two Super Bowls.

Green Bay Packer guard Jerry Kramer said that Buchanan was the defensive player who most worried the Packers when they prepared for Super Bowl II. The Packers won that game, 33–14, but the Kansas City defense dominated Super Bowl IV, when the Chiefs beat the Minnesota Vikings, 16–7.

Buchanan retired after the 1975 season. He later served as director of the Kansas Special Olympics and as an assistant coach with the New Orleans Saints and the Cleveland Browns.

★ Pro Football Hall of Fame

Buck, Jason O.

FOOTBALL
b. July 27, 1963, Moses Lake, Wash.

Buck attended Ricks College in Idaho and then transferred to Brigham Young University, where he was an All-American defensive tackle and winner of the Outland Trophy as the nation's outstanding collegiate lineman in 1986.

Chosen by the Cincinnati Bengals in the first round of the 1987 NFL draft, the 6-foot-4, 265-pound Buck was moved to defensive end as a professional. He played with Cincinnati through 1990 and then joined the Washington Redskins as an unrestricted free agent in 1991. Buck missed half of the season with an injury but played in Washington's 37–24 win over the Buffalo Bills in Super Bowl XXVI.

Bucyk, John P.

HOCKEY
b. May 12, 1935, Edmonton, Alta.

In 1956, the Boston Bruins traded one of hockey's all-time great goaltenders, Terry Sawchuk, to the Detroit Red Wings for the young Bucyk, who had spent two seasons with Detroit. It turned out to be a very good deal. Bucyk became one of the best scorers in Boston history, a durable and consistent player who was presented with a $1,000 bill when he played his 1,000th NHL game on December 11, 1970. He played seven more seasons and 540 more games.

The 6-foot, 215-pound Bucyk was a tough battler, but he was rarely penalized. In 1971, he won the Lady Byng Trophy for combining a high standard of play and gentlemanly conduct. Bucyk scored 556 goals and 813 assists in 1,540 regular season games, and he had 41 goals and 64 assists in 124 playoff games. He retired after the 1977–78 season.
★ Hockey Hall of Fame

Budge, Don (J. Donald)

TENNIS
b. June 13, 1915, Oakland, Calif.

He was not known for his grace, but Budge was known for hitting everything back. One frequent opponent, Sidney Wood, said, "Playing tennis against him was like playing against a concrete wall. There was nothing to attack." While he had a very good all-around game, he was most noted for his smooth, effortless backhand.

Budge learned to play tennis on the hard public courts of California starting when he was eight years old. Tall, gawky, and freckle-faced, he began playing on the eastern grass circuit in 1934 after winning the national junior championship.

In 1937, Budge swept the Wimbledon championships, winning the singles, the men's doubles with C. Gene Mako, and the mixed doubles with Alice Marble. He also won the U.S. National singles and the mixed doubles with Sarah Palfrey Fabyan.

By far his most famous match, though, came in the Davis Cup interzone finals that year. Budge had to beat Germany's Baron Gottfried von Cramm to get the U.S. team into the challenge round. Von Cramm won the first two sets, but Budge won the next two. After trailing 4–1 in the fifth set, he turned on his blistering serve to pull out an 8–6 win. The U.S. then beat England for its first Davis Cup since 1926.

He was named Associated Press athlete of the year and winner of the Sullivan Award as the nation's outstanding amateur athlete of the year. But he was even better in 1938, when he became the first player to win the grand slam of tennis — the Wimbledon title and the Australian, French, and U.S. national championships. The Associated Press again named him athlete of the year.

Budge joined the professional tour in 1939, when he had a 21–18 record against Ellsworth Vines and an 18–11 record versus Fred Perry. The great Bill Tilden rejoined the tour in 1941 but was well past his prime, and Budge won 51 of 58 matches against him. The tour was then suspended because of World War II, and Budge retired from competition.
★ International Tennis Hall of Fame

Bueno, Maria E.

TENNIS
b. Oct. 11, 1939, Sao Paulo, Brazil

Because of her flair, her grace, and her costumes, Bueno contributed immeasurably to the popularity of women's tennis internationally during the 1960s.

She never took a formal lesson as a youngster but learned by playing against boys and men starting when she was five. Bueno won the Brazilian women's championship at 14 and began playing on the international tour three years later.

In 1959, she became the first South American player ever to win the Wimbledon singles championship, and she also won the U.S. title that year. She was welcomed home to Buenos Aires with a parade and a 21-gun salute.

Bueno repeated at Wimbledon in 1960, but the following year she was stricken with hepatitis, and it took her a long time to regain her strength. However, she returned to win the U.S. singles title in 1963, 1964, and 1966 and the Wimbledon championship in 1964.

A hard server who liked to come to the net and volley, Bueno once said, "To me, tennis was more of an art than a sport." She enjoyed winning beautifully, and that included her tennis dresses, designed by Ted Tinling. In 1964, she astonished Wimbledon spectators by wearing a white dress with a shocking-pink lining that showed whenever she served or made a typically acrobatic shot.

Bueno won the Wimbledon doubles in 1958, 1960, 1963, 1965, and 1966 and the U.S. doubles in 1960, 1962, and 1966. She retired from competition after winning the U.S. amateur doubles and U.S. open doubles championships in 1968, the first year of open competition.
★ International Tennis Hall of Fame

Bunker, Paul D.
FOOTBALL
b. May 7, 1881, Mich.
d. March 16, 1943

Bunker was Army's first All-American and one of the very few players ever to be named to the All-American team at two positions. He was a tackle in 1901, a halfback in 1902. A remarkable combination of power and speed, Bunker scored two touchdowns in a 22–8 victory over Navy in his last game.

During his military career, Bunker was serving in the Philippines and met Ralph Strassburger, who had played for Navy in 1902. After they shook hands, Strassburger said, "Bunker, I hate you. Let's have a drink."
★ College Football Hall of Fame

Bunn, John W.
BASKETBALL
b. Sept. 26, 1898, Wellston, Ohio
d. Aug. 13, 1979

The first athlete to win ten letters at the University of Kansas, Bunn played basketball for "Phog" Allen at a time when the sport's inventor, James Naismith, was a professor of physical education at the school. Bunn stayed on as Allen's assistant for nine years after graduating in 1921 and then became basketball coach at Stanford in 1930.

Although Bunn emphasized defense, his team was best known for making the one-hand shot a powerful offensive weapon. Hank Luisetti was the player who did it, but Bunn was probably one of the few coaches of the era who would have allowed a player to use what was then a very unorthodox way of shooting.

Luisetti led the 1936–37 team to a 25–2 record. More important, Bunn brought his team to Madison Square Garden for a game against Long Island University in December 1936, the first time a West Coast team had played in New York. Stanford's 45–31 victory ended LIU's 43-game winning streak, and Luisetti's shooting style was soon adopted by other players.

In 1939 Bunn temporarily retired from coaching to become a college administrator. He returned as coach at Springfield, Massachusetts, College, basketball's birthplace, from 1947 through 1956, and he finished his coaching career at Colorado State at Greeley from 1956 through 1962. His overall record was 313 wins, 288 losses.

During his tenure at Springfield, Bunn was chairman of the Naismith Memorial Basketball Hall of Fame Committee. He served as official rules interpreter and editor of the *Basketball Guide* from 1959 through 1967 and wrote six books on the sport.
★ Basketball Hall of Fame

Burk, Joseph W.
ROWING
b. Jan. 17, 1914, Beverly, N.J.

Burk rowed on the University of Pennsylvania crew that won the Childs Cup in 1935 and 1936. He was the captain of the 1936 crew. But he's best known as a champion sculler and a college crew coach.

He won the national single sculls championship four years in a row, from 1937 through 1940, and he was the Diamond Sculls champion at the Henley-on-Thames Regatta in 1938 and 1939, when he set a course record and was named winner of the Sullivan Award as the outstanding amateur athlete of the year.

After serving in the Navy during World War II, Burk became freshman coach at Yale. In 1951 he returned to Pennsylvania as head crew coach. Burk took an analytical approach to coaching, developing a point system to rate his rowers and pioneering the development of an electronic dynamometer to measure the power of individual oarsmen. He left coaching after the 1969 season.

Burke, Thomas E.

TRACK AND FIELD
b. Jan. 15, 1875, Boston, Mass.
d. Feb. 14, 1929

Burke won two gold medals in 1896 at the first modern Olympics, in the 100-meter and 400-meter dashes. Spectators and athletes from other countries were fascinated by Burke's American crouch start, because at the time most runners from outside the U.S. used the standing start.

As a student at Boston University, Burke won the AAU 440-yard event in 1895, the IC4A 440-yard in 1896 and 1897 and the 880-yard run in 1898. He then attended Harvard Law School and won the IC4A 880-yard run in 1899.

After becoming a lawyer, Burke wrote about sports part-time for Boston newspapers, and he also coached track at Mercersburg Academy for a time.

Burkett, Jesse C.

BASEBALL
b. Feb. 12, 1870, Wheeling, W.Va.
d. May 27, 1953

The first player to bat over .400 three times, and one of only three to accomplish that feat, Burkett began his professional career as a pitcher. After a 3–10 record with the NL's New York Giants in 1890, he was sent to the minor leagues and moved to the outfield.

He joined the NL's Cleveland Spiders late in the 1891 season. The 5-foot-8, 155-pound Burkett was a left-handed hitter and a skilled bunter. He once boasted that he could hit .300 if he bunted every time up. When he swung away, he hit line drives to all fields, so he was exceptionally hard to defend against.

He batted only .275 in 1892, his first full season, but he then had averages of .348, .358, .409, .410, .383, and .341 with Cleveland, winning batting titles in 1895 and 1896. The franchise collapsed after the 1898 season, and Burkett went to the St. Louis NL team with several other Cleveland players.

In 1899, Burkett hit .396 without winning the batting championship. That went to Ed Delahanty, who had a .408 average. But Burkett did win the title in 1901, hitting .376.

Burkett jumped to the St. Louis AL team in 1902, but he was no longer the hitter he had been, largely because he didn't have the speed to get many bunt singles. St. Louis traded him to the Boston AL team in 1905, and Burkett was released after just one season there.

He bought the Worcester, Massachusetts, minor league franchise in 1906 and was player-manager of the team through 1913. Burkett later managed several other minor league teams, coached baseball at Holy Cross College from 1917 through 1920, and served as a coach and scout for the New York Giants.

In 2,066 games, Burkett batted .338 with 2,850 hits, including 320 doubles, 182 triples, and 75 home runs. He scored 1,720 runs and had 952 RBI.
★ Baseball Hall of Fame

Burns, George H.

BASEBALL
b. Jan. 31, 1893, Niles, Ohio
d. Jan. 7, 1978

The 6-foot-1½, 180-pound Burns was a right-handed first baseman who batted over .300 eight times, including marks of .352 and .358 without winning a batting title. However, he was named the AL's most valuable player in 1926, when he led the AL with 216 hits and 64 doubles. That was the season he batted .358.

Burns entered the major leagues with the Detroit Tigers in 1914. He went to the Philadelphia Athletics in 1918, when he had 178 hits to lead the league. Philadelphia traded him to the Cleveland Indians during the 1920 season. He went to the Boston Red Sox in 1922, returning to Cleveland in 1924.

He split the 1928 season between Cleveland and the New York Yankees, and he retired after playing in just 38 games for the Yankees and Athletics in 1929. He had a .307 career average with 2,018 hits, including 444 doubles, 72 triples, and 72 home runs. He scored 901 runs and had 951 RBI.

Burr, Leslie

EQUESTRIAN SPORTS
b. Oct. 1, 1956, Westport, Conn.

A member of the 1984 U.S. Olympic team, the first to win a gold medal in jumping, Burr was one of the country's top equestriennes beginning in 1979, when she won two Grand Prix events, riding Chase the Clouds. She rode on two winning Nations Cup teams the following year.

After Chase the Clouds died in 1982, Burr trained three horses. In 1983, she rode two of them in the American Gold Cup competition, finishing first on Albany and third on Corsair. They had the same first and third finishes in the Mercedes Grand Prix at the National Horse Show.

Burr won three consecutive Grand Prix events, a record, in 1983, when she was named Mercedes rider of the year and Albany was named horse of the year.

Burroughs, Jeffrey A.

BASEBALL
b. March 7, 1951, Long Beach, Calif.

Burroughs was with the AL's Washington Senators for parts of the 1970 and 1971 seasons, and he spent 22 games with the team in 1972, after it had moved to Texas and become known as the Rangers. He became a starter in 1973, playing mostly in the outfield with some stints at first base and as a designated hitter.

In 1974, Burroughs batted .302 with 25 home runs and 118 RBI to win the league's most valuable player award.

The 6-foot-1, 200-pound right-hander went to the Atlanta Braves in 1977 and led the NL in walks with 117 in 1978. He played for the Seattle Mariners in 1981 and the Oakland Athletics from 1982 through 1984 before ending his career as a designated hitter with the Toronto Blue Jays in 1985.

In 1,689 major league games, Burroughs had 1,443 hits, including 230 doubles, 20 triples, and 240 home runs. He scored 720 runs and drove in 882.

Burton, Michael J.

SWIMMING
b. July 3, 1947, Des Moines, Iowa

A pioneer of "mega-mileage" training, Burton swam 4,000 meters a day to build up his endurance. He was the AAU national outdoor 1,500-meter freestyle champion from 1966 through 1969 and in 1971. Indoors, he won the 500-yard championship in 1967 and the 1,650-yard title from 1966 through 1969.

Swimming for UCLA, he won NCAA championships in the 500-yard freestyle in 1970 and in the 1,650-yard event in 1967, 1968, and 1970. Burton was the first to swim 1,650 yards in less than 16 minutes and the first to break the $8\frac{1}{2}$-minute barrier in the 800-meter freestyle.

Burton was the favorite in the Olympic 1,500-meter in 1968. He not only won that event, he surprised most experts by also taking the gold medal in the 400-meter freestyle.

Because of a knee injury suffered in a bicycle accident when he was 12, Burton underwent surgery in 1970 and didn't compete in 1971. He returned in 1972 and barely qualified for the Olympic team. After leading for the first 600 meters, Burton was passed by Graham Windeatt of Australia, but he retook the lead at the 1,200-meter mark and became the only swimmer ever to win the Olympic 1,500-meter freestyle twice.

He retired from competition after the Olympics and became a coach. In 1980, he founded the Des Moines, Iowa, Aquatic Club.

Burton, Nelson, Jr.

BOWLING
b. June 5, 1942, St. Louis, Mo.

"Bo" Burton was named bowler of the year in 1970, when he led the PBA tour in scoring average. He won the ABC classic singles title in 1969 and 1973 and was a member of the Munsingwear team that won the 1976 and 1977 ABC classic championship.

Burton, son of Hall of Fame member Nelson Burton, Sr., joined the PBA tour in 1962 and won his first tour event two years later. His best season was 1978, when he won $67,003. He averaged 221 pins for 28 games in winning the 1976 ABC Masters championship, and he won the BPAA U.S. Open in 1978.

Since 1986, Burton has been on the tour only part time. He often does commentary on ABC bowling telecasts.

★ ABC Hall of Fame; PBA Hall of Fame

Bush, Lesley L.

DIVING
b. Sept. 17, 1947, Orange, N.J.

When Lesley Bush's parents heard reports that she had won a gold medal in platform diving at the 1964 Olympics, they didn't believe it until she phoned from Tokyo to give them the news. Bush, a 16-year-old high school student, was given no chance of beating the defending champion, Ingrid Engel-Kramer of Germany, but she went ahead on the first dive and led all the way.

Bush won her first national championship in the outdoor platform in 1965. She was the outdoor platform and indoor 1-meter springboard champion in 1967, when she won a gold medal in the platform competition at the Pan-American Games.

In 1968, Bush won the outdoor platform and the 3-meter springboard titles. At the Olympics that year, she had a poor first dive and failed to win a medal. She then retired from competition.

Butcher, Susan

SLED DOG RACING
b. Dec. 26, 1954, Cambridge, Mass.

Perhaps the most grueling sports event of all is the Iditarod Trail sled dog race, 1,162 miles across Alaska through temperatures as low as 50 degrees below zero. Butcher has won that race a record four times, from 1986 through 1988 and in 1990.

She set a record of 11 days, 1 hour, 53 minutes, and 23 seconds in her 1990 victory. Modest and soft-spoken, Butcher tends to downplay her accomplishments by saying she's only the coach, because the dogs do all the work.

Butkus, Dick (Richard M.)

FOOTBALL
b. Dec. 9, 1942, Chicago, Ill.

The Chicago Bears have often had one player who symbolized the team, usually a defensive player or a bruising fullback. Middle linebacker Dick Butkus was that player for nine seasons, from 1965 through 1973.

Butkus grew up in Chicago and decided as a youngster that he wanted to be a professional football player. He did it without moving far from his home town. A consensus All-American as a center and linebacker at the University of Illinois in 1963 and 1964, he joined the Bears the following season and won the starting linebacker job from a perennial All-Pro, Bill George.

At 6-foot-3 and 245 pounds, Butkus was mobile enough to cover backs on pass patterns and to cover virtually the entire width of the field on running plays. He was an All-Pro seven times and played in eight Pro Bowls.

A knee injury in 1970 slowed him somewhat, but he continued to star for the Bears until the knee was re-injured in 1973, forcing his retirement. During his pro career, he intercepted 22 passes, returning them for 166 yards, and recovered 25 fumbles, including 1 for his only NFL touchdown.

★ College Football Hall of Fame; Pro Football Hall of Fame

Butler, Brett M.

BASEBALL
b. June 15, 1957, Los Angeles, Calif.

A left-handed center fielder, the 5-foot-10, 161-pound Butler has been one of the best leadoff men in baseball for more than a decade. He was with the NL's Atlanta Braves for parts of the 1981 and 1982 seasons and became a starter in 1983, when he led the league with 13 triples.

The Braves traded him to the AL's Cleveland Indians in 1984. He led that league with 14 triples in 1986. Butler went to the San Francisco Giants as a free agent in 1988 and led the NL in runs scored with 109 in his first season there and in hits with 192 in 1990.

A free agent once more in 1991, Butler joined the Los Angeles Dodgers. He led the league with 112 runs and 108 walks that season. Butler is an outstanding defensive outfielder who went through two seasons, 1991 and 1993, without making an error. He led NL outfielders with 372 putouts and 380 total chances in 1991.

Through the 1994 season, Butler had a .290 career average with 2,089 hits, including 250 doubles, 118 triples, and 53 home runs. He had 503 stolen bases, 1,207 runs scored, and 524 RBI.

Button, Dick (Richard T.)
FIGURE SKATING
b. July 18, 1929, Englewood, N.J.

When Button was 11, he wanted a pair of skates for Christmas, and got them. But he was disappointed. His father had bought him hockey skates instead of figure skates. The skates were exchanged. At the time Button was a chubby 160 pounds at only 5-foot-2, and his first teacher said he would never be a good skater.

So his parents took him to another teacher, and within five years Button won the first of his seven straight national championships, 1946 through 1952. He also won five straight world championships, 1948 through 1952, and two Olympic gold medals, in 1948 and in 1952. He won the 1949 Sullivan Award as the nation's outstanding amateur athlete, the first time it had ever gone to a figure skater.

Never willing to rest on his laurels, Button consistently developed new moves during his championship years. At the 1948 Olympics, when he was a Harvard freshman, he did a double axel for the first time just two days before his free skating performance, and he did it flawlessly in competition to win first place from eight of the nine judges.

Button became the first skater ever to perform a triple jump in competition when he won his second gold medal in 1952. He combined precision in figures and a bold artistic style with his remarkable athleticism.

After retiring from amateur competition, Button toured with the Ice Capades while studying law at Harvard. He later formed a television production company and worked as an expert commentator for televised skating competitions.

Byron, Red (Robert)
AUTO RACING
b. 1916, Anniston, Ala.
d. Nov. 7, 1960

Byron was a pioneer of stock car racing, an Atlanta garage owner who prepared his own cars during the undocumented 1930s and won more than his share of races. An Air Force tail gunner during World War II, he was a founder of NASCAR after the war, and he won its first championship, which was run in modified cars, in 1947. The following year, the Grand National division was established, and Byron won that, too.

Poor health forced him out of driving but not out of racing. He worked for a time with Briggs Cunningham, who was trying to develop an American sports car that could win Grand Prix races, and then became manager of a Corvette team that had the same goal. Neither project succeeded, but Byron enjoyed sports cars. When he died of a heart attack at the age of 44, he was managing a team in Sports Car Club of America competition.

Cafego, George ("Bad News")

FOOTBALL
b. Aug. 30, 1915, Whipple, W.Va.

After one year at the University of Georgia, Cafego transferred to Tennessee in 1937. He became a three-year starter at tailback and an All-American in 1939. During his last two seasons, Tennessee won all 20 of its regular season games, beat Oklahoma, 17–0, in the 1939 Orange Bowl, and lost, 14–0, to Southern California in the 1940 Rose Bowl, when Cafego was injured.

His coach, Bob Neyland, said of him, "In practice, he couldn't do anything right, but for two hours on a Saturday afternoon he did everything an All-American is supposed to do."

The 5-foot-10, 183-pound Cafego combined breakaway speed with a high knee action that made him very difficult to tackle. He was also an excellent passer and punter and a strong defensive player. During his career, Cafego rushed 259 times for 1,589 yards, a 6.1 average; completed 49 of 105 passes for 550 yards; returned 64 punts for 883 yards, a 13.8 average; ran back 12 kickoffs for 391 yards, a 32.6 average; punted 115 times for a 38.3 average; and had 5 interceptions.

After playing for the NFL's Brooklyn Dodgers in 1940, Cafego spent two seasons in the Army. He was with the Dodgers and the Washington Redskins in 1943, and he finished his playing career with the Boston Yanks in 1944 and 1945.

Cafego became an assistant coach at Furman University in 1948 and later assisted at Wyoming, Arkansas, and Tennessee. He was also head baseball coach at Tennessee from 1955 through 1961.
★ College Football Hall of Fame

Cagle, Christian K.

FOOTBALL
b. May 1, 1905, DeRidder, La.
d. Dec. 26, 1942

His teammates usually called Cagle "Chris" or "Red," but sportswriters liked to call him "Onward Christian" because of his ability to advance the ball. In 1925, Cagle played at Southwestern Louisiana, where he scored 108 points to finish fifth in the nation.

He was appointed to the U.S. Military Academy in 1926 and was an All-American halfback three straight years, 1927 through 1929. A fast, deceptive runner, Cagle scored touchdowns on a 53-yard run and a pass reception in Army's 18–0 win over Notre Dame in 1927. In a 21–21 tie with Navy, Cagle had a 44-yard touchdown run and caught another touchdown pass.

In 1928, against Yale, Cagle had touchdown runs of 51 and 76 yards in an 18–6 win, and he scored on a 37-yard run in a 13–3 victory over Nebraska. Cagle captained the team in 1929, when he had five touchdown runs of 35 yards or more, including one of 70 yards.

Cagle had married secretly in August 1928, a violation of West Point rules. When his marriage was revealed after the 1929 season, he was forced to resign before graduating. He played in the NFL with the New York Giants from 1930 through 1932. In 1933, he and "Shipwreck" Kelly became co-owners of the league's Brooklyn Dodgers franchise, and Cagle played for the team in 1933 and 1934.

On December 23, 1942, Cagle was found unconscious in a Manhattan subway station. He died three days later of a fractured skull.

★ College Football Hall of Fame

Cahill, Mabel E.
TENNIS
b. April 2, 1863, Ireland
d. ?
Cahill learned to play tennis in her native Ireland and came to the U.S. in her mid-twenties. A very hard hitter, she won the national singles championship in 1891 and 1892, when she beat Elisabeth Moore in the first five-set match ever played by women in the national finals.

She also teamed with Mrs. W. Fellowes Morgan to win the 1891 women's doubles and with A. M. McKinley to win the 1892 doubles championship. Cahill and Clarence Hobart won the first national mixed doubles title in 1892.

★ International Tennis Hall of Fame

Caldwell, Charlie (Charles W.)
FOOTBALL
b. Aug. 2, 1902, Bristol, Tenn.
d. Nov. 1, 1957
Caldwell played center, fullback, linebacker, and wingback at Princeton from 1922 through 1924, but was better at baseball. A pitcher, he appeared in three games with the New York Yankees in 1925 before becoming an assistant coach at his alma mater.

He went to Williams College as head football coach in 1928 and had a 76–37–6 record in 17 seasons. The school dropped football in 1943 because of World War II, and Caldwell became an assistant coach at Yale for two years, then returned to Princeton as head football coach in 1945.

Caldwell was a major proponent of the single wing's buck lateral series, in which a back runs toward the line to divert the defense and then laterals the

ball to another back. Using that attack, Princeton went undefeated in 1950 and 1951, winning all 18 of its games, and had a 24-game winning streak.

Under Caldwell, Princeton won the Ivy League title in 1950, 1951, and 1955, and was "Big Three" champion six years in a row, from 1947 through 1952. Forced to retire because of ill health after the 1956 season, Caldwell died of cancer less than a year later. He had a 70–30–3 record in his 12 seasons at Princeton for an overall mark of 146 wins, 67 losses, and 9 ties.

★ College Football Hall of Fame

Calhoun, Lee Q.
TRACK AND FIELD
b. Feb. 23, 1933, Laurel, Miss.
d. June 22, 1989
Calhoun is the only athlete to win the 110-meter hurdles at two different Olympics. Going into the 1956 Olympics, his personal best in the event was 14.4 seconds, but he ran a 13.5 to win the gold medal, edging teammate Jack Davis with a lunge that just got his shoulder across the line in front. Ironically, he'd learned the maneuver from Davis.

Representing North Carolina College, Calhoun won the NCAA 120-yard hurdles in 1956 and 1957. He was the national outdoor hurdles champion in 1956, 1957, and 1959, and the champion in the indoor 60-yard hurdles in 1956 and 1957.

Calhoun was suspended in 1958 for receiving gifts on *Bride and Groom*, a television game show, and seemed to be past his prime for the 1960 Olympics. But he won the high hurdles again in a personal best 13.4 and shortly afterward he tied the world record with a 13.2.

★ National Track & Field Hall of Fame; Olympic Hall of Fame

Calnan, George C.
FENCING
b. Jan. 18, 1900, Boston, Mass.
d. April 4, 1933
He didn't begin fencing until he was a student at the U.S. Naval Academy, but within three years Calnan was captain of the school's fencing team, and

within five he was a member of the 1924 Olympic team. He won the national epee championship in 1923, the foil championship from 1925 through 1928 and in 1930 and 1931, and the three-weapon championship in 1927.

Calnan won the bronze medal in epee at the 1928 Olympics. In 1932, he took the oath of participation on behalf of all Olympic athletes and was on the bronze medal epee and sabre teams.

A career Navy officer, Calnan died in the crash of the dirigible *Akron*. The George C. Calnan Memorial Trophy is given to the national three-weapon championship team.

Camilli, Dolph (Adolph L.)

BASEBALL
b. April 23, 1907, San Francisco, Calif.

A left-handed first baseman, Camilli was named the NL's most valuable player in 1941, when he led the league with 34 home runs and 120 RBI while batting .285 for the pennant-winning Brooklyn Dodgers. However, Camilli batted .167 and had only one RBI in Brooklyn's five-game World Series loss to the New York Yankees.

Camilli joined the Chicago Cubs late in the 1933 season and was traded to the Philadelphia Phillies during the 1934 season. He hit .315 in 1936 and .339 in 1937 before being traded to Brooklyn. He went into the service during the 1943 season and returned to baseball with the Boston Braves for 63 games in 1945 before retiring.

In 1,490 games, Camilli had 1,482 hits, including 261 doubles, 86 triples, and 239 home runs. He scored 936 runs and drove in 950.

Camp, Walter C.

FOOTBALL
b. April 7, 1859, New Haven, Conn.
d. March 14, 1925

Camp almost single-handedly created American football from a rugby-like sport as a student at Yale University and later as a graduate member of the rules committee. He enrolled at Yale in 1875 and joined the school's new foot-

ball team, which was about to play Harvard for the first time. Other colleges were playing a type of soccer, but Harvard students had learned rugby and insisted on playing under the rules of that sport, with some minor variations.

After the Harvard-Yale game, other U.S. colleges began to play rugby instead of soccer. Camp graduated from Yale in 1880 but entered the medical school and continued to play, a common practice at the time. He captained the team in 1878, 1879, and 1881.

The first step toward transforming rugby into American football was taken in 1880, on a proposal by Camp. In rugby, when the ball goes out of bounds or a player is downed, possession is decided by a "scrummage" or "scrum," in which lines of players from each team push and shove against one another.

Camp proposed using a "scrimmage" instead, allowing the team that had the ball to retain possession and put it into play by snapping it back to the quarterback.

The trouble with the scrimmage was that it enabled a team to get possession of the ball indefinitely. Camp in 1882 came up with a solution to that problem, requiring a team to gain 5 yards or lose 10 in three scrimmages to retain possession.

Because he couldn't stand the sight of blood, Camp dropped out of medical school in 1882 and took a job at a New Haven clock factory. Even though he couldn't attend afternoon practices, he served as advisory coach to the Yale football team, meeting with the captain every night. After he married in 1888, his wife attended practices and took notes for Camp's review.

In 1884, Camp devised football's first numerical scoring system, assigning 1 point to a safety, 2 to a touchdown, 4 to a goal following touchdown (which we now call a conversion), and 5 to a field goal. Until then, there had often been disputes about who had won a game because some teams felt a field goal should beat a goal after touchdown; others felt it should work the other way around.

Yale appointed its first official head

football coach in 1893, but Camp continued to serve as an adviser through the 1906 season. During the period he was in that role, Yale won 218 games, losing only 11 and tying 8.

Camp was secretary of the rules committee from 1894 through 1905 and from 1911 until his death. He died of a heart attack while attending the committee's annual meeting in 1925.

Besides helping to shape the sport, Camp promoted football through many articles and a number of books. He helped Caspar Whitney select the first All-America team in 1889, and he chose All-America teams for *Collier's* magazine from 1898 through 1924.

★ College Football Hall of Fame

Campanella, Roy

BASEBALL
b. Nov. 19, 1921, Philadelphia, Pa.
d. June 26, 1993

Major league baseball's first black catcher, Campanella began playing professionally when blacks could hardly dream of ever being in the majors. In 1937, he was with the Bacharach Giants, a semipro team, but before the season ended he was the starting catcher for the Baltimore Elite Giants of the Negro National League.

Like many blacks, he played winter baseball in Latin America while he was with the Giants. Because he had two children, Campanella was granted a draft deferment during World War II. He went to the Mexican League in 1942 but returned to the Giants in 1944.

When Branch Rickey of the Brooklyn Dodgers was looking for a black player to integrate major league baseball, Campanella was among those considered. Jackie Robinson, of course, was chosen for that role, but Campanella also signed with the Dodgers soon afterward, in 1946.

After two seasons in the minor leagues, Campanella was with the Dodgers briefly at the beginning of the 1948 season. He was sent down to the minors, primarily to integrate the American Association, but was called back up for good after hitting 13 home runs in 35 games.

"Campy" played for four pennant winners in Brooklyn and was named the NL's most valuable player in 1951, 1953, and 1955. He hit .325 with 33 homers and 108 RBI in 1951. In 1953, he set a record for catchers with 41 home runs, led the league with 142 RBI, and batted .312. When the Dodgers won their first world championship in 1955, Campanella batted .318 with 32 home runs and 107 RBI.

Though known for his quiet demeanor off the field, Campanella could take charge on the field. A Dodger pitcher once shook off his sign and gave up a hit. Campanella told him angrily, "Don't ever shake me off again. You know I'm smarter than you are."

In the early morning of January 28, 1958, Campanella was driving from his Harlem liquor store to his home on Long Island when his car skidded on a patch of ice and hit a telephone pole. He suffered two broken vertebrae in his neck and was paralyzed from the chest down.

The Dodgers moved to Los Angeles that year. Campanella was honored before a pre-season game between the Dodgers and the Yankees, attended by a record crowd of 93,103 fans.

Campanella served as a spring training coach for the Dodgers for many years. His autobiography, *It's Good to Be Alive*, was adapted as a 1974 made-for-television movie.

In 1,215 games, Campanella batted .276, with 178 doubles, 18 triples, 242 home runs, 627 runs scored, and 856 RBI.

★ Baseball Hall of Fame

Campbell, David C.

FOOTBALL
b. Sept. 5, 1873, Waltham, Mass.
d. June 30, 1949

Campbell didn't enroll at Harvard until he was 25, after working for a number of years, and he didn't make the varsity as a freshman. But he was a three-time All-American end, from 1899 through 1901, and he was the 28-year-old captain of the undefeated 1901 team.

Although very slender, only 171 pounds on a 6-foot frame, Campbell was surprisingly strong and durable. In his era, teams usually massed blockers who locked their arms together to protect the ball carrier. Campbell was known for climbing right over the wall of blockers to grab the runner and pull him down.

As captain of the team in 1901, Campbell was virtually the coach. Against Army that season, he improvised a lateral play that won the game, 6–0, in the closing minutes.

★ College Football Hall of Fame

Campbell, Earl

FOOTBALL
b. March 29, 1955, Tyler, Tex.

A running back at the University of Texas, Campbell won the 1977 Heisman Trophy as the nation's outstanding college football player. Strong and powerful at 5-foot-11 and 230 pounds, he also had a surprising turn of speed that sometimes allowed him to run right past tacklers after getting through the line of scrimmage.

He joined the NFL's Houston Oilers as a first-round draft selection in 1978 and was named the American Football Conference player of the year by United Press International and *The Sporting News* after leading the league in rushing with 1,450 yards on 302 carries, a 4.8 average. He scored 12 touchdowns.

In 1979, Campbell won the Bert Bell Trophy as the NFL's most valuable player. He gained 1,697 yards on 368 attempts, a 4.6 average, to lead the league again, and he also led with 19 touchdowns.

Campbell set an NFL record by rushing for more than 200 yards in four different games in 1980, gaining 1,934 yards on 373 attempts, a 5.2 average, and scoring 13 rushing touchdowns to lead the league in all four categories.

Although he was the league's rushing leader for a fourth consecutive year in 1981, it was much harder. With defenses ignoring the pass and concentrating on Campbell, he averaged only 3.8 yards a carry, rushing 361 times for 1,376 yards and 10 touchdowns.

The workload he'd been carrying began to affect him in 1982, when injuries limited him to just 538 yards on 157 carries. Campbell bounced back with 1,301 yards in 322 carries, a 4.0 average, in 1983, and he was traded to the New Orleans Saints after the season.

A knee injury limited him to only 468 yards in 1984. The last time he carried the ball, in 1985, Campbell appeared to have broken away for a touchdown, but he pulled a thigh muscle, stumbled, was caught from behind, and fumbled the ball. He announced his retirement shortly afterward.

In seven NFL seasons, Campbell rushed for 9,407 yards in 2,187 attempts, a 4.3 average, and scored 74 touchdowns. He caught only 121 passes for 806 yards, a 6.7 average.

★ Pro Football Hall of Fame

Campbell, John

HARNESS RACING
b. April 4, 1955, London, Ont.

Although only fourth in career wins, Campbell is by far the top money-winning driver in harness racing history with over $118 million, more than $30 million ahead of Herve Filion, who is in second place.

Campbell began racing in 1972, primarily at Windsor Raceway in Ontario. When the track's racing secretary, Joe DeFrank, moved to the Meadowlands in New Jersey in 1975, Campbell made the same move, and won more that year than he had the previous three years combined.

His first big year was 1979, when he led in money won with $3,308,984. Campbell was the top money winner 8 of the next 14 years, setting a record with $11,148,565 in 1988. He broke that with $11,620,878 in 1990, when he won 543 races.

Through 1993, Campbell had driven 6,308 winners and earned $118,951,088. He was named harness driver of the year in 1983, 1988, and 1990.

Campbell, Milton

TRACK AND FIELD
b. Dec. 9, 1933, Plainfield, N.J.

Although best known as an Olympic champion decathlete, Campbell was also a world class hurdler. Representing the University of Indiana, he won the NCAA and AAU 120-yard hurdle championship in 1955 and on May 31, 1957, he tied the world record of 13.4 seconds in the event.

At 18, Campbell finished second to Bob Mathias in the 1952 Olympic decathlon, and he won the 1953 AAU championship in the event. He won the gold medal in 1956 with an Olympic record, but fell short of the world record because he pole vaulted only 11 feet, 1⅓ inches, far below his usual performance.

Campbell also played football at Indiana and, briefly, with the Cleveland Browns.

★ National Track & Field Hall of Fame

Campbell, Oliver S.

TENNIS
b. Feb. 25, 1871, Brooklyn, N.Y.
d. July 11, 1953

As a student at Columbia University, the 19-year-old Campbell won the U.S. national singles championship in 1890. He repeated after graduating in 1891 and won a third straight title in 1892, then retired from competition.

Campbell teamed with Val Hall to win the intercollegiate doubles championship in 1888 and with Empie Wright to win the 1889 title. He and Robert Huntington won the national doubles championship in 1891 and 1892.

A strong volleyer, Campbell went on a tour of Europe and England in late 1891 and early 1892, but he was unsuccessful against top British players.

★ International Tennis Hall of Fame

Canadeo, Tony (Anthony R.)

FOOTBALL
b. May 5, 1919, Chicago, Ill.

At 5-foot-11 and 195 pounds, Canadeo was neither fast nor particularly elusive, yet he became the first member of the Green Bay Packers and only the third NFL player to rush for more than 1,000 yards in a season.

Canadeo was a seventh-round draft choice in 1941 after playing for little Gonzaga University in Washington. He joined the team primarily as a backup to tailback Cecil Isbell, but became a starter in 1943. After spending 1945 in the service, he returned to the Packers as a running back in the newly installed T formation. His premier season was 1949, when he rushed 208 times for 1,052, a 5.1 average, and 4 touchdowns.

During his last three seasons, 1950 through 1952, Canadeo was usually used as blocking fullback and didn't carry the ball often. He retired after 1952 with an impressive set of statistics: 4,197 yards on 1,025 carries, a 4.1 average, and 26 touchdowns; 69 receptions for 579 yards and 5 touchdowns; 105 completions in 268 attempts for 1,642 yards and 16 touchdowns; 45 punt returns for 509 yards; 71 kickoff returns for 1,626 yards; 9 interceptions and 129 yards in returns; and 45 punts for a 37.0 average.

★ Pro Football Hall of Fame

Cann, Howard G.

BASKETBALL
b. Oct. 11, 1895, Bridgeport, Conn.
d. Dec. 18, 1992

When New York University won the national AAU basketball championship in 1920, Cann was the team's leading player. An AAU All-American forward, he was retroactively named college player of the year by the Helms Athletic Foundation. He also played football and was a member of the 1920 Olympic team as a shot putter.

He returned to the school as basketball coach for the 1923–24 season and remained for 35 years. His 1934–35 team won 19 of 20 games, outscored its opposition 740 to 489, and was selected as Helms national champion. Cann retired after the 1957–58 season with a record of 409 wins and 232 losses, a .638 percentage.

★ Basketball Hall of Fame

Cannon, Billy (William A.)

FOOTBALL
b. Feb. 8, 1937, Philadelphia, Pa.

Because of a tug of war between the established NFL and the new American Football League in 1960, Cannon was the most publicized football player of the year.

An All-American halfback at Louisiana State University in 1958 and 1959, Cannon won the Heisman Trophy as a senior. The 6-foot-1, 210-pounder was a fine all-around player who rushed for 1,867 yards, returned 31 punts for 349 yards, and caught 31 passes during his career. He was also LSU's punter.

The NFL's Los Angeles Rams secretly signed him to a $50,000 contract soon after the regular season ended. A few weeks later, Cannon also signed with the AFL's Houston Oilers for $100,000 a year. A court ruled that the Houston contract was binding.

Cannon spent four seasons with the Oilers. He led the league in rushing with 948 yards in 1961, when Houston won the AFL championship. Traded to the Oakland Raiders in 1964, Cannon was moved to tight end. He remained with the Raiders until 1970, when he played a final season with the Kansas City Chiefs.

During his 11 seasons as a professional, Cannon rushed 602 times for 2,455 yards, a 4.1 average, and 17 touchdowns. He caught 236 passes for 3,656 yards, a 15.5 average, and 29 touchdowns; returned 14 punts for 178 yards; and ran back 67 kickoffs for 1,704 yards and 1 touchdown.

Cannon was named all-AFL as a running back in 1961 and as a tight end in 1967. He practiced dentistry after retiring from football. In 1983, he was convicted of taking part in a counterfeiting operation and was sentenced to five years in prison.

Cannon, Jack (John J.)

FOOTBALL
b. April 19, 1907, Columbus, Ohio
d. Nov. 12, 1967

A happy-go-lucky player who refused to wear a helmet, Cannon was an All-American guard at Notre Dame in 1929, and he was named to the all-time All-American team selected by Grantland Rice ten years later. Cannon's greatest game was probably Notre Dame's 7–0 victory over Army at Yankee Stadium.

He kicked off three times and made the tackle each time, threw the block that enabled Jack Elder to run 96 yards with an interception to score the winning touchdown, and played brilliantly on defense. When the game ended, the Army players massed around Cannon to congratulate him on his play.

★ College Football Hall of Fame

Canseco, Jose, Jr.

BASEBALL
b. July 2, 1964, Havana, Cuba

Canseco played high school baseball in Miami and was chosen by the AL's Oakland Athletics in the 1982 free-agent draft. He joined the major league team late in the 1985 season and was named the league's rookie of the year by *The Sporting News* and the Baseball Writers Association of America in 1986, his first full season, when he batted only .240 but hit 33 home runs and had 117 RBI.

At 6-foot-4 and 240 pounds, Canseco is tremendously strong and has hit some mammoth home runs. An opposing player once said of him, "He'll hit the ball, and you'll say there's no way anybody can hit anything that far. Then he'll hit one farther." Despite his size, he's also very fast.

In 1988, Canseco became the first player to hit 40 or more home runs and steal 40 or more bases in the same season. His 42 home runs and 124 RBI led the league, and he had a career high .307 batting average to win the AL's most valuable player award.

An injury limited him to just 65 games in 1989, but he came back with 37 home runs and 101 RBI in 1990, then led the league in home runs for a second time with 44 in 1991, when he had 122 RBI.

The outspoken Canseco clashed with Oakland management, was frequently kept on the bench, and was finally traded to the Texas Rangers during the 1992 season.

A bizarre injury in 1993 threatened his career. With the Rangers losing badly to the Boston Red Sox on May 29 and the bullpen depleted, Canseco was brought in to pitch the ninth inning. He tore a ligament in his right elbow, and although he played sporadically for a month, he then underwent surgery that ended his season. There was some doubt that he could ever return, but he hit 31 home runs in the strike-shortened 1994 season.

In 1,143 major league games through 1994, Canseco had 1,154 hits, including 204 doubles, 11 triples, and 275 home runs. He had scored 732 runs and driven in 870.

Canzoneri, Tony

BOXING
b. Nov. 6, 1908, Slidell, La.
d. Dec. 9, 1959

Canzoneri began boxing as a young teenager in New Orleans. His family moved to Brooklyn in 1923, and the following year he won the New York state amateur bantamweight championship.

He turned professional early in 1925 and twice fought Bud Taylor for the world bantamweight title in 1927. Both fights were in Chicago. The first, on March 26, was a draw, and Taylor won a 10-round decision in the second, on June 24.

The 5-foot-4 Canzoneri, a nonstop puncher, moved up to the featherweight division in 1928 and won the world title on February 10 with a 16-round decision over Benny Bass in New York City. He lost the championship to Andre Routis of France on September 28, 1928, on a 10-round decision.

His next step was into the lightweight division. He lost a title fight to Sammy Mandell in 1929, but on November 14 of the following year he pulled a major upset by knocking out heavily favored Al Singer in the first round to win the championship. Canzoneri also became junior welterweight champion with a 3rd-round knockout of Jack "Kid" Berg on April 24, 1931.

He lost the junior welter title to Johnny Jadick on a 10-round decision on January 18, 1932, in Philadelphia, but regained it by winning a 10-rounder against Battling Shaw on May 21, 1933, in New Orleans.

Barney Ross easily outpointed Can-

zoneri to win both titles on June 23, 1933, in Chicago. After Ross vacated the lightweight title to become a welterweight, Canzoneri won a tournament, decisioning Lou Ambers in 15 rounds on May 10, 1935, to become champion once again. However, Ambers took the title from him on a 15-round decision on September 3, 1936.

Canzoneri's last fight was on November 1, 1939, when he was knocked out by Al Davis in the 3rd round. He won 139 of his 176 bouts, 44 by knockout; lost 24, 1 by knockout; and fought 10 draws and 3 no-decisions.

★ International Boxing Hall of Fame

Caponi, Donna M. (Mrs. Young)

GOLF
b. Jan. 29, 1945, Detroit, Mich.

Caponi joined the LPGA tour in 1965, and she won two consecutive U.S. Women's Open championships in 1969 and 1970. She also won the LPGA championship in 1979 and 1981.

Her best year was 1980, when she won five tournaments and $220,619. The following year, she won $193,916 and became the third woman to surpass $1 million in career earnings.

The 5-foot-5 redhead loves dancing and has been nicknamed the "Watusi Kid" and "Boogie D." She cut back on tour events in 1988 to spend more time as a golf commentator for ESPN.

Cappelletti, Gino R. M.

FOOTBALL
b. March 26, 1934, Keewatin, Minn.

A quarterback and kicker at the University of Minnesota, Cappelletti tried out with the NFL's Detroit Lions after graduating in 1955 but failed to make the team. He played Canadian football in 1958 and joined the Boston Patriots of the newly organized American Football League in 1960.

Cappelletti kicked the first field goal in AFL history in the Patriots' opening game against the Denver Broncos. Also used as a wide receiver during his early years with the Patriots, Cappelletti was named the league's player of the year in 1964, when he scored 155 points by catching 7 touchdown passes and kicking 25 field goals and 38 extra points.

He led the AFL in scoring in 1961 and from 1963 through 1966 and scored more than 100 points six straight seasons, 1961 through 1966. Cappelletti retired after the 1970 season and became a commentator on the Patriots' radio network.

During his 11 seasons, Cappelletti caught 292 passes for 4,589 yards, a 15.7 average, and 42 touchdowns. He kicked 342 of 353 extra point attempts and made 176 of 333 field goal attempts for a total of 1,130 points.

Cappelletti, John R.

FOOTBALL
b. Aug. 9, 1952, Upper Darby, Pa.

A defensive back as a freshman and sophomore at Penn State, Cappelletti was moved to running back in his junior year, 1972, and gained 1,117 yards. As a senior, he rushed for 1,522 yards, was a consensus All-American, and won the Heisman Trophy as the nation's outstanding college player.

The 6-foot-1, 219-pound Cappelletti joined the Los Angeles Rams in 1974 and was with them for five seasons. He missed 1979 with a knee injury and then spent three seasons with the San Diego Chargers before retiring.

In his eight professional seasons, Cappelletti rushed 824 times for 2,751 yards, a 3.3 average, and 24 touchdowns. He caught 135 passes for 1,233 yards and 4 touchdowns.

Capriati, Jennifer

TENNIS
b. March 29, 1976, Long Island, N.Y.

In 1990, the 14-year-old Capriati became the youngest player ever to reach the semifinals of a grand slam tennis tournament, the French Open, and she was also the youngest ever to win a match at Wimbledon.

Capriati spent a couple of difficult years on the tour. Usually effervescent, she often seemed sullen or unhappy after losing in the quarterfinals of three consecutive grand slam events in 1992, but

she was at her best in the Olympics, beating Steffi Graf to win the gold medal in singles.

"For two weeks, I was watching the other athletes up there who won gold medals and was thinking that it would be so cool to be up there," she said afterward. "Right now, this means more to me than any of the grand slams."

Late in 1993, Capriati left the tour to concentrate on her high school studies. Her tennis future was clouded by arrests for shoplifting in December of that year and for drug use in May of 1994.

Carbonneau, Guy

HOCKEY
b. March 18, 1960, Sept Iles, P.Q.

An outstanding defensive player, Carbonneau joined the NHL's Montreal Canadiens for just two games in 1980–81. After spending all of the following season in the minor leagues, he became a regular with Montreal in 1982–83.

The 5-foot-11, 184-pound Carbonneau is a center who's usually assigned to guard the opposition's best scorer. He won the Frank J. Selke Trophy as the league's best defensive forward in 1988, 1989, and 1992, and he played for Stanley Cup championship teams in 1986 and 1993.

Through the 1993–94 season Carbonneau had scored 221 goals and 326 assists for 547 points in 912 regular season games and had 73 points on 30 goals and 43 assists in 161 playoff games.

Carew, Rodney C.

BASEBALL
b. Oct. 1, 1945, Gatun, Panama

A right-handed thrower and left-handed hitter with excellent speed, Carew won seven AL batting titles. His .388 average in 1977 was the highest in the major leagues since Ted Williams hit .406 in 1941. (Williams also batted .388 in 1957.)

Carew joined the Minnesota Twins in 1957 as a second baseman and won his first batting championship with a .332 mark in 1969. He batted .366 the following year but didn't qualify for the championship because an injury limited him to only 191 at-bats.

Four of his titles came in consecutive seasons, with averages of .318 in 1972, .350 in 1973, .364 in 1974, and .359 in 1975. He slipped to .331 in 1976, when he began playing primarily at first base. Carew then had his finest season, winning the AL's most valuable player award by leading the league in batting average at .388, runs scored with 128, hits with 239, and triples with 16.

Carew's final batting championship came in 1978, when he hit .333. He was then traded to the California Angels. Although he hit over .300 the next five seasons, he didn't manage to win another batting title. Injuries limited him in 1984, when he batted only .295, and he retired after a .280 season in 1985.

In 2,469 games, Carew had 3,053 hits, including 445 doubles, 112 triples, and 92 home runs. He stole 353 bases, scored 1,424 runs, and drove in 1,015.

★ Baseball Hall of Fame

Carey, Max [Maximilian Carnarius]
BASEBALL
b. Jan. 11, 1890, Terre Haute, Ind.
d. May 30, 1976

A baseball and track star at Concordia College in Indiana, where he was studying to be a Lutheran minister, Maximilian Carnarius took the name Max Carey to protect his college eligibility when he began playing minor league baseball in 1909.

After graduating in 1910, he returned to professional baseball and played the last two games of the season with the Pittsburgh Pirates, collecting three hits in six at-bats.

The switch-hitting Carey became Pittsburgh's starting center fielder and leadoff man during the 1911 season. Never a great hitter, Carey could draw walks and was a great base stealer when he got on base.

Carey was one of the first stealers to study pitchers and their moves, rather than relying on sheer speed and abandon. He led the league in stealing ten times, the last time when he was 35 and not nearly as fast as he had once been.

Because of his speed and knowledge of how to play hitters, Carey led NL outfielders in putouts a record nine times. When he retired after the 1929 season, he held career records for stolen bases with 783, outfield putouts with 6,363, and outfield assists with 339.

Carey's best season was 1922, when he batted .329, stole 51 bases in 53 attempts, and scored 140 runs. When the Pirates won the 1925 NL pennant, he hit .343 and stole 46 bases. The Pirates beat the Washington Senators in a seven-game World Series in which Carey got 11 hits, batted .458, stole 3 bases, and scored 6 runs.

During the 1926 season, Carey had a dispute with the Pittsburgh front office. He was suspended and then released. The Brooklyn Dodgers signed him, and he played there through the 1929 season.

Carey managed the Dodgers to a 146–161 record in 1932 and 1933. He also managed several minor league teams and the Grand Rapids Chicks of the All American Girls Professional Baseball League.

In 2,476 games, Carey batted .285, with 419 doubles, 159 triples, and 70 home runs. He walked 1,040 times, stole 738 bases, scored 1,545 runs, and drove in 800.

★ Baseball Hall of Fame

Carey, Rick (Richard J.)
SWIMMING
b. March 13, 1963, Mt. Kisco, N.Y.

Carey was harshly criticized by the press after appearing angry and dejected despite winning a gold medal in the 200-meter backstroke at the 1984 Olympics. He had hoped to break his own world record in the event.

He went on to win the 100-meter event as well. This time he showed his happiness and issued a formal apology, saying, "I found it very difficult to smile when my performance didn't live up to my expectations. By not breaking the world record I felt I had not only let myself down, but also the crowd." Carey won a third gold medal as a member of the 4 x 100-meter freestyle relay team.

As a high school senior, Carey won

the national indoor 100- and 200-yard backstroke championships in 1981. He entered the University of Texas that fall and was the NCAA 200-meter backstroke champion from 1982 through 1984. He also won the 100-meter in 1983 and 1984.

In 1983, Carey set world records of 55.38 seconds in the 100-meter and 1:58.93 in the 200-meter backstroke, breaking marks set in 1976 by John Naber. At the Pan-American Games that year, he lowered the 100-meter record to 55.19, and he also won the 200-meter event.

Carey was the national outdoor 100-meter and 200-meter champion in the backstroke in 1985 and 1986; the indoor 100-yard champion in 1985; and the indoor 200-yard champion in 1985 and 1986 before retiring from competition.

Carideo, Frank (Francis F.)
FOOTBALL
b. Aug. 4, 1908, Mt. Vernon, N.Y.
d. March 17, 1992

Knute Rockne called the 5-foot-7 Carideo the best quarterback he ever saw. During Carideo's junior and senior years, 1929 and 1930, Notre Dame won all 19 of its games. A dangerous runner, good passer, and very intelligent signal caller, Carideo also excelled as a punter who could put the ball out of bounds near the opposition's goal line.

In 1929, Carideo had three touchdown runs of 65 yards or longer. For the 1930 team, generally considered Rockne's best, he salvaged an undefeated season by throwing a touchdown pass to beat Army, 7–6.

After graduating, Carideo served as an assistant coach at several colleges, and he was also basketball coach at Mississippi State from 1936–37 through 1938–39.
★ College Football Hall of Fame

Carlson, Doc (Henry C.)
BASKETBALL
b. July 4, 1894, Murray City, Okla.
d. Nov. 1, 1964

A three-sport star and winner of nine letters at the University of Pittsburgh,

Carlson was captain of the undefeated 1917 football team. He played end for the professional Cleveland Indians for one season while studying for his medical degree.

But his fame came as a basketball coach at his alma mater. Carlson began coaching in 1922 while working as a company doctor for Carnegie Steel. He developed the first patterned offense, the "Figure 8," and became the first coach to take his team across the continent in 1931–32, when Pittsburgh went on the road to beat Kansas University, the University of Colorado, Stanford, and Southern California.

His 1927–28 team was undefeated in 21 games, and his 1929–30 team had a 23–2 record. Both were selected as national champions by the Helms Athletic Foundation.

Carlson became director of student health services in 1932 and held that position until his retirement in 1964. He coached Pittsburgh through the 1952–53 season, compiling a record of 367 wins and 250 losses.
★ Basketball Hall of Fame

Carlton, Steven N.
BASEBALL
b. Dec. 22, 1944, Miami, Fla.

A fitness fanatic, Carlton trained by practicing kung fu, doing isometric exercises, and developing strength in his hands by working them in buckets of rice. It worked for him: the 6-foot-4, 210-pound left-hander became the only pitcher ever to win four Cy Young awards.

After pitching briefly for the NL's St. Louis Cardinals in 1965 and 1966, Carlton became a regular starter in 1967. It was the first of 17 seasons in which he made more than 30 starts. In 1968, Carlton added a nasty slider to an excellent fastball and fine control.

His first 20-victory season came in 1971, when he had a 20–9 record. His reward was a trade to the Philadelphia Phillies. Known simply as "Lefty" by his teammates, Carlton won his first Cy Young Award in Philadelphia in 1972, compiling a 27–10 record for a last-place team that won only 59 games. He led the NL in victories and in complete games with 30, innings pitched with 346, strikeouts with 310, and ERA with 1.97.

Carlton's performance won him a $167,000 salary, the highest ever for a pitcher at the time. After three sub-par seasons, he led the NL with a .741 winning percentage on a 20–7 record in 1976, then claimed his second Cy Young Award in 1977, when he led in victories with a 23–10 record.

After going 16–13 and 18–11, Carlton led the league in victories with a 24–9 record, in innings pitched with 304, and in strikeouts with 286 in 1980, when he had a 2.34 ERA and won another Cy Young Award. He claimed his fourth in 1982. That season, Carlton was the league leader in victories with a 23–11 record, in complete games with 19, in shutouts with 6, in innings pitched with 295, and in strikeouts with 286.

Despite a 15–16 record in 1983, Carlton again led in innings pitched with 283 and in strikeouts with 275. He began to slide in 1984, when he was 13–7 with a 3.58 ERA. In 1985, Carlton went on the disabled list for the first time, starting only 16 games and completing none.

Carlton pitched with little success for the Phillies and the San Francisco Giants in 1986, the Cleveland Indians and the Minnesota Twins in 1987. He retired after appearing in just four games for Minnesota in 1988.

In 24 seasons, Carlton had a 329–244 record, with 55 shutouts and a 3.22 ERA. He struck out 4,136 hitters while walking only 1,833 in 5,217⅓ innings.

★ Baseball Hall of Fame

Carner, JoAnne (Gunderson)
GOLF
b. April 4, 1939, Kirkland, Wash.

"The Great Gundy" won the U.S. Amateur championship five times, in 1957, 1960, 1962, 1966, and 1968. She even won a tournament on the professional tour in 1969; no amateur has done it since. She joined the tour in 1970 and won the U.S. Open the following year.

Although she was the Open cham-

pion again in 1976 and won the Vare Trophy for the lowest average round in 1974 and 1975, her best years as a pro came after she turned 40. She was named LPGA player of the year and Vare Trophy winner three years in a row, from 1981 through 1983, and she was the tour's leading money winner in 1982 and 1983.

Carner became the second LPGA player to pass $1 million in earnings in 1981; in 1988, she became the second to pass $2 million. She was also the first woman golfer to earn more than $200,000 in three consecutive years. Her last victory was the 1985 Safeco Classic, her 42nd, which ties her for sixth on the all-time list.

★ International Women's Sports Hall of Fame; LPGA Hall of Fame; World Golf Hall of Fame

Carnesecca, Lou (Luigi)
BASKETBALL
b. Jan. 5, 1925, New York, N.Y.

Carnesecca played basketball at St. John's University and was also an assistant coach as a student. After graduating in 1950, he became a teacher and coach at St. Ann's Academy in New York City and guided the school to three national Catholic high school championships in seven seasons.

In 1957, he returned to St. John's as an assistant coach and was named head coach in 1965. Carnesecca became general manager and coach of the ABA's New York Nets in 1970 but had only a 114–138 record in three seasons there, and went back to St. John's in 1973.

Carnesecca retired after the 1991–92 season with a 526–200 record. He ranks 27th all-time in victories, and his .725 winning percentage is 26th best in history.

★ Basketball Hall of Fame

Carnevale, Ben (Bernard L.)
BASKETBALL
b. Oct. 30, 1915, Raritan, N.J.

After playing for Howard Cann at New York University, where he captained the team in 1937–38, Carnevale had a brief professional career with the

New Jersey Reds and then entered coaching at Cranford, New Jersey, High School. His teams there won 75 games and three state championships in three years.

Carnevale served in the Navy during World War II and then became the coach at the University of North Carolina. The school began its rise to national prominence in his second season, 1945–46, winning 29 of 34 games. The Tarheels got into the final game of the NCAA tournament, losing 43–40 to Oklahoma A & M.

He then went to the U.S. Naval Academy, where he compiled a record of 257 wins and 158 losses over a 20-year period. His Navy teams played in five NCAA and two National Invitation tournaments.

Carnevale left Navy in 1967 to become athletic director at NYU. He held the same position at William and Mary from 1973 until retiring in 1981.
★ Basketball Hall of Fame

Carpenter, Bill (William S. Jr.)
FOOTBALL
b. Sept. 30, 1937, Woodbury, N.J.

Carpenter became famous as the "lonely end" at the U.S. Military Academy in 1958 and 1959. Army Coach "Red" Blaik devised the lonely end formation, in which Carpenter was split wide and never entered the huddle. Instead, plays were conveyed to him through hand signals from the quarterback.

As a junior in 1958, Carpenter caught 22 passes for 453 yards and 2 touchdowns. He was named an All-American in 1959, when he had 43 receptions for 591 yards and 4 touchdowns.

Although he had to enter military service after graduation, the 6-foot-2, 210-pound Carpenter was drafted by the Oakland Raiders of the AFL and the Baltimore Colts of the NFL, but he elected to became a career military officer, eventually rising to the rank of general.
★ College Football Hall of Fame

Carpenter, Connie (Mrs. Phinney)
CYCLING, ROWING, SPEED SKATING
b. Feb. 26, 1957, Madison, Wis.

Shortly before her fifteenth birthday, Carpenter finished seventh in the 1,500-meter speed skating event at the 1972 Olympics. She won the U.S. outdoor overall championship in 1976, but injured an ankle and missed the Olympics.

Like most speed skaters, Carpenter trained on a bicycle during the off-season. After her ankle injury, she began cycling competitively and won the national road and pursuit championships in 1976, 1977, and 1979.

Carpenter suffered a concussion in a fall and temporarily quit cycling to return to the University of California, Berkeley, where she took up rowing. She was a member of the crew that won the 1980 national collegiate championship in the four-oared shell with coxswain.

Carpenter returned to cycling in 1981 and won the national road and two-points championships that year. She was also the national two-points champion in 1982 and criterium champion in 1982 and 1983. Carpenter set a world record of 3:49.53 in winning the 1983 world pursuit championship. The following year, she became the first U.S. cyclist since 1912 to win an Olympic medal.

Rebecca Twigg of the U.S. took the lead in the Olympic road race with 50 meters to go, but Carpenter pulled even just 3 meters from the tape, then eased out of the saddle and threw her arms forward to propel her bike across the finish line less than half a wheel length ahead of Twigg. It was a trick she'd learned from her husband, Davis Phinney, who won a bronze in the team time trial.

Afterward, Carpenter said that the crowd of 200,000 people that lined the course in suburban Los Angeles definitely helped U.S. cyclists. "What made the Olympics special," she said, "was that a number of us had raced in the world championships several times where the support wasn't there, so we appreciated the support in the Olympics."
★ International Women's Sports Hall of Fame

Carr, Austin

BASKETBALL
b. March 10, 1948, Washington, D.C.

The second college player in history, after Pete Maravich, to score more than 1,000 points in each of two seasons, Carr was an All-American guard and player of the year for Notre Dame in 1971. In his three years as a starter, he scored 2,560 points, averaging 34.6 per game, hitting 1,107 of his 1,923 field goal attempts, and shooting .814 from the free throw line.

Carr was the first player chosen in the NBA college draft, by the Cleveland Cavaliers. He averaged 21.2 points per game as a rookie in 1971–72 and more than 20 points a game in each of the next two seasons. However, a knee injury late in 1974 cut his playing time and reduced his productivity.

After nine seasons with Cleveland, Carr was selected by the Dallas Mavericks in the 1980 expansion draft. He played just eight games with Dallas before being traded to the Washington Capitals, and he retired when the season ended.

In 682 regular season NBA games, Carr scored 10,473 points, an average of 15.4 per game, and had 1,878 assists. He scored 212 points in 18 playoff games.

Carr, Sabin W.

TRACK AND FIELD
b. Sept. 4, 1904, Dubuque, Iowa
d. Sept. 12, 1983

The first pole vaulter ever to clear 14 feet, Carr made that height exactly at the IC4A outdoor meet on May 25, 1927. Earlier in the year, he had set an indoor pole vault record of 13 feet, 7⅛ inches and raised that mark to 13 feet, 9¼ inches.

At the 1928 AAU indoor meet, Carr became the first to clear 14 feet indoors with a vault of 14 feet, 1 inch. Lee Barnes broke his world outdoor record that year, but Carr won the 1928 Olympic gold medal in the event, while Barnes finished fifth.

Representing Yale, Carr won the IC4A outdoor championship from 1926 through 1928; he tied for the indoor championship in 1927 and won it outright in 1928.

Carrigan, Bill (William J.)

BASEBALL
b. Oct. 22, 1883, Lewiston, Maine
d. July 8, 1969

A catcher, Carrigan played in only 709 games during his ten seasons with the Boston Red Sox, in 1906 and from 1908 through 1916, batting .257. Nicknamed "Rough," the 5-foot-9, 175-pounder was a scrappy player who became playing manager during the 1913 season.

Taking over a team in fifth place, Carrigan had a 40–30 record in his first season to bring the Red Sox into fourth. After a second-place finish in 1914, he guided them to consecutive pennants and world championships in 1915 and 1916.

Carrigan was Babe Ruth's first manager when Ruth arrived in the major leagues in 1914. Ruth later played for three managers who are in the Baseball Hall of Fame, but after he retired he said that Carrigan was the best manager he ever had.

After the 1916 World Series, Carrigan left baseball to go into banking. He was talked into managing the Red Sox in 1927, after Ruth was gone and the team had finished in last place 9 of the previous 11 seasons. Carrigan retired permanently after three more last-place finishes. He had a 489–500 record overall.

Carson, Jimmy (James)

HOCKEY
b. July 20, 1968, Southfield, Mich.

Carson began skating when he was six years old and played junior hockey in Canada for two seasons before joining the NHL's Los Angeles Kings in 1986, when he was only 18.

The 6-foot-1, 200-pounder set a record for a U.S.-born hockey player by scoring 107 points on 55 goals and 52 assists in the 1987–88 season. He then went to the Edmonton Oilers with another player, three draft choices, and $10 millon in a major trade that brought

Wayne Gretzky and two other players to Los Angeles.

In 1988–89, Carson scored an even 100 points on 49 goals and 51 assists. But he was unhappy in Edmonton, asked to be traded, and was sent to the Detroit Red Wings early in the 1989–90 season. Since then, Carson has been bothered by illness and injuries. He returned to Los Angeles in a trade in late January 1993 and was sent to the Vancouver Canucks a year later.

Through the 1993–94 season, Carson had scored 541 points on 265 goals and 276 assists in 577 regular season games, and he had added 17 goals and 15 assists for 32 points in 55 playoff games.

Carter, Donald J.

BOWLING
b. July 29, 1926, St. Louis, Mo.

A baseball and football star in high school, Carter served in the Navy during World War II and played minor league baseball as a pitcher and infielder for one season. He then returned to St. Louis to manage a bowling center.

Often referred to as "Mr. Bowling" because of his tireless promotion of the sport as well as his skill, Carter was named bowler of the year in 1953, 1954, 1957, 1958, 1960, and 1962. He won the 1962 Hickok Belt as the professional athlete of the year, the only bowler ever to achieve that honor.

A four-time winner of the All-Star tournament, in 1952, 1954, 1956, and 1958, Carter led the PBA in money won in 1960 and 1962 and had the top scoring average in 1962. He was named the best bowler of all time in a 1970 poll.

★ ABC Hall of Fame; PBA Hall of Fame

Carter, Joe (Joseph C.)

BASEBALL
b. March 7, 1960, Oklahoma City, Okla.

One of the most productive hitters in baseball today, Carter has driven in more than 100 runs in six consecutive seasons, from 1989 through 1994. A two-year college All-American as an outfielder at Wichita State University, the 6-foot-3, 225-pounder entered the major leagues briefly with the NL's Chicago Cubs in 1983.

The Cubs traded him to the AL's Cleveland Indians in 1984, when Carter hit 13 home runs in just 66 games. He became a starter in the outfield and at first base in 1986 and led the league with 121 RBI, batting .302 with 29 home runs. After RBI totals of 106, 98, and 105 over the next three seasons, Carter was traded to the NL's San Diego Padres.

He spent just one season in San Diego, collecting 115 RBI, before being sent to the AL's Toronto Blue Jays. With Toronto, he had 108 RBI in 1991, 119 in 1992, and 121 in 1993, and he helped lead the team to consecutive World Series victories in 1992 and 1993.

When the Blue Jays beat Philadelphia in six games in the 1993 Series, Carter hit a three-run home run in the ninth inning to win the final game 8–6. It was the first time in World Series history that a home run had brought a team from behind to win the deciding game.

Through the 1994 season, Carter had a career .263 average with 1,641 hits, including 322 doubles, 41 triples, and 302 home runs. He had scored 889 runs and driven in 1,097.

Cartwright, Alexander J.

BASEBALL
b. April 17, 1820, New York, N.Y.
d. July 12, 1892

Although Cartwright, not Abner Doubleday, is enshrined in the Hall of Fame as the inventor of baseball, some doubt has been raised about exactly what his role was in creating the modern version of the sport.

Cartwright joined the New York Knickerbocker Base Ball Club of New York in 1845. The club played a version of rounders or base ball called the "New York game" to distinguish it from the "Massachusetts game," which was also sometimes known as town ball.

Both were folk sports in the sense that rules were passed on orally, not written down. Cartwright suggested that the Knickerbocker club should be formally organized with a constitution and by-laws, which were the sport's first written rules.

The Knickerbocker rules of 1845 changed baseball in two major ways. First, the idea of fair and foul territory was established; previously, the batter could run the bases any time he hit the ball, as in cricket. Second, putting a runner out by hitting him with a thrown ball, the usual practice at the time, was disallowed.

The existing records don't indicate how important Cartwright was in drawing up these rules. He was one of four club members assigned the task. However, when a commission decided in 1907 that Doubleday had invented baseball in Cooperstown, New York, in 1838, Cartwright's son protested. Ironically, the Baseball Hall of Fame was founded in 1938, the centennial of the sport according to the Doubleday legend, yet Doubleday wasn't enshrined, and Cartwright was.

Cartwright didn't belong to the Knickerbocker club for long. He left New York on March 1, 1849, to join the gold rush, and went to Hawaii later that year. He spent the rest of his life in Hawaii, teaching baseball throughout the islands.

★ Baseball Hall of Fame

Case, Everett N.
BASKETBALL
b. June 21, 1900, Anderson, Ind.
d. April 30, 1966

Although he never played serious competitive basketball, Case became one of the most successful high school coaches in Indiana history. He compiled a record of 467 victories and only 124 defeats in 23 seasons, beginning at Connersville High, when he was only 18. His Frankfort High School teams won four state championships.

A 1923 graduate of the University of Wisconsin, Case served in World War II and was hired by North Carolina State in 1946. He quickly made the school a major basketball power, winning 20 or more games in each of his first ten seasons. The Wolfpack won seven straight regular season Southern Conference

championships and six straight tournament titles. The school moved into the newly formed Atlantic Coast Conference in 1954 and won four more postseason tournaments.

An 11–15 record in 1959–60, Case's first losing season, began a decline that resulted in his resignation just two games into the 1965–66 season. An ulcer, doubtless caused by emotional pressure, was a contributing factor. The ulcer became perforated in 1966, and Case died after surgery.

His estate totaled more than $200,000. He left $1,000 to Frankfort High School, $5,000 to the North Carolina State scholarship fund, and the rest of the estate was distributed among 57 of his former players.

★ Basketball Hall of Fame

Case, George W.
BASEBALL
b. Nov. 11, 1915, Trenton, N.J.
d. Jan. 23, 1989

He spent only 11 seasons in the major leagues, but Case won six AL base stealing titles, including five in a row. A right-handed outfielder, he joined the AL's Washington Senators late in the 1937 season, became a part-time player in 1938, and moved into a starting job in 1939, when he stole 51 bases to lead the league.

Case also led in steals with 35 in 1940, 33 in 1941, 44 in 1942, 61 in 1943, and 28 in 1948, when he was with the Cleveland Indians. He was the AL leader in runs scored with 102 in 1943. Case returned to the Senators in 1949 and retired after appearing in only 38 games that season.

In 1,225 major league games, Case had a .282 average with 1,415 hits, including 233 doubles, 43 triples, and 21 home runs. He stole 349 bases, scored 785 runs, and had 377 RBI.

Casey, Eddie (Edward L.)
FOOTBALL
b. May 16, 1894, Natick, Mass.
d. July 26, 1966

Though he weighed only 155 pounds, Casey was as solid on defense as he was dangerous on offense, often using a cross-body block to bring down opposing runners. He started at halfback for Harvard in 1916 and then served in the Navy for two years during World War I.

He returned to become an All-American as a senior in 1919, when he had a 40-yard touchdown run to tie Princeton, 10–10, and a 22-yard touchdown run to beat Yale, 10–3. Harvard was unbeaten that season, winning nine games while tying one, and went on to beat Oregon, 7–6, in the Rose Bowl.

Casey played for the NFL's Buffalo All-Americans in 1920. He coached Tufts to a 15–16–2 record from 1922 through 1925 and returned to Harvard as head coach from 1931 through 1934, winning 20 games, losing 11, and tying 1.

In 1935, Casey coached the Boston Redskins of the NFL to a 2–8–1 record.
★ College Football Hall of Fame

Casillas, Tony S.

FOOTBALL
b. Oct. 26, 1963, Tulsa, Okla.

An All-American defensive lineman in his junior and senior seasons at the University of Oklahoma, the 6-foot-3, 273-pound Casillas won the 1985 Lombardi Award as the nation's outstanding college lineman.

The second player chosen in the 1986 NFL draft, by the Atlanta Falcons, Casillas became a starter at nose tackle as a rookie but missed much of his second year with an injury and was also out for nearly half of the 1990 season.

In 1991, the Falcons traded him to the Dallas Cowboys, where Casillas has played on two NFL championship teams.

Casper, Billy (William E.)

GOLF
b. June 24, 1932, San Diego, Calif.

Casper will long be remembered as a great putter, perhaps the greatest ever. That reputation sometimes annoyed him, because he felt that people ignored the rest of his game. For 14 consecutive years, Casper was in the top 12 in PGA winnings. He was the leading money winner twice, in 1966 and 1968, and he

won five Vardon Trophies for the lowest average score, in 1960, 1963, 1965, 1966, and 1968.

But in his three biggest victories, the 1959 and 1966 U.S. Opens and the 1970 Masters, it was his putting that made the difference. In 1959, he was a chubby 212-pounder who shot 282 to beat Bob Rosburg by one stroke in the Open. He one-putted 31 of the 72 holes with an experimental, mallet-headed putter he'd never used before.

Seven years later, he was down to 185 pounds, thanks to a strange diet that included bear and buffalo meat. It didn't affect his putting. Trailing Arnold Palmer by seven shots with nine holes to play in the U.S. Open, Casper putted his way into a tie and then beat Palmer, 69–73, in a playoff. He used just 117 putts on the 90 holes and he shot under 70 for four of his five rounds.

Casper had another playoff in the 1970 Masters, against Gene Littler. He one-putted six of the first seven holes to take a five-stroke lead and won, 69–74. Casper had 51 wins on the PGA tour and has 9 on the Senior tour through 1993.
★ PGA Hall of Fame; World Golf Hall of Fame

Cassady, Howard ("Hopalong")

FOOTBALL
b. March 2, 1934, Columbus, Ohio

The most exciting college player of his era, Cassady was a starting halfback for four years at Ohio State. In his first game, he scored three touchdowns against the University of Indiana.

The 5-foot-10, 172-pound redhead was nicknamed for the popular movie cowboy played by William Boyd. Cassady starred on defense as well as offense and often played 60 minutes a game. His coach, Woody Hayes, said that Ohio State never gave up a long touchdown pass while Cassady was in the game on defense.

As a senior in 1955, Cassady rushed for 958 yards, scored 15 touchdowns, and led the team in both pass receptions and interceptions. A consensus All-American his last two seasons, Cassady not only won the Heisman and Maxwell trophies as college football's outstanding player, he was named Associated Press athlete of the year in 1955, beating out boxer Rocky Marciano and pro quarterback Otto Graham.

Cassady joined the NFL's Detroit Lions in 1956. After six seasons there, he played for the Cleveland Browns and Philadelphia Eagles in 1962, then returned to Detroit for a final year in 1963. During his eight professional seasons, he rushed for 1,229 yards on 316 carries, a 3.9 average, scoring 6 touchdowns; caught 111 passes for 1,601 yards, a 14.4 average, and 18 touchdowns; returned 43 punts for 341 yards, a 7.9 average; and ran back 77 kickoffs for 1,594 yards, a 20.7 average.

★ College Football Hall of Fame

Caulkins, Tracy

SWIMMING
b. Jan. 11, 1963, Winona, Minn.

The most versatile U.S. woman swimmer in history, Caulkins won a record 48 national championships in every type of stroke. She won her first titles in 1977, the AAU national 100- and 200-yard short-course breaststroke events and the 200- and 400-meter long-course individual medleys.

Caulkins became the youngest person ever to win the Sullivan Award as the nation's outstanding amateur athlete in 1978, when she took world championships in the 200-meter butterfly and both individual medleys as well as a silver medal in the 100-meter breaststroke. She was also the national champion in the long-course 200-meter butterfly and in the short-course individual medleys and both breaststroke events that year.

Going into the 1980 Olympics, Caulkins was considered likely to win as many as five gold medals, but the U.S. boycotted the Moscow Games that year. She surpassed Ann Curtis as the winningest women swimmer in history in 1981, and in 1982 she passed Johnny Weismuller's record of 36 national titles.

As a student at the University of Florida, Caulkins won a total of 12 NCAA championships from 1982 through 1984. She won the 1982 Honda Broderick Cup

as the nation's outstanding female college athlete, and she shared the 1984 award with basketball player Cheryl Miller.

Although Caulkins won both individual medleys at the 1983 Pan-American Games, her times were considerably slower than they had been two or three years earlier, and there were doubts about whether she could claim any gold medals at the 1984 Olympics.

Caulkins remarked, prophetically, "I think a lot of people have counted me out. They better watch out." She set an Olympic record of 2:12.64 in the 200-meter medley and also won golds in the 400-meter event and as a member of the 4 x 100-meter medley relay team. She announced her retirement immediately afterward.

★ International Women's Sports Hall of Fame; Olympic Hall of Fame

Cauthen, Steve

HORSE RACING
b. May 1, 1960, Covington, Ky.

Cauthen's father was a blacksmith, his mother a horse trainer, and he began riding horses at a gallop when he was five. As a young teenager, he decided he wanted to be a jockey. He made a pact with his parents that if weight became a problem, he'd give it up rather than go through starvation diets and steam rooms.

On May 12, 1976, he rode his first race. He won his fifth race on May 27, formally becoming an apprentice. Riding at River Downs, Cauthen set a track record by riding 94 winners in 50 days. He went from there to Arlington Park in Chicago, then east to Aqueduct and Belmont.

One racing columnist wrote of him, during his first year in the east, "He gets horses relaxed, feeling good. Even the real goof-offs seem to run for him." As a full-fledged jockey in 1977, Cauthen won a record $6.1 million in purses, was named the Eclipse Award winner as the nation's top rider, and was the Associated Press male athlete of the year.

In 1978, Cauthen became the youngest jockey to win the triple crown, riding

Affirmed to victories in the Kentucky Derby, Preakness, and Belmont. The Belmont win was one of the most exciting ever in triple crown history, as Cauthen whipped Affirmed across the finish line a bare head beyond Alydar.

Cauthen ran into problems in 1979, riding 110 consecutive races without a win, and then accepted an offer of well over $1 million to ride in England. He spent the rest of his career there and was the English champion in 1984, 1985, and 1987.

At the end of the 1985 season, Cauthen went into an alcohol dependency program in Cincinnati, worried that he might be drinking too much. He said later that he wasn't an alcoholic. In 1988, he broke his neck in a fall and spent seven months recuperating.

Cauthen retired from jockeying at the age of 33, recently married and about to become a father. He has worked as a television commentator and raises horses in his native Kentucky.

Cavanaugh, Frank W.

FOOTBALL
b. April 28, 1876, Worcester, Mass. d. Aug. 29, 1933

An end at Dartmouth, Cavanaugh graduated in 1898 and coached the University of Cincinnati to 5 wins, 1 loss, and 3 ties that fall. Among the victories was a 17–14 upset of his alma mater. He was player-coach of the Denver Athletic Club amateur team for the next four seasons, then returned to his native Worcester, Massachusetts, in 1903 as head coach at Holy Cross.

In three seasons there, his teams won 16 games while losing 10 and tying 2. Cavanaugh left in 1906 and practiced law for four years, working part-time as a coach at Worcester Academy in 1909 and 1910, and he then returned to Dartmouth as head coach in 1911.

He had six winning seasons at Dartmouth, compiling a 42–9–3 record, before leaving to serve as a major during World War I. Severely wounded by shrapnel, he was blind for a time but survived his injuries and won his nickname the "Iron Major."

Cavanaugh returned from the service to coach Boston College in 1919. His 1920 team won all eight of its games, and he had a 48–14–5 record in eight seasons before going to Fordham in 1927. One trademark of Cavanaugh's teams was strong defense, epitomized by the 1929 and 1930 Fordham lines that gave up just one rushing touchdown in 18 games. They became known as the "Seven Blocks of Granite," a nickname that was revived for the 1936 and 1937 Fordham lines.

Although he was listed as head coach in 1937, Cavanaugh was nearly blind, and the coaching was actually done by his assistant, William P. "Hiker" Joy. However, Cavanaugh did come to all the team's practices and was on the sidelines for every game. He died shortly before the 1938 season began.

A genuine innovator, Cavanaugh is credited with inventing the spot pass to a hooking end, and he used the T formation with a man in motion as early as 1929, 11 years before Clark Shaughnessy introduced that formation at Stanford.

★ College Football Hall of Fame

Cavaretta, Philip J.

BASEBALL
b. July 19, 1916, Chicago, Ill.

A great favorite with his hometown fans, Cavaretta joined the Chicago Cubs near the end of the 1934 season and became the team's starting first baseman the following year. He led the NL with 197 hits in 1944 and in hitting with a .355 average in 1945, when he was named the league's most valuable player.

The Cubs won the pennant that year, and Cavaretta hit .423 in the World Series, with 7 runs scored and 5 RBI, but the Detroit Tigers beat his team in seven games.

Cavaretta remained with the Cubs through 1953, becoming the team's playing manager during the 1951 season. After compiling a 169–213 record, he was let go by the Cubs, and he spent two final seasons as a part-time player across town with the White Sox.

In 22 seasons, Cavaretta had a .293

batting average on 1,977 hits, including 347 doubles, 99 triples, and 95 home runs. He scored 990 runs and drove in 920.

Cepeda, Orlando M.

BASEBALL
b. Sept. 17, 1937, Ponce, Puerto Rico

Cepeda's father, Pedro, was a big power hitter, Puerto Rico's version of Babe Ruth, nicknamed "Bull." Orlando became known as the "Baby Bull." The 6-foot-2, 210-pounder was a right-handed-hitting first baseman who arrived in the major leagues with the NL's San Francisco Giants in 1958 and won the rookie of the year award by batting .312 with 25 home runs, 96 RBI, and a league-leading 38 doubles.

After hitting 27 home runs in 1959 and 24 in 1960, Cepeda exploded in 1961, leading the league with 46 home runs and 142 RBI while batting .311. His great season was unfortunately overshadowed by the home run duel between Mickey Mantle and Roger Maris of the New York Yankees that culminated in Maris's hitting 61 home runs to break Babe Ruth's record.

Cepeda hit more than 30 home runs and batted over .300 each of the next three seasons, but a knee injury limited him to 33 games in 1965, and he was traded to the St. Louis Cardinals early in the 1966 season.

With St. Louis, Cepeda won the NL's most valuable player award in 1967, when he batted .325 with 25 home runs and a league-leading 111 RBI to help the Cardinals win the pennant. He hit only .107 with 1 RBI in the World Series, but St. Louis beat the Boston Red Sox in seven games.

After a sub-par season in 1968, Cepeda was traded to the Atlanta Braves. He hit 22 home runs with 88 RBI while batting only .257 in 1969, then had another fine season with a .305 average, 34 home runs, and 111 RBI.

The knee problem recurred, and he played only 71 games in 1971. After 28 games in 1972, the Braves traded him to the AL's Oakland A's, where he had just

three at-bats in three games. Cepeda had a final good season with the Boston Red Sox in 1973, hitting .289 with 20 home runs and 86 RBI. He retired after appearing in only 33 games with the Kansas City Royals in 1974.

In 17 major league seasons, Cepeda hit .297 with 2,351 hits, including 417 doubles, 27 triples, and 379 home runs. He scored 1,131 runs and had 1,365 RBI.

Cervi, Alfred N.

BASKETBALL
b. Feb. 2, 1917, Buffalo, N.Y.

One of the finest defensive players of his era, Cervi dropped out of high school during his junior year and played for a YMCA team before signing for $15 a game with the Buffalo Bisons of the new National Basketball League in 1937. A 5-foot-11½ guard, he was named the league's most valuable player in 1938–39.

After serving in the U.S. Army Air Corps from 1940 to 1945, Cervi joined the Rochester Royals of the NBL for the 1945–46 season. He led the league in scoring with a 14.4 average and was named most valuable player in 1946–47. When Rochester moved into the Basketball Association of America in 1948, Cervi joined the NBL's Syracuse team as player-coach.

The two leagues merged into the National Basketball Association the following season. Cervi retired as a player in 1953 but remained with Syracuse as coach through 1955–56. His team won the NBA championship in 1955, when he was named the league's coach of the year. He coached the Philadelphia Warriors in 1957–58.

From 1945–46 through 1952–53, Cervi averaged 10.2 points a game in 381 games. As a coach, he won 350 games and lost 267; his winning percentage of .573 is eleventh best in NBA history.

In an interview with Harold Peterson, Cervi explained his defensive philosophy: "I don't know what they're talking about today when they talk defense. Your hand has to be in your man's face. You don't let him get the ball. The first thing in good defense is to keep the ball from your man."

★ Basketball Hall of Fame

Chadwick, Florence

SWIMMING

b. Nov. 9, 1918, San Diego, Calif.

When Chadwick reached the shore of Dover, England, on August 8, 1950, after swimming the English Channel in a record 13 hours and 23 minutes, she said, "I feel fine. I am quite prepared to swim back."

She didn't do it right then, but a little more than a year later she was back in Dover waiting for a chance to swim the Channel from England to France, a much more difficult crossing because of adverse winds and tides. After 11 weeks of waiting for good weather conditions, she decided to start the swim in a heavy fog and against unfavorable winds.

She had to take medicine for sea sickness, but 16 hours and 22 minutes after entering the water, she was on the French shore, shaking hands with the mayor of Sangatte. Chadwick was the first woman to swim the channel from England to France; she did it again on September 4, 1953, in 14 hours and 42 minutes, and a third time on October 12, 1955, in a remarkable 13 hours and 55 minutes.

Chadwick performed two other major long-distance swims. In 1952 she swam the 21 miles from Catalina Island to Palos Verdes, California, in 13 hours, 47 minutes, and 32 seconds, breaking a record that had been set in 1927, and in 1953 she swam the Straits of Gibraltar in a record 5 hours and 6 minutes. In both cases, she broke records set by male swimmers.

Chaffee, Suzy (Susan)

SKIING

b. 1947, Rutland, Vt.

A pioneer in freestyle skiing, also known as "hot dog" skiing, Chaffee was originally an Alpine skier who took up the sport when she was three years old. She captained the 1968 women's Olympic team.

But she was also interested in free-style skiing, which features gymnastic moves and subjective judging of style, as in gymnastics and figure skating. When it became a professional sport in 1971, there was no women's division. Chaffee joined the pro tour anyway and won world championships from 1971 through 1973.

Because she encouraged more women to get involved — and perhaps also because she embarrassed men with her victories — a women's division was added when the International Freestyle Ski Association was formed in 1973. The association's rules put more emphasis on creativity of performance with musical accompaniment, as in figure skating.

Chaffee was named to the U.S. Olympic Committee's board of directors in 1976, and she worked hard to have freestyle skiing accepted as an Olympic sport. It was added to the Olympic program in 1992 after having been a demonstration sport in 1988.

Chamberlain, Wilton N.

BASKETBALL

b. Aug. 21, 1936, Philadelphia, Pa.

To critics who called him a "loser," Chamberlain retorted, "Take Jimmy Brown in football. Jimmy played seven years before he was on a winner. Did people call him a loser?"

Chamberlain didn't begin playing basketball until he was in the seventh grade. At 15, he grew four inches in three months, and he was 6-foot-11 when he entered high school. He became one of the most recruited players ever, with more than 200 colleges wooing him after he led Philadelphia's Overbrook High School to three public school championships and two all-city titles.

Already known as "Wilt the Stilt" and the "Big Dipper," two nicknames he hated, Chamberlain chose the University of Kansas and scored 52 points against Northwestern in his first game, a total he never surpassed as a collegian, partly because of the defenses used against him. He said later, "I was guarded so closely that I thought I was going to spend the rest of my life looking out at the world through wiggling fingers, forearms, and elbows."

Nevertheless, he averaged 29.9 points and 18.3 rebounds a game in three seasons and was twice named All-American center. Chamberlain left Kansas after his junior year and played with the Harlem Globetrotters for one season, then joined the Philadelphia Warriors of the NBA in 1959. The 7-foot-2, 275-pounder was rookie of the year and most valuable player, setting league records for most points with 2,707, most rebounds with 1,941, and most points per game with 37.6.

He broke his own records each of the next two seasons, peaking at an incredible 4,029 points, an average of 50.4 a game, in 1961–62. Chamberlain scored an NBA record 100 points against the New York Knicks on March 2, 1962.

He went with the Warriors when they moved to San Francisco for the 1962–63 season and then joined a new Philadelphia team, the 76ers, in 1964. Chamberlain's teams had lost five times to the Celtics in five playoff meetings, but they finally beat the Celtics and won the NBA championship in 1967.

Tired of criticism for being a mere scorer, Chamberlain changed his game in the 1967–68 season, when he concentrated on passing to the open man when he was double-teamed, and he led the league in assists, the only center ever to do so. He was the league's MVP for the third year in a row.

In 1968 he was traded to the Los Angeles Lakers. A knee injury limited him to just 12 games in 1969–70, but he returned full-time the following season, and in 1972 he played on his second NBA championship team, as the Lakers won 12 of their 15 playoff games, beating the Knicks four games to one in the final series. Chamberlain retired after one more season in Los Angeles.

He was often compared unfavorably to the Celtics' Bill Russell, a defensive standout, but Russell said, "Chamberlain is the greatest basketball player alive, no doubt about that. He has set the standards so high, his point totals are so enormous, that they've lost their impact."

Chamberlain was the first player to score more than 30,000 points. He led the NBA in scoring seven times, in rebounding 11 times, and in assists once, and he was the first-team all-star center seven times. In his 14 seasons, he played 1,045 games, scoring 31,419 points, an average of 30.1 a game, and had 23,924 rebounds. In 1972–73, he made 72.7 percent of his field goal attempts, an NBA record.

Often overlooked is the fact that Chamberlain was an excellent all-around athlete. At Kansas, he was the Big Eight Conference high jump champion three years in a row, he put the shot 56 feet, ran the 100-yard dash in 10.9 seconds, and triple jumped more than 50 feet. He turned down offers to become a professional boxer and football player, but after retiring from basketball he starred in the short-lived International Volleyball Association.
★ Basketball Hall of Fame

Chamberlin, Guy (Berlin Guy)

FOOTBALL
b. Jan. 16, 1894, Blue Springs, Nebr.
d. April 4, 1967

As a halfback at the University of Nebraska in 1914, Chamberlin returned a kickoff 95 yards against Michigan State and had a 70-yard touchdown run from scrimmage against Kansas. He played most of his senior season, 1915, at end. At that time ends were often moved into the backfield to run or pass. When Nebraska upset Notre Dame, 20–19, Chamberlin scored the first two touchdowns on runs of 20 and 10 yards, then completed two passes for a total of 49 yards and the winning touchdown.

Chamberlin made some All-American teams, but not Walter Camp's. Instead, Camp embarrassed himself thoroughly by naming Vic Halligan as a tackle on his third team to represent unbeaten Nebraska. Halligan had graduated in June and therefore didn't play in 1915.

After playing for the independent Canton Bulldogs in 1919, Chamberlin joined the Decatur Staleys when George Halas organized the team to play in the

American Professional Football Association (now the NFL). He and Halas were the starting ends. Chamberlin had a 70-yard interception return in 1920 and a 75-yard interception return in 1921, both for touchdowns.

He returned to Canton as player-coach in 1922. During the next two seasons, the Bulldogs won 21 games and tied 3 without suffering a loss to win two NFL championships. The franchise moved to Cleveland in 1924 and won a third straight title with 7 wins, 1 loss, and 1 tie.

Chamberlin became player-coach of the Frankford Yellowjackets in 1925. The team finished only sixth that year, despite winning 13 of 20 games, but went 14–1–1 in 1926 to bring Chamberlin his fourth championship in five seasons of coaching.

In 1927, he went to the Chicago Cardinals as a player for one season. He became the team's coach in 1928 and retired after they won only one game while losing six. His overall NFL coaching record was 56 wins, 14 losses, and 5 ties.

★ College Football Hall of Fame; Pro Football Hall of Fame

Chance, Dean (Wilmer Dean)

BASEBALL
b. June 1, 1941, Wayne, Ohio

A right-handed pitcher, Chance joined the AL's expansion Los Angeles (later California) Angels near the end of the 1961 season and established himself as the team's best pitcher the following year. In his first three years, he appeared in 100 games, starting 63, had a 27–30 record, and also picked up 11 saves.

Chance won the league's Cy Young Award in 1964, leading the league in victories with a 20–9 record, complete games with 15, shutouts with 11, innings pitched with 278, and ERA with 1.65.

After slipping to 15–10 and 12–17 the next two years, Chance was traded to the Minnesota Twins. He had a 20–14 record with them in 1967, leading the league in complete games with 18 and in

innings pitched with 283 while compiling a 2.73 ERA.

In 1968, Chance had just a 16–16 record despite a 2.53 ERA. The following year he developed arm problems and appeared in only 20 games. He joined the Cleveland Indians in 1970 and was used mostly in relief before being traded to the New York Mets of the NL near the end of the season. He retired after having a 4–6 record with the Detroit Tigers in 1971.

Chance had a career 128–115 record with 33 shutouts and a 2.92 ERA. He struck out 1,534 hitters and walked 739 in 2,147⅓ innings.

Chance, Frank L.

BASEBALL
b. Sept. 9, 1877, Fresno, Calif.
d. Feb. 15, 1924

The 6-foot, 190-pound Chance, nicknamed "Husk" for "husky" because of his size, joined the Chicago Cubs as a backup catcher in 1898. That was his role until the middle of the 1902 season, when he was moved to first base.

Chance didn't like changing positions, but his hitting improved when he became a starter. He batted .327 and led the league in stolen bases with 67 in 1903, and the following year he hit .310 and stole 42 bases.

Cubs manager Frank Selee contracted tuberculosis in 1904 and could manage the team only intermittently. Chance was named field captain, meaning that he took over as manager when Selee wasn't available. In July 1905, Chance formally became manager of the team.

In 1906, his first full year as a playing manager, the Cubs won a record 116 games. Chance batted .319, leading the league in stolen bases with 57 and in runs scored with 103. The Cubs lost the 1906 World Series to the Chicago White Sox, but they won pennants again in 1907 and 1908 and took the World Series from the Detroit Tigers both years.

Called the "Peerless Leader" by Chicago sportswriters, Chance guided the Cubs to a fourth pennant in 1910 but lost a five-game World Series to the Philadelphia Athletics. After the team finished second in 1911 and third in 1912, Chance was fired, enraging many Chicago fans.

He became playing manager of the New York Yankees in 1913 but was let go before the 1914 season ended. Chance owned and managed a minor league team in Los Angeles for two years, then remained out of baseball until 1923, when he managed the last-place Boston Red Sox.

Chance was the first baseman in the Tinker-to-Evers-to-Chance double play combination made famous by a poem written in 1910 by the New York newspaper columnist Franklin P. Adams. The three were inducted together into the Baseball Hall of Fame. Chance is probably the only one who could have made it on his own.

In 1,287 major league games, Chance batted .296, with 200 doubles, 79 triples, 20 home runs, 797 runs scored, and 596 RBI. He stole 401 bases.
★ Baseball Hall of Fame

Chandler, Jennifer B.

DIVING
b. June 13, 1959, Langdale, Ala.

Chandler won the AAU national indoor 1-meter springboard event in 1975 and was the springboard gold medalist at the Pan-American Games that year. She was the national indoor 3-meter champion in 1976.

At the 1976 Olympics, Chandler was the surprise gold medal winner in the springboard, taking the lead on the first dive over defending world champion Christine Kohler of East Germany and never relinquishing it.

After returning from the Olympics, Chandler entered the University of Alabama, but injuries forced her to retire from competition. She later did television commentary on diving events.

Chandler, Spud (Spurgeon F.)

BASEBALL
b. Sept. 12, 1907, Commerce, Ga.
d. Jan. 9, 1990

A right-handed pitcher, Chandler didn't make it to the major leagues until he was 29, and he had just two 20-vic-

tory seasons in his brief career. But he never had a losing season, and he turned in a remarkable career winning percentage and outstanding ERA.

Chandler was named the AL's most valuable player in 1943, when he helped take the Yankees to a pennant, leading the league in victories and winning percentage with a 20–4 record, in complete games with 20, in shutouts with 5, and in ERA with 1.64.

He had joined the Yankees during the 1937 season and had a 21–9 record during his first two years. Injuries limited his playing time for the next four seasons, yet he put together a composite 37–16 record before his MVP year.

Chandler missed almost all of the 1944 and 1945 seasons because of military service, but he came back to win 20 and lose only 8, with a 2.10 ERA in 1946. He retired after compiling a 9–5 record in the 1947 season.

In 11 major league seasons, Chandler had a 109–43 record for a .717 winning percentage, with 26 shutouts and a 2.84 ERA. He struck out 614 and walked 463 in 1,485 innings.

Chaney, John

BASKETBALL
b. Jan. 21, 1932, Jacksonville, Fla.

Chaney played basketball at Bethune–Cookman College in Florida. He graduated in 1953 and played in the Eastern Professional Basketball League for ten years before becoming head coach at Cheney State College in 1972.

In ten seasons at Cheney State, Chaney had a 225–59 record and guided the school to the NCAA Division II championship in 1978. He then took over at Temple University in 1982 and immediately began producing winners. Temple won four Atlantic 10 championships in Chaney's first 11 seasons. His 1987–88 team won 32 of 34 games and was ranked first in the nation after the regular season but didn't make the NCAA final four.

Although known for teaching tough defense, Chaney was a high scorer in his playing days at Bethune–Cookman, hitting a high of 57 points. His Temple teams are always a factor in NCAA tournament play because Chaney likes to play challenging non-conference teams away from home or on neutral courts early in the season, rather than fattening up a record against easy opposition.

Through the 1993–94 season, Chaney had a 501–164 record for a .753 winning percentage, twelfth best in history.

Chapman, Ben (William Benjamin)

BASEBALL
b. Dec. 25, 1908, Nashville, Tenn.

A four-time AL base-stealing champion, Chapman joined the New York Yankees as an infielder in 1930, when he batted .316, and was moved to the outfield the following year. He led the league with 61 stolen bases in 1931, 38 in 1932, and 27 in 1933, and played in the first three All-Star games, from 1933 through 1935.

The Yankees traded him to the Washington Senators during the 1936 season and he won his fourth stolen base title with 35 steals in 1937, when he was with the Senators and the Boston Red Sox. He also played for the Cleveland Indians and Chicago White Sox before leaving baseball temporarily in 1942.

Chapman returned to the majors as a pitcher with the NL's Brooklyn Dodgers in 1944. He had a 5–3 record with them. During the 1945 season, he went to the Philadelphia Phillies as a playing manager. He managed the Phillies into the 1948 season, when he was fired after compiling a 196–276 record.

In 1,717 major league games, Chapman batted .302 with 1,958 hits, including 407 doubles, 107 triples, and 90 home runs. He stole 287 bases, scored 1,144 runs, and had 977 RBI.

Chapman, John J.

HARNESS RACING
b. Nov. 25, 1928, Toronto, Ont.
d. May 2, 1980

A hockey player as a teenager, Chapman began training and driving harness horses in 1947. He was among the top 25 drivers for nine consecutive years, from 1949 through 1957. Chapman then became a trainer-driver for Alwood Stable,

where he developed Merrie Annabelle, who in 1958 was the first two-year-old filly ever to do a 2-minute mile.

The stable was destroyed in a 1962 fire, and Chapman went back into public training and onto the list of top drivers, averaging well over 100 victories a year, with a peak of 190 in 1966. He ranks 19th all-time with 3,915 career wins and 21st with $21,359,746 in winnings.

Charles, Ezzard M.

BOXING
b. July 7, 1921, Lawrenceville, Ga.
d. May 28, 1975

A clever boxer, Charles had a quiet, unassuming personality and lacked a big knockout punch. As a result, he was not a popular heavyweight champion during his brief reign.

Charles was undefeated in 42 amateur fights as a welterweight and middleweight. He became a professional shortly after winning the AAU national middleweight title in 1939, and he won 20 consecutive pro fights before losing a 10-round decision to former middleweight champion Ken Overlin on June 9, 1941.

He served in the Army during 1944 and 1945 and began fighting as a light heavyweight after World War II. Charles had three victories, one a knockout, over future champion Archie Moore in a three-year period, then moved into the heavyweight division.

After Joe Louis retired, Charles beat Jersey Joe Walcott on a 15-round decision on June 22, 1949, in Chicago to win the National Boxing Association version of the championship. Louis then came out of retirement, and Charles became world champion with a 15-round decision over him on September 27, 1950.

After three successful defenses, Charles lost the title on July 18, 1951, when Walcott knocked him out in the 7th round in Pittsburgh. Walcott won a 15-round decision in a rematch on June 5 of the following year.

Charles had two more shots at the title, both against Rocky Marciano in 1954. In the first fight, on June 17, Charles lost a 15-round decision. Marciano, who usually won by knockout, later said it was the toughest fight he ever had. On September 17, Marciano knocked Charles out in the 8th round.

Charles retired late in 1956 but returned to the ring in 1958. After losing four of six fights over a two-year period, he retired for good. He came down with Lou Gehrig's disease in 1966 and died nine years later.

He had 122 professional bouts and won 96, 58 by knockout. He lost 25, 7 by knockout, and fought 1 draw.

★ International Boxing Hall of Fame

Charleston, Oscar McC.

BASEBALL
b. Oct. 12, 1896, Indianapolis, Ind.
d. Oct. 5, 1954

Charleston's long baseball career began before black major leagues had been established and ended just as organized baseball was accepting its first black player of the twentieth century.

That career began in 1915, when he joined the Indianapolis ABCs as a center fielder. A left-handed hitter and thrower, the 5-foot-11 Charleston weighed about 185 pounds in his younger days, when he was an outstanding base runner and defensive outfielder; later, he grew to well over 200 pounds and became a first baseman.

He was, at various times, called the "black Tris Speaker" because of his fielding ability, the "black Ty Cobb" because of his aggressive base running, and the "black Babe Ruth" because of his power.

Charleston went to the Chicago American Giants in 1919, when he also began playing winter baseball in Latin America. In 1921, he joined the St. Louis Giants and hit four home runs in a post-season exhibition game against the NL's St. Louis Cardinals.

After serving as player and manager of the Harrisburg Giants from 1922 through 1927, he went to the Philadelphia Hilldales, where he batted .396 in 1929. He then joined the Homestead Greys for two seasons.

Charleston became player-manager of the great Pittsburgh Crawfords in 1932. He hit .363 with 19 triples and 13 home runs in his first year, when the team won 99 games and lost only 36. The Crawfords moved to Toledo in 1939. After one season there, Charleston went to the Philadelphia Stars, again as player-manager, and remained with them until joining the Brooklyn Brown Dodgers in 1945.

The Brown Dodgers, owned by the Brooklyn Dodgers, were a kind of a front for Branch Rickey's attempt to sign black players in order to integrate organized baseball. They lasted just one season, and Charleston then returned to the Philadelphia Stars for two more years before retiring.

★ Baseball Hall of Fame

Cheaney, Calbert N.

BASKETBALL
b. July 17, 1971, Evansville, Ind.

A 6-foot-7, 209-pound forward, Cheaney starred for four years at the University of Indiana, where he was frequently used at guard because of his ability to handle the ball and shoot from outside.

Cheaney was named college player of the year for the 1992–93 season, when he helped lead Indiana to 28–3 record and the top ranking at the end of the regular season. He averaged 22.4 points a game, hitting 47 of 110 three-point field goal attempts.

During his four years as a starter, Cheaney had an average of 19.8 points per game. He was chosen in the first round of the 1993 NBA draft by the Washington Bullets, and he averaged 12.0 points a game as a rookie.

Cheeks, Mo (Maurice E.)

BASKETBALL
b. Sept. 8, 1956, Chicago, Ill.

A virtual unknown coming out of West Texas State University, which had an 8–19 record in his senior year, Cheeks was chosen by the Philadelphia 76ers in the second round of the 1978 NBA draft, and he became the team's starting point guard as a rookie.

The 6-foot-1, 180-pound Cheeks specialized in assists and defense for his first several seasons with Philadelphia, but in the meantime he developed an accurate outside jump shot and began using his speed to drive to the basket, enabling him to average 15.4 points a game in 1985–86 and 15.6 in 1986–87.

The 76ers traded Cheeks to the San Antonio Spurs in 1989, and the Spurs sent him to the New York Knicks in February 1990. Injuries began to slow Cheeks in 1991–92, when he played only 56 games for the Atlanta Hawks. He was released by the Hawks after the season and signed as a free agent with the New Jersey Nets in January 1993.

He retired after the season with an NBA record of 2,310 career steals. A member of the league's all-defensive team four years in a row, from 1983 through 1986, Cheeks scored 12,195 points in 1,101 regular season games, an average of 11.1 per game, and had 7,392 assists. In 133 playoff games, he had 1,910 points, a 14.4 average, with 922 assists and 295 steals.

Cheeseborough, Chandra
TRACK AND FIELD
b. Jan. 10, 1959, Jacksonville, Fla.

In the space of less than an hour in 1984, Cheeseborough became the first woman ever to win gold medals in the 4 x 100-meter and 4 x 400-meter relays. She also won a silver medal in the 400-meter dash, finishing second to teammate Valerie Brisco-Hooks. Cheeseborough had won the Olympic Trials in an American record 49.28 seconds.

She won the national indoor 200-yard dash in 1979 and from 1981 through 1983. At Tennessee State, Cheeseborough was a member of national championship teams that set world indoor records of 1:08.9 in the 640-yard relay and 1:47.17 in the 880-yard sprint medley relay.

Cheevers, Gerry (Gerald M.)
HOCKEY
b. Dec. 7, 1940, St. Catharines, Ont.

The Toronto Maple Leafs owned the rights to Cheevers in 1965 and listed him as a forward, rather than a goalie, in an attempt to keep another team from drafting him. However, the Boston Bruins did, and after two years in the minor leagues, he became the team's starting goaltender in 1967–68.

Nicknamed "Cheesy" by his teammates, Cheevers was an outstanding clutch goalie who helped the Bruins win Stanley Cups in 1970 and 1972. After the 1971–72 season, Cheevers signed with Cleveland of the newly formed World Hockey Association.

In 418 regular season NHL games, Cheevers had 26 shutouts and gave up 1,175 goals, a 2.89 average. He had 8 shutouts in 88 playoff games, giving up 242 goals for a 3.30 average. Cheevers coached the Bruins to a 204–126–46 record from 1980–81 through 1983–84.
★ Hockey Hall of Fame

Chesbro, Jack (John D.)
BASEBALL
b. June 5, 1874, North Adams, Mass.
d. Nov. 6, 1931

After three mediocre seasons in the minor leagues, the right-handed Chesbro won 40 games while losing only 19 during the next season and a half, and was purchased by the Pittsburgh NL team in July 1899.

Chesbro became a star in 1901, leading the league in winning percentage with a 21–9 record and in shutouts with 6. In 1902, Chesbro added the spitball, then a legal pitch, to his repertoire and led the league in victories with a 28–6 record, including 8 shutouts. Pittsburgh won the NL pennant both years.

The troubled Baltimore AL franchise moved to New York in 1903 and began raiding the NL for players. Chesbro was among those who jumped. After going 21–15 in his first season, he had an incredible year in 1904. He completed 48 of his 51 starts, led the league in winning percentage with a 41–12 record, and struck out 240 hitters in a league-leading 454 innings. Chesbro and Ed Walsh are the only two pitchers to win more than 40 games in a season during the twentieth century.

Chesbro had a 19–13 record in 1905 and a 24–16 record in 1906. He had now pitched 1,407 innings over four seasons, and all that work took its toll. He was 10–10 in 1907, 14–20 in 1908, and New York released him during the 1909 season. He finished his career by pitching one game, a loss, for the Boston Red Sox.

In 1911, Chesbro coached baseball at Amherst College in Massachusetts, and he was briefly a coach for the Washington Senators in 1924. Chesbro appeared in 392 games during his 11 major league seasons, finishing 260 of 332 starts, and he had a 198–132 record, with 35 shutouts and a 2.68 ERA.

★ Baseball Hall of Fame

Chocolate, Kid [Eligio Sardinias]

BOXING
b. Jan. 6, 1910, Cerro, Cuba
d. Aug. 8, 1988

Chocolate reportedly won more than 100 fights as an amateur, and he had 21 knockouts in 21 professional fights in his native Cuba before coming to the United States in 1938.

Nicknamed the "Cuban Bon Bon" by sportswriters, he combined foot and hand speed with a powerful punch. He went undefeated in 45 fights before losing a decision to Jack "Kid" Berg on August 7, 1930. Chocolate fought Battling Battalino for the world featherweight title on December 12 of that year, but lost a 15-round decision.

On July 15, 1931, Chocolate won the world junior lightweight title with a 7th-round knockout of Benny Bass in Philadelphia. After losing to Tony Canzoneri for the world lightweight title, he won the New York State version of the featherweight championship by knocking out Lew Feldman in the 12th round on October 13, 1932.

Frankie Click won Chocolate's junior lightweight championship by knocking him out in the 7th round on December 26, 1933. Chocolate soon outgrew the featherweight division. He never had another championship fight and retired late in 1938. Chocolate then became a boxing instructor in Cuba, working for the government until Fidel Castro assumed power in 1959.

Chocolate won 145 professional fights, 64 by knockout, while losing only 10, 2 by knockout. He also fought 6 draws.

★ International Boxing Hall of Fame

Christian, David W.

HOCKEY
b. May 12, 1959, Warroad, Minn.

A member of America's foremost hockey family, Christian played right wing at the University of North Dakota but was used mostly on defense with the 1980 U.S. Olympic team that won a surprising gold medal in the Lake Placid Winter Games. The 6-foot, 195-pounder was big enough for the position, and his speed was a definite asset to the team. He didn't score a goal but had eight assists in the seven Olympic tournament games.

He was the fourth member of his family to play in the Olympics. His father, Bill, and uncle Roger had played for the 1960 gold medal team, and his uncle Gordon had played for the 1956 team that won a silver medal. The older members of the family operate a company that manufactures hockey sticks.

After the Olympics, Christian joined the NHL's Winnipeg Jets. He was traded to the Washington Capitals in 1983 and the Capitals sent him to the Boston Bruins during the 1989–90 season.

Christian was signed by the St. Louis Blues as a free agent in 1991, but the Bruins claimed he wasn't a free agent, and a trade was eventually worked out. After one season in St. Louis, he went to the Chicago Black Hawks in 1992. Through the 1992–93 season, Christian had scored 340 goals and 430 assists for a total of 770 points in 1,000 regular season games. He added 57 points on 32 goals and 25 assists in 101 playoff games.

Christiansen, Jack (John L.)

FOOTBALL
b. Dec. 20, 1928, Sublette, Kans.
d. June 29, 1986

Christiansen's left arm was badly injured in a shooting accident during his senior year in high school, so he concentrated on track and field as a freshman at Colorado State University in 1947.

Because of his speed, he was persuaded to go out for football as a sophomore, and he became a three-year starter at safety. At 6-foot-1 and only 185 pounds, Christiansen was generally considered too slight to play pro football, but he made the Detroit Lions in 1951 as a kick returner and was a defensive starter before the season ended.

An All-Pro from 1952 through 1958, his final season, Christiansen was always a threat to score returning interceptions or punts. He led the NFL in interceptions in 1953 with 12 and in 1957 with 10, and was tops in yards per punt return in 1952 with an average of 21.5.

In his eight seasons, he intercepted 46 passes and ran them back for 717 yards, a 15.6 average, and 3 touchdowns. Christiansen returned 85 punts for 1,084 yards, a 12.8 average, and 8 touchdowns, and he ran back 59 kickoffs for 1,329 yards, a 22.5 average. He also rushed for 143 yards on 20 attempts, a 7.2 average, and scored 2 rushing touchdowns.
★ Pro Football Hall of Fame

Clancy, King (Francis M.)
HOCKEY
b. Feb. 25, 1903, Ottawa, Ont. Nov. 10, 1986

Clancy had a dual reputation as a fighter during his 16-year NHL career. It was said he never backed away from a fight and never won one. Feisty, fast, and agile, he weighed only 150 pounds when he joined the Ottawa Senators in 1921 as one of the game's first great rushing defensemen.

The Toronto Maple Leafs acquired him from Ottawa in 1930 for an unprecedented price of $35,000 plus two players. Toronto owner Conn Smythe later called Clancy "probably the best all-around man, as far as morale, ability, and effort for his team is concerned, that ever was."

Clancy played with Toronto through the 1936–37 season, coached the Montreal Maroons for part of the 1937–38 sea-

son, then became an NHL referee. While working a game in Boston, Clancy got angry at a fan who was heckling him and offered to fight then and there. Fortunately for Clancy, the fan turned down the challenge: he was world heavyweight champion Jack Sharkey.

In 1950, Clancy returned to coaching with Toronto, remaining through the 1952–53 season. Later he worked in the Toronto front office as right-hand man to general manager and sometime coach Punch Imlach.

During his 16 seasons as a player, Clancy had 137 goals and 143 assists in 592 regular season games, with 13 goals and 17 assists in 61 playoff games.
★ Hockey Hall of Fame

Clapper, Dit (Aubrey V.)
HOCKEY
b. Feb. 9, 1907, Newmarket, Ont. d. Jan. 20, 1978

The first player to spend 20 seasons with the same NHL team, Clapper was an all-star both as a right wing and as a defenseman. An outstanding lacrosse player as a young teenager, he then decided to concentrate on hockey. After a half-season in the minor leagues, he joined the Bruins in 1927.

Clapper played on Boston's "Dynamite Line" with Cooney Weiland at center and Dutch Gainor at left wing. They led the Bruins to their first Stanley Cup in 1929. In 1929–30, Clapper had his finest scoring season with 41 goals and 20 assists in just 44 games, finishing third in the NHL in total points.

In 1937, the 200-pound Clapper became a defenseman. Two years later, the Bruins won their second Stanley Cup. Clapper was named a first-team all-star that year and the next two years. In 1942 he suffered a ruptured Achilles tendon and wasn't expected to play again, but he came back and was named to the all-star team once more in 1945.

Clapper became Boston's player-coach in 1945 and continued coaching through the 1948–49 season. When he retired as a player on February 12, 1947, a capacity crowd applauded as he received $7,500 worth of gifts. His uniform number, 5, was the first ever retired by the Bruins.

In 833 regular season games, he scored 228 goals and had 248 assists, with 13 goals and 19 assists in 89 playoff games.

★ Hockey Hall of Fame

Clark, Dutch (Earl H.)

FOOTBALL
b. Oct. 11, 1906, Fowler, Colo.
d. Aug. 5, 1978

The 1928 Associated Press All-American team listed a virtually unknown player from a virtually unknown school at quarterback: "Dutch" Clark of little Colorado College. One of the most versatile players in football history, Clark handled the ball on almost every play. He ran 135 times for 1,349 yards, an average of 10 yards a carry; completed 44 passes; and scored 103 points in only eight games, on 14 touchdowns, 16 points after, and 1 field goal. He had a 40-yard interception return for one of his touchdowns that season.

Clark wasn't quite as productive in 1929, when he captained the team, and he didn't repeat as an All-American, but he still had some outstanding games. His 50-yard run and two extra points gave Colorado a 14–13 victory over Colorado A & M, and he kicked a 33-yard field goal in the closing minutes to beat Denver University, 3–2. He also punted 11 times, averaging 45 yards a kick, to keep Denver out of scoring range in that game.

In 1930, Clark became backfield coach at Colorado and also coached basketball and basketball. He signed with the Portsmouth Spartans of the NFL in 1931 and remained with them for two seasons. He scored all of Portsmouth's points in a 19–0 win over the Brooklyn Dodgers as a rookie, and he led the league in scoring with 39 points in 1932. Clark was named All-Pro quarterback both seasons.

The Spartans had a problem paying his salary, $140 a game, so he left pro football in 1933 to coach all sports at the Colorado School of Mines. The following year, the Portsmouth franchise was

moved to Detroit, and Clark returned to the team. He was All-Pro quarterback four seasons in a row and he led the league in scoring twice, with 55 points in 1935 and 73 in 1936.

The 1935 team won the NFL championship, beating the New York Giants, 26–7, in the title game, when Clark had a 40-yard touchdown run. He became player-coach of the team in 1937. His final year as a player was 1938, when he carried the ball only seven times because of injuries. The Cleveland Rams hired Clark as coach in 1939, and he remained there for four seasons.

Clark went into business in 1943 but became football coach at the University of Detroit in 1951. His teams there won 13 games while losing 17 in three seasons before Clark left football for good to concentrate on business.

★ College Football Hall of Fame; Pro Football Hall of Fame

Clark, Ellery H.

TRACK AND FIELD
b. March 13, 1874, West Roxbury, Mass.
d. July 27, 1949

The only person to win the Olympic high jump and long jump, Clark did it in 1896, at the first modern Olympics in Athens. A Harvard student, he was given a leave of absence to compete because of his high grades — in contrast to another gold medal winner from Harvard, John B. Connolly.

Clark fouled on his first two attempts at the long jump but won the gold medal with his third and final jump. He never won a national championship in either jump, but he was the 1897 and 1903 AAU champion in the all-around, an event similar to the decathlon. Clark also competed in the 1904 Olympics in St. Louis, finishing fifth in the all-around.

★ National Track & Field Hall of Fame

Clark, Jimmy (James Jr.)

AUTO RACING
b. March 4, 1936, Kilmany, Scotland
d. April 7, 1968

Clark was already a well-established Grand Prix driver when he arrived at the Indianapolis Speedway to race in the 1963 Indy 500. But he was greeted with scorn and sarcasm. Clark was to drive a rear-engine Lotus-Ford, a special edition of the Formula One racing car, which looked like a toy next to the enormous Indy cars of the time.

But the car was fast in time trials, and there were complaints from Indy veterans. It was unsafe, they said. And the driver, though he had finished second to Graham Hill in the World Driving Championship the year before, might be unsafe as well. He had passed the test required of first-year Indy drivers, but some wanted him to be retested.

Clark was the fifth-fastest qualifier. After problems at the start, when the car in front of him stalled, he was well back in the pack, but he brought the Lotus-Ford into second place behind Parnelli Jones and was gaining when Jones's car suddenly started leaking oil. Two cars skidded out of the race on the oil slicks left behind, and Clark was forced to slow his charge to stay out of trouble. Jones could have been flagged off the course for endangering other drivers, but he wasn't. He won, and Clark was second.

The light, rear-engine car was at Indy to stay, though. After Indy, Clark won four straight Grand Prix races and the 1963 World Championship. He was leading at Indy in 1964 when a tire went. In 1965, he won at Indy — ahead of Jones, now driving a Lotus-Ford — and also won the world championship, an unprecedented double.

After two off years, Clark won his 25th Formula One race, a record at the time, on January 1, 1968. A little more than three months later he was racing at Heidelberg, in eighth place but gaining steadily, when something seemed to happen to his car's suspension. It veered off the course at about 175 mph, crashed into some trees, and Clark was killed instantly.

★ Indianapolis Speedway Hall of Fame

Clark, Steve (Stephen E.)

SWIMMING

b. June 17, 1943, Oakland, Calif.

Because of his lightning-fast turns, Clark was an exceptionally good short-course swimmer. He established nine world records during his career and would have had many more except that short-course times aren't accepted by the International Swimming Federation.

As a high school student, Clark made the 1960 U.S. Olympic team and swam in the heats of both freestyle relays but didn't compete in the finals. Representing Yale, he won the NCAA 100- and 200-yard freestyle events in 1964 and 1965. He was also the 50-yard freestyle winner and a member of the winning 400-yard freestyle relay team in 1965.

Clark won the national long-course 100-meter freestyle in 1961 and 1963, the short-course 100-yard in 1961, 1964, and 1965, and the short-course 220-yard in 1961. Because of shoulder tendinitis, he didn't qualify for any individual events in the 1964 Olympics, but he swam on relay teams that won gold medals and set world records for the 4 x 100-meter freestyle, 4 x 200-meter freestyle, and 4 x 100-meter medley.

Clark, Will (William N.)

BASEBALL

b. March 13, 1964, New Orleans, La.

Known for his tough "game face," his grim concentration on the pitcher, and a laid-back attitude off the field, Clark was an All-American at Mississippi State University for two years before signing with the NL's San Francisco Giants in 1985. After a year in the minor leagues, he entered the major leagues in 1986 but played only 111 games because of an injury.

A left-handed first baseman, Clark blossomed as a star in 1987, batting .308 with 35 home runs and 91 RBI. Although his average slipped to .282 the following season, he led the NL in games with 162, RBI with 109, and walks with 100.

Clark hit over .300 in three of the

next five seasons and had more than 100 RBI in two of them. A knee injury that kept him out of action during the stretch drive in 1993 may have cost the Giants the pennant, as they dropped out of first place during that period to finish a game behind the Atlanta Braves.

In two league championship series, Clark put up some amazing numbers. He batted .360 in 1987 and .650 in San Francisco's five-game victory over the Pittsburgh Pirates in 1989, setting series records for most hits with 13 and most total bases with 24. He also holds the single-game record for most RBI with 6.

Commenting on modern baseball salaries, Clark said to *Sports Illustrated* in 1990, "I haven't figured out how to spend $1 million yet. What do you do with the second and third million? Buy another hunting rifle? How many do you need?"

Clark joined the Texas Rangers as a free agent in November 1993. Through the 1994 season, he had 1,406 hits, including 273 doubles, 39 triples, and 189 home runs, with 760 runs scored and 789 RBI.

Clarke, Bobby (Robert E.)

HOCKEY
b. Aug. 13, 1949, Flin Flon, Man.

A center, the 5-foot-10, 180-pound Clarke was the leader of the Philadelphia Flyers teams known as the "Broad Street Bullies" which won consecutive Stanley Cups in 1974 and 1975.

Most NHL teams avoided him because he suffered from diabetes, but the Flyers took a chance on Clarke by choosing him in the second round of the 1969 amateur draft. He joined the team that year, and during his first four NHL seasons, Clarke missed only one game, because of a boil on his elbow.

A fiery, scrappy redhead, Clarke won the Hart Trophy as the league's most valuable player three times, in 1973, 1975, and 1976. He spent 15 seasons with the Flyers, retiring in 1984 to become the team's general manager.

Clarke scored 358 goals and had 852 assists for 1,210 points in 1,144 regular season games. In 136 playoff games,

he had 42 goals and 77 assists for 119 points.
★ Hockey Hall of Fame

Clarke, Fred C.

BASEBALL
b. Oct. 3, 1872, Winterset, Iowa
d. Aug. 14, 1960

The most successful player-manager in history, Clarke filled both roles for 19 of his 21 seasons in the major leagues and compiled Hall of Fame numbers in both.

Clarke, who threw right and batted left, was an outstanding hitter and outfielder. He began his major league career in 1894 with the Louisville NL team and went 5 for 5 in his first game, the only player ever to do so. He was named manager of the team during the 1897 season, when he hit .406 and stole 60 bases. The following year, he led the league with 66 stolen bases.

Despite Clarke, the Louisville team wasn't very successful, and the franchise was dissolved in 1900. Clarke went to Pittsburgh as player-manager. The team had finished seventh in 1899, but Clarke guided it to second place after an exciting race with Brooklyn.

The Pirates then won pennants from 1901 through 1903, with Clarke batting .316 in 1901 and .351 in 1903, when Pittsburgh lost to the Red Sox in the first modern World Series. After five first-division finishes, Pittsburgh won another pennant in 1909 and beat Detroit in an exciting seven-game World Series.

The strong-armed Clarke had four assists in a game in 1910, one of only eight outfielders to accomplish that, and he had ten putouts in a 1911 game, tying the major league record.

Although Clarke remained on the Pittsburgh roster through 1915, he played little after 1911. Near the end of the 1915 season, his last as a manager, Pittsburgh fans honored him with "Fred Clarke Day" at Forbes Field.

Clarke retired to his Little Pirate Ranch in Kansas for ten years, then returned to the Pirates as a coach in 1925. He became vice president and assistant manager the following year. His frequently harsh criticism led to a rebellion that resulted in the release of three players. Clarke returned to Kansas after the 1926 season.

In 2,242 games, Clarke had 2,672 hits and a .312 average, with 361 doubles, 220 triples, 67 home runs, 1,619 runs scored, and a 1,015 RBI. As a manager, he had a 1,602–1,181 record for a .576 winning percentage.

★ Baseball Hall of Fame

Clarkson, John G.

BASEBALL
b. July 1, 1861, Cambridge, Mass.
d. Feb. 4, 1909

In an era when the pitching distance was only 50 feet and most pitchers relied on sheer speed, Clarkson used a "drop curve," thrown directly overhand so that it broke straight down. The pitch had an unusually sharp break because Clarkson had very strong fingers: with a single twist, he could spin a billiard ball all the way around a table, hitting four banks.

Clarkson played for the Worcester NL team for part of the 1882 season, but the franchise folded, and he spent nearly two seasons in the minor leagues before joining the Chicago NL team late in 1884, when he had a 10–3 record.

Teams usually used just two starting pitchers at the time, and one of them started more often than the other. Clarkson became Chicago's chief pitcher in 1885. He completed 68 of his 70 starts, had a 53–16 record, struck out 318 while walking only 99 in 622 innings, and had 10 shutouts, including a no-hitter against Providence on July 27.

Clarkson went 36–17 in 1886 and 38–21 in 1887, but was sold to Boston in 1888 because of frequent clashes with Chicago manager Cap Anson. The price was $10,000. Boston also paid $10,000 for catcher King Kelly, giving the team the "$20,000 Battery."

For Boston, Clarkson was 33–20 in 1888, 49–19 in 1889, and 26–18 in 1890. He helped lead the team to the pennant in 1891, when he was 33–19. The following year, however, he developed arm trouble and was released after appearing in just 16 games. The Cleveland Spiders picked him up, and he ended the season with a combined 25–16 mark.

After going 16–17 and 8–10 the next two years, Clarkson left baseball. He suffered a nervous breakdown in 1906 and was in a mental institution most of the time until his death from pneumonia.

Clarkson had a career 328–178 record with 485 complete games and 37 shutouts in 518 starts. He struck out 1,978 hitters and walked 1,191 in 4,536 innings.

★ Baseball Hall of Fame

Cleary, Bill (William J. Jr.)

HOCKEY
b. Aug. 19, 1934, Cambridge, Mass.

At Harvard College, Cleary scored 42 goals and had 47 assists for 89 points during the 1954–55 season, then an NCAA record. After graduating, he played for the U.S. Olympic team that won a silver medal in 1956 and was also on the U.S. National team in 1957 and 1958 before a brief retirement.

When the 1960 Olympic hockey team was on tour, Cleary was called out of retirement to give the team more scoring punch. The move was controversial at the time, in part because Cleary insisted that his younger brother Bobby should also be added to the roster, but it was a key element in the surprise gold medal victory.

Cleary led the team in scoring with 12 points on 6 goals and 6 assists in the seven-game Olympic tournament, and he had the first goal in the key 3–2 victory over the Soviet Union — on an assist from brother Bobby.

In 1971, Cleary was named hockey coach at his alma mater. Under his guidance, Harvard won the 1989 NCAA championship, the only national title ever won by the school in any sport. He retired after the 1989–90 season with a 324–201–22 record for a .612 winning percentage.

★ U.S. Hockey Hall of Fame

Clemens, Roger (William Roger)

BASEBALL
b. Aug. 4, 1962, Dayton, Ohio

Nicknamed "Rocket" because of the fastball he throws at more than 90 miles an hour, Clemens also has a sharp-breaking slider, a good curve, and excellent control. That combination won him the AL Cy Young Award in 1986, 1987, and 1991.

The 6-foot-4, 215-pound Clemens grew up in Texas and helped take the University of Texas to the 1983 NCAA championship. He then entered the Boston Red Sox organization, joining the major league team during the 1984 season.

He missed much of 1985 with an injury, but came back to win the Cy Young Award in 1986, when he led the league in victories and winning percentage with a 24–4 record and in ERA at 2.46. Clemens set a major league record for a 9-inning game by striking out 20 Seattle Mariners on April 29. He was also named the league's most valuable player that season.

In 1987, he led the league in victories with a 20–9 record, in complete games with 18, and in shutouts with 7 to win his second Cy Young. After going 18–12 in 1988 and 17–11 in 1989, he led the AL with a 1.93 ERA in 1990, when he had a 21–6 record.

Clemens won his third Cy Young Award in 1991, leading the league in ERA with 2.62, in shutouts with 4, in innings pitched with 271⅓, and in strikeouts with 241, although he won only 18 games against 10 losses.

In 1992, Clemens led the league in ERA for the third consecutive season with a 2.41 average, and he was also the shutout leader with 5. A groin injury bothered him in 1993, when he went just 11–14 with a 4.46 ERA before going onto the disabled list with an inflamed elbow.

Through 1994, Clemens had a career 172–93 record with 36 shutouts and a 2.93 ERA. He had struck out 2,101 hitters while walking 690 in 2,393 innings.

Clemente, Roberto W.

BASEBALL
b. Aug. 18, 1934, Carolina, P.R.
d. Dec. 31, 1972

Clemente originally signed with the Brooklyn Dodgers for a $10,000 bonus in 1954, and he spent the season with their top farm club. He was used sparingly, because the Dodgers were trying to hide his skills from other teams.

At the time, a player who received a signing bonus could be drafted by another team if he wasn't placed on the major league roster after one season in the minors. The talent-laden Dodgers didn't put Clemente on their roster, and he was drafted by the Pittsburgh Pirates for $4,000.

Clemente became Pittsburgh's starting rightfielder during the 1955 season. He hit over .300 only once in his first five seasons, but he batted .314 with 16 homers in 1960, when the Pirates won the pennant, and he hit .310 in their seven-game win over the New York Yankees in the World Series.

In the next seven years, Clemente won four batting titles, hitting .351 in 1961, .339 in 1964, .329 in 1965, and .357 in 1967. He was named the NL's most valuable player in 1966, when he hit .317 with 29 home runs and 119 RBI. After slipping to .291 in 1968, Clemente hit .345, .352, .341, and .312 in the next four seasons.

Through most of his career, Clemente felt he was overlooked because of his Puerto Rican origin, and he was determined to impress the national television audience when the Pirates got into the 1971 World Series. He succeeded, batting .414 with 12 hits, including 2 doubles, 1 triple, and 2 home runs, and he made some outstanding plays in the field as Pittsburgh beat the Baltimore Orioles in seven games. Clemente easily won the most valuable player award for the series.

On September 30, 1972, Clemente got his 3,000th career hit. It was his last. In December, he was organizing relief missions for Managua, Nicaragua, which had been devastated by an earthquake. On New Year's Eve, a plane carrying supplies from Puerto Rico to Nicaragua exploded and crashed shortly after takeoff, killing Clemente and the four others aboard.

Puerto Rico observed an official

three-day mourning period. The usual five-year waiting period for induction into the Hall of Fame was waived, and Clemente was enshrined after a special election.

In 2,433 games, Clemente batted .317, with 440 doubles, 166 triples, 240 home runs, 1,416 runs scored, and 1,305 RBI.

★ Baseball Hall of Fame

Clotworthy, Bob (Robert L.)

DIVING
b. May 8, 1931, Newark, N.J.

Clotworthy won the 1956 Olympic springboard championship after having taken the bronze medal in 1952. He won the silver medal in the 1956 platform event, finishing just behind Joaquim Capilla of Mexico.

Diving for Ohio State University, Clotworthy was the NCAA springboard champion in 1952. He also won the national 3-meter springboard championship in 1951, 1953, and 1956 and the 1-meter championship in 1953 and 1956.

Clotworthy competed in the 1955 Pan-American Games in Mexico City, where he met Cynthia Gill, a member of the U.S. swimming team. They were married the following year. After retiring from competition, Clotworthy coached at Army, Dartmouth, Princeton, Arizona State, and Texas. From 1981 through 1984, he produced six NAIA champions at the University of Wisconsin–Eau Claire.

★ International Swimming Hall of Fame

Coachman, Alice (Mrs. Davis)

TRACK AND FIELD
b. Nov. 9, 1923, Albany, Ga.

Coachman was the first black woman to win an Olympic gold medal, in the 1948 high jump. She was also the only American woman to win a track and field event at the Olympics that year.

She would probably have won more medals if the 1940 and 1944 Olympics hadn't been canceled because of World War II, for she dominated the high jump

for a decade, and she was also a fine sprinter. Coachman won the AAU outdoor high jump championship from 1939 through 1948, and she was indoor champion in 1941, 1945, and 1946; there was no indoor competition from 1938 through 1940 or from 1942 through 1944.

She won the outdoor 50-meter dash from 1943 through 1947, the outdoor 100-meter in 1942, 1945, and 1946, and the indoor 50-meter dash in 1945 and 1946. Representing Tuskegee Institute, Coachman also ran on the national champion 4 x 100-meter relay team in 1941 and 1942.

★ National Track & Field Hall of Fame; International Women's Sports Hall of Fame

Coage, Allen J.

JUDO
b. Oct. 22, 1942, New York, N.Y.

Coage took up judo when he was 22, and in little more than a year he won the 1965 national heavyweight championship. He was also the champion in 1966, 1968, 1969, 1970, and 1975.

He won the bronze medal in the heavyweight class at the 1976 Olympic Games, becoming the first black to win an individual medal in a sport other than boxing or track. Coage was the Pan-American Games heavyweight champion in 1967 and 1975.

Since retiring from competition, he has often served as a bodyguard for Aretha Franklin and other entertainers.

Cobb, Tyrus R.

BASEBALL
b. Dec. 18, 1886, Narrows, Ga.
d. July 17, 1961

Some consider Cobb the greatest baseball player ever. He was certainly the most feared and most disliked. He played as if driven by demons. Hughie Jennings, who managed him for several years, said of Cobb, "When he was in his prime, he had half the American League scared stiff." Rube Bressler, who played against him, described Cobb as "the most feared man in the history of baseball."

Cobb once announced, "I would cut the heart out of my best friend if he ever tried to block the road." His apparent hatred for the world and almost everyone in it probably stemmed, at least in part, from his father's tragic death in 1905. Suspecting his wife of infidelity, W. H. Cobb climbed a ladder to look into her bedroom window one night, and Mrs. Cobb shot and killed him. She was tried for voluntary manslaughter but won acquittal, testifying that she had mistaken her husband for an intruder. Cobb, who was very close to his father, saw his mother only occasionally after that, and didn't attend her funeral.

On August 30 of that year, Cobb joined the AL's Detroit Tigers. From the beginning, he refused to room with anyone, ate his meals alone, and rarely spoke to any of his teammates off the field. But even the opponents who feared him soon had to respect his skills as a hitter and base runner.

After batting only .240 in his first season, Cobb hit .316 in 1906, the first of a record 23 seasons in which he had a batting average over .300. He won a record ten batting titles, hitting .350 in 1907, .324 in 1908, .377 in 1909, .420 in 1911, .409 in 1912, .390 in 1913, .369 in 1915, .383 in 1917, .382 in 1918, and .384 in 1919. Cobb also batted .401 in 1922 but lost the batting title to George Sisler, who hit .407 that season.

He also led in stolen bases with 49 in 1907, 76 in 1909, 83 in 1911, 96 in 1915, 68 in 1916, and 55 in 1917; in runs scored with 116 in 1909, 106 in 1910, 147 in 1911, 144 in 1915, and 113 in 1916; in hits with 212 in 1907, 188 in 1908, 216 in 1909, 248 in 1911, 226 in 1912, 208 in 1915, 225 in 1917, and 191 in 1919; in doubles with 36 in 1908, 47 in 1911, and 44 in 1917; in triples with 20 in 1908, 24 in 1911, 24 in 1917, and 14 in 1918; and in RBI with 119 in 1907, 108 in 1908, 107 in 1909, and 127 in 1911.

For good measure, Cobb was the league leader in home runs with nine in 1909, becoming the second player in AL history and the fourth in major league history to win the triple crown.

Cobb helped lead the Tigers to three consecutive pennants, 1906 through 1908. However, they lost the World Series all three years. Cobb hit .368 in the 1907 Series but only .200 in 1906 and .231 in 1908.

Despite the impressive numbers he compiled over the next 17 seasons in Detroit, the Tigers never won another pennant while he was there. Cobb became the team's playing manager in 1921, a move that surprised the baseball world because of the way even his teammates felt about him.

As a manager, he had moderate success, guiding the Tigers to a second-place finish in 1923 and two third-place finishes in six seasons. After the 1926 season, Detroit abruptly released him. It transpired that Ban Johnson, the league president, had been given two letters, one written by Cobb, that seemed to indicate he had been involved with Tris Speaker in fixing a 1919 game between Detroit and Cleveland.

Johnson declared that Cobb and Speaker would never play in the American League again, but Commissioner Kenesaw Mountain Landis cleared both players of the charges, and Johnson resigned shortly afterward.

Cobb went to the Philadelphia Athletics in 1927, hitting .357, and he retired after batting .323 in 95 games the following year. Wise investments, especially in the Coca-Cola Company, had made him a wealthy man, and he spent the rest of his life in lonesome retirement. Twice divorced, he was estranged from his six children. His autobiography, *My Life in Baseball*, consists largely of tirades against former teammates and opponents.

★ Baseball Hall of Fame

Cochran, Barbara Ann
SKIING
b. Jan. 4, 1951, Claremont, N.H.

The Cochrans were America's first family of skiing during the 1970s, and Barbara was probably the best of them. At one time all four of the Cochran children — Barbara, Linda, Marilyn, and Bob

— were on the U.S. national ski team, and their father, Mickey, was the coach.

Perhaps the most important thing Barbara learned from her father was how to save one-tenth of a second by getting the body moving forward in the starting gate before pushing open the mechanism that starts the timer, because that secret won her a gold medal. In the 1972 Olympic slalom, Barbara won in 1:31.24 to a time of 1:31.26 for Danielle Debernard of France. That race was run over a very difficult course at Sapporo, Japan; of the 42 entrants, only 19 completed both runs.

Barbara won two national championships, in the 1969 giant slalom and the 1971 slalom. She was second in the slalom in the 1970 world championships. After retiring from competition and graduating from the University of Vermont, she became a writer for the *Washington Post* and wrote a book, *Skiing for Women.*

Cochran, Bob (Robert)

SKIING
b. Dec. 11, 1952, Claremont, N.H.

A member of America's foremost skiing family, Bob learned to ski on "Cochran Hill" behind the family home in Richmond, Vermont, as did his three sisters. An outstanding technical skier, he won two national championships in every Alpine event.

He was the U.S. champion in the slalom in 1969 and 1970, the downhill in 1971 and 1973, the Alpine combined in 1971 and 1972, and the giant slalom in 1971 and 1974. Cochran and his two older sisters, Marilyn and Barbara, were on the 1972 Olympic ski team, which was coached by their father, Mickey.

He placed eighth in the downhill at the Olympics, but the following year he became the first U.S. male to win a World Cup giant slalom, and he was also the first to win the prestigious Hahnenkamm Alpine combined title in Austria.

Cochran, Jacqueline

AIR RACING
b. 1910, Pensacola, Fla.
d. Aug. 9, 1980

In 1934, Cochran became the first woman to take part in the London-to-Melbourne air race, and the following year she was the first to compete in the Bendix Trophy transcontinental race. She won the Bendix Trophy in 1938.

After competitive air racing lost its popularity, Cochran began competing against the clock. She was the first woman to fly faster than the speed of sound, in 1957, and she set a women's air speed record of 1,429 miles an hour on May 11, 1964.

During her career, she set a total of 33 national and international air speed records.

Cochrane, Mickey (Gordon S.)

BASEBALL
b. April 6, 1903, Bridgewater, Mass.
d. June 28, 1962

Cochrane was on the baseball, basketball, football, and track teams at Boston University, and he earned some of his tuition money by playing semipro baseball during the summers, using the alias "Frank King" to preserve his college eligibility.

When he graduated in 1923, Cochrane joined a minor league team in Dover, Delaware. The Portland team in the Pacific Coast League was interested in him but couldn't afford the $50,000 that Dover wanted for his contract.

Connie Mack of the Philadelphia Athletics bought the Portland team for $150,000 *and* paid the $50,000 for Cochrane, who spent the 1924 season with Portland and then became Philadelphia's starting catcher.

"Black Mike," as he was called by his teammates, hit .331 in his rookie year. He went on to bat over .300 nine times in his 13 seasons, and he caught more than 100 games each of his first 11 seasons.

He was not only a fine left-handed hitter, Cochrane was also outstanding on defense. During his early years, he was clearly the best catcher in baseball;

later, it was a tossup between him and Bill Dickey of the New York Yankees.

Cochrane was named the AL's most valuable player in 1928, when Philadelphia finished second to the Yankees. The award was largely a tribute to his defense and leadership, since he hit only .293 that season.

The Athletics won three consecutive pennants, from 1929 through 1931, with Cochrane hitting .331, .357, and .349. They won the World Series the first two years but lost to the St. Louis Cardinals in 1931.

As the Great Depression deepened, Mack began to sell off his high-salaried players. Cochrane went to the Detroit Tigers for $100,000 after the 1933 season, and became Detroit's player-manager.

The Tigers had finished fifth in 1933, but Cochrane guided them to pennants in 1934 and 1935 and a six-game victory over the Chicago Cubs in the 1935 World Series. In 1934, he won the most valuable player award for the second time.

During the 1936 season, Cochrane suffered a nervous breakdown. He returned as player-manager in 1937, but was hit in the head by a pitch on May 25 and lay in a coma for ten days. His playing career was over.

Cochrane managed the Tigers until August 1938, when he was replaced. He later served as a coach and, briefly, general manager of the Athletics, as a scout, and as vice president of the Detroit club from 1961 until his death from a respiratory ailment.

In 1,482 games, Cochrane batted .320, with 333 doubles, 64 triples, and 119 home runs. He scored 1,041 runs and drove in 832.

★ Baseball Hall of Fame

Coffey, Paul D.

HOCKEY
b. June 1, 1961, Weston, Ont.

The highest-scoring defenseman in NHL history, Coffey joined the Edmonton Oilers in 1980. He won the Norris Trophy as the league's outstanding defenseman in 1985 and in 1986.

Coffey played for Stanley Cup champions in 1984, 1985, and 1987, then was traded to the Pittsburgh Penguins, where he played on another Stanley Cup winner in 1991. The Penguins traded him to the Los Angeles Kings during the 1991–92 season, and he went to the Detroit Red Wings during the 1992–93 season.

The 6-foot, 200-pound Coffey holds a number of records for a defenseman, including most career goals, 344; most career assists, 934; most career points, 1,278; most goals in a season, 48 in 1985–86; most assists, 6, and most points, 8, in a game, set on March 14, 1986; most goals, 12, most assists, 25, and most points, 37, in the playoffs, set in 1985; and most points in a single playoff game, 6, set on May 14, 1985.

Coffin, Tad (Edmund)

EQUESTRIAN SPORTS
b. May 9, 1955, Toledo, Ohio

At the 1976 Olympics, Coffin became the first American rider ever to win a gold medal in the individual three-day equestrian event, and he was also a member of the winning U.S. team. He had previously won the individual event at the 1975 Pan-American Games.

Cohen, Tiffany

SWIMMING
b. June 11, 1966, Culver City, Calif.

Unusually tall and slender for a swimmer, at 5-foot-8 and 120 pounds, Cohen emerged as America's best woman distance racer during the early 1980s. She won her first major title in the 1981 national outdoor 400-meter freestyle race.

Cohen won the 500-, 1,000-, and 1,650-yard freestyle indoor titles in 1982. In 1983, she won all three of those championships again, along with the 200-meter race, was the national outdoor champion in the 800- and 1,500-meter freestyles, and won the 800- and 1,500-meter gold medals at the Pan-American Games.

After winning the indoor 400- and 800-meter events in 1984, Cohen won gold medals in both races at the Olympics. Her time of 4:7.10 in the 400 was the fastest since 1978.

Cohen entered the University of Texas in the fall of 1984. In her freshman season, she won the NCAA and national indoor titles in the 500- and 1,650-yard freestyles and was also the national indoor 1,000-yard champion.

In the 1986 outdoor championships, Cohen won the 400- and 800-meter freestyles and the 200-meter butterfly. She retired early in 1988 after finishing second to Janet Evans in the 400- and 800-meter races at the 1987 national outdoor meet.

Coleman, Georgia

DIVING
b. Jan. 23, 1912, St. Maries, Idaho
d. Sept. 14, 1940

Just six months after she had begun diving, Coleman won two medals in the 1928 Olympics, a silver in the platform and a bronze in the springboard. Four years later, she won two more medals, a gold in the springboard and another silver in the platform event.

An exceptionally athletic diver for her time, Coleman was the first woman to perform a 2½ forward somersault. She won the national outdoor springboard and platform championships from 1929 through 1931, the indoor 1-meter springboard in 1931, and the indoor 3-meter springboard from 1929 through 1932.

Coleman contracted polio in 1937. She learned to swim again, but she developed pneumonia as an aftermath of the polio and died at 28.

Coleman, Vincent M.

BASEBALL
b. Sept. 22, 1961, Jacksonville, Fla.

The 6-foot-1, 185-pound Coleman, a switch-hitter who throws right-handed, joined the NL's St. Louis Cardinals in 1985 and set a rookie record by stealing 110 bases. He was named the league's rookie of the year by the Baseball Writers Association of America and *The Sporting News.*

The Cardinals won the pennant that season, but Coleman missed the World Series with an injury suffered when an automatic tarpaulin rolled over his ankle during the league championship series.

Coleman led the league in stolen bases the next five years with 107 in 1986, 109 in 1987, 81 in 1988, 65 in 1989, and 77 in 1990. He then went to the New York Mets as a free agent but missed most of the 1991 and 1992 seasons with injuries, and he appeared in only 92 games in 1993 before joining the Kansas City Royals.

Through the 1994 season, Coleman had 1,280 hits in 1,217 games, had stolen 685 bases, and had scored 773 runs.

Collins, Eddie (Edward T.)

BASEBALL
b. May 2, 1887, Millerton, N.Y.
d. March 25, 1951

Nicknamed "Cocky" because of his aggressive demeanor and style of play, Collins was one of the few college-educated players of his era. He entered Columbia University in New York when he was 16 and starred as a football quarterback, playing semipro baseball during summers to earn tuition money.

After his junior year, Collins played briefly for the Philadelphia Athletics, using the name "Sullivan" to avoid losing his college eligibility. But when he returned to school in the fall of 1906, he found that he had been ruled ineligible for playing as a semiprofessional. Unable to play, he coached the Columbia baseball team during his senior year.

Collins had another brief stint with the Athletics in 1907 and joined the team for the entire 1908 season as a second baseman after having previously played shortstop and third base.

He became a full-time starter in 1909, batting .346 and stealing 67 bases. A left-handed hitter, Collins choked up on a heavy bat and hit line drives to all fields. Though he lacked power, he did hit a lot of triples because of his speed. An expert at getting on base and scoring runs, Collins usually batted second rather than leadoff because he was skilled at the hit and run play.

Collins hit .322 and led the league with 81 stolen bases in 1910, when

Philadelphia won the pennant, and he had 9 hits for a .429 average in a five-game World Series victory over the Chicago Cubs. He was also the stolen base leader with 33 in 1919, 47 in 1923, and 42 in 1924. He led in runs scored three years in a row, with 137 in 1912, 125 in 1913, and 122 in 1914, when he was named the AL's most valuable player.

The Athletics won pennants in 1911, 1913, and 1914, and were World Series champions in 1911 and 1913. But Collins threatened to jump to the Federal League, which had begun operating in 1914, and Mack sold him to the Chicago White Sox for $50,000.

In 1917, Collins hit just .289, but the White Sox won the pennant, and he batted .409 in a seven-game victory over the New York Giants in the World Series. He scored the winning run in the seventh game on a fluke play: he was caught in a rundown between third and home after a ground ball, but the Giants left home plate uncovered, and he crossed the plate with New York third baseman Heinie Zimmerman in vain pursuit.

The 1919 World Series was not so happy for the White Sox. Heavily favored, they lost to the Cincinnati Reds, five games to three. A year later, eight players were indicted for conspiring to throw the Series. Though acquitted, they were banned from organized baseball for life. Collins was among the honest White Sox who were bitter over the betrayal.

Collins became playing manager of the team in 1925. He hit .346 that season and .344 in 1926, but Chicago finished fifth both years, and he was released. He returned to the Athletics in 1927, when he batted .338. During the next three years, he was primarily a coach, appearing in only 48 games.

He retired as a player after the 1930 season and coached for two more years, then became vice president of the Boston Red Sox. On a 1937 scouting trip to the West Coast, Collins arranged for the purchase of Ted Williams from the San Diego minor league team and signed him to his first Red Sox contract.

Collins still holds records for most

games at second base, 2,650; most chances accepted, 14,156; and most assists, 7,630.

In 2,826 games, Collins had 3,312 hits, including 438 doubles, 186 triples, and 47 home runs. He stole 744 bases, scored 1,821 runs, and had 1,300 RBI.
★ Baseball Hall of Fame

Collins, Jimmy (James J.)
BASEBALL
b. Jan. 16, 1870, Niagara Falls, N.Y.
d. March 6, 1943

Though almost forgotten now, Collins invented modern third-base play. He was the first to play some distance from the base, allowing him to cut off grounders hit to the right of the shortstop, and the first to charge bunts and field them bare-handed. One sportswriter described him as charging "with a swoop like a chicken hawk."

Collins joined the Boston NL team in 1897 but was loaned for most of the season to Louisville, which was short of players. He was an outfielder at the time, but after Louisville's third baseman made four errors on bunts by the Baltimore Orioles, Collins was asked to try the position. The next four Oriole hitters bunted down the third-base line, and he threw all four of them out. From then on, he was a third baseman.

In 1896, Collins returned to Boston. He batted .346 in 1897 and .337 in 1898, when he led the league in home runs with 14. Boston won the NL pennant both seasons.

The Boston Red Sox of the new American League in 1901 offered Collins $4,000, twice what he was being paid by the NL team, to become player-manager. He hit .329 in 1901 and .325 in 1902, then guided the Red Sox to a pennant in 1903, when his average dropped to .296.

In the first modern World Series, Boston beat the favored Pittsburgh Pirates five games to three. The Red Sox won another pennant in 1904, but John McGraw, manager of the New York Giants, refused to play a post-season series.

Collins was replaced as manager during the 1906 season and was traded to the Philadelphia Athletics in 1907. He retired as a player after that season, then managed in the minor leagues for several years

In 1,726 games, Collins collected exactly 2,000 hits and a .294 batting average. He had 353 doubles, 116 triples, 65 home runs, 1,055 runs scored and 983 RBI.

★ Baseball Hall of Fame

Combs, Earle B.

BASEBALL
b. May 14, 1899, Pebworth, Ky.

Overshadowed by his power-hitting teammates Babe Ruth and Lou Gehrig, Combs was an outstanding hitter and leadoff man who scored 113 or more runs for eight straight seasons with the New York Yankees.

A fine defensive center fielder who threw right-handed and batted left-handed, Combs graduated from Eastern Kentucky State Teachers College in 1921 and was an elementary school teacher before entering professional baseball in 1923.

The Yankees bought his contract for $50,000 in 1924, and Combs had a .400 average in 24 games before suffering a broken ankle and missing the rest of the season. He came back to hit .342 in 1925. After slipping to .299 in 1926, he batted over .300 for the next eight seasons. Combs led the AL in hits with 231 in 1927 and in triples three times, with 23 in 1927, 21 in 1928, and 22 in 1929.

Combs had a fine record in the World Series. He hit .357 in New York's seven-game loss to the St. Louis Cardinals in 1926 and .313 in the 1927 Series, when he scored six runs in a four-game sweep of the Pittsburgh Pirates. A broken finger forced him to the bench in 1928, but he came to bat once as a pinch hitter and drove in a run with a sacrifice fly. In the Yankees' four-game sweep of the Chicago Cubs in 1932, Combs batted .375, scored 8 runs, and had 4 RBI.

Midway through the 1934 season, Combs suffered a fractured skull when he crashed into a fence while chasing a long drive. He was in a coma for hours and underwent brain surgery. He re-turned to the Yankees in 1935 but retired after batting .282 in just 89 games that season.

In his 12 major league seasons, Combs had 1,866 hits, including 309 doubles, 154 triples, and 58 home runs. He scored 1,186 runs and drove in 632.

★ Baseball Hall of Fame

Comiskey, Charles A.

BASEBALL
b. Aug. 15, 1859, Chicago, Ill.
d. Oct. 26, 1931

Comiskey began his long career in professional baseball in 1878, and he entered the major leagues with the American Association's St. Louis Browns in 1882. The 6-foot, 180-pounder originated modern first-base play by positioning himself some distance from the base so he had greater range to his right. Within a short time, most first basemen began following his example.

During the 1883 season, Comiskey became playing manager of St. Louis, and he guided the team to four consecutive pennants, from 1885 through 1888. After jumping to the Players' League in 1890, he returned to St. Louis for one year and then spent three seasons as player-manager of Cincinnati in the NL.

Comiskey became owner and player-manager of the St. Paul franchise in the minor Western League in 1895. The team moved to Chicago in 1900, when the WL became known as the American League. The following year, the American League claimed major league status and raided the established NL for a number of players. Comiskey lured star pitcher Clark Griffith away from the Chicago Cubs; the move helped the White Sox win the first AL pennant, with Griffith as player-manager.

Chicago won another pennant, as well as the World Series, in 1906, and in 1910 Comiskey built the first symmetrical stadium, Comiskey Park, which remained in use until replaced by a new Comiskey Park in 1991. After a third pennant and second world championship in 1917, Comiskey donated 10 percent of the team's 1918 gross receipts to the American Red Cross.

The move made him a philanthropist to the outside world, but it troubled his players, who were among the lowest paid in baseball despite their success on the field. Comiskey's tightfistedness helped lead to the Black Sox Scandal of 1919, when eight players conspired to throw the World Series. Though acquitted, the eight were banned from organized baseball for life.

Shortly afterward, Comiskey became ill and gave up active operation of the team. The White Sox didn't win another pennant until 1959.

★ Baseball Hall of Fame

Conacher, Charlie (Charles W.)

HOCKEY
b. Dec. 10, 1909, Toronto, Ont.
d. Dec. 30, 1967

During the 1930s, Conacher had the hardest shot in hockey, developed through hours of practice on the streets of the Toronto slums where he grew up. His long-time teammate, King Clancy, once got hit in the rear by a Conacher shot and said later, "It felt like somebody had turned a blow torch on me. I couldn't sit down for a week."

He joined the Toronto Maple Leafs near the end of the 1928–29 season and was put on the "Kid Line" with two other youngsters, Harvey "Busher" Jackson and Joe Primeau. All three are now in the Hockey Hall of Fame. In 1938, he was traded to the Detroit Red Wings, and he spent one season with the New York Americans before retiring in 1941.

Conacher won the Art Ross Trophy as the NHL scoring leader in 1934 and 1935 and he tied for the goal-scoring championship in 1932 and 1936. In 13 seasons, he scored 30 or more goals four times and 20 or more six times despite a number of serious injuries. He had an injured kidney removed in 1931. Later he suffered a broken collarbone, and he had both hands and both wrists broken at various times.

He became coach of the Chicago Black Hawks during the 1947–48 season and remained through the 1949–50 season. Conacher had 225 goals and 173 assists in 460 regular season games, with 17 goals and 18 assists in 49 playoff games.

★ Hockey Hall of Fame

Conacher, Lionel V.

HOCKEY
b. May 24, 1901, Toronto, Ont.
d. May 26, 1964

It would be hard to find a sport that Conacher didn't excel at, if he tried. He could run the 100-yard dash in 10.0 seconds when the world record was 9.8. He was the Canadian heavyweight boxing champion and the wrestling champion of Ontario. He played professional baseball in the International League, one step below the majors. He scored 15 points in the 1921 Grey Cup championship, when his Toronto Argonauts beat the Edmonton Eskimos, 23–0, for the Canadian football championship.

But his greatest fame was as a hockey player. He may not have been as skilled as his brother Charlie, but he was certainly rougher and tougher. In 1936, he and Charlie had a fight that started on the ice and moved up a ramp into the lobby of the rink, when Charlie finally gave up.

Lionel, known as "Big Train," entered the NHL with the Pittsburgh Pirates in 1925. He was traded to the New York Americans during the 1926–27 season, then went to the Montreal Maroons. After three seasons with them, he played for the Chicago Black Hawks for one season and returned to the Maroons for three more, retiring in 1937.

He scored 80 goals and had 105 assists, with 882 penalty minutes in 500 regular season games, and he added 2 goals, 2 assists and 34 penalty minutes in 35 playoff games.

After retiring from hockey, Conacher became a member of the Canadian Parliament. He died of a heart attack after hitting a triple in a sandlot baseball game.

★ Canadian Football Hall of Fame, Canadian Sports Hall of Fame

Cone, David B.

BASEBALL
b. Jan. 2, 1963, Kansas City, Mo.

A right-handed pitcher, Cone joined

the AL's Kansas City Royals briefly in 1986 and was then traded to the New York Mets. After going 5–6 in 1987, he had a brilliant 1988 season, leading the NL with an .870 winning percentage on a 20–3 record.

Cone won 14 games each of the next three seasons and led the league in strikeouts with 233 in 1990 and 241 in 1991. He set an NL record by striking out 19 hitters in a nine-inning game on October 6, 1991.

The Mets traded him to the Toronto Blue Jays near the end of the 1992 season and he returned to Kansas City as a free agent in 1993. Expected to be the team's ace, he had a disappointing 11–14 season despite a 3.33 ERA. The Royals scored only 18 runs in his 14 losses. He rebounded with a 16-5 record in the strike-shortened 1994 season.

Through 1994, Cone was 111–70 with 19 shutouts and a 3.12 ERA. He had struck out 1,550 hitters and walked 628 in 1,692⅔ innings.

Conerly, Charlie (Charles A.)

FOOTBALL
b. Sept. 19, 1921, Clarksdale, Miss.

A tailback at the University of Mississippi in 1941 and 1942, Conerly spent three years in the Marines during World War II. When he returned to Mississippi in 1946, he became quarterback in the newly installed T formation.

Conerly captained and quarterbacked the team to a 9–2–0 record in 1947, when Mississippi won its first Southeast Conference championship and beat Texas Christian, 13–9, in the Delta Bowl. He completed 133 of 233 passes for 1,367 yards and 27 touchdowns that season and was a consensus All-American.

In 1948, Conerly joined the NFL's New York Giants and was named rookie of the year. In a game against the Pittsburgh Steelers that season, he completed 36 of 53 passes. Conerly went on to help lead the Giants into championship games in 1956, 1958, 1959, and 1961. He threw two touchdown passes in New York's 47–7 victory over the Bears in 1956.

"Chuckin' Charlie," as sportswriters

liked to call him, retired after the 1961 season. As a professional, he completed 1,418 of 2,833 passes for 19,488 yards and 173 touchdowns. He also scored 10 rushing touchdowns.

★ College Football Hall of Fame

Conn, Billy (William D. Jr.)

BOXING
b. Oct. 8, 1917, E. Liberty, Pa.
d. May 29, 1993

Conn, nicknamed the "Pittsburgh Kid," is best known for his unsuccessful attempts to win the heavyweight championship from Joe Louis, but he was a very fine light heavyweight champion. In 1935, at a weight of 142 pounds, he left high school to begin fighting.

After a mediocre start, Conn won all 23 of his fights in 1936. Among them was a 10-round decision over Fritzie Zivic, who later became world welterweight champion. Conn won 15 of his next 18 fights before meeting Melio Bettina of Italy for the vacant world light heavyweight title on July 13, 1939. Conn won the championship with a 15-round decision.

A clever fighter without much of a knockout punch, Conn gave up the title in 1941 in order to meet Louis for the heavyweight championship. He led on all three scorecards after 12 rounds of the June 18 fight but was knocked out by Louis late in the 13th round. Conn became so celebrated in defeat that he starred in a Republic Pictures movie, *The Pittsburgh Kid,* later that year.

After serving in the Army during World War II, Conn had a rematch with Louis on June 19, 1946. The fight drew the second-biggest gate in history up to that time, nearly $2 million, and Conn earned $325,958. But he was rusty after more than three years without a serious fight, and Louis knocked him out in the 8th round.

Conn retired for a time, returned to the ring for three fights in 1948, and then quit for good. He won 63 of his 75 professional fights, 14 by knockout, while losing only 11, 2 by knockout, and he fought 1 draw.

★ International Boxing Hall of Fame

Conner, Bart
GYMNASTICS
b. March 28, 1958, Chicago, Ill.

An active, mischievous child, Conner was introduced to gymnastics when he was ten because his parents felt he needed a vent for his energy. He began competing in YMCA meets after just a year.

The U.S. Gymnastics Federation all-around champion in 1974, Conner entered the University of Oklahoma in 1976 and helped make the school a power in intercollegiate gymnastics. He won the NCAA all-around title in 1978, when Oklahoma won the team championship, and he tied for the floor exercise championship in 1979.

Conner won the world parallel bars championship in 1979. He was the high scorer in the 1980 Olympic trials, but the U.S. boycotted the Moscow Olympics that year, so he didn't get to compete.

A torn right biceps muscle in 1983 threatened his career. Because of the injury, he had to drop out of the 1984 national championships. Forty percent of the scores from the meet were to be used to choose the Olympic team. However, the U.S. Olympic Committee granted him a special waiver, and his performance at the Olympic trials won him a place on the team.

Conner got two perfect scores of 10.0 in winning the gold medal in the parallel bars, and he finished fifth in the floor exercise, the highest placing ever for an American in that event. He also won a gold medal as a member of the champion team.

He retired from competition after the Olympics to become a television commentator.

★ Olympic Hall of Fame

Conner, Dennis W.
YACHTING
b. Sept. 16, 1942, San Diego, Calif.

Someone once said that if a U.S. skipper ever lost the America's Cup, his head would replace the trophy at the New York Yacht Club. Conner did lose the cup, but he not only kept his head, he raced again and regained the trophy for the San Diego Yacht Club (SDYC).

Conner, who attended San Diego State University, won the Star Class world championship in 1971 and 1977 and finished second in 1978. He won the Congressional Cup in round-robin match race competition in 1973 and 1975, and in 1976 he was helmsman for the crew that won a bronze medal in the Tempest Class at the Olympics.

His first involvement in America's Cup competition came in 1976, when he was the helmsman for two boats in the preliminaries, but neither was chosen to defend the cup. However, Conner was skipper of *Freedom* in 1980, when she beat the challenger *Australia* in four of five races.

In 1983, *Australia II* won the America's Cup, defeating *Liberty*, skippered by Conner, in four of seven races. That ended the longest winning streak in the history of sports, 132 years, encompassing 25 challenges.

It seemed likely that Australia might hold the cup for a long time, since the defending crew benefits from experience of local waters and wind conditions. But Conner, now representing his own club, the SDYC, went to Australia in 1987 and regained the cup by guiding *Stars and Stripes* to a relatively easy four-race victory over *Kookaburra.*

New Zealand had planned to challenge in 1989, but the SDYC won a court ruling that the race should take place in 1988, when Conner skippered a new *Stars and Stripes,* a catamaran (two-hulled sailboat) to another easy victory over the poorly prepared challenger *Kiwi.*

Connolly, Harold V.
TRACK AND FIELD
b. Aug. 1, 1931, Somerville, Mass.

Connolly's left arm was slightly withered at birth, and he broke it several times playing football and wrestling, so he took up the hammer throw as a student at Boston College to strengthen it. His throw of 201 feet, 5 inches in June 1955 made him the first American to surpass 200 feet in the event, but Connolly went well beyond that in a short time.

The national AAU champion eight times, from 1955 through 1961 and in 1964 and 1965, Connolly set his first world record with a throw of 224–10 on November 2, 1956, shortly before the Olympics. Then he beat long-time world record holder Mikail Krivonosov to win a gold medal. Wearing ballet shoes to improve his footing, he trailed Krivonosov until his fifth and final throw, when he won with a distance of 207–3.

Connolly increased the record to 225–4 in 1958, 226–1½ in 1959, 230–9 in 1960, 231–10 in 1962, then to 233–2 and 233–9½ in 1965. He placed second in the 1960 Olympic trials but was injured before the Olympics and finished only eighth. In 1964, he placed sixth at the Olympics.

In 1957, Connolly married Olga Fikotova, who had won a 1956 gold medal in the discus for Czechoslovakia. She represented the U.S. at four Olympics, 1960, 1964, 1968, and 1972, but never won another medal. After their divorce in 1975, Connolly married Patricia Winslow, who had competed in the Olympic pentathlon in 1960, 1964, and 1968.

Connolly competed only sporadically after 1965, but he qualified for the 1968 Olympic team and placed fifth in the 1972 trials.

★ National Track & Field Hall of Fame

Connolly, James B.

TRACK AND FIELD
b. Nov. 28, 1868, S. Boston, Mass.
d. Jan. 20, 1957

On April 6, 1896, Connolly became the first athlete to win a gold medal in the modern Olympics, taking the triple jump. He later won a silver medal in the high jump and a bronze in the long jump.

Connolly never went to high school, but he educated himself before entering Harvard College as a 27-year-old freshman in 1895. When he heard about the Olympics in Athens, he asked for a leave of absence so he could compete. He was turned down, but he left school and went anyway, paying his own passage.

He didn't return to Harvard until years later, when he was invited to lecture on literature. In the meantime, he had become a journalist, a war correspondent for *Collier's* magazine, a novelist, and a short story writer.

Connolly, Maureen C. (Mrs. Brinker)

TENNIS
b. Sept. 17, 1934, San Diego, Calif.
d. June 21, 1969

In a tragically brief career that ended before she turned 20, Connolly won all nine grand slam tournaments that she entered and was the first woman to win the grand slam of tennis, all four major international championships in a single year.

Connolly loved horses, but her divorced mother couldn't afford a horse or riding lessons, so she began playing tennis when she was nine. Helen Wills saw her play when she was 12 and predicted, "That little girl will become the national champion in four years, and possibly the world's champion as well."

A tremendous baseline driver with great accuracy, Connolly more than fulfilled the prophecy. At 14, she won 56 straight matches and became the youngest player to win the national junior girls championship. Two years later, in 1951, she became the youngest U.S. women's champion, and she repeated in 1952 and 1953.

Nicknamed "Little Mo," Connolly won the Wimbledon singles title from 1952 through 1954, was the French champion in 1953 and 1954, and won the Australian championship in 1953, her grand slam year. She was named woman athlete of the year by the Associated Press three years in a row, from 1951 through 1953.

Just two weeks after she won the 1954 Wimbledon title, a cement truck brushed against Connolly's right leg while she was horseback riding. She was thrown to the ground, and the leg was seriously damaged, ending her competitive career.

Connolly married Norman Brinker, who had been on the 1952 Olympic equestrian team, and established the

Maureen Connolly Brinker Foundation to promote junior tennis. She died of cancer.

★ International Tennis Hall of Fame; International Women's Sports Hall of Fame

Connor, George
FOOTBALL
b. Jan. 21, 1925, Chicago, Ill.

After starting at tackle for Holy Cross in 1943, Connor spent two years in the Army and then went to Notre Dame, where he was an All-American in 1946 and 1947 and winner of the 1946 Outland Trophy as the nation's outstanding collegiate lineman.

His coach, Frank Leahy, said of Connor, "He had the agility to sort out the ball carrier and the toughness to break up the power play. He was indestructible."

Connor became a two-way tackle with the Chicago Bears in 1948 and was an All-Pro in 1949 and 1950. He continued to play both offense and defense even after NFL teams adopted the two-platoon system in 1951. He was a consensus All-Pro at both offensive tackle and defensive tackle that season.

The 6-foot-3, 240-pound Connor was moved to outside linebacker on defense in 1952. The Associated Press again named him an All-Pro offensive tackle, and the United Press named him an All-Pro linebacker in both 1952 and 1953. He played only linebacker in 1954 and 1955, his final season.

★ College Football Hall of Fame; Pro Football Hall of Fame

Connor, Roger
BASEBALL
b. July 1, 1857, Waterbury, Conn.
d. Jan. 4, 1931

Connor was major league baseball's career home run leader until Babe Ruth broke his record. Ironically, no one knew it until Hank Aaron broke Ruth's record in 1974.

A left-handed third baseman when he arrived in the major leagues with the NL's Troy, New York, team in 1880, Connor moved to first base after dislocating his shoulder early in the 1881 season, and he remained at that position for the rest of his career.

Connor led the league in triples with 18 in 1882 and with 20 in 1886. He was the home run leader only once, with 14 in 1890, when he was in the Players' League, but he had 11 or more home runs six times in an era when that was an unusual accomplishment.

The Troy team moved to New York City in 1883 and eventually became known as the Giants. Connor was the league's top hitter with a .371 average in 1885, and he hit .355 the following season. On May 9, 1888, he became the sixth player in history to hit three home runs in a game.

In 1890, Connor joined the New York team in the Players' League, but that league folded after one season, and he returned to the Giants in 1891. Traded to Philadelphia in 1892, he was back with the Giants the following year, then was traded again, to St. Louis, in 1894. He finished his major league career there by appearing in only 22 games in 1897.

Connor hit 138 career home runs, a record broken by Ruth in 1921. No one noticed that Ruth had broken a record, however. Only when Aaron surpassed Ruth, more than 50 years after Connor's death, did anyone wonder whose record Ruth had broken. The answer led to Connor's election to the Hall of Fame.

In 1,997 games, Connor batted .317 with 2,467 hits, including 441 doubles, 233 triples, and 138 home runs. He scored 1,620 runs, drove in 1,322, and stole 244 bases.

★ Baseball Hall of Fame

Connors, Jimmy (James S.)
TENNIS
b. Sept. 2, 1952, Belleville, Ill.

Connors began playing tennis when he was three years old, under the tutelage of his mother, Gloria, a teaching professional. When he was a young teenager, the family moved to California so he could receive advanced training from Pancho Gonzales and Pancho Segura.

After winning NCAA singles title as a student at UCLA in 1971, Connors left school to turn professional in 1972. He won the U.S. pro championship the following year.

A left-hander who uses the two-handed backhand, Connors was deprived of a shot at the grand slam in 1974. He won the Australian and U.S. Opens and the Wimbledon singles championship, but was banned from the French Open because he played in the World Team Tennis league. He won the U.S. Open again in 1976, 1978, 1982, and 1983, and he took his second Wimbledon title in 1982.

One of his opponents said of Connors, "Playing him is like fighting Joe Frazier. The guy's always coming at you. He never lets up." During the early part of his career, his personality matched his style of play. Connors had frequent clashes with judges and umpires, the players' union, Davis Cup officials, and other players.

Later, he mellowed. After his first Wimbledon victory, he declined to accept the commemorative medal emblematic of the championship. After his second, eight years later, he accepted it graciously and won over many British fans who had disliked him.

Ranked first in the world five years in a row, from 1974 through 1978, Connors had to yield that position to Bjorn Borg, John McEnroe, and Ivan Lendl for the rest of his career. Yet he gained popularity with American crowds. It reached a peak in 1989, when he played in his twentieth U.S. Open at the age of 37. Connors ignited the crowd with a fourth-round upset of Stefan Edberg before losing in the quarterfinals.

He retired in 1993 as the all-time leader with 109 tournament victories. Connors ranks fifth in money won with $8,498,820.

Conzelman, Jimmy (James G.)

FOOTBALL
b. March 6, 1898, St. Louis, Mo.
d. July 31, 1970

After playing quarterback at Washington University in St. Louis, Conzelman was a teammate of George Halas with the Great Lakes Naval Training Station team. When Halas organized the Decatur Staleys (now the Chicago Bears) in 1920, he hired Conzelman.

After one season with Decatur, Conzelman went to the Rock Island Independents in 1921 and became player-coach during the 1922 season. He also served as player-coach of the Milwaukee Badgers from 1923 through 1924, the Detroit Panthers from 1925 through 1926, and the Providence Steamroller from 1927 through 1929. Providence won the 1928 NFL championship.

Conzelman left football temporarily in 1930 but returned to coach at his alma mater from 1934 through 1939, compiling a 32–16–2 record. He became coach of the NFL's Chicago Cardinals in 1940, left after three disappointing seasons to join baseball's St. Louis Browns as an executive, then returned to the Cardinals for a second stint in 1946.

The team improved from a 1–9 mark in 1945 to 6–5 in his first season and won the NFL championship in 1947. The Cardinals were again division champions in 1948 but lost, 7–0, to the Philadelphia Eagles in the title game.

Conzelman retired after that season with an overall professional record of 82 wins, 69 losses, and 14 ties.

★ Pro Football Hall of Fame

Cook, Bill (William O.)

HOCKEY
b. Oct. 9, 1896, Brantford, Ont.
d. May 5, 1986

Cook was given land in Saskatchewan for serving in World War I and worked the land for several years before returning to hockey in 1922 with the Saskatoon Sheiks. He had been a good amateur player before the war, and he quickly became a good professional player, leading the Western Canada League in scoring three times before joining the New York Rangers of the NHL in 1926.

He was known as "Bad Bill" because of his frequent fights, but he was also a premier scorer. Cook led the NHL in scoring in 1926–27 with 37 points and in 1932–33 with 50 points. He scored the only goal in a 1–0 victory over Toronto that won the 1933 Stanley Cup for the Rangers.

Cook retired after the 1936–37 season. He scored 229 goals and had 138 assists in 475 regular season games. In 45 playoff games, he had 13 goals and 11 assists.

He returned to the Rangers as their coach in 1951, but lasted less than two seasons.

★ Hockey Hall of Fame

Cooper, Earl

AUTO RACING
b. 1886, Nebr.
d. Oct. 22, 1965

Cooper was a man ahead of his time, a race driver who took a methodical, scientific approach to his craft while most others just drove as fast as they could and hoped the car didn't break down. He tested cars and tires meticulously, worked closely with his mechanic to prepare cars, and helped develop hydraulic brakes and pressure lubrication.

A mechanic for a Maxwell dealership, Cooper began his racing career in 1908, when he won a San Francisco race in a borrowed car. He lost his job because one of the drivers he defeated was his boss, so he became a full-time auto racer. In 1912 he joined the Stutz team. The following year he won seven of eight major road races, finished second in the one he didn't win, and claimed his first national championship.

An injury kept him out most of the 1914 season, but he won the championship again in 1915 despite missing the first three months of the season because of illness. Stutz pulled out of racing in 1916, and Cooper again got a late start, finishing fifth in the championship standings. He won his third title in 1917, when the season was shortened because of World War I, and then he retired from racing, although he did enter the 1919 Indy 500.

He returned in October 1921 to replace Joe Thomas, who had broken an arm practicing for a 200-mile race in Fresno. Cooper won in a close finish with Jimmy Murphy. He was back full time in 1922, and in 1923 he won five races.

Cooper was dogged by bad luck and mechanical problems in the Indianapolis 500. The closest he came to victory was in 1924, when he led after 400 miles. Forced into the pit by a blown tire, he seemed about to take the lead back from Joe Boyer with 30 miles to go, but another tire blew, and he had to settle for second place. After two more unsuccessful starts at Indy and another year of retirement, he tried once more in 1928, then retired for good.

★ Indianapolis Speedway Hall of Fame

Cooper, Harry E.

GOLF
b. Aug. 4, 1904, Leatherhead, England

"Lighthorse Harry" grew up in Texas, where his family moved when he was young, and he learned to play golf there. A great player from tee to green, he was only an average putter, and he had terrible luck in the U.S. Open.

Cooper won two of the few tournaments on the tour in 1926, and he appeared to be the winner of the U.S. Open. In fact, he was changing clothes to appear at the presentation ceremony when word came that Tommy Armour had birdied two of the last six holes to tie for the lead. The next day, Cooper lost the playoff, 79–76.

Ten years later, Cooper again seemed to have won the Open. He was in the clubhouse with a 284, two strokes better than the former 72-hole record that had stood since 1916. Then a virtual unknown named Tony Manero shot a 67 on the last round for a 282. Cooper also finished second in the 1936 Masters after Horton Smith birdied three of the last five holes to win.

Cooper's best year was 1937, when he was the tour's top money winner and the winner of the Vardon trophy for fewest strokes per round. He was Canadian Open champion in 1932 and 1937. His last victory was in the Bing Crosby Pro-Am in 1942.

★ World Golf Hall of Fame

Cooper, Morton C.

BASEBALL
b. March 2, 1914, Atherton, Mo.
d. Nov. 17, 1958

After six years in the minor leagues and a brief stint with the NL's St. Louis Cardinals in 1938, Cooper became a regular starter in 1939 and was named the league's most valuable player in 1942. Pitching to his younger brother, catcher Walker Cooper, he led the league in victories with a 22–7 record, in shutouts with 10, and in ERA with a 1.78 mark.

He had an 0–1 record and a 5.54 ERA in the World Series, but the Cardinals beat the New York Yankees in five games. Cooper again led the league in victories with a 21–8 record and in winning percentage at .724 in 1943. This time, the Cardinals lost the World Series to the Yankees in five games, with Cooper compiling a 1–1 record and a 2.81 ERA.

Cooper posted a 22–7 record with a 2.46 ERA in 1944, leading the NL with 7 shutouts, as the Cardinals won their third straight pennant. He lost the first game of the World Series, 2–1, to the St. Louis Browns but came back to win the fifth, 2–0, and the Cardinals won in six games.

The Cardinals traded him to the Boston Braves early in the 1945 season. Arm trouble hampered him for the rest of his career. He was traded to the New York Giants during the 1947 season, missed all of 1948, and retired after a brief comeback attempt with the Chicago Cubs in 1949.

He had a career 128–75 record with 33 shutouts and a 2.97 ERA. Cooper struck out 913 hitters and walked 571 in 1,840⅔ innings.

Cooper, Tarzan (Charles T.)

BASKETBALL
Aug. 30, 1907, Newark, Del.
d. Dec. 19, 1980

The 6-foot-4, 215-pound Cooper was a big player for his era, and his long arms, which contributed to his nickname, made him an even bigger rebounder. After graduating from high school,

Cooper played with semiprofessional teams in Philadelphia for four years before joining the Harlem Renaissance team in 1929.

The all-black Rens, as they were called, had several fine shooters. Cooper brought the team rebounding and the ability to score from close in. During his 11 seasons, the Rens had 1,303 wins to 203 losses. When the Rens won the first world championship tournament in Chicago in 1939, Cooper was named the tournament's most valuable player. Cooper played for the Washington Bears when they won the tournament in 1943.
★ Basketball Hall of Fame

Copeland, Lillian

TRACK AND FIELD
b. Nov. 25, 1904, New York, N.Y.
d. July 7, 1964

The first great American woman weight thrower, Copeland won nine national AAU championships in three events. She was the shotput champion from 1925 through 1928 and in 1931, the discus champion in 1926 and 1927, and the javelin champion in 1926 and 1931.

Copeland set world records in the javelin in 1926, 1927, and 1928, but the women's javelin wasn't on the Olympic program in 1928. However, she did win a silver medal in the discus.

After entering the University of Southern California Law School in 1931, she competed very little before the 1932 Olympic trials. She barely made the team, finishing third in the discus trials, but she won the gold medal on her final throw. Copeland said afterward, "The only thing I could think of as I stood there waiting for my last throw of the day was Dr. [Patrick] O'Callaghan, who won the hammer throw on his last throw of the day."

She retired after the Olympics but returned in 1935 to win all three of her specialty events at the Second World Maccabiah Games in Palestine.

Corbett, James J.

BOXING
b. Sept. 1, 1866, San Francisco, Calif.
d. Feb. 18, 1933

Corbett began boxing as an amateur when he was 18 and within a year he won the championship of San Francisco's Olympic Athletic Club, which produced some fine fighters. Among them was Joe Choynski, a challenging stepping stone to the heavyweight title.

Using the name "Joe Dillon" to avoid losing his amateur status, Corbett fought professionals in Utah and Wyoming before returning to California in 1889 for three fights against Choynski. Corbett won two of them, one by knockout, and the third was stopped by the police after four rounds.

On May 21, 1891, Corbett fought Peter Jackson, an Australian who couldn't get a championship fight against the reigning John L. Sullivan because he was black. The match went 61 rounds before it was declared no contest because both boxers were too exhausted to continue.

Corbett met Sullivan on September 7, 1892, in New Orleans in the first championship fight using padded gloves under the Marquis of Queensbury Rules. He won the title by knocking Sullivan out in the 21st round.

The popular, dapper Corbett spent much of the rest of his career capitalizing on his championship without much fighting. He appeared in Broadway shows, fought an exhibition for the first boxing movie at Thomas Edison's laboratory, and toured England triumphantly after his first title defense, a 3-round knockout of Charley Mitchell on January 25, 1894.

Corbett lost the championship when Bob Fitzsimmons knocked him out in the 14th round on March 17, 1897, in Carson City, Nevada. He twice tried to regain the title against James J. Jeffries, but was knocked out both times, in the 23rd round on May 11, 1900, and in the 10th round on August 14, 1903.

"Gentleman Jim" is generally considered the first really scientific fighter because he used speed and knowledge of his opponent's strengths and weaknesses to develop a strategy for a fight, rather than depending on brawn and sheer volume of punches. He fought only 19 professionals bouts, winning 11,

7 by knockout, and losing 4, 3 by knockout. He also had 2 draws and 2 no-contests.

★ International Boxing Hall of Fame

Corbus, William

FOOTBALL
b. Oct. 5, 1911, San Francisco, Calif.

The 6-foot, 185-pound Corbus was nicknamed the "Baby-Faced Assassin" because his boyish appearance belied his devastating blocking and tackling as a three-year starter at Stanford. Although a guard, he was also a fine place-kicker.

An All-American in both 1932 and 1933, Corbus captained the 1933 team. There were nine sophomore starters on that team, known as the "Vow Boys," because they had vowed never to lose to Southern California. They never did, in part because Corbus kicked two field goals in the second half to beat Southern Cal, 13–7, that year.

★ College Football Hall of Fame

Cordero, Angel, Jr.

HORSE RACING
b. Nov. 8, 1942, Santurce, P.R.

The winner of two Eclipse Awards as jockey of the year, in 1982 and 1983, Cordero is third all-time in races won with 7,057 and second in winnings with $164,526,217.

He led the nation in wins in 1968 and was the top money-winning jockey in 1976, 1982, and 1983. Cordero has won six triple crown races: the 1974 Kentucky Derby aboard Cannonade, the 1976 Preakness and Belmont aboard Bold Forbes, the 1980 Preakness aboard Codex, the 1984 Preakness aboard Gate Dancer, and the 1985 Kentucky Derby aboard Spend a Buck.

In Breeder's Cup racing, Cordero has had 4 winners, 7 second places, and 7 third places in 48 starts. His victories came in the 1985 Distaff with Life's Magic, the 1988 Juvenile Fillies with Open Mind, the 1988 Sprint with Gulch, and the 1989 Sprint with Dancing Spree. Cordero's $6,020,000 in Breeder's Cup earnings is seventh best.

★ National Horse Racing Hall of Fame

Costello, Larry (Lawrence R.)

BASKETBALL
b. July 2, 1931, Minoa, N.Y.

As a guard at Niagara University, Costello averaged 15.0 points a game in three seasons as a starter. The 6-foot-1, 188-pounder joined the NBA's Philadelphia Warriors in 1954. After spending part of his first season and all of the 1955–56 season in the military service, Costello returned to the Warriors for the 1956–57 season.

He was sold to the Syracuse Nationals in October 1957. After the Warriors moved to California, the Syracuse franchise went to Philadelphia and became known as the 76ers in 1963. Costello retired after the 1967–68 season.

He became head coach of the Milwaukee Bucks in 1968, guiding them to first-place finishes in their division from 1970–71 through 1973–74 and in 1975–76. Costello was replaced after the team won only 3 of its first 18 games in 1976–77, and he took over the Chicago Bulls in 1978 but didn't finish the season.

In 1980, Costello went to Utica College, which was making the transition from NCAA Division III to Division I basketball. He had only one winning season there, and retired in 1987.

As a player, Costello scored 8,622 points in 706 regular season games, a 12.2 average, and had 3,215 assists. He added 592 points in 52 playoff games for an 11.4 average.

His professional coaching record was 430–300, a .589 winning percentage, in the regular season and 37–23 in the playoffs. Costello was 77–106 at Utica.

Costello, Paul V.

ROWING
b. Dec. 27, 1894, Philadelphia, Pa.

The first rower to win three consecutive Olympic gold medals in the same event, Costello won the double sculls in 1920, 1924, and 1928. He teamed with his cousin, John B. Kelly, Sr., for the first two victories and with Charles McIlvaine for the third.

Costello won the national championship single sculls in 1922, the association single sculls in 1919. He also teamed with Kelly and McIlvaine to win a number of national doubles sculls titles.

Counsilman, Doc (James E.)

SWIMMING
b. Dec. 28, 1920, Birmingham, Ala.

After he won the 1942 AAU outdoor 220-yard breaststroke championship, Counsilman's competitive swimming career at Ohio State was interrupted by World War II, in which he served as a bomber pilot. He returned to school as a junior after the war and was captain of the swim team in 1946 and 1947.

Counsilman received a master's degree from the University of Illinois in 1948 and a doctorate from the University of Iowa in 1951, then became swimming coach at Cortland State College in New York (now SUNY College at Cortland).

In 1957, he went to Indiana University, where his teams won six consecutive NCAA championships, from 1968 through 1973, and 20 straight Big Ten titles, from 1961 through 1980. Indiana once won 140 dual meets in a row. Counsilman coached the U.S. Olympic swimming teams in 1964 and 1976.

The scholarly Counsilman carefully analyzed all swimming strokes for his 1969 book, *The Science of Swimming*, and designed many types of training equipment for the sport. He also helped plan and design the Indiana University Natatorium, where the 1984 Olympic trials and the 1987 Pan-American Games swimming competition took place.

On September 14, 1979, Counsilman became the oldest person ever to swim the English Channel, at 58 years 260 days.

Counsilman retired in 1990 with a record of 267 victories, 36 losses, and 1 tie in dual meets.

Courier, Jim (James)

TENNIS
b. Aug. 17, 1970, Sanford, Fla.

A classmate of Andre Agassi at the Nick Bollettieri Tennis Academy, Courier was overshadowed by Agassi until

1991, when he won the French Open and ended the year ranked second in the world. He had never before been in the top ten.

Courier won the French Open again and also took the Australian Open to claim the world's top ranking in 1992. After winning the Australian Open for a second time in 1993, Courier lost in the finals of the French Open and the Wimbledon singles. He finished the year ranked second behind Pete Sampras.

Through 1994, Courier ranks fifth all-time in earnings with $9,061,864.

Cournoyer, Yvan S.

HOCKEY
b. Nov. 22, 1943, Drummondville, P.Q.

Opposition goalie Gerry Cheevers once jokingly asked Cournoyer if he could please slow down a little. "No, Gerry," Cournoyer laughed, "I have the tailwinds tonight."

It seemed that Cournoyer usually had the tailwinds. Small but fast and flashy, he joined the Montreal Canadiens in 1964 after only five games in the minor leagues and quickly became one of the most feared scorers in hockey. In his first season, other teams often intimidated him with rough play, but he took boxing lessons during the summer and could no longer be bullied.

Particularly dangerous on the power play because of his puck-handling ability, Cournoyer won the Conn Smythe Trophy as the most valuable player in the playoffs in 1973, when he scored 15 goals in Stanley Cup competition, including the goal that beat the St. Louis Blues in the final game.

In 16 seasons, all with the Canadiens, Cournoyer scored 428 goals and had 435 assists for a total of 863 points in 968 regular season games. He added 64 goals and 63 assists in 147 playoff games.
★ Hockey Hall of Fame

Courtney, Charles E.

ROWING
b. 1849, Union Springs, N.Y.
d. July 17, 1920

Undefeated in 88 races as an amateur,

Courtney won the national association single sculls championship in 1875 and the amateur championship at the 1876 Columbian Exposition in Philadelphia. He turned professional in 1878 to meet the great Canadian champion, Ned Hanlan, before 20,000 spectators at Lachine, Quebec. Hanlan won the 5-mile race and a $10,000 prize.

A rematch was scheduled at Lake Chautauqua, New York, for a $6,000 prize in 1879, but it never took place. Courtney's boat was sawed in half the night before the race, and he declined offers of other boats. Some thought that Hanlan's supporters had destroyed the boat, but others suspected Courtney had done it himself to avoid another loss.

The two finally met again on the Potomac River in 1880, resulting in another controversy. Hanlan took an enormous lead and Courtney dropped out, turning his boat around to return to the start/finish line before Hanlan reached the turning post. Many thought Courtney was winning, but Hanlan passed him once more and crossed the finish line ahead of him.

In 1884, Cornell University hired Courtney as rowing coach, drawing criticism from the *New York Times*, which editorialized, "If college boys cannot learn to row without associating with persons like Courtney, perhaps they would be quite as well off if they devoted a little more time to classics and mathematics and a little less to rowing."

The first full-time professional coach hired by any college, Courtney remained at Cornell through 1916. His crews won 98 meets and lost 46, including 14 of 24 championship races at the Intercollegiate Rowing Association Regatta, which was established in 1895.

Courtney, Tom (Thomas W.)

TRACK AND FIELD
b. Aug. 17, 1933, Newark, N.J.

As a junior at Fordham University, Courtney won the IC4A indoor 1,000-yard run in 1954 and the NCAA outdoor 800-meter run in 1955.

Courtney set a U.S. record of 1:46.4 in the 800-meter at the 1956 Olympic trials. He had a memorable duel with Derek Johnson of England in the Olympic final. Johnson took a narrow lead with 40 yards to go, but Courtney nipped him with a lunge at the tape, then collapsed with exhaustion.

He later wrote: "It was a new kind of agony for me. My head was exploding, my stomach ripping and even the tips of my fingers ached. The only thing I could think was, 'If I live, I will never run again.'" The medal ceremony had to be delayed for an hour while he and Johnson recovered.

Courtney did run again. He was the anchorman on the gold medal 4 x 400-meter relay team, and he also won the AAU national 880-yard championship in 1957 and 1958. He set a world record of 1:46.8 in the 880 on May 24, 1957.

★ National Track & Field Hall of Fame

Cousy, Bob (Robert J.)

BASKETBALL
b. Aug. 9, 1928, New York, N.Y.

The son of French-born parents, Cousy didn't learn to speak English until he was seven years old. He fell in love with basketball when he was 11 and was a New York City all-star as a high school senior. At Holy Cross in Worcester, Massachusetts, he played for an NCAA championship team as a freshman in 1947 and was an All-American in his senior year.

Cousy won a game against Loyola of Chicago as a junior when he got the ball with ten seconds to play, drove the length of the court, did a behind-the-back dribble to elude a defender, and made a layup. He said afterward, "I had never even thought of such a maneuver. It just came the moment the situation forced me into it. It was one of those cases when necessity is the mother of invention. I was amazed at what I had done."

The Chicago Gears of the NBA held the rights to Cousy, but the franchise folded before he played a game. The names of three Chicago players, Cousy, Andy Phillip, and Max Zaslofsky, were put into a hat to be drawn by three NBA teams. The New York Knicks drew Zas-lofsky, the Philadelphia Warriors drew Phillip, and the Boston Celtics got Cousy by default.

He was fourth in the league in assists as a rookie in 1950–51. After finishing second in assists the following season, Cousy led the NBA in that category eight years in a row. His 28 assists on February 27, 1959, against Minneapolis is an NBA record, since tied by Guy Rodgers, and he twice had a record 19 assists in a playoff game.

Cousy led the Celtics' fast break as they became one of the highest-scoring teams in the NBA, but they had little success in the playoffs until Bill Russell joined them in 1956–57. Then they won six championships in seven years. Cousy was named the league's most valuable player in 1957, their first championship season.

Nicknamed the "Houdini of the Hardwood" and the "Mobile Magician," Cousy bewildered opponents with his dribbling and passing skills. Sportswriter Jimmy Cannon once described him as "a thrilling dwarf among the frustrated giants." His exceptional peripheral vision enabled him to spot open teammates and openings in the defense, and his larger than average hands enabled him to get the ball exactly where he wanted it to go.

When Cousy retired in 1963, he held an NBA record for most assists with 6,949, was second in games played with 917, and was fourth in scoring with 16,955 points. He averaged 18.4 points and 7.5 assists per game. In his 13 seasons, he was a first-team all-star ten times and on the second team twice. Cousy was one of the ten players named to the NBA's silver anniversary team in 1971.

After coaching Boston College to 114 wins, 38 losses, and 5 appearances in the National Invitation Tournament in six seasons, 1963–64 through 1968–69, Cousy took over the NBA's Cincinnati Royals, who became the Kansas City–Omaha Kings in 1972. He played briefly in seven games during the 1969–70 season, scoring just five points.

Cousy left coaching after the 1973–74

season. He is now a television commentator for Celtics games.

★ Basketball Hall of Fame

Coveleski, Stanley A. [Stanislaus Kowalewski]

BASEBALL
b. July 13, 1889, Shamokin, Pa.
d. March 20, 1984

Because he signed with the Philadelphia Athletics, who had an outstanding pitching staff, Coveleski was trapped in the minors for a number of seasons, though he did pitch briefly for Philadelphia in 1912.

Coveleski developed a spitball, which was then legal, while pitching in the Pacific Coast League in 1915. He joined the Cleveland Indians the following season and won 20 or more games four years in a row, from 1918 through 1921, leading the AL in shutouts with 9 in 1917 and in strikeouts with 133 in 1920, when Cleveland won the pennant. Coveleski won three games, giving up just two earned runs, as the Indians beat the Brooklyn Dodgers in the World Series, five games to two.

Despite a league-leading ERA of 2.76 in 1923, Coveleski was only 13–14. After going 15–16 the following season, he was traded to the Washington Senators. He had an outstanding year with them, leading the league in winning percentage with a 20–5 record and in ERA at 2.84. However, he lost two games in the World Series, which was won by Pittsburgh.

Coveleski went 14–11 in 1926 and was released by the Senators early in 1927. He returned briefly to the major leagues with the New York Yankees in 1928, then played semipro baseball for several years.

In 14 major league seasons, Coveleski had a 215–142 record with 38 shutouts and a 2.89 ERA. He struck out 991 hitters and walked 802 in 3,082 innings.

★ Baseball Hall of Fame

Cowan, Hector W.

FOOTBALL
b. July 12, 1863, Hobart, N.Y.
d. Oct. 19, 1941

Cowan played guard and tackle at Princeton in an era when linemen often carried the ball. The 5-foot-10, 189-pound Cowan carried it often enough to score 79 touchdowns during his five-year career.

He had never played football before November 1884, when the captain of the Princeton team spotted him among students watching practice from the sidelines and had him put on a uniform. Cowan didn't play in a game that year, but he became a starting guard in 1885 and played every minute of every game for three seasons.

There was no limit on eligibility in those days. Cowan graduated in 1888, enrolled in the Princeton Theological Seminary, and kept playing football for the school. As team captain, he put himself at right tackle and installed a system of calling plays by number, the first time that was done at a major college.

In his last season, 1889, Cowan played right tackle and was named to the first All-America team. Princeton ended Yale's 49-game winning streak with a 10–0 victory in which Cowan ran 30 yards to set up one touchdown and recovered a fumble to set up the second. (Touchdowns were then worth only four points, with the conversion adding another point.)

Cowan went to the University of North Carolina campus in the spring of 1889 to organize that school's first football team. He became a Presbyterian minister and served as part-time athletic director and football coach at the University of Kansas from 1894 through 1896. His teams there won 15 games, lost 7, and tied 1.

★ College Football Hall of Fame

Cowens, David W.

BASKETBALL
b. Oct. 25, 1948, Newport, Ky.

Because he was only 6-foot-9, many thought Cowens would have to switch from center to forward when he entered the NBA with the Boston Celtics in 1970. But, as a center, he was named the league's most valuable player for the 1972–73 season.

Cowens was an All-American as a senior at Florida State, where he scored 1,479 points and had 1,340 rebounds. His offensive forte was a soft, left-handed jump shot from the 15- to 20-foot range. When bigger defenders moved out to try to stop that shot, Cowens would drive to the basket.

The fiery 230-pound redhead played aggressively on offense and defense. He shared rookie of the year honors with Geoff Petrie in 1970–71, when he was seventh in the league in rebounding and led in fouls with 350, a Celtics record. Cowens helped lead the Celtics to championships in 1974 and 1976. He became the team's player-coach for the 1978–79 season, but he quit coaching after a 24–41 record and stayed with the team for one more season as a player.

After two years of retirement, Cowens played a final season with the Milwaukee Bucks in 1982–83. He scored 13,516 points in 766 regular season games, an average of 17.6 per game. He also had 10,444 rebounds and 2,910 assists.

★ Basketball Hall of Fame

Cowley, Bill (William M.)
HOCKEY
b. June 12, 1912, Bristol, P.Q.

One of hockey's great playmakers, Cowley led the National Hockey League in scoring in the 1940–41 season. He scored only 17 goals but added 45 assists for a total of 62 points in just 44 games. He also won the Hart Trophy as the league's most valuable player.

Cowley was the first NHL player to score more than 60 points in a season. In 1942–43, he became the first to score more than 70 points, with 27 goals and 45 assists.

After joining the NHL with the St. Louis Eagles in 1934, Cowley went to the Boston Bruins in 1935 and remained with them through the 1946–47 season. He was the leading scorer in the Stanley Cup playoffs in 1939 with 11 assists and 14 points, both records at the time. In the first round of the playoffs, Boston's Mel Hill scored three times to win

games in overtime, and Cowley assisted on all three goals.

Cowley played 13 seasons in the NHL, scoring 195 goals and 353 assists for a total of 548 points in 549 games. He had 13 goals and 33 assists in 64 playoff games.

★ Hockey Hall of Fame

Coy, Ted (Edward H.)
FOOTBALL
b. May 24, 1888, Andover, Mass.
d. Sept. 8, 1935

A 6-foot, 195-pound fullback, Coy was an All-American at Yale in 1908 and 1909. He was a very strong runner and also surprisingly elusive. As a sophomore in 1907, he had touchdown runs of 60, 80, and 105 yards, and a 70-yard run against Army was wiped out by a penalty.

Coy was a particular nemesis of Princeton. Yale trailed Princeton, 10–0, at the half in 1907, but Coy scored two second-half touchdowns that won the game for Yale, 12–10. In the 1908 game, Coy started at end. With Princeton leading, 6–0, he moved to fullback and scored two more touchdowns in an 11–6 victory.

Because of an appendectomy, Coy missed the first four games of the 1909 season. He entered the game against Army in the second half with orders not to carry the ball, and he threw a touchdown pass to win the game.

After scoring a touchdown and a field goal in Yale's 17–0 victory over Princeton, Coy starred as a kicker against Harvard. His long, high punts continually gave Yale good field position, and he kicked two field goals in an 8–0 win that closed out an undefeated season. During his three years, Yale won 26 games while losing only 1 and tying 2.

★ College Football Hall of Fame

Crabbe, Buster (Clarence L.)
SWIMMING
b. Feb. 7, 1910, Oakland, Calif.
d. April 23, 1983

Crabbe's family moved to Hawaii when he was young, and he learned to swim there. The great Duke Kahanamoku became his idol. He swam for the University of Southern California but won just one NCAA championship, the 440-yard freestyle in 1931.

He was much more successful in the AAU national championships, winning the outdoor 440-yard freestyle in 1929 and 1931; the 880-yard from 1928 through 1931; the 1-mile from 1927 through 1931; and the 300-meter individual medley from 1928 through 1931. Indoors, he won the 220-yard freestyle in 1930; the 1,500-meter in 1932; and the 300-yard individual medley from 1930 through 1932.

At the 1932 Olympics, Crabbe had a great duel in the 400-meter freestyle with Jean Taris of France, who held the world record. Taris led most of the way, but Crabbe caught him about 25 meters from the finish and won by inches with a time of 4:48.4 to Taris's 4:48.5.

He said afterward, "That one-tenth of a second changed my life. It was then that [the Hollywood producers] discovered latent histrionic abilities in me." He retired from swimming after the Olympics and starred in 175 movies. He was best known for his serial roles as Buck Rogers and Flash Gordon, though he also appeared in more than 60 Westerns.

Crabbe was also involved in a number of business interests, including his own swimming pool company and television programs on physical fitness.

Craig, Jim (James D.)
HOCKEY
b. May 31, 1957, North Easton, Mass.

One of the most memorable television shots of the 1980 Olympics was the sight of Craig, wrapped in the American flag, looking into the stands at the Olympic hockey rink and asking, "Where's my father?"

A goaltender, Craig was one of the stars of the U.S. hockey team that won a surprising gold medal at the games. His 39 saves kept the team in the semifinal game against Russia, which finally ended in a 4–3 U.S. victory on two third-period goals, and the team went on to beat Finland, 4–2, in the championship game.

An All-American goalie at Boston University, Craig signed with the NHL's Atlanta Flames after the Olympics and did some television commercials with his father to capitalize on his fame. But things went downhill after that.

Media pressure and repeated injuries kept Craig from playing in the NHL as he had in the Olympics, and he appeared in just 27 games with Atlanta, the Boston Bruins, and the Minnesota North Stars, compiling a 3.69 goals-against average, before leaving professional hockey in 1981.

Craig, Ralph C.
TRACK AND FIELD
b. June 21, 1889, Detroit, Mich.
d. July 21, 1972

In just three years of competition, Craig won five major sprint events, including two Olympic gold medals, and twice tied a world record.

Competing for the University of Michigan, Craig was the IC4A 200-meter champion in 1910 and 1911, both times tying the record of 21.2 seconds for the straightaway race. He was also the 100-meter champion in 1911, running a collegiate record 9.8 seconds.

Howard Drew edged him in the 100-meter trials but strained a tendon in a heat and couldn't run in the Olympic final. Craig won the event in 10.8 seconds and took the gold medal in the 200-meter with a time of 21.7 seconds.

He retired from competition after the Olympics. In 1948, Craig was an alternate on the Olympic yachting team, and he carried the U.S. flag at the opening ceremonies in London.

Craig, Roger T.
FOOTBALL
b. July 10, 1960, Davenport, Iowa

Craig joined the NFL's San Francisco 49ers as a second-round draft choice in 1983 out of the University of Nebraska and was a vital member of the San Francisco offense during three Super Bowl championship seasons.

The 6-foot, 219-pound running back

set an NFL record for a running back with 92 pass receptions in 1985, gaining 1,016 yards. He also became the first player in history to gain more than 1,000 yards receiving and more than 1,000 yards rushing in a single season.

Craig was named the National Football Conference's offensive player of the year by United Press International in 1988, when he rushed for 1,502 yards and caught 76 passes for 534 yards.

He scored three touchdowns, two on pass receptions, when San Francisco beat the Miami Dolphins, 38–16, in Super Bowl XIX after the 1984 season. In two other championship seasons, 1988 and 1989, Craig averaged 133 yards a game in total offense during the playoffs. An All-NFL choice in 1988, he played in four Pro Bowls.

The Los Angeles Raiders signed him as a free agent after the 1990 season, when Craig was slowed by injuries. After one year as a backup in Los Angeles, he went to the Minnesota Vikings in 1992.

Craig retired after the 1993 season with 8,189 yards on 1,991 carries, a 4.1 average, and 56 rushing touchdowns. He caught 566 passes for 4,911 yards, an 8.7 average, and 17 touchdowns.

Cravath, Gavvy (Clifford C.)

BASEBALL
b. March 23, 1881, Escondido, Calif.
d. May 23, 1963

Virtually unknown today, Cravath led the NL in home runs six times in a seven-season period. Because he played in the dead ball era, his figures don't sound impressive today, but when he retired, he was ranked fourth all-time in home runs.

The 5-foot-10, 185-pound Cravath joined the AL's Boston Red Sox in 1908, playing in 94 games, but he appeared in only 23 games with the Chicago White Sox and Washington Senators in 1909. After two years in the minor leagues, he went to the Philadelphia Phillies in the NL in 1912 and became the team's starting right fielder.

A fine defensive player, Cravath led league outfielders with 34 assists in 1912. He had his best year in 1913, batting .341 and leading the league with 179 hits, 19 home runs, 126 RBI, and a .568 slugging percentage. He was the home run leader again with 19 in 1914. The following season, Cravath led in runs with 89, home runs with 24, RBI with 115, walks with 88, and slugging with a .510 percentage.

Cravath won the home run title three more seasons, hitting 12 in 1917, 8 in 1918, and 12 in 1919, when he played in only 83 games. He retired after hitting just 1 home run in 46 games in 1920.

In 1,220 games, Cravath had a .287 average on 1,134 hits, including 232 doubles, 83 triples, and 119 home runs. He drove in 719 runs and scored 575.

Crawford, Samuel E.

BASEBALL
b. April 18, 1880, Wahoo, Nebr.
d. June 15, 1968

"Wahoo Sam" was long overshadowed by teammate Ty Cobb, but he was one of the premier power hitters during his era. An outstanding defensive center fielder, he teamed for many years with Cobb in right and Bobby Veach in left to form one of the best outfields in baseball history.

Crawford entered the major leagues with the Cincinnati NL team late in the 1899 season and got five hits in eight at-bats during a doubleheader on his first day with the team. He remained with Cincinnati for three more full seasons, leading the league in home runs with 16 in 1901 and in triples with 22 in 1902.

A left-hander, the 6-foot, 190-pound Crawford was a solid line-drive hitter who specialized in triples because his hits often sped through the gaps between outfielders. His career total of 309 triples is a major league record.

Crawford jumped to the Detroit AL team in 1903, when he hit .335 and had 25 triples to lead the league. Cobb joined the team in 1905. The Tigers won three consecutive pennants, from 1907 through 1909, but lost the World Series each year.

In 1908, Crawford became the only player ever to lead both leagues in home runs, though he hit only seven that season. The following year, he led in doubles with 35, and in 1910 he led in triples again with 19 and in RBI with 120.

He spent the rest of his major league career with Detroit, leading the AL in triples three years in a row, 1913 through 1915, and in RBI two years in a row, 1914 and 1915, but the Tigers never won another pennant while he and Cobb were there.

After playing just 61 games in 1917, Crawford played in the Pacific Coast League for four seasons, then retired as a player. He was an umpire in the PCL from 1935 through 1938.

In 2,517 major league games, Crawford had a .309 batting average. He collected 2,961 hits, including 458 doubles, 309 triples, and 97 home runs; scored 1,391 runs while driving in 1,525; and stole 366 bases.

★ Baseball Hall of Fame

Crenshaw, Ben D.

GOLF
b. Jan. 11, 1952, Austin, Tex.

At the University of Texas, Crenshaw won the NCAA golf championship in 1971 and 1973 and tied with his teammate, Tom Kite, in 1972. After graduating, he won the qualifying competition for the PGA tour by 12 strokes, shooting a 30 on the last 9 holes.

He won the Texas Open, his first tournament as a professional, and it seemed as if a great career was getting underway. But, while Crenshaw won a fair share of tournaments and a lot of money, the major events eluded him until he won the 1984 Masters.

Crenshaw had a good chance to win the 1975 U.S. Open until he hit his tee shot into the water on the 71st hole. Similarly, he had a chance to win the 1978 British Open, but took a double bogey on the 71st hole to fall out of contention. And he tied David Graham for the 1979 PGA championship only to lose on the 3rd hole of the playoff.

In his Masters victory, Crenshaw opened with a 67 to take the lead, then shot 72 and 70, falling 2 strokes back. He tied for the lead after 8 holes of the final round, then birdied 3 of the next 4 holes to take over for good. He said afterward, "This is really a sweet, sweet win. I don't think there will ever be a sweeter moment."

Through 1993, Crenshaw had earned $5,448,507 on the tour, ninth on the all-time list.

Crisler, Fritz (Herbert O.)

FOOTBALL
b. Jan. 12, 1899, near Earlville, Ill.
d. Aug. 19, 1982

Although he never played football before entering the University of Chicago in 1918, Crisler was named to Walter Eckersall's All-American team as an end in 1921. He also played baseball and basketball at the school and had a brief tryout as a pitcher with the Chicago White Sox after graduating.

Crisler's college coach, Amos Alonzo Stagg, nicknamed him after a celebrated violinist whose name was spelled differently but pronounced the same, Fritz Kreisler. Crisler assisted Stagg for eight seasons, then became head coach at the University of Minnesota in 1930.

After a 10–7–1 record in two seasons, Crisler went to Princeton in 1932. He was viewed with some suspicion because he was the first nonalumnus ever to coach at the school. But, inheriting a team that had won only 1 game in 1931, he produced 35 victories against only 9 losses and 5 ties in six seasons.

In 1938, Crisler took over at the University of Michigan, where he installed the single-wing spinner series with buck laterals that he'd developed at Princeton. Led by halfback Tom Harmon, Michigan won 19 games while losing 4 and tying 1 in Crisler's first three seasons.

Crisler developed the two-platoon system at Michigan in 1945. His team was loaded with freshmen because most older players were in the service, while Army was loaded with talent. In an attempt to stop Army's powerful offense, Crisler trained eight defensive specialists and took them out of the game when Michigan had the ball. After three quarters, the score was tied 7–7, but Army scored three fourth-quarter touchdowns to win, 28–7.

Before the season ended, Michigan was platooning all 11 players. In 1946, most major colleges adopted the idea.

Crisler retired as a coach after his 1947 team won all nine regular season games and beat Southern California, 49–0, in the Rose Bowl. He remained as athletic director until 1968. In ten seasons at Michigan, his teams won 71 games, lost 16, and tied 3. His overall record was 116–32–9, a .768 winning percentage.
★ College Football Hall of Fame

Cromwell, Cy (Seymour L. II)

ROWING
b. Feb. 17, 1934, New York, N.Y.
d. May 2, 1977

Cromwell graduated from Princeton University in 1956 and did graduate work at both Harvard and the Massachusetts Institute of Technology. He won the national ¼-mile single sculls from 1961 through 1964, the 1½-mile in 1961 and 1962. After winning the Diamond Sculls at the Henley Regatta in 1964, Cromwell teamed with James Storm to take an Olympic silver medal in the double sculls event.

A naval architect, he helped design the 12-meter yacht *Nefertiti* and was one of her crew when she took part in the 1964 America's Cup trials. However, she wasn't chosen to defend.

Cromwell died of cancer.

Cromwell, Dean B.

TRACK AND FIELD
b. Sept. 29, 1879, Turner, Oreg.
d. Aug. 3, 1962

Cromwell played baseball and football and participated in track at Occidental College in California. He graduated in 1902 and then worked for the telephone company until 1909, when the University of Southern California hired him as football and track coach.

He compiled a 21–8–6 record in six seasons of football, but he made his mark as a track coach. Cromwell spent 39 years at USC, and his teams won 12 NCAA championships, including 9 in a row, from 1935 through 1943. They also won 9 IC4A titles. From 1930 through 1948, USC lost only three dual meets.

USC track athletes won gold medals every Olympic year from 1912 through 1948. They won 33 individual events in the NCAA championships, 39 in the IC4A, and 38 in the AAU nationals. In the process, they set 14 individual world records.

Cromwell retired in 1948 after coaching the U.S. Olympic team to 10 gold medals.
★ National Track & Field Hall of Fame

Cronin, Joseph E.

BASEBALL
b. Oct. 12, 1906, San Francisco, Calif.
d. Sept. 7, 1984

Cronin signed his first professional contract with the NL's Pittsburgh Pirates in 1925. He spent parts of the 1926 and 1927 seasons with Pittsburgh, but appeared in only 105 games, many of them as a pinch hitter, before being sold to the Kansas City team in the American Association.

Kansas City in turn sold him to the Washington Senators midway through the 1928 season. Cronin took over as the team's starting shortstop in 1929, and he became a star the following year, when he was named the AL's most valuable player. He hit .346 with 41 doubles, 127 runs scored, and 126 RBI.

The 6-foot, 180-pound Cronin, a right-hander, led the league in triples with 18 in 1932, when he batted .318 and was also the best fielding shortstop in the AL. He then became playing manager and guided the Senators to their last pennant in 1933. He led the league in doubles with 45 that season and again had the best fielding percentage among shortstops.

Washington lost the World Series to the New York Giants, then fell all the way to seventh place in 1934. The team also lost money, and Cronin was sent to the Boston Red Sox for $250,000 and another player.

Cronin played for the Red Sox until 1945, when he broke a leg early in the season, and he managed them through

1947. He led the league in doubles again with 51 in 1936, and as a part-time player in 1943, he had a record 5 pinch-hit home runs.

The Red Sox won the 1946 AL pennant but lost to St. Louis in the World Series. In 1948, Cronin became the team's general manager, and he was appointed president of the American League in 1959. He held that position until January 1974, when he became the league chairman, an honorary position.

★ Baseball Hall of Fame

Crow, John David
FOOTBALL
b. July 8, 1935, Marion, La.

A 6-foot-2, 218-pound running back at Texas A & M University, Crow was a consensus All-American and winner of the Heisman Trophy as the nation's best college player in 1957. In his three years as a starter, he carried the ball 296 times for 1,455 yards, a 4.9 average, and scored 19 touchdowns.

A first-round draft choice of the NFL's Chicago Cardinals in 1958, Crow was big enough to run between the tackles and fast and shifty enough to be a dangerous open-field runner. In his first regular season game as a professional, he ran 83 yards for a touchdown.

The Cardinals moved to St. Louis for the 1960 season, when Crow led the NFL in rushing average, with 5.9 yards per attempt. He was traded to the San Francisco 49ers in 1965 and retired after the 1968 season. Crow played in four Pro Bowls.

In his 11 years as a professional, Crow gained 4,963 yards on 1,157 attempts, a 4.3 average, and scored 38 touchdowns. He had 258 pass receptions for 3,699 yards, a 14.3 average, and 35 touchdowns.

Crow was football coach and athletic director at Northeast Louisiana University from 1975 through 1980, compiling a 20–34–1 record.

★ College Football Hall of Fame

Crowley, Jim (James H.)
FOOTBALL
b. Sept. 10, 1902, Chicago, Ill.
d. Jan. 15, 1986

The right halfback in Notre Dame's famous "Four Horsemen" backfield, Crowley played high school football in Green Bay, where his coach was "Curly" Lambeau, founder and long-time coach of the Packers. Crowley entered Notre Dame in 1921. He led the team in scoring in 1924, when he was named an All-American. During his three years as a starter, he averaged 6.3 yards per rushing attempt.

Nicknamed "Sleepy Jim" by Knute Rockne because of his heavy-lidded eyes, Crowley had a reputation for a quick and often caustic wit. Rockne, a native of Norway, once criticized him for missing an assignment during practice and asked rhetorically, "What's dumber than a dumb Irishman?" Crowley responded, "A smart Norwegian."

Crowley played pro football briefly with Green Bay and the Providence Steamroller in 1925. He became head coach at Michigan State in 1929 and had a 22–8–3 record in four seasons there, then went to Fordham in 1933.

Fordham had became a major football school under Frank Cavanaugh, and Crowley kept the tradition going. His 1937 team was undefeated but tied once in eight games. His last two teams both went to major bowls, losing to Texas A & M, 13–12, in the 1941 Cotton Bowl and defeating Missouri, 2–0, in the 1942 Sugar Bowl.

Crowley was the first commissioner of the All-America Football Conference when it was organized in 1945, but he resigned in 1947 to become part owner and co-coach of the league's Chicago Rockets. He left the team after winning only 1 of 14 games that season.

As a college coach, Crowley had a record of 78 wins, 21 losses, and 10 ties, a .761 winning percentage.

★ College Football Hall of Fame

Crum, Denny (Denzil E.)
BASKETBALL
b. March 2, 1937, San Fernando, Calif.

After attending Pierce Junior College, Crum played basketball for two years at UCLA. In 1959, he became a graduate assistant coach at the school and then returned to Pierce as head coach in 1961. His teams had an 84–40 record in eight seasons there.

Crum became John Wooden's assistant and chief recruiter at UCLA in 1968. He was also generally considered heir apparent to the head coaching job when Wooden retired, but in 1971 Crum became head coach at the University of Louisville.

Louisville has been a national power throughout Crum's tenure. He achieved his 300th victory in the second game of his thirteenth season at the school, a mark surpassed only by Everett Case at North Carolina State. Although he uses the zone press and fast break style he learned at UCLA, Crum generally allows his players more freedom to operate on their own.

Through the 1993–94 season, Crum had a 546–198 record for a .734 winning percentage. He ranks 26th all-time in victories and 21st in percentage.

Csonka, Larry (Lawrence R.)

FOOTBALL
b. Dec. 25, 1946, Stow, Ohio

An All-American fullback at Syracuse University in 1967, the 6-foot-3, 235-pound Csonka was nicknamed the "Lawnmower" because of his rugged, low-to-the-ground running style. With the Miami Dolphin teams that won three American Football Conference championships and two Super Bowls in the early 1970s, he was an integral part of the ball-control offense both as a punishing inside runner and as a blocker for halfbacks Jim Kiick and "Mercury" Morris.

Csonka put up pretty good numbers in his first three seasons with Miami, 1968 through 1970, then had three straight seasons of more than 1,000 yards rushing. He led the NFL with a 5.4-yard average in 1971, when he gained 1,051 yards.

The Dolphins won all 17 of their games in 1972, including the Super Bowl. Csonka and Morris became the first teammates ever to gain more than 1,000 yards apiece that season, and

Csonka led all rushers with 112 yards on 15 carries, a 7.5-yard average, in Miami's 14–7 win over the Washington Redskins in the Super Bowl.

He was named the game's most valuable player when the Dolphins beat the Minnesota Vikings in the Super Bowl the following year. He rushed for a Super Bowl record 145 yards on 33 carries and scored 2 touchdowns. Minnesota quarterback Fran Tarkenton said afterward, "In all my years, I've never seen any fullback play any better than he did."

Csonka, Kiick, and wide receiver Paul Warfield left the Dolphins to play for the Memphis Southmen in the World Football League in 1975, but a foot injury limited Csonka to just 99 carries that season. He returned to the NFL with the New York Giants from 1976 through 1978, but the foot still bothered him, and his career seemed to be at an end when he carried the ball only 91 times in his final season with the Giants.

However, Csonka returned to the Dolphins for one last season in 1979 and had a fine year, gaining 837 yards on 220 carries and scoring 12 touchdowns.

In his 11 AFL/NFL seasons, he gained 8,081 yards on 1,891 carries, a 4.3 average, and scored 64 touchdowns. He also caught 106 passes for 820 yards, a 7.7 average, and 4 touchdowns.

★ College Football Hall of Fame; Pro Football Hall of Fame

Cuellar, Mike (Miguel A.)

BASEBALL
b. May 8, 1937, Las Villas, Cuba

A clever left-handed pitcher with an excellent change-up, Cuellar played briefly with the NL's Cincinnati Reds in 1959, the St. Louis Cardinals in 1964, and the Houston Astros in 1965 before becoming a regular starter with Houston in 1966.

He was traded to the AL's Baltimore Orioles in 1969, when he tied with Detroit's Denny McLain for the league's Cy Young Award. Cuellar had a 23–11 record with 5 shutouts and a 2.38 ERA. He led the league in victories with a 24–8 record, winning percentage with .750, and complete games with 21 in 1970.

After going 20–9, 18–12, and 18–13 over the next three seasons, Cuellar led the league with a .688 winning percentage on a 22–10 record in 1974. Cuellar slipped to 14–12 in 1975 and 4–13 in 1976. He retired after appearing in just two games with the California Angels the following season.

Cumiskey, Frank J.
GYMNASTICS
b. Sept. 6, 1912, W. New York, N.J.

Cumiskey won 22 national gymnastics titles and was on three U.S. Olympic teams over a 16-year period. He began competition as a student at New York University and was a member of the Olympic team that won a silver medal for combined exercises in 1932, when he finished sixth in the pommel horse (now known as the side horse).

He won national championships in the all-around in 1934, 1936, 1945, 1946, and 1947; in the pommel horse in 1932, 1936, 1937, 1944, 1945, and 1947; in the horizontal bars in 1934, 1936, 1944, 1945, 1946, and 1948; in the parallel bars in 1944 and 1945; in the floor exercise in 1935; and in vaulting in 1945.

Cumiskey was not only a competitor in the 1948 Olympics, he served as team manager and was given the honor of accompanying the color guard as part of the opening ceremonies.

The long-time coach of the Swiss Turnverein of Hudson County, New Jersey, Cumiskey was also active in the administration of the sport as a judge and served as technical director of the U.S. Gymnastics Federation and technical director and president of the National Gymnastics Judges Association.

In addition to a manual for judges, Cumiskey wrote a *History of Gymnastics* and *Who's Who in Gymnastics.*

Cummings, Candy (William A.)
BASEBALL
b. Oct. 17, 1848, Ware, Mass.
d. May 16, 1924

Despite a losing record as a major league pitcher, Cummings is in the Hall of Fame because he is known as the inventor of the curve ball. That claim has occasionally been disputed, but it is now generally accepted by baseball historians.

Only 5-foot-9 and 120 pounds, Cummings supposedly got the idea for a new pitch when he threw a clamshell, saw it curve, and decided to try doing it with a baseball. After hours of practice, he perfected the pitch.

His most impressive performances came before the major leagues were established. Cummings played for the Brooklyn Excelsiors, one of the best amateur teams of the day, in 1866 and 1867. He soon won the nickname "Candy" which meant "the best" in the vernacular of the period.

In 1868, he joined the Brooklyn Stars, who called themselves the "championship team of the United States and Canada." Cummings beat the New York Mutuals in 1868 and 1871, and the Mutuals signed him in 1872. It was Cummings's debut as a professional.

The Mutuals belonged to the National Association, the first truly professional league, although it is not considered a major league for statistical purposes. Cummings went 33–20 and led the league with three shutouts in his first season. He was the shutout leader again with seven in 1875, when he pitched for Hartford. In four seasons, he won 124 games and lost 72.

The association was replaced by the NL in 1876. Cummings, still with Hartford, had a 16–8 record that season, but he was only 5–14 with Cincinnati in 1877. He later played briefly with semi-pro and amateur teams, but poor health forced him to give up the sport after 1884.

★ Baseball Hall of Fame

Cunningham, Billy (William J.)
BASKETBALL
b. June 3, 1943, Brooklyn, N.Y.

Known as the "Kangaroo Kid" because of his great jumping ability, Cunningham starred at the University of North Carolina and was named to a few All-American teams in 1965, though he was generally overshadowed by Bill Bradley and Rick Barry. He scored 1,709 points and had 1,062 rebounds in his college career.

The 6-foot-7, 220-pound forward was the first draft choice of the Philadelphia 76ers, who won the NBA championship in his second season, 1966–67. Cunningham jumped to the Carolina Cougars of the American Basketball Association in 1972 and was the league's player of the year in his first season there.

He returned to the 76ers in 1974 and was forced to retire after the 1975–76 season with a knee injury. He became coach of the team in 1977, remaining through 1984–85. In his 11 seasons, he scored 16,310 points, averaging 21.2 a game, and had 7,981 rebounds. He was named a first-team all-star three years in a row, from 1969 to 1971.

As a coach, Cunningham had 454 regular season victories against only 196 losses. His teams won 66 playoff games and lost 29.

★ Basketball Hall of Fame

Cunningham, Glenn V.

TRACK AND FIELD
b. Aug. 4, 1909, Atlanta, Kans.
d. March 10, 1988

When he was six, Glenn and his older brother Floyd had the chore of starting a fire in the schoolhouse stove every cold morning. One February morning in 1916, the kerosene container had accidentally been filled with gasoline. The stove exploded. Floyd was killed, and Glenn's legs were so badly burned it was feared he would never walk again.

After several weeks in bed, he was able to walk on crutches. Finally, he got rid of the crutches, but as he said later, "It hurt like thunder to walk, but it didn't hurt at all when I ran. So for five or six years, about all I did was run."

Cunningham became a miler in high school and set an interscholastic record of 4:24.7 in his last race. He entered the University of Kansas in 1931 and won the NCAA 1,500-meter championships in 1932.

He was given the Sullivan Award as the nation's outstanding amateur athlete in 1933, when he won the NCAA mile, the AAU 800- and 1,500-meter runs, and set a world record of 4:06.7 for the mile in the Princeton Invitational Meet.

The AAU 1,500-meter champion from 1935 through 1938, Cunningham finished fourth in the 1932 Olympic event. In 1936, he put on a burst of speed in the third lap to try to break away from the field, but took a silver medal behind New Zealand's Jack Lovelock, who ran a world record 3:47.8.

In 1938, Dartmouth University invited Cunningham to try for a world record on a new, high-banked indoor track. Paced by six Dartmouth runners, he turned in an incredible 4:04.4, which would have been the indoor world record until 1955. However, the mark wasn't recognized because it wasn't run in sanctioned competition.

Because of circulation problems caused by his childhood accident, Cunningham needed nearly an hour to prepare for a race. He first had to massage his legs, and he then required a long warmup period. Despite the fact that smoke bothered him, he turned in outstanding performances at Madison Square Garden, where he won 22 indoor miles.

Cunningham, who had a master's degree from the University of Iowa and a doctorate from New York University, retired from competition in 1940 and for four years was director of physical education at Cornell College in Iowa.

After spending two years in the Navy, Cunningham and his wife opened the Glenn Cunningham Youth Ranch in Kansas, where they helped to raise about 10,000 underprivileged children. A lay preacher, Cunningham periodically went on lecture tours to raise money for the ranch.

★ National Track & Field Hall of Fame

Cunningham, Randall

FOOTBALL
b. March 27, 1963, Santa Barbara, Calif.

Perhaps the best athlete ever to play quarterback in the NFL, Cunningham was chosen out of the University of Nevada–Las Vegas in the second round of the 1985 NFL draft by the Philadelphia Eagles.

After playing as a backup in 1985, he became the starter in his second season. The 6-foot-4, 205-pound Cunningham is a dangerous runner, the all-time leading ground gainer among quarterbacks, and a dangerous passer when scrambling out of the pocket, but he has been criticized at times for being too willing to run.

Cunningham passed for 3,400 or more yards in three straight seasons, 1988 through 1990, and had high touchdown to interception ratios all three years. He suffered a serious knee injury in the first 1991 regular season game and missed the rest of the season, and in 1992 he was benched for a game after a period of ineffectiveness, though he ended up completing more than 60 percent of his passes for the season.

After leading the Eagles to victories in their first four games of 1993, Cunningham broke his left leg early in the fifth game and missed the rest of the season. He returned in 1994 but was benched late in the year because of inconsistency.

Through 1993, Cunningham had completed 1,540 of 2,751 attempts for 19,043 yards and 131 touchdowns. He had also rushed 573 times for 3,986 yards, a 7.0 average, and 28 touchdowns.

Curtis, Ann E. (Mrs. Cuneo)
SWIMMING
b. March 6, 1926, Rio Vista, Calif.

One of the most popular woman athletes of her time, Curtis was taught to swim by nuns at the Ursuline Convent School in Santa Rosa, California. She then trained with Charlie Sava, coach of the Crystal Plunge Club of San Francisco.

She won the AAU girls' freestyle championship in 1937, but was held out of major seniors competition until 1943. Curtis dominated the freestyle events for the next six years. She was the AAU national outdoor champion in the 100-meter in 1944, 1945, 1947, and 1948; the 400-meter and 800-meter from 1943 through 1948; and the 1-mile in 1944 and 1946. She also swam on the cham-

pion 880-yard freestyle relay team from 1945 through 1948.

Indoors, Curtis won the 100-yard freestyle in 1945 and 1947; the 220-yard and 440-yard from 1944 through 1948. She was a member of the 300-yard medley relay team in 1945 and 1947 and the 400-yard freestyle relay team in 1945, 1947, and 1948. Her total of 31 national championships was a record for a woman swimmer until Tracy Caulkins broke it in 1981.

Curtis in 1944 became the first woman and the first swimmer of either sex to win the Sullivan Award as the nation's outstanding amateur athlete. She was also named Associated Press female athlete of the year.

World War II canceled the 1944 Olympic Games, but Curtis competed in 1948, winning a gold medal in the 400-meter freestyle and a silver in the 100-meter. She swam a great anchor leg to bring the U.S. a gold in the 4 x 100-meter freestyle relay. Curtis retired after the Olympics and opened a swimming school.

★ International Women's Sports Hall of Fame

Curtis, William B.
TRACK AND FIELD
b. Jan. 17 1837, Salisbury, Vt.
d. July 1, 1900

A founder of the New York Athletic Club in 1868, Curtis won the national hammer throw in 1876, 1878, and 1880, and he was the 56-pound weight throw champion in 1878.

Curtis has sometimes been called "the father of American amateurism" because he cowrote the first formal definition of professionalism. In 1872, the so-called "Schuylkill Navy," an organization of rowing clubs from the Philadelphia area, banned many rowers from its regatta on the grounds that they were professionals because they made bets on their races, a common practice at the time.

A major controversy resulted, and Curtis was asked to study the problem with James Watson, a Philadelphia newspaperman. They agreed that a professional is anyone who competes in the hope of winning any kind of cash prize. That definition was essentially accepted later by the Amateur Athletic Union and most other sports governing bodies.

Curtis died in a blizzard while climbing Mount Washington in New Hampshire with a friend.

★ National Track & Field Hall of Fame

Cuyler, Kiki (Hazen S.)

BASEBALL
b. Aug. 30, 1899, Harrisville, Mich.
d. Feb. 11, 1950

After briefly attending the U.S. Military Academy, Cuyler returned to Michigan and began playing minor league baseball in 1920. He was purchased by the NL's Pittsburgh Pirates after the 1921 season but spent most of 1922 and 1923 in the minors.

Cuyler became Pittsburgh's starting left fielder in 1924 and batted .354, fourth in the league. He moved to right field the following season and helped lead the Pirates to a pennant, leading the league in triples with 26 and runs scored with 144 while batting .357.

In the seventh game of the World Series against Washington, Cuyler made an outstanding catch to keep the game close, then hit a two-run double in the eighth inning to give Pittsburgh a 9–7 victory and the world championship.

After hitting .321 and leading the league with 35 stolen bases and 113 runs scored in 1926, Cuyler fell out of favor with manager Donie Bush. Moved to center field, a position he didn't like, and placed second in the batting order when he preferred to hit third, Cuyler sulked. He was fined $50 and removed from a game after failing to slide into second base in an August game, and he was benched for the rest of the season. He didn't make a single appearance in the World Series, when the Pirates lost to the New York Yankees in four straight games.

Cuyler was traded to the Chicago Cubs after the season. He led the league in stolen bases again in 1928, and his .360 average and league-leading 43 stolen bases helped the Cubs beat out the

Pirates for the 1929 pennant. They lost the World Series in five games to the Philadelphia Athletics.

He batted .355 and won his fourth stolen base title with 37 in 1930, and he had a .330 average in 1931. Although he slipped to .291, the Cubs won the 1932 NL pennant but were swept by the Yankees in the World Series.

An injury sidelined Cuyler for a large part of the 1933 season. He came back to hit .338 in 1934 but was released by the Cubs in July of the following year. He finished the season with Cincinnati.

Cuyler had one more good season, batting .326 in 1936. He was released by Cincinnati after hitting only .271 in 1937, and he finished his career as a part-time outfielder with the Brooklyn Dodgers in 1938.

After managing in the minor leagues for several years, Cuyler became a major league coach. He was with the Boston Red Sox when he died of a heart attack shortly before spring training began in 1950.

A right-hander, the 5-foot-11, 180-pound Cuyler was an outstanding defensive player, known for his strong throwing arm, as well as a fine hitter. In 1,879 games, he collected 2,299 hits, including 394 doubles, 157 triples, and 128 home runs. He scored 1,295 runs, drove in 1,065 runs, and stole 328 bases. His career average was .321.

★ Baseball Hall of Fame

Cyr, Louis

WEIGHTLIFTING
b. Oct. 11, 1863, St. Cyprien de Napierville, P.Q.
d. Nov. 10, 1912

Before he became a strongman, Cyr was a policeman in Montreal. After he disarmed two knife-wielding thugs and carried them to the police station, one under each arm, to be booked, he got considerable publicity.

Richard Kyle Fox, publisher of the *National Police Gazette,* then began managing Cyr, who was billed as "The Strongest Man in the World." He went on vaudeville and barnstorming tours, offering to pay $5,000 to anyone who could duplicate or surpass any of his weightlifting feats. No one ever won the prize.

Although he never formally competed, Cyr did a great deal to popularize weightlifting with his exploits. He once lifted a platform carrying 18 men, a total of 4,300 pounds, on his back. He set a record in 1896 by lifting a dumbbell of 258 pounds with his right hand and one of 254 pounds with his left for a total of 512 pounds. The same year, Cyr picked up a weight of $552\frac{1}{2}$ pounds using just the middle finger of his right hand.

Cyr retired in 1906 and died six years later of Bright's disease, a kidney ailment.

★ ★ D ★ ★

Daly, Charles D.

FOOTBALL
b. Oct. 31, 1880, Roxbury, Mass.
d. Feb. 12, 1959

Daly holds the distinction of being the only man to play for a Harvard team that beat Yale and an Army team that beat Navy, and he was an All-American quarterback at both schools. The 5-foot-9, 154-pound Daly was a versatile player who could run, kick, and play defense with the best in the game.

He entered Harvard in 1897 and became a starter as a sophomore. He was named an All-American three years in a row, 1898, 1899, and 1900. While he started at quarterback, Harvard won 32 consecutive games. An injured knee forced him out of his last game, against Yale, and Harvard lost, 28–0.

In 1901, Daly was appointed to the U.S. Military Academy at West Point. There was no limit on eligibility at that time, and Daly became Army's starting quarterback. Once again, he was named to most All-American teams. He scored all of Army's points in an 11–5 win over Navy by running back a kickoff 98 yards for a touchdown, kicking the conversion, and adding a 35-yard field goal.

There was much public criticism of his continuing to play, so Daly quit in 1902. He was persuaded to rejoin the team late in the season to get ready for the Navy game, in which he led Army to a 22–8 victory. Despite the fact that he appeared in only a few games, he was named third string on Walter Camp's All-American team.

Daly coached Army from 1913 through 1916, producing unbeaten teams in 1914 and 1916. After serving in World War I, he returned to the school for four more seasons and left coaching after having another unbeaten team in 1922. His overall record was 58 wins, 13 losses, and 3 ties.

★ College Football Hall of Fame

Daly, Chuck (Charles J.)

BASKETBALL
b. July 20, 1930, St. Mary's, Pa.

After playing basketball at St. Bonaventure University and Bloomsburg, PA, State College, Daly was a high school coach for seven years, then became an assistant at Duke University. He spent two years as head coach at Boston College, compiling a 26–24 record, before going to the University of Pennsylvania in 1971. Daly guided Penn to four Ivy League championships and two second-place finishes in six years.

In 1978, Daly joined the NBA's Philadelphia 76ers as an assistant coach. During the 1981 season, he was hired as head coach by the Cleveland Cavaliers, but had just a 9–32 record and was fired before the season ended. He then returned to the 76ers as a broadcaster.

The Detroit Pistons of the NBA hired Daly in 1983. The Pistons got into the playoffs every year he was there and reached the NBA finals three years in a row, winning two consecutive championships, in 1989 and 1990.

Daly was coach of the U.S. "Dream Team" that swept to an easy gold medal at the 1992 Olympics. He took over the NBA's New Jersey Nets that fall and had an 88-76 record in his first two seasons with that team.

Dancer, Stanley F.

HARNESS RACING
b. July 25, 1927, Edinburg, N.J.

Dancer entered harness racing as a groom in 1946 and drove a few winners for other owners before buying the eight-year-old gelding Candor in 1948 for $300. He began driving Candor at Roosevelt Raceway in 1949. When Yonkers Raceway opened in 1951, Dancer was the track's top driver.

During the 1960s, Dancer began racing on the Grand Circuit. He was the sport's top money-winning driver in 1961, 1962, 1964, and 1966, and he was named driver of the year in 1968.

He is the only driver to win two trotting triple crowns, with Nevele Pride in 1968 and Super Bowl in 1972, and he won the pacing triple crown with Most Happy Fella in 1970. Dancer is also the only driver to have won the Yonkers Trot six times, in 1959, 1965, 1968, 1971, 1972, and 1975; the Cane Pace/Futurity four times, in 1964, 1970, 1971, and 1976; and the Hambletonian five times, in 1974, 1976, 1977, 1980, and 1983.

He was pointing his own horse, Dancer's Crown, toward the 1983 Hambletonian, but the trotter died of intestinal problems three weeks before the race. Dancer was persuaded to drive Norman Woolworth's filly, Duenna, and won the race in straight heats.

His greatest horse was probably Nevele Pride, who won 26 of 29 starts in 1967 and was Harness Horse of the Year three times in a row, 1967 through 1969. Dancer also trained and drove Su Mac Lad, the 1962 Horse of the Year and the only trotter to win twice in two minutes or less on a half-mile track. Dancer's Noble Victory was the Aged Trotter of the Year in 1966, when he trotted the fastest race mile in history, a 1:55⅗ at DuQuoin, Illinois.

★ Hall of Fame of the Trotter

Dandridge, Raymond ("Hooks")

BASEBALL
b. Aug. 31, 1913, Richmond, Va.
d. Feb. 13, 1994

Considered black baseball's finest third baseman, Dandridge began his professional career with the Detroit Stars in 1933 and went to the Newark Dodgers in 1934. He spent most of his career with the Dodgers and the Newark Eagles, although he later played in the Mexican League for several seasons.

In 1949, Dandridge and pitcher Dave Barnhill were the first black players signed by the Minneapolis Millers in the AAA American Association. He batted .362 that season and .311 in 1950, when he was named the league's most valuable player. After hitting .324 with Minneapolis in 1951, he ended his playing career with two seasons in the Pacific Coast League.

Cum Posey, a long-time observer of black baseball, said of him, "There simply never was a smoother functioning master at third base than Dandridge, and he can hit that apple, too." After retiring, Dandridge worked as an East Coast scout for the San Francisco Giants.

★ Baseball Hall of Fame

Daniel, Beth (Elizabeth A.)

GOLF
b. Oct. 14, 1956, Charleston, S.C.

Daniel won consecutive U.S. Women's Amateur championships, in 1975 and 1976, while a student at Furman. She joined the LPGA tour shortly after graduating and was named rookie of the year in 1979. She was named LPGA player of the year in 1980, when she won four tournaments and more than $200,000 to lead the tour in winnings, and she led in winnings again in 1981.

Back problems hampered her swing and her play for several years, and she missed part of the 1988 season with mononucleosis, but came back strong, finishing in the top ten in 9 of the 18 tournaments she entered. She tied with Juli Inkster in the Atlantic City Classic, but lost on the first hole of a sudden death playoff.

Daniel won her first major tournament, the LPGA championship, in 1990, when she was named Associated Press female athlete of the year.

The 5-foot-11 Daniel generates tremendous power with a smooth, natural swing, and can hit the ball both high and far. She also has an excellent short game. Through 1994, she had 31 tournament victories, tenth on the all-time list, and $4,384,353 in earnings, to rank third all-time.

Daniels, Charles M.

SWIMMING
b. March 24, 1885
d. Aug. 8, 1973

One of the most important figures in the early history of competitive swimming, Daniels studied the new "Australian crawl" after it had been introduced to the United States in 1903. In the crawl, swimmers used a hand-over-hand stroke with a flutter kick, the legs moving up and down, alternately, in the water.

Daniels improved the stroke by emphasizing use of the full leg, from the hips down, and synchronizing the kick with the arm action, using six kicks per two-arm cycle. The "American crawl," as the new stroke became known, is still used by all freestyle swimmers, with some minor modifications.

He won eight Olympic medals, including five golds. He was the 1904 Olympic champion in the 220- and 440-yard freestyles and also swam on the champion 4 x 50-yard freestyle relay team. He won the Olympic 100-meter freestyle in 1906 and 1908, was the silver medalist in the 1908 100-meter, and won bronze medals in the 50-yard freestyle in 1904 and as a member of the 4 x 200-meter relay team in 1908.

From 1904 through 1911, Daniels won 31 AAU national championships, and at one time he held the world records at every distance from 25 yards to 1 mile. In 1905, he set 14 world records in one four-day period.

★ Olympic Hall of Fame

Danowski, Edward F.

FOOTBALL
b. Sept. 30, 1911, Jamesport, N.Y.

Danowski played tailback in the Notre Dame box formation at Fordham University and joined the NFL's New York Giants after graduating in 1934. He played behind Harry Newman most of the season but took over for the last three games after Newman suffered two broken vertebrae on November 18.

The 1934 NFL championship game was played on an icy field at the Polo Grounds. Trailing 10–3, the Giants came out wearing sneakers for better traction in the second half. They fell behind, 13–3, in the third quarter but scored 27 fourth quarter points to win, 30–13. Danowski threw a 28-yard touchdown pass and ran 6 yards for another touchdown.

As the starter in 1935, Danowski passed for 795 yards and 11 touchdowns and rushed for 335 yards. He threw a 42-yard touchdown pass for the team's only score in a 26–7 loss to the Detroit Lions in the championship game.

The Giants won the 1938 championship by beating the Green Bay Packers, 23–17, with Danowski throwing touchdown passes of 20 and 23 yards.

The 6-foot-1, 198-pound Danowski became a backup in 1939 and retired after that season. However, he returned to the Giants in 1941 before entering the service. Danowski took over as head coach at Fordham in 1946 and had a 29–44–3 record in nine seasons.

In his NFL career, Danowski completed 311 of 645 passes for 3,867 yards and 39 touchdowns. He rushed 455 times for 1,232 yards and 4 touchdowns.

Dantley, Adrian D.

BASKETBALL
b. Feb. 28, 1955, Washington, D.C.

A consensus All-American forward in his sophomore and junior years at Notre Dame, Dantley scored 2,223 points, second in school history only to Austin Carr. He was named player of the year by the U.S. Basketball Writers Association in 1976.

Dantley led the gold medal U.S.

Olympic team in scoring with 19.3 points per game. Passing up his senior year at Notre Dame, he then joined the Buffalo Braves of the NBA. He was named rookie of the year for the 1976–77 season, when he averaged 20.3 points a game.

Buffalo traded Dantley to the Indiana Pacers, who sent him to the Los Angeles Lakers in midseason. After a season and a half with Los Angeles, he was traded again, this time to the Utah Jazz. With Utah, Dantley twice led the NBA in scoring, averaging 30.7 points per game in 1980–81 and 30.6 in 1983–84. He also averaged more than 30 points a game in 1981–82 and 1982–83 but lost the scoring title to George Gervin and Alex English, respectively.

A good friend of Detroit Piston star Isiah Thomas, Dantley joined the Pistons in 1986. He became Detroit's sixth man, coming off the bench to add scoring punch. As a result, his per-game averages declined, but he led the team with 20.0 points a game in 1987–88.

Dantley was traded to the Dallas Mavericks during the 1989–90 season, and he played just ten games with the Milwaukee Bucks in 1990–91. He played professional basketball in Italy in 1991–92.

In 955 NBA games, the 6-foot-5, 210-pound Dantley scored 23,177 points, an average of 24.3 per game. He had 5,455 rebounds and 2,830 assists.

Daubert, Jake (Jacob E.)

BASEBALL
b. April 7, 1884, Shamokin, Pa.
d. Oct. 9, 1924

A left-handed first baseman, Daubert won two consecutive NL batting titles, hitting .350 in 1913 and .329 in 1914, and he won the Chalmers Award as the NL's most valuable player in 1913. The 5-foot-11, 160-pounder was unusually fast for a first baseman. He led the NL in triples with 15 in 1918 and 22 in 1922 and had more than 20 stolen bases six times.

Daubert joined the Brooklyn Robins in 1910 and played with them through 1918, then was traded to Cincinnati. He retired after the 1924 season. In 2,014 games, he had 2,326 hits and a .303 batting average, with 250 doubles, 165 triples, and 56 home runs. He stole 251 bases, scored 1,117 runs, and had 722 RBI.

Daugherty, Duffy (Hugh Duffy)

FOOTBALL
b. Sept. 8, 1915, Emeigh, Pa.
d. Sept. 25, 1987

As a guard at Syracuse University, Daugherty suffered a cracked vertebra in his neck in 1938, his junior year, and played the season wearing a protective collar. He captained the team in 1939, then became an assistant coach for a season before serving in the Army during World War II. He returned to Syracuse as line coach in 1946.

When head coach "Biggie" Munn went to Michigan State in 1947, Daugherty went with him and served as line coach until 1954, when Munn retired and Daugherty succeeded him. In 19 seasons as head coach, he had a 109–69–5 record and won two Big Ten championships.

His 1965 team won all ten regular season games and was consensus national champion, but lost, 14–12, to UCLA in the Rose Bowl. The 1966 squad was ranked second to Notre Dame in the wire service polls and tied with Notre Dame for first place in the National Football Foundation ranking.

Daugherty, who retired from coaching after the 1972 season, was a popular interviewee and after-dinner speaker because of his wit. He coined the often quoted phrase, "A tie is like kissing your sister."

★ College Football Hall of Fame

Davenport, Willie D.

TRACK AND FIELD
b. June 8, 1943, Troy, Ala.

An Army private in 1964, Davenport was the surprise winner in the 110-meter hurdles at the U.S. Olympic trials, and he suddenly became the favorite for the gold medal. A thigh injury hampered his form, however, and he lost in the Olympic semifinals.

Davenport was the national champion in the event the next three years, from 1965 through 1967, and he won his gold medal in 1968 in what he considered a perfect race. "From the first step, the gun, I knew I had won the race," he said afterward. "It was perhaps the only race I ever ran that way, but that first step was so perfect, right on the money." He finished fourth in the 1972 Olympics and came back to win the bronze medal in 1976.

His best event may actually have been the 60-yard hurdles, an indoor race that is not on the Olympic program. Davenport was national champion in that event five times, in 1966 and 1967 and from 1969 through 1971.

In 1980, Davenport was on the U.S. Olympic bobsled team, making him the fourth American to compete in both the summer and winter games.

★ National Track & Field Hall of Fame; Olympic Hall of Fame

Davidson, Bruce O.
EQUESTRIAN SPORTS
b. Dec. 31, 1949, Newburgh, N.Y.

The only American equestrian to win an individual medal at the 1974 world championships, Davidson took a gold in the three-day event on Irish Cap and was also a member of the gold medal three-day team. He won a team gold in the 1976 worlds and an individual gold in 1978, riding Mighty Tango.

At the 1975 Pan-American Games, Davidson won a silver medal in the three-day event and was a member of the silver medal team.

Davies, Bob (Robert E.)
BASKETBALL
b. Jan. 15, 1920, Harrisburg, Pa.
d. April 22, 1990

Although Bob Cousy is often considered the originator of the behind-the-back dribble, Davies actually deserves the credit. His Seton Hall coach, "Honey" Russell, once said, "He had such uncanny control of the ball behind his back that it never concerned me. He made it look as easy as the conventional dribble."

Davies entered Seton Hall in 1938 on a baseball scholarship, but Russell persuaded him to concentrate on basketball after seeing him practice once. Never a high scorer — his best college average was 11.8 points a game — Davies was a consummate passer and playmaker.

Known as the "Harrisburg Houdini," Davies led Seton Hall to 43 consecutive victories from 1939 into 1941. His spectacular skills helped attract the largest crowd in basketball history at the time, 18,403 people, to Madison Square Garden in March 1941, when Seton Hall beat Rhode Island in a quarterfinal game of the National Invitation Tournament.

An All-American guard in 1941 and 1942, Davies joined the U.S. Navy during World War II and led the Great Lakes Naval Training Station team to a 34–3 record before going overseas. After the war, he joined the Rochester Royals and played with them through the 1954–55 season. He was a first-team all-star four straight years, from 1949 through 1952, and he led the NBA in assists with 321 in 1948–49.

Davies coached Seton Hall in 1946–47, while playing with the Royals, and compiled a 24–3 record. After retiring as a player, he coached Gettysburg College for two seasons, winning 28 games while losing 19.

In his ten professional seasons, Davis scored 7,770 points, averaging 13.7 a game, and had 2,250 assists. He added 904 points and 182 assists in 67 playoff games. He was one of the ten players named to the NBA's silver anniversary team in 1971.

★ Basketball Hall of Fame

Davies, Thomas J.
FOOTBALL
b. 1901
d. Feb. 29, 1972

Old-time University of Pittsburgh fans think Davies was the best runner the school ever had, at least until Tony Dorsett came along. A single-wing tailback, the 150-pound Davies was not the classic triple threat, but he was an explosive runner and a pretty good passer, too.

As a freshman in 1918, he returned

punts for 60 and 50 yards for touchdowns, ran from scrimmage for 50 yards, and threw two touchdown passes in a 32–0 victory over Georgia Tech. He was named to Walter Camp's All-American team that year.

He was never again a first-team All-American, though he made Camp's second team in 1920 and 1921. It's hard to figure out why he wasn't on the first team at least one of those years. In 1920, he beat the University of Pennsylvania almost single-handed, returning a kickoff 90 yards for a touchdown, running 60 yards with an interception for another score, running 80 yards from scrimmage for a third and passing for a fourth in a 27–21 victory.

During his four-year career, Pittsburgh won 21, lost 6, and tied 4. Davies gained 4,625 yards rushing, an average of 149.2 yards per game. After graduating, he spent the 1922 season in the NFL with the Hammond, Indiana, Pros.
★ College Football Hall of Fame

Davis, Allen
FOOTBALL
b. July 4, 1929, Brockton, Mass.

After attending Wittenberg College in Ohio, Davis played baseball, basketball and football at Syracuse University, graduating in 1950. He was an assistant college coach and head coach of a U.S. Army team, then joined the staff of the Los Angeles Chargers of the new AFL in 1960.

In 1963, Davis went to the Oakland Raiders as the youngest general manager / head coach in pro football history. He adopted the motto "Pride and Poise," dressed his team in silver and black uniforms, and helped design a new logo, showing a pirate wearing an eye patch and a horned, Viking-like helmet.

One of Davis's chief goals was to turn the Raiders into a feared team, and he succeeded. In three seasons, he had a 23–16–3 record and was named AFL coach of the year in 1964, when Oakland went 10–4–0.

In April 1966, Davis was named commissioner of the league. He immediately set out to attack the rival NFL by signing its top quarterbacks to future contracts. That tactic was a major factor when the leagues agreed in July to a merger, which angered Davis because he felt the AFL could have succeeded without a merger.

He was also upset at being passed over for consideration as commissioner of the merged NFL. That was the beginning of a long feud with Commissioner Pete Rozelle. Davis could have remained as AFL commissioner until the merger formally took place in 1970, but he returned to the Raiders as managing general partner for the 1966 season and built teams that won the AFL title in 1967 and Super Bowls after the 1976, 1980, and 1983 seasons.

Davis was a maverick in NFL councils. Most owners and their representatives tended to work toward a consensus, under Rozelle's leadership, but Davis consistently fought such a consensus. When Oakland refused to add luxury box seats to its stadium, Davis signed a memorandum of agreement to move the team to the Los Angeles Coliseum in 1980.

Under league rules at the time, such a move was supposed to be approved by three-fourths of the other teams. Davis didn't get the approval, but tried to move anyway, only to be blocked by an injunction. However, he pressed an antitrust suit against the NFL, and a federal district court ruled in June 1982 that the move should be allowed, awarding $35 million in damages to the Raiders and nearly $15 million to the Los Angeles Coliseum.

Distrusted by many owners, Davis once told an interviewer that the secret to Oakland's success is simple: "Our way is to put fear in the opponent, baby, and outscore him." In another interview, he commented on his own single-minded approach, "It's tunnel vision, a tunnel life. I'm not really a part of society."
★ Pro Football Hall of Fame

Davis, Ernest
FOOTBALL
b. Dec. 14, 1939, New Salem, Pa.
d. May 18, 1963

Davis was recruited by Jimmy Brown to play football at Syracuse University, where he took Brown's number, 44, succeeded him as a running back, and broke most of his school rushing records.

Similar to Brown in size at 6-foot-2 and 220 pounds, in speed, and in elusiveness, Davis was the first black to win the Heisman Trophy as the nation's best college player, in 1961. He was also the first black player drafted by the NFL's Washington Redskins, who traded him to the Cleveland Browns, where he would be Jimmy Brown's teammate.

However, Davis never played pro football. While working out with the College All-Stars, he became ill and was diagnosed with leukemia. He went to Cleveland's training camp but never actually worked out with the team. After a brief remission, he died the following spring.

★ College Football Hall of Fame

Davis, Glenn A.

TRACK AND FIELD
b. Sept. 12, 1934, Wellsburg, W.Va.

Davis is the only man to win two Olympic gold medals in the 400-meter hurdles. Neither win was easy. In 1956, his U.S. teammate Eddie Southern led for the first half of the race. Then Davis caught him, and they ran evenly until the seventh hurdle, when Davis pulled away.

When competing at the 1960 Olympics, Davis couldn't catch his stride and was running third at the seventh hurdle. Then he finally got into stride, took the lead going over the tenth hurdle, and won by two yards.

His 1956 gold medal run was remarkable in that he ran his first hurdle race in April of that year. Two months later, he became the first to run faster than 50 seconds in the event, and a month after that, he set a world record of 49.5 seconds in the Olympic trials. He lowered the record to 49.2 in 1958, when he also set a world record of 49.9 for the 440-yard hurdles. He won the Sullivan Award as the top American amateur athlete that year.

Davis was also an exceptional 400-meter/440-yard sprinter. He set a world record of 45.7 seconds in the 440-yard dash in 1958, and he won a third gold medal as a member of the U.S. 4 x 400-meter relay team in 1960, running his leg in 45.4 seconds. One of the rare times he ran the 200-meter hurdles, Davis set a world record of 22.5 in 1960.

Representing Ohio State, Davis won the NCAA 440-yard hurdle championship in 1958. He was the AAU national champion from 1956 through 1958.

After leaving amateur competition, Davis was a wide receiver for the Detroit Lions in 1960 and 1961.

★ National Track & Field Hall of Fame; Olympic Hall of Fame

Davis, Glenn W.

FOOTBALL
b. Dec. 25, 1925, Claremont, Calif.

Called by the *Los Angeles Times* "the best athlete ever developed in southern California," Davis won 13 letters in four sports in high school before entering the U.S. Military Academy in 1943. As a freshman fullback, he gained 1,028 yards in 144 attempts.

"Doc" Blanchard joined the team in 1944 and became the starting fullback, with Davis moving to halfback. Nicknamed the "Touchdown Twins," they were probably the greatest pair of running backs ever to play together on the same college team. Davis, "Mr. Outside," had the speed and breakaway ability to run around the ends, while Blanchard, "Mr. Inside," liked to run between the tackles.

Davis had most of his best games against archrival Navy. In 1944, he had a 52-yard touchdown run and a touchdown-saving interception in a 23–7 victory. He ran for touchdowns of 33 and 49 yards in the 1945 game, when Army won, 32–13. And in the 1946 contest, he scored on a 40-yard run, caught a 30-yard pass, threw a 27-yard touchdown pass, and had 265 yards of total offense in a 21–18 win.

A three-time All-American, Davis won the Heisman Trophy and was named Associated Press athlete of the year in 1946. After three years in the

Army, he joined the NFL's Los Angeles Rams in 1950. Davis teamed with quarterback Bob Waterfield on an 82-yard touchdown pass, a championship game record, when the Rams lost the title game to the Cleveland Browns, 30–28.

Although he never had a serious football injury, ironically Davis tore a knee ligament while filming the 1946 movie *The Spirit of West Point*. The injury recurred in 1951, and he retired after seeing little action that season.

★ College Football Hall of Fame

Davis, Harold

TRACK AND FIELD
b. Jan. 5, 1921, Salinas, Calif.

Davis was one of the many athletes who lost a chance to win an Olympic medal because of World War II, and he is now almost forgotten. On June 6, 1941, Davis became the second man to run the 100-meter dash in 10.2 seconds. The first was Jesse Owens, who had done it in 1935. No one else tied the record until 1948, and it wasn't broken until 1956.

A student at the University of California, Davis won the NCAA 100-yard and 220-yard dashes in 1942 and 1943. He was the AAU national champion in the 100-meter dash in 1940, 1942, and 1943, and in the 200-meter dash from 1940 through 1943.

★ National Track & Field Hall of Fame

Davis, Harry H.

BASEBALL
b. July 19, 1873, Philadelphia, Pa.
d. Aug. 11, 1947

A right-handed-hitting first baseman, the 5-foot-10, 180-pound Davis won four consecutive AL home run titles during the dead ball era. He virtually had two major league careers. The first began with the NL's New York Giants in 1895. Traded to Pittsburgh during the 1897 season, Davis led the league with 28 triples in 1897.

He spent 1898 with Pittsburgh, Louisville, and Washington and then appeared in only 18 games with Washington in 1899, batting .188. Davis was out of baseball in 1900, but he began his sec-

ond career with the Philadelphia Athletics in the new American League in 1901.

Davis led the league with 43 doubles in 1902 and won his home run titles with 10 in 1904, 8 in 1905, 12 in 1906, and 8 in 1907. He also led the league in RBI with 83 in 1905 and 96 in 1906, in runs with 93 in 1905, and in doubles with 47 in 1905 and 37 in 1907.

He was with Philadelphia through 1911 and then became Cleveland's manager in 1912, when he appeared in two games. Davis returned to the Athletics as a coach in 1914, making occasional appearances as a pinch hitter before retiring after the 1917 season.

In 1,755 major league games, Davis had a .277 average with 1,841 hits, including 363 doubles, 145 triples, and 75 home runs. He stole 285 bases, scored 1,001 runs, and had 951 RBI.

Davis, John H., Jr.

WEIGHTLIFTING
b. Jan. 12, 1921, Smithtown, N.Y.

If there can be such a thing as a one-man dynasty, Davis was it. In 1938, when he was 17, he won the world light-heavyweight championship. From then until 1953, he never lost a weightlifting competition.

Davis repeated as world champion in 1939 and won the U.S. light-heavy championship in 1939 and 1940. The following year, he became a heavyweight and won three consecutive national championships. World championships weren't held during those years because of World War II, and there were no U.S. championships in 1944 and 1945.

After the war, Davis kept on winning. He was U.S. heavyweight champion in 1946, 1947, and 1948; missed the 1949 competition because of injury; and won four more titles from 1950 through 1953. He also won the world championship in 1946 and 1947. The world championship wasn't held in 1948. Davis then won it three consecutive years, from 1950 through 1952.

Davis also won Olympic gold medals in 1948 and 1952. In Olympic competition, he was never surpassed in any of the three lifts — the press, the snatch, and the jerk. Suffering from a thigh injury, Davis lost for the first time in the 1953 world championships and retired soon afterward.

He was the first lifter to jerk more than 400 pounds and the second to total more than 1,000 pounds for the three Olympic lifts. Davis also set unofficial records with some unusual stunts, such as jumping over a 30-inch-high table from a standing position while holding a 15-pound dumbbell in one hand and two 5-pound dumbbells in the other.
★ Olympic Hall of Fame

Davis, Mark W.
BASEBALL
b. Oct. 19, 1960, Livermore, Calif.

The left-handed Davis, a reliever in the best years of his major league career, was with the NL's Philadelphia Phillies briefly in 1980 and 1981 and joined the San Francisco Giants in 1983. The Giants used him primarily as a starter for two seasons, then put him in the bullpen.

He was traded to the San Diego Padres during the 1987 season, and he blossomed with San Diego in 1988, when he had 28 saves and a 2.01 ERA. The following year, he won the Cy Young Award by leading the league with 44 saves. He also had a 1.85 ERA.

Davis became a free agent after that season and went to the Kansas City Athletics in the AL. He had a terrible year in 1990, suddenly developing control problems, and his pitching arm was injured late in the season. He spent a good part of 1991 on the disabled list, then was traded to the NL's Atlanta Braves during the 1992 season.

He started the 1993 season with the Philadelphia Phillies but was released and picked up by the San Diego Padres in July. The Padres released him the following year.

Through 1994, Davis had a 51–84 record and 96 saves with a 4.15 ERA. He had struck out 993 hitters and walked 529 in 1,128⅔ innings.

Davis, Tommy (Herman Thomas)
BASEBALL
b. March 21, 1939, Brooklyn, N.Y.

A right-handed hitting outfielder, Davis won two consecutive batting titles with the NL's Los Angeles Dodgers, hitting .346 in 1962 and .326 in 1963. He also led the league with 230 hits and 153 RBI in 1962.

Davis joined the Dodgers for just one game in 1959 and became a starter the following year. He missed most of 1965 with a broken ankle but returned to hit .313 in 1966. He went to the New York Mets in 1967, batting .302.

During the next eight seasons, Davis was with eight different teams for varying periods of time. He ended his career as a designated hitter with the AL's Kansas City Royals in 1976. In 18 seasons, Davis batted .294 with 2,121 hits, including 272 doubles, 35 triples, and 153 home runs. He scored 811 runs and drove in 1,052.

Davis, Willie (William D.)
FOOTBALL
b. July 24, 1934, Lisbon, La.

The first player from Grambling College to be inducted into the Pro Football Hall of Fame, Davis was presented by his college coach, Eddie Robinson, who said of him, "For ten years, Willie was the standard of excellence by which defensive ends were judged."

The 6-foot-3, 245-pound Davis started his professional career with the Cleveland Browns in 1958. The Browns didn't quite know where to use him; he played defensive end, defensive tackle, and linebacker at one time or another without ever becoming a starter.

The Green Bay Packers needed help at defensive end, and Vince Lombardi decided that Davis was the answer. The Packers traded for him before the 1960 season, and he immediately became a starter.

Fast and agile, Davis was an outstanding pass rusher and was also a strong defender against the run. He was named to the All-Pro team in 1962 and from 1964 through 1967. He played 162 games without ever missing one before retiring after the 1969 season with 21 fumble recoveries, one less than the league record.

★ Pro Football Hall of Fame

Dawkins, Peter M.

FOOTBALL
b. March 8, 1938, Royal Oak, Mich.

One of the most celebrated college players of his time, not only because of his football skills but also because of his all-American boy image, Dawkins won the Heisman and Maxwell trophies as the nation's outstanding college player in 1958.

A versatile performer, Dawkins rushed for only 428 yards but scored 12 touchdowns on 78 carries that season. He also caught 16 passes for 491 yards and 12 touchdowns; returned 7 kickoffs for 132 yards; and ran back 10 punts for 162 yards.

A three-year letterman in hockey, Dawkins graduated seventh in his class and won a Rhodes Scholarship to Oxford University, where he starred in rugby. He then began an army career, and in 1983 he became the Army's youngest general at 45.

★ College Football Hall of Fame

Dawson, Andre N. ("Hawk")

BASEBALL
b. July 10, 1954, Miami, Fla.

Despite a long history of knee problems, Dawson has been a very productive offensive player and a surprisingly good defensive outfielder, the winner of eight Gold Glove awards.

The 6-foot-3, 195-pound Dawson, a right-hander, entered the major leagues with the NL's Montreal Expos late in the 1976 season. His best season with Montreal was 1983, when he led the league with 189 hits and had 32 home runs with 113 RBI and 104 runs scored.

Dawson was signed as a free agent by the Chicago Cubs in 1987. He was the NL's most valuable player that year, leading the league with 49 home runs and 137 RBI.

His production fell off significantly in 1988, and he appeared in only 118 games in 1989 because of injury. Daw-son came back with 27 home runs and 100 RBI in 1990, 31 home runs and 104 RBI in 1991.

He became a free agent once again after the 1992 season and signed with the Boston Red Sox. A broken wrist limited him to just 121 games, many of them as a pinch-hitter, and he hit only 13 home runs with 67 RBI in 1993.

Dawson, Lenny (Leonard R.)

FOOTBALL
b. June 20, 1935, Alliance, Ohio

As a 19-year-old sophomore at Purdue in 1954, Dawson threw 3 touchdown passes, kicked 3 extra points, and intercepted a pass in a 27–10 victory over Notre Dame, the only game the Irish lost that year. During his three years as a starting quarterback, he passed for 3,325 yards.

Dawson joined the NFL's Pittsburgh Steelers in 1957, then went to the Cleveland Browns in 1960. After five seasons in the NFL, he had attempted only 45 passes in regular season play. The Browns released him before the 1962 season, and he went to the Dallas Texans of the American Football League.

Under Coach Hank Stram, a guru of the passing game, Dawson suddenly became a great quarterback. He was named the AFL's player of the year by *The Sporting News* after his first season, when he won the passing championship and led the league in completion percentage, 61.0, and touchdown passes, 29. The Texans became the Kansas City Chiefs in 1963, and Dawson was Kansas City's starting quarterback for 13 more seasons.

He won AFL passing titles in 1964, 1966, 1968, led in completion percentage six years in a row, from 1964 through 1969, and led in touchdown passes in 1963, 1965, and 1966. He was named the most valuable player in Super Bowl IV, after the 1969 season, when he completed 12 of 17 passes for 142 yards and 1 touchdown in Kansas City's 23–7 win over the Minnesota Vikings.

Dawson retired after the 1975 season. He completed 2,136 passes in 3,741 attempts for 28,711 yards and 252 touchdowns during his professional career. He also ran for 9 touchdowns.

★ Pro Football Hall of Fame

Day, Ned (Edward P.)

BOWLING
b. Nov. 11, 1911, Los Angeles, Calif.
d. Nov. 26, 1971

The first genuinely famous bowler, Day toured widely during the 1940s and 1950s, visiting local bowling centers to play matches and give exhibitions, including a much publicized visit to the White House to give a demonstration for President Harry Truman in 1948. He starred in a series of movie shorts about bowling that were seen throughout the country and later rerun on television.

Day was bowler of the year in 1943 and 1944. He was the BPAA match play champion from 1938 through 1942, then presented the title to the All-Star tournament, which he won in 1944. He teamed with Rudy Pugel to win the 1944 match play doubles and with Buddy Bomar to win the title in 1951.

In addition to bowling on seven ABC championship teams, Day won the all-events championship in 1948 with a score of 1,979 for nine games. He had a 200-pin average in 28 years of ABC competition.

Day retired from competitive bowling after suffering a serious knee injury in 1958.

★ ABC Hall of Fame

Day, Patrick

HORSE RACING
b. Oct. 13, 1953, Brush, Colo.

During his 20-plus years as a jockey, there has always been at least one jockey to overshadow Day in the public eye. Yet Day has won four Eclipse Awards as the best jockey of the year, second only to Laffit Pincay's five.

His first Eclipse Award came in 1984, after he rode Wild Again to victory in the first Breeder's Cup Classic. He won the others in 1986, 1987, and 1991.

Day won a triple crown race for the first time in 1985, aboard Tank's Prospect in the Preakness. He took the Belmont on Easy Goer in 1989, the Preakness with Summer Squall in 1990, and the Kentucky Derby with Lil E. Tee in 1992. In 1994, he won two triple crown races, the Preakness and Belmont, aboard Tabasco Cat.

Through 1994, Day was the top jockey in Breeder's Cup races, winning 8 with 7 second-place and 2 third-place finishes. He was eighth all-time in races won with 6,239, and his earnings totaled $144,469,546, fourth best in history.

★ National Horse Racing Hall of Fame

Dean, Dizzy (Jay H.)

BASEBALL
b. Jan. 16, 1911, Lucas, Ark.
d. July 17, 1974

Dean was one of baseball's greatest pitchers and one of its greatest characters. The brash Dean, who never doubted his ability, was fond of saying, "It ain't braggin' if you can do it."

As a youngster, he and his brothers roamed through the Southwest with their father, picking cotton for 50 cents a day. Dean joined the Army in 1927, learned to pitch with a service team, and signed a professional contract after being discharged in 1930. He appeared in one game with the St. Louis Cardinals that season.

A right-hander, he joined the Cardinals to stay in 1932 and led the league in strikeouts with 191, in shutouts with 4, and in innings pitched with 286 while compiling an 18–15 record for a sixth-place team. He was the strikeout leader again with 199 in 1933, when he had a 20–18 record. On July 30, he set a record by striking out 17 Chicago Cubs in nine innings.

Dean's greatest year was 1934, when he had a 30–7 record, leading the NL in percentage, .811; shutouts, 7; and strikeouts, 195. He was named the league's most valuable player and the Associated Press's male athlete of the year. His younger brother Paul joined the team that year and had a 19–11 mark.

Going into the World Series against the Detroit Tigers, Dean predicted, "Me and Paul will win two games each." He was right. Paul won the second and sixth games while Dizzy won the first game and the deciding seventh game.

Dean had a 28–12 record in 1935, leading the league in strikeouts for the fourth year in a row as well as in victories, complete games, innings pitched, and strikeouts, and he went 24–13 in 1936, when he pitched three shutout innings in the All-Star game.

The 1937 All-Star game was his downfall, however. A line drive by Earl Averill broke the big toe on his left foot. Dean insisted on returning before it was completely healed. Unable to follow through properly, he seriously damaged his arm and was never the same.

He was traded to the Chicago Cubs after the season and won just 16 games for them before being released early in 1941. He then became a broadcaster for the St. Louis Cardinals and Browns. Dean made a final major league appearance with the Browns on the last day of the 1947 season.

When some teachers objected to his misuse of the language, particularly to his frequent employment of the word "ain't," Dean responded by quoting Will Rogers, "A lot of people who don't say 'ain't,' ain't eatin'." He was supported by thousands of listeners.

During the 1950s, he did network telecasts of the major league game of the week and became known to millions of fans who had never seen him pitch. He retired in the late 1960s.

In just 317 games, Dean had a 150–83 record with a 3.02 ERA. He struck out 1,163 hitters and walked 453 in 1,967 innings.
★ Baseball Hall of Fame

Dean, Everett S.

BASKETBALL
b. March 18, 1898, Livonia, Ind.
d. Oct. 28, 1993

A three-year starter at Indiana, Dean was named All-American center in 1921, his senior year. He also played football and baseball. After graduating, he coached basketball and baseball at Carleton College in Minnesota for three seasons, winning 45 games and losing only 4 in basketball.

He returned to Indiana in 1924 as baseball and basketball coach, remaining through the 1937–38 season. His basketball teams compiled a 162–93 record and tied for three Western Conference (now Big Ten) titles while his baseball teams won four conference championships.

In 1938, Dean went to Stanford, again to coach two sports. His 1942 basketball team won the NCAA championship, beating Dartmouth, 53–38, in the final game. He coached basketball through the 1950–51 season, winning 166 games and losing 120. Dean continued as baseball coach until his retirement in 1955.
★ Basketball Hall of Fame

DeBernardi, Red (Forrest S.)

BASKETBALL
b. Feb. 31, 1899, Nevada, Mo.
d. April 29, 1970

An All-American forward at Westminster, Missouri, College in 1920 and 1921, his freshman and sophomore years, DeBernardi played for the Kansas City Athletic Club in the 1921 AAU tournament and was named to the all-tournament team. In his junior year, he left the college team to play full time for Kansas City the next two seasons, and was an all-tournament player both of those years.

DeBernardi worked for the Hillyard Chemical Company in St. Joseph, Missouri, after graduating in 1923. He organized, played for, and coached the company's AAU team that won national championships in 1926 and 1927. He then joined the Cook Paint Company in Kansas City and won AAU titles there in 1928 and 1929.

In 11 AAU tournaments, DeBernardi was named to the all-tournament team seven times at three different positions. He was named the center on an all-time All-American team chosen by the Associated Press in 1938.
★ Basketball Hall of Fame

DeBusschere, David A.

BASKETBALL
b. Jan. 16, 1940, Detroit, Mich.
DeBusschere averaged 24.8 points per

basketball game at the University of Detroit and also starred as a pitcher on the school's baseball team. After graduating in 1962, he signed a baseball contract with the Chicago White Sox for a $70,000 bonus and a basketball contract with the Detroit Pistons for $15,000 a year.

After two seasons of playing both sports, compiling a 3–4 record with a 2.90 ERA as a major league pitcher, DeBusschere quit baseball in 1962 to become a player-coach with the Pistons at the age of 24.

His coaching record was only 79–143 when he was replaced late in the 1966–67 season. DeBusschere continued playing for Detroit until he was traded to the New York Knicks in December 1968.

DeBusschere became a key player on the New York teams that won NBA championships in 1970 and 1973. Never an exceptionally high scorer, the 6-foot-6, 235-pound forward starred on defense. He was named to the NBA all-defensive team six years in a row, from 1969 through 1974.

He retired after the 1973–74 season. In 875 regular season games, DeBusschere scored 14,053 points, an average of 16.1; he also had 9,618 rebounds and 2,497 assists.

★ Basketball Hall of Fame

Decker, Mary T. (Mrs. Tabb; Mrs. Slaney)

TRACK AND FIELD
b. Aug. 4, 1958, Flemington, N.J.

Shortly after her family moved to California when she was 11 years old, Decker discovered running. At 12, she ran a 440, an 880, a mile, a 2-mile, and a marathon in a single week, just before having an emergency appendectomy.

She won international attention in 1973 with a surprise victory in the 800-meter at a U.S. / U.S.S.R. dual meet in Minsk. Within a year, Decker held world records of 2:26.7 for 1,000 meters, 2:02.4 for 880 yards, and 2:01.8 for 800 meters.

Only 4-foot-10 and 86 pounds, the 15-year-old, inevitably known as "Little Mary Decker," was a great favorite with fans and media alike. But a long string of physical problems began to hamper her in late 1974 and eventually kept her from running competitively for the greater part of three years.

A sudden growth spurt of 6 inches and 25 pounds caused the most serious problem, compartment syndrome, in which the calf muscles grow too large for the sheath that contains them. Decker had an operation to cure that in 1977, and early the following year she broke her own 1,000-yard record with a 2:23.8 clocking.

After a bout with tendinitis, she set three world records in 1980, running 4:21.7 in the mile, 4:08.0 in the indoor 1,500-meter, and 1:59.7 in the 880-yard run. A sprained tendon then sidelined her for more than two months, but she came back to set an American record of 8:38.73 for the 3,000-meter in her first attempt at that distance.

Decker then tore an Achilles tendon, underwent two operations, and didn't return to form until 1982, her greatest single year. During the indoor season, she set world records in the mile, 2,000-meter, and 3,000-meter, then moved to longer distances outdoors. In June, she ran 5,000 meters in a world record 15:08.26. Then she went to Europe, won all five races she entered, and set another world record of 4:18.08 in the mile.

Late in the summer, Decker tried the 10,000-meter run for the first time and ran an extraordinary 31:35.23, setting a new world record and breaking the former U.S. record by 42 seconds. She was named female athlete of the year by the Associated Press, and she also won the Sullivan Award as the nation's outstanding amateur athlete.

Decker won the 1,500- and 3,000-meter runs at the first world championships in 1983 and qualified for both events at the 1984 Olympic trials. However, she decided to concentrate on the 3,000-meter. In the Olympic finals, she got tangled up with Zola Budd, a South African native who was running for Great Britain. Decker tripped, fell onto the infield, and injured her hip.

Putting her injury and disappointment behind, Decker set two more world records in 1985, a 5:34.2 in the indoor 2,000-meter and a 4:16.7 in the outdoor mile. She gave birth to a daughter in 1986, had a poor year in 1987, and finished a disappointing tenth in the 3,000-meter run at the 1988 Olympics. She then began pointing for the 1992 Games but failed to qualify for the U.S. team.

Described by Frank Shorter as a "remarkable combination of form and strength," Decker is unquestionably the greatest runner who never won an Olympic medal. Even though her best performances came more than a decade ago, she still holds U.S. records for 800 meters, 1,500 meters, 1 mile, 2,000 meters, and 3,000 meters.

Dedeaux, Rod (Raoul M.)

BASEBALL
b. Feb. 17, 1915, New Orleans, La.

Dedeaux played shortstop for the University of Southern California and had a very brief major league career, going 1 for 4 with the Brooklyn Dodgers in 1935.

He returned to his alma mater as baseball coach in 1942 and compiled an amazing record in 45 seasons, winning a record 1,331 games, 28 conference titles, and 10 NCAA tournament championships, in 1958, 1961, 1963, 1968, from 1970 through 1974, and in 1978.

Combining an emphasis on fundamentals with an impish sense of humor that helped keep his players relaxed, Dedeaux won six coach of the year awards. He retired after the 1986 season. More than 50 of his players, including Hall of Fame pitcher Tom Seaver, went on to major league careers.

Dedeaux coached the U.S. team at the 1964 Olympics, when baseball was offered as a demonstration sport, and he coached the U.S. silver medal team in 1984, when it was added to the program as a medal sport for the first time.

Degener, Richard K.

DIVING
b. March 14, 1912

With one dive to go in the 1936 Olympic springboard competition, De-gener was well behind teammate Marshall Wayne. He could have played it safe and settled for the silver medal. Instead, he went all out and performed a nearly perfect full twist with a one-and-a-half somersault for a score of 19.55. When Wayne came up short on his final dive, scoring only 15.54 points, Degener had the gold medal.

He was the bronze medalist in the springboard at the 1932 Olympics. Diving for the University of Michigan, he won the NCAA springboard championship in 1933 and 1934. Degener also won 12 national championships, in the outdoor springboard from 1933 through 1936; in the indoor 1-meter springboard in 1933 and 1934; in the indoor 3-meter springboard from 1932 through 1936; and in the outdoor platform in 1935.

DeGroot, Dudley S.

FOOTBALL, RUGBY,
SWIMMING
b. Nov. 10, 1899, Chicago, Ill.
d. May 5, 1970

DeGroot participated in a unique combination of four sports at Stanford: basketball, football, swimming, and water polo. He was the IC4A backstroke champion in 1923 and 1924, Stanford's football captain in 1922, and a member of the U.S. rugby team that won an Olympic gold medal in 1924.

He became head football coach at San Jose State in 1932 and compiled a 59–19–8 record in eight seasons there. His 1939 team won all 13 of its games, outscoring the opposition 324 to 29. DeGroot had a 24–6–0 record at the University of Rochester from 1940 through 1943 and then took over the NFL's Washington Redskins.

The Redskins won the Eastern Division title in 1945 but lost, 15–14, to the Cleveland Rams in the NFL championship game. DeGroot then went to the Los Angeles Dons of the new All-America Football Conference and had a 14–12–2 record in two seasons there.

He returned to college coaching at West Virginia University in 1948 and 1949, producing a 13–9–1 record, and he had a 13–17–0 record at the University of New Mexico from 1950 through 1952.

Dehnert, Dutch (Henry G.)

BASKETBALL
b. April 5, 1898, New York, N.Y.
d. April 20, 1979

Dehnert is often credited with "inventing" the pivot play when he was with the great Original Celtics team. Actually, it seems that the play had been used before, but Dehnert and his teammates brought it to near perfection. Nat Holman, a member of the team, later wrote, "The Original Celtics, with 'Dutch' Dehnert in the pivot position, developed this into the most damaging scoring play ever devised and did much to bring the play to its present state of comparative success."

The 6-foot-1, 210-pound Dehnert began playing professional basketball right out of high school for various teams in the New York State, Eastern, Pennsylvania State, and New England leagues. He joined the Celtics in 1919, their second year of existence.

He started using the pivot play when the Celtics came up against a team that used a "standing guard" who remained at his own foul line to prevent the other team from fast breaking. Some sources say the game was in Miami, others say Chattanooga. Dehnert recalled, "I volunteered to stand in front of him with my back to the basket, so that instead of the guard breaking up our passes, they could pass to me and I could give it back to them. We tried this, and in an effort to bat the ball out of my hands, the standing guard moved around to my right side. All I had to do was pivot to my left, take one step and lay the ball up."

After years of barnstorming success, the Celtics joined the American Basketball League in 1926 and won two straight championships. The team was forced to break up, Dehnert going to the Cleveland Rosenblums with Pete Barry and Joe Lapchick. Cleveland promptly won two titles. Dehnert then went to the Toledo Red Men. The ABL folded in 1931, and some of the Celtics, including Dehnert, got back together to continue barnstorming.

Dehnert later coached the Detroit Eagles for two seasons, winning the world professional tournament in 1941. After coaching Harrisburg of the new ABL in 1942–43, he went to the Sheboygan Redskins and won the National Basketball League's Western Division titles in 1944–45 and 1945–46. He coached the Cleveland Rebels in the new Basketball Association of America for part of the 1946–47 season.

★ Basketball Hall of Fame

Delahanty, Edward J.

BASEBALL
b. Oct. 31, 1867, Cleveland, Ohio
d. July 2, 1903

The best of five brothers who played in the major leagues, "Big Ed" was slender at 6 feet and only 170 pounds, but he swung a big bat. A right-hander, he played in 130 games with the NL's Philadelphia team in 1888 and 1889 before jumping to Cleveland in the Players' League in 1890.

After the Players' League folded, he returned to Philadelphia in 1891 and led the league in triples with 21 and in slugging percentage with .495 in 1892. Originally a second baseman, he became an outfielder that season, though he was also occasionally used at first base.

He then had a sensational five-year stretch, batting .368 in 1893, .407 in 1894, .404 in 1895, .397 in 1896, and .377 in 1897. Delahanty led the league in home runs with 19 in 1893 and 13 in 1896; in doubles with 49 in 1895 and 44 in 1896; in RBI with 146 in 1893 and 126 in 1896; and in slugging percentage with .583 in 1893 and .631 in 1896.

After tailing off to .334 in 1898, Delahanty had his best season the following year. His .410 average and .582 slugging percentage led the league, and he was also tops in hits with 238, doubles with 55, and RBI with 137.

Delahanty led the league in doubles once more with 38 in 1901, then jumped to the AL's Washington Senators for a $1,000 raise. He led the new league with a .376 average, 43 doubles, and a .590 slugging percentage in 1902.

A heavy drinker, Delahanty was suspended during the 1903 season. While traveling from Detroit to New York to be with his wife, Delahanty had several drinks and was put off the train near Niagara Falls for being rowdy. He tried to follow the train across the International Bridge, fell into the Niagara River, and was washed over the falls. His mangled body was found a week later.

In 1,835 games spanning 16 seasons, Delahanty batted .346, with 2,597 hits, 522 doubles, 185 triples, and 101 home runs. He stole 455 bases, scored 1,599 runs, and had 1,464 RBI.
★ Baseball Hall of Fame

Delahoussaye, Eddie (Edward)

HORSE RACING
b. Sept. 21, 1951, New Iberia, La.

A quarter-horse jockey in his early teens, Delahoussaye began riding thoroughbreds in 1968, and ten years later he was the top jockey in the nation with 384 wins.

Delahoussaye is one of only five jockeys to win the Kentucky Derby two years in a row, aboard Gato Del Sol in 1982 and Sunny's Halo in 1983. He had finished a close second on Woodchopper in 1981.

His other victories in triple crown races came aboard Risen Star in the 1988 Preakness and aboard AP Indy in the 1992 Belmont. Delahoussaye has also won four different events in the Breeders' Cup races. He won the 1989 turf championship with Prized and the 1991 juvenile filly championship with Pleasant Stage. In 1992, Delahoussaye rode AP Indy to victory in the Breeders' Cup Classic and Thirty Slews to the sprint championship.

In 25 years of racing through 1994, Delahoussaye has won 5,320 races, thirteenth all-time, and has collected purses of $135,850,323.
★ National Horse Racing Hall of Fame

Delvecchio, Alexander P.

HOCKEY
b. Dec. 4, 1931, Ft. William, Ont.

When Delvecchio replaced Sid Abel, centering Gordie Howe and Ted Lindsay on Detroit's "Production Line" in 1952, production actually improved. Howe and Lindsay were the NHL's two top scorers, and Delvecchio finished fifth with 16 goals and 43 assists. During his 24 seasons in the NHL, all with the Red Wings, he was among the league's top ten scorers 11 times, and he won the Lady Byng Trophy for combining skill and gentlemanly conduct three times, in 1959, 1966, and 1969.

The son of Italian immigrants, Delvecchio originally joined the Red Wings for one game in 1950, right out of junior hockey, but was then sent to the minor leagues for seasoning. He rejoined the team in 1951 and was there to stay until his retirement after the 1973–74 season.

In the seventh game of the 1955 Stanley Cup finals against Montreal, Delvecchio scored Detroit's first and last goals, assisting on the other, for a 3–1 victory.

Delvecchio had 456 goals and 825 assists in 1,549 regular season games with the Red Wings, and he scored 35 goals with 69 assists in 121 playoff games.
★ Hockey Hall of Fame

DeMar, Clarence H.

TRACK AND FIELD
b. June 7, 1888, Madeira, Ohio
d. June 11, 1958

He was called "Mr. DeMarathon." DeMar ran in the Boston Marathon 25 times and finished all of them. He won seven times, finished second four times, and was third twice. He might have won even more, but he took a five-year break from running because a doctor told him he had a heart problem. The problem was actually that medical science at the time didn't recognize that well-conditioned athletes often have very low pulse rates.

A graduate of the University of Vermont, DeMar entered the Boston Marathon for the first time in 1910, finishing second. He won in 1911, setting a course record. Then came his layoff. He returned and won three straight, from 1922 through 1924, two straight in 1927 and 1928, and he won once more in

1930. At 41, he is still the oldest winner in Boston Marathon history.

DeMar also won the AAU marathon from 1926 through 1928. He finished third in the 1924 Olympic marathon.

Demaret, Jimmy (James N.)

GOLF
b. May 10, 1910, Houston, Tex.

The genial, good-natured Demaret, probably Ben Hogan's best golfing friend, won the Texas PGA tournament five times in a row, from 1934 through 1938, before joining the professional tour full time. He became the first player to win the Masters Tournament three times.

In the 1940 Masters, Demaret played poorly on the first nine holes of the first round but shot a record 30 on the second nine. He was still three shots back, but he tied Lloyd Mangrum after the second round, shot a 70 in the third to take the lead, and finally beat Mangrum by four strokes.

Demaret was the top golfer on the pro tour in 1947, leading in money won, claiming the Vardon Trophy with an average of 69.9 strokes per round, and winning his second Masters by two shots over Byron Nelson and Frank Stranahan. He needed a great finish for his third Masters victory, in 1950. Australian Jim Ferrier had a four-shot lead going into the final round, but Demaret shot a 69 and Ferrier collapsed to a 75, giving Demaret a 283–285 win.

★ PGA Hall of Fame; World Golf Hall of Fame

Dempsey, Jack (William H.)

BOXING
b. June 24, 1895, Manassa, Colo.
d. May 31, 1983

At the age of 16, Dempsey was an itinerant miner who made extra money by challenging all comers in saloons and passing a hat after his victory. According to legend, he never lost one of these barroom brawls. He became a professional fighter in 1914, and two years later he went to New York City to seek his fortune as a boxer.

After breaking two ribs in a bout with a more experienced fighter, Dempsey went west again, hopping freights and picking up occasional bouts to earn some money. He met Jack "Doc" Kearns, a former fighter turned manager, in San Francisco. Kearns taught him how to box and matched him against a series of lesser fighters to build up his reputation and sharpen his skills.

Billed as the "Manassa Mauler" and the "toughest man ever to come out of the West," the 6-foot, 190-pound Dempsey met the 6-foot-6, 250-pound heavyweight champion Jess Willard on July 4, 1919, at Toledo, Ohio. Dempsey won on a 3rd-round knockout. Promoter Tex Rickard immediately began calling him "Jack the Giant killer" because Willard was known as the "Pottawatomie Giant."

During the next seven years, Dempsey defended his title only six times but made a lot of money in the process. His fight against Frenchman Georges Carpentier on July 2, 1921, at Jersey City, New Jersey, produced boxing's first $1 million gate. Rickard made Dempsey the villain because he had been accused of dodging the draft during World War I, while Carpentier was a war hero. Dempsey won on a 4th-round knockout.

His match against Luis Firpo of Argentina on September 14, 1923, also brought in more than $1 million. Dempsey was again the "Giant Killer" when facing the 6-foot-3, 220-pound Firpo. He knocked Firpo down seven times in less than two minutes of the 1st round, but then Firpo knocked Dempsey through the ropes and onto a sportswriter's typewriter. The dazed champion got back into the ring and lasted out the round. He knocked Firpo down twice more in the 2nd round before knocking him out.

Every time Firpo was knocked down, Dempsey stood over him so he could begin attacking again the instant Firpo got to his feet. As a result, New York boxing regulations were changed to require a boxer to go to a neutral corner after scoring a knockdown, and Illinois adopted the same rule.

After fighting only exhibitions and making vaudeville appearances for three years, Dempsey was matched against

Gene Tunney on September 23, 1926, at Philadelphia. Badly out of shape, he lost the title on a 10-round decision to the quick, clever Tunney.

In a rematch at Chicago on September 22, 1927, the only $2 million gate in boxing history, Dempsey knocked Tunney down in the 7th round. It took him several seconds to realize that he had to go to a neutral corner, and the count didn't start until he got there. Tunney got to his feet at the count of nine and went on to win a 10-round decision.

Observers estimated that Tunney was down for at least 15 seconds. An appeal was rejected by the Illinois Athletic Commission, and Dempsey announced his retirement. Named the greatest fighter of the half-century in a 1950 Associated Press poll, he won 60 professional fights, 49 by knockout; lost 7, 1 by knockout; and fought 7 draws, 5 no-decisions, and 1 no-contest.

★ International Boxing Hall of Fame

Dempsey, Jack (The Non-Pareil)
[John Kelly]
BOXING
b. Dec. 15, 1862, County Kildare, Ireland
d. Nov. 2, 1895

John Kelly, an immigrant barrel-maker from Ireland, went to watch the fights on Long Island on April 27, 1883. He volunteered to replace a fighter who didn't show up for one of the bouts, gave his name as "Jack Dempsey," and won in 21 rounds. So he became a professional boxer and was undefeated in his first 55 fights over the next five years.

On July 30, 1884, he beat George Fulljames of Canada in 22 rounds and was considered welterweight and middleweight champion because of the victory. Dempsey had 41 fights without a loss before meeting Johnny Reagan in his first genuine defense of the title on December 13, 1887. The bout took place outdoors on Long Island in heavy rain. By the 4th round, the ring was underwater, and the fight was moved 20 miles. The rain turned to snow. Dempsey finally won on a knockout in the 45th round.

His first "defeat" came on August 27, 1889, in a title fight against George Le-Blanche, who knocked Dempsey out in the 32nd round. However, LeBlanche used an illegal "pivot punch" and was over the weight limit anyway, so Dempsey was still considered the champion.

Dempsey lost the middleweight title on January 14, 1891, when he was knocked out by Bob Fitzsimmons in the 13th round at New Orleans. His health failing, he fought once in 1893 and once more in 1894. His final appearance was in a benefit for himself on January 18, 1895, when he lost a 3-round decision to Tommy Ryan.

Shortly afterward, Dempsey went to Portland, Oregon, hoping to regain his health, but he died before the end of the year.

He won 58 fights, 8 by knockout, and lost only 3, 2 by knockout. He also fought 8 draws and 4 no-decisions.

★ International Boxing Hall of Fame

Denny, John A.
BASEBALL
b. Nov. 8, 1952, Prescott, Ariz.

A right-handed pitcher, Denny struggled with arm problems through much of his career. But he was healthy in 1983, when he won the NL's Cy Young Award with a 19–6 record and a 2.37 ERA to help lead the Philadelphia Phillies into the World Series.

He won the first game of the series, 2–1, over the Baltimore Orioles. It was the only game the Phillies won. Denny was the losing pitcher in a 5–4 Baltimore win in the fourth game.

Denny entered the major leagues with the St. Louis Cardinals in 1974 and led the NL with a 2.52 ERA in 1976. He went to the Cleveland Indians in 1980 and was traded to Philadelphia near the end of the 1982 season. He finished his career with Cincinnati in 1986.

In 13 major league seasons, Denny had a 123–108 record, 18 shutouts, and a 3.59 ERA. He struck out 1,146 hitters and walked 778 in 2,148 innings.

Dent, Richard L.

FOOTBALL
b. Dec. 13, 1960, Atlanta, Ga.

Chosen by the Chicago Bears out of Tennessee State in the eighth round of the 1983 NFL draft, Dent became one of the anchors of the Chicago defense that helped take the team to two NFC championship games and a Super Bowl victory.

The 6-foot-5, 265-pound Dent is an outstanding pass rusher from his defensive end position because of his quickness and speed. He led the NFL with 17 quarterback sacks in 1985, when the Bears won the NFC championship and beat the New England Patriots, 46–10, in Super Bowl XX.

Dent joined the San Francisco 49ers as a free agent in 1994 but missed most of the season with an injury. Through 1994, Dent had 124½ sacks in 173 NFL games. He also intercepted 7 passes, returning them for 65 yards and 1 touchdown, and he recovered 13 fumbles. In 1990, he returned a fumble for 45 yards and a touchdown.

DePalma, Ralph

AUTO RACING
b. 1883, Italy
d. March 31, 1956

With just five laps to go, DePalma was leading the 1912 Indianapolis 500 when his car began leaking oil. He nursed it toward the finish, but it stopped on the track with less than a mile remaining. He and riding mechanic Rupert Jeffkins climbed out and pushed the car that last mile to the finish line. In the meantime, Joe Dawson passed them to win the race, and DePalma was disqualified, but he and Jeffkins won a standing ovation from the Indy crowd, and the newspaper photo of the gallant effort did as much as anything to glamorize the race to the American public.

DePalma's family came to America when he was ten years old. During a 25-year career that began early in the century, he won an estimated 2,000 races on every type of surface imaginable. Before formal championships had been established, he was considered the champion of dirt track racing, the sport's birthplace, from 1908 through 1911.

He won the American Automobile Association's national championship in 1912 and 1914. After retiring for some time, he returned to dirt track racing in 1929 and won the Canadian driving championship.

DePalma had a legendary rivalry with Barney Oldfield. He was once quoted as saying, "I would rather beat Oldfield than eat five plates of spaghetti in a row," a statement he later denied making. The rivalry began in 1914, when DePalma was in his second year as captain of the Mercer factory team preparing for the Vanderbilt Cup race in Santa Monica. Oldfield was signed by a Mercer executive to drive in the race, without DePalma's knowledge. When he found out about the deal, he resigned on the spot.

He then entered the race on his own, bringing an old Mercedes Grey Ghost out of retirement for the effort. Oldfield took the lead from DePalma with about ten laps to go in the 300-mile race, but couldn't pull away. With fewer than eight laps remaining, DePalma slowed and signaled to his crew that he was going to make a pit stop. Oldfield decided he could get off the track, too, to replace a badly worn tire. But DePalma never stopped. He took the lead and held off Oldfield's desperate charge to win the Vanderbilt Cup. The same old Grey Ghost won the 1915 Indy 500, erasing the disappointment of 1912.

DePalma's last major race was the 1925 Indy 500, when he finished seventh. But during the mid-1930s he drove stock cars to a number of records in time trials, and later he became honorary referee at Indy until 1954, two years before his death.

★ Indianapolis Speedway Hall of Fame

DePaolo, Peter

AUTO RACING
b. April 15, 1898, Roseland, N.J.
d. Nov. 26, 1980

DePaolo saw his first auto race in 1919, when his uncle, Ralph DePalma, beat Louis Chevrolet and Barney Oldfield. Less than a year later he was driving mechanic for DePalma in the 1920 Indianapolis 500. Then he turned to driving, wrecking five of the first six cars he drove. Nevertheless, he was invited to join the Duesenberg team in 1924. The following year, he averaged 101.13 mph to win the Indy 500, becoming the first to surpass the 100 mph barrier. He also won the National Championship that year.

In 1927, DePaolo formed his own racing team and qualified second at Indy. He was forced out of the race by mechanical problems, but he won major 250-mile races at Altoona, PA, and Salem, New Hampshire, to win his second driving championship.

He raced for seven more years without any major successes and retired after an accident in Spain put him in a coma for 11 days. But he was car owner and team manager for Kelly Petillo's 1935 victory in the Indy 500.

After World War II, DePaolo managed the Ford team effort in factory stock car racing, and he became director of industrial relations for the Michigan International Speedway when it opened in 1969.
★ Indianapolis Speedway Hall of Fame

DePietro, Joseph N.

WEIGHTLIFTING
b. June 8, 1914, Paterson, N.J.

DePietro was less than five feet tall, and his arms were so short that he could just barely raise a weighlifting bar above his head. But he won the world bantamweight championship in 1947 and was the Olympic champion in the weight class in 1948.

DePietro won nine U.S. weightlifting championships in a ten-year period, as a bantamweight in 1942 and 1943 and from 1946 through 1951 and as a featherweight in 1945. He also won a gold medal in the 1951 Pan-American Games and finished third in the 1949 world championships.

Desjardins, Pete (Ulise J.)

DIVING
b. April 10, 1907, St. Pierre, Man.
d. May 6, 1985

Desjardins grew up in Florida, where he began diving when he was 13. Only 5-foot-3, Desjardins was nicknamed the "Little Bronze Statue" by the press because of his stature and year-round Florida suntan.

A silver medalist in the 1924 Olympic springboard event, Desjardins was the national outdoor 3-meter and platform champion from 1925 through 1927, and he won the indoor 3-meter title in 1927 and 1928.

In the 1928 Olympics, Desjardins won both the springboard and the platform gold medals, the only diver to achieve that double victory until Greg Louganis in 1984. The platform event was held for the first time that year, and the outcome was controversial. Farid Samaiki of Egypt led on points and was proclaimed the winner at first. However, the judges then ruled that ordinals, not total points, should be the deciding factor, and Desjardins was awarded the gold medal.

He enrolled at Stanford University in 1927, but never won a collegiate championship, mainly because the AAU suspended him in 1929 for accepting too much expense money for an exhibition. He formally turned professional in 1931 and gave many exhibitions around the world, often with swimmer Johnny Weismuller.
★ International Swimming Hall of Fame

Desmarteau, Etienne

TRACK AND FIELD
b. 1877, Montreal, P.Q.
d. 1905

A Montreal policeman, Desmarteau asked for a leave of absence in 1904 so he could compete in the Olympics. His request was turned down, and when he decided to go anyway, he was fired.

Desmarteau won the 56-pound weight event with a throw of 34 feet, 4 inches. It was the first gold medal ever for Canada. When he returned to Montreal, he was welcomed as a hero, and his firing was forgotten. Less than a year later, he died of typhoid fever.
★ Canadian Sports Hall of Fame

Detmer, Ty H.

FOOTBALL
b. Oct. 30, 1967, San Marcos, Tex.

A two-time All-American quarterback at Brigham Young University, in 1990 and 1991, Detmer won the 1991 Heisman Trophy as a junior. In four years as a starter, Detmer completed 958 of 1,530 passes for 15,031 yards and 121 touchdowns with only 65 interceptions. He holds NCAA career records for attempts, completions, yards passing, and touchdown passes.

The 6-foot-tall, 183-pound Detmer was considered suspect by NFL scouts because of his slender frame, and he wasn't chosen until the ninth round of the 1992 college draft, by the Green Bay Packers. In three seasons with Green Bay, through 1994, he has thrown only five passes in regular season play.

Devaney, Bob (Robert S.)

FOOTBALL
b. April 13, 1915, Saginaw, Mich.

Devaney spent three years working in a foundry after graduating from high school and then entered Alma College in Michigan, where he played football. He graduated in 1939 and became a high school coach.

In 1953, he joined the coaching staff at Michigan State University. Devaney got his first job as a college head coach in 1957 at the University of Wyoming, where his teams won 35 games while losing only 10 and tying 5 through the 1961 season.

The University of Nebraska hired him in 1962 to rebuild a sad program. Devaney took a team that had gone 3–6–1 the previous year to a 9–2–0 record in his first season, and Nebraska beat the University of Miami, 36–34, in the Gotham Bowl.

Devaney's teams won national championships in 1970 and 1971, won eight Big Eight Conference titles, and compiled a 101–20–2 record in his 11 seasons. He retired from coaching after the 1972 season but remained at Nebraska as athletic director. His overall winning percentage of .806, on 136 victories, 30 losses, and 11 ties, is tenth best in the history of NCAA Division I football.
★ College Football Hall of Fame

de Varona, Donna E.

SWIMMING
b. April 26, 1947, San Diego, Calif.

A remarkably versatile swimmer, de Varona won national championships in the backstroke, butterfly, and individual medley. She was the 1964 Olympic gold medalist in the 400-meter individual medley, and she also swam on the 4 x 100-meter freestyle relay team that won a gold medal. For her accomplishment, she was named female athlete of the year by the Associated Press.

De Varona was a member of the 1960 Olympic team, when she was only 13, but failed to win a medal. She won AAU outdoor championships in the 100-meter backstroke in 1962, in the 200-meter individual medley in 1963 and 1964, and in the 400-meter individual medley in 1960, 1961, 1963, and 1964. Indoors, she won titles in the 100-yard backstroke in 1962, the 200-yard butterfly in 1964, the 200-yard individual medley in 1963 and 1964, and the 400-yard individual medley in 1963 and 1964.

She retired from competition after the 1964 Olympics, and in 1965 she became the first woman sportscaster on network television. de Varona was also the first woman to do television commentary on the Olympics, in 1968. A founder of the Women's Sports Foundation, de Varona was a member of the President's Commission on Olympic Sports.
★ International Swimming Hall of Fame; International Women's Sports Hall of Fame; Olympic Hall of Fame

Devers, Gail

TRACK AND FIELD
b. Nov. 19, 1966, Seattle, Wash.

As a student at UCLA, Devers competed in the 100-meter dash, 100-meter hurdles, long jump, and triple jump. She won a gold medal in the 100-meter dash at the 1987 Pan-American Games and was the NCAA champion in the event in 1988.

Devers became ill the following year, and the problem was eventually diagnosed as Graves' disease, a severe type of hyperthyroidism. It was thought for a time that her feet might have to be amputated. However, the illness was finally stabilized.

She returned to competition in 1992, winning a gold medal in the 100-meter at the Olympics. Devers was leading in the 100-meter hurdles when she stumbled and fell over the last hurdle, ending up fifth. In 1993, Devers won both events at the world championships.

Devine, Aubrey A.

FOOTBALL
b. Nov. 21, 1897, Des Moines, Iowa
d. Dec. 15, 1981

After graduating from high school in 1918, Devine briefly served in the Marines during World War I, then enrolled at the University of Iowa. Only 5-foot-9 and 170 pounds, he started at quarterback for three years, starring as a runner and kicker. Iowa won 17 games and lost 4 during those three years.

In his senior season, 1921, he dropkicked a 38-yard field goal for a 10–7 Iowa victory that ended Notre Dame's 20-game winning streak. Devine gained 1,961 rushing yards and scored 161 points during his career. He was an All-American in 1921.
★ College Football Hall of Fame

Devine, Daniel J.

FOOTBALL
b. Dec. 23, 1924, Augusta, Wis.

Devine served in the Army Air Corps during World War II and then went to the University of Minnesota at Duluth, where he was captain of the football and basketball teams as a senior in 1947. He coached high school football for three years, became an assistant at Michigan State University for five years, and then took over as head coach at Arizona State University in 1955.

Arizona State had its first undefeated season under Devine in 1957, winning all ten of its games, and he had a 27–3–1

record there before going to the University of Missouri in 1958.

In his second season at Missouri, Devine took the team to the Orange Bowl, losing 14–0 to Georgia. And in 1960, his third season, Missouri won 10 of 11 regular season games and beat Navy, 21–14, in the Orange Bowl.

Devine took on additional duties as athletic director in 1967. After compiling a 92–38–7 record in 13 seasons, he left Missouri to coach the NFL's Green Bay Packers in 1971. Although the Packers won a division championship in 1972, his stay in Green Bay was not successful, and he left with a 25–28–4 record in four seasons to become head coach at Notre Dame in 1975.

Notre Dame won 10 of 11 regular season games in 1977, then beat previously undefeated Texas, 38–10, in the Cotton Bowl to claim the national championship. Devine had a 53–16–1 record in six years at the school before retiring after the 1980 season because of his wife's ill health. His overall college record was 126–42–7, a .742 winning percentage.
★ College Football Hall of Fame

Devlin, Judy (Mrs. Hashman)

BADMINTON
b. 1935, Winnipeg, Man.

If badminton had ever won any standing with fans and media, Devlin would be accepted as one of the greatest female athletes in history. During a 15-year career, she won 56 national championships in the U.S., Canada, and England, and she also won the Dutch, German, Irish, Jamaican, Scottish, and Swedish titles at one time or another.

Devlin began playing when she was seven years old under the tutelage of her Irish-born father, J. Frank Devlin, who won the English singles championship six times. After winning six national junior girls titles, she moved into the senior ranks in 1953 and won the women's doubles championship with her sister, Susan.

In 1954, she won her first U.S. singles championship. She also won that title from 1956 through 1963 and from 1965 through 1967. Devlin won a record ten

All-England singles titles, in 1954, 1957, 1958, from 1960 through 1964, and in 1966 and 1967. (The All-England is badminton's equivalent of the Wimbledon tournament in tennis.)

She also won the national women's doubles 12 times, the national mixed doubles 8 times, the All-England women's doubles 7 times, the Canadian singles and women's doubles 3 times each, and the Canadian mixed doubles once.

DeWitt, John R.

FOOTBALL
b. Oct. 29, 1881, Phillipsburg, N.J. d. July 28, 1930

A 6-foot-2, 198-pound lineman at Princeton, DeWitt once warned an opponent at the beginning of a game, "There are two ways to play me: stay out of my way or get hurt." He became a starting tackle as a sophomore in 1901. He was also the team's kicker and often ran with the ball from kick formation. DeWitt's 50-yard touchdown run in the closing minutes beat Lafayette that season.

In 1902, he moved to guard, and he drop-kicked field goals of 45 and 50 yards that season. DeWitt became team captain in 1903. Princeton won its first ten games without giving up a point and then faced Yale in the final game of the season. Yale, also undefeated, was strongly favored, but DeWitt ran more than 50 yards with a blocked kick to score a touchdown, kicked the conversion, and added a 43-yard field goal in Princeton's 11–6 victory.

An All-American in 1902 and 1903, DeWitt was also an outstanding weight man on the track team. He won the IC4A hammer throw championship four years in a row, 1901 through 1904, and won a silver medal in the event at the 1904 Olympics. His throw of 164 feet, 10 inches in 1902 was the world record for 20 years.

★ College Football Hall of Fame

Dickerson, Eric D.

FOOTBALL
b. Sept. 2, 1960, Sealy, Tex.

The 6-foot-3, 230-pound Dickerson ran the 100-yard dash in 9.4 seconds as a high school student. At Southern Methodist University, he rushed 790 times for 4,450 yards and 48 touchdowns in four seasons and was a consensus All-American running back in 1982.

A first-round draft choice of the NFL's Los Angeles Rams, Dickerson was named rookie of the year by the Associated Press and National Football Conference player of the year in 1983, when he rushed for 1,808 yards to lead the league.

Dickerson gained 2,105 rushing yards, 2,244 combined rushing and receiving yards, and rushed for 100 or more yards in 12 games, all NFL records, in 1984.

The outspoken Dickerson held out for more money and missed the first two games of the 1985 season before coming to terms with the Rams. He led the NFL in rushing for a third time with 1,821 yards in 1986. But disputes with team management led to his trade to the Indianapolis Colts after the third game of the 1987 season in a major three-team deal that also sent rookie linebacker Cornelius Bennett to the Buffalo Bills.

With the Colts, Dickerson was the NFL rushing leader for the fourth time in 1988, and the following year he set a league record by gaining more than 1,000 yards rushing for the seventh season in a row. However, he again had difficulties with coaches and management, who accused him of exaggerating minor injuries. After playing in only 11 of 16 games in 1990, Dickerson was suspended for nearly a month in 1991 and was traded to the Oakland Raiders the following season.

Through the 1992 season, Dickerson had gained 13,168 yards on 2,970 attempts, a 4.4 average, and scored 90 rushing touchdowns. He had also caught 275 passes for 2,079 yards, a 7.6 average, and 6 touchdowns. Dickerson was traded to the Green Bay Packers in 1993 but retired after failing the team's physical examination.

A remarkable combination of speed and power, Dickerson was at his best starting wide and then cutting back against the defensive pursuit. He was criticized by some for not being a good short-yardage runner, despite his size, and for not being a good outside runner, despite his speed. Nevertheless, Dickerson was named an All-Pro five times and played in six Pro Bowls.

Dickey, Bill (William M.)

BASEBALL
b. June 6, 1907, Bastrop, La.
d. Nov. 12, 1993

After playing at Little Rock College for a year, Dickey entered professional baseball for a few games at the end of the 1925 season. He was called up to the New York Yankees for ten games in 1928, and he became the team's starting catcher the following year.

A left-handed hitter, Dickey was the link between two Yankee dynasties, the "Murderers' Row" teams of Lou Gehrig and Babe Ruth and the Joe Dimaggio-led teams of the late 1930s. He caught more than 100 games in each of 13 consecutive seasons, from 1929 through 1941, a major league record, and he batted over .300 in 11 of his 16 major league seasons.

He hit .324, .339, and .327 in his first three full seasons and set an AL record in 1931 by catching 130 games without allowing a passed ball. The Yankees won the pennant in 1932, when Dickey batted .310 during the regular season and .438 in a four-game sweep of the Chicago Cubs in the World Series.

Dickey hit .322 in 1933, when the Yankees won another pennant and beat the Washington Senators in a five-game World Series. He reached his peak from 1936 through 1939, hitting more than 20 home runs and driving in more than 100 runs each season, as the Yankees won four straight world championships. His .362 average in 1936 is still a record for catchers.

In 1940, Dickey slumped to .247. After hitting .284 in 1941, another pennant season, he became a part-time player. His two-run home run in the fifth game of the 1943 World Series gave the Yankees a 2–0 victory and another championship, Dickey's eighth and last.

He served in the Navy during 1944 and 1945, then returned to the Yankees for one more year. He guided the team to a 57–48 record as interim manager during the 1946 season.

Dickey managed briefly in the minor leagues, then became the link to yet another Yankee dynasty in 1949, when Casey Stengel hired him as a coach to help polish Yogi Berra's defensive skills. He remained as a coach through 1957, became a scout for two seasons, and then coached again in 1960 before retiring from baseball.

In 1,789 games, Dickey batted .313 with 1,969 hits. He had 343 doubles, 72 triples, and 202 home runs, scoring 930 runs and driving in 1,209. He led AL catchers in fielding percentage four times.

★ Baseball Hall of Fame

Diddle, Edgar A.

BASKETBALL
b. March 12, 1895, Gradyville, Ky.
d. Jan. 2, 1970

After playing football and basketball at Centre College in Kentucky, Diddle coached high school basketball for two years and then became coach at Western Kentucky University in 1923. He spent 42 seasons there, winning 759 games against 302 losses.

When he retired in 1965, he was the fourth winningest coach in college history and the only one to coach more than 1,000 games at a single school. The colorful Diddle constantly had a red towel which he used to cheer on his players. He often threw it into the air to protest an official's call, looped it around his neck like a noose when things were going bad, or buried his face in it when one of his players made a mistake.

Diddle's teams won or shared 32 conference championships, and they won 20 or more games 18 times, including ten seasons in a row, 1933–34 through 1942–43. They played in eight National Invitation Tournaments and three NCAA tournaments.

Western Kentucky's arena, built in 1963, is named for him.

★ Basketball Hall of Fame

Didrikson, Babe. *See* Zaharias, Babe Didrikson

Diegel, Leo

GOLF
b. April 27, 1899, Detroit, Mich.
d. May 8, 1951

"Eagle Diegel," as he was known after winning the Canadian Open with a 274 that included one round of 65, was a terribly nervous golfer who seemed able to relax during matches — he won the PGA championship in 1928 and 1929, when it was at match play — but not during major stroke play tournaments.

Diegel, who set a 72-hole record with a 275 in the 1922 Shreveport Open, finished among the top eight in the British and U.S. Opens 11 times without winning. He once bet he could shoot a 30 for nine holes, and won with a 29. A fellow golfer said that Diegel, given a week's practice, could probably break the course record anywhere — as long as he didn't have to wait for other foursomes or other players to get out of his way.

★ PGA Hall of Fame

Dihigo, Martin

BASEBALL
b. May 24, 1905, Havana, Cuba
d. May 20, 1971

During his more than 40 years in professional baseball, Dihigo played every position, including pitcher, and played them all well. Many former teammates and opponents have called him the greatest ever. But because he was a dark-skinned Cuban, he never got to the major leagues.

His professional career began in 1923, in the Cuban Winter League. The following season, he began playing for the Cuban Stars in the Eastern Colored League during the summer, returning to Cuba to play winter ball.

The 6-foot-1, 190-pound Dihigo was primarily an outfielder in the U.S., though he also played the infield at times and occasionally pitched. In Cuba and Mexico he was primarily a pitcher, compiling a record of 234 wins against only 117 losses.

With the Philadelphia Hillsdale Club in 1929, he batted .386 with 18 home runs and 21 stolen bases in just 65 games; he also had a 4–2 record as a pitcher. From 1931 through 1934, he played entirely in Cuba and Venezuela, then returned to the U.S. for two seasons with the New York Cubans in the Negro National League.

In the 1935 East / West All-Star game, Dihigo started in center field and batted third for the East, then came on as a relief pitcher in the late innings. He is credited with a .372 batting average that season.

Dihigo played in the Dominican Republic, Mexico, and Cuba during the late 1930s. He played one more season in the U.S. in 1945, then went back to Mexico, where he played through 1957. After Fidel Castro took power in Cuba in 1959, Dihigo was named minister of sports in his native country.

★ Baseball Hall of Fame

Dillard, Harrison (William Harrison)

TRACK AND FIELD
b. July 8, 1923, Cleveland, Ohio

When Cleveland honored the great Jesse Owens with a parade upon his return from the 1936 Olympics, the 13-year-old Dillard was one of the spectators. He later met Owens, who presented him with his first pair of running shoes.

Dillard became the only athlete ever to win Olympic gold medals in a sprint and a hurdle event. He was unquestionably the best hurdler of his time, winning 82 consecutive races from May 31, 1947, through June 26, 1948. However, he hit several hurdles in the Olympic trials and failed to qualify in his specialty, although he made the Olympic team by finishing third in the 100-meter dash.

In the Olympic final, Dillard and Barney Ewell finished in a virtual dead heat, and the photo showed that Dillard was the winner. He tied the world record of 10.3 seconds. Dillard qualified in the 110-meter hurdles in 1952 and won his second individual gold in that event. He was also on gold-medal 4 x 100-meter relay teams in both 1948 and 1952.

Known as "Bones" because of his tall,

lean frame, Dillard entered Baldwin-Wallace College in 1941 and two years later was drafted into the Army. He returned to college in 1946. He won the NCAA and AAU 120-yard and 220-yard hurdles in both 1946 and 1947, and he tied world records in both events with a 22.3 in the 220 in 1946 and a 13.6 in the 120.

Because of his great start, Dillard won the AAU indoor 60-yard hurdle event seven years in a row, 1947 through 1953, and again in 1955, his last year of competition. He was also the outdoor 110-meter high hurdle champion in 1952. Dillard was named Sullivan Trophy winner in 1953 as the nation's outstanding amateur athlete.

★ National Track & Field Hall of Fame; Olympic Hall of Fame

DiMaggio, Joseph P. [Giuseppe Paolo DiMaggio]

BASEBALL
b. Nov. 25, 1914, Martinez, Calif.

Casey Stengel summed up DiMaggio pretty well: "Joe did everything so naturally that half the time he gave the impression he wasn't trying. He had the greatest instincts of any ballplayer I ever saw. He made the rest of them look like plumbers."

DiMaggio left high school after one year to work in a fish cannery, then joined the San Francisco Seals of the Pacific Coast League in 1933. He hit safely in 61 consecutive games that season, an all-time record for professional baseball. The following year, he suffered a knee injury that made several major league teams lose interest in him.

However, the New York Yankees signed him late that year. After one more minor league season, DiMaggio joined the Yankees in 1936 as one of the most highly touted rookies in history. An ankle injury kept him out of the lineup early on in the season. When he finally made his debut on May 3, nearly 25,000 Italian-American fans showed up to wave Italian flags.

DiMaggio didn't disappoint anyone, leading the league with 15 triples and batting .323 with 29 home runs and 126 RBI. The Yankees won the first of four consecutive world championships that year. A right fielder for the first month of his career, DiMaggio moved to center field before the season ended and was soon recognized as one of the finest defensive players ever at that position.

In 1937, DiMaggio led the league with 46 home runs, 151 runs scored, and a .673 slugging percentage. After hitting .324 in 1938, he was named the league's most valuable player in 1939, when he was the AL's top hitter with a .381 average. He was batting .412 early in September, but an eye infection sent him into a slump during the last three weeks of the season.

DiMaggio won a second MVP award and was also named Associated Press male athlete of the year in 1941, when he had his legendary 56-game hitting streak. The streak ended in Cleveland, largely because of two outstanding defensive plays by third baseman Ken Keltner. DiMaggio then hit safely in his next 17 games. His 125 RBI led the league that season.

After hitting .305 in 1942, DiMaggio spent three years in the Army. He returned to the Yankees in 1946, batting just .290, but he won another MVP award in 1947, when he hit .315 with 31 doubles, 10 triples, 20 home runs, 97 runs scored, and 97 RBI.

"The Yankee Clipper" had an even better season in 1948, leading the league in home runs with 39 and RBI with 155. He became major league baseball's first $100,000 player the following year. However, a bone spur in his right heel limited him to just 76 games.

Despite continued pain, he batted .301 and hit 32 home runs, with 122 RBI, in 1950. After hitting only .263 in 1951, DiMaggio announced his retirement. Television appearances and commercials, along with his brief marriage to Marilyn Monroe in 1954, kept him in the limelight for many years, and his status as a legend was firmly established by the line, "Where have you gone, Joe Dimaggio," in a Simon and Garfunkel song featured in the 1967 movie *The Graduate*.

Two of DiMaggio's brothers, Dom and Vince, each played more than 1,000 major league games. Dom was an outstanding leadoff man and center fielder while Vince was noted for hitting with power but striking out too frequently.

In 1,736 games, DiMaggio batted .325, with 2,214 hits, 389 doubles, 131 triples, and 361 home runs. He scored 1,390 runs and drove in 1,537.

★ Baseball Hall of Fame

Dinneen, Bill (William H.)

BASEBALL
b. April 5, 1876, Syracuse, N.Y.
d. Jan. 13, 1955

A right-handed pitcher, Dinneen starred for the AL's Boston Pilgrims (now the Red Sox) in the first World Series in 1903, winning three games while losing one as Boston beat the Pittsburgh Pirates five out of eight games. Dinneen had two shutouts and a 2.01 ERA in the Series.

Nicknamed "Big Bill," the 6-foot-1, 190-pound Dinneen entered the majors with the NL Washington team in 1898 and was traded to the Boston NL team in 1900, when he had a 20–14 record. He jumped to the AL in 1902, when he was 21–21, and he had a 21–13 record to help lead Boston to the 1903 pennant.

Dinneen set a twentieth-century major league record in 1904 by pitching 37 consecutive complete games in 37 starts, compiling a 23–14 record. Quite possibly because of that streak, he was bothered by arm problems for the rest of his career. He ended his playing career with the St. Louis Browns, who released him in late August 1909.

Before the season ended, Dinneen was working as an AL umpire, and he became known as one of the best in the business at calling balls and strikes. He retired in 1937, having worked in eight World Series.

Dinneen pitched a no-hitter on September 27, 1905, and umpired six no-hitters during his career. As an umpire, he's a character in W. P. Kinsella's novel *Shoeless Joe*, on which the movie *Field of Dreams* was based.

In his 12 major league seasons, Din-neen had a 170–177 record with 23 shutouts and a 3.01 ERA. He struck out 1,127 hitters and walked 829 in 3,047⅔ innings.

Dionne, Marcel E.

HOCKEY
b. Aug. 3, 1951, Drummondville, P.Q.

After leading the Ontario Hockey Association in scoring two years in a row, despite the fact that he missed 14 games with a broken collarbone in 1970–71, Dionne was chosen by the Detroit Red Wings in the first round of the NHL's 1971 amateur draft.

Dionne spent four seasons with Detroit, winning the Lady Byng Trophy for combining skill with sportsmanlike play in 1975, when he had 121 points and only 14 penalty minutes. He went to the Los Angeles Kings before the 1975–76 season and won the Byng Trophy again in 1977.

A solid 5-foot-8, 190-pounder, Dionne was an excellent skater and stickhandler with very tricky moves near the net. He won the Art Ross Trophy as the league's scoring leader in 1980, with 137 points on 53 goals and 84 assists.

The Kings traded him to the New York Rangers during the 1986–87 season, and he played there through 1988–89 before retiring. In 1,348 games, Dionne had 1,771 points on 731 goals and 1,040 assists. He scored 45 points on 21 goals and 24 assists in 49 playoff games.

★ Hockey Hall of Fame

Ditka, Mike (Michael K.)

FOOTBALL
b. Oct. 18, 1939, Carnegie, Pa.

Captain of the Pittsburgh football team and an All-American end in 1960, Ditka was a first-round draft choice of the Chicago Bears in 1961, when he caught 56 passes for 1,076 yards and 12 touchdowns to win the NFL's rookie of the year award.

The 6-foot-3, 225-pound Ditka was not only an outstanding blocker but one of the best pass-catching tight ends in history. His 75 receptions in 1964 was a record for a tight end at the time. He started 84 consecutive games in his six seasons with the Bears and was named an All-Pro from 1961 through 1964.

A foot injury slowed him in 1965 and 1966, and he was traded to the Philadelphia Eagles. In his first season there, he suffered a partially torn knee ligament that further limited his effectiveness.

After two seasons in Philadelphia, Ditka was traded to the Dallas Cowboys in 1969. He finished his playing career with Dallas in 1972. Used mostly as a backup by the Cowboys, he showed something of his old form in 1971, catching 30 passes during the regular season and scoring a touchdown in the team's 24–3 Super Bowl victory over the Miami Dolphins.

Ditka returned to the Bears as head coach in 1982. He was consensus coach of the year in 1985, when the Bears won 15 of 16 regular season games and beat the New England Patriots, 46–10, in the Super Bowl.

Known for feuding with press, players, and even his assistants, the short-fused Ditka become increasingly irascible as the team's fortunes declined after that peak. He resigned after the Bears won only 5 games and lost 11 in 1992. His overall record was 112–68–0.
★ College Football Hall of Fame; Pro Football Hall of Fame

Dixon, George

BOXING
b. July 29, 1870, Halifax, N.S.
d. Jan. 6, 1909

The 5-foot-3½ Dixon weighed only 87 pounds when he began his professional boxing career in 1886, but he reached 122 pounds in his prime. The first black world champion in any weight class, Dixon was known as "Little Chocolate."

Although only 150 of his fights were recorded, it has been estimated that Dixon actually had as many as 800 bouts during a career that included exhibition tours in which he took on all comers.

Dixon claimed the world bantamweight title in 1888 and was officially considered the champion after knock-ing out Nunc Wallace of England in 18 rounds on June 27, 1890. However, Dixon soon outgrew the class. On May 31, 1891, he beat Cal McCarthy in 22 rounds to win the featherweight title.

He lost the championship to Solly Smith in a 20-round decision on October 4, 1897. Shortly afterward, Smith lost to Dave Sullivan, and Dixon regained the title when Sullivan was disqualified in the 10th round of their match on November 11, 1898.

Terry McGovern won the championship from Dixon with an 8th-round knockout on January 9, 1900, although Dixon claimed that McGovern was over the weight limit. He and Abe Attell fought twice within eight days for the vacated title in 1901. The first match was a 20-round draw, and Attell won a 15-round decision in the second.

Dixon retired from the ring after losing a 15-round decision to Monk Newsboy on December 1, 1906.

He won 78 fights, 30 by knockout, and lost 26, 4 by knockout. He also had 37 draws and 9 no-decisions.
★ International Boxing Hall of Fame

Dobie, Gilmour

FOOTBALL
b. Jan. 21, 1879, Hastings, Minn.
d. Dec. 23, 1948

He was known as "Gloomy Gil" because he was always pessimistic about his team's chances, but Dobie had an incredible coaching record, producing 14 unbeaten teams in 33 seasons.

Dobie played quarterback and end at the University of Minnesota, graduating in 1903, and spent two years as an assistant coach before becoming head coach at North Dakota Agricultural College (now North Dakota State) in 1906. He had a 6–0–0 record in two seasons there.

In 1908, Dobie went to the University of Washington. He spent nine seasons there and never lost a game, winning 58 while tying 3. From 1908 into 1914, Washington won 39 consecutive games.

At Navy from 1917 through 1919, Dobie had a 17–3–0 mark, then went to Cornell in 1920. He had unbeaten teams in 1921, 1922, and 1923 and was then given the first ten-year coaching contract in history. He spent a total of 16 seasons at Cornell, winning 82 games while losing 16 and tying 7.

After Cornell tightened its entrance requirements, Dobie had the first losing season of his career in 1934, and his 1935 team failed to win a game. The school paid him $11,000 to buy out the last two years of his contract. Dobie commented, "You can't win games with Phi Beta Kappas."

Dobie was seriously injured in an automobile accident in 1936 and never fully recovered. He became head coach at Boston College that fall and won 16 games while losing 6 and tying 3 in his three seasons there. He retired in 1938. His overall record was 179 wins, 45 losses, and 15 ties, a .780 percentage.
★ College Football Hall of Fame

Doble, Budd

HARNESS RACING
b. 1843, Philadelphia, Pa.
d. Sept. 3, 1919

Doble was such a celebrated harness racer that Oliver Wendell Holmes wrote a couplet about him: "Budd Doble, whose catarrhal name / So fills the nasal trump of fame."

He trained and drove some of the greatest harness horses of his time, starting in 1866, when he drove Dexter to 34 wins in 35 races. After a new owner took over Dexter in 1867, Doble bought Goldsmith Maid for $20,000. He sold her two years later for $37,000 but continued as her trainer and driver. In her 13-year career, campaigning throughout North America, Goldsmith Maid won 350 heats and 97 of 123 races. Her winnings were estimated at more than $364,000.

Beginning in 1890, Doble trained and drove Nancy Hanks, who was owned by J. Malcolm Forbes. She trotted a world record 2:04 at Terre Haute, Indiana, in 1892. The following year she ran a 2:08 at Hampden Park in Springfield, Massachusetts, breaking the track record by a full three seconds.

Doble was one of the first drivers to use the bicycle sulky, which was devel-

oped in 1892. The first one ever made was shipped to him, but Doble didn't try it until "Pop" Geers proved it was faster than the old high-wheeled sulky. When Nancy Hanks set her world record that year, she was pulling a bike sulky.
★ Hall of Fame of the Trotter

Doby, Larry (Lawrence E.)

BASEBALL
b. Dec. 13, 1924, Camden, S.C.

The first black to play in the AL, Doby made his debut with the Cleveland Indians on July 5, 1947, just three months after Jackie Robinson had broken the major league color barrier with the Brooklyn Dodgers.

The 6-foot-1, 182-pound Doby, who threw right but batted left, was soon recognized as one of the best center fielders in baseball. A good hitter with power, he was also a fine defensive player.

In 1948, his first full season, he batted .301 and helped the Indians win the World Series by hitting .318 with a game-winning home run. Named to the All-Star team every year from 1949 through 1955, Doby led the AL in home runs in 1952 and 1954, with 32 each season. He also led in runs scored with 104 in 1952 and in RBI with 126 in 1954.

The Indians traded him to the Chicago White Sox in 1956. Because of injuries, Doby became a part-time player in 1957, and he retired after splitting the 1959 season between the White Sox and the Detroit Tigers.

In 1978, Doby was named manager of the White Sox, becoming only the second black manager in major league history. He had a 37–87 record before being replaced late in the season.

Dodd, Bobby (Robert L.)

FOOTBALL
b. Nov. 11, 1908, Galax, Va.

Dodd is one of only two men enshrined in the College Football Hall of Fame both as a coach and as a player. The other is A. A. Stagg.

As a quarterback at Tennessee and a coach at Georgia Tech, Dodd was dedicated to the proposition that football should be fun. Ironically, Dodd wanted to play for Georgia Tech but was denied a scholarship, so he went to the University of Tennessee instead and became a starter in the fourth game of his sophomore season, 1928.

Dodd threw a touchdown pass in that game to tie Alabama, 13–13. Then he punted out of bounds inside the Alabama 1-yard line, and Tennessee got a safety on the next play to win, 15–13. In the 26 games Dodd started, Tennessee won 24, lost 1, and tied 1. He was named to Grantland Rice's All-American team in 1930.

After serving as an assistant to Bill Alexander at Georgia Tech for 15 years, Dodd became head coach in 1945. He believed in short, noncontact practices because he didn't want his players to get bored or stale and he insisted that they spend more time studying than practicing. Dodd was fond of telling parents, "We're not miracle workers, but if you send us a good boy to Georgia Tech, we will send you a good boy home."

He is usually credited with inventing the "belly series," in which the quarterback puts the ball in a running back's belly and reads the defense to decide whether to give the ball to him or pull it back and keep it. Dodd retired from coaching after the 1967 season and served as athletic director from 1968 through 1976.

In 23 seasons, his teams won 165 games, lost 64, and tied 8. He took Georgia Tech to 13 major bowl games, winning 9 of them, including 6 in a row.
★ College Football Hall of Fame

Dodds, Gilbert L.
TRACK AND FIELD
b. June 23, 1918, Norcatur, Kans.
d. Feb. 3, 1977

During a relatively brief career, Dodds established himself as one of America's finest indoor middle-distance runners. He studied for the ministry at Ashland College, Ohio, the Boston Theological Seminary, and Wheaton College in Illinois.

The AAU indoor mile champion in 1942, 1944, and 1947, Dodds set an American record of 4:06.5 in 1943, when he finished second to Gundar Haegg of Sweden in a Boston meet. He won the Sullivan Award as the nation's outstanding amateur athlete for his performances that year.

Dodds ran a world record indoor mile of 4:06.4, then retired after being undefeated during the indoor season. Hoping to make the 1948 Olympics, he returned to the track late in 1947 and ran a 4:06.8 mile at the Chicago Relays, then set a Madison Square Garden record of 4:07.1.

In 1948, he turned in his best time ever, a 4:05.3, in winning the Wanamaker Mile for a third time. However, he caught the mumps before the Olympic trials and was forced to retire permanently.

Doerr, Bobby (Robert P.)
BASEBALL
b. April 7, 1918, Los Angeles, Calif.

A nine-time AL all-star at second base, Doerr spent his entire major league career with the Boston Red Sox. A left-handed hitter, the 5-foot-11, 175-pound Doerr was a good hitter with surprising power as well as an outstanding defensive player who led the league's second basemen in fielding percentage four times.

Doerr joined the Red Sox in 1937 and became a full-time starter the following year. He had 22 home runs and 105 RBI in 1940 and 102 RBI in 1942. The Red Sox had a good chance at the 1944 pennant, but Doerr was drafted into the Army in August, and they ended up in fourth place. He led the league in slugging percentage that season at .528, with a .325 batting average.

He rejoined the team in 1946, when the Red Sox did win a pennant. Doerr hit 18 home runs and had 116 RBI during the regular season, and he batted .409 in the World Series, but Boston lost to the St. Louis Cardinals in seven games.

Doerr had 111 RBI in 1948, 109 in 1949, and 120 in 1950, when he led the league with 11 triples. An injury limited him to just 106 games and 402 at-bats in 1951, and he retired after that season.
★ Baseball Hall of Fame

Donahue, Michael J.
FOOTBALL
b. 1876, County Kerry, Ireland
d. ?

A quarterback at Yale, Donahue graduated in 1903 and became head coach at Auburn University in 1904. Emphasizing big linemen, solid defense, and a power offense, he built some of the first really good Southern teams. In 1913, Auburn won all eight of its games, and in 1914 the school won seven games and tied one without giving up a point. From 1913 into 1915, Donahue went 22 consecutive games without a loss.

In 19 seasons at the school, Donahue had a record of 101 wins, 37 losses, and 5 ties. He went on to Louisiana State in 1923 and had a 23–19–3 record in five seasons there. He retired after the 1927 season.

★ College Football Hall of Fame

Donelli, Buff (Aldo T.)
FOOTBALL, SOCCER
b. July 22, 1907, Morgan, Pa.
d. Aug. 9, 1994

The only person ever to coach college and professional football at the same time, Donelli was a soccer player as a teenager. He scored five goals in the championship game when the Heidelberg, Pennsylvania, Soccer Club won the 1929 National Amateur Challenge Cup.

Donelli played center for the Duquesne University football team as a freshman in 1926 and moved to halfback in 1927. He also did the team's place-kicking, but he used the standard straight-on approach, not the soccer-style kick.

He served as an assistant coach at Duquesne from 1931 through 1938, and he also played for the U.S. World Cup soccer team in 1934, when he scored all four goals in a preliminary 4–0 victory over Mexico.

In 1939, Donelli became head football coach at Duquesne, compiling a 29–4–2 record in four seasons. He was a pioneer of the wing T, a variation of the T formation in which one halfback moves to a wingback position behind and just outside an offensive end.

Owner Art Rooney of the Pittsburgh Steelers in 1941 gave Donelli a three-year, $30,000 contract to coach the team beginning in 1942. When Bert Bell resigned as Steeler coach after the second game of the 1941 season, Donelli took over while continuing to coach Duquesne.

The Steelers lost all five games under Donelli while Duquesne won its first six. Faced with a trip to California with the Duquesne team on a weekend when the Steelers were to play in Philadelphia, Donelli resigned the professional job under pressure from NFL Commissioner Elmer Layden, who had been his coach at Duquesne.

Donelli never did coach the Steelers again, but after Duquesne dropped football in 1944, he coached the NFL's Cleveland Rams to a 4–6–0 record. He serving in the Army in 1945, then coached Boston University to a 46–36–4 record from 1947 through 1956. Donelli ended his career at Columbia University, where he had a 30–67–2 record from 1957 through 1967.

Donoghue, Joseph
SPEED SKATING
b. Feb. 11, 1871
d. 1921

America's first champion speed skater, Donoghue won four world titles in 1891, the $\frac{1}{2}$-mile, 1-mile, 2-mile, and 5-mile. He was also the world 2-mile champion in 1889, and he won the first U.S. outdoor championships, in 1891 and 1892.

Donovan, Anne
BASKETBALL
b. Nov. 1, 1961, Ridgewood, N.J.

The 6-foot-8 Donovan succeeded Nancy Lieberman as the star of Old Dominion University's basketball team in 1980. She led NCAA Division I schools with an average of 14.7 rebounds per game as a junior in 1981–82, and her total of 504 rebounds in 35 games during the 1982–83 season is third highest all-time.

An All-American from 1981 through 1983, Donovan won the Wade and Naismith trophies as the nation's outstanding woman player after her senior year.

In her career she scored 2,719 points in 136 games, an average of 20.0 per game.

Donovan was named to the 1980 Olympic team that didn't compete because the U.S. boycotted the Moscow Games. She played for the gold medal Olympic team in 1984.

Donovan, Arthur, Jr.

FOOTBALL
b. June 5, 1925, Bronx, N.Y.

After entering Notre Dame on a football scholarship in 1942, Donovan enlisted in the Marines. He left the service in October 1945, and Notre Dame refused to renew his scholarship, so he went to Boston College and started as a two-way tackle for three years.

Donovan joined the Baltimore Colts in 1950. They became the New York Yanks in 1951 and the Dallas Texans in 1952. During those three seasons, the team won just three games. The franchise was reorganized in 1953 and returned to Baltimore, where only 13 of the Dallas players caught on. Donovan was one of them.

The 6-foot-3, 265-pound defensive tackle was smart and quick, able both to rush the passer and to move laterally to stop running plays. Donovan was an All-Pro from 1954 through 1957, and he anchored the defense for Baltimore's first championship team in 1958.

He was also a locker-room joker who helped ease tensions and build morale. Nicknamed "Fatso" by his teammates because he often came to training camp weighing 300 pounds or more, Donovan eventually had a clause in his contract calling for a fine if he weighed more than 270. He retired two weeks before the 1962 season began, and opening day was proclaimed Art Donovan Day in Baltimore.

★ Pro Football Hall of Fame

Dooley, Vincent J.

FOOTBALL
b. Sept. 4, 1932, Mobile, Ala.

An outstanding defensive back at Auburn University, Dooley captained the team in 1953 and played in the College All-Star game the following August.

He then served in the Marine Corps for two years.

In 1956, Dooley became an assistant coach at Auburn and was freshman coach at the school for three seasons before taking over as head coach at the University of Georgia in 1964.

Dooley coached at Georgia through the 1988 season, compiling a 201–77–10 record for a .715 winning percentage, including a 9–10–2 mark in post-season bowl games. He was consensus coach of the year in 1980, when Georgia won the national championship.

During his 25 years as coach, Georgia had only one losing season and won three Southeastern Conference championships. Dooley retired from coaching after the 1988 season but remains at the school as athletic director, a position he assumed in 1979. He ranks tenth all-time in NCAA Division I coaching victories.

Dorais, Gus (Charles E.)

FOOTBALL
b. July 2, 1891, Chippewa Falls, Wis.
d. Jan. 3, 1954

In the summer of 1913, Dorais and his Notre Dame teammate Knute Rockne worked at the Cedar Point Resort in Sandusky, Ohio. During their free time, they practiced passing on the beach with Dorais, a quarterback, throwing to Rockne, an end.

Rockne later wrote, "We mastered the technique of catching the football with hands relaxed and tried to master the more difficult feat of catching it with one hand."

After outscoring their first three opponents 169 to 7, Notre Dame traveled to West Point to face a heavily favored Army team. Dorais completed his first 12 passes, 3 of them for touchdowns, in a 35–13 victory. The win established Notre Dame as a genuine football power for the first time, and it also alerted other teams to the possibility of using the pass as a basic offensive weapon.

The 5-foot-7, 145-pound Dorais was a fast, elusive runner and dangerous kick returner as well as an accurate passer.

During his three years as a starter at Notre Dame, the school won 20 games and tied 2 without a loss.

Dorais played for several professional teams, including the Massillon Tigers, before the NFL was organized. He coached at Columbus (now Loras) College in Iowa from 1914 through 1917, at Gonzaga University from 1920 through 1924, and at Detroit University from 1925 through 1942. His overall record was 150 wins, 70 losses, and 13 ties. He had a 20–31–2 record with the NFL's Detroit Lions from 1943 through 1947.

★ College Football Hall of Fame

Dorsett, Tony (Anthony D.)

FOOTBALL

b. April 7, 1954, Rochester, Pa.

Dorsett piled up some incredible numbers as a college and professional running back. He was the first player in NCAA history to rush for more than 1,000 yards in each of four seasons at the University of Pittsburgh, where he gained a record 6,082 yards and scored 58 touchdowns in 1,133 attempts. As a junior in 1975, Dorsett gained 303 yards in 23 attempts against Notre Dame.

A consensus All-American in 1975 and 1976 and winner of the 1976 Heisman Trophy as the nation's outstanding college player, Dorsett was the first player chosen in the 1977 NFL draft, by the Dallas Cowboys.

The 5-foot-11, 185-pound Dorsett was named rookie of the year after gaining 1,007 yards in 208 attempts in 1977. He led all Super Bowl rushers with 66 yards on 15 carries when Dallas beat Denver, 27–10.

Ironically, the only time Dorsett led the league in rushing was the first time he failed to gain more than 1,000 yards, in the strike-shortened 1982 season, when he had 745 yards on 177 attempts in just nine games. In post-season play, he set an NFL record with a 99-yard touchdown run against the Minnesota Vikings.

Dorsett became an unhappy backup after Herschel Walker joined the Cowboys in 1987, and the following season he was traded to the Denver Broncos.

However, injuries limited his playing time with Denver, and he was forced to retire after suffering torn knee ligaments in the team's 1989 training camp.

In his 12 NFL seasons, Dorsett gained 12,379 yards, second only to Walter Payton, on 2,936 attempts, and he scored 77 rushing touchdowns while averaging 4.4 yards per carry. He caught 382 passes for 3,432 yards, a 9.0 average, and 14 touchdowns.

An All-Pro in 1981, Dorsett played in four Pro Bowls. In addition to great speed, he had an exceptional ability to cut away from tacklers. Dan Reeves, an assistant coach at Dallas and later Dorsett's head coach at Denver, once said of him, "Very few players have ever had the skill or balance to change direction without loss of speed . . . Tony does it so smoothly."

★ College Football Hall of Fame; Pro Football Hall of Fame

Douglas, Robert J.

BASKETBALL

b. Nov. 4, 1881, St. Kitts, B.W.I.

d. July 16, 1979

Douglas grew up in Harlem and played amateur basketball for a number of teams in and around New York City. In 1922, he decided to organize his own team, to be called the Spartans. The owners of the new Renaissance Casino in Harlem agreed to let the team play in the casino's second-floor ballroom, and Douglas renamed his team the Renaissance Big Five.

The Rens, as they were known, won 38 of 48 games in their first season, playing before crowds of fans dressed in evening clothes for the dancing that followed the basketball.

In 1925, Douglas signed three outstanding players, Clarence "Fat" Jenkins, James "Pappy" Ricks, and Eyre "Bruiser" Saitch, and the Rens began playing some games outside the casino. Charles "Tarzan" Cooper, John "Casey" Holt, "Wee Willie" Smith, and Bill Yancey joined the team during the next several years. By 1932, the Rens were primarily a barnstorming team, returning to the Renaissance Casino only during the Thanksgiving and Christmas holidays.

As a coach, Douglas emphasized sharp passing and tough defense, and he held an annual pre-season training camp to allow new players to try out. The Rens won more than 2,300 games in 22 years, including 14 straight seasons of more than 100 wins. In the 1932–33 season, they won 120 while losing only 8 and compiled an 88-game winning streak. They beat the Original Celtics 8 of 14 games that season. Their only other losses were to the New York Jewels and a Yonkers team, and the Rens beat each of those teams twice.

The Rens won the first world basketball championship in March 1939, beating the National Basketball League champions, the Oshkosh All-Stars, 34–25, in the final.

Douglas was the first black inducted into the Basketball Hall of Fame, and the Renaissance Big Five is one of four teams admitted to the Hall as a unit.

★ Basketball Hall of Fame

Doyle, Larry (Lawrence J.)

BASEBALL
b. July 31, 1886, Caseyville, Ill.
d. March 1, 1974

"Laughing Larry" won the Chalmers Award as the NL's most valuable player in 1912, when he batted .330, scored 98 runs, and had 90 RBI. A left-handed hitter, he played second base for New York Giants teams that won three straight pennants, from 1911 through 1913.

The ebullient Doyle is probably best known for exclaiming, "It's great to be young and a Giant." But he was a solid player, both offensively and defensively. Doyle joined the Giants in 1907 and led the league in hits with 172 in 1909. He was the triples leader in 1911 with 25.

Doyle's best year was 1915, when he won the batting title with a .320 average, also leading the league with 189 hits and 40 doubles. Late in the 1916 season he was traded to the Chicago Cubs, and he remained with them through 1917, then returned to the Giants for three more seasons before retiring.

In 1,766 games, Doyle had a .290 average on 1,887 hits, with 299 doubles, 123 triples, and 74 home runs. He stole 298 bases, scored 960 runs, and had 793 RBI.

Drabek, Douglas D.

BASEBALL
b. July 25, 1962, Victoria, Tex.

Drabek spent time in the minor leagues with four different organizations before joining the New York Yankees during the 1986 season. The following year, the Yankees traded him to the Pittsburgh Pirates.

He won the NL's Cy Young Award in 1990, when he led the league in victories with a 22–6 record and had a 2.76 ERA. Drabek won 15 games each of the next two years, and the Pirates won three consecutive Eastern Division titles.

Drabek wasn't so successful in postseason play, although he pitched well. In the 1990 league championship series, he had a 1.65 ERA, and in 1991 he allowed only one earned run in 15 innings, yet he had only a 1–1 record each year. He set a record by losing three games, all starts, in the 1992 LCS. Drabek went to the Houston Astros as a free agent in 1993. Through 1994, he has a 120–94 record.

Drahos, Nicholas

FOOTBALL
b. Dec. 6, 1918, Ford City, Pa.

The 6-foot-3, 210-pound Drahos was a starting tackle at Cornell University for three years and was named an All-American in 1939 and 1940. Very fast and agile for his size, he also served as the team's place-kicker. Cornell had a 19–3–1 record with Drahos as a starter, including an 8–0–0 mark in 1939.

Drahos played for the New York Americans of the American Football League in 1941 and was named to the all-league team. He entered military service in 1942 and never returned to football, except for a brief stint as freshman line coach at Cornell in 1947, when he was doing graduate work.

Drake, Bruce

BASKETBALL
b. Dec. 11, 1905, Gentry, Tex.
d. Dec. 2, 1983

Although he never played football in high school, Drake was the University of Oklahoma's starting quarterback for two years and was also a fine pole vaulter. But basketball was his strong suit. He played forward for three seasons, then switched to guard in his senior year, 1928–29, and was retroactively named to the Helms All-American team.

Drake became assistant coach to Bruce McDermott at Oklahoma after graduating, and he succeeded McDermott in 1938. His teams were usually small, nicknamed the "Roundball Runts," and Drake developed an offense using constant movement and screens to free his players against taller opponents. The offense became known as the "Drake shuffle."

When 7-foot-1 Bob Kurland of archrival Oklahoma State arrived on the scene in 1943, Drake began a campaign to ban goaltending. The Basketball Rules Committee adopted such a rule in 1945.

Drake's teams had 200 victories and 191 losses, and they won or shared six conference championships in his 18 seasons. He resigned after the 1954–55 season, then coached the U.S. Air Force team to the armed services championship. He also coached the Wichita Vickers to a tie for the National Industrial Basketball League title. His last coaching stint was as an assistant with the 1948 U.S. Olympic team.
★ Basketball Hall of Fame

Draves, Victoria (Manalo)

DIVING
b. Dec. 31, 1924, San Francisco, Calif.

Although she was generally at her best in the platform dive, Draves won gold medals in both the springboard and the platform event at the 1948 Olympics.

The child of a Filipino father and an English mother, she used her mother's maiden name, Draves, in order to train at swim clubs that would not have admitted someone with a Filipino name.

Draves won the AAU national outdoor platform championship from 1946 through 1948, and she was also the indoor 1-meter springboard champion in 1948. She retired after winning her Olympic medals.

Drexler, Clyde

BASKETBALL
b. June 22, 1962, New Orleans, La.

A member of the famed "Phi Slamma Jamma" team at the University of Houston, the 6-foot-7, 222-pound Drexler averaged 14.4 points a game in his three-year career there. He left school after his junior year to enter the NBA draft pool in 1983 and was chosen in the first round by the Portland Trail Blazers.

He was a part-time player as a rookie and became a starting guard in his second season, 1984–85. Drexler suddenly blossomed as a scorer in 1987–88, when he averaged 27.0 points a game. Very fast and agile despite his size, Drexler is a master on the fast break and also has a good outside shot.

Named to the All-NBA third team in 1990 and to the second team in 1988 and 1991, Drexler was a first team selection in 1992, when he averaged 25.0 points a game. He missed much of the 1992–93 season with a back injury.

Through 1994, he had scored 17,136 points in 826 regular season games, a 20.7 average, and he also had 1,721 steals, 4,725 assists, and 5,105 rebounds. In 94 playoff games, Drexler has scored 2,015 points, a 21.4 average, with 190 steals, 640 assists, and 670 rebounds.

Drillon, Gordie (Gordon A.)

HOCKEY
b. Oct. 23, 1914, Moncton, N.B.

Drillon and Syl Apps formed one of hockey's most prolific scoring combinations with the Toronto Maple Leafs during the late 1930s and early 1940s. One reason for their success was that they practiced together for hours, against goalie Turk Broda, with Apps shooting and Drillon deflecting the puck into the net. Drillon won the Art Ross Trophy as the NHL's top scorer in the 1938–39 season, when he had 52 points on 26 goals and 26 assists, many of the goals coming on deflections.

After playing minor league hockey in Pittsburgh and Indianapolis, Drillon joined the Maple Leafs in 1936. He played with them through 1941–42, then went to the Montreal Canadiens for one season before retiring. During his seven NHL seasons, he scored 155 goals and had 139 assists in regular season games and added 26 goals and 15 assists in seven playoff series. He was the league's all-star right wing in both 1937–38 and 1938–39.

★ Hockey Hall of Fame

Driscoll, Paddy (John L.)

FOOTBALL
b. Jan. 11, 1896, Evanston, Ill.
d. June 29, 1968

Although he is generally listed as a quarterback because he called his team's signals in college and professional football, Driscoll was actually a tailback. Only a fair passer, he was a great punter and drop-kicker and a fast, shifty runner. As a sophomore at Northwestern in 1915, he had an 85-yard kickoff return against Iowa.

Driscoll captained the team in his junior year and scored a touchdown and a field goal in a 10–0 win when Northwestern beat the University of Chicago for the first time since 1901. He entered the Navy in 1917, shortly after the U.S. got involved in World War I.

Playing for the Great Lakes Naval Training Station team that went undefeated in 1918, Driscoll starred in a 17–0 victory over the Mare Island Marines in the 1919 Rose Bowl game. He gained 236 yards in total offense, including a 32-yard touchdown pass to George Halas.

After playing for the independent Hammond, Indiana, Pros in 1919, Driscoll joined the Chicago Cardinals of the American Professional Football Association (now the NFL) in 1920. He scored 27 points on four touchdowns and three conversions against Rochester in 1923, a league record at the time. His 50-yard field goal against Milwaukee in 1924

tied the record set by Fats Henry. Against Columbus in 1925 Driscoll set a record by kicking 4 field goals, from 18, 23, 35, and 50 yards. His 11 field goals was the record for a season.

In 1926, he was traded to the Chicago Bears, and he remained with them through the 1929 season before retiring. He coached Marquette University from 1937 through 1940, winning 10 games while losing 23 and tying 1.

★ College Football Hall of Fame; Pro Football Hall of Fame

Drury, Morley E.

FOOTBALL
b. Feb. 15, 1903, Midland, Ont.
d. Jan. 22, 1989

"The noblest Trojan of them all," according to West Coast sportswriters, Drury was the first player from the University of Southern California to rush for more than 1,000 yards in a season and the first named to the College Football Hall of Fame.

Drury started at quarterback for three seasons and captained the USC team as a senior in 1927, when he was an All-American. During his career, the school won 27 games, lost 5, and tied 1. A strong runner and accurate passer, Drury was also an exceptionally smart signal-caller who could carry out Coach Howard Jones's game plans to perfection.

In 1969, Drury was named to the all-time Pacific Coast team.

★ College Football Hall of Fame

Dryden, Kenneth W.

HOCKEY
b. Aug. 8, 1947, Islington, Ont.

The Montreal Canadiens called Dryden up from the minor leagues to play goal near the end of the 1970–71 season. In six games, he gave up only nine goals, and he started for the Canadiens in the Stanley Cup playoffs. Although he had a couple of shaky games, he made some spectacular saves in the final series against the Chicago Black Hawks as the Canadiens won the Stanley Cup. Dryden won the Conn Smythe Trophy as the most valuable player in the playoffs.

The following season, he won the Calder Trophy as the NHL's outstanding rookie, and he went on to win the Vezina Trophy, awarded to the league's top goaltender, five times — in 1973 and from 1976 through 1979.

An All-American at Cornell, Dryden sat out the 1974–75 season to earn his law degree at McGill University in Montreal. He retired after the 1978–79 season to practice law.

In eight seasons, Dryden won 258 games to 57 losses and 74 ties. He had 46 shutouts and a 2.24 goals-against average. He appeared in 112 playoff games, winning 80, with 10 shutouts and a 2.40 average.

★ Hockey Hall of Fame

Drysdale, Donald S.

BASEBALL
b. July 23, 1936, Van Nuys, Calif.
d. July 3, 1992

A 6-foot-6, 216-pound right-hander who could terrorize right-handed hitters with his sidearm fastball, Drysdale spent his entire 14-year major league career with the Dodgers.

He joined them in 1956, when they were in Brooklyn, and went with them to Los Angeles in 1958. Drysdale led the league with four shutouts and 242 strikeouts in 1959 and was the strikeout leader again with 246 the following season.

His finest year was 1962, when he won the Cy Young Award with a 25–9 record, 2.83 ERA, and 232 strikeouts in 314 innings, leading the league in victories, strikeouts, and innings pitched. He had only one other 20-victory season, a 23–12 mark in 1965, but undoubtedly would have had more if he'd pitched for a team that scored more runs than the weak-hitting Dodgers.

Drysdale teamed with Sandy Koufax to form one of the best righty-lefty pitching combinations in history. He and Koufax staged a joint holdout after the 1965 season, asking for salaries of $175,000 apiece. At the time, only Mickey Mantle and Willie Mays earned more than $100,000. Drysdale finally

signed for $110,000, while Koufax got $130,000.

On May 14, 1968, Drysdale beat the Chicago Cubs, 1–0. It was the beginning of a streak of six consecutive shutouts and 58⅓ consecutive scoreless innings, breaking Walter Johnson's record of 56. (Drysdale's record was broken by another Dodger, Orel Hershiser, in 1988.)

The streak was aided by a controversial call. In the ninth inning of a game against the San Francisco Giants, the Giants loaded the bases with no one out, and a Drysdale pitch nicked a hitter, apparently forcing in a run. But umpire Harry Wendlestedt ruled that the hitter hadn't made an attempt to avoid the pitch. Drysdale then retired him and the next two hitters without giving up a run, stretching his streak to 45 innings.

Drysdale retired after the 1969 season and became a broadcaster for the Dodgers. He died of a heart attack while in Montreal to announce a game.

He had a career record of 209 wins and 166 losses, with an ERA of 2.95. Drysdale struck out 2,486 hitters and walked 855 in 3,432 innings.

★ Baseball Hall of Fame

Dudley, Bullet Bill (William McG.)

FOOTBALL
b. Dec. 24, 1921, Bluefield, Va.

Only 5-foot-10 and 176 pounds, Dudley wanted to play football at Virginia Polytechnic but was rejected because of his size. He went instead to the University of Virginia, where he was an All-American halfback in 1941.

He joined the Pittsburgh Steelers in 1942, led the NFL in rushing with 696 yards on 162 carries, and was named to the All-Pro team. After serving as a bomber pilot in World War II, Dudley returned to the Steelers for part of the 1945 season and again led the NFL in rushing in 1946 with 604 yards on 146 attempts.

Because of differences with Pittsburgh coach Jock Sutherland, Dudley was traded to the Detroit Lions. The remarkably versatile Dudley scored 13 touchdowns for the Lions in 1947, 7 on pass receptions, 4 on runs from scrimmage, 1 on a punt return, and 1 on a kickoff return, in addition to throwing 2 touchdown passes.

He played for Detroit through 1949, then joined the Washington Redskins for two seasons. Dudley sat out the 1952 season, returned to the Redskins briefly in 1953, then retired for good.

During his nine professional seasons, Dudley gained 3,057 yards on 765 rushing attempts, a 4.0 average, and scored 20 touchdowns; caught 123 passes for 1,383 yards and 18 touchdowns; returned 124 punts for 1,515 yards and 3 touchdowns; ran back 78 kickoffs for 1,743 yards and 1 touchdown; intercepted 23 passes and returned them for 459 yards and 2 touchdowns; and punted 191 times for a 38.2-yard average. He added 121 extra points and 33 field goals to his 44 touchdowns for a total of 484 points.

★ College Football Hall of Fame; Pro Football Hall of Fame

Duffy, Hugh

BASEBALL
b. Nov. 26, 1866, Cranston, R.I.
d. Oct. 19, 1954

Only 5-foot-7 and 168 pounds, Duffy arrived in the major leagues with the NL's Chicago team during the 1888 season and was accosted by legendary manager Cap Anson, who said, "We've got a bat boy. What are you doing here?"

The right-handed outfielder spent just a season and a half in the league before jumping the Chicago team in the new Players' League in 1890. He led the PL in runs scored with 161 and hits with 191.

The league folded after one season, and Duffy went to the Boston team in the American Association, then a major league, in 1891, and had 161 RBI to lead the league. The American Association merged into the NL in 1892, with Boston moving into the 12-team league.

After batting .301 and .363, Duffy had one of the greatest seasons in history in 1894. His .440 average that year is an all-time record. He also led the league in hits with 237, doubles with 51, home

runs with 18, RBI with 145, and slugging percentage with .694.

He never came close to such figures again, although he hit over .300 each of the next three seasons and again led the league in home runs with 11 in 1897.

Duffy became a part-time player in 1900. The following season, he helped organize a Boston team for the American League, which claimed major-league status for the first time. Duffy became playing manager of the league's Milwaukee team.

The team moved to St. Louis in 1902, but Duffy remained in Milwaukee as manager of a minor league team for two seasons, then became manager of the NL's Philadelphia franchise from 1904 through 1907. He played occasionally during his first three seasons in Philadelphia.

Duffy also managed the Chicago White Sox in 1910 and 1911 and the Boston Red Sox in 1921 and 1922. He later served the Red Sox as a scout.

In 1,737 games, Duffy batted .324, with 2,282 hits. He had 325 doubles, 119 triples, 106 home runs, 1,552 runs scored, 1,302 RBI, and 574 stolen bases.

★ Baseball Hall of Fame

Dumars, Joe III

BASKETBALL
b. May 24, 1963, Shreveport, La.

Dumars averaged 22.5 points a game in four years at little McNeese State College in Louisiana and was chosen in the first round of the 1985 NBA draft by the Detroit Pistons.

After a year as a backup, the 6-foot-3, 195-pound Dumars became a starter in 1986–87 and was soon recognized as one of the finest defensive guards in the league. He was named to the NBA's all-defensive team in 1989, 1990, 1992, and 1993.

He also worked on his shooting and became a very good scorer, averaging 20.4 points a game in 1990–92, 19.9 in 1991–92, and 23.5 in 1992–93. Dumars was named most valuable player of the 1989 NBA finals, when he scored 109 points and had 24 assists in a four-game victory over the Los Angeles Lakers.

Through the 1993–94 season, Dumars had scored 11,865 points in 695 regular season games, a 17.1 average, and he also had 3,274 assists and 663 steals. In 99 playoff games, he scored 1,591 points, a 16.1 average, with 478 assists and 84 steals.

Dumas, Charley (Charles E.)
TRACK AND FIELD
b. Feb. 12, 1937, Tulsa, Okla.

The first high jumper to surpass 7 feet, Dumas accomplished that at the 1956 Olympic trials, when he was only 19. He went on to win the gold medal in the event with an Olympic record of 6 feet, 11¼ inches.

As a student at the University of Southern California, Dumas surprisingly never won an NCAA championship, but he tied for the AAU championship with Ernie Shelton in 1955 and won the event the next four years, 1956 through 1959. After finishing sixth at the 1960 Olympics, he retired. He came back in 1964 and had a jump of 7 feet, ¼ inch, but failed to make the Olympic team and retired for good.
★ National Track & Field Hall of Fame

Dundee, Johnny [Joseph Corrara]
BOXING
b. Nov. 22, 1893, Sciacca, Italy
d. April 22, 1965

Considered one of the greatest featherweights of all time, Dundee had a problem staying under the weight limit and spent much of his career fighting as a lightweight, where he was not as successful.

He began boxing in 1910, when he won all 14 of his fights. On April 29, 1913, he fought Johnny Kilbane for the featherweight championship, but Kilbane retained the title with a 20-round draw. Dundee didn't get another championship fight until November 18, 1921, when he won the junior lightweight title from George Chaney on a foul in the 5th round.

After two successful defenses, Dundee lost the title to Jack Bernstein in a 10-round decision on May 30, 1923. However, he became world featherweight champion by decisioning Eugene Criqui in 15 rounds on July 26, and he regained the junior lightweight title by beating Bernstein in 15 rounds on December 17, becoming one of the few fighters ever to hold two championships at the same time.

Dundee lost the junior lightweight title to Kid Sullivan on June 20, 1924, and resigned the featherweight title shortly afterward because he couldn't make the weight. He fought lightweights for the rest of his career, retiring after a loss to Al Dunbar late in 1932.

In 321 fights, Dundee had 113 victories, 19 by knockout. He lost 31, 2 by knockout. He also fought 18 draws and 159 no-decisions.
★ International Boxing Hall of Fame

Duran, Roberto
BOXING
b. June 16, 1951, Guarare, Panama

Known as "Manos de Piedra," Spanish for "Hands of Stone," Duran learned to fight on the streets as a youngster, and he was a street fighter in the ring, unshaven and glaring, pounding opponents with nonstop punches. "I am not an animal outside the ring," he has said, "but when I am fighting, there is much animal in me."

He won his first 28 professional fights, 23 by knockout, before facing Ken Buchanan of Scotland for the world lightweight title on June 26, 1972, in Madison Square Garden. When the 13th round ended, Buchanan dropped, claiming he'd been hit by a low blow. But Duran was awarded the victory and the championship.

Duran held the title until February 1, 1979, when he resigned to fight as a welterweight. He won that championship on June 20, 1980, with a 15-round decision over Sugar Ray Leonard in Montreal.

His reputation lost much of its luster in the rematch with Leonard on November 28, 1980. Stung by Leonard's taunts and frustrated by his inability to land many punches on his speedier opponent, Duran suddenly dropped his hands in the 8th round and said, "No mas" —

"no more" in Spanish — though he was apparently not hurt.

In 1982, Duran began fighting as a light middleweight. He won the World Boxing Association version of that championship by knocking out Davey Moore in the 8th round on June 16, 1983, in New York City.

Since then, Duran's career has been stop-and-go. He's retired and come out of retirement several times and has moved up to the super middleweight class. Through 1994, he had won 90 of his 100 fights, 62 of them by knockout.

Durham, Dianne

GYMNASTICS
b. June 7, 1968, Gary, Ind.

The first black athlete to win a national gymnastics championship, Durham won the balance beam, floor exercise, vault, and all-around titles in 1983 and tied for second in the uneven bars. She also won the gold medal in the all-around and the silver in the uneven bars at the McDonald's International Championships that year, but injured a knee and couldn't compete in the other individual events.

After finishing third in the all-around at the Chunichi Cup competition in December 1983, Durham missed the finals of the 1984 American Cup competition and had to withdraw from the Olympic trials because of the recurring knee injury, which forced her premature retirement.

Durham, Bill (William R.)

HOCKEY
b. Jan. 22, 1915, Toronto, Ont.
d. Oct. 31, 1972

In seven seasons in the NHL, all with the Montreal Canadiens, Durnan won the Vezina Trophy as the league's best goaltender six times. He quit abruptly during the 1950 Stanley Cup series against the New York Rangers because his health was being destroyed by the emotional pressures of the position. He said afterward, "It got so bad that I couldn't sleep on the night before a game. I couldn't even keep my meals

down. I felt that nothing was worth that kind of agony."

The 6-foot-2, 200-pound Durnan was ambidextrous, and his ability to shift the goalie stick from one hand to another was a great asset throughout his career. He played amateur hockey for eight seasons before joining the minor league Montreal Royals in 1940. The Canadiens called him up in 1943–44, when he was 28 years old, and he won his first Vezina as a rookie that season. The only year he didn't win it while in the NHL was 1948, when it went to Turk Broda of Toronto.

In 383 regular season games, Durnan had 34 shutouts and a 2.35 goals-against average. He had 2 shutouts and a 2.20 average in 45 playoff games.
★ Hockey Hall of Fame

Durocher, Leo E.

BASEBALL
b. July 27, 1906, W. Springfield, Mass.
d. Oct. 7, 1991

Babe Ruth once called Durocher the "All-American out." He wasn't much of a hitter, compiling a career average of just .247 in 17 major league seasons with the New York Yankees, Cincinnati Reds, St. Louis Cardinals, and Brooklyn Dodgers, but he was a good shortstop and a scrappy, hustling player.

Durocher was known as "Leo the Lip" because he always had something to say, including "Nice guys finish last." He was playing manager of the Dodgers from 1939 through 1945, when he retired as a player but continued managing. The Dodgers won the NL pennant under his guidance in 1941, but lost to the New York Yankees in a five-game World Series.

Before the 1947 season, the Yankees hired two coaches, Charlie Dressen and Red Corriden, away from the Dodgers. An angry Durocher then accused Lee MacPhail, New York's general manager, of associating with gamblers. After an investigation, Durocher was suspended for a year for his statement.

He returned as manager in 1948. With the Dodgers mired in sixth place,

Durocher suddenly gave up the Brooklyn job and became manager of the crosstown New York Giants, stunning Dodger and Giant fans alike.

Durocher managed the Giants to pennants in 1951 and 1954. The 1951 pennant race is one of baseball's most famous. The Giants were 13½ games behind the Dodgers on August 12, but they tied them at the end of the season and won the playoff when Bobby Thomson hit his legendary home run off Ralph Branca in the ninth inning of the third and final game. The pennant drive became known as the "Little Miracle of Coogan's Bluff," named for the site of the Polo Grounds.

The Giants lost the World Series to the Yankees in six games that year, but in 1954 they swept the favored Cleveland Indians in four games.

Durocher retired after the Giants slipped to third place in 1955. However, he rejoined the Dodgers, now in Los Angeles, as a coach in 1961, and he was named manager of the Chicago Cubs in 1966. After being fired during the 1972 season, he took over the Houston Astros and managed them through 1973 before retiring for good.

In 24 seasons as a manager, his teams won 2,008 games and lost 1,709, a .540 winning percentage.

Durrance, Dick (Richard)

SKIING
b. Oct. 14, 1914, Tarpon Springs, Fla.

Durrance fell in love with skiing while attending Peekskill, New York, Academy, and he went to high school in New Hampshire to pursue the sport. He enrolled at Dartmouth College in 1934. There were no national intercollegiate championships at the time, but Durrance won the U.S. men's downhill, slalom, and Alpine combined in 1937, while still a student.

He repeated in all three events in 1939 and also won the slalom and combined titles in 1940 and the slalom for a fourth time in 1941. Durrance was a member of the 1936 Olympic ski team and was named to the 1940 team that didn't compete because of World War II.

In 1938, Durrance began working as a still and motion picture photographer at Sun Valley, Idaho, then a new ski resort. He trained para-ski troops during the war, and in 1947 he became manager of the resort in Aspen, Colorado. He later made commercial and industrial films and designed ski areas.

Dwight, James

TENNIS
b. July 14, 1852, Paris, France
d. July 14, 1917

Sometimes called "the Father of American Tennis," Dwight won the first recorded tournament in the U.S., played in 1876 on the property of his uncle, William Appleton, at Nahant, Massachusetts.

After graduating from Harvard in 1874, he traveled in Europe, saw the new sport of lawn tennis being played, and brought the necessary equipment home. Then he persuaded his uncle to mark out a court on his smooth front lawn so he could play a game with his cousin, Fred Sears.

That first attempt was disappointing. Dwight later wrote, "We voted the whole thing a fraud and put it away." About a month later they tried again, as a way of passing time on a rainy day. This time, tennis seemed much more interesting, even though they were wearing rubber boots and raincoats. The 1876 tournament was a neighborhood affair; by then, Dwight and Sears had taught the game to a number of people, including another cousin, Richard Sears, who went on to win the first seven national singles championships.

Dwight was one of the founders of the U.S. National Lawn Tennis Association in 1881, and he served as its president for 21 years. He never won the singles championship, but he did team with Richard Sears to take five national doubles titles, from 1882 through 1884 and from 1886 through 1887.

★ International Tennis Hall of Fame

Dye, Babe (Cecil H.)

HOCKEY

b. May 13, 1898, Hamilton, Ont.
d. Jan. 2, 1962

One of the greatest scorers in the early history of the NHL, Dye joined the Toronto St. Pats in 1919 and remained with them through the 1925–26 season. After one season with the Chicago Black Hawks, he broke a leg during training camp in 1927. The following year, he made a comeback with the New York Americans but retired after scoring only once in 41 games.

Dye was the league's top scorer in 1922–23 with 26 goals and 11 assists and in 1923–24 with 38 goals and 6 assists. He finished among the top 5 four other times. Twice he scored five goals in a game, and he scored four in a 5–1 victory over Vancouver that won the 1921 Stanley Cup for Toronto.

After retiring as a player, Dye coached the minor league Chicago Shamrocks and was an NHL referee for five years. In nine NHL seasons, Dye scored 202 goals and had 41 assists. He added 9 goals and 2 assists in three playoff series.
★ Hockey Hall of Fame

Dye, Patrick F.

FOOTBALL

b. Nov. 6, 1939, Augusta, Ga.

A starting guard at the University of Georgia from 1958 through 1960, Dye spent three seasons as a linebacker for the Edmonton Eskimos in the Canadian Football League, then served for two years in the Army.

After his discharge in 1965, Dye became an assistant to Bear Bryant at the University of Alabama. He took over as head coach at East Carolina University in 1974 and had a 48–18–1 record in six seasons there, then guided the University of Wyoming to a 6–5–0 mark in 1980.

In 1981, Dye was named head coach and athletic director at Auburn University. He resigned as athletic director after a former player charged that he'd received payments from alumni and assistant coaches. In the wake of the scandal, Auburn was put on probation by the NCAA, and Dye resigned his coaching job after the 1992 season.

He had a 99–39–4 record at Auburn and was 153–62–5 overall for a .707 winning percentage.

Dykstra, Lenny (Leonard K.)

BASEBALL

b. Feb. 10, 1963, Santa Ana, Calif.

Dykstra became the starting center fielder for the NL's New York Mets after being called up from the minor leagues midway through the 1985 season. A left-hander, the 5-foot-10, 195-pound Dykstra quickly impressed fans and writers with his aggressive playing style.

The Mets traded him to the Philadelphia Phillies during the 1989 season. After leading the league with 192 hits in 1990, when he had a .325 average, Dykstra spent much of the 1991 and 1992 seasons on the disabled list.

He rebounded in 1993, leading the league with 143 runs scored, 194 hits, and 129 walks to help the Phillies win the pennant. Dykstra batted .280 and scored 5 runs in Philadelphia's six-game victory over the Atlanta Braves in the NL championship series, and he hit .348 with 9 runs and 8 RBI in the World Series, but the Phillies lost in six games to the Toronto Blue Jays.

In 1,176 major league games, Dykstra has a .287 average with 1,196 hits, including 260 doubles, 39 triples, and 76 home runs. He has stolen 272 bases, scored 744 runs, and driven in 373.

★ ★ E ★ ★

Eagan, Eddie (Edward P. F.)

BOBSLEDDING, BOXING
b. April 26, 1897, Denver, Colo.
d. June 14, 1967

Frank Merriwell, the fictitious Yale hero-athlete, was Eagan's idol, but Eagan's own life was more like a Horatio Alger story. He came from a poor family, graduated from Yale, went to Oxford on a Rhodes scholarship, became a prominent lawyer, and rose to the rank of colonel during World War II.

He was also the only athlete ever to win gold medals at both the Summer and the Winter Olympics. Eagan's primary sport was boxing. He won the national amateur heavyweight championship in 1919 and his first Olympic gold medal in 1920 as a light heavyweight. He also won the British amateur heavyweight while attending Oxford, and he competed in the 1924 Olympics as a heavyweight boxer without winning a medal.

In 1932, Eagan was a member of Billy Fiske's four-man bobsled team that won the gold medal.
★ Olympic Hall of Fame

Earnhardt, Dale (Ralph Dale)

AUTO RACING
b. April 29, 1952, Kannapolis, N.C.

The son of Ralph Earnhardt, who won NASCAR's late model sportsman championship in 1956, Earnhardt was named rookie of the year on the Winston Cup circuit in 1979 and won the circuit championship the following year. In the process, he became only the third driver in history to win more than $500,000 in a single season.

A relentless, hard-charging driver who never lets up, Earnhardt is nicknamed "the Intimidator." He won Winston Cup championships in 1986, 1987, 1990, 1991, and 1993, and 1994, tying Richard Petty's record of seven titles.

Among major super-speedway races, Earnhardt won the Coca-Cola 600 at Charlotte, North Carolina, in 1986, 1992, and 1993; the Southern 500 at Darlington, South Carolina, in 1987, 1989, and 1990; and the Winston 500 at Talladega, Alabama, in 1990 and 1994.

Through 1994, Earnhardt is NASCAR's all-time leading money winner with $20,906,341 and is sixth in victories with 65.

Eastman, Benjamin B.

TRACK AND FIELD
b. July 19, 1911, Burlingame, Calif.

Representing Stanford University, Eastman won the IC4A 880-yard run in 1931. He set three world records in the spring of 1932, running the 440-yard in 46.4 seconds and the 880 in 1:51.3 and 1:50.9.

Eastman won his second IC4A half-mile title in 1932, but finished second to Bill Carr in the 400-meter at the Olympic trials and Olympic Games that year.

In 1933, Eastman began to specialize in the 800-meter/880-yard event. He won the 880-yard run at the IC4A meet again that year and was the 880 champion at the 1934 AAU nationals.

Eastman set world records in two indoor events in 1933, running the 500-meter in 1:02.0 and the 600-yard dash in 1:09.2. He lowered the world record for the 880 to 1:49.8 in 1934.

After retiring late in 1934, Eastman returned in 1936 in an attempt to make the Olympics, but he ran fifth in the 800-meter at the trials and retired permanently.

Easton, Bill (Millard E.)

TRACK AND FIELD
b. Sept. 13, 1906, Stinesville, Ind.

As a coach at Drake University from 1941 through 1947, Easton produced three consecutive NCAA champion cross-country teams, from 1944 through 1946. He also served as director of the Drake Relays while he was there.

In the fall of 1947, Easton went to Kansas University as track and cross-country coach. His Kansas teams won NCAA outdoor track championships in 1959 and 1960 and the cross-country title in 1953. Before his retirement in 1965, they won 39 Big Eight conference championships in cross-country and track.

Easton coached 32 All-American athletes and 8 Olympians, including Al Oerter, who won four Olympic gold medals in the discus throw.

★ National Track & Field Hall of Fame

Eaton, Mark E.

BASKETBALL
b. Jan. 24, 1957, Westminster, Calif.

The 7-foot-4, 286-pound Eaton played basketball at Cypress Junior College in California before enrolling at UCLA in 1980. He played only 196 minutes in two years there.

Eaton was chosen in the fourth round of the 1982 NBA draft by the Utah Jazz. He led the league in blocked shots four of five years, with 351 in 1983–84, 456 in 1984–85, 321 in 1986–87, and 304 in 1987–88. He was also the league leader in defensive rebounds with 720 in 1984–85.

Twice the NBA's defensive player of the year, in 1985 and 1989, Eaton was named to the league's all-defensive first team in 1985, 1986, and 1989, and to the second team in 1987 and 1988. His 456 blocks in 1984–85 is the league record.

Through 1992–93, Eaton had scored 5,216 points in 875 regular season games, an average of 6.0 per game. He had blocked 3,064 shots and pulled down 6,939 rebounds. In 74 playoff games, he had 454 points, 210 blocks, and 557 rebounds.

Eckersall, Walter H.

FOOTBALL
b. June 17, 1886, Chicago, Ill.
d. March 24, 1930

Small even for his era, at 5-foot-7 and 142 pounds, Eckersall had great speed and was a fine kicker. As late as 1951, 45 years after his senior season at the University of Chicago, he was listed at quarterback on the Associated Press all-time All-American team.

In high school, Eckersall tied the national interscholastic record for the 100-yard dash, at 10 seconds flat. He quarterbacked and captained the football team, which beat the University of Chicago in 1901, with a long run by Eckersall setting up the winning touchdown.

He enrolled at the university in 1903 and became a starter about halfway through the season. Eckersall couldn't be ignored in 1904. He had kickoff returns of 107 yards against Texas and 106 yards against Wisconsin, and he ran 95 yards from scrimmage for a touchdown against Iowa. In a 22–12 loss to Michigan, Eckersall had a 75-yard punt. Walter Camp chose a senior, Vincent Stevenson of Pennsylvania, as his All-American quarterback, but he put Eckersall on the team at end.

Against Illinois in 1905, Eckersall drop-kicked five field goals, a record at the time. He had two against Purdue, and his 23-yard field goal against Wisconsin was the only score of the game. Eckersall was Camp's All-American quarterback that season and again in 1906.

The forward pass was legalized in 1906, and Chicago's innovative coach, A. A. Stagg, installed an option play on which Eckersall could roll out around end and either run with the ball or throw it. The play helped Chicago whip Illinois, 63–0. Against Nebraska, Eckersall kicked five field goals to tie his own record in a 38–5 victory.

Eckersall graduated in 1907 and became a sportswriter with the *Chicago Tribune.* A professional team was organized around him that season, but he retired from the sport after a few games. He later officiated in many important college games and also worked as a boxing referee.

★ College Football Hall of Fame

Eckersley, Dennis L.

BASEBALL
b. Oct. 3, 1954, Oakland, Calif.

The right-handed Eckersley has had two very successful careers in baseball, as a starting pitcher from 1975 through 1986 and as a reliever from 1987 to the present.

Eckersley became a full-time starter with the AL's Cleveland Indians in 1975, his first major league season. After winning 40 games in three years, including a no-hitter against the California Angels on May 30, 1977, he was traded to the Boston Red Sox in 1978 and had a 20–8 record with a 2.99 ERA. He remained with Boston until 1984, when he was traded during the season to the NL's Chicago Cubs.

Arm trouble hampered him in 1985, and after he went 6–11 in 1986, Eckersley was written off by many baseball people. He was traded after that season to the AL's Oakland Athletics, who made him a relief pitcher.

From 1988 through 1992, Eckersley was the best closer in baseball. He led the league in saves with 45 in 1989 and with 51 in 1992, when he won the Cy Young Award and was named the AL's most valuable player. Eckersley had a 7–1 record, a 1.91 ERA, and 93 strikeouts against only 11 walks in 80 innings of work that season.

In the 1988 league championship series, Eckersley saved every game as Oakland swept Boston. Unfortunately, he may be best remembered for the game-winning home run he gave up to the

hobbled Kirk Gibson of the Los Angeles Dodgers in the first game of the World Series that year. The heavily favored Athletics lost the series in five games.

Colorful and at times controversial, Eckersley wore long hair and a moustache before such things became fashionable, and his demonstrative celebration after a strikeout often angered hitters. He has built his success on a good fastball, an excellent, hard-breaking slider, and superb control.

Through the 1994 season, Eckersley has a career record of 188–153, with 294 saves. He has struck out 2,245 hitters and walked just 705 in 3,082⅔ innings.

Edberg, Stefan

TENNIS
b. Jan. 19, 1966, Vastervik, Sweden

Ranked first in the world in 1990 and 1991, Edberg has won six grand slam titles: Wimbledon in 1988 and 1990, the U.S. Open in 1991 and 1992, and the Australian Open in 1985 and 1987.

A strong, solid baseline player, Edberg put on a dramatic performance in his 1992 U.S. Open victory. He was losing in the fifth set of three matches, against Richard Krajicek, Ivan Lendl, and Michael Chang, but he pulled out a victory in each. Then he lost the first set of his final match against Pete Sampras before rallying to win in four sets.

Through 1994, Edberg was ranked eighth all-time with 40 tournament victories, and he ranked second in money won with $16,749,250.

Ederle, Gertrude

SWIMMING
b. Oct. 23, 1906, New York, N.Y.

Two months before her 13th birthday, Ederle set a world record in the 880-yard freestyle swim. She won the U.S. outdoor 440-yard freestyle in 1922 and 1923, the 880-yard freestyle in 1923 and 1924, and the indoor 220-yard freestyle in 1923. At the 1924 Olympics she won a bronze medal in the 100-meter freestyle and swam a leg on the gold-medal 4 x 100-meter relay team.

But distance swimming was her real strength. The first time she ever competed at a distance greater than 220 yards, she won the 1921 J. P. Day Cup for a 3-mile race in New York Bay, beating a field of 50 top distance swimmers.

Ederle became a professional swimmer in 1925. A year later, she announced her plan to become the first woman, and only the sixth person, to swim the English Channel. The *London Daily News* thundered: "Even the most uncompromising champion of the rights and capacities of women must admit that in contests of physical skill, speed and endurance, they must remain forever the weaker sex."

Shortly after 7 A.M. on August 6, 1926, Ederle entered the water on the French shore. Fourteen hours and 31 minutes later, she arrived in England. It was the fastest channel swim ever by more than two hours, breaking the record set by a man. Her time was surpassed later that year, but it remained a record for women until 1964.

Ederle became a national hero. She was welcomed home by a ticker-tape parade in New York City that was attended by an estimated two million people. She toured the vaudeville circuit, performing in a huge collapsible swimming tank, for several years.

But she paid a price for her fame. Ederle became deaf because of water damage to her eardrums during the channel swim; she suffered a nervous breakdown in 1928; and she had to wear a cast for more than four years because of a back injury. But she recovered by 1933 and became a swimming instructor for deaf children.

Paul Gallico wrote of Ederle, "She was the demonstration of those times that courage, training, willpower and indomitable spirit comprise the secret weapon against seemingly unconquerable obstacles . . . but she went through hell."

★ International Women's Sports Hall of Fame

Edwards, R. Lavell

FOOTBALL
b. Oct. 11, 1930, Orem, Utah

A center, Edwards was captain of the Utah State University football team in 1951. He spent two years in the Army and coached high school football until 1962, when he became an assistant at Brigham Young University.

Edwards was named head coach in 1973. With his burly build and rugged features, he looks like a coach who would emphasize defense and the running game, but Edwards is one of college football's foremost teachers of the pro-style passing attack.

Brigham Young never had a consensus All-American player until 1979. Since then, the school has produced four All-American quarterbacks, Marc Wilson, Jim McMahon, Steve Young, and 1990 Heisman Trophy winner Ty Detmer.

Under Edwards, Brigham Young has led the nation in passing offense eight times, total offense five times, and scoring three times. Through 1994, he has a 207–76–3 record for a .729 winning percentage.

Edwards, Turk (Albert G.)

FOOTBALL
b. Sept. 28, 1907, Mold, Wash.
d. Jan. 12, 1973

Edwards starred at tackle for Washington State from 1929 through 1931 and was named to several All-American teams in 1930. The 6-foot-2, 260-pounder intercepted a pass in the key game against Oregon State that season and ran 26 yards for the winning touchdown that brought Washington State the conference championship. In his senior year he captained the team, but the Huskies won only six of ten games, and he didn't repeat as an All-American.

In 1932 he joined the Boston Braves of the NFL. The Braves became the Redskins in 1933, and in 1937 they moved to Washington. Edwards was an All-Pro tackle in 1932, 1933, 1936, and 1937, and he was second-team All-Pro in 1934 and 1938.

Early in the 1940 season, Edwards represented the Redskins for the coin toss before a game with the New York Giants. When he was returning to the bench, his left knee buckled because of repeated ligament damage, and he never played again. Edwards coached the Redskins from 1946 through 1948, winning 16 games, losing 18, and tying 1.

★ College Football Hall of Fame; Pro Football Hall of Fame

Elder, Lee E.

GOLF
b. July 14, 1934, Dallas, Tex.

The first black player to be invited to the Masters Tournament, Elder taught himself to play golf mostly by sneaking onto all-white courses at night. He never actually played a round until he was 16.

By his late teens, he was a golf hustler, often posing as a caddie. He led that uneasy existence until 1959, when he was drafted into the Army. Elder spent most of his military stint playing golf with his commanding officer at Fort Lewis in Washington State.

After being discharged in 1961, he joined the all-black United Golf Association tour. He dominated the tour, winning five UGA national championships. In one stretch, Elder won 21 of 23 tournaments.

In November 1967, Elder become one of the first black golfers on the PGA tour. The following year, he won some notice by tying Frank Beard and Jack Nicklaus for the lead in the American Golf Classic. Beard was out of the playoff after bogeying the first extra hole, but Elder and Nicklaus dueled evenly for four holes. Nicklaus finally won with a birdie on the fifth hole after Elder narrowly missed a long birdie putt.

Elder was invited by Gary Player to take part in the 1971 South African PGA Tournament, the first integrated tournament in that country's history. He accepted after insisting on some conditions: that the gallery be integrated and that he and his wife be allowed to stay at whatever hotel they chose, free to go wherever they wanted to go.

His first PGA victory came in the 1974 Monsanto Open, automatically winning an invitation to the 1975 Masters. Elder also won the Houston Open in 1976 and played in the 1977 Masters.

Elewonibi, Mohammed T. D.

FOOTBALL
b. Dec. 16, 1965, Lagos, Nigeria

The 6-foot-4, 282-pound Elewonibi grew up in Canada and went to Snow College in Utah before transferring to Brigham Young University. A guard in college, he won the 1989 Outland Trophy as the nation's outstanding lineman and was chosen by the Washington Redskins in the third round of the NFL's college draft.

The Redskins moved him to offensive tackle, but he missed all of the 1990 season and most of the 1991 season with injuries before becoming a starter in 1992. Surprisingly agile and mobile for a player his size, Elewonibi starred in soccer as a high school student and was chosen by British Columbia in the 1985 North American Soccer League draft of amateurs.

Eller, Carl L.

FOOTBALL
b. Jan. 25, 1942, Winston-Salem, N.C.

The 6-foot-6, 245-pound Eller played offensive and defensive tackle at the University of Minnesota and was named an All-American in 1963. A first-round selection of the Minnesota Vikings in the 1964 NFL draft, Eller was moved to defensive end as a pro.

He was an important member of the Minnesota front four nicknamed the "Purple People Eaters." Because of his speed and quickness, he teamed with tackle Alan Page to give the Vikings a ferocious pass rush. The strong Minnesota defense helped take the team to four Super Bowls, after the 1969, 1973, 1974, and 1976 seasons. However, the Vikings lost all four games.

Sometimes used as an extra blocker in short-yardage situations, Eller was named an All-Pro four straight years, from 1970 through 1973. He was with the Vikings through the 1978 season and retired after spending 1979 with the Seattle Seahawks.

Eller did some acting after retirement and then established a counseling program as part of the NFL's drug rehabilitation effort. He also operates a company involved in sports psychology.

Elliott, Bob (Robert I.)

BASEBALL
b. Nov. 26, 1916, San Francisco, Calif.
d. May 4, 1966

Nicknamed "Mr. Team" by Boston sportswriters because of his unselfish play, Elliott was the NL's most valuable player in 1947, when he batted .317 with 22 home runs and 113 RBI. It was one of six seasons in which he drove in 100 or more runs.

Elliott entered the major leagues as an outfielder with the Pittsburgh Pirates in 1939, but he played mostly at third base from 1942 on. Pittsburgh traded him to Boston in 1947. He finished his career with the New York Giants in 1952 and the AL's St. Louis Browns and Chicago White Sox in 1953.

The right-handed Elliott had a career average of .289, with 2,061 hits in 1,978 games, including 382 doubles, 94 triples, and 170 home runs. He scored 2,064 runs and drove in 1,195.

Elliott, Jumbo (James F.)

TRACK AND FIELD
b. Aug. 8, 1915, Philadelphia, Pa.
d. March 22, 1981

As a student at Villanova University, Elliott ran in the 220-, 440-, and 880-yard events. He graduated in 1935 and became the school's part-time track coach while working for a company that sold contracting equipment.

Elliott was best known for developing outstanding distance runners, including Ron Delaney, Marty Liquori, Eamonn Coghlan, and Sydney Maree. In 47 years of coaching, he produced 22 Olympians, including 5 gold medalists, 33 NCAA individual champions, and the winners of 203 IC4A titles.

Villanova won the NCAA outdoor team championship in 1957 and indoor titles in 1968 and 1971. Elliott retired shortly before his death in 1981.

★ National Track & Field Hall of Fame

Elliott, Sean M.

BASKETBALL
b. Feb. 2, 1968, Tucson, Ariz.

Highly recruited after averaging 33.4 points and 14.1 rebounds a game in his senior year at Tucson's Cholla High School, Elliott elected to go to the University of Arizona. A four-year starter at forward, he broke Lew Alcindor's Pacific 10 Conference scoring record with 2,555 points. Elliott was a consensus All-American in 1988 and 1989 and won the 1989 John Wooden Award as the college player of the year.

The 6-foot-8, 205-pound Elliott was the third player chosen in the NBA college draft and joined the San Antonio Spurs for the 1989–90 season. He was named to the league's all-rookie second team. In four NBA seasons, Elliott has scored 4,656 points in 315 games, an average of 14.8, with 1,514 rebounds and 643 assists. He has averaged 14.9 points in 27 playoff games.

Elliott, Wild Bill (William C.)

AUTO RACING
b. Oct. 8, 1955, Dawsonville, Ga.

Warm and personable, Elliott is a perennial winner of NASCAR's most popular driver award. He began racing in the Winston Cup circuit during the 1976 season but didn't claim his first victory until 1983, when he had 22 top-ten finishes in 30 races.

Elliott won 11 races in 1985, including the Daytona 500 and the Winston 500 at Talladega, Alabama, collecting $2,383,187 in winnings. He also won at Daytona in 1987 and was the Winston Cup champion in 1988.

Driving for a team that includes his father and two brothers, Elliott ranked twelfth all-time with 40 victories through the 1994 season and was second in earnings with $14,406,494.

Ellison, Pervis

BASKETBALL
b. April 3, 1967, Savannah, Ga.

Nicknamed "Never Nervous Pervis" by his teammates at the University of Louisville, Ellison was named the most outstanding player of the NCAA Division I tournament in 1986, the only freshman ever to win that honor. He was the top rebounder with an average of 9.5 a game during the tournament, helping to win the national championship for Louisville.

During his four years as the school's starting center, the 6-foot-10, 225-pounder scored 2,143 points and had 1,149 rebounds in 136 games. The Sacramento Kings made him the first pick overall in the 1989 NBA draft.

Ellison missed much of his rookie year with an injury and was sent to the Washington Bullets in 1990 in a three-team trade involving three other players and four draft choices.

After spending the 1990–91 season as a backup, Ellison became a starter the following year and was voted the league's most improved player after averaging 20.0 points a game. Used mostly at forward by Washington, Ellison also occasionally played center.

Another injury limited him to only 49 games in 1992–93. Shortly before the 1994-95 season, Ellison signed with the Boston Celtics as a free agent. Through 1993-94, he had scored 3,580 points in 272 regular season games, a 13.2 average. He has never appeared in a playoff game.

Elway, John A.

FOOTBALL
b. June 28, 1960, Port Angeles, Wash.

One of the few players ever chosen in the early rounds of baseball's amateur free agent draft and the NFL's draft of college players, Elway starred in both sports at Stanford University.

He was named to some football All-American teams as a sophomore in 1980 and was a consensus All-American in 1982, when he finished second in the Heisman Trophy voting. Elway set NCAA Division I career records for passing attempts, 1,246, completions, and most games with more than 200 yards passing, 30. He had a career total of 9,349 passing yards and 77 touchdown passes.

Elway was chosen by the New York Yankees in the second round of the 1981 baseball draft, and he batted .319 for the

Oneonta team in the New York–Pennsylvania League in 1982. The Baltimore Colts made him the first player picked in the 1983 NFL draft, but he refused to play for the Colts and was traded to the Denver Broncos for two players and a first-round draft choice.

Denver signed him to a six-year contract worth $12.7 million. A part-time starter as a rookie, he took the team into the playoffs, but the Broncos lost in the first round. Led by Elway, Denver went to the American Football Conference championship game four times, winning the title in 1986, 1987, and 1989 but losing the Super Bowl all three years.

His finest season to date was 1987, when he was named Associated Press player of the year and United Press International AFC offensive player of the year. Elway that season completed 224 of 410 passes for 3,198 yards and 19 touchdowns.

The strong-armed Elway has been criticized by some for not being able to throw soft touch passes and for a tendency to scramble out of the pocket too often. However, he's noted for his ability to win games by leading last-minute scoring drives.

Through the 1994 season, Elway had completed 3,030 passes in 5,384 attempts for 37,736 yards and 199 touchdowns. He also rushed for 2,282 yards on 494 attempts, a 4.6 average, and 22 touchdowns.

Emerson, Roy

TENNIS
b. Nov. 3, 1936, Kingsway, Australia

A long jump and high jump champion in high school, Emerson was one of the most athletic of tennis players. Big, strong, and fast, he covered the court almost effortlessly and depended more than most champions on his reflexes rather than any overall strategy to beat opponents.

Emerson won 12 singles titles in grand slam events, more than any other man. His first came in the 1961 Australian national championships, when he upset Rod Laver in the final match. After losing to Laver in the 1962 final, Emerson won the Australian title five years in a row, from 1963 through 1967.

He won the U.S. national singles championship in 1961 and 1963, the Wimbledon title in 1964 and 1965, and the French championship in 1963 and 1967. Emerson also won 16 doubles titles for a record total of 28 grand slam championships.

★ International Tennis Hall of Fame

Emery, Victor

BOBSLEDDING
b. June 28, 1933, Montreal, P.Q.

As a spectator at the 1956 Winter Olympics in Cortina, Italy, Emery discovered bobsledding. After returning to Canada, he organized the Laurentian Bobsledding Association with his brother John, a surgeon; Peter Kirby, who had been a competitive skier at Dartmouth College; and Douglas Anakin, a high school teacher.

None of them had ever tried bobsledding before, but they led from the first through the fourth and final run to win the gold medal at the 1964 Winter Olympics, the first time a Canadian team had ever entered. In 1965, Emery and Kirby teamed with Michael Young and Gerald Presley to win the world championship.

★ Canadian Sports Hall of Fame

Emtman, Steven C.

FOOTBALL
b. April 16, 1970, Spokane, Wash.

Red-shirted as a freshman because the Washington State coaching staff couldn't decide what position he should play, Emtman became a starting defensive tackle in 1989. The 6-foot-4, 300-pounder won the Outland and Lombardi trophies as the nation's outstanding collegiate lineman in 1991.

Though he still had a year of eligibility remaining, Emtman entered the NFL draft of college players in 1992, saying it wasn't for the money "but rather the opportunity to fulfill a lifelong dream of playing pro football."

The Indianapolis Colts made him the first player chosen in the draft, but Emtman spent most of the season on the disabled list with an injury to his right knee. Early in the 1993 season he injured the other knee and had to undergo a series of operations. Emtman finally got back into the lineup late in the 1994 season.

Endacott, Paul

BASKETBALL
b. July 13, 1902, Lawrence, Kans.

Endacott learned basketball from its inventor, James Naismith, at the Lawrence YMCA and then played for its first full-time coach, "Phog" Allen, at the University of Kansas. Allen later called him the greatest guard he'd ever coached.

The Helms Athletic Foundation named Endacott an All-American for 1923 and 1924 and college player of the year for 1923, when Kansas won 17 of 18 games and the mythical national championship.

After graduating with a degree in civil engineering, Endacott joined the Phillips Petroleum Company as an engineer, and he played for its AAU basketball team for two years. He was president of the company from 1951 until his retirement in 1967.

★ Basketball Hall of Fame

Engle, Rip (Charles A.)

FOOTBALL
b. March 26, 1906, Elk Lick, Pa.
d. March 7, 1983

After working in Pennsylvania coal mines for six years, beginning at the age of 14, Engle played baseball, basketball, and football at Western Maryland College, graduating in 1930.

Engle coached high school sports and did graduate work before becoming an assistant coach at Brown University in 1942. He took over as head coach in 1944.

His Brown teams had a 28–20–4 record in six seasons. Engle went to Penn State in 1950. He never had a losing season there, compiling a 104–48–4 record. Engle's teams won two Liberty Bowls, beating Alabama, 7–0, in 1953 and Oregon, 41–12, in 1960, and they won the

1961 Gator Bowl, 30–15, over Georgia Tech. Penn State suffered a 17–7 loss to Florida in the 1962 Gator Bowl.

Engle retired after the 1965 season with an overall record of 132 wins, 68 losses, and 8 ties.

★ College Football Hall of Fame

English, Alexander

BASKETBALL
b. Jan. 5, 1954, Columbia, S.C.

English scored 1,972 points in 111 games as a starting forward at the University of South Carolina, an average of 17.4 points per game. He was chosen in the second round of the 1976 NBA draft by the Milwaukee Bucks.

As a rookie, the 6-foot-7, 190-pound English averaged just over 10 minutes a game. That increased to almost 20 minutes in 1977–78. English then signed as a free agent with the Indiana Pacers, who had to compensate the Bucks with a first-round draft choice.

Indiana traded him to the Denver Nuggets during the 1979–80 season, and he blossomed as a scorer with Denver, averaging 23.8 points a game in 1980–81, 25.4 in 1981–82, and a league-leading 28.4 in 1982–83.

He continued to average 25 or more points a game for the next six seasons. English became a backup in 1989–90 and joined the Dallas Mavericks for his final NBA season in 1990–91. He then played in Italy for a year before retiring.

A very durable player despite his slender build, English was a quick, skilled performer around the basket and an excellent offensive rebounder.

In his 15 NBA seasons, English scored 25,613 points in 1,193 regular season games, an average of 21.5, and he also had 833 blocked shots and 6,538 rebounds. He added 1,661 points in 68 playoff games, an average of 24.4, with 371 rebounds.

Ervin, Frank

HARNESS RACING
b. Aug. 12, 1894, Pekin, Ill.
d. Sept. 30, 1991

Like many trainer/drivers, Ervin came from a harness racing family. He once drove in a race in which his father, grandfather, and two uncles were among the other drivers.

Ervin won more than 1,000 races after the U.S. Trotting Association began keeping official records in 1939. He may have had as many as 3,000 victories in his career, because he had raced for nearly 30 years before. He claimed his first victory at Charleston, Illinois, in early 1911, when he was 16.

Among the great horses he trained and drove were Bret Hanover, who won a record 35 races in a row and is the only harness horse to be named horse of the year three times, 1964 through 1966; Yankee Lass, the first two-year-old filly to break two minutes, in 1957; Sampson Hanover, who once won 22 consecutive races; and Good Time, the first pacer to win Horse of the Year honors, in 1949.

Ervin won the Hambletonian twice and the Little Brown Jug three times. His career earnings amounted to well over $4 million.

★ Hall of Fame of the Trotter

Erving, Julius W. II

BASKETBALL
b. Feb. 22, 1950, Roosevelt, N.Y.

Although he was only 6-foot-6, Erving starred as a center at the University of Massachusetts, averaging 27 points and 19 rebounds a game in his junior year. He then left school to sign a four-year, $500,000 contract with the American Basketball Association's Virginia Squires.

Known as "Dr. J" or simply "the Doctor" because of the way he could operate on defenses, Erving was cat-quick and had incredible leaping ability. He could soar through the air from the foul line to the basket, finishing the play with a slam dunk, and he could outjump taller opponents to grab rebounds.

He was an instant star as a professional, averaging 27.2 points and 15.7 rebounds as a rookie in 1971–72. After the season, he signed a contract with the NBA's Atlanta Hawks, but a court ordered him to play for the Squires.

Erving led the league with 31.9 points in his second year, when he had 22 rebounds per game. The financially troubled Squires then traded him to the New York Nets. In three years with the Nets, Erving led the league in scoring twice, in 1974 and 1976, was most valuable player both years, and shared the MVP award with George McGinnis in 1975. The Nets won the ABA championship in 1974 and 1976, and Erving was also the most valuable player in the playoffs both times.

The ABA was absorbed by the NBA in 1976, when Erving joined the Philadelphia 76ers. He remained with them until retiring after the 1986–87 season.

Erving was named the NBA's most valuable player in 1980–81. He was a first-team all-star five times and on the second team twice. In his final season, he became the third professional player, after Wilt Chamberlain and Kareem Abdul-Jabbar, to score more than 30,000 career points.

★ Basketball Hall of Fame

Esiason, Boomer (Norman J.)

FOOTBALL
b. April 17, 1961, West Islip, N.Y.

A left-handed quarterback, Esiason starred at the University of Maryland and was chosen by the NFL's Cincinnati Bengals in the second round of the 1984 college draft. He became the team's starter in 1985.

Esiason was the league's top quarterback in 1988 with a 97.4 rating, completing 223 of 388 passes for 3,572 yards and 28 touchdowns. The Bengals went to the Super Bowl after that season but lost, 20–16, to the San Francisco 49ers.

After subpar seasons in 1991 and 1992, Esiason was written off by Cincinnati and by many observers. Traded to the New York Jets for a third-round draft choice, he returned to form in 1993, completing 288 of 473 passes for 3,421 yards and 16 touchdowns.

Through the 1994 season, Esiason had thrown 2,440 completions in 4,291 pass attempts for 31,874 yards and 207 touchdowns. He had also rushed for 1,344 yards and 5 touchdowns.

Esposito, Philip A.

HOCKEY
b. Feb. 20, 1942, Sault Ste. Marie, Ont.

Early in his career, Esposito was regarded by some observers as a "garbage player" who scored easy goals simply by hanging around the net. As time went on and he was consistently among the top scorers in the NHL, he was finally recognized as one of the all-time great hockey players.

After dropping out of high school to play junior hockey, Esposito became a professional in 1961, and he joined the Chicago Black Hawks in 1963. He was the center on Bobby Hull's line in 1965–66, when Hull scored a record 54 goals.

Chicago traded Esposito to the Boston Bruins in 1967. He was the league's leading scorer and winner of the Hart Trophy in the record-shattering 1968–69 season, when three players went over the 100-point mark. Esposito had 126 points on 49 goals and 77 assists, while Hull scored 107 and Gordie Howe had 103 points.

Esposito was also the league's top scorer in 1970–71, with an incredible 152 points on 76 goals and 76 assists; in 1971–72, with 133 points on 66 goals and 67 assists; in 1972–73, with 130 points on 55 goals and 75 assists; and in 1973–74, with 145 points on 68 goals and 77 assists.

He helped lead the Bruins to Stanley Cup championships in 1970 and 1972. Esposito scored 23 points in the 1970 playoffs, then a record.

The New York Rangers acquired Esposito during the 1975–76 season, but injuries and a more conservative style of team play limited his scoring for the rest of his career. He retired as a player in 1981.

Esposito became general manager of the Rangers in 1986. Impatient with the team's progress, he replaced Coach Ted Sator with Tom Webster during the 1986–87 season, then fired Webster and took over himself shortly before the Stanley Cup playoffs. The Rangers lost in the first round. The following season he fired Michel Bergeron and again became coach. Esposito lost both jobs after the Rangers failed even to qualify for the playoffs.

The 6-foot-1, 210-pound Esposito was exceptionally strong and difficult to move once he took up a position near the net, as he liked to do, and his unusually long arms often allowed him to get the puck when it seemed out of reach.

In 1,282 regular season games, he scored 1,590 points on 717 goals and 873 assists. He had 137 points, on 61 goals and 76 assists, in 130 playoff games.
★ Hockey Hall of Fame

Esposito, Tony (Anthony J.)
HOCKEY
b. April 23, 1943, Sault Ste. Marie, Ont.

Tony Esposito learned to be a goaltender by stopping shots from his brother, Phil, in the family driveway. After playing at Michigan Tech, he turned professional in 1967 and joined the Montreal Canadiens for 13 games in the 1968–69 season.

The Canadiens left Esposito unprotected, and the Chicago Black Hawks drafted him. He rewarded Chicago by winning the Calder Trophy as the NHL's best rookie and the Vezina Trophy as its best goaltender in 1970. The following year, he missed the Vezina by just seven goals.

In 1972, Esposito and Gary Smith shared goaltending duties and the Vezina Trophy with a combined 2.12 goals-against average; Esposito's was a sparkling 1.76 in 48 games. Esposito and Philadelphia's Bernie Parent tied for the 1974 Vezina.

One of the first "flopping" goaltenders, frequently sprawling on the ice to make saves, Esposito candidly admitted that he didn't like his job. He retired after the 1983–84 season with a record of 423 wins, 307 losses, and 151 ties. He gave up 2,563 goals in 886 games, a 2.92 average, and had 76 shutouts.

Esposito became general manager of the Pittsburgh Penguins in 1988. He left to take the same position with an expansion team, the Tampa Bay Lightning, in 1988.
★ Hockey Hall of Fame

Evans, Chick (Charles Jr.)
GOLF
b. July 18, 1890, Indianapolis, Ind. d. Nov. 6, 1979

If Evans had mastered putting, there's no telling how many championships he might have won. But putting was such a problem for him that he often carried two putters in his golf bag and switched arbitrarily between them, hoping one of them would suddenly become a magic wand.

Evans won the Western Amateur in 1909 and went to the semifinals of the U.S. Amateur. The following year he won the Western Open. Still short of his 21st birthday, he went to England with his mother in 1911, reaching the fifth round of the British Amateur championship, then crossed the Channel and won the French Amateur.

His dream was to become the first amateur to win the U.S. Open, but Francis Ouimet beat him to it in 1913, and then amateur Jerry Travers won the 1915 Open. However, Evans did win both the Open and the U.S. Amateur in 1916, the first player ever to accomplish that. Evans had a one-shot lead in the Open when he hit a long drive on the 525-yard 13th hole. The green was protected by a creek that ran across the fairway, but Evans said to a friend, "I think I can afford to take a chance." He hit his second shot over the creek and onto the green, then two-putted for a birdie. His winning score of 286 was the Open record for 20 years.

Evans won the U.S. Amateur again in 1920. He also won four consecutive Western Amateurs, 1920 through 1923.
★ PGA Hall of Fame; World Golf Hall of Fame

Evans, Janet
SWIMMING
b. Aug. 28, 1971, Placentia, Calif.

Unusually slender for a swimmer, at 5-foot-5 and only 102 pounds, Evans dominated the 1987 U.S. championships by winning four events, the 400-, 800-, and 1,500-meter freestyle and the 400-meter individual medley. She was the first woman to break the 16-minute barrier for 1,500 meters.

Evans was one of the stars of the 1988 Seoul Olympics, winning gold medals in the 400- and 800-meter freestyle events and the 400-meter individual medley. Her time of 4:03.85 in the 400-meter freestyle was a world record.

In 1989, Evans won seven national championships. She took the 500- and 1,000-yard freestyle titles and the 400-yard individual medley at the short-course nationals, the 400- and 800-meter freestyles and the 200- and 400-meter medley events at the long-course nationals. Evans was given the Sullivan Award as the country's outstanding amateur athlete of the year.

Evans was the 200-, 400-, and 800-meter freestyle champion in the 1990 long course nationals, but she lost her 400-meter individual medley crown. She also won the 400- and 800-meter freestyle events at the 1991 world championships.

Swimming for Stanford University, Evans won the 500- and 1,650-yard freestyle events at the 1990 and 1991 NCAA championships, and she was the 400-yard individual medley titlist in 1990. However, she left school in 1991 because of a new NCAA rule limiting collegiate swimmers to only 20 hours of practice a week.

At the 1992 Olympics, Evans claimed two more medals, a gold in the 800-meter freestyle and a silver in the 400-meter. Entering 1995, she held world records in the 400-, 800-, and 1,500-meter freestyle swims.

Evans, Lee E.

TRACK AND FIELD
b. Feb. 25, 1947, Madera, Calif.

Undefeated in high school, Evans won his first AAU championship in 1966, shortly after graduating. He was the national 440-yard champion that year and in 1967, and he won the 400-meter title in 1968. Representing San Jose State, he was also the 1968 NCAA 400-meter champion.

Evans won the 1968 Olympic trials with a world record 44.0 seconds but found himself in a dilemma at the Mexico City Games. He was one of the militant black athletes who had threatened to boycott the Olympics, behind the leadership of Harry Edwards, a sociologist at San Jose State. Tommie Smith, gold medal winner in the 200-meter dash, and John Carlos, the bronze medalist, had been banished from the Olympic village for staging a "Black Power" protest during their medal ceremony. They were friends and San Jose State teammates.

Evans agonized for hours about whether he should run in the 400-meter final or pull out in protest. Carlos persuaded him to run. Evans responded with a new world record of 43.86 seconds, a record that still stands, more than 20 years later, with the notation that it was achieved at an altitude higher than 1,000 meters.

Evans won a second gold as the anchorman on the 1600-meter relay team, setting another world record of 2:56.1.

After winning the AAU 400-meter run in 1969 and 1972, Evans finished only fourth in the 1972 Olympic trials but was named a member of the 1600-meter relay team once more. However, the U.S. couldn't field a team because Vince Matthews and Wayne Collet were suspended, also for a demonstration at a medal ceremony.

Evans became a professional after the 1972 season. He was reinstated as an amateur in 1980 and ran a 46.5 in one of his few appearances that year, at the age of 33.

★ National Track & Field Hall of Fame; Olympic Hall of Fame

Evers, Johnny (John J.)

BASEBALL
b. July 21, 1881, Troy, N.Y.
d. March 28, 1947

Although a fiery, scrappy player who was on five pennant-winning teams, Evers is probably in the Hall of Fame only because he was the second baseman in the famous Tinker-to-Evers-to-Chance double-play combination. The three of them entered the Hall of Fame together as a gesture to history.

Evers joined the Cubs late in the 1902 season and became the team's starting second baseman the following year. The Cubs won three consecutive pennants, 1906 through 1908, and Evers played a key role in the third pennant with his head rather than his bat or glove.

At the time, a runner on first often didn't bother to advance to second base when the winning run scored. Evers, a student of the rules, knew that the runner could be forced out at second if he failed to advance in that situation.

In a September game, the New York Giants apparently beat the Cubs, 2–1, in the bottom of ninth, but Fred Merkle, who was on first base, trotted off the field without touching second. Evers called for the ball and finally got it after much confusion. When he touched second base, Merkle was called out, and the run disallowed. Fans then stormed onto the field, and the game couldn't be continued.

The Cubs and Giants ended in a tie, and the game was replayed, the Cubs winning, 4–2. Then they beat the Detroit Tigers in the World Series for the second year in a row. They won a fourth pennant in 1910, but Evers missed the World Series because of a broken leg.

Evers's best season was 1912, when he batted .341, a remarkable aberration; his second-best average was an even .300 in 1908. After managing the Cubs to a third-place finish in 1913, he was traded to the Boston Braves, and he promptly won the NL's most valuable player award. He batted .438 in Boston's four-game sweep of the Philadelphia As in the World Series.

Released by the Braves in 1917, Evers finished the season with the Philadelphia Phillies, then retired as a player, although he played one game in 1922 and another in 1929, when he was coaching.

Evers managed the Cubs once more for part of the 1921 season, and he was manager of the Chicago White Sox in 1924. He also served as a coach and scout with several teams and as a minor league manager and executive.

In 18 major league seasons, Evers batted .270 with 1,659 hits, including 216 doubles, 70 triples, and 12 home runs. He stole 324 bases, scored 919 runs, and drove in 778.

★ Baseball Hall of Fame

Evert, Christine M. [Mrs. Lloyd; Mrs. Mill]

TENNIS
b. Dec. 21, 1954, Ft. Lauderdale, Fla.

Nicknamed "Little Miss Icicle" for her imperturbable demeanor, Evert lacked the flair of Billie Jean King or Martina Navratilova, but she was a very steady, consistent baseline player who won 157 tournaments, second only to Navratilova, and $8,896,195, third all-time, in just under 18 years as a professional.

The daughter of tennis pro Jimmie Evert, who was ranked eleventh in the U.S. in 1943, she turned professional on her 18th birthday in 1972, after having passed up $50,000 in winnings that year to retain her amateur status.

Evert won her first major titles, the Wimbledon and French Open singles, in 1974. She also won at Wimbledon in 1976 and 1981 and was a finalist on five other occasions. Evert tied the record of Molla Mallory and Helen Jacobs by winning the U.S. Open four years in a row, from 1975 through 1978, and she won that title again in 1980 and 1982.

She was a finalist at the French Open ten years in a row, from 1973 through 1982, and won the championship in 1974, 1975, 1979, 1980, 1983, 1985, and 1986. With her Australian Open titles in 1982 and 1984, Evert had a total of 18 grand slam singles championships, third behind Margaret Smith Court and Helen Wills Moody.

When she was at her most consistent, Evert could put together some remarkable streaks. As an amateur in 1971, she won 46 consecutive matches before losing to King in the U.S. Open finals. Her 56-match winning streak in 1974 is a modern record for women. In 1981, she won 72 of 78 matches and swept to the Wimbledon title without losing a set. And from August 1973 to May 1979,

Evert won 125 straight matches on clay, a surface that favored her style.

The Associated Press female athlete of the year in 1974, 1975, 1977, and 1980, Evert had a career record of 1,304 victories and only 146 losses. Her last major tournament was the 1989 U.S. Open. After losing to Zina Garrison in the fifth round, Evert typically exited with a simple wave to the cheering crowd of more than 20,000. Garrison, not Evert, burst into tears.

Evert had a much publicized on-and-off romance with Jimmy Connors in 1974, but that ended, and she married British tennis pro John Lloyd in 1979. They were divorced in 1987, and she married Andy Mill, a former Olympic skier, the following year.

★ International Women's Sports Hall of Fame

Ewbank, Weeb (Wilbur C.)

FOOTBALL
b. May 6, 1907, Richmond, Ind.

A quarterback at Miami University of Ohio, Ewbank coached high school football after graduating in 1928. He entered the Navy in 1943 and became an assistant coach for Paul Brown with the Great Lakes Naval Training Station team.

After coaching the Brown University basketball team to an 8–12 record in 1946–47, Ewbank coached football for two seasons at Washington University in St. Louis, winning 14 games and losing only 4. He entered professional football in 1949 as the line coach for the Cleveland Browns, where he was reunited with head coach Paul Brown.

Ewbank was hired as head coach by the Baltimore Colts in 1954, their second year of existence. He gradually built a contending team that won 7 of 12 games in 1957 and then won consecutive NFL championships in 1958 and 1959. Baltimore's 23–17 title victory over the New York Giants in 1958, the first overtime game ever played, was a major factor in making professional football a popular television sport.

After a 7–7 record in 1962, Ewbank was fired by the Colts. He then took another rebuilding job with the New York Jets of the American Football League. Originally called the Titans, the team had declared bankruptcy before being purchased and completely reorganized by "Sonny" Werblin.

Under Ewbank, the Jets attained respectability with an 8–5–1 record in 1967 and won the AFL championship the following season. Led by quarterback Joe Namath, they became the first AFL team to win the Super Bowl, beating Ewbank's former team, the Colts, 16–7.

Ewbank retired after the 1973 season. Quiet and scholarly, he was known for virtually total recall of every game he ever coached. Baltimore owner Carroll Rosenbloom once referred to him as "my crew-cut IBM machine." His patience enabled him to mold two young players into Hall of Fame quarterbacks, Johnny Unitas at Baltimore and Namath at New York.

His professional coaching record was 134–130–7, but if the six rebuilding years are eliminated, it was 102–83–3. Ewbank was the only coach to win championships in both the AFL and the NFL.

★ Pro Football Hall of Fame

Ewell, Barney (Harold N.)

TRACK AND FIELD
b. Feb. 25, 1918, Harrisburg, Pa.

Ewell was the top sprinter in the world in 1940, when the Olympics were canceled because of World War II. He finally got his chance to compete in the Olympics in 1948. He won silver medals in the 100- and 200-meter dashes and ran on the gold medal 4 x 100-meter relay team.

As a student at Penn State, Ewell won both sprints at the NCAA meet in 1940 and 1941 and at the IC4A meet from 1940 through 1942. He was the AAU outdoor 100-meter champion in 1941, 1945, and 1948 and the 200-meter champion in 1939, 1946, and 1947.

He also won the long jump at the IC4A outdoor meet from 1940 through 1942; at the IC4A indoor meet in 1940 and 1942; and at the AAU indoor meet in 1944 and 1945.

Ewell tied the world record of 10.2 in the 100-meter dash at the 1948 AAU championship, which was also the Olympic trials.

★ National Track & Field Hall of Fame

Ewing, Buck (William)

BASEBALL
b. Oct. 17, 1859, Hoaglands, Ohio
d. Oct. 20, 1906

Baseball's first great catcher, Ewing entered the major leagues with the NL's Troy Haymakers in 1880. The Troy franchise folded after the 1882 season, and a number of its players, including Ewing, went to the New York Giants.

Ewing batted .303 and led the league in home runs with 10 in his first year with New York, and he was the league leader in triples with 20 the following season, 1884. More important than his hitting, though, were the contributions he made to the defensive side of the game.

He was the first catcher to throw from the crouch, rather than standing up, yet he made very accurate throws that were easy to catch. Ewing also pioneered the snap pickoff throw to catch a runner off base after a pitch.

A leadoff man for much of his career, the 5-foot-10, 188-pound Ewing was a fine base stealer despite a lack of great speed, because he was a student of pitchers and their deliveries.

The Giants won pennants in 1888 and 1889. Ewing then jumped to the New York team in the Players' League. That league lasted just one season, and Ewing returned to the Giants in 1891 but missed most of the season with an injury. He hurt his throwing arm in 1892, when he batted .310, and was traded to the Cleveland NL team.

Used primarily as an outfielder, he hit .344 in his first season in Cleveland, then slipped to .251 and was traded to Cincinnati. As Cincinnati's player-manager, Ewing became a first baseman. He batted .318 in 1895, his last full season as a player. Ewing appeared in only 67 games in 1896 and had just one at-bat in 1897 before retiring as a player. He managed Cincinnati for two more seasons.

Ewing played in 1,315 major league games, batting .303 with 1,625 hits, including 250 doubles, 178 triples, and 71 home runs. He scored 1,129 runs and had 883 RBI. Stolen bases weren't recorded until 1886; from then until the end of his career, he had 354 steals.

★ Baseball Hall of Fame

Ewing, Patrick A.

BASKETBALL
b. August 5, 1962, Kingston, Jamaica

When he was 13, Ewing's family moved from Jamaica to the United States, where he learned to play basketball. By the time he was a senior at Cambridge, Massachusetts, Rindge and Latin School, he was 7 feet tall, weighed 240 pounds, and was sought by many college coaches. He elected to go to Georgetown University in Washington, D.C. .

At Georgetown, he became one of the few players ever to win consensus All-America honors three times, in 1983, 1984, and 1985. Ewing was named the tournament's outstanding player when Georgetown won the 1984 NCAA championship, and he was presented with the Naismith Award, Eastman Award, and Rupp Trophy as college player of the year in 1985. He scored a total of 2,184 points and had 1,316 rebounds during his college career.

Ewing starred for the U.S. Olympic team that won the gold medal in 1984, blocking 18 shots during the Olympic tournament. The first player chosen in the 1985 NBA draft, by the New York Knicks, Ewing won the league's rookie of the year award by averaging 20.4 points a game.

Through the 1993–94 season, Ewing had scored 16,191 points in 680 regular season NBA games, an average of 23.8 per game. He also had 7,006 rebounds and 1,984 blocked shots. In 78 playoff games, he had scored 1,799 points, a 23.1 average, with 866 rebounds and 194 blocks.

Ewry, Raymond C.

TRACK AND FIELD
b. Oct. 14, 1873, Lafayette, Ind.
d. Sept. 29, 1937

Confined to a wheelchair by polio when he was a boy, Ewry exercised his legs until he could walk, then began jumping to increase their strength. He became the greatest competitor ever in the standing jumps, which were discontinued in 1913.

In 1890, Ewry entered Purdue University, where he played football and captained the track team. After receiving a graduate degree in engineering, he went to New York and joined the New York Athletic Club.

Ewry won a record ten Olympic gold medals, in the standing high jump and standing long jump in 1900, 1904, 1906, and 1908, and in the standing triple jump in 1900 and 1904, after which the event was dropped from the Olympic program. Three of the gold medals came on a single day, July 16, 1900. He also won 15 AAU national championships from 1898 through 1910.

★ Olympic Hall of Fame

Exendine, Albert A.

FOOTBALL
b. Jan. 7, 1884, near Bartlesville, Okla.
d. Jan. 4, 1973

One of several stars who played for "Pop" Warner at the Carlisle Indian Institute early in the century, Exendine had never played football before he entered the school. Four years after his first football game, he was named an end on Walter Camp's third-team All-American team in 1906.

In 1907, Exendine scored on a 50-yard pass to help beat the University of Chicago, 18–4. He became head coach at Otterbein College, Ohio, after leaving Carlisle in 1909, and had a 15–7–3 record there in three seasons. Exendine took over at Georgetown University in Washington, D.C., in 1914. After a losing season in his first year, he produced eight winning teams.

Exendine went to Washington State University in 1923, winning 6 games, losing 13, and tying 4 in three seasons. He then coached at Occidental College in California, Northwestern Oklahoma, and Oklahoma A & M (now Oklahoma State). Overall, he had a record of 93 victories, 60 losses, and 15 ties.

While coaching Georgetown, Exendine received a law degree from Dickinson College. He was a lawyer with the federal Bureau of Indian Affairs for many years.

★ College Football Hall of Fame

Eyser, George

GYMNASTICS
b. 1871
d. ?

It's too bad that so little is known about Eyser, because he is an intriguing figure in the history of sports: the only Olympic medal winner with a wooden leg. There's apparently no record of when or how he lost the leg, or even of which leg it was.

Confusion even surrounds the 1904 Olympics in which he competed. The Olympics were held in St. Louis that year, and not many foreign athletes took part. The U.S. was the only country represented in a number of sports, including gymnastics.

The AAU national gymnastics championships were held as part of the Olympics, and winners were considered Olympic champions. It's uncertain, however, which events were actually considered Olympic events. In the AAU competition, Eyser won the parallel bars and rope climb; tied for first with Anton Heida in the vault; finished second in the pommel horse and all-around; and placed third in the horizontal bar. His club, the Concordia Turnverein, won the team championship, bringing Eyser his third gold medal and seventh medal overall.

Eyser also competed for Concordia when the club won a 1908 international meet in Frankfurt, Germany, and a 1909 national meet in Cincinnati.

★ ★ F ★ ★

Faber, Red (Urban C.)

BASEBALL
b. Sept. 6, 1888, Cascade, Iowa
d. Sept. 15, 1976

It took Faber quite a while to get to the major leagues, but once he got there, he put in 20 seasons and was the last American League pitcher allowed to throw the spitball legally.

Faber learned the spitball in 1909, his first season as a professional. After five years in the minors, he joined the Chicago White Sox in 1914. He had a 24–14 record with a 2.55 ERA in his second season with Chicago.

Although his mark was only 16–13 in 1917, Faber had a 1.92 ERA. He appeared in four games in the World Series that year, winning three of them in Chicago's six-game victory over Cincinnati.

He had a 4–1 record in 1918 before enlisting in the Navy. After World War I, he returned to the White Sox, but injuries limited his playing time in 1919, when the team won another pennant, and he didn't appear in the "Black Sox" World Series.

With mediocre teams, Faber had an outstanding three-year period from 1920 through 1922, winning 69 games while losing 45. He led the league in ERA with 2.48 in 1921 and 2.81 in 1922.

The 6-foot-1, 180-pound right-hander was only an average pitcher after that and was used mostly as a reliever toward the end of his career. He retired after a 3–4 record in 1933. Faber then left baseball until 1946, when he became the White Sox pitching coach for three seasons.

In 669 games, Faber had a 254–213 record with 29 shutouts and a 3.15 ERA. He struck out 1,471 hitters and walked 1,213 in 4,086 innings.
★ Baseball Hall of Fame

Faggs, Mae (Heriwentha Mae)

TRACK AND FIELD
b. April 10, 1932, Mays Landing, N.J.

Faggs discovered running as a member of the New York City Police Athletic League and later became one of Tennessee State's many track stars. Although she won 12 national sprint championships, most of her international success came on sprint relay teams.

She won an Olympic gold medal for the 4 x 100-meter relay in 1952 and was on the bronze medal relay team in 1956. Faggs was also a member of the sprint relay team that won a gold at the 1955 Pan-American Games, where she finished second in the 200-meter dash.

In AAU outdoor national championships, Faggs won the 100-yard dash in 1955 and 1956, the 200-meter in 1954 and 1956, and the 220-yard in 1955. She was the indoor 100-yard champion in 1952 and the indoor 220-yard champion from 1949 through 1952 and in 1954 and 1956.
★ National Track & Field Hall of Fame

Fain, Ferris R.

BASEBALL
b. May 29, 1921, San Antonio, Tex.

A smooth-swinging left-handed first baseman, Fain won two consecutive AL batting titles with averages of .344 in 1951 and .327 in 1952, when he also led the league with 43 doubles.

Fain entered the major leagues with the Philadelphia Athletics in 1947 and remained with them through 1952, then was traded to the Chicago White Sox. He retired after spending the 1955 season with the Detroit Tigers and Cleveland Indians.

In 1,151 games, Fain had 1,139 hits, including 213 doubles, 30 triples, and 48 home runs. He scored 595 runs and drove in 570.

Faldo, Nick (Nicholas A.)

GOLF
b. July 18, 1957, Welwyn Garden City, England

Faldo took six golf lessons when he was 13 and played his first round at 14. He won a golf scholarship to the University of Houston in 1976 but left after only ten weeks and joined the European Professional Golfers' Association.

Although Faldo set a record by winning 140,751 pounds on the European tour, sportswriters were referring to him sarcastically as "Nick Fold-o" for his failures in major tournaments. He decided to change his swing entirely and went to work in the spring of 1985, hitting as many as 1,500 practice balls a day while working with an instructor.

Faldo won his first major tournament, the British Open, in 1987, shooting a 279 at Muirfield in Scotland. The following year, he and Curtis Strange tied for the lead in the U.S. Open, but Strange won the 18-hole playoff, 71–75. Scott Hoch and Faldo tied in the 1989 Masters, but this time Faldo won a sudden death playoff by shooting a birdie on the second hole.

In 1990, Faldo hired the first full-time woman caddie on the pro tour, Fanny Sunesson. He won two majors that year, repeating in the Masters by winning another playoff, over Ray Floyd, and shooting a 270 to take the British Open by 5 strokes. Faldo won the British Open for a third time in 1992 with a 272.

Farrell, Jeff (Felix Jeffrey)

SWIMMING
b. Feb. 28, 1937, Detroit, Mich.

An emergency appendectomy kept Farrell from competing in the 1960 Olympic trials, so he didn't have a chance to win any individual gold medals, but he was a member of the 4 x 200-meter freestyle and 4 x 100-meter individual medley relay teams that won golds.

Farrell won national long-course titles in the 100-meter and 200-meter freestyles in both 1959 and 1960 and was short-course champion in the 100-yard and 220-yard freestyles in 1960. He won a gold medal in the 100-meter freestyle at the 1959 Pan-American Games.

Farrington, Bob (Robert G.)

HARNESS RACING
b. July 15, 1929, Richwood, Ohio

A brick mason, Farrington began training a harness horse after work and driving on small Ohio tracks. Six years later, by 1961, training and driving had become a full-time job. Farrington became the first driver to win more than 200 heats in 1961, leading the nation in heats won that year and again in 1962.

In 1963, he performed the rare feat of winning all six races he started at Freehold, Ohio. Farrington didn't lead in wins that year, but in 1964 he became the first to win more than 300 heats, again leading all drivers. He was also the leader in heats won in 1965, 1966, and 1967.

Fator, Laverne

HORSE RACING
b. 1902, Hailey, Idaho
d. May 16, 1937

A cowboy as a young teenager, Fator became a professional jockey at Cuban tracks in 1918. He later rode for Rancocas Stable, the top breeding farm in the country during the early 1920s.

In just thirteen years as a jockey, Fator rode 1,121 winners and earned prizes of $2,408,720. His biggest victories came in consecutive Belmont Futurities, aboard Pompey in 1925 and with Scapa Flow in 1926, when he had 143 winners, earning $361,336.

Fator became a trainer in 1931. Blood poisoning caused by an infected appendix sent him into a delirium, and he died in a fall from his hospital window while awaiting an operation.

★ National Museum of Racing

Faurot, Donald B.

FOOTBALL
b. June 23, 1902, Mountain Grove, Mo.

A 1925 graduate of the University of Missouri, where he played quarterback, Faurot coached Northeast Missouri State to a 64–14–3 record from 1926 through 1934. His 1932, 1933, and 1934 teams won all of their games, compiling 26 consecutive victories.

Faurot returned to his alma mater as head coach in 1935. In 1941, a year after the modern T formation had been introduced by Clark Shaughnessy at Stanford, Faurot created a new version, the split T, so called because the offensive linemen split apart rather than being packed closely together, forcing similar splits in the defensive line.

Instead of turning away from center and bringing the ball back for handoffs, the quarterback in the split T slides along the line in either direction. There are only two basic plays, a handoff to a halfback diving into the line and an option. The quarterback watches the outermost defender, either an end or a linebacker. If the defender moves toward the quarterback, he pitches the ball to a trailing halfback. If the defender covers the halfback, the quarterback keeps the ball and cuts inside to run downfield.

The 1941 Missouri team led the nation in rushing yardage per game and won eight regular season games while losing only one, but lost to Fordham, 2–0, in the Sugar Bowl. Faurot served in the Air Force during World War II and coached the Iowa Pre-Flight team that was second in the nation in total offense in 1943.

He returned to Missouri in 1946 and coached there through 1956, compiling a record of 101 wins, 79 losses, and 10 ties in his 19 seasons.

Within a few years after its introduction, the split T became the most common offensive formation in college football, although professional teams never adopted it because it's not an effective passing formation. Other coaches had more success with it than Faurot because they had better material.

The split T's most productive proponent was Bud Wilkinson at the University of Oklahoma. Wilkinson said in 1950 that the formation was "the most original and significant contribution to offensive football in the past ten years." The idea of the option led to other types of option attacks such as the belly series, the wishbone T, and the veer.

★ College Football Hall of Fame

Favor, Suzy (Suzanne; Mrs. Hamilton)

TRACK AND FIELD
b. Aug. 8, 1968, Stevens Point, Wis.

Running for the University of Wisconsin, Favor became the first athlete of either sex to win the NCAA outdoor 1,500-meter/1-mile championship four times, from 1988 through 1991. She was also the 800-meter champion in 1990. At NCAA indoor meets, Favor won the 1-mile in 1987 and 1989, the 1-mile and 3,000-meter in 1990.

The 5-foot-3, 110-pound Favor won the 1990 Honda Broderick Cup as the nation's outstanding female collegiate athlete. She was named the Big Ten Conference's female athlete of the year three consecutive times, 1988 through 1990, and the conference's female athlete of the decade, 1981–1991.

As a collegian, Favor won 54 of 56 races, including 40 consecutive finals. She also won national championships in the outdoor 1,500-meter from 1989 through 1991 and the indoor 1-mile in 1991.

Fears, Tom (Thomas J.)

FOOTBALL
b. Dec. 23, 1923, Los Angeles, Calif.

A 6-foot-2, 215-pound end, Fears began his college career at Santa Clara University. After serving in the Air Force in

1944 and 1945, he played at UCLA for two seasons.

Fears joined the NFL's Los Angeles Rams in 1948 and began his professional career as a defensive back. He intercepted two passes, running one back for a touchdown, in his first game, and the Rams decided to move him back to offensive end.

Though not fast, Fears ran very precise pass routes and often used his size and strength to take passes away from defensive backs who seemed to have him covered. He led the league in receptions in each of his first three seasons, catching a total of 212 passes during that period. In 1949, Fears led in touchdown receptions with 9, and in 1950 he led in receiving yardage with 1,116. He caught 18 passes against the Green Bay Packers that season, still the NFL record.

Known for his clutch receptions, Fears caught three touchdown passes when Los Angeles beat the Chicago Bears, 24–14, in the 1950 Western Division championship game, and he caught a 74-yard touchdown pass to beat the Cleveland Browns, 24–17, for the 1951 league championship.

He retired after catching only five passes in 1956. During his eight NFL seasons, Fears had exactly 400 receptions for 5,397 yards, a 13.5 average, and 38 touchdowns.

Fears became the first coach of the New Orleans Saints when the team joined the NFL in 1967. He was replaced late in the 1970 season after winning only 1 game while losing 5 and tying 1. His overall record was 13–34–2.
★ Pro Football Hall of Fame

Feathers, Beattie (William Beattie)
FOOTBALL
b. Aug. 4, 1908, Bristol, Va.
d. March 11, 1979

Feathers became the first NFL player to rush for more than 1,000 yards as a rookie with the Chicago Bears in 1934, when he gained 1,004 yards in just 101 carries, an average of 9.9 yards per attempt, still the league record. He was greatly aided by the blocking ability of fullback Bronko Nagurski, who led him on many of his runs.

A triple-threat tailback at the University of Tennessee, Feathers was a consensus All-American in 1933. His finest college game was probably a 7–3 defeat of the University of Kentucky in 1932, when he punted 20 times for a 48-yard average and scored the winning touchdown.

The 5-foot-10, 185-pound Feathers then joined the Bears. After his outstanding rookie season, he was frequently hampered by injuries. He played for the NFL's Brooklyn Dodgers in 1938 and 1939 and went to the Green Bay Packers for a final season in 1940.

During his seven professional seasons, Feathers rushed for 1,979 yards on 360 carries, a 5.6 average, and scored 16 touchdowns. He also caught 14 passes for 222 yards, a 15.9 average, and 1 touchdown, and he threw 1 touchdown pass.

Feathers coached Appalachian State College to a 9–7–1 record in 1941 and 1942. In 1946, he became head baseball and football coach at North Carolina State University, where his teams won 37 games, lost 38, and tied 3 in eight seasons. He was also baseball coach at Wake Forest from 1972 through 1976.
★ College Football Hall of Fame

Feigner, Eddie
SOFTBALL
b. March 26, 1925, Walla Walla, Wash.

Named Myrle King by his adopted family, Feigner was a trouble-making child who was thrown out of school in his early teens. He served in the Marine Corps during World War II but was given a medical discharge after suffering a nervous breakdown.

He decided to start a new life by taking a new name — Feigner from his mother and Eddie from a friend. And he discovered he had a talent: he could pitch a softball faster than anyone. In 1946, he organized a four-man team, taking on all comers in the Pacific Northwest, and in 1950 he named the team "The King and His Court" and began touring the country, playing against nine-man teams.

Feigner, whose pitches have been clocked at 104 miles an hour, entertains crowds by pitching at times from behind his back and through his legs. In over 30 years of barnstorming, his team has traveled more than 3 million miles and played nearly 7,500 games before more than 15 million spectators.

Feller, Bob (Robert W. A.)
BASEBALL
b. Nov. 3, 1918, Van Meter, Iowa

Raised by his father to play baseball, Feller had a uniform and complete set of equipment, including a catcher's mitt and a fielder's glove, when he was ten. At 13, he was the shortstop and cleanup hitter for the Van Meter town team, and a year later he and his father laid out a diamond on the Feller farm and organized their own team.

Feller then became a pitcher, and at 16, was playing for a Dubuque semipro team, often striking out 20 hitters a game. He joined the Cleveland Indians in 1936. Although he appeared in only 14 games, with a 5–3 record, he tied Dizzy Dean's record of 17 strikeouts in a 9-inning game before going back to Van Meter to finish high school.

Arm trouble restricted him in 1937, but Feller led the AL in strikeouts in 1938, when he had a 17–11 record. He then had a great three-season stretch, leading the AL with records of 24–9, 17–11, and 25–13, and in strikeouts with 246, 261, and 260 from 1939 through 1941. He led the league with a 2.61 ERA in 1940. On April 16, 1940, he pitched the only opening-day no-hitter in history.

Feller joined the Navy after the 1941 season and didn't return to the Indians until late in 1945, when he had a 5–3 record. The next two seasons, he led the league in victories, with records of 26–15 and 20–11; shutouts, with 10 and 5; and strikeouts, with 348 and 196. His 348 strikeouts was a major league record at the time.

In 1948, Feller had a 19–15 record to help the Indians win the pennant. He lost a tough 1–0 decision to the Boston Braves in the first game of the World Series, then gave up 7 runs in $6\frac{1}{3}$ innings when the Indians lost the sixth game. However, Cleveland won the seventh game and the series.

After going 15–14 in 1949 and 16–11 in 1950, Feller had a 22–8 record in 1951, leading the league in percentage. He became a spot starter after that. He won 13 while losing only 3 in 1954, when the Indians won another pennant, but he didn't appear in the World Series. Feller retired after an 0–4 record in 1956.

Nicknamed "Rapid Robert," the 6-foot, 185-pound Feller threw some pitches clocked at 100 miles per hour. He could also tantalize hitters with a big, sweeping curve. He was the first pitcher to throw three no-hitters.

Feller pitched in 570 major league games, winning 266 and losing 162. He struck out 2,581 hitters and walked 1,764 in 3,827 innings and had a career ERA of 3.25.

★ Baseball Hall of Fame

Fenimore, Bob (Robert D.)
FOOTBALL
b. Oct. 6, 1925, Woodward, Okla.

Nicknamed the "Blond Bomber," the 6-foot-1, 188-pound Fenimore could run the 100-yard dash in 9.7 seconds. Sportswriter Homer Cooke called him "the greatest one-man offense in college football history."

A single-wing tailback at Oklahoma A & M, Fenimore led the nation in total offense per game two years in a row. In just eight games per season, he had 1,758 yards in 1944 and 1,641 yards in 1945, when he was a consensus All-American.

His biggest game was probably the school's 46–40 upset over Tulsa in 1944, when Fenimore ran for two touchdowns and threw two touchdown passes. The scores included a 72-yard run from scrimmage and a 50-yard pass that won the game.

Fenimore also rushed for 241 yards in a 19–14 victory over Arkansas and had 248 yards of total offense in a 26–12 win over Southern Methodist University in 1945. When Oklahoma A & M beat St. Mary's of California, 33–13, in the 1946 Sugar Bowl to conclude an unbeaten season, Fenimore scored two touchdowns and threw a touchdown pass.

Although a knee injury bothered him throughout his senior season, he was a first-round draft choice of the NFL's Chicago Bears in 1947. Fenimore spent just one season with the Bears, gaining 189 yards on 53 rushing attempts, a 3.8 average, and 1 touchdown and catching 15 passes for 219 yards, a 14.6 average, and 2 touchdowns.

★ College Football Hall of Fame

Ferguson, Tom (Thomas)
RODEO
b. Dec. 20, 1950, Tahlequah, Okla.

The 5-foot-11, 190-pound Ferguson is the only rodeo cowboy ever to win six consecutive national all-around championships, from 1974 through 1979, although he tied with Leo Camarillo for the 1975 title. In 1979, Ferguson became one of only four men ever to qualify for the national finals in three different events.

Ferguson was the national steer wrestling champion in 1977 and 1978 and the calf roping champion in 1974. He won more than $100,000 in the 1978 season, the first time that was ever accomplished, and in March 1986 he became the first cowboy to win more than $1 million during his career.

Ferrell, Barbara A.
TRACK AND FIELD
b. July 28, 1947, Hattiesburg, Miss.

In 1967, Ferrell twice tied the world record of 11.1 seconds for the 100-meter dash, the first time in winning the AAU national outdoor championship, the second time in winning the world title.

Running for Los Angeles State and the Los Angeles Mercurettes, Ferrell also won the national outdoor 100- and 220-yard championships in 1969, the indoor 60-yard dash in 1968 and 1969, and the rarely run 240-yard dash in 1969.

She won both sprints at the 1968 Olympic trials. After finishing second in the Olympic 100-meter, she won a gold medal as a member of the 4 x 100-meter relay team. Ferrell was also the gold medalist in the 100-meter at the 1967 Pan-American Games.

★ National Track & Field Hall of Fame

Ferrell, Rick (Richard B.)
BASEBALL
b. Oct. 12, 1905, Durham, N.C.

He never led a league in a single offensive category, but Ferrell was a solid hitter and one of the finest defensive catchers of his era. He entered the major leagues with the AL's St. Louis Browns in 1929, batting .306 in 1931 and .315 in 1932, then was traded to the Boston Red Sox during the 1933 season.

In 1934, Boston acquired his brother Wes, a right-handed pitcher. Throwing to Rick, Wes won 59 games during the next three seasons. The brothers were traded together to the Washington Senators early in the 1937 season.

Wes went to the New York Yankees in 1938, but Rick remained with Washington until May 1941, when he went back to the Browns. He returned to the Senators in 1944 and remained with them until retiring after the 1947 season.

In 1,884 games, Ferrell had a .281 batting average on 1,692 hits, including 324 doubles, 45 triples, and only 28 home runs. (Wes, one of the best-hitting pitchers of all time, hit 38 career home runs and had a .280 career average.)

★ Baseball Hall of Fame

Ferry, Danny (Daniel J. W.)
BASKETBALL
b. Oct. 17, 1966, Bowie, Md.

The son of Bob Ferry, a former NBA player who became general manager of the league's Washington Bullets, Danny was raised to play basketball. He was even sent to DeMatha High School in Washington, D.C., which has produced many outstanding basketball players. Ferry was one of the few white players in the history of the inner-city school.

Named the best high school player in the country by *Parade* magazine in 1985, Ferry entered Duke University. Averaging 19.1 points as a junior and 22.7 as a senior, he was named Atlantic Coast Conference player of the year twice. The

U.S. Basketball Writers Association and UPI selected him college player of the year in 1989, when he also won the Naismith Award.

Drafted by the NBA's Los Angeles Clippers, Ferry chose to play for the Il Messaggero team of Rome in the Italian League in 1989–90, when he averaged 29.3 points a game. In the meantime, the Cleveland Cavaliers acquired his rights, and Ferry joined them in 1990.

Through the 1993–94 season, Ferry had scored 1,966 points in 295 regular season NBA games, a 6.7 average, with 919 rebounds and 428 assists.

Fesler, Wesley E.

BASKETBALL, FOOTBALL
b. June 29, 1908, Youngstown, Ohio
d. July 30, 1989

Grantland Rice put Fesler at end on the all-time All-American team he named in 1939, and football's first historian, Parke Davis, wrote in 1931 that Fesler was "the most versatile end the game has ever known."

Fesler was a three-time All-American at Ohio State, from 1928 through 1930, and he was also on the Helms Athletic Foundation All-American basketball team in 1931.

He also coached both sports. His greatest success was in four seasons at Ohio State, 1947 through 1950, where his football teams won 21 games while losing 13 and tying 3. The 1949 squad won the Big Ten championship and beat California, 17–14, in the Rose Bowl.

Fesler coached football at Wesleyan in 1942, at Pittsburgh in 1946, and at Minnesota from 1951 through 1953. He also coached basketball at Harvard from 1933–34 through 1940–41 and at Princeton in 1944–45. His overall record was 18–36–8 in football and 39–55 in basketball.

★ College Football Hall of Fame

Fidrych, Mark S.

BASEBALL
b. Aug. 14, 1954, Worcester, Mass.

For a season, Mark "The Bird" Fidrych was one of the most popular players in baseball. A right-handed pitcher, he joined the AL's Detroit Tigers in 1976. Although he didn't get his first start until the middle of May, he had 19–9 season with a league-leading 2.34 ERA and 24 complete games in 29 starts.

But it wasn't just his skill that made him popular. Fidrych was a free spirit, animated on the mound, who talked to the baseball before throwing it and often rushed over to shake hands with a teammate who had made a good defensive play behind him.

Unfortunately, he hurt his arm after going 6–4 in 1977. After unsuccessful comeback attempts the next three seasons, he retired with a 29–19 record and a 3.10 career ERA.

Fielder, Cecil G.

BASEBALL
b. Sept. 21, 1963, Los Angeles, Calif.

The 6-foot-3, 230-pound Fielder was a part-time first baseman and designated hitter with the AL's Toronto Blue Jays from 1985 through 1988. A right-hander, he was used only against left-handed pitchers.

Displeased with his status, Fielder went to Japan to play for the Hanshin Tigers in 1989. He batted .302 and hit 38 home runs in just 106 games, missing the last month of the season with a broken finger.

The Detroit Tigers of the AL signed him in 1990. Used primarily at first base, Fielder led the major leagues with 51 home runs that season, and he also had a league-leading 132 RBI and .592 slugging percentage. He was the AL home run and RBI leader again in 1991, with 44 and 133.

In 1992, Fielder's home run total slipped to 35, but he led in RBI for the third straight year with 124. He had 30 home runs and 117 RBI in 1993, 28 home runs and 90 RBI in the strike-shortened 1994 season.

Through 1994, Fielder had 853 hits in 959 games, including 130 doubles, 5 triples, and 219 home runs. He had scored 500 runs while driving in 680.

Filion, Herve

HARNESS RACING
b. Feb. 1, 1940, Angers, P.Q.

Although he has never won any of harness racing's triple crown events because he prefers to drive in as many races as possible, Filion has compiled an incredible record during his career.

Only a handful of drivers have ever won more than 400 races in a year. Filion was the first to do it, with 407 in 1968, and he has done it 14 times since then. Filion has led in heats won 13 times, from 1968 through 1974, from 1976 through 1978, and from 1980 through 1982 (he tied with Carmine Abbatiello in 1981), and he was the leading money winner from 1970 through 1974 and in 1976.

Based on the Universal Driver Rating system, Filion has won the driver of the year award from the Harness Tracks of America 10 times since the award was instituted in 1968. He won from 1969 through 1974, in 1976, 1981, and 1989, and he and Abbatiello tied for the award in 1978.

In a 1990 interview with *Sports Illustrated*, Filion made driving sound very easy: "I sit down on the job. I let the horse do the work. I guide him. If the horse gets beat, it's not my fault. If he wins, it's not my fault."

Through the 1993 season, Filion was the all-time leader in races won with 14,084, nearly twice the number of Abbatiello, in second place. Filion is second in money won with $80,668,478.
★ Hall of Fame of the Trotter

Fincher, Bill (William E.)

FOOTBALL
b. Nov. 12, 1907, Spring Race. Ga.
d. July 17, 1978

Fincher played guard, tackle, and end at various times during his five-year career at Georgia Tech, when it became the first southern school to win national prominence. Coached by John W. Heisman, Fincher was a guard on the undefeated 1917 team that was considered the best in the country after beating Pennsylvania, 41–0, and Auburn, 68–7.

The 6-foot, 190-pound Fincher played mostly at end in 1918 and 1919, then moved to tackle for his final season. However, Walter Camp named Fincher an All-American at end that year, when Georgia Tech lost only to Pittsburgh. Grantland Rice put him at tackle when he named his all-time All-American team in 1939.
★ College Football Hall of Fame

Findlay, Conn F.

ROWING, YACHTING
b. April 24, 1930, Stockton, Calif.

Findlay began rowing on the University of California crew. After graduating in 1956, he got into sculling. He was a member of the Olympic pair-oared shell with coxswain teams that won gold medals in 1956 and 1964. He rowed with Dan Ayrault and coxswain Kurt Seiffert in 1956, with Ed Ferry and coxswain Kent Mitchell in 1964.

He was also a member of Dennis Conner's crew on the boat that took a bronze medal in Tempest Class yachting at the 1976 Olympics. Findlay served on Conner's crew in the 1974 America's Cup trials, was a mast man for Ted Turner's 1977 America's Cup defense, and crewed for John Kolius at the 1983 trials.

Fingers, Rollie (Roland G.)

BASEBALL
b. Aug. 25, 1946, Steubenville, Ohio

A remarkably long-lived relief pitcher, Fingers was a key member of the great Oakland Athletics teams of the early 1970s. After a brief stint with Oakland in 1968, he joined the team at the beginning of the 1969 season and was an unsuccessful starting pitcher until 1971, when he was moved into the bullpen.

Fingers later said that he worried so much about his starting assignments that he could never sleep the night before, so he pitched poorly. But he didn't seem to have a problem with worrying when he came out of the bullpen into a difficult situation.

From 1971 through 1976, Fingers appeared as a reliever in 346 games, compiling a 54–39 record with 105 saves. He led the league in games with 76 in 1974 and 75 in 1975. He also starred in post-season play. In 1972, he had a victory and two saves in Oakland's seven-game World Series win over the Cincinnati Reds. The following year, he lost one game but had two more saves and gave up only one earned run in 13⅔ innings as Oakland beat the New York Mets in seven games.

Fingers was named most valuable player of the 1974 World Series, when the As won their third straight championship with a five-game victory over the Los Angeles Dodgers; he picked up a victory and two more saves.

After a contract dispute, Oakland traded him to the NL's San Diego Padres in 1977, when he led the league with 78 appearances and 35 saves. Fingers also led in saves with 37 in 1978.

He was traded to the St. Louis Cardinals in 1981 but never pitched for them. Instead, he was sent on to the Milwaukee Brewers, and he was named the AL Cy Young Award winner and most valuable player, chalking up a 6–3 record with a league-leading 28 saves and a 1.04 ERA to help lead the Brewers into the East Division playoffs. Despite a victory and a save from Fingers, Milwaukee lost to the New York Yankees, three games to two.

Because of tendinitis, Fingers missed the entire 1983 season. He came back to have a good year with Milwaukee in 1984 but retired after an ineffective 1985 season.

Distinguished by his long handlebar moustache, Fingers had a good fastball, an excellent slider, and very good control. In 17 seasons, he had a 114–118 record with 341 saves, third best all-time, and a 2.90 ERA. He struck out 1,299 hitters and walked only 492 in 1,701 innings.
★ Baseball Hall of Fame

Fischer, Bill (William)
FOOTBALL
b. March 10, 1927, Chicago, Ill.

The 6-foot-2, 240-pound Fischer, called "Moose" by his teammates, was an All-American guard at Notre Dame

in 1947 and 1948, and he won the 1948 Outland Trophy as the nation's best collegiate lineman.

Fischer captained the 1948 team that went undefeated, winning nine games and tying one. During his four seasons as a starter, sometimes at tackle, Notre Dame won 33 games, lost 2, and tied 2, and had a 21-game victory streak.

The Chicago Cardinals chose Fischer in the first round of the 1949 NFL college draft. He spent five seasons with the Cardinals and was named an All-Pro in 1951 and 1952.
★ College Football Hall of Fame

Fish, Hamilton, Jr.
FOOTBALL
b. Dec. 7, 1888, Garrison, N.Y.
d. Jan. 18, 1991

After playing on the Harvard freshman team in 1906, Fish became the varsity's starting right tackle for three seasons and was named an All-American twice, in 1908 and 1909. He was known as a fine blocker but was probably even better on defense. At 6-foot-4 and 200 pounds, Fish was very quick and agile, and he was allowed to roam on defense rather than holding his position. Because of his size and large hands, Fish was often used as a pass receiver. In his senior year, he caught three passes in a victory over Army at a time when it was unusual for a team even to throw that many passes in a game. He captained the team that year.

After graduating, Fish often wrote about football for the *New York World*, and he played for and coached all-star teams in charity games in 1914 and 1915. As a U.S. congressman from 1919 to 1945, he was one of the isolationist Republicans denounced by Franklin Delano Roosevelt in his famous "Martin, Barton and Fish" speech of 1940.
★ College Football Hall of Fame

Fisher, Bud (Morris)
SHOOTING
b. May 4, 1892, Youngstown, Ohio
d. May 23, 1968

A remarkably nervous man for a rifle champion, Fisher played the violin to relax before his matches. He was once so nervous during a competition that he just stood and aimed for 20 minutes without firing. Finally he was ordered to fire, and his shot went wide; but the spell was broken, and he went on to win the match.

Fisher won five Olympic gold medals, in the free rifle, military rifle, and free rifle team in 1920, and in the individual free rifle and free rifle team in 1924. He won the national free rifle championship in 1923, the world prone position championship in 1923, and the world kneeling position championship in 1923 and 1924.

A gunnery sergeant in the U.S. Marine Corps from 1913 to 1934, Fisher was called back to duty as a shooting instructor during World War II.

Fisk, Carlton E.

BASEBALL
b. Dec. 26, 1947, Bellows Falls, Vt.

Nicknamed "Pudge" as a youngster, Fisk grew to be 6-foot-2 and 220 pounds, and he was one of the best catchers in baseball for more than 20 years.

After brief stints with the AL's Boston Red Sox in 1969 and 1971, Fisk became the team's starting catcher in 1972, when he led the league in triples with nine, batted .293, and was named rookie of the year.

He missed much of the 1974 season and the early part of the 1975 season with an injury, but he came back to help lead the Red Sox to a pennant, batting .331 with 10 home runs and 52 RBI in just 79 games. His winning home run in the twelfth inning of Game Six in the World Series has been often replayed, because Fisk watched the ball and used body English to try to keep it inside the foul pole. However, Boston lost to the Cincinnati Reds in the seventh game.

Fisk became a free agent after the 1980 season and signed with the Chicago White Sox, where he changed his number from 27 to 72 because, he said, "it represents a turn-around in my career." After a slow start in 1983, he came on strong in the second half of the season and ended with 26 home runs and 86 RBI

as Chicago won the AL's West Division title, only to lose to the Baltimore Orioles in the league championship series.

A torn abdominal muscle bothered him in 1984, when he appeared in only 102 games. He came back to have his most productive season in 1985, hitting 37 home runs and driving in 107 runs despite a .238 batting average.

After he had appeared in just 25 games in 1993, the White Sox abruptly released Fisk. The move brought much criticism from fans and sportswriters, who felt he should at least have been given the chance to retire gracefully.

In 2,499 major league games, Fisk had 2,356 hits, including 421 doubles, 47 triples, and 376 home runs. He scored 1,276 runs and drove in 1,330. He hit 350 of his home runs as a catcher, an AL record, and he holds AL catching records for most years, 24; most games, 2,201; most putouts, 11,612; and most chances accepted, 12,676.

Fiske, Billy (William M. L. III)

BOBSLEDDING
b. June 4, 1911, New York, N.Y.
d. Aug. 17, 1940

Born into a wealthy family, Fiske was at school in Europe in 1928 when he and a few other Americans formed a bobsled team to enter the Winter Olympics at St. Moritz, Switzerland. The fearless 17-year-old Fiske was chosen to drive the five-man sled, and he drove it to a gold medal.

Four years later, he won another gold medal as driver of the winning four-man sled in the Lake Placid Olympics. Fiske also won the Grand National championship on the famed Cresta Run in Switzerland in 1936 and 1938.

Fiske married the Countess of Warwick in 1938, and he joined the British Royal Air Force in 1939, shortly after World War II began. He was seriously wounded on a mission over Europe in June 1941. He landed his plane in England but died a short time later.

The Billy Fiske Memorial Trophy is awarded to the national champion four-man bobsled team.

Fittipaldi, Emerson

AUTO RACING

b. Dec. 12, 1946, Sao Paulo, Brazil

The son of a sportswriter who primarily covers auto racing, Fittipaldi fell in love with the sport at an early age and was racing before he was old enough to have a driver's license. He began Formula One racing with England's Lotus team in 1970, and two years later he became the youngest winner of the world driving championship. He won that title again in 1974, driving for Team McLaren.

In 1976 Fittipaldi and his brother Wilson formed a Brazilian-based Formula One team, and he retired from driving in 1980 to devote all his time to designing and manufacturing race cars. The extremely high inflation rate in Brazil made the project impractical, however, and Fittipaldi decided to try Indy-Car racing in 1984.

He placed fifth in his first race and finished second to Roberto Guerrero as rookie of the year. Fittipaldi's first Indy-Car victory came in the 1985 Michigan 500.

Fittipaldi won the Indy 500 in 1989 and 1993 and was national driving champion both years. Through 1994, he had 21 IndyCar victories, thirteenth all-time, and was third in career winnings with $13,272,875.

"To be a good racing driver," Fittipaldi has said, "you have to be brave and you have to be afraid. You have to balance the brave and the afraid."

Fitzsimmons, Bob (Robert L.)

BOXING

b. June 4, 1862, Helston, Cornwall, England
d. Oct. 22, 1917

A blacksmith, Fitzsimmons won the New Zealand amateur middleweight championship in 1880 by knocking out four opponents in one night, and he retained the title with five knockouts in 1881.

After fighting in Australia for several years, he sailed to San Francisco in 1890 and won the middleweight championship by knocking out Jack "the Nonpa-

reil" Dempsey in the 13th round of a fight at New Orleans on January 14, 1891.

Fitzsimmons never lost the middleweight title, but he moved up to the heavyweight class in 1896 and won that championship with a 14th-round knockout of James J. Corbett on March 17, 1897, in Carson City, Nevada. Outboxed for most of the contest, Fitzsimmons won by landing a paralyzing blow to Corbett's solar plexus.

Following the example of John L. Sullivan and Corbett, Fitzsimmons cashed in on his championship by fighting exhibitions, appearing in vaudeville, and starring in a Broadway play during the next two years. He lost the championship in his first defense, an 11th-round knockout by James J. Jeffries on June 9, 1899, at Coney Island.

Fitzsimmons was knocked out by Jeffries again, in the 8th round of a title fight on July 25, 1902. But he won the light heavyweight championship on November 25, 1903, with a 20-round decision over George Gardner in San Francisco. He was the first fighter ever to win championships in three different divisions.

Philadelphia Jack O'Brien took that title with a 13th-round knockout on December 20, 1905, also in San Francisco. Fitzsimmons did little fighting for the next several years. However, he won the Australian heavyweight title in 1909. After four more years of inactivity, he returned to the United States in 1914, fought two no-decisions, and retired from boxing.

Fitzsimmons won 40 of his 62 professional fights, 32 by knockout. He lost 11, 8 by knockout, and also had 10 no-decisions and 1 no-contest.

★ International Boxing Hall of Fame

Fitzsimmons, Sunny Jim (James)

HORSE RACING

b. July 23, 1874, Brooklyn, N.Y.
d. March 11, 1966

The house in which Fitzsimmons was born was torn down to make way for the Sheepshead Bay Race Track, where he began his long career in thoroughbred racing as a waterboy. After nearly ten unsuccessful years as a jockey, Fitzsimmons became too heavy for that job and began training horses.

Before he retired in 1963, just before his 89th birthday, he had saddled 2,428 winners with earnings of $13,082,911. Among the winners were Gallant Fox, who won the triple crown in 1930; Omaha, who won the 1935 triple crown; and Nashua, who won the Preakness and Belmont in 1955, then beat Kentucky Derby winner Swaps in a $100,000 match race.

Fitzsimmons also trained Granville, Horse of the Year in 1936, and Bold Ruler, Horse of the Year in 1955. He led trainers in money won in 1936, 1939, and 1955.

Most remarkably, Fitzsimmons was a public trainer through most of his career, yet wealthy owners who could afford their own trainers trusted their horses to him, beginning in 1914 with James Johnson of Quincy Stable, owner of 34 horses. Ten years later, Fitzsimmons took over the horses owned by William Woodward's Belair Stud. During one ten-year stretch, half of the winners at Belmont Park were Belair Stud horses trained by Fitzsimmons. When he retired, he was training horses for Wheatley Stable and Ogden Phipps.

★ National Horse Racing Hall of Fame

Flaherty, Raymond

FOOTBALL
b. Sept. 1, 1904, Spokane, Wash.
d. July 19, 1994

Though elected to the Hall of Fame as a coach, Flaherty was also a fine player. An end at Gonzaga University, he played for the Los Angeles Wildcats of the American Football League in 1926. The league folded after one season, and Flaherty went to the NFL's New York Yanks for two seasons before joining the New York Giants in 1928.

Flaherty temporarily retired after the 1929 season, but he returned to the Giants in 1931 and remained with them through 1935 before retiring for good. He led the NFL in receiving with 21 catches for 350 yards and 3 touchdowns in 1932, the first year official statistics were kept.

In 1936, Flaherty became coach of the Boston Redskins, who moved to Washington the following season. He guided the Redskins to NFL championships in 1937 and 1942, then entered the Navy.

After World War II, Flaherty coached the New York Yankees to division titles in the All-America Football Conference in 1946 and 1947, but they lost both championship games to the Cleveland Browns. He was fired after the team won only one of its first four games in 1948. He ended his coaching career with the AAFC's Chicago Hornets in 1949. His overall coaching record was 82–41–5.

★ Pro Football Hall of Fame

Flanagan, John J.

TRACK AND FIELD
b. Jan. 9, 1873, Kilbreedy, Ireland
d. June 4, 1938

Except for one two-year stretch, Flanagan held the world hammer throw record from 1896 until 1911. He set the record for the first time with a throw of 147 feet to win the 1896 British championship, then emigrated to the United States.

He was the first to surpass 150 feet (in 1897), 160 feet (1899), 170 feet (1901), and 180 feet (1909). His final world record throw was 37 feet, 8 inches longer than his first, and it made him the oldest athlete ever to break a world record in any track and field event.

Flanagan was the Olympic hammer throw champion in 1900, 1904, and 1908. He also won a silver medal in the 56-pound weight throw in 1904, when he was fourth in the discus. He was the AAU national champion in the hammer throw from 1897 through 1899 and in 1901, 1902, 1906, and 1907, and he won the 56-pound weight championship in 1899, 1901, 1904, 1906, and 1907.

Like many of the great Irish-American weight throwers of his time, Flanagan was a New York City policeman. He retired from the force in 1911 and returned to Ireland. Shortly afterward, he won the hammer throw for the Irish national team in its annual grudge match against Scotland.

Flanagan, Mike (Michael K.)

BASEBALL
b. Dec. 16, 1951, Manchester, N.H.

A left-handed pitcher who relied on the curve and change-up rather than the fastball, Flanagan became a full-time starter for the AL's Baltimore Orioles in 1977 after brief stints with the team the two previous seasons.

He won the league's Cy Young Award in 1979, when he led the AL in shutouts with five and in victories with a 23–9 record. It was his only 20-victory season, but he did reach double digits in wins seven other times.

Flanagan was troubled by injuries frequently from 1981 through 1986, and Baltimore traded him to the Toronto Blue Jays during the 1987 season. After three mediocre years in Toronto, he returned in 1991 to Baltimore, where he was used as a middle-inning relief pitcher for two seasons before his retirement.

He had a career 167–143 record, with 19 shutouts and a 3.90 ERA. Flanagan struck out 1,491 hitters and walked 890 in 2,770 innings.

Fleming, Peggy G.

FIGURE SKATING
b. July 27, 1948, San Jose, Calif.

Dick Button described Fleming as "a unique combination of athletic ability, technical control, great style, and immense musicality."

Fleming started skating competitively when she was 11. Two years later, her coach was among those killed when a plane carrying the U.S. figure skating team crashed in Belgium. She said later, "For a long time, I didn't feel like going out there to skate."

But she kept skating, and her parents did everything they could to advance her career. The family moved to Colorado Springs in 1965 so she could train with Carlo Fassi and prepare for the high altitude of Davos, Switzerland, where the next world championships were to be held. Her mother designed and sewed the dresses she wore in competition.

The 5-foot-3, 109-pound Fleming won five consecutive U.S. championships, from 1964 through 1968, and she was the world champion three years in a row, from 1966 through 1968. She won the only gold medal for the U.S. team at the 1968 Winter Olympics.

Named the Associated Press female athlete of the year for her 1968 triumphs, Fleming signed a long-term $500,000 contract shortly after the Olympics. She appeared in her own television specials and also performed with the Ice Follies and Holiday on Ice. Fleming later did figure skating commentary for ABC television.

★ International Women's Sports Hall of Fame; Olympic Hall of Fame

Flick, Elmer H.

BASEBALL
b. Jan. 11, 1876, Bedford, Ohio
d. Jan. 9, 1971

A virtually forgotten baseball player, Flick briefly achieved fame in 1963, when he was elected to the Hall of Fame, and again in 1968, when Carl Yastrzemski broke Flick's dubious record by winning a batting title with a .301 average. Flick had previously had the lowest average ever to lead a league, a .308 mark in 1905.

But Flick's lifetime average was 5 points better than that and 28 points better than Yastrzemski's lifetime average. And he once hit .367 without leading the league.

Flick became a major leaguer with the Philadelphia Phillies in 1898, batting .302. A left-handed hitter but right-handed thrower, he was an outfielder who occasionally played second base in his later years. He hit .342, .367, and .333 during his next three years and led the NL in RBI with 110 in 1900, when he also scored 106 runs.

In 1902, Flick jumped to the Philadelphia team in the AL, which was just a year old. However, a state court ruled that no member of the 1901 Phillies could play for any other team in the state, so Flick was sent to the Cleveland Indians, along with the better-known Napoleon Lajoie.

When he led the league with a .308 average in 1905, he was also the leader in triples with 18 and in slugging percentage with .462. The following year, he led in triples again with 22 and in runs scored with 98 while batting .311. And in 1907, he had a league-leading 18 triples.

A stomach problem that was never clearly diagnosed limited Flick to just nine games in 1908 and, in effect, ended his career. He appeared in 90 games the next two seasons with the Indians and then spent two years in the minor leagues before leaving baseball.

★ Baseball Hall of Fame

Flock, Fonty (T. Fontello)
AUTO RACING
b. March 21, 1921, Ft. Payne, Ala. d. July 15, 1972

Flock's roots were the roots of stock car racing: bootlegging. As a young teenager, he was delivering bootleg whiskey by bicycle. A little later, he was making auto trips from Atlanta to Dawsonville, Georgia, to pick up moonshine. "I used to deliberately seek out the sheriff and get him to chase me," he later recalled. "It was fun, and besides we could send to California to get special parts to modify our cars, and the sheriff couldn't afford to do that."

When stock car racing began to be organized, just before World War II, Flock was there, winning a 100-mile race at Lakewood Park in Atlanta in 1940. After four years in the Army Air Corps, he returned just as NASCAR was getting established. He won the association's first Northern race, at Providence, RI, in 1947, and was the first National Modified Champion in 1949, when he won 11 feature races.

During the early 1950s, Flock drove mostly in Grand National events. He finished second in the point standings in 1951, fourth in 1952, fifth in 1953, and tenth in 1955. He established an insurance agency in Nashville and raced only part-time beginning in 1954. In 1957 he entered only the beach-road race at Daytona, though he also drove in the Darlington 500 as relief for Herb Thomas, who had been injured in a practice crash. The car was also in bad shape. It blew

a tire on the sixth lap and got hit by two other cars. Flock fortunately walked away unhurt, and he also walked away from racing.

★ NASCAR Hall of Fame

Flock, Tim (Julius Timothy)
AUTO RACING
b. May 11, 1924, Ft. Payne, Ala.

The younger brother of Fonty Flock, Tim had a much briefer career. But it was very successful and more lucrative because he was in his prime when purses were bigger. Fonty and another older brother, Bob, also a racer, tried to talk Tim out of getting into stock car racing. But his older sister Ethel and her husband helped him get started in 1948.

Tim raced modified cars that year and did enough Grand National racing in 1949 to place eighth in the point standings — five places below Bob and three below Fonty. After an off year in 1950, when he spent considerable time in the hospital recovering from injuries suffered in a four-car crash at the Charlotte Speedway, he finished third in 1951 and won the championship in 1952.

Fonty and Tim were fifth and sixth, respectively, in the 1953 standings. In 1955, Tim had one of the greatest years in racing history with 17 victories, a NASCAR record, and he won another Grand National championship.

★ NASCAR Hall of Fame

Flood, Curtis C.
BASEBALL
b. Jan. 18, 1938, Houston, Tex.

Curt Flood was a very good defensive outfielder who batted over .300 six times in 12 full seasons in the major leagues, led the NL with 211 hits in 1964, played for three pennant-winning teams, and was selected to the All-Star team three times. But he's best known for his unsuccessful suit against baseball's reserve clause, which bound a player to his team even after his contract ran out.

Flood played in a total of eight games with the NL's Cincinnati Reds in 1956 and 1957 and then was traded to the St. Louis Cardinals, where he became a starter in 1958. He was with the Cardinals through 1969. When he was traded to the Philadelphia Phillies in 1970, Flood refused to report and filed suit, with the backing of the Major League Players' Association.

The suit charged major league baseball with violating antitrust laws and suggested that the perpetual reserve clause forced players into "involuntary servitude," a violation of the Thirteenth Amendment to the Constitution, which forbade slavery.

A federal court judge ruled against Flood on August 12, 1970, and the Supreme Court upheld the ruling in a 5–3 decision on June 18, 1972. In the meantime, Flood had spent a year out of baseball and retired permanently after playing just 13 games for the AL's Washington Senators in 1971.

Although Flood's suit was unsuccessful, the publicity surrounding led to a threat of legislative action that helped force team owners to accept outside arbitration of grievances. That ultimately led to the decision by arbitrator Peter Seitz in 1975 that the reserve clause is not binding.

In Flood's 15 major league seasons, he batted .293 with 1,861 hits, including 271 doubles, 44 triples, and 85 home runs. He scored 851 runs and had 636 RBI.

Flores, Tom (Thomas R.)

FOOTBALL
b. March 21, 1937, Fresno, Calif.

After graduating from the University of the Pacific in 1958, it took two years for Flores to make a professional football team. He was cut by the Calgary Stampeders of the Canadian Football League in 1958 and by the NFL's Washington Redskins in 1959.

Then the AFL was established in 1960, and Flores caught on with the Oakland Raiders. He became the team's starting quarterback early in the season and led the league by completing 54.0 percent of his passes, throwing for 1,738 yards and 12 touchdowns.

Flores had his most productive season in 1966. Although he completed only 49.3 percent of his attempts, he passed for 2,638 yards and 24 touchdowns in 14 games.

Oakland traded him to the Buffalo Bills in 1967. A backup with Buffalo, Flores was released early in the 1969 season and was picked up by the Kansas City Chiefs. He spent the 1970 season on Kansas City's taxi squad, then retired as a player.

After serving as an assistant coach with Buffalo and Oakland, Flores took over as head coach of the Raiders in 1979. The franchise moved to Los Angeles in 1982. In nine seasons, he directed the Raiders to three first-place division finishes and Super Bowl victories after the 1980 and 1983 seasons.

In 1988, Flores moved into the team's front office, but after a year he left to become president and general manager of the NFL's Seattle Seahawks. He named himself head coach in 1992.

As a player, Flores completed 838 of 1,715 passes for 11,959 yards and 92 touchdowns. He also rushed for 5 touchdowns. As a coach, he has a 99–85–0 record in regular season play and an 8–3 record in playoff games.

Flowers, Tiger (Theodore)

BOXING
b. Aug. 5, 1895, Camille, Ga.
d. Nov. 16, 1927

Flowers was an unusual boxer, especially for his time, a religious man and a steward in the Methodist Church who was nicknamed "Deacon." When World War I began, Flowers went to work in a Philadelphia shipyard. One day he visited a gym run by Philadelphia Jack O'Brien, decided to start sparring, and discovered he could hold his own with more experienced fighters.

After the war, Flowers returned to Georgia and got a job as a porter in an Atlanta gym, where he also continued his training. The 5-foot-10 left-hander won his first 28 professional fights, from 1918 until late 1921, when he was knocked out by Panama Joe Gans.

Flowers had 90 bouts in the next four years, losing only nine, to win a middleweight championship fight against Harry Greb on February 26, 1926. Flowers took the title with a 15-round decision, but he lost it to Mickey Walker in a 10-round decision on December 3.

In 1927, Flowers lost only 1 of 18 fights, with 3 draws, before going to the hospital for eye surgery. He died of an infection just four days after his last bout. Flowers won 115 of his 149 professional fights, 49 by knockout. He lost 13, 8 by knockout, and also fought 6 draws, 14 no-decisions, and 1 no-contest.

★ International Boxing Hall of Fame

Floyd, Raymond L.

GOLF
b. Sept. 4, 1942, Ft. Bragg, N.C.

Floyd's career has been a roller coaster ride with more downs than ups. Yet he won three of the four major tournaments over an 18-year period.

He joined the professional tour in 1961 and had just one victory going into 1969, when he won four tournaments, including the PGA championship. Then he virtually disappeared for several years; he didn't even finish among the top 60 in 1972 or 1973.

Floyd bounced back, winning more than $100,000 in both 1974 and 1975. Still, his name wasn't even on the leader board as a player to watch at the 1976 Masters until he shot a 32 on the first nine holes. He finished that round with a 65 and shot a 66 on the second day, setting a record of 131 for the first 36 holes of the Masters. He won the tournament easily, tying Jack Nicklaus's record of 271.

Ten years later, he was in the hunt for the U.S. Open championship. He had played the tournament 21 times before and had finished in the top ten only twice, most recently in 1971. Yet Floyd was just two shots behind Payne Stewart with six holes to play in the 1986 Open, and he hit two great shots to win. On the thirteenth hole, he hit a 6-iron to within four feet of the hole and putted for a birdie. Stewart bogeyed the hole, so they were tied. Hitting into the wind on the sixteenth hole, Floyd punched a low 8-iron shot that stopped ten feet from the cup, and his birdie putt gave him the lead for good. He was the oldest player ever to win the tournament.

Floyd suddenly reappeared in the news in February 1992, when fire destroyed his home near Miami. Three weeks later, he won the Doral-Ryder Open. That made him the second player in history to win tournaments in four different decades (Sam Snead was the other). More remarkably, he finished second in the Masters. Floyd also began playing on the PGA Senior circuit after turning 50 in September, won the second event he entered, and donated his winnings of $67,500 to the Hurricane Andrew Relief Fund.

★ World Golf Hall of Fame

Ford, Alan R.

SWIMMING
b. Dec. 7, 1923, Canal Zone, Panama

His career was interrupted by military service during World War II, so Ford didn't win as many championships as some other outstanding swimmers, but the times he turned in prove his greatness. In 1943, he swam the 100-yard freestyle in 50.7 seconds to break Johnny Weismuller's record, which had been set in 1927. Ford lowered the record five times in the next two years. His final mark of 49.4 seconds, set in 1945, stood until 1952. Ford also broke the world record for the 100-meter freestyle twice.

Competing for Yale in 1944, he became only the third swimmer to win three individual championships at the NCAA meet; he won the 50- and 100-yard freestyle events and the 150-yard backstroke. Ford was the national outdoor champion in the 110-yard freestyle in 1942 and 1943 and in the 220-yard freestyle in 1943. Indoors, he won the 220-yard championship in 1942, the 100-yard in 1943.

After serving in the Navy, he returned to competition briefly in 1948 — just long enough to win a silver medal in the Olympic 100-meter freestyle.

Ford, Danny L.

FOOTBALL
b. April 2, 1948, Gadsden, Ala.

The captain of the University of Alabama team as a senior in 1969, Ford played tackle and tight end. He served as an assistant coach at Alabama, Virginia Tech, and Clemson until December 1978, when he was named Clemson's head coach. He was the youngest coach at an NCAA Division I school at the time.

Because former coach Charley Pell had announced that he was moving to the University of Florida, Ford's first game was a 17–15 victory over Ohio State in the Gator Bowl. He compiled a 96–29–4 record in 11 seasons at Clemson, including a 12–0–0 record in 1981, when his team won the national championship, and he was consensus coach of the year.

Ford resigned in early 1989, shortly after it was announced that the NCAA was investigating recruiting violations at the school. He took over at the University of Arkansas in 1993.

Ford, Len (Leonard G. Jr.)

FOOTBALL
b. Feb. 18, 1926, Washington, D.C.
d. March 14, 1972

Ford played at Morgan State and at the University of Michigan before entering pro football with the Los Angeles Dons of the All-America Football Conference in 1948. He was an offensive end with the Dons, catching 67 passes for 1,175 yards, a 17.5 average, and 8 touchdowns in two seasons.

The AAFC folded in 1950, three of its teams moving into the NFL. Players from other teams were put into a special draft pool, and Ford was chosen by the Cleveland Browns, who moved him to defense. The 6-foot-5 Ford beefed up to 260 pounds and became one of the most feared pass rushers in the game.

In his first year on defense, Ford suffered a broken nose and two broken cheekbones and had to undergo extensive plastic surgery. Outfitted with a special helmet mask, he came back for Cleveland's 30–28 victory over the Los Angeles Rams in the NFL championship game. When the Browns beat the Detroit Lions, 56–10, in the 1954 title game, Ford had two interceptions.

Ford was named an All-Pro five years in a row, 1951 through 1955. He played with Cleveland through 1957 and spent a final season with the Green Bay Packers in 1958 before retiring. He died of a heart attack.
★ Pro Football Hall of Fame

Ford, Phil J., Jr.

BASKETBALL
b. Feb. 9, 1956, Rocky Mount, N.C.

A four-year starting guard at the University of North Carolina, the 6-foot-1, 185-pound Ford was an exceptionally quick and clever ball-handler who could also score. He averaged 20.8 points a game as a senior in 1977–78. A consensus All-American in both 1977 and 1978, he was named college player of the year by the U.S. Basketball Writers Association in 1978, when he also won the Eastman and Wooden awards.

After his sophomore season, Ford started for the U.S. Olympic team that won the gold medal in 1976.

Ford was the NBA rookie of the year with the Kansas City Kings in 1978–79. However, injuries and alcohol abuse shortened his career. He was traded to the Milwaukee Bucks in 1982 and went to the Houston Rockets in 1983. He retired in 1986 after failing to make the Golden State Warriors.

In 482 NBA games, Ford scored 5,594 points, an 11.6 average, and had 3,083 assists, an average of 6.4 per game. He later became a bank executive and spent much of his free time talking to students about alcohol and drug abuse. In 1988 he returned to North Carolina as an assistant coach.

Ford, Whitey (Edward C.)

BASEBALL
b. Oct. 21, 1928, New York, N.Y.

Although he was the ace of the New York Yankee pitching staff for 15 years, Ford was never really in the team's starting rotation for most of that time. Manager Casey Stengel used him when he thought Ford would be most effective, and Ford had his own preferences. For example, he hated to pitch in Boston's Fenway Park, and rarely did.

A clever left-hander who specialized in the curve ball and, as he later admitted, a trick pitch that involved cutting the ball to give it an unusual break, Ford was a high-percentage winner who specialized in big games.

Ford joined the Yankees during the 1950 season, won nine consecutive games down the stretch, and beat the Philadelphia Phillies in the deciding fourth game of the World Series.

After two years in the Army, Ford returned to the Yankees in 1953, when he had an 18–6 record. He led the AL in victories with an 18–7 mark in 1955, and in winning percentage, .760 on a 19–6 record, and ERA, with 2.47, in 1956. Ford was the ERA leader again in 1958 at 2.01, and he also led the league in shutouts with 7, though he had only a 14–7 record.

Although Ford pitched two shutouts in the 1960 World Series, the Yankees lost to the Pittsburgh Pirates in seven games, and Stengel was replaced by Ralph Houk, who made Ford his top pitcher. Ford responded by winning more than 20 games for the first time. He led the league in victories and percentage with a 25–4 record in 1961, when he won the Cy Young Award, and he led in both categories again with a 24–7 mark in 1963.

After going 17–6 in 1964 and 16–13 in 1965, Ford developed shoulder problems. He won just four games in limited action over the next two seasons and then retired. He coached with the Yankees for a year, then left to pursue business interests. However, he returned to the Yankees as pitching coach for the 1974 season and later became a spring training instructor with the team.

In 498 games, Ford had a 236–106 record, a .690 winning percentage, and a 2.75 ERA. He recorded 45 shutouts and struck out 1,956 hitters while walking 1,086 in 3,170 innings. When he retired, he held World Series records for most games, 22; most wins, 10; most losses, 8; most innings, 146; most strikeouts, 94; and most walks, 34.

★ Baseball Hall of Fame

Foreman, Chuck (Walter E.)

FOOTBALL
b. Oct. 26, 1950, Frederick, Md.

Originally a defensive back at the University of Miami in Florida, Foreman spent two years as a running back and was used mostly as a wide receiver in 1972, his senior year.

A first-round draft choice of the NFL's Minnesota Vikings, Foreman became a running back again as a professional but was often used as a receiver out of the backfield. He was a consensus choice as the National Football Conference rookie of the year in 1973, when he rushed for 801 yards on 182 attempts and caught 37 passes for 362 yards. Foreman rushed for 76 yards and one touchdown in Minnesota's 27–10 victory over the Dallas Cowboys in the conference championship game but was held to only 18 yards when the Vikings lost, 24–7, to the Miami Dolphins in the Super Bowl.

In 1975, the 6-foot-2, 210-pound Foreman came close to leading the NFC in receptions and rushing yardage. He caught 73 passes to lead the conference and finished just six yards behind Jim Otis of the St. Louis Cardinals in rushing. Foreman's 22 touchdowns tied Gale Sayers's former record, but O. J. Simpson scored 23 that season to break it.

Foreman was named conference player of the year by *The Sporting News* in 1974 and by United Press International in 1976. He was named to the All-Pro team in 1975 and 1976 and played in five consecutive Pro Bowls, 1973 through 1977.

A knee injury bothered him throughout the 1978 season, when he gained just 749 yards on 237 attempts, an average of only 3.2 per carry, and a rib injury forced him into a backup role in 1979. Foreman was then traded to the New England Patriots, where he spent the 1980 season before retiring.

Foreman rushed for 5,950 yards and 53 touchdowns in 1,556 carries, averaging 3.8 yards per attempt, and caught 350 passes for 3,156 yards, a 9.0 average, and 23 touchdowns.

Foreman, George

BOXING
b. Jan. 22, 1948, Marshall, Tex.

Foreman had only 18 amateur fights before he won the Olympic gold medal as a heavyweight in 1968. He also won immediate fame by parading around the ring holding a small U.S. flag after his victory; the scene was captured on live television from Mexico City, and the photo appeared in newspapers across the country.

He became a professional in June 1969 and won his first 34 fights to gain a shot at the heavyweight championship against Joe Frazier. Thirty-one of those victories came on knockouts, 29 of them before the 6th round.

Frazier was a 3–1 favorite in their January 22, 1973, fight in Kingston, Jamaica, but Foreman knocked the champion down six times in less than two rounds to win the title. After two defenses, Foreman suffered his first loss, an 8th-round knockout by Muhammad Ali on October 30, 1974, at Kinshasa, Zaire.

After a series of exhibitions in 1975, Foreman won his next five fights by knockout, but he retired after losing a 12-round decision to Jimmy Young in 1977. Ten years later, he came out of retirement and knocked out 13 opponents before meeting Evander Holyfield for the heavyweight title in 1991. Holyfield retained the championship with a 12-round decision.

Foreman retired once more in 1993 but remained very popular because of several television commercials in which he poked fun at himself for his eating habits. There were many doubts when he returned to the ring once more in 1994. However, he became the oldest champion ever in any weight division by knocking out Michael Moorer in the 10th round on November 6 to reclaim the heavyweight title.

He has won 73 of his 77 professional fights, 68 by knockout.

Fortmann, Daniel J.

FOOTBALL
b. April 11, 1916, Pearl River, N.Y.

After being tried at end and halfback,

Fortmann became a starting guard at Colgate in 1933, when he was only 17. He graduated as a Phi Beta Kappa at 20 and became the youngest player ever to sign an NFL contract, with the Chicago Bears in 1936.

The 6-foot, 210-pound Fortmann played a major role in the Bears' championship seasons in 1940, 1941, and 1943. They were also division champions in 1937 and 1942. Fortmann was a second-team All-Pro his first two seasons and was named to the first team six years in a row, from 1938 through 1943.

Though smaller than most guards even at that time, Fortmann was a deadly tackler and surprisingly strong blocker who was excellent at pulling out of the line to lead interference. He studied medicine in the off-season and retired after the 1943 season to begin practice as a surgeon in Los Angeles.

★ College Football Hall of Fame; Pro Football Hall of Fame

Fosbury, Dick (Richard D.)

TRACK AND FIELD
b. March 6, 1947, Portland, Oreg.

After Fosbury won the 1968 Olympic gold medal in the high jump, the U.S. coach, Payton Jordan, commented, "Kids imitate champions. If they try to imitate Fosbury, he'll wipe out an entire generation of high jumpers because they will all have broken necks."

Twelve years later, 13 of the 16 finalists in the Olympic high jump were using the "Fosbury flop," and there were no broken necks.

Fosbury began experimenting with the technique, in which the jumper goes over the bar headfirst and backward, when he was 16. In the next two years, his best jump improved from 5 feet, 3¾ inches to 6 feet, 6¾ inches.

As a student at Oregon State in 1968, he became the first ever to jump over 7 feet indoors, at the NCAA meet. He also won the NCAA outdoor championship that year and in 1969. Fosbury never won an AAU national championship, but he finished first in the 1968 Olympic trials.

At the Mexico City Olympics, he

missed on his first two attempts but made the third at 7 feet, 4¼ inches to set an Olympic and American record.

★ National Track & Field Hall of Fame

Foster, Bob (Robert W.)

BOXING
b. April 27, 1938, Albuquerque, N.Mex.

Like several other great light-heavyweights, Foster tried unsuccessfully to become the heavyweight championship. Two of his eight career defeats were in heavyweight fights.

Foster began his professional career with a knockout early in 1961. He had a fine record for his first five years, but it got even better. Beginning in 1966, he won 20 in a row, 19 by knockout. During that string, he won the light-heavyweight championship by knocking out Dick Tiger in the 4th round on May 24, 1968.

Foster's winning streak ended on November 18, 1970, when he fought Joe Frazier for the heavyweight championship. Frazier knocked him out in the 2nd round.

However, Foster retained his light-heavyweight title and won nine more in a row, eight by knockout, before facing former heavyweight champion Muhammad Ali. Ali knocked Foster out in the 8th round on November 21, 1972. After defending his light-heavy title three more times, on two decisions and a draw, Foster announced his retirement in 1974. But he returned to the ring less than a year later. He had five lackluster victories, then was knocked out twice in 1978 and retired for good.

Foster won 56 of his 65 professional fights, 46 of them by knockout. He lost 8, 6 by knockout, and had 1 draw.

★ International Boxing Hall of Fame

Foster, Bud (Harold)

BASKETBALL
b. May 30, 1906, Newton, Kans.

A forward and center at the University of Wisconsin, Foster captained the team as a senior in 1929–30. Wisconsin won 43 games and lost only 8 during his three years as a starter. He spent five seasons playing professional basketball with teams in Oshkosh, Milwaukee, and Chicago before succeeding Walter Meanwell as Wisconsin's basketball coach in 1935.

Foster basically used the deliberate ball-control offense he'd learned under Meanwell, but his teams were also taught to use the fast break when possible. During his 25 seasons, Wisconsin won 270 games while losing 264. He coached the Badgers to the NCAA championship in 1941 and to three Big Ten titles.

He retired from coaching after the 1958–59 season, remaining at the school as professor of athletics.

★ Basketball Hall of Fame

Foster, George A.

BASEBALL
b. Dec. 1, 1948, Tuscaloosa, Ala.

A right-hander, the 6-foot-1, 185-pound Foster was a clutch power hitter who became the chief RBI man for Cincinnati's "Big Red Machine" during the 1970s.

He had brief tryouts with the NL's San Francisco Giants in 1969 and 1970, then joined the team at the beginning of the 1971 season and was traded to Cincinnati after just 36 games with San Francisco. Injuries limited his playing time during the next three seasons, but he finally became a starting outfielder in 1975, and the following year he led the league with 121 RBI.

Foster was named the NL's most valuable player in 1977, when he batted .320 and led the league with 52 home runs, 149 RBI, 124 runs scored, and a .631 slugging percentage. He was the home run and RBI leader again in 1978 with 40 and 120, respectively.

His production began to tail off in 1979, and he was traded to the New York Mets in 1982. Media pressure to perform troubled him in his first season, when he hit only 13 home runs, his lowest total since 1974. He came back to hit 28, 24, and 21 over the next three seasons. During the 1988 season, the Mets traded him to the Chicago White Sox, and he retired after just 15 games with Chicago.

Foster had a career .274 batting average in 1,977 games, with 1,925 hits, including 307 doubles, 47 triples, and 348 home runs. He drove in 1,239 runs and scored 986.

Foster, Gregory

TRACK AND FIELD
b. Aug. 4, 1958, Chicago, Ill.

As a student at UCLA, Foster won the NCAA 200-meter championship in 1979 as well as the 110-meter hurdles in 1978 and 1980. After graduating in 1981, he concentrated on the hurdles.

Foster was ranked among the top ten in the world 15 times, a record for a running event. He won the world 110-meter championship in 1983, 1987, and 1991 and was the national outdoor champion in the event in 1981, 1983, 1986, and 1987.

His best Olympic performance was a silver medal in 1984.

Foster, Rube (Andrew)

BASEBALL
b. Sept. 17, 1879, Calvert, Tex. d. Dec. 9, 1930

A pitcher and manager in the early years of black baseball, Foster was the chief organizer of the National Negro League. At 17, the 6-foot-4, 210-pound right-handed Foster was starring for a barnstorming team.

He joined the new Chicago Union Giants in 1902, then went to the Cuban X Giants. Foster had four of the team's five wins when they beat the Philadelphia Giants in 1903 for the "colored championship of the world." He then went to the Philadelphia Giants in 1904 and had both their victories in a three-game championship series against the Cuban X Giants, striking out 18 in one game and pitching a two-hitter in the other.

Foster began pitching for the Leland Giants of Chicago in 1907 and took over as manager three years later, guiding them to an incredible 123–6 record. He and a white tavern owner organized the Chicago American Giants in 1911; Foster played for the team until 1915 and managed it until 1920, when the Negro National League was organized.

He served as league president and secretary and often seemed a tyrant because he had to be to keep the league going. As a salary, he collected five percent of the receipts from all league games, but he also used his own money to pay transportation and hotel bills for teams that got stranded without money, not an unusual problem.

In 1925, some team owners were unhappy with Foster, and he offered to resign. The owners backed down. A year later, he was hospitalized with mental illness. Without his leadership, the league struggled along for a while but folded after the 1931 season.
★ Baseball Hall of Fame

Fothergill, Dorothy

BOWLING
b. April 10, 1945, N. Attleboro, Mass.

Fothergill averaged 207 pins as an amateur in 1966 and turned professional the following year. She was the top money winner on the women's tour and bowler of the year in both 1968 and 1969. Fothergill won the women's All-Star tournament and the PWBA national championship both of those years.

In 1970, Fothergill won the WIBC all-events title with a record 1,984 pins for nine games, and she was also singles champion with a 695 series. She teamed with Mildred Martorella to win WIBC doubles titles in 1971 and 1973.

Her game began to decline in the late 1970s, and she retired from the tour in 1978 with 18 WIBC and tour victories in just 12 years. Fothergill returned to competition briefly in 1979 to win the first women's Great and Greatest tournament with Donna Adamek.
★ WIBC Hall of Fame

Fouts, Daniel F.

FOOTBALL
b. June 10, 1951, San Francisco, Calif.

A three-year starter at quarterback for the University of Oregon, Fouts was overlooked by All-American selectors because he played for mediocre teams that won only 15 games while losing 17 and tying 1.

Selected by the San Diego Chargers in the third round of the 1973 NFL college draft, Fouts became the team's starting quarterback before the end of his rookie season. He didn't emerge as a genuine star until Don Coryell became head coach during the 1978 season.

Coryell installed an offense featuring the pass that became known as "Air Coryell." During the next eight seasons, Fouts averaged 2,729 yards and 24 touchdown passes a year. He set an NFL record with 4,082 yards passing in 1979 and extended it to 4,715 yards in 1980 and to 4,802 yards in 1981.

Fouts was named the American Football Conference player of the year by *The Sporting News* and United Press International in 1979 and by UPI in 1982, when he was selected as the NFL player of the year by the Professional Football Writers Association.

He retired after the 1987 season and is now a broadcaster for NBC. During his 15 years in the NFL, Fouts completed 3,297 of 5,604 passes for 43,040 yards, second only to Fran Tarkenton, and 254 touchdowns, fourth on the all-time list. He also rushed for 13 touchdowns.
★ Pro Football Hall of Fame

Fox, Nellie (Jacob Nelson)
BASEBALL
b. Dec. 25, 1927, St. Thomas, Pa.
d. Dec. 1, 1975

Only 5-foot-9 and 150 pounds, Fox was a left-handed-hitting second baseman who could hit and field. His trademark was an enormous chaw of tobacco that always thrust out one of his cheeks. Some said the tobacco was bigger than he.

Fox played just ten games for the NL's Philadelphia Phillies in 1947 and 1948 and spent half of the 1949 season with Philadelphia before being traded to the Chicago White Sox of the AL in 1950.

He was named the league's most valuable player in 1959, when the White Sox won the pennant. Fox batted .306 that season, one of six times he hit better than .300, and he led AL second baseman in fielding percentage.

Fox led the league in hits four times, with 192 in 1952, 201 in 1954, 196 in 1957, and 198 in 1958, and he was the triples leader with 10 in 1960. He was the league's best-fielding second baseman six times.

In 1964, Fox was traded to the NL's Houston Astros. He retired after playing just 21 games for them in 1965.

Foxx, Jimmie (James E.)
BASEBALL
b. Oct. 22, 1907, Sudlersville, Md.
d. July 21, 1967

Foxx was six feet tall and 195 pounds, but he seemed bigger, probably because he could hit the ball so far. He joined the AL's Philadelphia Athletics in 1925 as a catcher but didn't play much during his first few seasons because Philadelphia already had the best catcher in baseball, Mickey Cochrane.

In his infrequent appearances, Foxx showed that he could hit, and in 1929 he became Philadelphia's starting first baseman. He hit .354 with 33 home runs and 117 RBI. It was the first in a record streak of 12 years in which he hit 30 or more home runs and drove in 100 or more runs.

Foxx had a .335 average with 37 home runs and 156 RBI in 1930, then batted .291 with 30 homers and 120 RBI in 1931, as the Athletics won their third straight pennant. In their three World Series appearances, Foxx hit .344 with 4 home runs, 11 runs scored, and 11 RBI.

Philadelphia owner-manager Connie Mack began to dismantle the team in 1932 because of financial problems. The Athletics started to slide, but Foxx didn't. He led the AL with 58 home runs and 169 RBI, batting .364. Foxx lost two home runs hit in games called by rain before they became official, keeping him from tying Babe Ruth's famous record of 60 in a season. He was also deprived of the triple crown because the batting title was awarded to Dale Alexander, even though Alexander didn't have the required 400 at-bats for the season.

In 1933, Foxx did win the triple crown, batting .356 with 48 home runs and 163 RBI. He won his second MVP award that season. Despite a pay cut, he hit .334 with 44 homers and 130 RBI in 1934. Foxx ended his career with Philadelphia by tying Lou Gehrig for the home run lead with 36 in 1935, when he hit .346 and had 115 RBI.

Mack then sent him to the Boston Red Sox in a trade that brought $150,000 to the Athletics, along with two inconsequential players. Foxx was an immediate favorite among Boston fans. He hit .338 with 41 home runs in 1936. After slipping to a .285 average and 36 home runs in 1937, he won his third most valuable player award in 1938 with a .349 average, 50 home runs, and 175 RBI. He led the league in average and RBI but finished second to Hank Greenberg in homers.

After leading the league in home runs with 35 in 1939, Foxx hit 36 in 1940, then declined to 19 in 1941. He got off to a poor start the following season and was released. The Chicago Cubs picked him up, but he was no more successful there, and he announced his retirement. The Cubs talked him into coming back in 1944, when players were scarce because of World War II, but he played in only 15 games, mostly as a pinch hitter. After appearing in 89 games for the Philadelphia Phillies in 1945, he retired for good.

He later coached and managed for a few years in the minor leagues. Known for drinking and for buying other people drinks, Foxx had little money left from his glorious baseball years. He suffered a heart attack in 1963 and choked to death while eating at his brother's house in Miami four years later.

In 2,317 games, Foxx batted .325 with 2,646 hits, including 458 doubles, 125 triples, and 534 home runs. He drove in 1,922 runs and scored 1,751.

★ Baseball Hall of Fame

Foyt, A. J. (Anthony Joseph)
AUTO RACING
b. Jan. 16, 1935, Houston, Tex.

The only driver to win the Indy 500 four times, Foyt had 34 starts and logged a record 11,785 miles in the race, winning $2,448,000. His victories came in 1961, 1964, 1967, and 1977.

A remarkably versatile driver, Foyt is the all-time leader in IndyCar victories with 67, and he won the national driving championship in 1960, 1963, 1964, 1967, 1975, and 1979. He also had 41 victories in U.S. Auto Club stock cars, 7 in NASCAR stock cars, 29 in sprint cars, 21 in midget cars, 7 in sports cars, and 2 in championship dirt cars.

Foyt is one of only three drivers to win races on oval speedways, road courses, and dirt tracks in a single season; he did that in 1968. And he's the only driver to win the Indy 500, the NASCAR Daytona 500, and the 24 Hours of LeMans. He won at Daytona in 1972 and at LeMans in 1968, 1983, and 1985.

He was the USAC dirt car champion in 1975 and the USAC stock car champion in 1968, 1978, and 1979.

Foyt began professional racing in 1953 in a midget car that his father built for him. He made his IndyCar debut in 1957 and qualified for the Indy 500 for the first time the following year. The personable Foyt has parlayed his winnings into a personal fortune. He owns the largest auto dealership in Texas and has extensive interests in oil wells, a hotel chain, and the largest funeral service business in the country.

★ Indianapolis Speedway Hall of Fame

Fralic, Bill (William)
FOOTBALL
b. Oct. 31, 1962, Penn Hills, Pa.

As a tackle at the University of Pittsburgh, Fralic was a consensus All-American in 1983 and 1984. He was the second player chosen in the 1985 NFL draft, by the Atlanta Falcons.

The 6-foot-5, 280-pound Fralic became a starting guard with Atlanta as a rookie. He was named to *The Sporting News* all-pro team in 1986 and 1987 and was selected for the Pro Bowl in 1986, 1987, 1988, and 1989.

In April 1993, Fralic signed with the

Detroit Lions as an unconditional free agent.

France, Bill (William H. G.)

AUTO RACING

b. Sept. 26, 1909, Washington, D.C.
d. June 7, 1992

A stock car driver in the 1930s, when the sport began with relatively informal competition, France called an organizational meeting of car owners, drivers, and mechanics in late 1947 to establish racing standards and regulations.

The meeting was held at Daytona Beach, Florida, the site of a popular track, part sand and part road. As a result, the National Association of Stock Car Auto Racing was incorporated in February 1948, with France as its president.

France ruled NASCAR from that point until 1972, building stock car racing into the richest, most popular of all motor sports. The 6-foot-5 France, known as "Big Bill," was often called a dictator. In response, he once smiled and said, "Well, let's make that a benevolent dictator. What I'm doing is best for the sport, not just me."

In 1959, France opened Daytona International Speedway, the first so-called superspeedway, a 2.5-mile, high-banked oval and the site of NASCAR's most prestigious race, the Daytona 500. By building it in Daytona, he signaled that the days of beach racing were over.

Within the next decade, other superspeedways were built at Atlanta, Charlotte, Dover (Delaware), Michigan, Pocono, and Rockingham. France opened another superspeedway, the 2.66-mile oval at Talladega, Alabama, in 1969.

When members of the newly established drivers organization, led by Richard Petty, proposed boycotting Talladega because tires might not be able to handle its 195-mile-per-hour speeds, France borrowed a car and did several laps at 176 miles an hour. "Surely the young pros can run 20 miles an hour faster than I can," he said, and the boycott fizzled.

After his retirement in 1972, France was replaced by his son, Bill France, Jr., but he remained active behind the scenes until shortly before his death.

Franco, John A.

BASEBALL

b. Sept. 17, 1960, Brooklyn, N.Y.

Franco joined the NL's Cincinnati Reds early in the 1984 season. He had a 12–3 record as a relief pitcher, with 12 saves and a 2.18 ERA in 1985. A left-hander, the 5-foot-10, 185-pounder Franco was named *The Sporting News* fireman of the year in 1988, when he led the league with 39 saves and had a 1.57 ERA.

Cincinnati traded him to the New York Mets in 1990, when he was the league leader in saves again with 33 to win his second fireman of the year award. After he had 30 saves in 1991, Franco began to suffer arm problems and missed large portions of the next two seasons. He became a full-time closer again in 1994, a strike-shortened season, when he once more had 30 saves.

Through 1994, Franco had a 63–51 record with 266 saves, a 2.63 ERA, and 559 strikouts in 770⅓ innings.

Franco, Julio C.

BASEBALL

b. Aug. 23, 1961, San Pedro de Macoris, Dominican Republic

Franco appeared in just 16 games with the NL's Philadelphia Phillies in 1982 and was then traded to the AL's Cleveland Indians. A right-hander, the 6-foot-1, 190-pound Franco took over as Cleveland's starting shortstop in 1983.

The Indians moved him to second base in 1988. After batting over .300 for three straight seasons, from 1986 through 1988, Franco went to the Texas Rangers. He led the AL with a .341 batting average in 1989.

Named the second baseman on *The Sporting News* AL all-star team from 1989 through 1991, Franco missed most of the 1992 season with a knee injury and was used entirely as a designated hitter in 1993. He joined the Chicago White Sox as a free agent the following year.

Through the 1994 season, Franco had a .301 average with 2,922 hits, including 299 doubles, 45 triples, and 120 home runs. He had stolen 237 bases, scored 964 runs, and driven in 861.

Frank, Clinton E.

FOOTBALL
b. Sept. 13, 1915, St. Louis, Mo.
d. July 7, 1992

In 1969, college football's centennial year, Frank was named to the "Best Backfield of the 1930s," along with Sammy Baugh, Marshall Goldberg, and Tommy Harmon. A quarterback at Yale, Frank was an All-American in 1937, when he narrowly edged "Whizzer" White for the Heisman Trophy.

Although Frank had poor eyesight, he was a very accurate passer. As a runner, he combined power with 10-second speed in the 100-yard dash, and he was also a fine defensive player. "Greasy" Neale, an assistant coach at Yale when Frank was playing, said of him, "He could do everything and do it brilliantly."
★ College Football Hall of Fame

Fraser, Gretchen (Kunigk)

SKIING
b. Feb. 11, 1919, Tacoma, Wash.
d. Feb. 18, 1994

Gretchen Kunigk's Norwegian-born mother was an enthusiastic skier who campaigned for the development of public skiing on Mount Rainier in Washington. In 1939, Gretchen married Donald Fraser, who had been on the 1936 Olympic ski team. A year later, she was named to the 1940 Olympic team, but the games were canceled because of World War II.

Fraser won the national downhill and Alpine combined championships in 1941 and was national slalom champion in 1942. She then retired from competition and taught riding, skiing, and swimming to disabled war veterans in Army hospitals while her husband served in the Navy.

After the war, he urged her to get back into competition and helped with her training. She was named to the 1948 Olympic team and became the first American skier ever to win a medal. Fraser won a gold in the slalom under very difficult circumstances. She had the fastest time in the first of two runs but had to wait in the starting gate for 17 minutes before her second run while a telephone line linking the top of the course to the bottom was repaired. When it was finally ready, she turned in the fastest time again to win the gold medal easily. She also won a silver in the Alpine combined event.

Fraser, Steven H.

WRESTLING
b. March 23, 1958, Detroit, Mich.

Very unusual among U.S. wrestlers in that he competed in both freestyle and Greco-Roman, which allows holds only above the waist, Fraser competed in football, track and field, and wrestling as a high school student.

He won a wrestling scholarship to the University of Michigan in 1976. Although he never won an NCAA title, Fraser continued in the sport after graduating. He won national Greco-Roman championships in the 198-pound division in 1982 and 1983, when he also won a gold medal at the Pan-American Games.

Fraser won the national freestyle title in 1984 but finished second in the Greco-Roman championship. However, he placed first in the 1984 Olympic trials and then became the first U.S. athlete ever to win an Olympic gold medal in Greco-Roman wrestling.

Fratianne, Linda S.

FIGURE SKATING
b. Aug. 2, 1960, Northridge, Calif.

A flashy, often spectacular skater with a remarkable repertoire of spins and jumps, Fratianne won four consecutive U.S. championships, but inconsistency and problems in the compulsory figures often troubled her in international competition.

She dueled Annet Potzsch of the German Democratic Republic five times and won only twice. After winning the world championship in 1977, Fratianne finished second to Potzsch in 1978. She won her second world championship in 1979, Potzsch finishing just behind.

At the 1980 Olympics, Fratianne turned in a brilliant free skating performance, but it wasn't quite good enough to overcome the big lead Potzsch had built up in the compulsories, and Fratianne had to settle for a silver medal. The story was much the same at the 1980 world championships.

Fratianne then left amateur skating to star in Walt Disney's World on Ice.

Frazier, Joseph

BOXING
b. Jan. 12, 1944, Beaufort, S.C.

Frazier dropped out of school at the age of 13 to become a mule driver, went to New York to work in the garment district at 16, and then became a butcher's apprentice in Philadelphia, where he began boxing.

Buster Mathis beat Frazier in the finals of the 1964 Olympic trials but hurt his thumb in the fight, and Frazier was his replacement. He won a gold medal with three knockouts and a unanimous decision in four Olympic fights.

The following year, Frazier turned professional. He won 19 consecutive fights, 17 by knockout, before meeting Mathis for the New York heavyweight championship on March 4, 1968. Frazier knocked Mathis out in the 11th round.

He won the vacant world heavyweight title by knocking out Jimmy Ellis in the 5th round on February 16, 1970. However, many fight fans still considered Muhammad Ali the champion. Ali had been stripped of his title for refusing induction into the U.S. Army in 1967.

Frazier and Ali, both undefeated as professionals, met in one of the most ballyhooed matches in boxing history on March 8, 1971, at Madison Square Garden. Frazier knocked Ali down with a left hook in the 15th round and won a unanimous decision that made him undisputed champion.

After two defenses, Frazier suffered a stunning 2nd-round knockout against George Foreman on January 22, 1973, at Kingston, Jamaica. The lightly regarded Foreman knocked Frazier down five times before the knockout.

Ali beat Frazier twice in the next two years, first on a 12-round decision and then on a 14th-round knockout. After being knocked out by Foreman in 1976,

Frazier retired. He toured and recorded for a time with a singing group called the Knockouts, returned to the ring for one lackluster fight in 1981, and then retired again to manage his son, Marvis, who lost a heavyweight title fight to Larry Holmes in 1983.

Known as "Smokin' Joe" because of his style of constantly boring in and throwing punches, Frazier didn't have a great knockout punch, but he wore down opponents with his relentless attack. He won 32 professional fights, 27 by knockout; lost 4, 3 by knockout; and fought 1 draw.

★ International Boxing Hall of Fame;
  Olympic Hall of Fame

Frazier, Walter II ("Clyde")

BASKETBALL
b. March 29, 1945, Atlanta, Ga.

After starring for two seasons at Southern Illinois University, Frazier had to sit out his junior year because he was academically ineligible. He returned to lead the team to the 1967 National Invitation Tournament championship. He was the tournament's most valuable player and was named to the Division II All-American team.

The 6-foot-4, 205-pound guard was the first-round draft choice of the New York Knicks. Although best known as an outstanding defensive player, Frazier averaged 21.7 points a game in 1970–71 to become the first guard ever to lead the team in scoring.

The Knicks won two NBA championships, in 1970 and 1973, during Frazier's ten seasons with the team. He tied an NBA playoff record with 19 assists in the 1970 championship game against the Los Angeles Lakers.

A snappy dresser, he was nicknamed "Clyde" by teammate Nate Bowman early in his career because he was wearing a derby hat that reminded Bowman of Warren Beatty as Clyde Barrow in the movie *Bonnie and Clyde*. The nickname was often lengthened to "Clyde the Glide" because of his smooth style of play.

Frazier was traded to the Cleveland Cavaliers in 1977, and he spent two seasons there before retiring. He was a first-team all-star four times and was named to the NBA's all-defensive first team seven years in a row, from 1969 through 1975.

He scored 15,581 points, an average of 18.9 per game, and had 5,040 assists, 6.1 per game, in 825 regular season games. Frazier added 1,927 points and 599 assists in 93 playoff games.

★ Basketball Hall of Fame

Freeman, David G.

 BADMINTON
b. 1920, Pasadena, Calif.

As a teenager, Freeman won the national junior singles tennis championship, but he later decided to concentrate on badminton. He was known primarily as a retriever who returned everything in his early years in the sport, but he later developed a strong attacking game as well.

Freeman dominated the sport in the U.S. for nearly 15 years. He was U.S. champion from 1939 through 1942 and in 1947, 1948, and 1953. There were no national championships from 1943 through 1946, so he actually won six in a row. He also won the men's doubles title five times with three different partners, and he was the All-England singles champion in 1949.

His colorful style, darting and whirling around the court to return his opponent's shots, was described by one spectator as resembling a Comanche war dance.

Friedman, Benny (Benjamin)

FOOTBALL
b. March 18, 1905, Cleveland, Ohio
d. Nov. 23, 1982

Probably the best player who isn't in the Pro Football Hall of Fame, Friedman openly campaigned for years to be elected. That created some resentment among the voters, which may be why he never made it. He certainly had the credentials. In 1928, Friedman led the NFL in both rushing touchdowns and touchdown passes; no other player has ever accomplished that. In 1929, he threw 20 touchdown passes, including 4 in one game, both NFL records for years.

Friedman played at the University of Michigan, where he was an All-American in 1925 and 1926. He and end Benny Oosterbaan formed one of the best passing combinations in college history. Although known as a passer, Friedman was also a fine runner and a fierce competitor. In a 21–0 victory over Wisconsin in 1926, he threw a touchdown pass on the first play of the game, returned a kickoff 85 yards for a second touchdown, and added another touchdown pass for Michigan's third score.

In 1927, Friedman joined the NFL's Cleveland Bulldogs. He moved to the Detroit Wolverines the following season. Tim Mara, owner of the New York Giants, bought the Detroit franchise in 1929 primarily to get Friedman. It was a good move. The Giants won 13 games, lost 1, and tied 1, and made a profit of $8,500 after having lost $40,000 the previous year.

The 5-foot-10, 180-pound Friedman was with the Giants through 1933 and played one game for the Brooklyn Dodgers in 1934 before retiring. The NFL didn't keep official statistics during most of his career, but incomplete figures credit him with nearly 7,500 yards and 68 touchdown passes as well as more than 2,000 rushing yards and 18 rushing touchdowns.

Friedman had unusually large hands, a distinct asset since the ball was much fatter than it is now, and he began lifting weights at an early age to strengthen his forearms. He was a deadly accurate passer who threw a soft, easy-to-catch ball. As sportswriter Paul Gallico described it, "The receiver merely has to reach up to take hold of it, like picking a grapefruit from a tree."

After retiring, Friedman coached football at City College of New York and was athletic director at Brandeis University for a time. His left leg was amputated because of a blood clot in 1979, and Friedman then developed shingles, a very painful skin condition. He shot himself with a pistol in 1979, leaving a suicide note that said he didn't want to end up as "the old man on the park bench."

★ College Football Hall of Fame

Friedman, Marty (Max)

BASKETBALL
b. July 12, 1889, New York, N.Y
d. Jan. 1, 1986

Friedman first played basketball with the University Settlement House team that won New York Metropolitan AAU championships from 1906 through 1908, when he was studying at the Hebrew Technical Institute.

Considered by many contemporaries as the finest defensive player of his era, Friedman became a professional with the New York Roosevelts in 1909. He played for a number of teams during the next several years, among them Newburgh, Hudson, Utica, and Albany in New York; Carbondale and Philadelphia in Pennsylvania; and Easthampton in Massachusetts.

He served in the Army during World War I. In 1919, after the war had ended, he organized the first international basketball tournament as part of the Inter-Allied Games for service teams. Friedman captained the U.S. team that beat France, 93–8, for the championship.

The 5-foot-8 Friedman in 1921 joined the New York Whirlwinds, the greatest professional team of the era before being superseded by the Original Celtics. He ended his career as player-coach of the Cleveland Rosenblums from 1923 through 1927. The Rosenblums won American Basketball League championships in his last two seasons.
★ Basketball Hall of Fame

Frisch, Frankie (Frank F.)

BASEBALL
b. Sept. 9, 1898, New York, N.Y.
d. March 12, 1973

At Fordham University, Frisch captained the baseball, basketball, and football teams and also took part in track. Walter Camp named him a second-team All-American halfback in 1918.

After graduating in 1919, Frisch signed a contract with the NL's New York Giants and immediately entered the major leagues. Originally a shortstop, he played second and third base with the Giants before settling in at second. A natural left-handed hitter, he taught himself to switch-hit. His speed soon won him a nickname, the "Fordham Flash," from sportswriters.

Frisch batted .341 and led the league with 49 stolen bases in 1921, when the Giants won the first of four consecutive pennants. He hit .327 the following season and .348 in 1923, when he had a league-leading 223 hits. Frisch tied for the league lead with 121 runs scored and had a .328 average in 1924.

The Giants fell to second place in 1925 and all the way to fifth in 1926. Frisch, the captain of the team, had a serious falling out with manager John McGraw and left the Giants for a time. After the 1926 season, he was traded to the St. Louis Cardinals with pitcher Jimmy Ring for Rogers Hornsby.

Hornsby was very popular in St. Louis, and fans were at first infuriated by the trade, but Frisch soon won them over with his all-around skill and his fiery, competitive style. After hitting .337 and leading in stolen bases with 48 in 1927, Frisch helped the Cardinals win the 1928 pennant with a .300 average and 107 runs scored.

The Cardinals also won pennants in 1930 and 1931, with Frisch hitting .346 and .311. He led the league in steals for a third time with 28 in 1931, when he was named the NL's most valuable player.

Chronic hamstring problems in both legs began to bother him in 1932, when he slipped below .300 for the first time since 1920. He was named playing manager during the 1933 season, and the following year he guided the famed "Gas House Gang" to a pennant. His double with the bases loaded was a key hit when the Cardinals scored seven runs in the third inning of the seventh game of the World Series to beat Detroit, 11–0.

Frisch began limiting his playing time in 1934 and appeared in only 17 games in 1937, his last season as a player. He was fired as manager late in the 1938 season. After a year as a radio broadcaster for the Boston Braves, he managed the Pittsburgh Pirates with little success from 1940 through 1946, returned to broadcasting for a year, served as coach with the Giants in 1948, and became manager of the Chicago Cubs in 1949. He was fired in midseason of 1951 and left baseball for good. Frisch died of injuries suffered in an automobile accident.

In 2,311 games, Frisch had a .316 average with 2,880 hits, including 466 doubles, 138 triples, and 105 home runs. He stole 419 bases, scored 1,532 runs, and had 1,244 RBI.

★ Baseball Hall of Fame

Fry, Hayden (John Hayden Jr.)

FOOTBALL

b. Feb. 28, 1929, Eastland, Tex.

After playing football at Baylor University, Fry spent four years in the Marine Corps, coached high school football for four years, and served as an assistant college coach for three seasons before becoming head coach at Southern Methodist University in 1962.

Fry took SMU to three bowl games, but those were his only three winning seasons, and he had a 50–68–1 record before being fired. He then had a 40–23–1 mark at North Texas State University from 1973 through 1978 and moved on to the University of Iowa.

Iowa has gone to the Rose Bowl three times under Fry's guidance, in 1982, 1986, and 1991, losing all three, but his teams have a 5–4–1 record in other bowl appearances. Through the 1994 season, Fry was 117–69–5 at Iowa and 206–158–9 overall. He ranks 17th all-time in NCAA Division I victories.

Ftorek, Robbie (Robert B.)

HOCKEY

b. Jan. 2, 1952, Needham, Mass.

Ftorek was an all-state high school star in both soccer and hockey. As a freshman, he set a new state hockey scoring record, and he improved the record every year until he graduated, then went to Canada to play junior hockey. The Detroit Red Wings signed him in 1972, after he played for the U.S. Olympic team that won a silver medal. But Ftorek was considered too small, at only 5-foot-6 and 140 pounds, to be an NHL star, and he spent most of his time in the minor leagues until he joined the Phoenix Roadrunners of the new World Hockey Association in 1974.

He was an instant star in the WHA, the league's most valuable player in 1977, and *The Sporting News* player of the year in 1979. After the WHA broke up, Ftorek joined the Quebec Nordiques of the NHL for the 1979–80 season. He was traded to the New York Rangers in 1981 and played with them until his retirement in 1984.

In his eight NHL seasons, Ftorek had 150 goals and 227 assists for 377 points in 334 regular season games. He added 9 goals and 6 assists in 19 playoff games. He became coach of the Los Angeles Kings during the 1987–88 season but resigned after coaching them to a 42–31–7 record in his only full year with the club.

★ U.S. Hockey Hall of Fame

Fuchs, Jim (James E.)

TRACK AND FIELD

b. Dec. 6, 1927, Chicago, Ill.

For a little more than two years, Fuchs was easily the best shot putter in the world. During that span, he won 88 consecutive meets and set four world records. Unfortunately, his peak period fell between Olympics, so he never won a gold medal, but he did win two bronze medals, in 1948 and 1952.

Competing for Yale, Fuchs won both the IC4A and NCAA championships in 1949 and 1950. He won the AAU national outdoor titles the same years and was the AAU indoor champion three years in a row, from 1950 through 1952.

During a 14-month period, Fuchs went on his world record spree. The first record was 58 feet, 4½ inches in June 1949 at Oslo, Norway. He extended it to 58–5½ on April 29, 1950, at Los Angeles; to 58–8¾ on August 20, 1950, at Visby, Sweden; and to 58–10¾ two days later at Eskilstuna, Sweden.

Fuchs was the discus champion at the 1951 Pan-American Games.

Fuhr, Grant

HOCKEY

b. Sept. 28, 1962, Spruce Grove, Alta.

The goalie on five Stanley Cup championship teams, Fuhr is one of a handful of black players to succeed in professional hockey and the only one to become a genuine star.

Fuhr joined Victoria of the World Hockey League in 1979, when he was only 17, and was named the league's top goaltender in both his seasons there before going to the NHL's Edmonton Oilers in 1981.

Injuries limited his playing time in his first couple of seasons with Edmonton, but he emerged as a star on the championship teams led by Wayne Gretzky: 1984, 1985, 1987, and 1988. Fuhr won the Vezina Trophy as the league's best goaltender for the 1987–88 season, when he set a record by playing 75 games.

Fuhr has been one of those clutch goaltenders who are at their best in the playoffs. After a 3.91 goals-against average in 1983–84, he gave up just 2.99 goals a game in the playoffs, compiling an 11–4 record. In the 1988 playoffs, he established records for most games by a goalie, 19, and most victories, 16.

His career took a dive because of injuries in 1989, and he was suspended for six months in 1990 for admitting to cocaine use. Edmonton traded him to the Toronto Maple Leafs in 1991, and Toronto sent him to the Buffalo Sabres during the 1992–93 season.

Through 1994, Fuhr had given up 1,991 goals in 578 regular season games, a 3.65 average, with 14 shutouts. In 119 playoff games, he had a 77–36 record and a 3.06 goals-against average, with 3 shutouts.

Fulcher, David D.

FOOTBALL
b. Sept. 28, 1964, Los Angeles, Calif.

An All-American defensive back at Arizona State University in 1984 and 1985, the 6-foot-3, 238-pound Fulcher was chosen by the Cincinnati Bengals in the third round of the 1986 NFL draft.

There were doubts about his ability to star in pro football because he seemed to many somewhat too small to play linebacker and somewhat too slow to play defensive back, but Fulcher soon established himself as one of the best strong safeties in the league.

Selected for the Pro Bowl from 1988 through 1990, Fulcher was named to *The Sporting News* all-pro team in 1989. He joined the Oakland Raiders in 1993 but missed much of that season because of an injury.

Through 1994, Fulcher had intercepted 31 passes and returned them for 246 yards, a 7.9 average, and 2 touchdowns. He had also recorded 8 ½ quarterback sacks on safety blitzes.

Fulks, Joseph

BASKETBALL
b. Oct. 26, 1921, Birmingham, Ky.

"Jumping Joe" was basketball's first modern jump shooter. While other players of his time usually released the shot from about eye level, Fulks leaped high and released the shot from over his head, making it virtually impossible to block. Although a forward, he often played in the pivot, and he developed the turnaround jumper to go with an accurate hook shot with either hand.

After starring for two seasons at Murray State in Kentucky, where he was a small-college All-American in 1943, Fulks left school to join the Marines. He was an all-service selection with the San Diego Marine team.

He left the service in 1946 and joined the Philadelphia 76ers of the new Basketball Association of America, which became the NBA in 1949. He led the league in scoring in its first season with 23.2 points per game, and Philadelphia won the first BAA championship. Fulks averaged 22.1 points in 1947–48 and 26.0 in 1948–49, finishing second both seasons. His 63 points against the Indianapolis Jets on February 10, 1949, was an NBA single-game record for ten years.

He retired after the 1953–54 season. In 1971, Fulks was named to the NBA's Silver Anniversary team. In 489 regular season games, he scored 8,003 points, an average of 16.4 per game. He added 588 points in 31 playoff games, a 19.0 average.

★ Basketball Hall of Fame

Fullmer, Gene

BOXING
b. July 21, 1931, West Jordan, Utah

A solid fighter but unexciting boxer, Fullmer wasn't a particularly popular middleweight champion. Other fighters and boxing experts had a very high opinion of him, however.

The 5-foot-8 Fullmer began his professional career in 1951 and won his first 29 fights, 19 by knockout, then won only three of his next six, as he began to meet better opponents. On January 2, 1957, he won the world middleweight championship with a 15-round decision over Sugar Ray Robinson. However, Robinson knocked him out in the 5th round less than four months later to regain the title.

On August 28, 1959, Fullmer knocked out Carmen Basilio in the 14th round to win the National Boxing Association version of the middleweight championship. He defended it successfully seven times, twice on draws, before losing to Dick Tiger in a 15-round decision on October 23, 1962. His last two fights were against Tiger for the championship. Tiger held on to the title with a draw in the first fight and knocked Fullmer out in the second.

Fullmer won 55 of his 64 professional fights, 24 by knockout; he lost 6, 2 by knockout; and he fought 3 draws.

★ International Boxing Hall of Fame

★ ★ G ★ ★

Gabelich, Gary

AUTO RACING
b. Aug. 29, 1940, San Pedro, Calif.

Gabelich did some hot rod racing in high school, and at 19 he traveled 356 mph at the Bonneville, Utah, Salt Flats in a jet car, probably a record for a teenager. Then he went to work in the mailroom at North American Rockwell, eventually becoming a test astronaut for the company.

He was offered a desk job because of budget cutbacks, but he decided to get back into racing, both on water and on land. He won the American Power Boat Association fuel hydro championship in 1968, set a National Drag Boat Association record of 200.44 mph in 1969, and also raced go-carts and automobiles.

Reaction Dynamics, Inc., was looking for a driver about that time for the Blue Flame, a 37-foot-long, 4,950-pound vehicle powered by a liquid natural gas–hydrogen peroxide rocket engine. Craig Breedlove, holder of the land speed record, wanted too much money. A drag racer, Chuck Suba, came to terms but was killed in a racing accident shortly thereafter. Gabelich was the third choice, and he jumped at the chance.

The Blue Flame's run for the land speed record at Bonneville was scheduled for September 1969, but it was postponed indefinitely. The first attempt finally took place a year later, on September 22, 1970. It was a dismal failure, reaching a speed of only 426 mph compared to Breedlove's five-year-old record of 600.601 mph. A lot of tinkering and testing took place.

Gabelich hit 609 mph on the first of two mandatory runs on October 15, but a mechanical problem prevented the second run. The same thing happened on October 23, when the first run reached 621 mph. Finally, on October 28, Gabelich and the Blue Flame averaged 617.602 mph on the first run and 627.207 on the second for a new land speed record of 622.407.

He said afterward that he thought the Blue Flame might be able to reach 750 mph, beyond the sound barrier. But Reaction Dynamics had no more plans for the Blue Flame, and Gabelich became a drag racer. Gabelich's right hand was severed in an accident early in 1972. It was sewed back on, but further racing was out of the question.

Gable, Daniel M.

WRESTLING
b. Oct. 25, 1948, Waterloo, Iowa

When Gable was named the outstanding wrestler after a 1972 meet in the Soviet Union, the Soviet national coach said, "Before the Olympics, we will find someone who can beat Gable." He was wrong. Despite a painful knee injury, Gable won the gold medal in the lightweight division without giving up a point in his six matches.

A completely dedicated workaholic, Gable trained for seven hours a day every day for three years in preparation for the Olympics. During high school and college, he was undefeated until 1970, when he lost in the finals of the NCAA 142-pound championship.

Wrestling for Iowa State, he was the NCAA champion at 130 pounds in 1968 and 137 pounds in 1969. Gable was AAU featherweight champion in 1969 and lightweight champion in 1970. He won the world and Pan-American 149.5-pound championships in 1971.

Gable competed infrequently after the Olympics and retired in 1973. He attempted a comeback in 1975 but was forced into retirement again by a pinched nerve. In 1977 he became wrestling coach at the University of Iowa, where his teams won nine consecutive NCAA championships, from 1978 through 1986.
★ Olympic Hall of Fame

Gabriel, Roman I., Jr.

FOOTBALL
b. Aug. 5, 1940, Wilmington, N.C.

Gabriel passed for 2,951 yards in three years as a starting quarterback at North Carolina State. A first-round draft choice of the NFL's Los Angeles Rams in 1962, he became a starter for a time during his rookie season, but was primarily a backup to Bill Munson in 1964 and 1965.

When George Allen took over as head coach in 1966, he made the 6-foot-4, 220-pound Gabriel the starter once more, and Gabriel responded by completing 217 of 397 passes for 2,540 yards and 10 touchdowns.

Gabriel was the consensus NFL player of the year in 1969, when he completed 217 of 399 attempts for 2,549 yards and 24 touchdowns while throwing only 7 interceptions. The Rams won the Coastal Division title that year but lost, 23–20, to the Minnesota Vikings in the first round of the playoffs.

Hampered by injuries during the next three seasons, Gabriel was traded to the Philadelphia Eagles in 1973. He had one fine year with the Eagles but was once more troubled by recurring injuries in 1974 and 1975. He underwent knee surgery in 1976 and retired after the 1977 season.

In his 16 years as a professional, Gabriel completed 2,366 of 4,498 passes for 29,444 yards and 201 touchdowns. He also rushed for 30 touchdowns.
★ College Football Hall of Fame

Gaidzik, George W.

DIVING
b. Feb. 22, 1885
d. ?

Germany and Sweden dominated international diving in the early years of the century, winning every Olympic championship but one before 1920. Gaidzik was America's best diver during that period. He tied for a bronze medal in the 1908 springboard event, preventing a complete German sweep. He also finished fifth in the "plain high dive," an obsolete event.

In 1912 Gaidzik competed in all three Olympic dives, but his best finish was only eighth place in the springboard. He was the AAA national platform champion three years in a row, from 1909 through 1911, and he won the indoor 3-meter springboard title in 1910 and 1912.

Gain, Bob (Robert)

FOOTBALL
b. June 21, 1929, Akron, Ohio

A two-way star at tackle for the University of Kentucky, Gain was a consensus All-American and winner of the Outland Trophy as the nation's outstanding collegiate lineman in 1950. He made a key play in the 1951 Sugar Bowl, forcing a fumble that set up Kentucky's first touchdown in a 13–7 upset of previously undefeated Oklahoma.

A first-round selection of the NFL's Green Bay Packers in 1951, Gain chose to play for the Ottawa Roughriders of the Canadian Football League. The Packers traded his rights to the Cleveland Browns, and in 1952 Gain signed with Cleveland, who made him a defensive tackle.

After serving in the Air Force for a year during the Korean conflict, Gain returned to the Browns in 1954 and remained with them through the 1964 season. The 6-foot-3, 230-pounder started for NFL championship teams in 1954, 1955, and 1964.
★ College Football Hall of Fame

Gaines, Clarence E.
BASKETBALL
b. May 21, 1923, Paducah, Ky.

Nicknamed "Big House," the 6-foot-4, 300-pound Gaines played football and basketball at Morgan State, graduating in 1945. He became an assistant coach at Winston-Salem State and took over as head basketball coach and athletic director in 1947.

In 47 seasons, Gaines coached the school to 828 victories, second only to Adolph Rupp, and 446 losses. Led by Earl "the Pearl" Monroe, Winston-Salem State won 31 of 32 games in 1966–67 and became the first predominantly black school to win an NCAA basketball championship, in the College Division.

Gaines was named College Division coach of the year in 1967. He retired after the 1992–93 season.
★ Basketball Hall of Fame

Gaines, Rowdy (Ambrose IV)
SWIMMING
b. Feb. 17, 1959, Winter Haven, Fla.

Although he was an age-group swimming champion before he was 10, Gaines gave it up for other sports, including baseball, basketball, and football, and didn't resume competitive swimming until his junior year in high school.

At Auburn University, Gaines won NCAA championships in the 50-yard freestyle in 1979 and in both the 100- and 200-yard freestyles in 1980 and 1981. He was the AAU long-course champion at 100 meters from 1979 through 1983 and at 200 meters from 1979 through 1982, and he won short-course championships in the 100- and 200-yard freestyles in 1980 and 1982.

Gaines was considered likely to win medals in both freestyle sprints and in one or more relays at the 1980 Olympics, but the U.S. boycotted the Moscow games that year because of the Soviet Union's invasion of Afghanistan. In 1984, he finished second in the 100-meter freestyle and only seventh in the 200-meter at the U.S. Olympic trials. However, he won three gold medals at the Los Angeles Olympics, in the 100-meter and as a member of the winning 4 x 100-meter freestyle and 4 x 100-meter medley relay teams.

Gaines set world records of 49.36 seconds in the 100-meter in 1981 and 1:49.93 in the 200-meter event in 1982. He won the 100-meter freestyle at the Pan-American Games in 1979 and 1983 and was a member of both winning freestyle relay teams in 1979.

Gainey, Bob (Robert M.)
HOCKEY
b. Dec. 13, 1953, Peterborough, Ont.

An outstanding defensive forward, the 6-foot-2, 195-pound Gainey was a key player on the Montreal Canadien teams that won four consecutive Stanley Cup championships, from 1976 through 1979, and he was still there when they won another title in 1986.

Gainey joined the Canadiens in the 1973–74 season after playing just six games in the minor leagues. A left-handed shooting left wing, he won the Frank J. Selke Trophy as the NHL's best defensive forward from 1978 through 1981. He also won the Conn Smythe Trophy as the most valuable player in the playoffs in 1979, when he scored 16 points in 16 playoff games.

In 1989, Gainey left Montreal to become player-coach of the Epinal Squirrels in France. He was named coach of the NHL's Minnesota North Stars in 1990 and guided them to the 1991 Stanley Cup finals, where they lost to the Pittsburgh Penguins. He remained with the team when it moved to Dallas and became known as the Stars for the 1993–94 season.

Through the 1993–94 season, Gainey had a coaching record of 137 wins, 148 losses, and 43 ties. As a player, he scored 501 points on 239 goals and 262 assists in 1,160 regular season games and had 73 points on 25 goals and 48 assists in 182 playoff games.
★ Hockey Hall of Fame

Gaither, Jake (Alonzo S.)

FOOTBALL

b. April 11, 1903, Dayton, Tenn.
d. Feb. 18, 1994

Gaither played football at Knoxville College, graduating in 1927. He did graduate work at several colleges, receiving a master's degree from Ohio State University in 1937. After military service during World War II, Gaither became head football coach at Florida A & M College.

The team is nicknamed the Rattlers, and Gaither became known as "Papa Rattler." Fond of saying, "I like my boys to be agile, mobile, and hostile," he turned Florida A & M into a major power among predominantly black colleges.

Under Gaither's guidance, Florida A & M won 20 Southern Intercollegiate Athletic Conference championships and shared another during his 25 seasons. He was voted small college coach of the year in 1962.

Gaither retired after the 1969 season with a 203–36–4 record. His .844 winning percentage is sixth best all-time, and he ranks nineteenth in victories.
★ College Football Hall of Fame

Galarraga, Andres J.

BASEBALL

b. June 18, 1961, Caracas, Venezuela

The 6-foot-3, 235-pound Galarraga joined the NL's Montreal Expos late in the 1985 season. He played in only 105 games in 1986 because of injury, but he established himself as the team's starting first baseman by hitting .305 in 1987.

A right-hander, Galarraga batted .302 in 1988 and led the league with 42 doubles and 184 hits. He also led in strikeouts for the first of three consecutive years. His average dropped to .257 and .258 the following two seasons, and he batted only .219 in 1991, when he was out for six weeks with an injury.

Montreal traded him to the St. Louis Cardinals before the 1992 season, and Galarraga again struggled with injury problems, spending part of the season on rehabilitation assignment to the minor leagues.

Galarraga was drafted by the expansion Colorado Rockies in 1993, and he responded in a big way, leading the NL in batting with a .370 average to win *The Sporting News* comeback player of the year award. Galarraga is a fine fielder who also won Gold Gloves at first base in 1989 and 1990.

Gale, Laddie (Lauren E.)

BASKETBALL

b. April 19, 1916, Gold Beach, Oreg.

As a senior at the University of Oregon, Gale starred on the team that won the first NCAA basketball tournament in 1939. The 6-foot-4 forward was named to the Helms Athletic Foundation All-American team. After missing much of his sophomore year with an injury, Gale averaged 12.5 points a game in 1937–38 and 11.6 in 1938–39, leading the Northern Division of the Pacific Coast Conference both seasons.

After playing part of the 1939–40 season with the professional Detroit Eagles, Gale served in World War II. He was player-coach of the Deseret Times team of Salt Lake City and of the Oakland Bittners after the war. In 1948, the Bittners went to the semifinals of the Olympic team trials, losing to the Phillips 66ers by one point. Gale left basketball in 1949 to go into real estate.
★ Basketball Hall of Fame

Galitzen, Michael R. ("Mickey Riley")

DIVING

b. Sept. 6, 1909
d. June 9, 1959

Michael Riley Galitzen created considerable confusion in the record books when he decided in 1931 that he wanted to be known as Mickey Riley. He won two Olympic medals under that name in 1932 after having won two as Michael Galitzen in 1928.

Galitzen was the national outdoor 3-meter springboard and platform champion in 1928 and 1929, the indoor 1-meter springboard champion in 1929, 1931, and 1932, and the indoor 3-meter champion from 1929 through 1931. Representing the University of Southern California, he won the 3-meter springboard championship in 1931 and 1932.

He won a silver medal in the 1928 Olympic springboard event and a bronze in the platform. In 1932 he won a gold in the springboard and a silver in the platform.

Gallagher, Edward C.

WRESTLING
b. 1887, Perth, Kans.
d. Aug. 8, 1940

When Oklahoma A & M (now Oklahoma State) University became the major power in intercollegiate wrestling during the 1920s and 1930s, it was because of Gallagher, who had never wrestled.

Gallagher played football and participated in track as a student at the school. In 1916, he was hired to coach wrestling. Despite his lack of practical experience in the sport, Gallagher used his engineering background to teach athletes how to use leverage to their advantage.

The NCAA established wrestling as a championship sport in 1928, and Oklahoma State won titles from 1928 through 1931, in 1934 and 1935, and from 1937 through 1940. The school tied with Iowa State for the 1933 championship.

Gallagher died of pneumonia in 1940, but his legacy was such that Oklahoma State won five NCAA team championships in the seven years after his death. In his 25 years of coaching, he produced three Olympic gold medal winners as well as the winners of 32 AAU national championships and 37 NCAA individual titles.

Gallatin, Harry J.

BASKETBALL
b. April 26, 1926, Roxana, Ill.

While a student at Northeast Missouri State, Gallatin was drafted into the U.S. Navy in 1945. He returned to school in 1946 and played basketball during his junior and senior years, averaging 13.2 points a game. He joined the New York Knickerbockers of the NBA in 1948.

Although nicknamed "the Horse," the 6-foot-6, 215-pound Gallatin was an agile forward who used his quickness to get to rebounds ahead of bigger men. He led the league in rebounding in 1953–54 with 1,098, an average of 15.3 a game. After ten seasons with New York, he went to the Detroit Pistons in 1957–58 and then retired. Gallatin played in 747 consecutive games, including playoffs, a record at the time.

After four years of coaching at Southern Illinois University–Carbondale, Gallatin took over the NBA's St. Louis Hawks in 1962. He was named the league's coach of the year in 1963, then went to the New York Knicks. He was fired during the 1964–65 season.

Gallatin returned to Southern Illinois as dean of students and later became a professor of physical education and the school's golf coach.
★ Basketball Hall of Fame

Galvin, Pud (James F.)

BASEBALL
b. Dec. 25, 1856, St. Louis, Mo.
d. March 7, 1902

The only pitcher in history to win more than 300 games *and* lose more than 300, the 6-foot, 200-pound Galvin played briefly with the St. Louis team in the National Association in 1875 but didn't become a full-time major leaguer until 1879, with the NL's Buffalo Braves.

Nicknamed "the Little Steam Engine" by sportswriters because of his durability, Galvin had a 46–29 record in 1883, when he led the league in complete games with 72, shutouts with 5, and innings pitched with 656, an all-time record. The following year, he led in shutouts again with 12 and had a 46–22 record.

Buffalo sold Galvin for $2,500 to Pittsburgh of the American Association, then a major league, during the 1885 season. The team moved into the NL in 1887. In his first four years with Pittsburgh, Galvin went 29–21, 28–21, 23–25, and 23–16.

He was with the Pittsburgh team in the short-lived Players' League in 1890, but was only 12–13. Galvin returned to the Pittsburgh NL club in 1891, when he had a 14–14 mark, and was traded to St. Louis during the 1892 season. He left the major leagues after winning only 10 games and losing 12 that year.

Galvin won 360 games and lost 308, with 56 shutouts. He struck out 1,799 hitters and walked 744 in 5,941 innings.
★ Baseball Hall of Fame

Gans, Joe [Joseph Gaines]
BOXING
b. Nov. 25, 1874, Philadelphia, Pa.
d. Aug. 16, 1910

A very clever fighter who was known as the "Old Master," Gans worked in a Baltimore fish market before becoming a professional boxer in 1891. He was undefeated in his first 30 fights, winning 16 of them by knockout. His first loss was a 15-round decision to Dal Hawkins in 1896.

Gans fought Frank Erne for the lightweight title on March 21, 1900, but threw in the towel after the 12th round because of an injury. On May 12, 1902, at Fort Erie, he knocked out Erne in the first round to become the first black lightweight champion.

His championship bout against Battling Nelson at Goldfield, Nevada, on September 3, 1906, was the first fight promoted by Tex Rickard. Gans won on a foul in the 42nd round. He lost the title when Nelson knocked him out in the 17th round at San Francisco on July 4, 1908. Gans was knocked out by Nelson again in a rematch on September 9. His next fight, a no-decision against Jabez White in 1909, was his last. Gans died of tuberculosis a little more than a year later.

He won 120 of his 156 fights, 55 of them by knockout, and lost only 8, 5 of them by knockout. He also fought 10 draws and 18 no-decisions.
★ International Boxing Hall of Fame

Garbisch, Edgar W.
FOOTBALL
b. April 7, 1900, Washington, Pa.
d. Dec. 13, 1979

His father wanted him to be a concert pianist but decided football was all right

when his son was carried off the field by his Army teammates after a 12–0 victory over Navy in 1924. "No matter how magnificent the performance of Paderewski," he said, "the audience does not sweep up on the stage and bear the artist off in triumph."

A starting center for three years, Garbisch was also an excellent kicker. His 47-yard field goal from a very difficult angle beat Navy, 17–14, in 1922, and his four field goals accounted for all of Army's points in that 12–0 win in 1924. The football captain in 1924, his senior season, Garbisch also captained the tennis team. He was named to Walter Camp's All-American team in 1922 and 1924.
★ College Football Hall of Fame

Gardiner, Chuck (Charles R.)
HOCKEY
b. Dec. 31, 1904, Edinburgh, Scotland
d. June 13, 1934

Although Gardiner said he became a goalie because he was a poor skater, he was known as the "Wandering Scotsman" because he was the first goaltender who consistently moved out of the net to cut down the shooter's angle.

His family moved to Canada in 1911, and Gardiner began playing intermediate hockey in 1919. He became a professional with the Winnipeg Maroons in 1926, and he joined the Chicago Black Hawks the following year. He won the Vezina Trophy as the NHL's best goaltender in 1932 and 1934 and was a first-team all-star both years.

In the 1934 Stanley Cup final against Detroit, Gardiner won the first two games and had a shutout after two periods of the third game when he suddenly became shaky and allowed five goals. There was concern about his health, but he insisted on starting the fourth game. Gardiner held Detroit scoreless in regulation, then was replaced by Mush March when the game went into overtime. Chicago won the game and the Stanley Cup. Less than two months later, Gardiner was admitted to a Winnipeg hospital, where he died of a brain tumor.

Gardiner had 43 shutouts and a 2.13 goals-against average in 316 regular season games. In 21 playoff games, he had 5 shutouts and a 1.67 average.

★ Hockey Hall of Fame

Gardiner, Herbert M.

HOCKEY
b. May. 8, 1891, Winnipeg, Man.
d. Jan. 11, 1972

A defenseman, Gardiner didn't get to the National Hockey League until he was 35, and he played only two full seasons. But he won the Hart Trophy as the league's most valuable player in 1926–27 and was elected to the Hockey Hall of Fame.

Gardiner worked as a surveyor for the Canadian Pacific Railroad from 1910 until serving in World War I. In 1920, he began playing for Calgary of the Western Canada League. The Montreal Canadiens acquired him in 1926. After two seasons in Montreal, he was loaned to Chicago to serve as the Black Hawks' manager; he returned to the Canadiens for the 1929 playoffs.

Gardiner later coached minor league teams in Philadelphia. In his NHL career, he scored ten regular season goals and 1 assist, with 1 goal and 1 assist in three playoff series.

★ Hockey Hall of Fame

Gardner, Jack (James H.)

BASKETBALL
b. March 29, 1910, Texico, N.Mex.

Gardner captained the University of Southern California team as a senior in 1931–32. While going to graduate school, he coached an AAU team for a season and then coached high school and junior college basketball for six years.

In 1940, Gardner became head basketball coach at Kansas State. He was in the armed services from 1943 to 1946, then returned to Kansas State. During his ten seasons there, his teams won three Big Seven championships and went to the final four of the NCAA tournament twice, in 1948 and 1951.

Gardner moved to the University of Utah in 1953. His emphasis on offense and the fast break won his Utah team the nickname "Runnin' Redskins." They won or shared six Skyline Conference championships and went to the final four in 1961 and 1966. Gardner is the only coach to take two different teams to the final four twice.

Gardner retired from coaching basketball after the 1970–71 season. His Kansas State teams won 147 games while losing 81, and his Utah teams were 339–154 for an overall record of 486 victories and 235 defeats, a .674 percentage.

★ Basketball Hall of Fame

Gardner, Robert

GOLF, RACQUETS, TRACK AND FIELD
b. April 9, 1890, Hinsdale, Ill.
d. June 21, 1956

Gardner is probably the only athlete to win national championships in three different sports. Best known as a golfer, he won the national amateur championship in 1909 and 1915, was runner-up in 1916 and 1922, and played on four Walker Cup teams. As a student at Yale, he became the first man to pole vault more than 13 feet with a height of 13–1 at the 1912 IC4A championships. And in 1926 he teamed with Howard Linn to win the national doubles championship in racquets.

Garlits, Donald G. ("Big Daddy")

DRAG RACING
b. Jan. 14, 1932, Tampa, Fla.

Considered "the father of drag racing" because of his innovations as well as his skill, Garlits became involved in the sport as a teenager, when races were often run on streets. He is credited with developing the rear-engine "top fuel" dragster, and he also designed the first full-body fire-resistant suit.

Garlits, a top competitor well into his fifties, won 35 top fuel events in National Hot Rod Association competition, fifth on the all-time list. He was the first driver to win three NHRA national titles, in 1964, 1965, and 1968, and he won world championships in

1975, 1985, and 1986, when he was 52 years old.

In 1964, Garlits became the first drag racer to surpass 200 miles an hour. He broke the 240 barrier in 1973, the 250 barrier in 1975, and the 270 barrier in 1986.

Garner, Mack (John Mack)
HORSE RACING
b. 1900, Centerville, Iowa
d. Oct. 28, 1936

In 1915, when he was just 15, Garner led the nation's jockeys in wins with 151 and in money won. He was also the top money winner in 1929, when his mounts collected purses of $314,975, a record at the time.

Garner won three triple crown races, the 1929 Belmont Stakes aboard Blue Larkspur, the Belmont again in 1933 aboard Hurry Off, and the Kentucky Derby with Cavalcade in 1934. In 21 years of racing, he rode 1,346 winners and 2,358 other mounts that finished in the money, collecting purses totaling $2,419,647.

His great-grandfather, grandfather, father, and five brothers were also jockeys. Garner died of a heart attack in Covington, Kentucky, shortly after riding in a race.

★ National Horse Racing Hall of Fame

Garrett, Bob (Robert)
TRACK AND FIELD
b. June 24, 1875, Baltimore County, Md.
d. April 25, 1961

The captain of the Princeton track team, Garrett was primarily a shot-putter, though he also competed in the jumping events. When he decided to compete in the first modern Olympics in 1896, Professor William Milligan Sloane suggested he also try the discus.

They consulted classical authorities to develop a drawing, and Garrett, who came from a wealthy family, hired a blacksmith to make a discus. It weighed nearly 30 pounds and was impossible to throw any distance, so he gave up on the idea. Garrett paid his own way to Athens to compete in the Olympics. When he discovered that a real discus weighed less than five pounds, he began practicing and decided to enter the event after all.

With his third and final throw, Garrett beat local favorite Panagiotis Paraskevopoulos in the discus. He also won the shot put and finished second in the long jump and high jump. In the 1900 Olympics, Garrett placed third in the shot put and the standing triple jump; he didn't take part in the discus throw because it was held on a Sunday.

Garrett was the IC4A shot put champion in 1897.

Garrett, Mike (Michael L.)
FOOTBALL
b. April 12, 1944, Los Angeles, Calif.

The 5-foot-9, 195-pound Garrett was a consensus All-American halfback at the University of Southern California and winner of the Heisman Trophy as the nation's outstanding college player in 1965, when he led NCAA Division I runners with 1,440 yards on 267 carries. His 3,221 career yards was a record at the time.

A first-round draft choice of the AFL's Kansas City Chiefs, Garrett signed a five-year, $450,000 contract in 1966 and led the league in yards per attempt, 5.5, as a rookie, gaining 801 yards and scoring 6 touchdowns on 147 attempts.

Although he was held to only 39 yards, Garrett scored a touchdown on a 5-yard run when Kansas City beat the Minnesota Vikings, 23–7, in Super Bowl IV after the 1969 season.

Garrett was traded to the San Diego Chargers during the 1970 season. He retired after the 1973 season. He carried the ball 1,308 times for 5,481 yards, a 4.2 average, and 35 touchdowns; caught 238 passes for 2,010 yards, an 8.4 average, and 13 touchdowns; returned 39 punts for 235 yards, a 6.0 average, and 1 touchdown; and ran back 14 kickoffs for 323 yards, a 23.1 average.

★ College Football Hall of Fame

Garrison, Snapper (Edward H.)

HORSE RACING
b. Feb. 9, 1868, New Haven, Conn.
d. Oct. 28, 1930

Garrison, who became a professional jockey when he was only 12 years old, pioneered the "Garrison finish," holding a horse back for most of the race and then coming on with a driving sprint in the stretch.

During his 17-year riding career, he won nearly 7,000 races and had total winnings of more than $2 million. He rode Foxford to victory in the 1891 Belmont Stakes, took the Suburban Handicap at Belmont in 1889 and 1892, and won the Withers Stakes in 1890 and 1892.

After retiring as a rider, Garrison worked as a trainer and racing official.
★ National Horse Racing Hall of Fame

Garvey, Steven P.

BASEBALL
b. Dec. 22, 1948, Tampa, Fla.

Compared by some to Lou Gehrig because of his good looks and quiet, courteous demeanor, Garvey set an NL record by playing in 1,207 consecutive games from September 3, 1975, until July 29, 1983 — still well behind Gehrig's major league record of 2,130.

A solid right-handed hitter and outstanding defensive first baseman, Garvey was named the league's most valuable player in 1974, when he batted .312 with 21 home runs and 111 RBI to help lead the Los Angeles Dodgers to a pennant. He hit .389 with 2 home runs and 5 RBI as the Dodgers beat the Pittsburgh Pirates three games to one in the league championship series, and he had a .381 average in their five-game loss to the Oakland Athletics in the World Series.

The muscular 5-foot-10, 192-pound Garvey joined the Dodgers at the end of the 1969 season and was a part-time player, mostly at third base, until 1973, when he was moved to first. He led the league in hits with 202 in 1978 and 200 in 1980.

The Dodgers traded him to the San Diego Padres in 1983, and he remained there until retiring after the 1987 season.

Garvey had 200 or more hits six times, 20 or more home runs six times, and more than 100 RBI five times. He led NL first basemen in fielding percentage five times, setting a record in 1984, when he didn't make any errors.

His "All-American Boy" image nettled some players and sportswriters, who sometimes referred to him as "Little Goody Two-Shoes." The image was tarnished somewhat in 1988, when Garvey agreed to pay support for an illegitimate child he'd fathered.

Gastineau, Mark

FOOTBALL
b. Nov. 20, 1956

Chosen out of East Central Oklahoma University by the New York Jets in the second round of the 1979 NFL draft of college players, Gastineau became one of the most feared defensive ends of the early 1980s, teaming with Joe Klecko to lead a line nicknamed "the New York Sack Exchange."

The 6-foot-5, 265-pound Gastineau used a combination of strength and quickness to get to quarterbacks before they could release the ball. He was named American Football Conference defensive player of the year in 1984, despite a disappointing season with the Jets, who lost their last six games to finish at 7–9–0.

Gastineau fell out of favor with his teammates in 1987 when he was pelted with eggs while crossing the players' association picket line during a midseason strike. He abruptly announced his retirement during the 1988 season, saying he wanted to offer support to his friend, model/actress Brigitte Nielsen, who had cancer.

Gates, Pop (William)

BASKETBALL
b. Aug. 30, 1917, Decatur, Ala.

One of the first blacks to play on an integrated professional team, Gates grew up in Harlem and was an all-city high school player. He briefly attended Clark College in Atlanta but returned home because, in those Depression years, there wasn't enough food on the school's training table. "I was hungry most of the time," he later told an interviewer.

The 6-foot-3 Gates joined the semiprofessional Harlem Yankees, playing for just a couple dollars a game. During a scrimmage against the Harlem Renaissance Big Five, he impressed owner-coach Bob Douglas, who signed him for $125 a month to play with the Renaissance. Gates was the team's high scorer when the Renaissance won the first world championship tournament in Chicago in 1939.

In 1946, Gates was signed by the Rochester Royals of the National Basketball League, becoming the league's first black player, and he was then sold to the Buffalo Bisons. He went with the Bisons when they became the Tri-Cities Blackhawks early in the season. During the 1950s, Gates played several seasons with the Harlem Globetrotters.
★ Basketball Hall of Fame

Gatski, Frank (Gunner)

FOOTBALL
b. March 13, 1922, Farmington, W.Va.

After graduating from high school, Gatski worked as a coalminer for a year and then was given a tryout with the Marshall University football team. He played at Marshall until entering the military service in 1943, and spent a year at Auburn University after his discharge in 1945.

Gatski joined the Cleveland Browns of the new All-America Football Conference in 1946 and played both offensive center and defensive linebacker in his rookie year. He had three interceptions and returned one of them for a touchdown.

In 1947, the 6-foot-3, 233-pound Gatski settled in as Cleveland's starting center and remained there for the next ten seasons. The AAFC folded after the 1949 season, and the Browns moved into the NFL, where Gatski was named to the All-Pro team from 1951 through 1953 and in 1955.

After the 1956 season, Gatski went to the Detroit Lions and spent a year there

before retiring. After having played in ten championship games with the Browns, he played in his eleventh with the Lions, and he helped them beat the Browns, 59–14, for the title.

Chuck Bednarik, another Hall of Fame player, referred to Gatski as "an immovable object" and said of him, "He was the best and toughest I ever played against."
★ Pro Football Hall of Fame

Gavilan, Kid [Gerardo Gonzalez]

BOXING
b. Jan. 6, 1926, Camaguey, Cuba

After turning professional in Cuba in 1943 and winning most of his fights there, Gavilan came to the United States late in 1946. He was matched against Sugar Ray Robinson for the world welterweight championship on July 11, 1949, but lost a 15-round decision.

The colorful Gavilan, known for his "bolo punch" (actually just a right uppercut), fought for the title again, this time against Johnny Bratton, who had won the National Boxing Association championship after Robinson became a middleweight. Gavilan decisioned Bratton in 15 rounds on May 18, 1951.

Charlie Humez was recognized as the welterweight champion in Europe, but he moved up to the middleweight class later in 1951, and Gavilan won worldwide recognition by beating Billy Graham in a 15-round decision on August 29.

He lost a bid for the middleweight title on April 2, 1954, when Carl "Bobo" Olson took a 15-round decision. In Gavilan's next fight, on October 20, he lost the welterweight championship to Johnny Saxton in another 15-round decision.

Gavilan fought for four more years, but he lost four of six fights in 1957, and he retired after losing two of three in 1958. He had 143 professional bouts and won 106 of them, 27 by knockout. He lost 30 decisions but was never knocked out. He also fought 6 draws and 1 no-contest.
★ International Boxing Hall of Fame

Gaylord, Mitchell J.
GYMNASTICS
b. March 10, 1961, Los Angeles, Calif.

The Los Angeles high school athlete of the year in 1979 for his skill in gymnastics, Gaylord entered UCLA after graduating. He left school for two years to train with Kurt Thomas and won the all-around championship at the 1982 National Sports Festival.

The first to perform the "Gaylord flip," a somersault on the high bar, the 5-foot-10, 160-pound athlete introduced "Gaylord II," a $1\frac{1}{2}$ somersault, in 1984, when he won the all-around titles at the NCAA and U.S. national championships. At the 1984 Olympics, he won a silver medal in the vault and bronzes in the parallel bars and rings and was a member of the gold medal U.S. team. His score of 59.45 in the team competition is a U.S. record.

He retired from competition after the Olympics and has since pursued a career as an actor, produced a fitness video, and coauthored a book, *Working Out Without Weights.*

Geers, Pop (Edward F.)
HARNESS RACING
b. 1851, near Lebanon, Tenn.
d. Sept. 3, 1924

Harness racing was centered almost entirely on trotting horses until Geers came north with some Tennessee pacers in the late 1870s. He soon demonstrated that pacers are naturally faster than trotters, and the number of pacing races increased rapidly during the 1880s.

Geers was also instrumental in the acceptance of the bicycle sulky. He tested one against the high-wheeled sulky in 1892 and discovered that one of his horses ran a full two seconds faster pulling the bike sulky. When Geers entered a race at Detroit with Honest George pulling one of the new sulkies, the crowd laughed at the sight. But Honest George won three of four heats and placed second in the other. The old high-wheeler was almost instantly obsolete.

Among the horses Geers trained was The Harvester, who was undefeated in 1908, and Single G, who won 262 of 434 heats from 1912 through 1926. His last champion was Peter Manning, who broke the half-mile track record with a time of $2:02\frac{1}{2}$ at South Bend, Indiana, on August 21, 1924.

Less than two weeks later, on September 3, Geers was killed when he was thrown from his sulky in a race at Wheeling, West Virginia. He landed on his head and died without regaining consciousness.

★ Hall of Fame of the Trotter

Gehrig, Lou (Henry Louis)
BASEBALL
b. June 19, 1903, New York, N.Y.
d. June 2, 1941

A high school star in baseball, basketball, football, and soccer, Gehrig played minor league baseball under an assumed name during the summer of 1921, before entering Columbia University. He played for the Columbia baseball team as a freshman, then was declared ineligible because his season as a professional was revealed.

New York Yankee scout Paul Krichell, who saw him hit a tremendous home run out of Columbia Stadium and onto the steps of Butler Library, across the street, told the team he'd found another Babe Ruth. Gehrig signed with the Yankees in 1923 and spent most of his first two seasons in the minor leagues.

In 1925, he was a backup until first baseman Wally Pipp took himself out of the lineup because of a headache. Gehrig took over and went on to establish a major league record of 2,130 consecutive games, winning the nickname "the Iron Horse."

Quiet and unassuming, Gehrig was one of the great RBI men in major league history, but he played in Ruth's shadow for many years. He led the league in triples with 20 in 1926, in doubles with 52 and RBI with 175 in 1927, in doubles with 47, RBI with 142, and slugging percentage with .467 in 1928. The Yankees won the pennant and World Series each year. Gehrig was named the league's most valuable player in 1927, although that was the season Ruth hit 60 home runs.

Gehrig led in RBI again with 174 in 1930 and 184 in 1931, when he hit 46 home runs to share the lead with Ruth. Gehrig was deprived of a 47th home run when he was called out for passing another runner on the base paths.

On June 3, 1932, Gehrig became the first twentieth-century player to hit four consecutive home runs in a game. In 1934, Ruth's last season with the Yankees, Gehrig won the triple crown with a .363 average, 49 home runs, and 165 RBI. He won his second most valuable player award in 1936, when he again led with 49 home runs and 130 RBI and was also the league leader with 167 runs scored.

Early in the 1939 season, Gehrig was obviously below par. He had lost weight and seemed slow and clumsy at bat and in the field. On May 2, he told manager Joe McCarthy that it was time to take a rest. No one knew it at the time, but his career was over. In June, it was discovered that he had amyotrophic lateral sclerosis, a hardening of the spinal cord, now often known as Lou Gehrig's disease.

On July 4, 1939, the Yankees held a day in his honor. Yankee Stadium was packed with 61,808 fans, who heard Gehrig say, "I may have been given a bad break, but I have an awful lot to live for. With all this, I consider myself the luckiest man on the face of the earth." He died less than two years later.

The 6-foot, 200-pound Gehrig, who batted and threw left-handed, played in 2,164 major league games. He hit .340 with 2,721 hits, including 534 doubles, 163 triples, and 493 home runs. Gehrig drove in 1,995 runs and scored 1,888.
★ Baseball Hall of Fame

Gehringer, Charlie (Charles L.)
BASEBALL
b. May 11, 1903, Fowlerville, Mich.
d. Jan. 21, 1993

Teammate and manager Mickey Cochrane once said of Gehringer, "He says hello on opening day and good-bye on closing day, and in between he hits .350." Nicknamed "the Mechanical Man" because of his durability and consistency, Gehringer hit over .300 in 13 seasons, scored 100 or more runs 12 times, drove in more than 100 runs 7 times, led AL second basemen in fielding percentage 7 times, and appeared in 150 or more games 9 times.

After brief appearances with the Detroit Tigers in 1924 and 1925, Gehringer became the team's starting second baseman in 1926 and stayed there for 16 seasons.

He hit .317 in 1927 and .320 in 1928 and then had a great season in 1929, batting .339 and leading the league in hits with 215, runs scored with 131, stolen bases with 27, doubles with 45, and triples with 19.

Gehringer hit .330 in 1930 and .311 in 1931, when an arm injury limited him to 101 games. After slipping to .298 in 1932, he hit .325, drove in 105 runs, and scored 103 to win a starting spot in the first All-Star game in 1933.

Cochrane took over as manager in 1934 and guided the Tigers to two straight pennants. Gehringer hit .356, led the league with 134 runs and 214 hits, and drove in 127 runs in 1934. He batted .330 with 19 home runs, 123 runs scored, and 108 RBI in 1935, then led the league in doubles with 60 the following season, batting .354.

Gehringer won his only batting title with a .371 average in 1937, when he was named the league's most valuable player. In 1938, he hit .306 with a career high 20 home runs.

Injuries again limited his playing time in 1939, though he batted .325 in 118 games. The Tigers won another pennant in 1940, when Gehringer had a .313 average. He dropped to .220 in 1941 and announced his retirement, but was persuaded to stay with the team as a backup in 1942, because of the player shortage caused by World War II.

The following year he entered the navy. Gehringer returned to baseball as Detroit's general manager in 1951 and 1952, then became a vice president of the team until 1959.

In 2,323 games, Gehringer batted .320 with 2,839 hits, including 574 doubles, 146 triples, and 184 RBI. He stole 181 bases, scored 1,774 runs, and drove in 1,427.

★ Baseball Hall of Fame

Gelbert, Charles S.

FOOTBALL
b. Dec. 24, 1871, Hawley, Pa.
d. Jan. 16, 1976

Gelbert was a three-time All-American end at the University of Pennsylvania, from 1894 through 1896, a period when the ends were often considered the most important players on a team. On defense they were responsible for protecting against long runs along the sideline, and on offense they were responsible for trying to create such runs.

Though he weighed only 160 pounds, Gelbert was often moved to guard in order to lead interference on a running play. During his career, Penn won 40 games while losing only 1.

★ College Football Hall of Fame

Genaro, Frankie [Frank Di Gennara]

BOXING
b. Aug. 26, 1901, New York, N.Y.
d. Dec. 2, 1966

As a youngster, Genaro worked as a stable boy and hoped to become a jockey. At 18, he became interested in boxing. Less than a year after taking up the sport, he won a gold medal in the flyweight class at the 1920 Olympics.

The 5-foot-2½, 112-pounder turned professional shortly after the Olympics and went 17 fights without a loss until Abe Goldstein beat him on a 4-round decision in 1922.

Genaro won the American flyweight championship with a 15-round decision over Pancho Villa on March 1, 1923. He lost that title when Fidel LaBarba took a 10-round decision on August 22, 1925.

The NBA flyweight championship became vacant in 1927, and Genaro fought Frenchy Belanger for that title on November 28, but Belanger won a decision. However, Genaro won the decision in a rematch on February 6, 1928.

Spider Pladner of France knocked out Genaro in the 1st round on March 2, 1929, but Genaro regained the title on April 18, when Pladner was disqualified for a foul in the 5th round.

Genaro got his only chance at the world title against Midget Wolgast on December 26, 1930. Wolgast held the New York championship, and the world championship was vacant. Ironically, the fight ended in a draw; each man kept his title while the world championship remained undecided.

On October 27, 1931, Young Perez knocked Genaro out in the 2nd round to win the NBA version of the title. Genaro had just eight more fights. He retired after being knocked out by Speedy Dado in the 3rd round on February 13, 1934.

In 129 professional bouts, Genaro had 83 victories, 19 by knockout, and he lost 22, 4 by knockout. He also fought 9 draws and 15 no-decisions.

Geoffrion, Bernard ("Boom Boom")

HOCKEY
b. Feb. 14, 1931, Montreal, P.Q.

One of the first players to use the slap shot as a primary scoring weapon, Geoffrion was a major player on the Montreal Canadiens' formidable power play during the 1950s. Usually a right wing, Geoffrion played the point on the power play because of his blistering shot. Even if it didn't go in the net, it was so hard for a goalie to control that the rebounds often set up easy shots for his teammates.

When he was 14, an assistant coach on his junior hockey team told him to forget the sport because he'd never make it to the NHL. That simply made Geoffrion more determined than ever, and five years later he went to the Canadiens without ever playing in the minor leagues.

After 18 games in 1950–51, Geoffrion won the Calder Trophy as the league's outstanding rookie the following season, and he won the Hart Trophy as the most valuable player in 1955. In 1960–61 he became the second player in history to score 50 goals in a season (the first was teammate Rocket Richard).

A freak injury in a 1958 practice session sent Geoffrion to the hospital with a ruptured bowel. He was given the last rites of the Catholic church, and after emergency surgery saved his life, he was told to forget about hockey until the following season. Less than six weeks later, he was on the ice for the Stanley Cup final series against Boston. In the sixth game, he scored the first Montreal goal, assisted on the second, and scored the winner in a victory that brought the Canadiens their third straight Stanley Cup.

Geoffrion retired in 1964 but returned to hockey with the New York Rangers in 1966 to play two more seasons. He became coach of the Rangers in 1968, but stomach problems forced him to quit before the season was over, and he moved into the front office. In 1972, he went to the expansion Atlanta Flames as head coach but again quit abruptly.

In his 16 NHL seasons, Geoffrion scored 393 goals and had 429 assists in 883 games. He had 58 goals and 60 assists in 132 playoff games.
★ Hockey Hall of Fame

George, Bill (William)
FOOTBALL
b. Oct. 27, 1930, Waynesburg, Pa.
d. Sept. 30, 1982

A tackle at Wake Forest, George went to the NFL's Chicago Bears in 1952 and became the first modern middle linebacker. He was playing defensive middle guard in a five-man line against the Philadelphia Eagles, who repeatedly completed short passes right over the middle early in the game.

George decided to move out of the line on obvious passing plays. The second time he did this, he made an interception, and he was a middle linebacker from then on. The 6-foot-2, 230-pound George had great speed for his size and was often used on blitzes in passing situations, but he was also good in coverage, and his lineman strength made him just as effective against the run.

He became Chicago's defensive signal caller in 1956, with the responsibility for running a very complex defense that used hundreds of schemes under defensive coordinator Clark Shaughnessy.

George was an All-Pro from 1955 through 1962, and he appeared in eight Pro Bowls. He was with the Bears through 1965 and spent the 1966 season with the Los Angeles Rams before retiring. He returned 18 interceptions 144 yards. George also kicked 14 extra points and 4 field goals for a career total of 26 points.
★ Pro Football Hall of Fame

George, Peter T.
WEIGHTLIFTING
b. June 29, 1929, Akron, Ohio

George won medals at three Olympics, and he was a five-time world champion. In 1948, he needed to clean and jerk 165 kilograms (363 pounds), 5 kilograms more than the world middleweight record, to beat Frank Spellman of the U.S. for the gold medal. George cleaned the weight but couldn't hold it over his head long enough, and settled for the silver medal.

He won the gold medal in 1952 and another silver medal in 1956. George was the U.S. lightweight champion in 1946, at only 17, and he won the middleweight championship from 1949 through 1952 and in 1957. From 1947 through 1956, he won five world championships and finished second twice, and he was the Pan-American Games middleweight champion in 1951 and 1955.

George graduated from Kent State University and received a degree in dentistry from Ohio State. After serving as a dentist in the U.S. Army, he moved to Hawaii to practice orthodontics.

Gerard, Eddie (Edward G.)
HOCKEY
b. Feb. 22, 1890, Ottawa, Ont.
d. Aug. 7, 1937

Gerard spent five years with the Ottawa Rough Riders in the Canadian Rugby Union before becoming a professional hockey player with the Ottawa Senators in 1917. A rushing defenseman, he scored 50 goals and had 30 assists in 128 regular season games; he added 7 goals and 1 assist in five playoff series.

In six seasons, Gerard played on four Stanley Cup champion teams, three of them with Ottawa. In 1922, manager Lester Patrick of Vancouver allowed the Toronto St. Pats to borrow Gerard from Ottawa as an emergency replacement during the Stanley Cup final, and he starred in two victories over Vancouver which won the cup for Toronto.

Gerard coached the Montreal Maroons to the Stanley Cup in 1926. He went to the New York Americans in 1930, returned to the Maroons in 1932, and took over the St. Louis Eagles in 1934, but quit halfway through the season.

★ Hockey Hall of Fame

Gervin, George

BASKETBALL
b. April 27, 1952, Detroit, Mich.

Known as the "Iceman" because of his cool demeanor, Gervin grew up in a Detroit ghetto and learned basketball on playgrounds. He won a scholarship to Long Beach State University but transferred after one semester to Eastern Michigan University.

Gervin was averaging 29.5 points a game in his second year at Eastern Michigan when he was suspended from the team for hitting an opposing player during a brawl. He was then expelled from school and began playing in the Continental Basketball League.

The Virginia Squires chose him in the first round of a special ABA draft during the 1972–73 season. Gervin was named to the league's All-Rookie team even though he played in only 30 games that season. The financially troubled Virginia team sold him to the San Antonio Spurs in January 1974.

San Antonio joined the NBA in a merger of the leagues in 1976. Gervin led the NBA in scoring four times, with averages of 27.2 in 1977–78, 29.6 in 1978–79, 33.1 in 1979–80, and 32.3 in 1981–82. He was named to the All-NBA team five straight times, from 1978 through 1982.

The spidery 6-foot-7, 185-pounder was basically a guard during his professional career but was also often used at forward. His speed, leaping ability, and long arms made him a dazzling performer driving to the basket and he could keep defenders honest by hitting the medium-range jump shot as well.

Gervin was traded to the Chicago Bulls in 1985. After one season with Chicago, he played in Italy in 1986–87.

During his ABA–NBA career, Gervin scored 26,595 points in 1,060 regular season games, an average of 25.1 per game. He also had 5,602 rebounds and 2,798 assists.

Gestring, Marjorie

DIVING
b. Nov. 18, 1922, Los Angeles, Calif.

At the age of only 13 years and 9 months, Gestring became the youngest individual gold medalist in Olympic history when she won the springboard diving championship in 1936. She may well have been deprived of another medal or two by World War II, which forced the cancellation of the 1940 and 1944 Olympics.

Gestring won the national outdoor 3-meter springboard championship in 1937, 1938, and 1940; the indoor 3-meter from 1936 through 1938; and the outdoor platform in 1939 and 1940. She made a comeback to compete in the 1948 Olympic trials but finished fourth and failed to qualify for the team.

Giacomin, Edward

HOCKEY
b. June 6, 1939, Sudbury, Ont.

A goaltender who was sometimes referred to as a third defenseman because of his excellent skating ability, Giacomin turned down baseball and football scholarships to play professional hockey.

After a long stay in the minor leagues, mostly with the Providence Reds, Giacomin joined the NHL's New York Rangers in 1965 and was an iron man for four seasons, playing 68, 66, 70, and 70 games before Gilles Villemure arrived in 1969 to share goaltending duties.

Giacomin and Villemure won the Vezina Trophy for the 1970–71 season, when Giacomin had a 2.15 goals-against average and Villemure was not much worse, at 2.29. Giacomin remained with the Rangers until 1975, when he was traded to the Detroit Red Wings. He retired after the 1977–78 season.

Giacomin had a 289–206–97 regular season record with 54 shutouts and a 2.82 goals-against average. In 65 playoff games, he gave up 180 goals, a 2.82 average, and had 1 shutout.

★ Hockey Hall of Fame

Gianulias, Nikki (Nicole)

BOWLING
b. Dec. 5, 1959, Vallejo, Calif.

The first woman to roll four 800 series on the Ladies Pro Bowlers Tour and one of only two women ever to accomplish that, Gianulias joined the tour in the 1979 season and was named rookie of the year.

She led the LPBT in scoring average in 1981, 1982, and 1986. Her average of 213.89 pins in 1986 is a record. Gianulias was named woman bowler of the year in 1982, when she was the top money winner with $45,875.

Though she never won a major tournament, she is third all-time with 18 tournament victories and fifth in career earnings with $442,896 through 1993. She has bowled in tour events only occasionally since 1986.

Giardello, Joey [Carmine O. Tilelli]

BOXING
b. July 16, 1930, Brooklyn, N.Y.

A very clever boxer with not much of a knockout punch, Giardello nevertheless had 11 knockouts in his first 17 professional fights. He turned professional in October 1948 and suffered his first loss, an 8-round decision, in January 1950 after 18 victories and 1 draw.

Giardello was involved in a very controversial fight against Billy Graham on December 19, 1952. He originally won a split decision, but two New York State boxing commissioners who were at the fight changed a judge's scorecard to give Graham the decision. A court later ruled that they had no authority to do so, and the original decision was restored.

Despite a fine record, Giardello didn't get a championship fight until April 20, 1960, when he met Gene Fullmer for the middleweight title in Bozeman, Montana. Fullmer retained the championship in a 15-round draw.

On December 7, 1963, Giardello won the world middleweight title by decisioning Dick Tiger in 15 rounds in Atlantic City. He defended the championship against Rubin Carter in 1964 but lost it to Tiger in a 15-round decision on October 21, 1965. Giardello retired two years later.

In 133 professional bouts, Giardello had 100 victories, 32 by knockout, and he lost 25, 4 by knockout. He also fought 7 draws and 1 no-decision.

★ International Boxing Hall of Fame

Gibbons, Mike (Michael J.)

BOXING
b. July 20, 1887, St. Paul, Minn.
d. Aug. 31, 1956

Though ranked by *Ring* magazine as one of the top ten middleweights of all time, Gibbons never got a title fight. Originally a wrestler, he switched to professional boxing in 1908. He won 12 of his first 13 fights, with 1 draw, and claimed the middleweight championship after Stanley Ketchel died in 1910, but he wasn't recognized as champion.

Known as the "St. Paul Phantom" because of his speed and elusiveness, Gibbons was never knocked out in 127 professional fights. His first fight was a knockout of Roy Moore on January 11, 1908. After losing a 10-round decision to Jimmy Clabby on March 12, 1910, Gibbons was undefeated until 1921. Nearly half of his fights were no-decision contests.

Because of eye damage suffered in the ring, Gibbons retired in 1922. He later operated a gym, managed some fighters, and promoted bouts. Gibbons also served on the Minnesota Boxing Commission.

Gibbons had 62 victories, 38 of them by knockout. He lost only 3 decisions, and he also had 4 draws and 58 no-decisions.

★ International Boxing Hall of Fame

Gibbons, Tommy (Thomas J.)

BOXING
b. March 27, 1891, St. Paul, Minn.
d. Nov. 19, 1960

Originally a middleweight like his older brother Mike, Tommy Gibbons began his professional boxing career in 1911. From then through 1920, most of his fights were no-decisions, but he did have 16 victories without a loss during that period.

In 1921, Gibbons became a light heavyweight or heavyweight, depending on whom he was fighting, and the additional weight gave him new punching power. He scored 27 knockouts and won 2 decisions with only 1 loss before meeting Jack Dempsey for the world heavyweight title on July 4, 1923, in Shelby, Montana.

Gibbons was a heavy underdog but surprised most observers by going the full 15 rounds. However, Dempsey won a decision. That fight was infamous because it virtually bankrupted the town of Shelby. The gate receipts didn't meet Dempsey's guarantee, so Gibbons didn't get paid at all.

After scoring 11 more knockouts in his next 12 fights, Gibbons was knocked out by Gene Tunney in 12 rounds on June 5, 1925, and retired from the ring. He served as sheriff of his native Ramsey County in Minnesota from 1934 until 1959.

In 106 professional bouts, Gibbons had 57 victories, 47 by knockout. He lost 4, 1 by knockout, and also fought 1 draw, 43 no-decisions, and 1 no-contest.
★ International Boxing Hall of Fame

Gibbs, Joe J.

FOOTBALL
b. Nov. 25, 1940, Mocksville, N.C.

Gibbs played football at San Diego State and served as a graduate assistant there while studying toward his master's degree, which he received in 1966. He spent the next 15 years as an assistant coach for several college and professional teams.

In 1981, he took over as head coach of the NFL's Washington Redskins. During 12 seasons there, he compiled a 124–60–0 record, produced five division champions, and won three Super Bowls, after the 1982, 1987, and 1991 seasons. His 1983 team also reached the Super Bowl but lost to the Los Angeles Raiders.

Known as a workaholic who paid little attention to anything other than football, Gibbs suddenly announced his retirement after the 1992 season, citing unspecified health problems and family considerations.

Gibbs was the chief architect of the so-called "one-back" offense, which sets up with just one running back behind the quarterback. The formation usually employs two tight ends, one of whom often goes in motion either to get into a pass pattern or to lead blocking for a running play.

Gibson, Althea

TENNIS
b. Aug. 25, 1927, Silver, S.C.

Something of a tomboy as a youngster in Harlem, Gibson played basketball, stickball, and paddle tennis. She won her age group in the New York City paddle tennis championship in 1939 and then began taking lessons at the Cosmopolitan Tennis Club.

In 1946, a well-to-do black doctor, Hubert Eaton of Wilmington, North Carolina, took her in to help advance her career. Barred from public courts because she was black, she practiced on Dr. Eaton's backyard court.

Gibson began playing in the all-black American Tennis Association tournaments in 1945 and won ten straight women's singles titles, from 1947 through 1956. She was the first black to play in the national indoor tournament, in early 1950, and she finished second, which should have won her an invitation to the U.S. National at Forest Hills.

No invitation came until after a letter from former champion Alice Marble appeared in the July issue of *American Lawn Tennis* magazine. Marble wrote, in part, "If Althea Gibson represents a challenge to the present crop of players, then it's only fair that they meet this challenge on the courts."

It took Gibson a while to adjust to

the stronger competition she was now facing, but she broke through by winning the French and Italian singles championships in 1956. She also teamed with Angela Buxton to win the women's doubles events at Wimbledon and in the French championship.

Gibson's big year was 1957, when she became the first black player to win the Wimbledon singles title and the first to win the U.S. national title. She also won the women's doubles at Wimbledon with Darlene Hard and the U.S. mixed doubles with Kurt Nielsen.

In 1957 Gibson became the first black to be named Associated Press female athlete of the year. She won the award again in 1958, when she repeated as singles champion both at Wimbledon and in the U.S. nationals and won her third straight Wimbledon women's doubles title, this time with Maria Bueno.

A powerful serve and volley player, the 5-foot-10 Gibson had the foot speed and reach for great court coverage, allowing her to return shots that seemed unreachable. A very popular champion, she received accolades from the press, fans, and fellow players for her accomplishments.

Late in 1958, she signed a $100,000 contract to play tennis exhibitions at halftime of Harlem Globetrotter games. She later played on the women's professional golf tour and pursued a career as a singer and actress.

★ International Tennis Hall of Fame;
International Women's Sports Hall of Fame

Gibson, Bob (Robert)
BASEBALL
b. Nov. 9, 1935, Omaha, Nebr.

Gibson had one of the greatest seasons ever for a pitcher in 1968. He set a major league record with a 1.12 ERA, had 13 shutouts in a 22–9 season, and led the NL in strikeouts with 268 in 304 innings while walking only 62. He won the NL's Cy Young and most valuable player awards.

That was just one season in a long stretch when Gibson was a dominating pitcher who helped lead the St. Louis

Cardinals into three World Series and two world championships. After appearing with St. Louis for parts of the 1959 and 1960 seasons, he became a full-time starter in 1961.

The right-handed Gibson led the league with five shutouts in 1962. He was 19–12 with a 3.01 ERA in 1964, when he set a World Series record with 31 strikeouts in 27 innings, winning two and losing one in the Cardinals' seven-game victory over the New York Yankees.

Gibson went 20–12 and 21–12 in the next two seasons, again leading the NL with five shutouts in 1966. He seemed on his way to another 20-victory season in 1967 before a line drive broke his right leg. However, he was ready for the World Series against the Boston Red Sox, winning three complete games and giving up just three runs.

After his incredible 1968 season, Gibson won the first and fourth games of the World Series against the Detroit Tigers, setting a record of seven consecutive series wins. Gibson also broke his own record with 35 strikeouts, but he lost the seventh game, 4–1, in part because of a misplayed fly ball that led to three Detroit runs.

Gibson won a second Cy Young Award in 1970, when he had a 23–7 record and a 3.12 ERA. He spent his entire career with the Cardinals, retiring after the 1975 season with a 251–174 record, 56 shutouts, and a 2.91 ERA. He struck out 3,117 hitters and walked 1,336 in 3,884 innings.

The 6-foot-2, 195-pound Gibson was an intimidating pitcher, always willing to throw inside to back a hitter off the plate. An outstanding all-around athlete, he played basketball with the Harlem Globetrotters once, had a career .206 batting average with 24 home runs, and won Gold Gloves for his fielding nine years in a row, from 1965 through 1973.

★ Baseball Hall of Fame

Gibson, Joshua
BASEBALL
b. Dec. 21, 1911, Buena Vista, Ga.
d. Jan. 20, 1947

Walter Johnson, who often saw Gibson play, said of him, "He hits the ball a mile and throws like a rifle." Satchel Paige called him "the greatest hitter who ever lived." But Gibson never played in the major leagues because he was black.

His family moved to Pittsburgh in 1924, and Gibson began playing semipro baseball in 1929. The 6-foot-1, 215-pounder occasionally played the outfield but was usually a catcher. He was in the stands that summer to watch the Kansas City Monarchs play Pittsburgh's Homestead Grays in a night game under a portable lighting system. The Homestead catcher refused to play because of the poor lighting, and Gibson was called out of the stands to replace him.

Within a short time, he was the starting catcher for the Grays. In 1931, he jumped to the Pittsburgh Crawfords, one of the greatest teams ever assembled. Among his teammates were Paige, Cool Papa Bell, Judy Johnson, and Oscar Charleston.

The Crawfords folded after 1936, and Gibson returned to the Homestead team for three seasons, went to the Mexican League in 1940 and 1941, then was forced back to the Grays by a lawsuit.

Gibson helped draw such large crowds when the Grays played in Washington that Clark Griffith, the owner of the Senators, considered signing him during the late 1930s but didn't. In part because of frustration from not being able to play in the major leagues, Gibson began drinking heavily after returning from Mexico, and his skills declined abruptly. He died of a stroke three months before Jackie Robinson made his debut with the Brooklyn Dodgers.

The Negro leagues didn't keep accurate records, but Gibson was credited with as many as 84 home runs in a season, which might include as many as 200 games, and he is believed to have hit nearly 800 in his 17 seasons. Although he was questionable on defense early in his career, he worked hard to become a fine catcher.

★ Baseball Hall of Fame

Gibson, Kirk H.

BASEBALL
b. May 28, 1957, Pontiac, Mich.

An All-American in both baseball and football at Michigan State, Gibson was drafted as a wide receiver by the NFL's St. Louis Cardinals in 1979, but he chose to play professional baseball.

He entered the major leagues with the AL's Detroit Tigers near the end of the 1979 season but was troubled by injuries until 1983, when he batted .282 with 27 home runs, 91 RBI, and 29 stolen bases.

The left-handed Gibson, at 6-foot-3 and 225 pounds, is an outfielder who has often been used as a designated hitter in the AL because of his chronic knee problems. He was signed as a free agent by the Los Angeles Dodgers in 1988 and was named the NL's most valuable player, batting .290 with 25 home runs, 76 RBI, and 31 stolen bases.

Gibson hit one of the most dramatic home runs in World Series history against the Oakland Athletics in 1988. Hobbled by injury, he wasn't expected to play in the series, but he was sent in to pinch hit in the ninth inning of the first game with a runner on, two outs, and the Dodgers losing, 4–3. Facing Dennis Eckersley, baseball's best relief pitcher, Gibson hit a home run to win the game. The television shot of Gibson pumping his fists as he rounded the bases has been shown over and over. The Dodgers went on to beat heavily favored Oakland in five games.

Injuries continued to hamper Gibson during the next two seasons. He went to the Kansas City Royals of the AL in 1991 and was released after playing in just 16 games for the Pittsburgh Pirates in 1992. Gibson returned to Detroit in 1993 and had a respectable season, hitting .261 in 116 games.

Through 1994, Gibson had 1,190 hits in 1,565 games, with 248 doubles, 49 triples, and 202 home runs. He had stolen 275 bases while scoring 948 runs and driving in 835.

Giegengack, Bob (Robert F.)

TRACK AND FIELD
b. Jan. 9, 1907, Brooklyn, N.Y.
d. May 25, 1987

Best known for producing middle distance runners, Giegengack was on the track team at Holy Cross College in Massachusetts. After graduating in 1929, he coached track at the high school level for nine years, then took over at Fordham in 1938, becoming the youngest track coach at a major university.

His 1941 team won the IC4A championship. Giegengack then served in the Navy, returning to Fordham in 1945, and in 1946 he became track coach at Yale. He held that position until retiring in 1972.

Giegengack guided Yale to four IC4A championships and a 186–121 record in dual and triangular meets. He coached the 1964 U.S. Olympic track team that won 20 medals, including 12 golds, and he also coached the first national team to go to mainland China, in 1975.

★ National Track & Field Hall of Fame

Gifford, Frank N.

FOOTBALL
b. Aug. 16, 1930, Santa Monica, Calif.

The versatile Gifford was a single-wing tailback at the University of Southern California. With the New York Giants, he played in the Pro Bowl seven times, as a defensive back, running back, and flanker.

Gifford joined the Giants in 1952, when he was used primarily on defense. He played both offense and defense in 1953 and also returned punts. But when Vince Lombardi took over as offensive coordinator in 1954, he insisted that Gifford should become a full-time member of the offense.

The 6-foot-1, 195-pound Gifford was named the NFL's player of the year by United Press International in 1956, when he rushed for 819 yards, caught passes for 603 yards, and scored 9 touchdowns. Gifford was named an All-Pro halfback from 1955 through 1957 and in 1959.

He retired after suffering a severe concussion in 1960 but returned to the Giants in 1961 and spent three seasons as a flanker before retiring for good. Gifford has become a prominent sportscaster, working ABC's Monday Night Football and also commenting on skiing events during the Winter Olympics.

In his 12 NFL seasons, Gifford rushed 840 times for 3,609 yards, a 4.3 average, and 34 touchdowns, and he caught 367 passes for 5,434 yards, a 14.8 average, and 43 touchdowns. Gifford also passed for 14 touchdowns on just 63 attempts and returned 2 interceptions for 112 yards and 1 touchdown.

★ College Football Hall of Fame; Pro Football Hall of Fame

Gill, Slats (Amory T.)

BASKETBALL
b. May 11, 1901, Salem, Oreg.
d. April 5, 1966

A Helms Athletic Foundation All-American forward at Oregon State in 1924, Gill returned to the school as head coach in 1929. In 35 seasons, his teams won 599 games, placing him 12th on the all-time list, while losing 392. They won or shared five Pacific Coast Conference titles and went to the NCAA final four twice, in 1949 and 1963.

Gill suffered a heart attack during the 1959–60 season and was replaced by Paul Valenti during his convalescence, but he came back as coach the following year. He retired from coaching after the 1963–64 season to become the school's athletic director, a position he held until his death from a stroke.

★ Basketball Hall of Fame

Gillman, Sidney

FOOTBALL
b. Oct. 26, 1911, Minneapolis, Minn.

An end at Ohio University, Gillman was chosen for the first college all-star game after graduating in 1934. He played for the NFL's Cleveland Rams in 1936 and then became an assistant college coach.

Gillman was named head coach at Miami University, Ohio, in 1944 and compiled a 31–6–1 record in four seasons. He spent a year as an assistant at Army, then took over at the University of Cincinnati in 1949. Cincinnati won 50 games while losing only 13 and tying 1, but the school was put on probation for recruiting violations in 1955, and Gillman moved on to the NFL's Los Angeles Rams.

The Rams won the Western Conference title in his first season, losing to the Cleveland Browns, 38–14, in the league championship game. He was fired after a 2–10 record in 1959.

Gillman became the first coach of the Los Angeles Chargers in the new American Football League in 1960. The Chargers, who moved to San Diego in 1961, won five Western Conference championships in six years and beat the Boston Patriots, 51–10, for the 1963 AFL title.

Ulcers forced Gillman to leave coaching after the Chargers lost four of their first nine games in 1969. He returned in 1971 but again left before the season was over. In 1973 Gillman was named general manager of the Houston Oilers. He replaced Bill Peterson as coach during the season and was named American Football Conference coach of the year in 1974, when the team had a 7–7 record. However, Gillman resigned in January of the following year. His overall record as a professional coach was 123–104–7.

A strong proponent of the passing game, Gillman designed pass patterns that almost always featured five receivers, with at least one of them going deep. He liked the threat of the long pass because it stretched defenses to the limit and made it easier to complete the shorter passes or to run the ball.

★ College Football Hall of Fame; Pro Football Hall of Fame

Gilmore, Artis

BASKETBALL
b. Sept. 21, 1949, Chipley, Fla.

After two years at Gardner-Webb Junior College, Gilmore went to Jacksonville University in 1969. He led NCAA Division I players with 22.2 rebounds per game in 1969–70 and 23.2 per game in 1970–71 and averaged 24.3 points per game in his two seasons at Jacksonville.

The 7-foot-2, 265-pound Gilmore joined the ABA's Kentucky Colonels as their first-round draft choice in 1971, and he was named both rookie of the year and player of the year after averaging 23.8 points a game and leading the league with 1,492 rebounds. He was also the league leader in rebounds each of the next four seasons.

The Kentucky franchise folded when the ABA and NBA merged in 1976, and Gilmore was chosen by the NBA's Chicago Bulls in a dispersal draft. After eight professional seasons without missing a game, he played in only 48 games in 1979–80 because of an injury. The Bulls traded him to the San Antonio Spurs in 1982, and the Spurs traded him back to Chicago in 1987.

After being waived by the Bulls during the 1987–88 season, Gilmore was signed by the Boston Celtics. Gilmore played in Italy in 1988–89 and then retired. The NBA leader in field goal percentage four consecutive seasons, from 1980–81 through 1983–84, he holds the league record for career field goal percentage, at .599.

During his 17 ABA/NBA seasons, Gilmore scored 24,041 points in 909 games, a 17.1 percentage, and pulled down 16,330 rebounds. He had 1,747 blocked shots in NBA games.

Gilmore, William E. Garrett

ROWING
b. Feb. 16, 1895, Wayne, Pa.
d. Dec. 5, 1969

Gilmore began rowing with the Bachelors Barge Club of Philadelphia in 1919. He won the national ¼-mile singles sculls in 1923, 1928, and 1932, the championship and 1½-mile races in 1924.

At the 1924 Olympics, Gilmore beat perennial British champion Jack Beresford in an early heat. That year, repechage was introduced, allowing heat losers a second chance to get into the finals. Beresford qualified and edged Gilmore for the gold medal, with Gilmore winning the silver.

In 1932, Gilmore teamed with Kenneth Myers to win a gold medal in the Olympic double sculls.

Gipp, George

FOOTBALL
b. Feb. 18, 1895, Laurium, Mich.
d. Dec. 14, 1920

Notre Dame sports historian Francis Wallace called Gipp "a most peculiar kind of saint," and sportswriter George Trevor compared him to a meteor because of his brilliant football career and short life.

After graduating from high school, Gipp played sandlot baseball and drove a taxi for three years, then accepted a baseball scholarship to Notre Dame in 1916. He was casually kicking a football on a practice field that fall when Knute Rockne, then an assistant coach, spotted him and talked him into playing for the freshman team. In one game that season, Gipp dropped into punt formation on his own 38-yard line, but instead of punting, he drop-kicked a 62-yard field goal.

Gipp quickly became known as a maverick. He defied Notre Dame rules by staying in a South Bend hotel instead of using his dormitory room, and he earned extra money by playing pool and poker. In September 1917, he left the school to enroll at the University of Wisconsin, but Rockne caught up to him and brought him back.

Gipp started at halfback that fall but suffered a broken leg in the sixth game and missed the rest of the season. Rockne succeeded Jess Harper as head coach in 1918. That was an abbreviated season because of World War I, and it didn't count against eligibility, so Gipp still had two years to play.

He came into his own in 1919, when Notre Dame went undefeated. After Army took a 9–0 lead in the first half, Gipp completed passes for a total of 75 yards to put the ball on Army's 10-yard line, then scored on a 7-yard touchdown run. Late in the game, he threw a long pass to Eddie Anderson to set up the winning touchdown.

Later that school year, Gipp was to be expelled for cutting classes. Rockne intervened with school authorities, who allowed Gipp to take a special examination. He passed and was allowed to remain in school. However, in the fall of 1920, Gipp again left campus, this time to attend the University of Michigan, and again Rockne had to persuade him to return to Notre Dame.

After scoring on runs of 95 yards against Purdue and 70 yards against Nebraska, Gipp turned in a spectacular performance against Army. He rushed for 124 yards, passed for 96, and ran back kicks for 112 yards in a 27–17 victory.

A dislocated shoulder forced Gipp out of the Indiana game, but with Indiana leading, 10–6, in the closing minutes and Notre Dame five yards from a touchdown, he talked Rockne into letting him go back in. He scored the winning touchdown on his second carry.

The following week, Gipp had a bad cold, and he was on the bench at the beginning of the game against Northwestern. With Notre Dame fans chanting his name, Rockne sent him into the game for a few minutes — just long enough to throw a 45-yard touchdown pass.

The cold turned out to be a streptococcus infection, and the weakened Gipp contracted pneumonia. He converted to Catholicism, and with Rockne sitting beside him and the entire Notre Dame student body kneeling in the snow outside his dorm to pray for him, he died in mid-December. He was posthumously named to Walter Camp's All-American team.

But Gipp was to haunt Army one more time. In 1928, Notre Dame had lost two games while Army was unbeaten. They played a scoreless first half. In the dressing room, Rockne told his players that Gipp, on his deathbed, had asked him to exhort the Notre Dame players to "win one for the Gipper" when they were involved in a tough game. Notre Dame did just that, scoring two touchdowns to win, 12–6. The deathbed scene, whether it happened or not, was recreated for the 1940 movie *Knute Rockne — All American*, in which Pat O'Brien played Rockne and Ronald Reagan played Gipp.

★ College Football Hall of Fame

Glass, Herman T.

GYMANSTICS
b. 1879, Chicago, Ill.
d. 1961

Glass took up gymnastics on a doctor's advice in order to strengthen his body when he was a teenager. After suffering a hand injury, he was forced to concentrate on the rings. He won both the U.S. and the Olympic championships in 1904.

Glavine, Tom (Thomas M.)

BASEBALL
b. March 25, 1966, Concord, Mass.

A baseball and hockey star in high school, Glavine was chosen by the Los Angeles Kings in the 1984 NHL draft of amateur players, but he chose to play professional baseball in the Atlanta Braves organization.

The left-handed pitcher joined the Braves late in the 1987 season and led the NL in losses with a 7–17 record in 1988. After winning a total of 24 games the next two years, Glavine had three straight 20-victory seasons, going 20–11 in 1981, 20–8 in 1992, and 22–6 in 1993. He won the Cy Young Award in 1991, when he led the league in complete games with 9 and had a 2.55 ERA.

Glavine boasts an excellent assortment of pitches: a fastball that can tail away or run in on a right-handed hitter, an excellent curve, and a good changeup. Through 1994, he had a career 108–75 record with 12 shutouts. Glavine had struck out 904 batters while walking only 513 in 1,552⅓ innings.

Glover, Richard E.

FOOTBALL
b. Feb. 6, 1950, Bayonne, N.J.

At 6-foot-1 and 234 pounds, Glover played defensive end in his first two football seasons at the University of Nebraska, 1970 and 1971. As a junior, he was moved to middle guard, where his quickness made him a star. Glover was named outstanding lineman in the Orange Bowl two years in a row. He was an All-American and winner of the Outland Trophy as the nation's outstanding collegiate lineman in 1972.

Glover spent the 1973 season with the NFL's New York Giants and another with the Shreveport team of the World Football League before retiring as a player to become a teacher and high school coach.

Goheen, Moose (Frank)

HOCKEY
b. Feb. 9, 1894, White Bear Lake, Minn.
d. Nov. 13, 1979

One of only three U.S.-born members of the Hockey Hall of Fame, Goheen learned to play hockey on outdoor rinks in Minnesota. He joined the St. Paul, Minnesota, Athletic Club team in 1915. After serving in World War I, he returned to the St. Paul team.

A rover — the seventh man in the era of seven-man hockey — Goheen played on the 1920 Olympic team that won a silver medal. In 1925, the league in which his St. Paul team played became a minor professional league. Despite frequent offers to play in the National Hockey League, Goheen remained with St. Paul until his retirement in 1932.
★ Hockey Hall of Fame; U.S. Hockey Hall of Fame

Gola, Thomas J.

BASKETBALL
b. Jan. 13, 1933, Philadelphia, Pa.

A multitalented player, Gola starred at LaSalle High School in Philadelphia and went on to nearby LaSalle University. In his freshman year, 1950–51, LaSalle won the National Invitation Tournament, and Gola shared the tournament's most valuable player award with teammate Norm Grekin.

A consensus All-American the next three seasons, Gola was named tournament MVP when LaSalle won the 1954 NCAA championship. The 6-foot-6, 220-pound Gola played all three positions at LaSalle, averaging 20.9 points and 18.7 rebounds a game during his four years as a starter. He averaged 24.1 points per game as a senior.

His college coach, Ken Loeffler, nicknamed Gola "Mr. All Around" and once said of him, "I have never seen one player control a game by himself as well as Gola does."

In 1955, Gola joined the Philadelphia Warriors of the NBA and averaged 10.8 points a game as the Warriors won the league championship. He entered military service after the season, returning to the Warriors in 1957. Wilt Chamberlain did most of the team's scoring, and Gola was used mainly as a play-making guard.

The Warriors moved to San Francisco in 1962, and Gola was traded to the New York Knicks in midseason. He finished his playing career with the Knicks in 1965–66. In 698 professional games, Gola scored 7,871 points, got 5,617 rebounds, and had 2,962 assists. He averaged 11.3 points, 8.0 rebounds, and 4.2 assists per game.

Gola coached LaSalle to a 23–1 record in 1968–69, when the team was ranked second in the nation, and he had a 14–12 record in his second and final season. He later served in the Pennsylvania State Legislature and as comptroller of the city of Philadelphia.

★ Basketball Hall of Fame

Goldberg, Marshall ("Biggie")

FOOTBALL
b. Oct. 24, 1917, Elkins, W.Va.

Goldberg was a member of two "Dream Backfields," as a college player at the University of Pittsburgh and as a professional player with the NFL's Chicago Cardinals. He became a starter at halfback as a sophomore in 1936 and was an All-American in 1937.

As a senior, Goldberg asked to be moved to fullback, a position that had been depleted by graduation. His coach, Jock Sutherland, warned that it would be difficult to repeat as All-American at a new position, but Goldberg was more interested in the good of the team.

That created the first "Dream Backfield," with Harold Stebbins at quarterback, Dick Cassiano and John Chickerneo at halfbacks. Pitt won eight of ten games that season, and Goldberg was named All-American fullback.

In 1939, Goldberg joined the NFL's Chicago Cardinals. He missed the 1944

and 1945 seasons while in military service during World War I, then returned to the Cardinals in 1946 and played through 1948. The team's 1946 "Dream Backfield" was made up of Paul Christman at quarterback, Goldberg and Elmer Angsman at halfbacks, and Pat Harder at fullback. In his last two seasons, Goldberg was replaced by Charlie Trippi but remained with the team as a valuable backup.

As a pro, Goldberg gained 1,644 yards on 476 carries and scored 11 touchdowns. He caught 60 passes for 775 yards and 5 touchdowns.

★ College Football Hall of Fame

Gomez, Lefty (Vernon L.)

BASEBALL
b. Nov. 26, 1908, Rodeo, Calif.
d. Feb. 17, 1989

At 6-foot-2, Gomez weighed only 173 pounds, but his long arms gave him the leverage to throw a very good fastball, and early in his major league career he developed an excellent slow curve that drove hitters crazy.

He had a 2–5 record in a brief stint with the New York Yankees in 1930 but became a regular starter the following season and had a 21–9 record with a 2.67 ERA. Gomez went 24–7 in 1932 and won the second game of the World Series, 7–2, as the Yankees swept the Cubs in four games.

After leading the league with 163 strikeouts in 1933, Gomez won the first of two pitching triple crowns. He was tops in the AL in victories and winning percentage with a 26–5 record, in strikeouts with 158, and in ERA with a 2.33 mark. He also led the league with 6 shutouts, despite the fact that he started only 33 games because of an arm injury late in the season.

The arm continued to bother him for the next two years, when he had a combined 25–22 record, but he won two games in the 1936 World Series. In 1937 he bounced back to win his second triple crown, leading in victories with a 21–11 record, in strikeouts with 194, and in ERA at 2.33. He also had a league-leading six shutouts. Gomez won two more games against the New York Giants in the World Series, giving up just three runs in 18 innings.

He had an 18–12 record in 1938 and won his sixth straight World Series game. Gomez's six victories without a loss in World Series play is a record. After a 12–8 mark in 1939, Gomez's recurring arm problem limited him to a 3–3 mark in 1940. He was used sparingly in 1941 yet led the league in winning percentage with a 15–5 record.

Gomez was only 6–4 in 1942 and retired after losing his only start with the Washington Senators the following year. He served as a minor league manager for two seasons, then began a second career as a speaker and frequent guest on radio shows. Known for his sense of humor, Gomez coined the phrase "I'd rather be lucky than good."

In 368 games, Gomez completed 173 of 320 starts and had a 189–102 record with 28 shutouts and a 3.34 ERA. He struck out 1,468 hitters and walked 1,095 in 2,503 innings.
★ Baseball Hall of Fame

Gonsalves, Billy (William A.)
SOCCER
b. Aug. 10, 1908, Tiverton, R.I.
d. July 17, 1977

Nicknamed "the Babe Ruth of soccer," Gonsalves is still considered by many the greatest soccer player ever produced by the United States. A brilliant scorer, he was also a fine passer and excellent defender.

Gonsalves learned the sport from English and Scottish textile workers as a youngster in Fall River, Massachusetts. He played for a number of different teams from 1922 until 1951.

Usually an inside right forward, Gonsalves led the Fall River Marksmen to the National Challenge Cup in 1930. The team moved to New York, became known as the Yankees, and won a second NCC in 1931.

Gonsalves played for four more NCC champions in the next four years: the New Bedford, Massachusetts, Whalers in 1932; the St. Louis Stix, Baer and Fuller Football Club in 1933 and 1934; and

the St. Louis Central Brewery Club in 1935.

After three seasons with an amateur team in White Plains, New York, Gonsalves joined the Hispano Football Club of Brooklyn, which won the NCC in 1943 and 1944. He spent his last four seasons with the German Sport Club of Newark, New Jersey. After retiring as a player, he coached for a time.

Gonsalves had extensive experience in international play. He was a member of the U.S. World Cup teams in 1930 and 1934, and he scored three goals in each of two upset victories by his Fall River team in 1931, a 5–2 win over an Argentinean club and a 4–3 victory over the Glasgow Celtics.
★ U.S. Soccer Federation Hall of Fame

Gonzales, Pancho (Richard A.)
TENNIS
b. May 9, 1928, Los Angeles, Calif.

When Gonzales was 12 years old, his mother gave him a 50-cent tennis racket for Christmas to discourage him from playing rougher sports. At 14, he was playing and frequently winning junior tournaments.

Gonzales quit school in the tenth grade and joined the navy as soon as he was old enough, in 1945. He was discharged in 1947, and less than a year later he became the second youngest player ever to win the national singles title.

Some thought his championship was tainted because defending champion Ted Schroeder didn't play in the 1948 tournament, but Gonzales beat him in the 1949 final. After losing the first two sets, 16–18 and 2–6, Gonzalez won the last three, 6–1, 6–2, and 6–4. He also won the 1949 Wimbledon singles championship.

Gonzalez then turned professional, joining Jack Kramer on a nationwide tour. He played badly, losing 96 matches while winning only 27, and was dropped in favor of Pancho Segura. After Kramer's retirement, Gonzalez rejoined the pro tour in 1954, and during the next eight years he consistently beat the best professionals around: Lew Hoad, Ken

Rosewall, Frank Sedgman, Segura, and Tony Trabert. The 6-foot-3 Gonzales was especially noted for his great serve, which was once clocked at 112 mph.

After retiring from competition, Gonzales became a top instructor and non-playing captain of the Davis Cup team. He had one last moment in the spotlight, though. In the 1969 Wimbledon tournament, which had been opened to professionals, the 41-year-old Gonzalez beat 25-year-old Charles Pasarell in a 112-game match that lasted 5 hours and 12 minutes, the longest in Wimbledon history. The scores were 22–24, 1–6, 16–14, 6–3, and 11–9.

★ International Tennis Hall of Fame

Goodell, Brian S.
SWIMMING
b. April 2, 1959, Stockton, Calif.

Known as a tireless worker who did extreme long-distance training, Goodell set world records in the 400- and 1,500-meter freestyle events at the 1976 Olympic trials, then broke his own records in both events at the Olympic games. In the 1,500-meter final, he did the final 100 meters in an incredible 57.73 seconds, which would have been good enough to win the national 100-meter championship 25 years before.

Goodell was a student at Mission Viejo High School at the time. He went to UCLA and won nine NCAA championships, in the 500- and 1,650-yard freestyles and in the 400-yard individual medley from 1978 through 1980. He made the 1980 Olympic team, but the U.S. boycott of the Soviet games deprived him of the chance for more medals.

Gooden, Dwight E.
BASEBALL
b. Nov. 16, 1964, Tampa, Fla.

A right-handed pitcher, Gooden won the NL's Cy Young Award in 1985, only his second major league season, when he led in victories with a 24–4 record, in ERA with 1.53, in complete games with 16, and in innings pitched with $276\frac{2}{3}$.

He was also named male athlete of the year by the Associated Press.

Gooden joined the New York Mets in 1984 and had a 17–9 record to win rookie of the year honors. Nicknamed "The Doctor," he throws a fastball at well over 90 miles an hour and has a big breaking curveball to go with it.

He missed the first month of the 1987 season while in a rehabilitation clinic for cocaine use, and injuries hampered him in 1989 and 1991. After a 10–13 record in 1992 and a 12–15 mark in 1993, some observers think a brilliant career may be approaching a premature finish.

Through 1994, Gooden had a 157–85 record with 23 shutouts. He had struck out 1,875 hitters and walked 651 in $2,169\frac{2}{3}$ innings.

Goodfellow, Ebbie (Ebenezer R.)
HOCKEY
b. April 9, 1907, Ottawa, Ont.

Goodfellow played for Detroit in the NHL for 14 seasons and two name changes. He joined the Detroit Cougars for the 1929–30 season. They became the Falcons the following season and the Red Wings in 1933.

He won the Hart Trophy as the league's most valuable player two years in a row, in 1939 and 1940, and he captained the team during his last five years. Goodfellow retired after the 1942–43 season, having scored 134 goals and 190 assists in the regular season. In eight playoff series, he had 8 goals and 8 assists.

Goodfellow was coach of the Chicago Black Hawks for two seasons, from 1950–51 through 1951–52.

★ Hockey Hall of Fame

Goodrich, Gail C., Jr.
BASKETBALL
b. April 23, 1943, Los Angeles, Calif.

Goodrich played for two of John Wooden's NCAA championship teams at UCLA, in 1964 and 1965. He scored 27 points against Duke University in the 1964 championship game and 42 against the University of Michigan in the 1965 final.

A consensus All-American in 1965, the 6-foot-1, 175-pound Goodrich was a fine outside shot who also had the quickness to drive past a defender to the basket if guarded too closely. He went to the NBA's Los Angeles Lakers as a territorial draft pick.

After spending three seasons as a backup guard with the Lakers, Goodrich went to the Phoenix Suns in the 1968 expansion draft. An immediate starter with Phoenix, he averaged 23.8 and 20.0 points per game in two seasons there, then was traded back to Los Angeles.

Even though the Lakers had Wilt Chamberlain and Jerry West, Goodrich led the team in scoring with 25.9 points per game in 1971–72, when Los Angeles won a record 69 regular season games and beat the New York Knicks in the NBA championship finals.

Goodrich played out his option and signed with the New Orleans Jazz as a free agent in 1976. He retired after the 1978–79 season.

In 1,031 regular season games, Goodrich scored 19,181 points, an average of 18.6, and had 4,805 assists. He added 1,450 points and 333 assists in 80 playoff games.

Goodwin, Budd (Leo G.)

SWIMMING
b. Nov. 13, 1883
d. May 25, 1957

Goodwin won gold medals in two different sports at the 1904 Olympics in St. Louis. He swam on the U.S. 4 x 50-yard freestyle relay team and played for the champion New York Athletic Club water polo team. Goodwin also won a bronze medal in plunge for distance.

He won the U.S. indoor 100-yard freestyle championship in 1903 and the outdoor 440-yard freestyle title in 1905. Because of blood poisoning, he nearly had an arm amputated in 1906, but he recovered and came back to win the outdoor 880-yard freestyle championship three years in a row, from 1910 through 1912.
★ International Swimming Hall of Fame

Goolagong, Evonne (Mrs. Cawley)

TENNIS
b. July 31, 1951, Griffith, Australia

One of eight children of part aboriginal background, Goolagong played cricket, rugby, and soccer with boys as a child and began playing tennis informally when she was 8 years old. Coach Vince Edwards recognized her potential when she was 13 and took her into his Sydney home to polish her game.

Goolagong began playing internationally in 1970. A year later she won the French and Wimbledon singles titles, and she also won the hearts of British fans by going on a shopping spree in King's Road, London, to celebrate her Wimbledon victory.

Named the female athlete of the year by the Associated Press in 1971, Goolagong won the Italian Open in 1973 and was the Virginia Slims circuit champion in 1974 and 1976. She won the Australian Open four times in five years, from 1974 through 1976 and in 1978. Although she never won the U.S. Open, she reached the finals there four years in a row, from 1973 through 1976.

Goolagong married English businessman Roger Cawley and had a daughter in 1977. She returned to competition in 1979, when she became the fifth woman to surpass $1 million in winnings. The following year, Goolagong won her second Wimbledon singles championship, matching Bill Tilden for the longest expanse of time between titles.

After giving birth to a son in 1981, Goolagong made a brief comeback attempt in 1982 before retiring. She is third on the all-time list with 88 tournament victories.
★ International Women's Sports Hall of Fame

Gordien, Fortune E.

TRACK AND FIELD
b. Sept. 9, 1922, Spokane, Wash.

Though he held the world discus record for ten years and competed in three Olympics, Gordien never won a gold medal. He finished third in 1948, fourth in 1952, and second in 1956.

Representing the University of Minnesota, Gordien won three consecutive NCAA championships, from 1946 through 1948, and he was the AAU national discus champion seven times, from 1946 through 1950 and in 1953 and 1954. Gordien claimed the world record for the first time with a throw of 185 feet, 2¾ inches in 1949. Later that year he extended the record to 186–11.

On August 22, 1953, Gordien became the first to throw the discus more than 190 feet, with a prodigious 194–6. That record stood until 1959.

Gordien was also a world class shotputter, though he never won a major championship in the event. He finished second in the national championships and third in the NCAA championships in 1947. His throw of 52 feet, 2¼ inches in the NCAA meet was the fifth best in the world that year.

★ National Track & Field Hall of Fame

Gordon, Joseph L. ("Flash")

BASEBALL
b. Feb. 18, 1915, Los Angeles, Calif.
d. April 14, 1978

Gordon is best known as the answer to a trivia question: Who won the AL's most valuable player award in 1942, when Ted Williams won the triple crown?

A right-handed-hitting second baseman, Gordon joined the New York Yankees in 1938 and was a starter on five pennant-winning teams in six seasons. Known primarily for his defense, he had an outstanding offensive season in 1942, hitting .322 with 18 home runs and 103 RBI.

That was the only season he batted over .300, but he hit 20 or more home runs seven times and had 100 or more RBI four times. Gordon was traded to the Cleveland Indians in 1947, and he finished his career with them in 1950.

In 11 seasons, Gordon had a .268 batting average, with 264 doubles, 52 triples, 253 home runs, 914 runs scored and 975 RBI.

Goslin, Goose (Leon A.)

BASEBALL
b. Oct. 16, 1900, Salem, N.J.
d. May 15, 1971

One of the finest clutch hitters of his era, Goslin hit seven home runs in his first 16 World Series games, all with the Washington Senators.

A left-handed-hitting outfielder who threw right-handed, the 5-foot-11, 185-pound Goslin arrived in the major leagues with the Senators at the end of the 1921 season and became a starter the following year, when he hit .324 in 101 games.

Goslin led the league in triples with 18 in 1923 and in RBI with 129 in 1924, batting .344, as the Senators won their first pennant. He had 11 hits, including three home runs, in Washington's seven-game World Series victory over the New York Giants.

The Senators won another pennant in 1925, when Goslin hit .334 and had a league-leading 20 triples. He batted .308 with another three home runs in the World Series, but Washington lost in seven games to the Pittsburgh Pirates.

After hitting .354 and .334 the next two seasons, Goslin was in a close race with Heinie Manush for the league batting lead going into the final game of 1928. He got a hit in his final time at bat to edge Manush, .379 to .378.

Goslin then slipped below .300 for two years and was traded to the St. Louis Browns during the 1930 season. He returned to the Senators for their last pennant in 1933 and hit his seventh and last World Series home run in the second game of a five-game loss to the Giants.

In three seasons with Detroit, Goslin hit over .300 twice, then became a part-time player in 1937. He returned to Washington for one last season in 1938, appearing in only 38 games, then became a minor league manager for several years before leaving baseball.

Goslin hit .316 in 2,287 games, with 2,735 hits, including 500 doubles, 173 triples, and 248 home runs. He drove in 1,609 runs and scored 1,483.

★ Baseball Hall of Fame

Gossage, Goose (Richard M.)

BASEBALL
b. July 5, 1951, Colorado Springs, Colo.

One of the best relief pitchers in baseball during the late 1970s and the early 1980s, the 6-foot, 226-pound Gossage had an intimidating look on the mound because of his size, his fierce scowl, and his cowboy-style moustache.

He entered the major leagues with the Chicago White Sox in 1972 and led the AL with 26 saves in 1975. The following season, the White Sox made him a starter, but he was only 9–17 with a 3.94 ERA, and Chicago sent him to the NL's Pittsburgh Pirates in a four-player trade after the season.

After just one season in Pittsburgh, Gossage signed with the AL's New York Yankees as a free agent in 1978, and he played an important role on three division championship teams during the next four years.

Gossage led the league with 27 saves in 1978 and 33 in 1980. His ERA in six seasons with the Yankees ranged from a low of 0.77 in 1981 to 2.64 in 1979, and he had 150 saves over that period.

In 1984, Gossage went to the NL's San Diego as a free agent. He recorded 72 saves during the next three seasons, but he began to experience arm trouble in 1987. Although generally ineffective since then, Gossage has pitched for the White Sox, San Francisco Giants, Yankees, Texas Rangers, Oakland Athletics, and Seattle Mariners for various periods. He spent the 1990 season with the Fukuoka Daiei Hawks in Japan.

Through the 1994 season, Gossage had a 124–107 record with 310 saves and a 3.01 ERA. He had struck out 1,502 batters while walking 732 in 1,809⅓ innings.

Gotch, Frank A.

WRESTLING
b. April 27, 1878, Humboldt, Iowa
d. Dec. 16, 1917

Gotch was the last of the genuine world champion professional wrestlers. Trained by the first great American champion, Martin "Farmer" Burns, Gotch lost a championship match to Tom Jenkins in 1903 but beat Jenkins the following year.

He lost the title briefly in 1906 when he banged his head against a ring post and was knocked out during a match against Freddie Beall. However, Gotch easily regained the championship in a rematch, and he held the title until his retirement in 1913.

The 5-foot-11, 200-pound Gotch won 154 of 160 professional matches. He had two celebrated bouts with European champion George Hackenschmidt. The first, on April 3, 1908, drew a crowd of more than 40,000 people to the Dexter Park Pavilion in Chicago. After more than two hours without a fall, Hackenschmidt quit and Gotch was awarded the victory. Three years later, they met again in Chicago. Hackenschmidt had suffered torn cartilage in his right knee during practice, and Gotch threw him twice in a short time to win again.

A national celebrity, Gotch toured the U.S. and Europe in a play to capitalize on his fame and never wrestled seriously again, though he gave some boxing exhibitions. He died at 39 of uremic poisoning.

Gottlieb, Eddie (Edward)

BASKETBALL
b. Sept. 15, 1898, Kiev, Russia
d. Dec. 7, 1979

His parents brought Gottlieb to the U.S. when he was a young child, and he was involved with basketball for most of the rest of his life. He began playing in 1910 with the Combine Club, a group of Jewish grade school boys. Many of them later played for South Philadelphia High School and, after graduating, with a team Gottlieb organized under the auspices of the South Philadelphia Hebrew Association.

Known as the Sphas, the team wore jerseys emblazoned with the Hebrew letters samech, pey, hey, and aleph. No longer a player, Gottlieb managed, coached, and promoted the team. Since they had no home court, they were sometimes called the "Wandering Jews."

In 1926, the Sphas beat the Original

Celtics twice in a three-game series. They also beat the great Harlem Renaissance team twice, and they defeated three American Basketball League teams, although they lost to the league champion Cleveland Rosenblums.

Renamed the Philadelphia Warriors and no longer all-Jewish, the team joined the ABL in 1926. Two years later they moved into the Eastern League, and in 1933 they joined a new American Basketball League.

In addition to his involvement with the Warriors, Gottlieb promoted black major league baseball and did scheduling for both the Negro National League and the Negro American League. He served as a business adviser to the Harlem Globetrotters and arranged their postwar international tours, and he also promoted professional wrestling.

When the new Basketball Association of America was organized in 1946, Gottlieb's Philadelphia Warriors joined the league and won the first championship. He coached the team and was part owner from 1946 through 1953, when he acquired full ownership. After selling the team to San Francisco owners in 1963, he became a consultant and schedule maker for the National Basketball Association.

Chairman of the NBA Rules Committee for 25 years, Gottlieb was instrumental in the adoption of the 24-second clock, the rule against zone defenses, and the bonus penalty shot.
★ Basketball Hall of Fame

Gould, Jay, Jr.

COURT TENNIS
b. 1889
d. Jan. 26, 1935

The son and grandson of multimillionaires who made most of their money in railroads, Gould learned to play court tennis on a private court in the family home. It was one of fewer than 100 courts in the country, most of them on private estates.

In 20 years of top-level competition, he lost only once in singles and once in doubles. He won the U.S. amateur championship for the first time in 1906,
when he was only 17, and he held it through 1925, except for 1918 and 1919, when there was no tournament.

In 1914, Gould became the first amateur ever to win the world championship. He held that title through 1922 without being challenged. Gould won a gold medal in the sport in the 1908 Olympics, when it was called *jeu de paume* on the official program.

He also teamed with W. T. H. Hugh to win eight national doubles championships and with Joseph Wear to win six doubles titles.

Governali, Paul V.

FOOTBALL
b. Jan. 5, 1921, New York, N.Y.

Governali was the top collegiate passer in the nation at Columbia University in 1942, when he completed 87 of 242 passes for 1,442 yards and 19 touchdowns. He was an All-American and won the Maxwell Trophy as the nation's outstanding college player. During his three years as a starter, he completed 175 passes in 384 attempts for 2,513 yards and 25 touchdowns. He also rushed for 856 yards.

After spending three years in the Marines during World War II, Governali joined the NFL's Boston Yanks 1946. The Yanks sent him to the New York Giants during the 1947 season. Governali played for the Giants in 1948, then retired as a player. During his professional career, he completed 218 passes in 500 attempts for 3,348 yards and 31 touchdowns.

While working as an assistant to Lou Little, his college coach at Columbia, Governali earned a doctorate from the school's teacher's college. His dissertation, submitted in 1951, was entitled "The Professional Football Player: His Vocational Status."
★ College Football Hall of Fame

Graf, Steffi (Stephanie M.)

TENNIS
b. June 14, 1969, Mannheim, Germany

Graf showed so much promise in tennis as a youngster that her father sold his business and started a tennis school, at which she was the prize pupil. At 13, she become the youngest player ever to win the West German 18-and-under championship.

When Billie Jean King saw her play as a young teenager, she correctly predicted that Graf would win the grand slam someday because of her strength, quickness, and tennis "instinct."

Graf won her first grand slam singles championship in the 1987 French Open. The following year, she became the third woman in history to win a true grand slam, taking the Australian, French, U.S., and Wimbledon singles titles. (The other two were Maureen Connolly and Margaret Court.)

In 1989, Graf won three legs of the grand slam, losing to Arantxa Vicario in the final match of the French Open. She won the Australian Open singles for the third straight time in 1990, but then Monica Seles began to dominate women's tennis.

Graf won at Wimbledon in 1991 and 1992, but Seles won the other grand slam singles titles both of those years. After winning the Australian Open championship in 1993, Seles was stabbed in the back by a crazed Graf fan during a tournament in Germany. Although the wound wasn't life threatening, Seles was out for the rest of the year.

In her absence, Graf won the French, U.S., and Wimbledon singles championships again, but she acknowledged that she missed Seles. "It sure helps if you have a player who pushes you more," she said.

Through 1993, Graf ranked fifth all-time with 14 grand slam singles titles. She also had one doubles title for a total of 15, placing her 18th on the all-time list.

Graham, Billy (William P. Jr.)

BOXING
b. Sept. 9, 1922, New York, N.Y.
d. Jan. 22, 1992

A. J. Liebling once wrote of Graham, "He was as good as a fighter can be without being a hell of a fighter." In 15 years and 126 professional fights, Graham was never knocked down. He had just two title fights, both against Kid Gavilan for the world welterweight championship. On August 29, 1951, Graham lost a controversial decision to Gavilan at Madison Square Garden. He lost another decision to Gavilan in Havana on October 5, 1952.

Graham retired in 1955 after losing four consecutive fights. He had 102 victories, 26 by knockout; 15 losses, all by decision; and 9 draws.

★ International Boxing Hall of Fame

Graham, James R.

TRAP SHOOTING
b. Feb. 12, 1873, Long Lake, Ill.
d. Feb. 18, 1950

Although he wasn't familiar with the international version of trap shooting, called clay pigeon shooting, Graham won an individual gold medal at the 1912 Olympics and also led the U.S. to the team championship. Graham, who once broke 432 consecutive targets, became a professional soon after his Olympic victory.

Graham, Otto E., Jr.

FOOTBALL
b. Dec. 6, 1921, Waukegan, Ill.

Graham went to Northwestern University on a basketball scholarship. When "Pappy" Waldorf saw him throwing a football in an intramural game, he got him to come out for the team as a sophomore, and Graham immediately became the starting tailback. He set a Big Ten record in 1942, his junior season, by completing 89 of 182 passes for 1,092 yards. As a senior, he was an All-American in both football and basketball.

After graduating, Graham spent two years in the Navy and then joined the Cleveland Browns of the new All America Football Conference, where he became a T formation quarterback for the first time. Using a "pass and trap" offense in which Graham's passing ability was employed to set up trap runs by other backs, Cleveland was the most successful team in pro football for the next decade.

The Browns won all four AAFC championships, winning 52 games while losing only 4 and tying 3. Graham led in touchdown passes with 17 in 1946 and 25 in 1947; in passing percentage in 1947 with 60.6; and in yardage with 2,753 in 1947, 2,713 in 1948, and 2,785 in 1949.

When the AAFC folded in 1950, the Browns entered the NFL. Most experts felt they would be overmatched against the stronger competition, but Cleveland won the NFL championship by beating the Los Angeles Rams 30–28, with Graham throwing four touchdown passes. Four years later, he passed for three touchdowns and ran for three in a 56–10 championship victory over the Detroit Lions.

Graham announced his retirement after that season, but he returned in 1955 after Cleveland got off to a slow start and led the Browns to yet another championship, passing for two touchdowns and running for two more to beat Los Angeles 38–14 in the title game.

All-league quarterback in all four AAFC seasons, Graham was also an NFL All-Pro in 1951, 1953, 1954, and 1955, and he was named the league's player of the year in 1953 and 1955. He led the NFL in completion percentage from 1953 through 1955; in yardage in 1952 and 1953; and in touchdown passes in 1952.

During his ten professional seasons, Graham completed 1,464 of 2,626 attempts for 23,584 yards and 174 touchdowns. He rushed 405 times for 882 yards, a 2.2 average, and 44 touchdowns.

In 1959, Graham became football coach at the Coast Guard Academy, where he produced an undefeated team in 1963. The Washington Redskins hired him as head coach in 1966 and he had a 17–22–3 record in four seasons there before returning to the Coast Guard Academy as athletic director in 1970. He retired in 1984.

★ College Football Hall of Fame; Pro Football Hall of Fame

Grange, Red (Harold E.)
FOOTBALL
b. June 13, 1903, Forksville, Pa.
d. Jan. 28, 1991

After winning 16 letters in four sports in high school, Grange entered the University of Illinois in 1922. He was one of more than 300 players who turned out for freshman football, and he decided he'd never make the team. But his fraternity brothers pressured him into going back to the practice field. He not only made the team, he scored two touchdowns in a scrimmage against the varsity, one of them on a 60-yard punt return.

Wearing the number 77 that he soon made famous, Grange started as a sophomore and scored three touchdowns, on runs of 12, 35, and 60 yards, in his first game. Against the University of Chicago, he returned an interception 43 yards to set up the winning touchdown — which he scored. He had a 92-yard interception return against Northwestern. After leading the Western Conference (now the Big Ten) in scoring, he was named an All-American halfback.

Early in the 1924 season, Illinois faced a University of Michigan team that had been unbeaten in 20 consecutive games. Michigan athletic director and former coach "Hurry-Up" Yost assured the press, "Mr. Grange will be carefully watched every time he takes the ball. There will be eleven clean, hard Michigan tacklers headed for him."

Grange responded by scoring touchdowns the first four times he touched the ball, in 12 minutes of the first quarter. He began with a 95-yard kickoff return, then had runs of 67, 56, and 45 yards from scrimmage. He was taken out until the third quarter, when he scored on a 12-yard run. Then he threw a 23-yard touchdown pass as Illinois won, 39–14.

After scoring three touchdowns in a 21–21 tie with the University of Chicago, Grange was injured during the game with Minnesota, and Illinois lost. He missed the final game of the season, a victory over Ohio State, but was still an All-American for the second year in a row.

Already known as the Galloping Ghost and the Illinois Flash, Grange captained the Illini in 1925. After the young team lost three of its first four games, he was moved to quarterback, and Illinois won the final four games. Grange's greatest performance came on a muddy field against Pennsylvania before 65,000 spectators. He gained 363 yards on 36 carries, scoring three touchdowns, in a 24–2 victory.

An All-American for the third time, Grange left college immediately after his final game to tour with the Chicago Bears. He actually had a personal services contract for more than $100,000 with promoter Charles C. "Cash and Carry" Pyle, who in turn sold his services to the Bears.

The tour was not totally successful. Grange missed several games with injury and played only briefly in several others. However, he attracted 65,000 fans in New York, by far the largest crowd to have seen a professional game at that time. That record was broken in January, when 75,000 turned out in Los Angeles to watch Grange and the Bears.

Pyle also got Grange a role in a football movie, *One Minute to Play*, and Grange later did a vaudeville tour and two other movies. One of Pyle's ambitions was to get a New York franchise in the NFL, but he was turned down, so he started the American Football League, with Grange playing for the New York Yankees. The AFL barely made it through the 1926 season, and the Yankees were then admitted into the NFL. Grange's knee was badly injured in a game against the Bears, and he was never again the same player.

After sitting out the 1928 season, he joined the Bears in 1929 and played with them through 1934. No longer an outstanding runner, he was still a very good player and a genuine defensive star. He was named to the first official All-Pro team chosen, in 1931, and was an All-Pro again in 1932.

When the Bears beat the Portsmouth Spartans for the 1932 NFL championship, Grange scored the only touchdown on a pass from Bronko Nagurski. And he saved the 1933 championship game against the New York Giants. With the Bears leading, 23–21, in the closing seconds, a Giant halfback broke loose and had a teammate trailing him, waiting for a lateral. Grange alertly pinioned the runner's arms to keep him from lateraling the ball and then threw him to the ground.

After missing the 1934 championship game with an injury, Grange played in a post-season exhibition game on January 27, 1935. He broke into the open on a 50-yard run but was caught from behind by a lineman. He decided it was time to retire.

★ College Football Hall of Fame; Pro Football Hall of Fame

Grant, Bud (Harold P.)
FOOTBALL
b. May 20, 1927, Superior, Wis.

Grant played football and basketball at the Great Lakes Naval Training Center after graduating from high school in 1945, and he then entered the University of Minnesota, where he starred in baseball, basketball, and football.

The first-round draft choice of the NFL's Philadelphia Eagles in 1950, the 6-foot-3, 195-pound Grant chose to play basketball with the Minneapolis Lakers of the NBA. He was a backup forward on the 1949–50 championship team. After another year with the Lakers, Grant joined the Eagles for the 1952 football season.

He spent his first season as a defensive end and was switched to offense in 1953, when he caught 56 passes for 997 yards and 7 touchdowns. Grant then went to the Winnipeg Blue Bombers of the Canadian Football League.

After leading the CFL in receptions three times in four seasons, Grant was named Winnipeg's head coach in 1957. He guided the team to four Grey Cup championships in ten years, compiling a 102–56–2 record.

Grant took over the NFL's Minnesota Vikings in 1966. He had a 3–8–3 record in his first season with the Vikings and then produced 11 Central Division champions, winning the NFL title in 1969 and

NFC championships in 1973, 1974, and 1976. The major blemish on Grant's coaching record was his failure to win a Super Bowl in four tries.

He retired after the 1983 season, came back for one more year in 1985, then retired permanently. In 18 seasons with the Vikings, Grant had a 168–108–5 record.

★ Pro Football Hall of Fame

Gray, Mel

FOOTBALL
b. March 16, 1961, Williamsburg, Va.

The 5-foot-9, 171-pound Gray spent two years at a junior college before going to Purdue University. He began his professional football career with the Los Angeles Express of the U.S. Football League in 1984.

A running back with Los Angeles, Gray rushed 258 times for 1,151 yards, a 4.5 average, and 4 touchdowns in two seasons. He joined the NFL's New Orleans Saints in 1986 and has been used primarily as a kick returner since then, with some time at wide receiver.

Gray led the NFL in punt return average in 1987, when he returned 24 punts for 352 yards, a 14.7 average. He became an unconditional free agent after the 1988 season and signed with the Detroit Lions.

In 1991, Gray led the league in punt and kickoff return average. He ran back 25 punts for 385 yards, a 15.4 average, and 1 touchdown, and returned 36 kickoffs for 929 yards, a 25.8 average. He was the kickoff return leader again in 1994, when he ran back 45 for 1,276 yards, a 28.4 average, and 3 touchdowns.

Through 1994, Gray had returned 181 punts for 2,084 yards, an average of 11.5 yards, and he had run back 309 kickoffs for 7,650 yards, an average of 24.8 yards. He had 3 touchdowns on punt returns and 6 on kickoff returns.

Grayson, Bobby (Robert H.)

FOOTBALL
b. Dec. 8, 1914, Portland, Oreg.
d. Dec. 21, 1981

Grantland Rice wrote of Grayson,

"Here is a big, fast back who can run an end, hit a line, kick, pass, block, and handle any assignment given him." An All-American fullback in 1934 and 1935, Grayson played at Stanford in "Pop" Warner's double wing, in which the fullback handled the ball on virtually every play and had to be a triple threat.

The 6-foot, 190-pounder could run the 100-yard dash in 9.8 seconds, so he had the power to run into the line and the speed to outrun defenders once he broke through it. In the 1935 Rose Bowl, a 7–0 loss to Columbia University, Grayson rushed for 151 yards, a bowl record for 20 years.

Grayson was the first draft choice of the NFL's Pittsburgh Pirates (now Steelers) in 1936, but he chose to go to law school rather than play professional football.

★ College Football Hall of Fame

Graziano, Rocky [Thomas Rocco Barbella]

BOXING
b. Jan. 1, 1922, New York, N.Y.

A product of New York City's tough Lower East Side, Graziano was continually in trouble during his teenage years. Drafted into the Army early in 1942, he soon went absent without leave and took the ring name of a friend, Tommy Rocky Graziano, to become a professional fighter.

He had eight fights in less than three months before the Army caught him. He was given a dishonorable discharge and sentenced to a year in military prison, where he joined the boxing team. Released in June 1943, he again became a professional boxer, still using his ring name.

A nonstop street fighter, Graziano had three historic bouts with Tony Zale. In the first, a middleweight championship fight on September 27, 1946, Zale seemed on the verge of collapse under Graziano's pounding, but he suddenly scored a 6th-round knockout to hold on to the title.

Though he was popular with fight fans because of his style, Graziano was not so popular with boxing officials. The

New York State Athletic Commission suspended his license in 1947 for allegedly failing to report a bribe attempt, so a rematch with Zale was moved to Chicago Stadium. The $422,918 gate was a record for an indoor fight.

Despite intense heat, neither fighter ever backed down. Graziano's right eye was almost closed and he had a bad cut next to his left eye when he knocked out Zale in the 6th round. He later wrote of the fight, "This was no boxing match. It was a war, and if there wasn't a referee, one of the two of us would have ended up dead."

Illinois then passed a law barring anyone with a dishonorable discharge from boxing. The third Graziano–Zale fight was held in Newark on June 10, 1948, and Zale regained the title with a 3rd-round knockout.

Graziano won 20 of his next 21 fights, but he was knocked out in the 3rd round by Sugar Ray Robinson in a middleweight championship fight on April 16, 1952. After losing a decision in his next bout, he retired.

He didn't leave the public eye, though. He appeared in television shows and movies, exhibited his paintings in galleries, and published a popular autobiography, *Somebody Up There Likes Me*, which was adapted into a successful movie starring Paul Newman.

In 83 professional fights, Graziano had 67 victories, 52 by knockout. He lost 10, 3 by knockout, and fought 6 draws.
★ International Boxing Hall of Fame

Greb, Harry (Edward Henry)
BOXING
b. June 6, 1894, Pittsburgh, Pa.
d. Oct. 22, 1926

The 5-foot-8, 158-pound Greb was a fearless, aggressive fighter known as the "Pittsburgh Windmill" because he threw punches in nonstop flurries. Though he fought mostly as a middleweight, Greb won the American light-heavyweight title by beating Gene Tunney on August 19, 1926. It was Tunney's only professional defeat.

Greb began fighting in 1913 and won the middleweight championship with a 15-round decision over Johnny Wilson on August 31, 1923. He defended the championship six times before losing it to Tiger Flowers in 15 rounds on February 26, 1926. He retired later that year after losing an August 19 rematch to Flowers. Greb died two months later while undergoing an eye operation.

He won 106 fights, 46 of them by knockout, and lost only 9, 2 by knockout. Greb also had 3 draws, 166 no-decisions, and 1 no-contest.
★ International Boxing Hall of Fame

Green, Roy
FOOTBALL
b. June 30, 1957, Magnolia, Ark.

A defensive back at little Henderson State College in Arkansas, the 6-foot-1, 195-pound Green played that position during his first two seasons with the NFL's St. Louis Cardinals, 1979 and 1980. Because of his speed and great hands, he was moved to wide receiver during the 1981 season.

Green led the league with 14 touchdown receptions in 1983, when he caught 78 passes for 1,227 yards. In 1984, he was the NFL leader in reception yardage with 1,555 on 78 catches.

The Cardinals moved to Phoenix in 1988. Green was traded to the Cleveland Browns before the 1991 season, but the Browns released him, and he was picked up by the Philadelphia Eagles. He retired after catching only eight passes in nine games in 1992.

Green caught 559 passes during his NFL career, gaining 8,965 yards, a 16.0 average, and scoring 66 touchdowns. He also rushed 23 times for 140 yards and 1 touchdown; returned 27 punts for 230 yards and 1 touchdown; and ran back 89 kickoffs for 2,002 yards and 1 touchdown.

Greenberg, Hank (Henry B.)
BASEBALL
b. Jan. 1, 1911, New York, N.Y.
d. Sept. 4, 1986

A right-handed first baseman, Greenberg put up some amazing RBI figures during his career and once challenged

Babe Ruth's record of 60 home runs in a season.

The 6-foot-3½, 210-pound Greenberg starred in basketball as well as baseball in high school, then signed a contract with the Detroit Tigers that allowed him to enter New York University in 1929. However, he left school in the spring of 1930 to pursue his baseball career.

Greenberg had just one at-bat with the Tigers that year and didn't rejoin the team until 1933, when he became a starter. He led the AL in doubles with 63 in 1934, when he hit .339 with 26 home runs and 139 RBI to help lead the Tigers into the World Series. Despite Greenberg's .321 average and 7 RBI, Detroit lost to the St. Louis Cardinals.

He was named the league's most valuable player in 1935. He hit .328 that season and led the league with 36 home runs and 170 RBI. The Tigers won the World Series, but Greenberg suffered a broken wrist in the second game.

The wrist was broken again early in the 1936 season, and Greenberg appeared in only 12 games. However, he came back with 40 home runs and 183 RBI, one short of Lou Gehrig's AL record, in 1937, and the following year he hit 58 home runs to tie Jimmy Foxx's record for a right-handed hitter.

After slipping to 33 home runs and 112 RBI in 1939, Greenberg was moved to the outfield to make room for Rudy York at first base. He responded by leading the league in doubles with 50, home runs with 41, RBI with 150, and slugging percentage with a .670 mark to win his second most valuable player award.

Drafted early in 1941, Greenberg became a captain in the Army Air Corps and took part in the first bombing raids on Tokyo in 1944. He rejoined the Tigers during the 1945 season and hit a ninth-inning grand-slam home run in the last game of the season to win another pennant for the Tigers. They went on to beat the Chicago Cubs in a seven-game World Series in which Greenberg batted .304 with 2 home runs, 7 RBI, and 7 runs scored.

After leading the league in home runs and RBI again, with 44 and 127 in 1946, Greenberg was sold to the NL's Pittsburgh Pirates. He retired after slipping to .249, 25 home runs, and 74 RBI in one season there, and became vice president and farm director for the Cleveland Indians. In 1959, he went to the Chicago White Sox as vice president, then retired to go into private business.

★ Baseball Hall of Fame

Greene, Mean Joe (Charles E.)
FOOTBALL
b. Sept. 24, 1946, Temple, Tex.

After playing defensive tackle at little North Texas State College, Greene was the surprise first-round draft choice of the NFL's Pittsburgh Steelers in 1969. He soon became the leader of the "Steel Curtain" defensive unit that helped the Steelers win four Super Bowls.

The 6-foot-4, 260-pound Greene was extremely fast off the ball, so much so that opponents sometimes accused him of being offside when he wasn't. He pioneered the technique of lining up at an angle, with one shoulder pointing at the gap between two offensive linemen rather than being square to the line of scrimmage.

The NFL's defensive rookie of the year in 1969, Greene was named an All-Pro eight consecutive years, from 1970 through 1977, and he was voted defensive player of the year in 1972 and 1974. One teammate said that having Greene on the squad "was like having a big brother around when the bullies were coming to fight you." Greene retired after the 1981 season and later became Pittsburgh's defensive line coach.

★ Pro Football Hall of Fame

Greene, Nancy C.
SKIING
b. May 11, 1943, Ottawa, Ont.

The winner of the first two women's World Cup competitions, in 1967 and 1968, Greene was the only North American to win the title until Tamara McKinney of the U.S. in 1983.

Greene won a gold medal in the Olympic giant slalom and a silver in the slalom at the 1968 Winter Olympics.

She also won four U.S. championships, the downhill in 1960, the downhill, giant slalom, and Alpine combined in 1965.

★ Canadian Sports Hall of Fame

Greenleaf, Ralph

BILLIARDS
b. Nov. 3, 1899, Monmouth, Ill.
d. March 15, 1950

Generally ranked second to Willie Mosconi among the all-time great pocket billiards players, Greenleaf won the world professional title 6 times and defended it 13 times.

He held the championship from 1919 through 1924 and also won it in 1926, 1928, 1929, 1931, 1932, and 1937. He set records in 1929 for high single-game average, 63, and high grand average, 11.02, on a 5- by 10-foot table.

A colorful showman, Greenleaf continued to attract spectators to exhibition matches until his death of a heart attack in 1950.

Greer, Frank B.

ROWING
b. 1879, East Boston, Mass.
d. May 7, 1943

In 1904 Greer became the first Olympic single sculls champion. He won the national 1½-mile championship from 1903 through 1905, and in 1908 and he was the Canadian champion from 1903 through 1905. Greer coached the Detroit Athletic Club rowing teams for several years after retiring from competition, then moved back to Boston and became the deputy sheriff in charge of the Suffolk County Jail.

Greer, Hal (Harold E.)

BASKETBALL
b. June 26, 1936, Huntington, W.Va.

The first black to play at Marshall University in West Virginia, Greer captained the team and averaged 23.6 points a game in his senior year, 1957–58. He played for Jules Rivlin, who had coached Paul Seymour at the University of Toledo. Rivlin recommended him to Seymour, then coaching the Syracuse Na-

tionals, who chose him in the second round of the NBA draft.

Gifted with exceptional speed and a fine outside shooting touch, Greer was unique in using a jump shot on his free throw attempts. A 6-foot-2, 175-pound guard, he played in the NBA for 15 seasons and averaged more than 20 points a game eight times.

The Nationals became the Philadelphia 76ers in 1963. Greer averaged 22.1 points per game in 1966–67, when the 76ers finally dethroned the Boston Celtics and won the NBA championship.

Greer retired after the 1972–73 season. In 1,122 games, he scored 21,586 points, an average of 19.2 per game, and had 4,540 assists. He scored 1,876 points and had 303 assists in 92 playoff games.

★ Basketball Hall of Fame

Gregg, Forrest (Alvin Forrest)

FOOTBALL
b. Oct. 18, 1933, Birthright, Tex.

Called by Vince Lombardi "the finest player I ever coached," Gregg was a two-way tackle at Southern Methodist University and expected to play defense with the Green Bay Packers when he joined them in 1956, but the Packers put him on offense.

Small for an offensive tackle at 6-foot-4 and 250 pounds, Gregg used intelligence and intensive study of game films to learn how to handle larger defensive ends by anticipating their moves. His speed made it possible for the Packers to design some plays that called for a tackle rather than a guard to pull out and lead interference, which was very unusual at the time.

Because of injuries, Gregg played extensively at guard in 1961 and 1965. He was named an All-Pro eight consecutive years, from 1960 through 1967. In 1965, United Press International named him an All-Pro tackle, and he was a guard on the Associated Press All-Pro team.

Gregg retired after the 1970 season but joined the Dallas Cowboys after that team suffered a series of injuries to offensive linemen. Having won two Super Bowl rings with the Packers, Gregg won a third with Dallas before retiring for good.

Gregg became head coach of the Cleveland Browns in 1975 and was fired with one game remaining in the 1977 season after compiling an 18–23 record. He took over the Cincinnati Bengals in 1980 and was named AFC coach of the year in 1981, when he took the Bengals to the Super Bowl, where they lost, 26–21, to the San Francisco 49ers. He had a 32–25 record in four seasons, then returned to Green Bay as head coach in 1984.

After compiling a 25–37–1 record in four seasons, Gregg went back to Southern Methodist. The school had been banned from playing football for two seasons because of recruiting violations, so he had to rebuild the program completely. He had a 3-19 record in 1988 and 1989, and then left coaching to become the school's athletic director.

★ Pro Football Hall of Fame

Gretzky, Wayne D.

HOCKEY
b. Jan. 26, 1961, Brantford, Ont.

He is, simply, the "Great One," a player of unsurpassed skills who dominated hockey as no other single player has ever dominated a team sport.

Gretzky began playing professionally when he was only 16. After two minor league seasons, he joined the Indianapolis Racers of the World Hockey Association in 1978 but was traded to the Edmonton Oilers after only eight games. He scored 46 goals and had 64 assists and was named the league's rookie of the year.

The WHA folded, and Edmonton moved into the NHL the following season, when Gretzky began putting up really big numbers: 137 points in 1979–80, 164 in 1980–81, 212 in 1981–82, 196 in 1982–83, 205 in 1983–84, 208 in 1984–85, 215 in 1985–86, 183 in 1986–87, leading the league each time.

A knee injury cut into his playing time in 1987–88, and he scored "only" 149 points, falling short of a ninth consecutive scoring title. Gretzky then announced that he no longer wanted to play for Edmonton, and he was sent to the Los Angeles Kings in a mammoth trade involving four other players, three first-round draft choices, and cash.

Gretzky led the NHL in scoring again with 142 points in 1989–90 and 163 in 1990–91. After slipping to 121 points in 1991–92, he underwent an operation for a herniated disc and missed the first 39 games of the 1992–93 season, when he scored 65 points in just 45 games.

A list of Gretzky's records would probably require more than a page. Among the highlights: most points, 2,458, most goals, 803, and most assists, 1,655, in a career; most goals in a season, 92, in 1981–82; most assists in a season, 163, in 1985–86; most points in a season, 215, in 1985–86; most goals, 110, most assists, 236, and most points, 346, in a playoff career; most games with 3 or more goals, 48; most seasons with 100 or more points, 14; highest average assists per game, 1.471, and points per game, 2.185.

The Associated Press male athlete of the year in 1982, Gretzky won the Hart Memorial Trophy as the league's most valuable player a record nine times, from 1980 through 1987 and in 1989, and the Ross Memorial Trophy as the top scorer a record nine times, from 1981 through 1987, in 1990, and in 1991.

Griese, Bob (Robert A.)

FOOTBALL
b. Feb. 3, 1945, Evansville, Ind.

A consensus All-American quarterback at Purdue as a junior in 1965, Griese completed 348 of 690 passes for 4,402 yards in three seasons. He joined the Miami Dolphins of the American Football League in 1967 and became the team's starter during his rookie season.

The 6-foot-1, 190-pound Griese was a very accurate short passer and sure ball handler who was the ideal leader for the ball control offense installed by Don Shula when he became head coach in 1970.

Griese quarterbacked the Dolphins to 17 wins in as many games during the 1972 season and completed 8 of only 11 passes for 88 yards in the 14–7 win over the Washington Redskins in Super Bowl VII. He was 6 of 7 for 73 yards when Miami crushed Minnesota, 24–7, the following year.

He played in six Pro Bowls and was named an All-Pro in 1971 and 1977. Griese retired after the 1980 season. In his 14 years as a professional, he completed 1,926 of 3,429 passes for 25,092 yards and 192 touchdowns. He also rushed for 7 touchdowns.

★ College Football Hall of Fame; Pro Football Hall of Fame

Griffey, Ken, Jr. (George Kenneth Jr.)
BASEBALL
b. Nov. 21, 1969, Donora, Pa.

Griffey's father, Ken Griffey, Sr., was a major league outfielder from 1973 through 1991. They were teammates during Ken Jr.'s first three seasons with the AL's Seattle Mariners, becoming the only father-son combination to play in the major leagues at the same time.

A left-handed outfielder, the 6-foot-3, 205-pound Griffey spent just two seasons in the minor leagues before joining the Mariners. After batting .264 as a rookie, he has hit .300 or better every season since, with a high of .327 in 1991. Griffey had career highs with 45 home runs and 109 RBI in 1993.

The winner of four consecutive Gold Glove awards, from 1990 through 1993, Griffey led the league's outfielders with ten assists in 1989. In 1993, he tied a major league record by hitting home runs in 8 consecutive games.

Through 1994, Griffey had a career .306 average with 972 hits, including 194 doubles, 19 triples, and 172 home runs. He had stolen 88 bases, scored 518 runs, and driven in 543.

Griffin, Archie M.
FOOTBALL
b. Aug. 21, 1954, Columbus, Ohio

Called by Ohio State coach Woody Hayes "the greatest player I've ever been associated with," Griffin is the only player ever to win the Heisman Trophy twice, in 1974 and 1975. He also won the 1975 Maxwell Trophy as the nation's outstanding college player.

Griffin set an NCAA record by rushing for more than 100 yards in 31 consecutive games. During four years as a starter, he gained 5,177 yards on 845 attempts, a 6.1 average. He was the first player to rush for more than 5,000 career yards.

He joined the NFL's Cincinnati Bengals in 1975 and played for them through the 1982 season, then retired because of injuries. Griffin made a brief comeback with the Jacksonville Bulls of the U.S. Football League in 1985 but retired again after carrying the ball only ten times.

In his eight NFL seasons, the 5-foot-9, 185-pound Griffin carried the ball 691 times for 2,808 yards, a 4.1 average, and 7 touchdowns. He caught 192 passes for 1,607 yards, an 8.4 average, and 6 touchdowns.

★ College Football Hall of Fame

Griffith, Clark C.
BASEBALL
b. Nov. 10, 1869, Clear Creek, Mo. d. Oct. 27, 1955

One of only two baseball players to become owners, Clark Griffith moved to Bloomington, Illinois, with his mother as a young teenager. He began pitching for a town team in 1887 and turned professional the following year.

Griffith entered the major leagues with the St. Louis team in the American Association, then was sold to Boston. He had a 17–7 combined record but developed a sore arm and was released.

At the end of the 1893 season, Griffith joined the NL's Chicago Cubs, where he became the team's ace, winning 21 or more games six consecutive seasons, from 1894 through 1899. When the AL was established as a major league in 1901, Griffith went across town to the White Sox, leading the league in winning percentage at .774 on a 24–7 record and in shutouts with 5.

In 1903, Griffith became player-manager of the AL's New York Highlanders. His pitching career effectively ended in 1907, though he made several more appearances over the next few years. Griffith managed the Cincinnati Reds from 1909 through 1911, then bought a 10 percent interest in the Washington Senators, managing the team from 1912 through 1920, when he increased his ownership share to 40 percent and became president of the team.

As a pitcher, the 5-foot-7, 156-pound Griffith achieved his success by doctoring the ball in a variety of ways, which was legal at the time. As an owner, he was a vigorous proponent of banning the spitball and other such pitches in 1920.

Griffith was the first to scout and sign Cuban players, as early as 1911, and he seriously considered signing the great black catcher, Josh Gibson, to a contract in the late 1930s. His family still ran the franchise after it was moved to Minnesota in 1961.

★ Baseball Hall of Fame

Griffith, Emile A.

BOXING
b. Feb. 3, 1938, St. Thomas, Virgin Islands

When he was 13, Griffith's family moved to New York City, and he got a job in a hat factory three years later. In his prime, Griffith was 5-foot-7½ and weighed 155 pounds but had a 26-inch waist. His physique caught the eye of the fight manager Howard Albert, who brought in trainer Gil Clancy to work with Griffith.

After two successful years as an amateur, Griffith had his first professional fight, a 4-round victory, on June 2, 1958. He won 21 of his next 23 bouts before being matched against Benny "Kid" Paret for the welterweight title at Miami Beach on April 1, 1961. Griffith won with a knockout in the 13th round.

He lost the title to Paret in a controversial 15-round split decision on September 30. Their third fight took place on March 24, 1962, in New York. Griffith trapped Paret against the ropes in the 12th round and pummeled him with a long series of punches. Paret went into a coma and died a week later.

Griffith lost the title again, to Luis Rodriguez, on March 21, 1963, and regained it on June 8. He tried to move up to the American middleweight champi-

onship against Don Fullmer on August 20, 1965, but lost a 12-round decision.

Nevertheless, Griffith fought for the world middleweight title on April 25, 1966, against Dick Tiger, and he won a 15-round decision, becoming the third fighter to hold both the welterweight and middleweight championships.

Griffith and Nino Benvenuti of Italy had a series of three fights in which the middleweight title changed hands, all 15-round decisions. Benvenuti used his longer reach to win on April 17, 1967. Griffith reclaimed the title on September 29, 1967, but lost it on March 4, 1968.

He lost his welterweight title to Jose Napoles on October 18, 1969, but continued fighting for another eight years. He retired after three consecutive losses in 1977.

Griffith used foot and hand speed to throw a lot of short, quick punches and combinations, but often seemed to lose his concentration and focus, even during important fights. Ironically, he was often accused of lacking the "killer instinct." He won 85 professional fights, 23 by knockout, and lost 25, 2 by knockout. He also fought 2 draws and 1 nocontest.

★ International Boxing Hall of Fame

Griffith-Joyner, Florence (Delorez Florence)

TRACK AND FIELD
b. Dec. 21, 1959, Los Angeles, Calif.

"Flo-Jo" entered California State at Northridge in 1979 and followed the track coach, Bob Kersee, to UCLA in 1981. She won the NCAA 200-meter championship in 1982 and the 400-meter title in 1983.

At the 1984 Olympics, Griffith took a silver medal in the 200-meter run. She married Al Joyner, gold medal winner in the triple jump, in 1987 and took the hyphenated name under which she became best known.

Griffith-Joyner set a world record of 10.49 seconds in the 100-meter dash at the 1988 U.S. Olympic trials, and she won the 200-meter in a U.S. record 21.77

seconds. She took three gold medals at the Olympics, in both individual sprints and in the 400-meter relay, running a world record 21.34 seconds in the 200-meter, and she also ran on the 1,600-meter relay team that won a silver.

After being named female athlete of the year by the Associated Press and winning the Sullivan Award as the nation's outstanding amateur athlete, Griffith-Joyner retired from competition. Known for her glamorous track outfits, she began designing and modeling clothes.

Griffo, Young [Albert Griffiths]
BOXING
b. March 31, 1871, Sydney, Australia
d. Dec. 7, 1927

Griffiths began fighting as a teenager on the Sydney waterfront. His first professional match was a bare-knuckle fight sometime before 1889. By 1889, he was using the ring name Young Griffo.

He was among a group of Australian fighters who boarded a ship to sail to the United States in 1892, but he changed his mind at the last minute, jumped off the ship, and swam back to shore. Griffo finally did come to America late in 1893.

The first loss of his career was a 10-round decision against lightweight champion Jack McAuliffe on August 27, 1894. The speedy, clever Griffo won the fight, according to many observers, but referee Maxie Moore was a friend of McAuliffe's, and he awarded him the decision.

Griffo's heavy drinking often affected his performances and, on one occasion, kept him from showing up for a fight. Although he had wins or draws against some of the best boxers of his time, including George Dixon, Joe Gans, Solly Smith, and George "Kid" Lavigne, he never had a title fight.

He retired after being knocked out in the first round by Tommy White in 1904, returned briefly for two fights in 1911, then retired for good. Of 107 recorded bouts, Griffo won 49, 5 by knockout; lost 9, 3 by knockout; and had 37 draws and 12 no-decisions.
★ International Boxing Hall of Fame

Grimes, Burleigh A.
BASEBALL
b. Aug. 18, 1893, Emerald, Wis.
d. Dec. 6, 1985

The last major league pitcher to throw the spitball legally, the right-handed Grimes joined the NL's Pittsburgh Pirates in 1916 and spent parts of two seasons there before being traded to the Brooklyn Robins in 1918.

Grimes led the league in winning percentage at .676 on a 23–11 record in 1920, and he led in victories with a 22–13 mark and in strikeouts with 136 the following season. Brooklyn traded him to the New York Giants in 1927, and after one season there he went back to Pittsburgh.

His best year was 1928, when he led in victories with a 25–14 record, complete games with 28, shutouts with 4, and innings pitched with 330⅔. He spent the 1930 season with the Boston Braves and St. Louis Cardinals, went to the Chicago Cubs in 1932, returned to the Cardinals during the 1933 season, and had a combined 4–5 record with the Cardinals, Pittsburgh, and the New York Yankees in 1934 before retiring.

When the spitball and other such pitches were made illegal in 1920, exceptions were made for 17 established major leaguers who used the pitch extensively. Grimes was unusual among spitballers in that he held the ball tightly, and he may have been the first to use slippery elm.

Known as "Old Stubblebeard" because he never shaved on a day he was pitching, Grimes managed extensively in the minor leagues and also scouted for major league teams until leaving baseball in 1971. He managed the Brooklyn Dodgers in 1937 and 1938.

Grimes had a 270–212 record, with 35 shutouts and a 3.53 ERA, in 19 seasons. He struck out 1,512 hitters and walked 1,295 in 4179⅔ innings.
★ Baseball Hall of Fame

Grissom, Marquis D.
BASEBALL
b. April 17, 1967, Atlanta, Ga.

Grissom led the NL in steals in his first two full seasons. He entered the league with the Montreal Expos in 1989, appearing in 26 games, and became a starter in 1990, but an injury limited him to just 98 games that season.

A right-handed outfielder, the 5-foot-11, 190-pound Grissom batted .267 in 1991 and stole 76 bases, and he had 78 steals in 1992, when he hit .276. Grissom improved greatly as a hitter in 1993, batting .295 with 19 home runs and 95 RBI. His stolen base total declined to 53, partly because he was moved from lead-off to the third spot in the batting order for much of the season.

Through 1994, Grissom had a .279 average on 747 hits, including 130 doubles, 23 triples, and 54 home runs. He had stolen 266 bases, scored 430 runs, and driven in 276.

Groat, Dick Richard M.

BASEBALL, BASKETBALL
b. Nov. 4, 1930, Swissvale, Pa.

A rare two-sport star, Groat played both major league baseball and professional basketball after graduating from college. After just one season of basketball, he decided to concentrate on his baseball career.

The 6-foot-1, 185-pound Groat was twice an All-American at Duke, in 1951 and 1952, and he was named Helms player of the year as a junior in 1951, when he set an NCAA record with 831 points. He was also a collegiate All-American shortstop in his junior and senior years.

Groat joined the Pittsburgh Pirates in 1952 without ever playing in the minor leagues and batted .284 in 95 games. He averaged 11.9 points per game in 26 games with the NBA's Ft. Wayne Pistons before being inducted into military service for two years.

He returned to the Pirates as their starting shortstop in 1955 and remained with them through the 1962 season. During that stretch, Groat batted over .300 four times and led the National League with a .325 average in 1960, when the Pirates beat the New York Yankees in the World Series. Groat was named the National League's most valuable player that year.

He was traded to the St. Louis Cardinals in 1963 and to the Philadelphia Phillies in 1966, his last year as a starter. After he had played 10 games with the Phillies in 1967, they traded him to the San Francisco Giants. Groat retired after that season.

He had a career batting average of .286, with 2,138 hits in 7,484 at-bats. He led the National League with 43 doubles in 1963.

Grossfeld, Muriel (Davis)

GYMNASTICS
b. 1941, Indianapolis, Ind.

Muriel Davis studied ballet for seven years before taking up gymnastics when she was 14. Because of her early training, she was an exceptionally graceful performer who won 17 national championships over a period of nine years.

She won the national all-around championship in 1957 and 1963; the floor exercise from 1956 through 1958 and from 1960 through 1964; the balance beam in 1957, 1959, and from 1962 through 1964; and the uneven parallel bars in 1960 and 1963.

A member of the U.S. Olympic team in 1956, 1960, and 1964, she married the gymnast Abie Grossfeld in 1960. Despite her accomplishments as a competitor, she became better known as a coach during a period when Americans were becoming more aware of gymnastics because of television coverage.

She began coaching in 1962 with her own club. She has also coached with the national training program for gymnastics, the women's Pan-American Games team, and the U.S. women's team in the North American championships. A tough disciplinarian, she was referred to by one journalist as "the tyrant of women's gymnastic coaches."
★ International Women's Sports Hall of Fame

Grove, Lefty (Robert M.)

BASEBALL
b. March 6, 1900, Lonaconing, Md.
d. May 22, 1975

Grove got to the major leagues late in life because he didn't enter professional baseball until he was 20, and then he spent 4½ years as the property of the minor league Baltimore Orioles, where he won 109 games while losing only 36.

In 1925, Baltimore finally sold him to the AL's Philadelphia Athletics for $100,600, $600 more than the Red Sox had paid Baltimore for Babe Ruth. After a slow start because he had trouble controlling his outstanding fastball, Grove won 20 or more games seven consecutive seasons, from 1927 through 1933.

Despite the early control problems, Grove led the AL in strikeouts the first seven years he was with Philadelphia, from 1925 through 1931. He led in victories with 24 in 1928, 28 in 1930, 31 in 1931, and 24 in 1933; in ERA with 2.51 in 1926, 2.81 in 1929, 2.54 in 1930, 2.06 in 1931, and 2.84 in 1932; and in shutouts with 4 each in 1931 and 1932.

Although he was primarily a starting pitcher, Grove was also excellent in relief when he had to be. In 1930, when he started 32 games and had 22 complete games, he actually led the AL with 9 saves.

The Athletics won three consecutive pennants, from 1929 through 1931, and he was the league's most valuable player in 1931. He picked up two saves in their five-game win over the Chicago Cubs in the 1929 World Series, and he had a 2–1 record with a 1.42 ERA in their six-game win over the St. Louis Cardinals in 1932. Grove was 2–1 again with a 2.42 ERA in 1931, when Philadelphia lost to the Cardinals in seven games.

Losing money during the Depression, the Athletics traded Grove to the Boston Red Sox in 1934. Arm trouble limited him to an 8–8 record that season. His fastball was no longer the same, but a good curve and his knowledge of how to pitch to hitters made him an effective pitcher for another five seasons, during which he led the league in ERA four times, with 2.70 in 1935, 2.81 in 1936, 3.08 in 1938, and 2.54 in 1939. He was also the league leader in shutouts with 6 in 1936 and in winning percentage at .789 in 1939, when he had a 15–4 record.

Grove struggled during his last two seasons with the Red Sox, but he won seven games in 1940 and in 1941 to reach the 300 mark, the eleventh pitcher to do so, before retiring.

During his 17 seasons, he had a 300–141 record with 35 shutouts and a 3.40 ERA. He struck out 2,266 hitters and walked 1,187 in 3,940⅔ innings.
★ Baseball Hall of Fame

Groza, Louis R.

FOOTBALL
b. Jan. 25, 1924, Martins Ferry, Ohio

Groza was a rarity, an outstanding offensive tackle who was also the finest kicker of his era and the first true kicking specialist. A starting tackle at Ohio State for two years, he joined the Cleveland Browns of the new All-America Football Conference in 1946 after military service in World War II.

Used primarily as a kicker in his rookie year, Groza led the league in scoring with 45 extra points and 13 field goals for a total of 84 points. He became Cleveland's starting tackle during the 1947 season and held the position until 1959.

The AAFC folded in 1950, and the Browns entered the NFL. They won the league championship that season when Groza kicked a field goal with 28 seconds remaining to beat the Los Angeles Rams, 30–28, in the title game.

Groza was an All-Pro tackle from 1951 through 1955 and in 1957. He led the NFL in field goals with 13 in 1950, 19 in 1952, 23 in 1953, 16 in 1954, and 15 in 1957. He was the league's leading scorer with 77 points in 1955.

A back injury forced Groza to miss the entire 1960 season, but he came back in 1961 as a kicker and played through 1967. In 21 seasons, all with the Browns, he converted 810 of 834 extra point attempts and 264 of 481 field goal attempts for a total of 1,608 points, a record at the time.
★ Pro Football Hall of Fame

Gruenig, Ace Robert F.

BASKETBALL
b. March 12, 1913, Chicago, Ill.
d. Aug. 11, 1958

An outstanding high school player in Chicago, the 6-foot-8, 230-pound Gruenig joined the Rosenburg-Avery AAU team after graduating in 1931. He became one of the all-time great players in a period when many of the nation's best players joined AAU teams rather than playing professionally.

Gruenig, a powerful rebounder who was one of the first hook shot specialists, played for the Denver Safeway team that won the national championship in 1937 and was named an All-American for the first time. In 1939, he joined the Denver Nuggets and led them to the championship. He played for a third national champion in 1942, the Denver Legion.

When he retired in 1948, he had been an AAU All-American 10 times in 11 seasons.

★ Basketball Hall of Fame

Guidry, Ronald A.

BASEBALL
b. Aug. 28, 1950, Lafayette, La.

Guidry's solid career as a winning pitcher was distinguished by four very good seasons. The 5-foot-11, 162-pound left-hander was with the New York Yankees briefly in 1975 and 1976, then joined them as a relief pitcher at the beginning of the 1977 season. He was soon moved into the starting rotation and had a 16–7 record, then won his only World Series start, 4–2, in the Yankees six-game victory over the Los Angeles Dodgers.

He won the AL's Cy Young Award and was named male athlete of the year by the Associated Press in 1978, when he led the league in victories with a 25–3 record, in winning percentage at .893, in shutouts with 9, and in ERA with 1.74.

Guidry won the fourth and deciding game of the AL championship series, 2–1, against the Kansas City Royals, and he won his only World Series start, 5–1, over the Los Angeles Dodgers in a six-game victory.

He won his second straight ERA title with a 2.78 mark in 1979 and had a 17–10 record the following year. Arm problems began to trouble him in 1981, but he was 21–9 in 1983 and 22–6 in 1985 to lead the league in victories and winning percentage at .786. The problems recurred after that season, and he went just 16–23 over the next three years before retiring.

Guidry ended with 170 wins and 91 loses, 26 shutouts, and a 3.29 ERA. He struck out 1,778 and walked 633 in 2,392 innings.

Gulack, George J.

GYMNASTICS
b. May 12, 1905, Riga, Latvia

A pole vaulter as well as a gymnast in his early years, Gulack came to the United States in 1922. He was the U.S. champion on the rings in 1928 and 1935, and he won the 1932 Olympic gold medal in the event.

As an administrator, Gulack helped bring U.S. gymnastics into the international arena after World War II. He helped the Amateur Athletic Union develop a set of rules meeting international standards, served as a judge at international meets, managed U.S. teams at the Olympics and Pan-American Games, and served as an honorary vice president of the International Gymnastics Federation.

Guldahl, Ralph

GOLF
b. Nov. 22, 1911, Dallas, Tex.
d. June 11, 1987

For a four-year period in the 1930s, Guldahl was one of the very best golfers in the world, winning two U.S. Opens and a Masters championship. Before and after that brief period, he played terrible golf and couldn't figure out why.

Guldahl first emerged at age 21, in the 1933 U.S. Open. Tied with Johnny Goodman, he needed a birdie on the final hole to win, a par to force a playoff. But he bogeyed the hole and finished second. Soon after that, his game fell apart, and he quit in disgust. He went back to Texas and sold cars for a while, then was asked to lay out a 9-hole course. That got him involved in golf once again, and he began playing quite well.

Back on the tour, he won the 1936 Radix Trophy with an average of 71.65 strokes per round. Guldahl became one of the few to win two consecutive Opens, in 1937 and 1938; his 1937 score of 281 was a record for the tournament. He also finished second in the Masters in both of those years, and he won the Masters in 1939, taking the lead with an eagle 3 on the 13th hole of the final round.

Guldahl teamed with Sam Snead to win the Inverness Four-Ball in 1940. That was his last victory. Suddenly his game fell apart once again. He played sporadically during World War II, then quit for good.

★ PGA Hall of Fame; World Golf Hall of Fame

Gurney, Daniel S.

AUTO RACING
b. April 13, 1931, Port Jefferson, N.Y.

Beginning as an amateur drag racer and sports car driver, Gurney became a sort of renaissance man of American auto racing. The drag racing began after his family moved to Riverside, California. As a high school student, he built himself a car that went 138 mph at the Bonneville, Utah, Salt Flats.

After serving in the Army during the Korean War, he bought a Porsche and won a couple races in 1956. Two years later, he was driving on the Grand Prix circuit. He won the French Grand Prix in 1962 and finished in the top five in the World Driving Championship standings four times in five years.

But he was interested in other types of racing, too. He returned to Riverside in January 1963 for a NASCAR stock car race on a road course. Gurney won it easily. He also finished seventh in the Indy 500 that year, driving one of the revolutionary rear-engine cars that were Indy versions of the Formula One cars he'd been racing in Europe.

Gurney formed his own Eagle team in 1965, hoping to win the World Driv-

ing Championship and the Manufacturers' Championship with an American-designed car. There were a lot of initial problems, but on June 18, 1967, Gurney won the Belgian GP in an Eagle. That year he became the first driver to win in all four major categories, Formula One, IndyCars, NASCAR stock cars, and sports cars.

His next step was to bring the Eagle back to America. His cars won three Indy 500s as well as national championships in 1968 and 1974.

Gurney retired from driving after the 1970 season. He had raced 25 makes of cars in 18 countries, and he had a total of 37 victories, seven in Formula One and IndyCars, 18 in sports cars, and 5 in stock cars. He remains in racing as owner of a new team that builds the All-American Eagle.

★ Indianapolis Speedway Hall of Fame

Guthrie, Janice

AUTO RACING
b. March 7, 1938, Iowa City, Iowa

It's easy to dismiss Janet Guthrie, the first woman to race in the Indy 500, as a novelty. That point of view ignores a harsh reality of auto racing: to be successful, a driver needs good cars, and she hardly ever got one. Most of her rides were in cars that were entered simply to fill out the field, like long shots in a horse race, and the record she compiled in such cars is a tribute to her racing skills.

Guthrie got her pilot's license at age 17. She majored in physics at the University of Michigan and was one of the first women astronaut candidates. She began racing in 1964, when she won two Sports Car Club of America races and finished sixth in the Watkins Glen 500. Going into 1971, she had nine consecutive finishes in endurance races.

She passed her rookie test at Indianapolis in 1976 but failed to qualify. Instead, she raced in NASCAR's World 600, finishing fifteenth. In 1977 she was top rookie finisher in two NASCAR Grand National events and placed third in Rookie of the Year voting.

Guthrie also got her first Indy 500

start in 1977 but was forced out early by engine trouble. She finished ninth at Indy in 1978. All told, she had 11 starts in IndyCar races and won $84,608. Her best finish was a fifth in the 1979 Milwaukee 200, her last major race.

★ International Women's Sports Hall of Fame

Guyon, Joseph N.
FOOTBALL
b. Nov. 26, 1892, White Earth Indian Reservation, Minn.
d. Nov. 27, 1971

A full-blooded Chippewa, Guyon attended Carlisle Indian School in Pennsylvania. He played tackle on the football team until Jim Thorpe left in 1912 and then replaced Thorpe at halfback for a season. He was named to Walter Camp's second-team All-American team in 1913.

Guyon went to Georgia Tech in 1917, where he played on a team that won all nine of its games, outscoring its opposition 491 to 17. His coach, John Heisman, later wrote, "I rate Guyon among the three or four greatest players of all time."

The 6-foot-1, 195-pound Guyon rejoined Thorpe with the Canton Bulldogs in 1919 and was with the team when it entered the new American Professional Football Association the following year. He followed Thorpe to the Cleveland Indians in 1921, the Oorang Indians in 1922 and 1923, and the Rock Island Independents in 1924.

Late in the 1924 season, Guyon went to the Kansas City Cowboys and played for them through 1925. He was out of football in 1926 but returned for one last season with the New York Giants. The versatile Guyon played guard, tackle, blocking back, and tailback as the Giants won the NFL championship with an 11–1–1 record.

A fast, dangerous runner and a crushing blocker and tackler, Guyon was also an outstanding kicker. As late as 1935, Ralph McGill wrote in the *Atlanta Constitution*, "There is no doubt in my mind that Joe Guyon is the greatest football player the South ever saw. He was almost a team all by himself."

★ College Football Hall of Fame; Pro Football Hall of Fame

Gwynn, Tony (Anthony K.)
BASEBALL
b. May 9, 1960, Los Angeles, Calif.

The left-handed Gwynn, who won four NL batting titles during the 1980s, is best known as a hitter, but he's also a dangerous base stealer and an excellent defensive outfielder who has won five Gold Glove Awards.

He joined the NL's San Diego Padres in the 1982 season but was on the disabled list for the last month, and he also missed the beginning of the 1983 season. In 1984, he stayed healthy and led the league with 213 hits and a .351 batting average.

Gwynn led the league in runs with 107 and hits with 211 in 1986. He then won three straight batting titles, hitting .370 in 1987, .313 in 1988, and .336 in 1989. He was the league leader in hits with 218 in 1987 and 203 in 1989.

Through 1994, Gwynn had hit over .300 in each major league season except his first. He had 2,204 hits, including 351 doubles, 79 triples, and 78 home runs. Gwynn had also stolen 525 bases, scored 991 runs, and driven in 714.

Hadl, John W.

FOOTBALL
b. Feb. 15, 1940, Lawrence, Kans.

After playing halfback on both offense and defense at the University of Kansas as a sophomore in 1959, Hadl became the offensive quarterback for his last two years.

The 6-foot-1, 210-pounder joined the AFL's San Diego Chargers in 1962. He was a backup until 1966, when he became San Diego's starting quarterback. Although Hadl put up impressive numbers, San Diego had limited success while he was there, and he was traded to the Los Angeles Rams before the 1973 season.

Hadl completed 135 of 258 passes for 2,008 yards and 22 touchdowns and was named player of the year as he led the Rams to 12 victories in 14 games. However, they lost, 27–16, to the Dallas Cowboys in the conference playoff game.

During the 1974 season, Hadl was traded to the Green Bay Packers for five draft choices. He spent two seasons in Green Bay and finished his playing career with the Kansas City Chiefs in 1976 and 1977.

During his 16 professional seasons, Hadl completed 2,363 of 4,687 attempts for 33,573 yards and 244 touchdowns. He coached the Los Angeles Wranglers of the U.S. Football League to a 3–15–0 record in 1985.

Hafey, Chick (Charles J.)

BASEBALL
b. Feb. 12. 1903, Berkeley, Calif.
d. July 2, 1973

One of the first outstanding players to emerge from a farm system, Hafey tried out with the NL's St. Louis Cardinals as a pitcher in 1923 but was moved to the outfield and sent to the minor leagues to learn the position. He joined the Cardinals late in the 1924 season.

After beginning the 1925 season in the minors, Hafey was called back up, batting .302 in 93 games. He missed much of the 1926 season with injuries, then began a streak of seven consecutive seasons in which he batted more than .300, including a league-leading mark in 1931. That was the closest batting race in major league history. Hafey's average was .3489; Bill Terry was second with .3486; and Jim Bottomley finished third at .3482.

A right-handed hitter, Hafey specialized in hitting line drives over third base and down the left field line, though he also demonstrated power at times. He batted .337 with 27 home runs and 111 RBI in 1928; .338 with 29 home runs and 125 RBI in 1929; and .336 with 26 home runs and 107 RBI in 1930.

Often bothered by injury and illness, Hafey had poor eyesight but didn't begin to wear glasses until 1930. He was also involved in several salary disputes with management. After holding out for $17,500 in 1932, he was traded to the Cincinnati Reds, who agreed to pay him $15,000. He hit .344 that year, but sinus problems limited him to just 83 games.

After batting .303 in 1933 and .293 in 1934, Hafey retired early in the 1935 season. He attempted a comeback with

Cincinnati in 1937 before retiring for good.

In 13 seasons, Hafey had 1,466 hits including 341 doubles, 67 triples, and 164 home runs. He drove in 833 runs and scored 777 in 1,283 games.

★ Baseball Hall of Fame

Hagan, Clifford O.

BASKETBALL
b. Dec. 9, 1931, Owensboro, Ky.

Hagan starred at the University of Kentucky for one of the greatest college teams ever assembled. Kentucky won the NCAA championship in 1951, Hagan's sophomore year. He was an All-American forward as a junior. Because of recruiting violations, the school was banned from competition in 1952–53.

Coach Adolph Rupp kept the team together, however. The players worked out all year, and in 1953 the Southeastern Conference granted Hagan, Lou Tsioropoulos, and Frank Ramsey an additional year of eligibility. Kentucky swept through the season, winning all 25 games, 24 of them by 12 points or more. However, the NCAA refused to allow the three to compete in the postseason tournament, so Kentucky declined to enter.

After two years in the service, during which he played for the Andrews Air Force Base team, Hagan joined the St. Louis Hawks of the NBA in 1957. He teamed with Clyde Lovellette and Bob Pettit to form an outstanding front line known as the "Unmatchables." The Hawks beat the Boston Celtics in a six-game final series to win the 1958 NBA championship.

Hagan was very quick at 6-foot-4 and 210 pounds, and he was strong for his size. He was a clever scorer near the basket, often lofting a quick, short hook shot over taller defenders.

He retired after the 1965–66 season but came back in 1967 to play with the Dallas Chaparrals of the American Basketball Association, and he became player-coach in 1968. He played just three games in 1969–70 and then resigned as coach. He served as athletic director at his alma mater from 1975 to 1988.

In 840 professional games, Hagan scored 14,870 points, an average of 17.7 per game. He averaged 20 or more points a game four consecutive seasons, from 1958–59 through 1961–62. As Dallas coach, he won 109 games and lost 90.

★ Basketball Hall of Fame

Hagen, Walter C.

GOLF
b. Dec. 21, 1892, Rochester, N.Y.
d. Oct. 6, 1969

"All the professionals who have a chance to go after the big money today should say a silent thanks to Walter Hagen each time they stretch a check between their fingers," Gene Sarazen once said. "It was Walter who made professional golf what it is."

Hagen was the most colorful and exciting golfer of his era. He had a loose swing and hit a lot of bad shots, but he always seemed to be able to make the great shot under pressure when he needed it.

After finishing fourth in the 1913 U.S. Open, behind a three-way tie for first, Hagen won the tournament in 1914. He shot a course record 68 on the first round and never trailed. In the 1919 Open, he was five strokes behind Mike Brady going into the final round, but he managed a tie and then beat Brady, 77–78, in the playoff.

Hagen also won four British Opens, in 1922, 1924, 1928, and 1929. The 1924 victory showed Hagen at his best as a showman. He had to sink a six-foot putt on the final hole to win. Without bothering to line up the putt, he strode to the ball, hit it, and turned his back on the shot, tossing the putter to his caddie. The putt dropped in, of course, and the British gallery loved it.

His greatest accomplishment was probably winning five LPGA championships, including four in a row, when it was a match-play tournament. He won in 1921, didn't play in 1922, lost to Gene Sarazen in the final in 1923, then won each year from 1924 through 1927. During those six years of competition, he lost just one match against the best professionals in the United States.

Hagen's 11 major championships rank him third on the all-time list, behind Jack Nicklaus and Bobby Jones. Since he got to play in only three of the six tournaments that have been considered majors, that 11 may well be better than Jones's 13 and very close to, if not better than, Nicklaus's 20.

The impact Hagen had on professional golf goes far beyond the tournaments he won. He was a star who commanded amazing amounts of money for playing exhibitions, and he spent the money freely and conspicuously. He toured the country in a caravan of automobiles with suitcases full of cash. He dressed handsomely, and he threw champagne parties to celebrate victories.

During the 1920s, Hagen's celebrity status brought the spotlight to professional golf, and he helped bring professionals out of the shadow by refusing to accept second-class treatment. Professional golfers at the time weren't allowed to use locker rooms at exclusive country clubs. In fact, they were treated much like servants, especially in England.

Hagen helped to change that status. He embarrassed promoters of the 1920 British Open by parking outside the clubhouse in his limousine and changing his clothes in the car. The same year, he and British professional George Duncan said they would boycott the French Open unless professionals were allowed into the locker room, and they won their case because tournament promoters knew they needed golfers like Hagen and Duncan to draw spectators.

★ PGA Hall of Fame; World Golf Hall of Fame

Hagler, Marvin
BOXING
b. May 23, 1954, Newark, N.J.

After winning 57 amateur fights and the 1973 AAU national middleweight championship, Hagler became a professional and won 26 consecutive bouts, including 19 knockouts. The 5-foot-9½, 160-pound left-hander shaved his head and used a menacing glower to intimidate opponents in pre-fight confrontations.

Hagler fought a draw against Sugar Ray Seales late in 1974 and didn't lose a fight until January 13, 1976, when Bobby Watts won a 10-round decision. On November 30, 1979, Hagler met Vito Antuofermo for the world middleweight championship in Las Vegas, but Antuofermo retained his title with a 15-round draw.

He got his second title fight against Alan Minter in London on September 27, 1980, and this time Hagler won the championship with a 12th-round knockout. After two successful defenses, Hagler was stripped of the WBC version of the title because his 1981 fight against Mustafa Hamsho was scheduled for 15 rounds instead of 12. However, the championship was restored after Hagler knocked out Hamsho in the 11th round.

Hagler won nine more championship bouts but lost the WBA title in 1986 because he hadn't fought one of that association's top-ranked contenders during a nine-month period. In one of the most celebrated middleweight fights of all time, Hagler lost the WBC title to Sugar Ray Leonard on a 12-round split decision in April 1987 in Las Vegas. Hagler earned $12 million for the bout, which brought the largest purse in history.

Nicknamed Marvelous Marvin, Hagler had his first name legally changed to "Marvelous" while he was champion. He retired in June 1988 with a record of 61 wins, 51 by knockout, 3 losses, and 2 draws.

★ International Boxing Hall of Fame

Hahn, Archie (Archibald)
TRACK AND FIELD
b. Sept. 14, 1880, Dodgeville, Wis. d. Jan. 21, 1955

The "Milwaukee Meteor" was the first person to win the sprint double at the Olympics. In fact, Hahn won a sprint triple, the 60-meter, 100-meter, and 200-meter dashes, at the 1904 Games, a feat that's no longer possible because the 60-meter dash has been dropped from the

Olympic program. He repeated as 100-meter champion at the "intercalated" Olympics of 1906.

Hahn tied the world record of 9.8 seconds in the 100-yard dash in 1901, and he set a world record of 21.6 seconds for the 200-meter straightaway in 1904. He was the AAU national 100-yard and 220-yard champion in 1903, and he won the 220-yard championship again in 1905.

He received a law degree from the University of Michigan, but Hahn never practiced. Instead, he worked with individual runners and also coached the Princeton and University of Virginia teams. His book, *How to Sprint,* is considered a track and field classic.

★ National Track & Field Hall of Fame

Haines, Jackson

FIGURE SKATING
b. 1840, Troy, N.Y.
d. 1879

Figure skating was a stiff, even awkward exercise in its early years. Skaters simply performed figures with no attempt at grace or style.

Haines changed all that. After studying dance in Europe as a young teenager, he returned to the United States when he was 17, and he began to incorporate dance movements into skating with musical accompaniment.

His ideas met with little enthusiasm until he founded a skating school in Vienna in 1863. Haines's colorful, theatrical approach to figure skating became known as the "international style." Among his many pupils was Louis Rubinstein of Canada, who popularized the style in North America.

Haines died in Finland and was buried there. His tombstone refers to him as "the American Skating King."

Haines, Jesse J.

BASEBALL
b. July 22, 1893, Clayton, Ohio
d. Aug. 5, 1978

Haines was on the roster of the Detroit Tigers briefly in 1915 and 1916 but never appeared in a game for the team. In 1918, he pitched five innings for the Cincinnati Reds, then was sent back to the minors. He finally made it in 1920 with the St. Louis Cardinals, who bought his contract for $10,000, a sizable sum at the time.

A right-hander, the 6-foot, 190-pound Haines had a 13–20 record as a rookie, despite a 2.98 ERA and 4 shutouts. He then had three straight winning seasons, topped by a 20–13 mark in 1923.

On July 7, 1924, Haines pitched a no-hitter to beat the Boston Braves, 5–0, one of the few bright spots in an 8–19 season, and he was 13–14 in 1925. Then Rogers Hornsby took over as the St. Louis manager. He used Haines as a spot starter and occasional reliever in 1926, resulting in a 13–4 record that helped the Cardinals get into the World Series against the New York Yankees.

After relieving in a first-game loss, Haines shut out the Yankees, 4–0, in the third game. He had a 3–2 lead in the seventh inning of the seventh game when he developed a blister on his pitching hand. Grover Cleveland Alexander relieved him with the bases loaded and two outs and struck out Tony Lazzeri to end the inning. Alexander went on to pick up a save while Haines was the winning pitcher.

Haines had his finest season in 1927, leading the NL in complete games with 25 and in shutouts with 6 while compiling a 24–10 mark and a 2.72 ERA. He went 20–8 in 1928, but arm trouble began to bother him. Nevertheless, he had three straight winning seasons, going 13–10 in 1929, 13–8 in 1930, and 12–3 in 1931, when he appeared in only 19 games.

Haines, who was primarily a knuckleball pitcher, was used mostly in relief for the last six years of his career. He retired after the 1937 season, at the age of 44, with a lifetime record of 210–158, 24 shutouts, and a 3.64 ERA. He struck out 981 hitters and walked 871 in 3,208⅔ innings.

★ Baseball Hall of Fame

Hainsworth, George

HOCKEY
b. June 26, 1895, Toronto, Ont.
d. Oct. 9, 1950

Hainsworth succeeded Georges Vezina as the Montreal Canadien goaltender after Vezina's tragic death in 1926, and he won the first three Vezina Trophies, from 1927 to 1929.

However, he didn't really win the respect of the tough Montreal fans until halfway through his third season. During a pregame practice, he was hit in the face by a shot that knocked him out and broke his nose. With one eye virtually swollen shut, he held Toronto to a 1–1 tie and was rewarded with a standing ovation.

In that 1928–29 season, Hainsworth gave up only 43 goals in 44 games and had an incredible 22 shutouts. He was traded to Toronto in 1933 and returned to Montreal briefly at the end of the 1936–37 season before retiring.

Hainsworth had 94 shutouts, second on the all-time list, and he had a record 1.91 goals-against average in 465 regular season games. In 52 playoff games, he recorded eight shutouts and a 2.15 average.

★ Hockey Hall of Fame

Halas, George S.
FOOTBALL
b. Feb. 2, 1895, Chicago, Ill.
d. Oct. 31, 1983

Halas played end at the University of Illinois, graduating in 1918, and was with the Great Lakes Naval Training Station team that lost to the Mare Island Marines in the 1918 Rose Bowl. After playing briefly as an outfielder with the New York Yankees in 1919, Halas was hired in 1920 by the Staley Starch Company of Decatur, Illinois, primarily to organize a company football team.

The Decatur Staleys, with Halas as player-coach, joined the new American Professional Football Association (APFA). The team moved to Chicago in 1921. The Staley company didn't renew the franchise in 1922, but Halas and his partner Dutch Sternaman did. They renamed the team the Bears. At the annual league meeting in January 1922, Halas suggested that the APFA should also be given a new name, the National Football League, and other owners agreed.

"Papa Bear," as Halas became known, was associated with the team until his death in 1983. He was player-coach through 1929. After he retired as a player, Halas hired Ralph Jones as coach for three seasons, but with the team losing money during the Depression, he took over again in 1933 because, as he said, "I came cheap."

Halas entered the Navy during the 1942 season and returned as coach in 1946, after World War II ended. He retired for two seasons, 1956 and 1957, then took over coaching again and retired permanently after the 1967 season, remaining with the team as a consultant.

During his 40 seasons as the Bears' coach, Halas won 325 games, lost 151, and tied 31. The Bears won NFL championships in 1921, 1933, 1934, 1937, 1940, 1946, and 1963. They were also champions under Jones in 1932 and under co-coaches Luke Johnsos and Hunk Anderson in 1943.

Halas had an almost quixotic commitment to the T formation for a 20-year period, when most other teams were using the single wing or Notre Dame shift. During the late 1930s, Clark Shaughnessy of the University of Chicago also worked as an adviser for the Bears, and he helped develop a modernized version of the formation, with one end split wide and a back going in motion to the other side.

Shaughnessy introduced this formation at Stanford University in 1940. That season, the Bears won the Western Division championship and beat the Washington Redskins, 73–0, for the NFL title. The overwhelming victory, combined with Stanford's unbeaten season, began a revolution. Within a decade, virtually every professional and major college team was using some version of the T formation.

But Halas's success as a coach owed more to his personality than to strategy or tactics. He was a tough disciplinarian who expected his teams to play hard and physically punish their opponents. Because of that approach, the Bears were known as "the Monsters of the Midway" during their best years under Halas.

★ Pro Football Hall of Fame

Haley, Charles L.
FOOTBALL
b. Jan. 6, 1964, Gladys, Va.

After playing for little James Madison College in Virginia, Haley was drafted by the San Francisco 49ers in the fourth round of the 1986 NFL draft. The very quick 6-foot-5, 245-pounder was used primarily as a pass rushing specialist at linebacker and occasionally at defensive end, recording 12 sacks in 16 games as a rookie.

Haley was named the National Football Conference defensive player of the year by United Press International in 1990, when he had 16 sacks. After several well-publicized clashes with the San Francisco coaching staff, he was traded to the Dallas Cowboys before the 1992 season. The Cowboys have also used him mostly as a pass rusher, at defensive end. A back problem limited his playing time until 1994, when he had 12½ sacks.

Through 1994, Haley had 86 sacks in 135 NFL games, and he had also recovered 7 fumbles and intercepted 1 pass. He has played for three Super Bowl champions, two in San Francisco and one in Dallas.

Hall, Evie (Evelyne R.; Mrs. Adams)
TRACK AND FIELD
b. Sept. 10, 1909, Minneapolis, Minn.

In the 80-meter hurdles at the 1932 Olympics, Hall led Babe Didrikson going over the final hurdle but just barely lost on the run to the tape. They were both timed in a world record 11.7 seconds.

Hall was the AAU outdoor 80-meter hurdles champion in 1930, and she won the indoor 50-yard/50-meter hurdles in 1931, 1933, and 1935. She ran on the Illinois Women's Athletic Club relay team that won national championships from 1931 to 1933, setting a world record of 49.4 seconds in 1932.

She retired from competition after failing to make the 1936 Olympic team and went into coaching. Hall coached the U.S. women's track team at the first Pan-American Games in 1951, and for many years she served as chairman of the U.S. Olympic women's track and field committee.

★ National Track & Field Hall of Fame

Hall, Gary W.
SWIMMING
b. Aug. 7, 1951, Fayetteville, N.C.

The first swimmer ever to break the four-minute mark in the 400-meter individual medley, Hall was a member of three U.S. Olympic teams, in 1968, 1972, and 1976. He won a silver in the 400-meter medley event in 1968, as a high school student, and entered Indiana University the following year.

Hall won seven NCAA championships, in the 400-meter medley from 1970 through 1972, the 200-meter medley in 1971 and 1972, the 200-meter backstroke in 1971, and the 200-meter butterfly in 1973.

He was the AAU national outdoor champion in the 200-meter backstroke in 1969, the 200-meter butterfly in 1970, the 200-meter individual medley from 1969 through 1971, and the 400-meter medley from 1968 through 1971. Indoors, Hall won the 200-yard backstroke from 1969 through 1970, the 100-yard butterfly in 1975, the 200-meter butterfly from 1969 through 1971, the 200-yard medley in 1970 and 1972, and the 400-yard medley from 1968 through 1970 and in 1972.

Hall captained the Olympic swim team in 1972, when he won a silver in the 200-meter butterfly, and in 1976, when he won a bronze in the 100-meter butterfly. He was chosen to carry the U.S. flag in the 1976 opening ceremonies.

After graduating from Indiana, Hall attended medical school at the University of Cincinnati and became an ophthalmologist.

★ International Swimming Hall of Fame

Hall, Glenn H.

HOCKEY
b. Oct. 3, 1931, Humboldt, Sask.

Hall usually threw up before a game because of nervousness, and sometimes he had to leave the ice to vomit during a game. He often threatened to quit because of his nervous stomach, and several times he won bigger contracts with his threats.

He once told a reporter, "Playing goal is a winter of torture for me. I often look at those guys who can whistle and laugh before a game and shake my head. You'd think they didn't have a care in the world. Me? I'm just plain miserable before every game."

Yet he played goal in 906 regular season games, including a record 502 in a row, and he was in net for 115 playoff games. He had 94 regular season shutouts and 8 playoff shutouts, and he won or shared three Vezina Trophies as the NHL's best goalie, in 1963, 1967, and 1969.

After playing briefly with the Detroit Red Wings in 1952–53 and 1954–55, Hall joined the team as a starter in 1955–56 and won the Calder Trophy as the league's outstanding rookie. He was traded to Chicago in 1957 and went to the St. Louis Blues in the 1967 expansion draft. Hall retired after the 1970–71 season.

Hall had a great semifinal series against defending champion Montreal in the 1961 Stanley Cup playoffs. He had three shutouts, including a 1–0 victory that went into two overtimes. During one stretch, he held the powerful Canadiens scoreless for 135 minutes and 26 seconds of play. Against Detroit in the final series, he gave up just 12 goals in six games as the Black Hawks won their first Stanley Cup since 1938.

In regular season play, Hall had a 2.51 goals-against average, with a 2.79 average in the playoffs.
★ Hockey Hall of Fame

Ham, Jack R.

FOOTBALL
b. Dec. 23, 1948, Johnstown, Pa.

One of many fine linebackers developed at Pennsylvania State University,
Ham was a consensus All-American in 1970 and a second-round choice of the Pittsburgh Steelers in the 1971 NFL college draft.

The 6-foot-1, 225-pound Ham used speed, intelligence, and determination to become one of the best in the business, an All-Pro outside linebacker from 1973 through 1979 and the NFL's defensive player of the year in 1975.

Ham was known for his ability to make the big play. A skilled punt blocker, he had 32 career interceptions, and he recovered 19 opposition fumbles. When the Steelers beat the Oakland Raiders, 24–13, for the 1974 American Football Conference championship, Ham had two interceptions. Pittsburgh went on to the first of four Super Bowl victories after that season.

Quiet and shy of publicity, Ham retired after the 1982 season. He returned his 32 interceptions 218 yards, a 6.8 average, and scored one touchdown.
★ Pro Football Hall of Fame

Hamill, Dorothy

FIGURE SKATING
b. July 26, 1956, Chicago, Ill.

The favorites for the 1976 Olympic figure skating championship were Dianne de Leeuw of the Netherlands, who had beaten Hamill in the 1975 world championships, and Christine Errath of East Germany, the 1974 world champion.

However, Hamill took the lead in the compulsory figure program, increased it with a perfect score of 6.0 on her short program, and turned in a solid free skating performance to win the gold medal. She also won the world championship later that year.

The U.S. champion from 1974 through 1976, Hamill developed a new move, a spin that turns into a sitz-spin, which became known as the "Hamill camel." The bobbed hairstyle that she wore during her Olympic performance started a fad.

Hamill retired from competition after 1976 and skated with the Ice Capades. She married Dean-Paul Martin, son of the singer Dean Martin.
★ Olympic Hall of Fame

Hamilton, Billy (William R.)

BASEBALL

b. Feb. 16, 1866, Newark, N.J.
d. Dec. 16, 1940

"Sliding Billy" was the premier base stealer of his era. He stole more than 100 bases in three consecutive seasons and scored a remarkable 1,690 runs in only 1,591 games. A left-handed hitter and right-handed thrower, the 5-foot-6, 165-pound Hamilton joined the Kansas City team in the American Association, then a major league, during the 1888 season. He led the association with 111 stolen bases in 1889, his first full year.

In 1890, Hamilton joined the Philadelphia Phillies of the NL and led that league in stolen bases with 102. His best all-around year was 1891, when he was the league leader in five categories, with 141 runs scored, 179 hits, 102 walks, a .340 batting average, and 111 stolen bases.

He dropped off to 57 stolen bases in 1892. Despite missing more than 50 games with typhoid fever the following season, he led the league with a .380 batting average and stole 43 bases in just 82 games.

Hamilton had another outstanding season in 1894. He led the league in walks with 126 and steals with 98, and he set an all-time record for runs scored with 192. He also tied a major league record by stealing seven bases in a game. In 1895, he won his fifth and final stolen base title with 97, again leading in runs scored with 166 and in walks with 96.

Philadelphia traded him to the NL's Boston Beaneaters (later the Braves) in 1896. His league-leading 105 walks and 152 runs scored helped lead Boston to the 1897 pennant. Leg injuries bothered him for the last four years of his career, and his stolen base totals declined significantly, but he batted over .300 in three of those years. Hamilton left the major leagues after hitting only .287 in 1901, and he served as a playing manager in the minors through 1909.

In 14 major league seasons, Hamilton had a .344 batting average with 2,158 hits, including 242 doubles, 94 triples, and 40 home runs. His 912 stolen bases was the major league record until 1978, when it was broken by Lou Brock.

★ Baseball Hall of Fame

Hamilton, Brutus K.

TRACK AND FIELD

b. July 19, 1900, Peculiar, Mo.
d. Dec. 28, 1970

The national decathlon champion in 1920, Hamilton won the silver medal in the event at the Olympics that year, when he was a sophomore at the University of Missouri.

He graduated in 1922 and became track coach at Westminster College in Missouri in 1924, then returned to his alma mater in 1927. The University of California hired him in 1932, and he remained there until his retirement in 1965.

Hamilton was decathlon coach for the U.S. Olympic team in 1932 and 1936. Americans James Bausch and Glenn Morris won gold medals in the event at those Olympics. Hamilton was head coach of the men's track team that won 14 gold medals at the 1952 Olympics.

Among the collegiate athletes he coached were milers Glenn Cunningham at Kansas and Don Bowden at California. Bowden was the first American to break four minutes in the one-mile run.

★ National Track & Field Hall of Fame

Hamilton, Scott

FIGURE SKATING

b. Aug. 28, 1958, Toledo, Ohio

Hamilton, who was adopted, stopped growing when he was two years old. He was eventually diagnosed with Swachman-Diamond syndrome, a partial paralysis of the intestinal tract that prevents the body from absorbing nutrients, and a special diet and exercise program cured the problem. However, he grew to only 5-foot-2½, and he weighed only 108 pounds during his peak skating years.

After trying gymnastics briefly, Hamilton took up figure skating when he was nine but didn't become a champion until he was 22. Then he became unbeatable, winning 16 consecutive competitions, including the U.S. and world championships from 1981 through 1984 and the gold medal at the 1984 Winter Olympics.

Although he was a brilliant free skater at his best, his excellence in the compulsories often gave him a nearly insurmountable lead. In the 1984 Olympics, Brian Orser of Canada had higher scores in the short and long programs but couldn't overcome the advantage Hamilton had gained in the compulsory figures.

Hamilton became a professional after the 1984 season.

★ Olympic Hall of Fame

Hannah, John A.

FOOTBALL
b. April 4, 1951, Canton, Ga.

A consensus All-American at offensive guard for Alabama in 1972, the 6-foot-3, 265-pound Hannah also lettered in wrestling and track, where he was a shot-putter and discus thrower.

The first draft choice of the NFL's New England Patriots, Hannah immediately became a starter in 1973 and remained with the team until he retired after the 1985 season because of surgery on both shoulders and his left knee.

Hannah was named an All-American Football Conference guard in 1974, 1976, 1978, and 1979, and was chosen for the All-NFL team in 1980, 1981, 1984, and 1985. He was also selected for the quarter-century AFL-NFL team for the 1960–1984 period.

★ Pro Football Hall of Fame

Hannum, Alexander M.

BASKETBALL
b. July 19, 1923, Los Angeles, Calif.

Hannum attended the University of Southern California on a basketball scholarship in 1941. After serving in the Army from 1943 to 1946, he returned to school and graduated in 1948. During three seasons on the varsity, he averaged 9.2 points a game.

The 6-foot-7, 225-pound Hannum played for the Oshkosh All-Stars of the National Basketball League in 1948–49

and then joined the NBA's Syracuse Nationals. His playing career ended in 1956–57, when he went to the St. Louis Hawks as player-coach in midseason.

Hannum guided the Hawks to two consecutive division championships and the 1958 NBA title, then left coaching for a year. He returned to Syracuse in 1960 and went to the San Francisco Warriors for the 1963–64 season, when they won the Western Division title.

The Syracuse franchise moved to Philadelphia in 1964 and became known as the 76ers. Hannum took over that team in 1966 and directed it to a 68–13 regular season record and the NBA championship.

After coaching Philadelphia to a 62–20 record and an Eastern Division title in 1967–68, Hannum went to the Oakland Oaks of the ABA. Led by Rick Barry, Oakland won the league championship, making Hannum the only coach ever to win titles in both the NBA and the ABA.

He returned to the NBA with the San Diego Clippers during the 1969–70 season and brought the team from seventh to third place, then became general manager and coach of the ABA's Denver Nuggets. He retired from coaching after the 1973–74 season to devote all his time to his construction business in California.

As a professional player, Hannum scored 3,443 points in 578 regular season games, a 6.0 average. As a coach, he had a 649–564 record in regular season play and a 61–46 record in the playoffs.

Hanson, Victor A.

BASKETBALL, FOOTBALL
b. July 30, 1903, Watertown, N.Y.
d. April 10, 1982

Named the best amateur athlete in New York State history in 1953, Hanson starred in four sports in high school but dropped track and participated in only three, baseball, basketball, and football, at Syracuse University. He captained all three teams as a senior.

Hanson was an All-American forward three times, in 1925, 1926, and 1927, and the Helms Athletic Foundation named him player of the year for 1927. Syracuse had a 48–7 record over his three seasons, and in 1925–26 the team was Helms national champion, winning 19 games while losing only 1.

An end, the 5–10, 160-pound Hanson was also a football All-American in 1926. In 1952, Grantland Rice named him to his all-time All-American football team, and Helms placed him on the all-time All-American basketball team.

After graduating in 1927, Hanson joined the Cleveland Rosenblums, who won the American Basketball League championship, and he played baseball for a season in the New York Yankee system. He coached football at Syracuse from 1930 through 1936, winning 33 games, losing 21, and tying 5. He was later a high school teacher and coach.
★ Basketball Hall of Fame; College Football Hall of Fame

Harbert, Chick (Melvin R.)
GOLF
b. Feb. 20, 1915, Dayton, Ohio
d. Sept. 1, 1992

World War II undoubtedly deprived Harbert of quite a few tournament victories. As an amateur, he won the 1937 Michigan Open with a score of 268. He also won the Trans-Mississippi Amateur and went to the quarterfinals of the U.S. Amateur before joining the professional tour.

After winning three tournaments in two years, Harbert spent four years in the Army Air Corps. He had six more victories after the war; the biggest was the 1954 PGA championship, when he beat Walter Burkemo, 4 and 3. Harbert also reached the finals of the PGA championship in 1947 and 1952.
★ PGA Hall of Fame

Hard, Darlene R.
TENNIS
b. Jan. 6, 1936, Los Angeles, Calif.

The irrepressible Hard, who was known for a strong serve and her volleying ability, won the French and U.S. championships in 1960 and was also U.S. champion in 1961.

Because of an erratic forehand, she

was at her best as a doubles player. With eight different partners, she won a total of 14 doubles titles in grand slam tournaments: the U.S. from 1958 through 1962 and in 1969, Wimbledon in 1957, 1959, 1960, and 1963, and the French title in 1955, 1957, and 1960. Her last doubles title, at the U.S. Nationals in 1969, came five years after she had retired from serious competition to become a tennis instructor.

Hard once said, "I was the last of the amateurs. In our day, I won Forest Hills and got my airfare from New York to Los Angeles. Whoopee." But, she added, "I was happy. I loved it. I loved tennis."
★ International Tennis Hall of Fame.

Harder, Pat (Marlin M.)
FOOTBALL
b. May 6, 1922, Milwaukee, Wis.

The 5-foot-11, 205-pound Harder was a very versatile player, a hard-running fullback, powerful blocker, fine pass receiver, and excellent kicker who also played defensive linebacker at times. A starter at the University of Wisconsin as a sophomore in 1942, Harder was in military service from 1943 until 1945.

After World War II ended, Harder elected to play pro football with the NFL's Chicago Cardinals. He was the first player in history to score more than 100 points three seasons in a row, leading the league with 102 in 1947, 110 in 1948, and 102 in 1949. The Cardinals beat the Philadelphia Eagles, 28–21, to win the 1947 NFL championship, with Harder kicking 4 extra points.

Harder was traded to the Detroit Lions in 1951. In Detroit's 31–21 victory over the Los Angeles Rams in the 1952 National Conference championship game, he scored 21 points on 2 touchdowns, 1 field goal, and 4 conversions.

He retired after the 1953 season and served as an NFL official from 1965 to 1982. In his 8 seasons, Harder rushed 740 times for 3,016 yards, a 4.1 average, and 33 touchdowns; caught 92 passes for 864 yards and 5 touchdowns; kicked 35 field goals in 69 attempts; and made 198 of 204 conversion attempts for a total of

531 points. He was named All-Pro full-back from 1947 through 1949.

★ College Football Hall of Fame

Hardin, Glenn F.

TRACK AND FIELD
b. July 1, 1910, Derma, Miss.
d. March 6, 1975

Although he finished second to Robert Tisdall of Ireland in the Olympic 400-meter hurdles in 1932, Hardin was credited with tying the world record in 52.0 seconds, while Tisdall's time of 51.8 wasn't recognized under the rules of the day because he knocked over the last hurdle.

Hardin lowered the record to 51.8 in the 1934 AAU national championships, then turned in a remarkable 50.6 during a meet in Stockholm later that year. That record stood for 19 years.

The tall, lanky Hardin won the 400-meter hurdles event at the 1936 Olympics. He was the AAU champion in the 440-yard hurdles in 1933, 1934, and 1936. Representing Louisiana State, he was the NCAA 440-yard dash champion in 1933 and 1934.

★ National Track & Field Hall of Fame

Hardwick, Billy (William B.)

BOWLING
b. July 25, 1941, Florence, Ala.

Hardwick joined the PBA tour in 1961 and was named bowler of the year by *The Sporting News* in 1963, when he won four tournaments, including the PBA National, and averaged 210.346 pins to win the George Young Memorial Award for high average.

The Bowling Writers Association of America voted him bowler of the year in 1964 and again in 1969, when he had the tour's highest average with 212.957 pins. He won the All-Star event and five other tournaments that year and led the PBA in earnings with $64,160.

Hardwick retired after the 1976 season with a total of 17 tournament victories. He now operates a bowling center in Memphis.

★ ABC Hall of Fame; PBA Hall of Fame

Hardwick, Tack (Huntington R.)

FOOTBALL
b. Oct. 15, 1892, Quincy, Mass.
d. June 26, 1949

Hardwick was probably the best player on Harvard's best teams, coached by Percy Haughton to 23 victories, 0 losses, and 2 ties from 1912 through 1914. Haughton called him "the most valuable player who ever played football at Harvard."

A halfback as a sophomore in 1912, the 6-foot, 174-pound Hardwick had a 60-yard touchdown run against Amherst. Hardwick was moved to end in 1913 but was often used as a runner on the end-around play. He also did most of the team's punting.

Hardwick captained the 1914 team. He began the season as an end but was moved into the backfield against Washington and Jefferson because of injuries, and he scored all of Harvard's points in a 10–9 victory. He also scored the only touchdown and kicked the extra point in a 7–0 win over Michigan that season, caught two touchdown passes and kicked two conversions against Yale, and had a touchdown reception and two extra points against Princeton.

After being named to some All-American teams in 1913, Hardwick was a unanimous choice in 1914. He also starred in baseball, batting .357 for the 1915 Harvard team that beat the New York Giants in an exhibition.

★ College Football Hall of Fame

Hare, T. Truxton

FOOTBALL
b. Oct. 12, 1878, Philadelphia, Pa.
d. Feb. 2, 1956

Walter Camp said that Hare was the only football player who could have been an All-American at any position. He played guard at the University of Pennsylvania, but he was also the team's signal caller, punter, and drop-kicker, and he was often used to run the ball from coach George Woodruff's guards-back formation.

A four-time All-American, from 1897 through 1900, Hare captained the team for his final two seasons. In the last game of his college career, he ran 35 yards for a touchdown against Harvard, dragging five defenders across the goal line. At 6-foot-2, Hare weighed just under 200 pounds, but he was remarkably strong. He won the silver medal in the hammer throw at the 1900 Olympics, and in 1904 he placed third in the AAU national all-around championship, an event similar to the decathlon.

★ College Football Hall of Fame

Harlan, Bruce I.

DIVING
b. Jan 2, 1926
d. June 22, 1959

Shortly after graduating from high school in 1944, Harlan joined the Navy. He was stationed at the Jacksonville, Florida, Naval Training Center when he won his first AAU title, in the 3-meter springboard, in 1946. After being discharged, he went to Ohio State.

Harlan won the NCAA 1-meter championship in 1948, and he won both the 1-meter and the 3-meter championships in 1949 and 1950. He was the AAU 3-meter springboard and platform champion in 1947 and 1948. Indoors, he won both the 1-meter and the 3-meter in 1949 and 1950. He won a gold medal in the springboard and a silver in the platform at the 1948 Olympics.

After retiring from competition, he became diving coach at the University of Michigan. He was killed in a fall from a diving tower while dismantling the scaffolding after an exhibition in Norwalk, Connecticut.

Harley, Chic (Charles W.)

FOOTBALL
b. Sept. 15, 1895, Chicago, Ill.
d. April 21, 1976

Ohio State's first All-American, Harley was largely responsible for turning the school into a football power. When he played at Columbus East High School, the annual game between Columbus East and Columbus North drew bigger crowds than Ohio State did. Harley never played on a losing team until his last high school game in 1914.

The 145-pound halfback was a fast, exciting runner who delighted crowds. Many of the fans who had watched him in high school became Ohio State fans when he became a starter at the university in 1916. Harley promptly led the school to its first Western Conference (Big Ten) championship and was named to Walter Camp's All-American team.

Ohio State repeated as champion in 1917, and Harley was again an All-American. After serving in the Army in 1918, he returned to the school for a third All-American season and starred in Ohio State's first victory over Michigan, a 13–3 win. During his three years as a starter, Ohio State won 21 games while losing only 1 and tying 1.

Harley played professional football with George Halas's Chicago Staleys in 1921.

★ College Football Hall of Fame

Harlow, Dick (Richard C.)

FOOTBALL
b. Oct. 19, 1889, Philadelphia, Pa.
d. Feb. 19, 1962

As a tackle at Penn State, Harlow distinguished himself by blocking five punts in 1911. He remained as an assistant coach for three seasons and was named head coach in 1915. After compiling a 20–8–0 record in three seasons, Harlow entered the service in 1918.

He returned to Penn State as an assistant in 1919, then went to Colgate in 1922. His 1925 team was undefeated, winning seven games and tying two, and he had a record of 24–9–3 in four seasons before going to Western Maryland in 1926.

Harlow produced three more unbeaten teams, in 1929, 1930, and 1934. The 1929 team won all 11 of its games; the 1930 and 1934 teams each had one tie. Harlow's nine-year record of 61 wins, 13 losses, and 7 ties caught the attention of Harvard athletic director Bill Bingham. In 1935, Harlow became the first non-alumnus ever to coach at Harvard.

The lack of material haunted him. He had just three winning teams in his first eight seasons before entering the Navy in 1943. He became ill while in the service and was put on a lifelong diet of rice and fruit juice. However, he returned to coaching at Harvard in 1945 and had his best team there in 1946, winning seven of nine games.

He retired after the 1947 season on his doctor's advice. In his 11 seasons, Harvard won 45 games, lost 39, and tied 7. His overall record was 150–68–17.

Although an amateur, Harlow was an expert in oology, the study of birds' eggs. In 1939, he was named curator of oology at the Harvard Museum of Comparative Zoology, and he remained in that position until 1954.

Harlow pioneered modern defensive schemes. Because his teams were often greatly outweighed, he taught his linemen and linebackers to use coordinated stunts and loops to get around or between blockers. His offense was similarly based on deception and timing rather than power, using a wide variety of shifts, reverses, and lateral passes.

★ College Football Hall of Fame

Harmon, Thomas D.

FOOTBALL
b. Sept. 28, 1919, Gary, Ind.

One of the last of the triple-threat single-wing tailbacks, Harmon was named to the All-1930s team in a 1969 poll marking college football's centennial year. Amos Alonzo Stagg said he was better than Red Grange because he was more versatile. "Harmon was superior to Grange in everything but running," Stagg said. "I'll take Harmon on my team and you can have all the rest."

An All-American at Michigan in 1939 and 1940, Harmon won the Heisman Trophy in 1940 and was also named Associated Press Athlete of the Year. His most spectacular game was a 41–0 victory over the University of California in 1940, when he scored on runs of 72, 80, 86, and 94 yards.

During his three years as a starter, Harmon gained 2,338 yards on 398 carries, an average of 5.9 yards. He scored 237 points and also threw 16 touchdown passes.

Harmon played for the New York Americans in the American Football League in 1941 and then served in the Air Force during World War II. Although he suffered serious burns on both legs when his plane was shot down over China, he played two more seasons of professional football with the Los Angeles Rams in 1946 and 1947, but was obviously not the player he had been before the war.

He went on to have a successful career as a radio and television sportscaster.

★ College Football Hall of Fame

Harper, Chandler

GOLF
b. March 10, 1914, Portsmouth, Va.

When Harper was hot, he was very, very hot. He used only 20 putts over one 18-hole round when he won the Tucson Open in 1950. And he shot a PGA record of 189 for the last 54 holes to win the 1954 Texas Open.

Harper won the Virginia Amateur in 1930, 1932, and 1933 and the Virginia Open in 1932 and 1941 before joining the pro tour after World War II. He won the 1950 PGA championship, and he was also Virginia Open champion again in 1952 and 1960.

His most famous tournament, though, was probably his heartbreaking loss in the 1953 "World Championship," then the biggest money event on the tour. Harper was in the clubhouse with a comfortable two-shot lead over Lew Worsham, who had just one hole to play. But Worsham holed a wedge shot for an eagle on that final hole to win the $25,000 first prize.

★ PGA Hall of Fame

Harper, Donald De W.

DIVING, GYMNASTICS
b. June 4, 1932, Redwood City, Calif.

Although diving obviously contains elements of gymnastics, Harper is the only athlete to have won national championships in both sports. At a time when trampoline was part of the standard gymnastics program, Harper won the Pan-American Games trampoline title in 1955. He was also the NCAA trampoline champion in 1956 and 1958.

Representing Ohio State, he won three NCAA diving championships, in the 1-meter springboard in 1958 and in the 3-meter in both 1956 and 1958. He was the AAU outdoor 3-meter springboard champion in 1955, the platform champion in 1961, the indoor 1-meter champion in 1957, and the indoor 3-meter champion in 1956 and 1958. Harper won a silver medal in 1956 Olympic springboard competition.

Harper, Jesse C.

FOOTBALL
b. Dec. 10, 1883, Pawpaw, Ill.
d. July 31, 1961

After graduating from the University of Chicago, where he played halfback and quarterback for Amos Alonzo Stagg, Harper became head coach at Alma College in Michigan and had a 10–4–4 record from 1906 through 1908. At Wabash College in Indiana from 1909 through 1912, Harper used the forward pass more than most coaches of his time and compiled a 14–8–1 record.

He went to Notre Dame in 1913. The school first became known for football that year because Harper lined up a game against powerful Army, and Notre Dame pulled a 35–13 upset by featuring the forward pass, often out of a short punt or spread formation.

Harper's greatest coaching contribution, though, was the development of the Notre Dame shift in 1914, with the help of his assistant and former player, Knute Rockne. The offense lined up in a T formation, and the backs then shifted into one of three different formations, with the ball being snapped immediately to keep the defense from adjusting. Harper also had his ends shift at times, usually moving farther away from the offensive tackle in order to get good blocking angles.

In five seasons at Notre Dame, Harper won 33 games, lost only 5, and tied 1. He resigned after the 1917 season to go into ranching and was succeeded by Rockne. Harper returned for two

years as athletic director in 1931 after Rockne's death in a plane crash.
★ College Football Hall of Fame

Harpster, Howard

FOOTBALL
b. 1907

Harpster starred at Carnegie Tech in Pittsburgh when that school was an Eastern football power. A quarterback, he led Carnegie to upset victories over Notre Dame in 1926 and in 1928, when he was named an All-American.

A dangerous runner, excellent kicker, and accurate passer, Harpster was also a signal caller who liked to surprise the defense. He often threw a long pass on second down with less than a yard to go. In the 1928 victory over Notre Dame, he ran 35 yards on a quarterback sneak when it was third down and 15.

In 1933, Harpster became head coach at his alma mater, but material had grown much thinner by then. He won only 12, lost 20, and tied 3 in four seasons of playing some of the best teams in the country.
★ College Football Hall of Fame

Harris, Archie (Archibald)

TRACK AND FIELD
b. July 3, 1918, Urbanna, Va.

As a student at the University of Indiana, Harris set a world record of 174 feet, 9 inches, in the discus throw in 1941, becoming the first black athlete to hold a world record in any weight event. Harris was the NCAA discus champion in 1940 and 1941, and he also won the AAU national title in 1941.

Harris, Bucky (Stanley R.)

BASEBALL
b. Nov. 8, 1896, Port Jervis, N.Y.
d. Nov. 8, 1977

The 5-foot-9, 156-pound Harris played briefly for the AL's Washington Senators in 1919 and became the team's starting second baseman the following year, when he batted an even .300, the best average of his career.

Never a star player, Harris was a dependable performer who, beginning in 1922, teamed with veteran shortstop

Roger Peckinpaugh to form the league's best double-play combination.

Although he was the youngest starter on the team, Harris received a telegram offering him the job of manager while he was golfing in Florida during the winter of 1924. Harris wired back, "I'll take that job and win Washington's first American League pennant."

The message was prophetic. The Senators, who had finished 23½ games out of first place in 1923, weren't expected to do much, but the "Boy Manager" guided them to first place, beating the Yankees by two games. Then he led them to victory over the New York Giants in a seven-game World Series, hitting .333 with two home runs and setting records for chances, putouts, and double plays by a second baseman.

Washington also won the 1925 pennant but lost a seven-game World Series to Pittsburgh. The team then began to decline, and Harris was traded after the 1928 season to Detroit, where he took over as manager. His playing career was essentially over; he appeared in just seven games with the Tigers in 1929 and in only four in 1931.

For the rest of his career, Harris managed some poor teams: Detroit through 1933 and from 1955 through 1956, the Boston Red Sox in 1934, Washington again from 1935 through 1942 and from 1950 through 1954. He managed the Philadelphia Phillies for part of the 1943 season but was fired in July after calling the team's owner "a jerk."

He took over the New York Yankees in 1947 and guided them to a World Series victory but was replaced by Casey Stengel after the team finished just 2½ games out in 1948. Harris also served at various times as a minor league manager, a scout, and a major league executive. He retired from baseball in 1971 after a nine-year stint, primarily as a scout, with the expansion Washington Senators.

In 29 managerial seasons, Harris had a record of 2,157 wins and 2,218 losses, a .493 percentage. As a player, he batted .274, with 1,297 hits in 1,263 games.

★ Baseball Hall of Fame

Harris, Franco

FOOTBALL
b. March 7, 1950, Ft. Dix, N.J.

As a fullback at Penn State, Harris received much less attention than halfback Lydell Mitchell, but in three years he rushed 380 times for 2,002 yards, a 5.3 average, and scored 24 touchdowns.

A first-round draft choice of the NFL's Pittsburgh Steelers in 1972, he was named the league's rookie of the year by *The Sporting News* and United Press International after gaining 1,055 yards on 188 carries, a 5.6 average. He rushed for 10 touchdowns and scored 3 on pass receptions.

Harris was involved in one of pro football's most famous plays, the "immaculate reception," in the American Football Conference playoffs after that season. Pittsburgh was trailing the Oakland Raiders, 7–6, with five seconds to play when a Terry Bradshaw pass caromed off the shoulder pad of Oakland defensive back Jack Tatum. Harris grabbed the ball and ran it in for the winning touchdown.

Although he made All-Pro only once, in 1977, Harris was chosen for nine consecutive Pro Bowls, from 1972 through 1980, and he broke Jim Brown's record by rushing for more than 1,000 yards in eight seasons. His running ability gave Pittsburgh a powerful ball control offense that combined with a strong defense to win four Super Bowls, after the 1974, 1975, 1978, and 1979 seasons. He was the most valuable player in Super Bowl IX, after the 1974 season, when he rushed for 158 yards on 34 carries in a 16–6 win over the Minnesota Vikings.

Harris played with the Steelers through 1983 and then spent one final season with the Seattle Seahawks before retiring.

At 6-foot-2 and 225 pounds, Harris was similar in running style to Jim Brown, though he didn't quite have his speed. He had the ability to cut quickly to avoid direct hits by defenders, which often allowed him to break through arm tackles and gain extra yardage.

In his 13 professional seasons, Harris gained 12,120 yards on 2,949 carries, a 4.1 average, and scored 91 rushing touchdowns. He caught 307 passes for 2,287 yards, a 7.4 average, and 9 touchdowns.

★ Pro Football Hall of Fame

Harris, Lucy (Lusia M.)

BASKETBALL
b. Feb. 10, 1955, Minter City, Miss.

The first woman drafted by a men's professional basketball team, Harris was a three-time All-American at Delta State University in Mississippi in 1975, 1976, and 1977, as Delta State won the AIAW championships all three years. The 6-foot-3, 185-pound center scored 1,060 points in 1976–77, averaging 31.2 a game, with a high of 58 points against Tennessee Tech. She also averaged 15 rebounds a game.

Harris became Delta State's first black homecoming queen in 1975, a year in which she starred for the U.S. teams in the World University Games and the Pan-American Games. She also played for the 1976 silver medal Olympic team.

In 1977, Harris won the Broderick Award as the nation's best collegiate basketball player and the Honda Broderick cup as the best collegiate athlete in any sport. She was chosen by the New Orleans Jazz in the seventh round of the 1977 NBA draft but made no effort to play for the team. She did play for the Houston Angels of the Women's Professional Basketball League in 1980 but left when she became pregnant.

She later returned to Delta State as admissions counselor and assistant basketball coach while studying for her master's degree, which she received in 1984.

★ Basketball Hall of Fame

Harroun, Ray

AUTO RACING
b. Jan. 12, 1879, Spartansburg, Pa. d. Jan. 19, 1968

If Ray Harroun is remembered at all, it is for winning the first Indy 500 in 1911. In fact, he may not have won that race (see the Ralph Mulford entry for details), but as a pioneer driver and de-signer of cars, Harroun still deserves his place in the Indianapolis Speedway Hall of Fame.

After serving as a driving mechanic for a time, he began racing in 1906 and won the national championship in 1910, then joined the Marmon automobile company in Indianapolis as chief engineer. The company asked him to design and drive a car in the new 500-mile race. Harroun came up with a revolutionary design.

Racecars of the period were usually heavy two-seaters that carried the driver and a mechanic, who kept the driver informed about what was happening behind him. Harroun designed a light, streamlined one-seater with a pointed tail and a stabilizer. To replace the mechanic, he added a rearview mirror. Whether or not the car actually finished first at Indy, it performed exceptionally well, averaging 74.602 mph.

That was Harroun's last race. He later invented a carburetor that was a forerunner of modern fuel injection systems. He also developed a kerosene-burning Maxwell racecar in 1914 that ran on tracks for nearly 15 years.

★ Indianapolis Speedway Hall of Fame

Harshman, Marvin

BASKETBALL
b. Oct. 4, 1917, Eau Claire, Wis.

After winning 13 letters in four sports at Pacific Lutheran College, Harshman played briefly for the Seattle–Tacoma Mountaineers in the Northwest Professional Basketball League before joining the Navy in 1942. Upon his discharge in 1946, he began his 40-year career as a college basketball coach, a career divided almost evenly among three different schools.

It began at his alma mater, where Harshman also coached football and track for several years. In 13 seasons, his basketball teams won 236 games while losing 111. He was hired in 1958 to revive Washington State University's basketball program. It took a while, but he finally had five consecutive winning seasons at the school. His best record was 19 wins and 7 losses in 1969–70.

Overall, his teams won 155 games but lost 181 in 13 seasons.

Harshman went to the University of Washington in 1971 and spent 14 seasons there before retiring in 1985. His 1983–84 team had a 24–7 record, winning Harshman the National Basketball Coaches Association coach of the year award. His record at Washington was 251 wins and 156 losses for an overall record of 642–448. His victory total is the twelfth highest of all time.
★ Basketball Hall of Fame

Hart, Doris

TENNIS
b. June 20, 1925, St. Louis, Mo.

Soon after she learned to walk, Hart developed a serious infection in her right knee, and a specialist recommended amputation. The leg was saved, but the knee bothered her throughout her career and beyond.

When she was 10 years old, Hart discovered tennis by watching people play from her hospital window after an operation. She and her older brother Bud got involved in the sport, practicing together and taking lessons at a public court. (Bud was ranked twentieth nationally in 1943.)

Despite her bad knee, Hart developed a fluid style and a solid all-court game to go with an excellent serve. She was sometimes criticized for using frequent half-volleys from the baseline, but she explained she had great confidence in the shot because her brother had trained her never to retreat more than a couple of feet behind the baseline.

Hart's first grand slam singles title came in the 1949 Australian championships. She went on to win the French singles in 1950 and 1952, Wimbledon in 1951, and the U.S. singles in 1954 and 1955. In 1951, she beat her long-time doubles partner, Shirley Fry, 6–1, 6–0, in the Wimbledon finals, taking just 34 minutes to do so.

She had even more success in doubles, winning the women's doubles at Wimbledon in 1947 and from 1951 through 1953, at the French championships in 1948 and from 1950 through

1953, at the U.S. championships from 1951 through 1954, and in Australia in 1950. Hart won most of those titles with Shirley Fry, but she teamed with Pat Canning Todd for two and with Louise Brough Clapp for another.

In mixed doubles, Hart won championships at Wimbledon from 1951 through 1956 and at the U.S. Nationals from 1951 through 1955, giving her a total of 34 grand slam titles. Her mixed doubles partners were Frank Sedgman in 1951 and 1952 and Vic Seixas from 1953 through 1956, her last year of serious competition.

Hart lost only one match in ten consecutive years of Wightman Cup play, from 1946 through 1955.
★ International Tennis Hall of Fame

Hart, Jim (James W.)

FOOTBALL
b. April 29, 1944, Evanston, Ill.

Although Hart put up impressive numbers at Southern Illinois University, passing for 3,779 yards and 34 touchdowns, he was ignored by NFL teams because he played at a small school that won only eight games in his three seasons.

The St. Louis Cardinals signed him as a free agent in 1966, and he became the team's starting quarterback the following season, when Charlie Johnson was drafted into the Army. He was named the NFL player of the year after the 1974 season for guiding the Cardinals to the Eastern Division championship. The 6-foot-1, 210-pound Hart completed 200 of 388 passes for 2,411 yards and 20 touchdowns that season.

Hart lost the starting job in 1981 and was released by the Cardinals after the 1983 season. He played one more season with the Washington Redskins and then retired. In his 19 professional seasons, he completed 2,593 passes in 5,076 attempts for 34,665 yards and 209 touchdowns. He also ran for 16 touchdowns.

Hart, Leon J.

FOOTBALL
b. Nov. 2, 1928, Turtle Creek, Pa.

In 1949 the mammoth Hart became

only the second lineman in history to win the Heisman Trophy as the nation's outstanding college football player. He also won the Maxwell Award and was named Associated Press athlete of the year.

An end at the University of Notre Dame, the 6-foot-5 Hart weighed 245 pounds as a freshman and played frequently, though he wasn't a starter. He did take over the starting job as a sophomore. By his senior year, he weighed 265 pounds and was feared as a blocker, receiver, and defender. Because of his quick start and overall speed, he was often used as a fullback in short yardage situations.

Hart was a consensus All-American in 1948 and 1949. During his four years at Notre Dame, the team won 36 games and tied 2 without a loss, and Hart caught 49 passes for 742 yards and 13 touchdowns. He also rushed for 2 touchdowns.

In 1950, Hart joined the Detroit Lions of the NFL. Although professional teams were generally using the two-platoon system, he played both offense and defense for his first two seasons, and in 1951 he was named All-Pro as an offensive end by the Associated Press and as a defensive end by United Press International. He became an offensive specialist in 1952.

Hart spent eight seasons with the Lions, playing on NFL championship teams in 1952, 1953, and 1957. He retired after the 1957 season. During his professional career, he caught 174 passes for 2,499 yards, a 14.4 average, and 26 touchdowns. He also carried the ball from the fullback position 143 times for 612 yards, a 4.3 average, and 5 touchdowns.
★ College Football Hall of Fame

Hartack, Bill [William J. Jr.]

HORSE RACING
b. Dec. 9, 1932, Colver, Pa.

Often called "Willie" early in his career, Hartack resented the diminutive and insisted on being called "Bill" after he became a successful jockey. The very intelligent Hartack was noted for his pride, honesty, and outspokenness, to the point where some considered him arrogant.

During the 1950s, Hartack joined Eddie Arcaro and Willie Shoemaker in a triumvirate of great jockeys. He led the nation in victories from 1955 through 1957 and in 1960, and he was the leading money winner in 1956 and 1957. His $3,060,501 in 1957 was a record for ten years.

Hartack and Arcaro are the only jockeys ever to win five Kentucky Derbies. Hartack did it aboard Iron Liege in 1957, Venetian Way in 1960, Decidedly in 1962, Northern Dancer in 1964, and Majestic Prince in 1969. He also won the Preakness three times, with Fabius in 1956, Northern Dancer in 1964, and Majestic Prince in 1969, and he had one Belmont Stakes winner, Celtic Ash in 1960.

A rider for the famous Calumet Farms through most of the 1950s, Hartack lost that position in 1958 because of continued arguments with management and trainers over the handling of horses. Hartack liked to take a horse to the lead and hold it throughout a race, while trainers often preferred to have him rein the horse back for a time and win with a stretch drive.

In 1978, Hartack went to Hong Kong and raced there for three years. After his retirement in 1981, he served as a television commentator and racing official.
★ National Horse Racing Hall of Fame

Hartnett, Gabby (Charles L.)

BASEBALL
b. Dec. 20, 1900, Woonsocket, R.I.

When Hartnett was in the New York Giants' farm system, a scout reported that he would never be a major league catcher because his hands were too small, and he was sold to the Chicago Cubs for $2,500 after the 1921 season.

Hartnett was a backup catcher with the Cubs in 1922 and 1923 and took over as the starter in 1924. Because of an arm injury, he missed most of the 1929 season, when the Cubs won the pennant, but he had his best offensive year in 1930, batting .339 with 37 home runs and 122 RBI.

The Cubs won another pennant in 1932, when Hartnett hit .271, but they lost to the New York Yankees in a four-game World Series — the series in which Babe Ruth supposedly called his shot by pointing to the center field bleachers and then hitting a home run there. Hartnett, who was behind the plate, said it didn't happen like that, that Ruth merely held up a finger and said, "It only takes one to hit."

Hartnett had a great streak of three seasons from 1935 through 1936, hitting .344, .307, and .354, though his home run and RBI totals were much lower than in 1930. With the Cubs in third place during the 1938 season, Hartnett became playing manager. He guided the team to a 44–27 record and a pennant, but they were again swept by the Yankees in the World Series.

After the Cubs finished fourth in 1939 and fifth in 1940, Hartnett was released. He spent a final season as a part-time player and coach for the New York Giants in 1941, hitting an even .300.

In 20 major league seasons, Hartnett batted .297, with 1,912 hits, including 396 doubles, 64 triples, and 236 home runs. He scored 867 runs and had 1,179 RBI in 1,990 games, and he led NL catchers in fielding percentage six times.
★ Baseball Hall of Fame

Harvey, Douglas N.

HOCKEY
b. Dec. 19, 1924, Montreal, P.Q.

The only criticism anyone could make of Doug Harvey was that he didn't shoot enough. He had a simple explanation: "I didn't have a bonus for goals, so why not set up the guys who needed them?"

A master at establishing the pace of a game, Harvey could lead a rush when his team needed to score or protect a lead by bringing the puck slowly up the ice and killing time by moving back and forth at the opposition's blue line.

In 14 seasons with the Montreal Canadiens, he played for six Stanley Cup champions, won the Norris Trophy as the NHL's outstanding defenseman six times, and was a ten-time all-star. And that wasn't his entire career: he played five more seasons with the New York Rangers, the Detroit Red Wings, and the St. Louis Blues, winning another Norris Trophy with the Rangers.

Harvey joined the Canadiens in 1947. Because of his casual, phlegmatic style, he was never very popular with the Montreal fans, yet hockey experts recognized his value as a team player on a squad of individualistic stars such as Rocket Richard and Bernie Geoffrion.

When he became active in the new NHL Players Association in 1961, Harvey was sent to the Rangers as player-coach, but he quit coaching after one season to concentrate on playing. "When I was a coach," he explained, "I couldn't be one of the boys. This way, if I want a beer with them, I get a beer."

He left the Rangers in 1964 to play with the minor league Quebec Aces, then went to the Detroit Red Wings in the 1966–67 season. After joining the St. Louis Blues for the 1968 playoffs, he had one full season as a player and assistant coach before retiring for good in 1969.

Harvey played in 1,113 regular season games, scoring 88 goals and 452 assists. He had 8 goals and 64 assists in 137 playoff games.
★ Hockey Hall of Fame

Haselrig, Carlton L.

FOOTBALL, WRESTLING
b. Jan. 22, 1966, Johnstown, Pa.

Wrestling for the University of Pittsburgh–Johnstown, Haselrig won NCAA heavyweight championships in both Division I and Division II from 1987 through 1989, becoming the only man ever to win six titles. During his college career, he won 143 matches while losing only 2 and tying 1.

Though he hadn't played football in college, Haselrig was chosen by the Pittsburgh Steelers in the twelfth round of the 1989 NFL draft. He spent a season on the team's developmental squad and was on the regular roster as a nose tackle in 1990.

The 6-foot-1 Haselrig wrestled at 275 pounds and increased that to 290 as a pro football player. The Steelers moved him to offensive guard in 1991 and he was chosen to play in the 1992 Pro Bowl.

Haugen, Anders

SKIING
b. Oct. 24, 1888, Oslo, Norway
d. April 17, 1984

Haugen was awarded an Olympic bronze medal 50 years after he won it because a scoring mistake was discovered. He had been placed fourth in the special jumping event at the 1924 Winter Olympics, behind Norway's Thorleif Haug, who was credited with 18.000 points to Haugen's 17.916.

In preparation for a reunion of the Norwegian team, a sports historian discovered that Haug actually had only 17.821 points. Notified of the error, the International Olympic Committee scheduled a special ceremony in Oslo on September 17, 1974, and Haugen was given his medal by Haug's daughter.

Haugen and his brother Lars were America's first outstanding ski jumpers. Haugen won the U.S. championship in 1910, 1920, 1923, and 1926, and Lars was the champion in 1912, 1915, 1918, 1922, 1924, 1927, and 1928.

In 1920, Anders jumped 214 feet at Dillon, Colorado, setting a U.S. record that stood until 1932.

Haughton, Percy D.

FOOTBALL
b. July 11, 1876, Staten Island, N.Y.
d. Oct. 27, 1924

A second-team All-American tackle at Harvard in 1898, Haughton coached Cornell to a 17–5–0 record from 1899 through 1900 and then went into business. He returned to Harvard as head coach in 1908 and was an immediate success, winning nine games and tying one without a loss.

Haughton created the modern coaching staff. At the time, most teams had just one coach or, at most, one assistant. Haughton had a backfield coach, a line coach, and an end coach as well as coaches who worked with passers and

kickers. He also established a system of scouting opponents.

He scheduled his practices to the minute, and he was one of the first coaches to use specialists. In Harvard's 4–0 victory over Yale in 1908, the winning field goal was kicked by Vic Kennard, who was put into the game for that one play. (A field goal was worth four points at that time.) Later in the game, a player named Sprague was sent in to punt 60 yards from behind the Harvard goal line, keeping Yale out of scoring range.

At a time when most teams emphasized power on offense, Haughton emphasized deception. He developed plays similar to those used in the modern T formation, with the quarterback often taking a direct snap from center, spinning, and faking or making handoffs to another back. As one writer described it, "Rivals chased will-o'-the-wisps, only to discover somebody else had the ball."

Haughton is often credited with inventing the mousetrap play, on which a defensive player is allowed to cross the line of scrimmage and is then blocked from the side. When sportswriter Grantland Rice remarked to Haughton that Yale had large, fast linemen, Haughton responded, "I only wish they were twice as fast. We'll let 'em through and then cut 'em down."

He was also probably the first coach to use a five-man line with three linebackers. Since his teams were often undersized, that defense, like Haughton's offense, put a premium on speed. Harvard's defenders were taught to read offensive keys and respond quickly to a developing play, with the object of getting three defenders to the point of attack.

In nine seasons at Harvard, Haughton won 71 games while losing only 7 and tying 3. His 1912 and 1913 teams both won all nine of their games. Haughton entered the service in 1917 and returned to private business after World War I ended. He coached Columbia to a 4–4–1 record in 1923 and died of a cerebral hemorrhage after the school had won four of its first five games in 1924.
★ College Football Hall of Fame

Haughton, William R.

HARNESS RACING
b. Nov. 2, 1923, Gloversville, N.Y.
d. July 15, 1986

No harness driver was better than Haughton in the big races. He was one of only three drivers to win the Hambletonian four times, the only driver to win the Little Brown Jug five times, and the only one to win the Messenger Stakes seven times.

After racing on fairground tracks in upstate New York for several years, Haughton finished tenth in the nation in heats won and winnings in 1949. He led in heats won for six straight years, from 1953 to 1958, and was the leading money-winner 12 times, from 1952 to 1959, 1963, 1965, 1967, and 1968.

Haughton trained primarily for other owners until the early 1960s, when he began developing his own stable. His Rum Customer won the trotting triple crown in 1968, and Green Speed was named harness horse of the year in 1977. Haughton drove Meadow Paige to a world record 1:55$\frac{2}{5}$ in a time trial at Lexington in 1967. Among his other top horses were Belle Action, Galophone, Speedy Count, and Carlisle.

Haughton's oldest son, Peter, was a top driver who died in an auto accident in early 1980. Another son, Tom, was the winning driver in the 1982 Hambletonian. Haughton died of head injuries suffered in an accident at Yonkers Raceway.

★ Harness Racing Hall of Fame

Havens, Frank B.

CANOEING
b. Aug. 1, 1924, Arlington, Va.

Havens's father was a member of the Yale crew that was chosen to row for the United States in the 1924 Olympics. But his wife was pregnant, and he decided not to go to the Paris Games. He was replaced by an alternate, and the crew won a gold medal. Frank Havens was born shortly after the closing ceremonies.

Frank chose canoeing as his sport. He won two Olympic medals in the 10,000-meter canoe singles, a silver in 1948, and a gold in 1952. He won the national canoeing championship in 1950, 1951, 1952, 1954, 1956, 1957, and 1961. His older brother, William Havens, Jr., was national champion in 1947.

Havlicek, John ("Hondo")

BASKETBALL
b. April 8, 1940, Lansing, Ohio

Although he was an All-American in 1962, Havlicek was overshadowed at Ohio State by Jerry Lucas, a three-time All-American center. Lucas and Havlicek led Ohio State into three straight NCAA tournament finals, winning in 1960 and losing to the University of Cincinnati in both 1961 and 1962.

Havlicek never played college football, but he was drafted by the Cleveland Browns of the NFL as well as by the NBA's Boston Celtics. He tried out as a wide receiver but was cut, and then joined the Celtics for the 1962–63 season.

He was the second of the Celtics' sixth men, replacing Frank Ramsey in that role. At 6-foot-5 and 205 pounds, Havlicek could come off the bench either as a guard or as a forward to add instant offense. He was quick and clever around the basket and could score from the 18- to 20-foot range with his unusual jump shot, christened the "leaping leaner" by Johnny Most, the announcer for the Celtics. Instead of leaping vertically, Havlicek jumped up and forward, inclining his body toward the basket as he shot.

Havlicek was like a perpetual motion machine, constantly running up and down the court at full speed. He became a starter at forward in 1966–67 and was a key man on the Celtic fast break because of his running, along with his scoring and passing ability.

He played for six championship teams in his first seven seasons, went through a few years when the Celtics were down, and then played for two more championship teams before retiring after the 1977–78 season. He was named most valuable player in the 1974 playoffs.

Havlicek could score — he averaged

28.9 points a game in 1968–69 and was the first NBA player to score 1,000 or more points for 16 consecutive seasons — but he was also a fine defensive player, named to the NBA all-defensive team eight times.

In his 16 seasons, Havlicek played 1,270 regular season games and scored 26,395 points, an average of 20.8 per game. He had 8,007 rebounds and 6,114 assists.

★ Basketball Hall of Fame

Hawerchuk, Dale

HOCKEY
b. April 4, 1963, Toronto, Ont.

A 5-foot-11, 190-pound center, Hawerchuk played just two seasons of junior hockey before joining the NHL's Winnipeg Jets in 1981. He won the Calder Trophy as the league's rookie of the year after scoring 103 points on 45 goals and 58 assists. At 18 years, 351 days, he was the youngest player ever to have more than 100 points in a season.

After slipping to 91 points in his second year, Hawerchuk had 100 or more points in five consecutive seasons, from 1983–84 through 1987–88. On March 6, 1984, he set an NHL record with 5 assists in one period.

The Jets traded Hawerchuk to the Buffalo Sabres in 1990 for three players. Through the 1993–94 season, he had 1,298 points on 484 goals and 814 assists in 1,032 regular season games. He added 25 goals and 58 assists for 83 points in 66 playoff games.

Hawkins, Connie (Cornelius L.)

BASKETBALL
b. July 17, 1942, Brooklyn, N.Y.

Hawkins was a playground basketball legend as a teenager in the tough Bedford–Stuyvesant area of Brooklyn. Jerry Harkness, who played for the NBA's Indiana Pacers, remembered seeing Hawkins in a pickup game against Wilt Chamberlain when he was still in high school: "Believe me, Connie more than held his own. . . . He was doing all the Doctor J moves 15 years before anyone ever heard of Julius Erving."

After leading Brooklyn Boys High

School to two city championships, he won a scholarship to the University of Iowa in 1960. But he lost his scholarship in his freshman year because of alleged links to a gambler convicted of fixing games. The NCAA wouldn't allow another school to give him a scholarship, and the NBA wouldn't allow him to play for any of its teams, though no criminal charge was ever brought against him.

Hawkins joined the Pittsburgh Rens of the new American Basketball League for the 1961–62 season, averaging 27.5 points a game, leading the team to the ABL championship, and winning the league's most valuable player award. Then the ABL folded during its second season, and he went to the Harlem Globetrotters.

When the American Basketball Association was formed in 1967, Hawkins left the Globetrotters for the ABA's Pittsburgh Pipers. He averaged 26.8 points a game, his team again won the league championship, and he was again named most valuable player.

In the meantime, Hawkins had filed a suit against the NBA for not letting him play. The suit was settled out of court in 1969. He got $1 million and the right to play in the NBA. He joined the league's Phoenix Suns after averaging 30.2 points a game with his ABA team, which had moved to Minnesota.

At 27, Hawkins had an outstanding "rookie" season in the NBA. He was the first Phoenix player ever named a first-team all-star, and he averaged 24.6 points a game, sixth in the league. But his knees were going bad, in part no doubt because of all the games he'd played on hard playground pavements. Hawkins played six more seasons before retiring. Despite his knee problems, he appeared in four NBA All-Star games.

In 616 professional games, Hawkins scored 11,628 points, an average of 18.9 a game, and had 5,450 rebounds.

★ Basketball Hall of Fame

Hawkins, Hersey R., Jr.

BASKETBALL
b. Sept. 29, 1966, Chicago, Ill.

A four-year starter at guard for Bradley University, Hawkins led NCAA Division I scorers with an average of 36.3 points a game in 1987–88 and was consensus college player of the year. In his career, he scored 3,008 points in 125 games, an average of 24.1 per game.

Chosen by the Los Angeles Clippers in the first round of the 1988 NBA draft, Hawkins was traded to the Philadelphia 76ers before the season. He made the league's all-rookie team, averaging 15.1 points a game.

Hawkins's best season was 1990–91, when he averaged 22.1 points per game. Philadelphia traded him to the Charlotte Hornets before the 1993–94 season.

Through 1993–94, he had scored 8,837 points in 485 NBA games, an average of 18.2, and he also had 1,833 rebounds, 1,580 assists, and 857 steals. An excellent outside shot, the 6-foot-3, 190-pound Hawkins hit 554 of 1,407 three-point attempts, a .394 average, in six seasons.

Hayes, Bob (Robert L.)

FOOTBALL, TRACK & FIELD
b. Dec. 20, 1942, Jacksonville, Fla.

"World's Fastest Human" is the label that has long been attached to whoever happened to be the best sprinter in the world at the moment. Hayes may have had more right to the title than anyone. Though not a great starter, Hayes was the first to run better than 6.0 seconds in the 60-yard dash, where the start is usually all-important, and he was the first to run 9.1 seconds in the 100-yard dash.

In 1963, he tied the world record of 20.6 seconds in the 220-yard dash, running against an 8-mph wind. But his sheer speed was probably best displayed in relays, where he got a running start. As the anchor man for the U.S. in the 1964 Olympics 4 x 100-meter relay, he took the baton 4 meters behind and won by 3 meters; the team set a world record of 39.0 seconds. His leg was estimated at 8.6 seconds for 100 meters and 7.7 seconds for the 100-yard portion.

Hayes also won the gold medal in the 1964 100-meter dash. He was the AAU

100-yard champion from 1962 to 1964, and running for Florida A & M, he won the NCAA 200-meter dash in 1964.

After the Olympics, Hayes joined the Dallas Cowboys of the NFL as a wide receiver. In 12 seasons with the Cowboys, he caught 371 passes for 7,414 yards, an average of 20.0 per catch, and 71 touchdowns. He returned 104 punts for 1,158 yards, an 11.1 average, and 3 touchdowns, and had 23 kickoff returns for 581 yards, a 25.3 average.

★ National Track & Field Hall of Fame

Hayes, Elvin E.

BASKETBALL
b. Nov. 17, 1945, Rayville, La.

The "Big E" was a prolific scorer who averaged 35 points a game during his high school career in Rayville, Louisiana, before becoming one of the first two black players, with Don Chaney, to play for the University of Houston.

Not very tall for a center, at 6-foot-9½, Hayes was both bulky — 235 pounds — and quick, and he could hit the short- to medium-range jump shot against opponents who stayed near the basket to try to defend against him close in.

At Houston, he was a consensus All-American in 1967 and 1968, but was listed as a forward because Lew Alcindor (later Kareem Abdul-Jabbar) was the All-American center both years. Hayes scored 2,888 points during his college career, averaging 31.0 a game, and had 1,602 rebounds.

Hayes and Alcindor met in one of the most publicized games in college basketball history on January 5, 1968, when Houston met UCLA at the Astrodome before 52,693 spectators, the largest crowd ever to watch a basketball game in the U.S. Hayes had 39 points and 15 rebounds in Houston's 71–69 victory, which ended UCLA's winning streak at 47 games. However, UCLA eliminated Houston, 101–69, in the semifinals of the NCAA tournament.

As a rookie with the San Diego Rockets, Hayes led the NBA in scoring with 28.4 points a game in 1968–69. He went with the Rockets when they moved to Houston in 1971 and was traded to the

Baltimore Bullets in 1972. In 1981, he returned to Houston and played for the Rockets until his retirement in 1984.

When the Bullets won the NBA championship in 1978, Hayes was named most valuable player of the championship series.

In his 16 NBA seasons, Hayes scored 27,313 points, third on the all-time career list, and averaged 21.0 per game. He had 16,279 rebounds, an average of 12.5 a game. He led the league in rebounds in 1969–70 and 1973–74.

★ Basketball Hall of Fame

Hayes, Woody (Wayne Woodrow)

FOOTBALL

b. Feb. 13, 1913, Clifton, Ohio
d. March 12, 1987

Hayes played tackle at Denison University in Ohio, graduating in 1935, and then became a high school teacher and coach. After serving in the Navy during World War II, he returned to Denison as head football coach in 1946 and produced unbeaten teams in 1947 and 1948.

Miami University of Ohio hired Hayes in 1949. His 1950 Miami team won nine of ten regular season games and beat Arizona State, 34–21, in the Salad Bowl. Hayes then became coach at Ohio State University, where he won 205 games while losing 68 and tying 10 in 28 seasons.

His teams featured the "three yards and a cloud of dust" offense, with big, powerful lines and usually a hard-running fullback. In 1954, Ohio State won all nine regular season games, beat Southern California, 20–7, in the Rose Bowl, and was consensus national champion. The Buckeyes were also named national champion by United Press International in 1957, and Hayes was voted coach of the year after an 8–1–0 regular season and a 10–7 victory over Oregon in the Rose Bowl.

A student of military history whose idol was George S. Patton, Hayes was a fiery, volatile leader who took a paternal interest in his players but who frequently fought with those outside his football family. When the Ohio State faculty committee voted to turn down a bid for the 1962 Rose Bowl, Hayes gave an impromptu speech at a rally in which he said he respected the integrity but not the intelligence of the committee members.

From that time on, his relations with the administration and faculty were strained, but strong support from alumni and players gave him job security. The end of his coaching career came after the 1978 Gator Bowl. A Clemson linebacker intercepted a pass near the end of the game to preserve a 17–15 victory over Ohio State, ran out of bounds, and was attacked by Hayes before a national television audience. Hayes was forced to resign shortly afterward.

During his 33 years as a head coach, Hayes had 238 wins, fifth on the all-time list, while losing 72 and tying 10. His .759 winning percentage is twenty-seventh best in history.

★ College Football Hall of Fame

Haynes, Abner

FOOTBALL

b. Sept. 19, 1937, Denton, Tex.

Probably the American Football League's most exciting player, Haynes was a starting halfback for North Texas State University for three years. He rushed for 1,864 yards and 25 touchdowns in 345 attempts and caught 46 passes for 579 yards and 6 touchdowns during his collegiate career.

Haynes joined the Dallas Texans of the new American Football League in 1960. He was named both rookie of the year and player of the year after leading the league in rushing with 875 yards on 156 carries and in punt returns with 215 yards on 14 runbacks, a 15.4 average.

The Dallas team moved to Kansas City and became known as the Chiefs in 1963. The following year, Haynes was traded to the Denver Broncos. He played for the Miami Dolphins and New York Jets in 1967 before retiring.

The 6-foot-1, 200-pound Haynes, who had great speed and dazzling moves in the open field, set AFL records with 5 touchdowns in a game and 19 touchdowns in a season in 1961, and with 46 career rushing touchdowns. During his eight professional seasons, Haynes carried the ball 1,036 times for 4,630 yards, a 4.5 average; caught 287 passes for 3,535 yards, a 12.3 average, and 20 touchdowns; returned 85 punts for 875 yards, a 10.3 average, and 1 touchdown; and ran back 121 kickoffs for 3,025 yards, a 25.0 average, and 1 touchdown. His 12,065 combined yards is the AFL record.

Haynes, Marques O.

BASKETBALL
b. Oct. 3, 1926, Sand Springs, Okla.

As a guard at Oklahoma's Langston University, the 6-foot, 160-pound Haynes orchestrated a victory over the Harlem Globetrotters. His skills, and especially his incredible dribbling ability, won him a job with the Kansas City Stars, who toured with the Globetrotters.

After a half season with the Stars, Haynes joined the Globetrotters in early 1947. His displays of dribbling were a major part of the team's act; the Globetrotters had become so good that they had to be showmen to keep spectators entertained.

Haynes left the Globetrotters in 1953 to tour with his own team, the Fabulous Magicians. After a brief return to the Globetrotters in 1972, he and Meadowlark Lemon toured with a team called the Bucketeers.

Haynie, Sandra J.

GOLF
b. June 4, 1943, Ft. Worth, Tex.

Haynie won the Texas Amateur championship two years in a row, in 1958 and 1959, and then joined the LPGA tour. Over a 16-year period, 1961–76, she won 39 tournaments, and in 1974 she became only the second golfer to win the U.S. Women's Open and the LPGA championship in the same year.

However, arthritis limited her playing time from 1977 through 1980. She entered only 14 tournaments during that period. Haynie rejoined the tour full-time in 1981. The following year she won her third major tournament, the Peter Jackson Classic, and earned $245,232. In 1988, Haynie became the sixteenth woman golfer to earn more than $1 million in her career.
★ LPGA Hall of Fame

Hazzard, Walter R., Jr.

BASKETBALL
b. April 15, 1942, Wilmington, Del.

Hazzard was the key player on the 1963–64 UCLA team that won all 30 of its games and the NCAA championship, the start of coach John Wooden's dynastic streak when UCLA won ten titles in 12 years. The 6-foot-3, 185-pound guard was named the tournament's most valuable player. He was also a consensus All-American, and he was selected by the U.S. Basketball Writers Association as college player of the year.

After playing for the U.S. team that won the 1964 Olympic gold medal, Hazzard joined the Los Angeles Lakers of the NBA. He never became as big a star as he was in college, although he averaged 23.9 points a game in 1967–68.

After three seasons with the Lakers, he went to the Seattle Supersonics in 1967, then played for the Atlanta Hawks from 1968–69 through 1970–71 and the Buffalo Braves from 1971–72 through 1972–73. After a brief stint with the Golden State Warriors, he returned to Seattle for the 1973–74 season before retiring.

Hazzard became a Muslim late in his career and adopted the name Mahdi Abdul-Rahmad. In his ten NBA seasons, he scored 9,087 points, averaging 12.6 a game, and had 3,555 assists. He coached UCLA from 1984–85 through 1987–88, winning 77 games and losing 48.

Healey, Edward F., Jr.

FOOTBALL
b. Dec. 28, 1894, Indian Orchard, Mass.
d. Dec. 9, 1978

Healey played end at Dartmouth but never made an All-American team. After working in Nebraska for four years, he tried out with the NFL's Rock Island Independents and made the team as a tackle.

In 1922, Healey faced end George Halas, co-owner and coach of the Chicago Bears as well as a player. Halas was so impressed with the 6-foot-3, 220-pound Healey that he paid Rock Island $100 for his services after the game. No money actually changed hands because the Independents owed the Bears $100 for playing in Rock Island.

Halas later called Healey "the most versatile tackle" in history. Along with size and strength, he had speed. He once caught up to a Bear halfback who was running the wrong way with an intercepted pass and tackled him to prevent a safety.

Healey was named to unofficial All-Pro teams in 1921 and 1923. He retired after the 1927 season.

★ Pro Football Hall of Fame

Hearns, Thomas

BOXING
b. Oct. 18, 1958, Memphis, Tenn.

As an amateur, Hearns won 147 of 155 fights and took the AAU national and Golden Gloves 147-pound championships in 1977. The 6-foot-1 Hearns had only 11 knockouts in his amateur career, but after turning professional in November 1977, he became known as the "Hit Man" because of his newfound punching ability.

Hearns won 28 straight professional bouts going into a WBA welterweight championship fight against Pipino Cuevas in Mexico on August 2, 1980. He knocked out Cuevas in the 2nd round to win the title, and he was named fighter of the year on the strength of that match.

On September 16, 1981, Hearns met WBC champion Sugar Ray Leonard and was leading after 12 rounds. But Leonard knocked Hearns down in the 13th and won on a technical knockout in the 14th round.

Hearns won the WBC super welterweight championship in 1982 by beating Wilfred Benitez, and he was named fighter of the year again in 1984 after knocking out Roberto Duran to win the WBA version of the title.

He then stepped up to the middleweight class but lost to Marvin Hagler in a 1985 championship fight. However, in 1987 Hearns knocked out Dennis Andries to win the WBC light heavyweight title, and Juan Roldan to take the WBC middleweight crown. After he won the middleweight victory, the WBC stripped him of the welterweight championship.

Hearns won his fifth championship, in the new super middleweight division, by beating James Kinchen in 1988. He had a rematch with Leonard in 1989, knocking him down twice, but the fight resulted in a controversial draw. In 1991, Hearns began fighting exclusively as a light heavyweight. He won the WBA championship in June, beating Virgil Hill in a 12-round decision. Hearns lost the title to Iran Barkley in a 12-round split decision on March 20, 1992.

He became a champion for the seventh time by winning the NABF heavyweight title with a 1st-round knockout of Dan Ward on January 1, 1994. Hearns has won 52 of his 56 professional fights, 41 by knockout, with 4 losses and 1 draw.

Hebner, Harry J.

SWIMMING
b. June 15, 1891
d. Oct. 12, 1968

The backstroke didn't become a separate swimming event until the early part of the century. Hebner was its first great competitor. He won the national indoor 150-yard backstroke championship seven years in a row, from 1910 to 1916, and he held the world records at every backstroke distance during those years and beyond.

Hebner won the gold medal in the Olympic 100-meter backstroke in 1912, after having won the bronze in 1908. He was also a fine freestyle swimmer; he won the national outdoor 440-yard championship in 1914, the indoor 100-yard championship in 1913–14, and the indoor 220-yard in 1914. He was a member of the 4 x 200-meter relay team that won an Olympic silver medal in 1912.

At the 1920 Olympics, Hebner was the U.S. flag bearer during opening ceremonies, this time as a member of the country's water polo team, which failed to win a medal.

Heenan, John C.

BOXING
b. May 2, 1833, Troy, N.Y.
d. Oct. 28, 1873

Heenan went to Benicia, California, at 17 and became known as the "Benicia Boy" after he began prize fighting. He returned to New York in 1857, and on October 20, 1858, he met John Morrissey at Long Point, Canada, for a $10,000 side bet and the American heavyweight championship. In the 1st round, Heenan broke his hand, but he managed to go 10 more rounds before being knocked out.

Morrissey refused a rematch and retired, so Heenan claimed the title. He went to England and fought Tom Sayers, the British title claimant, on April 17, 1860. After 42 rounds the crowd broke into the ring, and the fight was ruled a draw. American newspapermen felt the spectators had stopped the fight because Heenan was winning, but British journalists naturally thought Sayers had the upper hand.

Like Morrissey, Sayers retired immediately afterward. Heenan challenged the new British titlist, Tom King; their fight, on December 18, 1863, was also controversial. King couldn't come "up to scratch" in the required 30 seconds after the 18th round, but he was given additional time to recover, and Heenan was forced to give up after 25 rounds. It was his last fight.

Heffelfinger, Pudge (William W.)

FOOTBALL
b. Dec. 20, 1867, Minneapolis, Minn.
d. April 5, 1954

Despite his nickname, the 6-foot-3 Heffelfinger weighed only 178 pounds when he entered Yale in 1888. Within a year he was up to about 205 pounds, and he was the best college lineman in the country. He was a guard on the first All-American team selected, in 1889, and he was named to the team again in 1890 and 1891.

Yale in 1890 developed a new kind of play to take advantage of Heffelfinger's speed and strength. Instead of simply blocking the defensive player across

from him at the line of scrimmage, he was asked to pull out of the line to lead interference for the runner. The pulling guard has been a standard feature of American football ever since.

During Heffelfinger's four-year career at Yale, the school won 54 games while losing only 2. There were no limits on eligibility at that time, and a student newspaper led a campaign to get him to play a fifth season, using the slogan, "Linger, oh linger, Heffelfinger," but he chose to play for the Chicago Athletic Association instead.

On November 12, 1892, Heffelfinger played a game for the Duquesne Athletic Club of Pittsburgh. He was paid $500, the first time a player was known to be given money, although there may well have been under-the-table payments before that. Heffelfinger forced a fumble, picked up the ball, and ran 35 yards for the only touchdown as Duquesne beat the archrival Allegheny Athletic Association.

Heffelfinger coached Lehigh University to a 6–8–0 record in 1894 and had a 7–3–0 record at the University of Minnesota in 1895. He then became a stockbroker but occasionally helped with the coaching at Minnesota. In 1916, he returned to Yale to coach the linemen, but in his exuberant demonstration of how the game should be played, he knocked two of them out of action.

At 54, Heffelfinger captained an all-star team that played a 1922 game against the Ohio State alumni to raise money for charity. He was on the field for 51 minutes in a 16–0 victory. On November 11, 1933, a few weeks before his 65th birthday, he played nine minutes in another charity game, his final appearance in a football uniform.

★ College Football Hall of Fame

Heida, Anton

GYMNASTICS
b. 1878
d. ?

Heida won five gold medals and a silver at the 1904 St. Louis Olympics. He tied with Edward Hennig in the horizontal bar and with George Eyser in the vault; he won the pommel horse and the four-event combined championship outright; he was a member of Turngemeinde Philadelphia team that won the gold in combined exercises; and he won a silver in the parallel bars.

He was the national champion in the vault in 1902. His victories at the Olympics were also considered national championships.

Heiden, Beth (Elizabeth L.)

CYCLING, SKIING, SPEED SKATING

b. Sept. 27, 1959, Madison, Wis.

Although overshadowed by the brilliant speed skating performances of her brother Eric, Heiden was a remarkable athlete who excelled in a number of sports. As a high school student, she played tennis and soccer and set a national age group record for the mile run.

In 1979, she won world championships at all four speed skating distances, from 500 meters to 3,000 meters, and became the first American women to win the world overall championship. An ankle injury troubled her during the 1980 Olympics, where she won only one medal, a bronze in the 3,000-meter race.

Like many speed skaters, Heiden competed in cycling as a means of off-season training. She won the U.S. and national road race championships, as well as the prestigious Coors International Classic, in 1980.

Heiden took up cross-country skiing in 1981, while attending the University of Vermont. Two years later, she won the first NCAA women's championship in the sport.

Heiden, Eric A.

SPEED SKATING

b. June 14, 1958, Madison, Wis.

Heiden was a hero in Europe before his name was well known in the United States. One of the most popular songs in Norway in 1979 was "The Ballad of Eric Heiden."

At 18, he won the 1977 world junior overall, senior overall, and sprint championships, an unprecedented sweep. He repeated the sweep in 1978. A year later,

he won the world sprint title again and captured all four events at the world overall championships, setting a record of 14:43.11 in the 10,000-meter race. In 1980, he won the world sprint and overall championships for the fourth straight year, setting world records of 1:13.60 in the 1,000-meter race and 1:54.79 in the 1,500-meter race.

Entering the 1980 Winter Olympics just a week later, Heiden was expected to win at least two gold medals and perhaps as many as four. He astonished almost everyone by winning five.

In the 500-meter race, his weakest event, he set a world record of 38.03 seconds. After setting Olympic records in the 1,000-, 1,500-, and 5,000-meter races, he watched the U.S. Olympic hockey team beat the Soviet Union. The win so excited him that he found it hard to sleep. Awaking late the next morning, he had a couple of slices of bread for breakfast, hurried to the speed skating rink, and won the 10,000-meter race in 14:28.13, breaking the world record by 6.20 seconds.

Heiden won the Sullivan Award as the nation's outstanding amateur athlete of 1980. When he announced his retirement after the Olympics, Heiden said, "Maybe if things had stayed the way they were, and I could still be obscure in an obscure sport, I might want to keep skating. I really liked it best when I was a nobody."

★ Olympic Hall of Fame

Heilmann, Harry E.

BASEBALL

b. Aug. 3, 1894, San Francisco, Calif.

d. July 9, 1951

A four-time AL batting champion, Heilmann was a 6-foot-1, 195-pounder who specialized in line drives. Although he could hit the ball a long way, he was more likely to hit the fence than to drive the ball over it. As a result, he had three times as many doubles as home runs during his major league career.

Heilmann joined the Detroit Tigers of the AL as an outfielder during the 1914 season but spent 1915 in the minor leagues. He returned to the Tigers in 1916 and was a good hitter but not a great one, until Ty Cobb became the team's manager in 1921. Cobb had Heilmann move his feet closer together, and with the new stance, Heilmann responded with a league-leading .394 average and 237 hits that season.

During the next nine seasons, Heilmann batted .356, .403, .346, .393, .367, .398, .328, .344, and .333, winning batting titles in 1923, 1925, and 1927.

He had dramatic finishes in two of those seasons. Tris Speaker was the league leader going into September 1925, about 15 points ahead, but Heilmann caught fire in the last month while Speaker was on the bench with an injury. He finished by getting six hits in nine at-bats in a doubleheader to beat Speaker, .393 to .389.

In 1927, Heilmann could have won the batting championship by sitting out a doubleheader on the last day of the season. Instead, he got seven hits in nine at-bats to beat out Al Simmons, .398 to .392.

Heilmann played for Detroit through 1928, then was traded to Cincinnati. He missed the 1930 season with arthritis and retired after a brief comeback attempt in 1932. He was the Tigers' radio announcer from 1933 until June 1951, when he had to quit because of lung cancer. He died less than a month later.

In 2,148 games, Heilmann had a career average of .342 on 2,660 hits, including 542 doubles, 151 triples, and 183 home runs. He scored 1,291 runs and had 1,539 RBI.

★ Baseball Hall of Fame

Hein, Melvin J.

FOOTBALL
b. Aug. 22, 1909, Redding, Calif.
d. Jan. 31, 1992

On Pearl Harbor Day, December 7, 1941, Mel Hein of the New York Giants was taken to a hospital in an ambulance after suffering a broken nose and a concussion in a game against the Brooklyn Dodgers. It was the only time he was permanently removed from a game be-

cause of injury in 15 seasons of professional football.

Hein played all three interior line positions at Washington State from 1928 through 1930 and was named an All-American at all three by various selectors in 1930, when he captained the team.

There was no NFL draft of college players at that time, and Hein signed a contract with the Providence Steamroller for $135 a game. Then the Giants offered him $150. Hein immediately sent a telegram to the Providence postmaster, asking that the envelope containing his contract be returned to him. It was, and he joined the Giants.

The 6-foot-2, 225-pound Hein settled in as a center in New York. He was named a second-team All-Pro his first two seasons and was a first-team All-Pro the next eight years in a row, 1933 through 1940. When the Giants won the NFL championship in 1938, Hein won the Joe Carr Trophy as the league's most valuable player.

Remarkably fast for his size, Hein excelled as a linebacker both against the run and the pass. He once had a 50-yard interception return against the Green Bay Packers.

He announced his retirement after the 1941 season to coach at Union College in Schenectady, but the Giants persuaded him to keep playing because of the World War II manpower shortage. For the last four years of his career, Hein coached in Schenectady during the week, then played for the Giants on Sunday without practicing. He retired for good after the 1945 season, when the war was over.

★ College Football Hall of Fame; Pro Football Hall of Fame

Heinsohn, Thomas W.

BASKETBALL
b. Aug. 26, 1934, Union City, N.J.

As a center at Holy Cross in Massachusetts, Heinsohn was noted for his low, line-drive hook shots that somehow went into the basket most of the time. He was an All-American in his senior year, 1955–56, when he scored 740 points, an average of 27.4 a game. In his three-year college career Heinsohn scored 1,789 points and averaged 22.1 a game.

He joined the Boston Celtics for the 1956–57 season and was moved to forward. At that position, he developed a low, line-drive jump shot that also went into the basket a good deal of the time. Heinsohn was named rookie of the year after averaging 16.2 points a game and pulling down 705 rebounds.

The 6-foot-7, 220-pounder was an aggressive player and a strong rebounder. Along with Bill Russell, he excelled at getting the defensive rebound and making the good outlet pass to set up the Boston fast break. In his nine seasons, the Celtics won eight NBA championships.

Heinsohn's best season was 1961–62, when he averaged 22.3 points a game. Bothered by injuries in 1964–65, he played in only 67 games and averaged only 13.6 points, and he retired after the season. He had a total of 12,194 career points, an average of 18.6 a game, and 5,749 rebounds. In 104 playoff games, he scored 2,058 points, a 19.8 average.

He returned to the Celtics as head coach in 1969. Heinsohn was named NBA coach of the year in 1973, when the Celtics won 68 games and lost only 14, the best record in the team's history. They won NBA championships under Heinsohn in 1974 and 1976. He resigned after the 1977–78 season with a record of 427 victories and 263 losses.
★ Basketball Hall of Fame

Heisman, John W.
FOOTBALL
b. Oct. 25, 1869, Cleveland, Ohio
d. Oct. 3, 1936

Heisman played football at Brown University from 1887 through 1889 and at the University of Pennsylvania in 1890 and 1891. He coached in 1892 at Oberlin College. It was only the second year of football at the school, but Heisman's team won all seven of its games, including a victory over Michigan and two over Ohio State.

He went 5–2–0 at Akron University in 1893, returned to Oberlin for a 4–3–1 season in 1894, and then took over at Auburn University for five seasons, winning 12 games, losing 4, and tying 2.

In 1900, Heisman became coach at Clemson. His first team won all six of its games, and he had a 19–3–2 record there in four seasons before moving on to Georgia Tech, where he had the longest stay of his 36-year career.

Heisman turned Georgia Tech into a football power. His 1915, 1916, and 1917 teams were all unbeaten, contributing to a 32-game undefeated streak, including 2 ties. Tech outscored its opponents 1,592 to 62 during that stretch. Its 222–0 victory over Cumberland in 1916 is the highest score ever recorded.

In 16 seasons at Georgia Tech, Heisman had a 100–29–6 record. He returned to Pennsylvania as coach in 1920 and had a 16–10–2 record in three seasons there. After a 7–2–0 mark at Washington and Jefferson in 1923, he finished his coaching career with four seasons at Rice Institute, where he was 14–18–3.

One of the sport's chief innovators, Heisman developed one of the first shifts, which was named for him. He was probably the first coach to have both guards pull to lead an end run, a forerunner of the Green Bay Packer power sweep of the 1960s. And he may have been the first to have the center toss the ball back instead of rolling or kicking it, though others claimed that honor.

An early advocate of legalizing the forward pass, Heisman was also a proponent of dividing the game into quarters instead of halves. He was a founder and twice president of the American Football Coaches Association.

After retiring from coaching, he became athletic director of the Downtown Athletic Club in New York City. The club in 1935 began awarding a trophy to college football's outstanding player. After Heisman died in 1936, the award became known as the Heisman Memorial Trophy.
★ College Football Hall of Fame

Heiss, Carol E. (Mrs. Jenkins)

FIGURE SKATING

b. Jan. 20, 1940, New York, N.Y.

For four years, Heiss was eclipsed by Tenley Albright. She finished second to Albright in the U.S. figure skating championships from 1953 through 1956, in the 1953 and 1955 North American championships, in the 1955 world championship, and in the 1956 Olympics.

Two weeks after the Olympics, she beat Albright for the first time to win the world title. Albright then retired, and Heiss succeeded her as the best in the world. She won the U.S. and world championships each year from 1957 through 1960, was the North American champion from 1957 through 1959, and climaxed her career by winning the Olympic gold in 1960, fulfilling a promise she'd made to her mother.

Heiss began skating when she was five years old, and she immediately showed talent. At seven, she started taking lessons from Pierre and Andre Brunet of the Skating Club of New York. Pierre assured Carol's mother, "In ten years, your daughter can be the best in the world."

To pay for the lessons, Mrs. Heiss worked as a freelance fabric designer, working on drawings in the Skating Club rink while Carol practiced. When they traveled to Cortina, Italy, for the 1956 Winter Olympics, Mrs. Heiss was suffering from terminal cancer. She died in October of that year, after Carol had promised to keep competing until she won a gold medal.

Heiss was chosen to take the Olympic oath on behalf of all the athletes in the 1960 Winter Games. After winning her gold, she had a brief professional career. In 1961, she married another champion figure skater, Hayes Alan Jenkins.

★ International Women's Sports Hall of Fame

Held, Bud (Franklin)

TRACK AND FIELD

b. Oct. 25, 1927, Los Angeles, Calif.

Injuries prevented Held from winning an Olympic medal, but he was the first to throw the javelin more than 260 feet, and he came close to 270 feet. He also improved everyone else's performances by designing a javelin that had a lighter point and better balance than the old model.

Competing for Stanford, Held won the NCAA javelin championship three years in a row, 1948–50. He was the AAU national champion six times, in 1949, 1951, 1953–55, and 1958. In a meet at Pasadena on August 8, 1953, Held threw the javelin 263 feet, 10 inches, breaking a world record that had been set in 1938. He extended the record to 268 feet, $2\frac{1}{2}$ inches in 1955.

Held competed in the 1952 Olympics but was suffering from a shoulder injury and finished ninth. Another injury kept him out of the 1956 Olympics. He retired from competition after winning the 1958 national title.

★ National Track & Field Hall of Fame

Hencken, John F.

SWIMMING

b. May 29, 1954, Culver City, Calif.

After a knee operation, Hencken took up swimming as physical therapy in his early teens. He became an outstanding breaststroker during the 1970s. Hencken won gold medals in the 200-meter breaststroke at the 1972 Olympics and the 100-meter in 1976, when he won a silver in the 200-meter. He was also a member of the gold medal 4 x 100-meter medley relay team in 1976.

Hencken's first major victory came in the AAU national outdoor 100-meter breaststroke in 1972. He entered Stanford University that fall and won NCAA championships in the 100-yard breaststroke in 1975 and 1976, the 200-yard in 1974 and 1975.

He was also the national outdoor champion in the 100-meter and 200-meter breaststroke in 1973, 1974, and 1976. He won indoor titles in the 100-yard in 1974 and in both the 100- and 200-yard events in 1975. Hencken won the world 100-meter breaststroke championship in 1973 and finished second in the 200-meter.

Hencken set a total of 11 world records in the two breaststroke distances. He retired from competition after the 1976 Olympics.

Henderson, Rickey H.

BASEBALL
b. Dec. 25, 1958, Chicago, Ill.

Considered by many experts the greatest leadoff hitter in history, Henderson has a rare combination of hitting ability, power, and speed. He has led the AL in stolen bases 11 times, including seven seasons in a row, in walks three times, and in runs scored five times. Henderson holds major league records for most career stolen bases with 1,117, most steals in a season with 130 in 1982, and most home runs leading off a game, 63.

He joined the Oakland Athletics during the 1979 season. In 1980, his first full season, he led the league with 100 stolen bases. Henderson had a league-leading 89 runs scored, 135 hits, 56 stolen bases, and 327 outfield putouts in 1981, when a player strike shortened the season.

With Oakland, Henderson also led in steals with 130 in 1982, 108 in 1983, and 66 in 1984. He was then traded to the New York Yankees. Despite missing nearly a month of the 1985 season with an injury, he again led in stolen bases with 80, and repeated with 87 in 1986.

An injury limited him to only 95 games in 1987, but he bounced back with a league-leading 93 steals in 1988. The Yankees traded him back to Oakland during the 1989 season, when he led in steals with 77, runs scored with 113, and walks with 126.

Henderson was named the league's most valuable player in 1990. He had his highest batting average that season, .325, with a league-leading 119 runs scored and 65 steals in only 75 attempts. Although he slipped to a .268 average in 1991, he was the stolen base leader again with 58.

In 1992, Henderson was on the disabled list three times and appeared in only 117 games. During the following season, Oakland traded him to the Toronto Blue Jays, and he helped lead Toronto to a second consecutive world championship. He returned to Oakland in 1994.

The 5-foot-10, 190-pound Henderson is a rarity in that he throws left but bats right-handed. Through 1994, he had 2,216 hits in 2,080 games, including 364 doubles, 56 triples, and 226 home runs. He had stolen 1,117 bases and scored 1,652 runs.

Henderson has been a consistently good performer in post-season play. In the 1989 AL championship series, he stole a record 8 bases and tied a record by scoring 8 runs, and he was named most valuable player in the World Series, batting .474 with 3 stolen bases, 4 runs scored, and 3 RBI in four games. He hit .333 with 3 more steals, 2 runs, and 1 RBI in the 1990 World Series.

Hendricks, Ted (Theodore P.)

FOOTBALL
b. Nov. 1, 1947, Guatemala City, Guatemala

As a defensive end at the University of Miami, Hendricks was named to some All-American teams as a sophomore in 1966 and was a consensus All-American choice in 1967 and 1968. The 6-foot-7, 220-pounder was named college lineman of the year by United Press International as a senior.

Hendricks was moved to outside linebacker when he joined the NFL's Baltimore Colts as a second-round draft choice in 1969. Nicknamed "the Mad Stork" because of his frame and his style of play, he distinguished himself as a pass rusher and kick blocker.

When the new World Football League was organized in 1974, its teams signed a number of players to future contracts, to begin playing after their NFL contracts expired. Hendricks was among them. When the announcement was made, the Colts traded him to the Green Bay Packers for the 1974 season.

Because of the WFL's financial problems, Hendricks never played in the league. Instead, he was signed as a free agent by the Oakland Raiders in 1975. He retired after the 1983 season.

An All-Pro from 1971 through 1974

and in 1980 and 1982, Hendricks was selected for the Pro Bowl nine times.

★ College Football Hall of Fame; Pro Football Hall of Fame

Henie, Sonja

FIGURE SKATING
b. April 8, 1912, Oslo, Norway
d. Oct. 12, 1969

A fine all-around athlete, Henie competed in tennis, swimming, and skiing, and she also studied ballet before she took up figure skating. The combination of grace and athleticism that she brought to the sport transformed skating into a popular spectacle.

Henie won the Norwegian championship when she was ten years old and competed in her first Winter Olympics in 1924, two months before her twelfth birthday. She finished second in the world championships when she was 13, and then won the title ten years in a row, from 1927 through 1936.

She is the only skater ever to win three Olympic titles, in 1928, 1932, and 1936. Her first two Olympic victories came easily. Her third was much more difficult. Henie announced her intention to retire after the 1936 Winter Games and then found herself in a close contest with a young English skater, Cecilia Colledge. Henie won by just 3 points.

Petite, blond, and button-nosed, Henie proved even more successful as a professional performer and businesswoman. She starred in her own show, the Hollywood Ice Revue, and in ten Twentieth Century Fox movies. In her first full year as a professional, 1937, she earned more than $200,000. When she died of leukemia aboard an ambulance plane carrying her from Paris to Oslo in 1969, she was worth more than $47 million.

★ International Women's Sports Hall of Fame

Henke, Tom (Thomas A.)

BASEBALL
b. Dec. 21 1957, Kansas City, Mo.

Henke was with the AL's Texas Rangers for parts of the 1982, 1983, and 1984 seasons before being chosen by the Toronto Blue Jays in a special compensation draft in 1985. He immediately established himself as an outstanding relief pitcher.

A right-hander, the 6-foot-5, 225-pound Henke had 20 or more saves every year from 1986 through 1993, with a league-leading 34 in 1987. He became a free agent after the 1992 season and returned to Texas, where he had a career high of 40 saves.

Henke appeared in four AL championship series with the Blue Jays and had a 2–0 record with 3 saves and a 1.65 ERA in 12 appearances. He had 2 saves and a 2.70 ERA in Toronto's six-game victory over the Atlanta Braves in the 1992 World Series.

Through the 1994 season, Henke had a 40–41 record with 275 saves and a 2.73 ERA. He had struck out 813 hitters and walked 237 in 735⅓ innings.

Hennig, Edward A.

GYMNASTICS
b. 1880, Cleveland, Ohio
d. Aug. 28, 1960

At 62, Hennig was the oldest candidate ever for the Sullivan Award as the nation's outstanding amateur athlete. He finished third in the 1942 voting.

Hennig got involved in gymnastics, particularly Indian clubs, on the advice of a doctor, because he was a sickly youngster. He won two gold medals in the 1904 Olympics, in club swinging and the horizontal bar, where he tied with Anton Heida of the United States.

Over a period of nearly 50 years, Hennig won the national club swinging championship 13 times; his last championship came when he was 71 years old, just nine years before his death. He was also national champion in the horizontal bars in 1911.

Henning, Anne

SPEED SKATING
b. Sept. 6, 1955, Raleigh, N.C.

A great sprinter, Henning won the 500-meter event in both the world championships and the world sprint championships in 1971, and she was the Olympic gold medalist in 1972.

She entered the Olympics holding

world records in both the 500- and 1,000-meter. In the 500-meter race, she was paired with Sylvia Burka of Canada. At the crossover point, where the skaters change lanes, they were about to have a collision when Henning slowed to let Burka cross. She probably lost a full second, yet skated an Olympic record 43.70.

Burka was disqualified, and Henning was allowed another attempt. Skating alone, she improved her time to 43.33 seconds. The second run may have hurt her chances in the 1,000-meter, however; she won the bronze medal in that event and said afterward that her legs felt "dead."

Hennings, Chad W.

FOOTBALL
b. Oct. 20, 1965, Elberton, Iowa

The 6-foot-6, 267-pound Hennings won the 1987 Outland Trophy as the nation's outstanding collegiate lineman. A defensive tackle at the Air Force Academy, he was chosen by the Dallas Cowboys in the 1988 NFL draft but was required to serve in the Air Force for four years. After his discharge in 1992, he joined the Cowboys and was a part-time defensive lineman in their victories in Super Bowls XXVII and XXVIII.

Henry, Fats (Wilbur F.)

FOOTBALL
b. Oct. 31, 1897, near Mansfield, Ohio
d. Feb. 7, 1952

"Fats" Henry, also known as "Pete," was 5-foot-10 and weighed 230 pounds as a college player at Washington And Jefferson, where he became the first student to letter in baseball, basketball, football, and track. He looked fat but was remarkably fast and agile; sportswriter Grantland Rice once described him as "a human rubber ball."

A starting tackle for five years, beginning when he was a 17-year-old freshman in 1915, Henry was a second-team All-American in 1918 and a first-team selection in 1919. He was exceptionally strong both as a blocker and as a defender, and because of his strength and speed, he was a master at blocking kicks.

In a 1919 game, he charged into the opposition's backfield so quickly that he grabbed the ball before it hit the punter's foot and ran 36 yards for a touchdown.

Henry joined the Canton Bulldogs of the NFL in 1920 and played for them through 1923. Because of a salary dispute, he went to the independent Pottsville Maroons in 1924 and was with the Akron Pros in the NFL the following season.

In 1925, Henry returned to Canton as a player and co-coach for two seasons. He began the 1927 season with the New York Giants but went back to Pottsville to reorganize and coach the Maroons. He retired after the 1928 season but was persuaded to play with the Staten Island Stapletons in 1930.

Henry was a prodigious kicker. For a long time, he was credited with an NFL record 94-yard punt against the Akron Pros on October 28, 1923. Recent research has shown that the kick traveled "only" 83 yards before rolling dead on the Akron two-yard line. His 50-yard field goal on November 13, 1922, is the league record for a drop kick, later tied but never broken. Henry also holds the NFL record for most consecutive conversions by drop kick with 49.

Grantland Rice chose Henry for his all-time All-American team in 1952. The same year, Roger Treat named him to an all-time All-Pro team.
★ College Football Hall of Fame; Pro Football Hall of Fame

Henry, Jim (James E.)

DIVING
b. Sept. 4, 1948, San Antonio, Tex.

As a student at the University of Indiana, Henry won three consecutive NCAA springboard titles, from 1968 through 1970. He was the national outdoor champion on the 1-meter springboard from 1967 through 1970 and on the 3-meter springboard from 1969 through 1971. He also won indoor titles in the 1-meter from 1968 through 1970 and in the 3-meter event in 1970.

Henry was leading with three dives to go in the 1968 Olympic springboard competition, but he finished third to win a bronze medal.

Henry, Kenneth C.

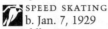
SPEED SKATING
b. Jan. 7, 1929

Oddly, Henry never won a national championship, but he was the world 500-meter speed skating champion in 1949 and 1952, and he also won the Olympic gold medal in the event in 1952. He also competed in the 1948 and 1956 Olympics without winning a medal. On exceptionally fast ice at Cortina, Italy, in 1956, he easily broke the former Olympic record, but finished only seventeenth.

At the 1960 Winter Games, Henry became the only American to carry the Olympic torch into the stadium during opening ceremonies. The torch was relayed to him by former skiing gold medalist Andrea Mead Lawrence, and Henry took one lap around the rink before lighting the Olympic flame.

Henry coached the 1968 Olympic speed skating team.

Herber, Arnie (Arnold)

FOOTBALL
b. April 2, 1910, Green Bay, Wis.
d. Oct. 14, 1969

The first great long passer in pro football history, Herber teamed with Don Hutson to give the Green Bay Packers the most dangerous passing combination in the NFL during the late 1930s.

While starring as a high school basketball and football player, Herber sold programs at Packer games. He went to the University of Wisconsin as a freshman, then transferred to Regis College in Colorado, but was forced to drop out of school because of the Depression.

Herber joined his hometown Packers in 1930 and played for championship teams in his first two seasons. He was named All-Pro tailback in 1932, when he threw nine touchdown passes.

When the Packers beat the Boston Redskins, 21–6, in the 1936 championship game, Herber threw a 43-yard touchdown pass to Hutson, and his 52-yard pass to Johnny "Blood" McNally set up another touchdown. He also threw a touch-

down pass in the Packers' 27–0 victory over New York Giants in the 1939 title game.

Herber retired after the 1940 season, but he joined the Giants in 1944 because of the World War II manpower shortage and threw 15 touchdown passes in two seasons before retiring permanently.

The 6-foot, 200-pound Herber had unusually small hands and used an unorthodox grip, putting his thumb rather than his fingers on the laces of the football. Nevertheless, he could throw accurately at ranges of up to 60 yards.

The NFL passing leader in 1932, 1934, and 1936, Herber completed 487 of 1,174 passes for 8,033 yards and 79 touchdowns during his last 11 seasons. Statistics are not available for 1930 and 1931.

★ Pro Football Hall of Fame

Herman, Billy (William J.)

BASEBALL
b. July 7, 1909, New Albany, Ind.
d. Sept. 5, 1992

One of the best-hitting second basemen in history, Herman spent nearly four years in the minor leagues before being purchased by the NL's Chicago Cubs late in the 1931 season. He became a starter in 1932.

Although he wasn't fast, his reflexes and lateral quickness gave him great defensive range. He led NL second basemen in putouts a record seven times, in assists three times, and in fielding percentage three times.

He batted .314 in his first full season, collecting 206 hits and 102 runs to help lead the Cubs to a pennant. However, the team lost the World Series in four games to the New York Yankees. After slipping to .279 in 1933, he hit over .300 the next four seasons, leading the league with 227 hits and 57 doubles in 1935, when the Cubs again won the pennant.

Herman batted .333 against the Detroit Tigers in the World Series, but the Cubs again lost. They won another pennant in 1938, again losing to the Yankees in the Series, when Herman hit only .188.

He led the NL in triples with 18 in 1939, then was traded early in the 1941 season to the Brooklyn Dodgers, where he played on another pennant winner but batted just .125 in a five-game World Series loss to the Yankees.

After serving in the Navy in 1944 and 1945, Herman returned to the Dodgers in 1946. He was traded during the season to the Boston Braves, and in 1947 he became manager of the Pittsburgh Pirates, appearing in only 15 games. He was fired the day before the last game of the season.

Herman managed in the minors and coached in the major leagues for several years before becoming manager of the AL's Boston Red Sox for the last two games of 1964. He was replaced late in the 1966 season.

During his 15 years in the major leagues, Herman had a .304 average on 2,345 hits, including 486 doubles, 82 triples, and 47 home runs. He scored 1,163 runs and drove in 839. As a manager, he had a 189–274 record.

★ Baseball Hall of Fame

Herman, Pete [Peter Gulotta]

BOXING
b. Feb. 12, 1896, New Orleans, La. d. April 13, 1973

Herman became a professional boxer in 1912, when he was only 16, and had several fights that are not officially recorded. On February 7, 1916, he met Kid Williams for the world bantamweight championship, but Williams retained his title with a 20-round draw.

They met again on January 9, 1917. This time Herman won a 20-round decision and the championship. After serving in the Navy during World War I, Herman lost the title to Joe Lynch in a 15-round decision on December 22, 1920.

Herman opened 1921 with five consecutive knockouts. He took a 15-round decision from Lynch on July 25 to reclaim the title, then lost it to Johnny Buff in a 15-round decision on September 23.

After five more fights, Herman was forced to retire because of failing eyesight caused by a ring injury. He went blind shortly afterward but operated a successful café in his native New Orleans until his death.

Herman won 71 of his 148 professional bouts, 19 by knockout, and lost 12, 1 by knockout. He also fought 10 draws and 57 no-decisions.

Hernandez, Keith

BASEBALL
b. Oct. 20, 1953, San Francisco, Calif.

A left-handed first baseman with the St. Louis Cardinals, Hernandez tied with Willie Stargell of the Pittsburgh Pirates for the 1979 NL MVP award. Hernandez led the league in hitting at .344, in runs scored with 116, and in doubles with 48 that season.

He joined the Cardinals near the end of the 1974 season, played part-time in 1975, and became a starter the following year. An excellent hitter with a good batting eye, he was also a very good defensive player, the winner of 11 Gold Gloves.

Hernandez led the league in runs scored again in 1980. He was traded to the New York Mets during the 1983 season and remained with them through 1989, leading the league in walks with 94 in 1986.

He finished his 17-year career with the AL's Cleveland Indians in 1990. Hernandez had a career average of .296 with 2,182 hits, including 426 doubles, 60 triples, and 162 home runs. He scored 1,124 runs and drove in 1,071.

Hernandez, Willie (Guillermo)

BASEBALL
b. Nov. 14, 1954, Aguada, P.R.

A left-hander with an explosive fastball, Hernandez won the AL's Cy Young Award and was named the league's most valuable player in 1984, when he appeared in a league-leading 80 games for the Detroit Tigers, compiling a 9–3 record, 32 saves, and a 1.92 ERA.

Hernandez also had a fine post-season, appearing in all three games and picking up a save in Detroit's league playoff victory over the Kansas City Royals, then saving two games with a 1.69 ERA in three appearances during a five-game World Series win against the San Diego Padres.

He entered the major leagues with the Chicago Cubs of the NL in 1977. His best season there was 1982, when he had ten saves and a 3.00 ERA. He went to the Philadelphia Phillies during the 1984 season, then to the Tigers in 1984.

After a total of 55 saves in 1985 and 1986, Hernandez began to suffer arm trouble. He retired after the 1989 season with a 70–63 record, 147 saves, and a 3.38 ERA. He struck out 788 hitters and walked 349 in 1,044 innings.

Herschberger, Clarence

FOOTBALL
b. 1877, Chicago, Ill.
d. Dec. 14, 1936

Herschberger was the first All-American player chosen by Walter Camp from outside the Ivy League, in 1898. A fullback at the University of Chicago, Herschberger was college football's outstanding kicker at a time when kicking was probably the most important element of the game.

He caught Camp's attention in a 23–11 loss to the University of Pennsylvania. Explaining his All-American selections, Camp wrote, "Against Penn this year, Herschberger exhibited the best all-around kicking of the season, punting, place-kicking, and drop-kicking with equal accuracy and facility . . . He is also a fine runner."

★ College Football Hall of Fame

Hershiser, Orel L.

BASEBALL
b. Sept. 16, 1958, Buffalo, N.Y.

Nicknamed "the Bulldog" by Tommy Lasorda, his long-time manager with the NL's Los Angeles Dodgers, Hershiser has demonstrated toughness throughout his career, as the nickname suggests.

He won the league's Cy Young Award and was named male athlete of the year by the Associated Press in 1988, when he led the NL in victories with a 23–8 record, in complete games with 15, in shutouts with 8, and in innings pitched with 267.

A right-hander, Hershiser has three

good, but not superior, pitches, a fastball, curve, and slider. His success has come from being able to throw the right pitch in the right place at the right time — when the hitter is expecting something else.

Hershiser joined the Dodgers for eight appearances at the end of the 1983 season and became a regular starter in 1984. He led the league in winning percentage in 1985, at .884, going 19–3. For the next two years, he pitched at exactly .500, at 14–14 and 16–16, and then had his Cy Young Award season.

In 1988, Hershiser had a strange season. Pitching for a weak-hitting team, he led the league in losses with 15. He also had 15 wins, set a major league record with 59 consecutive scoreless innings, led the league in innings pitched for the third consecutive year, and posted a 2.31 ERA.

Then arm problems set in. Hershiser missed most of the 1990 and 1991 seasons and hasn't had a winning record since then, although he was 6–6 in the strike-shortened 1994 season.

Through 1994, Hershiser had a 134–102 record with 23 shutouts and a 3.00 ERA. He had struck out 1,443 hitters while walking 653 in 2,156 innings.

Heston, Willie (William M.)

FOOTBALL
b. Sept. 9, 1878, Galesburg, Ill.
d. Sept. 9, 1963

"Hurry-Up" Yost, his coach at the University of Michigan, once said that Heston had scored at least 100 touchdowns in his four-year career, but Heston modestly admitted to only 93.

Heston first played guard at San Jose Normal, now San Jose State, in California. He captained the team in 1900. Yost, then coaching Stanford, was asked to help coach San Jose for its big game against Chico State. He moved Heston to halfback, and San Jose won the game.

In 1901, Yost took over at Michigan and persuaded Heston to attend law school there. There were no eligibility limits at the time, so he could also play football. In his first game, he broke into the opposition backfield, intercepted a lateral pass, and ran for a touchdown. He scored four touchdowns in his second game. Undefeated Michigan beat Stanford, 49–0, in the first Rose Bowl, with Heston gaining 180 yards in 17 attempts.

Heston was both very strong and very fast. He was 5-foot-8 and weighed 184 pounds, and it was said that he beat Michigan's sprint champion, Archie Hahn, in the 40-yard dash. In the open field he was shifty, and he often leaped clear over an opponent who was getting set to tackle him.

Against the University of Chicago in 1903, Heston gained 237 of Michigan's 260 total yards. He ran 37 times for 240 yards against Chicago the following season. An All-American in 1903 and 1904, Heston was named to most all-time All-American teams until Red Grange arrived at the University of Illinois.

Heston coached Drake University to a 4–4–0 record in 1905 and played one game for the Canton Bulldogs, for a record $600. The following season, he had a 3–1–4 record coaching North Carolina State, and again he played a professional game at the end of the season, with a group of college all-stars. He suffered a serious leg injury and retired from football.

★ College Football Hall of Fame

Hewitt, Bill (William E.)

FOOTBALL
b. Oct. 8, 1909, Bay City, Mich.
d. Jan. 14, 1947

After starring as an end for two years at the University of Michigan, Hewitt was moved to fullback in 1931, his senior season, which probably cost him All-American recognition. The 5-foot-11, 195-pounder ran 57 yards against Minnesota for the only score of the game.

He joined the Chicago Bears in 1932 and was an All-Pro end in 1933, when the Bears won the NFL championship. They were trailing the New York Giants, 21–16, in the title game, when Hewitt caught a pass from Bronko Nagurski and lateraled the ball to Bill Karr, who scored a touchdown to win the game, 23–21.

Known for playing without a helmet until NFL rules required headgear in 1939, Hewitt was a solidly built player who was once described as "three parts gorilla and one part Englishman." He had such a quick start that he was nicknamed "the Offside Kid."

After another All-Pro season in 1934, Hewitt had an off year in 1935 and was sold to the Philadelphia Eagles, where he was an All-Pro again in 1936 and 1937. He was the first player to be selected as an All-Pro with two different teams.

Hewitt retired after the 1939 season, but he played sparingly with the merged Philadelphia-Pittsburgh team in 1943 because of the World War II manpower shortage. In his NFL career, he caught 101 passes for 1606 yards, a 15.9 average, and 24 touchdowns.

★ Pro Football Hall of Fame

Hextall, Bryan A.

HOCKEY
b. July 31, 1913, Grenfell, Sask.

After playing amateur hockey in Manitoba, Hextall became a professional with the Vancouver Lions in 1934 and joined the New York Rangers of the NHL in 1936. When the Rangers beat Toronto four games to two for the 1940 Stanley Cup, Hextall scored the goal that gave the Rangers a 3–2 overtime victory in the final game of the series.

Hextall won the Art Ross Trophy as the league's top scorer for the 1941–42 season, when he had 24 goals and 32 assists for 56 points. He was among the top ten scorers three other times, and he was named the league's All-Star center three straight years, from 1940 to 1942.

Hextall retired after the 1947–48 season. In 447 regular season games, all with the Rangers, he had 187 goals and 175 assists. He scored 8 goals and 9 assists in 37 playoff games.

His sons, Bryan Lee and Dennis, also played in the NHL.

★ Hockey Hall of Fame

Hextall, Ronald

HOCKEY
b. May 3, 1964, Winnipeg, Man.

After six rather undistinguished seasons in the minor leagues, Hextall joined the NHL's Philadelphia Flyers in 1986 and had an outstanding season. He won the Vezina Trophy as the league's top goaltender, was named rookie of the year, and went on to win the Conn Smythe Trophy as the most valuable player in the Stanley Cup playoffs.

His consistency is shown by the fact that he played in 66 regular season games and had a 3.00 goals-against average with only one shutout. He was even better in Stanley Cup play, with two shutouts and a 2.77 goals-against average in 26 games.

1986 was his best year to date. Hextall missed most of the 1989–90 season and much of the 1990–91 season with a series of injuries. He was traded to the Quebec Nordiques in 1992 and to the New York Islanders in 1993.

Through the 1993–94 season, he had a 3.27 goals-against average with 9 shutouts in 400 regular season games, and a 3.31 average with 2 shutouts in 54 playoff games.

Heyman, Arthur B.

BASKETBALL
b. June 29, 1941, Rockville Centre, N.Y.

One of the finest players in Duke's glorious history, Heyman was an All-American forward and won all the player of the year awards in 1963. He was also named most valuable player in the NCAA final tournament, although Duke lost to the eventual champion, Loyola of Chicago, in a semifinal game.

During his three years as a starter, Heyman scored 1,984 points and averaged 25.1 per game, both school records at the time. The first draft choice of the NBA's New York Knicks, Heyman never became a professional star, although he averaged 15.4 points a game and made the league's all-rookie team in 1963–64.

The Knicks used him sparingly in his second season. In 1965–66 he was with both the Cincinnati Royals and the Philadelphia 76ers, but appeared in only 17 games.

After sitting out the 1966–67 season, Heyman joined the New Jersey Nets in the new American Basketball Association. The Nets traded him to the Pittsburgh Pipers shortly after the season started. Heyman had his best year as a professional, averaging 18.5 points a game, as Pittsburgh won the ABA championship.

Heyman went with the Pipers when they moved to Minnesota in 1967–68. He played just 19 games in 1969–70 with the Pittsburgh Condors and the Miami Floridians before a back injury forced his retirement. In 310 professional games, Heyman scored 4,030 points, an average of 13.0 points a game.

Hickcox, Charles B.

SWIMMING
b. Feb. 6, 1947, Phoenix, Ariz.

Hickcox was the surprise winner of three gold medals at the 1968 Olympics, in the 200- and 400-meter individual medleys and in the 4 x 100-meter medley relay. He also won a silver medal in the 100-meter backstroke.

Best known as a backstroker, Hickcox won only one national championship in the individual medley. He and Indiana University teammate Gary Hall swam stroke for stroke in the 400-meter event at the Olympics and Hickcox touched out to win by .3 second.

At Indiana, he won seven NCAA championships, in the 100-yard backstroke in 1967 and 1968, the 200-yard backstroke from 1967 through 1969, and the 200-yard individual medley in 1968 and 1969.

He won AAU national outdoor championships in the 100- and 200-meter backstroke events in 1966 and 1967. Indoors, he won the 100-yard backstroke in 1968, the 200-yard backstroke in 1966 and 1968, and the 200-yard individual medley in 1968.

After graduating from Indiana in 1969, Hickcox retired from competition. He later worked as a television commentator and swimming coach.

Hickey, Edgar S.

BASKETBALL
b. Dec. 20, 1902, Reynolds, Nebr.
d. Dec. 7, 1980

Hickey played football and basketball at Creighton University, and as a senior law student in 1926–27, he coached basketball at Creighton University High School, also known as Creighton Prep. He had planned to become an attorney with his father's real estate firm, but his father was killed in a car accident, and Hickey remained at Creighton Prep after receiving his degree, coaching track and football as well as basketball.

He became the Creighton University basketball coach in 1935. His 1943 team won the National Invitation Tournament, after which Hickey entered the U.S. Navy. He returned to Creighton after his discharge in 1946 and coached there one more season before moving to St. Louis University in 1947.

Led by "Easy Ed" Macauley, St. Louis won the 1948 NIT. Hickey remained at the school until 1958, when he became basketball coach and athletic director at Marquette University. His first team won the 1959 NCAA championship, and Marquette won the title again in 1961. Hickey retired after the 1963–64 season.

His overall record was 435 wins and 222 losses. Hickey developed the modern three-lane fast break, in which the player with the ball heads down the middle of the floor toward the basket, flanked by two wing men.

★ Basketball Hall of Fame

Hickman, Herman M.

FOOTBALL
b. Oct. 1, 1911, Johnson City, Tenn.
d. April 25, 1958

Hickman was both a great football player and a great entertainer. Only 5-foot-10, he weighed about 240 pounds in his prime, and although he looked chubby, he was very fast. His line coach at the University of Tennessee said that Hickman consistently finished second only to a halfback in the team's wind sprints.

He entered Tennessee in 1929 and became a starting tackle as a sophomore but was moved to guard before the season ended. Largely because of his brilliant performance in a 13–0 win over New York University at Yankee Stadium, he was named to Grantland Rice's 1931 All-American team.

After graduating, Hickman became a professional wrestler and also played for the NFL's Brooklyn Dodgers for three seasons. He was named All-Pro at left guard in 1933. Hickman retired from football after the 1934 season but kept wrestling for several years, eventually taking part in more than 500 bouts.

He worked as an assistant coach at a number of colleges, meanwhile developing a reputation as an after-dinner speaker. He used his Tennessee drawl to great effect in telling anecdotes and reciting poetry.

In 1948, he became head coach at Yale. In four seasons there, his teams won just 16 games while losing 17 and tying two. He resigned after the 1951 season. During the last several years of his life, he frequently appeared on radio and television panel shows.

★ College Football Hall of Fame

Hickok, William O.

FOOTBALL, TRACK & FIELD
b. Aug. 23, 1874, Harrisburg, Pa.
d. Sept. 4, 1933

As a senior, Hickok captained the Yale football and track teams. He was an All-American guard in 1894 and 1895. During those two seasons, Yale won 29 games and tied 2 without a loss. He was also a starter on the 1893 team that won 10 and lost 1.

Hickok won the IC4A shot put and hammer throw championships three years in a row, from 1893 through 1895, and was the AAU national shot put champion in 1895. He coached Carlisle School for Indians to a 4–5–0 record in 1896.

★ College Football Hall of Fame

Hicks, John C., Jr.

FOOTBALL
b. March 21, 1951, Cleveland, Ohio

Hicks started at offensive tackle as a sophomore at Ohio State University in 1970, then missed the entire 1971 season with a knee injury. He came back the following season and was a consensus All-American in 1973, when he won the Outland Trophy and the Lombardi Trophy as college football's outstanding lineman of the year.

The NFL's New York Giants moved Hicks to guard when he joined the team in 1974. The 6-foot-2, 260-pounder was named offensive rookie of the year. Hicks was traded to the Pittsburgh Steelers in 1978 and retired after the 1979 season.

Higgins, Bob (Robert A.)
FOOTBALL
b. 1894
d. June 6, 1969

After playing at Penn State from 1914 through 1916, Higgins entered the service during World War I and was named an end on Grantland Rice's all-Army team. He returned to captain the Penn State team to a 7–1–0 record in 1919 and was a Walter Camp All-American. In a 20–0 victory over Pittsburgh that season, Higgins caught a short pass from Walter Hess and turned it into a 92-yard gain.

Higgins coached at West Virginia Wesleyan in 1920 and from 1922 through 1924, then went to Washington University in St. Louis for three seasons. He returned to Penn State as head coach in 1930 and remained there for 19 seasons, winning 91 games while losing 57 and tying 9.

Penn State won all nine of its games in 1947 and tied Southern Methodist University, 13–13, in the Rose Bowl. The school continued unbeaten through the first six games of 1948 before suffering a 7–0 upset by Pittsburgh that ended hopes for another bowl bid.

Ill health forced Higgins's retirement after the 1948 season, but he remained at Penn State as a special assistant in the Physical Education Department until November 1951. His overall coaching record was 123–80–17.

★ College Football Hall of Fame

Hill, Drew
FOOTBALL
b. Oct. 5, 1956, Newman, Ga.

The 5-foot-9, 172-pound Hill played college football at Georgia Tech and was chosen by the Los Angeles Rams in the twelfth round of the 1979 NFL draft. He was used primarily as a kick returner with the Rams, catching only 60 passes in five seasons.

Hill, who missed the entire 1983 season with a back injury, was traded to the Houston Oilers in 1985. He became a starting wide receiver in Houston's pass-oriented offense. Despite his lack of size, he was a very durable player, missing only six games in seven seasons with the Oilers.

His best year was 1991, when he caught 90 passes for 1,109 yards and 4 touchdowns. Hill became a free agent after that season and signed with the Atlanta Falcons. Released in early 1994, he announced his retiremnt.

In 14 NFL seasons, Hill had 634 receptions for 9,831 yards, a 15.5 average, and 60 touchdowns. He returned 172 kickoffs for 3,460 yards, a 20.1 average, and 1 touchdown.

Hill, Phil
AUTO RACING
b. April 20, 1927, Miami, Fla.

The first American ever to win the World Championship of Drivers in Formula One racing, Hill joined the Ferrari racing team in 1956 after driving sports cars for seven years. He got his first Formula One start in 1958 and his first victory in 1960, in the Grand Prix of Europe.

In 1961, Hill won the Grand Prix of Belgium and Grand Prix of Italy and finished second in the Grand Prix of Holland and Grand Prix of England to win the world title.

Hillebrand, Doc (Arthur R. T.)
FOOTBALL
b. March 9, 1877, Freeport, Ill.
d. Dec. 16, 1941

An All-American tackle at Princeton in 1898 and 1899, Hillebrand was a particular star on defense because of his speed and agility. Princeton in those years had three heavy but not very mobile players in the center of the line, so Hillebrand had to roam all over the field to make tackles. During those two seasons, Princeton won 23 games while tying 1 and losing 1. He captained the 1899 team. In 1903, Hillebrand returned to Princeton as head coach for three seasons, compiling a 27–4–0 record.

★ College Football Hall of Fame

Hillman, Harry L.

TRACK AND FIELD
b. Sept. 8, 1881, Brooklyn, N.Y.
d. Aug 9, 1945

Hillman scored a unique triple victory at the 1904 Olympics, winning the 200-meter and 400-meter hurdles and the 400-meter run. He had Olympic record times in all three events, but his time in the 400-meter hurdles wasn't admitted as a record because he knocked over the last hurdle.

En route to Greece for the "intercalated" Olympics of 1906, Hillman was one of a half-dozen athletes who were injured by an enormous wave that washed over the deck of the ship. He finished fifth in the 400-meter run, his only event that year. Hillman won a silver medal in the 400-meter hurdles at the 1908 Olympics. He and Charley Bacon of the U.S. went over the last hurdle simultaneously, but Bacon won the run to the tape to win in a world record 55.0 seconds.

On April 24, 1909, Hillman and Lawson Robertson set a record that has never been equalled, running the 100-yard three-legged race in 11.0 seconds.

The track coach at Dartmouth from 1910 until his death, Hillman advised hurdlers to swallow raw eggs, which he believed to be "excellent for the wind and stomach." He was on the Olympic track and field coaching staff in 1924, 1928, and 1932.

★ National Track & Field Hall of Fame

Hines, Jim (James R.)

TRACK AND FIELD
b. Sept. 10, 1946, Dumas, Ark.

The U.S. 4 x 100-meter relay team was in third place in the 1968 Olympic finals when Hines took the baton for the last leg. He carried the team to a victory and a world record time of 38.2 seconds. Hines was timed at 8.2 seconds for his anchor leg. He also won the 100-meter dash, tying his own pending world record of 9.9 seconds.

As a student at Texas Southern, Hines was the 100-yard champion at both the National Association of Intercollegiate Athletics championship meet and the AAU national meet. He tied the world record of 9.1 seconds in the AAU championships.

Four days after the Olympics ended, Hines signed a contract with the Miami Dolphins of the American Football League. He played just one season with the Dolphins.

★ National Track & Field Hall of Fame

Hinkey, Frank A.

FOOTBALL
b. Dec. 23, 1871, Tonawanda, N.Y.
d. Dec. 30, 1925

Hinkey was an All-American end at Yale four years in a row, from 1891 through 1893, but he was one of the strangest and least likely of football stars. At 5-foot-9 and only 157 pounds, he was small even for his era. As a child, he'd been told to refrain from strenuous sports because of lung trouble, and he was described as "cadaverous looking" by one writer.

Yet Hinkey was the most feared player of his day. On defense, he seemed impossible to block. Walter Camp wrote that Hinkey "drifted through the interference like a disembodied spirit." He was a ferocious tackler who clasped the ball carrier around the knees, lifted him into the air, and threw him headfirst to the ground.

One opponent said that Hinkey "played like a fiend, but played clean." Other opponents and many sportswriters disagreed. After the brutal 1894 Harvard-Yale game, the *New York Post* said that "no father or mother worthy of the name would permit a son to associate with the set of Yale brutes on Hinkey's football team," and Harvard refused to play Yale the following year.

Because of Hinkey's reputation, other teams tried to retaliate, often ganging up on him. But he had to leave a game because of injury only once, and it was the only game Yale lost during his four years as a starter.

Hinkey became the head coach at Yale in 1914 and installed a lateral passing offense derived from Canadian rugby. Yale went 7–3–0 that year. After a poor start the following season, Hinkey was replaced by Tom Shevlin.

★ College Football Hall of Fame

Hinkle, Clarke (William Clarke)

FOOTBALL
b. April 10, 1910, Toronto, Ohio
d. Nov. 9, 1988

Hinkle led Bucknell to a 20–5–3 record from 1929 through 1931, scoring 128 points, and he was the outstanding back in the 1932 East-West Shrine Game, where Green Bay Packer coach "Curly" Lambeau scouted him and signed him immediately after the game.

The 5-foot-11, 205-pound Hinkle was devastating both as a runner and as a linebacker. He had some notable confrontations with Bronko Nagurski, his counterpart with the Chicago Bears, who outweighed him by 30 pounds.

On one occasion, Hinkle carried the ball through the line and was knocked into the backfield by Nagurski. But he didn't go down, and he ran back through the hole and past Nagurski for a 56-yard touchdown.

Hinkle played for championship teams in 1936 and 1939 and was named an All-Pro from 1936 through 1938 and in 1941, his final season. He carried the ball 1,079 times for 3,545 yards, a 3.3 average, and 31 touchdowns; caught 47 passes for 561 yards, an 11.9 average, and 9 touchdowns; and punted 234 times for a 37.6 average. Hinkle also kicked 28 extra points and 28 field goals for a career total of 367 points.

★ College Football Hall of Fame; Pro Football Hall of Fame

Hinkle, Tony (Paul D.)

BASKETBALL
b. Dec. 9, 1899, Logansport, Ind.
d. Sept. 21, 1992

Hinkle won nine letters in three sports at the University of Chicago, where he captained the basketball team for two years and was an All-American guard in 1920. After graduating, he went to Butler University in Indiana to coach baseball, basketball, and football.

His teams won more than a thousand games in the course of nearly 50 years. Except for three years when he was in the Navy during World War II, he coached basketball through the 1969–70 season, compiling 561 wins and 393 losses. While in the Navy, Hinkle coached the Great Lakes Naval Training Station team to 98 victories and the 1942–43 national service championship.

At one time, 55 of Hinkle's former players were coaching basketball in Indiana. Butler's 10,800-seat gym was renamed Hinkle Fieldhouse in his honor in 1965, and when he coached his last game in 1970, more than 17,000 people crowded in to pay him tribute.

★ Basketball Hall of Fame

Hirsch, Crazylegs (Elroy L.)

FOOTBALL
b. June 17, 1923, Wausau, Wis.

A halfback, Hirsch was ninth in the nation in rushing at the University of Wisconsin in 1942, when he averaged 5.5 yards a carry. His coach, Harry Stuldreher, said of him, "Hirsch is one of the best athletes I ever saw — fast, smart, dead game, and hard to bring down."

He was transferred to the University of Michigan because of military training, and he played there in 1943. After leaving the service in 1946, he signed with the Chicago Rockets of the All America Football Conference. In 1948, his skull was fractured just behind the right ear when he carried the ball into the line. He missed the rest of the season, and it was suspected he would never play again.

However, Hirsch joined the NFL's Los Angeles Rams in 1949 and wore a special protective helmet for the rest of his career. He played sparingly as a running back during his first season, but in 1950 coach Joe Stydahar installed the three-end offense, with Hirsch as a flanker and pass receiver, and he caught 42 passes for 687 yards and 7 touchdowns.

Hirsch had a sensational 1951 season, catching 66 passes for 1,495 yards, a 22.7 average, and 17 touchdowns to lead the NFL in each category. His average touchdown reception that year covered 47.8 yards. Boasting the league's highest scoring offense, the Rams beat the Cleveland Browns, 24–17, to win the NFL championship.

After the 1954 season, Hirsch announced his retirement, but he returned in 1955 because the Rams were depleted by injuries, and he played three more seasons. He caught a total of 387 passes for 7,029 yards, an 18.2 average, and 60 touchdowns. He also rushed for 3 touchdowns, scored 1 on a punt return, and 1 on an interception return.

Hirsch had a brief career in the movies and then served as Wisconsin's athletic director from 1969 to 1987.
★ Pro Football Hall of Fame

Hirsch, Maximilian J.
HORSE RACING
b. July 12, 1880, Fredericksburg, Tex.
d. April 3, 1969

When he was ten years old, Hirsch began riding quarter horses. He rode in a railroad boxcar to Maryland when he was 12 and worked as an exercise boy, then spent five years as a jockey before becoming a trainer.

In 60 years of training horses, Hirsch produced the winners of 1,933 races and $12,203,270 in purses. Among his champions were Assault, who won the triple crown in 1946; Bold Venture, winner of the Kentucky Derby and Preakness in 1936; Middleground, who won the Kentucky Derby and Belmont in 1950; and Belmont Stakes winners Vito (1928) and High Gun (1954).

Rugged and raspy-voiced, Hirsch was outgoing and well liked. His home, a cottage between horse barns at Belmont Park, was a gathering place for trainers and other horse people, and Hirsch freely offered advice, counsel, and even money to younger trainers. One writer referred to him as "the softest touch on the race track."
★ National Horse Racing Hall of Fame

Hitchcock, Jimmy (James F.)
FOOTBALL
b. June 28, 1911, Inverness, Ala.
d. June 23, 1959

In 1932, Hitchcock became Auburn University's first All-American. A 5-foot-11, 175-pound halfback, he captained Auburn to a 9–0–1 record as a senior. A triple-threat tailback, Hitchcock was particularly noted as a runner and kicker. In a 19–17 win over Tulane, he had touchdown runs of 55 and 65 yards.

Hitchcock led the Southern Conference in scoring in 1932, and in three seasons as a starter, he punted 232 times without having one blocked. After graduating, he played professional baseball for seven seasons, including 28 games as an infielder with the Boston Braves in 1938. His brother, Billy, also a football star at Auburn, played nine seasons of major league baseball and later managed the Baltimore Orioles and Atlanta Braves.
★ College Football Hall of Fame

Hitchcock, Tommy (Thomas Jr.)
POLO
b. Feb. 11, 1900, Aiken, S.C.
d. April 19, 1944

He was nicknamed "Ten-Goal Tommy" because he was given a ten-goal rating, the highest possible in polo's handicapping system, 18 times in his 22 years as an active player. His father, Thomas Sr., played in the first Westchester Cup match in 1886.

Hitchcock played for the Meadow Brook team that won the national junior championship in 1916. The following year, he tried to enlist as an aviator in World War I but was rejected because of his age, and he joined the French army. He was later transferred to the U.S. Army Air Corps and was shot down behind German lines.

Hitchcock jumped out of a train while being transferred from one prison camp to another and escaped by walking 100 miles to the Swiss border in eight nights of travel.

After the war, he took up polo again and quickly became the country's outstanding player. Though not quite as skilled as others, he was an aggressive, fearless rider and an accurate long hitter, which fit well into the American style of play: advancing the ball through long passes.

Hitchcock played for four National Open champions, Meadow Brook in 1923, Sands Point in 1927, and Greentree in 1935 and 1936. He played on U.S. teams that beat Great Britain in 1921, 1924, 1927, 1930, and 1939, and he was on the national teams that beat Argentina in 1928 and lost to Argentina in 1936. He also played for the silver medal Olympic team in 1924.

During World War II, he served in the Army Air Corps again, as assistant air attache to the U.S. Embassy in London. Hitchcock was killed in the crash of an Army plane near Salisbury, England.

Hobson, Howard A. ("Hobby")

BASKETBALL
b. July 4, 1903, Portland, Oreg.
d. June 9, 1991

The first coach to win major conference championships on both coasts, Hobson was captain of the basketball and baseball teams at the University of Oregon for two years. After coaching high school basketball in Oregon and Washington for two years, he became head coach at Southern Oregon College in 1928.

He returned to his alma mater in 1935 and remained there through the 1946–47 season. Oregon won the first NCAA tournament under Hobson in 1939 and claimed three straight Pacific Coast Conference championships, from 1937 through 1939.

In 1948, he became basketball coach at Yale, where he won or tied for five Big Three championships in nine seasons. Hobson left coaching after the 1955–56

season with a record of 495 wins and 291 losses.

★ Basketball Hall of Fame

Hodge, Daniel A.

BOXING, WRESTLING
b. May 13, 1932, Perry, Okla.

Hodge spent two years in the Navy after graduating from high school and then entered the University of Oklahoma in 1953. He won three consecutive NCAA wrestling championships in the 177-pound class, from 1955 through 1957, and he won AAU 180½-pound titles in 1953, 1954, and 1956.

A silver medalist at the 1956 Olympics, Hodge became an amateur boxer in 1958, winning 17 consecutive fights and the national Golden Gloves heavyweight championship. He won eight of ten professional bouts and then went into professional wrestling.

A serious injury suffered in a 1976 auto accident forced his retirement.

Hodges, Gil [Gilbert R. Hodge]

BASEBALL
b. April 4, 1924, Princeton, Ind.
d. April 2, 1972

A right-handed first baseman, Hodges was a 6-foot-1½-inch, 200-pound power hitter who fielded his position with surprising grace. He played in just one game with the Brooklyn Dodgers in 1943, joined the team for good at the end of 1947 season, and became a starter in 1948.

Hodges drove in more than 100 runs for seven consecutive years, from 1949 through 1955, and hit 22 or more home runs 11 seasons in a row, from 1949 through 1959, with a high of 42 in 1954. He was with the Dodgers when they moved to Los Angeles in 1958, and he spent two seasons with the expansion New York Mets in 1962 and early in 1963 before retiring as a player to become manager of the AL's Washington Senators.

A member of seven pennant-winning teams, six in Brooklyn and one in Los Angeles, Hodges was unfortunately known for performing poorly in the World Series in his early years, especially after going hitless in 21 at-bats against the Yankees in 1952. However, he batted .364 in 1953, .292 with 5 RBI in 1955, when Brooklyn won its only world championship, .304 with 8 RBI in 1956, and .391 with a triple and a home run in 1959, when Los Angeles won its first world title.

Hodges managed Washington through 1967, then took over the Mets. He did an outstanding job of platooning in guiding the 1969 Mets to a pennant and World Series victory. Hodges died of a heart attack during spring training in 1972.

In 18 seasons as a player, Hodges had a .273 average with 1,921 hits, including 295 doubles, 48 triples, and 370 home runs. He scored 1,105 runs, had 1,274 RBI, and led NL first basemen in fielding percentage three times. As a manager, he had a 660–753 record.

Hodgins, Clinton T.

HARNESS RACING
b. June 18, 1907, Clandeboye, Ont. d. Oct. 22, 1979

A trainer and driver, Hodgins won more than 1,500 heats after the U.S. Trotting Association began keeping official records in 1939, and he had many more in a dozen years of driving before that.

In 1949, Hodgins led the nation in dashes won with 128 and in money won with $184,108. Fourteen years later, he drove horses that won $205,031, but that was good only for 25th in the year's rankings.

Among the outstanding harness horses he handled were Proximity, Horse of the Year in 1950, and Bye Bye Byrd, Horse of the year in 1959. He also drove Adios Butler to a world record 1:55⅘ in 1959.
★ Hall of Fame of the Trotter

Hodgson, George

SWIMMING
b. 1890, Canada

Hodgson won gold medals in the 400- and 1,500-meter freestyle races at the 1912 Olympics, but his finest performance came the year before at the Festival of Empire Games in London. In the first heat of the 1,500-meter event, Hodgson

set a world record of 22:23.0. He lowered that to 22:00.0 in the final. Along the way, he also set a world record in the 1,000-meter, and he continued past the finish to the 1-mile mark, setting a third world record at that distance.
★ Canadian Sports Hall of Fame

Hogan, Ben (William Benjamin)

GOLF
b. Aug. 13, 1912, Dublin, Tex.

It took Hogan a relatively long time and hours of practice to reach the top, but once he did, he became a remarkably consistent golfer, even after an auto accident almost took his life.

Hogan began caddying at 12, when he discovered it paid more than delivering newspapers. He became a professional in 1931 but didn't win a big event until 1940, when he set a tournament record in the North and South Open. In 1941, Hogan entered 26 stroke-play tournaments, won five of them, and was never lower than sixth. He was the tour's top money winner and the winner of the Vardon Trophy for the lowest strokes per round average from 1940 through 1942.

After serving in the Army Air Corps during World War II, Hogan rejoined the tour in 1945 and won 35 tournaments in the next 4½ years, including the PGA championship in 1946 and 1948 and the U.S. Open in 1948.

In February 1949, Hogan and his wife, Valerie, were returning from a tournament when a bus hit their car head-on. Hogan probably saved his wife's life by throwing his body in front of her just before impact. He suffered a double fracture of the pelvis, a broken collarbone, a broken left ankle, and was almost killed by blood clots during an operation.

He had to learn how to walk and how to swing a golf club again. But just 11 months after the accident, he tied Sam Snead for first in the Los Angeles Open, though he lost the playoff. In the 1950 U.S. Open, Hogan struggled with pain and lost three shots on the last round to tie Lloyd Mangrum and Tom Fazio for the lead, then won the playoff with a 69.

Forced to limit his playing schedule, Hogan continued to turn in brilliant performances in major tournaments. He won the Open and the Masters in 1951 and was named male athlete of the year by the Associated Press in 1953, when he won the U.S. Open, the Masters, and the British Open.

From 1940 through 1960, Hogan finished among the top ten in every U.S. Open he entered, and he was never lower than seventh in the Masters from 1941 through 1956. His British Open victory came the only time he ever entered that tournament.

Hogan retired from competition in 1960 after shooting a record 30 on the back nine of the Masters. Nicknamed the "Wee Ice Mon" by the Scots and the "Mechanical Man" by U.S. sportswriters, he was known for his outward lack of emotion. Will Grimsley once wrote of Hogan, "He was a cold, detached artisan on the course, likened by some observers to an undertaker weaving a shroud of defeat for his adversaries."

★ PGA Hall of Fame; World Golf Hall of Fame

Hogan, James J.
FOOTBALL
b. Nov. 1, 1876, Glenbane, County Tipperary, Ireland
d. March 20, 1910

An All-American tackle at Yale three years in a row, from 1902 through 1904, Hogan has often been cited as an example of "professionalism" in the early years of intercollegiate sports. As captain of the team in 1904, Hogan lived free of charge in luxurious Vanderbilt Hall, ate free meals at the University Club, had his tuition paid by the Yale Athletic Association, and was given a two-week vacation in Cuba, all expenses paid, when the season was over.

His family moved from Ireland to Torrington, Connecticut, when he was young, and Hogan played several seasons of sandlot football before entering Yale at the age of 25. The 5-foot-10, 210-pounder was often used as a ball carrier from the tackle back formation. One opponent called him "the strongest tackle I ever saw."

Hogan was also an excellent student

who graduated with honors and then earned a law degree from Columbia University. He died of a kidney disease.

★ College Football Hall of Fame

Hogshead, Nancy L.
SWIMMING
b. April 17, 1962, Iowa City, Iowa

In the only dead heat in Olympic swimming history, Hogshead and U.S. teammate Carrie Steinseifer tied in the 100-meter freestyle in 1984 and shared the gold medal. Hogshead won two other golds, on the 4 x 100-meter freestyle and the 4 x 100-meter medley relay teams. She also won a silver in the 200-meter individual medley.

Hogshead had given up swimming for nearly three years after the U.S. boycott of the 1980 Moscow Olympics. She won three national butterfly championships, in the 100-yard and 200-meter in 1977 and the 200-yard event in 1978. When she came back in 1983, she had switched to freestyle, and she won the 1984 indoor 220-yard event.

Holland, Brud (Jerome H.)
FOOTBALL
b. Jan. 9, 1916, Auburn, N.Y.
d. Jan. 13, 1985

One of 13 children, Holland was called "Brudder" by one of his younger siblings and a shortened form of the nickname stuck for the rest of his life. A 6-foot, 215-pound end with sprinter speed, he was an All-American at Cornell in 1938. Often used to carry the ball on the end-around play, Holland scored three touchdowns in a 40–7 victory over Colgate in 1937.

Holland taught and coached football at Lincoln University for four years after graduating. He worked for a shipbuilding company during World War II and then became a teacher and football coach at Tennessee A & I from 1946 to 1951, meanwhile earning a doctorate from the University of Pennsylvania.

Holland later served as president of Delaware State College and Hampton Institute. In 1970, he was named U.S. ambassador to Sweden. He resigned from that post in 1972 and was appointed the first black director of the New York Stock Exchange.

★ College Football Hall of Fame

Hollenback, Bill (William M.)

FOOTBALL
b. Feb. 22, 1886, Blue Ball, Pa.
d. March 12, 1968

"Pudge" Heffelfinger called Hollenback "indestructible," which may not have been an overstatement. A halfback at the University of Pennsylvania, he once played an entire game with a slight fracture of the leg that wasn't discovered until afterward.

Known as "Big Bill," Hollenback was 6-foot-1 and 185 pounds. Originally a tackle, he was moved to halfback in 1906, and he captained the team in 1907 and 1908. During those two seasons, Penn won 22 games, lost 1, and tied 1. Walter Camp named him a first-team All-American in 1908 after having placed him on the second team in 1906 and 1907.

After receiving a degree in dentistry, Hollenback coached at Penn State in 1910 and from 1912 through 1914, at Missouri in 1911, at Pennsylvania Military College in 1915, and at Syracuse in 1916.

★ College Football Hall of Fame

Holm, Eleanor G.

SWIMMING
b. Dec. 6, 1913, New York, N.Y.

The original glamour girl of swimming, Holm once turned down a chance to join the Ziegfeld Follies in order to continue competing. She won her first national championship in 1927, when she was 13; her last in 1936.

Holm was the AAU national outdoor 300-meter individual medley champion from 1927 through 1930 and the 220-yard backstroke champion from 1929 through 1933. She won the indoor 100-yard backstroke title from 1930 through 1932 and from 1934 through 1936 and was the indoor 300-yard individual medley champion from 1928 through 1932.

A member of the U.S. Olympic team in 1928, when she finished fifth in the 100-meter backstroke, Holm won a gold medal in the event in 1932. She was also selected for the 1936 team but was suspended after being found, according to the team doctor, "in a deep slumber which approached a state of coma" after an all-night drinking party.

Holm was involved in show business beginning in 1932, when she signed an acting contract with Warner Brothers. The following year, she married the musician Art Jarrett, a fellow alumnus of Brooklyn's Erasmus Hall High School, and sang with his band. In 1938, she played Jane in the movie *Tarzan's Revenge*, with the Olympic decathlon gold medalist Glenn Morris as Tarzan.

After divorcing Jarrett, she starred in Billy Rose's Aquacade, and she married Rose in 1939. They were divorced in 1954 after a messy court battle, called the "War of the Roses" by the press. Holm later worked as an interior decorator and retired to Miami Beach.

★ International Swimming Hall of Fame; International Women's Sports Hall of Fame

Holman, Marshall

BOWLING
b. Sept. 29, 1954, Medford, Oreg.

The all-time leading money winner on the PBA tour through 1993 with $1,606,961, Holman is fourth in tournaments won with 21, including the U.S. Open in 1981 and 1985. Considered the tour's most consistent bowler during the 1980s, Holman had the PBA's highest scoring average in 1982, 1984, and 1987. His 1987 performance was unusual in that he didn't win a tournament that year.

A right-hander, Holman ran into problems in 1989 when the tour adopted new lane-dressing procedures that favored left-handed bowlers.

★ PBA Hall of Fame

Holman, Nat (Nathan)

BASKETBALL
b. Oct. 18, 1896, New York, N.Y.

Often referred to as "Mr. Basketball" because of his long association with the sport, Holman played his first professional game in 1916 with a Hoboken,

New Jersey, team. He scored 23 points in Hoboken's 28–25 victory.

A 5-foot-11 guard, Holman played for several professional teams during the next few years. In 1920, he joined the New York Whirlwinds, one of the best teams of the era. The Whirlwinds played a long-awaited series against the Original Celtics in 1921. They won the first game, 40–27, with Holman scoring 22 points, but lost the second, 26–24. The third game was never played.

Jim Furey, owner of the Celtics, persuaded Holman and two other Whirlwind stars to play for his team. For the next decade, the Celtics dominated professional basketball. Holman captained the team, which was equivalent to coaching it. Known as an outstanding floor general, he also had an accurate two-handed set shot.

A graduate of the Savage School of Physical Education, Holman became a professor at City College of New York in 1917 and he began coaching the school's basketball team in 1920. He retired from playing in 1933 to concentrate on coaching.

CCNY won both the NCAA tournament and the National Invitation Tournament in 1950, the only school to accomplish that. A year later, players from seven colleges were implicated in a point-shaving scandal, and two CCNY players were convicted. The school reacted by de-emphasizing basketball, and Holman resigned after the 1951–52 season. However, he returned as coach in 1955–56 and 1959–60. His record was 422 victories and 188 defeats.

★ Basketball Hall of Fame

Holmes, Larry
BOXING
b. Nov. 3, 1949, Cuthbert, Ga.

In 1973 the 6-foot-3, 215-pound Holmes turned professional after winning 19 of 22 amateur fights. Quick of foot and hand, Holmes was an excellent boxer with a very good left jab but not much of a knockout punch, though he scored many knockouts by wearing his opponents down.

Holmes won the WBC heavyweight championship on June 9, 1978, with a 15-round decision over Ken Norton in Las Vegas. He defended the title 17 times through 1983, then abruptly gave it up because of a dispute with promoter Don King, and was recognized as IBF champion.

He defended that title three times before losing it to Michael Spinks on a 15-round decision on September 21, 1985. Spinks won a 15-round split decision in a rematch on April 19, 1986, and Holmes then retired. He made a brief comeback attempt on January 22, 1988, but Mike Tyson knocked him down three times in the 4th round to win by a knockout.

Holmes won 48 of his 51 professional fights, 34 of them by knockout.

Holmgren, Paul H.
HOCKEY
b. Dec. 2, 1955, St. Paul, Minn.

Holmgren played at the University of Minnesota in 1974–75, scoring 31 points in 37 games, and then joined the Minnesota Fighting Saints of the World Hockey Association. The team folded late in the season, and Holmgren went to the NHL's Philadelphia Flyers for one game.

A defenseman, the 6-foot-3, 210-pound Holmgren became a regular with the Flyers in 1976–77 and was traded to the Minnesota North Stars late in the 1983–84 season. A recurring separated shoulder, which was operated on twice, forced his retirement in 1985, when he became an assistant coach with the Flyers.

Holmgren took over as the team's head coach in 1988 and was replaced early in the 1991–92 season. The following year, he became head coach of the Hartford Whalers. He was fired early in the 1992–93 season with a 137–189–39 record.

In 527 regular season NHL games, Holmgren scored 323 points on 144 goals and 179 assists and had 1,648 minutes in penalties. He added 19 goals and 32 assists for 51 points in 82 playoff games.

Holovak, Mike (Michael J.)

FOOTBALL
b. Sept. 19, 1919, Lansford, Pa.

Holovak was a three-year starter at Boston College at both halfback and fullback from 1940 through 1942. As a senior, he gained 965 yards in 174 carries and was a consensus All-American fullback.

After spending nearly four years in the Navy during World War II, the 6-foot-1, 210-pound Holovak played for the NFL's Los Angeles Rams in 1946 and for the Chicago Bears in 1947 and 1948. Never a starter as a professional after his long absence from football, Holovak gained just 720 yards in 136 carries and scored 6 touchdowns.

In 1951, Holovak became head coach at Boston College, where he had a 49–29–3 record in nine years. When the Boston Patriots were organized to join the new American Football League in 1960, Holovak was director of player personnel. He was named the team's head coach in 1961.

The Patriots won the AFL Eastern Division title in 1963 but lost, 51–10, to the San Diego Chargers in the league's championship game. Holovak resigned in 1968 after two poor seasons but worked in the front office for several professional teams afterward.

★ College Football Hall of Fame

Holtz, Louis L.

FOOTBALL
b. Jan. 6, 1937, Follansbee, W.V.

The undersized Holtz was a 5-foot-10, 150-pound backup linebacker at Kent State University in Ohio, graduating in 1959. He was an assistant coach at several colleges before becoming head coach at William and Mary in 1969.

Holtz had a 13–19–0 mark there but guided the team to the Southern Conference championship in 1970. He took over at North Carolina State in 1972 and had a 31–11–2 record in four seasons. His team played in four bowl games, winning two, losing one, and tying one.

The NFL's New York Jets hired Holtz in 1976, but he quit after the Jets won only 3 of their first 13 games. Holtz re-turned to college coaching at the University of Arkansas in 1977. He spent seven years there, compiling a 60–21–2 record and taking the Razorbacks to six bowl games.

Holtz's next stop was the University of Minnesota in 1984. The school had won only four games in the previous two seasons, but in his second year Holtz took his team to the Independence Bowl, where Minnesota beat Clemson, 20–13.

When Holtz took the job at Minnesota, he said he would spend the rest of his career there unless he had a chance to become head coach at Notre Dame. That happened in 1986. Again Holtz quickly rebuilt a program that had been struggling. Notre Dame was ranked first in the nation in 1988, winning all 11 regular season games and beating third-ranked West Virginia, 34–21, in the Fiesta Bowl.

Through 1994, Holtz's Notre Dame teams have won 83 games while losing only 23 and tying 2. Overall his record is 199–88–7, a .689 winning percentage.

The slender, bespectacled Holtz is known for a quick wit and the ability to inspire players, but he is also a stern disciplinarian. At Arkansas, he suspended three starting players for breaking rules shortly before the 1977 Orange Bowl. Nevertheless, Arkansas beat heavily favored Oklahoma, 31–6.

Holum, Diane

SPEED SKATING
b. May 19, 1951, Chicago, Ill.

As a competitor and a coach, Holum was a leader of the revival of U.S. speed skating that began in the late 1960s. She competed in the 1966 world championships at 14, the youngest competitor ever, and the following year she placed third overall. She followed that performance with a bronze in the 1,000-meter race at the 1968 Olympics and a remarkable three-way tie with two teammates, Jennifer Fish and Mary Meyers, for the silver medal in the 500-meter.

Holum was the world 1,000-meter champion in 1971, and in 1972, she won the 500-meter at the world championships, the 1,000-meter at the world sprint championships, and the 1,500-meter in the Olympics. She also won an Olympic silver medal at 3,000 meters.

At 22, she retired from competition and began coaching. Among her prize pupils were Beth and Eric Heiden.

Holyfield, Evander
BOXING
b. Oct. 19, 1962, Atmore, Ala.

Holyfield was considered the favorite to win the light-heavyweight championship at the 1984 Olympics but was the victim of one of the controversial decisions that plagued boxing at the Seoul Games. He had apparently knocked out his opponent in a semifinal bout, but the referee ruled the punch had been thrown after the bell, and Holyfield lost on a questionable decision.

He became a professional after the Olympics and won the WBA and IBF junior heavyweight championships on July 12, 1986, with a decision over Dwight M. Qawi in Atlanta. Holyfield added the WBC junior heavyweight title by knocking out Carlos DeLeon in the 8th round on April 9, 1988.

Holyfield became world heavyweight champion with a 3rd-round knockout of Buster Douglas on October 25, 1990. He was then scheduled to fight Mike Tyson, who had been upset by Douglas, but the fight was postponed when Tyson suffered an injury, and it was canceled entirely after Tyson's conviction for rape.

After three defenses, Holyfield lost the title to Riddick Bowe in a unanimous decision on November 13, 1992. It was his first loss in 29 professional fights.

Holzman, Red (William)
BASKETBALL
b. Aug. 10, 1920, New York, N.Y.

After a year at the University of Baltimore, Holzman played for Nat Holman at the City College of New York. He joined the U.S. Navy in 1942 and was with the Norfolk, Virginia, Naval Base team for two years.

Holzman joined the Rochester Royals of the National Basketball League after being discharged in 1945, and the team won the NBL championship in his first season. The Royals moved into the National Basketball Association in 1949, when the NBL merged with the Basketball Association of America, and they won the NBA championship in 1951.

A 5-foot-10 guard, Holzman was an excellent defensive player and a good playmaker. He played for the Royals through the 1952–53 season, then went to the Milwaukee Hawks as player-coach.

Holzman retired as a player after only one season but remained as coach. The Hawks moved to St. Louis in 1955, and Holzman was fired after the team lost 19 of its first 33 games in 1956–57.

After ten years as an assistant with the New York Knicks, Holzman became head coach in 1967. The team made the playoffs for eight straight years and won NBA titles in 1970, when Holzman was named coach of the year, and in 1973. As a coach, Holzman emphasized a switching team defense and unselfish offense. The Knicks' unofficial team slogan was "Hit the open man."

Holzman was replaced by his former player Willis Reed in 1977, but he returned to replace Reed early in the 1978–79 season. He retired in 1982 with an overall record of 696 wins and 604 losses. His teams won 58 of 105 playoff games.
★ Basketball Hall of Fame

Hooper, Harry B.
BASEBALL
b. Aug. 24, 1887, Bell Station, Calif.
d. Dec. 18, 1974

A left-handed hitter who threw right-handed, Hooper was a member of one of the all-time great outfields with the Boston Red Sox. He played right field on a team that had future Hall of Famer Tris Speaker in center and Duffy Lewis in left.

Hooper hoped to be an engineer rather than a professional baseball player. Red Sox owner John Taylor lured him to Boston with an offer of $2,800 a year plus a chance to help design Fenway Park, which was soon to be constructed.

However, Hooper found he enjoyed major league baseball and never did do any engineering work.

He joined the team during the 1909 season and remained with the Red Sox through 1920, then went to the Chicago White Sox for five years, retiring after the 1925 season.

A line drive hitter with speed, Hooper was a fine leadoff man and an exceptional defensive player. In the eighth game of the 1912 World Series against the New York Giants, he fell into the Fenway Park stands after making a leaping catch to rob Larry Doyle of a home run. The Red Sox won the game, 3–2, in ten innings.

Although he hit only 2 home runs during the 1915 season and only 75 in his career, Hooper hit 2 in the final game of Boston's five-game victory over the Philadelphia Phillies in the 1915 World Series. The first tied the score in the third inning, and the second won the game, 5–4.

He batted .333 and scored 6 runs when Boston beat the Brooklyn Robins in a five-game World Series in 1916, but he hit only .200 in the six-game 1918 World Series victory over the Chicago Cubs.

Hooper played one season, 1927, in the Pacific Coast League after leaving the majors, and he coached baseball at Princeton University in 1931 and 1932, then became postmaster of Capitola, California, for 25 years.

In 2,309 major league games, Hooper had a career average of .281 on 2,466 hits, including 389 doubles, 160 triples, and 75 home runs. He stole 375 bases, scored 1,429 runs, and had 817 RBI.
★ Baseball Hall of Fame

Hoppe, Willie (William F.)
BILLIARDS
b. Oct. 11, 1887, Cornwall-on-Hudson, N.Y.
d. Feb. 1, 1959

When he was five years old, Hoppe began playing billiards by climbing up on a box to reach the table at the hotel his father operated. He became known as the "Boy Wonder" when he was 9, and

he began playing professionally before he was 14.

Hoppe won the world 18.1 balkline championship by beating Maurice Vignaux of France on January 15, 1906. He also held that title in 1908, from 1909 through 1911, and from 1914 through 1926. After losing the championship to Jake Schaefer, Jr., in 1926, Hoppe regained it in 1927, the last year competition took place in that form of billiards.

The world 18.2 balkline champion in 1907, from 1910 through 1920, from 1923 through 1924, and in 1927, Hoppe began concentrating on three-cushion billiards in the 1930s. He won world championships in 1936, from 1940 through 1944, and from 1947 until his retirement in 1952.

Many of Hoppe's records still stand, including an unbelievable run of 622 in 18.2 balkline during an exhibition in 1912. He set records with runs of 20 points in three-cushion league play in 1927 and three-cushion match play in 1945, and he ran a record 25 points in a 1928 exhibition against Charles C. Peterson. His grand tournament average of 1.33 in 1950 is also a record.

Horn, Ted (Eylard Theodore)
AUTO RACING
b. Feb. 27, 1910, Cincinnati, Ohio
d. Oct. 10, 1948

If the fable of the tortoise and the hare could conceivably be applied to auto racing, Ted Horn was the tortoise. He began racing in a $12 jalopy when he was 15, but he wasn't a genuine success at the sport until he was 35.

After a serious crash when he was 18, his parents urged him to find a safer job, and he did, for a while. He entered another race when he was 21, crashed again, but returned to racing once more as soon as he got out of the hospital. Through the 1930s he had moderate success, finishing second in the 1936 Indy 500 and third in the championship point standings for the year. He was third at Indy in 1937, fourth in 1938, 1939, and 1940, third again in 1941.

Horn was rejected for military service in World War II because of his past injuries. Racing resumed on a limited scale in 1945, and Horn was suddenly a winner, placing first in all seven races he entered. There was no national championship that year, but he won the title in 1946, 1947, and 1948, becoming the first three-time winner. He also placed third, third, and fourth in the Indy 500 during those years, giving him 10 straight finishes in the top four.

He clinched the 1948 championship with a third-place finish at the track in DuQuoin, Illinois, in September. A month later he was racing at DuQuoin again. He crashed on the second lap and died in a hospital a short time later.

★ Indianapolis Speedway Hall of Fame

Horner, Red (George R.)

HOCKEY
b. May 29, 1909, Lynden, Ont.

The first real bad boy of professional hockey, Horner once spent 17 minutes in the penalty box during the first period of a game. He led the NHL in penalty minutes eight seasons in a row, from 1932–33 through 1939–40, and in 1935–36 he set a record with 167 penalty minutes in 43 games. The record was broken in 1956 by Lou Fontinato, who had 202 penalty minutes — but it took him 70 games.

Horner was a defensive mainstay of the Toronto Maple Leafs for 12 seasons, beginning in 1928. For much of that time, he was paired with King Clancy, an attacking defenseman, and Horner had to guard against opposition rushes when Clancy went deep into the offensive zone. He also had to protect the small but feisty Clancy and other Maple Leafs from aggressive opponents.

When Boston's Eddie Shore almost killed Ace Bailey with a vicious body check in 1933, Horner knocked Shore down and out with a single punch that sent him to the ice with his head in a widening pool of blood. While Bailey was rushed to a hospital for emergency surgery, Shore was in the Boston dressing room having 18 stitches taken in his head.

Horner played with Toronto through the 1939–40 season. He had 42 goals, 110 assists, and 1,254 penalty minutes in 490 regular season games, with 7 goals, 10 assists, and 166 penalty minutes in 71 playoff games.

★ Hockey Hall of Fame

Hornsby, Rogers

BASEBALL
b. April 27, 1896, Winters, Tex.
d. Jan. 5, 1963

Probably the greatest right-handed hitter in baseball history, Hornsby joined the NL's St. Louis Cardinals toward the end of the 1915 season. Used primarily at third base and shortstop, he hit over .300 in three of his first four full seasons, with a high of .327 in 1917, when he led the league with 17 triples.

After being moved to second base in 1920, Hornsby won six straight batting titles, beginning with a .370 average. He had an incredible five-year stretch from 1921 through 1925, hitting .397, .401, .384, .424, and .403. His average over that period was .402, with 1,078 hits, despite the fact that he missed more than 50 games with an injury in 1923.

Hornsby led the league in hits with 218 in 1920, 235 in 1921, 250 in 1922, and 227 in 1924; in doubles with 44 in 1920, 44 in 1921, 46 in 1922, and 43 in 1924; in triples with 18 in 1921; in home runs with 42 in 1922 and 39 in 1925; in RBI with 94 in 1920, 126 in 1921, 152 in 1922, and 143 in 1925; and in runs scored with 131 in 1921, 141 in 1922, and 121 in 1924.

In July 1925, Hornsby replaced Branch Rickey as St. Louis manager. He won the league's most valuable player award that year, though the team finished fourth, and in 1926 he guided St. Louis to the pennant, despite the fact that his average tumbled to .317. The Cardinals then beat the Yankees in a seven-game World Series.

Brash and outspoken, Hornsby had an argument with Cardinal management after the season and was traded to the New York Giants for Frankie Frisch, another future Hall of Fame second baseman, and pitcher Jimmy Ring. He hit .361 and led the league with 133 runs scored but was traded again, this time to the Boston Braves. Hornsby won his seventh and last batting title with a .387 average in 1928.

The Braves were in financial trouble, and Hornsby was sent to the Chicago Cubs in 1929 for five players and $200,000. He won his second most valuable player award in Chicago, hitting .380 with 39 home runs and 149 RBI and leading the league with 156 runs scored and a .679 slugging percentage. However, he batted only .238 in a five-game World Series loss to the Philadelphia Athletics.

He was named manager of the Cubs late in the 1930 season and began limiting his own playing time. He appeared in just 100 games in 1931 and only 19 in 1932. Fired during the 1932 season, Hornsby went back to the Cardinals the following year but left them to take over as manager of the St. Louis Browns in the AL before the season was over.

Hornsby remained with the Browns until July 20, 1937, appearing only occasionally, primarily as a pinch hitter. After coaching and managing in the minors for 15 years, he returned as manager of the Browns in 1952, was fired on June 9. He took over the Cincinnati Reds on August 1. After being fired by Cincinnati late in the 1953 season, Hornsby coached and scouted for the Chicago Cubs and New York Mets for several seasons.

In 2,259 games, Hornsby had a .358 average on 2,930 hits, including 541 doubles, 169 triples, and 301 home runs. He drove in 1,584 runs and scored 1,579. His career average is an NL record, and his .424 average in 1924 is a major league record for the twentieth century. As a manager, he had a 701–812 mark.
★ Baseball Hall of Fame

Hornung, Paul V.

FOOTBALL
b. Dec. 23, 1935, Louisville, Ky.

A fullback as a sophomore at Notre Dame, Hornung was moved to quarterback in 1955 and was a consensus All-American. As a senior in 1956, he became the only player ever to win the Heisman Trophy with a losing team.

And, ironically, he wasn't an All-American that season.

Although he was a fair passer, his strengths were running the ball in the split T offense and place-kicking. When he joined the Green Bay Packers as the bonus draft choice in 1957, the team didn't know quite what to do with him. He saw playing time at quarterback, halfback, fullback, and even tight end until Vince Lombardi took over the team and made him the starting left halfback in 1959.

The 6-foot-2, 220-pound Hornung responded with a sensational season in 1960, scoring 176 points on 15 touchdowns, 41 extra points, and 15 field goals. Set in just 12 games, that is an NFL record that has survived the increases to 14-game and 16-game seasons. Hornung rushed for 671 yards and also threw two touchdown passes on the halfback option that year.

He was in the Army in 1961 but was able to get weekend leave to play on Sunday. He again led the league in scoring with 146 points. In Green Bay's 37–0 victory over the New York Giants in the NFL championship game, Hornung set a record by scoring 19 points. He won the Bert Bell Trophy as the league's player of the year.

Hornung missed much of the 1962 season with injuries. On April 17, 1963, he and Alex Karras of the Detroit Lions were suspended indefinitely for betting on games and associating with undesirable persons. The suspension was lifted in 1964, when Hornung came back with 107 points. However, recurring injuries in 1965 and 1966 forced his retirement.

Known as a money player who got better as the goal line got closer, Hornung made contributions that can't be measured entirely in statistics. He and fullback Jim Taylor blocked exceptionally well for one another.

In his nine seasons, Hornung rushed 893 times for 3,711 yards, a 4.2 average, and scored 50 touchdowns. He caught 130 passes for 1,480 yards, an 11.4 average, and 12 touchdowns, and scored a total of 760 points on 62 touchdowns,

190 extra points, and 66 field goals. He also threw 5 touchdown passes.

★ College Football Hall of Fame; Pro Football Hall of Fame

Horvath, Leslie

FOOTBALL
b. Sept. 12, 1921, South Bend, Ind.

The versatile Horvath was primarily a single-wing tailback at Ohio State, but he also played wingback and quarterback at times. He excelled as a broken-field runner and pass receiver. A starter in 1941 and 1942, Horvath missed the 1943 season because he was in an Army training program.

He returned in 1944 to gain 905 yards rushing, scoring 12 touchdowns in just nine games, to lead Ohio State to a 9–0–0 season. He was named an All-American halfback and won the Heisman Trophy as the nation's outstanding college football player.

After receiving a degree in dentistry in 1945, Horvath entered the Navy and assisted his former Ohio State coach, Paul Brown, with the Great Lakes Naval Training Station team. In 1946, he coached a U.S. Marine team in Hawaii.

Horvath played professionally with the Los Angeles Rams in 1947 and 1948 and the Cleveland Browns in 1949. He finished third in the NFL in returning punts in 1948, with 203 yards on 13 runbacks, an average of 15.6 yards.

★ College Football Hall of Fame

Hotchkiss, Hazel V. [Mrs. Wightman]

TENNIS
b. Dec. 20, 1886, Healdsburg, Calif.
d. Dec. 5, 1974

Because she was frail and sickly as a child, Hotchkiss's brothers were told by a doctor to include her in their games to help build her strength. As she grew stronger in her teen years, her parents decided she was too old to play with boys and urged her to take up tennis, which was considered more genteel.

Women's tennis in the early part of the century at the time was dominated by the five Bundy sisters, led by May and Florence. The saying was, "It takes a Bundy to beat a Bundy." That eventually became "It takes a Hotchkiss to beat a Bundy."

Hotchkiss won the national singles, women's doubles, and mixed doubles championships from 1909 through 1911. She married George Wightman of Boston in 1912 and retired from competition to raise children, although she won the national women's and mixed doubles championships in 1915. She returned in 1919 to win another national singles title, her last.

However, she remained an outstanding doubles player for many years, winning national women's doubles championships in 1924 and 1928 and mixed doubles titles in 1918 and 1920. She also won the Olympic women's doubles with Helen Wills and the mixed doubles with R. Norris Williams in 1924.

Later, she won a number of senior championships, her last in 1954, when she was 68. All told, she won 45 national titles. She was also the U.S. squash racquets champion in 1930.

Hotchkiss's contributions to tennis extended far beyond her play. In 1923, she donated a trophy for international competition among women's teams, usually referred to as the Wightman Cup, and until her death she frequently gave advice, on courtesy as well as technique, to younger players.

★ International Tennis Hall of Fame; International Women's Sports Hall of Fame

Houbregs, Bob (Robert J.)

BASKETBALL
b. March 12, 1932, Seattle, Wash.

The son of a professional hockey player, Houbregs couldn't take part in sports as a boy because he suffered a severe case of rickets when he was 3, and his legs had to be broken and set so they would grow straight.

But he played basketball in high school and fell in love with the hook shot, which he practiced 300 times a day during his career. His accuracy, at distances of up to 25 feet, won him his alliterative nickname, "Hooks" Houbregs.

As a 6-foot-8, 225-pound center at the University of Washington, he was an All-American and the Helms Athletic Foundation player of the year in 1953. In three years, he scored 1,774 points, the school record until 1988.

Houbregs joined the Baltimore Bullets of the NBA after graduating, but back problems limited his playing time and finally resulted in his retirement after playing only 17 games with Detroit in the 1957–58 season. He had also played with Ft. Wayne and Boston. In 281 NBA games, he averaged 9.3 points per game.

★ Basketball Hall of Fame

Houk, Ralph G.

BASEBALL
b. Aug. 9, 1919, Lawrence, Kans.

After serving in the Marine Corps during World War II, which won him his nickname, the Major, Houk spent eight seasons as a backup catcher with the AL's New York Yankees but appeared in only 91 games and had just 158 at-bats during that time. He retired from playing after the 1954 season and became a minor league manager.

In 1961, he took over the Yankees and guided them to three consecutive pennants and World Series victories in his first two seasons. After losing the 1963 World Series, however, he was replaced by Yogi Berra.

Houk returned to the Yankees in 1966, but the team was in the second division for most of the next eight seasons, and Houk left to take over the Detroit Tigers in 1974. He retired after the 1978 season but came out of retirement three years later to manage the Boston Red Sox. After a fourth-place finish in 1984, he retired permanently.

In 20 seasons, his teams won 1,619 games and lost 1,531, a .514 percentage.

Houser, Bud (Lemuel C.)

TRACK AND FIELD
b. Sept. 25, 1901, Winnigan, Mo.

Houser was the last athlete to win both the shot put and the discus in the Olympics, in 1924, when he was a student at Southern California. He carried the U.S. flag at the opening ceremonies of the Amsterdam Games in 1928; he was then a practicing dentist, and he was competing only in the discus throw. He almost failed to qualify for the finals because he fouled on the first attempt and the discus slipped out of his hand on the second. But he made a good throw on his third and final attempt, then went on to win the gold medal.

Houser won the IC4A discus throw in 1925 and both the discus throw and shot put in 1926. He was the NCAA discus champion in 1926. He won national championships in the discus in 1925, 1926, and 1928, and in the shot put in 1921 and 1925.

On April 3, 1926, he set a world record with a discus throw of 158 feet, 1¾ inches. The record stood until 1929.

★ National Track & Field Hall of Fame

Houston, Kenneth R.

FOOTBALL
b. Nov. 12, 1944, Lufkin, Tex.

A linebacker at Prairie View A & M in Texas, Houston became a strong safety when he joined the American Football League's Houston Oilers as a ninth-round draft choice in 1967. The 6-foot-3, 198-pound Houston was a natural for the position. He had the speed to be an excellent pass defender and the strength to support the run defense.

In his third game as a starter, against the New York Jets, he scored two touchdowns, one on a 43-yard interception return and the other on a 45-yard run with a block field goal attempt. He went on to set a professional record by returning nine interceptions for touchdowns.

Houston, who once said that he originally started playing football in high school because the football players had all the girlfriends, was traded to the Washington Redskins after the 1972 season. He retired after becoming a backup player in 1980.

He was named to the American Football Conference All-Pro team in 1971 and to the National Football Conference squad from 1974 through 1977. In 14 professional seasons, he returned 49 interceptions for 898 yards, an 18.3 average, and 9 touchdowns. He also returned 51 punts for 333 yards, a 6.5 average, and 1 touchdown.

★ Pro Football Hall of Fame

Howard, Desmond K.

FOOTBALL
b. May 15, 1970, Cleveland, Ohio

After catching a touchdown pass against Ohio State in the last regular season game of his college career at Michigan, Howard struck a Heisman Trophy pose for photographers and cameramen. It was prophetic. He did indeed win the Heisman that year. He is one of only three wide receivers ever to win the award.

Although he played for a team that emphasized the run, Howard caught 19 touchdown passes in 11 games as a senior and had 30 touchdowns in 33 career games.

Drafted in the first round of the 1992 NFL draft by the Washington Redskins, Howard was used sparingly as a rookie, catching only three passes for a total of just 20 yards. He saw more action toward the end of the 1993 season, when the stumbling Redskins began to look at some of their younger players for the future.

Howard, Elston G.

BASEBALL
b. Feb. 23, 1929, St. Louis, Mo.
d. Dec. 14, 1980

The first black to play for the New York Yankees, Howard joined the team in 1955. He was used primarily in the outfield during his first five seasons while also playing first base on occasion and serving as backup catcher to Yogi Berra.

In 1960, Howard took over as the team's starting catcher, with Berra backing him up and frequently playing the outfield. Howard had his best overall offensive season in 1961, hitting .348 with 21 home runs and 77 RBI. He was named the AL's most valuable player in 1963, when he batted .287, hit 28 home runs, and had 85 RBI.

He was traded to the Boston Red Sox during the 1967 season and played on his tenth pennant-winning team in 13 years. Howard retired as a player after the 1968 season and returned to the Yankees as a coach.

In 1,605 games, Howard had 1,471 hits, including 218 doubles, 50 triples, and 167 home runs. He scored 619 runs and drove in 762.

Howard, Frank J.

FOOTBALL
b. March 25, 1909, Barlow Bend, Ala.

Howard played guard at the University of Alabama in 1929 and 1930 and was called by his coach, Wallace Wade, "a great competitor and fine player all around." The team was known as the "Herd of Red Elephants" because of its overall size; Howard, at only 180 pounds, was called the "Little Giant."

After graduating in 1931, he became an assistant coach at Clemson and took over as head coach in 1940. He spent 30 years at Clemson, winning 165 games, losing 118, and tying 12. His 1948 team won all ten of its regular season games and beat Missouri, 24–23, in the Gator Bowl. Howard's 1950 team won eight of nine, tying the ninth, and won the Orange Bowl, 15–14, over Miami of Florida.

Howard retired after the 1969 season but remained as athletic director until 1972. A homespun humorist much in demand as a speaker, he pretended to be something of a country bumpkin but was, in fact, a Phi Beta Kappa.

★ College Football Hall of Fame

Howard, Frank O.

BASEBALL
b. Aug. 8, 1936, Columbus, Ohio

Variously known as "Hondo," "the Capital Punisher," and "the Gentle Giant," Howard played baseball and basketball at Ohio State University before entering professional baseball in 1956. He had brief stints with the Los Angeles Dodgers in 1958 and 1959 and joined the team full-time in 1960, when he was named the NL's rookie of the year. He had a .268 average with 23 home runs and 77 RBI in 117 games that season.

The 6-foot-7, 255-pound Howard was

traded to the Washington Senators before the 1965 season. He led the AL in home runs twice, with 44 in both 1968 and 1970, and he was also the league leader in slugging percentage at .552 in 1968 and in RBI with 126 in 1970.

Howard went with the team when it moved to Texas and became known as the Rangers in 1972, but he was traded to the Detroit Tigers near the end of that season. He finished his playing career with Detroit in 1973.

In 1981, Howard managed the San Diego Padres to a 41–69 record. He took over the New York Mets during the 1983 season and had a 52–64 record with them. Howard has also served as a coach with several major league teams.

In 1,895 games, he had a .273 batting average with 1,774 hits, including 245 doubles, 35 triples, and 382 home runs. He scored 864 runs and drove in 1,119.

Howard, John
CYCLING
b. 1947, Springfield, Mo.

In a single race, Howard helped rejuvenate competitive cycling in the United States. As a member of the Army cycling team, Howard competed in the 200-kilometer road race at the 1971 Pan-American Games in Cali, Colombia. It was the last event on the program, so it drew more attention from U.S. media than a bicycle race normally would have, and an estimated one million spectators lined the road to watch.

Despite a broken spoke in his rear wheel that caused the rim to rub against the brake, Howard broke away from the pack with Luis Carlos Florez, and with about 50 yards to go, he took the lead and beat Florez by four lengths.

The *New York Times* headlined the story of his victory, "U.S. Wins Cycling Breakthrough." That was accurate, because the U.S. Olympic Committee had considered abandoning cycling, but Howard's victory gave the sport new prestige, and with increased financial support, American cyclists began to win world and Olympic championships during the 1970s.

Howard was the national road racing champion in 1968, 1972, 1973, and 1975.

Howe, Gordon
HOCKEY
b. March 31, 1928, Floral, Sask.

No one else, in any sport, ever performed at as high a level for as long a time as Gordie Howe. In 25 seasons with the Detroit Red Wings, he won the Hart Trophy as the NHL's most valuable player 6 times and was a first-team all-star 12 times and a second-team all-star 9 times.

He retired in 1971 but returned two years later, at the age of 45, to play with the World Hockey Association's Houston Aeros as a teammate with his sons Marty and Mark. He won that league's most valuable player award in 1974, when he scored 100 points on 31 goals and 69 assists. When the Houston team folded in 1977, Howe returned to the NHL with the Hartford Whalers and played three more seasons before retiring in 1980 at the age of 52.

Howe joined the Red Wings in 1946 after a year in the minor leagues. For three seasons he seemed to be little more than a steady journeyman. But in 1949–50 he finished third in scoring, and he was among the top six scorers in the league for 20 more seasons.

During a 1950 Stanley Cup playoff game against Toronto, Howe suffered a serious head injury when he was checked into the boards. He underwent surgery to relieve pressure on his brain, but there was some permanent damage that caused an uncontrollable blink and facial spasms at times. His teammates began calling him "Blinky," and Howe never objected.

He came back to lead the NHL in scoring for the next four seasons. After finishing second in 1955–56, he was the scoring leader again in 1956–57 and 1962–63. But Howe was more than a scorer. He was also an outstanding defensive forward who was usually on the ice when Detroit was short-handed or on the power play. During an eight-year period, 1957–64, he averaged more than 40 minutes a game, twice the playing time of most forwards.

Although seasons have lengthened and scoring totals have become inflated since Howe's peak years, he still ranks first in regular season games played (2,186) and goals scored (975) and is second to Wayne Gretzky in assists (1,383) and total points (2,358), including WHA totals for both. Howe also played in 157 NHL playoff games, scoring 68 goals and 92 assists. He won the Hart Trophy in 1952, 1953, 1957, 1958, 1960, and 1963.

Rocket Richard, his long-time rival with the Montreal Canadiens, said, "Howe is a better all-around player than I was." Richard's teammate, Jean Beliveau, went a little farther: "Gordie Howe is the best hockey player I have ever seen." And Bill Gadsby, who played with Howe and against him, said, "Gordie Howe was not only the greatest hockey player I've ever seen, but the greatest athlete."

★ Hockey Hall of Fame

Howe, Mark S.
HOCKEY
b. May 28, 1955, Detroit, Mich.

As a six-year-old, Howe often skated in practice sessions with the Detroit Red Wings, the team his famous father, Gordie Howe, starred for. At 16, he played for the U.S. team that won a silver medal in the 1972 Winter Olympics.

In 1973, Howe joined the Houston Aeros of the new World Hockey Association with his brother Marty, and father Gordie came out of retirement to play with his sons. A left wing, Mark scored 79 points on 38 goals and 41 assists and was named rookie of the year.

Howe had 76 points in 1974–75 and was the top scorer in the WHA playoffs with 10 goals and 12 assists for 22 points, leading Houston to the championship. After two more seasons with Houston, the franchise folded, and all three Howes went to the New England Whalers. Mark had his best offensive season in 1978–79, scoring 42 goals and adding 65 assists for 107 points.

The team became known as the Hartford Whalers in 1979–80, after moving into the NHL. The 5-foot-11, 180-pound Howe was put on defense that year but remained a scoring threat because of his fine wrist shot, puck-handling skill, and skating speed, scoring 80 points on 24 goals and 56 assists.

Hartford traded Howe to the Philadelphia Flyers in 1982. He suffered the first of a series of back injuries in January 1990 and eventually underwent surgery for a herniated disc. From 1989–90 through 1991–92, he played in only 101 games, and he signed with the Detroit Red Wings as a free agent in July 1992.

Through the 1993–94 season, Howe had 196 goals and 540 assists for 736 points in 911 NHL regular season games. He added 10 goals and 51 assists for 61 points in 98 playoff games.

Howe, Steven R.
BASEBALL
b. March 10, 1958, Pontiac, Mich.

While playing for the University of Michigan, Howe was named the left-handed pitcher on *The Sporting News* college All-American team in 1979. He was chosen by the NL's Los Angeles Dodgers in the free agent draft that year and joined the team in 1980.

It was the beginning of a checkered career. Howe became a relief pitcher for the Dodgers and had 56 saves during the next four seasons. However, he was suspended on September 23, 1983, for cocaine use.

Howe missed the entire 1984 season. He returned to the Dodgers in 1985 but was ineffective. They released him in July. The Minnesota Twins picked him up but released him in September.

In 1986, Howe began the season with a minor league team before being suspended for a relapse in July. He pitched in the Mexican League early in 1987 before joining the AL's Texas Rangers for 24 appearances.

Howe was out of baseball in 1988 and 1989, reappeared in ten minor league games in 1990, and joined the New York Yankees in 1991. He spent a month of that season on the disabled list and was suspended once more in June 1992, but he returned to the Yankees in 1993.

Through all of the turmoil, Howe has compiled a 41–37 record with 88 saves and a 2.75 ERA. He struck out 295 hitters and walked 116 in 540⅓ innings.

Howell, Dixie (Millard F.)

FOOTBALL
b. Oct. 12, 1913, Hartford, Ala.
d. March 2, 1971

An All-American halfback at Alabama in 1934, Howell saved his most brilliant performance for the 1935 Rose Bowl. In a 29–13 victory over Stanford, Howell scored touchdowns on runs of 5 and 67 yards and threw two touchdown passes to Don Hutson. He had 10 completions in 13 attempts for 210 yards, and he also returned 4 punts a total of 74 yards.

In his three years as a starter, Alabama had a 26–2–1 record as Howell passed for 3,947 yards and 43 touchdowns. He played for the NFL's Boston Redskins in 1936. They became the Washington Redskins in 1937, when they added Sammy Baugh, forcing Howell to the bench.

He coached Arizona State to a 23–15–4 record from 1938 through 1941. After four years in the service, Howell compiled a 13–20–1 record at the University of Idaho from 1947 through 1950.
★ College Football Hall of Fame

Howell, Harry (Henry V.)

HOCKEY
b. Dec. 28, 1932, Hamilton, Ont.

After one game in the minor leagues, Howell joined the New York Rangers in 1952 and spent 21 seasons in the NHL. When he finally won his only Norris Trophy as the league's best defenseman in 1967, Bobby Orr's rookie year, Howell said, "I'm glad I won this award now because I expect it's going to belong to Bobby Orr from now on."

Like many of the best defensemen, Howell was solid but unspectacular, and his consistent play was not often appreciated by fans, especially since he never played for a Stanley Cup champion. After 17 seasons as a regular with the Rangers, Howell underwent spinal fusion surgery in the summer of 1967 and

was sold to the California Seals. He finished his career with the Los Angeles Kings in 1972–73.

Howell scored 94 goals and had 324 assists in 1,411 regular season games and added 3 goals and 3 assists in 38 playoff games.
★ Hockey Hall of Fame

Howell, Lida (Scott)

ARCHERY
b. Aug. 23, 1859
d. Dec. 20, 1933

Howell was by far the finest woman archer of her time. In her only chance at international competition, she won two gold medals in the 1904 Olympics, in the double national round and double Columbia round. She won 17 national championships in 25 years of competition. And she set scoring records in 1895 that stood until 1931.

As Lida Scott, she won Ohio state championships in 1881 and 1882. She married Millard C. Howell in 1883 and won her first national title that year. Her other national championships came in 1885–88, 1890–93, 1895–96, 1898–1900, 1902–05, and 1907.

Hoyt, Beatrix

GOLF
b. 1880, Westchester County, N.Y.
d. Aug. 14, 1963

Hoyt won the U.S. Women's Amateur championship in 1896, the first year she entered. At age 16, she was the youngest champion until Laura Baugh won in 1971. Hoyt also won the title in 1897 and 1898; she is one of only four golfers to win three amateur championships in a row. She was low scorer in the tournament's qualifying round five years in a row, from 1896 through 1900. Hoyt retired from serious competition after losing in the semifinals of the 1900 tournament.

Hoyt, La Marr (Dewey La Marr)

BASEBALL
b. Jan. 1, 1955, Columbia, S.C.

A right-handed pitcher, Hoyt had two fine seasons with the Chicago White Sox, climaxing with the AL's Cy Young

Award in 1983, when he led the league in victories with a 24–10 record. He had also led in victories with a 19–10 record in 1982.

The White Sox won the AL Western Division in 1983, and Hoyt pitched them to a 2–1 victory in the first game of the league championship series against the Baltimore Orioles, but Chicago lost the next three games, and Baltimore took the pennant.

After a 13–18 record in 1984, Hoyt was traded to the NL's San Diego Padres. He was 16–8 in 1985, but arm troubles shortened his season and ended his career the following year.

In eight major league seasons, Hoyt had a 98–68 record and a 3.99 ERA, with 681 strikeouts and 279 walks in 1,311 innings.

Hoyt, Waite C.

BASEBALL
b. Sept. 9, 1899, Brooklyn, N.Y.
d. Aug. 25, 1984

Nicknamed "Schoolboy" during the early part of his major league career because of his baby face, Hoyt pitched one game for the NL's New York Giants in 1918 and joined the Boston Red Sox in the AL the following year. His chief claim to fame with Boston was that he replaced Babe Ruth in the starting rotation when Ruth was moved to the outfield in 1919.

After having just a 10–12 record in two seasons, he rejoined Ruth on the New York Yankees in 1921. With the powerful Yankees, Hoyt became a star on the field and a celebrity off the field. A fun-loving playboy, he often celebrated victories and drowned defeats with Ruth.

Hoyt's best seasons were 1927, when he led the league in victories with a 22–7 record and in winning percentage with .759, and 1928, when he had a 23–7 record and a league-leading 8 saves in 42 appearances.

A very popular player, Hoyt went on the vaudeville circuit after the season. His lifestyle and the many innings he had pitched during the previous eight seasons then began to catch up with him. After a 10–9 record in 1929, he was traded to the Detroit Tigers early in the 1930 season.

He did a lot of traveling for the rest of his career, pitching for Detroit and the Philadelphia Athletics in 1931, for the Brooklyn Dodgers and the New York Giants in 1932, for the Pittsburgh Pirates from 1933 through 1936, for Pittsburgh and Brooklyn in 1937, and finishing with an 0–3 record for Brooklyn in 1938.

Hoyt spent the next 26 years as a radio broadcaster, the first 2 with Brooklyn, the next 24 with the Cincinnati Reds. He retired in 1966 but returned to the microphone for the 1972 season.

In 21 major league seasons, Hoyt had a 237–182 record, with 26 shutouts, 52 saves, and a 3.59 ERA. He struck out 1,206 hitters and walked 1,003 in 3,762 innings.

★ Baseball Hall of Fame

Huarte, John G.

FOOTBALL
b. May 20, 1943, Anaheim, Calif.

Huarte started at quarterback only in his senior season at Notre Dame, but it was a great season. He completed 114 of 205 pass attempts for 2,062 yards and 16 touchdowns, leading Notre Dame to a 9–1 season and a third-place finish in the 1964 national championship polls. Huarte was a consensus All-American and winner of the Heisman Trophy as the nation's best collegiate player.

However, the 6-foot-1, 200-pound Huarte was not highly regarded by professional scouts. He wasn't chosen until the sixth round of the NFL draft, by the Philadelphia Eagles, and he chose to play for the New York Jets of the American Football League, who offered him a $200,000 contract.

The Jets paid twice that amount to another rookie quarterback, Joe Namath, who became the team's starter, while Huarte spent most of the 1966 season on the taxi squad before being released and then picked up by the Boston Patriots.

Huarte played for Boston through 1967, spent 1968 with the NFL's Philadelphia Eagles, 1970 and 1971 with the AFL's Kansas City Chiefs, and finished his professional career with the Chicago Bears of the NFL in 1972. As a professional, he completed just 19 of 48 passes for 230 yards and 1 touchdown.

Hubbard, Cal (Robert Calvin)

FOOTBALL
b. Oct. 31, 1900, Keytesville, Mo. d. Oct. 17, 1977

At 6-foot-5 and somewhere around 250 pounds, Hubbard was football's first giant and the first lineman to consistently knock down passes almost as soon as they were thrown. He played tackle for "Bo" McMillin at little Centenary College in Louisiana for three seasons beginning in 1922.

When McMillin went to Geneva, Pennsylvania, College in 1925, Hubbard left school for a year. But he showed up at Geneva to play one more college season in 1926, when he was used mostly at end. He then signed with the New York Giants of the NFL.

The Giants won the league championship in his first season, allowing only 20 points in 13 games. However, Hubbard didn't like the big city, and he joined the Green Bay Packers in 1929. The Packers won three straight NFL championships in his first three years with the team, 1929 through 1931.

Other teams stopped running at Hubbard early in his professional career, so he developed the habit of moving out of the line and chasing the play wherever it went — in effect, becoming a linebacker. On offense, he was a devastating blocker, and the Packers often used him as a receiver on the tackle play. He caught at least two touchdown passes as a professional and also had at least six interceptions. (The NFL didn't keep official statistics until 1932.)

Hubbard was named to the first official All-Pro team in 1931 and was an All-Pro again in 1932 and 1933. He left football in 1934 to pursue a career as a minor league baseball umpire but returned to the Packers for the 1935 season.

In 1936, Hubbard became an American League umpire. He played one game for the New York Giants and then was traded to the NFL's Pittsburgh Pirates (later the Steelers), where he finished his football career that season.

Amiable and mild-mannered off the field, Hubbard was a very tough player and just as tough as an umpire. He once said to a rookie teammate, "You see those two holes over the ears in the helmet? Well, they're not to hear through. They're for you to stick your fingers in his helmet and jerk his face down when you raise your knee up."

Hubbard became supervisor of umpires for the American League in 1958. He is the only man enshrined in three major sports halls of fame.

★ Baseball Hall of Fame; College Football Hall of Fame; Pro Football Hall of Fame

Hubbard, John H.

FOOTBALL
b. Feb. 6, 1886, Putney, Vt. d. April 2, 1978

The only player from Amherst College to be named an All-American, Hubbard was a remarkably durable player. In four seasons, from 1903 through 1906, he started all 33 of his team's games at halfback and played every minute in 31 of them.

An All-American in 1905, the 185-pound Hubbard ran the 220-yard dash in 22.0 seconds. He was strong enough to run into the line and fast enough to get around the ends, and he was also an excellent kicker who never missed an extra point during his last three seasons at Amherst.

★ College Football Hall of Fame

Hubbard, William DeHart

TRACK AND FIELD
b. Nov. 25, 1903, Cincinnati, Ohio d. June 23, 1976

Hubbard was the first black to win an individual Olympic gold medal, in the 1924 long jump. The following year, he set a world record of 25 feet, 10⅞ inches in the event at the NCAA championships. And in 1926 he tied the world record of 9.6 seconds in the 100-yard dash.

Competing for the University of Michigan, Hubbard won the NCAA long jump championship in 1923 and both the 100-yard dash and the long jump in 1925. He was the AAU triple jump champion in 1922–23 and the long jump champion six consecutive years, from 1922 to 1927.

In 1927, Hubbard had his best long jump, 26 feet, 2¼ inches, but the mark wasn't recognized because the takeoff board was an inch higher than the landing pit.

★ National Track & Field Hall of Fame

Hubbell, Carl O.

BASEBALL
b. June 22, 1903, Carthage, Mo.
d. Nov. 22, 1988

"King Carl" learned to throw the screwball in the minor leagues in 1925. But when he went to spring training with the Detroit Tigers in 1926 and 1927, he was told not to use the pitch because it might injure his arm. He never made the Detroit roster.

The NL's New York Giants bought his contract for $30,000 in late July 1928, and he had a 10–6 record with a 2.83 ERA that season. After four more winning seasons, the left-handed Hubbell became a genuine star in 1933, leading the league with 23 victories, 10 shutouts, 308 innings pitched, and a 1.66 ERA. He was named the league's most valuable player, and the Associated Press voted him male athlete of the year.

The Giants won the pennant, and Hubbell won two games, 4–2 and 2–1, in their five-game World Series victory over the Washington Senators. His most celebrated performance, though, came in the 1934 All-Star game, when he struck out Babe Ruth, Lou Gehrig, Jimmy Foxx, Al Simmons, and Joe Cronin in succession.

In 1934, Hubbell led the league in complete games with 25, in saves with 8, and in ERA with 2.30, and he had a 23–12 record in 1935. He was named the league's most valuable player for a second time in 1936, when he went 26–6 to lead the league in victories, winning percentage, and ERA at 2.31. He finished the season with 16 consecutive victories and won the first game of the World Se-

ries. However, he lost the fourth in a six-game defeat by the New York Yankees.

His last outstanding year was 1937. Hubbell won his first 8 games to make it 24 consecutive regular season victories, a major league record. He ended with a 22–8 record, leading the league again in victories and winning percentage and also winning his only strikeout title with 159.

Arm trouble began to bother him in 1938. He remained with the Giants through 1943 and had only one losing season in that stretch but never again won more than 13 games. After retiring as a player, Hubbell became director of the team's farm system and later player development director.

In 16 major league seasons, Hubbell had a 253–154 record, with 36 shutouts, 33 saves, and a 2.98 ERA. He struck out 1,677 hitters and walked 725 in 3,590⅓ innings.

★ Baseball Hall of Fame

Huber, Vicki

TRACK AND FIELD
b. May 29, 1967, Wilmington, Del.

As a freshman at Villanova University, Huber won the NCAA 3,000-meter run, both indoors and outdoors, in 1987. She repeated in both events in 1988, when she also won the NCAA outdoor 1-mile and the national outdoor 1,500-meter championships.

The 5-foot-6, 111-pounder finished second in the 3,000-meter run at the 1988 Olympic trials and placed sixth at the Olympics. She won the 1989 Honda Broderick Cup as the nation's outstanding female college athlete for winning the NCAA cross-country title in addition to both 3,000-meter events.

Huber was hampered by injuries as a senior in 1990. Her best finish that year was a third in the national indoor 3,000-meter. She retired in 1991 because of recurring physical problems.

Huff, Sam (Robert L.)

FOOTBALL
b. Oct. 4, 1934, Morgantown, W.V.

A tackle at the University of West

Virginia, Huff was moved to middle linebacker when he joined the NFL's New York Giants in 1956, and within a short time he was one of the best-known players in football, the subject of a 1960 CBS television special "The Violent World of Sam Huff."

At 6-foot-1 and 230 pounds, Huff had speed enough to be good on pass defense and the strength to stop the run. His duels with running backs Jimmy Brown of the Cleveland Browns and Jimmy Taylor of the Green Bay Packers were celebrated.

Huff was named an All-Pro in 1958 and 1959, and he played in five Pro Bowls. The Giants traded him to the Washington Redskins in 1964, and he played there through 1967. After one season of retirement he returned to the Redskins in 1969 and then retired for good.

During his 13 NFL seasons, Huff intercepted 30 passes, returning them for 381 yards, a 12.7 average, and 2 touchdowns. He also scored 3 touchdowns on fumble recoveries.

★ Pro Football Hall of Fame

Huggins, Miller J.

BASEBALL
b. March 27, 1880, Cincinnati, Ohio
d. Sept. 25, 1929

A good but not outstanding major league infielder for 12 seasons with the Cincinnati Reds and St. Louis Cardinals, Huggins became one of baseball's finest managers. Only 5-foot-4 and 140 pounds, Huggins was a switch-hitting infielder who joined the Reds in 1904, after receiving a law degree from the University of Cincinnati.

Huggins started at second base until 1909, when he played in only 57 games. He was then traded to the Cardinals, and he became the team's playing manager in 1913. He retired as a player after 16 games in 1916, replacing himself with young Rogers Hornsby.

In five seasons, Huggins guided St. Louis to two third-place finishes, the best the team had done since 1876, but

the franchise was sold in 1918, and he was replaced by Branch Rickey.

The New York Yankees then hired him. After finishing fourth in 1918 and third in 1919, they had a chance to acquire Babe Ruth from the Boston Red Sox. After Huggins met with Ruth to work out contract terms, the deal was made.

Even with Ruth, the team finished third again in 1920, but they then won three consecutive pennants and beat the New York Giants in six games in 1923 for their first World Series victory.

The Yankees slipped into second place in 1924. The following season, Ruth was badly out of shape and was doing even more carousing than usual. He didn't hit a home run until June 11. In August, Huggins suspended him indefinitely and fined him $5,000. The furious Ruth poured obscenities on his tiny manager, and Huggins told him he wouldn't be reinstated until he apologized.

After nine days, Ruth apologized, paid his fine, and began playing again. The Yankees fell all the way to seventh place that season, but they came back to win consecutive pennants from 1926 through 1928 and world championships in 1927 and 1928.

A worrier, Huggins fretted about his team's performance in 1929 and began losing weight. A carbuncle developed below his right eye. It was a symptom of erysipelas. He missed several games because of illness and entered a hospital late in September after turning the team over to coach Art Fletcher. He died five days later.

As a player, Huggins batted .265, led the NL in walks four times, and was the league's best-fielding second baseman in 1913 with a .977 percentage. As a manager, he had 1,413 wins and 1,134 losses, a .555 percentage.

★ Baseball Hall of Fame

Hull, Bobby (Robert M.)

HOCKEY
b. Jan. 3, 1939, Point Anne, Ont.

Hull's skills are sometimes defined in terms of speed. He could skate 28.3 mph with the puck and 29.7 mph without it; his slap shot was timed at 118.3 mph, his wrist shot at 105 mph, his backhand shot at 96 mph. But he was also an exceptionally strong player with a nearly perfect athlete's body at 5-feet-10 and a solid 195 pounds.

"The Golden Jet" joined the Chicago Black Hawks in 1957. He scored only 31 goals in his first two seasons, but then he perfected his slap shot. Hull won the 1960 Ross Trophy as the NHL's leading scorer with 39 goals and 43 assists for a total of 82 points. He also won the trophy in 1962 and 1966. Hull scored 50 goals to tie the league record in 1961–62; he broke the record with 54 goals in 1965–66 and extended it to 58 in 1968–69.

He won the Hart Trophy as the league's most valuable player in 1965 and 1966, and he holds the record for left wings with 12 all-star selections, including 10 as a first team all-star.

Hull was as strong-minded as he was strong-bodied. He demanded $100,000, an unprecedented amount, in 1968, and sat out the first 11 games of the season before settling for $60,000. When the NHL proposed banning curved sticks in 1971, he threatened to boycott the playoffs. The result was a compromise allowing curvature but limiting it to a half inch.

The World Hockey Association won instant respect when it signed Hull for the Winnipeg Jets in 1972. The price was a $1 million signing bonus, $1 million for four years as a player, and $100,000 a year for six years with the team's management. He was the new league's most valuable player in its first season, 1973–74, and again in 1974–75.

Hull remained with the Jets when they entered the NHL in 1979 but went to the Hartford Whalers for the last part of the season. He retired in 1980.

In 23 seasons, Hull played 1,474 regular season games, scoring 913 goals with 895 assists. His total of 1,808 points is third behind Wayne Gretzky and Gordie Howe. In 119 NHL playoff games, he had 62 goals and 67 assists.

★ Hockey Hall of Fame

Hull, Brett
HOCKEY
b. Aug. 9, 1964, Belleville, Ont.

The son of the great Bobby Hull, Brett is a pretty good scorer in his own right. He joined the NHL's Calgary Flames for just two games in the 1986 Stanley Cup playoffs and was called up from the minors again late in the 1986–87 season.

In March 1988, Hull was traded to the St. Louis Blues. He won the 1990 Lady Byng Trophy for combining skill and sportsmanship and the Hart Memorial Trophy as the league's most valuable player for the 1990–91 season, when he set a record for left wings with 86 goals, adding 45 assists for a total of 131. It was the second of four consecutive seasons in which he had 100 or more points.

Through the 1993–94 season, Hull had scored 413 goals and 287 assists for a total of 700 points in 540 regular season games. He had 52 goals and 34 assists for 86 points in 72 playoff games.

Hunt, Joseph R.
TENNIS
b. Feb. 17, 1919, San Francisco, Calif.
d. Feb. 2, 1945

What might have been a great tennis career was unfortunately cut short by World War II, as Hunt was able to compete in few tournaments while serving in the U.S. Navy. He was killed when his fighter plane crashed into the ocean during training in Florida.

The 6-foot, 165-pound Hunt was one of many tennis players of his era who learned to play on public courts in California. An outstanding volleyer, he won the U.S. boys championship in 1934 and the U.S. junior title in 1937. He also won junior doubles championships from 1935 through 1937 with three different partners.

Hunt spent a year at the University of Southern California and transferred to the U.S. Naval Academy in 1938. He entered the Navy after graduating in 1941. Two years later, Hunt won the national singles title. It was one of only four tournaments he entered while in service.

★ International Tennis Hall of Fame

Hunter, Catfish (James A.)

BASEBALL
b. April 8, 1946, Hertford, N.C.

Hunter was signed by the AL's Kansas City Athletics in 1964, shortly after his eighteenth birthday and less than a year after he had accidentally shot off his right big toe in a hunting accident. He joined the big league team early in the 1965 season. Asked by a sportswriter what his hobbies were, Hunter replied, "Fishing for catfish," earning himself a new nickname.

The Athletics moved to Oakland in 1968, when Hunter had a 13–13 record, including a perfect game against the Minnesota Twins. From 1971 through 1974, he won more than 20 games each season, helping to lead the As to four consecutive pennants and three consecutive world championships.

Hunter led the league in winning percentage with a 21–7 record in 1972 and a 21–5 record in 1973. He won the Cy Young Award in 1974, when he had a 25–12 record, leading the league in victories and in ERA with 2.49.

After a salary dispute with Oakland owner Charles O. Finley, Hunter went to arbitration and was awarded free agency on a technicality: Finley had failed to deliver a life insurance policy required under Hunter's previous contract. He then signed the biggest contract in baseball history at the time, a five-year, $3.75 million deal with the New York Yankees.

In 1975, Hunter again led the league in victories with a 23–14 record, as well as in complete games with 30 and innings pitched with 328. However, he fell off to 17–15 in 1976 and then began to suffer arm problems. After winning just 23 games and losing 18 over the next three seasons, he retired.

Hunter combined a good fastball, a good slider, and excellent control to keep hitters off balance. In his 15 major league seasons, he had a 224–166 record with 42 shutouts and a 3.26 ERA. He struck out 2,012 hitters and walked 954 in 3,449⅓ innings.

★ Baseball Hall of Fame

Hurley, Marcus L.

CYCLING
b. 1885, New York, N.Y.
d. March 28, 1941

Cycling was an unofficial sport at the 1904 Olympics in St. Louis. Hurley won all four races, at distances ranging from a quarter-mile to a mile. The national amateur sprint champion four years in a row, from 1901 through 1904, he won the world championship in 1904.

A basketball star at Columbia University, Hurley captained the team as a senior in 1907–08. He was also captain of a New York Athletic Club team that won the Metropolitan championship tournament in 1905.

Hurst, Bruce V.

BASEBALL
b. March 24, 1958, St. George, Utah

A clever left-handed pitcher, the 6-foot-3, 220-pound Hurst signed with the AL's Boston Red Sox organization in 1976 and had brief stints with the team in 1980 and 1981. He became a full-time starter in 1982, when he struggled to a 3–7 record with a 5.77 ERA.

Never blessed with a great fastball despite his size, Hurst developed a slow curve and change-up. Combined with excellent control, those pitches made him a consistent winner from 1986 on, but recurring physical problems have prevented him from being a 20-game winner.

Hurst's best season was 1988, when he had an 18–6 record with a 3.66 ERA. He starred in post-season play in 1986, the Red Sox pennant season, going 1–0 in the league championship series and 2–0 with a 1.96 ERA in the World Series, but Boston lost to the New York Mets in seven games.

After the 1988 season, Hurst became an unrestricted free agent and signed with the NL's San Diego Padres. He led the league with 10 complete games in 1989 and with 4 shutouts in 1990. San Diego traded him to the expansion Colorado Rockies during the 1993 season, but Hurst spent most of that year on the disabled list. He pitched only briefly with the Texas Rangers in 1994.

Through that season, he had a 145–113 record with 23 shutouts and a 3.92 ERA. He had struck out 1,689 hitters and walked 774 in 2,417⅔ innings.

Hutchison, Jock

GOLF
b. June 6, 1884, St. Andrews, Scotland
d. ?

Hutchison came to the United States in his late teens and settled in the Pittsburgh area. He won the Western Pennsylvania Open five times between 1909 and 1915. Runner-up in both the U.S. Open and the PGA championship in 1916, Hutchison won the PGA in 1920 and tied for second in the U.S. Open. He returned to his native St. Andrews in 1921 to win the British Open. His last victory on the PGA tour came in the 1928 Belleair Open. Hutchison tied for first in the PGA Senior tournament in 1946 and won it outright in 1947.
★ PGA Hall of Fame

Hutson, Donald M.

FOOTBALL
b. Jan. 31, 1913, Pine Bluff, Ark.

As a freshman at the University of Alabama, Hutson was 6 feet tall and weighed only 160 pounds. Many thought he was too skinny ever to be a good football player, but he became one of the greatest pass receivers in history.

He could run the 100-yard dash in 9.8 seconds, and he had a long effortless stride that often fooled defenders into thinking he wasn't running very fast. Hutson was a master of the change of pace, turning on a sudden, unexpected burst of speed to get into the open. He also had a variety of fakes and great hands.

He didn't start for Alabama till near the end of his junior year, but he was an All-American in his senior season, 1934. In Alabama's 29–13 Rose Bowl victory over Stanford, Hutson caught six passes for 165 yards and two touchdowns.

There was no NFL draft of college players when Hutson graduated. Only two teams really wanted him, the Brooklyn Dodgers and the Green Bay Packers. Hutson signed contracts with both teams. NFL president Joe Carr decided that the team that mailed its contract to the league office first would get Hutson. Both contracts were postmarked the same day, but the Packer postmark was 17 minutes earlier.

Hutson later said it was the best thing that happened to him, because the Packers featured a passing attack and the Dodgers didn't. He was held out of the Packers' opening game in his rookie year, but he started in the second game, against the Chicago Bears, and caught an 83-yard touchdown pass on his first play as a professional.

In his 11 seasons with the Packers, he was an All-Pro nine times, and he set records that weren't broken until longer seasons and more pass-oriented offenses came along. He led the NFL in receptions eight times, in yards six times, and in touchdown receptions nine times. During the 1940s, Hutson also kicked extra points and short field goals.

When he retired after the 1945 season, he held virtually every NFL pass receiving record: most receptions in a game, 14, in a season, 74 in 1942, and in a career, 489; most touchdown receptions in a game, 4, in a season, 17 in 1942, and in a career, 99; most yards receiving in a game, 237, in a season, 1,211 in 1942, and in a career, 8,010; and most touchdown receptions in championship playoff games, 9.

Hutson also held three major scoring records: most consecutive games scoring at least one point, 41; most points in a season, 138; and most points in a career, 825. He scored 31 points in one game, the second-highest total in NFL history.
★ College Football Hall of Fame; Pro Football Hall of Fame

Hyatt, Chuck (Charles)

BASKETBALL
b. Feb. 18, 1908, Syracuse, N.Y.
d. May 8, 1978

Inducted into the Basketball Hall of Fame the first year it opened, Hyatt was a three-time All-American forward, from 1928 through 1930, and was named the Helms Athletic Foundation player of the year as a senior. During his three years, Pittsburgh won 60 games and lost only 7, as Hyatt scored 880 points. He had 28 points in a 37–35 win over Montana State in his sophomore year, and he won the game with a basket with ten seconds to play.

Hyatt led the nation in scoring his last two seasons at Pittsburgh and then joined an AAU team, the Phillips 66 Oilers. He was an AAU All-American eight times, and he was player-coach when the Oilers won the AAU national championship in 1940.

★ Basketball Hall of Fame

Hyer, Tom (Thomas)
BOXING
b. Jan. 1, 1819, New York, N.Y.
d. June 26, 1864

Hyer's father, Jacob, was generally considered America's boxing champion on the basis of one fight, an 1816 draw with Tom Beasley in the first recorded boxing match in the U.S.

Tom Hyer won general recognition as American champion after beating Country McCloskey (George McChester) on September 9, 1841. In early 1848, he and English boxer Yankee Sullivan clashed briefly in a New York saloon. That led to a match between the two on February 7, 1849.

This was the first widely publicized bout in the country. Hyer won easily in just 17 minutes and 18 seconds, when Sullivan failed to answer the call for the 17th round. (At the time, a round ended when one of the fighters went down.)

The U.S. press proclaimed Hyer the world champion on the basis of that vic-tory, which led to an enormous increase in boxing. Genuine boxing matches had been rare until then, but they became regular events in New York City during the 1850s.

Hyer never fought again. He was challenged by England's William Perry, known as the "Tipton Slasher," in 1851, but nothing came of it. When John Morrissey challenged him, Hyer demanded a $5,000-per-side bet, and Morrissey couldn't come up with the money.

A saloon operator for most of his adult life, he became a supplier to the Union Army during the Civil War. Hyer died of dropsy and rheumatism probably brought on by sleeping on the ground.

Hyman, Flo (Flora)
VOLLEYBALL
b. July 29, 1954, Inglewood, Calif.
d. Jan. 24, 1986

An All-American volleyball player at the University of Houston from 1974 through 1976, the 6-foot-5 Hyman left school in 1976 to concentrate on playing for the U.S. national team. She helped lead the team to a silver medal in 1984, the highest finish ever for American women.

Hyman was voted best hitter at the World Cup Games in Tokyo in 1981 and became the first American woman to be named to the All–World Cup team. Her coach, Arie Selinger, called her "a leader on the court," adding, "if Flo plays well, the team follows."

In 1986, Hyman was playing professionally in Japan when she collapsed on the bench and died of Marfan's Syndrome, a congenital defect of the aorta.

★ International Women's Sports Hall of Fame

Iba, Hank (Henry P.)

BASKETBALL
b. Aug. 6, 1904, Easton, Mo.
d. Jan. 15, 1993

Iba played basketball for two years at Westminster, Missouri, College, then transferred to Maryville Teachers College, now Northwest Missouri State. After graduating in 1929, he played AAU basketball with the Hillyards of St. Joseph, Missouri, and Sterling Milk of Oklahoma City.

He coached Classen High School in Oklahoma City to 51 victories in three seasons, then returned to Maryville as head coach. The team won its first 43 games under Iba before he suffered his first collegiate loss. He compiled a record of 101 wins and 14 losses in four seasons, and his 1932 team finished second in the AAU national tournament.

Iba coached Colorado University in the 1933–34 season and then went to Oklahoma A & M (Oklahoma State), where he spent 35 years. Led by 7-foot-1 Bob Kurland, the Aggies became the first school to win two consecutive NCAA tournaments, in 1945 and 1946.

Under Iba's guidance, Oklahoma State won or tied for 15 conference championships. Iba is the only man to coach two Olympic gold medal teams, in 1964 and 1968. He also coached the 1972 team that suffered a controversial loss to the Soviet Union in the championship game.

A believer in a slow, ball-control offense, Iba taught a tenacious switching man-to-man defense. Fittingly, the Henry Iba Corinthian Award, established in 1987, is presented by the National Association of Basketball Coaches to the outstanding collegiate defensive player of the year.

His overall college coaching record was 767 wins and 338 losses. Iba's brother, Clarence, was a long-time coach at the University of Tulsa, and his son, Moe, coached at Memphis State and the University of Nebraska.

★ Basketball Hall of Fame; Olympic Hall of Fame

Igaya, Chick (Chiharu)

SKIING
b. 1936, Japan

As a student at Dartmouth College, Igaya won a record six NCAA skiing championships, the downhill in 1955, the slalom from 1955 through 1957, and the Alpine combined in 1955 and 1956. He also won five national titles, the slalom in 1954, the downhill in 1955, the Alpine combined in 1954 and 1955, and the giant slalom in 1960.

Racing for his native Japan, Igaya won a silver medal in the slalom at the 1956 Winter Olympics.

Imlach, Punch (George)

HOCKEY
b. March 15, 1918, Toronto, Ont.
d. Dec. 1, 1987

The abrasive, hard-driving Imlach was player personnel director with the Boston Bruins in 1958, when Conn Smythe of the Toronto Maple Leafs offered him a job. Imlach said he wanted to be general manager. Since no one in the Toronto organization held that title, Smythe agreed.

Early in the season, Imlach fired coach Billy Reay and took over the job himself. During the next ten years, Toronto won the Stanley Cup four times. Imlach constantly strengthened his team by acquiring veteran players, often at the expense of giving up promising youngsters, and he worked his players hard, criticizing them profanely and abusively for bad plays.

By 1968–69, many of his players were tired of his methods, particularly Frank Mahovlich, the high-scoring left wing. Imlach sent Mahovlich and two others to the Detroit Red Wings for four players. The move was widely criticized by press and fans, and after the Maple Leafs were eliminated in the first round of the playoffs, Imlach was fired.

He became general manager and coach of the expansion Buffalo Sabres in 1970 but suffered a severe heart attack in 1971 and gave up coaching for three months, then resigned after the 1971–72 season. Imlach returned to coaching Toronto for part of the 1979–80 and 1980–81 seasons.

His overall record was 423 wins, 373 losses, and 163 ties. In Stanley Cup play, his teams won 44 games and lost 48.
★ Hockey Hall of Fame

Inkster, Juli (Simpson)
GOLF
b. June 24, 1960, Santa Cruz, Calif.

Inkster won the U.S. Women's Amateur three years in a row, from 1980 through 1982. She is one of only three golfers to accomplish that. The others were Glenna Collet Vare and Virginia Van Wie.

She joined the LPGA tour late in 1983, winning one of the eight tournaments she entered. The following year, Inkster beat Pat Bradley on the first hole of a sudden death playoff to win the Nabisco Dinah Shore, and she shot a 67 on the last round to win the du Maurier Classic by one shot. The only rookie ever to win two major tournaments, she

earned $186,501 and was named the tour's rookie of the year.

Inkster won the Nabisco Dinah Shore again in 1989. Her best financial season to date was 1986, when she finished third in winnings with $285,293. She is considered one of the most complete players on the LPGA tour, with virtually no weaknesses except for an occasional outburst of temper when she hits a poor shot.

Insko, Delmer M.
HARNESS RACING
b. July 10, 1931, Amboy, Minn.

A member of a harness racing family, Insko drove in his first race on July 4, 1946, six days before his fifteenth birthday. Insko was the leading driver in dashes won with 156 in 1960, when he was named driver of the year, and he led in money won with $1,635,463 in 1969.

Insko did most of his driving on tracks in the New York City area, though he occasionally picked up rides on the grand circuit. He drove Speedy Rodney to a world trotting record of 1:58⅗ on a half-mile track in 1966, and he was also the driver for Henry T. Adios, Josedale Go Lucky, Bye and Large, Overcall, and Merrie Gesture in many of their victories.

During his career, Insko won 4,558 heats and $27,601,984.

Irvin, Dick (James Dickenson)
HOCKEY
b. July 19, 1892, Limestone Ridge, Ont.
d. May 16, 1957, Montreal

As a rookie with the Chicago Black Hawks, Irvin finished second in NHL scoring in 1926–27 with 18 goals and 18 assists. A fractured skull ended his playing career in 1929, but Irvin went on to become one of the league's most successful coaches.

Irvin coached the Chicago Black Hawks to the Stanley Cup finals in 1931 but was fired because of a clash with owner Frederic McLaughlin at the beginning of the 1931–32 season. Then he took over the Toronto Maple Leafs, who had lost their first six games, and guided them to their first Stanley Cup championship. The Leafs beat the New York Rangers, 6–4, 6–2, 6–4, in the best-of-five final series. It became known as "the tennis series," because those were the same scores by which France's Jean Borotra beat Ellsworth Vines in Davis Cup competition that year.

Irvin went to the Montreal Canadiens in 1940 and remained there through the 1954–55 season, winning three more Stanley Cups, in 1944, 1946, and 1953.

A perfectionist who worked his players hard to get them into shape, Irvin was an excellent judge of talent. He discovered Maurice "Rocket" Richard and brought him to Montreal in 1943. He put the French-speaking Richard on a line with Elmer Lach, who spoke only English, and the bilingual Toe Blake. The Punch Line, as it was called, scored 82 goals as the Canadiens lost only five games and won the regular season NHL championship by 15 points.

Irvin coached the Chicago Black Hawks for just one season, 1955–56, before retiring. He holds the record for most NHL games coached, 1,437, and is second in victories with 690. His teams won an even 100 games while losing 88 and tying 2 in Stanley Cup play.

★ Hockey Hall of Fame

Irvin, Michael J.

FOOTBALL
b. March 5, 1966, Ft. Lauderdale, Fla.

The 6-foot-2, 199-pound Irvin was chosen out of Miami University in the first round of the 1988 NFL draft by the Dallas Cowboys. A wide receiver, he caught 32 passes for 654 yards, a 20.4 average, and 5 touchdowns as a rookie.

Irvin suffered a knee injury in the sixth game of 1989 and missed the rest of that season and the first month of the 1990 season, when he was a backup. However, he became a starter in 1991 and led the NFL in reception yardage with 1,523 yards on 93 catches, a 16.4 average, scoring 8 touchdowns. He caught 78 passes for 1,396 yards in 1992 and 88 for 1,330 yards in 1993.

A major factor in the Cowboys 1992 and 1993 NFL championships, Irvin

functions as a possession receiver who is willing to catch the ball over the middle to pick up the first down, but he also has exceptional running ability that often allows him to turn a short reception into a long gain.

Through the 1994 season, Irvin had 417 receptions for 6,935 yards and 40 touchdowns.

Irvin, Monte (Monford)

BASEBALL
b. Feb. 25, 1919, Columbia, Ala.

Although he had only a brief major league career, Irvin was named to the Baseball Hall of Fame by the Committee on the Negro Leagues for his total career, including eight seasons in the Negro National League, a season in the Mexican League, and a season in the Cuban Winter League, as well as eight years in the National League.

Irvin grew up in Orange, New Jersey, and was all-state in baseball, basketball, football, and track as a high school student. While a student at Lincoln University in Pennsylvania, he began playing professional baseball under the name "Jimmy Neilson" with the Newark Eagles of the Negro National League in 1937.

Branch Rickey of the Brooklyn Dodgers, who was looking for a player to integrate major league baseball, considered Irvin a candidate in the early 1940s, but Irvin entered the U.S. Army after playing in the Mexican League in 1942, and Jackie Robinson was chosen in 1946, shortly before Irvin returned to the Newark Eagles.

The Dodgers claimed him in 1948, when the Eagles disbanded, but the team owner, Effie Manley, insisted she still had a contract with Irvin, and the Dodgers withdrew their claim at the request of Commissioner Happy Chandler.

Irvin then played in the Cuban Winter League until 1949, when the New York Giants offered him a contract. After playing most of the season in the International League, he was called up to the Giants in July but appeared in only 36 games.

He began the 1950 season in the International League again but rejoined the Giants early in the season. Used mostly in left field and at first base, he batted .299.

In 1951, Irvin helped lead the Giants to a pennant, hitting .312 with 24 home runs and a league-leading 121 RBI. He had a sensational World Series, batting .458 with 11 hits, but the Giants lost in six games to the New York Yankees.

After missing most of 1952 with a broken ankle, Irvin rebounded with a .329 average, 21 home runs, and 97 RBI in 1953. The Giants won another pennant in 1954, Irvin contributing 19 home runs and 64 RBI, but he hit only .222 in their World Series victory over the Cleveland Indians.

He hit only .253 in 51 games in 1955, then spent a final season with the Chicago Cubs before retiring. Irvin later worked as a scout for the New York Mets and as a public relations representative in the commissioner's office.

★ Baseball Hall of Fame

Irwin, Hale S.

GOLF
b. June 3, 1945, Joplin, Mo.

Irwin was a quarterback and defensive back on the University of Colorado football team that was ranked twentieth in the nation in 1966, and he won the 1967 NCAA golf championship. After graduating in 1968, Irwin joined the PGA tour.

His first tour victory came in the 1971 Heritage Classic. Irwin won the 1974 U.S. Open with a 287. At the 1979 Open, he held a 6-stroke lead after rounds of 74, 68, and 67, and won by 2 shots over Gary Player despite a 75 on the final day.

Irwin won his third U.S. Open in 1990, beating Mike Donald in the longest playoff in the tournament's history. They were tied for first place at 280 after 72 holes, and they both shot 74 in an 18-hole playoff. Then they went to sudden death, and Irwin won by shooting a

birdie 3 to Donald's par on the 1st hole. Irwin is the only golfer to win three U.S. Opens; four players have won it four times.

In 1982, Irwin became the fifth golfer in history to surpass $2 million in earnings. Through 1994, Irwin was seventeenth all-time with $5,599,462.

An exceptionally consistent golfer, the 6-foot, 180-pound Irwin has earned more than $100,000 every year since 1972. He once made the cut in 86 consecutive tournaments, placing him third behind Jack Nicklaus and Byron Nelson.

Issel, Daniel P.
BASKETBALL
b. Oct. 25, 1948, Batavia, Ill.

An All-American at the University of Kentucky in 1970, the 6-foot-9, 240-pound Issel scored 2,138 points and had 1,078 rebounds in four seasons as a starter, averaging 25.8 points a game. He was chosen in the first round of the ABA's draft by the Kentucky Colonels.

Issel was named rookie of the year after leading the league in scoring with 2,480 points in 1970–71, and he established an ABA record with 2,538 points the following season. Shortly before the 1974–75 season, Issel went to the Denver Nuggets in a three-team trade. The Nuggets entered the NBA after the ABA folded in 1976, and Issel remained with them until his retirement after the 1985 playoffs. He became head coach of the team in 1992.

A rugged performer around the basket, Issel had a soft touch on a medium range jump shot that was most effective from around the foul line. In 15 professional seasons, he scored 27,413 points, fifth best in history, averaging 18.3 per game. He also had 11,133 rebounds. Issel added 2,936 points and 1,255 points in 133 playoff games.

In 1992, Issel was named head coach of the Denver Nuggets. He had a 36–46 record in his first season.

★ Basketball Hall of Fame

★ ★ J ★ ★

Jack, Beau [Sidney Walker]
BOXING
b. April 1, 1921, Atlanta, Ga.

Beau Jack began fighting at 15 in battles royal, in which a half-dozen or so blindfolded fighters swung wildly at one another until only one was left standing. The fighters were usually black, and the spectators were often well-to-do whites who put up a purse for the winner.

In 1936, Beau Jack won $1,000 in a battle royal at the Augusta National Golf Club, home of the Masters Tournament. As a further reward, he was given a job as a shoeshine boy at the club.

Nicknamed "Beau Jack" by his maternal grandmother, who raised him, he went to New England after she died in 1940, and he began boxing professionally. After winning 22 of 28 fights, 15 by knockout, he moved on to New York in August 1941. He quickly became a popular, crowd-pleasing fighter.

On December 18, 1942, he won the vacant New York lightweight championship by knocking out Tippy Larkin in the 3rd round. He lost the title to Bob Montgomery in a 15-round decision on May 21, 1943, but won it back on November 19.

Jack faced Montgomery again on March 3, 1944, in a bout for recognition in New York as world champion. Montgomery won another 15-round decision.

After serving in the Army, Beau Jack returned to boxing in December 1945. In his last title fight, he was knocked out in the 6th round by Ike Williams on July 12, 1948. He retired in 1951 but made a comeback in 1955. Beau Jack retired permanently after being knocked out by Williams again in a nontitle fight on August 12, 1955.

His 21 matches in Madison Square Garden alone drew more than 355,000 fans and receipts of $1,578,069. Beau Jack lived well during his fighting years, but after leaving the ring he became a shoeshine boy again, at the Fontainebleu Hotel in Miami.

He won 83 of his 112 professional bouts, 40 by knockout; lost 24, 4 by knockout; and fought 5 draws.
★ International Boxing Hall of Fame

Jackson, Bo [Vincent E.]
BASEBALL, FOOTBALL
b. Nov. 30, 1962, Bessemer, Ala.

One of the few athletes ever to participate in two professional sports, Jackson may have been the best of all — certainly the best since the great Jim Thorpe.

At Auburn University, Jackson won the 1985 Heisman Trophy as the nation's outstanding college player. A 6-foot-1, 228-pound running back with speed, he gained 4,303 yards in 650 attempts and scored 43 touchdowns during his four years as a starter.

The Tampa Bay Buccaneers made him the first choice overall in the 1986 NFL draft, but he chose to play professional baseball instead. After spending most of the 1986 season in the minor leagues, he joined the AL's Kansas City Royals.

Although he batted only .235, he demonstrated substantial power with 22 home runs in just 116 games in 1987. When the season was over, he joined the NFL's Los Angeles Raiders, who had chosen him in that year's draft, rushing for 554 yards in 81 carries, a 6.8 average, and scoring 4 touchdowns in 7 games.

Jackson continued to play both sports through 1990, but he suffered a serious hip injury in a post-season game with the Raiders, ending his football career and threatening his baseball career. After surgery and a rehabilitation assignment to the minor leagues, he played in 23 games with the Chicago White Sox in 1991.

The following year, Jackson had an artificial hip implanted, and he missed the entire 1992 season. However, he returned to the White Sox in 1993, batting .232 with 16 home runs in 85 games. He joined the California Angels as a free agent in 1994.

During his NFL career, Jackson carried the ball 515 times for 2,782 yards, a 5.4 average, and scored 16 rushing touchdowns. He caught 40 passes for 352 yards, an 8.8 average, and 2 touchdowns.

Through 1994, he had 598 hits in 694 major league games, with 86 doubles, 17 triples, and 141 home runs.

Jackson, Busher (Harvey)

HOCKEY
b. Dec. 15, 1911, Toronto, Ont.

Shortly after his eighteenth birthday, in December 1929, Jackson become the youngest member of Toronto's "Kid Line," with 20-year-old Charlie Conacher and 22-year-old Joe Primeau. During their seven seasons together, the three combined for 836 points.

A left wing, Jackson was a flashy, spectacular player who led the NHL in scoring in 1932–33 with 53 points on 28 goals and 25 assists, and he was among the top ten scorers in the league five other times. On November 20, 1934, he became the first NHL player to score four goals in one period.

Jackson went to the New York Americans in 1940, but after just one season, he held out for more money and was sold to the Boston Bruins for $7,500. He remained with the Bruins until his retirement in 1944.

He played 636 regular season games, scoring 241 goals with 234 assists. In 71 playoff games, he had 18 goals and 12 assists.

★ Hockey Hall of Fame

Jackson, Jim (James A.)

BASKETBALL
b. Oct. 14, 1970, Toledo, Ohio

The 6-foot-6, 220-pound Jackson was an All-American guard as a junior at Ohio State University in 1992, when he was named college player of the year by United Press International. Jackson averaged 22.4 points that season and 19.2 for his three-year career.

He then left school to enter the NBA draft and was chosen by the Dallas Mavericks in the first round. Limited to only 28 games by an injury, Jackson averaged 16.3 points as a rookie, with 131 assists and 40 steals.

In Jackson's first two NBA seasons, he scored 2,033 points in 110 games, an 18.5 average, with 505 assists and 127 steals.

Jackson, Keith J.

FOOTBALL
b. April 19, 1965, Little Rock, Ark.

An All-American tight end at the University of Oklahoma in 1986, the 6-foot-2, 249-pound Jackson was used primarily as a blocker in the run-oriented Sooner offense. He was chosen by the Philadelphia Eagles in the first round of the 1988 NFL draft.

Jackson quickly demonstrated that he could catch as well as block. He had 81 receptions for 869 yards and 6 touchdowns to win the *Sporting News* rookie of the year award.

In 1990, Jackson held out for two games in a contract dispute and fell into disfavor with Philadelphia Coach Buddy Ryan. He won his free agency after the 1991 season and signed with the Miami Dolphins.

Jackson was named to *The Sporting News* all-pro team from 1988 through 1990 and in 1992. Through the 1994 season, he had caught 349 passes for 4,023 yards, an 11.5 average, and 32 touchdowns.

Jackson, Mark A.

BASKETBALL
b. April 1, 1965, Brooklyn, N.Y.

As a senior guard at St. John's University in 1986–87, the 6-foot-3, 192-pound Jackson led the nation with an average of 9.11 assists per game. He also averaged 18.9 points per game.

The New York Knicks chose him in the first round of the 1987 NBA draft. An immediate starter, Jackson set a rookie record with 868 assists and averaged 13.6 points per game to win the rookie of the year award.

After averaging 16.9 points in his second season, Jackson slipped badly in 1989–90, when he had only 604 assists and 9.9 points per game. He became a backup the following season but returned to the starting lineup in 1991–92.

The Knicks traded him to the Los Angeles Clippers in 1992. Through the 1993–94 season, Jackson had 6,734 points and 4,639 assists in 550 regular season games. He added 401 points and 283 assists in 42 playoff games.

Jackson, Philip D.

BASKETBALL
b. Sept. 17, 1945, Deer Lodge, Mont.

After averaging 19.9 points a game in three seasons at the University of North Dakota, the 6-foot-8, 230-pound Jackson became a hard-working journeyman NBA player, joining the New York Knicks in 1967 as a second-round draft choice.

Jackson missed the entire 1969–70 season with an injury and was traded in 1978 to the New Jersey Nets, where he became a player and assistant coach. He retired in 1980, remained as an assistant coach for a season, then became a broadcaster for the team.

From 1982 through the 1986–87 season, Jackson coached the Albany team in the Continental Basketball Association, then returned to the NBA as an assistant coach with the Chicago Bulls in 1987. He became head coach in 1989.

After a second-place division finish in 1989–90, Jackson guided the Bulls to three consecutive NBA championships, the first time that had been accomplished since 1966.

As a player, Jackson averaged 6.7 points a game. As an NBA head coach, he has a record of 295 wins and 115 losses, a .720 percentage, in regular season play, and a 61–23 record, a .726 percentage, in the playoffs through the 1993–94 season.

Jackson, Reggie (Reginald M.)

BASEBALL
b. May 18, 1946, Wyncote, Pa.

Nicknamed "Mr. October" for his World Series heroics, the outspoken Jackson joined the Kansas City Athletics during the 1967 season. In 1968 the team moved to Oakland and changed its name to the A's, and Jackson led the AL in runs scored with 123 and in slugging percentage with .608 in 1969, when he had 47 home runs and 118 RBI.

From 1971 through 1975, Jackson helped lead the A's to five straight division titles, four pennants, and three consecutive world championships, from 1972 through 1974. He was named the league's most valuable player in 1973, when he led the league with 99 runs scored, 32 home runs, 117 RBI, and a .531 slugging percentage. Jackson was the home run leader again with 36 in 1975.

Jackson missed the 1972 World Series with a pulled hamstring, but he batted .310 with 1 home run and 6 RBI when the A's beat the New York Mets in seven games in 1973. In 1974, he hit .286 with 1 home run, 1 RBI and 3 runs scored in their five-game victory over the Los Angeles Dodgers.

He was traded to the Baltimore Orioles in 1976, when he led the league with a .502 slugging percentage, and he then went to the New York Yankees. Announcing "I'm the straw that stirs the drink" when he arrived, Jackson stirred the anger of team captain Thurman Munson and had frequent clashes with manager Billy Martin, but he helped lead the Yankees to the world championship in 1977, their first since 1962.

After hitting 32 home runs and driving in 110 runs during the regular season, Jackson hit .450 with 5 home runs, 8 RBI, and 10 runs scored when the Yankees beat the Dodgers in a six-game World Series. He set a Series record by hitting home runs in four consecutive at-bats. The first came in his last time up in the fifth game. After walking in his first appearance in the sixth game, Jackson homered in the fourth, fifth, and eighth innings. Each home run came on the first pitch.

The Yankees beat the Dodgers in six games again in 1978, with Jackson batting .391 with 2 home runs, 2 runs scored, and 8 RBI. He led the league in home runs for a third time with 41 in 1980. Bothered by injuries in 1981, he appeared in only 94 games and then went to the California Angels as a free agent.

Jackson won his fourth and last home run title in 1982 with 39. In 1987, he returned to Oakland for a final season before retiring. Although he had a strong arm, Jackson was a poor defensive outfielder and was often used as a designated hitter from 1973 on.

In 21 major league seasons, he had 2,584 hits, including 463 doubles, 49 triples, and 563 home runs, sixth all-time. He scored 1,551 runs and drove 1,702.
★ Baseball Hall of Fame

Jackson, Shoeless Joe (Joseph J.)

BASEBALL
b. July 16, 1889, Pickens County, S.C.
d. Dec. 5, 1951

Because of his alleged involvement in the 1919 "Black Sox Scandal," Jackson is not in the Baseball Hall of Fame, though he belongs there on the basis of his playing skills.

A left-handed hitting outfielder who threw right-handed, Jackson had brief appearances with the Philadelphia Athletics in 1908 and 1909, then was traded to the Cleveland Indians and played for them briefly in 1910 before becoming a starter the following season.

A graceful outfielder with a strong throwing arm, Jackson was an exceptional hitter who never won a batting title even though he hit over .370 four times. In 1911, his first full season with Cleveland, he batted .408 yet finished second to Ty Cobb, who hit .420.

Jackson led the league with 226 hits and 26 triples in 1912, when he batted .395 and was the league leader with 197 hits, 39 doubles, and a .551 slugging percentage in 1913, when he hit .373.

After slipping to .338 in 1914, Jackson was traded to the Chicago White Sox during the 1915 season, and he again led in triples with 21 in 1916. He hit .301 in the 1917 regular season and .304 in the World Series, scoring 4 runs and driving in 2 in Chicago's six-game victory over the New York Giants.

Jackson's wartime work in a shipyard limited him to just 17 games in 1918. When he returned the following season, many of the White Sox were disgruntled with owner Charles Comiskey because of their low salaries. They won the pennant again, with Jackson batting .351, but they lost the World Series to the Cincinnati Reds in eight games. (At that time, the Series was a best-five-of-nine affair.)

In 1920, Jackson hit .382 with a league-leading 20 triples. After the season, a grand jury investigated charges that eight of the White Sox, including Jackson, had been bribed to throw the World Series the previous year. They were indicted but acquitted of all charges. However, Commissioner Kenesaw Mountain Landis banned them all from baseball.

If Jackson was in on the fix, he evidently reneged, because he batted .375 and made several outstanding defensive plays in the Series. And it's doubtful that he ever received any money. He returned to his South Carolina home and operated a liquor store for the rest of his life.

In 13 major league seasons, Jackson had a .356 average on 1,772 hits, including 307 doubles, 168 triples, and 54 home runs. He stole 202 bases, scored 873 runs, and had 785 RBI.

Jackson, Travis C.

BASEBALL
b. Nov. 2, 1903, Waldo, Ark.
d. July 27, 1987

The 5-foot-10½, 160-pound Jackson played briefly with the NL's New York Giants in 1922, spent most of the 1923 season with them, playing three infield positions, and became the team's starting shortstop in 1924.

An unsteady fielder at first, he eventually became a very good one, leading the league in fielding percentage in 1928 and 1930. He was also a good hitter with some power. Jackson hit over .300 six times and had 21 home runs and 94 RBI in his best power year, 1929, when he batted .294.

Jackson didn't fare well in the World Series. Used only as a pinch hitter in 1923, he batted just .074 in 1924 and .222 in 1933. However, he scored 4 runs and had 2 RBI in the Giants' 1933 victory over the Washington Senators in five games.

Jackson was moved to third base in 1935, when he began to lose his range. He retired after the 1936 season and became a long-time minor league manager with occasional stints as a major league coach.

★ Baseball Hall of Fame

Jacobs, Helen Hull

TENNIS
b. Aug. 8, 1908, Berkeley, Calif.

A fine tennis player in her own right, Jacobs is unfortunately best known for her long rivalry with Helen Wills. It began when the 17-year-old Wills beat the 14-year-old Jacobs in a practice set, 6–0, that took just seven minutes. Jacobs wanted to play another set, but Wills refused and left the court.

Jacobs lost to Wills in the finals at the 1928 U.S. Nationals, the 1929 and 1932 Wimbledon tournaments, and the 1930 French Nationals. When Wills planned a European tour in 1929, she chose the third-ranked Edith Cross as her playing partner, passing over Jacobs, who was ranked second. That fueled speculation that there was a feud between the two, although both persistently denied it.

The two met again in the finals at the U.S. Nationals in 1933, when Wills was suffering from a bad back. Jacobs won the first set, 8–6, and Wills won the second, 6–3. With Jacobs leading 3–0 in the third set, Wills suddenly went to the umpire's stand and announced she couldn't continue, thereby defaulting the match to Jacobs.

In 1933 Jacobs became the first tennis player to win the Associated Press female athlete of the year award. She also won the U.S. Nationals singles title in 1932, 1934, and 1935, but Wills didn't compete in the tournament in any of those years.

In the 1935 Wimbledon finals, Jacobs had match point in the second set when she returned a lob into the net, then lost four straight games and the match. Jacobs won her only Wimbledon title the following year, when Wills didn't enter. They met for the last time in the Wimbledon finals in 1938, but it was no contest. Jacobs had torn the sheath of an Achilles tendon in a quarterfinal match, and though she couldn't run, she refused to default. Wills won again, 6–4, 6–0.

The outgoing Jacobs was a very popular player, usually a crowd favorite against Wills, whose cold demeanor did not charm fans. She had an excellent backhand drive and was a fine volleyer. Jacobs was also a fashion leader, the first woman player to wear shorts at Wimbledon, in 1933.

In addition to her five major singles championships, Jacobs won national doubles titles with Sarah Palfrey in 1932, 1934, and 1935, and with Billie Yorke in 1939, and she teamed with George M. Lott, Jr., to win the mixed doubles championship in 1934. She retired from serious competition in 1940.

★ International Tennis Hall of Fame

Jacobs, Hirsch

HORSE RACING
b. April 8, 1904, New York, N.Y.
d. Feb. 13, 1970

The trainer of more thoroughbred winners than anyone else in history, Jacobs originally trained racing pigeons in partnership with Johnny Ferraro. In

1924, Ferraro acquired a horse, and Jacobs became his trainer.

Jacobs's specialty during the next 20 years was claiming horses and turning them into big winners. He formed a partnership with Isidore Bieber in 1928, with Bieber serving as money man and owner while Jacobs did the training. He led all trainers in winners every year from 1933 through 1944 except 1940.

A new phase of his career began when he claimed Stymie for $1,500. Stymie became one of the all-time great thoroughbreds, winning 35 races and $918,-485, a record at the time. He was handicap horse of the year in 1945.

With some of the money earned by Stymie, Bieber and Jacobs set up their own breeding farm, Stymie Manor. From 1946 through 1969, Jacobs worked with horses that won more than $30 million. As a trainer, he led in earnings in 1946, 1960, and 1965. Stymie Manor led all breeders in winnings from 1964 through 1967.

After suffering a stroke in 1966, Jacobs became less active, and his son, John, took over much of the responsibility for training Stymie Manor's best horses. Jacobs died of a heart attack in 1970.

He trained a record 3,596 winners that earned $15,340,534. Among his best horses were Hail to Reason, the two-year-old champion in 1960; Regal Gleam, champion two-year-old filly in 1966; Straight Deal, the champion handicap mare in 1967; and Affectionately, champion sprinter in 1965. Pimlico Race Track in Baltimore in 1975 memorialized him with the Hirsch Jacobs Stakes.

★ National Horse Racing Hall of Fame

Jacobs, Mike (Michael S.)
BOXING
b. March 10, 1890, New York, N.Y.
d. Jan. 25, 1953

Jacobs discovered the value of tickets when he was a young newsboy. Given two passes to a sold-out fight, he was offered money for them outside the door, and he made a $2 profit. Jacobs began buying tickets to shows and sports events and scalping them on the street.

In the late 1890s, he became legitimate by opening a ticket brokerage. Jacobs also invested his money in several other successful enterprises, including real estate development, Enrico Caruso's concert tour, a series of lectures by British suffragette Emily Panhurst, and a river steamboat line.

He became involved in fight promotion in 1921, when Tex Rickard needed money for the Jack Dempsey–Georges Carpentier heavyweight championship bout. Jacobs raised $100,000 in cash in just eight hours by offering other ticket brokers good seats at the fight in exchange for their backing. The result was the first $1 million gate in boxing history.

Jacobs continued as an unofficial adviser and financier for Madison Square Garden promotions after Rickard's death in 1929. But he broke away in 1933 to promote a card at the Bronx Coliseum for the Milk Fund. After 10,000 people had to be turned away for lack of seating, Jacobs and three Hearst sports reporters formed the Twentieth Century Boxing Club.

In 1935, black heavyweight contender Joe Louis signed a contract giving Jacobs the right to promote all of his fights. Two years later, Jacobs persuaded champion Jim Braddock to break a contract with Madison Square Garden in order to fight Louis in Chicago. Louis won the title on an 8th-round knockout.

Because of his control over the new champion, Jacobs quickly became the most powerful promoter in New York City, with exclusive rights to boxing at Madison Square Garden, the Polo Grounds, and Yankee Stadium. As a result, other fighters signed contracts with him, including Billy Conn, Rocky Graziano, and Sugar Ray Robinson.

Jacobs reportedly built a $10 million fortune during the 15 years he promoted Louis's fights. He nearly died of a stroke in 1946; three years later he sold most of his holdings to Jim Norris of the International Boxing Club and retired to Florida.

★ International Boxing Hall of Fame

Jaffee, Irving W.

SPEED SKATING
b. Sept. 15, 1906, New York, N.Y.
d. March 20, 1981

Jaffee never won a national championship, but he won three gold medals at the Winter Olympics, though his first victory was considered unofficial. In 1928, Jaffee beat Bernt Evensen of Norway in the first heat of the 10,000-meter event. After six more heats, with three remaining, the temperature in St. Moritz, Switzerland, suddenly went up, melting the ice.

Officials planned to cancel the results and rerun all the heats after the temperature dropped again. But the Norwegian skaters, the only threats to Jaffee, decided they couldn't beat him since he'd already defeated their champion, and they left. Jaffee had also won a silver medal in the 5,000 meters. In 1932, he won both the 5,000-meter and 10,000-meter events.

The winter sports director at Grossinger's Resort in the Catskills, Jaffee set a marathon record there on January 27, 1934, by skating 25 miles in 1 hour, 26 minutes, and 0.1 seconds, breaking the old record of 1:31:00. He had never before skated more than 10,000 meters.

Jameson, Betty (Elizabeth M.)

GOLF
b. May 19, 1919, Norman, Okla.

Jameson had a very successful career even before she became a professional golfer. She won the Texas Publinx championship at the age of 13, and she was the Southern Amateur champion at 15; she won the National Amateur championship in 1939 and 1940, the Western Amateur in 1940 and 1942.

As an amateur, she also won the 1938 Texas Open and the 1942 and 1944 Western Opens. Jameson became a professional in 1945, and she was a founding member of the LPGA in 1948. She shot a 295 to win the U.S. Women's Open in 1947, becoming the first woman golfer to score lower than 300 in a 72-hole tournament. Her best year as a professional was 1955, when she won four events.

In 1952, Jameson donated the Vare Trophy, named for Glenna Collet Vare, which is awarded annually to the LPGA player with the lowest average strokes per round.

★ LPGA Hall of Fame

Janney, Craig H.

HOCKEY
b. Sept. 26, 1967, Hartford, Conn.

A 6-foot-1, 190-pound center, Janney was an NCAA East All-American at Boston College in 1986–87, when he led the conference with 55 assists and 83 points. He had 70 points in 52 games with the U.S. national team and 4 points in five games with the Olympic team in 1987–88, then joined the NHL's Boston Bruins near the end of the season.

An excellent puck handler and passer, Janney is very effective on the power play. He likes to operate behind the net, keeping the puck away from defensemen until he can make a quick, accurate pass to a teammate in good scoring position.

The Bruins traded Janney to the St. Louis Blues in February 1992. Through the 1993–94 season, he had 509 points on 131 goals and 378 assists in 440 regular season games. He added 20 goals and 74 assists for 94 points in 90 playoff games.

Janowicz, Victor F.

FOOTBALL
b. Feb. 26, 1930, Elyria, Ohio

As a sophomore halfback at Ohio State University, Janowicz missed much of the 1949 season with an injury, but he played at defensive back in the school's 17–14 victory over the University of California in the Rose Bowl. His coach, Wes Fesler, described his play in that game as "brilliant."

Janowicz became starting tailback in the single wing in 1950 and was just as brilliant on offense. The 5-foot-9, 187-pounder ran for 2 touchdowns, passed for 4, and kicked 10 extra points in an 83–21 rout of Iowa that season. A consensus All-American, he became the third junior to win the Heisman Trophy as the nation's outstanding college player.

Woody Hayes became the school's coach in 1950 and installed the T formation, which didn't use Janowicz's triple-threat skills, and he had an average season as a part-time starter. After a year of military service, he played professional baseball for two seasons, batting .214 as a catcher and third baseman for the Pittsburgh Pirates of the National League.

Janowicz entered pro football in 1954 with the NFL's Washington Redskins. He finished second in the league in scoring with 88 points in 1955 but suffered a brain injury in an auto accident the following year. Though he recovered from the injury, his football career was over.

During his brief professional football career, Janowicz carried the ball 99 times for 410 yards and 4 touchdowns; caught 12 passes for 148 yards and 3 touchdowns; kicked 10 field goals and 37 extra points.
★ College Football Hall of Fame

Jansen, Dan (Daniel)
SPEED SKATING
b. 1969, West Allis, Wis.

In his last race at the 1994 Winter Olympics, Jansen may have had more people rooting for him to win than any other athlete in history. He had entered the 1988 Winter Games as the favorite in both the 500- and 1,000-meter speed skating events. His older sister, Jane, died of leukemia seven hours before he raced in the 500-meter.

Even though her death had been expected, Jansen was obviously shaken. Just ten seconds into the race, he fell rounding a turn and was out of the competition. Three nights later, he fell again while on a winning pace in the 1,000-meter race.

"I'll be back," he told reporters. But at the 1992 Olympics, Jansen missed a bronze medal in the 500-meter by 0.16 second and skated poorly in the 1,000-meter, finishing 26th.

He might have retired from competition then, but the next chance for a medal was just two years away because

the International Olympic Committee had decided the Winter and Summer Olympics should no longer take place in the same year. Jansen kept skating and set a world record of 35.76 seconds in the 500-meter. Entering the 1994 Games in Norway, he was only skater ever to break the 36-second mark.

Heavily favored in the short sprint, Jansen slipped again. He didn't fall, but the slip cost him time, and he finished in 36.68 seconds, placing eighth. That left him only the 1,000-meter, not his best event. Millions of Americans, well acquainted with his story, watched on television; the Norwegian spectators and even some of his competitors were hoping Jansen would win at least some kind of medal.

Skating at a world record pace, Jansen slipped slightly with 200 meters to go, but he managed to gather himself with little loss of momentum and finished in the world record time of 1:12.43. In the locker room, every skater cheered at the announcement. The lights in the arena were turned out and a spotlight followed Jansen as he skated a victory lap, carrying his infant daughter, Jane, while the crowd gave him a standing ovation.

Norwegian skater Adne Sondral said afterward, "If anyone deserves a gold medal, it must be him . . . The world and the sport would be unfair if he hadn't won."

Jarrett, Ned M.
AUTO RACING
b. Oct. 12, 1932, near Newton, N.C.

Growing up in stock car country, Jarrett saw a lot of races as a youngster. He debuted as a driver in 1952, finishing tenth, but his parents disapproved. For a time, he raced under another driver's name, but after several victories in the sportsman class, his secret was revealed.

But he kept racing, under his own name now, and won the national sportsman championship in 1957 and 1958. The following year he entered his first Grand National race. As an independent, he won five races in 1960, and he also got a sponsor, enabling him to run better equipment.

In 1961, Jarrett won only one race but finished in the top ten 34 times in 46 starts to win the GN title. He was third in the point standings in 1962, fourth in 1963. His best year may have been 1964, when he won 15 GN races but finished second to Richard Petty in the championship.

Jarrett claimed his second GN title in 1965, with 13 victories and 42 top-five finishes in 54 races. During the 1966 season, Ford suddenly pulled out of NASCAR racing, leaving Jarrett without sponsorship. He announced his retirement. Later he promoted races at North Carolina tracks.

A master of the short track, Jarrett had 50 Grand National victories, only two of them on super speedways.

★ NASCAR Hall of Fame

Jaworski, Ronald V.

FOOTBALL
b. March 23, 1951, Lackawanna, N.Y.

After starring at little Youngstown State University in Ohio, Jaworski was chosen in the second round of the 1973 NFL draft by the Los Angeles Rams. He spent his first season on the team's taxi squad and was added to the roster as backup quarterback in 1974.

He was traded to the Philadelphia Eagles before the 1977 season and became the starter there. Nicknamed the "Polish Rifle" because of his strong arm, the 6-foot-2, 198-pound Jaworski was named the National Football Conference player of the year by United Press International in 1980, and he also won the Bert Bell Trophy as the NFL's outstanding player.

He completed 257 of 451 passes for 3,529 yards and 27 touchdowns, with only 12 interceptions, that season, and took the Eagles into the Super Bowl, where they lost, 27–10, to the Oakland Raiders.

Jaworski played with Philadelphia through 1986 and finished his career as a backup with the Miami Dolphins in 1987. During his NFL career, he completed 2,142 of 4,042 passes for 27,682 yards and 176 touchdowns.

Jeannette, Buddy (Harry E.)

BASKETBALL
b. Sept. 15, 1917, New Kensington, Pa.

After graduating from Washington and Jefferson College in 1938, Jeannette was paid $150 a month to play for a professional team that was sometimes the Warren, Pennsylvania, Penns of the National Basketball League and sometimes the Elmira, New York, Indians of the New York–Penn League.

In 1939, the 5-foot-11, 175-pound Jeannette joined the Detroit Eagles of the NBL. He was with the Sheboygan Redskins briefly during the 1942–43 season, then went to the Ft. Wayne Zollner Pistons.

Jeannette retired as a player to coach the Baltimore Bullets of the American Basketball League to a 31–3 record in 1946–47. The Bullets entered the new Basketball Association of America in 1947, and Jeannette served as player-coach through 1949–50, his last season as a player. He was replaced as coach during the following season.

From 1952–53 through 1955–56, Jeannette coached Georgetown University to a 49–49 record. After three years out of basketball, he became coach of the Baltimore franchise in the Eastern Basketball League from 1959–60 through 1960–61. He was named general manager and coach of the NBA's Baltimore Bullets in 1964 but was replaced during the 1965–66 season. He also coached the Pittsburgh Pipers of the American Basketball Association in 1969–70.

During his ten professional seasons, Jeannette scored 2,317 points in 300 games, a 7.7 average. He coached Baltimore to the first BAA championship, in 1948, and he also produced an EBL champion in 1961.

★ Basketball Hall of Fame

Jeffires, Haywood F.

FOOTBALL
b. Dec. 12, 1964, Greensboro, N.C.

The name looks like a misprint, but

it isn't. Despite the spelling, it is pronounced *Jeffries*. After playing at North Carolina State University, the 6-foot-2, 201-pound Jeffires was chosen by the Houston Oilers in the first round of the 1987 NFL draft.

A wide receiver, he caught only nine passes in his first two seasons, in part because of an injury that limited him to only two games in 1988. The following year, he established himself as an excellent possession receiver who excels at going over the middle and outfighting defenders for the ball when necessary.

Jeffires led the league with 100 pass receptions in 1991, and he had 90 in 1992. Injuries cut into his playing time in 1993, when he caught just 66 passes. Through the 1994 season, Jeffires had 454 receptions for 5,435 yards, a 12.0 average, and 39 touchdowns.

Jeffries, James J.

BOXING
b. April 15, 1875, Carroll, Ohio
d. March 3, 1953

The first really big heavyweight champion, at 6-foot-2½ and 220 pounds, Jeffries was known as the "Boilermaker" because he worked in iron foundries when he was a youth, and as the "California Grizzly" because of his size.

His family moved to California in 1881, and he began boxing there as an amateur while in his teens. Jeffries won his first professional fight with a 14th-round knockout of Hank Griffin in 1896.

A clumsy fighter who scarcely bothered to defend himself, Jeffries could take enormous amounts of punishment while he stalked an opponent, looking for a chance to land one of his powerful punches. He was an enormous underdog when he met Bob Fitzsimmons for the heavyweight championship at Coney Island on June 9, 1899. But Jeffries won the title on an 11th-round knockout.

He retained the championship with a decision in a brutal 25-round fight against Tom Sharkey, who was taken to a hospital with two broken ribs and severe lacerations when the bout ended. Jeffries defended his title six times before retiring in 1905, including a knock-out of Fitzsimmons and two knockouts of former champion Jim Corbett.

Because of the public clamor for a "Great White Hope" to defeat black champion Jack Johnson, Jeffries came out of retirement to fight Johnson on July 4, 1910, in Reno, Nevada. Johnson gave him a terrible beating before Jeffries's corner threw the sponge into the ring as a symbol of surrender in the 15th round.

He won 18 of his 21 professional fights, 15 by knockout, and fought 2 draws. His knockout by Johnson was his only defeat.

★ International Boxing Hall of Fame

Jenkins, Charles L.

TRACK AND FIELD
b. Jan. 7, 1934, New York, N.Y.

Running for Villanova University, Jenkins won the IC4A outdoor 440-yard championship in 1955 and 1957 and was the indoor 600-yard champion from 1955 through 1957. He also won the AAU outdoor 440-yard dash in 1955 and the indoor 600-yard event in 1957 and 1958.

Jenkins was a surprise winner in the 400-meter at the 1956 Olympics, beating U.S. teammate Louis Jones, who had set a world record of 45.2 seconds in the Olympic trials. After winning the gold medal with a time of 46.7, Jenkins told reporters, "Jones is still the champ. That 45.2 is it." He was also a member of the gold medal 1,600-meter relay team.

Jenkins, David W.

FIGURE SKATING
b. June 29, 1936, Akron, Ohio

The younger brother of Hayes Jenkins, David won 12 major championships in the four-year period from 1957 through 1960. He succeeded his brother as U.S. and world figure skating champion in 1957, when he also won the North American title, and he repeated in all three championships in 1958 and 1959.

He finished only second in the 1960 world championships, but he won the Olympic gold medal and both the U.S. and North American titles again. Jenkins trailed Karol Divin of Czechoslovakia after the compulsories at the Olympics but put on a brilliant exhibition of free skating to win the first-place ranking from all nine judges.

After graduating from Colorado College, Jenkins went to medical school and became a specialist in internal medicine.

Jenkins, Ferguson A.

BASEBALL
b. Dec. 13, 1943, Chatham, Ont.

A basketball and hockey star in high school, Jenkins chose a career in professional baseball and became the only pitcher in major league history to strike out more than 3,000 batters while walking fewer than 1,000, and he is one of only four pitchers to win more than 100 games in each major league.

He played briefly for the Philadelphia Phillies in 1965 and appeared in one game for them in 1966 before being traded to the Chicago Cubs. With the weak-hitting Cubs, he won 20 or more games six consecutive seasons, from 1967 through 1972, despite losing five 1–0 games in 1968. The durable Jenkins led the NL in complete games with 20 in 1967, 24 in 1970, and 30 in 1971; in strikeouts with 273 in 1969; and in victories with 24 and innings pitched with 325 in 1971. He won the NL's Cy Young Award in 1971.

After slipping to a 14–16 mark in 1973, Jenkins was traded to the Texas Rangers of the AL. He led that league in victories with a 25–12 record and in complete games with 29 in 1974 to win the comeback player of the year award. Jenkins went to the Boston Red Sox in 1976, returned to Texas in 1978, and finished his career with the Cubs in 1982 and 1983.

Gifted with a live fastball and excellent control, Jenkins had a career record of 284 wins and 226 losses with 49 shutouts and a 3.34 ERA. He struck out 3,192 hitters while walking only 997 in 4,500⅔ innings.

★ Baseball Hall of Fame

Jenkins, Hayes Alan

FIGURE SKATING
b. March 23, 1933, Akron, Ohio

The young Jenkins skated in the shadow of Dick Button for several years, but after Button retired, he was unbeaten in major competition for four years. He won the U.S. and world championships from 1953 through 1956 and took an Olympic gold medal in 1956.

Although he lacked the flair of some other great skaters, Jenkins usually took a lead in the compulsory figures and held on to it with outstanding technique in his free skating. A graduate of Colorado College, he received a law degree from Harvard University and married Carol Heiss, the women's singles gold medalist in 1960.

Jenner, Bruce (William Bruce)

TRACK AND FIELD
b. Oct. 28, 1949, Mt. Kisco, N.Y.

Probably no other athlete became more famous or made more money by winning a single event than Jenner. A high school letterman in basketball, football, and track, Jenner was also a three-time Eastern States water ski champion.

He went to Graceland College in Iowa on a football scholarship, but a knee injury prevented him from playing after his freshman year. He did play basketball, however, and he discovered the decathlon in 1971. A year later, he qualified for the Olympic team and placed tenth at Munich.

For the next four years, Jenner concentrated on winning a gold medal in 1976 while his wife, Christie, worked as an airline hostess. He won the AAU decathlon in 1974 and 1976 and was the 1975 Pan-American Games champion.

The favorite going into the Montreal Games, Jenner had a virtually unsurpassable lead after the eighth event. Leonid Litvinenko of the Soviet Union congratulated him at that point and then asked, "Bruce, you going to be a millionaire?" Jenner's answer is not recorded, but "Yes" would have been correct. He ran his best time ever in the final event, the 1,500-meter run, to set a world record of 8,618 points. Jenner was named Associated Press athlete of the year and won the Sullivan Award as the nation's best amateur athlete.

Immediately after the Olympics, Jenner began to cash in on his fame. The handsome, 6–2, 195-pounder and the attractive, blue-eyed, blond Christy were widely promoted as the All-American couple, and they did a number of commercials and public appearances together.

Their divorce in 1980 was almost as widely publicized as Jenner's Olympic victory. The following year, he married Linda Thompson, a former girlfriend of Elvis Presley.

★ National Track & Field Hall of Fame; Olympic Hall of Fame

Jennings, Hugh A.

BASEBALL
b. April 2, 1869, Pittston, Pa.
d. Feb. 1, 1928

The 5-foot-9, 165-pound Jennings originally hoped to make it in baseball as a catcher, but he became a shortstop in 1890 and joined Louisville of the American Association, then a major league, the following season.

During the 1893 season, Jennings went to the Baltimore Orioles of the NL and became one of many stars on a team that won four straight pennants from 1894 through 1897. Jennings hit .335, .386, .401, and .355, scored 125 or more runs each year, drove in more than 100 runs three times, and led the league's shortstops in fielding all four years.

In 1899, Jennings began the season with the Brooklyn Superbas, returned to the Orioles for two games, then went back to the Superbas. He helped lead Brooklyn to the 1900 pennant although he batted only .272 in 115 games that season.

Jennings went to the Philadelphia Phillies in 1901 and returned to Brooklyn briefly in 1903 before becoming a minor league manager. In 1907, he took over as manager of the Detroit Tigers and guided them to three consecutive pennants from 1907 through 1909. How-

ever, they lost the World Series each year.

He remained with the Tigers through 1920, then became a coach with the New York Giants under his former Baltimore teammate, John McGraw. Jennings managed the Giants for 44 games in 1924, when McGraw was ill. In 1925, Jennings had a nervous breakdown and spent some time in a sanitarium.

Although he'd had no formal education before his baseball career, Jennings had received a law degree from Cornell University while playing, and he left baseball to practice law in Pennsylvania.

As a player, Jennings had a .311 career average with 1,527 hits, including 232 doubles, 88 triples, and 18 home runs. He stole 359 bases, scored 994 runs, and had 840 RBI. His record as a manager was 1,163–984, a .542 winning percentage.

★ Baseball Hall of Fame

Jennings, Morley (William Morley)

FOOTBALL
b. Jan. 23, 1890, Holland, Mich.
d. May 13, 1985

After a year at Albion College in Michigan, Jennings went to Mississippi A & M (now Mississippi State), where he starred in baseball, basketball, football, and track. He graduated in 1912 and played minor league baseball for eight years while also coaching college football.

Jennings had a 72–17–12 record at Ouachita College in Arkansas from 1912 through 1925 and then became head coach at Baylor. Many Southwest Conference schools emphasized the passing attack at that time, and Jennings was a pioneer in using a five-man defensive line in order to get seven players in the pass defense.

He coached at Baylor through 1940, compiling an 83–60–6 record. In 1941, Jennings became athletic director at Texas Tech. He left that position in 1950 but remained at the school as head of the physical education department until his retirement in 1965.

★ College Football Hall of Fame

Jensen, Jackie (Jack E.)

BASEBALL, FOOTBALL
b. March 9, 1927, San Francisco, Calif.
d. July 14, 1982

An All-American halfback as a junior at the University of California in 1948, the 5-foot-11, 195-pound Jensen scored a touchdown in the team's 20–14 loss to Northwestern in the 1949 Rose Bowl. He was also an All-American pitcher in baseball, helping California win the 1947 NCAA championship.

He left college after his junior year to play professional baseball and joined the New York Yankees as an outfielder in 1950. During the 1952 season, Jensen was traded to the Washington Senators, and he went to the Boston Red Sox in 1954.

Jensen won the AL's most valuable player award in 1958, when he batted .286 with 35 home runs and a league-leading 116 RBI. He also led the league in RBI with 116 in 1955 and 112 in 1959, and in triples with 11 in 1956.

Primarily because he feared flying, Jensen retired after the 1961 season. He later coached baseball at California and the University of Nevada and was a minor league manager for a year.

In 11 major league seasons, Jensen batted .279 with 1,463 hits, including 259 doubles, 45 triples, and 199 home runs. He stole 143 bases, scored 810 runs, and had 929 RBI.

★ College Football Hall of Fame

Jewtraw, Charles

SPEED SKATING
b. May 5, 1900, Lake Placid, N.Y.

Jewtraw was the first athlete ever to win a gold medal at the Winter Olympics. He won the 500-meter speed skating championship, the first event at the 1924 "Olympic winter carnival" in France, which was approved by the International Olympic Committee.

He was the national outdoor champion in 1921 and 1923. Jewtraw, who once held the U.S. record at 9.4 seconds for 100 yards on skates, became a representative for the Spalding Sporting Goods Company after winning at the Olympics.

Jochim, Alfred A.

GYMNASTICS
b. June 12, 1902, New York, N.Y.
d. 1981

Jochim won a record 34 national gymnastics championships and is the only male gymnast ever to win at least one national title on every type of apparatus. He also won a silver medal in the vault at the 1932 Olympics and was a member of the U.S. team that won a silver in combined exercise.

He was the national all-around champion seven times, from 1925 through 1930 and in 1933. Jochim won titles on the parallel bars in 1926, 1928–29, 1931, and 1933–34; in the vault 1930–34; on the horizontal bar in 1926 and 1928–30; in free exercise in 1923 and 1928–34; on the side horse in 1926–28 and 1933; and on the flying rings in 1929.

Joesting, Herbert W.

FOOTBALL
b. April 17, 1905, Little Falls, Minn.
d. Oct. 2, 1963

The 6-foot-1, 196-pound Joesting was a bruising runner and blocker for three seasons at the University of Minnesota, and he was named All-American fullback twice, in 1926 and 1927. He captained the 1927 team that went undefeated, winning six games and tying two. His fourth-quarter touchdown pass salvaged a 7–7 tie against Notre Dame.

Joesting was player-coach of the NFL's Minneapolis Red Jackets in 1929. The team had a 1–9–0 record. He gave up coaching duties and began the 1930 season as the Minneapolis fullback but was traded to the Frankford Yellow Jackets. He played for Frankford and the Chicago Bears in 1931 and finished his career with the Bears in 1932, when they won the NFL championship.

He retired because of injuries after that season. Complete statistics aren't available for the period in which he played, but partial statistics credit him

with 1,092 yards on 239 attempts, a 4.6 yard average.
★ College Football Hall of Fame

Johnson, Albert

HORSE RACING
b. Nov. 18, 1900, Spokane, Wash.
d. Sept. 18, 1966

The fifth jockey in history to win the Kentucky Derby twice, Johnson did it with Morvich in 1922 and Bubbling Over in 1926. He won two straight Belmont Stakes, aboard American Flag in 1925 and Crusader in 1926.

Johnson began jockeying in 1917 and was the top money-winning jockey with $345,054 in 1922, when he won 43 of 297 races. Among the outstanding horses he rode during his career was Exterminator in 1922.

In 1928, Johnson had trouble keeping his weight down. He went to Europe to try steeplechasing, but he was unsuccessful. After his return to the U.S., he returned to jockeying briefly and then became a trainer. He later served as a racing official.

Johnson was killed after being hit by a train. In just 12 full seasons as a jockey, his mounts earned $1,304,570. Johnson had 503 wins in 3,199 races, with 473 seconds and 481 third-place finishes.
★ National Horse Racing Hall of Fame

Johnson, Benjamin S., Jr.

TRACK AND FIELD
b. Dec. 30, 1961, Falmouth, Jamaica

Running for Canada, Johnson set a world record of 9.83 seconds in the 100-meter dash at the 1987 world championships, and he apparently won a gold medal in the event at the 1988 Olympics in another record time of 9.79 seconds. However, he tested positive for steroid use, and the gold medal was awarded to Carl Lewis of the U.S., who had finished second.

After Johnson admitted that he'd begun using steroids as early as 1981, his 1987 world record was also revoked, and he was suspended for life. The suspension was lifted in January 1991, after he had evidently been drug-free for $2\frac{1}{2}$

years, but he performed poorly. He tested positive for steroid use after a Montreal meet in January 1993 and received another life suspension.

Johnson had tied the world record of 10.00 in the 1985 World Cup meet, and he won the 100-meter at the 1986 Commonwealth Games with a meet record of 10.07. He was named male athlete of the year by the Associated Press in 1987.

Johnson, Bill (William D.)

SKIING
b. March 30, 1960, Los Angeles, Calif.

Johnson learned to ski in Idaho, where his family moved when he was seven, and he began competing in Oregon when he was 11. After graduating from high school in 1977, he attended a ski academy in Washington State.

He joined the U.S. ski team in 1979 but was dropped in 1982. After rejoining the team in 1983, Johnson finished sixth in his first World Cup downhill event. He won the U.S. championship that year and finished second in the North Americans.

Early in 1984, Johnson became the first American to win a World Cup downhill event, and he then became the first male American skier to win a gold medal in the Olympic downhill, with a time of 1:45.59. He won the U.S. national championship again and two more World Cup events to place third in the overall standings.

Johnson had off years in 1985 and 1986. Late in 1986, he suffered a severe knee injury in a car crash. He returned to competition during the 1987–88 season but with little success, and he failed to make the 1988 Olympic team.

Johnson, Bob (Robert)

HOCKEY
b. March 4, 1931, Minneapolis, Minn.
d. Nov. 26, 1991

Although he was from Minnesota, Johnson was nicknamed "Badger Bob" because of his long tenure as hockey coach at the University of Wisconsin, from 1967 through the 1981–82 seasons.

He coached Wisconsin to NCAA championships in 1973, 1977, and 1981.

After playing hockey at the Universities of North Dakota and Minnesota, Johnson coached at the high school level from 1956 until 1963, when he took over at Colorado College. He then moved on to Wisconsin, where he had a 367–175–23 record. While he was at Wisconsin, Johnson coached the U.S. national teams in 1973, 1974, 1975, and 1981, and was also coach of the 1976 Olympic team.

Johnson became coach of the NHL's Calgary Flames in 1982, where he had a 193–155–52 record, guiding the team to five consecutive Stanley Cup playoffs, including an appearance in the finals in 1986, when they lost in five games to the Montreal Canadians.

After the 1986–87 season, Johnson became executive director of the Amateur Hockey Association of the U.S., which became known as U.S.A. Hockey while he was in charge. He left that job to take over as coach of the NHL's Pittsburgh Penguins in 1990. Johnson took the Penguins to their first Stanley Cup championship in his first season.

Early in the 1991–92 season, he developed a brain tumor and was replaced by Scotty Bowman. Johnson, who liked to say "It's a great day for hockey," died two months later.
★ Hockey Hall of Fame; U.S. Hockey Hall of Fame

Johnson, Ching (Ivan W.)
HOCKEY
b. Dec. 7, 1897, Winnipeg, Man.
d. June 16, 1979

Johnson didn't begin playing hockey seriously until he was in his early twenties. He served in the Canadian Army during World War I and began playing with a semiprofessional team in Winnipeg after the war. When the New York Rangers were organized in 1926, he won a tryout with them, lying about his age and insisting on a three-year contract.

He once said about his early career, "I couldn't skate very well. I looked like an elephant on skates. But after a while I started to get the hang of it." What he may have lacked in skating ability, the 6-foot, 210-pound Johnson made up for with determination and solid body checking.

He played with the Rangers through 1937, then joined the New York Americans for the 1937–38 season, retiring when he was 40. The Rangers won two Stanley Cups during his tenure, and Johnson was an all-star defenseman four times. He scored 38 goals and 48 assists in 435 regular season games and had 5 goals and 2 assists in 60 playoff games.

Johnson later worked as a linesman in minor league hockey. He once bodychecked a player who was breaking in alone on the goal. "The old habit was too deep within me," he explained. "I forgot where I was and what I was doing."
★ Hockey Hall of Fame

Johnson, Cornelius
TRACK AND FIELD
b. Aug. 21, 1913, Los Angeles, Calif.
d. Feb. 15, 1940

Hitler's supposed snub of Jesse Owens at the 1936 Olympics has become part of sports mythology, but if a black athlete was snubbed in Berlin, Johnson was the victim. On the first day of competition, Hitler personally congratulated the winners of the first three events, who happened to be Germans and Finns. After all the German high jumpers had been eliminated, he left his box, so he wasn't on hand to congratulate Johnson for winning the gold medal in the high jump. It seems likely Hitler went home because it was getting dark and threatening rain, but the truth will never be known.

Johnson had competed in the 1932 Olympics, while still a high school student. He and three other jumpers tied at the same height, but Johnson was given fourth place because he had more misses. Under the modern tie-breaking procedure, he would have won the silver medal.

The 6-foot-5 Johnson set a world indoor record at 6 feet, $8^{15}/16$ inches early in 1936, and he and David Albritton both cleared 6 feet, $9^{3}/4$ inches at the Olympic trials that year to tie for the world record. Johnson won the AAU outdoor championship in 1933 and 1935 and tied in 1932, 1934, and 1936. He was the indoor champion in 1935 and tied in 1936 and 1938.

Johnson, Davey (David A.)

BASEBALL
b. Jan. 30, 1943, Orlando, Fla.

The starting second baseman for the AL's Baltimore Orioles from 1966 through 1972, Johnson was traded to the NL's Atlanta Braves after hitting only .221 in his final season with Baltimore. He set a record for second basemen by hitting 43 home runs for Atlanta in 1973 to win the comeback player of the year award.

Johnson was released by the Braves early in the 1975 season. He played in Japan for two years and finished his playing career with the Philadelphia Phillies and Chicago Cubs in 1978.

After winning three pennants in three seasons as a minor league manager, Johnson took over the NL's New York Mets in 1984. He guided the team to two second-place finishes, then to the 1986 pennant and a seven-game World Series victory over the Boston Red Sox.

The Mets won the 1988 Eastern Division title but lost in the league championship series, and Johnson was replaced after a 20–22 start in 1990. He was out of baseball for more than two years before becoming manager of the Cincinnati Reds early in the 1993 season.

As a player, Johnson batted .261 with 1,252 hits, including 242 doubles, 18 triples, and 136 home runs. His managerial record through 1994 is 714–540 for a .568 winning percentage.

Johnson, Dennis W.

BASKETBALL
b. Sept. 16, 1954, San Pedro, Calif.

"D.J." played at Los Angeles Harbor Junior College for two years and then spent one year at Pepperdine before being chosen by the Seattle SuperSonics as a so-called hardship case in the second round of the 1976 NBA draft.

Johnson was named most valuable player in the 1979 NBA finals, when he helped lead Seattle to the league championship, averaging 20.9 points and 4.0 assists per game in the playoffs.

Seattle traded him to the Phoenix Suns in 1980. He had a falling-out with coach John MacLeod during the 1982–83 season and was relegated to a backup role. The Suns sent him to the Boston Celtics for journeyman center Rick Robey after that season. It was a great deal for the Celtics.

In Boston, Johnson started for two NBA championship teams, in 1984 and 1986. He retired after the 1989–90 season. A fine all-around player, the 6-foot-4, 202-pound Johnson was best known for his defensive skills. He was named to the all-NBA defensive first team from 1979 through 1983 and in 1987, and he made the second team from 1984 through 1986.

Johnson scored 15,535 points in 1,100 regular season games, an average of 14.1 per game, and he also had 5,499 assists and 1,477 steals. He added 3,116 points, 1,006 assists, and 247 steals in 180 playoff games.

Johnson, Donald

BOWLING
b. May 19, 1940, Kokomo, Ind.

The bowler of the year in 1971 and 1972, Johnson began bowling when he was 15 and joined the PBA tour when he was 22. He won at least one tournament for 12 consecutive years, from 1964 through 1975, a PBA record.

Nicknamed the "Kokomo Kid" by bowling writers, Johnson had a herky-jerky motion, yet he rolled 16 sanctioned perfect games and won more than 30 championships, including ABC doubles and team events. He won the BPAA U.S. Open in 1972, when he was the tour's leading money winner with $56,648. Johnson led the tour in average pins with 213.98 in 1971 and 215.29 in 1972. He won the 1970 Tournament of Champions with a 299 in the final game.

Johnson teamed with Bill Tucker in 1968 and with Paul Colwell in 1976 to win ABC classic doubles titles, and he was a member of the Columbia 300 team that won the 1977 team championship.

★ ABC Hall of Fame; PBA Hall of Fame

Johnson, Gail (Mrs. Buzonas)

SYNCHRONIZED SWIMMING
b. 1954

Johnson won a total of 11 national championships in synchronized swimming, including four consecutive outdoor solo titles, from 1972 through 1975. She was the indoor solo champion in 1972 and 1975, she teamed with Teresa Andersen to win indoor and outdoor duet titles in 1972 and 1973, and in 1974 she and Sue Baross won the outdoor duet championship.

In 1975, Johnson won the world solo title and a gold medal in the solo event at the Pan-American Games.

Johnson, Harold

BOXING
b. Aug. 9, 1928, Manayunk, Pa.

After turning professional in 1946, Johnson won his first 5 bouts and 13 of his first 17 by knockout. He was undefeated until April 26, 1949, when Archie Moore took a 10-round decision from him.

The 5-foot-10 Johnson, who fought at a weight between 170 and 177 pounds, suffered his first knockout in the 14th round of a fight against future heavyweight champion Jersey Joe Walcott on February 8, 1950. He fought another future heavyweight titlist, Ezzard Charles, on September 8, 1953, and won a 10-round decision.

Johnson and Moore split two decisions in 1951. Moore went on to win the light heavyweight championship, and Johnson challenged him on August 11, 1954, but Moore won with a 14th-round knockout. After the NBA vacated Moore's title, Johnson won the vacant championship by knocking out Jesse Bowdry in the 9th round on February 7, 1961.

He defended the NBA version of the title twice and then won recognition as world champion by taking a 15-round decision from Doug Jones on May 12,

1962. He lost the championship to Willie Pastrano in a 15-round decision on June 1, 1963.

During the next several years, Johnson fought only sporadically. He was inactive for all of 1965, 1969, and 1970, and he retired after being knocked out by Herschel Jacobs in 1971.

Johnson won 76 of his 87 professional fights, 32 by knockout. He lost 6 decisions and was knocked out 5 times.

★ International Boxing Hall of Fame

Johnson, Howard M.

BASEBALL
b. Nov. 29, 1960, Clearwater, Pa.

A switch hitter, "Ho-Jo" has been a major league starter at four positions. He joined the AL's Detroit Tigers during the 1982 season, batting .316 in 54 games, but was with the team for only 27 games in 1983.

Johnson was used as a utility player and pinch hitter by the Tigers in 1984, when he saw time at first base, third base, shortstop, and the outfield. He hit only .248 that year and was traded to the NL's New York Mets.

In 1987, Johnson suddenly became a power hitter. Playing third base, shortstop, and the outfield, he batted .287 with 36 home runs and 99 RBI to go with 32 stolen bases. He was the fourth member of the "30–30 Club," players who have hit more than 30 home runs and stolen more than 30 bases in the same season.

After slipping to .230 in 1988, Johnson hit .287 the following season, with 36 home runs, 101 RBI, 41 stolen bases, and a league-leading 104 runs scored. His finest year to date was 1991, when he stole 30 bases and led the league with 38 home runs and 117 RBI.

Johnson's playing time was limited by injuries the next two seasons. He became a free agent in October 1993 and signed with the Colorado Rockies.

Through the 1994 season, Johnson had a .251 average with 1,196 hits, including 243 doubles, 21 triples, and 221 home runs. He had stolen 230 bases, scored 734 runs, and driven in 938.

Johnson, Jack (John Arthur)

BOXING
b. March 31, 1878, Galveston, Tex.
d. June 10, 1946

The first black heavyweight champion, Johnson began boxing as a teenager. His first recorded professional fight was a 4th-round knockout of Jim Rocks in Galveston. He won the so-called Negro heavyweight championship on February 3, 1903, with a 20-round decision over Denver Ed Martin at Los Angeles.

But Johnson was determined to become world champion. He took a major step toward the title by knocking out former champion Bob Fitzsimmons in the 2nd round on July 17, 1907. Tommy Burns, who had won the championship the previous year, went on a tour of England and France. Johnson followed him.

He finally caught Burns in Australia, where a promoter named Hugh D. "Huge Deal" McIntosh put up a guarantee of $30,000 for a Burns–Johnson match. Burns accepted. McIntosh refereed the fight, which took place on December 26, 1908 — Boxing Day in Australia.

The 6-foot-1, 200-pound Johnson had a large advantage in reach over Burns, who was the shortest heavyweight champion ever at only 5-foot-7. Johnson gave Burns a thorough battering before a police inspector stepped into the ring to stop the fight in the 14th round.

When Johnson returned to the United States, a search began for a "Great White Hope" who could win the title from him. Former champion James J. Jeffries was finally persuaded to come out of retirement, but he was out of shape, and Johnson toyed with him before knocking him out in the 15th round on July 4, 1910, at Carson City, Nevada. The victory sparked race riots across the country; 19 people were killed.

Johnson's second wife committed suicide in September 1912, and he married a young white woman three months later. That was the last straw for white authorities. Johnson was sentenced to a year in prison for violating the Mann Act, which forbade transportation of a woman across state lines for immoral purposes.

While his conviction was being appealed, Johnson fled to Canada and then to France. On April 5, 1915, he lost his title when Jess Willard knocked him out in the 26th round in Havana, Cuba. Johnson claimed in his autobiography that he deliberately lost the fight because he'd been promised a pardon if he did so.

Johnson lived in Spain and Mexico until 1920, when he returned to the United States and surrendered to authorities. He spent nearly a year in federal prison and then resumed his boxing career. He fought sporadically through 1933 and returned to the ring for two exhibitions in 1945. He was killed when his car crashed in North Carolina while he was driving to New York to see the Joe Louis–Billy Conn championship fight.

A superb defensive boxer, Johnson did little serious training, rarely extended himself in the ring, and enjoyed taunting opponents. He won 78 of his 113 professional fights, 44 by knockout. He lost 7, 5 by knockout, and he also fought 14 draws and 14 no-decisions.
★ International Boxing Hall of Fame

Johnson, Jimmy (James E.)

FOOTBALL
b. March 31, 1938, Dallas, Tex.

The brother of decathlon champion Rafer, Johnson was a two-way player, as a defensive back and as a wingback in the single wing at UCLA. He also won the NCAA 110-meter hurdle championship as a junior in 1960. The 6-foot-2, 188-pound Johnson was one of three first-round draft choices of the NFL's San Francisco 49ers in 1961.

After playing defense as a rookie, he was moved to wide receiver in 1962, when he caught 34 passes for 627 yards and 4 touchdowns. Then he returned to left cornerback and remained at that position for the rest of his career.

An NFC Western Conference all-star in 1966 and 1969, Johnson was named to the NFC all-star team three years in a row, from 1970 through 1972. He retired after the 1976 season with 47 career interceptions, which he returned for 615 yards and 2 touchdowns.
★ Pro Football Hall of Fame

Johnson, Jimmy (James W.)

FOOTBALL
b. July 16, 1943, Port Arthur, Tex.

The co-captain of the undefeated University of Arkansas team in 1964, Johnson was an assistant coach at several schools before becoming head coach at Oklahoma State in 1979. He won 30 games, lost 25, and tied 2 in five seasons there before going to the University of Miami, Florida, in 1984.

He built a remarkable record at Miami, winning 52 games with just 9 losses in five seasons. His undefeated 1987 team was ranked first in the nation after winning all 11 regular season games and beating Oklahoma, 20–14, in the Orange Bowl. The 1986 team was ranked first after the regular season, when it won all 11 games, but dropped to second because of a 14–10 loss to Penn State in the Fiesta Bowl. Johnson's 1988 squad was also rated second.

Jerry Jones, the other Arkansas co-captain in 1964, bought the NFL's Dallas Cowboys in 1989 and hired Johnson as head coach, replacing the legendary Tom Landry, who had been the team's only coach until then. The move was criticized in many circles, and criticism continued after the Cowboys had a 1–15–0 record in Johnson's first season.

The Cowboys improved to 7–9–0 in 1990, 11–5–0 in 1991, and 13–3–0 in 1992, when they went on to beat the Buffalo Bills, 52–17, in the Super Bowl. Johnson coached Dallas to a second straight Super Bowl victory over Buffalo by a 30–13 score following the 1993 season. Because of a series of disagreements with Jones, Johnson abruptly resigned early in 1994 and became a television analyst.

A believer in speed rather than size, Johnson has often been considered primarily an offensive coach who is very good with the passing game. However, attacking defenses at both Miami and Dallas were important to his successful record. The Cowboys had the top-rated defense in the NFL in 1992.

Johnson, John Henry

FOOTBALL
b. Nov. 24, 1929, Waterproof, La.

After playing at St. Mary's College in California and Arizona State University, Johnson was a second-round draft choice of the NFL's Pittsburgh Steelers in 1953. He chose to play for the Calgary Roughriders of the Canadian Football League, and he was named the league's most valuable player as a rookie.

The Steelers traded negotiating rights to the San Francisco 49ers, who signed him for the 1954 season. The 6-foot-2, 225-pound Johnson became the fullback in the "Million Dollar Backfield," with quarterback Y. A. Tittle and halfbacks Hugh McElhenny and Joe Perry. All four are now in the Pro Football Hall of Fame.

The 6-foot-2, 225-pound Johnson was probably the least celebrated. A crushing blocker, he was also a very good runner with a surprising burst of speed. He finished second in the NFL in rushing as a rookie with 681 yards.

Injuries bothered him during the next two seasons, and he was traded to the Detroit Lions in 1957. After three troubled years there, he went to the Pittsburgh Steelers in 1960, where he had his finest seasons, rushing for 1,141 yards in 1962 and 1,048 yards in 1964.

Johnson retired after the 1966 season. In 13 years in the NFL, he gained 6,803 yards in 1,571 carries, a 4.3 average, and scored 48 touchdowns. He also caught 186 passes for 1,478 yards, a 7.9 average, and 7 touchdowns.
★ Pro Football Hall of Fame

Johnson, Judy (William J.)

BASEBALL
b. Oct. 26, 1899, Snow Hill, Md.
d. June 13, 1989

The 5-foot-11, 145-pound Johnson was considered the greatest third baseman ever to play in black baseball before blacks were admitted to the major leagues. Sure-handed and strong-armed, Johnson was a line-drive hitter who consistently batted over .300.

He became a professional in 1918, collecting $5 a game from the Bacharach Giants, and he went to the Hilldale Club of Philadelphia in 1920. During his nine years there, he often spent the winters playing for hotel teams in Florida and in the Cuban Winter League. After serving as playing manager of the Homestead Grays in 1930 and the Darby, Pennsylvania, Daisies in 1931, Johnson was with the Pittsburgh Crawfords from 1932 until retiring after the 1937 season.

Johnson was the top Hilldale hitter with a .341 average in the first Negro World Series in 1924, and in 1929 he led the American Negro League in hits. Unofficially, he is credited with a career batting average of .344.

In 1954, Johnson became a coach and scout with the Philadelphia Athletics, and he later scouted for the Boston Braves and Philadelphia Phillies before retiring in 1973.

★ Baseball Hall of Fame

Johnson, Junior

AUTO RACING
b. 1930

Johnson began his NASCAR career on dirt tracks, and for some years he seemed to scorn the Grand National circuit, never running enough races to finish very high in the point standings. But in 1962 he suddenly began racing mostly in super-speedway events. When he retired in 1966 he had 50 GN victories to his credit, which is still eighth on the all-time list, although he never won the national championship.

His biggest wins came in the second Daytona 500, in 1960; the 1963 Dixie 400 at Atlanta; the 1962 and 1963 National 400 at Charlotte; and the 1965 Rebel 300 at Darlington. That Darlington victory was one of 13 in 1965. It gave him exactly 50 for his career, and he abruptly announced his retirement from driving to become a car owner. His first driver was Bobby Allison, who won ten races and $271,395 in Johnson's car in 1972 to become driver of the year. That was just the beginning. Through 1992, Johnson had won more than $12 million as an owner.

★ NASCAR Hall of Fame

Johnson, Larry D.

BASKETBALL
b. March 14, 1969, Tyler, Tex.

After averaging 26.0 points a game in two seasons at Odessa, Texas, Junior College, Johnson entered the University of Nevada–Las Vegas in 1989. He won the 1991 Wooden and Naismith awards as college player of the year and was also named player of the year by *The Sporting News* and the Basketball Writers Association of America.

Johnson averaged 22.7 points a game as a senior and 20.6 for his two-year career at UNLV. A forward, the 6-foot-7, 250-pounder was made the first choice in the 1991 NBA draft by the Charlotte Hornets. He was named the league's rookie of the year in 1992 after averaging 19.2 points a game, and he raised that to 22.1 in the 1992–93 season. However, he missed much of the 1993–94 season with an injury.

In three NBA seasons, Johnson has scored 4,220 points in 215 games, a 19.6 average. He also has 2,211 rebounds and 829 assists.

Johnson, Magic (Earvin Jr.)

BASKETBALL
b. Aug. 14, 1959, E. Lansing, Mich.

Johnson played just two years of basketball at Michigan State University, leading the school to the NCAA championship in 1979, when he was named outstanding tournament player and a first-team All-American at guard. He averaged 17.1 points per game in his collegiate career.

The 6-foot-9, 225-pound Johnson was a charismatic figure on and off court. His remarkable all-around basketball skills, combined with his infectious smile and enthusiasm, made him one of the best-known professional athletes of his time.

He was chosen by the Los Angeles Lakers in the first round of the 1979 NBA draft and was named to the league's All-Rookie team in 1980, when he helped lead the Lakers to an NBA championship. After missing much of the 1980–81 season with a knee injury, Johnson played for four more championship teams, in 1982,

1985, 1987, and 1988, and he was named the league's most valuable player in 1987, 1989, and 1990.

Johnson led the league in assists per game four times, with 10.5 in 1982–83, 13.1 in 1983–84, 12.6 in 1985–86, and 12.2 in 1986–87, and he holds the record for most career assists with 9,921. He also led in steals with 3.43 per game in 1980–81 and 2.67 in 1981–82. Unlike most guards with high assist totals, however, Johnson was also a prolific scorer, four times averaging more than 20 points a game.

His finest performance probably came during the 1980 NBA playoffs. After starting center Kareem Abdul-Jabbar went down with a knee injury, Johnson took over at center in the final game against the Philadelphia 76ers, scored 42 points, and was named most valuable player in the playoffs. He also won that award in 1982 and 1987.

A first-team All-NBA performer nine years in a row, from 1983 through 1991, Johnson shocked the sports world in 1991 when he announced that he had contracted the AIDS virus through heterosexual contact. He retired from the Lakers, but he played for the 1992 "Dream Team" that won an Olympic gold medal.

In 874 regular season games, Johnson scored 17,239 points, an average of 19.7 per game. He also had 6,376 rebounds, 9,921 assists, and 1,698 steals. He appeared in 186 playoff games, scoring 3,640 points, a 19.6 average, with 1,431 rebounds, 2,320 assists, and 358 steals. He holds career playoff records for most assists and most steals.

Johnson, Mark E.

HOCKEY
b. Sept. 22, 1957, Madison, Wis.

Johnson starred at the University of Wisconsin, where his father, Bob, was the coach, in 1977–78 and 1978–79, leading the Western Collegiate Hockey Association in goals both years with 48 and 41 and in total points with 90 in 1978–79, when he was named WCHA player of the year.

He then joined the U.S. national team and had five goals and six assists in seven games when the team won the gold medal at the 1980 Winter Olympics. In the key game against the Soviet Union, Johnson scored the tying goal at 8:39 of the third period, and shortly afterward Mike Eruzione scored a goal to win, 4–3.

After the Olympics, Johnson joined the NHL's Pittsburgh Penguins. The 5-foot-10, 170-pound left wing was traded to the Minnesota North Stars late in the 1981–82 season and went to the Hartford Whalers the following season. Hartford traded him to the St. Louis Blues in 1984–85, and he was with the New Jersey Devils from the 1985–86 season through 1988–89.

In 606 NHL games, Johnson had 187 goals and 276 assists for a total of 463 points. He scored 16 goals and 12 assists for 28 points in 35 playoff games.

Johnson, Marques K.

BASKETBALL
b. Feb. 8, 1956, Natchitoches, La.

Johnson's family moved to Los Angeles when he was young, and urged on by his father, he became a high school basketball star. Recruited by more than 200 colleges, he elected to stay at home with UCLA. Under coach John Wooden's general policy of using upperclassmen as starters and bringing younger players along slowly, Johnson was a substitute forward in his freshman year. Although he started as a sophomore in 1974–75, when UCLA won the NCAA championship, his playing time was limited, and he averaged just 11.6 points per game.

In his junior year, Johnson came into his own. The 6-foot-7, 225-pounder used quick, agile moves around the basket and an accurate short-range jump shot to average 17.3 points. In his final season at UCLA, 1976–77, his average was 21.4, and he also had more than 10 rebounds a game. He was a consensus All-American and a unanimous player of the year selection.

Johnson was on the NBA All-Rookie team with the Milwaukee Bucks, with a 19.5 point-per-game average, and he scored more than 20 points a game in each of the next three seasons. The Bucks traded him to the Los Angeles Clippers in 1984, and back problems began to hamper his play, but he was named the league's comeback player of the year when he scored 20.3 points a game in 1985–86.

Still, the back problems recurred. Johnson could play only ten games in 1986–87, and he retired for two seasons. After a brief comeback with the Golden State Warriors in 1989, he retired for good. In his 11 NBA seasons, Johnson scored 13,892 points, an average of 20.1 per game.

Johnson, Rafer L.

TRACK AND FIELD
b. Aug. 18, 1935, Hillsboro, Tex.

Decathletes, by definition, are outstanding all-around athletes, but Johnson proved it in several sports. He was the star halfback on the Kingsburg, California, High School football team that won three state championships; he batted over .400 for the baseball team; he averaged more than 17 points a game for the basketball team; and he was an outstanding sprinter and long jumper on the track team.

But his athletic future was decided when, as a high school junior, he saw Bob Mathias in a decathlon meet. "I could have beaten most of those guys in that meet," he told his high school track coach on the way home. Less than a month later, he won the state junior decathlon championship. In his fourth attempt at the event, in 1955, he set a world record of 7,985 points.

Johnson won the decathlon at the 1955 Pan-American Games. In 1956, he qualified for the Olympic team in the long jump and the decathlon, but because of an injury, he withdrew from the long jump competition. He finished second to Milt Campbell in the decathlon and was never again beaten.

In the 1958 dual meet between the U.S. and the Soviet Union, Johnson beat Valeri Kuznyetsov with a world record 8,302 points. However, he suffered a severe back injury in an automobile accident in 1959, and while he was in the hospital, Kuznyetsov set a new record of 8,357 points. Unable to train for more than a year and a half, Johnson returned in 1960 and extended the record to 8,683 points, beating his UCLA teammate C. K. Yang of Formosa.

Johnson became the first black to carry the American flag at the Olympic ceremonies in 1960, and he went on to win a close duel with Yang. After nine events, Johnson led by only 67 points, and the 1,500-meter run, the final event, was one of his weakest. If Yang could run ten seconds faster than Johnson, he'd win the decathlon — and since Yang's personal best was 18 seconds better than Johnson's, there was a good chance that would happen.

But Johnson hung on doggedly and ran a personal best of 4:49.7, finishing just a second behind Yang to claim the gold medal with a score of 8,392 to Yang's 8,334. He was named Associated Press athlete of the year for his accomplishment.

In 1984, Johnson was selected to light the torch at the opening ceremonies of the Los Angeles Olympics.
★ National Track & Field Hall of Fame; Olympic Hall of Fame

Johnson, Randy (Randall D.)

BASEBALL
b. Sept. 10, 1963, Walnut Creek, Calif.

The 6-foot-10, 225-pound Johnson is an overpowering left-handed pitcher who has shown signs of approaching greatness as his control improves.

He joined the NL's Montreal Expos during the 1988 season and was traded to the AL's Seattle Mariners in late May 1989. Johnson led the league in walks three years in a row, with 120 in 1990, 152 in 1991, and 144 in 1992.

He was also the league leader with 241 strikeouts in 1992 and 308 in 1993. Johnson cut his walks down to 99 in 1993, when he had a 19–8 record with 3 shutouts and a 3.24 ERA. He was 13–6 in the strike-shortened 1994 season.

Through 1994, he has an 81–62 record with 94 shutouts and a 3.70 ERA. Johnson has struck out 1,330 hitters and walked 690 in 1,245⅓ innings. He pitched a 2–0 no-hit victory over the Detroit Tigers on June 2, 1991.

Johnson, Skinny (William C.)

BASKETBALL
b. Aug. 16, 1911, Oklahoma City, Okla.
d. Feb. 5, 1980

Johnson, who had great leaping ability, was a key player in the era when there was a jump ball after each score. He led the University of Kansas to three consecutive Big Seven championships, from 1931 through 1933, and he was named an All-American center in his senior year.

After graduating, Johnson played AAU basketball with the Southern Kansas Stage Lines. His team won the national AAU championship in 1935, and Johnson was an AAU All-American in all three seasons he played there. In 1947–48, he coached Cleveland Chiropractic College to a 16–2 record.

★ Basketball Hall of Fame

Johnson, Tish (Patricia)

BOWLING
b. June 8, 1962, Oakland, Calif.

Johnson, who began bowling when she was only six years old, won the 1980 Albert E. Crowe Star of Tomorrow Award as the sport's most promising female newcomer. Two years later, she had the high average in the WIBC national tournament with 224 pins.

She was named the Ladies Professional Bowling Tour bowler of the year in 1990 and 1992. Johnson led the tour in winnings both years, with $94,420 in 1990 and $96,872 in 1992, when she won two major tournaments, the Women's Open and the Sam's Town Invitational.

Through 1993, Johnson was third on the all-time money list with earnings of $515,690.

Johnson, Walter P.

BASEBALL
b. Nov. 6, 1887, Humboldt, Kans.
d. Dec. 10, 1946

Johnson joined the AL's Washington Senators in 1907 directly out of semipro baseball without ever playing in the minor leagues. The 6-foot-1, 200-pound, right-handed pitcher soon won the nickname "Big Train" from sportswriter Grantland Rice because of the speed of his fastball. His teammates often called him "Barney" after auto racer Barney Oldfield because of the way Johnson drove a car.

In 1908, Johnson set a record by pitching shutouts in three consecutive games against the New York Yankees, on September 4, 5, and 7. (There was no game on September 6.) But he had the misfortune of pitching for poor teams through most of his career; his record was only 14–14 that year, despite 6 shutouts, and in 1909 he slipped to 13–25, although he had a 2.21 ERA.

From 1910 through 1919, Johnson won 20 or more games each year. He led the league in strikeouts for the first time with 313 in 1910. He led in shutouts with 6 in 1911, 11 in 1913, 9 in 1914, and 7 in 1915, and he was the ERA leader at 1.39 in 1912, 1.14 in 1913, 1.27 in 1918, and 1.49 in 1919.

Johnson topped the AL in strikeouts eight consecutive years, from 1912 through 1919. He was the league leader in victories and winning percentage with a 36–7 record and an .837 percentage in 1913, when he won the most valuable player award. The Senators finished second that season with 90 victories. However, from 1910 through 1920, they averaged only 76 wins a year, and Johnson averaged 26.

He led the league in victories the next three seasons, with 28 in 1914, 27 in 1915, and 25 in 1916, and again in 1918 with 23. After a 20–14 mark in 1919, he developed a sore arm that limited him to an 8–10 record the following season, but he pitched the only no-hitter of his career, a 1–0 victory over the Boston Red Sox.

It seemed that Johnson's career might have been just about over as he had records of 17–14, 15–16, and 17–12 the next three seasons. But in 1924 he led the league in victories and percentage with a 23–7 record, in shutouts with 6, in strikeouts with 158, and in ERA with 2.72. The Senators won their first pennant that year, and Johnson won his second most valuable player award. He lost his two starts in the World Series but picked up a victory in relief in the seventh and final game as Washington beat the New York Giants.

His last good season was 1927, when he was 20–7 and the Senators won another pennant. Johnson was 2–1 in a seven-game World Series loss to the Pittsburgh Pirates. After going 15–16 and 5–6 the next two years, he became a minor league manager for one season, then took over the Senators in 1929. After four seasons there, he became manager of the Cleveland Indians during the 1933 season and was fired in August 1935.

He then retired to a farm in Maryland, although he spent one season as a radio announcer for the Senators.

In 21 major league seasons, Johnson had 417 victories, second only to Cy Young, 279 losses, 110 shutouts, and a 2.16 ERA. He struck out 3,509 hitters and walked 1,363 in 5,923 innings.
★ Baseball Hall of Fame

Johnston, Bill (William M.)

TENNIS
b. Nov. 2, 1894, San Francisco, Calif.
d. May 1, 1946

Nicknamed "Little Bill" in contrast to his nemesis, "Big Bill" Tilden, Johnston won the U.S. national singles title in 1915 and 1919. His best stroke was a powerful forehand, and he was good at scrambling to retrieve shots, but his serve and backhand were little better than average.

From 1919 through 1925, Johnston and Tilden met in the finals of the U.S. Nationals every year but 1921. Johnston won in 1919 but lost to Tilden in their other meetings. In 1921 they met early in the tournament, and Johnston was eliminated. Tennis fans were outraged. As a result, seeding was adopted for the first time in 1922 to prevent an early-round match between top players.

While Tilden was the better player of the two, Johnston was better than most other players in the world. In 1923,

Tilden didn't play at Wimbledon, and Johnston won the singles title easily, losing only one set. They were ranked 1–2 in the U.S. and the world from 1920 through 1923 and in 1925; Johnston slipped to third, behind Vincent Richards, in 1924.

In addition to his U.S. and Wimbledon singles titles, Johnston teamed with Clarence J. Griffin to win the U.S. men's doubles in 1915, 1916, and 1920, and with Mary K. Browne to win the mixed doubles championship in 1921.
★ International Tennis Hall of Fame

Johnston, Neil (Donald Neil)

BASKETBALL
b. Feb. 4, 1929, Chillicothe, Ohio

After playing basketball at Ohio State for two seasons, Johnston signed with the Philadelphia Phillies organization as a pitcher in 1949. He spent two summers playing in the minor leagues while getting his degree but could no longer play college sports because he was competing as a professional.

The Philadelphia Warriors of the NBA signed Johnston in 1951. He was used only as a substitute in his first year but then became a starter and averaged more than 20 points a game for five consecutive seasons, leading the NBA in scoring three years in a row, 1953–55. He also led in field goal accuracy three times and was the league's top rebounder in 1954–55.

The 6-foot-8, 200-pound center did most of his scoring with an accurate and virtually unstoppable hook shot. He was an NBA first-team all-star four times. A knee injury during the 1958–59 season ended his playing career, but he became coach of the Warriors for two seasons, starting in 1960, winning 95 games and losing 59.

In 1961, Johnston became player-coach of the Pittsburgh Condors in the American Basketball League. However, he played just five games because of his bad knee. Johnston had 53 wins and 50 losses before being fired during the 1962–63 season.
★ Basketball Hall of Fame

Joiner, Charley (Charles Jr.)

FOOTBALL
b. Oct. 14, 1947, Many, La.

A defensive back at Grambling State University, the 5-foot-11, 180-pound Joiner was drafted by the AFL's Houston Oilers in 1969. Houston converted him to wide receiver and traded him to the Cincinnati Bengals in 1972, and the Bengals sent him to the San Diego Chargers in 1976.

During his first seven professional seasons, Joiner was often used as a third receiver in passing situations because his speed made him a deep threat. In San Diego's offense, though, Joiner demonstrated his all-around skills as a starting receiver.

Sure-handed, precise at running patterns, and a very intelligent reader of defenses, Joiner was also amazingly durable for someone his size, playing in 180 consecutive games during a professional career that lasted 17 seasons.

In 1984, Joiner caught his 650th pass, breaking the NFL record. He retired after the 1986 season with 750 receptions for 12,162 yards, an average of 16.2 per catch, and 65 touchdowns. Since retiring, he has been the receivers coach for the Chargers.

Joliat, Aurel

HOCKEY
b. Aug. 29, 1901, Ottawa, Ont.

Though he weighed only 135 pounds, Joliat was a football star with the Ottawa Rough Riders until a broken leg ended his career, and he then went into professional hockey. He played for the Saskatoon Sheiks in the Pacific Hockey League until 1922, when the Montreal Canadiens acquired him in a trade for Newsy Lalonde.

Known as the "Mighty Atom," Joliat was a clever stick-handler and passer who teamed with the speedy Howie Morenz to form a powerful one-two scoring punch. He was among the NHL's top ten scorers eight times, and he won the Hart Trophy as the league's most valuable player in 1934. Joliat retired after the 1937–38 season.

In 654 regular season games, Joliat scored 270 goals and had 190 assists. He had 14 goals and 19 assists in 54 playoff games.

★ Hockey Hall of Fame

Jones, Benjamin A.

HORSE RACING
b. Dec. 31, 1882, Parnell, Mo.
d. June 13, 1961

After more than 20 years of training and breeding horses on his own, Jones was hired by Woolford Farm in 1932. He trained Lawrin, winner of the 1938 Kentucky Derby, and then went to Calumet Farm, where he was in charge of breeding as well as training.

Under his direction, Calumet became the greatest stable ever, leading the nation in earnings 11 times in the 18-year period from 1941 through 1958. Jones saddled Whirlaway, the triple crown winner in 1941; Pensive, Kentucky Derby winner in 1944; Citation, the 1948 triple crown winner; Ponder, the 1949 Kentucky Derby Winner; and Hill Gail, the 1952 Kentucky Derby winner.

Jones is the only trainer ever to saddle six winners of the Kentucky Derby and the only one to produce two triple crown champions. He became general manager of Calumet Farm in 1948, and his son, Horace A. "Jimmy" Jones, took over as head trainer. Jimmy was trainer of record for the winners of two consecutive Kentucky Derbies, Iron Liege in 1957 and Tim Tam in 1958.

★ National Horse Racing Hall of Fame

Jones, Bertram H.

FOOTBALL
b. Sept. 7, 1951, Ruston, La.

The son of William A. "Dub" Jones, a halfback with the Cleveland Browns from 1948 through 1955, Jones was a starting quarterback at Louisiana State in 1972 and 1973. He was a consensus All-American in 1972, and although he didn't finish high in the Heisman Trophy voting as a senior, he was named college player of the year by *The Sporting News*.

The strong-armed, 6-foot-2, 220-pounder was the first-round draft choice of the NFL's Baltimore Colts in 1973. He spent most of his rookie year as a backup but won the starting job during the 1974 season, when he lost a memorable passing duel to Joe Namath and the New York Jets. The Jets won the game, 45–38, but Jones set an NFL record by completing 17 consecutive passes.

He led the Colts to three straight Eastern Division titles in the American Football Conference, from 1975 through 1977. Jones was named the league's most valuable player by the NFL Players' Association in 1976, when he completed 207 of 343 passes for 3,104 yards and 24 touchdowns.

Jones remained with the Colts through 1981 and spent the 1982 season with the Los Angeles Rams before retiring because of a chronic back problem. During his ten seasons in the NFL, he completed 1,430 of 2,551 passes for 18,190 yards and 124 touchdowns. He also rushed for 11 touchdowns.

Jones, Biff (Lawrence McC.)

FOOTBALL
b. Oct. 8, 1895, Washington, D.C.
d. Oct. 10, 1954

A 6-foot-3, 200-pound tackle, Jones played at Army in 1915 and 1916. He was elected captain of the 1917 team but missed the season while serving in France during World War I. Jones returned to West Point as an assistant coach in 1919, and he became head coach in 1926.

In four seasons at his alma mater, Jones had a 30–8–2 record. He served as a field artillery officer in 1930 and 1931, then became head coach at Louisiana State University. He was also appointed an instructor in military science so he could remain in the Army.

Jones had a 20–5–6 record in three seasons at LSU, and his 1933 team was unbeaten, winning seven and tying three. He left the school for the University of Oklahoma in 1935, in large part because of a conflict with Governor Huey Long.

After a 9–6–3 record in two seasons, Jones retired from the Army and became head coach at Nebraska in 1937. His 1940 squad won eight games in a row after losing its opener and became the first Nebraska team to play in a bowl game, losing 21–13 to Stanford in the Rose Bowl.

Jones retired after the 1941 season. Overall, he had a 87–33–15 record, a .700 winning percentage, in 14 seasons.
★ College Football Hall of Fame

Jones, Bobby (Robert T. Jr.)

GOLF
b. March 17, 1902, Atlanta, Ga.
d. Dec. 18, 1971

Considered by many the greatest golfer ever, Jones was certainly the greatest amateur of all time. He began playing when he was five years old, beat a 16-year-old to win a junior tournament when he was nine, broke 80 before he was 12, and won the Georgia amateur championship in 1916, when he was 14, to win his first trip to the National Amateur.

Wearing secondhand Army shoes that he'd screwed spikes into, Jones won his first two matches and led defending champion Robert Gardner by one stroke after 18 holes of the 36 holes in his third match, but lost.

During the next several years, however, Jones was held back by his terrible temper, leading British professional George Duncan to comment, "Jones will never be a champion . . . Only the perfect shot ever suits him."

Jones eventually learned to control his temper and made a breakthrough by winning the 1923 U.S. Open. That ended what his biographer, O. B. Keeler, called "the seven lean years" and began seven years of plenty. From 1923 through 1930, Jones finished worse than second in the Open only once, winning again in 1926, 1929, and 1930.

He also won the U.S. Amateur in 1924, 1925, 1927, 1928, and 1930; the British Open in 1926, 1927, and 1930; and the British Amateur in 1930 to complete the only grand slam ever accomplished. He won the 1930 Sullivan Award as the nation's outstanding amateur athlete.

Jones graduated from Georgia Tech and Harvard Law School but never practiced. He retired from serious competition after his sensational year in 1930, saying, "14 years of intensive tournament play in this country and abroad have given me about all I want in the way of hard work in the game."

He then did a series of pioneering instructional movie shorts, worked as a consultant and representative for Spalding Sporting Goods, and helped design the Augusta, Georgia, National Course. He and Clifford Roberts established the Masters Tournament there in 1934, and Jones played in the tournament every year until 1947, when he was forced to withdraw after two rounds because of a sore shoulder.

Originally diagnosed as bursitis, the shoulder problem turned out to be the first symptom of a spinal ailment that confined him to a wheelchair in his later years. Herbert Warren Wind once wrote of Jones, "As a young man he was able to stand up to just about the best that life can offer, which isn't easy, and later he stood up with equal grace to just about the worst."

★ PGA Hall of Fame; World Golf Hall of Fame

Jones, Calvin J.

FOOTBALL
b. Feb. 7, 1933, Steubenville, Ohio
d. Dec. 9, 1956

A two-time All-American at guard for the University of Iowa, in 1954 and 1955, Jones won the 1955 Outland Trophy as the nation's outstanding collegiate lineman. He was the first black player to win the trophy and the first to captain an Iowa team.

The 6-foot, 220-pounder was chosen by the Detroit Lions in the NFL's 1956 college draft, but he chose to play for the Winnipeg Blue Bombers in the Canadian Football League. He was killed in a plane crash while returning from the CFL's All-Star game after his rookie season.

★ College Football Hall of Fame

Jones, Deacon (David)

FOOTBALL
b. Dec. 9, 1938, Eatonville, Fla.

After playing at two small, predominantly black colleges, South Carolina State and Mississippi Vocational, Jones joined the NFL's Los Angeles Rams as a fourteenth-round draft choice in 1961.

Flamboyant and confident to the point of cockiness, Jones invented his nickname, "Deacon," for no particular reason except that he felt David Jones was not a memorable name. He also coined the term "sack" for the tackle of a quarterback before he can get the pass away.

Jones was the premier sacker of his day. Playing left end for the Rams' famous "Fearsome Foursome" defensive line, the 6-foot-5, 260-pounder had 26 sacks in 1967 alone. A consensus All-Pro six years in a row, from 1965 through 1970, he played in eight Pro Bowls and was voted the NFL defensive player of the year in 1967 and 1968.

In 1972, Jones went to the San Diego Chargers and spent two seasons there before finishing his career with the Washington Redskins in 1974. He missed only three games in his 14-season career.

★ Pro Football Hall of Fame

Jones, Hayes W.

TRACK AND FIELD
b. Aug. 4, 1938, Starkville, Miss.

At less than six feet tall, Jones was short for a hurdler, but his outstanding speed, great start, and nearly perfect technique won him an Olympic gold medal in the 110-meter hurdles in 1964, along with many other championships.

Because a fast start is so important in short hurdles races, Jones was a master of the indoor events; he won 55 in a row from March 1959 until his retirement after the 1964 Olympics. He was the AAU outdoor high hurdles champion in 1958, 1960, and 1961, the indoor champion in 1958 and 1960–62. Representing Eastern Michigan, he won the NCAA title in 1959, when he was also the Pan-American Games champion.

Jones ran on a 4 x 100-meter sprint relay team that set a world record in 1961. After retiring from competition, he became New York City's director of recreation.

★ National Track & Field Hall of Fame

Jones, Howard H.

FOOTBALL
b. Aug. 23, 1885, Excello, Ohio
d. July 27, 1941

Although he spent his early years of coaching in the East and Midwest, Jones became best known for turning the University of Southern California into a national power, beginning in 1925. He was nicknamed "the King of the Rose Bowl" because five of his teams played in the bowl, and all of them won.

Jones played end at Yale and coached Syracuse to a 6–3–1 record after graduating in 1908. He returned to Yale for one season, producing a 9–0–0 team that didn't give up a single point, and then coached Ohio State to a 6–1–3 mark in 1910.

After the 1910 season, Jones went into business. He interrupted his career to coach Yale to a 5–2–3 record in 1913, and he left business for good in 1916 to concentrate on coaching at the University of Iowa.

Jones had unbeaten teams in 1921 and 1922; his 1921 team ended Notre Dame's 21-game unbeaten streak with a 10–7 victory. In eight seasons, Iowa won 42 games while losing 17. Jones went to Southern California in 1925.

Until his arrival, the school had played almost exclusively against West Coast teams. Jones changed that, adding rivals such as Iowa, Notre Dame, Idaho, Utah, Colorado, Pittsburgh, and Georgia to the schedule over the years.

He remained at Southern Cal until his death of a heart attack after the 1940 season. The 1928 team was undefeated, with one tie in ten games, and the 1932 team won all nine of its regular season games. The Trojans beat four different teams in their five Rose Bowl victories: Pittsburgh, 47–14, in 1930; Tulane, 21–12, in 1932; Pittsburgh, 35–0, in 1933; Duke, 7–3, in 1939; and Tennessee, 14–0, in 1940.

Jones's record in 16 seasons at Southern Cal was 121–36–13. Overall, his teams won 194 games, lost 64, and had 21 ties, a .733 winning percentage. His younger brother, Tad, also played at Yale and was a successful college coach.
★ College Football Hall of Fame

Jones, Jimmy (Horace A.)

HORSE RACING
b. Nov 24, 1906, Parnell, Mo.

The son of Ben Jones, Jimmy worked as an assistant trainer with his father for many years, chiefly at Calumet Farm. He helped develop two triple crown winners, Whirlaway in 1941 and Citation in 1948.

His father became general manager of Calumet in 1948, and Jones took over as head trainer. Among the outstanding horses he produced were Iron Liege, winner of the 1957 Kentucky Derby, and Tim Tam, who was named the top 3-year-old in 1958 after winning the Kentucky Derby and Preakness.

Jones led all trainers in winnings from 1947 through 1949 and in 1957 and 1961. His horses won a total of 1,034 races and earned $12,792,676. He became director of racing at Monmouth Park in New Jersey in 1964.
★ National Racing Hall of Fame

Jones, K. C.

BASKETBALL
b. May 25, 1932, San Francisco, Calif.

He may be the poorest shooter in the Basketball Hall of Fame, but Jones was a great defensive player. He teamed with Bill Russell to lead the defense-minded University of San Francisco to 55 consecutive victories and two straight NCAA championships, in 1955 and 1956. Later they played together on Boston Celtics teams that won eight NBA championships.

The 6-foot-1, 200-pound guard entered USF in 1951, a year ahead of Russell, but he played in only one game as a junior because of an emergency appendectomy, so he was granted another year of eligibility. USF lost only one game the following season and defeated LaSalle, 77–63, in the NCAA championship. The key to the victory was that Jones held LaSalle's high-scoring All-

American forward Tom Gola scoreless for the first 21 minutes of the game, even though Gola was five inches taller.

USF went undefeated in 1955–56 and won a second NCAA title. After playing for the U.S. gold medal Olympic team, Jones served in the Army for two years. He had a tryout as a defensive back with the Los Angeles Rams, who had chosen him in the NFL draft, then rejoined Russell with the Celtics.

At first a backup behind Bob Cousy and Bill Sharman, Jones became a starter after Sharman retired in 1961. His defense and play-making were key ingredients in the Celtics' success during his nine seasons with the team. He retired in 1968 to become head coach at Brandeis University for three years, winning 34 games while losing 32.

Jones took over the San Diego Conquistadors in the American Basketball Association in 1972, then coached the Capitol Bullets of the NBA for three seasons. He returned to the Celtics as head coach in 1983 and guided them to two NBA championships in his first three years. He left after the 1987–88 season. Jones then took over the Seattle Supersonics in 1990–91 and 1991–92.

As a player, Jones scored 4,999 points in 675 regular season games, a 7.4 average, and had 2,904 assists. He won 552 games and lost 306 as a professional coach and had an 81–57 record in playoff competition.

★ Basketball Hall of Fame

Jones, Parnelli (Rufus Parnell)

AUTO RACING
b. Aug. 12, 1933, Texarkana, Ark.

In a quiet kind of way, Jones won just about everything he set out to win. It seemed that he always needed a new challenge. He began as a jalopy racer on the West Coast, then won the Midwestern sprint car championship in 1960. He was rookie of the year at the Indy 500 in 1961, when he qualified fifth and finished twelfth. He also won the national sprint championship that year and again in 1962.

In 1963 he won the Indy 500 and set a record for a stock car in the Pikes Peak Climb, breaking the old record by more than 30 seconds. He broke that record in 1964, when he also won seven races and shared an eighth with his teammate, Rodger Ward, to claim the USAC stock car championship.

After placing second in the 1965 Indy 500, Jones failed to finish the race in 1966 because of mechanical problems, and he announced his retirement from IndyCar racing. Then came another challenge, the chance to drive Andy Granatelli's turbine car in the Indy 500. Jones qualified sixth and was in the lead by the end of the first lap. Rain stopped the race on the 18th lap, and the race resumed the next day. Jones and the turbine car had an unbeatable lead with just three laps to go — and then the car died.

Jones really retired from IndyCar driving after that race. But he became a car owner, drove at times in off-road racing and the Trans-Am series, and won more money with his Vel's-Parnelli team, hiring drivers such as Al Unser and Mario Andretti, than he ever had as a driver.

★ Indianapolis Speedway Hall of Fame

Jones, Randy (Randall L.)

BASEBALL
b. Jan. 12, 1950, Fullerton, Calif.

Though he batted right, Jones was a left-handed pitcher who won the NL's Cy Young Award in 1976, when he led the league in victories with a 22–14 record, in complete games with 25, and in innings pitched with 315. He had also led the league in ERA with 2.24 in 1975, when he had a 20–12 record.

Jones joined the San Diego Padres in 1973. With a poor team, he won only 15 games while losing 28 in his first two seasons. After his Cy Young year, he developed arm trouble and never had another winning season. San Diego traded him to the New York Mets in 1981, and he pitched there for two years before retiring.

Jones, Samuel

BASKETBALL
b. June 24, 1933, Wilmington, N.C.

As a boy, Jones played neighborhood

football games with future tennis great Althea Gibson. But his future was in basketball. Though he was virtually unheard of as a player at little North Carolina College, the Boston Celtics made him their number-one pick in the 1957 NBA draft.

Jones became one of the Celtics' top scorers after a three-year apprenticeship as a substitute. He averaged more than 20 points in four consecutive seasons, his best in 1964–65, when he scored 25.9 points a game. The 6-foot-4, 205-pound guard liked to bank his jump shots off the backboard from an angle, 15 to 20 feet away from the basket. One of the fastest players in the NBA during his prime, he also excelled on Boston's fast break.

In his 12 seasons with the Celtics, Jones played for ten championship teams. In his last playoff series before retiring, the 1969 NBA finals against the Los Angeles Lakers, he hit what was probably the most important shot of his career. The Celtics were down, two games to one, and losing 88–87 at home with seconds remaining when Jones hit an off-balance, 18-foot jump shot to win the game. The Celtics went on to win the championship, and Jones retired when it was over.

In 872 regular season games, Jones scored 15,380 points, an average of 17.6 per game. He added 2,909 points in 154 playoff games. Jones was one of the ten players named to the NBA silver anniversary team in 1971. After retiring as a player, he coached at Federal City College in Washington, D.C., and at North Carolina A & T University.

★ Basketball Hall of Fame

Jones, Stanley P.

FOOTBALL
b. Nov. 24, 1931, Altoona, Pa.

An offensive and defensive tackle at the University of Maryland, Jones was an All-American in 1953, when he won the Knute Rockne Award as the nation's outstanding collegiate lineman. Because his original college class had already graduated, Jones had been chosen by the

Chicago Bears in the 1953 NFL draft, and he joined the team in 1954.

Jones became an immediate starter at offensive tackle, moving to guard in his second season. He was an All-Pro in 1955, 1956, 1959, and 1960, and played in seven straight Pro Bowls, from 1955 through 1961. The 6-foot-1, 250-pounder was moved to defensive tackle in 1963, when the Bears won the NFL championship game, 14–10, over the New York Giants.

In 1966, Jones was traded to the Washington Redskins, and he retired after that season. One of the first football players to embark on a weightlifting program, Jones began lifting as a high school freshman and gained 20 pounds a year during the next eight years. He became one of the sport's first strength coaches with the Denver Broncos in 1967, went to the Buffalo Bills in the same position from 1972 through 1976, then returned to Denver through 1988. He became the Cleveland Browns' strength and conditioning coach in 1989 and went to the New England Patriots in 1991.

★ Pro Football Hall of Fame

Jones, Tad (Thomas A. D.)

FOOTBALL
b. Feb. 22, 1887, Excello, Ohio
d. June 19, 1957

Jones quarterbacked Yale for three seasons, 1905 through 1907, and was named an All-American as a senior. While he called the signals Yale won 28 of 30 games, tying 2. Princeton led at halftime of their 1907 game, 10–0, but Jones helped bring Yale back for a 12–10 victory with a 40-yard punt return to set up a touchdown.

He coached Syracuse University to a 9–9–1 record in 1909 and 1910, then taught and coached at prep schools until 1916, when he returned to Yale as head coach. Yale hadn't beaten Harvard since 1909, but Jones's first team did it, 6–3, and had an 8–1–0 record. The 1917 team played only three games because of World War I, winning all of them.

After the season, Jones went to Seattle to help build ships for the war effort, and he remained there until 1920, when he returned to Yale. He coached at Yale through 1927. His 1923 team won all eight of its games, and the 1924 squad was also undefeated, winning six and tying two. Jones's last team won seven of eight games.

During his nine seasons at Yale, the school won 60, lost 15, and tied 4, beating Harvard six times while losing three.

★ College Football Hall of Fame

Jordan, Lee Roy

FOOTBALL
b. April 27, 1941, Excel, Ala.

A center and linebacker at the University of Alabama, Jordan played for teams that won 29 games while losing only 2 and tying 2 over a three-year period. He was a consensus All-American in 1962 and was named the outstanding player in the 1963 Orange Bowl, when he made 31 tackles in Alabama's 17–0 win over Oklahoma.

Jordan became a defensive specialist as a middle linebacker with the NFL's Dallas Cowboys in 1963. The 6-foot-1, 220-pounder had great speed, which gave him the ability to close quickly on running plays and to drop back quickly into pass defense. He intercepted three passes in a 1973 game.

A consensus All-Pro in 1973 and 1975, Jordan played in five Pro Bowls. He retired after the 1976 season. During his 14 years with the Cowboys, he intercepted 34 passes and returned them for 472 yards, a 13.9 average, and 3 touchdowns. He also recovered 16 fumbles.

Jordan, Michael J.

BASKETBALL
b. Feb. 17, 1963, Brooklyn, N.Y.

Jordan first became known as a freshman at the University of North Carolina, when he hit the winning shot with seconds to play in the school's 63–62 win over Georgetown University in the final game of the 1982 NCAA championship tournament. He was named college player of the year in 1984 after averaging 19.6 points as a junior, then decided to leave school and enter the NBA draft.

The Chicago Bulls chose him in the first round of the draft, and Jordan joined the team after leading the U.S. Olympic team in scoring en route to a gold medal. He averaged 28.2 points a game and was named rookie of the year.

A 6-foot-6, 198-pound guard, Jordan may have been the finest all-around player in history. He is the only athlete ever to win the most valuable player award and the defensive player of the year award in the same season, 1988, and he was also named the NBA's MVP in 1991 and 1992.

He holds the record for most consecutive seasons leading the league in scoring, seven, from 1986–87 through 1992–93, and he led in steals three times, with 259 in 1987–88, 227 in 1989–90, and 221 in 1992–93. He is the only player ever to lead in scoring and steals in a single season. In 1986–87, Jordan became the first player to have more than 200 steals and more than 100 blocked shots, and he did it again the following season.

Jordan led the Bulls to three straight NBA championships, from 1991 through 1993, and was named the most valuable player in the playoffs all three years. He set a record by averaging 41.0 points per game during the final playoff series in 1993.

A month after that series ended, Jordan's father, James, was found murdered near the border between North Carolina and South Carolina. There was speculation that his death might have been linked somehow to an unpaid gambling debt, allegedly more than $1 million, that Michael had incurred in high stakes golf matches. However, two 18-year-old suspects were arrested, and the motive was apparently robbery.

In October, shortly before the NBA season began, Jordan announced his retirement. He had played just nine NBA seasons but had scored 21,541 points in 667 regular season games, an average of 32.3. He also had 4,219 rebounds, 3,935 assists, 1,1815 steals, and 684 blocked shots. In 111 playoff games, he averaged 34.7 points, a record, while getting 741 rebounds, 738 assists, 258 steals, and 109 blocked shots.

Jordan, Shug (Ralph J.)

BASKETBALL, FOOTBALL
b. Sept. 25, 1910, Selma, Ala.
d. July 17, 1980

Jordan played baseball, basketball, and football at Auburn University, graduating in 1932. He began coaching basketball at the school in 1935 and had an 84–63 record before joining the Army in 1942.

He had a 7–9 record as Auburn basketball coach in the 1945–46 season and then became an assistant football coach with the All America Football Conference's Miami Seahawks. In 1947, Jordan became basketball coach at the University of Georgia, where his teams won 40 games and lost 35 in three seasons.

His alma mater hired him to coach football in 1951, and he spent 25 seasons there, compiling a 175–83 record. His 1957 team was undefeated in ten games and won the national championship. However, the school was ineligible for post-season play because it was on probation for recruiting violations. Auburn did play in 12 bowl games during Jordan's tenure.

He retired after the 1975 season. Auburn's football stadium is now named for him.

★ College Football Hall of Fame

Joss, Addie (Adrian)

BASEBALL
b. April 12, 1880, Woodland, Wis.
d. April 14, 1911

Although he was unquestionably a great pitcher, Joss was kept out of the Hall of Fame for years because of the requirement that a player had to have spent ten years in the major leagues to qualify. The only reason Joss didn't was that he died at age 31.

Joss spent his entire career with the Cleveland Indians, joining them in 1902, when he led the league in shutouts with five and had a 17–13 record. He had the league-leading ERA, 1.59, in 1904. A right-hander, the 6-foot-3, 185-pounder won 20 or more games four consecutive seasons, from 1905 through 1908, leading in victories with a 27–11 record in

1907 and in ERA a second time with a sparkling 1.16 in 1908.

In 1909, he slipped to a 14–13 record despite a 1.71 ERA, and arm trouble limited him to a 5–5 record in 1910. Joss fainted during an exhibition game in Chattanooga before the 1911 season but came north with the team for an exhibition series in Toledo, his adopted hometown, where he was partner in a poolroom and wrote sports stories for the local newspaper in the off-season.

Joss remained in Toledo while the Indians went north to begin the season. He died two days after his thirty-first birthday. Billy Sunday, a ballplayer turned evangelist, delivered the eulogy at his funeral, which was one of the largest in Toledo history. The Cleveland game scheduled for that day was postponed so the team could attend.

During his brief career, Joss had a 160–97 record with 45 shutouts and a 1.89 ERA. He struck out 920 hitters and walked 364 in 2,327 innings.

★ Baseball Hall of Fame

Joyce, Joan

SOFTBALL
b. Aug. 1, 1940, Waterbury, Conn.

Although she is not nearly as well known, Joyce has to be ranked very close to Babe Didrikson Zaharias as the greatest woman athlete of all time. She made her name as a softball player. Before she was 14, she joined the Raybestos Brakettes of Stamford, Connecticut. During her 20 seasons with the team, the Brakettes won 11 national championships, including four in a row. Joyce pitched 105 no-hitters and 33 perfect games, winning 509 games while losing only 33. When not pitching, she played first base and had a .327 career batting average. An All-American 18 years in a row, she was named most valuable player of the National Softball Association tournament eight times.

The 5-foot-9 Joyce averaged 25 points a game in AAU basketball competition and was a three-time All-American. She was also a fine volleyball player, and three months after she started bowling, she won the Connecticut state championship.

Joyce announced her retirement from softball after the 1973 season and was given the Gold Key award by the Connecticut Sportswriters Association for outstanding achievement. She was not only the first woman to win the award, she was the first ever invited to the awards banquet.

But she didn't stop there. Joyce joined the Ladies' Professional Golf Association tour in 1975. Though never a champion, she did win more than $30,000 in 1984, when she shot a 66 for one round of the S & H Golf Classic.

During her softball career, Joyce's pitches were sometimes clocked at more than 116 mph. In exhibition games, she struck out Ted Williams in 1962 and Hank Aaron in 1978.

★ International Women's Sports Hall of Fame

Joyner-Kersee, Jackie (Jacqueline)

TRACK AND FIELD
b. March 3, 1962, E. St. Louis, Ill.

A high school All-American in both basketball and track, Joyner went to UCLA on an athletic scholarship in 1980 and was a four-year starter in basketball. She also set college records of 22–11½ in the long jump and 6,718 points in the pentathlon in 1985, when she won the Broderick Cup as the nation's outstanding female college athlete.

The NCAA pentathlon champion in 1982 and 1983, Joyner won the national championship in 1982 and set an American record of 6,520 points in the 1984 Olympic trials. She won a silver medal in the pentathlon in the Los Angeles Olympics, missing the gold by just five points, and she finished fifth in the long jump.

Joyner married her coach, Bob Kersee, early in 1986. That year she became the first American woman to hold the pentathlon world record by scoring 7,148 points at the Goodwill Games in Moscow. She extended the record to 7,158 points in the U.S. Olympic Sports Festival, where she won all seven events.

Joyner-Kersee was presented with the Sullivan Award as the country's top amateur athlete of the year.

In 1987, Joyner-Kersee competed extensively in the high hurdles and long jump. She won 5 of 8 hurdles races and 11 of 12 long jump competitions. At the national outdoor championships, she won the pentathlon and the long jump, and she tied the world long jump record of 24–5½ at the Pan-American Games.

Her season culminated at the world championships, where she again won both the pentathlon and the long jump, becoming the first woman ever to win an individual event and a multievent in Olympic-level competition, and the first athlete to do it since Harold Osborne in 1924. She was named female athlete of the year by the Associated Press and amateur sportswoman of the year by the Women's Sports Foundation.

Joyner-Kersee won gold medals in the long jump and the heptathlon at the 1988 Olympics. She repeated in the heptathlon in 1992, when she won a bronze in the long jump. She was the first woman to win multievent titles at two Olympics and the first athlete of either sex to win multievent medals in three Olympics. She was also the world long jump champion in 1991, when she had to drop out of the pentathlon competition because of an injury.

Julian, Doggy (Alvin F.)

BASKETBALL
b. April 5, 1901, Reading, Pa.
d. July 28, 1967

After winning ten letters in three sports at Bucknell University, Julian played minor league baseball and semiprofessional football for several years before going to Schuylkill (now Albright) College in Pennsylvania as football coach in 1925. Two years later, he became baseball and basketball coach as well.

In 1936, Julian became football and basketball coach at Muhlenberg College. He spent ten seasons there before moving to Holy Cross as basketball coach in 1945. His 1946–47 team won the NCAA championship. A year later, Holy Cross again went to the final four but lost to the University of Kentucky in the semifinals.

Julian was persuaded to take over the Boston Celtics in 1948 but won only 47 games while losing 81 with a team that lacked both talent and money. He then returned to college coaching at Dartmouth, where he won three Ivy League titles. Julian suffered a stroke midway through the 1966–67 season and died six months later.

His overall college record was 386 wins and 343 losses.

★ Basketball Hall of Fame

Jurgensen, Sonny (Christian A. III)

FOOTBALL
b. Aug. 23, 1934, Wilmington, N.C.

Perhaps the greatest quarterback who never started for an NFL champion team, Jurgensen starred at Duke University before joining the NFL's Philadelphia Eagles in 1957. He was a backup to Norm Van Brocklin for four seasons, including 1960, when the Eagles won the league title.

He took over as Philadelphia's starter in 1961, after Van Brocklin retired, and had a sensational year, passing for a record 3,723 yards and tying the NFL record with 32 touchdown passes.

A series of injuries limited his playing time in 1963, and the Eagles traded him to the Washington Redskins the following season. In 1967, Jurgensen broke his own record by passing for 3,747 yards, and he also set NFL records for attempts, 508, and completions, 288. He was the league's passing champion.

He missed much of the 1968 season because of broken ribs and elbow surgery but won the passing championship again in 1969. Injuries again bothered him in 1971 and 1972, and for his last two seasons in Washington he was Billy Kilmer's backup, but he played in a number of games.

The 1974 Redskins got into the playoffs by tying for first place in the Eastern Division. Jurgensen relieved Kilmer in the Washington's 19–10 first-round loss to the Los Angeles Rams, completing 6 of 12 passes but throwing 3 interceptions. It was his last game and the first playoff game in which he'd ever appeared.

The All-Pro quarterback in 1961 and 1969, Jurgensen played in five Pro Bowls. During his career, he completed 2,433 of 4,262 passes for 32,224 yards and 255 touchdowns. He also ran for 15 touchdowns.

★ Pro Football Hall of Fame

Justice, Charles ("Choo Choo")

FOOTBALL
b. May 18, 1924, Asheville, N.C.

Fresh out of high school, Justice joined the Navy during World War II and became the youngest player on the Bainbridge, Maryland, Naval Training Station football team. He entered the University of North Carolina in 1946 and was the school's starting single-wing tailback for four years.

Nicknamed the "Scintillating Sicilian" by sportswriters, the 5-foot-10, 175-pound Justice rushed for 3,774 yards and passed for 2,362, setting what was then an NCAA record with 6,136 yards of total offense during his college career. He scored 39 touchdowns and also punted for a 42.6-yard average.

His college coach, Carl Snavely, said of him, "Justice was a great open-field runner and exceptional kicker . . . In addition to his skill, speed, and other qualities, Justice was a spirited leader, and he possesses amazing stamina." He missed only one game during his four years at North Carolina.

Justice was chosen by the Washington Redskins in the NFL's 1950 college draft, but he was out a good part of the season in a contract dispute. He held out for all of 1951, when he was an assistant coach at North Carolina, then returned to the Redskins in 1952 and spent three more seasons with them before retiring.

During his four years as a professional, Justice gained 1,284 yards on 266 attempts, a 4.8 average, and scored 3 rushing touchdowns. He also caught 63 passes for 962 yards, a 15.3 average, and 7 touchdowns, and punted 94 times for a 40.4-yard average.

★ College Football Hall of Fame

Justice, David C.

BASEBALL
b. April 14, 1966, Cincinnati, Ohio

Justice was with the NL's Atlanta Braves briefly in 1989 and joined the team to stay early in the 1990 season, when he was named rookie of the year after hitting .282 with 28 home runs and 78 RBI in 127 games.

He missed a month of the 1991 season with an injury and had 21 home runs in 109 games. After batting .256 in 1992, Justice had his finest season in 1993, when he hit .270 with 40 home runs and 120 RBI.

A left-hander, Justice played first base for much of the 1990 season but was moved to right field the following year. Through 1994, he had a .276 average with 637 hits, including 101 doubles, 14 triples, 130 home runs, 379 runs scored, and 419 RBI.

K

Kahanamoku, Duke P.

SURFING, SWIMMING
b. Aug. 24, 1890, Honolulu, Hawaii
d. Jan. 22, 1968

Kahanamoku left Hawaii to begin competing on the mainland in 1912, and many were surprised to see he used the American crawl stroke, which had only recently been developed by Charles M. Daniels. The stroke had been used by Hawaiian natives for a long time, possibly for centuries, and Kahanamoku had learned it as a child.

After winning the national indoor championship in the 100-yard free style in 1912, Kahanamoku won a gold medal in the 100-meter at the Olympics and was also a member of the 4 x 200-meter relay team. He was the national outdoor 100-yard champion in 1916, 1917, and 1920.

World War I canceled the 1916 Olympics, but Kahanamoku won two gold medals in 1920, in the 100-meter freestyle and in the 4 x 200-meter relay. He set a world record of 1:00.4 in the 100-meter finals, which took place on his birthday.

In 1924, at the age of 34, Kahanamoku won a silver medal in the 100-meter, and his brother Sam won the bronze. The gold medalist was Johnny Weismuller. Kahanamoku was an alternate on the Olympic water polo teams in 1928 and 1932.

An excellent surfer, Kahanamoku is believed to have invented windsurfing, also known as board-sailing, in which a small sail is attached to a surfboard, and he was the first to wake-surf behind a motorboat. As a Red Cross instructor in water safety, he traveled all over the world and introduced surfing to many countries.

Kahanamoku had a small career in the movies, usually playing Polynesian chiefs. He later returned to Hawaii and was the sheriff of Honolulu for 20 years.
★ International Swimming Hall of Fame; Olympic Hall of Fame

Kaline, Albert W.

BASEBALL
b. Dec. 19, 1934, Baltimore, Md.

In only his second major league season, 1955, Kaline became the youngest player ever to win a batting title, finishing the season at .340 just two months before his twenty-second birthday. He also led the AL in hits that season with 200.

That was his only batting championship, but Kaline hit over .300 or better in eight other seasons, and he was an outstanding defensive player with a strong throwing arm.

Kaline joined the Detroit Tigers in 1953, playing in just 30 games, primarily as a late-inning defensive replacement and pinch hitter. He became the team's starting right fielder in 1954. He led the league in slugging percentage at .530 in 1959 and in doubles with 41 in 1961. Kaline was also the AL leader in outfield assists with 18 in 1956 and 23 in 1958, and he led the league's outfielders in fielding percentage with .993 in 1966 and 1.000 in 1971.

As he slowed down in his later years, Kaline was often used at first base to get his bat into the lineup. He spent 22 seasons in the major leagues, all with the Tigers. Soft-spoken and modest, he was extremely popular with Detroit fans, and he joined the team as a broadcaster when he retired as a player after the 1974 season.

In 2,834 major league games, Kaline had 3,007 hits, including 498 doubles, 75 triples, and 399 home runs. He scored 1,622 runs and drove in 1,583.

★ Baseball Hall of Fame

Kamenshek, Dottie (Dorothy)

BASEBALL
b. Dec. 21, 1925, Cincinnati, Ohio

Like many players in the All-American Girls Professional Baseball League, Kamenshek grew up playing softball. At 17, she joined the Rockford, Illinois, Peaches in 1943, the league's first year. At that time, it was the All-American Girls Softball League, and aside from the fact that stealing was permitted, it used softball rules and the 12-inch diameter ball.

Originally an outfielder, Kamenshek moved to first base early in the season and stayed there for the rest of her nine-year career. Above all, Kamenshek was a hitter. She led the AAGPBL in batting two years in a row, with .316 in 1946 and .306 in 1947. In those seasons, the ball was 11 inches in diameter.

The league went to a 10-inch ball in 1949, and batting averages immediately went up. Kamenshek hit .334 in 1950 and .345 in 1951, her final season, despite the fact that she had to wear a brace because of a back injury. Her career average was .292, one of the best among players who had started when the AAGPBL used a softball.

Kamenshek was also a fine fielder at first base. Wallie Pipp, the former New York Yankee first baseman, called her the fanciest fielder he had ever seen at the position.

After retiring, Kamenshek entered college and became a physical therapist.

Karras, Alexander G.

FOOTBALL
b. July 15, 1935, Gary, Ind.

A fullback in high school, Karras was moved to tackle when he entered the University of Iowa in 1954. He was a consensus All-American in 1957, his senior season, and he won the Outland Trophy as the nation's outstanding college lineman.

Karras was the first-round draft choice of the NFL's Detroit Lions in 1958. He immediately became a starting defensive tackle. Smaller than most other tackles, at 6-foot-2 and 248 pounds, Karras used intelligence, agility, and aggressiveness to become an All-Pro three consecutive years, from 1960 through 1962.

On April 17, 1963, Karras and Green Bay Packer halfback Paul Hornung were suspended indefinitely for betting on games. Karras took a defiant attitude at first. Ordered to stay away from a bar called Lindell's AC, he instead bought a one-third interest in the business and worked there as a bartender. He also wrestled professionally.

Karras finally agreed to sell his share in January 1964 and made a public apology, saying, "Everybody always wanted me to be sorry, I guess, and I am. And I'm tired of it. And I want to play football and, well, if I can't I'll have to do something else."

The suspension was lifted before the 1964 season. Karras returned to the Lions and played with them through 1970 before retiring. Since then, he spent three years working as an analyst on *Monday Night Football*, and he has done a considerable amount of acting in movies and television.

Kavanaugh, Kenneth W.

FOOTBALL
b. Nov. 23, 1916, Little Rock, Ark.

The 6-foot-3, 204-pound Kavanaugh was a fast, sure-handed receiver. He led the nation in receptions as a senior at Louisiana State University in 1939, catching 30 passes for 469 yards in nine games. Kavanaugh was named an All-American end and was the first winner of the Knute Rockne Memorial Trophy as the top collegiate lineman in the country.

Kavanaugh joined the NFL's Chicago Bears in 1940. After military service from 1942 through 1944, he returned to the Bears in 1945 and played with them until his retirement after the 1950 season. He was named to the United Press All-Pro team in 1946 and was a consensus All-Pro in 1947.

In his eight professional seasons, Kavanaugh caught 162 passes for 3,622 yards, a 22.4 average, and 50 touchdowns.

★ College Football Hall of Fame

Kaw, Eddie (Edgar L.)

FOOTBALL
b. Jan. 18, 1898, Houston, Tex.
d. Dec. 13, 1971

A dangerous runner and fine punter, Kaw was an All-American at fullback for Cornell in 1921 and at halfback in 1922. In a 41–0 win over Pennsylvania in 1921, Kaw scored five of his team's six touchdowns, one of them on a 50-yard run. He also had touchdown runs of 35 and 70 yards against Columbia that season, when he scored 15 touchdowns in eight games.

The 6-foot-3, 185-pound Kaw also won three letters in baseball. He played for the NFL's Buffalo Bisons in 1924.

★ College Football Hall of Fame

Kazmaier, Dick (Richard W., Jr.)

FOOTBALL
b. Nov. 23, 1930, Toledo, Ohio

Most major college teams had switched to the T formation by the early 1950s, but Princeton was still using the single wing, and from 1949 through 1951 Dick Kazmaier shone as the school's triple-threat tailback. In those three years, he ran, passed, and kicked for a total of more than 4,000 yards, scored 20 touchdowns, and threw 35 touchdown passes.

A slim 170 pounds at 5-foot-11, Kazmaier had his greatest day in a 53–15 victory over Cornell in 1951. He ran for 124 yards and two touchdowns and completed 15 of 17 passes for 236 yards and three touchdowns. Kazmaier was named an All-American halfback and won both

the Heisman and Maxwell trophies as college player of the year. He was also named Associated Press athlete of the year.

The Chicago Bears made him their first draft choice in 1952, but he opted not to play pro football.

★ College Football Hall of Fame

Kealoha, Warren P.

SWIMMING
b. March 3, 1904
d. Sept. 8, 1972

The first day he practiced for competitive swimming, Kealoha unofficially broke the world record in the 100-yard backstroke. As a member of a Hawaiian swimming team that included the great Duke Kahanamoku, Kealoha toured the mainland United States in 1920 before competing in the Olympics.

Kealoha set a world record of 1:14.8 in a 100-meter backstroke heat at the Olympics, then won the event in 1:15.2, which was also better than the previous world record. Because he used an unusual stroke, which has since become standard, judges debated for some time about whether to allow the victory. They eventually decided that his stroke was legal.

In October 1922, Kealoha lowered his world record to 1:12.6. He won a second gold medal in the event at the 1924 Olympics, clocking an Olympic record 1:13.2, and he lowered the world record to 1:11.4 in June 1926. However, Walter Laufer of the U.S. broke that record the following day while competing in Europe.

After suffering his first loss, in a very close race with Johnny Weismuller in 1926, Kealoha retired from competition.

★ International Swimming Hall of Fame

Keaney, Frank W.

BASKETBALL
b. June 5, 1886, Boston, Mass.
d. Oct. 10, 1967

As a coach at little Rhode Island College, now the University of Rhode Island, Keaney was a pioneer of modern basketball offense. His teams ran and ran and ran. To keep the running game going, Keaney introduced conditioning programs to help his players remain in top shape. He was also the first to use a full-court press throughout a game to get quick turnovers and easy scores.

Keaney played four sports at Bates College in Maine, graduated in 1911, then coached at high schools in New England until 1920, when he and his wife, Winifred, went to Rhode Island. Keaney taught chemistry, coached five sports, and was athletic director; Winifred coached all the women's teams for 13 years and was a physical education instructor.

Although Rhode Island scored 87 points in the first game Keaney coached, he didn't begin to refine his "run and shoot" offense until the late 1920s, and it didn't reach fruition until the 1930s. His first "point a minute team" averaged 48.6 points a game in 1935. The average reached 70.7 in 1938–39 and 80.7 in 1942–43.

Keaney never won a major championship, but his teams went to four National Invitation Tournaments and barely lost, 46–45, to the University of Kentucky in the 1947 NIT. He retired in 1948 with a record of 403 wins and 124 losses.
★ Basketball Hall of Fame

Kearns, Jack [John Leo McKernan]
BOXING
b. Aug. 17, 1882, Waterloo, Mich.
d. June 17, 1963

His family moved from Michigan to North Dakota and then to Seattle when he was young, and at 15, John L. McKernan went to the Klondike region of Alaska, where he worked in saloons and met Herbert Hoover, Jack London, Tex Rickard, and Robert Service.

After playing semipro baseball for a time, he began boxing as a lightweight and welterweight under the ring name "Young Kid Kearns." Kearns spent a year in prison and then began working as a boxing manager and promoter, using the name "Jack Kearns."

In 1917, he met Jack Dempsey in a San Francisco bar. Dempsey had been boxing professionally for three years, mostly in small Western mining towns for small purses. Kearns taught him to box and kept him busy fighting, at first in San Francisco and then in the East.

Kearns also began a tireless publicity campaign for his fighter. It resulted in a heavyweight championship fight against Jess Willard, promoted by Kearns's old Klondike friend, Rickard. Willard was heavily favored, but Dempsey knocked Willard out in the 3rd round on July 4, 1919, at Toledo to win the title.

Rickard also promoted Dempsey's first defense, against Georges Carpentier of France, which brought boxing's first $1 million gate. Then Kearns went off on his own, persuading the town of Shelby, Montana, to host Dempsey's fight against Tom Gibbons for a guarantee of $300,000. However, ticket sales brought only about $200,000, and Kearns took over the box office the day of the fight. After Dempsey won a 15-round decision, he and Kearns left with all the money, leaving Gibbons with nothing.

After Dempsey married actress Estelle Taylor in 1926, he dropped Kearns. However, Kearns had signed welterweight champion Mickey Walker, and he made a good deal of money during the next several years by matching Walker against heavier fighters.

At one time or another, he also handled Jackie Fields, Joey Maxim, Battling Nelson, Benny Leonard, and Abe Attell. His last champion was Archie Moore, the light heavyweight titlist who had two shots at the heavyweight crown.
★ International Boxing Hall of Fame

Keefe, Timothy J.
BASEBALL
b. Jan. 1, 1857, Cambridge, Mass.
d. April 23, 1933

After playing semipro baseball for four years, Keefe entered the minor leagues in 1879, and he joined the Troy team in the NL during the following season. A workhorse with a poor team, he had records of 18–27 in 1881 and 17–26 in 1882 before going to New York in the American Association, then a major league.

At the time, pitchers threw underhand from 50 feet away. (The modern distance is 60 feet, 6 inches.) Keefe had a 41–27 record in 1883, leading the league with 68 complete games in 68 starts, 619 innings pitched, and 361 shutouts. When the overhand delivery was legalized in 1884, he kept throwing underhand and had a 37–17 record.

Keefe joined the NL New York team in 1885. In his second season there, he led the league in victories with a 42–20 record, in complete games with 62, and in innings pitched with 535. New York won the 1888 pennant, with Keefe leading in victories with a 35–12 record, in winning percentage at .745, in shutouts with 8, and in strikeouts with 335.

His last big season was 1889, when he was 28–13 on another pennant-winning team. He jumped to the New York team in the Players' League in 1890 and had a 17–11 record. That league folded after one season; Keefe returned to the NL with New York but was released early in the season, and he then went to Philadelphia.

After a 5–11 mark, he bounced back with a 19–16 record in 1892 and retired after going 10–7 in 1893. Keefe then spent two seasons as an umpire.

At a time when most pitchers relied on a fastball and an occasional curve, Keefe specialized in the change-up. His advice to young pitchers was to learn control first and let speed come later.

★ Baseball Hall of Fame

Keeler, Wee Willie (William H.)

BASEBALL
b. March 3, 1872, Brooklyn, N.Y.
d. Jan. 1, 1923

Known for his dictum "Keep your eye clear and hit 'em where they ain't," the 5-foot-4, 140-pound Keeler was one of the finest hitters of his day, collecting singles in bunches.

He entered the major leagues with the New York NL team for a brief stint in 1892 and was traded to Brooklyn early in the 1893 season, when he appeared in only 27 games. After playing mostly at third base, he became an outfielder in 1894 with Baltimore, where he fit perfectly into an offense built around singles, stolen bases, and the hit and run play.

Keeler was good at bunting for base hits, and he also became an expert at the "Baltimore chop," bouncing the ball off the hard infield dirt so it would go over the heads of charging infielders. After batting .371, .377, and .386 in his first three seasons with Baltimore, he led the league in hitting with a .424 average in 1897 and a .385 average in 1898. He also led in hits both seasons, with 239 and 216.

Despite four pennants in five seasons, the Baltimore team was dismantled after the 1898 season, and Keeler went to Brooklyn with manager Ned Hanlon and several other teammates. He led the league with 140 runs in 1899 and with 204 hits in 1900, when Brooklyn won the pennant.

After hitting .339 and .333 in the next two seasons, Keeler was offered $10,000 to play for the AL's New York Highlanders (now the Yankees), making him baseball's highest-paid player. He hit over .300 each of his first four seasons in New York, then suddenly fell to .234 in 1907. He became a part-time player, batting .263 in 1908 and .264 in 1909, then returned to the New York NL team as a pinch hitter for manager John McGraw, a former Baltimore teammate. After getting three hits in ten at-bats in 1910, Keeler played in the minor leagues for a season and then retired. He later scouted for the NL's Boston Braves.

In 19 seasons, Keeler had a .341 average with 2,932 hits, including 241 doubles, 145 triples, and 33 home runs. He stole 495 bases, scored 1,719 runs, and had 810 RBI.

★ Baseball Hall of Fame

Kell, George C.

BASEBALL
b. Aug. 23, 1922, Swifton, Ark.

Best known for his hitting, Kell was also an outstanding defensive player who led AL third basemen in fielding percentage seven times in 11 full seasons in the major leagues. He played in just one game for the Philadelphia Athletics in 1943, then joined the team full-time in 1944.

During the 1946 season, Kell was traded to the Detroit Tigers. He hit .322 that year, .320 in 1947, and .304 in 1948, then won his only batting title with a .343 average in 1949.

Kell led the league in hits and doubles each of the next two seasons, with 218 and 56 in 1950, 191 and 36 in 1951. After 39 games of the 1952 season, Detroit traded him to the Boston Red Sox. He hit .311 that year and .307 in 1953, his only full season with Boston.

Traded to the Chicago White Sox in 1954, he dropped to .276 in only 97 games but came back with a .312 average in 1955. He was batting .313 after 21 games with Chicago in 1956, when he was traded to the Baltimore Orioles. He dropped all the way down to a .271 average that season and retired after batting .297 in 99 games with Baltimore in 1957.

In 1,795 games, Kell had 2,054 hits, including 385 doubles, 50 triples, and 78 home runs. He scored 881 runs and had 870 RBI.

★ Baseball Hall of Fame

Kelley, Joe (Joseph J.)

BASEBALL
b. Dec. 9, 1871, Cambridge, Mass.
d. Aug. 14, 1943

Primarily a pitcher in his first professional season in 1891, Kelley was bought by the Boston NL team during the season and used as an outfielder in 12 games. He returned to the minors in 1892, played entirely in the outfield, and was purchased by Pittsburgh. After hitting only .239 in 56 games, he was sold to the Baltimore NL team near the end of the season.

Kelley came into his own with Baltimore in 1893, hitting .305. It was the first of 12 consecutive seasons in which he batted over .300. The 5-foot-11, 190-pound Kelley worked hard under manager Ned Hanlon to develop his defensive skills. Gifted with a strong throwing arm, he soon became known for using his great speed to make running catches, robbing opponents of extra base hits.

Only once did Kelley lead the league in an offensive category, with 87 steals in 1896. But he scored more than 100 runs and had more than 100 RBI in five of his six seasons with Baltimore, helping lead the team to pennants from 1894 through 1897.

Despite that success, the Baltimore franchise was in financial trouble, and it folded in February 1899. Hanlon went to the Brooklyn Superbas, taking Kelley, Wee Willie Keeler, and Hugh Jennings with him. Those three players are all now in the Baseball Hall of Fame.

Kelley hit .325, .319, and .307 for Brooklyn before going back to Baltimore, this time with an AL team, in 1902. He managed the team for a short time, then returned to the NL with Cincinnati, where he again became playing manager. His combined average was .321 that season.

He gave up managing after the 1905 season but remained as a player through 1906, then spent a season as a playing manager in the minor leagues. He was named manager of the Boston NL team in 1908, when he played in his final 73 major league games.

In 1909, Kelley returned to the minor leagues as a manager, remaining through 1914. He was later a scout for the New York Yankees and a coach with the Brooklyn Dodgers.

Kelley played 1,853 games and had 2,220 hits, including 358 doubles, 194 triples, and 65 home runs. He stole 443 bases, scored 1,421 runs, and had 1,194 RBI.

★ Baseball Hall of Fame

Kelley, John J.

TRACK AND FIELD
b. Dec. 24, 1930, Norwich, Conn.

Called "Young John" by Boston sportswriters to distinguish him from John A. Kelley, another marathoner who is not related to him, Kelley attended Boston University and won the IC4A cross-country championship in 1953.

After graduating in 1954, he joined the Boston Athletic Association, which conducts the Boston Marathon. Kelley won the AAU marathon title from 1956 through 1963. His record time of

2:20:13.6 in 1960 stood until 1974. Kelley also won the AAU 15-kilometer run in 1957 and 1962, the 20-kilometer run from 1956 through 1960, the 25-kilometer from 1956 through 1959, and the 30-kilometer in 1959.

He captured the Boston Marathon in 1957 after finishing second the previous year. In 1959, he became the first American runner to win a gold medal in the Pan-American Games marathon.

★ National Track & Field Hall of Fame

Kelley, Larry (Lawrence M.)

FOOTBALL
b. May 30, 1915, Conneaut, Ohio

One of only two linemen ever to win the Heisman Trophy (the other was Leon Hart), Kelley was an All-American end at Yale in his senior year, 1936, when he captained the team and scored 91 points.

Kelley had the rare distinction of scoring at least one touchdown against Harvard and Princeton in each of his three years as a starter. He had a 54-yard touchdown reception in Yale's 14–13 win over Harvard in 1936 and a 46-yard touchdown catch that year in a 26–23 win over Princeton.

In 1937, Kelley played for the Boston Shamrocks of the American Football League.

★ College Football Hall of Fame

Kelley, Snooks (John)

HOCKEY
b. July 11, 1907, Cambridge, Mass.
d. April 11, 1986

Kelley played hockey at Boston College, graduating in 1930, and became a high school teacher. He agreed to serve as unpaid volunteer coach at his alma mater in 1933, after the sport had been dropped for a time because of the Depression.

Except for four years in the U.S. Navy during World War II, Kelley coached Boston College until 1975, when he retired. Unlike other major college hockey coaches, he refused to recruit Canadian players, and BC in 1949 became the first team to win the NCAA championship with a roster made up entirely of U.S. players.

Named coach of the year in 1959 and 1972, Kelley had a 501–242–15 record. He coached the U.S. national team in 1972.

★ U.S. Hockey Hall of Fame

Kelly, George L.

BASEBALL
b. Sept. 10, 1895, San Francisco, Calif.
d. Oct. 13, 1984

A 6-foot-4, 190-pound first baseman, Kelly was nicknamed "Highpockets" when he joined the NL's New York Giants during the 1915 season. He played only 17 games that year, and 49 in 1916, then was sold to the Pittsburgh Pirates during the 1917 season on the condition that he could be returned if he didn't make the team.

He didn't make it, and the Giants sent him to the minor leagues in 1918. Recalled toward the end of the 1919 season, he finally became a starter in 1920, when he led the league with 94 RBI.

Kelly was the home run leader with 23 in 1921, when he hit .308 and had 122 RBI, second in the league. He hit .328 with 107 RBI in 1922, .307 with 103 RBI in 1923, and .324 with a league-leading 136 RBI in 1924. The Giants won four straight pennants during those years.

Blessed with a strong arm and unusual range for a first baseman, Kelly was often used in the outfield, at second base, and at third base by the Giants after Bill Terry joined the team in 1925. He was traded to the Cincinnati Reds for another future Hall of Famer, center fielder Edd Roush, in 1927.

Although he wasn't at first happy with the trade, he was glad to be a full-time first baseman again. In three full seasons with Cincinnati, however, he failed to hit .300, and his home run figures dropped into single digits. During the 1930 season, he was sent to the Chicago Cubs after a short stay in the minors. He batted .308 that year, then spent a season in the minors. He ended his major league career after hitting only .243 in 64 games with Brooklyn in 1932.

Kelly later coached with Cincinnati and the Boston Braves, scouted for several teams, and was a minor league manager for one season.

In 1,622 games, Kelly had 1,778 hits, including 337 doubles, 76 triples, and 148 home runs, with 819 runs scored and 1,020 RBI.

★ Baseball Hall of Fame

Kelly, Jim (James E.)

FOOTBALL
b. Feb. 14, 1960, Pittsburgh, Pa.

Chosen in the first round of the 1984 NFL draft by the Buffalo Bills out of the University of Miami, Kelly elected to play for the Houston Gamblers in the new U.S. Football League. He was named the league's rookie of the year by *The Sporting News* after completing 370 of 587 passes for 5,219 yards and 44 touchdowns in 18 games.

The league folded in August 1986, and Kelly joined the Bills, becoming a starter immediately. He was put in charge of a hurry-up, no-huddle offense in which the quarterback calls the plays after sizing up the defensive alignment. That offense, and Kelly's skill at running it, took the Bills to four consecutive AFC championships, from 1990 through 1993. However, Buffalo lost in all four Super Bowls.

Kelly led the NFL with a 63.3 completion percentage and a rating of 101.2 in 1990, and he had a league-leading 33 touchdown passes in 1991. A very tough competitor who has often played despite injury, Kelly has missed some time with a chronic knee problem.

Through the 1994 season, he had completed 2,397 passes in 3,942 attempts for 29,527 yards and 201 touchdowns.

Kelly, John B., Jr.

ROWING
b. May 24, 1927, Philadelphia, Pa.
d. May 2, 1985

Kelly's father, John B. Sr., wasn't allowed to compete in the 1920 Henley Regatta because the English racing authorities considered him a professional. John B. Jr. got some sort of revenge for the family by winning the Diamond Sculls at Henley in 1947 and 1949.

His 1947 victory helped him win the Sullivan Award as the nation's outstanding athlete of the year.

Kelly won the national 1½-mile single sculls championship in 1946, 1948, and 1950, and from 1952 through 1956. He competed in four Olympics without winning a medal, but he won two gold medals at the Pan-American Games, in the single sculls in 1955 and in the doubles with William Knecht in 1959.

Kelly served as president of the AAU, as a vice president of the U.S. Olympic Committee, and as president of the International Swimming Hall of Fame. He died of a heart attack.

Kelly, John B., Sr.

ROWING
b. Oct. 4, 1889, Philadelphia, Pa.
d. June 26, 1960

Kelly began rowing with the Chamonix and Montrose Boat Clubs when he was 18, and the following year, 1909, he was admitted to Philadelphia's Vesper Boat Club, the outstanding club in the country at the time.

He scored an unusual double victory two years in a row, winning the national ¼-mile and 1½-mile singles sculls in 1919 and 1920.

In 1920, he went to England for the Diamond Sculls race at the Henley Regatta, but he wasn't allowed to compete. The Vesper Boat Club had previously been accused of professionalism, and Kelly, a bricklayer at the time, didn't meet English standards of amateurism because he worked as a laborer, which was considered to give him an advantage over "gentleman amateurs."

A few weeks afterward, Kelly won the gold medal in single sculls at the Olympics, beating Jack Beresford, who had won the Diamond Sculls competition. Thirty minutes later, he teamed with his cousin, Paul V. Costello, to win the double sculls gold medal. Kelly and Costello also won the double sculls at the 1924 Olympics.

Kelly later became a wealthy contractor. His daughter, Grace, starred in movies before becoming the Princess of

Monaco, and his son, John B. Jr., won the Diamond Sculls at Henley twice.
★ Olympic Hall of Fame

Kelly, King (Michael J.)
BASEBALL
b. Dec. 31, 1857, Troy, N.Y.
d. Nov. 8, 1894

The most colorful, most popular player of the 1880s, Kelly played with the Cincinnati NL team in 1878 and 1879, when he hit .348, then went to Chicago, where the fans began calling him "King" because of his dandyish off-the-field apparel, which featured a London silk hat, jeweled ascot, and patent leather shoes.

Primarily an outfielder, Kelly was a versatile player who handled every position, including pitcher, at one time or another. He spent most of the 1879 season at third base, played shortstop for most of 1882, and in his later years worked as a catcher.

Though not particularly fast, he was a good base stealer because he invented the hook slide, which often allowed him to avoid a fielder's tag, and he may also have been the first to use the headfirst slide. The chant of Chicago fans, "Slide, Kelly, slide," when he got on base, was adopted by Boston fans when he played for the Beaneaters, and it later became the title of a popular song.

Kelly led the league in doubles with 27 in 1881 and 37 in 1882, and he was the batting champion in 1884 with a .354 average and in 1886 with a .388 average. He also led in runs scored three years in a row, with 120 in 1884, 124 in 1885, and 155 in 1886.

After he demanded more money before the 1887 season, he was sold to Boston for an unprecedented $10,000. National League owners that year established a salary limit of $2,000. When Kelly refused to accept that amount, the Beaneaters offered him another $3,000, supposedly for the use of his photograph in advertising.

The Boston fans loved the "$10,000 Beauty" even more than the Chicago fans had. After he hit .322 and stole 84 bases in his first season there, they gave

him a house and a carriage, drawn by two white horses, in which he could ride to the park.

After hitting .318 in 1888 and .294 in 1889, when he led the league with 41 doubles, Kelly became playing manager of the Boston team in the new Players' League. The league lasted just one season. In 1891, he went to Cincinnati in the American Association, then a major league. The Cincinnati franchise didn't last the season, and Kelly returned to Boston with the American Association team there. After just four games, though, he jumped back to the Beaneaters.

A heavy drinker, Kelly was rapidly losing his baseball skills. He batted only .189 in 78 games in 1892. The following season, he went to the New York NL team and was ordered to take a Turkish bath before every game to remove the alcohol from his system. He was suspended early in the season for passing up too many of his Turkish baths.

Kelly was still popular in Boston, and he was offered a chance to appear on stage there. While taking the boat from New York, he caught a severe cold, and he died a few days later of pneumonia. As his body lay in state at the Elks Hall, 5,000 loyal fans turned out to pay him a final tribute.

In 1,455 games, Kelly had 1,813 hits, including 359 doubles, 102 triples, and 69 home runs. He had 950 RBI, and he scored 1,357 runs. Stolen base figures weren't kept during the early part of his career, but he had 368 steals from 1886 through 1893.
★ Baseball Hall of Fame

Kelly, Leroy
FOOTBALL
b. May 20, 1942, Philadelphia, Pa.

A four-year starter as a halfback at Morgan State College, Kelly joined the NFL's Cleveland Browns as an eighth-round draft choice in 1964. He was used primarily as a kick returner during his first two seasons. Kelly led the league in punt returns in 1965, running back 17 kicks for 265 yards, a 16.5 average, and two touchdowns.

He became a starter at running back when Jim Brown retired after that season. The 6-foot, 205-pound Kelly had such a fast start that he was repeatedly penalized for illegal motion during his first several games, but the Browns sent films to the league office to prove that he wasn't moving too soon, and officials stopped penalizing him improperly.

Kelly won the rushing "triple crown" in 1967, leading the NFL in yards with 1,205, average with 5.1 yards per carry, and rushing touchdowns with 11. Only seven other players have ever accomplished that. He won the Bert Bell Trophy as the league's player of the year in 1968, when he led the league once more with 1,269 yards and 16 touchdowns.

Slowed by a leg injury early in the 1969 season, Kelly was never quite the same. He retired after the 1973 season. A consensus All-Pro in 1967 and 1968, he played in six Pro Bowls. During his ten years in the NFL, Kelly gained 7,274 yards and scored 74 touchdowns on 1,727 rushing attempts. He caught 190 passes for 2,281 yards, a 12.0 average, and 12 touchdowns; returned 94 punts for 990 yards, a 10.5 average, and 3 touchdowns; and ran back 76 kickoffs for 1,784 yards, a 23.5 average.
★ Pro Football Hall of Fame

Kelly, Pamela R.
BASKETBALL
b. March 17, 1960, Columbia, La.

A three-time All-American at Louisiana Tech, from 1980 through 1982, Kelly won the Wade Trophy and the Broderick Award as the nation's outstanding woman college basketball player in 1982. She led the school to the top ranking in the nation in her junior and senior years.

In her four seasons as a starter, Kelly scored 2,979 points in 153 games, an average of 19.5 per game, and pulled down 1,511 rebounds. She shot a remarkable .623 from the field, with 1,193 field goals in 1,916 attempts.

Kelly, Red (Leonard P.)
HOCKEY
b. July 9, 1927, Simcoe, Ont.

Beginning in 1947, Kelly spent 12½ seasons with the Detroit Red Wings as a great rushing defenseman who was among the top ten scorers in the NHL three times. He won the first Norris Trophy as the league's best defenseman in 1954, and he won the Lady Byng Trophy, symbolic of combining skillful play with gentlemanly conduct, four times, in 1951, 1953, 1954, and 1961. Detroit won four Stanley Cup championships during his tenure.

Then Punch Imlach, general manager and coach of the Toronto Maple Leafs, decided he needed a center who could play defense, primarily to stop Jean Beliveau of the Montreal Canadiens. Kelly refused to report to the New York Rangers after a trade in the middle of the 1959–60 season, so Imlach acquired him, gave him the money he wanted, and moved him to center.

Kelly not only did the defensive job Imlach wanted, he became a fine playmaker. The moody young Frank Mahovlich increased his goal scoring from 18 to 48 in his first full season playing on Kelly's line, and Toronto won four Stanley Cups in Kelly's seven and a half seasons with them.

After the 1966–67 season, Kelly retired as a player to become coach of the expansion Los Angeles Kings, and he guided them to a surprising second-place finish in the Western Division. Two years later, he was fired by the Kings and hired by the Pittsburgh Penguins. The Penguins finished second in 1969–70, and Kelly won the Adams Trophy as the league's coach of the year.

He was fired again in the middle of the 1972–73 season, and seven months later he returned to Toronto as head coach. After four seasons there, he retired.

In his 20 seasons as a player, Kelly was in 1,316 games and scored 281 goals with 542 assists. He had 33 goals and 59 assists in 164 playoff games. He was in the playoffs 19 times, an NHL record he shares with Gordie Howe. As a coach, he had 278 victories, 330 defeats, and 134 ties.
★ Hockey Hall of Fame

Kennedy, Cortez

FOOTBALL

b. Aug. 23, 1968, Osceola, Ark.

After attending Northwest Mississippi Community College, Kennedy won a football scholarship to the University of Miami and was named an All-American at defensive tackle in 1989.

The Seattle Seahawks made him the third player chosen in the 1990 NFL draft. He stayed out of training camp while his contract was being negotiated and finally signed just two days before the season began.

As a result, Kennedy got off to a slow start, but in 1991 he went to the Pro Bowl, and the following season he was named to *The Sporting News* All-Pro team after recording 14 quarterback sacks. A nose tackle with Seattle, the 6-foot-3, 293-pound Kennedy has amazing quickness as well as strength and usually occupies at least two blockers.

Kennedy, Theodore S. ("Teeder")

HOCKEY

b. Dec. 12, 1925, Humberstone, Ont.

When he was only 16, Kennedy was invited to training camp with the Montreal Canadiens, but he got homesick and left. The Canadiens traded him to the Toronto Maple Leafs, and he began his NHL career in the 1942–43 season, when he was 18.

He starred for the 1947 Stanley Cup champions, the youngest team ever to win the NHL championship. They beat the Montreal Canadiens in the finals, with Kennedy scoring the winning goal in the final game. The following season he was named Toronto captain, and the Leafs won two more Stanley Cups in a row.

Kennedy was involved in one of hockey's ugliest incidents in 1950, during the Stanley Cup semifinals against the Detroit Red Wings. In the first game, Kennedy avoided a check from Detroit's Gordie Howe, and Howe suffered a serious head injury when he crashed into the boards. The Red Wings thought Kennedy had deliberately injured Howe with his stick.

In the second game, one of the Red Wings tripped Kennedy and was whistled for a penalty. As Kennedy was getting up, Detroit's Ted Lindsay cross-checked him. In the meantime, Leo Reise of the Red Wings attacked a Toronto defenseman with his stick, left him lying bloody on the ice, and then went after Kennedy. Backed into the boards, Kennedy was grabbed from behind by a Detroit fan who held him while two Red Wings pummeled him. Fortunately, he wasn't seriously hurt.

Detroit went on to win the series and the cup, but Toronto won again in 1951, beating Montreal in the only series in which every game went into overtime, Kennedy scoring one of the winning goals as the Maple Leafs won in five games.

Kennedy won the Hart Trophy as the league's most valuable player in 1955, then retired. However, he returned to the team for the second half of the 1956–57 season because the Maple Leafs were depleted by injuries.

In 696 regular season games, Kennedy had 231 goals and 329 assists. He scored 29 goals, with 31 assists, in 78 playoff games.

★ Hockey Hall of Fame

Keogan, George E.

BASKETBALL

b. March 8, 1890, Detroit Lakes, Minn.

d. Feb. 17, 1943

While Knute Rockne was coaching great football teams at Notre Dame, Keogan was quietly beginning to build a marvelous record as a basketball coach. A graduate of the University of Minnesota's School of Dentistry, he coached at high schools in Illinois and then at small colleges before arriving at Notre Dame in 1923.

Keogan is credited with inventing the shifting man to man defense, although he may have adapted it from the Original Celtics, since he was a student of the professional game. He taught a deliberate offense, using continual cuts and screens until a player had a clear path to the basket, or a clear shot at it.

His teams won Helms Athletic Foundation championships in 1927 and 1936 and went through some remarkable stretches, winning 38 games out of 40 at one point and 42 of 47 at another. Keogan died of a heart attack during the 1942–43 season and was replaced by "Moose" Krause. His record at Notre Dame was 327 wins and 96 losses, a .773 percentage. Keogan's overall collegiate record was 385–117, and his percentage of .767 is seventh best of all time.

★ Basketball Hall of Fame

Keon, David M.
HOCKEY
b. March 22, 1940, Noranda, P.Q.

A clever skater and stick handler, Keon left St. Michael's College to play professional hockey and joined the Toronto Maple Leafs for the 1960–61 season, scoring 20 goals to win the Calder Cup as the NHL's rookie of the year.

Keon won the Lady Byng Trophy for combining excellent play with sportsmanship in 1962 and 1963. When Toronto won the 1967 Stanley Cup, he was named most valuable player in the playoffs. He had just one goal and one assist in the six-game victory over the Montreal Canadiens but turned in an outstanding defensive performance as the Maple Leafs held Montreal to just four goals in their four victories.

The long-time Maple Leaf captain, Keon ended his career with the Hartford Whalers in 1981–82. He scored 986 points on 396 goals and 590 assists in 1,296 regular season games and added 32 goals and 36 assists for 68 points in 92 playoff games.

★ Hockey Hall of Fame

Keough, Harry J.
SOCCER
b. Nov. 15, 1927, St. Louis, Mo.

A fine all-around athlete who excelled at soccer, Keough was this country's most successful college soccer coach. He played for the St. Louis Raiders when they won the National Challenge Cup in 1952 and for the Kutis Football Club of St. Louis which won

the NCC six years in a row, 1956 through 1961.

Keough started at fullback for the U.S. World Cup teams in 1950, 1954, and 1958 and was the captain of the U.S. Olympic soccer team in 1952 and 1956. He became coach at St. Louis University in 1967. He produced four NCAA champions (in 1969, 1970, 1972, and 1973) and one co-champion (in 1967) in 16 seasons there. Keough retired after the 1982 season with a record of 213 wins, 50 losses, and 23 ties.

Kerr, Andy (Andrew)
FOOTBALL
b. Oct. 7, 1878, Cheyenne, Wyo.
d. Feb. 12, 1969

A long-time assistant to the legendary "Pop" Warner, Kerr didn't become a genuine head coach until he was 48, but he then compiled an excellent record at three colleges.

Kerr was a 130-pound quarterback at Dickinson College, where he also played baseball and was a high jumper on the track team. He studied law after graduating in 1900, went into teaching for a time, and coached high school football.

He became track coach at the University of Pittsburgh in 1914 and began assisting Warner with football the following season. In 1922, Warner agreed to coach at Stanford, but he was under contract with Pittsburgh until 1924. Kerr went to Stanford to install Warner's complex double wing attack and had an 11–7–0 record in two seasons.

After assisting Warner at Stanford for two more seasons, Kerr took over at Washington and Jefferson in 1926. His 1927 team was undefeated, winning seven games and tying two. He was hired at Colgate in 1929 and spent 18 seasons there, compiling a 95–50–7 record. His 1932 team won all nine of its games, outscoring the opposition, 264–0.

Kerr retired briefly after the 1946 season but returned to coaching at little Lebanon Valley College in Pennsylvania for three more seasons, 1947 through 1949. His teams there won 15 games while losing eight and tying two. Kerr's overall record was 137–71–13.

His teams played a wide open, razzle-dazzle style of offense featuring many lateral passes. To develop the lateral attack, Kerr learned from Stanford rugby coaches and players and from a Canadian rugby coach. His teams spent long hours practicing laterals to reduce the possibility of fumbling.

★ College Football Hall of Fame

Kerr, Red (John G.)

BASKETBALL
b. Aug. 17, 1932, Chicago, Ill.

A 6-foot-9, 230-pound center, Kerr averaged 25.3 points a game as a senior at the University of Illinois and 18.6 points for his three-year career. He was chosen by the Syracuse Nationals in the first round of the 1954 NBA draft.

Rather than playing near the basket like most pro centers, Kerr liked to station himself near the foul line, where he could use his soft jump shot and excellent passing ability.

He helped take Syracuse to the NBA championship in his rookie season. Kerr remained with the team when it moved to Philadelphia and became known as the Warriors in 1963. He was traded to the Baltimore Bullets in 1965 and spent his final season as a player with them.

The Chicago Bulls chose Kerr in the 1966 expansion draft, and he became the team's first coach. The Bulls were the first expansion team ever to go to the playoffs in its first season of existence. Kerr was named NBA coach of the year for that accomplishment.

In 1968, Kerr took over another expansion team, the Phoenix Suns. He was replaced after a 15–23 start in 1969–70.

Kerr scored 12,480 points in 905 regular season games, a 13.8 average, and had 10,103 rebounds and 2,005 assists. He added 933 points, 827 rebounds, and 152 assists in 76 playoff games. As a coach, he had a 93–190 record.

Ketcham, Henry H.

FOOTBALL
b. June 17, 1891, Highwood, N.J.

One of the first "roving centers," a kind of early version of the modern linebacker, Ketcham was an All-American at Yale in his junior season, 1912. The following season he was moved to guard, and he made second-team All-American at that position.

Ketcham was six feet tall and weighed only 175 pounds, but he was very fast and had a wiry strength that could surprise opposing blockers. As captain in 1913, Ketcham appointed Yale's first paid coach, Howard Jones. Up until then, the previous year's captain had always returned as a volunteer coach. Ketcham's move was, in part, a response to Harvard's having hired Percy Haughton as its first professional coach in 1908.

★ College Football Hall of Fame

Ketchel, Stanley [Stanislaus Kiecal]

BOXING
b. Sept. 14, 1887, Grand Rapids, Mich.
d. Oct. 15, 1910

Orphaned at 14, when his parents were murdered, Ketchel became a hobo and often fought with other hobos for food. He began boxing professionally in 1903. During an eight-month stretch in 1905, he knocked out 14 opponents in a row, winning his nickname, the "Michigan Assassin."

Ketchel won the vacant world middleweight title on February 22, 1908, when he knocked out Mike "Twin" Sullivan in the 1st round at Colma, California. After three defenses, he lost the championship to Billy Papke on September 7, 1908, in Los Angeles. When the fighters met in the center of the ring for the traditional handshake before the bout, Papke knocked Ketchel down. Fighting in a daze, Ketchel was knocked down three more times in the first round, but he managed to last into the 12th round, when he was knocked out.

In a rematch on November 28 in San Francisco, Ketchel won the title back with an 11th-round knockout. He defended the championship four times and then met Jack Johnson for the heavyweight title on October 16, 1909. Outweighed by about 50 pounds, Ketchel more than held his own for 11 rounds. He knocked Johnson down with the first punch of the 12th round, but Johnson got up and knocked Ketchel out with a tremendous right hand.

Ketchel was training on a farm in Conway, Missouri, for a 1910 fight when he became involved with a female cook. He was shot to death by a jealous farmhand, Walter Dipley.

Ketchel won 53 bouts, 50 of them by knockout; lost 4, 2 by knockout; and fought 4 draws and 4 no-decisions.

★ International Boxing Hall of Fame

Kidd, Billy (William W.)

SKIING
b. April 13, 1943, Burlington, Vt.

America's first real world-class male skier, Kidd attended the University of Colorado. He was on the 1962 national ski team but missed most of the 1963 season with a chronic sprained ankle.

In 1964, he became the first American male to win an Olympic medal in Alpine skiing, taking a silver in the slalom and a bronze in the Alpine combined. He was the U.S. national giant slalom champion that year.

Kidd and the great Jean-Claude Killy of France had a number of duels on the European circuit in 1966, and Kidd won several of them. He missed the 1967 season with a broken leg, and the chronic ankle sprain bothered him during much of 1968. However, he beat Killy in a World Cup slalom in Colorado that year and managed to finish fifth in the Olympic giant slalom.

After winning his second World Cup Slalom, at Squaw Valley in 1969, Kidd won the world Alpine combined event in 1970. It was the first world championship ever for an American male skier. He then joined the professional International Ski Racing Association and won the giant slalom and alpine combined events at the ISRA world championships.

Recurring injuries forced his retirement in 1972. He became ski director at Steamboat Springs, Colorado, did television commentary, helped coach the U.S.

team, and wrote two instructional books on the sport.

Kiefer, Adolph G.

SWIMMING
b. June 27, 1918, Chicago, Ill.

The first swimmer to break the 1-minute barrier in the 100-yard backstroke, Kiefer won a gold medal in the 100-meter event at the 1936 Olympics. He continued competing until 1946 and probably would have won more medals, except that there were no Olympic Games in 1940 or 1944 because of World War II.

Kiefer won the AAU outdoor 100-meter backstroke nine years in a row, from 1935 through 1943, and was the 220-yard freestyle champion in 1938. He also won the 300-meter individual medley event in 1938, 1939, and 1943.

Indoors, he won AAU championships in the 150-yard backstroke from 1935 through 1937, from 1939 through 1942, and in 1944 and 1945, and in the 300-yard individual medley from 1940 through 1942 and in 1944 and 1945.

After he retired from swimming, Kiefer was put in charge of swimming instruction for the U.S. Navy because of the number of deaths by drowning that occurred during the war. He also owned a company that manufactured swimming-related items and pool accessories.

Kiesling, Walter A.

FOOTBALL
b. May 27, 1903, St. Paul, Minn.
d. March 2, 1962

After playing guard at little St. Thomas College in Minnesota, the 6-foot-2, 245-pound Kiesling became a professional with the NFL's Duluth Eskimos in 1926. He remained with the Eskimos through 1927, played for the Pottsville Maroons in 1928, and then settled down with the Chicago Cardinals for five seasons. He was named to the 1932 All-Pro team.

After spending 1934 with the Chicago Bears, Kiesling played for the Green Bay Packers in 1935 and 1936. There he was reunited with a long-time friend, Johnny "Blood" McNally; they had been teammates in Duluth and Pottsville.

When McNally went to Pittsburgh as player-coach in 1937, Kiesling went with him as assistant coach and part-time player, and he became head coach when McNally left in 1939, remaining through 1940.

Kiesling, who retired as a player after the 1938 season, had an unusual coaching career. He said he preferred being an assistant coach, his usual role, but he was pressed into service as a head coach three times. An assistant with Pittsburgh in 1941, he became head coach again for the last game of the season and took the team to a 7–4–0 record in 1942.

Because of the World War II manpower shortage, the Pittsburgh and Philadelphia teams merged in 1943, when Kiesling and "Greasy" Neale served as co-coaches. Pittsburgh and the Chicago Cardinals merged in 1944, and Kiesling was again a co-coach, with Phil Handler.

After serving as an assistant in Green Bay for four seasons, Kiesling returned to Pittsburgh as an assistant in 1949 and was made head coach once again just before the 1955 season started. He retired after the 1956 season because of poor health. His overall record was 30–55–5.
★ Pro Football Hall of Fame

Killebrew, Harmon C.
BASEBALL
b. June 29, 1936, Payette, Idaho

Nicknamed "Killer" because of his power, the 5-foot-11, 213-pound Killebrew was a right-handed first baseman who won six AL home runs championships and was the league's RBI leader three times.

He spent parts of five seasons with the Washington Senators, from 1954 through 1958, before becoming a full-time player in 1959. Although he batted only .242 in 1959, he led the league with 42 home runs and also had 105 RBI.

Killebrew was used mostly at third base that season but was moved to first the following year because of his defensive liabilities. The franchise moved to Minnesota and became known as the Twins in 1961. In Minnesota, Killebrew won three consecutive home run titles

with 48 in 1962, 45 in 1963, and 49 in 1964. He was also the league leader in RBI with 126 in 1962 and in slugging with a .555 percentage in 1963.

Despite being walked a league-leading 131 times in 1967, Killebrew was again the home run leader with 44, and he had 113 RBI. He played in only 100 games, many as a pinch hitter, because of injury in 1968, but in 1969 he won the league's most valuable player award. His 49 home runs and 140 RBI led the league, as did his 145 walks.

After hitting 41 home runs with 113 RBI in 1970, Killebrew's home run totals began to decline. Still, he was the league's leader with 119 RBI in 1971. Killebrew spent three more injury-laden seasons in Minnesota and finished his career with the Kansas City Royals in 1975, when he batted only .199 with 14 home runs in 106 games.

In 2,435 games, Killebrew batted .256 with 2,086 hits, including 290 doubles, 24 triples, and 573 home runs. He had 1,584 RBI and scored 1,283 runs.
★ Baseball Hall of Fame

Killinger, Glenn
FOOTBALL
b. 1900

Hugo Bezdek called Killinger the greatest athlete he coached during his 12 seasons at Penn State. A quarterback, Killinger was an outstanding runner, especially on Bezdek's spinner play from the single wing. He had a 90-yard touchdown run against Georgia Tech and a 70-yard run against North Carolina State in 1921, when he was named an All-American.

Killinger played for the NFL's New York Giants in 1926.
★ College Football Hall of Fame

Kilpatrick, John Reed
FOOTBALL
b. June 15, 1889, New York, N.Y.
d. May 7, 1960

An All-American end at Yale in 1909 and 1910, the 5-foot-10, 190-pound Kilpatrick was best known for his play on a strong defensive team that didn't allow a single point in 1909. He captained the team in 1910, when he caught a touchdown pass to beat Princeton, 5–3; it was the only time Princeton was scored on that season.

A sprinter and hurdler, Kilpatrick was also captain of the school's track team as a senior. He later continued his involvement with sports as president of Madison Square Garden from 1933 until his death.

★ College Football Hall of Fame

Kimbrough, John A.

FOOTBALL
b. 1918, Haskell, Tex.

"Jarrin' Jawn" was a 6-foot-2, 222-pound fullback with speed, an All-American at Texas A & M in 1939 and 1940. He starred in the school's 14–13 win over Tulane in the 1940 Sugar Bowl, gaining 152 yards on 26 runs and scoring both touchdowns against one of the nation's strongest defensive lines. Tulane had given up only 46 points in nine regular season games.

During the 1940 season, Kimbrough gained 658 yards on 158 carries, scored 7 touchdowns, caught 9 passes, and had 6 interceptions. In the Cotton Bowl, Fordham used a defense meant specifically to stop Kimbrough, but he gained 75 yards in 18 runs, scored the winning touchdown, and blocked an extra point try that would have tied the game.

After serving in the Army during World War II, Kimbrough played with the Los Angeles Dons of the All-American Football Conference from 1946 through 1948. As a professional, he carried the ball 329 times for 1,224 yards, a 3.7 average, and scored 17 rushing touchdowns. He also caught 35 passes, 6 for touchdowns.

★ College Football Hall of Fame

Kinard, Bruiser (Frank)

FOOTBALL
b. Oct. 23, 1914, Pelahatchie, Miss.
d. Sept. 7, 1985

Though he weighed only 190 pounds, Kinard was an iron man at tackle at the University of Mississippi, averaging 55 minutes a game in 34 games as a starter. In 1936, he played 562 consecutive minutes and 708 out of a possible 720 minutes for the season.

Kinard captained the team in 1937, when he was named an All-American by some selectors. He also played guard on the basketball team and ran the 440-yard dash and threw weights on the track team.

He joined the NFL's Brooklyn Dodgers in 1938, and his weight eventually went to 215 pounds — still light for a tackle, but he retained his iron-man reputation, often playing 60 minutes a game. During his nine-year professional career, he missed just one game, when a hand infection turned into gangrene, and doctors refused to let him play.

Kinard played for the Dodgers through 1944, spent a year in the Navy, and then joined the New York Yankees of the All-American Football Conference for two seasons before retiring. He was named an All-Pro in 1940, 1941, 1943, and 1944.

★ College Football Hall of Fame; Pro Football Hall of Fame

Kiner, Ralph McP.

BASEBALL
b. Oct. 27, 1922, Santa Rita, N.Mex.

In a relatively brief career, Kiner hit a lot of home runs. He once told a sportswriter, "Singles hitters drive Fords and such. Home run hitters drive Cadillacs." After becoming the NL's first $100,000 player, he did drive a Cadillac.

The 6-foot-2, 195-pound outfielder, who batted right-handed, joined the Pittsburgh Pirates in 1946 and led the league in home runs each of his first seven seasons, with 23 in 1946, 51 in 1947, 40 in 1948, 54 in 1949, 47 in 1950, 42 in 1951, and 37 in 1952.

He also led in RBI with 127 in 1949; in runs with 124 in 1951; in walks with 117 in 1949, 137 in 1951, and 110 in 1952; and in slugging percentage with .639 in 1947, .658 in 1949, and .627 in 1951.

Kiner was traded to the Chicago Cubs during the 1953 season, and he was forced to retire because of chronic back problems after playing for the AL's Cleveland Indians in 1955. His ratio of a home run for every 7.1 times at bat is second only to Babe Ruth's.

In 1,472 games, Kiner batted .279 with 1,451 hits, including 216 doubles, 39 triples, and 369 home runs. He had 1,015 RBI and scored 971 runs.

★ Baseball Hall of Fame

King, Bernard

BASKETBALL
b. Dec. 4, 1956, Brooklyn, N.Y.

After averaging 25.8 points per game in three years as a starter at the University of Tennessee and leading NCAA Division I schools with a .622 field goal percentage as a sophomore, King left school after his junior year to enter the 1977 NBA draft.

He was chosen in the second round by the New Jersey Nets and averaged 24.2 points per game to make the all-rookie team. A 6-foot-7, 205-pound forward, King was traded to the Utah Jazz in 1979 but missed most of the season with a knee injury and was sent to the Golden State Warriors.

King was named comeback player of the year after averaging 21.9 points a game in 1980–81. Golden State traded him to the New York Knicks in 1982. With New York, King led the NBA in scoring with 32.9 points a game in 1984–85.

Because of a career-threatening knee injury, King missed all of the 1985–86 season and played in only six games in 1986–87. He was released by the Knicks and signed with the Washington Bullets in 1987.

The recurring knee problem forced him out for all of the 1991–92 season, but King returned to appear in 32 games with New Jersey in 1992–93. In 874 regular season games, he scored 19,655 points, an average of 22.5 per game, and he added 687 points in 28 playoff games, a 24.5 average.

King, Betsy (Elizabeth)

GOLF
b. Aug. 13, 1955, Reading, Pa.
King was a member of the national

intercollegiate championship golf team at Furman University in 1976. She joined the LPGA tour after graduating in 1977 but didn't win her first tournament until 1984, when she had three wins.

The 5-foot-6 blonde was the tour's leading money-winner in 1984 with $266,771, and she also took the player of the year award.

King claimed her first major victory in 1987, when she holed a bunker shot on the 70th hole of the Dinah Shore to tie Patty Sheehan, and she then beat Sheehan in a playoff.

In 1989, King won her first U.S. Women's Open and set a record by winning $654,132 to claim her second player of the year award. She repeated in the Open in 1990 and also won her second Dinah Shore championship that year.

King was the tour's money leader and player of the year again in 1993. Through that season, she had won 29 tournaments and was second all-time with $4,502,635 in earnings.

King, Billie Jean (Moffitt)

TENNIS
b. Nov. 22, 1943, Long Beach, Calif.

Billie Jean Moffitt loved softball as a girl, but her father decided that sport was unladylike, and he persuaded her to take tennis lessons when she was 11. She fell in love with the new sport and began playing in tournaments.

At 16, she was ranked nineteenth in the country, and the great Alice Marble began coaching her. Marble later recalled that when the teenager stayed with her on weekends, "She was so crazy about tennis, I'd have to lock her in her room to do her homework."

Under Marble's tutelage, King went from nineteenth to fourth in less than a year. In 1961, she won her first Wimbledon title, the women's doubles with Karen Hantze. The following year, she upset Margaret Smith, the top seed, in the first round of the singles tournament, and the British press began calling her "Little Miss Moffitt."

She was to become better known under her married name, though. In 1965, she married Larry King, a law student who became her business manager.

As Billie Jean King, she won her first major singles title at Wimbledon in 1966. She went on to win that championship five more times, in 1967, 1968, 1972, 1973, and 1975. She won the U.S. Open in 1967, 1971, 1972, and 1974; the Australian Open in 1968; and the French Open in 1972.

Coming into her own when the sport was becoming a television staple, King helped transform the popular image of women's tennis with her athletic, aggressive style of play. One sportswriter described her style: "She buzzes the net like a torpedo approaching for the blast."

King's influence extended beyond her on-court performance. After the middle-aged Bobby Riggs struck a blow for male chauvinism by beating Margaret Court on Mother's Day, 1973, King struck back by beating him at the Houston Astrodome on September 30. Billed as the "Battle of the Sexes," the match drew the largest crowd ever to watch tennis, 30,472, and was also a major television event.

After defeating Riggs, 6–4, 6–3, 6–3, King told the media, "This is the culmination of a lifetime in the sport. Tennis has always been reserved for the rich, the white, the males — and I've always been pledged to change all that."

King was one of the cofounders of the Virginia Slims Circuit, created in 1970 to increase prize money for women players, and of the Women's Tennis Association, which was instrumental in getting the U.S. Open to award equal prizes to men and women. She was also a founder of the Women's Sports Foundation and of _WomenSports_ magazine.

In 1976, King teamed with Martina Navratilova to win the women's doubles at Wimbledon, giving her a record 20 Wimbledon championships. In addition to 12 grand slam singles titles, sixth on the all-time list, and 39 overall grand slam championships, third all-time, King won 29 Virginia Slims events. She ranks fifth in tournament victories with 71.

King was the Associated Press female athlete of the year in 1967 and 1973. Largely because of her victory over Riggs, _Sports Illustrated_ didn't name its annual "Sportsman of the Year" for 1973. Instead, King was on the magazine's cover as "Sportswoman of the Year."

★ International Tennis Hall of Fame; International Women's Sports Hall of Fame

King, Micki (Maxine J.)
DIVING
b. July 26, 1944, Pontiac, Mich.

King began diving when she was ten. When she entered the University of Michigan in 1962, she went out for water polo and was twice an All-American goalie. She also played for two AAU national champions with the Ann Arbor Swim Club.

Dick Kimball, Michigan water sports coach, encouraged King to take up competitive diving again. After graduating, she enlisted in the Air Force, worked with the Michigan ROTC unit, and trained under Kimball. King won the national outdoor 3-meter championship in 1965, 1967, 1969, and 1970, and was also the 1-meter champion in 1967 and the platform champion in 1969. Indoors, King won the 3-meter event in 1971 and 1972, the platform event in 1965 and 1971.

A favorite going into the 1968 Olympics, she was leading in the springboard finals after eight dives, but she broke her left forearm when she hit the board on the ninth dive. Nevertheless, she performed her tenth and final dive, dropping to fourth place.

She won her gold medal in 1972, taking the lead with her eighth dive and finishing with the same reverse 1½ somersault that she'd broken her arm on. King wept at the medal ceremony and commented afterward, "I've been diving longer than the girl who came in second has lived."

King retired from competition after the Olympics and became diving coach at the Air Force Academy. She was transferred to Tacoma in 1978 and worked with young divers in her spare time there before returning to the academy as men's and women's diving coach in 1983.

★ International Women's Sports Hall of Fame

King, Phillip

FOOTBALL
b. March 16, 1872, Washington, D.C.
d. Jan. 7, 1938

King was only 5-foot-6, but he weighed 190 pounds, most of it muscle. In four years as a starting back at Princeton, he scored 50 touchdowns and kicked 56 conversions. During that period, 1890 through 1893, the team won 46 games while losing only four and tying one.

As a senior in 1893, King was the Princeton captain. At that time, the captain really coached the team, and King developed an open style of offense featuring long laterals, often two or three on a single play. Princeton won all 11 of its games that season, outscoring the opposition, 270 to 14.

An All-American at quarterback in 1891 and 1893 and at halfback in 1892, King coached the University of Wisconsin from 1896 through 1902 and in 1905, compiling a 63–11–2 record. He coached Georgetown to a 7–3–0 record in 1903.

★ College Football Hall of Fame

King, Stacey (Ronald Stacey)

BASKETBALL
b. Jan. 29, 1967, Lawton, Okla.

An All-American and *The Sporting News* college player of the year in 1989, after averaging 26.0 points for the University of Oklahoma, King was chosen by the Chicago Bulls in the first round of the NBA draft.

The 6-foot-11, 230-pound King was a center in college but became a backup power forward and center with the talent-laden Bulls and saw little playing time. His performance was generally disappointing. He was traded to the Minnesota Timberwolves during the 1993–94 season. Through his first five seasons, he scored 2,491 points in 362 regular season games, an average of 6.9, and had 263 points in 60 playoff games, a 4.4 average.

Kingdom, Roger

TRACK AND FIELD
b. Aug. 26, 1962, Unadilla, Ga.

Kingdom won scholarships in football and track to the University of Pittsburgh in 1981. He won the NCAA outdoor 110-meter high hurdles championship in 1983 and the indoor 55-meter hurdles in 1984.

The 6-foot-3, 180-pounder won his first international championship at the 1983 Pan-American Games, in the 110-meter event. After placing third in the 1984 Olympic trials, Kingdom upset the favorite, Rod Foster, to win the gold medal in a very close finish. Kingdom thought he'd finished second until he looked up at the giant video screen to see the slow-motion replay, and he then began jumping up and down in joy.

After winning the national outdoor title in 1985, Kingdom was troubled by injuries, but he went undefeated in 1988, winning the national championship, the Olympic trials, and his second gold medal in an Olympic record 12.98 seconds.

On August 16, 1989, Kingdom ran a world record 12.92 seconds. He also won the national and World Cup championships in the 110-meter and the world indoor title in the 60-meter high hurdles. He retired from competition after winning the 110-meter event at the national outdoor meet and at the Goodwill Games.

Kinnick, Nile

FOOTBALL
b. Oct. 6, 1902, Adel, Iowa
d. June 2, 1943

His great football ability, combined with an early death as a wartime fighter pilot, made Kinnick one of college football's brightest legends. A 5-foot-9, 175-pound quarterback, Kinnick led the University of Iowa to a surprising 6–1–1 record in 1939. He was named an All-American, won the Heisman Trophy as the outstanding college player of the year, and was named the Associated Press athlete of the year.

He began the season by scoring 23 points on 3 touchdowns and 5 conversions in a 41–0 win over South Dakota.

The following week, Iowa beat Indiana for the first time since 1921 when Kinnick decided to pass on fourth down rather than trying a field goal to tie the game. He threw for a touchdown to win the game, 29–26.

After a loss to powerful Michigan, Kinnick threw three touchdown passes to beat Wisconsin, 19–13. Against previously unbeaten Notre Dame, Kinnick punted 16 times for an average of nearly 46 yards to keep the game close, ran for Iowa's only touchdown, and kicked the conversion to win the game, 7–6.

Iowa was trailing Minnesota, 9–0, in the fourth quarter, but Kinnick threw two touchdown passes of 45 and 28 yards for a 13–9 win. After having played 402 consecutive minutes, Kinnick suffered a shoulder injury in the final game of the season, against Northwestern. Iowa was winning, 7–0, when he left, but the game ended in a 7–7 tie.

During that remarkable season, Kinnick accounted for 998 yards of total offense, a record for an eight-game schedule. Either scoring or throwing touchdown passes, he was involved in 107 of Iowa's 130 points. He also had eight pass interceptions and returned kicks for a total of 377 yards.

His coach, Eddie Anderson, said of Kinnick, "He was a perfectionist, never satisfied unless he could come as close as he could to absolute perfection in any move he made."

Kinnick was a U.S. Navy fighter pilot during World War II. He was killed when his plane crashed in the Caribbean after its engine died.

★ College Football Hall of Fame

Kinsella, John P.

SWIMMING
b. Aug. 26, 1952, Oak Park, Ill.

While still a high school student in 1970, Kinsella set world records for the 400-meter and 1,500-meter freestyle and American records for the 200-, 500-, and 1,650-yard freestyle events. He was the first swimmer to break 16 minutes for the 1,500-meter, with a time of 15:57.1. Kinsella was given the Sullivan Award as the outstanding amateur athlete of 1970.

Swimming for Indiana University, Kinsella won the NCAA 500-yard and 1,650-yard championships three years in a row, 1971 through 1973. He was the AAU outdoor 400-meter and 1,500-meter champion in 1970. Indoors, he won the national 200-yard title in 1970 and the 500-yard and 1,650-yard championships from 1970 through 1972.

A silver medalist in the 1,500-meter freestyle at the 1968 Olympics, Kinsella was a member of the gold medal 4 x 200-meter relay team in 1972.

He became a professional long-distance swimmer after graduating from college in 1974 and won 26 of 29 races. In 1979, his last year of competition, he set a record of 9 hours and 9 minutes for the English Channel swim.

Kiphuth, Bob (Robert J. H.)

SWIMMING
b. Nov. 17, 1890, Tonawanda, N.Y.
d. Jan. 7, 1967

Though he supposedly couldn't swim a stroke, Kiphuth became one of the all-time great swimming coaches. Originally a physical educator at the Tonawanda, New York, YMCA and then at Yale University, Kiphuth became Yale's swim coach in 1918.

Because of his background in physical education, Kiphuth was the first coach to emphasize land training for his swimmers, who spent two months doing exercises and working out on apparatus before entering the water. He also pioneered interval training, in which short, all-out sprints to build speed are mingled with distance training to build endurance.

During his 42 years at Yale, his teams won 528 of 540 dual meets, including 165 in a row from 1924 to 1937. Yale won NCAA team championships in 1942, 1944, 1951, and 1953. Kiphuth also coached the New Haven Swim Club to AAU national indoor championships in 1949, 1951, 1953, 1954, 1955, and 1957. His remarkable record led other coaches to adopt his methods.

Kiphuth retired from coaching in

1959. He died of a heart attack after attending a swim meet at which Yale beat the U.S. Military Academy.

★ International Swimming Hall of Fame

Kipke, Harry G.

FOOTBALL
b. March 26, 1899, Lansing, Mich.
d. Sept. 14, 1972

Named an All-American halfback in 1922 primarily because of his great punting ability, Kipke was a fine all-around back at the University of Michigan, where he also lettered in baseball and basketball. His ability to punt out of bounds near the opposition's goal line helped Michigan to a 19–1–2 record from 1921 through 1923, when he captained the team.

After serving as an assistant coach at the University of Missouri for four years, Kipke coached Michigan State to a 3–4–1 record in 1928 and then returned to his alma mater as head coach.

He had a very successful four-year period from 1930 through 1933, when Michigan won 31 games while losing only 1 and tying 3. Kipke called his system "a punt, a pass, and a prayer" in a 1933 article for the *Saturday Evening Post*. He also coined the phrase, "A great defense is a great offense."

The system didn't work so well during his last four years at Michigan, when he won only 12 games and lost 22. He resigned after the 1937 season.

★ College Football Hall of Fame

Kiraly, Karch

VOLLEYBALL
b. Nov. 3, 1960, Jackson, Mich.

The best volleyball player the U.S. has produced and quite possibly the best in the history of the sport, Kiraly learned the game from his father, Laszlo, a former member of the Hungarian national team who escaped from Hungary during the 1956 revolution.

California's most valuable player as a high school senior, he entered UCLA in 1979 and led the school to three NCAA championships, in 1979, 1981, and 1982, and to a second-place finish in 1980.

UCLA won 123 of 128 games during his career.

The 6-foot-3, 190-pound Kiraly was a member of the U.S. national team from 1981 to 1989. During that period, the team won gold medals at the 1984 and 1988 Olympics, at the 1982 and 1986 world championships, and at the 1987 Pan-American Games.

Kiraly was named the best player in the world after being selected for the all-tournament team in the 1986 world championships, and he was most valuable player of the 1988 Olympic tournament, in which he had 137 kills, 16 block stuffs, 15 block assists, and a 60 percent kill percentage.

After leaving the national team, Kiraly played for Il Messaggero in Italy and was named most valuable player and best digger when the squad won the 1991 club world championship.

Kiraly has also starred in beach volleyball, winning 42 open tournaments. He was named "king of the beach" after winning six tournaments in 1991, and in 1992 he teamed with Kent Steffens to win the U.S. beach championship.

Kirk, Oliver L.

BOXING
b. 1880
d. ?

By a rather strange fluke, Kirk became the only man ever to win two gold medals in boxing at a single Olympics. In the 1904 Games at St. Louis, there were only two competitors in each division. Kirk knocked out George Finnegan to win the bantamweight title. Hungry for more action, the crowd clamored for a fight between Kirk and the featherweight champion, Frank Haller. Kirk won a decision in that bout and was awarded both titles.

Kirksey, Morris M.

RUGBY, TRACK AND FIELD
b. Sept. 13, 1895, Waxahachie, Tex.
d. Nov. 25, 1981

One of only four athletes to win gold medals in two different sports, Kirksey was a member of the gold medal 4 x

100-meter relay team, and he played on the gold medal U.S. rugby team at the 1920 Olympics. He also won a silver medal in the 100-meter dash.

Representing Stanford, Kirksey won the IC4A 100-yard championship in 1922 and 1923.

Kite, Tom (Thomas O. Jr.)

GOLF
b. Dec. 9, 1949, Austin, Tex.

Kite and his University of Texas teammate Ben Crenshaw tied for the NCAA golf championship in 1972. He joined the PGA tour late that year and was named the tour's rookie of the year in 1973.

He spent 18 years on the tour before he won a major tournament, but Kite was the PGA's top money winner in 1981 and 1989, and his career total of $8,500,729 through 1993 is the highest ever, ahead of Jack Nicklaus and Tom Watson.

Kite won the 1981 Vardon Trophy for the fewest strokes per round, 69.80, and he was named player of the year in 1989, when he won the Tournament Players Championship.

The 5-foot-8, 155-pounder was often called "the best player who never won a major tournament" until 1992, when he won the U.S. Open at Pebble Beach. Asked afterward how he would describe his emotions, Kite replied, "I don't know. We're talking about dreams that have been around many, many years. And there are an awful lot of dreams left."

Kiviat, Abel R.

TRACK AND FIELD
b. June 23, 1892, New York, N.Y.
d. Aug. 24, 1991

Only 5-foot-3 and 120 pounds, Kiviat didn't begin competing in track and field until he was a senior in high school, but within two years, he was the top middle-distance runner in the country.

He won the AAU outdoor 1-mile championship in 1911, 1912, and 1914, the indoor 600- and 1,000-yard runs in 1911 and 1913, and the indoor 1,000-yard again in 1914. He was also national cross-country champion in 1913.

Kiviat set a world record of 3.55.8 in the 1,500-meter run at the Olympic trials in 1912, then continued on to the mile post, finishing in 4:15.6, just .2 seconds above the world record for that distance. A favorite going into the Olympics, he placed second in one of the closest finishes ever. Arnold Strode Jackson beat Kiviat by .1 second, and Kiviat edged Norman Taber of the U.S. for second place in a photo finish.

★ National Track & Field Hall of Fame

Klein, Chuck (Charles H.)

BASEBALL
b. Oct. 7, 1904, Indianapolis, Ind.
d. March 28, 1958

A left-handed hitter who threw right-handed, Klein was a 6-foot, 185-pound outfielder who had one of the most productive five-year periods in baseball history from 1929 through 1933. During that period, he collected 1,118 hits, scored 658 runs, hit 180 home runs, and had 693 RBI.

Klein joined the NL's Philadelphia Phillies during the 1928 season, batting .360 and hitting 11 home runs in just 64 games. Then he began his five-year tear. He led the league in home runs with 43 in 1929, when he batted .356 and had 145 RBI. In 1930, he scored 158 runs and hit 59 doubles to lead the league in both categories, with a .386 average, 40 home runs, and 170 RBI.

His 121 runs, 31 home runs, and 121 RBI led the league in 1931. The following year, Klein was named the league's most valuable player, leading in runs with 152, hits with 226, home runs with 38, and stolen bases with 20. He topped it all off by winning the triple crown in 1933 with a .368 average, 28 home runs, and 120 RBI. Klein also led the league with 223 hits and 44 doubles that season.

The strong-armed Klein had 44 assists in 1930, still the major league record for an outfielder, and his 43 home runs in 1929 was an NL record at the time.

The financially troubled Phillies sold

Klein to the Chicago Cubs in 1934, and he never again produced such amazing numbers. However, after returning to the Phillies in 1936, he hit four home runs in a game against Pittsburgh. He is one of only a dozen players in baseball history to accomplish that.

Klein went to the Pittsburgh Pirates during the 1939 season but was back in Philadelphia the following year. For the last five years of his career, he was a part-time player, often used as a pinch hitter. He retired after getting one hit in seven at-bats in 1944.

In 1,753 games, Klein had a .320 batting average with 2,076 hits, including 398 doubles, 74 triples, and 300 home runs. He drove in 1,201 runs and scored 1,168.

★ Baseball Hall of Fame

Knapp, Willie (William)

HORSE RACING
b. 1888, Chicago, Ill.
d. Oct. 26, 1972

Knapp is probably best known for being the winning jockey in one of the greatest upsets in racing history, when the appropriately named Upset beat Man o'War in the 1919 Sanford Stakes. It was the only loss of Man o'War's career.

Man o'War's jockey, Johnny Loftus, was suspected of having thrown the race and was denied a jockey's license in 1920 as a result, but in fact Upset won because of Knapp's clever tactics. He took his horse out fast but, instead of taking the lead, hung alongside Golden Broom to keep Man o'War boxed in along the rail. When the favorite finally moved to the outside to get around the two leading horses, Knapp drove Upset to victory in the ¾-mile sprint.

Knapp became a jockey when he was only 13, and he began riding in New York when he was 17. He led the nation in winners and money won in 1911. For the Willis S. Kilmer Stable, Knapp won the 1918 Kentucky Derby with Exterminator, a 30–1 shot.

Exterminator went on to become one of the great horses in history. Knapp became his trainer in 1920. Known as "Old Bones" because of his lean conformation, Exterminator won 50 races in 100 starts and finished in the money 34 other times, though he usually carried the top weight in handicap events.

Knapp later worked as a timer. He died of injuries suffered when a car hit him as he was crossing a street.

★ National Horse Racing Hall of Fame

Knecht, William J.

ROWING
b. March 10, 1930, Camden, N.J.

Knecht began rowing with the Vesper Boat Club of Philadelphia when he was 16 and continued with the club during and beyond his college years at Villanova. He won the national ¼-mile single sculls championship in 1955, 1956, and 1960.

Knect won gold medals at three consecutive Pan-American Games. Knecht was a member of the champion eight-oared shell in 1955. He teamed with John B. Kelly, Jr., to win the double sculls championship in 1959 and with Robert C. Lea to win the same title in 1963.

The 6-foot, 200-pound Knecht also rowed in the U.S. crew that won an Olympic gold medal in the 1964 eight-oared shell event.

Knight, Bobby (Robert)

BASKETBALL
b. Oct. 25, 1940, Orville, Ohio

Knight earned ten letters in three sports at Ohio State University. He was a sophomore substitute on the team that won the 1960 NCAA championship, and he also played for the teams that lost in the finals of the 1961 and 1962 NCAA tournaments.

After graduating, Knight entered the Army and became assistant basketball coach at the U.S. Military Academy at West Point. Two years later, he was named head coach at 24, the youngest basketball coach at a Division I school in history.

His emphasis on solid team defense soon became obvious. He spent five years at West Point; three of his teams led the nation in defense, and the other two finished second. Knight compiled a record of 102 wins against 50 losses before going to Indiana University in 1971.

At Indiana, he was thrust into the national spotlight and was frequently criticized by media and fans for his courtside behavior. Knight often grabbed players and shouted angrily at them. He once threw a chair onto the floor to protest an official's decision. And he was involved in international controversy twice, once for allegedly striking a security guard in Puerto Rico while coaching the 1979 Pan-American Games team, the other time for pulling his Indiana team off the floor after he had been ejected from a game against the Soviet Union.

But, while a few players transferred from Indiana to other schools, most of his players defended him. At a time when a number of college basketball programs were tainted by recruiting violations, there was never a hint of scandal at Indiana, and Knight's players had a consistently high graduation rate.

They also produced on the court. Under Knight, Indiana won three NCAA championships, in 1976, 1981, and 1987, and the 1975–76 team won all 32 of its games. Knight got his 300th career victory in 1979, at the age of 39, the youngest coach ever to reach that figure. Through the 1993–94 season, he had a 640–223 record. His .742 winning percentage is sixteenth-best all-time, and he is tied for twelfth in career victories.
★ Basketball Hall of Fame

Knox, Chuck (Charles R. Sr.)
FOOTBALL
b. April 27, 1932, Sewickley, Pa.

Knox has a long history of getting NFL teams into the playoffs without winning a championship. After graduating from Juniata College in Pennsylvania, he served as an assistant coach at the school in 1954, then became a high school coach.

He moved on to assistant coaching positions with college and professional teams before becoming head coach of the Los Angeles Rams in 1973. Knox guided the Rams to five NFC Western Division titles in five years but lost three straight NFC championship games, from 1974 through 1976.

In 1978, he went to the Buffalo Bills and took them from a 5–11–0 record to 11–5–0 and a division title in his third season. However, the Bills lost in the first round of the 1980 playoffs.

Knox took over the Seattle Seahawks in 1983. In his nine seasons there, Seattle made the playoffs four times and advanced to the AFC championship in 1983 before losing to the Los Angeles Raiders. In 1992, Knox returned to the Rams for three unsuccessful seasons.

An old-school conservative coach, Knox emphasizes the running game, defense, and ball control, and he likes to keep the score down. In his 22 years as an NFL head coach, he has a 184–133–1 record for a .580 winning percentage in regular season games, and he was 7–11 in playoff games.

Koch, Bill (William)
SKIING
b. June 7, 1955, Brattleboro, Vt.

The first world-class cross-country skier from the U.S., Koch originally began competing in the Nordic combined, which also includes ski jumping, but he then decided to concentrate on cross-country racing.

In 1974, he became the first American ever to win a medal in top-level international competition by placing third in the European junior championships. He was also the first American to win an Olympic medal in his sport, taking a silver in the 30-kilometer event in 1976.

The media attention, along with exercise-induced asthma, bothered Koch for several years afterward. He was the top American hope at the 1980 Winter Olympics, but he skied poorly and finished far out of medal contention in all three races.

After the Olympics he developed a new technique that resembled skating with skis, and in 1982 he won the Nordic World Cup in cross-country, another first. Koch led the World Cup competition for much of the 1983 season before placing third.

Kolb, Claudia A.

SWIMMING
b. Dec. 19, 1949, Hayward, Calif.

Kolb burst into prominence in 1964, when she was 14, by winning the AAU outdoor 100- and 200-meter breaststroke championships and the indoor 100-yard breaststroke title. She repeated in both outdoor breaststroke championships in 1965, when she also won the 200-meter individual medley.

Although she had set a world record of 1:17.9 in the 100-meter breaststroke in 1964 and won a surprising silver medal in the 200-meter event at the Olympics, Kolb in 1966 decided to concentrate on the individual medley races.

She was the AAU outdoor 200-meter champion from 1966 through 1968 and the 400-meter champion in 1966 and 1967. Indoors, she won the 200-yard title in 1967 and the 200- and 400-yard championships in 1968.

Going into the 1968 Olympics, Kolb held world records of 2:23.5 in the 200-meter individual medley and 5:04.7 in the 400-meter, and she was a heavy favorite to win gold medals in both events. She didn't disappoint, taking both races easily. Her 20-meter margin in the 400-meter was the most decisive Olympic victory by a woman swimmer since 1928.

Kolb has coached swimming in South Bend, Indiana, and Santa Clara, California, since her retirement from competition after the Olympics.
★ International Swimming Hall of Fame

Konno, Ford H.

SWIMMING
b. Jan. 1, 1933, Honolulu, Hawaii

Shortly after graduating from high school in 1951, Konno set a world record of 9:30.7 in the 800-meter freestyle swim. He also won that event and the 1,500-meter freestyle at the AAU outdoor championships that year.

Konno entered Ohio State University in the fall of 1951. He had an outstanding year in 1952, winning the NCAA and AAU 440-yard and 1,500-meter freestyle championships and the AAU indoor 220-yard, 440-yard, and 1,500-meter titles. At the Olympics, he won gold medals in the 1,500-meter freestyle and the 4 x 200-meter relay. He was also the silver medalist in the 400-meter race.

He won only one major title, the AAU outdoor 400-meter, in 1953, but in 1954 he again took the NCAA 440-yard and 1,500-meter championships along with the AAU outdoor 200-, 400-, and 1,500-meter titles and the indoor 220-, 440-, and 1,500-meter events. Konno set world records of 2:03.9 in the 200-meter and 4:26.7 in the 400-meter freestyle during 1954 college meets.

Konno won the NCAA 440-yard and 1,500-meter championships for a third time in 1955. He was also the AAU outdoor champion in the 200- and 400-meter events, and he won the indoor 220- and 440-yard titles. In 1956, his last year of competition, Konno won a silver medal as a member of the Olympic 4 x 200-meter relay team.
★ International Swimming Hall of Fame

Kono, Tommy T.

WEIGHTLIFTING
b. June 27, 1930, Sacramento, Calif.

The only weightlifter ever to set world records in four different weight classes, Kono suffered from asthma as a child. During World War II, he and his parents were among the Japanese-Americans interned at Tule Lake, California, where his health improved markedly because of the dry desert air.

Beginning in 1952, Kono was an important member of the U.S. national team because of his ability to move up or down in weight without losing strength, allowing him to compete in the classification where the team needed help.

He was the AAU national champion as a lightweight in 1952, as a middleweight in 1953 and from 1958 through 1960, and as a light heavyweight in 1954, 1955, 1956, and from 1961 through 1964. Kono won Olympic gold medals as a lightweight in 1952 and as a light heavyweight in 1956, and he was silver medalist as a middleweight in 1960.

The world middleweight champion in 1953 and from 1957 through 1959, Kono won world light heavyweight titles in 1954 and 1955. He also won the 1954 Mr. World contest and the 1955 and 1957 Mr. Universe championships.

Kono was known for his ability to "psych out" opponents. Fyodor Bogdanovasky of the Soviet Union once said of him, "When Kono looks at me from the wings, he works on me like a python on a rabbit."

★ Olympic Hall of Fame

Konstanty, Jim (Casimir James)

BASEBALL
b. March 2, 1917, Strykersville, N.Y.
d. June 11, 1976

A right-handed pitcher, the 6-foot-1½, 202-pound Konstanty looked as if he should be throwing fastballs, but instead he was a knuckleball specialist.

Konstanty had one great season as a relief pitcher for the Philadelphia Phillie "Whiz Kids" who won the NL pennant in 1950. He appeared in 74 games, had a 16–7 record with 22 saves and a 2.66 ERA, and won the league's most valuable player award. He was also named male athlete of the year by the Associated Press.

Because Philadelphia's pitching had been depleted by a pennant race that came down to the last game of the season, Konstanty was the surprise starter in the first game of the World Series against the New York Yankees. He gave up only four hits in eight innings but lost, 1–0, and the Yankees went on to a four-game sweep.

Konstanty had joined the Cincinnati Reds briefly during the 1944 season and was with the Boston Braves for ten appearances in 1946 before landing with Philadelphia in 1948. He had one more fine year with Philadelphia, going 14–10 in 1953, when he was a part-time starter as well as a reliever. Philadelphia sent him to the Yankees during the 1954 season, and he had a 7–2 record with 11 saves and a 2.32 ERA in 1955.

He retired after pitching for the Yankees and the St. Louis Cardinals in 1956. His career record was 66–48 with 74 saves and a 3.46 ERA.

Koufax, Sandy [Sanford Braun]

BASEBALL
b. Dec. 30, 1935, Brooklyn, N.Y.

"If there was ever a better pitcher, it was before my time," Dodger manager Walter Alston said of Koufax. Yet it took Koufax years to become a genuine star, and that stardom lasted only a short time because of physical problems.

His parents divorced when he was 3 years old, and he took the name of his mother's second husband, Irving Koufax, when she remarried. Koufax starred in basketball in high school, though he played sandlot baseball during the summer, usually as a first baseman.

The 6-foot-2, 200-pound Koufax went to the University of Cincinnati on a basketball scholarship in 1953 and averaged ten points a game as a freshman. He also pitched for the baseball team, and after striking out 51 hitters in 32 innings, he left college to sign with the NL's Brooklyn Dodgers for a $140,000 bonus.

A left-hander, Koufax was an exceptionally hard thrower, and that was his problem for a long time. In his second major league start in 1955, he pitched a two-hitter. He said later that performance hurt him, explaining, "I threw real hard in the game, and it worked . . . It took me a long time to learn that it was wrong."

During his first six seasons with the Dodgers, who moved to Los Angeles in 1958, Koufax won just 36 games while losing 40. The turning point in his career came during an exhibition game against the Chicago White Sox in 1961. With the bases loaded and no outs, catcher Norm Sherry came to the mound and told him, "Don't force your fastball. That's when you get real wild. Throw it easy."

Koufax decided to try it, retired the next three hitters without giving up a run, and became a different pitcher. During the next six seasons, his last in the majors, he had a 129–47 record. He went 18–13 in 1961, leading the league with

269 strikeouts in only 255⅔ innings, and he was 14–7 in 1962 with a league-leading 2.54 ERA.

In 1963, Koufax won his first Cy Young Award and was named the league's most valuable player and the Associated Press male athlete of the year. He led the NL in victories with a 25–5 record, 11 shutouts, 306 strikeouts, and a 1.88 ERA to lead the Dodgers to the pennant. In a four-game World Series sweep of the New York Yankees, he had a 2–0 record with a 1.50 ERA, and he set a record with 23 strikeouts in 18 innings.

Koufax was the league leader in winning percentage at .792 on a 19–5 record, in shutouts with 7, and in ERA with 1.74 in 1964. He followed that with two consecutive Cy Young Award seasons. In 1965, he was 26–8, a .765 winning percentage, with 27 complete games, 335⅔ innings pitched, 382 strikeouts, and a 2.04 ERA, leading the league in every category including victories.

He almost duplicated that in 1966 with a 27–9 record, 27 complete games, 5 shutouts, 323 innings pitched, 317 strikeouts, and a 1.73 ERA. Koufax didn't lead in winning percentage that season, but he did lead in shutouts.

The Dodgers won pennants both years. Koufax was 2–1 with a 0.38 ERA and a record 29 strikeouts in 24 innings when Los Angeles beat the Minnesota Twins in seven games in 1965. Despite a 1.50 ERA, he lost his only decision in 1966, when the Baltimore Orioles swept the Dodgers in four games.

During his last three seasons, Koufax pitched in almost constant pain because of arthritis in his pitching arm. He announced his retirement after the 1966 World Series, saying, "I don't regret for one minute the twelve years I've spent in baseball, but I could regret one season too many."

The first pitcher to have four no-hitters, Koufax threw a perfect game against the Chicago Cubs on September 9, 1965. Leading 1–0, he struck out the last six hitters he faced. Although famed for his explosive fastball, Koufax often got his strikeouts with a devastating curve that broke sharply down at the last moment.

In 12 major league seasons, Koufax had a 165–87 record with 40 shutouts and a 2.76 ERA. He gave up 1,754 hits, walked 817, and struck out 2,396 hitters in 2,324 innings.

★ Baseball Hall of Fame

Kraenzlein, Alvin C.
TRACK AND FIELD
b. Dec. 12, 1876, Milwaukee, Wis. d. Jan. 6, 1928

Until Kraenzlein, hurdlers simply jumped over the hurdles as well as they could. He developed the modern technique of going over the hurdle with a straight front leg and the trailing leg tucked under. A very versatile athlete, he once won seven events in a high school meet, and he is the only athlete ever to win four individual track and field gold medals at a single Olympics.

Kraenzlein entered the University of Wisconsin in 1895. His first major championship came in the AAU national 220-yard hurdles in 1897. In September of that year, he transferred to the University of Pennsylvania to study dentistry.

He won the 120- and 220-yard hurdles at the AAU national championships in 1898 and 1899 and was also the 1898 long jump champion. Running for Penn, Kraenzlein captured IC4A championships in both hurdles events for three straight years, 1898 through 1900. He won the IC4A long jump in 1898, and he scored a record 18 points in the 1899 meet, when he also won the 100-yard dash and finished second in the long jump to lead Penn to the team championship.

In 1900, Kraenzlein missed the AAU meet because he was in England, preparing for the Paris Olympics. He won British championships in the 120-yard hurdles and the broad jump while he was there. Then he went on to the Olympics, where he won gold medals in the 60-meter dash, the 110-meter hurdles, the 220-meter hurdles, and the long jump.

Kraenzlein retired from active competition with world records in the 60-meter dash, the 110-meter and 120-yard high hurdles, the 200-meter and 220-

yard low hurdles, and the long jump. His record of 23.6 seconds in the 220-yard hurdles stood for 26 years.

He practiced dentistry for five years after graduating from Penn in 1901, then devoted most of the rest of his life to coaching. He was the track coach at the University of Michigan from 1910 until 1913, when he was hired to prepare the German team for the 1916 Olympics. The games were postponed because of World War I, and he returned to the United States. After serving in the Army, he was assistant coach at Penn until 1922. He died of heart disease.

★ National Track & Field Hall of Fame; Olympic Hall of Fame

Kramer, Frank L.

CYCLING
b. Nov. 20, 1880, Evansville, Ind.
d. Oct. 8, 1958

It was feared that Kramer might have tuberculosis in his early teens, so his parents bought him a bicycle for exercise and later sent him to live with friends in East Orange, New Jersey, for the sea air. He began racing when he was 15 and won the League of American Wheelmen's national sprint championship in 1898. The following year, he won the National Cycling Association title.

The great black cyclist Major Taylor persuaded Kramer to turn professional in 1900. Ironically, Taylor beat Kramer in the finals of the national sprint championship that year, but Kramer went on to win the title 16 years in a row. After losing in 1917, he switched to a larger gear and won the championship again in 1918 and 1921. He also won the world championship the only time he entered, in 1912, when it was held in Newark.

By 1905, Kramer had become so well known that he was invited to race in Europe. He subsequently made three other European tours, winning 50 of 62 races, including two victories in the Grand Prix de Paris. He further enhanced his international reputation in 1908, when Australian champion Jackie Clark came to the United States specifically to test Kramer. In the national championships at Madison Square Gar-

den, Kramer beat Clark in both the ½-mile and 1-mile sprints.

Kramer studied and trained assiduously. He went to bed so punctually at nine P.M. that his neighbors set their clocks when he turned off his bedroom light. The stress of racing finally caught up to him 1922, when he began suffering from insomnia. In his last appearance, he tied the world record of 15.4 seconds in the ⅙-mile time trial in front of more than 20,000 cheering fans at the Newark Velodrome.

Kramer remained active in cycling as a referee until 1937, and he also held various positions with the National Cycling Association. Two years before his death in 1958, he handed out the prizes at the Tour of Somerville.

Kramer, Jack (John A.)

TENNIS
b. Aug. 1, 1921, Las Vegas, Nev.

As a boy, Kramer loved playing sandlot football, but after a variety of injuries, his father suggested he should take up tennis instead. He won the national boys' singles when he was 15 and in 1940 and 1941 he teamed with Ted Schroeder to win the men's doubles at the U.S. Nationals.

Kramer reached the national singles final in 1943 but came down with ptomaine poisoning and lost. He then served in the Coast Guard during World War II, returning to tennis in 1946, when he won his first national singles title.

He also went to the singles final at Wimbledon that year. Suffering from a blister on his racket hand, he lost to Jaroslav Drobny. When a reporter suggested the blister had caused his defeat, Kramer snapped, "Nonsense. The injury didn't beat me. Drobny did."

In December of 1946, Kramer and Schroeder went to Australia and won the Davis Cup. After Kramer became the singles champion at Wimbledon in 1947, he was offered a chance to turn professional and tour with Bobby Riggs, but he decided he wanted to win one more national singles title first. He reached the final match against Frank Parker, lost the first two sets, then came back to win the last three, 6–1, 6–0, 6–3.

His goal accomplished, Kramer signed a contract and thoroughly dominated Riggs, winning 69 of 89 matches. A hard hitter and excellent volleyer with a big serve, Kramer was described by Riggs as "a merciless competitor," and *Time* magazine said, "He is always boring in, always making the other fellow feel he is doomed unless he does something tremendous."

He continued to dominate the tour for the next five years, winning 96 of 123 matches against Pancho Gonzales in 1949 and 1950, 64 of 92 against Pancho Segura in 1951 and 1952, and 54 of 95 against Frank Sedgman in 1953.

Kramer then retired from competition to become the tour promoter. Australians were dominating tennis, and Kramer proceeded to sign several of the best Australian players, including Ken Rosewall, Lew Hoad, Ashley Cooper, and Malcolm Anderson.

His involvement in tennis went beyond the tour, though. Kramer worked with young players at clinics, helped to coach the country's Davis Cup players, and constantly worked for open tennis, which would allow professionals to compete against amateurs. He finally won that point in 1968, when the U.S. National became the U.S. Open Tournament.

★ International Tennis Hall of Fame

Kramer, Ronald J.

FOOTBALL
b. June 24, 1935, Girard, Kans.

Twice an All-American end at the University of Michigan, in 1955 and 1956, Kramer also starred as a center on the basketball team and as a high jumper and weight thrower on the track team. During his three years as a starter in football, he caught 53 passes for 880 yards and 9 touchdowns, kicked 43 extra points and 2 field goals, punted 31 times for a 40.6-yard average, and excelled on defense.

The 6-foot-3 Kramer weighed 220 pounds as a college player but beefed up to 240 pounds as a professional tight end

with the NFL's Green Bay Packers in 1957. He served in the Air Force in 1958 and returned to the Packers the following year. A strong blocker, Kramer was also a sure-handed receiver who was often used on short routes to pick up first down yardage.

Kramer played for two NFL champions in Green Bay, in 1961 and 1962. He starred in the Packers' 37–0 victory over the New York Giants in the 1961 title game, catching 4 passes for 80 yards and 2 touchdowns. He was named an All-Pro by the Associated Press in 1962.

The Packers traded Kramer to the Detroit Lions in 1965, and he spent three seasons there before retiring. In his ten NFL seasons, he caught 229 passes for 3,272 yards and 16 touchdowns.

★ College Football Hall of Fame

Krause, Moose (Edward W.)

BASKETBALL, FOOTBALL
b. Feb. 2, 1913, Chicago, Ill.
d. Dec. 10, 1992

The 6-foot-3, 215-pound Krause was a starting tackle on the Notre Dame football team for three seasons. He also lettered in track and played baseball for a year, but his best sport was basketball. He was a prolific scorer for his time, and he was also an excellent passer from the pivot position and a strong, surprisingly agile rebounder.

Notre Dame won 54 games and lost just 12 during his three years as a starter. He scored 547 career points and averaged 10.1 a game in 1932–33, both school records at the time. Krause captained the team as a senior and was named a Helms Athletic Foundation All-American in 1934.

After graduating, Krause became basketball coach and athletic director at little St. Mary's, Minnesota, College for six seasons. He then went to Holy Cross, where his teams won 11 games and lost 14 from 1939–40 through 1941–42.

Krause returned to Notre Dame in 1942 as an assistant in both basketball and football. He served as interim basketball coach for part of the 1942–43 season, when George Keogan was ill, and again in 1943–44, after Keogan's death.

Notre Dame had two other head coaches in each of the next two seasons, and then Krause took over again in 1946, compiling a 20–4 record in his first season. He resigned in 1950 to devote full time to his duties as athletic director. His Notre Dame teams won a total of 98 games and lost 48.

★ Basketball Hall of Fame

Kremer, Ray (Remy P.)

BASEBALL
b. March 23, 1893, Oakland, Calif. d. Feb. 8, 1965

Kremer's career as a major league pitcher barely lasted ten seasons, but he was the NL leader eight times in five different categories during that time. A right-hander, the 6-foot-1, 190-pound Kremer joined the Pittsburgh Pirates in 1924, when he had an 18–10 record and led the league with 41 games and 4 shutouts.

The Pirates won the 1925 pennant, and Kremer had a 2–1 record with a 3.00 ERA in their seven-game World Series victory over the Washington Senators. He led the league with 20 victories, a .769 winning percentage, and a 2.61 ERA in 1927, and he was the ERA leader again with a 2.47 mark in 1928.

In 1930, Kremer had a league-leading 20 victories and 276 innings pitched. Arm trouble set in the following season, when he was only 11–15 in 30 appearances. He appeared in just 11 games in 1932 and 7 in 1933 before retiring.

Kremer had a career 143–85 record with 14 shutouts and a 3.76 ERA. He struck out 516 hitters and walked 483 in 1,954⅔ innings.

Krone, Julie

HORSE RACING
b. July 24, 1963, Benton Harbor, Mich.

When Krone became the first woman jockey to win one of the triple crown races by riding Colonial Affair to victory in the 1993 Belmont Stakes, she had already established herself as one of the best jockeys in the business, regardless of sex.

Krone began to ride in equestrian events at an early age, winning her first competition in a county fair horse show when she was 5. At 13, she decided she wanted to be the best jockey in the world.

She entered thoroughbred racing as a groom but soon became an exercise rider and then a jockey, riding her first winner at Tampa Bay Downs in 1983. From 1987 through 1989, Krone was among the top five jockeys in the nation in races won, and on August 20, 1993, she had five wins at Saratoga, tying the track record. Krone was the nation's top female jockey in 1983 and from 1986 through 1993.

Shortly afterward, Krone suffered a serious ankle fracture in a fall at Saratoga and missed the rest of the 1993 season. Through 1993, she had ridden more than 2,300 winners and collected more than $30 million in earnings.

Krzyzewski, Mike (Michael W.)

BASKETBALL
b. Feb. 13, 1947, Chicago, Ill.

The name is pronounced *Roo-shevski,* but his players call him "Coach K." Krzyzewski played basketball for Bobby Knight at the U.S. Military Academy, graduating in 1969. He coached service teams during his stint in the Army, then became head coach at the U.S. Military Academy Prep School for three seasons.

He rejoined Knight as an assistant coach at Indiana in 1975 and then became head coach at Army. In five seasons there, his teams won 73 games, losing 59, and twice went to the National Invitation Tournament.

Krzyzewski was named coach at Duke University in 1981. After two years of rebuilding the program, the team won 20 games in 1983–84 and went to the NCAA tournament. Duke has won 20 or more games and played in the NCAA every year since then, with seven appearances in the final four and two championships, in 1991 and 1992. The 1985–86 team set an NCAA record with 37 victories.

Kummer, Clarence

HORSE RACING
b. Aug. 8, 1899, New York, N.Y.
d. Dec. 18, 1930

Best known as Man o'War's jockey in 1920, Kummer took over after Johnny Loftus was denied a license because he was suspected of having thrown a race, Man o'War's defeat by Upset in the 1919 Sanford Stakes.

Kummer rode Man o'War to nine wins in nine starts, including the Preakness and the Belmont. (The horse didn't run in the Kentucky Derby.) He had 78 other victories that year and led all jockeys in winnings with $292,376. Kummer also won the 1925 Preakness aboard Coventry and the 1928 Belmont aboard Vito.

Because of weight problems, Kummer didn't have any rides in 1929. He died of pneumonia, possibly because he had weakened his constitution by losing weight for a comeback attempt.

★ National Horse Racing Hall of Fame

Kundla, John A.

BASKETBALL
b. July 3, 1916, Star Junction, Pa.

Kundla played baseball and basketball at the University of Minnesota, graduating in 1939, and spent a year in minor league baseball before becoming a grade school and high school basketball coach.

After one season as head coach at St. Thomas College in Minnesota, where he had an 11–11 record, Kundla took over the Minneapolis Lakers of the National Basketball League in 1947. The team joined the Basketball Association of America (now the NBA) the following season.

Kundla guided the great Minneapolis teams, led by George Mikan, that won championships in 1949, 1950, 1952, 1953, and 1954. When the Lakers moved to Los Angeles in 1959, Kundla took over at the University of Minnesota.

He retired after the 1967–68 season with a collegiate record of 121 wins and 116 losses. As a professional coach, he had a 423–302 mark for a .583 winning percentage in regular season play and a 61–37 record in playoff games.

Kurland, Bob (Robert A.)

BASKETBALL
b. Dec. 23, 1924, St. Louis, Mo.

Basketball's first seven-footer, Kurland starred at Oklahoma A & M (now Oklahoma State) from 1943–44 through the 1945–46 season. Under Coach Henry Iba, the team emphasized defense and played a ball-control offense that featured a lot of patient passing to set up a good shot.

Iba said, "Kurland made our type of game go. We knew he would get us the ball so we never had to rush into a bad shot." As a sophomore, Kurland often leaped above the rim to grab opponents' shots before they went in. As a result, the NCAA in 1945 adopted a rule against goaltending.

Led by Kurland, Oklahoma A & M became the first team to win two consecutive NCAA championships, in 1945 and 1946. He scored 22 points in a 49–45 win over New York University in the 1945 championship and 23 points in a 43–40 victory over North Carolina in the 1946 title game, and he was named the tournament's most valuable player both years. The Helms Athletic Foundation named him college player of the year as a senior, when he led the nation in scoring with 19.5 points per game.

After graduating, Kurland went to work for the Phillips Oil Company and played for its AAU basketball team, the 66ers. In his six seasons of AAU play, the 66ers won three national championships, and Kurland was named an AAU All-American six times.

He was the first player to perform for two gold medal Olympic basketball teams, in 1948 and 1952. Kurland said the biggest thrill of his life was carrying the American flag at the opening ceremony of the Olympics in 1952.

★ Basketball Hall of Fame

Kurri, Jarri

HOCKEY
b. May 18, 1960, Helsinki, Finland

The 6-foot-1, 195-pound Kurri joined

the NHL's Edmonton Oilers in 1980 after playing for the Finnish Olympic team. He scored more than 100 points five seasons in a row, from 1982–83 through 1986–87, with a high of 135 points in 1984–85.

Kurri led the NHL with 68 goals in 1985–86. A sharpshooter and excellent passer, he was a linemate of Wayne Gretzky, and some critics felt he owed a great deal of his success to the "Great One." However, after Gretzky went to the Los Angeles Kings in 1988, Kurri scored 102 points.

He left Edmonton in a contract dispute and played in Italy during the 1990–92 season, then rejoined Gretzky in Los Angeles. A first-team All-Star in 1985 and 1987, Kurri won the 1985 Lady Byng Trophy for combining a high standard of play and sportsmanship.

Through the 1993–94 season, Kurri had 555 goals and 712 assists for 1,267 points in 990 regular season games. He had 222 points on 102 goals and 120 assists in 174 playoff games. Kurri was on Stanley Cup championship teams in 1984, 1985, 1987, 1988, and 1990.

Kurtsinger, Charles E.

HORSE RACING
b. Nov. 16, 1906, Shepherdsville, Ky.
d. Sept. 24, 1946

Nicknamed the "Dutchman," Kurtsinger won the Kentucky Derby twice, aboard Twenty Grand in 1931 and War Admiral in 1937. With Kurtsinger aboard, War Admiral also won the Preakness and Belmont to become the fourth triple crown winner in history.

Twenty Grand also won the 1931 Belmont but finished second in the Preakness. After losing by a nose in the Kentucky Derby, Kurtsinger rode Head Play to victory in the 1933 Preakness.

After a fall in 1938, Kurtsinger retired to become a trainer, although he rode briefly in 1939. He died of complications from pneumonia. Kurtsinger was the leading money winner in 1931 and in 1937.

★ National Horse Racing Hall of Fame

Kurys, Sophie M.

BASEBALL
b. May 14, 1925, Flint, Mich.

Kurys was by far the greatest base stealer and possibly the greatest player in the All-American Girls' Professional Baseball League, which was virtually unknown until the 1992 movie *A League of Their Own.*

In eight seasons, all with the Racine Belles, she stole 1,114 bases, an average of 139 a year. She had an astounding record in 1946, when she reached base 215 times and stole 201 bases in 203 attempts. Kury's batted .286 that year, had a league record 93 walks in 113 games, and set another league record for fielding percentage by a second baseman, at .973. She led the league in runs scored with 117 and was named most valuable player.

Kurys entered the league when it was organized in 1943 and led in stolen bases six times. She was an all-star second baseman four years in a row, from 1946 through 1949. The Racine franchise folded after the 1950 season, and she played professional softball for four more years before retiring.

While her stolen base totals were enhanced by the fact that AAGPBL baselines were only 72 feet long, compared to 90 feet in major league baseball, Kurys faced a hindrance that major league runners don't have to worry about. She played in a short skirt that offered absolutely no protection to her legs when she slid into a base. In such a uniform, it took uncommon courage to slide as often as she did during her career.

Kusner, Kathy (Kathryn H.)

EQUESTRIAN SPORTS, HORSE RACING
b. March 21, 1940, Gainesville, Fla.

A world-class dressage rider, Kusner was also the first woman ever given a jockey license. She began riding when she was ten years old. A member of the gold medal three-day event teams at the 1963 Pan-American Games and the 1964 Olympics, Kusner won the 1966 International Grand Prix aboard Untouchable. The following year, she became the first rider ever to win the event two years in a row on the same horse.

In November 1967, Kusner applied for a jockey license in Maryland and was turned down. She told reporters, "Horse riding is more a game of technique and skill than strength. It's the same as playing chess with men, so I don't intend to give up the fight." A year later, a judge ruled that she had been denied a license because of sex discrimination and ordered the Maryland Racing Commission to license her.

A broken leg delayed her debut as a jockey, but she began racing in 1969 and rode her first winner at Pocono Downs that September. Her career as a jockey was rather brief because she began to have problems making the weight. However, Kusner continued riding as an amateur equestrian and was a member of the U.S. team that won a silver medal in the 1972 Olympics.

Kwalick, Ted (Thaddeus J.)

FOOTBALL
b. April 15, 1947, McKees Rocks, Pa.

An All-American tight end at Penn State University in 1968, the 6-foot-4, 226 pound Kwalick was a first-round draft choice of the NFL's San Francisco 49ers. After two seasons as a backup, he became a starter in 1971, catching 52 passes for 664 yards and 5 touchdowns.

Kwalick was named to the NFC all-star team by *The Sporting News* in 1973, when he caught 47 passes for 729 yards and 5 touchdowns. He fell out of favor in San Francisco the following year because he announced he was playing out his option to join the Philadelphia Bell of the World Football League. Kwalick was relegated to the bench and caught only 13 passes in 1974.

The WFL folded in November 1975, and Kwalick was signed by the Oakland Raiders but saw little action. He retired after the 1977 season. Kwalick had 168 career receptions for 2,570 yards, a 15.3 average, and 23 touchdowns. He also carried the ball 19 times for 175 yards, a 9.2 average.

Lach, Elmer J.

HOCKEY
b. Jan. 22, 1918, Nokomis, Sask.

Twice the NHL's leading scorer, Lach was the center for Rocket Richard and Toe Blake on the Montreal Canadiens' famous "Punch Line." When he led in scoring for the first time with 80 points in 1944–45, Richard was second with 73, and Blake was third with 67. Lach also won the Ross Trophy as the league's most valuable that year.

He won his second scoring title in 1947–48 with 61 points on 30 goals and 31 assists, and he was among the top ten four other times. On November 8, 1952, he scored his 200th goal and assisted on Richard's 325th, an NHL career record at the time.

Lach joined the Canadiens in 1940 after playing amateur hockey in Saskatchewan. He retired after the 1953–54 season. He scored 215 goals and had 408 assists in 664 regular season games, with 19 goals and 45 assists in 76 playoff games.
★ Hockey Hall of Fame

Lachey, Jim (James M.)

FOOTBALL
b. June 4, 1963, St. Henry, Ohio

Lachey graduated from Ohio State in 1985 and was chosen by the San Diego Chargers in the first round of the NFL draft that year. He was a starter for three seasons and then was traded to the Oakland Raiders in 1988.

He played just one game with the Raiders before being traded again, to the Washington Redskins. The 6-foot-6, 294-pound Lachey became a free agent in 1992 but resigned with Washington. He missed more than a month of the season with a knee injury that forced him out of the lineup several times during the 1993 season.

Named to *The Sporting News* all-pro team from 1989 through 1991, Lachey played in the 1987, 1990, and 1991 Pro Bowls.

Lackie, Ethel

SWIMMING
b. Oct. 27, 1907, Chicago, Ill.

Lackie was the first woman to swim the 100-yard freestyle in less than 1 minute and the first to break the 1-minute, 10-second barrier in the 100-meter freestyle.

She won two gold medals at the 1924 Olympics, in the 100-meter freestyle and as a member of the U.S. 4 x 100-meter freestyle relay team. Trailing in the individual event with 25 meters to go, Lackie put on a spectacular burst of speed to win.

Lackie won the national outdoor 100-yard freestyle in 1924 and the 100-meter event in 1926. She was the indoor 100-yard freestyle champion in 1925, 1926, and 1928.

Ladewig, Marion

BOWLING
b. Oct. 30, 1914, Grand Rapids, Mich.

Ladewig became interested in bowling as a young teenager, when she got a job cashiering, cleaning up, and occasionally setting pins at a Grand Rapids bowling center for $2.50 a day. At the peak of her career, in the early 1960s, she was earning $25,000 a year giving exhibitions and clinics, writing a syndicated column, and serving as a sportswear design consultant.

The woman bowler of the year a record nine times, from 1950 through 1955 and in 1958, 1959, and 1963, Ladewig was named the greatest of all time in a 1973 poll. A vivacious 5-foot-4, 124-pound blonde, she won the Women's All-Star tournament from 1949 through 1952 and in 1954, 1956, 1959, and 1963.

She achieved her 1951 All-Star victory by averaging 247.5 pins over an eight-day period, which would have won the men's title that year. Ladewig's other championships included the 1960 WPBA National, the WIBC all-events in 1950 and 1955, the 1955 WIBC doubles with Wyllis Ryskamp, and the 1950 WIBC team title with the Grand Rapids Fanatorium Majors.

Ladewig announced her retirement from competitive bowling in November 1965, after winning the World Invitational for a record fifth time.

★ International Women's Sports Hall of Fame; WIBC Hall of Fame

Laettner, Christian D.

BASKETBALL
b. Aug. 17, 1969, Angola, N.Y.

A four-year starter at Duke University, the 6-foot-11, 235-pound Laettner set an NCAA Division I record for most games, 148, and he played for two NCAA tournament champions, in 1991 and 1992. He averaged 16.6 points for his collegiate career and 21.5 as a senior, when he was an almost unanimous choice as college player of the year.

Although a center at Duke, Laettner is not the standard post-up, back-to-the-basket player. He prefers facing the basket and shooting. In his college career, he hit 45.5 percent of his 3-point shots (79 of 163). His 17-foot shot while double-teamed with time running out in overtime beat Kentucky, 104–103, to get Duke into the final four in 1992.

Laettner was the only non-NBA player on the U.S. "Dream Team" that easily won the gold medal at the 1992 Olympics. A first-round draft choice of the Minnesota Timberwolves, he averaged 17.5 points per game in his first two NBA seasons, through 1993–1994.

Lafleur, Guy D.

HOCKEY
b. Sept. 20, 1951, Thurso, P.Q.

After he scored an incredible 209 points in 62 games with the Quebec Ramparts junior team in the 1970–71 season, Lafleur was chosen in the first round of the NHL draft by the Montreal Canadiens.

The 6-foot, 185-pound Lafleur was a fast, tricky skater, a great puck-handler, and an accurate passer. He was also strong, able to ward off defenders with one arm while he shot with the other.

Lafleur had more than 50 points in each of his first three seasons with Montreal, but he exploded in 1974–75, collecting 119 points on 53 goals and 66 assists during the regular season and adding 12 goals and 7 assists in 11 playoff games.

In 1975–76, Lafleur won the Art Ross Trophy as the league's leading scorer with 56 goals and 69 assists for 125 points. He had two game-winning goals when Montreal swept the Philadelphia Flyers in the Stanley Cup finals.

Lafleur was even better in 1976–77, winning the Ross Trophy again with 136 points on 56 goals and 80 assists. He also won the Hart Trophy as the league's outstanding player and the Conn Smythe Trophy as the most valuable player in the playoffs, with 10 goals and 11 assists for 21 points in 15 games.

The Ross and Hart trophies went to Lafleur again in 1977–78, when he had 132 points on 60 goals and 72 assists, with 10 goals and 11 assists for 21 total points in the playoffs.

After he scored 129 points in 1978–79 and 125 in 1979–80, Lafleur's numbers began to decline with his declining speed. He announced his retirement after injuries limited him to only 19 games in 1984–85.

Elected to the Hockey Hall of Fame

in 1988, Lafleur decided to come out of retirement, signing with the New York Rangers. Though not nearly the threat he had been, he still put up above-average numbers with 45 points on 18 goals and 27 assists in 67 games.

In 1,028 regular season games, Lafleur had 1,291 points on 536 goals and 755 assists. He scored 58 goals and 76 assists for 134 points in 128 playoff games.

★ Hockey Hall of Fame

LaFontaine, Patrick

HOCKEY
b. Feb. 22, 1965, St. Louis, Mo.

The New York Islanders made LaFontaine the third player chosen in the 1983 NHL draft. At the time, it was the highest choice ever devoted to a U.S.-born player.

Before joining the Islanders, LaFontaine scored 111 points in 56 games for the U.S. national team and 8 points in 6 games for the U.S. Olympic team. In 15 NHL games, he had 19 points in the 1983–84 season.

His best season with the Islanders was 1989–90, when he had 54 goals and 51 assists for a total of 105 points. LaFontaine wanted his contract renegotiated in 1991, and he held out at the beginning of the season. The Islanders sent him to the Buffalo Sabres in a multiplayer deal.

The 5-foot-10, 177-pound LaFontaine had his best professional season with Buffalo in 1992–93, when he scored 148 points on 53 goals and 95 assists. He missed most of the following season with a broken jaw.

In 687 regular season NHL games, LaFontaine has scored 391 goals and 434 assists for 825 points. He added 58 points on 24 goals and 34 assists in 64 playoff games.

Laird, Ronald

TRACK AND FIELD
b. April 31, 1938, Louisville, Ky.

Although he holds the record for the most national titles won in track and field with 65, Laird is virtually unknown because he was a race walker, and race walking gets no media attention in the United States.

He began competing in 1958, and at one time or another he won championships and held American records for every race walking distance from 3,000 meters to 50 kilometers. Laird won a gold medal in the 20-kilometer walk at the 1967 Pan-American Games. He retired in 1976.

★ National Track & Field Hall of Fame

Lajoie, Napoleon

BASEBALL
b. Sept. 5, 1875, Woonsocket, R.I.
d. Feb. 7, 1959

Known as "Larry" or "Nap," Lajoie was a hard-hitting, graceful, sure-handed second baseman who batted over .300 15 times and led in fielding percentage 6 times. He used a specially designed bat that had two knobs, one partway up the handle, allowing him to used a split-handed grip for better bat control.

After just three months of minor league baseball, Lajoie joined the Philadelphia Phillies late in the 1896 season. Used mostly at first base, he led the NL with a .569 slugging percentage in 1897. He was then moved to second, where he spent the rest of his career.

Lajoie was the league leader with 43 doubles and 127 RBI in 1898. After batting .378 and .337 during the next two seasons, he jumped to the Philadelphia Athletics in the new AL and had a sensational year, leading the league with 145 runs, 232 hits, 48 doubles, 14 home runs, 125 RBI, a .426 batting average, and a .643 slugging percentage. He was the third player in history to win the triple crown, and his .426 average is a record for the twentieth century.

The Phillies got an injunction prohibiting him from playing for any either Philadelphia team, effective in 1902. After appearing in just one game for the Athletics that season, he went to Cleveland in June. He was so popular in Cleveland that the team became known as the "Naps" while he was there.

Lajoie's .378 in 1902 would have won the batting title, but he didn't qualify because he'd missed so much of the season. However, he did lead the league in hitting and slugging the next two years, with .344 and .518 in 1903, .376 and .552 in 1904, when he also led in hits with 208, doubles with 49, and RBI with 102.

He became Cleveland's playing manager in 1905. Because of a spike wound in his foot that led to blood poisoning, Lajoie played in only 65 games that year, batting .329. He bounced back to .355 in 1906, leading the AL with 214 hits and 48 doubles, but his average dropped to .299 and .289 the next two seasons.

Late in the 1909 season, Lajoie resigned as manager, feeling that the pressure was affecting his play. The following year, he won another batting title with a .384 average, also leading the league in hits with 227 and doubles with 51.

After hitting .365, .368, and .335 the next three seasons, Lajoie began to decline. He slipped to .258 in 1914, then spent two seasons back with the Athletics. He left the major leagues after hitting only .246 in 1916 and became a minor league playing manager for two seasons before leaving baseball entirely.

In 2,480 games, Lajoie batted .338 with 3,242 hits, including 657 doubles, 163 triples, and 83 home runs. He stole 380 bases, scored 1,504 runs, and had 1,599 RBI.

★ Baseball Hall of Fame

Lalonde, Newsy (Edouard)
HOCKEY, LACROSSE
b. Oct. 31, 1887, Cornwall, Ont.
d. Nov. 21, 1970

Lalonde played in the NHL for only four seasons, but he led the league in scoring twice, was second once, and finished fourth in his other season.

Nicknamed "Newsy" because he worked as a linotype operator as a youth, Lalonde didn't begin skating until he was 13. An outstanding lacrosse player, he took up hockey at 16 with his hometown team, and in 1911 went to Vancouver, where he was paid $6,500, by far the highest hockey salary of the time. In 1912, he scored 60 goals in just 12 games.

Lalonde joined the Montreal Canadi-

ens when they were organized in 1913. They played in the National Hockey Association at the time and moved into the National Hockey League when it was organized in 1917. Lalonde was fourth in scoring in the league's first season with 23 goals. He led in 1918–19 with 32 points on 23 goals and 9 assists and in 1920–21 with 41 points on 33 goals and 8 assists.

He retired from playing after that season but returned for two seasons with the New York Americans in 1925, then retired for good. Lalonde coached the Canadiens from 1932 into the 1934–35 season.

In 99 regular season games, Lalonde had 124 goals and 210 assists. He added 22 goals and 1 assist in 12 playoff games.

★ Hockey Hall of Fame

Lambeau, Curly (Earl L.)
FOOTBALL
b. April 9, 1898, Green Bay, Wis.
d. June 1, 1965

As a fullback at Notre Dame in 1918, Lambeau was the only freshman to win a letter. However, he had to leave school because of tonsillitis, and he got a job with the Indian Packing Corporation in Green Bay.

Lambeau talked his employer into putting up $500 to buy uniforms and equipment for a semiprofessional football team called the Packers. Organized in 1919, the team in 1921 entered the American Professional Football Association, which became the National Football League the following year.

As player-coach, Lambeau emphasized the forward pass much more than most professional coaches of the time. In 1929, after retiring as a player, he signed guard Mike Michalske, tackle Cal Hubbard, and halfback Johnny "Blood" McNally, all of whom are now in the Pro Football Hall of Fame. The Packers won the first of three consecutive championships that season. From 1929 through 1931, they won 34 games, lost only 5, and tied 2.

The Packers also won championships under Lambeau in 1936, 1939, and 1944. But after World War II the team had little success, and Lambeau resigned under fire in January 1951. He coached the Chicago Cardinals for two seasons, then went to the Washington Redskins for two more seasons. He left football after the 1954 season with an overall record of 229–134–22.

★ Pro Football Hall of Fame

Lambert, Jack (John H.)

FOOTBALL
b. July 8, 1952, Mantua, Ohio

After playing defensive end as a freshman at Kent State University in Ohio, Lambert was moved to middle linebacker, and he started at that position for three years.

A second-round draft choice of the NFL's Pittsburgh Steelers in 1974, the 6-foot-4, 220-pound Lambert was the only rookie to start for the Pittsburgh team that beat the Minnesota Vikings, 16–6, in Super Bowl IX. He was named the league's defensive rookie of the year.

Lambert also started for three other Super Bowl champions, after the 1975, 1978, and 1979 seasons. He was selected as the NFL's defensive player of the year in 1976, when he recovered seven opposition fumbles, two shy of the league record. An All-American Football Conference selection in 1975, 1976, and 1978, Lambert played in nine consecutive Pro Bowls, from 1975 through 1983.

A toe injury forced him out of the lineup in 1984, and he retired after that season. He had 28 career interceptions in his 11 NFL seasons, all with the Steelers.

★ Pro Football Hall of Fame

Lambert, Piggy (Ward L.)

BASKETBALL
b. May 28, 1888, Deadwood, S.D.
d. Jan. 20, 1958

After playing three sports at Wabash College in Indiana, Lambert did graduate work at the University of Minnesota, then began coaching high school basketball. He became head coach at Purdue University in 1916.

Military service in World War I interrupted his career, but he returned to Purdue in 1919 and remained there through the 1945–46 season. His teams won 371

games and lost only 152, a winning percentage of .710. His 1931–32 team, which won 17 of 18 games, was named national champion by the Helms Athletic Foundation.

Lambert became commissioner of the professional National Basketball League for two years, then returned to Purdue as coach of freshman basketball and football.

A pioneer of the fast break, Lambert coached nine All-Americans, including two future Hall of Fame members, Charles "Stretch" Murphy and John Wooden.

★ Basketball Hall of Fame

Lamonica, Daryle

FOOTBALL
b. July 17, 1941, Fresno, Calif.

Known as the "Mad Bomber" because his long passes stretched opposing defenses to the limit, Lamonica joined the AFL's Buffalo Bills out of Notre Dame University in 1963. The 6-foot-2, 215-pound quarterback became one of the league's top stars after being traded to the Oakland Raiders in 1967.

In his first season with the Raiders, he helped take them to the AFL championship and was named the league's player of the year. Lamonica that season completed 220 of 425 passes for 3,228 yards and 30 touchdowns.

Although he completed only 10 of 24 passes in Oakland's 40–7 championship victory over the Houston Oilers, two went for touchdowns. Oakland lost Super Bowl II to the Green Bay Packers, 33–14.

Lamonica was named player of the year again in 1969 with very similar numbers: he completed 221 of 426 attempts for 3,302 yards and 32 touchdowns. However, the Raiders lost the AFL championship game, 17–7, to the Kansas City Chiefs.

The AFL merged into the NFL in 1970, and Lamonica remained with the Raiders until his retirement after the 1974 season. For his career, he threw 1,288 completions in 2,601 attempts for 19,154 yards and 164 touchdowns. He also scored 14 rushing touchdowns.

La Motta, Jake (Giacobe)

BOXING

b. July 10, 1921, New York, N.Y.

Nicknamed the "Bronx Bull" because of his aggressive, charging style, La Motta learned to box while serving time in the Coxsackie Correctional Institute as a teenager. He had his first professional fight on March 3, 1941, winning a 4-round decision over Charley Mackley.

La Motta put together an impressive record during the next two years and reached prominence when he won a 10-round decision over Sugar Ray Robinson on February 5, 1943. It was Robinson's first loss as a professional. La Motta and Robinson fought six times, La Motta winning only that one bout, but they were always interesting to fight fans because of the matchup of stand-up slugger versus skilled boxer.

On June 16, 1949, La Motta won the world middleweight championship when Marcel Cerdan of France couldn't come out for the 10th round. A rematch was scheduled for later that year, but Cerdan was killed in an October plane crash en route to begin training in the United States.

La Motta defended his title twice but lost it when Robinson knocked him out in the 13th round on February 14, 1951. Although badly battered, La Motta avoided being knocked down by hanging onto the ropes while he was counted out.

Knocked out in two of his next seven fights, La Motta didn't box in 1953 but came back for three fights in 1954 before retiring. He co-authored an autobiography, *Raging Bull*, which was adapted as a very successful 1981 movie starring Robert DeNiro, and he also appeared in several stage shows.

La Motta won 83 fights, 30 by knockout, and lost 19, 4 by knockout. He also fought 4 draws.

★ International Boxing Hall of Fame

Landis, Kenesaw Mountain

BASEBALL

b. Nov. 20, 1866, Millville, Ohio
d. Nov. 25, 1944

As a federal district judge, Landis demonstrated his feeling for baseball in 1914, when an antitrust suit filed by the upstart Federal League against organized baseball came before him. Landis was known as being tough on antitrust violations, but he remarked during the trial that "any blows at the thing called baseball would be regarded by this court as a blow to a national institution." The Federal League folded in 1915, before Landis had made a ruling in the case.

In 1920, eight members of the Chicago White Sox were accused of having taken bribes to throw the 1919 World Series to the Cincinnati Reds. The major league owners decided to replace the three-man National Commission with a single, powerful commissioner. They chose Landis, giving him authority to investigate any act detrimental to the interests of baseball and to impose any punishment he considered necessary on players, teams, or officers of teams.

One of Landis's first acts was to ban the eight "Black Sox" permanently from baseball, although one of them wasn't even tried and the other seven were acquitted. He also banned a number of other players for various reasons, among them Benny Kauff of the New York Giants, who was indicted for car theft. Kauff, too, was acquitted, but Landis refused to lift his ban.

The extent of Landis's power was demonstrated in 1922, when he suspended Babe Ruth and two other players for going on a barnstorming tour after having played in the World Series. Although team owners begged him to reduce the six-week suspension because Ruth drew so many fans, Landis let his original decision stand.

Landis could be as tough on owners as he was on players. A fierce opponent of gambling, he ordered two part owners of the Giants, Horace Stoneham and John McGraw, to divest themselves of their interest in a Havana race track and casino. In 1943, William Cox, owner of the Philadelphia Phillies, admitted betting on his own team. Landis made him sell the team and then banned him permanently from baseball.

While his dictatorial tactics did help

rid baseball of the gambling specter, Landis wasn't successful in his other major crusade, against farm systems. While he spoke out against the practice and was occasionally able to free a player for a technical rules violation, he was unable to use his powers to get rid of farm systems.

★ Baseball Hall of Fame

Landry, Tom (Thomas W.)
FOOTBALL
b. Sept. 11, 1924, Mission, Tex.
One of the most successful coaches in NFL history, Landry played quarterback and fullback at the University of Texas after serving in the Army Air Corps in World War II. He co-captained the team as a senior in 1948.

Landry became a defensive back and punter for the New York Yankees of the All-America Football Conference in 1949. The AAFC folded after that season, and the Yankees moved into the NFL. In compensation for having their territory invaded, the New York Giants were allowed to select five players from the Yankee roster, and Landry was one of them.

He played for the Giants through 1955. An All-Pro in 1954, Landry had 31 career interceptions and punted 389 times for a 40.9 average. He served as an assistant coach during his last two seasons as a player and became the Giants' defensive coach in 1956.

When the Dallas Cowboys entered the NFL as an expansion team in 1960, Landry was named head coach. He coached the Cowboys through the 1988 season, compiling a 250–162–6 record in regular season play and winning 20 of 36 in playoff competition. Landry guided the team to five Super Bowls, a record, winning two of them. During his 29 years, Dallas won 14 division championships and had 21 consecutive winning seasons.

Landry developed the "flex defense," in which one tackle plays slightly off the line of scrimmage in order to read and react to the offensive play. He also pioneered in bringing the shotgun formation back into the offense on passing downs after it had been developed and then abandoned by the San Francisco 49ers.

He was named National Football Conference coach of the year in 1975. Unfortunately, he suffered three losing seasons in a row, from 1986 through 1988, and was summarily replaced by Jimmy Johnson, formerly of the University of Miami, when Jerry Jones bought the team before the 1989 season.

Lane, Alfred P.
SHOOTING
b. Sept. 26, 1891, New York, N.Y.
d. Jan. 11, 1940
Known as the "Boy Wonder" after he won the U.S. Revolver Association championship in 1911, before his twentieth birthday, Lane won five gold medals and one bronze at two Olympics.

At the 1912 Stockholm Olympics, Lane won the free pistol and rapid-fire pistol and was a member of the winning U.S. teams in both events. In 1912, at the Antwerp Games, he was on the gold medal free pistol team and took a bronze in the individual free pistol event.

Lane was the U.S. Revolver Association champion three years in a row, from 1913 through 1915. He worked for many years in the advertising department of the Remington Firearms Company.

Lane, Dick (Richard)
FOOTBALL
b. April 16, 1928, Austin, Tex.
Selected the best cornerback of the NFL's first 50 years in a 1969 poll of sportswriters, Lane was an unlikely prospect when he walked into the Los Angeles Rams training camp in 1952 and asked for a tryout. He had played at little Scottsbluff Junior College in Nebraska and had then spent two years in the Army.

The Rams were impressed with his size — 6-foot-2, 210 pounds — and his speed, so they tried him at wide receiver. To learn the position, he spent hours talking to veteran Tom Fears, who constantly played "Night Train," a hit record of the time, on his phonograph. Lane got the nickname "Night Train" as a result.

Finally coach Joe Stydahar moved Lane to defensive back, and he was an instant sensation. As a rookie, he intercepted 14 passes in 12 games, still the NFL record, running them back for 298 yards and 2 touchdowns.

After an off year in 1953, Lane was traded to the Chicago Cardinals, and he responded by again leading the league in interceptions with 10. He remained with the Cardinals through 1959, then went to the Detroit Lions. He retired after the 1965 season.

An All-Pro in 1956, 1960, 1961, 1962, and 1963, Lane had 68 interceptions in his 14 NFL seasons, returning them for 1,207 yards and 5 touchdowns.

★ Pro Football Hall of Fame

Langer, Jim (James J.)

FOOTBALL
b. May 16, 1948, Little Falls, Minn.

No professional teams drafted Langer after he finished his college career at South Dakota State University. He tried out with the NFL's Pittsburgh Steelers in 1970, was cut, and the Miami Dolphins signed him.

Langer spent two seasons as a backup center and guard before becoming Miami's starting center in 1972. The Dolphins won 17 games that year, including the Super Bowl, and Langer was in on every offensive play of every victory.

The 6-foot-2, 255-pound Langer had the strength to block defensive tackles one-on-one and the speed to move through the line and take out linebackers. He was also a very good pass blocker.

An All-Conference center for six consecutive years, from 1973 through 1978, Langer was traded to the Minnesota Vikings in 1980. He retired after the 1981 season.

★ Pro Football Hall of Fame

Langford, Sam

BOXING
B. March 4, 1886, Weymouth, N.S.
d. Jan. 2, 1956

Though basically a lightweight or welterweight, Langford fought in every division up to heavyweight. He went to Boston when he was 13 and won his first professional fight in 1902.

Known as the "Boston Tar Baby," Langford never had a world championship fight. He lost a 15-round decision in 1906 to Jack Johnson, who became the first black heavyweight champion two years later. Langford did knock out middleweight champion Philadelphia Jack O'Brien in 1911, but it was a nontitle fight.

Langford never had a title fight and spent much of his career fighting other black boxers who also never got championship bouts. He met Harry Wills 22 times, Sam McVey 15 times, and Joe Jeannette 14 times. His career was ended by blindness, probably caused by fight injuries, in 1924. In 252 recorded fights, he won 137, 99 by knockout; lost 23,4 by knockout; and had 31 draws, 59 no-decisions, and 2 no-contests.

In 1944, the destitute Langford was found by New York sportswriter Al Laney living in a Harlem tenement. Laney's story in the *Herald-Tribune* brought in $11,000 in contributions that helped him live the rest of his life in relative comfort.

★ International Boxing Hall of Fame

Langston, Mark E.

BASEBALL
b. Aug. 20, 1960

A 6-foot-2, 190-pound left-hander, Langston led the AL in strikeouts three of his first four seasons in the league. He joined the Seattle Mariners in 1984 and had a 17–10 record, a 3.40 ERA, and a league-leading 204 strikeouts in 225 innings. A sore arm put him on the disabled list for six weeks in 1985, when he was only 7–14.

In 1986, Langston became one of the few pitchers ever to have more strikeouts than innings pitched, fanning 245 hitters in 239⅓ innings, but he had only a 12–14 record, largely because of control problems. In 1987, he went 19–13 with a league-leading 262 strikeouts.

After a 15–11 record in 1988, Langston was traded to the NL's Montreal

Expos early in the 1989 season, and he went to the AL's California Angels as a free agent in 1990. Cutting down on both walks and strikeouts, he had his best season in 1991 with a 19–8 record and a 3.00 ERA.

Langston slipped to 13–14 in 1992, then came back with a 16–11 record and 3.20 ERA in 1993. He has been inconsistent in part because of recurring arm problems. Through 1994, he had a 151–134 record and a 3.74 ERA with 2,110 strikeouts and 1,081 walks in 2,448$\frac{1}{3}$ innings.

Langway, Rod C.
HOCKEY
b. May 3, 1957, Taiwan

The son of a career Navy officer, Langway grew up in Massachusetts and played hockey at the University of New Hampshire. The Montreal Canadiens chose him in the 1977 NHL draft, but Langway elected to sign with the Birmingham Bulls of the World Hockey Association.

In 1978, Langway signed with the Canadiens as a free agent and played 18 games in the minors before entering the NHL. A rock-solid defenseman, he helped Montreal win the 1979 Stanley Cup. After three more seasons with the Canadiens, he asked for a trade.

He was traded to the Washington Capitals before the 1982–83 season and spent the rest of his career there. In 1983, he became the first U.S. player ever to win the Norris Trophy as the league's outstanding defenseman, and he repeated the following year.

After a variety of injuries from 1987 through 1992, Langway announced his retirement during the 1992–93 season.

In his career, he scored 329 points on 51 goals and 278 assists in 994 regular season NHL games. He added 5 goals and 22 assists for 27 points in 104 playoff games.

Lanier, Bob (Robert J. Jr.)
BASKETBALL
b. Sept. 10, 1948, Buffalo, N.Y.

Because his coordination couldn't keep pace with his rapid growth, Lanier didn't make his high school basketball team until his junior year. He eventually grew to 6-foot-11 and 250 pounds, and wore size 21 sneakers.

Lanier starred at center for St. Bonaventure University and was a consensus All-American in 1970. In his three seasons as a starter, he scored 2,067 points, averaging 27.5 a game. St. Bonaventure won the NCAA Eastern Regional tournament in his senior year, but Lanier suffered torn knee ligaments in the championship game, and the team lost in the national semifinals without him.

He joined the Detroit Pistons in the 1970–71 season and made the NBA All-Rookie team. The Pistons traded Lanier to the Milwaukee Bucks in February 1980, and he played in Milwaukee until his retirement after the 1983–84 season.

In his 14 NBA seasons, he was an All-Star eight times. Lanier scored 19,248 points in 949 games, an average of 20.1 per game, and had 9,698 rebounds.
★ Basketball Hall of Fame

Lanier, Willie E.
FOOTBALL
b. Aug. 21, 1945, Clover, Va.

A Little All-American as a linebacker at Morgan State, Lanier was a remarkable physical specimen, 6-foot-1 and 245 pounds, with a 50-inch chest and 34-inch waist. He joined the Kansas City Chiefs of the American Football League in 1967, and in 11 seasons he was named All-AFL or All-American Football Conference seven times, and he appeared in eight Pro Bowls.

Lanier was a very hard hitter with a nose for the ball. In addition to 27 interceptions, he recovered 15 fumbles. When the Chiefs became the second AFL team to win the Super Bowl, beating the Minnesota Vikings, 23–7, after the 1969 season, he had one of the team's three interceptions. That was the last game played by an AFL team, since the leagues merged in 1970.

Because of his hard hits, Lanier suffered several concussions in his first couple of seasons and had to be outfitted with a helmet with special padding to prevent the problem. And, he said later in explaining the role of the middle linebacker, "You must learn to control your aggression."

The first black player to star at middle linebacker, Lanier retired after the 1977 season. He ran back his 27 interceptions for 440 yards, a 16.3 average, and 2 touchdowns.

★ Pro Football Hall of Fame

Lapchick, Joseph B.
BASKETBALL
b. April 12, 1900, Yonkers, N.Y. d. Aug. 10, 1970

Lapchick left school to help support his family, working as a machinist, and played his first professional basketball game when he was 15. At 6-foot-5 and 185 pounds in his prime, he became a much sought player as one of the sport's first big athletes, often appearing for four or five different teams in the course of a season.

He told an interviewer that he learned to get good pay by pitting one owner against another in the era when players were hired and paid for one game at a time. "The first thing I knew, I was selling myself to the highest bidder for $75 a game," he said. "Like the rest of the fellows, I'd play where the money was."

In 1923, Lapchick joined the Original Celtics, the first team to sign its players to contracts for an entire season. The Celtics were the best team in basketball during his tenure, in part because Lapchick could usually win the center jump that followed every score at the time.

The team entered the American Basketball League in 1926 and won two league championships. The ABL forced the Celtics to break up in 1928, and Lapchick went to the Cleveland Rosenblums, who won the next two championships.

After one season with the ABL's Toledo Red Men, Lapchick joined the reorganized Celtics, now owned by singer Kate Smith, for six years of barnstorming basketball.

Lapchick became head coach at St. John's University in New York in 1937. His teams won the National Invitation Tournament in 1943 and 1944. He left

the school to coach the NBA's New York Knickerbockers in 1948 and compiled a record of 326 wins and 247 losses, then returned to St. John's in 1957. After two more NIT victories, in 1959 and 1965, he retired because of a heart problem. His overall record at St. John's was 335 wins against 129 losses.

★ Basketball Hall of Fame

Laperriere, Jacques (Joseph Jacques Hugues)
HOCKEY
b. Nov. 22, 1941, Rouyn, P.Q.

After playing for the Junior Canadiens for four seasons, Laperriere became a professional and spent one season in the minor leagues, joining Montreal for six games in 1962–63. He won the 1964 Calder Trophy as the NHL's rookie of the year and the 1966 Norris Trophy as the best defenseman in the league.

Laperriere was often injured, and he often played despite pain. During the 1972 Stanley Cup playoffs, he didn't miss a game despite a cracked bone in his left arm. The Canadiens won six Stanley Cup championships during his 12 seasons in Montreal.

He scored 40 goals and had 242 assists in 691 regular season games, and he added 9 goals and 22 assists in 88 playoff games.

★ Hockey Hall of Fame

Largent, Steve M.
FOOTBALL
b. Sept. 28, 1954, Tulsa, Okla.

At Tulsa University, Largent caught 126 passes for 2,385 yards and 32 touchdown in three seasons as a starter. He led the nation in touchdown passes caught with 14 in both 1974 and 1975.

The NFL's Houston Oilers drafted him in 1976, but he was traded to the Seattle Seahawks before the season began. The 5-foot-11, 185-pound Largent lacked great speed, but he ran very precise pass routes and was very sure-handed and remarkably durable despite his size.

Every year from 1978 through 1986, except for the strike-shortened 1982 season, he caught at least 66 passes and gained more than 1,000 yards on receptions.

An All-Pro in 1985 and 1987, Largent played in seven Pro Bowls. He missed six games with a broken elbow in 1989 and retired after that season, holding NFL records for most consecutive games with a reception, 177; most seasons with 50 or more receptions, 8; most passes caught, 819; most yards on receptions, 13,089; and most touchdown passes, 100.
★ Pro Football Hall of Fame

Larkin, Barry L.

BASEBALL
b. April 28, 1964, Cincinnati, Ohio
An All-American shortstop at the University of Michigan in 1985, the 6-foot, 196-pound Larkin joined the NL's Cincinnati Reds during the 1986 season. After hitting .296 in 1988, he missed much of the 1989 season with an injury.

Larkin came back strong in 1990 and hit over .300 each of the next four seasons. He led the league's shortstops with 469 assists in 1990. *The Sporting News* named Larkin to its NL All-Star team five years in a row, from 1988 through 1992.

Larkin starred in Cincinnati's four-game World Series victory over the Oakland Athletics in 1990, batting .353 and handling 15 chances without an error.

Larned, Bill (William A.)

TENNIS
b. Dec. 30, 1872, Summit, N.J.
d. Dec. 16, 1926
Larned won the intercollegiate singles championship in 1892, when he was a student at Cornell. However, he was unsuccessful in the national championships until 1901, when he won the singles title at the age of 28. He went on to win six more national championships, in 1902 and from 1907 through 1911, tying him with Dick Sears and Bill Tilden with seven singles titles.

He was forced to retire after 1911 because of rheumatic fever, which he had contracted while serving in Cuba with Teddy Roosevelt's "Rough Riders" in 1898.

An all-around athlete, Larned cap-

tained the St. Nicholas hockey team in 1896–97 and was also a fine horseman, golfer, and rifle shot. He invented the steel-framed racket in 1922 and founded a company to manufacture it. Partially paralyzed by spinal meningitis, he committed suicide shortly before his fifty-fourth birthday.
★ International Tennis Hall of Fame

Larrieu, Francie (Frances)

TRACK AND FIELD
b. Nov. 28, 1952, Palo Alto, Calif.
The sixth of nine children, Larrieu has an older brother, Ron, who ran for the U.S. Olympic team in 1964. Francie began racing at 13 and won the first competition she ever entered, a 660-yard race for junior girls.

As a tiny 16-year-old, the 5-foot, 100-pound Larrieu was a crowd favorite, much like Mary Decker. But, also like Mary Decker, she was hampered by a series of injuries, possibly caused by intensive training at too early an age.

By 1972, she had grown to 5–4 and 135 pounds and had increased her stamina. She scored an unusual double that year, winning AAU national titles in the 1,500-meter and the cross-country, and she repeated in 1973, winning the 1-mile and cross-country championships.

After missing most of the 1974 season with an injury, Larrieu came back in 1975 to set a world record of 4:28.5 in the mile at the U.S.–Soviet Union indoor meet.

The national champion in the 1,500-meter in 1976, 1977, 1979, and 1980, Larrieu began racing at longer distances in 1979, when she won the national 3,000-meter title. She was also the 3,000-meter champion in 1982. As Francie Larrieu-Smith, she won the 10,000-meter event in 1985, her final competitive season.

Larsen, Don J.

BASEBALL
b. Aug. 7, 1929, Michigan City, Ind.
Larsen had a losing record, but he spent 14 seasons in the major leagues because of his great promise, and he will always live in baseball history because

he is the only pitcher to have thrown a perfect game in the World Series.

A 6-foot-4, 227-pound right-hander, Larsen joined the St. Louis Browns of the AL in 1953 and had a 3–21 record after the franchise moved to Baltimore and became known as the Orioles in 1954. The Orioles traded him to the New York Yankees in 1955. He had his finest years there as a spot starter and occasional reliever.

In 1956, Larsen was 11–5 with a 3.26 ERA. He started the second game of the World Series against the Brooklyn Dodgers but lasted less than two innings. With the Series tied at two games apiece, he got another chance in the fifth game. Jackie Robinson of the Dodgers hit a line drive off the third baseman's glove in the second inning, but was thrown out by the shortstop. In the fifth inning, Gil Hodges hit a long drive to left center, and Mickey Mantle made a fine backhanded catch.

That was as close as the Dodgers came to getting a hit. Larsen, usually wild, went to three balls on only one hitter that afternoon. No Dodger reached base; the Yankees won, 2–0, and they went on to win the World Series in seven games.

Larsen was 10–4 in 1957, 9–6 in 1958, and 6–7 in 1959. The Yankees then traded him to the Kansas City Athletics. He also pitched for the Chicago White Sox, San Francisco Giants, Houston Astros, Baltimore Orioles, and Chicago Cubs before retiring after the 1967 season. He had an 81–91 record with 11 shutouts and a 3.78 ERA. Larsen struck out 849 hitters and walked 725 in 1,546 innings.

LaRussa, Tony (Anthony Jr.)
BASEBALL
b. Oct. 4, 1944, Tampa, Fla.

An infielder, LaRussa appeared in only 132 major league games in six different seasons from 1963 through 1973. After receiving a law degree, he began managing in the minor leagues in 1978 and took over the AL's Chicago White Sox during the 1979 season.

LaRussa was named manager of the year in 1983, when the White Sox won the Western Division championship, but they were defeated by the Baltimore Orioles in the league championship series.

After a 26–38 record in 1986, the White Sox replaced LaRussa. He was hired a short time later to manage the Oakland Athletics, who were in seventh place at the time. LaRussa brought them into a third-place tie. They finished third again in 1987, then won three consecutive pennants and the 1989 world championship.

LaRussa won the manager of the year award in 1988 and in 1992, when Oakland won another division title, losing to Toronto in the league championship series.

Through 1994, LaRussa has a record of 1,253 wins and 1,106 losses in regular season play. He is 20–16 in post-season play.

Lary, Yale (Robert Yale)
FOOTBALL
b. Nov. 24, 1930, Ft. Worth, Tex.

After starring at Texas A & M, Lary joined the NFL's Detroit Lions as a safety man in 1952 and he became the team's punter in 1953. Lary spent two years in the Army during the Korean conflict, then returned to the Lions in 1956 and played nine more seasons.

The 5-foot-11, 189-pounder was very fast and had great anticipation. Detroit quarterback Bobby Layne once said of him, "He was smart, but the big thing was his quickness and his ability to recover and intercept after lulling the quarterback into thinking he had an open receiver."

An All-Pro from 1956 through 1958 and in 1962, Lary led NFL punters with averages of 47.1 yards in 1959, 48.4 yards in 1961, and 48.9 yards in 1963. He retired after the 1964 season.

Lary returned 50 interceptions for 787 yards, a 15.7 average, and 2 touchdowns; he ran back 126 punts for 758 yards, a 6.0 average, and 3 touchdowns; and he punted 503 times for a 44.3 yard average.

★ Pro Football Hall of Fame

Lash, Donald

TRACK AND FIELD
b. Aug. 15, 1913, Bluffton, Ind.
d. Sept. 19, 1994

Running for the University of Indiana, Lash was the NCAA 5,000-meter champion and the AAU 3-mile and 6-mile champion in 1936. He set a world record of 8:58.4 in the 2-mile on June 13 of that year.

Lash also won the AAU 6-mile championship in 1940 and the indoor 3-mile titles in 1938 and 1939. He was the national cross-country champion seven consecutive years, from 1934 through 1940. He won the Sullivan Award as the nation's outstanding amateur athlete in 1938.

Lasorda, Tommy (Thomas C.)

BASEBALL
b. Sept. 22, 1927, Norristown, Pa.

A left-handed pitcher, Lasorda spent most of his 14-year career in the minor leagues, appearing in only 26 major league games with the Brooklyn Dodgers and Kansas City Athletics. After retiring as a player, he became a scout for the Dodgers and then managed in the minor leagues.

Lasorda joined the Dodgers as a coach in 1972 and managed the team at the tail end of the 1976 season, after Walter Alston announced his retirement. The Dodgers promptly won pennants under Lasorda's guidance in 1977 and 1978, but they lost the World Series in six games each year.

Because of a player strike, the 1981 season was shortened and split into halves. The Dodgers won the first half, beat the Houston Astros in the division playoff, won the league championship series over Montreal, and then defeated the Yankees in a six-game World Series.

Los Angeles won the division in 1983 and 1985 but lost in the league championship series both years. In 1988, Lasorda took the Dodgers to another pennant, and they then beat the heavily favored Oakland Athletics in a five-game World Series.

A fiery leader known for his loyalty to the Dodger organization — he has often exhorted his players to "bleed Dodger blue" — Lasorda has sometimes been derided by the press as a clown whose success has resulted largely from having superior talent. But, like Casey Stengel, who once had a similar image, he is respected by baseball people for knowing the game and for his ability to handle and inspire players.

Lattner, Johnny (John J.)

FOOTBALL
b. Oct. 24, 1932, Chicago, Ill.

The only player ever to win the Maxwell Award twice as college football's outstanding player, Lattner also won the Heisman Trophy in 1953, his senior year at Notre Dame. The versatile 6-foot-2, 195-pounder was a T-formation halfback, but he performed like a single-wing tailback, passing on the run and from punt formation, kicking, running, and returning kicks.

A marvelous clutch performer, Lattner as a junior scored the winning touchdowns against the University of Pennsylvania and the University of Southern California. In his senior year, he rushed for 567 yards on 118 carries, returned 8 kickoffs for 321 yards and 2 touchdowns, caught 13 passes for 180 yards, intercepted 4 passes, and punted 28 times for a 34.5 average. He scored 4 touchdowns in Notre Dame's 48–14 win over Southern California.

Lattner was a first-round draft choice of the NFL's Pittsburgh Steelers in 1954 but played with them for only one season. He entered the Air Force in 1955 and suffered a severe knee injury in a service game. He rejoined the Steelers in 1957 but quit during training camp because of the bad knee.
★ College Football Hall of Fame

Laufer, Walter

SWIMMING
b. July 5, 1906, Cincinnati, Ohio

Although overshadowed by Johnny Weismuller and Buster Crabbe, Laufer was one of the most versatile swimmers of his era. He won 11 national championships in three different strokes over a five-year period.

Laufer won a silver medal in the 100-meter backstroke at the 1928 Olympics and was a member of the U.S. 4 x 200-meter freestyle relay team, which won a gold. One of his best events, the individual medley, wasn't on the Olympic program at that time.

Laufer won the national indoor 100-yard freestyle in 1926, 1929, and 1930; the 220-yard freestyle in 1929; the 150-yard backstroke in 1926, 1928, 1930, and 1931; and the 300-yard individual medley in 1926, 1928, and 1929. He was the national outdoor champion in the 220-yard backstroke in 1925.

The high point of his career may have been his 1926 European tour, when he won all but one race while competing in 21 cities over a 23-day period. At one time, he held world backstroke records at both 100 and 200 meters.

Lavelli, Dante B. J.

FOOTBALL
b. Feb. 23, 1923, Hudson, Ohio

A halfback as a freshman at Ohio State, Lavelli played only three games at end in 1942 before being drafted. But his coach, Paul Brown, must have seen something he liked. When Brown was putting together the Cleveland Browns team in the new All-American Football Conference in 1946, he asked Lavelli to try out.

He became the team's starting right end, led the AAFC in receptions with 40 and in reception yardage with 843, and he caught the winning touchdown pass from Otto Graham when the Browns beat the New York Yanks, 14–9, for the league championship.

"Glue Fingers," as his teammates called him, was sure-handed, a precise runner of routes, and a great clutch performer. One of his finest outings came in the Browns' 30–28 victory over the Los Angeles Rams in the 1950 NFL championship game. Lavelli caught 11 passes and scored 2 touchdowns.

Lavelli was an All-AAFC end in 1946 and 1947. That league folded after the 1949 season, and the Browns joined the NFL, where Lavelli was named an All-Pro in 1951 and 1953. He retired after

the 1956 season with 386 receptions for 6,488 yards, a 16.8 average, and 62 touchdowns. All but 20 of the passes he caught were thrown by Graham.
★ Pro Football Hall of Fame

Laver, Rodney G.

TENNIS
b. Aug. 9, 1938, Rockhampton, Australia

Only five tennis players have ever won all four grand slam singles championships — the Australian, French, U.S., and Wimbledon titles — in a single year. Laver is the only person to do it twice, in 1962 and 1969.

Nicknamed "Rocket" because of the speed with which he hit the ball, the left-handed Laver popularized the forehand topspin drive. Not many players used it before he came along, but Laver's success persuaded many others to begin using it. (A top-spin shot tends to rise somewhat at first, making it more likely to clear the net, but it then drops rapidly and takes a long, skidding bounce when it hits the court.)

Laver's first major title was the Australian Open in 1960, and he won at Wimbledon the following year. After his first grand slam, he went through a long fallow period before winning Wimbledon again in 1968 and taking the grand slam for the second time the following year.
★ International Tennis Hall of Fame

Laviolette, Jean B. ("Jack")

HOCKEY
b. July 27, 1879, Belleville, Ont. d. Jan. 10, 1960

A hockey and lacrosse star with the Montreal Nationales in the early part of the century, Laviolette in 1904 joined the professional team in Sault. Ste. Marie, Michigan. In 1909, he organized a team of French Canadians; that team became the Montreal Canadiens in 1913.

Originally a defenseman, Laviolette moved to forward in the latter part of his career. He played with the Canadiens during their first season in the NHL, 1917–18, and then retired. Laviolette lost a foot in an accident the following year, yet he later became a referee.

Records are incomplete for his one NHL season. He played in 18 games and is credited with 2 goals.

★ Hockey Hall of Fame

Law, Vernon S.

BASEBALL
b. March 12, 1930, Meridian, Idaho

Nicknamed "the Preacher" by his teammates because of his deep religious beliefs, Law was a right-handed pitcher who was generally unappreciated because he spent most of his career with losing teams.

However, he was the ace of the staff when the Pittsburgh Pirates won the 1960 NL pennant. Law, who had a 20–9 record with 3 shutouts, a 3.08 ERA, and a league-leading 18 complete games, was named the NL's Cy Young Award winner that season. In Pittsburgh's seven-game World Series victory over the New York Yankees, Law had a 2–0 record and a 3.44 ERA.

He spent his entire 16-year career with the Pirates, from 1950 through 1951 and from 1954 through 1967. Law had a 162–145 record with 28 shutouts and a 3.77 ERA. He struck out 1,092 hitters and walked 597 in 2,672 innings.

Lawrence, Andrea (Mead)

SKIING
b. April 19, 1932, Rutland, Vt.

The only American skier to win two gold medals at the Winter Olympics, Andrea Mead learned the sport at a very early age because her parents owned a ski center.

When she was 15, she qualified for the 1948 Olympic slalom. She didn't win any medals, but she did meet David Lawrence of the men's ski team. They were married in Switzerland in 1951, when the U.S. national team was touring Europe. She had a very successful tour, winning 10 of 16 races and finishing second in 4.

Her new husband had to learn not to wish her good luck; she preferred being told to have fun. "Everybody wants to win but, honestly, I don't care," she once said. "I just want to do my best."

At the 1952 Olympics, Mrs. Lawrence was the first medal winner, in the giant slalom, the day before the opening ceremonies. She followed that with an incredible victory in the slalom. She fell on the first of her two runs but got up quickly and flashed down the course to finish fourth. Her second run was two seconds faster than anyone else's to put her in first place overall.

She had a chance for a third gold medal, but she fell again while turning in the best split times in the downhill race. This time, there was no way to make up for it, and she finished seventeenth.

She had three children in the next four years. The third was born just four months before the Olympics, but she again qualified for the U.S. team and finished in a tie for fourth in the giant slalom, just .1 second behind the bronze medal winner.

Mrs. Lawrence won the national downhill, slalom, and Alpine combined championships in 1949, 1952, and 1955, and she was the giant slalom champion in 1953.

★ International Women's Sports Hall of Fame

Lawrence, Janice

BASKETBALL
b. June 7, 1962, Lucedale, Miss.

Lawrence won the Wade Trophy as the nation's outstanding women's college basketball player for the 1983–84 season, when she averaged 20.7 points and 9.1 rebounds per game, also leading her Louisiana Tech team in steals.

During her career, Lawrence scored 2,403 points in 135 games, a 17.8 average, hitting 934 of 1,577 field goal attempts for a 59.2 percentage. She also had 1,097 rebounds, an average of 8.1 per game.

An All-American in 1983 and 1984, Lawrence was named outstanding player of the NCAA championship tournament in 1982, when she was a sophomore. She led all scorers with an average of 22.8 points per game, and Louisiana Tech won the national title.

After starting for the U.S. Olympic team that won a gold medal in 1984, Lawrence played for the New York franchise in the short-lived Women's American Basketball Association.

Layden, Elmer F.

FOOTBALL
b. May 4, 1903, Davenport, Iowa
d. June 30, 1973

Known later in life as "the Thin Man," the 5-foot-11 Layden played fullback in Notre Dame's Four Horsemen backfield, though he weighed only 162 pounds. In Knute Rockne's style of offense, speed was much more important than power, and Layden was noted not only for speed but for his very quick start.

He was a substitute halfback early in the 1922 season but moved to fullback after the starter broke a leg, and he stayed there for the next two seasons. Layden starred in Notre Dame's 27–10 victory over Stanford in the 1925 Rose Bowl. He ran back two interceptions for touchdowns of 70 and 80 yards and scored another on a 7-yard run. When his 55-yard punt was fumbled by a Stanford player, Notre Dame recovered the ball for its fourth touchdown of the day.

In 1925, Layden became football coach at Columbia (now Loras) College in Dubuque, Iowa. His teams won eight, lost five, and tied two in two seasons. He went to Duquesne in 1927. The small Pittsburgh school had only 11 numbered football jerseys and a difficult schedule, yet Layden had a 48–16–6 record in seven seasons, and his 1933 team beat Miami, 33–7, in the Festival of Palms post-season game, the forerunner of the Orange Bowl.

Layden returned to Notre Dame as football coach and athletic director in 1934. He remained there for seven seasons, winning 47 games while losing 13 and tying 3, first on a two-year contract, then a five-year contract. When he was offered a contract for only one year after the 1940 season, Layden refused.

Shortly afterward, he signed a five-

year contract for $20,000 a year to serve as commissioner of the NFL. He left that position when the contract expired, and he became a sales executive.

Layden's overall coaching record in 16 seasons was 103 wins, 34 losses, and 11 ties, a percentage of .733.

★ College Football Hall of Fame

Layne, Bobby (Robert L.)

FOOTBALL
b. Dec. 19, 1926, Santa Ana, Tex.
d. Dec. 1, 1986

Layne was the starting tailback at the University of Texas as a freshman in 1944. He served in the Merchant Marines and missed the first part of the 1945 season, but he returned to lead Texas to four straight victories, the Southwest Conference championship, and a 40–27 victory over Missouri in the Cotton Bowl.

After leading the conference in passing in 1946, Layne became a T formation quarterback in 1947 and was an All-American at the new position as Texas won nine of ten regular season games and beat Alabama, 27–7, in the Cotton Bowl. During his college career, he completed 210 of 400 passes for 3,145 yards and 25 touchdowns. He also had a 39–7 record as a baseball pitcher.

Layne joined the Chicago Bears in 1948 and became a starter with the New York Bulldogs the following season. His finest years were spent with the Detroit Lions from 1950 through 1958. The Lions won three straight divisional titles, from 1952 through 1954, and they were NFL champions in 1952 and 1953.

He scored one of Detroit's two touchdowns in a 17–7 championship win over the Cleveland Browns in 1952. The 1953 championship game showed Layne at his best. The Lions were losing to the Browns, 16–10, when they took over at their own 20-yard line with a final chance to win. Layne completed four of six passes, the last a 33-yard touchdown to Jim Doran, for a 17–16 victory.

Detroit lost, 56–10, to the Browns in the 1954 championship game. Layne helped lead the Lions to another division title in 1957, but he suffered a broken leg late in the season and was replaced by Tobin Rote, who quarterbacked Detroit to a 59–14 championship win over Cleveland.

Coach Buddy Parker had left the Lions for the Pittsburgh Steelers before the 1947 season. He traded for Layne in mid-season of 1958. Layne promised to take the Steelers to a championship, but he couldn't make good. He retired after the 1962 season.

In 15 years of pro football, Layne completed 1,814 of 3,700 passes for 26,768 yards and 196 touchdowns. He also ran for 25 touchdowns, kicked 34 field goals, and converted 120 extra point attempts for a total of 372 points. He was named an All-Pro in 1952 and 1956.

A confident, fiery team leader, Layne wasn't a great passer but he seemed to be able to complete passes when he had to, and he was a master of the late, game-winning touchdown drive. Otto Graham once said of him, "He's not as good a pure passer as some, but he more than makes up for it. He's always been able to fire up a team."

★ Pro Football Hall of Fame

Lea, Langdon ("Biffy")

FOOTBALL
b. May 11, 1874, Germantown, Pa.
d. Oct. 4, 1937

When Lea was a sophomore at Princeton, the sportswriter and All-America selector Caspar Whitney already thought he was the best tackle in college football. He wrote, "Biffy's all-around tackle play — his blocking and tackling — were unsurpassed."

A four-year starter, Lea was an All-American three times, from 1893 through 1895. While he started, Princeton won 41 games, lost 5, and tied 1. When he captained the team as a senior in 1895, they won 10, lost 1, and tied 1. The legendary coach "Pop" Warner, who played for Cornell in 1893 and 1894, named Lea to his all-time All-American team in 1920.

★ College Football Hall of Fame

Leahy, Frank (Francis W.)

FOOTBALL
b. Aug. 22, 1908, O'Neill, Nebr.
d. June 21, 1973

Leahy played tackle at Notre Dame in 1929 and 1930 but suffered a torn knee cartilage early in the 1931 season, ending his playing career. It was actually good fortune, for Coach Knute Rockne liked Leahy, sat next to him on the bench, and shared football knowledge with him. When Rockne had to go to the Mayo Clinic for an operation after the season, he took Leahy with him for his knee operation, and they shared a room for two weeks.

After graduating in 1932, Leahy became line coach for one of Rockne's former players, "Sleepy Jim" Crowley, at Fordham University. There he forged a powerful line that was christened the "Seven Blocks of Granite."

In 1939, Leahy became head coach at Boston College, where he had a 19–1–0 record in two seasons. His 1939 team lost to Clemson, 6–3, in the Cotton Bowl, but in 1940 Boston College won all ten of its regular season games and beat Tennessee, 19–13, in the Sugar Bowl.

Leahy was rewarded with the head job at Notre Dame in 1941, and he proceeded to compile a record that would have made Rockne proud. His first three teams won 24 games while losing 3 and tying 3. Leahy shocked some long-time fans by scrapping the shift from the T into the Notre Dame box in favor of the new T formation, but he liked the scoring possibilities of the T, and he got the results he wanted.

After spending two years in the Navy during World War II, Leahy returned to Notre Dame in 1946. In his first four postwar seasons, the school won 36 of 38 games with 2 ties. Then came a three-year slump during which the record was 18–8–3.

In Leahy's final season, 1953, Notre Dame won nine games and tied one without a loss. Leahy collapsed because of a pancreas attack at halftime of the Georgia Tech game and announced his retirement on January 31, 1954.

A hard-working perfectionist who stressed fundamentals, Leahy was also an inspiring speaker from the standpoint of his players, but he was known to sportswriters for his often stilted speech. He once summed up his team's prospects by saying, "Notre Dame hopes to field a representative aggregation."

★ College Football Hall of Fame

Lee, Sammy (Samuel)

DIVING
b. Aug. 1, 1920, Fresno, Calif.

The first diver ever to win two gold medals in the Olympic platform diving event, Lee was born of Korean-American parents. As a student at Occidental College, he won the AAU national platform and 3-meter springboard championships in 1942, then retired to study medicine at the University of Southern California.

He returned to competition in 1946 and won the national platform title again. He was a doctor in the U.S. Army Medical Corps when he won his first gold medal in the 1948 Olympics. He also took a bronze in springboard diving.

Lee competed only occasionally during the next four years. He never won another national title, but he qualified for the 1952 Olympic team, and on his thirty-second birthday, he captured his second gold medal in platform diving. The victory brought him the 1953 Sullivan Award as the nation's outstanding amateur athlete.

A specialist in ear diseases, Lee was a fine coach who produced a number of champions. Among them was Bob Webster, who became the second diver to win two gold medals in the platform event. Lee coached the 1960 U.S. Olympic diving team and the 1964 Japanese and Korean teams.

★ Olympic Hall of Fame

Leemans, Tuffy (Alphonse E.)

FOOTBALL
b. Nov. 12, 1912, Superior, Wis.
d. Jan. 19, 1979

Because he was constantly getting into fights, and usually winning them, when other boys teased him about his given name, Leemans won the nickname "Tuffy" when he was young, and it stuck with him. After spending a year at the University of Oregon, Leemans became a starting fullback at George Washington University, where he gained 2,382 yards on 490 carries during his career.

He was named the most valuable player in the 1936 College All-Star game and then joined the NFL's New York Giants. Leemans led the league in rushing with 830 yards on 206 attempts and was the only rookie named to the All-Pro team, at right halfback. He was also an All-Pro in 1939.

Leemans scored New York's first touchdown on a 6-yard run when the Giants beat the Green Bay Packers, 23–17, in the 1938 NFL championship game. As a tailback and sometimes fullback in the single wing, Leemans was also a passer and occasionally a pass receiver.

The Giants honored him with a "Tuffy" Leemans day at the Polo Grounds on December 7, 1941, which also turned out to be Pearl Harbor Day. U.S. Postmaster General James Farley presented him with $1,500 in defense bonds.

Leemans was waiting to be called into the Navy's V-12 training program in 1942 when he suffered a head injury against the Chicago Bears and lost the hearing in one ear, which kept him out of the service. He retired after the 1943 season.

In his eight seasons with the Giants, Leemans carried the ball 919 times for 3,142 yards, a 3.4 average, and 17 touchdowns. He completed 167 of 383 passes for 2,324 yards and 25 touchdowns and caught 28 passes for 422 yards, a 15.1 average, and 3 touchdowns.

★ Pro Football Hall of Fame

Leetch, Brian J.

HOCKEY
b. March 3, 1968, Corpus Christi, Tex.

A defenseman, the 5-foot-11, 190-pound Leetch was named to the NCAA All-American East team as a freshman at Boston College in 1986–87, when he scored 47 points in 37 games. He had 74 points in 60 games for the U.S. national team and 6 points in 6 games with the 1988 U.S. Olympic team.

Leetch joined the NHL's New York Rangers for 17 games at the end of the 1987–88 season and won the Calder Trophy as the league's rookie of the year the following season, when he set a record for a rookie defenseman by scoring 23 goals.

In 1991–92, Leetch scored 102 points on 22 goals and 80 assists and was awarded the James Norris Trophy as the NHL's best defensemen. He missed most of the 1992–93 season with a broken ankle, but came back to win the Conn Smythe Trophy as the outstanding player in the 1994 Stanley Cup playoffs, when he had 34 points in 23 games to lead the Rangers to the NHL championship.

Leetch has scored 103 goals and 343 assists for 446 points in 437 regular season games, and he added 58 points on 19 goals and 39 assists in 46 playoff games.

Lemieux, Mario

HOCKEY
b. Oct. 5, 1965, Montreal, P.Q.

Just when everyone thought no one would ever surpass Wayne Gretzky as a hockey player, Mario Lemieux came along. Lemieux hasn't surpassed Gretzky yet and perhaps never will, but he has come close, and in the process he has proven himself to be a remarkably courageous player.

The 6-foot-4, 210-pound Lemieux averaged more than four points a game in his final season of junior hockey before joining the NHL's Pittsburgh Penguins in 1984. He scored an even 100 points in his first season to win the Calder Trophy as the league's outstanding rookie.

After scoring 141 and 107 points in his next two seasons, Lemieux won the Art Ross Trophy as the league's scoring leader two seasons in a row. He had 70 goals and 98 assists for 168 points in 1987–88, 85 goals and 114 assists for 199 points in 1988–89. Lemieux also won the Hart Memorial Trophy as the player of the year in 1987–88.

Lemieux missed the last 21 games of the 1989–90 season because of a herniated disc, but he still had 123 points. There was doubt about whether he would ever play again after undergoing an operation for the disc problem.

He missed the first 50 games of the 1990–91 season, but Lemieux came back to score 45 points in 26 regular season games and 44 points in 23 playoff games, leading Pittsburgh to the Stanley Cup and winning the Conn Smythe Trophy as the most valuable player in the playoffs.

Although back spasms and a broken hand forced him out of action several times in 1991–92, Lemieux scored 131 points in 64 games to lead the league and was again the top scorer in the playoffs, with 34 points in 15 games, to win his second Conn Smythe Trophy.

Early in 1993, Lemieux was being treated for continued back problems when it was discovered that he had Hodgkin's disease, cancer of the lymphatic system. He missed 20 games while undergoing radiation treatment but came back once again to win the Ross Trophy with 160 points in just 60 games. Because of recurrent back trouble, he missed most of the following season.

Through the 1993–94 season, Lemieux had 494 goals and 717 assists for 1,211 points in 599 regular season games. He had 122 points on 56 goals and 66 assists in 66 playoff games. His average of .825 goals a game is a career record.

Lemon, Bob (Robert G.)

BASEBALL
b. Sept. 22, 1920, San Bernardino, Calif.

A number of major league players, most notably Babe Ruth, have made a successful transition from pitching to an everyday position. Lemon was one of the very few to go the other way.

He entered professional baseball in 1938 and played shortstop, third base, and the outfield, briefly joining the AL's Cleveland Indians in 1941 and 1942 as a third baseman. After three years in the U.S. Navy during World War II, he was Cleveland's starting center fielder in 1946.

Lemon was hitting only .180 when manager Lou Boudreau moved him into the bullpen because of his strong arm. In 1947, he played a few games in the outfield, but he was primarily a pitcher, used both as a starter and as a reliever. The following season, he became a full-time starter, had a 20–14 record, and led the league with 10 shutouts, 20 complete games, and 193⅔ innings pitched. Among his victories was a no-hitter against the Detroit Tigers.

When the Indians beat the Boston Braves in a six-game World Series that year, Lemon won the second and sixth games, compiling a 1.65 ERA.

After a 22–10 record in 1949, Lemon led the league in victories with a 23–11 record, complete games with 22, innings pitched with 288, and strikeouts with 170 in 1950. He had a 17–14 record in 1951, then posted three more 20-victory seasons, leading the league in wins with a 23–7 record in 1954, when the Indians won another pennant. However, they were swept by the New York Giants in the World Series, and Lemon lost both his starts.

Lemon led the AL in victories for a third time with an 18–10 record in 1955, and he was 20–14 in 1956. Leg and elbow injuries combined to end his playing career after the 1958 season. He then spent several seasons as a pitching coach before becoming manager of the Kansas City Athletics in 1970. He was fired during the 1972 season.

After managing in the minors and coaching in the majors, Lemon became manager of the Chicago White Sox in 1977. He was fired during the 1978 season but took over the New York Yankees, replacing Billy Martin, and the Yankees won the pennant and the World Series.

Lemon also managed the Yankees for parts of the 1979, 1981, and 1982 seasons. As a manager, he had a record of 430 wins and 403 losses, a .516 winning percentage. As a pitcher, he had a 207–128 record with 31 shutouts and a 3.23 ERA. He struck out 1,277 hitters and walked 1,251 in 2,850 innings.

★ Baseball Hall of Fame

Lemon, Meadowlark (Meadow G. III)

BASKETBALL

b. April 25, 1933, Lexington, S.C.

Nicknamed the "Clown Prince of Basketball," Lemon was a fine basketball and football player in high school, but his goal was to play for the Harlem Globetrotters, and he spent extra hours working on ball handling and tricky maneuvers to reach that goal.

Lemon entered Florida A & M University after graduating from high school in 1952. His college career was cut short by two years in the Army. He was stationed in Germany while the Globetrotters were playing there, and he got an audition with the team.

After his discharge in 1954, he joined the Globetrotters and quickly became one of their most popular players with his skilled antics. At a time when the best black players were being admitted into the NBA rather than forced into playing for barnstorming teams, Lemon may well have been the salvation of the Globetrotters, since playing for them was his only ambition.

LeMond, Gregory J.

CYCLING

b. June 26, 1961, Lakewood, Calif.

Skiing was originally LeMond's sport, but he became interested in bicycle racing when the course of a road race happened to go past his home. Two years later, he had to get special permission to enter the Tour of Fresno because he was only 16. He finished in second place, just six seconds behind the winner.

In 1979, LeMond became the first road racer ever to win three medals at the junior world championships, taking a gold in the 120-kilometer road race, a silver in the 3,000-meter pursuit race, and a bronze in the team 70-kilometer time trial.

The following year, LeMond joined the Renault-Gitane team in Europe. His French teammate Edouard Hinault predicted shortly afterward, "Greg will be the next champion after me." LeMond got his first major victory in 1983, a 169-mile race in Switzerland, winning by a margin of 1 minute, 11 seconds. He won the world professional road racing championship later that year.

LeMond joined the La Vie Claire team in 1985, finishing second to Hinault in the Tour de France, and in 1986 he became the first American to win the race, beating Hinault by more than three minutes.

After missing most of the 1987 seasons, first with injuries caused by cycling accidents and then with serious wounds from a hunting accident, LeMond returned to win the Tour de France in 1989. He also won the world professional road racing championship for a second time and was named sportsman of the year by *Sports Illustrated.* In 1990, LeMond won the Tour de France for the third time and the second year in a row.

Lendl, Ivan
TENNIS
b. March 7, 1960, Ostrava, Czechoslovakia

A solid baseline player who rarely goes to net, Lendl was long viewed as a very good player who wasn't quite great because he couldn't win the big tournaments. He grew up playing tennis — his mother was ranked second in Czechoslovakia, his father, twentieth — and he turned professional in 1979 after having won the French, Italian, and Wimbledon junior titles in 1978.

Lendl took the Australian Open singles championship in 1983 and the French Open in 1984 but lost in the finals of the U.S. Open three years in a row, from 1982 through 1984, and never reached the Wimbledon finals during the early 1980s. However, he made a breakthrough in 1985, winning the U.S. Open and claiming the Number 1 world ranking for the year. He held on to that ranking in 1986, winning the U.S. and French Opens and finally reaching the final at Wimbledon, only to lose to Boris Becker in straight sets.

In 1987, Lendl won his third straight U.S. Open title and his third French Open. Again he lost in the finals at Wimbledon, to the unheralded Pat Cash, but he retained the top ranking. After slipping to second behind Mats Wilander in 1988, Lendl was back atop the rankings in 1989, when he won the Australian Open but lost in the finals of the U.S. Open.

Younger players then began to pass him. Lendl dropped to third in 1990, fifth in 1991, eighth in 1992, and fifteenth in 1993. He won just one major tournament during that period, the 1990 Australian Open.

Through 1993, Lendl was the top money winner in history with $19,516,-503, and his 92 victories was second only to Jimmy Connors. With eight grand slam singles titles, he's tied for fifth all-time with Jimmy Connors.

Lenglen, Suzanne
TENNIS
b. May 24, 1899, Compiegne, France
d. July 4, 1938

Because she was a frail child, her father decided that Lenglen should learn to play tennis to gain strength. He wasn't a player himself, but he was the secretary of a tennis club in Nice and a keen student and observer of the game.

The fiery Lenglen was outstanding at getting to shots that seemed out of reach, through a combination of speed and determination. She once explained her style, "I just throw dignity to the winds and think of nothing but the game."

In 1919, she won her first major title, the Wimbledon singles, in a classic 44-game match against six-time champion Dorothy Douglass Chambers. Lenglen won, 10–8, 4–6, 9–7. She also won at Wimbledon the next four years, from 1920 through 1923, and in 1925.

The French singles champion from 1920 through 1923 and in 1925 and 1926, Lenglen wasn't so fortunate on her first trip to the United States, in 1921, to play a series of exhibition matches against the U.S. champion, Molla Bjurstedt Mallory, to raise money for French war relief.

Her father opposed the trip because she was suffering from asthma, and he made her agree not to enter the U.S. national championship because of the strain it could be on her health. However, tournament officials were already advertising that she would be playing, and she finally agreed to enter.

Lenglen faced Mrs. Mallory in the first match. After losing the first set, 6–2, and the first two points of the second set, Lenglen began coughing, burst into tears, and walked off the court. She was savagely attacked by American sportswriters.

A few days later, she withdrew from her first exhibition with Mrs. Mallory, saying her doctor had ordered her not to play, and she was attacked even more savagely. She sailed back to France shortly afterward.

Lenglen did get some measure of revenge in 1920. Now healthy, she beat Mallory, 6–2, 6–0, in the singles final at Wimbledon and later that year she defeated her, 6–0, 6–0, in a tournament at Nice.

In addition to her singles victories, Lenglen won the women's doubles at Wimbledon from 1919 through 1923 and in 1925; the Wimbledon mixed doubles in 1920, 1922, and 1925; and the French women's doubles and mixed doubles in 1925 and 1926.

Late in 1926, promoter C. C. Pyle offered Lenglen $50,000 to tour the United States in a series of matches against Mary K. Browne. Although four men also joined the tour, Lenglen got top billing. It was so successful that Lenglen received a $25,000 bonus. Browne was paid $25,000, and the four men shared $77,000.

Lenglen retired from serious competition after the tour. She died of pernicious anemia at the age of 39.

★ International Women's Sports Hall of Fame; International Tennis Hall of Fame

Leonard, Benny [Benjamin Leiner]

BOXING
b. April 7, 1896, New York, N.Y.
d. April 18, 1947

Nicknamed the "Ghetto Wizard" because of his boxing skill, Leonard learned to fight as a youngster growing up in a Jewish neighborhood bordering Irish and Italian neighborhoods. He was

knocked out in his first professional fight in 1911, but he went on to become one of the greatest lightweights in history.

Billy Gibson, later manager of heavyweight champion Gene Tunney, took over Leonard's career in 1914 and guided him toward the title. Leonard fought two no-decisions against world lightweight champion Freddy Welsh in 1916. At the time, New York didn't allow decisions, and the only way to win a fight was by knockout.

On May 28, 1917, Leonard won the title by knocking out Welsh in the 9th round, and he held the championship until his retirement in 1925. Leonard fought Jack Britton for the welterweight title on June 26, 1922, but lost on a foul in the 13th round.

Leonard's biggest fight was just over a month later, on July 27, when Lew Tendler almost knocked him out in the 8th round. Leonard managed to stay on his feet, dazed, and he recovered to last through 12 rounds of a no-decision contest. The fight drew more than 80,000 spectators. Leonard won a rematch in 15 rounds the following year.

He announced his retirement on January 15, 1925. After losing much of his money in the stock market crash, Leonard returned to the ring as a welterweight in 1931. He retired after Jimmy McLarnin knocked him out in the 6th round on October 7, 1932.

In 1943, Leonard became a referee. He died of a heart attack while working a fight in St. Nicholas Arena four years later. Leonard won 89 bouts, 71 by knockout, and lost only 5, 4 by knockout. He also fought 1 draw and 115 no-decisions.

★ International Boxing Hall of Fame

Leonard, Buck (Walter F.)

BASEBALL
b. Sept. 8, 1907, Rocky Mount, N.C.

A left-handed first baseman, Leonard played semipro baseball until 1933, when he began playing for the all-black Baltimore Stars at the age of 25. The team folded during the season, and he joined the Brooklyn Royal Giants.

In 1934, Leonard went to the Homestead Grays. He spent 17 seasons with the team, one of the best in baseball history, and for many of those seasons he batted fourth behind the legendary Josh Gibson, another Hall of Famer. They were black baseball's answer to Ruth and Gehrig.

The Negro National League didn't do a meticulous job of keeping statistics, but by all accounts Leonard usually hit in the high .300s. He led the league with a .391 average in 1948, when the statistics were accurate. Leonard was also renowned for his great range and strong throwing arm.

The Homestead team folded after the 1950 season, and Leonard began playing in the Mexican League. He was offered a chance to join the AL's St. Louis Browns in 1952; he turned it down because he knew he was past his prime, and he didn't want to be embarrassed. However, he didn't retire until after the 1955 season, when he was 48 years old.

Leonard later became a director and vice president of the Class A minor league team in his home town of Rocky Mount.

★ Baseball Hall of Fame

Leonard, Sugar Ray (Ray Charles)

BOXING
b. May 17, 1956, Wilmington, N.C.

His mother wanted him to be a singer, so she named him Ray Charles Leonard. Instead, he became a successful boxer and was nicknamed after Sugar Ray Robinson.

Leonard won 145 of 150 amateur bouts, was the AAU welterweight champion in 1974 and 1975, and won gold medals at the 1975 Pan-American Games and the 1976 Olympics. He had his first professional fight on February 5, 1977, when he won a 6-round decision over Luis Vega.

After winning his first 23 professional fights, Leonard met Pete Ranzany for the North American Boxing Federation welterweight championship on Au-

gust 12, 1979, at Las Vegas. Leonard knocked out Ranzany in the 4th round. He won the world title with a 15th-round knockout of Wilfred Benitez on November 30, also at Las Vegas.

Leonard lost the championship to Roberto Duran on a 15-round decision on June 20, 1980, in Montreal. He regained it in a strange fight on November 25 in New Orleans. During the 8th round, Duran suddenly lowered his hands, said "No mas" ("No more" in Spanish), and walked back to his corner, though he hadn't apparently been hurt.

On June 25, 1981, Leonard won the world junior middleweight title by knocking out Ayub Kalule in the 9th round at Houston. Later that year, he won an estimated $10 million, then the highest single paycheck ever for an athlete, by knocking out Tommy Hearns in the 14th round to defend his welterweight championship.

A detached retina forced Leonard's retirement in 1982. He returned for one fight in 1984, then retired again. On April 7, 1987, Leonard won a split decision over Marvin Hagler in Las Vegas to claim the World Boxing Council's middleweight title. He broke his own record by collecting an $11 million purse.

A month later, he retired once more, but Leonard returned again to win the WBC light heavyweight and super middleweight titles in November 1988, when he knocked out Don Lalonde of Canada. Leonard retired for good after being badly beaten by Terry Norris on February 9, 1991.

★ Olympic Hall of Fame

Levy, Marvin D.

FOOTBALL
b. Aug. 3, 1928, Chicago, Ill.

Levy played football at Coe College, graduating in 1950, and then received a master's degree in English history from Harvard in 1951. After coaching St. Louis Country Day School to a 13–0–1 record in two seasons, he returned to Coe as an assistant football coach. He became an assistant at the University of New Mexico in 1956 and took over as head coach in 1958.

After compiling a 14–6–0 record in two seasons there, he went to the University of California but was fired in 1964 after winning only 8 games while losing 29 and tying 2. Levy was then hired by William & Mary College, where he had a 23–25–2 record in five seasons.

From 1969 through 1972, Levy served as an assistant NFL coach. He took over the Montreal Alouettes of the Canadian Football League in 1973 and guided them to two Grey Cup championships, in 1974 and 1977. His CFL record was 43–31–4 in five seasons.

Levy became head coach of the NFL's Kansas City Chiefs in 1978. He made a respectable team of them, going 9–7–0 in 1981, but was replaced after the Chiefs won only three of their first nine games the following season. After a year out of football, Levy took over the Chicago team in the U.S. Football League, where he had a 5–13–0 record.

That league folded after the 1984 season, and Levy spent another year out of football before being hired by the NFL's Buffalo Bills during the 1986 season. He has had his greatest success with Buffalo, guiding the Bills to a 79–39–0 regular season record, an 11–6 record in the playoffs, and four consecutive American Football Conference championships, from 1990 through 1993. However, Buffalo lost all four Super Bowls.

Levy developed the no-huddle offense into a powerful weapon for Buffalo, allowing quarterback Jim Kelly to call his own plays at the line of scrimmage most of the time. The "hurry-up" offense, as it is also called, prevents defenses from making situational substitutions.

Lewis, Bill (William H.)

FOOTBALL
b. Nov. 30, 1868, Berkeley, Va.
d. Jan. 1, 1949

The first black ever named to an All-American team, Lewis was the son of former slaves who moved to New England when he was young. He had an unusual college football career: he graduated from Amherst College, where he was a starter at center for three years and team captain in his senior season, 1891,

and then played for Harvard in 1892 and 1893 while attending law school.

Casper Whitney selected him as an All-American after both of his seasons at Harvard. Though slender, at 5-foot-11 and 177 pounds, Lewis was deceptively strong. As a defender, he was noted for his ability to diagnose offensive plays as they unfolded. In 1903, he wrote the chapter on defense for Walter Camp's *How to Play Football.*

Lewis was the first black admitted to the American Bar Association, in 1911. He served as an assistant attorney general of the United States for some years and was the first black member of the Massachusetts State Legislature.

★ College Football Hall of Fame

Lewis, Carl (F. Carlton)

TRACK AND FIELD
b. July 1, 1961, Birmingham, Ala.

Lewis, who grew up in Willingboro, New Jersey, was a small child who suddenly had such a growth spurt at age 15 that he had to walk on crutches for nearly a month to allow his body to adjust. A year later, he ran the 100 meters in 10.6 seconds and did 23 feet, 9 inches in the long jump.

After graduating from high school in 1979, Lewis entered the University of Houston. He won the NCAA long jump championship in 1980, and in 1981 he won the NCAA and national outdoor 100-meter and long jump titles.

Lewis left school in 1981 to join the Santa Monica Track Club and concentrate on training. After winning the national 100-meter and long jump championships again in 1982, Lewis established himself as the best athlete in the world in 1983. He won the 100- and 200-meter dashes and the long jump at the U.S. nationals, the first to accomplish that since 1936, and he also took world championships in the 100-meter and long jump.

At the 1984 Olympic Games, the 6-foot-2, 175-pound Lewis duplicated Jesse Owens's 1936 feat by winning gold medals in the 100- and 200-meter, the long jump, and the 4 x 100-meter relay. Never a great starter, he showed an amazing finishing burst in the 100-meter; he was clocked at 28 miles an hour when he hit the tape, and he won by 8 feet, the largest margin in the history of the Olympic event.

An injury kept Lewis out of action for most of 1985, but he returned in 1986 to win national titles in the 100-meter and long jump once again. In 1987, he repeated his triple victory at the national championships and won the long jump in the world championships, where he finished second to Ben Johnson of Canada in the 100-meter.

He was just behind Johnson again at the 1988 Olympics, but the Canadian sprinter was disqualified when he tested positive for steroids, and Lewis was awarded the gold medal. His time was a world record 9.93 seconds. He also won the long jump and ran on the gold medal 4 x 100-meter relay team.

Often outspoken, Lewis boycotted the 1989 national championships, criticizing The Athletics Congress for not doing enough to stop drug use by track and field athletes. He also cut down on his sprint schedule and began to concentrate on the high jump in the hope of breaking Bob Beamon's 1968 world record of 29 feet, 2½ inches.

However, that record fell to Mike Powell at the 1991 world championships. Although Lewis turned in the greatest three-jump series in history, surpassing 28 feet easily on each attempt, he couldn't beat Powell's leap of 29–4½. But he did win the world championship in the 100-meter.

By the 1992 Olympics, Lewis's star seemed to be in decline. He failed to qualify for either of the sprints and won a spot on the 4 x 100-meter relay team only because another runner was injured. However, he won his seventh and eighth gold medals, in the long jump and the relay. For the fifth time in his career, he anchored a team to a world record in the 4 x 100.

His performance spurred Mel Rose, the coach of the U.S. team, to comment, "I've said it all along: Carl is the greatest athlete I have ever seen, and he proves it time and time again." Lewis said he'd like to be back for the 1996 Olympics, but it seemed doubtful after his difficult 1993 season. A chronic back injury, aggravated by an auto accident, kept him out of the long jump for most of the year, he didn't win a 100-meter race all year, and his only medal in the world championships was a bronze in the 200-meter.

The Associated Press male athlete of the year in 1983 and 1984, Lewis won the Sullivan Award as the nation's outstanding amateur athlete of 1981.
★ Olympic Hall of Fame

Lewis, Guy V.
BASKETBALL
b. March 19, 1922, Arp, Tex.

After serving in the Army Air Corps in World War II, Lewis played basketball at the University of Houston, graduating in 1947. He became an assistant coach at the school in 1953 and took over as head coach in 1956.

A colorful dresser who flourished a red and white towel on the sideline, Lewis remained at Houston through the 1985–86 season. The school had 27 straight winning seasons and 14 seasons with 20 or more wins during his tenure.

Lewis guided 14 teams into the NCAA tournament, and 5 of them reached the final four. However, Houston lost both times it reached the final game, to North Carolina State in 1983 and to Georgetown in 1984.

In his 30 seasons, Lewis had a 592–279 record for a .680 winning percentage. He is 20th on the all-time NCAA Division I victory list.

Lewis, Reggie (Reginald)
BASKETBALL
b. Nov. 21, 1965, Baltimore, Md.
d. July 27, 1993

The 6-foot-7, 195-pound Lewis starred at Northeastern University in Boston, averaging 22.2 points a game in four years as a starter. He was chosen in the first round of the 1987 NBA draft by the Boston Celtics.

He missed a good part of his rookie season with an injury and was a backup during the next two seasons, but he averaged over 30 minutes a game because he could be used at small forward or shooting guard. Very quick, Lewis could score by driving to the basket or by shooting from outside.

Lewis became a starter in 1990–91, when Larry Bird was out much of the year with an injury, and he was named the team's captain after Bird's retirement in 1992. He averaged 20.8 points a game in both 1991–92 and 1992–93.

In Boston's first game of the 1993 playoffs, Lewis collapsed and had to be taken to a hospital. Displeased when a team of doctors told him he would have to give up basketball because of a heart disease, Lewis changed hospitals and doctors in the middle of the night. He was then advised that his heart was healthy and that he could begin training again, under medical supervision. He died of a heart attack while taking part in an unsupervised workout.

Lewis, Ted Kid [Gershon Mendeloff]
BOXING
b. Oct. 24, 1894, London, England
d. Oct. 14, 1970

Lewis began boxing professionally in England in 1909 and won the European featherweight championship on February 2, 1914, when Paul Til fouled him in the 12th round. Late that year, Lewis came to the United States.

Over a six-year period beginning in 1915, Lewis had a series of 20 fights with Jack Britton, most of them no-decision bouts. Lewis won the world welterweight title with a 12-round decision over Britton on August 31, 1915, and retained the title in a rematch on September 27.

Britton regained the title with a 20-round decision on April 24, 1916; Lewis won it back with a 20-round decision on June 25, 1917; and Britton reclaimed it by knocking Lewis out in the 9th round on March 17, 1919.

Lewis returned to England in December 1919. He later won the British welterweight, middleweight, and light heavyweight titles. He won 170 bouts, 70 by knockout; lost 31, 7 by knockout; and fought 13 draws and 66 no-decisions.
★ International Boxing Hall of Fame

Lieberman, Nancy [Mrs. Cline]
BASKETBALL
b. July 1, 1958, Brooklyn, N.Y.

Lieberman fell in love with basketball when she was young and developed her skills on New York City playgrounds, playing with and against boys. As a high school junior, she was a member of the U.S. team in the Pan-American Games in 1975, and a year later she was the youngest member of the team that won a silver medal in the Olympics.

An outstanding shooter and ball handler, Lieberman entered Old Dominion University in Virginia in 1976. The school won two straight national championships in 1979 and 1980, and Lieberman won both the Wade Trophy and the Broderick Award as the nation's best collegiate woman basketball player both years. In 1979, she was awarded the Honda Broderick Cup as the outstanding woman athlete in any sport.

Lieberman played on the 1979 Pan-American Games team and was chosen for the 1980 Olympic team that didn't play because of the U.S. boycott of the Soviet Union Games. During her collegiate career, she averaged 18.1 points and more than 9 rebounds a game, along with 961 assists and 561 steals.

The first draft choice of the Dallas Diamonds in the Women's Professional Basketball League, Lieberman was named rookie of the year after averaging 26.3 points a game, but the league folded. As trainer and manager, she helped tennis player Martina Navratilova revive her game during the early 1980s, then signed a three-year $250,000 contract with Dallas of the new Women's American Basketball Association in 1984.

That league also collapsed, and in 1986 Lieberman signed with the Springfield, Massachusetts, team in the U.S. Basketball League, becoming the first woman to play in a men's professional league. A year later, she became the first woman to play for the Washington Generals, the team that tours with the Harlem Globetrotters.

Lightbody, Jim (James D.)

TRACK AND FIELD
b. March 15, 1882, Pittsburgh, Pa.
d. March 2, 1953

As a student at the University of Chicago, Lightbody didn't win any major races, but he won four medals, including three golds, at the 1904 Olympics in St. Louis.

He began with a victory in the 2,500-meter steeplechase, beating heavily favored John D. Daly of Ireland. Three days later, Lightbody was given little chance to win the 800-meter, but after a very fast pace began to wear out most of the competitors, he sprinted through the stretch to take the lead 50 yards from the tape, and won going away.

After a day off, Lightbody won the 1,500-meter run in a world record 4:05.4. That race was in the morning; in the afternoon, he ran in the 4-mile team race for the Chicago Athletic Association, which won the silver medal.

Lightbody won the AAU national 800- and 1,500-meter runs in 1905. To celebrate the tenth anniversary of the modern Olympics, Athens hosted an "intercalated" Olympic Games in 1906. Lightbody repeated as the 1,500-meter champion and won a silver in the 800-meter, finishing just inches behind Paul Pilgrim of the U.S.

Lilly, Bob (Robert L.)

FOOTBALL
b. July 26, 1939, Olney, Tex.

An All-American tackle at Texas Christian University in 1960, Lilly was the first player ever chosen in the NFL college draft by the Dallas Cowboys when they entered the league in 1961.

The Cowboys used the 6-foot-5, 260-pound Lilly at defensive end at first, but he was then moved to tackle in Tom Landry's flex defense. Playing slightly off the line of scrimmage, Lilly had to read the play quickly and then react to it. His size and speed made him the key player in the famed "Doomsday Defense."

Quick to the ball, Lilly recovered 16 of the opposition's fumbles and returned them for 109 yards and 3 touchdowns.

He also had a touchdown on a 17-yard interception return. In a 24–3 victory over the Miami Dolphins in Super Bowl VI, Lilly set a record by tackling Miami quarterback Bob Griese for a 29-yard loss.

Lilly was an All-Pro eight times, from 1964 through 1969 and from 1971 through 1972. He played in 292 games, including playoff games, and missed only one before retiring after the 1974 season.
★ Pro Football Hall of Fame

Lind, Joan L.

ROWING
b. Sept. 26, 1952, Long Beach, Calif.

Lind began rowing in 1971, when she was a freshman at Long Beach State University. After competing in double sculls and four-oared shells, she moved into single sculls racing in 1973 and won five national championships.

At the 1976 Olympics, Lind took a silver medal, finishing just .65 of a second behind the winner. She won silver medals in two major European races, at Lucerne and Amsterdam, in 1980, when she again made the Olympic team. However, the U.S. boycotted the Moscow Games that year because of the Soviet invasion of Afghanistan.

Lind then retired from rowing to get her master's degree from St. Thomas College in Minnesota, but she came out of retirement in 1984 to row on the U.S. team that won a silver medal in the quadruple sculls event.

Lindsay, Ted (Robert Blake Theodore)

HOCKEY
b. July 29, 1925, Renfrew, Ont.

"Terrible Tempered Ted" was a hockey rarity, a fierce brawler who was also an outstanding scorer. When he retired, he held NHL records for most goals and most assists by a left wing and for most minutes spent in the penalty box by any player.

The son of a rink operator in Kirkland Lake, Ontario, Lindsay played amateur hockey there until joining the Detroit Red Wings in 1944. For most of his career with Detroit, he was on the "Production Line" with Gordie Howe at right wing and Sid Abel, followed by Alex Delvecchio at center.

Lindsay led the league in scoring with 23 goals and 55 assists in 1948–49 and was among the top ten scorers seven other times. Though only 5-foot-8 and 160 pounds, he acquired the nickname "Scarface" because of his frequent fights; he once said he stopped counting his stitches when he got to four hundred.

Traded to the Chicago Black Hawks in 1957, Lindsay retired in 1960 but returned to Detroit for one more season in 1964–65. During his first stint with the Red Wings, they won eight regular season championships and four Stanley Cup titles. In his comeback season, they won their first regular season championship in eight years.

Lindsay scored 379 goals and had 427 assists in 1,068 regular season games and had 47 goals and 49 assists in 133 playoff games.

★ Hockey Hall of Fame

Lindstrom, Freddy (Frederick C.)

BASEBALL
b. Nov. 21, 1905, Chicago, Ill.
d. Oct. 4, 1981

Lindstrom began playing major league baseball at the triple-A level in 1922, when he was only 16. He joined the NL's New York Giants late in the 1924 season to replace starting third baseman Heinie Groh, whose season had been ended by a knee injury.

The Giants won the pennant, and Lindstrom, aged 18 years and 10 months, become the youngest player ever to appear in the World Series. Batting leadoff, he hit .333 with 10 hits, including 2 doubles, in New York's seven-game loss to the Washington Senators.

Despite his hitting, the decisive seventh game was a personal embarrassment to Lindstrom. The Giants were leading, 3–1, in the eighth inning when a grounder hit a pebble and flew over Lindstrom's head, bringing in the tying runs. In the twelfth inning, the Senators had a runner on second when another grounder to Lindstrom hit a pebble and went over his head to score the run that

won the series for the Senators. Lindstrom wasn't given an error on either play, but he was heartbroken.

Lindstrom hit over .300 in 6 straight seasons, from 1926 through 1931, with a high of .379 in 1930. He led the league in hits with 231 in 1928, when his average was .358, and he was also the NL's best fielding third baseman that year.

In 1931, Lindstrom was moved to center field. A broken leg limited him to just 78 games and a .300 average. After slipping to .271 in 1932, Lindstrom was traded to the Pittsburgh Pirates. He had averages of .310 and .290 in two seasons there, then went to the Chicago Cubs. He was a part-time player with the Cubs in 1935 and the Brooklyn Dodgers in 1936 before retiring.

Lindstrom later did a sports radio program, managed in the minor leagues, and served as baseball coach at Northwestern University from 1947 through 1960.

In 1,438 games, Lindstrom had 1,747 hits, including 301 doubles, 81 triples, and 103 home runs. He scored 895 runs and had 779 RBI.

★ Baseball Hall of Fame

Liquori, Martin

TRACK AND FIELD
b. Sept. 11, 1949, Montclair, N.J.

Liquori made the U.S. Olympic team in 1968, when he was a 19-year-old freshman, and he reached the finals of the 1,500-meter run but suffered a stress fracture and finished last.

In 1969, he won the NCAA and AAU outdoor 1-mile championships and finished second to Jim Ryan in the NCAA indoor meet. He repeated in the AAU outdoor in 1970 and had his best year in 1971, winning the NCAA and AAU outdoor titles, a gold medal in the 1,500-meter at the Pan-American Games, and running a personal best 3:54.6 in the mile at the Martin Luther King Games in Philadelphia.

Late in the year, however, he injured his left heel while running cross-country. He didn't return to competition until 1973 and had indifferent success until 1975, when he ran a personal best 3:52.2

in the mile, finishing second to Gilbert Bayi, and set a U.S. record of 8:17.12 in the 2-mile.

Liquori qualified for the 1976 Olympic team by running a 13:33.6 in the 5,000 meters early in the year. Unfortunately, he missed the Olympics again because of a severe hamstring pull at the AAU national outdoor meet, and he was forced to retire.

Since then, Liquori has worked for a number of sportswear companies, including his own, and he has also done frequent television commentary on track and field.

Liston, Sonny (Charles)
BOXING
b. May 8, 1932, Forest City, Ark. d. Dec. 30, 1970

Titled "the Heavyweight Champion Nobody Wanted" by his biographer, Liston learned to box while serving a five-year prison sentence for robbery. He won the U.S. and international Golden Gloves heavyweight championships in 1953.

The 6–1, 220-pound Liston turned professional shortly afterward and knocked out Don Smith with his first punch as a pro. He won 14 of 15 fights before serving a nine-month sentence for assaulting a police officer in 1957.

Early in his career, Liston came under the control of two racketeers, Frankie Carbo and Blinky Palermo. He was denied a Pennsylvania boxing license until he hired an independent manager, George Katz, in 1961. New York State, however, turned down his license application with the statement, "The history of Liston's past associations provides a pattern of suspicion."

As a result, his fight with heavyweight champion Floyd Patterson took place in Chicago rather than New York. On September 25, 1962, Liston won the title by knocking out Patterson in the 1st round, and a rematch in Las Vegas on July 22, 1963, had the same result.

After an exhibition tour of Europe, Liston fought the lightly regarded Cassius Clay in Miami Beach on February 25, 1964. Clay won when Liston failed to come out for the 7th round, claiming a shoulder injury. They met again on May 25, 1965, in Lewiston, Maine, and Liston was knocked out in the 1st round by a phantom punch that few observers saw. His criminal background and associations led many to think both fights were fixed.

Liston fought Leotus Martin for the vacant North American Boxing Federation title on December 6, 1969, and was knocked out in the 9th round. He was found dead in the swimming pool of his home several months after his last fight, a 10th-round knockout of Chuck Wepner.

Liston won 50 professional fights, 39 by knockout. He lost 4, 3 by knockout.
★ International Boxing Hall of Fame

Little, Larry C.
FOOTBALL
b. Nov. 2, 1945, Georgetown, Ga.

Little played tackle at Bethune-Cookman College in Florida and wasn't selected in the 1967 AFL or NFL drafts. He signed as a free agent with the AFL's San Diego Chargers and was traded to the Miami Dolphins in 1969.

The 6-foot-1, 265-pound Little became a star as a guard with Miami, leading the Dolphins' powerful running attack. He was named to the All-AFC team four years in a row, from 1971 through 1974. Miami won all 17 games in the 1972 season, including a 14–7 win over the Washington Redskins in the Super Bowl, and they repeated as Super Bowl champions the following year.

Little retired after the 1980 season.
★ Pro Football Hall of Fame

Little, W. Lawson
GOLF
b. June 23, 1910, Newport, R.I. d. Feb. 1, 1968

Generally considered the greatest amateur golfer since Bobby Jones, Little accomplished something Jones didn't: he won both the U.S. and British Amateur championships two years in a row, in 1934 and 1935. During that two-year period, he won 34 consecutive matches against the best amateur players in the world. Little was presented with the 1935 Sullivan Award as the outstanding U.S. amateur athlete of the year.

He became a professional in 1936 but never reached the heights some had expected him to. His one major championship was the 1940 U.S. Open, when he beat Gene Sarazen, 70–73, in a playoff after the two had tied at 287.

★ PGA Hall of Fame; World Golf Hall of Fame

Little, Lou (Luigi Piccolo)

FOOTBALL
b. Dec. 6, 1893, Boston, Mass.
d. May 28, 1979

Although he had only five winning teams in his last 20 seasons of coaching, Little was recognized by his peers as one of the finest college coaches of his time. The problem was that he spent most of his career at Columbia University, where good football players were rare.

Little played tackle for one year at the University of Vermont, then transferred to Pennsylvania in 1916. After serving in World War I, he played at Penn again in 1919, then joined the NFL's Buffalo All-Americans for two seasons. He was one of several Buffalo players who also performed for the independent Philadelphia Quakers in 1921; the Quakers played on Saturdays, the All-Americans on Sundays.

In 1924, Little became head coach at Georgetown University and compiled a 39–12–4 record in six seasons. He went to Columbia in 1930. His first seven seasons there were very successful. His teams won 43 games while losing 15 and tying 3 during that period, and his 1933 team upset Stanford, 7–0, in the Rose Bowl. The winning touchdown came on a trick play, a bootleg by the fullback after a fake reverse that became famous in the newspapers as "KF-79."

After 1936, Columbia fell on hard times. The school gave no full athletic scholarships and simply couldn't keep up even with other Ivy League schools. Little did rally the team for three seasons after World War II, winning 21 games while losing 6 from 1945 through

1947, but he had only one more winning season before retiring in 1957.

His last game, though, was an 18–12 victory over Rutgers in 1956. Four players from his first team, the 1924 Georgetown squad, were in the Columbia locker room to congratulate him afterward.

★ College Football Hall of Fame

Littler, Gene (Eugene A.)

GOLF
b. Nov. 16, 1920, San Diego, Calif.

After winning the U.S. Amateur, the California Amateur, and the California Open in 1953, Littler joined the PGA tour. He won the first tournament he entered, the 1954 San Diego Open, and he finished second in the U.S. Open.

Littler won five tournaments in 1955, then went into a three-year slump. He came out of it with five more victories in 1959, when he finished second in winnings.

His only major victory came in the 1961 U.S. Open, when he shot a 68 in the final round to overtake Doug Sanders. Littler lost playoffs in two other major tournaments, to Bill Casper in the 1970 Masters and to Lanny Wadkins in the 1977 PGA championship.

★ PGA Hall of Fame; World Hall of Fame

Litwack, Harry

BASKETBALL
b. Sept. 10, 1907, Galicia, Austria

Litwack captained the Temple University team in 1928–29 and 1929–30, then played for the Philadelphia SPHAs for six years. After coaching the Temple freshman team for 20 seasons, he spent a year as an assistant coach of the NBA's Philadelphia Warriors, then returned to Temple as head basketball coach in 1952.

In 21 seasons, Litwack had just one losing season. He was named coach of the year by the New York Basketball Writers Association in 1958, after his team won 27 of 30 games. Temple won the 1969 National Invitation Tournament and twice went to the final four in the NCAA tournament, finishing third both times.

Known for getting the very most out of the limited talent available to him, Litwack coached four All-Americans. His teams won 373 games while losing only 193.

★ Basketball Hall of Fame

Lloyd, Marion [Mrs. Vince]
FENCING
b. April 16, 1906, Brooklyn, N.Y.
d. Nov. 2, 1969

The national women's foil champion in 1928 and 1931, Lloyd in 1932 became the first American woman to reach the finals at the Olympics. She placed ninth. Lloyd was a member of the Salle Vince team, directed by her husband, Joseph Vince, which won ten consecutive national team championships in the 1920s and 1930s.

Lloyd, Pop (John H.)
BASEBALL
b. April 15, 1884, Palatka, Fla.
d. March 19, 1965

A shortstop, Lloyd was often referred to as "the Black Wagner." The great Honus Wagner commented on the nickname, "I am honored to have John Lloyd called the Black Wagner. It's a privilege to have been compared to him." Like Wagner, the 5-foot-11, 180-pound Lloyd had long arms, big hands, great speed for his size, and great lateral range. Unlike Wagner, he batted left-handed.

Although he was a soft-spoken, easygoing man who genuinely loved baseball, Lloyd was also a fierce competitor on the field, and he was continually moving from one team to another to get a raise. "Wherever the money was, that's where I was," he once said.

Lloyd played second base in his first professional season with the Cuban X Giants in 1906 but was moved to shortstop when he joined the Philadelphia Giants the following year. After three seasons there, he went to the Chicago Leland Giants with several teammates, and the Philadelphia team folded.

During the winters, Lloyd usually played in Cuba, where he was known as "El Cucharo" — the Shovel — because he often came up with pebbles and pieces of the infield dirt when he scooped up a grounder. In 1910, his Cuban team played a 12-game exhibition series against the Detroit Tigers, led by Ty Cobb. Lloyd hit .500 to Cobb's .370.

In 1911, Lloyd went to the Lincoln Giants in New York, and he moved back to Chicago, with the American Giants, in 1913. He stayed there through the 1917 season, then became player manager of the Brooklyn Royal Giants in 1918.

From that time on, Lloyd began to play first base more often than shortstop. He played for and managed several teams before retiring from professional baseball in 1931, at the age of 47. However, he continued managing and sometimes playing for semipro teams in Atlantic City until 1942, and he later served as commissioner of the city's Little League.

★ Baseball Hall of Fame

Locke, Gordon C.
FOOTBALL
b. August 3, 1898, Denison, Iowa

An All-American quarterback at the University of Iowa in 1922, the 165-pound Locke was sometimes a fullback who could hit the line with surprising power. When he played quarterback, he was actually a tailback who was expected to pass and kick as well as run.

Locke starred for Iowa teams that won 17 consecutive games, including undefeated seasons in 1921 and 1922. He captained the 1922 team.

★ College Football Hall of Fame

Loeffler, Kenneth D.
BASKETBALL
b. April 14, 1902, Beaver Falls, Pa.
d. Jan. 1, 1975

Loeffler entered the newspaper business in 1924 after playing basketball at Penn State, then became head coach at little Geneva College in 1929. He earned a law degree from the University of Pittsburgh while coaching Geneva to 95 wins against 55 losses in six seasons.

He moved to Yale in 1936 but had

just one winning season there before joining the Army Air Corps in 1942. After World War II, he coached Denver University for one season and then took over the St. Louis Bombers of the new Basketball Association of America. The Bombers won 67 games and lost 42 in his two seasons, and the BAA's Providence Steamroller had a 12–48 record in Loeffler's one season of coaching.

Loeffler returned to college coaching at LaSalle in 1950. His 1951–52 team, led by freshman Tom Gola, won the National Invitation Tournament, and in 1954 LaSalle won the NCAA championship, beating Bradley, 92–76, in the final game to set a tournament record for points in a single game.

After winning 145 games against only 30 losses in six seasons, Loeffler went to Texas A & M in 1956. His teams won just 13 of 48 games in two seasons. Accused of recruiting violations, Loeffler resigned in 1958 and became a college law teacher.

★ Basketball Hall of Fame

Lofton, James D.

FOOTBALL
b. July 5, 1956, Fort Ord, Calif.

The all-time NFL leader in reception yardage, Lofton was an All-American wide receiver at Stanford University in 1977, when he caught 68 passes for 1,216 yards and 16 touchdowns. The 6-foot-3, 190-pound Lofton was also a track star. He won the NCAA long jump championship in 1978 and was timed at 20.7 seconds in the 200-meter dash.

Lofton joined the NFL's Green Bay Packers as their first-round draft choice in 1978 and was named rookie of the year after catching 46 passes for 818 yards and 6 touchdowns. He led the league in yards per reception with 22.4 on 58 catches in 1983 and 22.0 on 62 catches in 1984.

Accused of sexual assault in 1986, Lofton was suspended from the final game of the season and was then traded to the Oakland Raiders. The Raiders released him after two seasons, and he signed with the Buffalo Bills in 1989, when he caught only 8 passes. However, he became a frequent starter with the Bills for the next three seasons, catching 35, 57, and 51 passes, and scoring 18 touchdowns over that span.

Lofton became a free agent after the 1992 season and played for the Los Angeles Rams and the Philadelphia Eagles the following year before retiring. Because of his speed and athletic ability, Lofton was often used on the end-around play, rushing for 246 yards and 1 touchdown on 32 carries, a 7.7 average. He also threw a 43-yard touchdown pass on a trick play in 1982.

Through the 1993 season, Lofton had 764 receptions, fourth all-time, with a career record 14,004 yards. His 75 touchdown receptions tied him for tenth on the all-time list.

Loftus, Johnny (John P.)

HORSE RACING
b. Oct. 13, 1896, Chicago, Ill.
d. March 20, 1976

Loftus's brief, brilliant career as a jockey unfortunately ended under a cloud of suspicion when the Jockey Club refused to issue him a license in 1920. No official explanation was given, but there is no question that race stewards suspected Loftus of throwing the 1919 Sanford Stakes, when Man o'War suffered the only loss of his career, finishing second to Upset.

Actually, Loftus was probably the victim of circumstances. After a false start, he was still bringing Man o'War back to the line when the starting signal was given, so he had to turn the horse around to get into the race. He was then boxed in behind Upset, the eventual winner, and Golden Broom. Loftus was forced to take Man o'War two horses wide for a stretch drive, and in the ¾-mile sprint, he just didn't have enough track left to catch Upset.

Loftus began jockeying in 1912, and his first major victory came in the 1916 Kentucky Derby aboard George Smith. He rode War Cloud to a win in the 1918 Preakness, and in 1919 he became the first jockey to win the triple crown, guiding Sir Barton to victories in the

Kentucky Derby, Preakness, and Belmont.

In 1919, he also rode Man o'War to nine wins in ten starts, and he led in earnings with $252,707, winning 65 of 177 starts.

When his career as a jockey ended with the loss of his license, Loftus became a fairly successful trainer and jockey instructor. He was technical adviser for the 1950 movie *Man o'War*.

★ National Horse Racing Hall of Fame

Lombardi, Ernie (Ernest N.)
BASEBALL
b. April 6, 1908, Oakland, Calif.
d. Sept. 26, 1977

The 6-foot-3, 230-pound Lombardi was one of the biggest, strongest players of his era, and quite likely the slowest of all time, which makes his lifetime .306 average all the more remarkable. Lombardi never beat out an infield hit and in fact shortstops played him very deep because of his lack of speed. He was often thrown out on hard-hit balls that would have been singles for anyone else.

A catcher, Lombardi also had an exceptionally strong throwing arm and often caught runners trying to steal second without even coming out of his crouch.

He began his major league career with the Brooklyn Dodgers during the 1931 season but was traded to the Cincinnati Reds in 1932. He led the NL in hitting with a .342 average in 1938, when he had 19 home runs and 95 RBI to win the league's most valuable player award.

Although he slipped to .287 in 1939, he hit 20 home runs, his career high, to help lead the Reds to the pennant. However, Cincinnati was swept by the New York Yankees in the World Series, with Lombardi hitting only .214. He had a .319 average in 1940, when the Reds won the pennant again. This time, he batted .333 in the World Series, as Cincinnati beat the Detroit Tigers in seven games.

Lombardi was traded to the Boston Braves in 1942, when he hit .330, and he had a .305 average with the New York

Giants in 1943. After hitting .307 in 1945, Lombardi became a back-up catcher and frequent pinch hitter. He retired after the 1947 season.

In 1,853 games, Lombardi had a .306 average with 1,792 hits, including 277 doubles, 27 triples, and 190 home runs. He drove in 990 runs and scored 601.

★ Baseball Hall of Fame

Lombardi, Vincent T.
FOOTBALL
b. June 11, 1913, Brooklyn, N.Y.
d. Sept. 3, 1970

A guard at Fordham, Lombardi was one of the "Seven Blocks of Granite," the school's second line with that nickname, in 1935 and 1936. After graduating *magna cum laude* in 1937, he taught and coached at St. Cecilia's High School in New Jersey until 1947, when he became an assistant coach at Fordham. He went to the U.S. Military Academy as an assistant under Earl Blaik in 1949.

Lombardi was hired as offensive coordinator by the New York Giants in 1954. In that role, he developed a powerful rushing attack, based on the principles of the single wing that he'd learned in college, with double-team blocks, cross-blocking, and pulling guards leading a so-called sweep that was actually a version of the old single-wing cutback play.

During his five years with the Giants, they won four division titles and one NFL championship. The Green Bay Packers hired Lombardi as coach and general manager in 1959. Taking over a team that had won only one game the year before, he had a 7–5–0 record.

In his second season, the Packers won the Western Division title but lost to the Philadelphia Eagles, 17–13, in the league's championship game. It was the last time a Lombardi team was beaten in post-season play.

During 1961 and 1962, the Packers had a 24–4–0 record, winning two NFL championships. They missed the playoffs in 1963 and 1964, then won three consecutive championship games and the first two Super Bowls, beating the

Kansas City Chiefs, 35–10, and the Oakland Raiders, 33–14.

Lombardi retired as coach but remained as Green Bay's general manager in 1968. However, he soon decided to return to coaching — "I miss the fire on Sunday," he said — and became executive vice president, general manager, and head coach of the Washington Redskins.

He began to turn that team around, too, from a 5–9–0 record to 7–5–2 in his first year. But he developed cancer in the summer of 1970 and died shortly after the Redskins opened the season.

A hard-driving disciplinarian, Lombardi believed that success in anything depended on 100 percent effort at all times. "If you cheat on the practice field, you'll cheat in the game," he said, "and if you cheat in the game, you'll cheat the rest of your life."

In his ten seasons as a head coach, his NFL teams had a 105–35–6 regular season record and won nine of ten playoff games.

★ Pro Football Hall of Fame

Lonborg, Dutch (Arthur C.)

BASKETBALL
b. March 16, 1899, Horton, Kans.
d. Jan. 31, 1985

One of many coaches who played for "Phog" Allen at the University of Kansas, Lonborg also took part in baseball and football. He was an AAU All-American guard with the Kansas City Athletic Club in 1921 and then became coach of all team sports at McPherson College in Kansas. He had a record of 23 wins and 4 losses in two seasons and then went to Washburn University in Topeka.

Washburn won the 1925 AAU national championship, the last college team to accomplish that, as Lonborg compiled a 63–15 record in four seasons before becoming head coach at Northwestern University in 1927.

Northwestern had its first successful seasons under Lonborg, winning the 1931 Western Conference (now Big Ten) championship and tying for the 1933 title. He had a record of 237 wins and 198 losses at the school for an overall mark of 324–225. In 1950, he became athletic

director at Kansas. Lonborg retired in 1964.

★ Basketball Hall of Fame

Lonborg, Jim (James R.)

BASEBALL
b. April 16, 1942, Santa Maria, Calif.

The 6-foot-5, 210-pound Lonborg, a right-handed pitcher, joined the AL's Boston Red Sox in 1965 and had a 19–27 record in his first two seasons. But with the pennant-winning "Impossible Dream" team of 1967, he had a 22–9 record with a 3.16 ERA and a league-leading 246 strikeouts to win the league's Cy Young Award.

Lonborg pitched a one-hit, 5–0 victory over the St. Louis Cardinals in the second game of the World Series and won the fifth game, 3–1, on a three-hitter. However, facing Bob Gibson on just two days' rest in the seventh game, he lost 7–2.

A broken leg in a skiing accident nearly ended Lonborg's career. On and off the disabled list because of the injury, He won just 17 games while losing 22 over the next three seasons. After going 10–7 in 1971, he was traded to the Milwaukee Brewers, who sent him to the Philadelphia Phillies the following year.

Lonborg pitched for Philadelphia, with limited success, until retiring after the 1979 season. He had a 157–137 record with 15 shutouts and a 3.86 ERA. He struck out 1,475 hitters and walked 823 in 2,464 innings.

Lopez, Alfonso R.

BASEBALL
b. Aug. 20, 1908, Tampa, Fla.

During the 1950s, the New York Yankees won eight of ten AL pennants. The other two were won by the Cleveland Indians in 1954 and the Chicago White Sox in 1959. Lopez managed both teams.

He began his professional baseball career as a catcher in 1925 and had a brief stay with the Brooklyn Dodgers at the end of the 1928 season. He joined the Dodgers in 1930 as their starting catcher, batting .309.

A solid defensive catcher and intelligent handler of pitchers, Lopez led the NL in fielding percentage at his position four times. He remained with the Dodgers through the 1935 season, then was traded by manager Casey Stengel to the Boston Braves. In 1938, Stengel became manager of the Braves, and during the 1940 season he traded Lopez again, to the Pittsburgh Pirates. Later, Lopez and Stengel became rival managers in the American League, but they were also very close friends.

In 1945, Lopez became a backup catcher with the Pirates. He retired as a player after appearing in 61 games for the Cleveland Indians in 1947.

Lopez managed in the minor leagues for three years and took over the Indians in 1951. Cleveland finished second to the Yankees, managed by Stengel, three years in a row before a sensational 111–43 season and the pennant in 1954. However, the New York Giants beat the Indians four games straight in the World Series.

After finishing second in 1955 and 1956, Lopez resigned and planned to retire. But the Chicago White Sox hired him in 1957. They finished second twice before winning the 1959 pennant, then lost the World Series to the Los Angeles Dodgers in six games.

Chicago slipped to third in 1960, the first time a Lopez team hadn't finished first or second, then dropped to fourth place in 1961 and fifth place in 1962 before finishing second three more times. Lopez retired after the 1965 season. He managed the team again at the end of the 1968 season and the beginning of the 1969 season before retiring for good.

In 1,950 games as a player, Lopez had a .261 batting average on 1,547 hits, including 206 doubles, 43 triples, and 51 home runs. He scored 613 runs and drove in 652. As a manager, he had a 1,410–1,004 record, a .584 winning percentage. He is eighteenth all-time in victories and third in percentage.
★ Baseball Hall of Fame

Lopez, Nancy
GOLF
b. Jan. 6, 1957, Torrance, Calif.

Lopez began playing golf when she was 8, under the tutelage of her father, and she won the New Mexico Women's Amateur championship when she was 12. An 18-year-old student at Tulsa University, she entered the 1975 U.S. Women's Open as an amateur and finished second.

The winner of the 1976 AIAW collegiate championship, Lopez left school after her junior year to join the LPGA tour. She played in just six tournaments in 1977, but in 1978 she won nine events, including a record five in a row, and was named rookie of the year, player of the year, and Associated Press female athlete of the year. Among her victories was the LPGA championship.

She followed that outstanding rookie year with eight tournament wins in 1979. Lopez won the Vare Trophy in both 1978 and 1979 with averages of 71.76 and 71.20 strokes per round, both records.

Although her victory pace slowed during the next three years, she had eight wins, including the 1981 Dinah Shore, where she shot a 64 for one round. Lopez married major league baseball player Ray Knight in 1982 and played in only 12 events the following year because of pregnancy, but she won 2 of them.

Lopez took 2 of 16 tournaments in 1984 and then won her second player of the year award and second Associated Press athlete of the year award in 1985. She set records with winnings of $416,472, an average of 70.73 strokes per round, 25 birdies in a single tournament, and a 268 to win the Henredon Classic. Among Lopez's victories that year was her second LPGA championship.

After missing almost all of the 1986 tour because of a second pregnancy, Lopez won 2 tournaments in 18 starts in 1987. The following year, she became the fourth woman golfer to surpass $2 million in career earnings, and she was again named player of the year. In 22 starts, she finished in the top five 12 times, including three victories. She also tied for the lead in two other tournaments but lost playoffs.

Lopez won her third LPGA championship in 1989. To date, those are her only victories in a major tournament. Through 1993, she was sixth all-time in wins with 47 and fourth all-time in earnings with $3,866,851.

Another Hall of Fame golfer, Carol Mann, once said of Lopez, "She plays by feel. All her senses come into play. That's when golf is an art."

★ LPGA Hall of Fame; World Golf Hall of Fame

Lott, Ronnie (Ronald M.)

FOOTBALL
b. May 8, 1959, Albuquerque, N.M.

An All-American defensive back at the University of Southern California in 1980, Lott was chosen by the San Francisco 49ers in the first round of the 1981 NFL draft. He started at cornerback for six seasons, leading the league with ten interceptions in 1986.

The 6-foot-1, 203-pound Lott, a very hard hitter, was moved to free safety the following season. He became a free agent in 1991 and signed with the Oakland Raiders, who used him at strong safety. Lott again led the NFL in interceptions with eight in 1991.

He joined the New York Jets as a free agent in 1993. Besides his obvious physical skills, Lott is much respected as a team leader. He has been an All-Pro at three positions, as a cornerback in 1981, a free safety in 1987 and 1990, and a strong safety in 1991.

Through 1994, Lott had intercepted 60 passes and returned them for 695 yards, an 11.6 average, and 5 touchdowns.

Louganis, Gregory E.

DIVING
b. Jan. 29, 1960, San Diego, Calif.

Unquestionably the greatest diver in history, Louganis was virtually unbeatable for nearly a decade. Of Samoan and Swedish ancestry, he was given up for adoption by his teenaged mother, and he had a difficult childhood. Called "nigger" by classmates because of his dark skin and "retarded" because he suffered from dyslexia, he turned to drugs and alcohol in his early teens.

Diving became his outlet because he could practice in solitude. Sammy Lee, twice a gold medalist, coached Louganis for six months in 1976, when the youngster won a silver medal in the Olympic platform event.

Louganis emerged as a premier diver in 1978, winning the world platform championship and the AAU indoor 1-meter and 3-meter titles. He entered the University of Miami in Florida that year but transferred to the University of California–Irvine in 1981.

In 1979, Louganis won gold medals in both the springboard and the platform at the Pan-American Games. He was favored to win the double at the 1980 Olympics, but the U.S. boycott of the Russian games forestalled him. Louganis did win both events at the 1982 world championships.

In 1984, Louganis became the first male diver to win both gold medals since 1928, and he was given the Sullivan Award as the country's amateur athlete of the year. He repeated as a double winner in the 1986 worlds, the 1987 Pan-American Games, and the 1988 Olympics, despite suffering a severe gash in his head after hitting the board on his ninth dive in the Olympic platform event.

The muscular 5-foot-9, 160-pounder won the incredible total of 45 national championships before retiring in 1989. He was the NCAA 1-meter springboard champion in 1979 and the 3-meter champion in 1979 and 1980. Louganis won the 1-meter, 3-meter, and platform events at the national indoor and outdoor championships for five years in a row, from 1982 through 1986, and he was the springboard and platform champion at the U.S. Olympic Festival six years in a row, from 1982 through 1987. He also won the 3-meter springboard and the platform dive at the 1987 outdoor championships, the 1988 national indoor platform, and all three events at the 1988 national outdoor championships.

★ Olympic Hall of Fame

Loughran, Beatrix S.

FIGURE SKATING
b. June 30, 1900, New York, N.Y.
d. Dec. 7, 1975

She never won a gold, but Loughran is the only American figure skater to win medals at three different Olympics, and she did it in two different events. After a 1924 silver and a 1928 bronze in the women's singles, she teamed with Sherwin Badger to win a silver in the pairs in the 1932 Winter Olympics.

Loughran won the U.S. singles title from 1925 through 1927. She and Badger won the national pairs title from 1930 through 1932, and they also captured the North American championship in 1930.

Loughran, Tommy (Thomas)

BOXING
b. Nov. 29 1902, Philadelphia, Pa.
d. July 7, 1982

A quick, clever boxer who lacked a knockout punch, Loughran had his first professional fight in 1919 and was undefeated until he lost a 15-round decision to Harry Greb on January 30, 1923, in a match for the light heavyweight championship.

Loughran won the title with a 15-round decision over Mike McTigue on October 7, 1927, in New York City. He vacated the championship in 1929 after five defenses to campaign as a heavyweight. Among the fighters he beat in title bouts were Mickey Walker and Jim Braddock, who was later heavyweight champion.

He fought for the heavyweight title on March 1, 1934, against Primo Carnera, but lost a 15-round decision. Loughran retired in 1937. A very religious man who went to Mass every day, Loughran was successful in business after leaving the ring, and he was also a sought-after speaker.

Loughran won 95 bouts, 18 by knockout; lost 23, 2 by knockout; and fought 8 draws and 2 no-decisions.

★ International Boxing Hall of Fame

Louis, Joe [Joseph Louis Barrow]

BOXING
b. May 13, 1914, Lafayette, Ala.
d. April 12, 1983

When he was ten years old, Louis moved with his mother and stepfather to Detroit, where, as a teenager, he developed his physique by delivering 50-pound blocks of ice. At 18, he learned that a boxing club paid fighters in food. He won $7 worth of food in a match but was knocked down seven times in two rounds, and he swore he'd never fight again.

However, a short time later a professional fighter, Holman Williams, gave him some lessons and persuaded him to enter Golden Gloves competition. He won 50 of 54 amateur fights, 41 by knockout, and was the AAU national light heavyweight champion in 1934.

Louis turned professional later that year. He became a genuine contender after knocking out Primo Carnera, King Levinsky, Max Baer, and Paulino Uzcudun in 1935, when he was named Associated Press athlete of the year.

He suffered his first professional defeat on June 19, 1936, a 12th-round knockout by Max Schmeling of Germany. Despite the loss, Louis was selected over Schmeling to meet heavyweight champion Jim Braddock on June 22, 1937, in Chicago. He knocked out Braddock in the 8th round to become the second black heavyweight champion.

Nicknamed the "Brown Bomber," Louis was taught by manager John Roxborough, a black lawyer, and trainer Joe Blackburn to be quiet and modest in demeanor, unlike the first black champion, Jack Johnson. As a result, Louis was a very popular champion among whites as well as blacks.

His popularity reached a peak after he knocked out Schmeling in the 1st round of a title fight on June 22, 1938. Schmeling was viewed by many as a tool of Hitler and Nazism, while Louis was seen as the champion of the American way. A crowd of 70,000 watched the fight in Yankee Stadium, and millions more listened to the radio broadcast.

Louis defended his title 25 times in

five years, knocking out 23 of his opponents. He entered the Army in 1942 and was used basically as a goodwill ambassador. His service included an appearance in a movie, *The Negro Soldier,* an attempt to boost morale among black fighting men. He also fought exhibitions throughout the country.

After World War II ended, he defended his championship five more times. Louis announced his retirement in 1949, but he owed more than $1 million in back taxes, and he resumed fighting in 1950. He was outpointed by Ezzard Charles on September 27 in an attempt to reclaim his title. In his last fight, he was knocked out by champion Rocky Marciano in the 8th round on October 26, 1951.

Louis won 67 professional bouts, 53 of them by knockout, and lost 3, 2 by knockout. He spent several months in a psychiatric hospital in 1970 and then became the official greeter at a Las Vegas casino.

★ International Boxing Hall of Fame

Lovellette, Clyde E.
BASKETBALL
b. Sept. 7, 1929, Terre Haute, Ind.

He was awkward as a boy because of his size, but his mother made him jump rope and do exercises to develop agility, and Lovellette gave her credit for his success as a basketball player. He was the first of four players to be a member of an Olympic gold medal team and NCAA and NBA championship teams.

Lovellette was also one of the first big, high-scoring centers. At 6-foot-9 and 235 pounds, he could score from close to the basket, and he also had a fine jump shot. Twice an All-American at the University of Kansas, in 1951 and 1952, he led the nation in scoring with a 28.4 average and was named college player of the year in 1952. Kansas won the NCAA championship that year, and Lovellette was named the tournament's most valuable player, scoring a record 141 points in four games, including a single-game record of 44.

After playing AAU basketball for a season, Lovellette joined the NBA's Min-

neapolis Lakers in 1953. They won the NBA championship in his first season. He also played for two Boston Celtics teams that won NBA titles, in 1963 and 1964.

Lovellette was with the Cincinnati Royals for one season, 1957–58, and the St. Louis Hawks from 1958–59 through 1961–62 before joining the Celtics for two seasons. He retired in 1964 with a total of 11,947 points in 704 games, an average of 17.0 a game. He had 7,220 career rebounds.

★ Basketball Hall of Fame

Lowe, Paul E.
FOOTBALL
b. Sept. 27, 1936, Homer, La.

The second-highest ground gainer in American Football League history, Lowe played at Oregon State and joined the Los Angeles Chargers as a free agent in 1960. He quickly became one of the biggest stars in the offense-oriented AFL, averaging 6.3 yards a carry while gaining 855 yards and scoring 9 touchdowns.

The Chargers moved to San Diego in 1961, when Lowe led the league with 9 rushing touchdowns. After missing the 1962 season with an injury, he gained 1,010 yards on 177 rushing attempts, a 5.7 average, and scored 8 rushing touchdowns in 1963.

The 6-foot, 180-pound Lowe was named the league's player of the year in 1965, when he had a record 1,121 yards in 222 carries, a 5.1 average, with 7 touchdowns rushing. He went to the Kansas City Chiefs in 1968 and spent two seasons there before retiring.

In his ten years, Lowe rushed 1,026 times for 4,995 yards, a 4.9 average, and 40 touchdowns. He also caught 111 passes for 1,045 yards, a 9.4 average, and 7 touchdowns.

Lucas, Jerry R.
BASKETBALL
b. March 30, 1940, Middletown, Ohio

Lucas scored 2,466 points for Middletown, Ohio, High School, breaking Wilt Chamberlain's career record. As a 6-foot-9 sophomore center, he led Ohio State to the 1960 NCAA championship, and he starred for the gold medal U.S. Olympic team that summer. Oscar Robertson and Jerry West were on that team, but Olympic coach Pete Newell called Lucas "the greatest player I've ever coached."

Ohio State also went to the NCAA finals in 1961 and 1962 but lost to the University of Cincinnati both times. During Lucas's three-year career, Ohio State won 78 of 84 games. Lucas was a three-time All-American and college player of the year in both 1961 and 1962. He led the nation in field goal percentage three times and in rebounding twice.

Lucas signed with the Cleveland Pipers of the American Basketball Association in 1962, but the ABL folded before he could play a game. He joined the NBA's Cincinnati Royals for the 1963–64 season and was the league's rookie of the year, averaging 17.7 points a game.

Cincinnati traded him to the San Francisco Warriors during the 1969–70 season. He ended his career with the New York Knicks from 1971–72 through 1972–73, when New York won its first NBA championship. In 685 games, he scored 12,894 points, an average of 18.8 per game, and had 12,942 rebounds. He was the third player in history to average more than 20 points and more than 20 rebounds a game in 1964–65, and he is one of a small number to have more than 10,000 points and more than 10,000 rebounds in his NBA career.
★ Basketball Hall of Fame

Luckman, Sidney

FOOTBALL
b. Nov. 21, 1916, Brooklyn, N.Y.

The first of the modern professional T-formation quarterbacks, Luckman was a triple threat as a single-wing tailback at Columbia University. George Halas, the Bears' coach, handpicked him to play quarterback, in large part because of his intelligence.

Luckman played sparingly in his rookie year, 1939, but became a starter in 1940, when the Bears fully modernized the formation by using a split end to one side and a man in motion to the other. Their 73–0 victory over the Wash-

ington Redskins in the NFL championship game started a virtual stampede toward the T. The *New York Times* wrote of his performance, "No field general ever called plays more artistically. He was letter perfect."

The 6-foot, 200-pounder was also an excellent ball handler and an accurate passer. In 1943, when he was named the league's player of the year, a Sid Luckman Day was held at the Polo Grounds, and Luckman responded by throwing seven touchdown passes in a 56–7 rout of the New York Giants. In the Bears' 41–21 win over Washington for the league championship that season, he passed for 276 yards and 5 touchdowns.

In a 21–14 victory over the Giants for the 1946 championship, Luckman scored the winning touchdown in the fourth quarter when he faked to George McAfee running to the left and bootlegged the ball to the right for a 19-yard run.

He became a backup to Johnny Lujack in 1949 and retired after the 1950 season. During his career, he completed 904 of 1,744 passes, a 51.8 percentage, for 14,683 yards and 137 touchdowns. He also punted 230 times for a 38.4-yard average, rushed for 2 touchdowns, and returned 14 interceptions for 293 yards and 1 touchdown.
★ Pro Football Hall of Fame

Luisetti, Hank (Angelo J.)

BASKETBALL
b. June 16, 1916, San Francisco, Calif.

Luisetti grew up in the Telegraph Hill area of San Francisco, an Italian-American neighborhood where future New York Yankee stars Frank Crosetti, Joe DiMaggio, and Tony Lazzeri also lived as youngsters. Learning to play basketball against boys who were bigger than he, Luisetti developed an unusual one-handed shot, usually released while he was on the run.

He entered Stanford University in 1934. In December of his sophomore year, Stanford played Long Island University at Madison Square Garden and ended LIU's 43-game winning streak with a 45–31 game in which Luisetti scored 15 points.

The *New York Times* wrote of his performance, "Some of his shots would have been foolhardy if attempted by another player, but with Luisetti doing the heaving, these were accepted by the crowd as a matter of course." Within a couple of years, high school and college players throughout the country were abandoning the two-hand set shot for the one-handed shot.

A three-time All-American, the 6-foot-3, 184-pound Luisetti was an excellent dribbler and passer as well as a scorer. His career total of 1,596 points, an average of 16.5 a game, was a college record at the time. The Helms Athletic Foundation named him college player of the year in 1937 and 1938, and in a 1950 poll of Associated Press sportswriters, he finished second to George Mikan as the best basketball player of the half century.

Luisetti starred in a 1938 movie, *College Confessions,* and his amateur status was suspended for a year as a result. He set an AAU tournament scoring record in 1940, but a knee injury limited his playing time the following season. While serving in the Navy during World War II, he averaged more than 30 points a game with the St. Mary's Pre-Flight School team.

In 1944, Luisetti nearly died of spinal meningitis and was told by doctors to give up basketball. However, he coached Stewart Chevrolet of San Francisco to the 1951 AAU championship.
★ Basketball Hall of Fame

Lujack, Johnny (John C. Jr.)

FOOTBALL
b. Jan. 4, 1925, Connellsville, Pa.

As a sophomore at Notre Dame in 1943, Lujack started at halfback but was moved to quarterback when starter Angelo Bertelli was called into service. In his first game at that position, he completed 8 of 15 passes for 237 yards and 2 touchdowns and scored a touchdown rushing in a 26–0 upset of Army.

The following year, Lujack himself was in the service. He returned to Notre Dame as the starting quarterback in 1946. In a scoreless tie against the powerful Army team led by Doc Blanchard and Glenn Davis, the 6-foot-1, 180-pound Lujack saved the game with an open-field tackle of Blanchard to prevent a touchdown.

Lujack led Notre Dame to an 8–0–1 record in his senior season, 1947, when he completed 61 of 109 passes for 777 yards and 9 touchdowns. A two-time All-American, he won the 1947 Heisman Trophy as the nation's best college player and was also named athlete of the year by the Associated Press. In his Notre Dame career, he completed 144 of 280 passes for 2,080 yards. He also won letters in baseball, basketball, and track during his sophomore year.

A first-round draft choice of the Chicago Bears in 1948, Lujack was used primarily as a defensive back in his rookie year and was named to the All-Pro team at that position. He took over as starting quarterback in 1949 and was an All-Pro again in 1950. Bad knees forced his retirement after the 1951 season.

In his four years as a pro, Lujack completed 404 passes in 808 attempts for 6,925 yards and 41 touchdowns. He set an NFL record against the Chicago Cardinals in 1949 by passing for 458 yards and 6 touchdowns.
★ College Football Hall of Fame

Lukas, Wayne (Darrell Wayne)

HORSE RACING
b. September 2, 1935, Antigo, Wis.

Lukas dealt in quarterhorses while a student at the University of Wisconsin. He became a high school coach after graduating, returned to Wisconsin as assistant basketball coach while working for his master's degree, and he then coached high school basketball.

He left coaching to go into quarter horse training in 1968. Lukas trained Dash for Cash, quarter horse of the year in 1976 and 1977, and then began training thoroughbreds. He was the top money winner among trainers from 1983 through 1990, and he won the Eclipse Award from 1985 through 1987.

Lukas has trained two horses of the

year, Lady's Secret in 1986 and Criminal Type in 1990. He won the 1988 Kentucky Derby with Winning Colors, only the third filly in history to take that race. He has also trained two Preakness winners, Codex in 1980 and Tank's Prospect in 1985.

In Breeders' Cup racing, Lukas leads all trainers with ten victories. He won the juvenile division with Capote in 1986, Success Express in 1987, and Is It True in 1988; the distaff division with Life's Magic in 1985, Lady's Secret in 1986, and Sacahuista in 1987; the juvenile fillies division with Twilight Ridge in 1985; the sprint with Gulch in 1988; and the 1-mile with Steinlen in 1989.

In 1993, Lukas came under fire for his training techniques. Amid rumors that the empire he had painstakingly built was falling apart because of the 1990 death of Eugene Klein, his chief patron, Lukas predicted that his Union City had a very good chance to win the Kentucky Derby. After the horse ran fifteenth, Lukas decided to give him another chance in the Preakness, two weeks later, without any serious workouts. Union City broke down on the backstretch of the race and had to be destroyed.

However, Lukas won his fourth Eclipse Award as trainer of the year in 1994.

Lumley, Harry

HOCKEY
b. Nov. 11, 1926, Owen Sound, Ont.

"Apple Cheeks" Lumley entered the NHL with the New York Rangers in 1943. After one season in goal there, he went to the Detroit Red Wings, where he starred for eight seasons. In the 1950 Stanley Cup playoffs, Lumley had three shutouts and gave up an average of just two goals a game to lead Detroit to the championship.

He was then traded to Chicago, where he had two mediocre seasons, but he rebounded in Toronto after being traded to the Maple Leafs in 1952. In two of his four seasons there, Lumley averaged fewer than two goals a game,

and he won the Vezina Trophy as the league's best goalie in 1954, when he had a record 13 shutouts.

Lumley finished his NHL career with three seasons in Boston, retiring in 1960. He played 804 regular season games, with 71 shutouts and a 2.75 goals-against average. He had 7 shutouts and a 2.62 average in 76 playoff games.
★ Hockey Hall of Fame

Lund, Pug (Francis L.)

FOOTBALL
b. April 8, 1913, Pico Lake, Wis. d. May 26, 1994

Although sometimes regarded only for his blocking ability, Lund starred in every possible way for the 1934 Minnesota team that won all eight of its games. An All-American fullback that season, Lund rushed for 657 yards, threw a touchdown pass that gave Pittsburgh its only loss of the year, and consistently got off long punts to pin the opposition deep in its own territory. Bernie Bierman thought that was the best team he'd ever coached, and he gave Lund much of the credit: "He was our sparkplug. As a ball carrier, passer, kicker, blocker and tackler, he carried out every heavy assignment we gave him."
★ College Football Hall of Fame

Luque, Dolph (Adolfo D.)

BASEBALL
b. Aug. 4, 1890, Havana, Cuba d. July 3, 1957

The first Cuban-born player to reach the major leagues, Luque was a right-handed pitcher who had brief tryouts with the NL's Boston Braves in 1914 and 1915 before joining the Cincinnati Reds in 1918.

He led the league in victories with a 27–8 record, winning percentage with .771, shutouts with 6, and ERA in 1923. Luque was also the league leader with 4 shutouts and a 2.63 ERA in 1925, though his record was only 16–18 that season.

In 1930, the Reds traded him to the Brooklyn Dodgers. After two years with Brooklyn, he went to the New York Giants in 1932. He worked mostly as a relief pitcher with the Giants and retired after the 1935 season.

In his 20 seasons, Luque played for just one pennant-winning team, the 1933 Giants. He relieved Hal Schumacher in the fifth and deciding game of the World Series and picked up the victory in a 4–3 New York win.

Lyle, Sparky (Albert W.)

BASEBALL
b. July 22, 1944, DuBois, Pa.

The left-handed Lyle, who threw a lively fastball and a nasty slider, joined the AL's Boston Red Sox as a relief pitcher in 1967. They won the pennant that year, but Lyle wasn't on the World Series roster.

After a 21–15 record with 64 saves over the next four seasons, Lyle was traded to the New York Yankees in 1972, when he led the AL with 35 saves. He led the league again with 23 in 1976 and won the league's Cy Young Award the following season, when he had a 13–5 record with 26 saves in a league-leading 72 appearances.

Arm problems began to bother Lyle in 1978, and he went to the Texas Rangers the following year. The Rangers sent him to the Philadelphia Phillies during the 1980 season. He spent one full season there, then retired after splitting the 1982 season between Philadelphia and the Chicago White Sox.

Lyle appeared in 899 games without a start. He had a 99–76 record with 238 saves and a 2.88 ERA. He struck out 873 hitters and walked 481 in 1,390⅓ innings.

Lyman, Link (William Roy)

FOOTBALL
b. Nov. 30, 1898, Table Rock, Nebr.
d. Dec. 16, 1972

The 6-foot-2, 240-pound Lyman didn't play football until he entered the University of Nebraska in 1917. He started for the next two seasons, then left school for a year to earn his tuition money and returned in 1921, when Nebraska lost only to Notre Dame. Despite his size, he had enough speed to be used frequently as a runner on the tackle-around play.

He entered pro football with the Canton Bulldogs of the NFL in 1922. They won two league championships, then moved to Cleveland in 1924 and won a third consecutive title. The Bulldogs returned to Canton in 1925, and Lyman was traded to the Frankford Yellowjackets in midseason.

When the Chicago Bears went on their barnstorming tour with Red Grange after the season, Lyman joined them, and he remained with the team through 1928. After a year of playing semipro football, he returned to the Bears in 1929. He took another season off in 1932 for business reasons, then rejoined the Bears for two more seasons. The Bears won the 1933 NFL championship and were division champions in 1934, Lyman's last season.

Lyman is credited with being the first defensive lineman to shift his position frequently, sometimes moving inside to play between the offensive guard and tackle, at other times moving out between the tackle and the end. He usually shifted at the last second, just before the ball was snapped. Steve Owen, an opponent who later coached the New York Giants, said, "It was difficult to play against him because he would vary his moves, and no matter how you reacted, you could be wrong."
★ Pro Football Hall of Fame

Lynn, Fred (Fredric M.)

BASEBALL
b. Feb. 3, 1952, Chicago, Ill.

After playing 15 games with the AL's Boston Red Sox at the end of the 1974 season, batting .419, Lynn became the team's starting center fielder in 1975. He helped lead Boston to a pennant, leading the league in runs with 103, doubles with 47, and slugging with a .566 percentage.

Lynn batted .331 that year with 21 home runs and 105 RBI and also played outstanding defense. He not only won the league's most valuable player award, he was named Associated Press male athlete of the year. He hit .364 in Boston's victory over the Oakland A's in the league championship series and .280 with three runs and five RBI in a seven-game loss to the Cincinnati Reds in the World Series.

After hitting only .260 in 1977 and .298 in 1978, Lynn won the AL batting title with a .333 average in 1979, and he was also the league's top slugger with a .637 percentage. He batted .301 in 1980, then went to the California Angels as a free agent.

A left-hander, Lynn had prospered at Fenway Park by slicing singles and doubles off the short left field fence. Once he left Boston, he wasn't the same hitter, though he was still a fine defensive outfielder. He never hit over .300 again, and he retired after batting only .240 for the NL's San Diego Padres in 1990.

In 1,969 games, Lynn hit .283 with 1,960 hits, including 388 doubles, 43 triples, and 306 home runs, with 1,063 runs scored and 1,111 RBI.

Lynn, Janet [Janet Lynn Nowicki]

FIGURE SKATING
b. April 6, 1953, Chicago, Ill.

A genuine prodigy, Lynn began skating before she was 3. Her parents enrolled her in a dancing class when she was a young girl, but she hated it because she was so shy. In the meantime, she taught herself to skate backwards, and dancing lessons were abandoned for skating lessons.

She entered a competition for the first time when she was seven. A year later she won the Upper Great Lakes novice championship. From that time, she moved steadily up the competitive ladder and was almost always one level above her age. She won the national junior championship when she was 12, finished fourth in the national senior championship at 13, and was a member of the 1968 U.S. Olympic team at 14.

By then she had dropped her family name, Nowicki. Skating as Janet Lynn, she won five consecutive U.S. senior titles, from 1969 through 1973. However, she suffered misfortune in international competition. She won a bronze medal at the 1972 Olympics after falling during her free skating program, and she fell

twice during her short program at the 1973 world championships and finished second as a result.

Lynn signed a three-year, $1.4 million contract with the Ice Follies in 1973. Respiratory problems, which had troubled her throughout her career, forced her retirement before the term of the contract. After she married and had three children, doctors discovered that she suffered from a variety of allergies. The problem was brought under control, and Lynn returned to skating. She won the first U.S. professional championship in 1983.

Lyon, George S.

GOLF
b. July 28, 1858, Richmond, Ont.
d. May, 1938

Lyon set a Canadian record in the pole vault and also played baseball, cricket, and tennis before taking up golf when he was 38. He then won eight Canadian amateur championships.

At 46, Lyon competed in the St. Louis Games in 1904, the only time golf was actually on the Olympic program. A colorful figure, he told jokes, sang songs, and occasionally did handstands while going around the course in the match-play elimination tournament. After beating Chandler Egan of the U.S. in the final, Lyon walked on his hands to the ceremony at which he was presented with a $1,500 silver trophy.
★ Canadian Sports Hall of Fame

Lyons, Ted (Theodore A.)

BASEBALL
b. Dec. 28, 1900, Lake Charles, La.
d. July 25, 1986

After having a 10–2 record as a freshman pitcher at Baylor University in 1920, Lyons was offered contracts by the AL's Cleveland Indians and Philadelphia Athletics. He chose to remain in college and learned how to throw the knuckleball in his sophomore year.

He signed with the Chicago White Sox immediately after graduating in 1923. A right-handed thrower who was a switch hitter, Lyons led the league in victories with a 21–11 record and in shutouts with 5 in 1925. He was the league leader in victories again in 1927 with a 22–14 record, when he also led in complete games with 30 and innings pitched with 307²⁄₃.

Playing most of his career with poor teams, Lyons had just one more 20-win season, in 1930, when he was 22–15 with a league-leading 29 complete games and 297²⁄₃ innings pitched.

He injured his pitching shoulder in 1931 and appeared in only 21 games that year, but he began concentrating on the knuckleball to prevent strain on his arm.

For the rest of his career, Lyons consistently won between 10 and 15 games a year, but he lost more than he won several times. However, he led the league in shutouts with 4 in 1940, when he had a 12–8 record and a 3.24 ERA, and he was the league leader with a 2.10 ERA in 1942.

After serving in the Marines during World War II, Lyons returned to the White Sox in 1946 and pitched briefly before being named manager. That was the end of his pitching career. He managed Chicago through the 1948 season, then served as a coach for several major league teams.

In 21 seasons, Lyons had a 280–230 record with 27 shutouts and a 3.87 ERA. He struck out 2,073 hitters and walked 1,121 in 4,161 innings.

★ Baseball Hall of Fame

★ ★ M ★ ★

McAdoo, Bob (Robert A.)

BASKETBALL
b. Sept. 25, 1951, Greensboro, N.C.

McAdoo spent two years playing junior college basketball in Indiana before entering North Carolina University in 1971. He averaged 19.5 points a game and was a consensus All-American center in his only season before entering the 1972 NBA draft as a so-called hardship case.

The Buffalo Braves chose him in the first round, and the 6-foot-9, 225-pounder led the league in scoring his first three seasons with averages of 30.6 in 1972–73, 34.5 in 1974–75, and 31.1 in 1975–76. He also led the NBA with 1,155 rebounds in 1974–75, when he was named the league's most valuable player.

Although he usually played center, with occasional stints at power forward, McAdoo got most of his points from outside, hitting a soft, accurate jump shot from 15 to 18 feet away and driving to the basket only to keep defenders honest.

Buffalo traded him to the New York Knicks during the 1976–77 season, and the Knicks sent him to the Boston Celtics during the 1977–78 season. He went from Boston to the Detroit Pistons in 1978.

A knee injury limited McAdoo to only 16 games in 1980–81, when he was with Detroit and the New York Nets, and it forced him to become a part-time player for the rest of his career.

McAdoo was traded to the Los Angeles Lakers in 1981, and he spent four seasons with them. He retired after playing in only 29 games with the Philadelphia 76ers in 1985–86.

In 852 regular season games, McAdoo scored 18,787 points, a 22.1 average, and had 8,048 rebounds. He added 1,718 points and 711 rebounds in 94 playoff games.

McAfee, George A.

FOOTBALL
b. March 13, 1918, Ironton, Ohio

Nicknamed "One Play" because he was a threat to score any time he touched the ball, McAfee was an All-American halfback at Duke University in 1939. During his three years as a starter, the team won 24 of 28 games.

Though he was celebrated for his breakaway running, coach Wallace Wade said of McAfee, "He was really a one-man offense and practically unstoppable. He was a great kicker, great runner, great passer, and one of the best receivers I've ever seen."

There were doubts about whether the slender 6-foot, 177-pounder could make it with the Chicago Bears when he joined the team in 1940, but McAfee erased those doubts by returning a punt 75 yards for a touchdown in his first exhibition game and running back a kickoff 93 yards in his first regular season game.

The Bears had a bunch of outstanding backs in 1940 and 1941, so McAfee was used as a spot player, but he scored 12 touchdowns in 1941 to tie Don Hutson's record. After serving in the Navy for nearly four years, McAfee played part of the 1945 season. A heel injury limited his playing time in 1946, but he came back strong in 1947 and spent three more seasons with the Bears before retiring.

McAfee was particularly dangerous as a punt returner. He led the NFL in punt return yardage in 1948 with 417 yards, and his career average of 12.8 yards per return was a league record for many years.

During eight seasons with the Bears, McAfee gained 1,685 yards on 341 attempts, a 4.9 average, scoring 22 touchdowns; caught 85 passes for 1,357 yards, a 16.0 average, and 10 touchdowns; and returned 112 punts for 1,431 yards and 2 touchdowns. He also had 21 interceptions, returning them for 294 yards and 1 touchdown.

★ College Football Hall of Fame; Pro Football Hall of Fame

McAtee, Linus (John Linus)

HORSE RACING
b. 1897, Frenchtown, N.J.
d. Nov. 15, 1963

While still an apprentice, McAtee rode Damrosch to victory in the 1916 Preakness. Known as a master of pace and timing, McAtee often won races by the narrowest of margins under perfectly judged stretch drives.

Nicknamed "Pony," McAtee won two Kentucky Derbies, aboard Whiskey in 1927 and Clyde Van Dusen in 1929. He scored three victories in what was then the nation's richest race, the Belmont Futurity, with Mother Goose in 1924, High Strung in 1928, and Jamestown in 1930.

McAtee was the nation's leading money winner in 1928 with $301,295. He retired in 1932, and a brief comeback attempt in 1935 was ended by a foot injury. He had 930 career victories in 5,742 starts and was in the money on another 1,679 mounts, for total earnings of $2,442,682.

★ National Horse Racing Hall of Fame

Macauley, Easy Ed (Charles Edward Jr.)

BASKETBALL
b. March 22, 1928, St. Louis, Mo.

Although he was a two-time All-American and a professional star for nine seasons, Macauley will probably be best remembered as one of the two players traded by the Boston Celtics to the St. Louis Hawks for the draft rights to Bill Russell. (The other was Cliff Hagan.)

The 6-foot-8, 185-pound center was nicknamed "Easy Ed" because of his fluid, effortless style of play. At St. Louis University, he was the national collegiate leader with a .524 shooting percentage in 1946–47. Macauley was named an All-American the next two years and was the Associated Press player of the year in 1949.

He played for the St. Louis Bombers in the NBA for one season and joined the Boston Celtics in 1950 after the St. Louis franchise folded. In six years with the Celtics, he averaged more than 20 points a game twice and was named an all-star four years in a row, from 1951 to 1954.

The Hawks drafted Russell in 1956, but he was going to miss half of the season while with the U.S. Olympic team, and St. Louis management felt he was going to sign with the Harlem Globetrotters, so the trade was made with Boston. Macauley played for the Hawks against the Celtics in two championship series, the Celtics winning in 1957, the Hawks winning in 1958.

Injuries limited Macauley's playing time in 1958–59, and he retired after the season to become the Hawks' coach and general manager. After winning two Western Division titles in two years, he retired from the sport but later worked as a St. Louis sports announcer.

In his nine NBA seasons, Macauley scored 11,234 points in 641 games, an average of 17.5 per game. As a coach, he had a record of 157 wins and 108 losses.

★ Basketball Hall of Fame

McCann, Terry (Terrence J.)

WRESTLING
b. March 23, 1934, Chicago, Ill.

At the University of Iowa, McCann

was the NCAA 125½-pound wrestling champion in 1955 and 1956, losing only three matches in three years. He won AAU national championships in the weight class from 1957 to 1959 and was named the outstanding wrestler in the 1959 national tournament.

McCann won a gold medal at the 1960 Olympics, then retired from competition. In 1963, he began coaching wrestling for the Mayor Daley Youth Foundation in Chicago. Under his guidance, the team won six AAU national freestyle wrestling championships and five Greco-Roman titles.

McCann was a founder of the U.S. Wrestling Federation in 1965.

McCarron, Christopher
HORSE RACING
b. March 27, 1955, Boston, Mass.

Although ranked as one of the nation's leading jockeys since 1974, McCarron didn't win a triple crown race until 1986, when he rode Danzig Connection to a victory in the Belmont Stakes.

The following year, he captured the Kentucky Derby and the Preakness with Alysheba, who won the Eclipse Award as three-year-old of the year despite a fourth-place finish in the Belmont, a sixth-place finish in the Travers Stakes, and a narrow defeat in the Breeders' Cup Classic. Alysheba, under McCarron, did win the $1 million Super Derby in 1987 and the Breeders' Cup Classic in 1988.

McCarron won the Classic for a second straight time aboard Sunday Silence in 1989. His first Breeders' Cup victory came in the 1985 sprint race, with Precisionist. In 1992, he won the juvenile race with Gilded Time and the distaff race with Paseana. He also rode Pine Bluff to victory in the 1992 Preakness for his third win in a triple crown race.

After working as a groom and horse walker, McCarron began riding in 1974 and got his first victory in March. Racing mostly at Bowie Race Track in Maryland and Penn National in Pennsylvania, he set records for both winners, with 547, and mounts, with 2,199, in 1974. He

won the Eclipse Award as the best jockey of the year.

McCarron led in victories again with 648 in 1975 but didn't really come into his own until he 1977, when he began riding against better competition at Hollywood Park. Accepting fewer mounts but riding in more prestigious races, McCarron led in victories with 405 and money won with $7,663,300 to claim his second Eclipse Award.

He was the top money winner again in 1981, with $8,397,604; in 1984, with $12,045,813; and in 1991, with $14,456,073. In 1983, he became the youngest jockey ever to achieve $50 million in career earnings and more than 3,000 career wins. Through 1994, McCarron ranked second all-time in earnings with $167,129,960 and eleventh in victories with 6,092.

★ National Horse Racing Hall of Fame

McCarthy, Joseph V.
BASEBALL
b. April 21, 1887, Philadelphia, Pa.
d. Jan. 13, 1978

McCarthy spent 15 seasons as a minor league infielder, several of them as a playing manager. He quit playing after the 1921 season, when he guided the Louisville Colonels to the American Association pennant, but he continued managing in the minors until 1926, when the NL's Chicago Cubs hired him.

In 1929, McCarthy guided the Cubs to the pennant, but they lost to the Philadelphia Athletics in five games. However, McCarthy was unhappy throughout the 1930 season because he felt Rogers Hornsby, the great second baseman, was trying to undermine him. McCarthy resigned with four games left in the season and was replaced by Hornsby.

The AL's New York Yankees signed McCarthy after the 1930 World Series. Some of the players didn't like the move, notably Babe Ruth, who coveted the managerial job.

McCarthy, who was a tough disciplinarian, worked to instill a sense of pride in his players. He made them wear jackets and ties in public, forbade card playing in the clubhouse, and told them to shave at home or in the hotel before games. "This is your job," he said. "Shave before you come to work."

While Ruth was playing well, McCarthy pretty much let the big slugger do what he wanted. But a problem arose after the 1934 season, when McCarthy still had a year left on his five-year contract. Ruth told writers that he wanted to be a manager and that he wouldn't play for McCarthy anymore. McCarthy offered to resign but was told to sit tight, and shortly afterward the Yankees sold Ruth to the Boston Braves.

McCarthy won just one pennant in his first five years with the team, in 1932, finishing second the other four seasons. That 1932 flag made him the first manager to win pennants in both leagues, and the Yankees beat the Cubs in four straight games in the World Series that year.

After his contract was renewed in 1936, the Yankees won seven pennants and six World Series in eight years. They became the first team to win four straight world championships, from 1936 through 1939, and they lost only three games in the process. They also won the World Series in 1941 and 1943, losing only in 1942.

McCarthy resigned early in the 1946 season because of a gall bladder problem, although some suspected that friction with the new team president, Lee MacPhail, was the real reason. He took over the Boston Red Sox in 1948, when they finished in a tie for first but lost a playoff to the Cleveland Indians. After a second-place finish in 1949, he resigned during the 1950 season.

In 24 years as a manager, McCarthy had a 2,125–1,333 record, a winning percentage of .615.

★ Baseball Hall of Fame

McCarthy, Tommy (Thomas F. M.)
BASEBALL
b. July 24, 1864, S. Boston, Mass.
d. Aug. 5, 1922

McCarthy was something of an innovator during the formative years of major league baseball. He and Hugh Duffy, known as the "Heavenly Twins," per-

fected the hit and run and the double steal in the early 1890s, and McCarthy was a pioneer at faking a bunt to draw the opposing third baseman and then slapping the ball past him for a hit.

A right fielder, McCarthy also developed a defensive trick. Because of his great speed, he played shallow. With a runner on first base, McCarthy would often charge a line drive and deliberately trap it, then throw to second to start a double play.

While playing sandlot ball in 1884, McCarthy was signed by the Boston team in the rebel Union Association. The league folded after one season, and he joined the Boston NL team, then played briefly with Philadelphia in 1886 and 1887, never hitting better than .200.

McCarthy caught on with the St. Louis team in the American Association, then a major league, in 1888. He hit .274, stole 93 bases, and scored 107 runs in 131 games to help St. Louis win a pennant. He led the league with 83 steals in 1890, when he batted .350, and he had a .310 average in 1891.

The American Association folded after the 1891 season, and McCarthy returned to the Boston NL team. Duffy also joined the team in 1892 to play center field. McCarthy hit only .242, but he stole 53 bases and scored 119 runs for a pennant-winning team.

He batted .346 and .349 the next two seasons. After dropping to .290 in 1895, he was traded to Brooklyn. He retired after hitting only .249 in 1896. He later served as a scout, a minor league manager, and a baseball coach at Boston College, Dartmouth, and Holy Cross.

In 13 major league seasons, McCarthy had a .292 average, with 1,496 hits, including 192 doubles, 53 triples, and 44 home runs. He stole 468 bases, scored 1,069 runs, and had 666 RBI.

★ Baseball Hall of Fame

McClung, Bum (Thomas Lee)
FOOTBALL
b. March 26, 1870, Knoxville, Tenn.
d. Dec. 19, 1914

Though not very fast, McClung was

a smart, shifty runner who scored somewhere around 500 points in four years as a starting halfback at Yale. He captained the 1891 team, which won all 13 of its games, outscoring the opposition 488 to 0.

The captain at that time was virtually a coach. McClung is credited with designing the cutback play, in which the runner looks as if he's going to go around the end and then cuts back over the tackle. The cutback later became a standard play in the single wing.

In 1892, McClung became the first football coach at the University of California. The team had won two, lost one, and tied one in his only season there. McClung was U.S. treasurer from 1909 to 1912.

★ College Football Hall of Fame

McColl, Bill (William F. Jr.)
FOOTBALL
b. April 20, 1930, San Diego, Calif.

While he was playing at Stanford, the 6-foot-4, 240-pound McColl was called by sportswriter Curley Grieve "a giant end stamped with greatness." A consensus All-American in 1950 and 1951, he played both offense and defense and was sometimes used at tackle because of his size and at linebacker because of his speed.

McColl joined the NFL's Chicago Bears in 1952 and studied toward a medical degree at the University of Chicago. He received the degree in 1955 and retired from football after the 1959 season to practice medicine.

During his eight-year professional career, McColl caught 301 passes for 2,815 yards, a 9.4 average, and 25 touchdowns. Two of his sons, Duncan and Milton, played football at Stanford and also played professional football.

★ College Football Hall of Fame

McCormack, Mike (Michael)
FOOTBALL
b. June 21, 1930, Chicago, Ill.

An unsung player out of the University of Kansas, McCormack played both offensive tackle and linebacker for the NFL's New York Yanks in 1951 and had an outstanding game against the Cleveland Browns.

He entered the Army in 1952 and was still in service the following year when the Browns acquired him in a complex trade involving 15 players. McCormack joined the Browns in 1954 and played defensive middle guard that season, then was moved to offensive tackle.

The 6-foot-4, 250-pound McCormack was the Browns' offensive captain from 1956 until his retirement after the 1962 season. Although he never made the All-Pro team, he played in the Pro Bowl six times.

McCormack coach the Philadelphia Eagles to a 16–25–1 record from 1973 through 1976 and had a 9–23–0 record with the Baltimore Colts in 1980 and 1981. He was named director of football operations for the Seattle Seahawks in 1982, serving as interim coach briefly. He became the team's general manager in 1984.

★ Pro Football Hall of Fame

McCormick, Frank A.
BASEBALL
b. June 9, 1911, New York, N.Y.
d. Nov. 21, 1982

A right-handed first baseman, McCormick led the NL in hits three consecutive years, with 209 in 1938 and in 1939 and 191 in 1940. He also led with 128 RBI in 1939 and with 44 doubles in 1940, when he was named the league's most valuable player. McCormick had a .309 batting average with 93 runs scored and 127 RBI for the Cincinnati Reds that season.

The Reds won pennants in 1939 and 1940. McCormick batted .400 in a four-game World Series loss to the New York Yankees in 1939. He hit only .214 in the 1940 World Series, but with Cincinnati trailing, 1–0, in the seventh inning of the final game, he started the winning rally with a leadoff double and scored the tying run. The Reds won the game, 2–1, and the Series four games to three.

The 6-foot-4, 205-pound McCormick wasn't much of a power hitter despite his size. He specialized in hard-hit line drives and only once hit 20 home runs, in 1944. McCormick had brief trials with the Reds in 1934 and 1937 before becoming a starter in 1938. He was traded to the Philadelphia Phillies in 1946 and went to the Boston Braves during the 1947 season. He retired after batting .250 for Boston in 1948.

In 1,534 games, McCormick had a .299 average on 1,711 hits, including 334 doubles, 26 triples, and 128 home runs. He scored 722 runs and had 951 RBI.

McCormick, Mike (Michael F.)

BASEBALL
b. Sept. 29, 1938, Pasadena, Calif.

An unspectacular journeyman pitcher for most of his career, the left-handed McCormick led the NL with a 2.70 ERA in 1960 and won the league's Cy Young Award in 1967, when he led the league in victories with a 22–10 record, posting five shutouts and a 2.85 ERA for the San Francisco Giants.

McCormick pitched briefly for the Giants in 1956 and 1957 and became a regular starter in 1958, when he was 11–8. He developed arm trouble in 1962 and was traded to the Baltimore Orioles the following year. After appearing in only 4 games with Baltimore in 1964, he went to the Washington Senators for two seasons, then returned to San Francisco and had his Cy Young season.

He had a record of 12–14 in 1968 and was 11–9 in 1969. He pitched for both the Giants and the New York Yankees in 1970 and finished his career with the Kansas City Athletics in 1971.

In 16 seasons, McCormick had a 134–128 record with 23 shutouts and a 3.73 ERA. He struck out 1,321 hitters and walked 795 in 2,380⅓ innings.

McCormick, Patricia J. (Keller)

DIVING
b. May 12, 1930, Seal Beach, Calif.

In 1951, McCormick went to a doctor because she was exhausted. Her schedule called for five hours of diving practice, two hours of housework, shopping, and cooking, and another three hours of practice. The doctor found lacerations on her arms and legs, welts across her back, a loosened jaw, scars in her scalp

and on her back, a healed rib fracture, and a healed finger fracture. "I've seen worse casualty cases," he said, "but only where a building caved in."

McCormick performed difficult, dangerous dives usually attempted only by men in her era and outlawed for women in international competition until 1952, when she won gold medals in the Olympic springboard and platform events. She also won both events in 1956, just eight months after birth of her first child. The first diver of either sex to win the springboard and platform at two Olympics, McCormick was voted the Sullivan Award recipient as the nation's outstanding amateur athlete.

Her first national championship came in the national outdoor platform dive in 1949. She also won that event in 1950, 1951, 1954, and 1955. McCormick was the outdoor 1-meter and 3-meter springboard champion in 1950, 1951, and from 1953 through 1956. Indoors, she won the 1-meter five years in a row, from 1951 through 1955, and the 3-meter in 1951, 1952, 1954, and 1955.

She retired from competition after the 1956 Olympics and operated a diving camp for a number of years. In 1984, she was a member of the escort for the U.S. flag at the Olympic opening ceremonies. Her daughter, Kelly, won a silver medal in the springboard that year.

★ International Women's Sports Hall of Fame; Olympic Hall of Fame

McCovey, Willie Lee

BASEBALL
b. Jan. 10, 1938, Mobile, Ala.

"Stretch" McCovey was a 6-foot-4, 210-pound left-handed first baseman who could hit the ball about as hard and as far as anyone could. He joined the NL's San Francisco Giants in July 1959 and went four for four in his first game, including two triples, against future Hall of Famer Robin Roberts. Although he played in only 52 games, he hit 13 home runs and was named the league's rookie of the year.

Because the Giants had right-handed slugger Orlando Cepeda at first base, McCovey was only a part-time player for the next three seasons. He hit 20 home runs and had 54 RBI in just 229 at-bats in 1962, when the Giants won the pennant but lost the World Series to the New York Yankees in seven games. In the ninth inning of the final game, McCovey came up with two outs, runners on second and third, and the Giants trailing, 1–0. He hit a vicious line drive toward right field, but it was snared by Yankee second baseman Bobby Richardson, and the Series was over.

In 1963, the Giants moved McCovey to the outfield to get his bat into the lineup every day. He responded by leading the league with 44 home runs, batting .280, and driving in 102 runs while scoring 103. After being hampered by injuries in 1964, McCovey hit 39, 36 and 31 home runs during the next three seasons.

He won two straight home run titles, with 36 in 1968 and 45 in 1969, and he also led in RBI both years, with 105 and 126. He was the league's slugging leader three years in a row, with percentages of .545 in 1968, .656 in 1969, and .612 in 1970.

Nagging injuries cut into his playing time for most of the rest of his career. He went to the San Diego Padres in 1974 and was traded to the Oakland Athletics during the 1976 season. Then he returned to San Francisco in 1977 and had his best year since 1970, batting .280 with 28 home runs and 86 RBI in 141 games. He retired after the 1980 season.

In 2,588 games, McCovey had a .270 average on 2,211 hits, including 353 doubles, 46 triples, and 521 home runs. He drove in 1,555 runs and scored 1,229.
★ Baseball Hall of Fame

McCoy, Charles Kid [Norman Selby]
FOOTBALL
b. Oct. 13, 1873, Rush County, Ind.
d. April 18, 1940

McCoy's life story sounds like the scenario for a bad movie. Married ten times to seven different women, at various times he starred in silent films, operated a detective agency, was accused of

jewel theft, and was convicted of murder.

He probably began boxing in Montana as a teenager, but his first recorded fight was a 4-round decision over Pete Jenkins on June 2, 1891, in St. Paul, Minnesota. McCoy went undefeated in 19 fights before being knocked out by Billy Steffers in the 1st round on May 10, 1894. He avenged that loss by winning a 10-round decision over Steffers on August 29, 1894.

McCoy claimed the welterweight title after knocking out champion Tommy Ryan in the 15th round on March 2, 1896, but Ryan was generally still considered the titlist. After outgrowing the division, he also claimed the vacant middleweight championship when he knocked out Dan Creedon in the 15th round on December 17, 1897.

He had only one recognized title fight, for the light heavyweight championship on April 22, 1903, but he lost a 10-round decision to Jack Root. That year Lionel Barrymore starred in a Broadway play, *The Other Girl*, that was based on McCoy's life.

McCoy fought only six times in the next seven years, but he had five fights in 1911 and two more in 1912 before being arrested in London on a charge of stealing jewels from an Austrian princess. He reportedly fought as the "Masked Marvel" for the next three years because of the notoriety he had created.

While serving in the National Guard, he had a final recorded fight in Mission, Texas, in 1916. Between 1919 and 1924 McCoy lived in Los Angeles and was in a number of movies. He was arrested in August 1924 for murdering his girlfriend and attempting to kill three other people. McCoy spent eight years in prison, then became a gardener in Detroit. In 1940 he committed suicide by taking an overdose of sleeping pills.
★ International Boxing Hall of Fame

McCracken, Branch (Emmett Branch)
BASKETBALL
b. June 9, 1908, Monrovia, Ind.
d. June 4, 1970

In three seasons of basketball at Indiana University, the 6-foot-4 McCracken scored 525 points, more than 30 percent of the points scored by the team during that period. He was named an All-American forward for 1929–30, his senior season, when he set a Western Conference (Big Ten) record with 147 points.

After graduating, he became basketball coach at Ball State University in Indiana. In seven seasons, his teams won 93 games while losing 41. He returned to his alma mater as coach in 1938, and the team soon became known as the "Hurrying Hoosiers" because of McCracken's emphasis on the fast break.

McCracken entered the Navy in 1943 and returned to Indiana after being discharged in 1947. He retired in 1965. His Indiana teams won two NCAA championships, in 1940 and 1953, and won or shared four Big Ten titles. Indiana won 364 and lost 174 during his 22 seasons at the school.

★ Basketball Hall of Fame

McCracken, Jack D.

BASKETBALL
b. June 11, 1911, Chickasha, Okla.
d. Jan 5, 1958

A 6-foot-2 center, "Jumping Jack" starred for Hank Iba at Maryville College, now Northwest Missouri State, when the team won 43 straight games. The 1930–31 squad won all 31 of its regular season games. In 1932, Maryville lost in the finals of the AAU national tournament, and McCracken was named to the AAU All-American team.

McCracken played on several Denver AAU teams, including the Denver Safeway team that won the 1937 AAU championship and lost in the finals in 1938. He became player-coach of the Denver Nuggets, who won the 1939 championship. Before retiring in 1945, he coached and played for two more AAU champions, the Denver American Legion in 1942 and the Phillips 66ers in 1945.

McCracken was an eight-time AAU All-American at both forward and guard. In 1939, he was chosen the greatest AAU player of all time.

★ Basketball Hall of Fame

McCreary, Conn (Cornelius)

HORSE RACING
b. 1921, St. Louis, Mo.
d. June 29, 1979

Although he begin riding in 1937, McCreary didn't have a major victory until 1941, when he rode Our Boots to an upset over Whirlaway in the Blue Grass Stakes. In 1944, he won the Kentucky Derby and the Preakness aboard Pensive, but fell short of the triple crown by a half-length in the Belmont.

McCreary's greatest ride was undoubtedly his win in the 1951 Kentucky Derby with Count Turf. Running sixteenth and apparently hopelessly blocked by a large field, McCreary somehow threaded his way through the pack to take fourth at the beginning of the stretch, and he then took Count Turf to the outside and drove to a four-length victory.

He won his fourth triple crown race with Blue Man in the 1952 Preakness. McCreary retired from riding in 1957 and later worked as a trainer and track publicity man.

★ National Horse Racing Hall of Fame

McCutchan, Arad A.

BASKETBALL
b. July 4, 1912, Evansville, Ind.

McCutchan played four years of basketball at Evansville College, graduating in 1934, and received a master's degree from Columbia University Teachers College. He coached high school basketball for nine seasons, then served in the U.S. Navy for three years during World War II.

In 1946, he became head coach at Evansville and developed a perennial college division power. His teams won a record five college division (now Division II) NCAA championships, in 1959, 1960, 1964, 1965, and 1971, and McCutchan was named college division coach of the year in both 1964 and 1965.

The 1964–65 team, which starred Jerry Sloan, had a perfect 29–0 record and beat the University of Iowa, Louisiana State, Northwestern, and Notre Dame. Sloan became an NBA player and coach. McCutchan retired in 1972 with a record of 433 wins, a college division record at the time, and 259 losses.

★ Basketball Hall of Fame

McCutcheon, Floretta (Doty)
BOWLING
b. July 22, 1888, Ottumwa, Iowa
d. Feb. 2, 1967

"Mrs. Mac" didn't begin bowling until she was 35, and her competitive career lasted little more than a decade, yet she had a profound impact on the sport. It's been estimated that she introduced more than 250,000 people, most of them women and children, to bowling through her clinics, exhibitions, and lessons.

She rolled a 69 in her first game in 1923. After a season of league bowling, she quit, but she resumed in 1926 and blossomed quickly. In 1927, she beat the great Jimmy Smith, 704 to 697, in a three-game series.

McCutcheon then began touring, and in 1930 she opened the Mrs. McCutcheon School of Bowling. When she retired in 1939, she had bowled 10 perfect 300 games, 11 800 series, and more than a hundred series of 700 or better, despite the fact that most of her games were rolled on unfamiliar lanes throughout the country.

Most of her records are not recognized because they were made in exhibitions or unsanctioned matches. However, her average of 206 in a sanctioned league during the 1938–39 season was a recognized record for a woman bowler until 1964.

After retiring from competition, she taught bowling in New York City until 1944 and in Chicago until 1954, when she retired and moved to California.

★ WIBC Hall of Fame

McDaniel, Mildred L.
TRACK AND FIELD
b. Nov. 4, 1933, Atlanta, Ga.

McDaniel played basketball and was a high jumper at Tuskegee Institute from 1953 through 1956. She was the AAU outdoor champion in 1953, and she won both the outdoor and the indoor championships in 1955 and 1956.

She won a gold medal at the 1955 Pan-American Games with a meet record jump of 5 feet, 6½ inches. McDaniel set a world record of 5 feet, 7 inches in winning the 1956 Olympic high jump. She beat Iolanda Balas of Romania, the former world record holder. Later that year, McDaniel extended the record to a remarkable 5 feet, 8¾ inches.

After graduating from Tuskegee in 1957, McDaniel retired from competition and became a physical education teacher.

★ National Track & Field Hall of Fame

McDermott, Bobby (Robert)
BASKETBALL
b. Jan. 7, 1914, Whitestone, N.Y.
d. Oct. 3, 1963

Al Cervi, a great defensive player who often had to guard him, said of McDermott, "Oh, he could shoot! If he shot ten times from 30 feet, I'd guarantee he'd make eight in game conditions."

A 5-foot-11 guard, Bobby McDermott dropped out of high school and became a legendary playground star before joining the Brooklyn Visitations of the American Basketball League. Brooklyn won the 1934–35 ABL championship, and McDermott led the league in scoring.

After a year in the New York Professional League, where he set a record with 32 points in a playoff game, he was with the reorganized Original Celtics for three seasons. He went back to the ABL and was again the league's scoring leader, returned to the Celtics for another season, then settled down for a while with the Ft. Wayne Zollner Pistons of the National Basketball League in 1941.

Led by McDermott, the Pistons won three consecutive NBL titles from 1944 through 1946, and they also won the world professional championship tournament in Chicago all three years. McDermott was named to the all-tournament team each year, and he was the tournament's most valuable player in 1944. In 1944–45, he set an NBL record with 36 points in a game.

McDermott was player-coach of the Pistons in 1946–47, then took the same position with the Chicago Gears, who won the NBL championship. He went to the Tri-Cities Blackhawks in 1947–48, to the Hammond Buccaneers the following season, and finished his career with the Wilkes-Barons in 1950.

The NBL in 1946 named McDermott the greatest player in league history, and *Collier's* magazine chose him for an "All-World" team in 1950. McDermott died of injuries suffered in an automobile accident.

★ Basketball Hall of Fame

McDermott, John J., Jr.

GOLF
b. Aug. 8, 1891, Philadelphia, Pa.
d. Aug. 2, 1971

McDermott was one of the truly tragic figures in sports. Cocky and brash, he tied Alex and MacDonald Smith in the 1910 U.S. Open but lost the playoff to Alex. He told Alex that the outcome was a mistake that would be rectified the following year, and it was. McDermott won the Open in 1911, the youngest winner ever, and repeated in 1912; he is one of only five golfers who have won two Opens in a row. A great iron player who could reputedly drop a shot onto a newspaper, McDermott was the first golfer to break par for 72 holes.

In 1914, McDermott went to England to compete in the British Open, but missed a ferry boat and arrived late. Officials offered to let him play, but he declined, saying it would be unfair to the other golfers. He sailed back to the U.S. on the *Kaiser Wilhelm II*, which collided with another ship, and McDermott spent some time in a lifeboat before being rescued. When he finally got home, he discovered that he'd lost most of his money in the stock market.

Shortly afterward, he blacked out when entering the clubhouse in Atlantic City, where he was the club pro. McDermott spent the rest of his life in mental hospitals and rest homes or living with his family in Philadelphia, the victim of mental illness. He never played golf again.

★ PGA Hall of Fame

McDermott, Terry (Richard Terrance)

SPEED SKATING
b. Sept. 20, 1940, Essexville, Mich.

The only U.S. gold medal in the 1964 Winter Olympics went to McDermott, in the 500-meter speed skating event. McDermott's victory was a major upset and a major sports story. Fans throughout the country who had never paid any attention to speed skating before read about the 23-year-old barber who had raced on skates borrowed from the team coach, Leo Freisinger, wearing a good luck pin given to him by Mrs. Freisinger.

McDermott probably deserved a gold medal in 1968, but he skated in the last pairing on ice that was melting under the midday sun and finished in a tie for second. Erhard Keller of Germany, who won the gold medal, said later, "If he had started in the earlier heats while the ice was still good, I'd have lost. It's as simple as that."

McDermott won the national indoor speed skating championship in 1960, the North American indoor title in 1961. He later became a speed skating official and took the Olympic oath on behalf of all officials at the opening ceremonies of the 1980 Winter Games.

McDonald, Babe (Patrick J.)

TRACK AND FIELD
b. July 29, 1878, County Clare, Ireland
d. May 16, 1954

The family name in Ireland was McDonnell, but it was misspelled by an immigration official when his older sister arrived in the U.S., and all members of the family who arrived afterward accepted the new version.

McDonald originally aspired to be a hammer thrower, following the example of such great Irish-American athletes as John Flanagan, Matt McGrath, and Martin Sheridan, but he discovered he was better at the shot put and weight throw.

He won gold medals in the shot put at the 1912 Olympics and the 56-pound weight throw at the 1920 Olympics, when he was 42 years old, making him the oldest Olympic track champion ever. McDonald also won the silver medal in

1912 in an obsolete event, the two-handed aggregate shot put.

A New York City policeman from 1905 until his retirement in 1946, McDonald won AAU outdoor shot put championships in 1911, 1912, 1914, 1919, 1920, and 1922, and he was the indoor champion in 1916 and 1917 and from 1919 through 1921.

When McDonald won the AAU 56-pound weight throw in 1933, less than a month before his 57th birthday, he became the oldest national track champion in history. He had previously won the event in 1911 and 1914, from 1919 through 1921, and from 1926 through 1929.

MacDonald, Irene

DIVING
b. Nov. 22, 1933, Hamilton, Ont.

The winner of 15 Canadian diving championships from 1951 through 1961, MacDonald won a bronze medal in the springboard competition at the 1956 Olympics. She was the U.S. outdoor 1-meter and 3-meter springboard champion in 1959, and she also won indoor titles in the 1-meter in 1959 and in the 3-meter in 1960.

After retiring from competition in 1962, MacDonald became a very successful coach. She coached the Canadian women's diving team for the 1966 Commonwealth Games, the 1971 European tour, and the world championships from 1973 through 1975.

★ Canadian Sports Hall of Fame

McDonald, Tommy (Thomas F.)

FOOTBALL
b. July 26, 1934, Roy, N.Mex.

As a running back at the University of Oklahoma, McDonald helped lead his team to a 30-0-0 record from 1954 through 1956. Called by Bud Wilkinson "the best halfback I've ever coached," the 5-foot-9, 168-pounder rushed for 1,683 yards, averaged 6.8 yards per carry, and completed 28 of 44 passes on the halfback option.

He was a consensus All-American in 1956 and won the Maxwell Award as the nation's outstanding college player. He finished third in the Heisman Trophy voting to Paul Hornung and Johnny Majors.

McDonald wasn't selected until the third round of the 1957 NFL draft because of his size. The Philadelphia Eagles moved him to flanker, where he was a three-time All-Pro. A star on the Eagle championship team of 1960, McDonald played for the Dallas Cowboys in 1964, the Los Angeles Rams in 1965 and 1966, the Atlanta Falcons in 1967, and the Cleveland Browns in 1968.

During his 12 NFL seasons, McDonald caught 495 passes for 8,410 yards, a 17.0 average, and 84 touchdowns. He returned 73 punts for 404 yards, a 5.5 average, and 1 touchdown, and ran back 51 kickoffs for 1,055 yards, a 20.7 average.

★ College Football Hall of Fame

McDowell, Jack B.

BASEBALL
b. Jan. 16, 1966, Van Nuys, Calif.

Nicknamed "Black Jack" by his teammates because of his dark beard, McDowell is a 6-foot-5, 188-pound right-handed pitcher who attended Stanford University before entering professional baseball in 1987.

He was with the AL's Chicago White Sox briefly that season, compiling a 3–0 record and a 1.93 ERA, and he became a full-time starter in 1988. However, McDowell spent some time in the minor leagues the following season, when he was ineffective with Chicago.

Since 1990, McDowell has been a consistent winner. He led the league in complete games with 15 in 1991 and 13 in 1992 and won the Cy Young Award as the league's outstanding pitcher in 1993. That season, McDowell was the league leader in victories with a 22–10 record and in shutouts with 4.

Through 1994, McDowell had a 91–58 record with 10 shutouts and a 3.50 ERA. He had struck out 978 hitters and walked 419 in 1,343⅔ innings.

McDowell, Samuel E. T.

BASEBALL
b. Sept. 21, 1942, Pittsburgh, Pa.

"Sudden Sam," as he was known because of his great fastball, was a left-handed pitcher who led the AL in strikeouts five times in a six-year period. Wildness and the tendency to fall in love with other pitches that weren't as effective for him, such as the curve and the change-up, unfortunately prevented him from becoming a great pitcher.

After brief stints with the Cleveland Indians in 1961, 1962, and 1963, McDowell became a regular starter in 1964, when he had an 11–6 record and a 2.70 ERA. The following year, he led the league with 325 strikeouts and a 2.18 ERA while compiling a 17–11 record.

The 6-foot-5, 218-pound McDowell had some arm trouble in 1966 but was still the AL strikeout leader with 225 in only 194⅓ innings. He led in strikeouts three years in a row, with 283 in 1968, when he was 15–14 with a 1.81 ERA; with 279 in 1969, when he was 18–14 with a 2.94 ERA; and with 304 in 1970, when he had a 20–12 record and a 2.92 ERA.

McDowell began to decline in 1971, when his ERA increased to 3.40 and his record dropped to 13–17. He went to the NL's San Francisco Giants in 1972, to the New York Yankees during the 1973 season, and to the Pittsburgh Pirates in 1975. He spent one season in Pittsburgh before retiring.

In 15 seasons, McDowell had a 143–134 record with 23 shutouts and a 3.17 ERA. He struck out 2,453 hitters and walked 1,312 in 2,492⅓ innings.

McElhenny, Hugh E., Jr.

FOOTBALL
b. Dec. 31, 1928, Los Angeles, Calif.

Speed, quick cuts, and great peripheral vision made McElhenny one of the most dangerous runners in history. As a junior at the University of Washington in 1950, he scored five touchdowns in a 52–21 win over Washington State.

A first-round draft choice of the NFL's San Francisco 49ers in 1952, McElhenny had the league's longest run from scrimmage, 89 yards, and longest punt return, 94 yards. He led the league with 7.0 yards per rushing attempt and

was a consensus choice as rookie of the year.

The San Francisco organization was in financial trouble when the 6-foot-1, 198-pound McElhenny arrived, but his exciting running style drew fans, and general manager Lou Spadia referred to him as the "franchise saver."

A knee injury limited his playing time in 1954, but he scored 6 rushing touchdowns on only 64 carries and again led the NFL with 8.0 yards per attempt. After three solid seasons, the knee began to bother him again in 1959 and the 49ers let him go to the Minnesota Vikings in the 1961 expansion draft.

McElhenny had a fine year with the Vikings, gaining a total of 1,067 yards rushing, receiving, and returning kicks. In 1963, he went to the New York Giants and was a spot player on their NFL championship team. He retired after spending the 1964 season with the Detroit Lions.

An All-Pro in 1952 and 1953, McElhenny played in six Pro Bowls. During his 13 professional seasons, he rushed 1,124 times for 5,281 yards, a 4.7 average, and 38 touchdowns; caught 264 passes for 3,247 yards, a 12.3 average, and 20 touchdowns; returned 126 punts for 920 yards, a 7.3 average, and 2 touchdowns; and returned 83 kickoffs for 1,921 yards, a 23.1 average.
★ Pro Football Hall of Fame

McElmury, Audrey (Phleger)

CYCLING
b. 1943

An avid surfer as a teenager, McElmury took up cycling to strengthen a leg she had broken while skateboarding. She graduated from the University of California at San Diego in 1965, got married, had a son, and then returned to competition. She won the U.S. road racing and pursuit championships in 1966.

In 1969, McElmury won the women's world road race title. She was the first American to win a world cycling championship since Frank Kramer, the professional sprint champion in 1912. Her victory was so unexpected that the award ceremony had to be held up for half an hour while officials searched for a recording of the National Anthem.

McElmury repeated as national road racing and pursuit champion in 1970. She and her first husband, Scott McElmury, were divorced shortly afterward, and she married another cyclist, Michael Levonas, in 1971. They both raced extensively in Europe that year. She then began coaching cyclists in Boulder, Colorado, but retired from the sport after suffering a concussion in a crash. She and her second husband wrote a book, *Bicycle Training for Triathletes.*

McEnroe, John P.
TENNIS
b. Feb. 16, 1959, Wiesbaden, Germany

A superb tennis player, McEnroe is unfortunately best known for his terrible temper tantrums and profane outbursts at officials, which won him such nicknames as "Superbrat," "Mac the Strife," and "the Incredible Sulk."

As a student at Stanford University in 1977, McEnroe became the youngest man ever to reach the semifinals at Wimbledon. After winning the 1978 NCAA singles title, McEnroe became a professional and won the first of three consecutive U.S. Open singles championships in 1979. He also won the Grand Prix Masters and World Championship Tennis (WCT) finals that year.

McEnroe had an off year in 1980, although he won his second U.S. Open title, and he had a great year in 1981. He won the U.S. Open, Wimbledon, the Grand Prix Masters, and the WCT finals, and he was named AP male athlete of the year.

However, the achievement was marred by his behavior at Wimbledon, where he was fined £5,000 for an angry outburst in his first match. McEnroe refused to attend the traditional champions' dinner, and for the first time in history, the All-England Tennis Club didn't extend an honorary membership to the men's singles champion.

In 1982, McEnroe reached the Wimbledon finals but was badly bothered by an ankle injury. His game performance in struggling through a five-set loss to Jimmy Connors won McEnroe his All-England honorary membership.

McEnroe won the Wimbledon singles for the second time in 1983, and he won at both Wimbledon and the U.S. Open in 1984. In addition to his seven singles championships, he won eight doubles titles in grand slam tournaments.

Through 1994, McEnroe was third all time with 77 career victories and fourth in winnings with $12,227,622.

McEver, Gene (Eugene T.)
FOOTBALL
b. Sept. 15, 1908, Bristol, Va.
d. July 12, 1985

As a halfback, McEver scored an incredible 130 points for the University of Tennessee in just 10 games in 1929 and was named an All-American. He had a 90-yard touchdown run against Centre and eight other touchdown runs of 25 or more yards that season, as Tennessee went undefeated, winning nine games and tying one.

After missing the entire 1930 season with a knee injury, he returned as a fullback in 1931. Forced to wear a knee brace, he lacked his former speed and mobility but still received some All-American mention at the new position, and Tennessee again went 9–0–1.

The first All-American from Tennessee and the first player from the school inducted into the College Football Hall of Fame, McEver coached Davidson College of North Carolina to a 16–43–4 record from 1937 through 1943, and he had a 1–7–1 record as interim coach at the University of North Carolina in 1944.
★ College Football Hall of Fame

McEwan, John J.
FOOTBALL
b. Feb. 18, 1893, Alexandria, Minn.
d. Aug. 9, 1970

A 6-foot-4, 200-pound center, McEwan was a Walter Camp All-American as a sophomore in 1914 but was relegated to Camp's third team in 1915 and to the second team in 1916, when he captained Army to a 9–0–0 record.

Remarkably fast for his size, McEwan was one of the early "roving centers," playing five yards back of the defensive line and moving to meet the play. On offense, he was one of the first centers to use the spiral pass to the deep back.

McEwan coached Army to an 18–5–3 record from 1923 through 1925. He had 19 wins, 12 losses, and 2 ties at the University of Oregon from 1926 through 1929 and was 21–6–3 at Holy Cross from 1930 through 1932. In 1933 and 1934, McEwan coached the NFL's Brooklyn Dodgers, who had a 9–11–1 record during that period.

★ College Football Hall of Fame

McFadin, Bud (Lewis P.)

FOOTBALL
b. Aug. 21, 1928, Iraan, Tex.

An All-American guard at the University of Texas in 1950, the 6-foot-4, 240-pound McFadin served in the Air Force during the Korean conflict, then joined the NFL's Los Angeles Rams as a middle guard and linebacker during the 1952 season. He was moved to defensive tackle in 1955.

McFadin retired from football after being injured in a freak shooting accident in 1956. When the American Football League was established in 1960, he came out of retirement to play for the Denver Broncos. In 1964, he went to the Houston Oilers. He spent two seasons there before retiring to become the team's defensive line coach. He was named to the All-AFL team in 1960 and 1961.

★ College Football Hall of Fame

McFarland, Packey (Patrick)

BOXING
b. Nov. 1, 1888, Chicago, Ill.
d. Sept. 23, 1938

Probably the greatest fighter who never held a championship, McFarland built an incredible record during his 12-year career but never even got a title shot.

He began fighting professionally in 1904 and was knocked out by Dusty Miller in the 5th round in his last fight

that year. It was the only loss he ever suffered. The 5-foot-8 McFarland, who fought at between 130 and 140 pounds, had a devastating punch. From 1905 to 1907, he won 36 fights in a row, 27 by knockout.

In 1908, he won a decision over Freddie Welsh, who later became lightweight champion, and he also had no-decisions against Welsh in 1909 and 1910. His last fight was a no-decision in 1915 against Jack Britton, who later won the world welterweight title.

McFarland then retired from boxing and became a successful businessman in Joliet, Illinois. He won 64 bouts, 47 by knockout; lost only 1, by knockout; and fought 5 draws and 34 no-decisions.

★ International Boxing Hall of Fame

McGee, Willie D.

BASEBALL
b. Nov. 2, 1958, San Francisco, Calif.

A switch-hitting, right-handed throwing outfielder, McGee has had an up-and-down major league career. In 12 seasons, he has hit over .300 just four times, but he has won two NL batting titles.

McGee joined the NL's St. Louis Cardinals in 1982. He had his best year in 1985, when he led the league with 216 hits, 18 triples, and a .353 batting average. He stole 56 bases, scored 114 runs, and was named the league's most valuable player.

The next time McGee hit over .300 was in 1990, when he won another NL batting title at .335, even though he finished the season in the other league. After playing the first 125 games of the season with St. Louis, McGee was traded to the AL's Oakland As for their drive to the pennant, but he still had enough plate appearances for his average to stand up.

McGee joined the NL's San Francisco Giants as a free agent in 1991. Through the 1994 season, he had 1,876 hits in 1,637 games, including 288 doubles, 84 triples, and 66 home runs. He also had 320 stolen bases, 845 runs scored, and 706 RBI.

McGinnity, Joseph J. [McGinty]

BASEBALL
b. March 19, 1872, Rock Island, Ill.
d. Nov. 14, 1929

McGinnity got the nickname "Iron Man" because he worked in his father-in-law's iron factory during the off-season. It turned out to be appropriate for a pitcher who led the NL in innings four times, twice working more than 400 innings.

A 5-foot-11, 206-pounder, McGinnity depended primarily on a blazing fastball in his minor league career, but he retired because of a bad arm to run a saloon after the 1894 season. He began pitching again in semipro baseball, and he developed a slow underhand curveball that he called "Old Sal." It was so effective that he got back into professional baseball and joined the NL's Baltimore Orioles in 1899.

He led the league in victories with a 28–16 record that season, then went to Brooklyn. McGinnity helped lead the team to a pennant, leading the NL in victories again with a 28–8 record, in winning percentage with .778, and in innings pitched with 343.

When the AL became a major league in 1901, McGinnity was the first player to sign a contract, joining the Baltimore team. He led that league with 39 complete games and 382 innings pitched, compiling a 26–20 record in the process.

During the 1902 season, Baltimore manager John McGraw jumped to the New York Giants, taking McGinnity and several other players along. McGinnity had a league-leading 31 victories, 44 complete games, and 434 innings pitched in 1903. He proved himself a real iron man in August of that season, winning complete game victories in both games of a doubleheader three times.

His best season was 1904, when he was tops in the league with an .814 winning percentage, 35 victories, 9 shutouts, 5 saves, 408 innings pitched, and a 1.61 ERA. When the Giants won the pennant the following season, he was 21–15 with a 2.87 ERA. Although he didn't give up an earned run in New York's five-game World Series victory over the Philadelphia Athletics, he had a 1–1 record, losing the second game, 3–0, and winning the fifth game, 1–0.

McGinnity led the NL in victories for the fifth and last time in 1906, when he had a 27–12 record and a 2.25 ERA. After going 18–18 in 1907 and 11–7 in 1908, he was released at his own request so he could manage in the minor leagues. He continued to pitch during his managing career. At the age of 54, in 1925, he had a 6–6 record with a Dubuque team of which he was part owner as well as manager.

★ Baseball Hall of Fame

McGovern, John F.

FOOTBALL
b. Sept. 15, 1887, Arlington, Minn.
d. Dec. 14, 1963

The first University of Minnesota player to be named an All-American, McGovern was a three-year starter at quarterback. Working in Henry L. Williams's innovative shift, he was vitally important as a signal caller, but he could also run, pass, and kick.

McGovern drop-kicked three field goals in a 20–6 win over the University of Chicago in 1909, his All-American season. As a senior in 1910, he was a third-team member of Walter Camp's All-American squad. During his career, Minnesota won 15 games, lost 4, and tied 1.

★ College Football Hall of Fame

McGovern, Terry (John Terrance)

BOXING
b. March 9, 1880, Johnstown, Pa.
d. Feb. 26, 1918

One of the first fighters to use persistent body blows to set up an opponent for a knockout, McGovern became a professional boxer in 1897. His only loss in four years of fighting came on July 23 1898, when he was disqualified for fouling Tim Callahan. The foul was deliberate and came after Callahan had insulted "Terrible Terry," who was so nicknamed because of his temper.

McGovern won the vacant world bantamweight championship by knocking out British titlist Pedler Palmer in the 1st round on September 12, 1899, at Tuckahoe, New York. Before the end of the year, McGovern could no longer make the weight limit, and he relinquished the title.

On January 9, 1900, McGovern became world featherweight champion with an 8th-round knockout of George Dixon in New York City. Later that year, he knocked out lightweight champion Frank Erne in a nontitle fight.

An extremely popular fighter, McGovern starred in several shows in 1900 and 1901, including *The Bowery After Dark* and *Terry on the Spot.* He briefly quit boxing for the stage in the summer of 1901, then fought only two short exhibitions before facing Young Corbett in a title fight on November 28.

Corbett taunted McGovern by calling him names, and the infuriated champion became an easy target. He was knocked out in the second round. He suffered a nervous breakdown shortly afterward and was in and out of mental institutions for much of the rest of his life. He had just 13 fights during the next five years. After being inactive for all of 1907, he fought two no-decisions in 1908 and then retired from the ring.

McGovern won 69 bouts, 34 by knockout; lost 4, 2 by knockout; and fought 4 draws and 10 no-decisions.

★ International Boxing Hall of Fame

McGrath, Matthew J.

TRACK AND FIELD
b. Dec. 18, 1878, Nenagh, Ireland
d. Jan. 29, 1941

One of the "Irish whales," most of them New York policemen, who excelled as weight throwers in the early part of the century, McGrath came to the United States when he was 21.

He didn't win his first national championship until he was 37, but he went on to win 13 national titles, and he competed in four Olympics, winning three medals.

McGrath was the AAU national hammer throw champion in 1908, 1912, 1918, 1922, 1925, and 1926. He won the 56-pound weight throw in 1913, 1916, 1918, and from 1922 through 1925. He

won a silver medal in the hammer throw at the 1908 Olympics.

The 5-foot-11, 240-pound McGrath set a world record of 40 feet, 6⅜ inches in 1911, and he also had a world record hammer throw of 187 feet, 4 inches that year.

At the 1912 Olympics, McGrath dominated the hammer throw. The shortest of his six throws was 173 feet, 4 inches. His best throw, 179–6, was an Olympic record until 1936. Duncan Gillis of Canada won the silver medal with a throw of only 158–9.

An injured knee forced McGrath to withdraw from the 1920 Olympics after only two attempts, and he finished fifth in the hammer throw, but he won a silver medal in the event in 1924. He was so popular among New York Irish-Americans that they raised money for him to go to the Amsterdam Olympics in 1928 after he failed to qualify for the U.S. team. McGrath did sail to Amsterdam, but he wasn't allowed to compete.

McGraw, John J.

BASEBALL
b. April 7, 1873, Truxton, N.Y.
d. Feb. 25, 1934

As a boy, McGraw spent as much time reading about baseball as he did playing it. When he joined the local town team at the age of 16, he knew how to throw a curve, an uncommon skill at the time, and he knew more about the rules of baseball than any of the older players.

In 1890, McGraw began his professional career as a minor league shortstop and sometime pitcher. He joined the Baltimore Orioles in the American Association, then a major league, in August of 1891. The Orioles entered the NL after the American Association disbanded in 1892.

After playing 79 games that season, mostly in the outfield, McGraw became Baltimore's starting third baseman in 1893 and batted .321. It was the first of nine consecutive seasons in which he hit better than .300. The 5-foot-7, 155-pound McGraw, a left-handed hitter, led the league in runs scored with 143 in 1898 and 140 in 1899.

McGraw also became known as a belligerent player who would take on teammates as well as opponents, especially if he was called "Mugsy," a nickname he hated.

In 1899, McGraw was Baltimore's playing manager. He went to the St. Louis NL team as a player only the following season, then returned to Baltimore in 1901 to serve as playing manager of a team in the new American League. Although he continued to play occasionally through the 1906 season, McGraw was primarily a manager from this time on.

Ban Johnson, the AL founder and president, was a strong backer of the league's umpires and their authority. McGraw, an umpire baiter, had several clashes with Johnson, and in July 1902 he left Baltimore to become manager of the NL's New York Giants, taking several players with him.

The first World Series was played in 1903, after the rival leagues reached a truce. The Giants won the 1904 pennant, but McGraw refused to play a postseason series against the Boston Red Sox because he still nursed a grudge against the other league. However, he changed his mind in 1905, when the Giants won another pennant and beat the Philadelphia Athletics in the second World Series.

Nicknamed "Little Napoleon," McGraw was an autocrat who sometimes went too far with verbal abuse of his players. Yet he could also be very patient while working with younger players, and he often gave money to former Giants who had fallen on hard times.

Under McGraw, the Giants won pennants from 1911 through 1913, in 1917, and from 1921 through 1924. They had only three losing seasons from 1903 through 1931, his last full season as manager. On June 3, 1932, McGraw abruptly resigned, hiring first baseman Bill Terry as his replacement.

Although he still owned part of the team, McGraw never again visited the clubhouse or involved himself in management. When the first All-Star Game was played in 1933, he came out of retirement to manage the NL team. It was his last public appearance.

As a player, McGraw had a career batting average of .334. He stole 436 bases and scored 1,024 runs in 1,099 games. As a manager, he won 2,784 games and lost 1,959, a .587 winning percentage.
★ Baseball Hall of Fame

McGriff, Frederick S.
BASEBALL
b. Oct. 31, 1963, Tampa, Fla.

The 6-foot-3, 215-pound McGriff joined the AL's Toronto Blue Jays for three games in 1988 and became a part-time starter at first base the following season, when he hit 20 home runs in 107 games.

Since then, the left-handed McGriff has hit 31 or more home runs each season and has also established himself as an outstanding defensive player and a team leader. Toronto traded him to the NL's San Diego Padres in 1991, and San Diego sent him to the Atlanta Braves during the 1993 season.

McGriff was a major factor in Atlanta's stretch drive to the Western Division championship. When he joined the team in July, the Braves were ten games behind the San Francisco Giants and they ended up edging the Giants by one game.

He batted .435 with one home run, six runs scored, and four RBI in the 1993 NL championship series against the Philadelphia Phillies, but the Braves lost in six games.

McGriff led the AL with 36 home runs in 1989 and the NL with 35 in 1992. Through 1994, he had a .285 average with 1,136 hits, including 202 doubles, 16 triples, and 262 home runs. He had scored 703 runs and driven in 710.

McGugin, Daniel E.
FOOTBALL
b. July 29, 1879, Tingley, Iowa
d. Jan. 19, 1936

McGugin played football at Drake for one season, then transferred to the University of Michigan, where he was a starting guard in 1902 and 1903. His Michigan coach, "Hurry Up" Yost, later became a good friend and McGugin's brother-in-law. Yost was best man when McGugin married Virginia Fite. He met Virginia's sister, Eunice, at the wedding and married her a year later.

In 1904, McGugin was appointed head coach at Vanderbilt. He remained there through the 1934 season, although he spent 1918 serving in World War I. Under McGugin, Vanderbilt became the first Southern school to play intersectional games.

Though coaching was only a part-time job — he was a successful corporate lawyer — McGugin produced some outstanding teams. His very first team won all eight of its games, outscoring the opposition 452 to 4, and his 1910, 1921, and 1922 squads were unbeaten, though each had one tie.

A pioneer in the use of the forward pass, McGugin could motivate players in a quiet, soft-spoken way. Before the 1922 game against an unbeaten and heavily favored Michigan team, McGugin pointed to the military cemetery just outside Vanderbilt's football field. "In that cemetery sleep your grandfathers," he intoned, and then, pointing to the Michigan players, he said, "and down on that field are the grandsons of the damn Yankees who put them there." The game ended in a scoreless tie.

In his 30 seasons at Vanderbilt, McGugin won 197 games, lost 55, and had 19 ties, a winning percentage of .762. He retired because of poor health and died two years later.

★ College Football Hall of Fame

McGuire, Alfred J.

BASKETBALL
b. Sept. 7, 1928, New York, N.Y.
McGuire was captain of the St. John's University team that won 26 of its 31 games in 1950–51. He spent four years in the NBA, with the New York Knicks from 1950–51 through 1952–53 and with the Baltimore Bullets in 1953–54, averaging 3.9 points in 191 games, then became an assistant coach to "Doggy" Julian at Dartmouth in 1955.

In 1958, McGuire took over as head coach at Belmont Abbey College in North Carolina. His teams won 109 games while losing 64 in seven seasons, and McGuire went to Marquette University as basketball coach and athletic director in 1964. The school had won just 5 of its 26 games the previous season. After an 8–18 record in his first year, McGuire brought Marquette to national prominence.

From 1969–70 into the 1970–71 season, Marquette won 39 consecutive games, including the 1970 National Invitation Tournament. In his last coaching season, 1976–77, the team won the NCAA tournament. McGuire was named coach of the year by UPI, the Associated Press, and the U.S. Basketball Writers Association in 1971, and he won the 1974 coach of the year award from the National Association of Basketball Coaches.

After retiring as a coach, McGuire became an excellent television analyst, combining his knowledge of the sport with wit and wisecracks to entertain and inform fans. He popularized the phrase, "The opera isn't over until the fat lady sings."

★ Basketball Hall of Fame

McGuire, Dick (Richard J.)

BASKETBALL
b. Jan. 25, 1926, Huntington, N.Y.
Known as "Tricky Dick" because of his clever ball-handling, McGuire enrolled at St. John's University in New York in 1943. He played 16 games for the school's basketball team but entered the Navy before his freshman year was over and played five games at Dartmouth while in a special training program.

McGuire returned to St. John's in 1946 and graduated in 1949 with an average of 9.6 points per game during his four years. He was chosen by the New York Knickerbockers in the first round of the NBA draft. The 6-foot, 180-pound McGuire led the NBA with 386 assists as a rookie.

He was traded to the Detroit Pistons in 1957 and became the team's player coach during the 1958–59 season. Mc-

Guire retired as a player in 1960, remaining as coach through 1962–63. After a season out of basketball, he returned to the Knicks as head coach in 1965 but was replaced during the 1967–68 season.

During his 11 NBA seasons, McGuire scored 5,921 points in 738 regular season games, an 8.0 average, and had 4,205 assists. He added 521 points and 350 assists in 63 playoff games. As a coach, he had a 197–260 record.

★ Basketball Hall of Fame

McGuire, Edith M. (Mrs. Duvall)

TRACK AND FIELD
b. June 3, 1944, Atlanta, Ga.

As a 16-year-old high school student, McGuire finished fourth in the 100-yard dash at the 1960 AAU national championships. She entered Tennessee State University in the fall of 1961.

At the 1964 Olympics, McGuire won a gold medal in the 200-meter dash, running a 23.0 to break Wilma Rudolph's Olympic record. She finished second to college teammate Wyomia Tyus in the 100-meter and won a second silver medal as a member of the 4 x 100-meter relay team.

McGuire won the AAU national 100-meter in 1963 and was the 200-meter champion in 1964 and 1965. She also won a gold medal in the 100-meter at the 1963 Pan-American Games.

After graduating from college in 1966, McGuire retired from competition and became a teacher in Atlanta. She later worked with underprivileged children in Detroit.

★ National Track & Field Hall of Fame

McGuire, Frank J.

BASKETBALL
b. Nov. 8, 1914, New York, N.Y.
d. Oct. 11, 1994

McGuire was instrumental in making the Atlantic Coast Conference a major force in basketball, largely through his ability to recruit so-called "Yankee Rebels" from the metropolitan New York area.

He won four letters in both baseball and basketball at St. John's University and captained both teams in his senior

year. After graduating in 1936, he became baseball coach at his high school alma mater, Xavier High in New York City, and he also played pro basketball with the Brooklyn/New York Visitations.

McGuire entered the U.S. Navy during World War II. He returned briefly to Xavier before becoming basketball coach at St. John's in 1947. In five seasons there, he won 103 games while losing 35, and his teams went to two National Invitation Tournaments and two NCAA tournaments.

The University of North Carolina hired McGuire in 1952. The school had won just 24 games, losing 30, during the previous two seasons. McGuire quickly produced winners, culminating with the 1956–57 team that won all 32 of its games, beating Kansas and Wilt Chamberlain to win the NCAA championship.

McGuire left North Carolina to coach the NBA's Philadelphia Warriors to a 49–31 record in 1962–63. He returned to the ACC with the University of South Carolina in 1964 and built a successful program there. After two losing seasons, South Carolina had 20 or more victories for six consecutive seasons and went to four straight NCAA tournaments.

McGuire retired in 1980. He was the first coach to win 100 or more games at three different schools. His overall college record was 550 wins and 235 losses, a .701 winning percentage. Two of his St. John's players, Lou Carnesecca and Al McGuire, became very successful college coaches.

★ Basketball Hall of Fame

McGwire, Mark D.

BASEBALL
b. Oct. 1, 1963, Pomona, Calif.

McGwire was named *The Sporting News* college player of the year in 1984, when he played for the U.S. Olympic team before entering professional baseball. The 6-foot-5, 225-pounder was used mostly at third base in the minor leagues and in a brief stint with the AL's Oakland Athletics in 1986, but when he joined Oakland to stay in 1987, he was installed at first base.

A very powerful right-hander, McGwire was named rookie of the year after leading the league with 49 home runs, a record for a first-year player. He batted .289 and had 118 RBI that year.

McGwire is also an adept fielder who won a Gold Glove in 1990 and led the league's first basemen with 101 assists in 1991. After hitting 22 or more home runs each season from 1988 through 1992, he spent most of the 1993 season on the disabled list, and he also missed much of the 1994 season with injuries.

Through 1994, McGwire had a .249 average with 834 hits, including 137 doubles, 5 triples, and 238 home runs. He had scored 546 runs and driven in 657.

McHale, Kevin E.

BASKETBALL
b. Dec. 19, 1957, Hibbing, Minn.

McHale averaged 15.2 points per game and had 950 rebounds in 112 games during his four seasons at the University of Minnesota. He was chosen in the third round of the 1980 NBA draft by the Boston Celtics.

A center in college, the 6-foot-10, 225-pound McHale became a power forward with Boston. For most of his first six professional seasons, he specialized in coming off the bench to give the team added scoring power and rebounding. He won the league's "sixth man award" for that role in 1984 and 1985.

A very clever low post player with a wide variety of moves, McHale also developed a good turnaround jump shot as a professional, and his unusually long arms made him an outstanding defender. He was named to the NBA's all-defensive team from 1986 through 1988.

During his first five seasons, McHale played in 413 consecutive games, including the playoffs. His most productive season was 1986–87, when he averaged 26.1 points per game and led the league with a .604 field goal percentage. He was also the league leader with an identical .604 percentage the following season, when he averaged 22.6 points per game.

McHale played for three NBA championship teams, in 1981, 1984, and 1986. A broken foot suffered early in 1987 bothered him frequently during the rest of his career, and he retired after playing in pain throughout the 1992–93 season. Very popular with fans, teammates, and media, McHale was honored at a roast in Boston, and his uniform number was retired by the Celtics.

In 971 regular season games, McHale scored 17,335 points, an average of 17.9 per game, pulled down 7,122 rebounds, and blocked 1,690 shots. He scored 3,182 points in 169 playoff games, an 18.8 average, and had 1,253 rebounds and 281 blocks.

MacInnis, Allan

HOCKEY
b. July 11, 1963, Inverness, N.S.

A high-scoring defenseman, the 6-foot-2, 196-pound MacInnis won the 1989 Conn Smythe Trophy as the most valuable player in the Stanley Cup playoffs. He scored 31 points on 7 goals and 24 assists in 22 games that year, and he set a record for defensemen by scoring in 17 consecutive playoff games to lead the Calgary Flames to the championship.

MacInnis, universally recognized as having the hardest shot in hockey, scored two game-winning goals on slapshots in Calgary's six-game win over the Montreal Canadiens in the final series.

He played for the Flames briefly in the 1981–82 and 1982–83 seasons, then joined the team to stay early in 1983–84. Twice a first-team All-Star, MacInnis has scored 822 points on 213 goals and 609 assists in 803 regular season games through the 1993–94 season. He added 25 goals and 77 assists for 102 points in 95 playoff games.

Mack, Connie [Cornelius A. McGillicuddy]

BASEBALL
b. Dec. 22, 1862, E. Brookfield, Mass.
d. Feb. 8, 1956

Mack was involved in major league baseball, as a player, manager, and owner, for far longer than anyone else in the sport's history. He joined the NL's Washington team as a catcher at the end of the 1886 season and remained through 1889, then jumped to Buffalo in the Players' League in 1890.

The league folded after just one season, and Mack went to the Pittsburgh NL team. He was named Pittsburgh's manager late in the 1894 season and remained through 1896, when he was fired. That was also his last season as a player. The 6-foot-1, 150-pound Mack was a good defensive catcher but not much of a hitter. He had a career average of .251 in 723 major league games.

In 1897, Mack began managing the Milwaukee team in the minor Western League, which was presided over by Ban Johnson. Johnson turned it into the American League in 1901 and gave Mack a 25 percent interest in the league's new Philadelphia franchise.

At a time when most managers were tough, brawling, profane men, Mack was a distinct exception. He didn't smoke, drink, or use profanity, and he wore a business suit, necktie, and hat while managing from the dugout. Because he didn't wear the standard uniform, Mack was not allowed to step onto the playing field.

The Athletics won a pennant in 1902, a year before the World Series began. They were also pennant winners in 1910, 1911, 1913, and 1914, and they took the World Series every year except 1913. Despite that success, however, the franchise had financial problems, and Mack had to sell off his best players to raise cash.

After seven straight last-place finishes, Philadelphia got back into the first division in 1925 and won three consecutive pennants, from 1929 through 1931, capturing the World Series in 1929 and 1930. Because of the Depression, the franchise was again losing money. Mack sold four future Hall of Famers, Mickey Cochrane, Jimmy Foxx, Lefty Grove, and Al Simmons, to pay off $500,000 in debts.

Until 1940, Ben Shibe was the team's majority owner and Mack was the manager. After Shibe's death, Mack bought enough stock from his widow to become majority owner, with 58 percent of the team. He continued managing through 1950, when he was honored with a ticker-tape parade in New York and an invitation to the White House.

Mack then retired, giving control of the team to his three sons. In 1954, he sold the franchise to Arnold Johnson, who moved it to Kansas City. Mack's record as a manager reflects the fact that the Athletics had more hard times than good during his tenure: he won 3,731 games and lost 3,948, a winning percentage of .486.

★ Baseball Hall of Fame

McKay, John H.
FOOTBALL
b. July 5, 1923, Everettsville, W.Va.

After serving in the Army Air Corps during World War II, McKay entered Purdue University and then transferred to the University of Oregon, where he started at halfback in 1948 and 1949.

He served as an assistant coach at Oregon and the University of Southern California before becoming USC head coach in 1960. McKay's teams were distinguished by a powerful running attack out of the I formation, with occasional passes to keep the defense off balance. Among the outstanding tailbacks he produced were Heisman Trophy winners O. J. Simpson and Mike Garrett.

Under McKay, Southern California won national championships in 1962, 1967, 1972, and 1974, and were undefeated in 1962, 1969, and 1972. He is the only coach to take a team to the Rose Bowl four years in a row, from 1967 through 1970.

During his 16 seasons, Southern California won 127 games while losing 40 and tying 8. He left the school in 1975 to become head coach of the NFL's expansion Tampa Bay Buccaneers. The team lost 28 consecutive games in its first two seasons but reached the playoffs by winning the 1979 Central Division title. The Buccaneers also won the division in 1981 and qualified for the playoffs as a wildcard team in 1982.

McKay retired after the 1984 season with a professional record of 44 wins, 88 losses, and 1 tie.

★ College Football Hall of Fame

McKechnie, Bill (William B.)

BASEBALL
b. Aug. 7, 1886, Wilkinsburg, Pa.
d. Oct. 29, 1965

A competent infielder but not much of a hitter, McKechnie appeared in just 846 games in 11 major league seasons. Yet Frank Chance, his manager in 1913, called him "one of my most valuable players" because of his knowledge of the game. When Chance needed advice, he said, he usually sought out McKechnie.

After retiring in 1921, McKechnie became a coach with the NL's Pittsburgh Pirates, and he took over as manager in July 1922. In 1925, he guided the Pirates to a pennant and a seven-game victory in the World Series.

McKechnie was an unusual kind of manager for his era. A very religious man, he didn't smoke, drink, or use profanity. When he had a problem player who was likely to go out carousing, McKechnie's simple solution was to room with him.

Because of a dispute with management, McKechnie left Pittsburgh after the 1926 season and became a coach with the St. Louis Cardinals. He was named manager of the team in 1928 and promptly won another pennant, but St. Louis lost to the New York Yankees in a four-game World Series.

As punishment for that defeat, Cardinal owner Sam Breadon sent McKechnie to manage a minor league farm club in 1929, but he returned to the Cardinals before the end of the season, then took over the Boston Braves in 1930.

After eight years in Boston, including a brief period as interim president of the franchise, McKechnie was hired by the Cincinnati Reds in 1938. The team finished fourth that year, then won pennants in 1939 and 1940. The Reds lost the 1939 World Series but won in 1940. Released by Cincinnati after a sixth-place finish in 1946, McKechnie became a coach and adviser to Lou Boudreau, the young playing manager of the Cleveland Indians, for three years.

The first manager to win pennants with three different teams, McKechnie won 1,896 games and lost 1,723, a .524 winning percentage.

★ Baseball Hall of Fame

Mackey, John

FOOTBALL
b. Sept. 24, 1941, New York, N.Y.

When Mike Ditka became the first tight end inducted into the Pro Football Hall of Fame in 1988, he asked why Mackey wasn't there ahead of him. The answer was simple: Mackey's involvement in the NFL Players' Association had alienated the pro football establishment. He was finally inducted in 1992.

Mackey was a halfback in his first two seasons at Syracuse University but was moved to end as a junior in 1961. He was chosen in the second round of the 1963 NFL draft by the Baltimore Colts. The 6-foot-2, 220-pound Mackey was lighter than most tight ends, but he was a crushing blocker, and he had a good turn of speed that often enabled him to get open for a pass deep down the middle of the field. He averaged more than 20 yards per catch in 1963 and 1965.

An All-Pro from 1966 through 1968, Mackey lost some speed after a knee operation in 1970, but he made the biggest play in Super Bowl V after that season, scoring a 75-yard touchdown on a tipped pass in Baltimore's 16–13 win over the Dallas Cowboys.

Also in 1970, Mackey became president of the Players' Association and was a major force behind the strike of 1971. He brought a suit against the NFL that resulted in the "Rozelle rule" being voided. (The rule required a team to compensate another team for acquiring a player who had played out his option year.)

Mackey ended his career in 1972 with the San Diego Chargers. In his ten seasons in the NFL, Mackey had 331 receptions for 5,238 yards, a 16.2 average, and 39 touchdowns. He also carried the ball ten times for 103 yards.

★ Pro Football Hall of Fame

McKinney, Frank E., Jr.

SWIMMING
b. Nov. 3, 1938, Indianapolis, Ind.
d. Sept. 11, 1992

The son of a former owner of the NL's Pittsburgh Pirates, McKinney was the youngest member of a U.S. team that set a world record in the 4 x 100-meter medley relay at the 1955 Pan-American Games. The 16-year-old high school student also won a gold medal in the 100-meter backstroke.

McKinney won a bronze medal in the 200-meter backstroke at the 1956 Olympics and then entered Indiana University. He won the NCAA 100- and 200-yard backstroke championships in 1959 and was a member of the winning 4 x 100-yard medley relay team in 1960.

The AAU outdoor 100-meter backstroke champion from 1957 through 1959, McKinney also won the indoor 220-yard backstroke from 1956 through 1959 and the indoor 100-yard backstroke in 1958.

At the 1959 Pan-American Games, McKinney again won gold medals in the 100-meter backstroke and the 4 x 100-meter medley relay. He won a silver medal in the 100-meter backstroke at the 1960 Olympics and swam on the medley relay team that won a gold medal in a world record 4:05.4.

McKinney retired from competition after graduating from Indiana in 1961 and went into banking. He was the president of an Indianapolis bank when he died in the collision of two small planes.

McKinney, Rick (Richard)

ARCHERY
b. 1955, Muncie, Ind.

McKinney and Darrell Pace grew up less than a hundred miles apart, and they had a long rivalry as competitive archers. In 1975, McKinney failed to make the U.S. national team, finishing one point behind Pace in the trials. Pace went on to win the world championship.

In 1977, McKinney beat Pace to win his first national title, and he also won the world championship that year. Pace reclaimed the U.S. championship in 1978, but McKinney won the next five years in a row, from 1979 through 1983. He and Pace went to the last arrow in the 1983 world championship, with McKinney hitting a 10 to Pace's 9 to win the title.

After finishing second to Pace in the national championship and the Olympics in 1984, McKinney won three more national titles, from 1985 through 1987, and then retired from competition.

McKinney, Tamara

SKIING
b. Oct. 16, 1962, Lexington, Ky.

A seven-time winner of the U.S. slalom championship, from 1982 through 1984 and from 1986 through 1989, McKinney is the only American woman ever to win the World Cup for Alpine skiing.

The 5-foot-4, 117-pound McKinney generates tremendous speed and attacks courses with a boldness that verges on recklessness. At the 1980 Olympics, she was considered a medal contender, but she fell in both the slalom and the giant slalom, failing to place.

McKinney came back in 1981 to win the World Cup championship in the giant slalom. She was overall World Cup champion in 1983 and the slalom World Cup winner in 1984.

McLain, Denny (Dennis D.)

BASEBALL
b. March 24, 1944, Chicago, Ill.

In 1968, McLain became the first major league pitcher to win 30 or more games since Dizzy Dean in 1934. He had a 31–6 record and a 1.96 ERA and was the league leader in victories, winning percentage (.838), complete games (28), and innings pitched (336). That performance won him the AL's Cy Young and most valuable player awards, and he was also named male athlete of the year by the Associated Press.

The Detroit Tigers won the pennant behind McLain's effort. He had a 1–2 record and a 3.24 ERA in the World Series, but Detroit beat the St. Louis Cardinals in seven games.

A right-hander, McLain led the league in victories with a 24–9 record, in shutouts with 9, and in innings pitched with 325 in 1969, when he shared the Cy Young Award with Mike Cuellar of the Baltimore Orioles.

Early in 1970, word leaked that McLain was being investigated by a Detroit grand jury for possible involvement with gamblers. After he admitted investing money in a bookmaking operation, he was suspended indefinitely by Commissioner Bowie Kuhn. The suspension was lifted in July, but he was suspended by the Tigers twice during the season for several bizarre actions, including dumping a bucket of ice water on two sportswriters, carrying a gun on a commercial airliner, and threatening a parking lot attendant.

After a miserable 10–22 record with the Washington Senators in 1971, McLain pitched briefly for the Oakland Athletics and the Atlanta Braves in 1972. That was the end of his meteoric major league career. In 1985, he was sentenced to 23 years in prison for racketeering, loan sharking, extortion, and possession of cocaine with intent to distribute. He served 30 months before winning an appeal and his freedom.

McLain had a career 131–91 record with 2 shutouts and a 3.39 ERA. He struck out 1,282 hitters and walked 548 in 1,886 innings.

McLane, Jimmy (James P. Jr.)

SWIMMING

b. Sept. 13, 1930, Pittsburgh, Pa.

In 1944, McLane became the youngest AAU men's champion in history by winning the outdoor long-distance race at the age of 13, and he won the event again in 1945. He was also the AAU outdoor champion in the 800-meter freestyle from 1945 through 1948; the 1,500-meter freestyle from 1945 through 1947; and the 400-meter freestyle from 1946 through 1948.

McLane won an Olympic gold medal in the 1,500-meter freestyle in 1948, when he was a member of the gold medal 4 x 200-meter relay team. He also won a silver medal in the 400-meter freestyle.

In 1949, McLane enrolled at Yale,

where he was overshadowed by teammate John Marshall of Australia. However, McLane won the AAU indoor 440-yard and 1,500-meter freestyle events, and he was also the NCAA 220-yard and 1,500-meter champion that year. McLane's last year of competition was 1955, when he won gold medals at the Pan-American Games in the 400- and 1,500-meter freestyle races and in the 4 x 200-meter freestyle relay.

★ International Swimming Hall of Fame

McLarnin, Jimmy (James A.)

BOXING

b. Dec. 17, 1905, Inchacore, Ireland

McLarnin grew up in Vancouver, British Columbia, and began boxing professionally there in 1923. After winning ten fights, he went to California in 1924 with his shrewd manager, Pop Foster, to face better competitors. He beat most of them, including Fidel LaBarba, Jackie Fields, Pancho Villa, and Bud Taylor.

On May 21, 1928, McLarnin fought Sammy Mandell for the world lightweight championship in New York City but lost a 15-round decision. He beat Mandell twice in the next two years in nontitle bouts.

McLarnin moved into the welterweight division in 1932 and won the world title by knocking out Young Corbett III in the 1st round on May 29, 1933 in Los Angeles. He lost the title to Barney Ross in his first defense, on May 28, 1934; won it back from Ross on September 17, 1934; and lost it again on May 28, 1935. All three fights were 15-round decisions.

After splitting a pair of decisions with Tony Canzoneri and winning a decision over Lou Ambers in 1936, McLarnin retired. During his career, he had 21 victories over titleholders and future champions. Overall, he won 63 bouts, 20 by knockout; lost 11, 1 by knockout; and fought 3 draws.

★ International Boxing Hall of Fame

McLaughlin, Jimmy (James)

HORSE RACING
b. Feb. 22, 1861, Hartford, Conn.
d. Jan. 19, 1927

Though his racing career ended more than a hundred years ago, McLaughlin still holds the record for most victories in the Belmont Stakes with six. He won with Forester in 1882, George Kinney in 1883, Panique in 1884, Inspector B in 1886, Hanover in 1887, and Sir Dixon in 1888. McLaughlin also won the 1881 Kentucky Derby aboard Hindoo and the 1885 Preakness aboard Tecumseh.

A homeless orphan as a young teenager, McLaughlin was informally adopted by thoroughbred trainer William Daly, who taught him how to ride. He began his jockeying career when he was 15. Among his best mounts was Luke Blackburn, one of the finest thoroughbreds of the era, who won 22 of 24 races.

Weight problems forced McLaughlin to retire from riding in 1892, and he then became a successful trainer. He later served as a race official.

★ National Horse Racing Hall of Fame

McLaughry, Tuss (DeOrmond)

FOOTBALL
b. 1883
d. ?

After playing guard, tackle, and end at Michigan State for two seasons, McLaughry transferred to Westminster College and captained the 1914 team. He coached there in 1916 and 1917, spent two years in the service, and returned for two more seasons of coaching in 1920 and 1921.

At Williams College from 1922 through 1925, McLaughry had a 21–8–3 record. He went to Brown University in 1926 and remained there for 15 seasons, winning 76 games, losing 58, and tying 5. His 1926 team went undefeated, winning its first 9 games and playing a scoreless tie with Colgate in the final game of the season.

All 11 starters played 60 minutes in consecutive games against Yale and Dartmouth. They became known as the "Iron Men." In the third game, against Harvard, they played the first 55 minutes before McLaughry made a substitution.

In 1941, McLaughry moved on to Dartmouth. Except for 1943 and 1944, when he was in the Marines, McLaughry coached there through 1954. His Dartmouth teams won 44, lost 58, and tied 3. In 1955, he was named professor of physical education. He held that post until retiring in 1960.

★ College Football Hall of Fame

McLendon, John B., Jr.

BASKETBALL
b. April 4, 1915, Hiawatha, Kans.

At Kansas City Junior College and the University of Kansas, McLendon couldn't play basketball because he was black. While a student at the university, he coached a nearby high school, and he also served as an adviser to James Naismith, the sport's inventor.

After receiving a master's degree from the University of Iowa, McLendon became basketball coach at North Carolina College, winning four conference championships in a dozen seasons. He spent two seasons at Hampton Institute, 1952–53 and 1953–54, then went to Tennessee A & I, where he had his greatest success. His teams won three straight NAIA (small college) championships from 1957 through 1959. Among his players were Sam Jones and Dick Barnett, both of whom became NBA stars.

In 1959, McLendon took over the Cleveland Pipers of the National Industrial Basketball League. The Pipers won the 1961 NIBL and AAU national championships and then joined the professional American Basketball League, making McLendon the first black coach of a major professional team. The ABL soon folded, however. McLendon then coached three seasons each at Kentucky State and Cleveland State before going to the Denver Rockets of the ABA in 1969. He resigned after winning just 9 of 28 games.

The NAIA coach of the year in 1958, McLendon had a college record of 523 victories and 165 losses. His .760 winning percentage is one of the highest in collegiate history.

★ Basketball Hall of Fame

McLoughlin, Maurice

TENNIS
b. Jan. 7, 1890, Carson City, Nev.
d. Dec. 10, 1957

In a relatively brief career at the top, the "California Comet" had a major impact on tennis. He learned to play on hard, fast cement and asphalt courts that put a premium on speed, so he developed a cannonball serve and an aggressive volleying game.

Until McLoughlin arrived, many considered tennis an effete, sissyish sort of game for the upper set. McLoughlin's style of play showed that it could be a strenuous, manly sport, which helped persuade many boys and men that they should try it. The fact that he came from a middle-class family also helped popularize tennis.

The red-headed, freckle-faced McLoughlin first won attention in 1909, when he came east to win the national interscholastic championship. In 1912, he won the national singles title, becoming the first champion from west of the Mississippi, and he repeated as singles champion in 1913. McLoughlin also won three doubles titles with Thomas C. Bundy, from 1912 through 1914.

★ International Tennis Hall of Fame

McMichael, Steve D.

FOOTBALL
b. Oct. 17, 1957, Houston, Tex.

Chosen out of the University of Texas by the New England Patriots in the third round of the 1980 NFL draft, McMichael missed most of his rookie season with a back injury and was released.

The Chicago Bears picked him up during the 1981 season. McMichael became a starter at defensive tackle in 1985 and was a key player in the outstanding defense that helped the Bears win the 1985 NFL championship by beating the Patriots, 46–10, in Super Bowl XX.

A fierce competitor, McMichael is 6-foot-2, 268 pounds, and quite agile. Through the 1993 season, he had recorded 86$\frac{1}{2}$ quarterback sacks, 12 fumble recoveries, 1 interception, and 3 safeties.

McMichael was named to *The Sporting News* all-pro team and played in the Pro Bowl in 1986 and 1987.

McMillan, Daniel

FOOTBALL
b. 1885
d. ?

After playing football at the University of Southern California in 1916 and 1917, McMillan entered military service during World War I. He returned to college at the University of California in 1919.

McMillan captained the 1921 team that won all nine of its games and played a scoreless tie against Washington and Jefferson in the Rose Bowl. He was an All-American tackle that season. During his three seasons at the school, California won 23 games while losing only 2 and tying 1. The 1920 team beat Ohio State, 28–0, in the Rose Bowl.

★ College Football Hall of Fame

McMillin, Bo (Alvin N.)

FOOTBALL
b. Jan. 2, 1895, Prairie Hill, Tex.
d. March 31, 1952

Known for his speed and ability to pass on the run, McMillin starred as a 5-foot-9, 170-pound quarterback at Centre College of Kentucky from 1919 through 1921. The "Praying Colonels" won 27 of 30 games during that period. McMillin kicked the only field goal of his career to beat the University of Kentucky, 3–0, in 1919, and he ran 32 yards for a touchdown in Centre's "Upset of the Century" over Harvard, 6–0, in 1921.

McMillin played in the NFL with the Milwaukee Badgers in 1922 and with the Badgers and Cleveland Indians in 1923, coaching Centenary College at the same time. He also coached Centenary in 1924 and had a 26–3–0 record during that period, but he wasn't rehired when the school was threatened with loss of accreditation because McMillin earned more than the college president.

He went on to Geneva College in 1925 and won 22 games while losing 5 and tying 1 in three seasons there, then put together a 29–21–1 record in six years at Kansas State University.

The University of Indiana gave McMillin a ten-year contract in 1934. Despite four losing seasons, he received another ten-year contract in 1944 and guided Indiana to an undefeated season in 1945, when the team won nine games and tied one.

McMillin jumped from Indiana to the NFL's Detroit Lions in 1948. He won only 12 games while losing 24 in three seasons before being fired. The Philadelphia Eagles hired him in 1951, but he coached only two regular season games before resigning because he was diagnosed with cancer. He died of a heart attack less than a year later.

★ College Football Hall of Fame

McNally, John V., Jr. ("Johnny Blood")
FOOTBALL
b. Nov. 27, 1903, New Richmond, Wis.
d. Nov. 28, 1985

McNally played football for the first time at little St. John's College in Minnesota, and he attended Notre Dame briefly but didn't make the team there because the coaches wanted him to play tackle, and he wanted to play halfback.

In 1924, he and a friend were riding on McNally's motorcycle on their way to try out for a semipro team in Minneapolis. Since they both had college eligibility left, they needed assumed names. When they passed a theater where the Rudolph Valentino movie, *Blood and Sand*, was playing, McNally said to his friend, "That's it. I'll be Blood and you be Sand." For the rest of his long career in football, he was known as Johnny Blood.

He entered the NFL with the Milwaukee Badgers in 1925, played with the Duluth Eskimos in 1926 and 1927, and spent the next season with the Pottsville Maroons. In 1929, McNally joined the Green Bay Packers and was a key player when the Packers won three straight championships from 1929 through 1931.

The 6-foot-1, 190-pound McNally had sprinter speed and great leaping ability. Though best known as a pass receiver, he was an outstanding all-around player who could run, pass, kick, and play defense. In 1931, he caught 10 touchdown passes, still a record for a running back, intercepted 6 passes and returned 1 for a touchdown, scored 2 touchdowns from scrimmage, and threw a touchdown pass. His 78 points on 13 touchdowns led the league.

McNally was named to the first official All-Pro team that season. He was also on unofficial All-Pro teams from 1928 through 1930.

The flamboyant McNally was celebrated for his off-the-field exploits. He rode the rods on a train to get to Green Bay for the 1932 season, and a Milwaukee sportswriter wanted to nickname him the "Hobo Halfback." Packer coach "Curly" Lambeau objected, and the sportswriter changed it to the "Vagabond Halfback."

Lambeau sent McNally to the Pittsburgh Pirates (now the Steelers) in 1934, but he returned to the Packers in 1935 and played for another championship team the following season. McNally became player-coach at Pittsburgh in 1937 and remained there into the 1939 season, when he was replaced.

His 15 seasons in the NFL is a record for the one-platoon era. Complete statistics are not available for his early years, but he is credited with at least 297 points.

★ Pro Football Hall of Fame

McNamara, Julianne L.
GYMNASTICS
b. Oct. 11, 1966, Flushing, N.Y.

McNamara was the first American woman ever to win an individual gold medal in an Olympic gymnastics event, but she was hardly noticed because Mary Lou Retton was the focus of attention at the 1984 Los Angeles Games.

On the parallel bars, her best event, McNamara performed daring moves attempted by few women. That was the event in which she won her 1984 gold medal. She was also the first American woman to win a silver medal in the floor exercise, ahead of Retton, who won the bronze. They led the U.S. team to a silver medal. McNamara, who once said, "I'm striving for a ten every time out," did achieve five perfect scores of ten during the Olympics, a record for an American gymnast.

She began competition when she was ten years old and won the national vault and all-around championships in 1980, shortly after her fifteenth birthday. McNamara won the American Cup all-around title and was named female gymnast of the year in 1981 and 1982. She was named female gymnast of the year a third time in 1984 after winning the national and American Cup championships in the parallel bars. McNamara teamed with Jim Hartung to win the international mixed pairs title that year.

After the 1984 Olympics, McNamara retired from gymnastics competition to go into acting.

Macpherson, Wendy

BOWLING
b. Jan. 28, 1968, Walnut Creek, Calif.

Macpherson was the youngest woman bowler ever to roll a perfect 300 game, at 14, and at 18 she was named the 1986 rookie of the year on the LPBT tour. She won two major championships in her first three years on the tour, the U.S. Women's Open in 1986 and the WIBC Queens tournament in 1988. Macpherson, who carries a two-dollar bill for good luck, led the LPBT with a 211.11 average in 1987.

Madden, John E.

FOOTBALL
b. April 10, 1936, Austin, Minn.

Madden went to high school in California and spent two years at the College of San Mateo before entering California Polytechnic at San Luis Obispo, where he was a starting tackle for two years. Drafted by the NFL's Philadelphia Eagles,

he injured a knee during the team's 1959 training camp, ending his playing career.

He became an assistant coach at Allen Hancock College while studying for his master's degree at his alma mater. In 1962, Madden took over as head coach and had a 12–6–0 record in two seasons at Hancock, then moved on to San Diego State as an assistant from 1964 through 1966.

The AFL's Oakland Raiders hired Madden as an assistant in 1967 and made him head coach two years later. Madden was immediately successful, taking the team to a 12–1–1 regular season record and winning the league's coach of the year award. However, Oakland lost, 17–7, to the Kansas City Chiefs in the AFL championship game.

The Raiders won seven Western Division titles during Madden's ten seasons. They won 13 of 14 regular season games in 1976, beat the Pittsburgh Steelers for the AFC title, and won Super Bowl XI, 32–14, against the Minnesota Vikings.

At 6-foot-4 and anywhere from 250 to 275 pounds, Madden was a colorful figure on the sidelines, exhorting his players and often confronting officials when he disagreed with their calls. He retired from coaching after the 1978 season with a 112–39–7 record, a .731 winning percentage.

Madden became a very popular television commentator with CBS, displaying the same kind of exuberance and enthusiasm that he had as a coach. When the Fox Network won rights to NFL games for the 1994 season, Madden was signed to do commentary.

Maddux, Gregory A.

BASEBALL
b. April 14, 1966, San Angelo, Tex.

Maddux won two consecutive NL Cy Young Awards, with the Chicago Cubs in 1992 and the Atlanta Braves in 1993. His records for the two years showed a remarkable consistency. In 1992, he was 20–11, with a 2.18 ERA, 199 strikeouts, and 70 walks in 268 innings. In 1992, he went 20–10, with a 2.36 ERA, 197 strikeouts, and 52 walks in 267 innings.

A 6-foot, 175-pound right-hander, Maddux entered the major leagues with the Cubs late in the 1986 season and was with them for a time in 1987 before being sent to the minors for further seasoning. He became a full-time starter in 1988 and had records of 18–8, 19–12, 15–15, and 15–11 before winning his first Cy Young Award.

Through 1994, Maddux had a 131–91 record with 17 shutouts and a 3.02 ERA. He had struck out 1,190 hitters while walking 538 in 1,911 innings.

Madigan, Slip (Edward P.)

FOOTBALL
b. Nov. 18, 1896, Ottawa, Ill.
d. Oct. 10, 1966

A colorful and controversial coach, Madigan was a Knute Rockne disciple. He played center at Notre Dame under Jess Harper in 1916 and was a guard in 1917, when Rockne was Harper's assistant. After spending a year in the Army during World War II, Harper returned to Notre Dame in 1919, when Rockne was in his second season as head coach.

Madigan received a law degree in 1920 and coached high school football that year. He was then named head coach at little St. Mary's College in California. The administration wanted to publicize the school by producing winning football teams, which was not uncommon at the time, and Madigan did the job.

Like Rockne, though in a somewhat smaller way, Madigan developed "suicide schedules," pitting St. Mary's against some of the best teams on the West Coast. His 1924 club went 9–1–0, with a victory over the University of Southern California, and in 1926 St. Mary's was 9–0–1 with a 26–7 win over the University of California.

In 1928, St. Mary's was ranked ninth in the nation after tying California and beating UCLA, the University of Oregon, and the University of San Francisco to finish with an 8–0–1 mark.

Madigan set out to conquer New York City in 1930, when he scheduled a game against Fordham University at the Polo Grounds. St. Mary's won, 20–12, to end Fordham's 15-game unbeaten streak. The game became an annual event, and Madigan made it a major media event with his team rolling into the city in luxury railroad cars.

Outgoing and witty like Rockne, Madigan had a contract that called for him to receive a percentage of the team's gate receipts in addition to his salary. The school withheld that bonus for several years, however, and Madigan took St. Mary's entire $100,000 share of receipts from the 1939 game against Fordham. He was fired as a result, although he wasn't forced to make restitution.

Madigan had a 116–45–12 record in his 19 years at St. Mary's. After leaving the school, he worked for a San Francisco racetrack for two years and then coached the University of Iowa to a 2–13–1 record in 1943 and 1944. He later became a successful contractor.
★ College Football Hall of Fame

Madison, Helene E.

SWIMMING
b. June 19, 1913, Madison, Wis.
d. Nov. 27, 1970

Madison was virtually unbeatable at any distance in freestyle swimming during her brief career. Nicknamed the "Queen of the Waters" by sportswriters, she won every AAU national freestyle championship in 1930, her first year of senior competition: the outdoor 100-meter, 440-yard, 880-yard, and 1-mile, and the indoor 100- and 220-yard events.

She was named female athlete of the year by the Associated Press in 1931, when she repeated that feat and set three world records in the span of less than two weeks. Madison didn't compete in the 1932 AAU outdoor meet, but she again won both indoor freestyle titles.

At the 1932 Olympics, Madison won three gold medals. After an easy victory in the 100-meter freestyle, she had a close duel with teammate Lenore Kight in the 400-meter event. Kight took the lead with about 75 meters to go, but Madison just caught her at the finish, winning in a world record 5:28.5 to Kight's 5:28.6. The bronze medalist was nearly 20 seconds behind. Madison won her third gold as a member of the 4 x 100-meter relay team, which also set a world record.

During her three years of top competition, the 5-foot–10½, 154-pound Madison set world records at 20 distances from 100 yards to 1 mile. She appeared in an unsuccessful 1933 movie, *The Warrior's Husband*, then embarked on an unsuccessful career as a nightclub singer. She later taught swimming and clerked in a department store. Married and divorced three times, she died of cancer.

★ International Swimming Hall of Fame

Madlock, Bill

BASEBALL
b. Jan. 2, 1951, Memphis, Tenn.

A four-time NL batting champion, the 5-foot-11, 185-pound Madlock had a brief tryout with the AL's Texas Rangers in 1973 and became the starting third baseman for the Chicago Cubs the following season, when he hit .313. He then won two consecutive batting titles with averages of .354 in 1975 and .339 in 1976.

Madlock was traded to the San Francisco Giants in 1977, and the Giants sent him to the Pittsburgh Pirates during the 1979 season. He hit .328 in 85 games with the Pirates to help them win the NL pennant, and he batted .375 in their seven-game victory over the Baltimore Orioles in the World Series.

After hitting .277 in 1978, Madlock won his third batting championship with a .341 average in 1981, and he took his fourth title two years later with a .323 average. Pittsburgh traded him to the Los Angeles Dodgers near the end of the 1985 season. In just 34 games with the Dodgers, Madlock hit .360. Los Angeles won the Western Division title but lost the league championship series in six games to the St. Louis Cardinals, despite Madlock's .333 average and 7 RBI.

Madlock hit .280 for the Dodgers in 1986 and ended his career after the 1987 season, when he played for the Dodgers and the Detroit Tigers. In 1,806 games, he had a .305 average on 2,008 hits, including 348 doubles, 34 triples, and 163 home runs. He stole 174 bases, scored 920 runs, and had 860 RBI.

Magee, Sherry (Sherwood R.)

BASEBALL
b. Aug. 6, 1884, Clarendon, Pa.
d. March 13, 1929

A switch-hitting outfielder who threw right-handed, Magee won a batting championship and led the NL in RBI four times in the early part of the century. He joined the Philadelphia Phillies early in the 1904 season and won his first RBI title with 85 in 1907.

Magee's finest year was 1910, when he led in hitting with a .331 average, in slugging with a .507 percentage, in runs with 110, and in RBI with 123.

The following year, on July 10, Magee threw his bat into the air after being called out on strikes. Umpire Bill Finneran threw him out of the game. Magee hit Finneran in the mouth, cutting him badly. He was escorted from the park by police while Finneran was taken to a hospital. Magee was fined $200 and suspended for the rest of the season. However, he was reinstated in the middle of August because the Philadelphia roster had been depleted by injuries.

In 1914, after he led the league in hits with 171, doubles with 39, and RBI with 103, Magee was traded to the Boston Braves. During the 1917 season, the Braves sent him to the Cincinnati Reds. He won his fourth and last RBI title with 76 in 1918, when the season was shortened because of World War I.

Magee retired after the 1919 season. In 2,087 games, he batted .291 with 2,169 hits, including 425 doubles, 166 triples, and 83 home runs. He stole 441 bases, scored 1,112 runs, and had 1,176 RBI.

Mahan, Larry (Lawrence)

RODEO
b. Nov. 21, 1943, Salem, Oreg.

Mahan got involved in rodeo when he was a youngster in Oregon. He won his first prize, $6 and a belt buckle, when he was 12. In 1962, he was the Arizona high school all-around champion, and he joined the Professional Rodeo Cowboy Association the following year.

Nicknamed "Bull" because of his strength and because his best event is bull riding, Mahan won the national finals all-around championship a record 5 consecutive times, from 1966 through 1970. After being hampered by injuries in 1971 and 1972, he won a record sixth title in 1973.

He was also national bull riding champion in 1965 and 1967, when he became the first cowboy ever to reach the finals in three different events, finishing third in saddle bronc riding and fifth in bareback riding. He set a record with $51,996 in winnings that year; he broke the record with $64,447 in 1973.

Of his specialty Mahan has said, "On a horse you can sometimes make a mistake and pick up in time to save yourself, but a bull usually won't give you a second chance." He retired from competition in 1979. Mahan now breeds horses and cattle and works as a rodeo broadcaster.

Mahan, Ned (Edward W.)
FOOTBALL
b. Jan. 19, 1892, Natick, Mass.
d. July 22, 1975

Harvard's last three-time All-American, Mahan starred at fullback in 1913, 1914, and 1915. The great Jim Thorpe called Mahan the best back he ever played against.

As a sophomore, he missed a game with an infected spider bite and didn't start against Princeton, but his 52-yard run set up the winning field goal in a 3–0 victory. Mahan passed for a touchdown against Brown, and his long, high punts kept Yale out of scoring range in Harvard's 15–5 victory.

Mahan missed five games with injuries in 1914 but still made Walter Camp's All-American team with outstanding performances in important contests. He kicked two field goals and punted for a 45-yard average in Harvard's 20–0 win over Princeton, and in a 36–0 victory against Yale he returned a punt 45 yards, threw a touchdown pass, and kicked a 20-yard field goal.

As captain in 1915, Mahan kicked field goals of 13, 25, and 41 yards to beat the University of Virginia, 9–0. His 25-yard run set up Harvard's only touchdown against Princeton, and he kicked the extra point and a field goal to win that game, 10–6. Mahan's greatest individual game was his last, a 41–0 victory over Yale, when he scored 29 points on 4 touchdowns and 5 extra points.

Also a fine baseball player, Mahan was the pitcher when Harvard beat the Boston Red Sox, 1–0, in the spring of 1916. The Red Sox went on to win the World Series that fall.

★ College Football Hall of Fame

Maher, William P.
ROWING
b. June 25, 1946, Detroit, Mich.

Rowing for Northeastern University and the Detroit Boat Club, Maher won national 1½-mile single sculls championships in 1965, 1967, and 1969, and he teamed with John Nunn to take a bronze medal in double sculls at the 1968 Olympics. He was also a member of the Detroit crew that won the national eight-oared shell championship in 1963.

Mahre, Philip
SKIING
b. May 10, 1957, White Pass, Wash.

Phil and his twin brother, Steve, who was born four minutes later, had a long, friendly rivalry that culminated at the 1984 Winter Olympics, when Phil won the gold medal in the slalom and Steve won the silver.

The twins were known as rebels who preferred racing motorcycles during the summer to following the training regimen recommended by the U.S. ski team. But no one could argue with their results, especially Phil's. He was national giant slalom champion in 1975, 1977, 1978, and 1979, and he also emerged as a genuine threat in World Cup races, finishing second overall in 1978 and third in 1979.

However, in March 1979 he suffered a severely broken left ankle in a race at Lake Placid, New York. The U.S. ski team doctor called it "the ultimate broken ankle, a break of both the ankle and the lower leg." A metal plate and seven screws had to be inserted. Mahre began skiing less than six months after the injury, and less than a year later he won a silver medal in the slalom at the 1980 Winter Olympics.

In 1981, Mahre became the first American male to win the World Cup overall championships, and he repeated in 1982 and 1983, becoming the third skier to win three straight titles. He also won the national slalom title in 1983.

Both Mahre brothers had a difficult time during the 1983–84 season, and there seemed little chance that either could win a medal. Phil had finished 62nd in the World Cup standings, and he was concerned about his wife, who was due to have a baby in the United States while the Winter Olympics were going on in Sarajevo, Yugoslavia.

After the first of two slalom runs, Steve was in first place and Phil was third. But Phil had a great second run to become the first American male skier to win a gold medal; Steve won the silver. On the way to the medal ceremony, Phil learned his wife had given birth to their second child and first son. "Heck," he said, "there she was doing all the work while I was out there playing."

Both Mahre brothers retired from competition shortly after the Olympics.

Majors, Johnny (John T.)

FOOTBALL
b. May 21, 1935, Lynchburg, Tenn.

A triple-threat tailback at the University of Tennessee, one of the last schools to use the single wing rather than some version of the T formation, Majors was an All-American in 1956. He played for the Montreal Alouettes of the Canadian Football League in 1957 and then became an assistant coach at several schools.

Majors was named head coach at Iowa State University in 1968. He had only a 24–30–1 record in five seasons there, but his 1971 and 1972 teams both went to bowl games. In 1973, he went to the University of Pittsburgh, which had had nine straight losing seasons. His 1976 team won all 11 regular season games, beat Georgia, 27–3, in the Sugar Bowl, and was ranked first in the nation.

After compiling a 33–13–1 record in four seasons at Pittsburgh, Majors returned to his alma mater as head coach in 1977. He had a 116–62–8 record in just over 15 seasons there. A heart attack forced him to miss the last four games of the 1992 season, and he was replaced, though he wanted to keep the job.

Majors was rehired by Pittsburgh in 1993.

★ College Football Hall of Fame

Malone, Joe (Maurice Joseph)

HOCKEY
b. Feb. 28, 1890, Quebec, P.Q.
d. May 15, 1969

The greatest scorer in the early history of the NHL, Malone began playing professional hockey in 1909. He became captain and coach of the Quebec Bulldogs in 1911 and promptly led them to two consecutive Stanley Cup championships. He scored 9 goals in one of the 1913 playoff games.

After the Quebec team folded, Malone joined the Montreal Canadiens in the NHL's first season, 1917–18. He scored 5 goals in their first game and ended the season with 44 goals in 20 games. The Quebec franchise resumed play in 1919, and Malone returned to the team. On January 31, 1920, he scored 7 goals in a game, still the NHL record, and he had 6 goals in the last game of the season. He led the league for the second time with 48 points on 39 goals and 9 assists.

Malone returned to Montreal for one season, went to Hamilton, Ontario, for another, then played with Montreal again in 1922–23. He retired after just nine games the following season. He played 125 regular season games in the NHL, scoring 146 goals with 21 assists. In nine playoff games, he had 5 goals.

★ Hockey Hall of Fame

Malone, Karl

BASKETBALL
b. July 24, 1963, Summerfield, La.

Nicknamed "the Mailman" because of his ability to deliver the ball to the basket, the 6-foot-9, 256-pound Malone averaged 18.7 points in three years as a starter at Louisiana Tech and was chosen by the Utah Jazz in the first round of the 1985 NBA draft.

His strength, explosive first step, and leaping ability make Malone especially effective around the basket, and he often delivers points with thunderous slam-dunks. Malone is also one of the best rebounding forwards in the NBA.

He averaged only 14.9 points per game coming off the bench as a rookie, but since then his lowest average has been 21.7 points a game, with a high of 31.0 in 1989–90. Malone led the league in free throws attempted and free throws made for five consecutive seasons, from 1988–89 through 1992–93. He was also the league leader in defensive rebounds with 731 in 1990–92.

Named to the all-NBA team from 1989 through 1994, Malone was a second-team choice in 1988, when he was also selected for the league's all-defensive second team.

Through the 1993–94 season, Malone had scored 19,050 points in 734 regular season games, a 26.0 average, with 8,058 rebounds. He had 2,018 points and 859 rebounds in 74 playoff games.

Malone, Moses E.

BASKETBALL
b. March 23, 1955, Petersburg, Va.

Petersburg High School won 50 consecutive games and two state championships while Malone was playing there. In 1974, he became the first player in modern times to go directly from high school to professional basketball, signing a five-year, $3 million contract with the Utah Stars of the American Basketball Association.

A 6-foot-10, 250-pound center, Malone averaged 18.8 points a game as a rookie, but the franchise folded, and he joined the St. Louis Spirits in 1975. After missing a good part of the season with a broken foot, he jumped to the NBA, playing for the Portland Trailblazers, the Buffalo Braves, and the Houston Rockets in his first year.

Malone was named the league's most valuable player for the 1978–79 season, when he averaged 24.8 points and 17.6 rebounds per game, and again in 1981–82, when he averaged 31.1 points and 14.7 rebounds. He signed with the Philadelphia 76ers after that season and won his second straight MVP award and third overall in 1983. In 1984–85, he led the NBA in rebounding for the fifth year in a row.

The 76ers traded him to the Washington Bullets after the 1985–86 season. Malone went to the Atlanta Hawks in 1988 and the Milwaukee Bucks in 1991. He retired after playing in only 11 games with the Bucks in 1992–93, but came back as a backup center with the Philadelphia 76ers the following year, and then went to the San Antonio Spurs as a free agent.

In 18 NBA seasons, Malone scored 27,360 points in 1,312 regular season games, an average of 20.9, and had 16,166 rebounds. He added 2,077 points and 1,295 rebounds in 94 playoff games. Malone was named to the all-NBA team in 1979, 1982, 1983, and 1985.

Mangrum, Lloyd E.

GOLF
b. Aug. 1, 1914, Trenton, Tex.
d. Nov. 17, 1973

Although Mangrum became a professional golfer at 15, he didn't play in his first PGA tournament until he was 19, and he didn't win his first tournament until 1938, when he was 24. He served in the Army during World War II and was wounded at the Battle of the Bulge.

His most successful years came after the war. He tied with Byron Nelson and Vic Ghezzi in the 1946 U.S. Open and won the 36-hole playoff. In 1950, he and Ben Hogan tied in the Open, but Hogan won that playoff.

During his career, Mangrum won 34 PGA tournaments. His best year was 1948, when he won eight tournaments and $45,898, second to Hogan.

★ PGA Hall of Fame

Mann, Carol A. [Mrs. Hardy]

GOLF
b. Feb. 3, 1941, Buffalo, N.Y.

Mann played 21 seasons on the LPGA tour, beginning in 1960, and she won two or more tournaments in eight of them. She was the U.S. Women's Open champion in 1965, and in 1968 she won ten titles and the Vare Trophy for fewest average strokes per round. Her average of 72.04 was a record until 1978, when Nancy Lopez broke it. Mann's 23 rounds under 70 was also a record, broken by Amy Alcott in 1980.

The tour's leading money winner in 1969, Mann had 38 career victories, and she won more than $500,000. She began doing golf commentary on television in 1979, and her tournament activity gradually diminished. After playing in 14 events in 1981, she left the tour entirely. She has been active in drug abuse programs for male and female athletes and has served as a trustee of the Women's Sports Foundation since 1979.

The 6-foot-3 Mann was a very fashion-conscious golfer, one of the few to wear culottes on the tour. She once said, "We should all try to look more ladylike on the course. Being thought of as anything but a woman definitely frosts me."
★ International Women's Sports Hall of Fame; LPGA Hall of Fame

Mann, Shelley I.

SWIMMING
b. Oct. 15, 1937, New York, N.Y.

Stricken by polio when she was six years old, Mann began swimming to strengthen her limbs. She entered competitive swimming when she was 12, and within a few years was one of the most versatile swimmers in the world. At one time she held world records in the 100- and 200-meter butterfly, the 100-meter freestyle, and the 400-meter individual medley, and she also won national championships in the backstroke.

As a student at American University in Washington, D.C., Mann joined the Walter Reed Swim Club and trained at dawn in a hospital pool used later in the day for patient rehabilitation.

One of the most heralded American swimmers going into the 1956 Olympics, Mann won a gold medal in the 100-meter butterfly, and was a member of the 4 x 100-meter freestyle relay team that won a silver medal. She also qualified for the finals of the 100-meter freestyle, finishing sixth.

Mann won national outdoor championships in the 100-meter backstroke and 100-meter butterfly in 1954; and in the 110-yard butterfly, 220-yard butterfly, and 440-yard individual medley in 1956. She was indoor champion in the 100-yard backstroke, 100-yard butterfly, and 400-yard individual medley in 1954; in the 100-yard freestyle, 250-yard freestyle, and 400-yard individual medley in 1955; and in the 100-yard and 200-yard butterfly in 1956.

Manning, Archie (Elisha Archie Jr.)

FOOTBALL
b. May 19, 1949, Drew, Miss.

A very athletic quarterback, the 6–3, 212-pound Manning played at the University of Mississippi and was chosen by the New Orleans Saints in the first round of the 1971 NFL college draft.

He became a starter before the end of his rookie season, and in his second year, 1972, he led the league with 448 passing attempts and 230 completions. Playing for a poor team, Manning had to pass a great deal, which probably caused the severe tendinitis in his right shoulder that kept him on the sidelines for the entire 1976 season.

United Press International named Manning the National Football Conference player of the year in 1978, when he completed 291 of 471 passes for 3,416 yards and 17 touchdowns.

During the 1982 season, Manning was traded to the Houston Oilers, and he went to the Minnesota Vikings the following year. He retired after the 1984 season. Manning completed 2,011 of 3,642 passes for 23,911 yards and 125 touchdowns. He rushed 346 times for 2,197 yards, a 6.4 average, and 18 touchdowns.

Manning, Danny (Daniel R.)

BASKETBALL
b. May 17, 1966, Hattiesburg, Miss.

A four-year starter at the University of Kansas, where his father was an assistant coach, Manning set a Big Eight record with 2,951 career points. The 6-foot-10, 234-pound forward won the Wooden, Naismith, and Eastman awards as the college player of the year in 1988. In Kansas's 83–79 victory over the University of Oklahoma for the NCAA championship, Manning had 31 points, 18 rebounds, and 5 steals and was named most valuable player in the tournament.

Manning played for the U.S. team that won a bronze medal at the 1988 Olympics and then joined the NBA's San Diego Clippers. He played only 26 games as a rookie because of a knee injury that required surgery, but he returned for the 1989–90 season. His best year as a pro was 1992–93, when he averaged 22.8 points a game and played in the NBA All-Star game.

He was traded to the Atlanta Hawks during the 1993–94 season. Through that season, Manning had scored 7,529 points in 399 games, an 18.9 average. He also had 2,568 rebounds, 1,217 assists, 594 steals, and 431 blocked shots.

Manning, Madeline

TRACK AND FIELD
b. Jan. 1, 1948, Cleveland, Ohio

The first world-class American woman in the 880-yard/800-meter run, Manning set a world record of 2:18.4 as a student at Tennessee State in 1967, when she won the AAU indoor 880-yard run. She also set an American record of 2:02.3 when she won the 800-meter at the Pan-American Games that year.

Manning won the gold medal in the 800-meter at the 1968 Olympics, running an Olympic record 2:00.9. She retired from competition in 1970 but returned in 1972. After losing in the Olympic semifinals of the 800-meter, she ran the second leg on the silver medal 4 x 400-meter relay team.

She retired once more after the Olympics, began competing again in

1975, and became the first American woman to break 2 minutes in the 800-meter, running a 1:59.8 at the 1976 Olympic trials. She again failed to make the Olympic finals and retired for a third time.

Manning was back on the track in 1979, and she won the 800-meter in the Olympic trials for the fourth time in 1980, but the U.S. boycott of the Moscow games prevented her from trying for another medal. Manning retired permanently after the 1981 season.

Though her career spanned 14 years, she actually competed in only 8 of those years. She won the national outdoor championship in her event in 1967, 1969, 1972, 1975, 1976, 1980, and 1981, and she was the indoor champion in 1967, 1968, 1969, 1972, and 1980.
★ International Women's Sports Hall of Fame; National Track & Field Hall of Fame

Mantle, Mickey C.

BASEBALL
b. Oct. 20, 1931, Spavinaw, Okla.

Elvin "Mutt" Mantle worked in lead and zinc mines, played semipro baseball, and wanted his son to be a major league player. Named after Hall of Famer Mickey Cochrane, the young Mantle had a complete uniform when he was three and learned to switch-hit at five.

He played football as well as baseball in high school. A halfback, he suffered an injury to his left shin that resulted in osteomyelitis, a condition that weakens bones and muscles and can cause lifelong pain.

After graduating from high school in 1949, Mantle began playing minor league ball as a shortstop in the New York Yankees' farm system. When he joined the Yankees in 1951, he was announced as the heir apparent to center fielder Joe DiMaggio, but he was placed in right field because DiMaggio was still playing. After a slow start, he was sent back to the minors for a while, but he returned to the Yankees in August.

Mantle tore knee cartilage in the World Series that year and had to undergo surgery. The knee, and the osteomyelitis from his high school football injury, bothered him throughout his career. By the time he was 30, both legs had to be heavily taped before every game.

Mantle led the AL with 129 runs in 1954, and he was the leader in slugging with a .611 percentage, triples with 11, home runs with 37, and walks with 113 in 1955. He had an even better year in 1956, winning the triple crown with a .353 average, 52 home runs, and 132 RBI, and also leading the league with 132 runs and a .705 slugging percentage.

He won the league's most valuable player award that year and again in 1957, when he hit .365 with 34 home runs, 121 runs scored, and 94 RBI. He was the home run leader for a third time with 42 in 1958, and he also led in runs with 127 and walks with 129.

Mantle's average slid to .285 in 1959 and .275 in 1960, but he won the home run title with 40 and again led the league with 119 runs scored. In 1961, he and teammate Roger Maris, "the M and M Boys," had a season-long race for the home run championship, and as the season neared its end, they both had a chance to break Babe Ruth's legendary record of 60 in a season. Mantle ended with 54 home runs, a career high, but Maris broke Ruth's record with 61. Mantle led the league with a .687 slugging percentage, 132 runs scored, and 126 walks that season.

His last outstanding year was 1962, when he won his third most valuable player award. Mantle hit .321 with 30 home runs and 89 RBI, leading the league with 12 walks and a .605 slugging percentage.

A broken foot limited him to 65 games in 1963. After a .303 average in 1964, Mantle never again hit over .300. He retired after batting only .237 in 1968. When retirement ceremonies were held for him at Yankee Stadium early in the 1969 season, a sellout crowd gave him a ten-minute standing ovation.

Those fans hadn't always appreciated Mantle, in part because they didn't realize how much he was bothered by his physical problems, even in his early years. People in the clubhouse knew, however. Manager Casey Stengel called him "the best one-legged player I ever saw," and teammate Joe Pepitone once said, "Sometimes you feel tired and low. Then you think about Mickey and what he must be going through with the pain and you say to yourself, 'If he can do it the way he feels and the way he must be hurting, then I can do it, too.'"

Mantle hit .298 in 2,401 games, with 2,415 hits, including 344 doubles, 72 triples, and 536 home runs. He had 1,509 RBI and 1,677 runs scored. In his 18 seasons with the Yankees, they won 12 pennants. Mantle is the all-time World Series leader with 18 home runs, 42 runs, 40 RBI, and 123 total bases.

★ Baseball Hall of Fame

Manush, Heinie (Henry E.)

BASEBALL
b. July 20, 1901, Tuscumbia, Ala.
d. May 12, 1971

Manush joined the Detroit Tigers in 1923 as the team's starting left fielder. A left-hander, the 6-foot-1, 200-pound Manush hit .334 in his rookie year. After batting .289 and .302 in the next two seasons, he won the 1926 batting title with a .378 average. Manush got six hits in nine at-bats during a doubleheader on the last day of the season to edge Babe Ruth.

The Tigers traded him to the St. Louis Browns in 1928, when he batted .378, led the league in hits with 241, and tied Lou Gehrig for the doubles lead with 47. Manush hit .355 in 1929 and was traded to the Washington Senators during the 1930 season, when he batted .350.

The Senators won the AL pennant in 1933, aided by Manush's .336 average, with a league-leading 221 hits and 17 triples. The World Series was embarrassing to him, however. After being called out on a close play at first base, he grabbed umpire Charlie Moran's bow tie, which was on an elastic band, pulled it out, and let it snap back against Moran's Adam's apple. He was thrown out of the game and fined $50. Manush batted only .111 for the Series.

He hit .349 in 1934 but dropped to .273 the following season and was traded to the Boston Red Sox. They released him in September 1936, and he went to the Brooklyn Dodgers the following season, batting .333. He played only 32 games with Brooklyn and Pittsburgh in 1938 and left the major leagues after appearing in only 10 games, most of them as a pinch hitter, in 1939.

Manush later managed several minor league teams and served as a scout and coach in the major leagues. He batted .330 in 2,008 games, with 2,524 hits, including 491 doubles, 160 triples, and 110 home runs. He had 1,183 RBI and 1,287 runs scored.

★ Baseball Hall of Fame

Maranville, Rabbit (Walter J.)

BASEBALL
b. Nov. 11, 1891, Springfield, Mass.
d. Jan. 5, 1954

Though most scouts dismissed him as too small for major league baseball — he was only 5-foot-5 and 155 pounds — Maranville set an NL record by playing for 23 seasons, and he is sixth all-time with 2,153 games at shortstop.

Not an outstanding hitter, Maranville was one of those players who contributed to their teams with good defense, smart base running, and overall intelligent play. He was also a colorful character who often took a pet monkey on road trips. Maranville once swam across a river rather than walk ten blocks to a bridge, and on another occasion he jumped, fully clothed, into a hotel fountain to win a bet.

Maranville entered the major leagues with the Boston Braves in 1912 and played for the "Miracle Braves," who won the 1914 pennant after being in last place on July 4. He batted only .246 that season but set a record for NL shortstops by handling 981 chances. In Boston's four-game sweep of the Philadelphia Athletics in the World Series, Maranville hit .308.

In 1921, Boston traded him to Pittsburgh. He had his best batting averages in his first two seasons there, .294 in

1921 and .295 in 1922. He went to the Chicago Cubs in 1925, the Brooklyn Dodgers in 1926, and the St. Louis Cardinals in 1927 after spending most of the season in the minor leagues and giving up alcohol, which had begun to interfere with his play.

The Cardinals won the pennant in 1928, and Maranville again hit .308 in a losing cause in the World Series. He returned to the Braves in 1929 and was named manager of the team in July. After the season, he demanded a five-year contract to manage but was turned down, so he dropped that job but continued as a player.

A broken leg in spring training forced Maranville to miss all of the 1934 season, and he retired after playing only 23 games in 1935. He later managed in the minor leagues.

In 2,670 games, Maranville had a .258 average on 2,605 hits, including 380 doubles, 177 triples, and 28 home runs. He stole 291 bases, scored 1,255 runs, and had 884 RBI.

★ Baseball Hall of Fame

Maravich, Pistol Pete (Peter P.)

BASKETBALL
b. June 22, 1948, Aliquippa, Pa.
d. Jan. 5, 1988

Although he was a flashy ball-handler and passer, Maravich was best known for his scoring, as his nickname indicates. He shot early and often with enough success to become college basketball's first and only point-a-minute scorer. Playing for his father, Press Maravich, at Louisiana State University, he scored 3,667 points in 83 games for an average of 44.2 a game over his three-year career.

Maravich led the nation in scoring all three years, with averages of 43.8 in 1967–68, 44.2 in 1968–69, and 44.5 in 1969–70. He was a three-time All-American guard, and he won the Rupp Trophy and Naismith Award as the college player of the year in 1970.

The 6-foot-5 200-pounder delighted crowds at home and away, dashing up and down the court with his mop of hair flopping and his socks hanging down over his shoes. He joined the Atlanta Hawks of the NBA in 1970, averaged 23.2 points a game, and was named to the league's all-rookie team.

Mononucleosis slowed him in his second season, but he averaged 26.1 points a game in 1972–73 and finished second in scoring with a 27.7 average the following season. Maravich went to an expansion team, the New Orleans Jazz, in 1974. The team moved to Salt Lake City and become known as the Utah Jazz in 1979. Maravich was released in early 1980 and signed with the Boston Celtics. He played out the season with them and then retired.

Maravich led the NBA in scoring with 31.1 points per game in 1976–77. He was twice a first-team all-star and twice named to the second team. He retired in 1980 and died of a heart attack after a pickup game.

★ Basketball Hall of Fame

Marble, Alice

TENNIS
b. Sept. 28, 1913, Beckworth, Calif. d. Dec. 13, 1990

When she was eight years old, Marble was the mascot and ball girl of the minor league San Francisco Seals. Joe DiMaggio, who played for the team, later recalled, "She had a pretty good arm." Before games, she entertained fans by going into the outfield to catch fly balls.

She learned to play tennis on public courts, with little formal instruction. Because she didn't have much confidence in her ground strokes, she began rushing the net, and she became the first aggressive serve-and-volley player in women's tennis.

Her career got off to a slow start, though. In 1933, matches in a Long Island tournament were postponed by rain, and it was decided to hold the singles and doubles semifinals and finals on the same day. Marble won her singles match in the morning, won the doubles match with Helen Wills Moody, then lost in both finals. After playing 108 games in temperatures of more than 100 degrees, she passed out.

It took her a long time to recover, but she went to France with a U.S. women's team in 1934 and fainted during her first match before finishing a set. She was finally diagnosed as having tuberculosis, and she went into a sanitarium. After several months, coach Eleanor Tennant got her out of the sanitarium and put her on a program of exercise and diet to rebuild her strength.

Marble won her first major championship, the national singles, in 1936, when she also won the mixed doubles. From 1938 through 1940, she swept the U.S. titles, winning in the singles, women's doubles, and mixed doubles. She won the Wimbledon singles title in 1939, the women's doubles in 1938 and 1939, and the mixed doubles from 1937 through 1939. She was named female athlete of the year by the Associated Press in 1939 and 1940.

★ International Tennis Hall of Fame

Marchetti, Gino J.

FOOTBALL
b. Jan. 2, 1927, Smithers, W.Va.

One of the few defensive linemen ever to be named player of the year, Marchetti was voted the best defensive end of the NFL's first 50 years in a 1969 poll of sportswriters.

After graduating from high school, Marchetti served in the Army during World War II and then organized a semi-pro football team in Antioch, California. He attended Modesto Junior College and the University of San Francisco and was chosen by the New York Yanks in the second round of the 1952 NFL draft.

The Yanks became the Dallas Texans before his rookie season and folded a year later. Marchetti went to the new Baltimore Colts franchise in 1953 and played in the Pro Bowl after the season, one of 11 Pro Bowl appearances.

Best known as a pass rusher, the 6-foot-4, 245-pound Marchetti was also a solid defender against the run. He was named an All-Pro six seasons in a row, from 1957 through 1962. When the Colts won the 1958 NFL championship, Marchetti was named player of the year by the Associated Press.

He retired after the 1964 season but

returned to play four games with Baltimore in 1966, when the team was depleted by injury.

★ Pro Football Hall of Fame

Marciano, Rocky [Rocco F. Marchegiano]

BOXING
b. Sept. 1, 1923, Brockton, Mass. d. Aug. 31, 1969

Marciano hoped to be a major league baseball player when he was a teenager. He was a catcher for sandlot teams while holding various jobs after dropping out of high school at 16. Drafted into the Army in 1943, he was challenged by a bully to enter the camp boxing tournament at Fort Lewis, Washington..He not only beat the bully, he won the tournament.

After World War II ended, Marciano had a tryout with a minor league team, but he developed a sore arm and was released. In 1947, manager Al Weill agreed to become his manager and hired Charley Goldman to train Marciano, who was a powerful swinger. Goldman taught him how to defend himself and how to use his left hand to set up his right. In the process of training, the 5-foot-11 Marciano also slimmed down from 200 pounds to 185.

Nicknamed the "Brockton Blockbuster," Marciano won 42 consecutive fights, 37 of them by knockout, before meeting Jersey Joe Walcott for the heavyweight championship on September 23, 1952, at Philadelphia. Walcott knocked him down in the 1st round, and at the end of the 12th, Marciano's left eye was badly swollen, but he won with a knockout in the 13th.

Always well conditioned, Marciano liked to keep moving forward and attacking, often absorbing much punishment but also handing out a lot. His second title defense, against Roland LaStarza on September 24, 1953, was typical Marciano. He relentlessly pounded away at LaStarza's biceps until the challenger could barely lift his arms, then knocked him out in the 11th round.

After defending his title just six times, Marciano announced his retirement in 1956. He won all 49 of his professional fights, 43 by knockout. The winner of an estimated $4 million, he lost some of his money in bad investments but was still able to live comfortably. He died in a plane crash in Iowa while traveling to a business meeting.

★ International Boxing Hall of Fame

Marichal, Juan A.

BASEBALL
b. Oct. 20, 1937, Laguna Verde, Dominican Republic

The right-handed Juan Marichal was known as the "Dominican Dandy," not for his style of dress but for his style of pitching. He threw a fastball, slider, curve, and screwball from a whole assortment of angles, using a high leg kick to further throw off the hitter's timing.

Marichal had a number of brilliant seasons with the San Francisco Giants during the 1960s. His misfortune was that there always seemed to be one other pitcher, usually Sandy Koufax, who had an even better year and so won the Cy Young Award.

After joining the Giants midway through the 1960 season, Marichal became a regular starter in 1961. He had an 18–11 record in 1962, when they won the pennant, but he pitched only four innings in their seven-game World Series loss to the New York Yankees.

Marichal became San Francisco's ace the following season, leading the league in victories with a 25–8 record and in innings pitched with 321. He had a 2.41 ERA that year. He led the league with 22 complete games in 1964, when he had a 21–8 record and a 2.48 ERA, and in 1965 he had a league-leading 10 shutouts en route to a 22–13 record and a 2.13 ERA.

In 1966, Marichal led the NL in winning percentage at .806 on a 25–6 record with a 2.23 ERA. An injury limited him to 26 starts and a 14–10 mark in 1967, but he came back the following year to lead the league in victories with a 26–9 record, in complete games with 30, and in innings pitched with 326.

His last 20-victory season was 1969, when he had a 21–11 record and a league-leading 8 shutouts and 2.10 ERA. It was the seventh season in a row in which he had an ERA well under 3. Marichal was only 12–10 in 1970, but he bounced back with an 18–11 record and a 2.94 ERA in 1971, when his team won the Western Division title. Marichal gave up only two runs in eight innings but lost his only start in the league championship series, won in four games by the Pittsburgh Pirates.

Marichal was only 17–31 during the next two seasons. He went to the Boston Red Sox briefly in 1974 and retired after appearing in two games with the Los Angeles Dodgers in 1975.

In 16 seasons, Marichal had a 243–142 record, a .631 winning percentage, with 52 shutouts and a 2.89 ERA. He struck out 2,303⅓ hitters while walking only 709 in 3,507 innings.
★ Baseball Hall of Fame

Marino, Daniel C.

FOOTBALL
b. Sept. 15, 1961, Pittsburgh, Pa.

Named to some All-American teams as a junior quarterback at the University of Pittsburgh in 1981, Marino was considered a major candidate for the Heisman Trophy the following year but had a disappointing season. Nevertheless, he set a school career record for total offense with more than 8,500 yards.

Although he was chosen in the first round of the 1983 NFL college draft, there were five quarterbacks selected ahead of him. He went to the Miami Dolphins, who had the 27th pick.

The 6-foot-3, 220-pound Marino became Miami's starter for the last 11 games of his rookie season and was so impressive that he became the first rookie quarterback ever to start in a Pro Bowl.

Gifted with a strong arm and an amazingly quick release, Marino is very difficult to sack, despite his lack of mobility. During a period from 1988 to 1989, Marino threw 759 consecutive passes without being trapped for a loss.

Marino was awarded the Bert Bell Trophy as the NFL player of the year in 1984, when he completed 362 of 564 passes for 5,084 yards and 48 touchdowns. He was the first quarterback to pass for more than 5,000 yards in a season, and he shattered the old record of 36 touchdown passes. In a 38–16 loss to the San Francisco 49ers in Super Bowl XIX after that season, Marino completed 29 of 50 passes, both records.

Through the 1994 season, Marino had completed 3,604 of 6,049 passes for 45,173 yards and 328 touchdowns while throwing only 185 interceptions. He had also rushed for 6 touchdowns. He holds NFL records for most game with 400 or more passing yards, 10; most seasons with 4,000 or more passing yards, 5; most seasons with 3,000 or more passing yards, 10; most games with 400 or more passing yards, 4 in 1984; and most games with 4 or more touchdown passes, 6 in 1984.

Named an All-Pro by *The Sporting News* from 1984 through 1986, Marino has been selected for seven Pro Bowls.

Marion, Marty (Martin W.)

BASEBALL
b. Dec. 1, 1917, Richburg, S.C.

Known as "Slats" or the "Octopus" because of his long arms and great range, the 6-foot-2, 170-pound Marion was a mainstay at shortstop with the St. Louis Cardinals for 11 seasons. The Cardinals won four pennants during that time; Marion led NL shortstops in fielding three times, and he was named the most valuable player in 1944, when he batted only .267 but had a league-leading .972 fielding percentage.

Named to the All-Star team six times, Marion was traded to the St. Louis Browns to become their playing manager in 1952. He retired as a player after the 1953 season but remained as manager for one more year. He also managed the AL's Chicago White Sox from the tail end of the 1954 season through 1956.

In 1,572 games, Marion had a .263 average with 1,448 hits, including 272 doubles, 37 triples, and 36 home runs. He scored 602 runs and drove in 624.

Maris, Roger E. [Maras]
BASEBALL
b. Sept. 10, 1934, Hibbing, Minn.

Instead of becoming a hero for hitting 61 home runs in 1961 to break Babe Ruth's long-standing single season record, Maris was despised, even hated, by many fans. Soft-spoken and modest, he didn't respond well to the media pressure than engulfed him as he approached the record, and he was often curt and discourteous with sportswriters.

Unfortunately, that single season also obscured his all-around ability. He wasn't a great baseball player, perhaps, but he was a very good one, an excellent defensive right fielder with an outstanding arm, and a power hitter as well. He did win the most valuable player award twice, a feat accomplished by only a handful of players.

Maris joined the Cleveland Indians in 1957 and was traded to the Kansas City Athletics during the 1958 season. The Athletics sent him to the New York Yankees in 1960. He promptly led the league with 112 RBI and a .581 slugging percentage, hitting 39 home runs. He won his first MVP award that year.

In 1961, Maris and teammate Mickey Mantle had a long duel for the home run title. Mantle faded toward the end of the season and finished with 54, but Maris, despite the pressure, hit his 61st on the last day of the season. He also led the league with 132 runs scored and 142 RBI to win the MVP award for the second year in a row, and he was named male athlete of the year by the Associated Press.

Maris struggled with a variety of injuries during the next four seasons and went to the NL's St. Louis Cardinals in 1967. He played on two pennant winners in two seasons there, retiring in 1968.

In 12 major league seasons, Maris batted .260 with 1,325 hits, including 195 doubles, 42 triples, and 275 home runs. He scored 826 runs and had 851 RBI.

Mariucci, John P.
HOCKEY
b. May 8, 1916, Eveleth, Minn.

Mariucci played both football and hockey at the University of Minnesota and was a star defenseman on the hockey team that went undefeated in the 1939–40 season. He became a professional with the Chicago Black Hawks in 1940.

After serving in the Coast Guard from 1942 through 1945, Mariucci returned to the Black Hawks and played there through the 1947–48 season. He then spent three seasons in the minor leagues.

In 1953, Mariucci was named coach at his alma mater. He had a 215–148–18 record in 14 seasons there before joining the NHL's Minnesota North Stars as a scout in 1966. Mariucci coached the silver medal U.S. Olympic team in 1956.
★ Hockey Hall of Fame; U.S. Hockey Hall of Fame

Marolt, Bill (William)
SKIING
b. Sept. 1, 1943, Aspen, Colo.

Marolt lettered in both football and skiing in high school and entered the University of Colorado in 1961. He won NCAA championships in the downhill in 1965 and in the slalom and the Alpine combined in 1966, and he also won three national titles, the downhill in 1963, the slalom in 1964, and the giant slalom in 1965. Marolt skied on the national teams that competed in the 1962 and 1966 world championships and the 1964 Olympics.

He graduated with a degree in engineering in 1967 and was named ski coach at his alma mater the following year. Marolt guided Colorado to eight consecutive NCAA team championships, from 1971 through 1978 (including a tie with Dartmouth in 1976), and produced 30 All-Americans in 10 years. He was also instrumental in establishing a women's ski team at the school.

In 1979, Marolt became Alpine director of the U.S. ski team in Park City, Utah. His 1984 team won five medals, including three gold medals, at the Winter Olympics. Marolt returned to the University of Colorado as athletic director in August 1984.

Marquard, Rube (Richard W.)
BASEBALL
b. Oct. 9, 1889, Cleveland, Ohio
d. June 1, 1980

His father wanted Marquard to be an engineer, and when he left home at 16 to play professional baseball, he was told never to return. They didn't see one another for ten years, but then his father paid a surprise visit to the New York Giants' clubhouse, and they were reunited.

Marquard rode freight trains to get to that first job in pro baseball, in Iowa, but he ended up playing in Canton, Ohio, not far from Cleveland. His last minor league start was a no-hitter; immediately afterward, the NL's New York Giants bought him for $11,000, and Marquard joined the Giants at the end of the 1908 season.

New York sportswriters dubbed him the "$11,000 Lemon" after he went 5–13 in 1909, and a 4–4 record the following year didn't help. Then he broke through, leading the league with a .774 winning percentage on a 24–7 record and in strikeouts with 237 in 1911.

In 1912, he won his first 19 decisions, a modern major league record, en route to a 26–11 mark, leading the league in victories. He was 23–10 in 1913, when the Giants won their third straight pennant. Marquard was 0–1 in the 1911 World Series, 2–0 in 1912, and 0–1 in 1913, as the Giants lost all three.

He slumped to 12–22 in 1914 and was traded to the Brooklyn Dodgers during the 1915 season. He never won 20 games again, but he did have some good years in Brooklyn, including a 13–6 record and a 1.58 ERA in 1916 and a 19–12 record with a 2.55 ERA in 1917. The Dodgers sent him to Cincinnati in 1921, when he was 17–14. It was his last winning season. He ended his career with the Boston Braves from 1922 through 1925.

After retiring as a player, Marquard managed in the minor leagues for several years and then became a parimutuel clerk at Maryland racetracks.

In 18 seasons, he had a 201–177 record with 30 shutouts and a 3.08 ERA. He struck out 1,593 hitters and walked 858 in 3,306⅔ innings.
★ Baseball Hall of Fame

Marsh, Henry
TRACK AND FIELD
b. March 15, 1954, Boston, Mass.

The top steeplechaser in the U.S. during the 1980s, Marsh attended Brigham Young University. He never won an NCAA championship, finishing second in 1976 and third in both 1977 and 1978, but he won the national 3,000-meter steeplechase championship ten years in a row, from 1978 through 1987.

Marsh's time of 8:09.17 in 1985 is an American record. His best international finish was second place in the World Cup competition that year. Marsh finished fourth in the 1979 World Cup, fourth at the 1984 Olympics, and sixth in the 1987 World Championships.

Marshall, Mike (Michael G.)
BASEBALL
b. Jan. 15, 1943, Adrian, Mich.

Marshall played minor league baseball while studying exercise physiology at Michigan State University, graduating in 1965. He got his master's degree in 1967. Shortly afterward, he began his major league pitching career by appearing in 37 games with the Detroit Tigers of the AL.

Marshall spent 1968 in the minor leagues and joined the AL's Seattle Mariners the following season. He started the 1970 season with the Houston Astros in the NL but was traded to the Montreal Expos before the season ended.

With Montreal, Marshall became a top relief pitcher. He led the league in appearances with 65 in 1972 and 92 in 1973 and in saves with 31 in 1973. He was then traded to the Los Angeles Dodgers, where he won the 1974 Cy Young Award, appearing in a record 106 games, leading the league with 21 saves, and compiling a 15–12 record with a 2.42 ERA.

The Dodgers traded him to the Atlanta Braves during the 1976 season, and he went to the Texas Rangers in 1977, to the Minnesota Twins in 1978. With Minnesota, he set the AL record for appearances with 90 in 1979, when he also led the league with 32 saves. Marshall appeared in 18 games for Minnesota in 1980 and in 20 games with the New York Yankees in 1981 before retiring.

Marshall received his Ph.D. in 1978 and has taught and coached baseball at St. Leo College in Florida and Henderson State University in Arkansas.

In 14 seasons, he had a 97–112 record with 188 saves and a 3.14 ERA. He struck out 880 hitters and walked 514 in 1,368⅔ innings.

Martin, Billy (Alfred M.)

BASEBALL
b. May 16, 1928, Berkeley, Calif.
d. Dec. 25, 1989

As a player, Martin was known as a feisty competitor who, in the words of one opponent, "couldn't do anything but beat you." He played part-time for the AL's New York Yankees in 1950 and 1951 and became the team's starting second baseman in 1952. After missing most of the 1955 season with an injury, he made his only All-Star game appearance in 1956.

The Yankees traded him to the Kansas City Athletics during the 1957 season; he went to the Detroit Tigers in 1958, the Cleveland Indians in 1959, and the Cincinnati Reds in 1960. He retired after playing for the Milwaukee Braves and the Minnesota Twins in 1961. Although only a .257 career hitter, Martin set a record for a six-game World Series in 1953 by collecting 12 hits for a .500 average. He scored 5 runs and drove in 8 during New York's six-game victory over the Brooklyn Dodgers.

Martin went on to have a checkered managing career. He guided Minnesota to a Western Division title in 1969 but left because of a dispute with management. He took over the Detroit Tigers in 1971, won an Eastern Division championship the following year, was fired during the 1973 season, and managed the Texas Rangers for the last 23 games.

After bringing Texas from sixth place to second in 1974, Martin was again fired in 1975, with the team in fourth place. He was then hired by the New York Yankees, where he had a 30–26 record for the rest of the season.

Martin's ever-changing status with the Yankees and owner George Steinbrenner became something of a joke, especially when it was complicated by the arrival in 1977 of outfielder Reggie Jackson.

The Yankees won a pennant in 1976 and a world championship in 1977, when Martin and Jackson had a confrontation that almost flared into a fight on national television. Steinbrenner fired Martin during the 1978 season but almost immediately announced that he would be rehired in 1979.

Martin did return in 1979 but was fired again because of a much-publicized fight in an elevator with a marshmallow salesman who criticized the team's performance.

He then went to the Oakland Athletics, guided them to a division title in 1981, and was fired after the 1982 season. Though it seems hard to believe, Martin returned to the Yankees in 1983, was fired after the season, and went back for a fourth time in 1985. He spent three years out of baseball before one last try at managing the Yankees for 68 games in 1988.

Martin was killed in the crash of a friend's pickup truck under icy conditions. His overall managerial record was 1,253–1,013 for a .553 winning percentage.

Martin, Marianne

CYCLING
b. 1961, Fenton, Mich.

Martin was the surprise winner of the first Tour de France for women in 1984, covering the 616-mile course in 29 hours, 39 minutes, and 2 seconds. Because the race conflicted with the Los Angeles Olympic Games, the U.S. Cycling Federation didn't send a team, but the North Jersey Women's Bicycle Club did. A French company supplied bicycles and jerseys, since the six riders couldn't wear U.S. national team jerseys.

Because she'd been suffering from anemia and riding poorly in the early part of the year, Martin had to talk her way onto the team. In fact, she said later, "I begged and pleaded to get on the team."

An excellent climber, Martin took the lead for the first time after the fourteenth stage, which covered only 20 miles but climbed nearly a mile. She led the rest of the way and cycled triumphantly into Paris, where more than two million spectators lined the streets. As Martin did her victory lap along the Champs Élysées, she was surprised to hear a familiar voice in the crowd: her father had flown in from Michigan to watch the finish.

Martin, Pepper (John L. R.)

BASEBALL
b. Feb. 29, 1904, Temple, Okla.
d. March 5, 1965

Martin was named Associated Press athlete of the year in 1931, primarily for his performance in the World Series. A right-handed center fielder, Martin played his first full season with the NL's St. Louis Cardinals that year, batting .300.

In the World Series, he got 12 hits in 24 at-bats, stole five bases and scored five runs, as the Cardinals beat the Philadelphia Athletics in seven games. Martin got three hits and stole a base in the first game, but St. Louis lost, 6–2. He scored both runs in a 2–0 victory in the second game and scored two more runs in a 5–2 win in the third.

The Cardinals lost the fourth game, 3–0, on a two-hitter, with Martin getting both hits. He went three for four with a home run and four RBI when St. Louis won the next game, 5–1. Although he didn't get a hit in the last two games, Martin saved the Cardinals' 4–2 victory in the seventh game of the Series by making a great running catch of a line drive with two runners on for the final out.

The 5-foot-8, 170-pound Martin rarely bothered to shave, and his uniform

was usually dirty and often torn because of the way he played. Not especially fast, Martin was nevertheless a terror as a runner because he threw himself wildly into bases and fielders.

Nicknamed "the Wild Bull of the Osage" by sportswriters, Martin played briefly with St. Louis in 1928 and 1930 before becoming a starter in 1931. An injury limited him to just 85 games in 1932, but he led the league with 122 runs scored and 26 stolen bases in 1933, when he batted .316. That year he played third base, where he usually fielded balls by stopping them with his body.

Martin led the league in stolen bases twice more, with 23 in both 1934 and 1936. From 1937 on, he was a part-time player because of a variety of injuries. He retired after the 1944 season with a .298 average on 1,227 hits, including 270 doubles, 75 triples, and 59 home runs. He stole 146 bases, scored 754 runs, and had 501 RBI.

Martin, Slater N. ("Dugie")

BASKETBALL
b. Oct. 22, 1925, El Mina, Tex.

While the great Minneapolis Laker front line of George Mikan, Jim Pollard, and Vern Mikkelsen did most of the scoring and got most of the publicity, Slater was an outstanding play-making guard and an even better defender. He once held another Hall of Fame guard, Bob Davies, scoreless.

Slater was a four-year starter at the University of Texas, beginning in the 1943–44 season. He then served in the Navy during World War II and returned to Texas in 1947. He scored 984 points in his career, once had 49 points in a game against Texas Christian, and averaged 16 points per game as a senior, when he was named to the Helms Athletic Foundation All-American team.

Nicknamed "Dugie" for his supposed resemblance to a character of that name in the *Mutt and Jeff* comic strip, Martin joined the Lakers in 1949. They won NBA championships in four of his first five seasons. The 5-foot-10 Martin went to the New York Knickerbockers in 1956 and was traded in midseason to the St.

Louis Hawks, who won the 1957–58 NBA title.

Martin retired in 1959. In his ten NBA seasons, he scored 6,940 points in 681 games, an average of 10.2.

★ Basketball Hall of Fame

Maryland, Russell

FOOTBALL
b. March 22, 1969, Chicago, Ill.

The 6-foot-2, 275-pound Maryland was clocked at 4.98 for 40 yards during his career as the University of Miami, where he was a unanimous All-American nose tackle and winner of the Outland Trophy as the nation's outstanding collegiate lineman in 1990.

The first pick overall in the 1991 NFL draft, Maryland was selected by the Dallas Cowboys. He started at defensive tackle as a rookie and returned a fumble recovery for a touchdown. Maryland played for the Cowboy teams that won the 1992 and 1993 NFL championships.

Mathews, Eddie (Edwin L.)

BASEBALL
b. Oct. 13, 1931, Texarkana, Tex.

His apple-cheeked, baby-faced looks didn't deceive NL pitchers for very long. They soon realized that Mathews was a dangerous hitter. The only man to play for the Braves in Boston, Milwaukee, and Atlanta, Mathews was also a good fielding third baseman with a rifle arm.

A left-handed hitter, he joined the Braves in 1952, their last season in Boston, and hit 25 home runs. Mathews hit 40 or more home runs in each of the team's first three seasons in Milwaukee, leading the league with 47 in 1953. He had a league-leading 109 RBI in 1955, when he had 41 home runs.

The Braves won pennants in 1957 and 1958, with Mathews and Henry Aaron forming the most feared 1–2 punch in baseball. Aaron usually batted third, Mathews fourth, and he later said he benefited from hitting behind Aaron. "If the pitcher got him out, he was so tired from the effort he might make a mistake with me."

Mathews hit only .225 but scored four runs and had four RBI in Milwau-

kee's seven-game World Series victory over the New York Yankees in 1957. He batted only .160 when they lost to the Yankees in seven games the following year.

In 1959, Mathews won his second and last home run title with 46. He also hit .306, scored 118 runs, and had 114 RBI that year. He hit 23 or more home runs each of the next six seasons and had 32 or more three times.

After playing with the Braves for one season after they moved to Atlanta in 1966, Mathews was with the Houston Astros and Detroit Tigers in 1967. He ended his major league career with the Tigers in 1968. Mathews became a coach with the Braves after retiring. He took over as manager during the 1972 season and was fired during the 1974 season.

In 2,391 games, Mathews had 2,315 hits, including 354 doubles, 72 triples, and 512 home runs. He had 1,453 RBI and scored 1,509 runs. During their years as teammates, Mathews and Aaron teamed for 1,267 home runs, 60 more than Babe Ruth and Lou Gehrig hit together.

★ Baseball Hall of Fame

Mathewson, Christy (Christopher)

BASEBALL
b. Aug. 12, 1880, Factoryville, Pa.
d. Oct. 7, 1925

In an era when the public perceived major league players as tough, brawling, hard-drinking profane ruffians, Mathewson was the All-American boy. Well dressed and clean-cut, he had starred in baseball, basketball, and football at Bucknell University, where he was class president and a member of the glee club and literary society. Grantland Rice once wrote of Mathewson, "He handed the game a certain . . . indefinable lift in culture, brains, personality."

Mathewson dropped out of college to play professional baseball in 1899. A right-handed pitcher, he developed a pitch called the "reverse curve" or "fadeaway," now usually known as the screwball, a pitch that breaks in on a right-handed hitter rather than away from him. Later in his career, he came up with another unusual pitch that he called a "dry spitter," which was probably a knuckleball.

He joined the NL's New York Giants during the 1900 season and had an 0–3 record before being sent back down to the minor leagues. But he was back to stay in 1901, and during the next 14 seasons he won 20 or more games 13 times and 30 or more 4 times.

Mathewson led the league in strikeouts from 1903 through 1905 and had 30 or more victories each year, going 30–13, 33–12, and 31–9 over that period. He led the league in wins, shutouts (8), and ERA (1.28) in 1905, when the Giants won the pennant. In New York's five-game World Series victory over the Philadelphia Athletics, Mathewson had three shutouts, giving up just 14 hits and walking one while striking out 18 in 27 innings.

After a 22–12 record in 1906, Mathewson led the league with 24 victories, 8 shutouts, and 178 strikeouts in 1907. He followed that with his greatest season, when he won 37 games, an NL record for the twentieth century, with a league-leading 34 complete games, 11 shutouts, 5 saves, 390⅔ innings pitched, 259 strikeouts, and a 1.43 ERA.

Mathewson again led the NL with a 1.14 ERA in 1909, and he also had the best winning percentage, .806 on a 25–6 record. He was the leader in victories with a 27–9 record in 1910.

The Giants won three straight pennants from 1911 through 1913, with Mathewson going 26–13, 23–12, and 25–11 and leading the league in ERA with 1.99 in 1911 and 2.06 in 1913. However, the Giants lost all three World Series, and Mathewson had a 2–5 record despite a 1.51 ERA.

After a 24–13 mark in 1914, Mathewson was only 8–14 the following season. Late in 1915, the Giants traded him to Cincinnati so he could become the Reds' manager. He appeared in just one game for Cincinnati, finishing with a 4–4 record. Mathewson managed the team until he was drafted during the 1918 season.

His lungs were severely damaged by poison gas while he was serving in Europe. When he returned after World War II, he coached with the Giants for three years, then went into a sanitorium with tuberculosis. Mathewson was released in 1923 and became the president of the Boston Braves. A little more than two years later, he was back in the sanitorium, and he died while the Pittsburgh Pirates and Washington Senators were playing the first game of the 1925 World Series.

Mathewson had a 373–188 record and a .665 winning percentage with 79 shutouts and a 2.13 ERA. He struck out 2,502 hitters and walked only 844 in 4,780⅔ innings.

★ Baseball Hall of Fame

Mathias, Bob (Robert B.)
TRACK AND FIELD
b. Nov. 19, 1930, Tulare, Calif.

After he became the youngest person ever to win a gold medal in the decathlon at the 1948 Olympics, Mathias was asked what he would do to celebrate. The 17-year-old replied, "I'll start shaving, I guess."

Mathias averaged almost 9 yards a carry in football and 18 points a game in basketball during his high school years. At a high school track meet, he once won the shot, discus, and high hurdles, anchored the winning sprint relay team, and finished second in the high jump. His track coach suggested he should try the decathlon, even though it isn't usually a high school event. A month later, Mathias won his first competition, the Pacific Coast Games, and two weeks after that he finished first in the Olympic trials, beating Irving Mondschein, a three-time national champion.

At the Helsinki Games, Mathias was the youngest member ever of a U.S. Olympic track team. He was in third place after the first day of competition, but he took the lead with a discus throw of 144 feet, 4 inches on the second day and still held the lead after finishing the 1,500-meter run at 10:35 that night.

When he returned to his hometown, the plane had to circle the airport until the runway was cleared of the crowds who had come to welcome him back. Mathias won the Sullivan Award as the nation's outstanding amateur athlete for his feat. He also received more than 200 marriage proposals.

He enrolled at Stanford University after graduating from high school. A fullback on the football team, he played in the 1952 Rose Bowl, a 40–7 loss to Illinois, and then finished first in the Olympic decathlon trials again.

At 6-foot-3 and 205 pounds, Mathias was 3 inches taller and 15 pounds heavier than he had been in 1948, and this time he won the gold medal easily, setting a world record of 7,887 despite a badly pulled thigh muscle. His margin of victory, more than 900 points, is the largest in Olympic decathlon history, and he is the only athlete ever to win the Olympic event twice.

Mathias won all 11 decathlons he entered, including the AAU national championships from 1948 through 1950 and in 1952. He appeared in four movies, including *The Bob Mathias Story*, in which he played himself; served as a U.S. congressman; and then became director of the Olympic Training Center in Colorado Springs.

★ National Track & Field Hall of Fame; Olympic Hall of Fame

Matson, Ollie (Oliver A.)

▲ FOOTBALL
b. May 1, 1930, Trinity, Tex.

At the University of San Francisco, Matson set an NCAA record by rushing for 3,166 yards in three years as a starter. He led the nation with 1,566 yards and 21 touchdowns in 1951, his senior season.

The 6-foot-2, 220-pound Matson ran on the U.S. silver medal 4 x 400-meter relay team in the 1952 Olympics and won an individual bronze in the 400-meter run. Right after the Olympics, he joined the NFL's Chicago Cardinals.

Matson was named an all-pro defensive back in his rookie year, though he was also used on offense and ran back 20 kickoffs for 624 yards, a 31.2 average, and 2 touchdowns. He spent the 1953 season in the Army, then returned to the Cardinals in 1954 and was used primarily as a running back.

In 1958, Matson led the NFL in kickoff returns, running back 14 kickoffs for 497 yards, a 35.5 average, and 2 touchdowns. He was traded to the Los Angeles Rams after that season and spent four years there. The Rams sent him to the Detroit Lions in 1963, and after a year there, he finished his career with the Philadelphia Eagles from 1964 through 1966.

Matson played 14 NFL seasons, and only twice was he on a winning team. Yet he piled up impressive numbers. He gained 5,173 yards on 1,170 carries, a 4.4 average, and 40 touchdowns; caught 222 passes for 3,285 yards, a 14.8 average, and 23 touchdowns; returned 143 kickoffs for 3,746 yards, a 26.2 average, and 6 touchdowns; and ran back 65 punts for 595 yards, a 9.2 average, and 3 touchdowns.

★ College Football Hall of Fame; Pro Football Hall of Fame

Matson, Randy (James Randel)

TRACK AND FIELD
b. March 5, 1945, Kilgore, Tex.

When Matson entered Texas A&M University, he was good-sized at 6 feet, 6½ inches and 215 pounds, but track coach Emil Mamaliga advised him to put on more weight if he wanted to be a champion shot-putter. Mamaliga explained, "You can't fire a 16-inch shell from a PT boat. You have to have a big, heavy ship."

So Matson began lifting weights. Within seven months, he had gained 30 pounds and was throwing the shot six feet farther than he ever had before. He won the national championship in 1964 and finished second to Dallas Long in the Olympics.

After putting on another ten pounds, Matson broke Long's world record with a throw of 70 feet, 7¼ inches on May 8, 1965. He was not only the first man to break the 70-foot barrier, he was the only man to do it until 1972. Matson extended the record to 71 feet, 5½ inches on April 22, 1967.

The NCAA champion in both the discus and shot put in 1966 and 1967, Matson was the national shot put champion in 1964 and from 1966 through 1971. He won the gold medal in the event at the 1967 Pan-American Games. Matson won the Sullivan Award as the nation's outstanding amateur athlete in 1967.

A fine all-around athlete, Matson averaged 15 points a game as a high school basketball player, did the 100 meters in 10.2 seconds, and once had a 50-yard touchdown run in football. When he graduated from college, he was drafted by teams in the National Football League, the National Basketball Association, and the American Basketball Association. However, he chose to stay in track and field. He retired after finishing fourth in the 1972 Olympic Trials.

★ National Track & Field Hall of Fame

Matthews, Bruce R.

FOOTBALL
b. Aug. 8, 1961, Arcadia, Calif.

The son of a former end with the San Francisco 49ers and the brother of NFL linebacker Clay Matthews, Bruce was an All-American guard at the University of Southern California and was chosen in the first round of the 1983 draft by the Houston Oilers.

The 6-foot-5, 291-pound Matthews was named *The Sporting News* All-Pro team as a guard from 1988 through 1990 and in 1992. He moved to center in 1993 and was also an All-Pro at that position.

Mattingly, Donald A.

BASEBALL
b. April 20, 1961, Evansville, Ind.

After his first six full seasons in the major leagues, Mattingly looked like a shoo-in for the Hall of Fame. Then injuries struck, and he suddenly looked like a rather ordinary player.

A left-handed first baseman, Mattingly appeared in seven games with the AL's New York Yankees in 1982 and was

with the team for more than half the 1983 season. In 1984, his first full season in the majors, he led the league with 207 hits, 44 doubles, and a .343 batting average.

Mattingly was named the league's most valuable player in 1985, when he hit .324 with a league-leading 48 doubles and 145 RBI. He led the AL in 1986 with 238 hits, 53 doubles, and a .573 slugging percentage.

After batting .327, .311, and .303 during the next three seasons, Mattingly suffered a back injury and missed more than 50 games in 1990. After he returned, the recurring back problem hampered his swing. Mattingly hit only .288 in 1991 and .287 in 1992, totaling just 23 home runs over those two seasons.

In 1993, Mattingly began to rebound, batting .291 in 134 games, and he had a .304 average in 1994. In 1,707 games, he has 2,021 hits, including 410 doubles, 18 triples, and 215 home runs. He has driven in 1,050 runs and scored 948.

May, Mark E.

FOOTBALL
b. Nov. 2, 1959, Oneonta, N.Y.

An All-American as an offensive tackle at the University of Pittsburgh in 1980, the 6-foot-6, 300-pound May won the Outland Trophy as the outstanding college lineman of the year. He was chosen by the Washington Redskins in the first round of the 1981 NFL draft, the twentieth pick overall.

May was a starter on the Redskin teams that won Super Bowls after the 1982 and 1987 seasons, and he was named to the Pro Bowl team after the 1988 season. However, he missed the second half of 1989 and all of the 1990 season with a knee injury. The San Diego Chargers signed him as a free agent in 1991, and he went to the Phoenix Cardinals in 1992.

May, Scott G.

BASKETBALL
b. March 19, 1954, Sandusky, Ohio
A 6-foot-7, 210-pound forward, May

starred at Indiana University in 1974–75, when the Hoosiers were undefeated during the regular season. However, he cracked a bone in his left arm in the last game of the season and played sparingly, wearing a cast, in NCAA tournament action. Indiana lost in the regional finals to the University of Kentucky.

In his senior year, May averaged 23.3 points as Indiana swept through the season and the NCAA tournament without losing a game. He co-captained the team with Quinn Buckner, was named an All-American, and won the Rupp Trophy and the Naismith Award as 1976 college player of the year.

After playing on the gold medal U.S. Olympic team, May joined the Chicago Bulls. He played with them for five seasons and went to the Milwaukee Bucks in 1981. He began the 1982–83 season with the Detroit Pistons but was released before the season ended. May then played six years of professional basketball in Italy. During his NBA career, he scored 690 points, an average of 10.4 per game.

Mayasich, John E.

HOCKEY
b. May 22, 1933, Eveleth, Minn.

An All-American three years in a row at the University of Minnesota, Mayasich won the Western Collegiate Hockey Association title in 1954 and 1955. He set the NCAA tournament record for the most points in a game with seven against Boston College in 1954.

Mayasich turned down a number of offers from NHL teams and remained an amateur, playing mostly with the Green Bay, Wisconsin, Bobcats. He played on more national teams than any other U.S. player. He was a member of the 1956 Olympic team that won the silver medal and the 1960 team that won the gold medal. He also played in the world championship tournaments in 1957, 1958, 1961, 1962, 1966, and 1969.

The University of Minnesota gives the John Mayasich Award annually to the best student-athlete on the hockey team.

★ U.S. Hockey Hall of Fame

Mayer, Helene

FENCING
b. 1911, Offenbach, Germany
d. Oct 15, 1953

Mayer won a fencing gold medal at the 1928 Olympics, representing Germany, and she was the European champion in 1929 and 1931. After finishing fifth at the 1932 Los Angeles Games, she remained in the U.S. to study at the University of Southern California.

The daughter of a Jewish father and Christian mother, Mayer became a *cause célebrè* in 1933 when she was expelled from the Offenbach Fencing Club as part of a Nazi purge of Jewish athletes. Shortly afterward, the AAU voted to boycott the 1936 Olympics, to be held in Berlin, unless Jews were allowed to take part in the German trials and compete for Germany in the Olympics.

As a gesture of compliance, the German Olympic Committee invited Mayer to join the national team. She accepted and won a silver medal, then won the world women's championship in 1937.

Mayer won the U.S. national foil championship in 1934, 1935, 1937, 1938, 1939, 1941, 1942, and 1946.

Maynard, Donald R.

FOOTBALL
b. Jan. 25, 1937, Crosbyton, Tex.

One of the chief joys of New York Jet fans during the 1960s was that the player who caught a lot of long passes from quarterback Joe Namath had been cut by the hated New York Giants. His name was Don Maynard.

Maynard played at Texas Western College and was with the Giants in 1958, but caught only five passes. After being released, he went to the Hamilton Tiger-Cats of the Canadian Football League for one season, then signed with the New York Titans of the new American Football League in 1960.

He became a starter immediately and caught a total of 171 passes in his first three seasons. In 1963, the team was renamed the Jets, and Namath became the starting quarterback. During the next ten years, Maynard averaged more than 20 yards per catch four times.

Maynard's biggest game was the AFL championship playoff against the Oakland Raiders in 1968, when he caught six passes for 118 yards and two touchdowns in a 27–23 victory. The Jets went on to become the first AFL team to win the Super Bowl.

The fast 6-foot-1, 185-pound Maynard led the AFL in touchdown receptions with 14 in 1965; in yardage with 1,434 in 1967; and in average yards per catch with 20.2 in 1967 and 22.8 in 1968. He played the 1973 season with the St. Louis Cardinals before retiring.

During his 15 professional seasons, Maynard caught 633 passes for 11,834 yards, an 18.7 average, and 18 touchdowns. Although he was named to the All-AFL team only once, in 1969, he was chosen as an all-time All-AFL wide receiver.

★ Pro Football Hall of Fame

Mays, Rex

AUTO RACING
b. 1913, Glendale, Calif.
d. Nov. 6, 1949

The tall, handsome, mustached Mays could have been a stand-in for Errol Flynn, and he drove race cars the way Flynn might have. He never won the Indianapolis 500, largely because his hard-charging style generally wore cars out before they could finish the race. He failed to finish at Indy in 9 of his 12 starts, but he did place second in 1940 and 1941, and he was the fastest qualifier four times.

Mays began racing midget cars in California at 18. He was the Midwestern sprint car champion in 1936 and 1937 and won the national driving championship in 1940 and 1941. Paradoxically, Mays refused to wear a safety belt but was an outspoken advocate of driver safety and welfare. In 1946, he deliberately crashed his car into the wall at the Milwaukee Speedway to avoid hitting Duke Densmore, who had been thrown out of his car onto the track.

Mays was killed in a crash at Del Mar, California.

★ Indianapolis 500 Hall of Fame

Mays, Willie H.

BASEBALL
b. May 6, 1931, Westfield, Ala.

Mays brought more than just great skill to the game of baseball. He also brought a rare exuberance and excitement to the sport, prompting Leo Durocher to say, "Willie is without doubt the most dynamic, most dramatic, most fantastic, most exciting performer in action today. He is Joe Louis, Jascha Heifetz, Sammy Davis, and Nashua rolled into one."

At 16, he was playing for the Birmingham Black Barons. The New York Giants paid $15,000 for his contract in 1950 and gave Mays a $6,000 signing bonus. After a season at the Class B level, he jumped to Minneapolis in the Triple-A American Association, where he batted .477 in the first 35 games of the 1951 season.

The Giants then brought him up. Mays went hitless in his first 21 major league at-bats, but he ended up batting .274 with 20 home runs and 68 RBI in 121 games and fielding sensationally to help win a pennant.

Mays missed most of the 1952 season and all of the 1953 season while serving in the Army. He returned in 1954 to help lead the Giants to another pennant, leading the league in hitting with a .345 average, in slugging with a .667 percentage, and in triples with 13. He also had 41 home runs, 110 RBI, and 119 runs scored, won the league's most valuable player award, and was named male athlete of the year by the Associated Press.

In New York's four-game World Series sweep of the heavily favored Cleveland Indians, Mays batted .286, scoring four runs and driving in three. But the unforgettable play of that World Series was his catch — "the Catch" — in the eighth inning of the first game. With the score tied, 2–2, Cleveland had two men on and nobody out when Vic Wertz hit a tremendous drive to center field. Racing toward the fence, Mays made an over-the-shoulder catch about 425 feet from home plate, then somehow recovered to make a strong throw back to the infield, holding the runners. The Giants went on to win the game, 5–2, on Dusty Rhodes's three-run homer in the tenth.

Mays led the league with 13 triples, 51 home runs, and a .659 slugging percentage in 1955; with 20 triples and a .626 slugging percentage in 1957; and with 121 runs scored in 1958, the team's first season in San Francisco. It wasn't a happy move for Mays. He encountered racial prejudice when he bought a home in a formerly all-white section of the city, and San Francisco fans at first preferred a younger hero, Orlando Cepeda.

But his 1962 performance won over most of the fans. He led the league with 49 home runs, batted .304, scored 130 runs, and had 141 RBI to help San Francisco win its first pennant. However, he hit only .250 in a seven-game World Series loss to the New York Yankees.

Mays won two more home run titles, with 47 in 1964 and 52 in 1965. He also led the league in slugging both years with percentages of .607 and .645, and he won the 1965 most valuable player award. That was the last season in which he batted over .300.

Early in the 1972 season, Mays went back to New York to play for the Mets. He hit just .250 that year, and he retired after batting only .211 in 66 games in 1973.

Mays had a career .302 average with 3,283 hits, including 523 doubles, 140 triples, and 660 home runs. He stole 338 bases, scored 2,062 runs, and had 1,903 RBI.

★ Baseball Hall of Fame

Meagher, Mary T.

SWIMMING
b. Oct. 27, 1964, Louisville, Ky.

A phenomenal butterfly swimmer, Meagher set her first world record before her fifteenth birthday, beating former record holder Tracy Caulkins by seven yards in the 200-meter event at the 1979 Pan-American Games. The following April, she set a world record of 59.26 seconds in the 100-meter butterfly.

Meagher qualified for five events, including two relays, at the 1980 U.S. Olympic trials, but the U.S. boycotted the Moscow Games that year. Her quali-

fying times at the trials would have won gold medals. She thought about retiring because of her disappointment but decided instead to look ahead to the 1984 Olympics.

At the 1981 national long-course championships, Meagher lowered both of her world records, winning the 100-meter butterfly in 57.93, the 200-meter in 2:05.96. Those are still world records, more than 12 years later.

She entered the University of California in 1982 and won the NCAA 200-yard butterfly as a freshman at the 1983 meet. Her decision to continue competing was rewarded with three gold medals at the 1984 Olympics, in the two butterfly events and as a member of the 4 x 100-meter medley relay team. Her 2:06.90 in the 200-meter gave her the seven fastest times ever in that event. She was also the national indoor champion in both butterfly races and in the 200-meter freestyle in 1984.

Meagher won the NCAA 200-yard butterfly three years in a row, from 1985 through 1987, and was the 100-yard champion in 1985 and 1987, when she won the Honda Broderick Cup as the nation's outstanding female college athlete. Her time of 54.42 in the 100-yard event in 1987 was another world record.

In 1985, Meagher won both national butterfly championships in the short-course and long-course meets. She was world champion in the 200-meter butterfly in 1986, and she also won silver medals in the 100-meter butterfly and the 4 x 100-meter medley relay, along with a bronze in the 400-meter freestyle. She closed out her career with a bronze medal in the 200-meter butterfly at the 1988 Olympics.

Meanwell, Doc (Walter E.)

BASKETBALL
b. Jan. 26, 1884, Leeds, England
d. Dec. 2, 1953

Meanwell's only serious basketball experience was with the Rochester, New York, Athletic Club, but he became an innovative and very successful college coach. He received an M.D. from the University of Maryland in 1909. Because of his interest in health through physical training, he became Baltimore's supervisor of recreation and coached a team in the Baltimore Public Athletic League.

At the University of Wisconsin in 1912–13, Meanwell developed one of the sport's first continuity offenses, the "criss cross," which featured players constantly cutting through the foul lane from one side and the other. The offense emphasized short passes, which was very unorthodox at the time. His Wisconsin teams won 29 consecutive games during one period.

After receiving a doctorate in public health from Wisconsin, Meanwell served in the Army Medical Corps during World War I and then coached at the University of Missouri for two seasons, winning Missouri Valley Conference championships both years. He returned to Wisconsin in 1920 and coached there for another 14 years, also serving as the school's athletic director from 1933 to 1935. His overall record was 290 wins and 101 losses.

Meanwell coached two future Hall of Famers, "Bud" Foster and Harold Olson. He helped to develop the modern, laceless basketball with a hidden valve, and, with Notre Dame football coach Knute Rockne, he wrote *Training, Conditioning, and the Care of the Injuries,* one of the first books of its kind.

★ Basketball Hall of Fame

Meany, Helen

DIVING
b. Dec. 15, 1904

Meany was the first American diver to compete in three Olympics. After failing to win a medal in the platform event in 1920 and 1924, she won a gold medal in springboard diving in 1928.

She won 14 AAU national titles, in the outdoor 3-meter springboard in 1921, 1922, 1926, and 1927; in the outdoor platform from 1921 through 1923 and in 1925 and 1927; in the indoor 1-meter springboard from 1926 through 1928; and in the indoor 3-meter springboard in 1925 and 1927.

Meany lost her amateur status after the 1928 Olympics for participating in a Miami Beach water show, not sanctioned by the AAU, with Pete DesJardins, Martha Norelius, and Johnny Weissmuller.

Mears, Rick R.

AUTO RACING
b. Dec. 3, 1951, Wichita, Kans.

The only driver to win the pole position at the Indianapolis 500 six times, Mears won the race in 1979, 1984, 1988, and 1991 and was the national driving champion in 1979, 1981, and 1982.

Mears began his career by racing motorcycles in 1968, then switched to off-road dune buggy racing because his mother was concerned about his safety. He won the Firecracker 250 off-road race in 1972 and had seven off-road wins in 1973, when he also started driving stock cars.

He moved into IndyCar racing in 1976 and was named rookie of the year, then joined the Roger Penske racing team. At first primarily a substitute for Mario Andretti, he became the team's top driver in 1979.

Mears had a bad crash in September 1984, suffering severe injuries to both feet, and didn't return to racing full time until 1986. He retired after the 1992 season with 29 IndyCar victories and $11,050,087 in winnings.

Medica, Jack C.

SWIMMING
b. Oct. 5, 1914, Seattle, Wash.

Swimming for the University of Washington, Medica won NCAA championships in the 220-yard, 440-yard, and 1,500-meter freestyle three years in a row, from 1934 through 1936. His record of nine championships was tied several times before John Naber broke it in 1977.

At the 1936 Olympics, Medica won a gold medal in the 400-meter freestyle. Trailing Japan's Shumpei Uto most of the way, he put on a burst of speed to take a fingertip-length lead with about ten yards to go and held on for the victory. Medica also won silver medals in the 1,500-meter freestyle and as a member of the 4 x 200-meter freestyle relay team.

Medica won AAU outdoor championships in the 440-yard and 880-yard freestyle races in 1933 and 1934 and was the 1-mile champion in 1934. Indoors, he won the 220-yard freestyle in 1935 and 1936. He retired after the 1936 Olympics and later coached swimming at Columbia University and the University of Pennsylvania.

★ International Swimming Hall of Fame

Medwick, Joseph M.

BASEBALL
b. Nov. 24, 1911, Carteret, N.J.
d. March 21, 1975

Medwick dreamed of playing football at Notre Dame and took the name "Mickey King" to protect his amateur standing when he entered professional baseball in 1930. After hitting .419 in the minor leagues, he decided baseball was his calling, and he began using his real name.

He joined the NL's St. Louis Cardinals late in the 1932 season. The 5-foot-10, 187-pound Medwick liked the nickname "Muscles," but he was more often called "Ducky" by his teammates because they thought he walked like a duck.

The Cardinals of his era were known as the Gas House Gang because of their aggressive style on and off the field. Medwick was a charter member, often engaging in clubhouse fights with teammates. He led the league in triples with 18 in 1934, when he hit .319, scored 110 runs, and had 106 RBI to help take St. Louis to the pennant.

In the seventh inning of the seventh game of the World Series, against the Detroit Tigers, Medwick slid hard into Detroit third baseman Marv Owen after hitting a triple. When Medwick took the field in the top of the eighth, Detroit fans showered him with garbage and bottles. Baseball Commissioner Kenesaw Mountain Landis finally ordered Medwick to leave the game for his own protection. Since St. Louis was winning,

11–0, at the time, there was little protest.

Medwick led the league with 223 hits, 64 doubles, and 138 RBI in 1936, and he won his only batting title with a .374 average in 1937, when he was also the league leader with 11 runs, 237 hits, 56 doubles, 31 triples, 154 RBI, and a .641 slugging percentage. He was the tenth man in baseball history to win a triple crown; no NL player has done it since. Medwick also led NL outfielders in fielding percentage that season and was an easy winner of the most valuable player award.

During the 1940 season, Medwick was traded to the Brooklyn Dodgers. He hit .318 when they won the pennant in 1941 but batted only .235 in their five-game loss to the New York Yankees in the World Series. The Dodgers sent him to the New York Giants in July 1943, and he was traded to the Boston Braves during the 1945 season.

Released by the Braves early in 1946, Medwick sat out the early part of the season before signing with the Dodgers. He was released again in October and returned to the Cardinals as a part-time player in 1947 and 1948. Medwick then became a playing manager in the minor leagues for several years. He was the Cardinals' minor league hitting instructor when he died of a heart attack during spring training of 1975.

★ Baseball Hall of Fame

Meggett, Dave (David L.)

FOOTBALL
b. April 30, 1966, Charleston, S.C.

Meggett played football at Morgan State and Towson State and was chosen by the New York Giants in the fifth round of the 1989 NFL draft.

Only 5-foot-7 and 180 pounds, Meggett has been a versatile performer for the Giants as a kick returner and pass receiver out of the backfield, especially on third-down situations.

Meggett led the NFL in punt return yardage with 582 yards in 1989 and 467 yards in 1990, when he was named to *The Sporting News* All-Pro team. He played for the Giants in their victory in Super Bowl XXV.

Through the 1993 season, he had returned 176 punts for 1,907 yards, a 10.8 average, and 4 touchdowns; run back 93 kickoffs for 2,038 yards, a 21.9 average, and 1 touchdown; caught 161 passes for 1,582 yards, a 9.8 average, and 10 touchdowns; and rushed 111 times for 601 yards, a 5.4 average, and 1 touchdown.

Mehnert, George N.

WRESTLING
b. Nov. 3, 1881, Newark, N.J.
d. July 8, 1948

During his eight years as a top amateur wrestler, Mehnert lost only two matches, one of them to George Dole in the finals of the 1907 AAU national bantamweight championship. Mehnert was national flyweight champion from 1902 through 1904 and in 1908, and he won the bantamweight title in 1905 and 1906.

Mehnert won an Olympic gold medal as a flyweight in 1904 and was the Olympic bantamweight champion in 1908, when a London sportswriter reported that he "undoubtedly was the most scientific, both in attack and defense, of any wrestler taking part in the Games."

After wrestling professionally in 1909 and 1910, Mehnert served as president of the Newark, New Jersey, National Turnverein Club and as chief clerk of the AAU's national wrestling committee.

Melges, Buddy (Harry C. Jr.)

YACHTING
b. Jan. 26, 1930, Elkhorn, Wis.

Melges won the Mallory Cup, emblematic of the North American sailing championship, a record three years in a row, 1959 through 1961. With William Bentsen and William Allen as crew members, he took the gold medal in the soling class at the 1972 Olympics, finishing first in three of the six races with a second-, a third-, and a fourth-place finish to score 8.7 points to 31.7 for the silver medalist.

He and Bentsen had won a bronze in the Flying Dutchman Class in 1964. Melges was coskipper, with Bill Koch, of *America*³ when she defended the America's Cup against the Italian challenger *Il Moro di Venezia* in 1992.

Meredith, Ted (James E.)

TRACK AND FIELD
b. Nov. 14, 1892, Chester Heights, Pa.
d. Nov. 2, 1957

Meredith had his greatest year in 1912, when he was a senior at Mercersburg Academy. He set interscholastic records of 49.2 seconds in the 440-yard run and 1:55.0 in the 880-yard.

After graduating, Meredith qualified for the U.S. Olympic team and won a gold medal in the 800-meter run with a world record 1:51.9. He ran on to the 880-yard mark and also set a world record for that distance, with a 1:52.5. He finished only fourth in the 400-meter, but he won a second gold medal as a member of the 4 x 400-meter relay team.

That fall, Meredith entered the University of Pennsylvania. He was the IC4A 400-meter champion from 1914 through 1916 and the 880-yard champion in 1914 and 1915. He also won the AAU 440-yard title in 1914 and 1915. In 1916, he set a world record in the 440 of 47.6 seconds, which wasn't broken until 1928. His world record time in the 800-meter, set at the 1912 Olympics, stood until 1926.

Meredith retired from competition in 1917 and served in the Army during World War I. He made a comeback for the 1920 Olympics, where he was eliminated in the 400-meter trials and ran on the 4 x 400-meter relay team that finished fourth.

★ National Track & Field Hall of Fame

Merrell, Mary E. (Brennan)

ROLLER SKATING
b. Nov. 24, 1938, Miami, Fla.

Merrell started skating at the age of nine and won her first important title, the Southern regional junior girls' speed skating championship, when she was 14. She went on to win a record six national seniors titles, from 1959 through 1961 and in 1964, 1966, and 1967.

The wife of Grady Merrell, who coached U.S. roller skating teams in the 1980 and 1981 world championships, she has a daughter, Diane, national junior girls speed skating champion in 1975, and a son, Grady Jr., who won the national artistic skating title in 1977.

Messier, Mark D.
HOCKEY
b. Jan. 18, 1961, Edmonton, Alta.

A tough, scrapping center who can put on a surprising burst of speed when he needs to, the 6-foot-1, 202-pound Messier had a brief tryout with the Indianapolis Racers of the World Hockey Association before joining the Cincinnati Stingers of the WHA during the 1978–79 season. He had 58 penalty minutes but just 11 points in 47 games with Cincinnati.

Messier joined the NHL's Edmonton Oilers early in the 1979–80 season. He blossomed as a scorer with 50 goals and 38 assists for 88 points in 1981–82, and he had 106 and 101 points in the next two seasons. When the Oilers won the 1984 Stanley Cup, Messier won the Conn Smythe Trophy as most valuable player in the playoffs, scoring 26 points on 8 goals and 18 assists in 19 games.

After winning the Hart Trophy as the league's most valuable player in 1990, Messier suffered a knee injury and played only 53 games in the 1990–91 season. He then held out for more money and was traded to the New York Rangers in October 1991. Messier won a second Hart Trophy in 1992 after scoring 107 points on 35 goals and 72 assists for the Rangers.

A first-team all-star in 1982, 1983, 1990, and 1992, Messier holds the NHL record for most short-handed goals in the playoffs with 11. In 1,081 NHL games through the 1993–94 season, he has 478 goals and 838 assists for 1,316 points, and he has scored 259 points on 99 goals and 160 assists in 200 playoff games.

Metcalfe, Ralph H.
TRACK AND FIELD
b. May 29, 1910, Atlanta, Ga.
d. Oct. 10, 1978

One of those unfortunate athletes who peaked between Olympics and therefore never quite got the recognition he deserved, Metcalfe grew up in Chicago and entered Marquette University in 1930.

Metcalfe won the NCAA 100- and 200-meter dashes in 1932 and was the 100- and 220-yard champion in 1933 and 1934. He also won the AAU national 100-yard championship from 1932 and 1934, the 200-meter title from 1932 through 1936.

A very fast finisher who lacked a great start, Metcalfe finished second to Eddie Tolan in the 100-meter at the 1932 Olympics. The race was so close that judges studied the photo-finish picture for hours before deciding on a winner. In the 200-meter dash, Metcalfe ran third to Tolan and George Simpson. It was discovered afterward that his lane was about two meters too long, but he didn't protest because he was content with a U.S. sweep of the medals.

At the 1936 Olympics, Metcalfe finished second to Jesse Owens in the 100-meter and ran on the gold medal 4 x 100-meter relay team that set a world record of 39.8 seconds.

Metcalfe tied the world record of 10.3 in the 100-meter dash eight times, though only three of the marks went into the record book. He also tied the 20.6-second world record in the 200-meter.

He retired from competition after the 1936 Olympics. Metcalfe served on the Chicago City Council from 1949 through 1971 and was a U.S. congressman from 1971 until his death in 1978.
★ National Track & Field Hall of Fame

Metheny, Linda J.
GYMNASTICS
b. Aug. 12, 1947, Olney, Ill.

Metheny began competing as a gymnast in 1962. Two years later, she made the U.S. Olympic team. The national all-around champion in 1966, 1968, 1970, 1971, and 1972, she won the NCAA all-around title in 1967 as a member of the University of Illinois team.

At the 1967 Pan-American Games, Metheny won a record five gold medals, taking every event including the all-around championship. She became the first American woman ever to qualify for the Olympic finals in an individual event in 1968, when she finished fourth in the balance beam.

A member of the 1972 Olympic team that placed fourth, Metheny suffered an injury and was unable to compete in the individual finals. She retired from competition after the Olympics and married her longtime coach, Dick Mulvihill. In 1973, they opened a gymnastics academy in Eugene, Oregon. Among their students were U.S. Olympians Julianne McNamara and Tracee Telavera and Canadian Olympian Keri Kelsall.

Meyer, Debbie (Deborah E.)

SWIMMING
b. Aug. 14, 1952, Annapolis, Md.

Because Meyer had asthma, her family moved to California when she was a young teen, and she began competitive swimming there in 1965. Within two years, she was one of the best in the world.

Meyer won AAU national titles in the 400- and 1,500-meter freestyle from 1967 through 1970, and she was the 400-meter individual medley champion in 1969. Indoors, she won the 1,650-yard freestyle five years in a row, from 1967 through 1971, and was the 200-yard champion in 1968, the 500-yard champion in 1968, 1970, and 1971, and the 400-yard individual medley winner in 1970.

She set world records in the 400- and 800-meter freestyles at the Pan-American Games in 1967, when she was named woman athlete of the year by TASS, the Soviet news agency. At the 1968 Olympic trials, Meyer set world records of 2:06.7 in the 200-meter, 4:24.5 in the 400-meter, and 9:10.4 in the 800-meter. Although dysentery and the high air of Mexico City slowed her times at the Olympics, she won all three events,

becoming the first swimmer to claim three gold medals at a single Olympics.

Winner of the 1968 Sullivan Award as the amateur athlete of the year, Meyer was also voted woman athlete of the year by Associated Press sportswriters in 1969, when she set another world record of 17:19.9 in the 1,500-meter freestyle.

Meyer had hoped to compete in the 1972 Olympics, but recurring bursitis in her left shoulder forced her retirement after the 1971 season.

★ International Women's Sports Hall of Fame; Olympic Hall of Fame

Meyer, Dutch (Leo R.)

FOOTBALL
b. Jan. 15, 1898, Ellinger, Tex.
d. Dec. 3, 1982

Meyer entered Texas Christian University in 1917 but was sent to Transylvania College in Kentucky as an ROTC instructor because of World War I. He returned to TCU in 1918 and became a starter at end. However, he didn't play in his senior season, 1921, because of a falling out with the coach.

After playing minor league baseball as a pitcher for a short time, he became a high school coach in Ft. Worth, then returned to TCU to coach baseball and freshman football in 1923. Oddly enough, he recruited Sammy Baugh after seeing him play sandlot baseball in 1932. When Meyer became head football coach in the 1934, he installed Baugh as his starting tailback.

To take advantage of Baugh's great arm, Meyer designed a double-wing formation in which the ends and wingback were split wider than usual, allowing them to get into pass routes quickly. With Baugh throwing from the "Meyer spread," as the formation became known, TCU had a 27–7–2 record over the next three seasons. The Horned Frogs beat LSU, 3–2, in the 1936 Sugar Bowl and Marquette, 16–6, in the 1937 Cotton Bowl.

After Baugh graduated, Meyer had little Davey O'Brien to replace him. Not quite as great a passer as Baugh, O'Brien was a fast, elusive runner and an outstanding field general. With O'Brien leading the way, Meyer's 1938 team won all ten of its games, outscoring opponents 254 to 53, and beat Carnegie Tech, 15–7, in the Sugar Bowl.

After a couple of lean years, Meyer's 1941 team went to the Orange Bowl, losing, 40–26, to Georgia, and his 1944 team lost, 34–0, to Oklahoma A & M in the Cotton Bowl. His 1951 team was beaten, 20–7, by Kentucky in the Cotton Bowl.

Meyer retired after the 1952 season. His record in 19 seasons, all at TCU, was 109 wins, 79 losses, and 13 ties.
★ College Football Hall of Fame

Meyer, Raymond J.
BASKETBALL
b. Nov. 18, 1913, Chicago, Ill.
At Notre Dame, Meyer captained the basketball team to 40 victories in 46 games during his junior and senior seasons, 1937 and 1938. After two years as a social worker, he returned to Notre Dame as an assistant coach, and in 1942 he become head coach at DePaul University in Chicago. He was there for 42 seasons, second only to "Phog" Allen for the longest tenure at a major college.

Meyer had 37 winning seasons; his teams won 20 or more games 20 times. DePaul won the 1945 National Invitation Tournament and played in 13 NCAA tournaments under Meyer. When his son, Joey, succeeded him as coach in 1984, Meyer had compiled a record of 724 victories, fifth all-time, and 354 losses. He was named coach of the year by the National Association of Basketball Coaches in 1979, and was consensus coach of the year in 1984.
★ Basketball Hall of Fame

Meyers, Ann E. (Mrs. Drysdale)
BASKETBALL
b. March 26, 1955, San Diego, Calif.
The first nationally prominent woman basketball player, the 5-foot-9, 140-pound Meyers had hopes of being an Olympic high jumper when she was in high school, where she won letters in seven sports. But she decided to focus on basketball after becoming the first high school student to play for a U.S. national team, in 1974.

Meyers was the first woman to win a full athletic scholarship to UCLA. She was a four-time All-American, and she won the Broderick Award as the nation's best woman collegiate player in 1978, when UCLA won the national championship. Her coach, Billie Moore, said of her, "I've never seen anyone have more impact on a team than Annie did."

An outstanding all-around player, Meyers starred for the 1975 national team that won the Pan-American Games and world championships, the 1976 Olympic team that won a silver medal at Montreal, the team that finished second in the 1977 World University games, and the 1979 Pan-American Games champion. She was selected to carry the U.S. flag at the Pan-American opening ceremonies.

In 1979, Meyers became the first woman to sign an NBA contract, with the Indiana Pacers. She didn't make the team, but she got a job as commentator on their televised games. With the New Jersey Gems of the Women's Professional Basketball League, she tied for most valuable player honors in 1979–80, when she led the league in steals and averaged 22.2 points a game.

Meyers won the made-for-television Women Superstars competition three years in a row, 1980–82. She then became a full-time broadcaster. Her brother, Dave, was an All-American at UCLA and played in the NBA, and she was married to former Dodger pitcher and broadcaster Don Drysdale, who died in 1993.
★ Basketball Hall of Fame; International Women's Sports Hall of Fame

Michaels, Louis A.
FOOTBALL
b. Sept. 28, 1935, Swoyersville, Pa.
A defensive tackle and left-footed place-kicker at the University of Kentucky, Michaels was an All-American in 1956 and 1957, and he won the 1957 Knute Rockne Trophy as the nation's outstanding collegiate lineman.

Michaels joined the NFL's Los Angeles Rams in 1958. Though sometimes used as a defensive end, the 6-foot-2, 235-pound Michaels was primarily a kicker during his professional career. He was traded to the Pittsburgh Steelers in 1961, was with the Baltimore Colts from 1964 through 1970, and played one season with the Green Bay Packers in 1971.

His 26 field goals in 1962 was an NFL record at the time. In his 14 NFL seasons, Michaels scored 955 points by kicking 187 of 341 field goal attempts and converting 386 of 402 extra point attempts.

★ College Football Hall of Fame

Michalske, Mike (August M.)

FOOTBALL
b. April 24, 1903, Cleveland, Ohio
d. Oct. 26, 1983

After starring at guard for two years at Penn State, Michalske was moved to fullback in 1925, his senior season. He scored both of his team's touchdowns in a 13–6 victory over Michigan State.

Michalske was back at guard with the New York Yankees of the American Football League in 1926. The league folded after that season, and the Yankees moved into the NFL. When the team disbanded after the 1928 season, Michalske joined the Green Bay Packers. He was one of their outstanding players when they won three consecutive NFL championships in his first three seasons.

He was named to unofficial All-Pro teams in 1929 and 1930 and was the left guard on the first official All-Pro team in 1931. Michalske was named an All-Pro right guard in 1935. The 6-foot, 210-pounder was strong, fast, and a very intelligent defender who was particularly good at rushing the passer. He retired in 1936 but returned to the Packers for one more season, in 1937.

Michalske coached Iowa State from 1942 through 1946, winning 18 games while losing 18 and tying 3.

★ Pro Football Hall of Fame

Middlecoff, Cary (Emmett Cary)

GOLF
b. Jan. 6, 1921, Halls, Tenn.

After receiving his degree as a doctor of dental surgery in 1944, Middlecoff served in the U.S. Army Dental Corps. As an amateur, he won the 1945 North and South Open and was named to the Walker Cup team. He declined in order to join the PGA tour, giving himself two years to succeed. He never practiced dentistry again.

Middlecoff was the most successful golfer on the tour during the 15 years after World War II, winning 37 tour events. He was the U.S. Open champion in 1949 and 1956, and he won the Masters by seven strokes in 1955. He won the 1956 Vardon Trophy for the fewest average strokes per round.

A long driver, Middlecoff was known as the fastest walker and slowest player on the pro tour. After hitting the ball, he would head toward it as if he couldn't wait to take his next shot, and then he'd spend minutes agonizing over it. During the early 1960s, back problems and putting woes troubled his game and eventually forced his retirement. Middlecoff frequently did golf commentary on television, and he also wrote several books on golf.

★ PGA Hall of Fame; World Golf Hall of Fame

Mikan, George L., Jr.

BASKETBALL
b. June 18, 1924, Joliet, Ill.

There were other big players before and during Mikan's prime, but he was the first truly dominant big man. A professional teammate, Bob Calihan, said he had never seen defenses double-team a player before Mikan came along. Joe Lapchick, a pretty good big man in his own right, commented, "Everyone forgets that Mikan is also the best feeder from the pivot this game has ever seen. Cover him normally and he kills you with his scoring. Cover him abnormally and he murders you with passes."

His size was a major problem before he entered college. He didn't play high school basketball because he was awkward, and a badly broken leg kept him in bed, convalescing, for a year and a half. When he entered Chicago's DePaul University in 1942, he was 6-foot-10, weighed 245 pounds, and wore thick glasses.

First-year DePaul coach Ray Meyer transformed him into a confident, aggressive player by working closely with him on exercises and drills and teaching him how to make hook shots accurately with either hand. Meyer later said, "As soon as George stopped feeling sorry for himself and realized his height was something to be admired, he was on his way to being great."

Mikan became a three-time All-American and was college player of the year in 1945 and 1946. He led the nation in scoring with 23.9 points per game in 1944–45 and 23.1 in 1945–46. When DePaul won the 1945 National Invitation Tournament, Mikan was named most valuable player, scoring 120 points in three games, including 53 points in a 97–53 win over Rhode Island.

As soon as the 1945–46 college season was over, Mikan signed with the Chicago American Gears of the National Basketball League. He played seven games with them at the end of the season, leading the team to the championship of the World Basketball Tournament. Mikan was tournament MVP with 100 points in five games.

He left the Gears for six weeks during the 1946–47 season in a contract dispute but returned to lead them to the NBL playoff championship after they finished third in the league's Western Division. The Gears folded, and Mikan then joined the Minneapolis Lakers. He led the league in scoring with a 21.3 average, was named MVP, and the Lakers won the NBL playoffs.

In 1948, the NBA was formed by a merger of the NBL and the Basketball Association of America. Mikan led the new league in scoring its first three years, and Minneapolis won five of the first six NBA championships, missing out only in 1951. The physical beatings he'd been taking persuaded Mikan to retire after the 1953–54 season, when he was only 30. He had broken both legs, both feet, his right wrist, three fingers, a thumb, and his nose at various times.

He returned for just 37 games in 1955–56, scoring only 390 points, then retired for good. However, he coached the Lakers for part of the 1957–58 season, winning only 9 of 39 games, and he was commissioner of the American Basketball Association when it was organized in 1967. The ABA's distinctive red, white, and blue striped ball was his idea.

In 520 pro games, Mikan scored 11,764 points, an average of 22.6 per game, and he was a six-time first-team all-star. He was named the best player of the first half century by the Associated Press in 1950, was one of ten players selected for the NBA Silver Anniversary Team in 1972, and was on the Helms Athletic Foundation all-time All-American team, chosen in a 1952 poll.
★ Basketball Hall of Fame

Mikita, Stan [Stanley Gvoth]
HOCKEY
b. May 20, 1940, Sokolce, Czechoslovakia

Although he was often overshadowed by his flamboyant, high-scoring teammate, Bobby Hull, Mikita was a great hockey player, an excellent stick handler, and a brilliant passer who won four scoring titles and outscored Hull five times during a six-year period.

In his early years in the NHL, he compensated for his lack of size with belligerent play, winning the nickname "Le Petit Diable" (The Little Devil) from Montreal fans. However, he did a complete turnaround and won the 1967 Lady Byng Trophy for combining a high level of play with gentlemanly conduct.

Mikita spent his entire 22-year NHL career with the Chicago Black Hawks, beginning in the 1958–59 season. In 1963–64, he and Hull had the first of their battles for the scoring championship. Hull scored more goals, 43 to 39, but Mikita had 50 assists to win the Ross Trophy. He led again in 1964–65 with 87 points yet he wasn't even named a first-team all-star.

In 1966–67, Mikita became the first triple crown winner in NHL history. He set a record with 62 assists, tied Hull's record of 97 points, and won the Ross Trophy as leading scorer, the Hart Trophy as the league's most valuable player, and the Byng Trophy. This time he was the NHL's first-team all-star center.

Mikita won all three trophies and was a first-team all-star again in 1967–68. The following year, he again had 97 points, but Phil Esposito, Gordie Howe, and Hull all had more than 100 points, so Mikita finished fourth in scoring.

Injuries troubled Mikita throughout the rest of his career, and he never again hit such scoring heights. After a serious head injury, Mikita began wearing a helmet designed especially for him, and he went into the helmet manufacturing business. He was also slowed by a chronic bad back, and in 1973 a broken heel sidelined him for six weeks. Nevertheless, he played through the 1979–80 season and kept scoring consistently.

In 1394 regular season games, Mikita had 541 goals and 926 assists, averaging more than a point a game. He scored 59 goals and had 91 assists in 155 playoff games.

★ Hockey Hall of Fame

Milburn, Rodney, Jr.

TRACK AND FIELD
b. May 18, 1950, Opelousas, La.

As a freshman at Southern University in Baton Rouge, Milburn won the 120-yard hurdle event at the 1970 NAIA championship meet. He had a brilliant 1971 season, winning the high hurdles at the NAIA, NCAA College Division, NCAA University Division, and AAU championships, where he set a world record of 13.0 seconds. He was also the Pan-American Games champion in the 110-meter hurdles.

After winning 27 consecutive races, Milburn had a problem in the 1972 Olympic trials. He hit two hurdles and barely qualified for the team by finishing third. However, he returned to form at the Olympics and led all the way to win a gold medal in the 110-meter hurdles, tying the world record of 13.2 seconds. Milburn set a new record of 13.1 on July 6, 1973, at a Zurich meet. He won his second NCAA University Division championship that year.

The AAU outdoor champion in 1971

and 1972 and indoor champion in 1972 and 1973, Milburn turned professional in 1974. His string of 31 consecutive victories was ended by Leon Coleman in a 50-meter race in April. Milburn regained his amateur status in 1980 and retired after the 1983 season.

Millard, Keith

FOOTBALL
b. March 18, 1962, Pleasonton, Calif.

Millard was named the 1989 National Football Conference defensive player of the year by United Press International after he had a league-leading 18 sacks. He also intercepted a pass and returned it 48 yards.

A 6-foot-5, 263-pound defensive tackle, Millard played at Washington State University and spent his first professional season with the Arizona Wranglers of the U.S. Football League in the spring of 1985. He then signed with the NFL's Minnesota Vikings and had 21½ sacks in his first two seasons there.

Hampered by injuries in 1987 and early in 1988, Millard came back to play the entire 1989 season for the Vikings. However, he suffered a serious knee injury in the fourth game of the 1990 season and missed all of 1991. The Vikings then traded him to the Seattle Seahawks, who released him after two games in 1992. He played two more games that season with the Green Bay Packers and spent 1993 with the Philadelphia Eagles before retiring.

Miller, Cheryl D.

BASKETBALL
b. Jan. 3, 1964, Riverside, Calif.

Known as "Silk" because of her smooth manner of play, Miller was the only athlete ever to be named to *Parade* magazine's high school All-American team four times, from 1979 through 1982. In her 90 games at Riverside, California, Polytechnic High School, she scored 3,026 points, an average of 32.8 per game, grabbed 1,353 rebounds, and had 368 assists. She once scored 105 points in a game and was the first female player to dunk a basketball in competition.

She never missed a beat at the University of Southern California, where she was a four-time All-American and three-time college player of the year, in 1984, 1985, and 1986. Miller won the Naismith Trophy and the Broderick Award as the nation's outstanding woman basketball player all three years, was the Wade Trophy winner in 1985, and shared with swimmer Tracy Caulkins the 1984 Honda Broderick Cup as the outstanding college athlete in any sport.

During her four years and 128 games at Southern Cal, she scored 3,018 points, grabbed 1,534 rebounds, and had 462 steals in 128 games. She led the school to NCAA championships in 1983 and 1984 and was named the tournament's outstanding player both years. After Southern Cal beat defending champion Louisiana Tech in the final game in 1983, losing coach Leon Barmore said of Miller, "She is one of the few women who can singlehandedly turn the tide of the game."

Miller starred for several U.S. national teams. She was the top scorer on teams that won gold medals in the 1983 Pan-American Games and the 1984 Olympics, and on the team that finished second in the 1983 World University Games. She was also on the team that won gold medals at the 1986 Good Will Games and the world basketball championship.

A severe knee injury that required surgery effectively ended her basketball career in 1987. She was unable to play on the Pan-American Games team that year, and she failed in the trials for the 1988 Olympic team. A sports information major, she went into broadcasting.
★ International Women's Sports Hall of Fame

Miller, Delvin G.

HARNESS RACING
b. July 5, 1913, Woodland, Calif.

Miller has been successful in every aspect of harness racing during his long career. He began driving horses on fairgrounds tracks in 1930, moved to the Grand Circuit in 1947, and was the nation's top money winner with $306,813 in 1950 and $567,282 in 1960.

In 1948, Miller established Meadowlands Farm in Pennsylvania and bought Adios as his breeding stallion. Adios became the leading sire in the history of the sport. His progeny won nearly $20 million during the next 20 years. Miller sold a two-thirds interest in Adios to Hanover Shoe Farms in 1955, but the stallion continued to stand at Meadow Lands.

Miller trained and drove two harness horse of the year winners, Stenographer in 1954 and Delmonica Hanover in 1974. Stenographer won 23 of 32 starts, earning $123,741.32 over a two-year period. Another Miller-trained horse, Arndon, set a world record for trotters in 1982 by running a 1:54 time trial.

The president of the Grand Circuit in 1967 and 1968, Miller founded the Meadows harness track near his breeding farm in 1963, when parimutuel betting was legalized in Pennsylvania.

Through 1993, Miller had recorded 2,434 victories, with $10,920,921 in winnings, since the U.S. Trotting Association began keeping records in 1939.
★ Hall of Fame of the Trotter

Miller, Ralph H.

BASKETBALL
b. March 9, 1919, Chanute, Kans.

Nicknamed "Cappy" in high school because he captained the basketball team for three years, Miller was also a football and track star. He went to the University of Kansas, starring as a football quarterback and as a forward on the basketball team, which he captained in his senior year, 1941–42.

After three years in the Army Air Corps during World War II, Miller coached East High School in Wichita, Kansas, for three years, winning 63 games and losing 17. His 1951 squad won the state championship. Miller then began his 38-year college coaching career at Wichita State University.

Miller brought with him the concept of the full-court zone press, later adapted by John Wooden at UCLA to help establish a dynasty. With the press creating turnovers all over the floor, his teams were taught to attack with a passing fast break. If they were unable to break, they generally went to a slow ball-control offense.

After 13 seasons at Wichita State, Miller went to Iowa in 1965 and then to Oregon State in 1971. He was noted for getting fine performances out of teams that weren't always long on talent. He had 33 winning seasons and went to the National Invitation Tournament five times and to the NCAA tournament nine times.

Miller was named consensus coach of the year in 1982 and the Associated Press coach of the year in 1983. He is one of a handful of coaches to have been named coach of the year twice in three different conferences: in the Missouri Valley Conference in 1954 and 1964, in the Big Ten in 1968 and 1970, and in the Pacific Ten in 1975 and 1981.

His teams won 657 games, seventh on the all-time list, and lost 382.
★ Basketball Hall of Fame

Miller, Shannon

GYMNASTICS
b. March 10, 1977, Edmond, Okla.

At the 1992 Olympics, Miller won five medals, two silver and three bronze, to lead all female athletes. Her silver medals came in the all-around and the balance beam, her bronzes in the floor exercise, uneven bars, and team competition.

Miller grew an inch to 4-foot-10 and went from 69 to 79 pounds before the 1993 world championships, where she won gold medals in the all-around, floor exercise, and uneven bars, despite the fact that she felt ill during her warmups and had serious problems with her balance beam routine during the all-around competition.

Miller, Walter [Walter Goldstein]

HORSE RACING
b. 1890, New York, N.Y.

Miller is known chiefly for riding an incredible 388 winners in 1906, a record that stood until 1952. The feat won him the nickname "Marvelous Miller" from the press. Among his victories that year was the Preakness, aboard Whimsical. There were usually just six races on a card at that time, and Miller won all six on three different occasions.

He was the jockey for Colin in most of that horse's races in 1907, when the two-year-old went undefeated. Miller won 334 races in 1907 and 194 in 1908, then began riding in Australia and Europe, where weight restrictions are less rigorous.

Later Miller suffered from mental illness and a variety of physical problems, and he disappeared from sight. It is not known when or where he died.
★ National Horse Racing Hall of Fame

Millner, Wayne V.

FOOTBALL
b. Jan. 31, 1913, Roxbury, Mass.
d. Nov. 19, 1976

A starter at end for Notre Dame from 1933 through 1935, Millner figured in one of college football's most dramatic plays as a senior when he caught a touchdown pass from Bill Shakespeare in the closing seconds to beat Ohio State, 18–13.

When the Boston Redskins of the NFL signed Millner in 1936, coach Ray Flaherty said he'd resign if the team didn't win the championship. They lost to the Green Bay Packers in the title game that year, but the following year they moved to Washington and beat the Chicago Bears, 28–21, for the championship. Millner played a big role in the victory, catching touchdown passes of 55 and 78 yards from Sammy Baugh.

Millner entered the Navy in 1942. He returned to the Redskins for one final season in 1945. During his seven years, he caught 124 passes for 1,578 yards, a 12.7 average, and 12 touchdowns. He was a ferocious blocker and a fine defensive player as well as a sure-handed receiver.
★ Pro Football Hall of Fame

Mills, Billy (William M.)

TRACK AND FIELD
b. June 30, 1938, Pine Ridge, S.Dak.

Mills grew up on the Oglala Sioux Reservation and went to Haskell Institute in Kansas after being orphaned at age 12. He began running to get into shape for boxing, but after losing a couple of fights, he decided to concentrate on running for its own sake.

He ran distance events at the University of Kansas, graduating in 1962, then joined the Marine Corps. Mills returned to competition in 1964 and scored one of the biggest upsets in Olympic history. He led the 10,000-meter run in the home stretch but was passed by Mohamed Gamoudi of Tunisia and world record holder Ron Clarke of Australia, and seemed to be out of the running.

However, Mills turned on a tremendous sprint, passed the two leaders with about 50 yards to go, and won by 3 yards in an Olympic record 28:24.4. He said of his victory, "I'm flabbergasted. I can't believe it. I suppose I was the only person who thought I had a chance." A virtual unknown entering the Olympics, Mills was suddenly a hero as the first American ever to win a gold medal in the event.

Mills also ran fourteenth in the Olympic marathon. The following year, he set a world record of 27:11.6 in the 6-mile, winning the AAU championship in a rare photo-finish over Gerry Lindgren. He retired from competition after injuries kept him out of the 1968 Olympics.

★ National Track & Field Hall of Fame; Olympic Hall of Fame

Mills, Samuel D., Jr.

FOOTBALL
b. June 3, 1959, Neptune, N.J.

Although he is only 5-foot-9, which is usually considered much too short for a middle linebacker, the 225-pound Mills has played in four Pro Bowls and was named to *The Sporting News* all-pro team in 1991 and 1992.

Mills played football at Montclair State College in New Jersey and was signed by the NFL's Cleveland Browns as a free agent in 1981, but the Browns released him during training camp.

In 1982, he went to camp with the Toronto Argonauts of the Canadian Football League, again failing to make the squad. He finally caught on with the Philadelphia Stars of the U.S. Football League in 1983. Mills spent three seasons with the team, which moved to Baltimore in 1985. He intercepted 9 passes, returning them for 69 yards and 1 touchdown, had 14 quarterback sacks, and recovered 10 fumbles.

The USFL went out of business in 1986, and Mills joined the New Orleans Saints of the NFL. In nine years with the Saints, Mills has intercepted 3 passes, recorded 9½ sacks, and recovered 16 fumbles. He returned two of the recoveries for touchdowns.

Milstead, Century A.

FOOTBALL
b. Jan. 1, 1900, Rock Island, Ill.
d. June 1, 1963

Milstead got his unusual first name because of his birth date, since his father had the common misconception that the new century began in 1900, not 1901. After starring at tackle for Wabash, Indiana, College in 1921, he transferred to Yale.

The 6-foot-4, 220-pounder had to sit out a season before becoming eligible for football, but he got into a scrimmage against the varsity before the 1922 Princeton game and threw the ball carrier for consecutive losses of 5 and 10 yards, then was ordered to the sidelines so he wouldn't hurt anyone.

As a senior in 1923, Milstead helped lead Yale to an 8–0–0 record and was named an All-American.

★ College Football Hall of Fame

Milton, Tommy (Thomas W.)

AUTO RACING
b. 1893, Mt. Clemens, Mich.
d. July 10, 1962

Milton was the first driver to win the Indianapolis 500 twice, in 1921 and 1923. He was also the first to win the national driving championship two years in a row, in 1920 and 1921.

He began racing on dirt tracks in the Midwest in 1914 and won his first major victory at Providence, Rhode Island, in

1917. Milton won five of nine championship races in 1919 before suffering severe burns when his car burst into flames in a race at Uniontown, New Jersey.

In 1920, he not only won the driving championship, he set a new land speed record of 156.046 in a special Duesenberg that he helped to design. He retired from competition after the 1925 season. Milton became chief steward of the Indianapolis 500 in 1949.

★ Indianapolis Speedway Hall of Fame

Minds, Jack (John H.)
FOOTBALL
b. 1871, Clearfield County, Pa.
d. Dec. 31, 1963

Probably the first player ever to score on a place kick, Minds was a four-year starter at the University of Pennsylvania, from 1894 through 1897. The school won 55 of 56 games during that period.

Named an All-American halfback in 1897, the 5-foot-11, 175-pound Minds also played guard, tackle, end, and fullback at various times. He captained the 1897 team to a 15–0–0 record.

★ College Football Hall of Fame

Minoso, Minnie (Saturnino O. A.)
BASEBALL
b. Nov. 29, 1922, Havana, Cuba

Largely as a publicity stunt, Minoso in 1980 became the fourth person in major league history to play in four different decades. An attempt by the Chicago White Sox to activate him again in 1990 in order to make it a record five decades was not allowed by Commissioner Fay Vincent.

Minoso was much more than a publicity stunt as a player. He appeared in just nine games with the Cleveland Indians in 1949 and in eight games in 1951 before being traded to the White Sox. Minoso led the league with 31 stolen bases and 14 triples, finishing second in batting with a .326 average and in runs scored with 112.

A right-handed outfielder who occasionally played third base, the 5-foot-10, 175-pound Minoso was one of the leaders of the "Go Go Sox" who relied on speed rather power and perennially finished second to the New York Yankees through most of the 1950s. He led the AL in steals with 22 in 1952 and 25 in 1953, in triples with 18 in 1954 and 11 in 1956, in doubles with 36 in 1957, and in hits with 184 in 1960.

Minoso was traded back to Cleveland in 1958 but returned to the White Sox in 1960. He played for the NL's St. Louis Cardinals in 1962 and with the AL's Washington Senators in 1963.

The White Sox rehired him as a player-coach in 1964. He retired as a player after that season but remained with the team as a coach. Minoso was reactivated as a player for three games in 1976 and for two games in 1980.

In 1,835 games, Minoso batted .298 with 1,963 hits, including 336 doubles, 83 triples, and 186 home runs. He stole 205 bases, scored 1,136 runs, and had 1,023 RBI.

Mitchell, Bobby (Robert C.)
FOOTBALL
b. June 6, 1935, Hot Springs, Ark.

Mitchell was a running back at the University of Illinois and in his first three NFL seasons, with the Cleveland Browns. The 6-foot-0, 195-pounder had sprinter speed and was a threat to score every time he touched the ball. He had a 98-yard kickoff return as a rookie in 1958, and the following year he returned a punt 78 yards for a touchdown and had 232 yards rushing in one game.

The Browns traded him to the Washington Redskins in 1962 for the draft rights to Ernie Davis of Syracuse University. Mitchell became the first black star for Washington, the last NFL team to be integrated.

Moved to wide receiver, Mitchell led the league in receptions with 72 and reception yardage with 1,384 yards in his first season with the Redskins. He caught 58 or more passes each of the next five years. Mitchell retired after catching only 14 passes in 1968.

An All-Pro in 1962 and 1964, Mitchell played in four Pro Bowls. During his career, he caught 521 passes for 7,954 yards, a 15.3 average, and 65 touchdowns; rushed 513 times for 2,735 yards, a 5.3 average, and 18 touchdowns; returned 102 kickoffs for 2,690 yards, a 26.4 average, and 5 touchdowns; and ran back 69 punts for 699 yards, a 10.1 average, and 3 touchdowns.

★ Pro Football Hall of Fame

Mitchell, Kevin D.

BASEBALL
b. Jan. 3, 1962, San Diego, Calif.

A tremendously powerful right-handed hitter, the 5-foot-11, 210-pound Mitchell was named the NL's most valuable player in 1989, when he batted .291 and led the league with 47 home runs, 125 RBI, and a .635 slugging percentage.

He helped take the San Francisco Giants to the Western Division title that year and hit .353 with two home runs, seven RBI, and five runs scored in their five-game victory over the Chicago Cubs in the league championship series. The Giants lost the World Series in four games to the Oakland Athletics, although Mitchell hit .294 with one home run.

Mitchell entered the major leagues with the New York Mets late in the 1984 season and spent all of 1985 with the Mets, playing the outfield, shortstop, third base, and first base. The Mets traded him to the San Diego Padres in 1986, and the Padres traded him to San Francisco in midseason.

After splitting his time between the outfield and third base, Mitchell became a full-time outfielder in 1990, when he hit .290 with 35 home runs and 93 RBI. An injury limited him to 113 games in 1991, but he still hit 27 home runs and drove in 69 runs.

He missed much of the 1992 season with an injury after being traded to the AL's Seattle Mariners. Mitchell joined the Cincinnati Reds in 1993 and had two fine seasons with them, despite injuries that limited his playing time.

Through the 1994 season, Mitchell had a .286 average with 1,070 hits in 1,088 games, including 201 doubles, 24 triples, 220 home runs, 582 runs scored, and 689 RBI.

Mix, Ronald J.

FOOTBALL
b. March 10, 1938, Los Angeles, Calif.

A unanimous choice as an offensive tackle on the all-time American Football League team chosen in 1969, Mix was surprisingly fast for a 6-foot-4, 255-pound player. He was often able to make his initial block at the line of scrimmage and then get downfield to make another block in the secondary. When his San Diego Charger teammate Paul Lowe ran 56 yards for a touchdown in the 1963 AFL championship, Mix took out three Boston Patriot defenders to pave the way.

After starting at the University of Southern California for three years, Mix joined the Chargers in 1960, the AFL's first season. The team was then in Los Angeles, but it moved to San Diego in 1961.

Mix was named to the All-AFL team nine years in a row, from 1960 through 1968. He retired after the 1969 season but returned to play a final season with the Oakland Raiders in 1971. Christened "the Intellectual Assassin" by sportswriters because he was intelligent and articulate, Mix was called for holding only twice during his 11-season career.

★ Pro Football Hall of Fame

Mize, Johnny (John R.)

BASEBALL
b. Jan. 7, 1913, Demorest, Ga.
d. June 2, 1992

Asked to name the ideal designated hitter, long-time manager Ralph Houk picked Johnny Mize without a moment of thought. A left-handed hitter, the 6-foot-2, 215-pound Mize was nicknamed the "Big Cat," but not for his agile fielding. He got the nickname from a teammate who saw him lying, half asleep, in the sun before a game. The teammate commented, "He looks just like a big cat."

Mize joined the NL's St. Louis Cardinals as a first baseman during the 1936 season. He led the league with 16 triples and a .614 slugging percentage in 1938, when he batted .337 with 27 home runs and 102 RBI.

In 1939, Mize was the league leader with 28 home runs, a .349 batting average, and a .626 slugging percentage. He led in home runs with 43, RBI with 137, and slugging with a .636 percentage in 1940, when he batted .314.

After hitting 39 doubles to lead the league in 1941, Mize was traded to the New York Giants. He led the league with 110 RBI and a .521 slugging percentage in 1942 and then spent three years in the service during World War II.

When he returned to the Giants in 1946, Mize became the only player ever to hit more than 50 home runs while striking out fewer than 50 times. His 51 home runs, 137 runs scored, and 138 RBI led the league, and he had only 42 strikeouts. After leading the league in home runs for a fourth time with 40 in 1948, Mize was traded to the AL's New York Yankees during the 1949 season.

With the Yankees, Mize was usually platooned against right-handed pitchers, and he was often used as a pinch hitter. He hit 25 home runs with 72 RBI in only 90 games in 1950, his last big season. Mize retired after going to bat only 104 times in 81 games in 1953. During his 15-year career, he hit a home run in every major league park.

Mize had a career .312 average with 2,011 hits in 1,884 games, including 367 doubles, 83 triples, and 359 home runs. He scored 1,118 runs and drove in 1,337. ★ Baseball Hall of Fame

Mochtie, Dottie (Dorothy Pepper)

GOLF
b. Aug. 17, 1965, Saratoga Springs, N.Y.

The low amateur in the U.S. Women's Open in 1984, when she was a freshman at Furman University, Mochtie was a three-time All-American. She finished second in the 1985 NCAA championships and also became the first amateur to win a tournament on the LPGA Futures Tour that year.

After graduating in 1987, she spent a season on the Futures Tour and then joined the LPGA tour. Mochtie had just

two victories in her first four years as a pro, but in 1992 she won four tournaments, including the Dinah Shore, where she beat Juli Inkster in a sudden-death playoff. Mochtie was the top money winner with $693,335, the winner of the Vare Trophy with a 70.80 strokes per round average, and player of the year.

She won the World Championship of Women's Golf in 1993 with a 283, 5 under par.

Modzelewski, Dick (Richard)

FOOTBALL
b. Feb. 16, 1931, West Natrona, Pa.

The 6-foot-2, 260-pound Modzelewski was nicknamed "Little Mo" only because his older brother, Ed, was known as "Mighty Mo." Modzelewski started at tackle for the University of Maryland for four seasons and was an All-American and winner of the Outland Trophy as the nation's outstanding college lineman in 1952.

He played defensive tackle for the Washington Redskins in 1953 and 1954, then signed a contract with the Calgary Stampeders of the CFL. However, the Stampeders and Redskins reached an agreement that allowed Modzelewski to stay in Washington.

"Little Mo" went to the Pittsburgh Steelers in 1956, played for the New York Giants from 1956 through 1963, and then joined the Cleveland Browns. He retired after the 1966 season.

Modzelewski, who once started 180 consecutive games, played for two NFL champions, the 1956 Giants and the 1964 Browns. After retiring, Modzelewski served as a scout, defensive line coach, and defensive coordinator for several NFL teams. He was interim coach of the Cleveland Browns for part of the 1977 season.

Moffat, Alexander

FOOTBALL
b. 1862
d. Feb. 23, 1914

Moffat was never named an All-American simply because he played at Princeton from 1881 through 1883, before there were All-American teams. In an era when kicking was preeminent, he was the best kicker in football. Amos Alonzo Stagg credited him with inventing the spiral punt in 1881, and Moffat could also drop-kick with either foot.

In a 26–7 win over Harvard in 1883, Moffat kicked four field goals, two with his left foot and two with his right foot. He also kicked a conversion after a touchdown. Moffat kicked 16 field goals and 7 extra points that season, in addition to scoring 7 touchdowns, as he captained Princeton to a 7–1–0 record. During his three seasons, he had a total of 36 field goals.

★ College Football Hall of Fame

Molitor, Paul L.

BASEBALL
b. Aug. 22, 1956, St. Paul, Minn.

For years, the 6-foot, 185-pound Molitor was recognized as a very good baseball player. After he was named most valuable player in the 1993 World Series, people suddenly began to think he might well be a future member of the Hall of Fame.

Molitor joined the AL's Milwaukee Brewers in 1978 and hit .273 in 125 games, playing second base, third base, and shortstop. After hitting .322 in 1979 and .304 in 1980, he spent much of the 1981 season on the disabled list but came back to lead the league with 136 runs scored in 1982, when he batted .302. Molitor hit .316 with two home runs, four runs scored, and five RBI when the Brewers beat the California Angels in a five-game league championship series, and he had a .355 average with five runs and three RBI in their seven-game loss to the St. Louis Cardinals in the World Series.

In 1983, Molitor settled in at third base for the Brewers and spent most of the next seven seasons at that position. He had his best year in 1987, when he hit .353 and led the league with 41 doubles and 114 runs scored.

Molitor moved to first base in 1991, when his 133 runs, 216 hits, and 13 triples led the league. He hit .325 that season and .320 in 1992 and then went to the Toronto Blue Jays as a free agent. Molitor responded with a .332 average, 121 runs, a career-high 22 home runs, 111 RBI, and 22 stolen bases during the regular season.

Against the Philadelphia Phillies in the World Series, Molitor played third base and first base and was Toronto's designated hitter at various times. He got 12 hits in 24 at-bats, scored 10 runs, and drove in 8 runs. He singled in the bottom half of the ninth inning in the sixth and final game of the Series and scored the winning run on Joe Carter's homer.

Through 1994, Molitor had a .307 average with 2,647 hits in 2,121 games, including 472 doubles, 95 triples, 196 home runs, 454 stolen bases, 1,482 runs scored, and 976 RBI.

Molter, Willie (William Jr.)

HORSE RACING
b. 1910, Fredericksburg, Tex.
d. April 2, 1960

Originally a quarter horse jockey, Molter outgrew that occupation and became a trainer in 1935. He led the nation in winners saddled four consecutive years, from 1946 through 1949, setting a record of 155 in 1947, and he led trainers in winnings in 1954, 1956, 1958, and 1959.

Molter trained Determine, who won the 1954 Kentucky Derby, and Round Table, horse of the year in 1958. During his career, he saddled 2,160 winners and won $11,983,635 in purses.

★ National Horse Racing Hall of Fame

Molyneux, Tom

BOXING
b. March 27, 1784
d. Aug. 4, 1818

The first American to fight for the London Prize Ring championship, Molyneux was a slave who was reportedly given his freedom after winning a match on which his owner, Algernon Molyneux, had placed a large bet. He went to New York City, where he worked on the docks for several years.

Molyneux sailed to England in 1809 to become a professional prize fighter. In London, he met another black American, Bill Richmond, a former boxer who became his trainer. After victories over Bill Burrows and Tom Blake, Molyneux met the British champion, Tom Cribb, on December 18, 1810. He seemed to be winning handily, and in the 23rd round he apparently knocked out Cribb. However, Cribb's corner claimed he had been fouled, and the long argument that ensued gave the champion a chance to regain his senses.

In the 30th round, Molyneux again knocked Cribb down, but Molyneux slipped and banged his head against a ring post. Both fighters were unconscious for some time. After they were revived, they fought on until Cribb won on a knockout in the 33rd round.

It was discovered later that Molyneux had fractured his skull. He and Cribb fought again on September 28, 1811. Cribb broke Molyneux's jaw in the 10th round and knocked him out in the 11th. Molyneux had four more fights in the next two years, winning two while losing one and drawing one.

While giving sparring exhibitions during a tour of Ireland in 1818, Molyneux became seriously ill as the result of tuberculosis and heavy drinking. He was taken in by the black members of a British Army regiment stationed in Galway, and he died in their barracks.

Monk, Arthur

FOOTBALL
b. Dec. 5, 1957, White Plains, N.Y.

A running back at Syracuse University, Monk was drafted by the Washington Redskins in the first round of the 1980 NFL draft. The 6-foot-3, 210-pounder was moved to wide receiver.

Monk went on to set a record for career receptions with 934 for 12,607 yards, a 13.5 average, and 68 touchdowns. He led the league in 1984 with 106 catches, a record at the time, for 1,372 yards and 7 touchdowns.

An All-Pro in 1984 and 1985, Monk played in three Super Bowls. He caught only one pass for 28 yards in Washing-ton's 38–9 loss to the Oakland Raiders after the 1983 season, and he caught one pass for 40 yards when the Redskins beat the Denver Broncos, 42–10, for the 1987 NFL championship.

In Washington's 37–24 Super Bowl victory over the Buffalo Bills after the 1991 season, Monk had 7 receptions for 113 yards, a 16.1 average.

Monroe, Earl (Vernon Earl)

BASKETBALL
b. Nov. 21, 1944, Philadelphia, Pa.

"Earl the Pearl" had one of the most spectacular seasons in college basketball history at Winston-Salem State in 1966–67. He scored 1,329 points, averaging 44.5 per game, both small-college records. An uncanny shooter when he was on a hot streak, he made 22 of 24 field goal attempts and 14 of 16 free throws in a game against North Carolina College that season. His school won the NCAA College Division championship, and Monroe was named the division's player of the year.

During his four-year college career, he scored 2,935 points, averaging 26.6 a game. A fast, inventive, acrobatic player, Monroe originated the 360-degree spin move to the basket while flying down the free throw lane.

A 6-foot-3, 185-pound guard, Monroe was the number-one draft pick of the NBA's Baltimore Bullets in 1967 and was the league's rookie of the year, averaging 24.3 points a game. He averaged more than 21 points a game in each of the next three seasons, then was traded to the New York Knicks during the 1971–72 season.

Knee problems limited him to just 63 games that year, and he had difficulty fitting into the Knicks' team concept at first, but in 1972–73 he was an important member of New York's NBA championship team, averaging 15.5 points and using his quickness to become a good defender and ball stealer. He remained with the Knicks through the 1979–80 season, then retired because of recurring knee problems. In 926 NBA games, he scored 17,454 points, 18.8 per game.

★ Basketball Hall of Fame

Montana, Joseph C., Jr.

FOOTBALL
b. June 11, 1956, Monongahela, Pa.

Considered by some the greatest professional quarterback of all, Montana had a strange career at Notre Dame. Not always a starter, he won acclaim for his ability to come off the bench and rally the team to victory, most notably in the 1979 Cotton Bowl, when he brought Notre Dame back from a 23-point deficit in the fourth quarter to win, 35–34.

A third-round choice of the San Francisco 49ers in the 1979 NFL college draft, Montana took over as the starter in his second season and led the league in completion percentage with 64.5. The following year, he helped lead the 49ers to the Super Bowl and was its most valuable player, completing 14 of 22 passes for 157 yards and a touchdown. He also ran for a touchdown in San Francisco's 26–21 win over the Cincinnati Bengals.

In Super Bowl XIX, after the 1984 season, Montana was again MVP. He completed 24 of 35 passes for 331 yards and two touchdowns and ran five times for 59 yards and another touchdown as the 49ers overwhelmed the Miami Dolphins, 38–16.

The 49ers also won Super Bowls XXIII and XXIV, after the 1988 and 1989 seasons. Montana was MVP in the latter game, when he completed 22 of 29 pass attempts for 297 yards and five touchdowns. He is the only player to be named Super Bowl MVP three times, and he was one of only five to play on all four San Francisco champions.

A very mobile quarterback with an uncanny ability to complete passes while on the run, Montana didn't often put up really big numbers because the 49ers complemented their passing with a strong running attack. However, he led the NFL in completion percentage five times, with a high of 70.2 percent in 1989. He was also the leader in touchdown passes with 17 in 1982 and 31 in 1987; in yards per attempt with 9.12 in 1989; and in quarterback rating with 102.1 in 1987 and a record 112.4 in 1989.

Montana was named the NFL player of the year by *The Sporting News* in 1989, and he was the Associated Press athlete of the year in 1989 and 1990. He was selected for seven Pro Bowls.

An elbow injury sidelined him for the entire 1991 season and most of the 1992 season, when he returned for just one game. He was traded with defensive back David Whitmore to the Kansas City Chiefs for two draft choices in April 1993.

Through the 1994 season, Montana had completed 3,409 of 5,391 passes, 63.2 percent, for 40,551 yards and 273 touchdowns. He also ran 414 times for 1,595 yards, a 3.9 average, and 20 touchdowns.

Montgomery, Jim (James P.)

SWIMMING
b. Jan. 24, 1955, Madison, Wis.

At the 1976 Olympics, Montgomery won his semifinal heat of the 100-meter freestyle in 50.39, setting a world record, and in the final he became the first swimmer to break the 50-second barrier, doing a 49.99 to win the gold medal. He won two other gold medals as a member of the 4 x 200-meter freestyle and the 4 x 100-meter medley relay teams, and he also took a bronze in the 200-meter freestyle.

Swimming for the University of Indiana, Montgomery won the NCAA 200-yard freestyle in 1974 and 1976. He was the AAU outdoor 100-meter freestyle champion in 1973 and 1975, and he won the indoor 100- and 200-meter events in 1976.

Montgomery won gold medals in the 100- and 200-meter freestyles at the 1973 world championships, where he also swam on three winning relay teams.

Moon, Warren

FOOTBALL
b. Nov. 18, 1956, Los Angeles, Calif.

Moon wasn't drafted by any NFL team after his senior year at the University of Washington, and he signed with the Edmonton Eskimos of the Canadian Football League in 1978. A 6-foot-3, 212-pound quarterback, Moon took Edmonton to six consecutive Grey Cup championships, from 1978 through 1983. He completed 1,369 of 2,382 attempts for 21,228 yards and 144 touchdowns.

In 1984, he went to the NFL's Houston Oilers and immediately became the team's starting quarterback. To use Moon's passing skills to the utmost, coach Jerry Glanville in 1986 installed an offense called the "run and shoot," which generally uses four wide receivers and no tight end.

Moon led the NFL with 584 attempts, 362 completions, 4,689 yards, and 33 touchdown passes in 1990. The following year, he set records with 655 attempts and 404 completions, also leading the league with 4,690 yards and 21 interceptions.

Because of a broken collarbone suffered in the first game of the 1992 season, Moon missed five games that year, and he was briefly benched after the Oilers won only one of their first five games in 1993. Moon then led the team to 11 consecutive victories and a berth in the playoffs, where Houston was eliminated by the Kansas City Chiefs. He joined the Minnesota Vikings as a free agent in 1994.

Through 1994, Moon had completed 3,003 of 5,147 passes for 37,949 yards and 214 touchdowns during his NFL career. He had also rushed for 1,396 yards on 391 carries, a 3.6 average, and 20 touchdowns.

Moore, Archie (Archibald Lee Wright)
BOXING
b. Dec. 13, 1913, Benoit, Miss.

Mystery surrounds Moore's early career and even his birthdate. He claimed to have been born in 1916; his mother said it was 1913. Most authorities accept his mother's version. Whichever is correct, he was the oldest fighter ever to hold a world championship.

His first recorded fight was a 2nd-round knockout of Piano Man Jones in 1935. Moore built up an impressive record, including a lot of knockouts, as a middleweight and light heavyweight during the next ten years, and he briefly held the California middleweight title in 1943.

After World War II, Moore was generally considered a light heavyweight contender, but he couldn't get a title fight until he began a public relations campaign on his own behalf. On December 17, 1952, Moore won a 15-round decision over Joey Maxim in St. Louis to win the championship.

He defended the title four times, twice against Maxim, and then tried for the heavyweight title against Rocky Marciano on September 21, 1955. Marciano knocked him out in the 9th round. After Marciano retired, Moore fought Floyd Patterson for the vacant heavyweight championship on November 30, 1956, but was knocked out in the 5th round.

The National Boxing Association withdrew recognition of Moore's title in 1960 and awarded it the following year to Harold Johnson. Other boxing authorities didn't follow suit because Moore had already beaten Johnson four times in five meetings. However, Johnson beat European champion Gustav Scholz in 1961, and both the New York State Athletic Commission and the European Boxing Union formally named him the titlist on February 10, 1962. At 46 or 49 years of age, Moore was no longer champion.

He had six more fights before retiring in 1965. In 234 recorded bouts, he knocked out 145 opponents, a record, and won 54 other fights by decision. He lost 26, 7 by knockout, and also fought 8 draws and 1 no-contest.
★ International Boxing Hall of Fame

Moore, Bernie H.
FOOTBALL
b. 1885, Jonesboro, Tenn.

A football and track star at Carson-Newman College in Tennessee, Moore graduated in 1917. He was football coach at Mercer College in Georgia from 1925 through 1927.

In 1935, Moore took over as football and track coach at Louisiana State University, and he was very successful in both roles. His football teams won 83 games, lost 39, and tied 6 in 13 seasons, but lost 3 straight in the Sugar Bowl: 3–2 to Texas Christian in 1936, 21–14 to

Santa Clara in 1937, and 6–0, again to Santa Clara, in 1938. The 1936 team won 9 regular season games and tied 1 without a loss.

Moore's track teams won 9 of the first 10 Southeastern Conference championships. In 1933, Moore drove five athletes in his car to Chicago, where his team won the NCAA outdoor championship. Moore left coaching in 1947 to become SEC commissioner.

★ College Football Hall of Fame

Moore, Dickie (Richard W.)

HOCKEY
b. Jan. 6, 1931, Montreal, P.Q.

Although he had chronic problems with both legs because of an accident suffered in childhood, Moore played in the NHL for 14 seasons and led the league in scoring twice.

He joined the Montreal Canadiens during the 1951–52 season but was little more than a supporting player on that star-laden team until the 1957–58 season. Rocket Richard and Jean Beliveau both missed much of the season with injuries, and Moore stepped forward to become a leader.

Playing the last five weeks with a cast on his wrist, he won the Ross Trophy as the league's scoring champion with 84 points. The following season, he set an NHL record with 96 points and was named first-team all-star left wing for the second year in a row.

Moore was traded to the Toronto Maple Leafs in 1964. After one season in Toronto he sat out a year, then went to the expansion St. Louis Blues for his final season. In 719 regular season games, he had 262 goals and 347 assists, with 46 goals and 64 assists in 135 playoff games. Moore tied an NHL playoff record with 6 points, on 2 goals and 4 assists, against Boston in a 1954 Stanley Cup game.

★ Hockey Hall of Fame

Moore, Elisabeth H.

TENNIS
b. March 5, 1876, Brooklyn, N.Y.
d. Jan. 22, 1959

Moore began playing competitive tennis in the 1890s, when women played best three-out-of-five sets in major tournaments, as men still do. She once won a marathon match, 4–6, 1–6, 9–7, 9–7, 6–3, and remarked afterward that her opponent "didn't have much strength left after the fourth set." The next day, she won another five-set match.

When the format was changed to best two-out-of-three for the U.S. national championship in 1902, Moore recorded that it was "to considerable expressed dissatisfaction of the leading women players, including myself."

Moore won national singles titles in 1896, 1901, 1903, and 1905. She teamed with Juliette P. Atkinson to win the women's doubles in 1896 and with Carrie B. Neely to win the title in 1903. Moore and Wylie C. Grant won the mixed doubles championship in 1902 and 1904.

★ International Tennis Hall of Fame

Moore, Lenny (Leonard E.)

FOOTBALL
b. Nov. 25, 1933, Reading, Pa.

A running back at Penn State, the 6-foot-1, 198-pound Moore was the first draft choice of the NFL's Baltimore Colts in 1956. He went on to a remarkable 12-year career with the Colts, playing both at running back and at flanker, and he was one of the very best at both positions.

Moore was named rookie of the year after leading the league in yards per rushing attempt, 7.5, with 649 yards and 8 touchdowns on just 86 carries. When the Colts won the 1958 NFL championship, Moore had 1,633 combined yards, scored 14 touchdowns, and was named an All-Pro for the first time. In the overtime 23–17 championship win over the New York Giants, he caught 6 passes for 101 yards.

In 1961, Moore was moved from flanker to split end, and his production dropped. Injuries limited him to only seven games in 1963, but he rebounded with one of his finest seasons in 1964, when he set a record by scoring 20 touchdowns.

An All-Pro from 1958 through 1961

and in 1964, Moore played in seven Pro Bowls. He retired after the 1967 season with 363 receptions for 6,039 yards, a 16.6 average, and 42 touchdowns. He carried the ball 1,069 times for 5,174 yards, a 4.8 average, and 63 touchdowns, and he also returned 49 kickoffs for 1,180 yards, a 24.1 average, and 1 touchdown.

★ Pro Football Hall of Fame

Mora, Jim (James E.)

FOOTBALL
b. May 24, 1935, Glendale, Calif.

A tight end at Occidental College in California, Mora played three years of service football after graduating and then became an assistant coach at his alma mater in 1960. He moved up to head coach four years later.

Mora, who received a master's degree in education in 1967, left Occidental after compiling an 18–9 record in three seasons and served as an assistant coach at several colleges until 1978, when he became defensive line coach for the NFL's Seattle Seahawks.

When the U.S. Football League was organized in 1983, Mora was named head coach of the Philadelphia Stars, who moved to Baltimore in 1985. He guided the team to a 48–13–1 record and two USFL championships. Mora was named coach of the year in 1984.

The league folded after the 1985 season, and Mora took over the NFL's New Orleans Saints. After going 7–9–0 in his first year, Mora guided the Saints to a 12–3–0 record and the first playoff appearance in the team's history. He won the NFL coach of the year award for that accomplishment.

A conservative coach who believes in a running game and defense, Mora has been criticized by some despite his fine overall record, because his New Orleans teams have had no success in post-season play. But every time there are reports that he might be fired, there are also reports that several other NFL teams are waiting eagerly to hire him.

Through 1994, Mora had a 78–49–0 regular season record with the Saints for a .614 winning percentage. His overall professional record was 119–61–1.

Moran, Uncle Charley (Charles B.)

FOOTBALL
b. Feb. 22, 1879, Nashville, Tenn.
d. June 13, 1949

Moran played football for the University of Tennessee in 1897 but left after one year to go to Bethel College, where he coached football as well as played it. After graduating, he became an assistant to Pop Warner at Carlisle Indian Institute and played minor league baseball.

In 1903, Moran joined the NL's St. Louis Cardinals as a pitcher but hurt his arm after appearing in just three games. He returned to the Cardinals as a catcher in 1908, when he played in 21 games.

Moran began a football coaching career in 1909 at Texas A & M, where he had a 38–8–4 record in six seasons while also working as an umpire in the minor leagues. He became an NL umpire in 1916 and left coaching until 1919, when he took over the "Praying Colonels" of Centre College. Centre had one of the greatest upsets in college football history in 1921, beating Harvard, 6–0. Moran's Centre teams had a 42–6–1 record in five seasons and went undefeated in 1919 and 1921.

At Bucknell, Moran had a 20–9–2 record from 1924 through 1926. He was co-coach with Ed Weir of the NFL's Frankford Yellowjackets in 1927 but left after the team went only 6–9–3. His final coaching stint was at Catawba College in South Carolina, where he had a 23–10–5 mark from 1930 through 1933.

Moran continued umpiring in the NL through the 1939 season, and he was chosen to work four World Series, in 1927, 1929, 1933, and 1938. He then retired to farming before dying of a heart attack.

Two of his Centre College players, Alvin "Bo" McMillin and Madison Bell, went on to become outstanding coaches. Moran had an overall college record of 122 wins, 33 losses, and 12 ties for a .766 winning percentage, twentieth best all-time.

Morenz, Howie (Howarth W.)

HOCKEY

b. Sept. 21, 1902, Mitchell, Ont.
d. March 8, 1937

His nicknames say a lot about Morenz. He was known as the "Stratford Streak," the "Mitchell Meteor," the "Swift Swiss," and, finally, as the "Babe Ruth of Hockey." In 1950, he was voted Canada's greatest hockey player of the half century.

A teammate, Toe Blake, called him "a man with remarkable skills who laughed hard and played hard." A longtime opponent said of him, "When Howie skates full speed, everyone else on the ice seems to be skating backwards."

Morenz played amateur hockey in Stratford, where his family had moved when he was 14. After he scored nine goals in an amateur game, the Montreal Canadiens gave him a $1,000 signing bonus, and he joined them for the 1923–24 season. He scored three goals in the first game of the Stanley Cup semifinals and added another in the second game as the Canadiens beat the Calgary Tigers. They went on to win the cup with a two-game victory over Vancouver.

The league's top scorer in 1927–28 and 1930–31, Morenz won the Hart Trophy as most valuable player in 1928, 1931, and 1932. He was traded to Chicago in 1934 and went to the New York Rangers the following season. He was unhappy with both teams, and his performance showed it. Morenz returned to Montreal in 1936. He had scored 20 goals by January 28, 1937, when he collided with another player and suffered four broken bones in his left leg and ankle.

Despondent because he would never play hockey again, Morenz had a nervous breakdown and died of a heart attack in the hospital less than six weeks after the injury. His funeral was held at center ice in the Montreal Forum. An estimated 25,000 fans showed up to pay their last respects.

Morenz scored 273 goals and had 197 assists in 550 regular season games, with 21 goals and 11 assists in 47 playoff games.

★ Hockey Hall of Fame

Morgan, Joe L.

BASEBALL

b. Sept. 19, 1943, Bonham, Tex.

Only 5-foot-7 and 160 pounds, Morgan was a good fielding second baseman with surprising power at the plate. He entered the major leagues with the NL's Houston Astros for brief trials in 1963 and 1964, then became a starter in 1965. He led the league with 97 walks that year.

After hitting a league-leading 11 triples in 1971, Morgan was traded to Cincinnati, where he became recognized as an outstanding player with the great "Big Red Machine" teams. Morgan led the NL with 115 walks and 122 runs scored in his first season with the Reds.

He led the league in walks again with 132 in 1975, when he batted .327, scored 107 runs, hit 17 home runs, and had 94 RBI to win the NL's most valuable player award. Morgan was the hero of Cincinnati's seven-game World Series victory over the Boston Red Sox. He singled with the bases loaded in the tenth inning to win the third game, 6–5, and his RBI single in the ninth inning won the seventh game, 4–3.

Morgan won his second straight MVP award in 1976, when he had his finest all-around season, batting .320 with a career high 27 home runs, leading the league in slugging with a .576 percentage, scoring 113 runs, and driving in 111. He batted .333 with 3 runs and 3 RBI when the Reds swept the New York Yankees in a four-game World Series.

Cincinnati traded Morgan back to Houston in 1980, and he went to the San Francisco Giants as a part-time player in 1981. He finished his career with the Philadelphia Phillies in 1982 and the AL's Oakland Athletics in 1983.

In 22 seasons, Morgan had 2,517 hits in 2,649 games, including 449 doubles, 96 triples, and 268 home runs. He stole 689 bases, scored 1,650 runs, and had 1,133 RBI.

★ Baseball Hall of Fame

Morley, William

FOOTBALL
b. 1879, N.Mex.
d. 1932

Columbia University dropped football in 1892. When the sport was revived in 1899, the school had an 8–3–0 record, including its first victory over Yale, led by the "chain lightning backfield" that had Morley and Harold Weekes at halfback. Morley was most noted because of his blocking for the speedy Weekes, but he was also a hard, slashing runner. He was named to Walter Camp's All-American team in 1900 and was a third-team selection in 1901.

★ College Football Hall of Fame

Morrall, Earl E.

FOOTBALL
b. May 17, 1934, Muskegon, Mich.

As the quarterback in Michigan State's multiple offense in 1954 and 1955, Morrall was noted for his clever ball-handling and intelligent play-calling. He was also a good runner on the split-T option play. Though not often called on to pass, he was exceptionally accurate; in 1955 he completed 42 of 68 attempts for 941 yards and 5 touchdowns.

Morrall also played defense as a senior and set a school record with a 90-yard return of a fumble for a touchdown. He led his team to a 9–1 regular season record and a last-second, 17–14 victory over UCLA in the 1956 Rose Bowl.

The first choice of the NFL's San Francisco 49ers in the 1956 college draft, Morrall was rarely a genuine starter during his 21 seasons in pro football, but he was one of the greatest backup quarterbacks in history.

He played for San Francisco in 1956, the Pittsburgh Steelers in 1957 and 1958, the Detroit Lions from 1958 through 1964, the New York Giants from 1965 through 1967, the Baltimore Colts from 1968 through 1971, and the Miami Dolphins from 1972 through 1976.

Filling in for the injured Johnny Unitas, Morrall was named the NFL's player of the year in 1968 after leading the Colts to the NFL championship. However, they lost, 16–7, to the New York

Jets in Super Bowl III. Morrall replaced Unitas again in Baltimore's 16–13 win over Dallas Cowboys in Super Bowl V.

When Miami starter Bob Griese was hurt during the 1971 season, Morrall guided the Dolphins to 12 of their wins in an unprecedented 17–0 season and was named American Football Conference player of the year.

During his professional career, Morrall completed 1,379 of 2,689 passes for 20,809 yards and 61 touchdowns.

Morris, Betty

BOWLING
b. May 10, 1948, Sonora, Calif.

The woman bowler of the decade for the 1970s, Morris won the 1973 WPBA National, the 1977 Women's Open, the WIBC all-events in 1976 and 1979, and the WIBC singles in 1979 and 1980.

Morris was named bowler of the year in 1974, when she entered 15 tournaments, won 3, and finished second in 8 others to earn $30,037, a record at the time. She was again bowler of the year and top money winner with $23,802 in 1977.

After a long slump during the 1980s, which she ascribed to the fact that she was working too hard at her real estate business, Morris returned to her previous form in 1987, when she earned $55,095, the second highest ever at the time, and she was selected bowler of the year for the third time.

Through the 1993–94 season, Morris was tied for sixth in career titles with 17 and was eleventh on the all-time earnings list with $335,417. She is the only woman ever to have bowled two perfect 300 games on the same day, on June 2, 1976, when she set a six-game record of 1,546 in the BPAA Women's Open.

★ WIBC Hall of Fame

Morris, Glenn E.

TRACK AND FIELD
b. June 18, 1912, Simla, Colo.
d. Jan. 31, 1974

Morris competed in just three decathlons during his brief career, but he won all three, set two world records, and earned an Olympic gold medal in the process.

After playing football and competing in track at Colorado State University, Morris became an assistant coach at the school in 1934 and began training for the decathlon. In April 1936, he won his first competition with a U.S. record of 7,575 points.

In June, Morris won the Olympic trials with a world record 7,880 points, and he went on to win the gold medal with another world record, 7,900 points. That record stood until 1950. He won the Sullivan Award as the outstanding amateur athlete of the year.

He retired from competition to become a radio announcer for NBC. Morris played Tarzan in the 1936 movie *Tarzan's Revenge,* with former Olympic swimmer Eleanor Holm as Jane. He also played professional football with the NFL's Detroit Lions in 1940.

Morris, Jack (John S.)

BASEBALL
b. May 16, 1955, St. Paul, Minn.

A battler who often wins games despite a relatively high ERA, the 6-foot-3, 210-pound Morris holds the AL record for most consecutive starts with 492. A right-hander, he played for Brigham Young University before entering professional baseball in 1976.

Morris was with the AL's Detroit Tigers for seven appearances in 1977 and was used mostly as a relief pitcher in 1978. After starting the 1979 season in the minor leagues, he rejoined the Tigers and had a 17–7 record.

In the strike-shortened 1981 season, Morris led the AL in victories with a 14–7 record. He helped lead the Tigers to the AL pennant in 1994, when he was 19–11, and he had a 2–0 record with a 2.00 ERA when the Tigers beat the San Diego Padres in a five-game World Series.

Morris led the AL with six shutouts and had a 21–8 record in 1986. He suffered from arm trouble in 1989, when he was 6–14, and he became a free agent after a 15–18 record in 1990.

The Minnesota Twins signed him in 1991, and Morris rebounded with an 18–12 record. He was 2–0 in the AL championship series and 2–0 with a 1.17 ERA in Minnesota's seven-game World Series victory over the Atlanta Braves.

Morris joined the Toronto Blue Jays as a free agent in 1991. He led the league in victories with a 21–6 record despite a 4.04 ERA, but the following season he was only 7–12, and Toronto released him. He joined the Cleveland Indians in 1994 and was released once more shortly before the players went on strike that season.

A pioneer in using the split-finger fastball, Morris often fools catchers as well as hitters with the pitch. He holds the AL record for most career wild pitches with 193.

Through 1994, Morris had a 254–186 record with 28 shutouts and a 3.90 ERA. He had struck out 2,478 hitters and walked 1,390 in 3,824⅔ innings.

Morrison, Ray (Jesse Ray)

FOOTBALL
b. Feb. 28, 1885, Switzerland County, Ind.
d. Nov. 19, 1982

The coach who created college football's first "aerial circus" at Southern Methodist University, Morrison played football at Vanderbilt from 1908 through 1911, then became a high school math teacher and coach.

When SMU opened in 1915, Morrison was the school's first football coach. His first stint wasn't successful. SMU won just 2 games while losing 13 and tying 2. After serving in the Army and filling in at Vanderbilt in 1918, Morrison returned to SMU as freshman coach in 1920 and became varsity coach again in 1922.

After a 6–3–1 record in his first season, SMU won all nine of its games in 1923, outscoring the opposition, 207 to 9. His 1926 team was also undefeated, winning eight and tying one, and his 1929 team won only six games but tied four without losing.

SMU astounded the East on October 6, 1928, by completing 16 of 30 passes in a 14–13 loss to Army. Army attempted only four passes. On the last play of the game, SMU's Redman Hume threw a completion to a wide-open Sammy Reed, but Reed fell down and didn't score. Despite the loss, Morrison's team had demonstrated that the pass could be an effective offensive weapon rather than a desperate tactic.

Morrison left SMU for Vanderbilt in 1935. He had three winning seasons in his first four years but resigned after a 2–7–1 record in 1939 and went to Temple, where he had just one winning season in five. Morrison finished his coaching career at Austin College from 1946 through 1950. His overall record was 143–108–27.

★ College Football Hall of Fame

Morrissey, John

BOXING, HORSE RACING
Feb. 12, 1831, Templemore, Ireland
d. May 1, 1878

Morrissey's family emigrated to Canada in 1834 and moved to Troy, New York, shortly afterward. As a teenager, he went to New York City and joined a political gang as a "shoulder hitter," earning a reputation for his fighting ability.

The gold rush lured Morrissey to California in 1851, and he learned something about the casino business as a faro dealer in San Francisco. He also had his first professional fight, against George Thompson on August 31, 1852. The ring was surrounded by Morrissey's armed backers, and Thompson deliberately lost on a foul in the 11th round.

Morrissey had another questionable victory in his next fight, against the English champion Yankee Sullivan on October 12, 1853. Sullivan was winning handily when a group of Morrissey supporters began rioting at ringside, threatening Sullivan. He left the ring and fought some of them, and was disqualified for not returning when the next round was called.

Morrissey's third and last formal match was against John Heenan on October 20, 1858. Heenan broke his hand on a ring post early in bout and was forced to concede in the 11th round, but he claimed the American championship after Morrissey's retirement.

In 1860, Morrissey invested his ring earnings in a gambling house in New York City. Four years later he established a horse track at Saratoga, New York, and he opened a luxurious casino there in 1867, turning Saratoga from a stylish spa into America's first gambling resort.

After serving as a U.S. congressman, Morrissey was elected to the State Senate in 1877, but he never took the seat because of illness brought on by his strenuous campaign.

Morrow, Bobby Joe

TRACK AND FIELD
b. Oct. 15, 1935, Harlingen, Tex.

The fast-starting Morrow was almost unbeatable in the short sprints from 1955 through 1958. As a student at Abilene Christian, he won the 1955 AAU 100-yard dash championship and had 30 consecutive victories in the event until losing to Dave Sime at the 1956 Drake Relays.

Morrow won the AAU 100-meter and the NCAA 100- and 200-meter dashes in 1956. He also finished first in both events at the Olympic trials, and at the Melbourne Olympics he became the first runner since Jesse Owens in 1936 to win gold medals in both short sprints and as a member of the 4 x 100-meter relay team that set a world record of 39.5 seconds. He tied the world 220-yard record of 20.6 seconds three times during the season.

In 1957, Morrow again won both NCAA short sprints. He tied the 100-yard dash record of 9.3 seconds three times that year and was the anchorman on the Abilene Christian 4 x 100-yard relay team that set a world record of 40.6 seconds. Morrow was given the Sullivan Award as the nation's outstanding amateur athlete of the year.

Morrow's last major victories came in the AAU short sprints in 1958. Injuries began to plague him after that, and he retired after finishing fourth in the 200-meter at the 1960 Olympic trials.

A devout Christian, Morrow dedicated himself to making the most of his God-given ability during his competitive years, getting 11 hours of sleep every night to preserve his strength. He felt that relaxation was the key to victory, and once said, "Whatever success I have had is due to being so perfectly relaxed that I can feel my jaw muscles wiggle."

★ National Track & Field Hall of Fame; Olympic Hall of Fame

Morton, Craig (Larry Craig)

FOOTBALL
b. Feb. 5, 1943, Flint, Mich.

As a quarterback at the University of California, Morton completed 355 of 641 passes for 4,501 yards and 36 touchdowns. He was a first-round draft choice of the NFL's Dallas Cowboys in 1965, and he became the team's starter in 1969.

The 1970 Cowboys went to the Super Bowl but lost, 16–13, to the Baltimore Colts. Morton became a backup to Roger Staubach in 1971 and was traded to the New York Giants in 1974.

He went to the Denver Broncos in 1977 and was named the American Football Conference player of the year after completing 131 of 254 passes for 1,929 yards and 14 touchdowns. The Broncos lost, 27–10, to the Dallas Cowboys in Super Bowl XII.

Morton retired after the 1982 season. During his 18 years in the NFL, he had 2,053 completions in 3,786 attempts for 27,908 yards and 183 touchdowns.

★ College Football Hall of Fame

Mosbacher, Bus (Emil Jr.)

YACHTING
b. April 1, 1922, Mt. Vernon, N.Y.

The son of a wealthy family, Mosbacher began sailboat racing as a young teenager. After graduating from Dartmouth College and serving in the Navy during World War II, he won eight consecutive world International Class championships, from 1947 through 1955.

Nicknamed "Bus" for "Buster," he skippered *Vim* in the 1958 America's Cup trials. *Vim* was a much slower boat than

Columbia, which became the defender, but Mosbacher's tactical skills made for close races.

As a result, the New York Yacht Club asked Mosbacher to skipper its 1962 America's Cup boat, *Weatherly.* Australia challenged with *Gretel,* generally considered the faster of the two, but Mosbacher won four of five races to retain the cup. He also skippered *Intrepid* to a four-race victory over Australia's *Dame Pattie* in 1967.

Mosbacher has said of match racing, "the idea is to find your opponent's Achilles' heel — and sink your teeth into it."

Mosconi, Willie (William J.)

BILLIARDS
b. June 27, 1913, Philadelphia, Pa.
d. Sept. 16, 1993

Mosconi's father owned a billiards parlor but wouldn't let his son play, so Willie began sneaking in at night when he was five years old, practicing with a broomstick and potatoes.

He entered his first major tournament in 1937 and won the world pocket billiards championship in league play in 1941 and in tournament play the following year. After losing the championship in a match with Andrew Ponzi in 1943, he regained the title by beating Ponzi in 1944 and held it until 1946, when Irving Crane won a world championship tournament.

Mosconi reclaimed the championship by beating Crane in a 1947 match. from 1950 through 1953 and in 1956 and 1957, Mosconi won annual tournaments to become world champion. He retired from competition after suffering a stroke in 1957.

In 1954, Mosconi ran a record 526 balls during an exhibition in Springfield, Ohio. He also set a record for highest run in a single game, 127 balls, in 1945, and his high grand tournament average of 18.34 balls in 1950 is the record for a 4½ by 9-foot table.

Even after his retirement from formal competition, Mosconi was an enthusiastic promoter of pocket billiards for the Brunswick company, giving exhibitions and appearing in televised matches. He was technical adviser for the 1961 movie *The Hustler*, which starred Paul Newman and Jackie Gleason.

Moseley, Mark D.

FOOTBALL
b. March 12, 1948, Lanesville, Tex.

Moseley, a place-kicker who attended Texas A & M University and Stephen F. Austin College, was drafted by the Philadelphia Eagles in the fourteenth round of the 1970 NFL draft. The Eagles released him after one season, and the Houston Oilers picked him up in 1971 but cut him early in the 1972 season.

After a year out of football, Moseley was signed by the Washington Redskins in 1974, and he handled their kicking through the 1986 season. He set an NFL record in 1983 by scoring 161 points, kicking 62 of 63 extra points and 33 of 47 field goal attempts.

In 17 NFL seasons, Moseley scored 1,382 points, converting 482 of 511 extra point attempts and hitting 300 of 457 field goal attempts. He ranks fifth all-time in scoring.

Moses, Edwin C.

TRACK AND FIELD
b. Aug. 31, 1958, Dayton, Ohio

When he entered Morehouse College in Atlanta in 1973 as an engineering and physics major, Moses was primarily a 400-meter-dash man who also ran the 110-meter high hurdles. Encouraged by his coach to point toward the 1976 Olympics, Moses began practicing the 400-meter hurdle event and became the first athlete to use just 13 strides between hurdles.

Moses ran the event for the second time in late March 1976. Four months later, he won an Olympic gold medal in a record 47.64 seconds; his margin of victory, 1.05 seconds, is the largest in Olympic history of the event.

That was no fluke. After the next two years, Moses was generally recognized as the greatest 400-meter hurdler ever. The 6-foot-2, 165-pounder lost to Harald Schmid of Germany on August 26, 1977. A week later, he beat Schmid by 15 yards,

beginning a 102-race winning streak, including 89 finals, that stretched through nearly 10 years and 22 countries.

Moses probably would have won a gold at the 1980 Olympics, but the U.S. boycotted the Moscow Games that year because of the Soviet invasion of Afghanistan. He did win a second gold in 1984, leading all the way. By that time, the 48-second barrier in the event had been broken 32 times, and Moses had done it 27 times. He also had the nine fastest clockings ever, including a world record 47.02 in August 1983. (That has since been broken by Kevin Young.)

The winner of the 1983 Sullivan Award as the nation's outstanding amateur athlete, Moses won world championships in 1983 and 1987 and was the national outdoor champion in 1976, 1977, 1979, 1981, 1983, and 1987. Because of injuries, he was out of competition for nearly two years, from August 1984 to June 1986. Moses retired after finishing third at the 1988 Olympics.
★ Olympic Hall of Fame

Motley, Marion

FOOTBALL
b. June 5, 1920, Leesburg, Va.

His family moved from Virginia to Canton, Ohio, when he was young, and Motley played high school football against Paul Brown's Massillon teams. After going to South Carolina State College and the University of Nevada at Reno, Motley entered the service and played for Brown with the Great Lakes Naval Training Station team that beat Notre Dame, 39–7, in 1945.

Motley rejoined Brown with the Cleveland Browns of the newly formed All-America Football Conference in 1946. The 6-foot-1, 238-pound fullback became a cornerstone in the Browns' powerful offense.

A strong blocker, sometimes called "Otto Graham's bodyguard" because of his ability to keep defensive linemen away from Cleveland's quarterback, Motley was also a fast, powerful runner who was often used on draw plays in the Browns' pass-and-trap offense. He was the leading rusher in the four-year history of the AAFC, gaining 3,024 yards on 489 carries, a 6.2-yard average.

Motley was also an excellent linebacker during his first two seasons with the Browns, but he became an offensive specialist when the two-platoon system was adopted in 1948.

The Browns joined the NFL in 1950, and Motley led the league with 810 yards on 140 carries. Knee injuries limited Motley's playing time during the next three years. After missing the entire 1954 season, he attempted to come back in 1955 but retired after carrying the ball just twice.

During his nine professional seasons, Motley rushed 828 times for 4,720 yards, a 5.7 average, and 31 touchdowns. He caught 85 passes for 1,107 yards, a 13.0 average, and 7 touchdowns. He also returned 48 kickoffs for 1,122 yards, a 23.4 average.

Motley and guard Bill Willis, also of the Browns, were the only two black players in the AAFC in 1946. That season, the Los Angeles Rams had Woody Strode and Kenny Washington, the first blacks to play in the NFL since 1933.

★ Pro Football Hall of Fame

Mourning, Alonzo

BASKETBALL
b. Feb. 8, 1970, Chesapeake, Va.

Very similar in style to the great Bill Russell, the 6-foot-10, 240-pound Mourning is an intimidating defensive center because of his size, reflexes, and leaping ability.

At Georgetown University, he averaged 16.7 points per game and led NCAA Division I schools with 169 blocked shots in 1988–89 and 160 in 1991–92. Mourning was chosen by the expansion Charlotte Hornets in the first round of the 1992 NBA draft. He was the second player selected.

Mourning was named to the league's all-rookie team in 1993. Through the 1993–94 season, he had scored 2,926 points in 138 NBA games, an average of 21.2, and he had 1,415 rebounds and 459 blocked shots.

Muldowney, Shirley (Roques)

DRAG RACING
b. June 19, 1940, Schenectady, N.Y.

Shirley Roques dropped out of high school at 17 to marry Jack Muldowney, an amateur hot rodder. She began drag racing for grocery money in a 1940 Ford coupe with a Cadillac engine. When she decided to become a professional drag racer in 1972, her marriage broke up.

Conrad "Connie" Kalitta, a colorful racer, became her agent and gave her the nickname "Cha Cha," which she didn't like. But with Kalitta's help, Muldowney became a top driver in "funny cars," which are dragsters with fiberglass bodies made to look like ordinary street cars.

In 1974, Muldowney moved into top fuel dragsters. Driving a hot pink car that became her trademark, she won three consecutive national events in 1977 and became the first woman to win the Winston world championship.

There were those who thought Kalitta, as her crew chief, was the main reason for her success, so Muldowney went off on her own. With her son, John, as a crew member, she won the 1980 Winston title. She was the first driver of either sex to win two world championships, and she won a third in 1982, when she also beat Kalitta to win the U.S. Nationals for the first and only time.

A movie about her life, *Heart Like a Wheel*, was produced in 1983, with Muldowney as creative consultant. The following year, she suffered terrible injuries when a tire blew while she was traveling 50 miles an hour. She spent 18 months in rehabilitation, learning to walk again, but she returned to drag racing in 1986.

Mulford, Ralph K.

AUTO RACING
b. 1884
d. Oct. 23, 1973

Mulford may have won the first Indianapolis 500, in 1911, but he didn't get credit for it. He was given the checkered flag before Ray Harroun, and he took three extra laps as a precaution. When he finished the third lap, Harroun was in the winner's circle, and Mulford's protests were largely ignored.

The following year, bonus money was offered to the first 12 finishers at Indy. Mulford was running tenth and last with more than 100 miles to go when Joe Dawson won the race. He was told he actually had to finish the 500 miles to collect the bonus money, so he took his time, at one point stopping to have a fried chicken dinner. Mulford finished the race nearly nine hours after it had started.

Known as the "Gumdrop Kid" because he ate gumdrops throughout his races, Mulford was the national driving champion in 1911 and 1915. A superb engineer, he dreamed of building his own passenger car but was swindled out of more than $200,000 in one attempt to form a manufacturing company. Mulford retired from racing on tracks after 1922 but for some years continued to compete in hill climbs. At one time he held the record for both the Mount Washington and Pikes Peak climbs.
★ Indianapolis Motor Speedway Hall of Fame

Muller, Brick (Harold P.)

FOOTBALL
b. June 12, 1901, Dunsmuir, Calif.
d. May 17, 1962

More than anyone, the 6-foot-2, 215-pound Muller brought West Coast football into national prominence. An end at the University of California, Muller was an outstanding pass receiver who could catch the much fatter ball of his time with one hand. He was also an outstanding passer.

In the 1921 Rose Bowl, when Muller was a sophomore, California was an underdog against unbeaten Ohio State. Muller caught five passes, had two interceptions, recovered three fumbles, and threw three completions in a 28–0 upset. He also got downfield under punts so fast that Ohio State couldn't return any kicks.

One of the passes he threw made Ripley's "Believe It or Not" newspaper series, which reported that it traveled 70 yards through the air. A sportswriter on the scene, however, said it went "only" 53 yards.

Muller and tackle Dan McMillan were the first California players to be named to the All-American team, in 1921, and Muller repeated in 1922 even though he missed much playing time because of an infected leg. A fine all-around athlete, Muller won a silver medal in the high jump at the 1920 Olympics.

He played for the NFL's first West Coast team, the Los Angeles Buccaneers, in 1926, and was an assistant coach at his alma mater while working for his medical degree. He was the head physician for the 1956 Olympic team.
★ College Football Hall of Fame

Mullin, Christopher P.

BASKETBALL
b. July 30, 1963, New York, N.Y.

The quintessential "gym rat," Mullin spent much of his boyhood practicing shooting and playing pickup games in gyms and on playgrounds. He grew into a 6-foot-7, 220-pounder who could make NBA three-point shots.

At St. John's University, Mullin set school records with 2,440 points, 211 steals, and an .848 free throw percentage. He was a consensus All-American in 1984–85, when he won the Wooden Award as the top college player of the year, and he was also voted player of the year by UPI and the U.S. Basketball Writers Association. As a college junior, he starred on the 1984 gold medal Olympic team.

In 1985, he joined the NBA's Golden State Warriors. He was named to the All-NBA team in 1992. Through the 1993–94 season, Mullin had scored 13,767 points in 628 regular season games, an average of 21.9. He had 2,917 rebounds, 2,486 assists, and 1,101 steals. In 33 playoff games, he scored 685 points, an average of 20.8.

Mullin was one of 11 NBA players chosen for the 1992 Olympic dream team, and he won his second gold medal.

Munn, Biggie (Clarence L.)
FOOTBALL
b. Sept 11, 1908, Crow Township, Minn.
d. March 18, 1975

An All-American guard and captain at the University of Minnesota in 1931, Munn served as an assistant coach at the school under Bernie Bierman for three years before becoming head coach at Albright College in Pennsylvania in 1935. He had a 13–2–1 record there in two seasons.

Munn then served as an assistant at Syracuse University in 1937 and at the University of Michigan from 1938 through 1945. He returned to Syracuse as head coach, winning four games and losing five, before taking over at Michigan State in 1946.

While other major colleges were adopting the T formation, Munn installed a multiple offense at Michigan State. His teams used the single wing along with the winged T and split T formations, keeping defenses constantly off balance.

Michigan State won all nine of its games in both 1951 and 1952, and the winning streak stretched to 28 in 1953 before a 6–0 upset by Purdue. Munn was voted coach of the year in 1952, when his team was ranked first in the country.

The school had joined the Big Ten Conference in 1949 but wasn't allowed to contend for the championship until 1953, when Michigan State and Illinois tied for the title. The conference voted to send Munn's team to the Rose Bowl, where it beat UCLA, 28–20.

Munn was named athletic director in 1954, and he resigned his coaching job. His record in seven seasons was 54–9–2.
★ College Football Hall of Fame

Munoz, Anthony (Michael Anthony)
FOOTBALL
b. Aug. 19, 1958, Ontario, Calif.

Considered by many the greatest tackle ever to play pro football, the 6-foot-6, 285-pound Munoz played at the University of Southern California, where he blocked for the 1979 Heisman Trophy winner Charles White.

The Cincinnati Bengals made him the third player chosen in the first round of the 1980 NFL draft. Munoz immediately became a starter, and he was named an All-Pro in his second season. He was also an All-Pro from 1984 through 1986 and in 1988, 1989, and 1991, and he was selected for the Pro Bowl nine times.

Because of a sprained shoulder and a knee injury, Munoz missed half of the 1992 season. As an unconditional free agent, he signed with the Tampa Bay Buccaneers in 1993. Munoz retired after that season to become a television analyst.

Munson, Thurman L.
BASEBALL
b. June 7, 1947, Akron, Ohio
d. Aug. 2, 1979

In 1976, Munson was formally named captain of the New York Yankees, the first player to hold the position since Lou Gehrig. He responded by batting .302 and driving in 105 runs to win the AL's most valuable player award. Munson hit .529 in the World Series, but the Yankees lost in four straight games to the Cincinnati Reds.

Munson joined the Yankees late in the 1969 season and was named rookie of the year in 1970, when he batted .302. The following year, he led the league's catchers in fielding percentage. From 1975 through 1977, Munson batted over .300 and had more than 100 RBI each year, becoming the first player to do that since Al Rosen in 1954.

When the Yankees beat the Dodgers in a six-game World Series in 1977, Munson batted .320 with four runs scored and three RBI. They repeated that feat in 1978, when Munson again hit .320, driving in seven runs and scoring five.

A three-time Gold Glove winner, Munson was killed when his twin-engine plane crashed while he was practicing takeoffs and landings.

Murdock, Margaret L. (Thompson)
SHOOTING
b. Aug. 25, 1942, Topeka, Kans.

When Murdock shot a 391 score to

win a gold medal in the small-bore rifle competition at the 1967 Pan-American Games, it was a historic occasion, though little noted by the media. Her score was a world record, and it marked the first time a woman ever surpassed the men's record in any sport. Murdock also won the gold medal in small-bore rifle at the 1975 Pan-American Games.

At the 1976 Olympics, Murdock and Lanny Bassham of the U.S. tied for first place in the small-bore three-position event. After examining the targets, judges determined that Bassham's shooting had been slightly better, and they decided to award him the gold medal, with Murdock taking the silver. Bassham was unhappy with the decision; at the medal ceremony he put his arms around Murdock and shared the victory platform with her while the national anthem was played.

A 1965 graduate of Kansas State University, Murdock is a registered nurse who specializes as an anesthesiology. She won the national women's small-bore three-position and prone position championships in 1969 and the prone position title in 1972. She also won the small-bore standing position event at the world championships in 1970, when she was four months pregnant.

★ International Women's Sports Hall of Fame

Murphy, Calvin J.
BASKETBALL
b. May 9, 1948, Norwalk, Conn.

After averaging an eye-opening 48.9 points a game for the Niagara University freshman team, the 5-foot-9, 165-pound Murphy was a three-year starter for the varsity, averaging 33.1 points, fourth best in NCAA Division I history.

Because of his size, he wasn't chosen until the second round of the 1970 NBA draft, by the San Diego Rockets, who moved to Houston in 1971–72. Very quick, Murphy was an excellent outside shot and an outstanding free throw shooter. He was named to the league's all-rookie team after averaging 15.8 points a game in 1970–71.

Murphy averaged 20.4 points a game

in 1973–74, the first of five seasons in which his average was above 20 points. His finest season was 1977–78, when he averaged 25.6 points a game. Murphy led the NBA in free throw shooting percentage with .958 in 1980–81, an NBA record, and .920 in 1982–83, his last season as a player.

His career free throw percentage of .892 is second only to Rick Barry in NBA history. In 1,002 regular season games, Murphy scored 17,949 points, an average of 17.9 per game, and had 4,402 assists and 1,165 steals. He added 945 points, 213 assists, and 79 steals in 51 playoff games.

★ Basketball Hall of Fame

Murphy, Charles C. ("Stretch")
BASKETBALL
b. April 10, 1907, Marion, Ind.
d. Aug. 24, 1992

One of college basketball's first really tall players, at 6-foot-6, Murphy had the defensive skill and rebounding ability to key the Purdue fast break, leading to some unusually high scores for the era, such as a 60–14 victory over Ohio State. He could also score. In the 1928–29 season, he set Western Conference (Big Ten) records with 26 points in a game and 143 for the conference season.

He was Purdue's first three-time All-American, from 1928 through 1930. In his senior year, he captained the team and, with sophomore guard John Wooden, led the school to an undefeated season and the Western Conference championship.

★ Basketball Hall of Fame

Murphy, Dale B.
BASEBALL
b. March 12, 1956, Portland, Oreg.

Nolan Ryan once said of Murphy, "I can't imagine that Joe DiMaggio was a better all-around player than Dale." The 6-foot-5, 215-pound Murphy was with the NL's Atlanta Braves as a catcher for brief periods in 1976 and 1977. He became a regular first baseman in 1978 and was moved to center field because of his speed in 1980.

Murphy was named the league's most

valuable player in 1982, when he batted .281 with 36 home runs, 113 runs scored, and a league-leading 109 RBI. He led the league in RBI again, with 121, and in slugging with a .540 percentage in 1983 to win the MVP award again. Murphy hit .302 that season with 36 home runs, 131 runs scored, and a career high 30 stolen bases.

In 1984 and 1985, Murphy won titles with 36 and 37 home runs, respectively. He also led the league in slugging with a .547 percentage in 1984, in runs with 118, and in walks with 90 in 1985.

Murphy's best home run year was 1987, when he hit 44 but failed to lead the league. During the 1990 season, he was traded to the Philadelphia Phillies. After missing most of the 1992 season with an injury, he was traded to the expansion Colorado Rockies. He retired on May 27, 1993.

In 2,180 games, Murphy had 2,111 hits, including 350 doubles, 39 triples, and 398 home runs, with 1,266 RBI, 1,197 runs scored, and 161 stolen bases. He won five consecutive Gold Glove Awards, from 1982 through 1986.

Murphy, Isaac [Isaac Burns]
HORSE RACING
b. April 16, 1861, Frankfort, Ky.
d. Feb. 12, 1896

The first jockey elected to the National Museum of Racing's Hall of Fame, Murphy won 628 of his 1,412 starts. His 44 percent victory rate has never been equaled.

His father died when he was young, and Murphy grew up with his mother and his grandfather, Green Murphy, whose name he took. He had his first race in 1878 and won his first major victory the following year, the Phoenix Hotel Stakes aboard Falsetto.

At the time, jockeys usually just ran their horses as fast as they could for the length of the race. Murphy was probably the first to hold his horse off the pace, conserving energy for a stretch run, and many of his victories were by narrow margins. One racetrack observer commented, "No man with a touch of heart disease should ever back his mounts."

Murphy won three Kentucky Derbies, aboard Buchanan in 1884, Riley in 1890, and Kingman in 1891. That record was tied by Earl Sande in 1930 and broken by Eddie Arcaro in 1948. He also took the American Derby four times in five years and the Latonia Derby five times, still a record for that race.

Murphy was the winning jockey in the most celebrated match race of the period, Salvator against Tenny at the Sheepshead Bay course on June 25, 1890. Each owner put up $5,000 for the winner-take-all race. Murphy, aboard Salvator, won by half a head over "Snapper" Garrison on Tenny.

When his career was at its peak, most jockeys were black, and they were usually paid flat fees for racing, though owners sometimes gave bonuses for important victories. As prize money increased and jockeys began to collect a share of the horse's winnings, whites began to take over the profession. During the early 1890s, Murphy found it harder to get rides. He also faced weight problems and alcoholism.

He died of pneumonia and is buried in Lexington, Kentucky, near the grave of the great thoroughbred, Man o'War.
★ National Horse Racing Hall of Fame

Murphy, Jimmy (James A.)
AUTO RACING
b. 1895, San Francisco, Calif.
d. Sept. 22, 1924

In a career that lasted only five years, Murphy established himself as one of the greatest drivers ever, winning 17 races and 2 national driving championships. He entered racing as Tommy Milton's riding mechanic in 1918 and drove in his first race in late 1919.

One of Murphy's biggest victories was the French Grand Prix in 1921, the year he won his first driving championship. It was the last time an American driver won a Grand Prix in an American-built car until Dan Gurney did it in 1968.

Murphy won the 1922 Indy 500 and finished third in both 1923 and 1924. After clinching his second driving championship in 1924, Murphy planned to retire from competition. However, he had promised the promoter of dirt track races in Syracuse, New York, to enter a race there in September. His car hit the wooden inside rail and a splinter pierced his heart, killing him instantly.

★ Indianapolis Motor Speedway Hall of Fame

Murray, Bill (William D.)

FOOTBALL

b. Sept. 9, 1908, Rocky Mount, N.C.

d. March 29, 1986

A halfback at Duke University, Murray graduated in 1931. He had a 69–9–3 record at the Methodist Children's home in Winston-Salem, North Carolina, from 1931 through 1940, and then went to the University of Delaware, where he coached undefeated teams in 1941 and 1942. After three years of military service, Murray had another undefeated season in 1946. His record was 49–16–2 in seven seasons at Delaware.

Murray returned to Duke as head coach in 1951, and his 1952 team won the Southern Conference championship. Duke moved into the new Atlantic Coast Conference in 1953 and won or shared six ACC titles through 1965. Murray retired with a 93–51–9 record after the 1965 season.

★ College Football Hall of Fame

Murray, Eddie C.

BASEBALL

b. Feb. 24, 1956, Los Angeles, Calif.

A switch hitter who throws right-handed, Murray entered professional baseball in 1973 and became a starter as an outfielder and first baseman with the AL's Baltimore Orioles in 1977, when he batted .283 with 27 home runs to win the league's rookie of the year award.

After playing first base and third base in 1978, Murray settled in permanently as a first baseman the following season. He led the AL with 22 home runs and 78 RBI in the strike-shortened 1981 season, when he batted .294.

Murray was with Baltimore until 1989, when he was traded to the NL's Los Angeles Dodgers. He had his best career average, .330, with the Dodgers in 1990, but he slipped to .260 in 1991.

The New York Mets signed Murray as a free agent in 1992. He became a free agent again, after hitting 27 home runs with 100 RBI in 1993, and joined the AL's Cleveland Indians.

Through 1994, Murray had a .288 batting average with 2,930 hits, including 511 doubles, 34 triples, and 458 home runs. He had scored 1,477 runs and driven in 1,738.

Murray, R. Lindley

TENNIS

b. Nov. 3, 1892, San Francisco, Calif.

d. Jan. 17, 1970

A 1914 graduate of Stanford University, Murray played tennis competitively only part-time because of his job as an engineer. A left-hander, he won the 1917 "Patriotic" tournament, a World War I substitute for the national championship.

In 1918, he began practicing just eight days before the reinstated national tournament and beat Bill Tilden in the final match. He was eliminated in the 1919 quarterfinals and played only rarely after that.

Tall and slender at 6-foot-1½ and 155 pounds, Murray was a strong, accurate volleyer who liked to rush the net behind his sharp-breaking serve.

★ International Tennis Hall of Fame

Musial, Stanley F.

BASEBALL

b. Nov. 21, 1920, Donora, Pa.

As a boy, the left-handed Musial dreamed of becoming a major league pitcher. He signed his first professional contract with the St. Louis Cardinals in 1938 and pitched in the minor leagues, occasionally playing the outfield, until he injured his left arm late in the 1940 season.

Moved permanently to the outfield, he came up to the Cardinals late in the 1941 season and batted .426 in 12 games. The following year, he became the team's starting left fielder, and he batted

315. It was the first of 16 consecutive seasons in which he hit over .300.

Musial led the league in 1943 with a .357 average, 220 hits, 48 doubles, 20 triples, and a .562 slugging percentage to win the NL's most valuable player award. He was the league leader with 197 hits, 51 doubles, and a .549 slugging percentage in 1944, when he batted .347.

After serving in the Navy in 1945, Musial returned to the Cardinals to win another batting title with a .365 average. He also led with 124 runs, 228 hits, 50 doubles, 20 triples, and a .587 slugging percentage to win his second MVP award.

In 1948, Musial changed to an odd "peek-a-boo" batting stance, with his back almost to the pitcher and his bat held straight up. It increased his power without hurting his average. Musial's previous home run high was 19 in 1947; from 1948 through 1955, he hit 30 or more home runs six times.

Musial won four batting titles in the five years from 1948 through 1952, hitting .376 in 1948, .346 in 1950, .355 in 1951, and .338 in 1952. He led the league in runs scored with 135 in 1948, 124 in 1951, 105 in 1952, and 120 in 1954; in hits with 230 in 1948, 207 in 1949, and 194 in 1952; in doubles with 46 in 1948, 41 in 1949, 42 in 1952, 53 in 1953, and 41 in 1954; in triples with 18 in 1948, 13 in 1949, and 12 in 1951; in RBI with 131 in 1948 and 109 in 1956; in walks with 105 in 1953; and in slugging percentage with .702 in 1948, .596 in 1950, and .538 in 1952.

The league's MVP for a third time in 1948, Musial frequently played first base from that year on, and in 1957 he became a full-time first baseman, though he moved back to the outfield in 1959. He won his seventh and last batting title with a .351 average in 1957. He retired after batting .255 in 1963.

Nicknamed "Stan the Man" by Brooklyn fans because he had a career average of .356 in Ebbets Field, Musial was a modest, well-liked man who was honored in every NL park during his farewell season. The sportswriter Ed Linn once said, "It is difficult to write about Stan Musial without sounding as if you were delivering the nominating address at a presidential convention."

After retiring, Musial continued to run a very successful St. Louis restaurant which he'd opened during his playing days, and he served as a vice president of the Cardinals. In 3,026 games, Musial had an average of .331 with 3,630 hits, including 725 doubles, 177 triples, and 475 home runs. He drove in 1,951 runs and scored 1,949.

★ Baseball Hall of Fame

Musso, George F.
FOOTBALL
b. April 8, 1910, Collinsville, Ill.

Musso played college football at little James Millikin College, a Presbyterian school in Illinois, where he started at tackle for four years. One of the biggest players of his time, he was 6-foot-2 and 255 pounds in college and grew to 270 pounds during his peak professional years.

Owner-coach George Halas of the Chicago Bears saw Musso in an all-star game and sent him $5 in expense money to come to the Bears' camp in 1933 for a tryout. He not only made the team, he became a starting tackle before the season was over and was named a second-team All-Pro.

"Big Bear" was a first-team All-Pro in 1935 and then moved to guard, where he was an All-Pro in 1937. A devastating blocker and a defensive standout as a middle guard, where he usually occupied two or three blockers, Musso became the Bears' captain in 1936 and held the job until he retired after the 1944 season. During his 12 seasons, the Bears won four NFL championships, in 1933, 1940, 1941, and 1943.

★ Pro Football Hall of Fame

Myers, Lon (Lawrence E.)
TRACK AND FIELD
b. Feb. 16, 1858, Richmond, Va.
d. Feb. 15, 1899

At his peak from 1879 through 1887, Myers was virtually unbeatable at every distance from 100 yards to 1 mile, and he was never beaten at the 440-yard run.

Sickly as a boy, he began running to build up his strength. In 1879, he set the first of his seven world records, running the 440 in 49.2 seconds. It was the first time anyone had broken the 50-second barrier.

Myers also set a world record of 1:56 in the half-mile in 1881. He lowered it to 1:55.4 in 1884 and matched that twice in 1885. The 5-foot-8, 114-pounder won national championships in the 220-, 440-, and 880-yard runs in 1879; in the 100, 220, 440, and 880 in 1880; in the 100, 220, and 440 in 1881; in the 220, 440, and 880 in 1884; and in the 440 in 1882 and 1883.

In 1884, Myers was charged with professionalism because he held a paid position with the Manhattan Athletic Club, accepted money to judge a race and to write a sports column, and had won a $20 gold piece at a meet. Although the charges were dismissed by the National Association of Amateur Athletes of America, which then supervised amateur track and field, the incident led to the formation of the Amateur Athletic Union, which replaced the NAAAA.

Myers became a professional in 1886 to run against Walter George of England in a contest billed the "Middle Distance Championship of the World" at Madison Square Garden. Myers beat George at 1,000 yards, 1,320 yards, and 1 mile to collect the $3,000 purse.

A similar contest was held in Australia in 1887. After Myers won the first two races, George sailed home to England in chagrin without running the third race. Myers then returned to the U.S. and became a bookmaker, which was then legal. He died of pneumonia.
★ National Track & Field Hall of Fame

Myers, Paula Jean (Mrs. Pope)

DIVING
b. Nov. 11, 1934, La Verne, Calif.

Myers won four medals in diving at three different Olympics. Shortly after graduating from high school, she won a silver in the 1952 platform event. As a student at the University of Southern California, she won a bronze medal in platform diving at the 1956 Olympics. And she won silver medals in both the springboard and the platform in 1960, when she was Paula Jean Myers-Pope and the mother of two children.

Myers also won 11 AAU national championships, in the outdoor 1-meter and 3-meter springboard events in 1957 and 1958; in the outdoor platform in 1953 and from 1957 through 1959; in the indoor 3-meter springboard in 1953; and in both indoor springboard events in 1957.

She also won gold medals in both springboard and platform diving at the 1959 Pan-American Games.

★ ★ N ★ ★

Naber, John P.

SWIMMING
b. Jan. 20, 1956, Evanston, Ill.

When John Naber was nine years old, his family visited Olympia while on a trip to Greece, and he told his parents that he would be an Olympic champion some day. Although he didn't begin swimming competitively until he was 13, Naber made good on his prophecy in 1976, winning gold medals in the 100- and 200-meter backstroke events, the 4 x 200-meter freestyle relay, and the 4 x 100-meter medley relay. He also won a silver medal in the 200-meter freestyle.

The 6-foot-6, 195-pound Naber swam world record times in both backstrokes, 55.49 seconds in the 100-meter and 1:59.19 in the 200-meter, making him the first swimmer to break the 2-minute barrier in that event. His world records stood until 1983, an unusually long period in modern swimming.

Swimming for the University of Southern California, Naber won the 500-yard freestyle in 1974 and 1975 and both backstroke events from 1974 through 1977. He also swam on five winning relay teams. His 10 individual titles was the NCAA record until 1987, and his total of 15 championships is still the record.

Naber won a total of 18 national individual championships and was on seven relay champions. He won three gold medals at the 1975 Pan-American Games. He was named winner of the Sullivan Award as the outstanding amateur athlete of 1977.

★ Olympic Hall of Fame

Nagurski, Bronko Bronislaw

FOOTBALL
b. Nov. 3, 1908, Rainy River, Ont.
d. Jan. 7, 1990

Grantland Rice once wrote of Nagurski, "Bronko is the only man who ever lived who could lead his own interference," and long-time New York Giants coach Steve Owen said, "There's only one defense that could stop Nagurski — shoot him before he leaves the dressing room."

The 6-foot-2, 225-pounder usually played fullback on offense and tackle on defense at the University of Minnesota. He was named an All-American at both positions by the *New York Sun* in 1929, although most other selectors listed him as a tackle.

Nagurski joined the Chicago Bears in 1930 and played the same dual role for most of his professional career. He was a bruising runner who could rarely be brought down by a single tackler, and offensive teams usually had to use at least two blockers on him, as well.

Although he wasn't a great passer, he was effective when he ran toward the line as if on a plunge. As defenders massed to stop him, Nagurski would stop, take a step or two back, and throw the ball. He threw a 2-yard touchdown pass to Red Grange on that kind of play to beat the Portsmouth Spartans in the 1932 NFL championship game, and the following year he threw two touchdown passes in a 23–21 championship victory over the New York Giants.

When Beattie Feathers, a small, fast

halfback, joined the Bears in 1934, Nagurski was used primarily as a decoy and a blocker. Feathers became the first NFL player in history to gain more than 1,000 yards in a season, and he gave Nagurski much of the credit.

From 1935 through 1937, Nagurski was often used as a tackle on offense as well as on defense. He retired in 1938 to go into professional wrestling and was briefly the world champion, losing the title to Jim Londos. The Bears talked him into playing football again in 1943, because of the manpower shortage caused by World War II. He played most of that season at tackle but was moved to fullback in the final regular season game, when the Bears were losing, 24–14, to the Chicago Cardinals. Nagurski scored one touchdown and made a key fourth-down run to set up a second as the Bears pulled out a 28–24 victory.

He also scored the touchdown that put the Bears ahead to stay in a 41–21 win over the Washington Redskins in the NFL championship game. He retired for good after that game.

Nagurski was named All-Pro fullback three consecutive years, from 1932 through 1934.

★ College Football Hall of Fame; Pro Football Hall of Fame

Nagy, Steve J.

BOWLING
b. Aug. 10, 1913, Shoaf, Pa.
d. Nov. 10, 1966

At 17, Nagy was managing the bowling alleys at a club in Cleveland for which his father was caretaker. There was no professional tour during his younger years, so his serious competitive career began with the 1939 ABC tournament.

After World War II, Nagy was well enough known as a bowler to become a member of Brunswick's promotional team. He was named bowler of the year in 1952, when he won the ABC all-events championship, teamed with John Klares for the doubles title, and joined the ABC championship team.

Nagy frequently appeared on filmed television matches, and in 1954 he became the first bowler ever to roll a perfect 300 game on television. He was chosen bowler of the year for the second time in 1955, after winning the BPAA All-Star tournament.

When the PBA was organized in 1958, Nagy was one of the 33 charter members, but he was past his prime and never won a tour event. Nagy suffered several strokes in the two years before his death.

★ ABC Hall of Fame; PBA Hall of Fame

Naismith, James

BASKETBALL
b. Nov. 6, 1861, near Almonte, Ont.
d. Nov. 28, 1939

After working as a lumberjack for five years, Naismith went back to high school, graduating when he was 21, and then he earned a degree at McGill University in Montreal, where he played rugby. In 1891, he went to the International YMCA Training School in Springfield, Massachusetts, as a student and part-time instructor.

The director of the school, Luther H. Gulick, asked Naismith to develop an indoor sport that would keep students occupied and interested during the winter. Naismith eventually decided that such a sport should have a high, horizontal goal, at which a ball had to be lofted, and he felt that running with the ball would have to be forbidden to avoid dangerous physical contact between players on the hardwood floors of a gymnasium.

He first thought of using boxes as goals, but no suitable boxes were handy, so he used peach baskets. The exact date of the first game is not known, but it wasn't long before Christmas of 1891. There were 18 students in the class that tried the new sport, so each team had nine players.

Basketball, as it was later named, was an immediate success among the students. Because the school's graduates took it with them as they went to work at YMCAs across the country and in other nations, it spread rapidly. In the early years, Naismith and Gulick worked together to refine the rules, but in 1895 Naismith went to the Denver YMCA, and he had little influence on the sport's development after that.

However, he introduced basketball at the University of Kansas when he went there as a physical education instructor in 1899, and he coached the Kansas team for ten years, winning 53 games while losing 55. One of his students and players was "Phog" Allen, who became the sport's first genuine coach.

In keeping with Gulick's ideas, which became YMCA principles, Naismith favored sport as a pleasurable means of physical improvement and frowned on intense, all-out competition. In his later years, he wasn't fond of what had happened to the sport he had invented.

Naismith received international recognition in 1936, when basketball became an Olympic sport. He tossed up the ball for the opening tipoff of the first Olympic game and presented the medals to the winning teams.

★ Basketball Hall of Fame

Namath, Joe (Joseph W.)
FOOTBALL
b. May 31, 1943, Beaver Falls, Pa.

As quarterback for the University of Alabama, Namath was edged out as consensus All-American in 1964 by John Huarte of Notre Dame, who won the Heisman Trophy that year. The New York Jets of the American Football League drafted both of them.

Huarte was with the Jets for only one season. Namath led the team to headlines, respectability, and the AFL's first victory ever in the Super Bowl.

The headlines began when he signed with the Jets for a reported $400,000. They continued to come throughout his career, sometimes for his play and sometimes for his off-the-field exploits, which earned him the nickname "Broadway Joe."

He was named the AFL's rookie of the year in 1965 after passing for 2,220 yards and 18 touchdowns. Namath led the league in passing yardage with 3,379 in 1966 and a professional record of 4,007 yards in 1967.

The Jets won the Eastern Division title in 1968, when Namath was named player of the year. In the AFL championship game, he completed only 19 of 49 passes, but three of them went for touchdowns as the Jets won, 27–23, over the Oakland Raiders.

The NFL's Green Bay Packers had won the first two Super Bowls with relative ease, and the Baltimore Colts were favored by 18 points over the Jets in Super Bowl III. In a talk three days before the game, Namath brashly "guaranteed" a victory. Then he produced it.

Abandoning the Jets' usual long passing attack for a ball-control offense that featured short passes and off-tackle runs by fullback Matt Snell, Namath kept the Colts off balance throughout the game. He completed 17 of 28 passes for 206 yards in a 16–7 win and was named the game's most valuable player.

The AFL merged into the NFL and became the American Football Conference in 1970. Knee problems limited Namath's playing time in his first two NFL seasons, but he led the league with 2,816 passing yards and 19 touchdown passes in 1972. He underwent his fifth knee operation midway through the 1976 season, his last with the Jets, and he retired after playing for the Los Angeles Rams in 1977.

Namath was the quarterback on the All-AFL team in 1968 and on the All-AFC team in 1972. During his 13 professional seasons, he completed 1,886 of 3,776 passes for 27,663 yards and 173 touchdowns. He also rushed for seven touchdowns and scored one on a fumble recovery.

★ Pro Football Hall of Fame

Nance, Jim (James S.)
FOOTBALL
b. Dec. 30, 1942, Indiana, Pa.
d. June 16, 1992

A three-year starter at fullback for Syracuse University, Nance won the NCAA heavyweight wrestling championship in 1963 and 1965. The powerful, 6-foot-1 Nance played at 235 pounds in college but was nearly 260 pounds when he joined the Boston Patriots of the

American Football League in 1965, and he never really got into form.

In 1966, at 240 pounds, Nance led the AFL in rushing with 1,458 yards on 299 carries, both all-time league records, and scored 11 rushing touchdowns. He was named the AFL's player of the year. The following season, he again led the league with 1,216 yards in 269 attempts.

The Patriots traded Nance to the Philadelphia Eagles in 1972, but he refused to play and temporarily retired. He returned to football with the New York Jets in 1973 and ended his career with the World Football League's Memphis Southmen in 1974. During his eight AFL/NFL seasons, he gained 5,461 yards in 1,341 attempts and scored 45 rushing touchdowns. He caught 133 passes for 870 yards, a 6.5 average, and 1 touchdown.

Navratilova, Martina

TENNIS
b. Oct. 8, 1956, Prague, Czechoslovakia

Navratilova's stepfather began giving her tennis lessons when she was six, and she entered her first tournament when she was eight, reaching the semifinals against girls as old as 12. She won the Czech women's singles title in 1972 and came to the U.S. for the first time the following year.

Czech officials criticized her for being "too Americanized" after her return and only reluctantly allowed her to compete in the 1975 U.S. Open. After losing in the semifinals, she asked for political asylum and defected.

Navratilova won six tournaments in 1977. She took her first Wimbledon singles title in 1978 and repeated the following year. By the early 1980s, she had emerged as the best woman player in the world, surpassing Chris Evert, who was two years older.

Interestingly, they both won 18 singles championships in the grand slam tournaments, and they had many classic duels on the court, with Navratilova's athletic, aggressive, serve and volley style contrasting with Evert's consistent ground strokes from the baseline.

In 1982, Navratilova began an unprecedented run at Wimbledon, winning the first of six consecutive singles championships. She also won the U.S. Open in 1983, 1984, 1986, and 1987, the French Open in 1982 and 1984, and the Australian Open in 1981, 1983, and 1985. Just when it seemed she was past her prime, she won her ninth Wimbledon title in 1990.

A fine doubles player because of her great volleying ability, Navratilova also won 31 women's doubles titles in grand slam tournaments, many of them with Pam Shriver, and 6 mixed doubles championship for a total of 55 grand slam titles, second only to Margaret Court Smith's 66.

She was named Associated Press female athlete of the year in 1983, when she won 86 of 87 matches, and in 1986, when she was ranked number one in the world for the sixth consecutive year. Navratilova retired from the tour at the end of the 1994 season with a record 161 singles championships. She also ranks first in money won with $19,052,570 through 1993.

★ International Women's Sports Hall of Fame

Neale, Greasy (Alfred Earle)

BASEBALL, FOOTBALL
b. Nov. 5, 1891, Parkersburg, W.Va.
d. Nov. 2, 1973

As an end at West Virginia Wesleyan, Neale caught 14 passes when the school upset the University of West Virginia, 19–14, in 1912. He graduated in 1914 and played for the Canton Bulldogs in the pre-NFL days, then went to Muskingum College as football coach in 1915.

Neale returned to West Virginia Wesleyan to coach in 1916 and 1917. After military service in World War I, he coached at Marietta College in 1919 and 1920; Washington and Jefferson in 1921 and 1922; the University of Virginia from 1923 through 1928; and West Virginia University from 1931 through 1933. His overall college record was 78–55–11.

In 1934, Neale became an assistant coach at Yale, where he worked mainly on offensive strategy. When Alexis Thompson bought the NFL's Philadelphia Eagles in 1941, he hired Neale as coach. Neale immediately installed the modern T formation, which had been developed just a year earlier by the Chicago Bears and Stanford University.

Under Neale's guidance, the Eagles had three straight second-place division finishes, from 1944 through 1946. They beat the Pittsburgh Steelers, 21–0, for the Eastern Division championship in 1947, but lost, 28–21, to the Chicago Cardinals in the league title game.

The Eagles then won two straight NFL championships with shutouts, beating the Cardinals, 7–0, in 1948 and the Los Angeles Rams, 14–0, in 1949. Neale's "chug" defense was a major reason for the victories. To combat the T formation's passing attack, he assigned linebackers to hold up the opposition's receivers at the line of scrimmage, preventing them from getting into pass patterns quickly.

Despite his success, Neale was fired after the Eagles slipped to a 6–6–0 record in 1950. His overall record in 10 seasons was 71 wins, 48 losses, and 6 ties.

Neale also played eight seasons as a major league outfielder, mostly with the Cincinnati Reds. In 768 games, he batted .259. Neale hit .357 for the Reds in the 1919 World Series, as Cincinnati beat the Chicago White Sox, 5 games to 3. A year later, eight Chicago players were banned from baseball for allegedly conspiring with gamblers to throw the series.
★ College Football Hall of Fame; Pro Football Hall of Fame

Neely, Jess C.

FOOTBALL
b. Jan. 4, 1898, Smyrna, Tenn.
d. April 9, 1983

Neely played end and halfback at Vanderbilt University from 1920 through 1922. As a senior, he captained the 1922 squad that won eight and tied one without a loss.

Neely went to Southwestern College in Memphis, Tennessee, in 1924 as athletic director and coach of all sports. He became baseball coach and end coach at the University of Alabama in 1928, before taking over as head football coach and athletic director at Clemson in 1931.

In nine seasons with Clemson, Neely had a 43–35–7 record. His 1939 team beat Boston College, 6–3, in the Cotton Bowl. Neely went to Rice University in 1940 and spent 27 seasons there, compiling a record of 144 wins, 124 losses, and 10 ties. His Rice teams won six Southwestern Conference championships, and they were 3–3 in bowl games.

Although he was known as a conservative coach who stressed a running attack, Neely developed an excellent passing team when he had quarterback Tobin Rote and end "Froggy" Williams. They led the 1949 team to a 9–1–0 regular season record and a 27–13 win over North Carolina in the Cotton Bowl.

Neely left coaching after the 1966 season to become athletic director at Vanderbilt. He retired from that position in 1970.
★ College Football Hall of Fame

Nehemiah, Renaldo

TRACK AND FIELD
b. March 24, 1959, Newark, N.J.

Running for the University of Maryland, Nehemiah won the NCAA indoor 60-yard high hurdles in 1978 and 1979 and the outdoor 110-meter hurdle championship in 1979. He was also the AAU 110-meter hurdle champion in 1978 and 1979, and he won the event at the 1979 Pan-American Games and in World Cup competition.

Nehemiah set four world records in 1979. He ran the indoor 50-meter hurdles in 6.36 seconds and the 60-yard hurdles in 6.89 seconds. After setting a record of 13.16 seconds in the 110-meter hurdles, he lowered it to exactly 13.00 seconds.

Nicknamed "Skeets," Nehemiah signed a contract with an athletic shoe company in 1980, losing his college eligibility though retaining his amateur standing. He won the national outdoor 110-meter hurdles that year.

In 1981, Nehemiah lowered his

world records to 5.98 seconds in the 50-yard hurdles and to 12.93 seconds in the 110-meter event, becoming the first hurdler to break the 13-second barrier. He ran two more world record times, 5.92 in the 50-yard and 6.82 seconds in the 60-yard, in 1982.

Nehemiah joined the NFL's San Francisco 49ers as a wide receiver in 1982. He spent three seasons with them, catching 43 passes for 754 yards, a 17.5 average, and 4 touchdowns.

Nelson, Battling [Oscar Nielson]
BOXING
b. June 5 1882, Copenhagen, Denmark
d. Feb. 7, 1954

"The Durable Dane" was an unscientific attacker who took punishment in order to give it out. In his first fight, he knocked out Wallace's Kid in Hammond, Indiana, on September 3, 1896. He followed that with a number of early-round knockouts but also suffered some losses during the next ten years.

Nelson faced Joe Gans for the lightweight championship on September 3, 1906. It was the first fight promoted by the legendary Tex Rickard. Nelson was guaranteed $23,000, Gans, $11,000. The fight went 42 rounds before Nelson was disqualified after Gans doubled over and fell to the canvas because of a low blow.

The two met again in San Francisco on July 4, 1908. This time Nelson won the championship on a knockout in the 17th round. He also knocked out Gans in the 21st round in a rematch on September 9.

Nelson and Ad Wolgast fought a bitter, bloody 10-round no-decision contest in a nontitle fight in 1909. They agreed to meet in a 45-round grudge match for the championship. No fouls were to be called, and the referee wasn't supposed to stop the fight unless a boxer was completely unable to carry on.

It took place on February 22, 1910, at Point Richmond, California. Nelson was helpless and bleeding badly from the mouth in the 40th round, when the fight was stopped.

Nelson fought on through 1915. He was inactive in 1916 but had one fight the following year. He returned for two exhibitions in 1923 before retiring for good. He won 59 fights, 38 by knockout; lost 19, 2 by knockout; and fought 19 draws and 35 no-decisions.

★ International Boxing Hall of Fame

Nelson, Byron (John Byron Jr.)
GOLF
b. Feb. 4, 1912, Ft. Worth, Tex.

Nelson had the most incredible streak in golfing history in 1945, when he won 11 consecutive tournaments and a total of 19 tour events. The performance has been disparaged by some because most of the other top professional golfers were serving in World War II. (Nelson wasn't qualified for military service because he had hemophilia.)

That, however, is a simplistic view. For one thing, Nelson's scores would have beat just about anybody. He averaged an almost unbelievable 68.33 strokes per round for 31 tournaments that year, and at the Seattle Open, he shot a record 62 for 18 holes and 259, 29 shots under par, for 72 holes. For another, there were other good golfers playing in 1945. Sam Snead played in 27 tournaments, winning 6; Ben Hogan, discharged from the Army Air Corps, played in 19 and won 4; and Jimmy Demaret and Craig Wood were on the tour for the entire year.

Nelson had established his credentials as a great golfer before the war. He won the U.S. Open in 1939, the PGA championship in 1940, and the Masters in 1937 and 1942, when he beat Hogan, 69–70, in a playoff. By the end of 1945, he had finished in the money in 113 consecutive tournaments.

After winning six more tournaments in 1946, Nelson retired from the tour because of the strain of competition and bought a ranch in Texas. He competed in just a few tournaments a year after that but tied for second in the 1947 Masters and won the 1955 French Open.

Nelson was named male athlete of the year in 1944, when he won seven tournaments and averaged 69.67 strokes for 85 rounds, and again after his remarkable 1945 season.

★ PGA Hall of Fame; World Golf Hall of Fame

Nelson, Cindy (Cynthia)

SKIING
b. Aug. 19, 1955, Lutsen, Minn.

Nelson became a member of the U.S. national ski team in 1971, when she was 15. She won the national downhill championship in 1973 and 1978, the slalom in 1975 and 1976, and the Alpine combined in 1978.

Injuries hampered her in Olympic competition. She missed the 1972 Olympics with a dislocated hip. After winning a bronze medal in the downhill in 1976, Nelson was disappointing at the 1980 Olympics, tying for seventh place in the downhill for her best finish.

In 1984, Nelson couldn't compete in the Olympic downhill event because of a serious injury to her right knee. Skiing with a brace on the knee, she could do no better than nineteenth in the slalom. The injury forced her to retire after the Olympics.

Nelson, Maud [Clementina Brida]

BASEBALL
b. Nov. 17, 1881, Italy
d. Feb. 15, 1944

Something of a mystery woman, Clementina Brida came to America with her family when she was young. She learned to play baseball when she was a child and took the name "Maud Nelson." Before she was 16, she was pitching for the Boston Bloomer Girls, who traveled across the country in 1897. She started virtually every day, though she often pitched only a few innings and then moved to third base for the rest of the game.

Nelson played for several teams during her career, including the otherwise all-male Cherokee Indian Base Ball Club in 1908. There she met her first husband, John B. Olson, Jr., the team's manager. They organized the Western Bloomer Girls in 1911. Despite the name, the team usually had three male starters.

Olson died in 1917, and Nelson rejoined the Boston Bloomer Girls. She also played for the American Athletic Girls and the Star Bloomers at various times. She retired as a player after the 1922 season and organized yet another team, the All Star Ranger Girls, which she managed until the Great Depression made barnstorming unprofitable. She then retired to Chicago with her second husband, Constante Delacqua.

Nevers, Ernie (Ernest A.)

FOOTBALL
b. June 11, 1903, Willow Grove, Minn.
d. May 3, 1976

The 6-foot-1, 205-pound Nevers played fullback at Stanford in "Pop" Warner's double wing formation, in which the fullback was the triple threat tailback who handled the ball on virtually every play. Warner, who had coached the great Jim Thorpe, said that Nevers was the better football player because he had all of Thorpe's skills, and he tried harder.

A starter as a sophomore, Nevers was named to Walter Camp's third All-American team in 1923. However, he missed the first six games the following season with a broken ankle, and when he finally got back into the lineup, he broke the other ankle.

Stanford faced Notre Dame and the Four Horsemen in the 1925 Rose Bowl. With his ankles wrapped in bandages and deadened by Novocain, Nevers played all 60 minutes. He gained 114 yards rushing and, according to one sportswriter, made three quarters of Stanford's tackles, but Notre Dame won, 27–10.

That performance brought him national attention, and he was an All-American in his senior season, when Stanford lost just one game. Like "Red" Grange, Nevers began playing professional football shortly after the college season ended. In January 1926, he was with the Jacksonville All-Stars when they played Grange and the touring Chicago Bears. The Bears won, 19–6, but Nevers outplayed Grange, rushing for 46 yards, completing 8 of 16 passes, punting for a 53.3 yard average, and intercepting two passes. He scored Jacksonville's only touchdown.

In the fall, he joined the Duluth Eskimos of the NFL for $15,000, the highest salary in league history at that time. The Eskimos played 29 games, 28 of them on the road, and Nevers missed just 27 minutes. The team won 19, lost 7, and tied 3.

The Eskimos weren't as successful in 1927, and the franchise folded. Nevers didn't play in 1928, then spent the next three years with the Chicago Cardinals. On November 28, 1929, he scored all of his team's points in a 40–6 victory over the Bears, still the league record for a single game. A week later, he scored all of the points in a 19–0 win over Dayton.

Nevers retired after the 1931 season, but he made a final appearance in an all-star game for charity in January 1932. Before leaving the game with a broken wrist, Nevers again scored all of his team's points in a 26–14 win.

★ College Football Hall of Fame; Pro Football Hall of Fame

Neves, Ralph

HORSE RACING
b. Aug. 26, 1918, Cape Cod, Mass.

Nicknamed the "Prince of Busted Bones" by sportswriters because of his many spills, Neves was nevertheless one of best jockeys on the West Coast during the 1940s and 1950s. Among his major victories were the 1940 Santa Anita Derby aboard Sweepida, the 1949 Hollywood Gold Cup aboard Solidarity, and the 1957 Santa Anita Handicap aboard Corn Husker. He also won the Sunset Handicap at Hollywood Park in 1939, 1954, and 1957.

Neves began riding in 1934. He was the top rider at Bay Meadows in 1936, despite a terrible fall. Trampled by four horses, Neves was pronounced dead and was put in a cold storage area to await transportation to the morgue. He recovered consciousness, took a taxi back to the track, and was riding again the next day.

Later in his career, Neves suffered a fractured skull, broken back, shattered rib cage, and numerous other broken bones, along with an eye injury that left him with only 70 percent vision.

He retired in 1964 after winning 173 stakes races and earning more than $14 million.

★ National Horse Racing Hall of Fame

Newcombe, Donald

BASEBALL
b. June 14, 1926, Madison, N.J.

The first black pitcher to star in the major leagues, Newcombe was with the Newark Eagles of the Negro National League in 1944 and 1945 before signing with the NL's Brooklyn Dodgers. He spent three seasons in the minor leagues and joined the Dodgers in 1949.

The 6-foot-4, 225-pound Newcombe had a 17–8 record and led the league with 5 shutouts in his first season. Despite a 3.09 ERA in the World Series, he lost both starts as the New York Yankees beat the Dodgers in five games.

After a 19–11 record in 1950, Newcombe went 20–9 and led the NL in strikeouts with 164 in 1951. An injury limited him to 29 starts in 1954, but he came back with a league-leading .800 winning percentage in 1955, when he won 20 and lost 5. He lost his only start in the World Series, but the Dodgers beat the Yankees in 6 games.

In 1956, Newcombe won the first Cy Young Award as the best pitcher in baseball and was named the league's most valuable player. He led the league in victories with a 27–7 record and in winning percentage with .794, striking out 139 hitters while walking only 46 and compiling a 3.06 ERA.

Newcombe suffered from arm trouble and was only 11–12 in 1957, and the Dodgers traded him to Cincinnati during the 1958 season. He came back with a 13–8 record and a 3.16 ERA in 1959, but retired after going just 6–9 with Cincinnati and the AL's Cleveland Indians in 1960.

Newell, Marshall

FOOTBALL
b. April 2, 1871, Clifton, N.J.
d. Dec. 24, 1897

At Harvard, Newell was called "Ma,"

partly because it was an abbreviation of his first name but mostly because he took younger students and players under his wing. He was only 5 feet, 7 inches tall, but he weighed a solid 168 pounds, and he was named an All-American tackle four times, from 1890 through 1893.

Newell also rowed on the Harvard crew. After graduating, he became Cornell's first football coach, winning 9 games, losing 8, and tying 2 in his two seasons there. He was killed in a train crash, and Harvard named one of the entrances to its football stadium, Soldier's Field, after him.

★ College Football Hall of Fame

Newell, Peter F.

BASKETBALL
b. Aug. 31, 1915, Vancouver, B.C.

Newell played basketball at Loyola University of Los Angeles, graduating in 1939, and he served in the Navy during World War II. After the war he began his college coaching career at the University of San Francisco, emphasizing team defense and a controlled offense.

His USF teams won 25 of 30 games and the 1949 National Invitation Tournament. Newell had a 70–37 record in four seasons, then went to Michigan State in 1950. After indifferent success there, a 45–42 record in four seasons, he moved on to the University of California in 1952.

Newell took California to the NCAA championship game in 1959 and 1960, winning the title the first year and losing to Ohio State in the second. He coached the U.S. Olympic team to a gold medal in 1960, becoming the first coach ever to win an NIT, an NCAA tournament, and Olympic gold. In six seasons at California, he won 118 games and lost 44.

His overall college record was 233 wins and 123 losses. Newell later served as general manager of the San Diego Rockets and the Los Angeles Lakers of the NBA.

★ Basketball Hall of Fame

Newhouser, Hal (Harold)

BASEBALL
b. May 20, 1921, Detroit, Mich.

A left-handed pitcher, Newhouser put together a remarkable three-year stretch, from 1944 through 1946, leading the AL in victories each year and winning 80 games while losing only 27 during the period.

Newhouser appeared in just one game with the AL's Detroit Tigers in 1939 and became a regular the following year. After going 34–51 in his first four full seasons, he won the league's most valuable player award in 1944. He led the league in victories with a 29–9 record and in strikeouts with 187, and he had six shutouts and a 2.22 ERA.

The big difference for the hard thrower was improved control. In 1943, he walked 111 hitters in 195⅔ innings; in 1944, he walked only 102 in 312⅓ innings.

Newhouser led the league in victories again in 1945, with a 25–9 record, and was also the league leader with a .735 winning percentage, 29 complete games, 8 shutouts, 313⅓ innings pitched, 212 strikeouts, and a 1.81 ERA. He was rewarded with his second MVP award.

He wasn't at his best in the World Series, but he had a 2–1 record as the Tigers beat the Chicago Cubs in seven games.

In 1946, Newhouser led the AL in victories for the third year in a row, with a 26–9 record, and in ERA for the second year in a row, at 1.94. After going 17–17 in 1947 with a league-leading 27 complete games, he led in victories again with a 21–12 mark in 1948.

Newhouser went 18–11 and 15–13 in the next two years and then began to have arm problems. The Tigers traded him to the Cleveland Indians after he appeared in only seven games in 1953. He made a bit of a comeback in 1954, going 7–2 with seven saves and a 2.51 ERA, but he retired the following season after appearing in just two games.

In 17 seasons, Newhouser had a 207–150 record with 33 shutouts and a 3.06 ERA. He struck out 1,796 hitters and walked 1,249 in 2,993 innings.

★ Baseball Hall of Fame

Newman, Harry L.

FOOTBALL
b. Sept. 5, 1909, Detroit, Mich.

An All-American quarterback at the University of Michigan in 1932, the 5-foot-7, 170-pound Newman joined the NFL's New York Giants in 1933 and was named to the All-Pro team after completing 53 of 136 passes for 973 yards and 9 touchdowns to lead the league.

Newman threw touchdown passes of 29 and 8 yards in New York's 23–21 loss to the Chicago Bears in the NFL championship game. He missed the Giants' 30–13 victory over the Bears in the 1934 title game. In 1935, Newman played sparingly as a backup to Ed Danowski. He played with the New York Yanks and Brooklyn Tigers of the American Football League in 1936 and ended his career with the AFL's Rochester Tigers in 1937.
★ College Football Hall of Fame

Neyland, Bob (Robert R. III)

FOOTBALL
b. Feb. 17, 1892, Greenville, Tex.
d. March 28, 1962

In 1969, football's centennial year, Neyland finished second only to Knute Rockne as the greatest college coach in a poll of coaches. He coached 21 seasons, all at the University of Tennessee, winning 173 games while losing only 31 and tying 12. His .829 winning percentage is fifth all-time.

Neyland's teams owned much of their success to defense. He once explained that an offense can score only three ways, while a defense can score in four ways, on an interception, a fumble, a blocked kick, or a kick return. He added, "The psychological shock of being scored on in any of those ways is so profound that a team so scored on rarely is able to rally for victory."

A career Army officer, Neyland graduated from West Point in 1916 and served in Europe during World War I. He arrived at Tennessee in 1925 as an assistant football coach and ROTC instructor. He became head coach in 1926. During much of his career at the school, he was involved in work for the Tennessee Valley Authority as an officer in the Army Corps of Engineers.

Success came quickly. His first team won eight of nine games, and the next three were undefeated, though each was tied once. In 1930, his fifth season, Tennessee won nine of ten games. During that period, the school went 33 consecutive games without a loss. Neyland also produced unbeaten teams in 1938, 1939, 1940, and 1951, when Tennessee won the national championship.

Neyland missed the 1935 season because of Army duty, and he served overseas during World War II. He retired after the 1952 season. Four of his players, Bobby Dodd, Murray Warmath, Bob Woodruff, and Bowden Wyatt, became Hall of Fame coaches.
★ College Football Hall of Fame

Nichols, Kid (Charles A.)

BASEBALL
b. Sept. 14, 1869, Madison, Wis.
d. April 11, 1953

Even in an era when pitchers were expected to put in a lot of work, Nichols was unusually durable. In his first 10 years in the major leagues, he won 20 or more games every season, 30 or more seven times, and his innings pitched ranged from a low of $343\frac{1}{3}$ to a high of 453.

A right-hander, the 5-foot-10, 175-pounder joined the NL's Boston team in 1890 and had a 27–19 record, leading the league with seven shutouts. During the next four years, from 1891 to 1894, he was 30–17, 35–16, 34–14, and 32–13. In 1894 he led the league with three shutouts.

After going 26–16 in 1895, Nichols was the NL leader in victories three years in a row, with records of 30–14 in 1896, 31–11 in 1897, and 31–12 in 1898. He also led the league in saves twice, with 3 in 1897 and 4 in 1898, and he was tops in innings pitched with 368 in 1897.

Nichols had records of 21–19 in 1899, 13–16 in 1900, and 19–16 in 1901. Then he acquired part ownership of a minor league team in Kansas City and became its playing manager for two seasons.

The St. Louis Cardinals hired Nichols as manager in 1904, and he had a 21–13 record as a pitcher. The team finished fifth, though, and he left early in the 1905 season to join the Philadelphia Phillies. He was 10–6 with Philadelphia but retired with an 0–1 record in 1906 when back problems forced him to retire. Nichols later coached amateur teams in Kansas City, where one of his pupils was Casey Stengel.

Nichols used a fast ball and excellent control to build a 361–208 major league record, with 48 shutouts and a 2.95 ERA. He struck out 1,868 hitters and walked only 1,268 in 5,056 innings.

★ Baseball Hall of Fame

Nicholson, Bill (William B.)

BASEBALL
b. Dec. 11, 1914, Chestertown, Md.

Nicknamed "Swish" because of his mighty swing, which often missed the ball, Nicholson was twice the NL home run and RBI leader. He played briefly for the AL's Philadelphia Athletics in 1936, then spent two years in the minors before joining the Chicago Cubs in 1939.

A left-handed hitter and right-handed thrower, the 6-foot, 205-pound Nicholson became Chicago's starting left fielder in 1940. He had his finest season in 1943, batting .309 with a league-leading 29 home runs and 128 RBI. In 1944, his average slipped to .287, but he again led the league with 33 home runs and 122 RBI and was also the leader in runs scored with 116.

The Cubs won the 1945 NL pennant, but Nicholson hit only .243 with 13 home runs that season. Though he batted just .214 in the World Series, he had 8 RBI in Chicago's seven-game loss to the Detroit Tigers.

In 1949, Nicholson was traded to the Philadelphia Phillies, where he became a part-time player and frequent pinch hitter. He retired after the 1953 season. In 1,677 games, Nicholson batted .268 with 1,484 hits, including 272 doubles, 60 triples, and 235 home runs. He scored 837 runs and drove in 948.

Nicklaus, Jack W.

GOLF
b. Jan. 21, 1940, Columbus, Ohio

Very slowly, Nicklaus was accepted as a great golfer. Part of his problem was that he came along when Arnold Palmer was the darling of galleries and sportswriters. The other part was that he was chubby and he dressed colorlessly, which didn't endear him to the new and growing television audience for golf in the early 1960s.

Nicklaus won the Ohio Open when he was 16, was the U.S. Amateur champion in 1959 and 1961, and finished second in the U.S. Open as an amateur in 1960, when he was only 20. He joined the pro tour in 1962, finished in the top ten in 16 of the 26 tournaments he entered, and won $61,868.95, more than any other rookie in history. Among his wins was a victory over Palmer in an 18-hole playoff for the U.S. Open Championship.

From there, Nicklaus just kept winning, especially major tournaments. In 1963, he won the Masters and PGA championship; in 1965 he shot a 271 to win another Masters, breaking the course record of 274 that had been set in 1953, and led the tour in winnings with $113,284; In 1966 he won his third Masters and first British Open.

Nicklaus also changed his image. He lost at least 20 pounds, let his hair grow and had it styled, and began to wear colorful clothes. With the charismatic Palmer fading as a competitor, Nicklaus began to attract his own fans in the late 1960s, though they were never as fervent as "Arnie's Army" had been.

A student of golf history, Nicklaus focused from the beginning on winning major championships and, in particular, on Bobby Jones's record of 13 major championships. He surpassed that by winning 21. In addition to his two U.S. Amateur titles, Nicklaus won a record six Masters, in 1963, 1965, 1966, 1972, 1973, and 1986; five PGA championships, in 1963, 1971, 1973, 1975, and 1980; four U.S. Opens, in 1962, 1967, 1972, and 1980; and three British Opens, in 1966, 1970, and 1978.

(Without detracting from Nicklaus's record, it should be noted that "major championship" had been redefined. In Jones's day, the so-called Grand Slam comprised the U.S. and British Amateur championships and the U.S. and British Opens. As an amateur, Jones never competed in the PGA championship, and Jones himself helped to create the Masters Tournament after he'd retired from competition.)

Like most golfers, Nicklaus seemed to be in the twilight of his career after he turned 40. But at 46 he came up with what was probably his most amazing victory. Tied for eighth place after three rounds of the 1986 Masters, he shot a 65, with a 35 on the front nine and a record-tying 30 on the back nine, to pick up his last victory in a major tournament.

Nicklaus was the PGA's top money winner in 1964, 1965, 1967, from 1971 through 1973, and in 1975 and 1976, and he was named player of the year in 1967, 1972, 1973, 1975, and 1976. He won 70 PGA tournaments, second to Sam Snead, and his $5,309,130 in earnings is seventh all-time.

Although he didn't seem very enthusiastic at the time, Nicklaus began to play some events on the senior PGA Tour when he turned 50 in 1990. He won the PGA Seniors championship in 1991, the U.S. Seniors Open in 1991 and 1993, and the Tradition in 1990 and 1991.
★ World Golf Hall of Fame

Nieder, Bill (William H.)
TRACK AND FIELD
b. Aug. 10, 1933, Hempstead, N.Y.

Nieder grew up in Kansas and was the first high school athlete to break the 60-foot barrier with the 12-pound shot. At the University of Kansas, he became the first college athlete to surpass 60 feet with the 16-pound shot.

Overshadowed by Parry O'Brien and Dallas Long, Nieder won only two national championships, the NCAA outdoor title in 1955 and the AAU outdoor title in 1957. However, he set world records four times, at 62–2 in 1959 and at 63–10, 65–7, and 65–10 in 1960. Nieder took a silver medal behind O'Brien at the 1956 Olympics and the gold medal in 1960, when he set an Olympic record of 62–6¼.

The 6-foot-3, 225-pounder retired from competition after the 1960 Olympics and tried professional boxing but was knocked out in his only bout.

Nieman, Nancy (Mrs. Baranet)
CYCLING
b. 1933, Detroit, Mich.

A pioneer woman cyclist, Nieman got involved in bicycling in 1951 by taking an American Youth Hostel tour. She then began training for competitive racing and won the national women's road championship in 1953 and 1954.

At the time, she was racing in what was called the "girls' division." Nieman complained to officials that she was 21 and no longer a girl, and the name was changed to "women's division."

Nieman went to Europe in 1955 because there were few opportunities for women to race in the United States, and she tied the world record for the 200-meter sprint, 14.4 seconds. She returned to Europe to compete in a major eight-day stage race in France, finishing fourteenth among 40 finishers out of 87 starters.

After winning the U.S. women's road race again in 1956 and 1957, Nieman retired from competition. She served as the only woman officer of the American Bicycle League from 1956 through 1983, and she wrote two books, *The Turned Down Bar*, about her racing experiences in Europe, and *Bicycling*, a manual on recreational cycling.

Nighbor, Frank
HOCKEY
b. 1893 Pembroke, Ont.
d. April 13, 1966

Known as the "Pembroke Peach" because he was such a smooth player, Nighbor became a professional with Toronto in 1913, played for the Vancouver Millionaires when they won the Stanley Cup in 1914, then went to the Ottawa Senators. They were then part of the National Hockey Association, which was reorganized as the National Hockey League in 1917.

An expert at stealing the puck, Nighbor won the first Hart Trophy as the league's most valuable player in 1924, and he was the first winner of the Lady Byng Trophy for combining skillful play with gentlemanly conduct in 1925. He also won the Byng Trophy in 1926.

Nighbor played for Stanley Cup champions with Ottawa in 1920, 1921, 1923, and 1927. He was traded to the Toronto Maple Leafs during the 1928–29 season and retired when the season ended.

In 13 NHL seasons, Nighbor played 348 games, scored 135 goals, and had 61 assists. He had 11 goals and 9 assists in 36 playoff games.

★ Hockey Hall of Fame

Nitschke, Raymond E.
FOOTBALL
b. Dec. 29, 1936, Elmwood Park, Ill.

Nitschke's father died when Raymond was three years old, and his mother died ten years later. Adopted by an older brother, he was often involved in street fights before discovering football. He later said that the sport probably saved him from prison.

He played fullback and linebacker at the University of Illinois and joined the Green Bay Packers of the NFL in 1958. Nitschke took over as the team's starting middle linebacker before his rookie season ended.

The 6-foot-3, 235-pound Nitschke was named an All-Pro from 1964 through 1966. He was chosen most valuable player in the 1962 NFL championship game, when the Packers beat the New York Giants, 16–7, on an icy field at Yankee Stadium.

Nitschke retired after the 1972 season. During his 13 years with the Packers, he intercepted 25 passes and returned them for 385 yards and 2 touchdowns.

★ Pro Football Hall of Fame

Nitz, Leonard Harvey
CYCLING
b. Sept. 30, 1956, Hamilton, Ohio

Nitz was among the top U.S. cyclists for longer than anyone since the early part of the century. He won the national 4,000-meter individual pursuit championship five times, in 1976 and from 1980 through 1983, the 1-kilometer time trial in 1982 and 1984, and the criterium in 1986.

He also raced for the national team pursuit champions from 1980 through 1984 and in 1986, 1988, and 1989.

In international competition, Nitz was a member of the team pursuit champion at the Pan-American Games in 1983 and 1987. He won a bronze in the world points championship in 1986 and took a silver medal in team pursuit and a bronze in the individual pursuit event at the 1984 Olympics.

Nobis, Tommy (Thomas H. Jr.)
FOOTBALL
b. Sept. 20, 1943, San Antonio, Tex.

A center and linebacker at the University of Texas, Nobis was especially noted for his defensive ability. The 6-foot-4, 240-pounder had the speed to be a dangerous pass rusher and a good pass defender. His blitzes against Joe Namath helped Texas upset top-ranked Alabama, 21–7, in the 1965 Orange Bowl. Nobis was a consensus All-American and winner of the Outland Trophy as the nation's best collegiate lineman in 1965.

The first college player chosen by the Atlanta Falcons, an expansion team, in the NFL's 1966 draft, Nobis signed for a bonus reported at $400,000. He was rookie of the year in 1966, an All-Western Conference linebacker in 1966 and 1968, and a member of four Pro Bowl teams. Because of knee surgery, Nobis retired after the 1976 season. Nobis had 11 interceptions as a pro, returning them for 177 yards and 2 touchdowns.

★ College Football Hall of Fame

Noll, Chuck (Charles H.)
FOOTBALL
b. Jan. 5, 1932, Cleveland, Ohio

After captaining the University of Dayton football team in 1952, Noll joined the NFL's Cleveland Browns. Originally a linebacker with the Browns, the 6-foot-1, 218-pounder later became one of the "messenger guards" bringing plays in from coach Paul Brown.

Noll retired as a player after the 1959 season and became an assistant coach with the AFL's Los Angeles (later San Diego) Chargers and the NFL's Baltimore Colts. He took over as head coach of the Pittsburgh Steelers in 1969.

A defensive specialist as an assistant, Noll painstakingly built the Steelers into a winning team by emphasizing aggressive defense and a strong running game, using occasional long passes to loosen opposition defenses.

Led by the "Steel Curtain" defense, the running of fullback Franco Harris, and quarterback Terry Bradshaw's leadership and accurate passing, Pittsburgh had 13 straight winning seasons and appeared in the playoffs 11 times from 1972 through 1984.

Pittsburgh won its first ever NFL championship in 1974, beating the Minnesota Vikings, 16–6, in Super Bowl IX. The following year, the Steelers defeated the Dallas Cowboys, 21–17, in the Super Bowl.

Noll became the first coach to guide a team to three Super Bowl victories when Pittsburgh beat Dallas, 35–31, in Super Bowl XIII after the 1978 season. He added a fourth championship in 1979, when the Steelers defeated the Los Angeles Rams, 31–19.

Named the "Team of the Decade" for the 1970s, the Steelers began to decline in 1985. Noll retired after the 1991 season with a record of 193–148–1 in regular season games and a 16–8 mark in the playoffs.

★ Pro Football Hall of Fame

Nomellini, Leo

FOOTBALL

b. June 19, 1924, Lucca, Italy

His family came to the United States when Nomellini was an infant, and settled in Chicago. He worked in a foundry while going to a high school and didn't play football until he joined the Marines in 1942, when he was recruited for the Cherry Point, North Carolina, base team.

After serving in the South Pacific during World War II, Nomellini was given a football scholarship at the University of Minnesota. As a freshman in 1946, Nomellini was a starting guard. He was moved to tackle in his sophomore season and was named an All-American in 1948 and 1949.

The 6-foot-3, 284-pound Nomellini was the San Francisco 49ers' first draft choice in 1950. He played offensive tackle for his first three professional seasons and was an All-Pro in 1951 and 1952. He then moved to defensive tackle and was named to the All-Pro team at that position in 1953, 1954, 1957, and 1959.

Nomellini retired after the 1963 season. In 14 years as a professional, he never missed a game.

★ College Football Hall of Fame; Pro Football Hall of Fame

Norelius, Martha

SWIMMING

b. Jan. 20, 1908, Stockholm, Sweden

d. Sept. 23, 1955

Originally coached by her father, who had been a member of Sweden's team at the 1906 "intercalated" Olympics, Norelius grew up in New York City and competed for the New York Women's Swimming Association. She was the first woman ever to win the same swimming event at two different Olympics, taking gold medals in the 400-meter freestyle in 1924 and 1928. She was also a member of the winning 4 x 100-meter freestyle relay team in 1928.

Norelius swept every national freestyle championship in 1927, winning the outdoor 100-meter, 440-yard, 880-yard, and 1-mile titles and the indoor 100- and 220-yard events. She was also the outdoor 440- and 880-yard and the indoor 220-yard champion in 1926 and 1928.

She was suspended from amateur competition in 1929 for giving an exhibition in the same pool with professional swimmers, so she turned professional and won the $10,000 Wrigley Marathon in Toronto. There Norelius met Joe Wright, who had won a silver medal for Canada in the 1928 Olympic double sculls event. They were married the following year.

North, Andy

GOLF
b. May 9, 1950, Thorp, Wis.

In an injury-plagued career, North had only three victories on the PGA tour, but two of them came in the U.S. Open. North joined the tour in 1973. His first victory was in the 1977 Westchester Open.

In the 1978 U.S. Open, North led Jack Nicklaus by two shots after the second round and had a one-shot lead over Gary Player after three rounds. The final round was anticlimactic: North shot a 74 but won as Player dropped out of contention with a 77.

North shot a 65 in the second round of the 1985 Open after an opening 70 but still trailed T. C. Chen by one stroke. He shot a 70 in the third round and was two strokes back. The fourth round was a four-player contest among Chen, North, Dave Barr, and Payne Stewart, with the lead changing on almost every hole. North hit his tee shot into a bunker on the par-three 17th hole but made a great sand shot to within four feet of the pin and sank the putt to take the lead and, eventually, the victory.

Norton, Homer H.

FOOTBALL
b. June 15, 1891, Birmingham, Ala.
d.   May 26, 1965

Norton starred in four sports at Birmingham–Southern College and played minor league baseball for three years before becoming football coach at Centenary College in 1919. He had a record of 5–7–0 in three seasons. In 1922, a new college president asked him to step down to become an assistant to Bo McMillin.

McMillin left in 1926, and Norton took over again. His 1927 team won all ten of its games, and he also had unde-

feated teams in 1932 and 1933, beating Texas A & M both years, along with Southern Methodist and Arkansas.

Texas A & M hired Norton in 1934. It took him two years to rebuild the program, but his 1937 team won eight games, lost three, and tied one, and in 1939 the Aggies won all ten of their regular season games, beat Tulane, 14–13, in the Sugar Bowl, and were named national champions.

During the next two season, Texas A & M won 17 of 19 games and went to the Cotton Bowl both times, beating Fordham 13–12 and losing to Alabama, 29–21. Norton's 1943 team won seven, lost one, and tied one, but lost to Louisiana State, 19–14, in the Cotton Bowl.

Norton won only three games in 1947 and lost to the University of Texas for the eighth straight time. He was fired after the season. His record at Texas A & M was 82 wins, 53 losses, and 9 ties in 14 seasons. Overall, he was 137–69–17.
★ College Football Hall of Fame

Norton, Kenneth H.

BOXING
b. Aug. 9, 1945, Jacksonville, Ill.

While serving for four years in the Marine Corps, Norton won three all-Marine championships. He became a sparring partner for Joe Frazier after being discharged. Norton's first professional fight was a 9th-round knockout of Grady Brazell in San Diego on November 14, 1967.

The angular 6-foot-3, 210-pound Norton had a powerful punch and an awkward boxing style that often puzzled opponents. He won 16 straight fights, 15 by knockout, before being knocked out by Jose Luis Garcia on July 2, 1970. He then won 13 more matches to earn a fight against Muhammad Ali for the North American Boxing Federation version of the heavyweight championship.

In a stunning upset, Norton took a 12-round decision from the former world champion on March 31, 1973. After the fight, it was learned that he had broken Ali's jaw in the 7th round. Ali reclaimed the NABF title with a 12-round decision on September 10.

George Foreman knocked out Norton in the 2nd round of a match for the world championship on March 26, 1974, in Caracas, Venezuela. After Ali won the title from Foreman, Norton faced Ali for the third time on September 28, 1976. He put up a good fight but lost a 15-round decision.

The title fell into confusion less than two years later. After Michael Spinks beat Ali to win the championship, Norton was ranked as the top contender by the World Boxing Council. Spinks signed for a rematch with Ali instead of fighting Norton, and the WBC stripped him of his crown and proclaimed Norton champion on March 29, 1978. Norton lost the title in his first defense, on June 9, 1978, when Larry Holmes won a 15-round decision in Las Vegas.

In 50 professional fights, Norton had 42 victories, 33 by knockout. He lost 7, 4 by knockout, and also had 1 draw. His son, Ken Jr., played football at UCLA and was a starting linebacker for the Dallas Cowboys when they won Super Bowl XXVII after the 1992 season.

★ International Boxing Hall of Fame

Norton, Ray

TRACK AND FIELD
b. Sept. 22, 1937, Tulsa, Okla.

The top sprinter in the world in 1959 and 1960, Norton suffered through a terribly embarrassing Olympics. He was given a good chance of winning three gold medals, in both sprints and in the sprint relay. He didn't win any medals at all. Norton finished dead last in the sprints and was on the receiving end of an illegal baton pass that resulted in the disqualification of the U.S. 4 x 100-meter relay team.

Running for San Jose State, Norton won the NCAA 220-yard dash in 1959, and he was the AAU outdoor 100- and 200-meter champion in 1959 and 1960. On April 4, 1959, he ran the 100 meters in 10.1 seconds, and later that year he tied the world record of 9.3 seconds in the 100-yard dash. In the spring of 1960, he twice ran the 200-meter in 20.6 seconds to tie the world record. After the record had been lowered to 20.5, he tied

that in a preliminary heat at the Olympics.

Norton did win gold medals in the sprints and sprint relay at the 1959 Pan-American Games.

Notter, Joseph A.

HORSE RACING
b. June 21, 1890, Brooklyn, N.Y.
d. April 10, 1973

Something of a specialist at riding two-year-olds because of his easy riding style and ability to evaluate horses, Notter won the Hopeful Stakes, a juvenile race, three times. One of his winners in that race was the filly Regret, in 1914.

Notter persuaded trainer Jimmy Rowe to enter Regret in the 1915 Kentucky Derby, and she led all the way to win. She was the only filly to win that prestigious race until Genuine Risk in 1980.

His only other victory in a triple crown race came aboard Colin in the 1908 Belmont. Notter led jockeys in winnings that year with a record $464,322.

In 1923, Notter retired from riding with 56 major stakes victories and became a successful trainer. Notter later served as a racing official.

★ National Horse Racing Hall of Fame

Novara-Reber, Sue (Susan)

CYCLING
b. Nov. 22, 1955, Flint, Mich.

Nicknamed "Navajo Sue" because of her long ponytail, Novara originally planned to be a speed skater, but she switched to cycling when she was 13.

In 1975, Novara became the youngest cyclist ever to win the world sprint cycling championship. She had placed second in a photo-finish the year before. She was also second three years in a row, from 1976 through 1978, and she won the championship again in 1980.

Novara had a series of exciting duels with Sheila Young in the national match sprint championships. She finished second to Young in 1971, beat her in 1972, finished second to her in 1973, beat her in 1974 and 1975, and finished second to her once more in 1976. Novara then won the championship four years in a row, from 1977 through 1980.

When women's cycling was added to the Olympic program for the 1984 games, the only event was the road race. Hoping for a medal, Novara switched from track racing to road racing in 1982 and won the national championship. However, she failed to win a medal in the Olympics.

In her last race, Novara won the 1984 Central Park Grand Prix in New York City. She then retired from competition. In March 1986, the U.S. Cycling Federation hired her to coach the U.S. women's team preparing for the 1987 world championships. Under Novara's direction, the team won four medals, including a gold.

Nunes, Leo G.

FENCING
b. Jan. 29, 1892, Leghorn, Italy

Nunes won the Rome epee championship in 1914, shortly before coming to the U.S. He won the U.S. national epee title in 1917, 1922, 1924, 1926, 1928, and 1932, the saber championship in 1922, 1926, and 1929, and the foil championship in 1924.

In 1928, Nunes was the winner of the President's medal as the top scorer in three-weapon competition.

Nyad, Diana

SWIMMING
b. Aug. 22, 1949, New York, N.Y.

Nyad won three Florida state championships in the 100-meter backstroke during her high school years. She dreamed of swimming in the 1968 Olympics, but in 1966 she spent three months in bed with endocarditis, an infection of the heart, and when she began swimming again, she had lost her speed.

Buck Dawson, director of the International Swimming Hall of Fame in Florida, introduced her to marathon swimming later in her teens, and she began training at his camp in Ontario, Canada. She set a woman's world record of 4 hours and 22 minutes in her first race, a 10-mile swim in Lake Ontario in July 1970, finishing 10th overall.

While attending Emory University in Atlanta and Lake Forest College in Illinois, Nyad found time to train and to enter major marathon races throughout the world. In the 22-mile bay of Naples race in June 1974, she set another women's record of 8 hours, 11 minutes.

Nyad then begin swimming solo marathons. In 1974, she attempted a two-way crossing of Lake Ontario, 32 miles in each direction. After crossing successfully in 18 hours and 20 minutes, Nyad lost consciousness on the return swim and had to be pulled out of the water.

Heavy tides ended her first attempt to swim around Manhattan Island in September 1975, but she set a record of 7 hours and 57 minutes for the 28 miles on October 6.

Nyad announced plans to swim 130 miles from Havana, Cuba, to Marathon Key, Florida, in August 1977. The effort was delayed by the Cuban government. She finally set out in October but was unable to finish. However, she set a world distance record by swimming 89 miles from the Bahamas to Florida in 27 hours, 38 minutes in 1978.

Nyad then retired from marathon swimming. She wrote a book about her experiences, *Other Shores.*

★ ★ O ★ ★

Oakley, Annie [Annie Moses]

SHOOTING

b. Aug. 13, 1860, Greenville, Ohio
d. Nov. 3, 1926

Annie Moses learned to shoot game as a young girl to help feed her family. Aware of her shooting prowess, her neighbors raised money to send her to Cincinnati in 1895 for a match against Frank Butler, a marksman who had a traveling show.

She won the match, and Butler added her to his troupe, giving her the stage name Annie Oakley. Later they were married. In 1884, Buffalo Bill Cody signed them to travel with his Wild West Show. Oakley quickly became the show's biggest star.

Although known for her trick shots, Oakley was also a great trapshooter. Between 1867 and 1922, when she was 62 years old, she broke 100 targets in a row many times.

Among her feats were hitting a dime thrown into the air, splitting a playing card held on edge from 30 paces, and shooting a cigarette from Butler's lips. Oakley's most spectacular trick was to lie on her back and have someone throw six glass balls into the air simultaneously. Using three double-barreled shotguns, she would break all six before they hit the ground.

The Irving Berlin musical, *Annie Get Your Gun*, was based on her life, and free passes are still called "Annie Oakleys" because of the holes that are punched in them so that they won't be counted as paid admissions.

Oberlander, Swede (Andrew J.)

FOOTBALL

b. Feb. 17, 1905, Chelsea, Mass.
d. Jan. 1, 1968

Oberlander played tackle at Dartmouth in 1924 and was moved to the backfield the following season because of his strong passing arm. He threw 12 touchdown passes to lead Dartmouth to victory in all eight of its games, and he was named an All-American.

He once explained, "My secret of timing was to whisper to myself, 'Ten thousand Swedes jumped out of the weeds at the Battle of Copenhagen.' After reciting that jingle to myself, I'd let the ball go, confident my ends would be downfield by then."
★ College Football Hall of Fame

O'Brien, Davey (Robert David)

FOOTBALL

b. June 22, 1917, Dallas, Tex.
d. Nov. 18, 1977

The 5-foot-7, 150-pound O'Brien succeeded Sammy Baugh as the tailback in Texas Christian University's pass-oriented spread offense in 1937. The team got off to a slow start that season, but O'Brien led them to three victories in a row, over Texas, Rice, and Southern Methodist, for a 4–4–2 record.

In 1938, "Slingshot Davey" really came into his own. TCU won all ten regular season games, then beat Carnegie Tech, 15–7, in the Sugar Bowl, when O'Brien completed 17 of 28 passes for 225 yards. He was not only a great passer but a fast, elusive runner, as he demonstrated in a 20–7 win over Southern Methodist. He returned a punt 39 yards to set up a 37-yard touchdown pass that put the game out of reach.

During his career at Texas Christian, O'Brien completed 197 of 432 passes for 2,659 yards. He was named an All-American in 1938 and became the first person ever to win the Camp, Heisman, and Maxwell awards as the nation's outstanding college player.

O'Brien joined the Philadelphia Eagles of the NFL in 1939, finished second in the league in passing, and was named an All-Pro. In his last game, on December 1, 1940, he completed 33 of 60 passes against the Washington Redskins for 316 yards. O'Brien then retired from football to become an FBI agent.

★ College Football Hall of Fame

O'Brien, Joseph C.

HARNESS RACING
b. June 25, 1917, Alberton, P.E.I.
d. Sept. 29, 1984

O'Brien trained and drove Scott Frost, the harness horse of the year in 1955 and 1956. The first horse to win the trotting triple crown — the Hambletonian, Kentucky Futurity, and Yonkers Futurity — Scott Frost won 23 of 28 races in 1955 and earned $186,101, a record at the time.

In 1956, Scott Frost finished a close second to Galophone in his first two races and then won 17 in a row. He had seven clockings of less than 2 minutes in the mile; his best time was 1:58³/₅ at Hollywood Park in 1956.

O'Brien began driving on fairground tracks when he was 13. In 1946, he started racing on the grand circuit and soon became one of its top drivers. He won the Kentucky Futurity four times, the Hambletonian twice, and was the second driver to have more than 2,000 official victories. His career winnings surpassed $7 million.

All of the pacers O'Brien trained wore shadow rolls because he had the unusual theory that if they saw they were wearing hobbles, they would think their legs were tied together and would fall down as a result.

★ Hall of Fame of the Trotter

O'Brien, Parry (William Parry Jr.)

TRACK AND FIELD
b. Jan. 28, 1932, Santa Monica, Calif.

O'Brien revolutionized shot putting in the early 1950s by starting with his face toward the back of the ring and going through a 180-degree turn to build up momentum. On May 8, 1954, just two days after Roger Bannister had become the first to run the mile in less than 4 minutes, O'Brien became the first to put the shot more than 60 feet. Within a short time, virtually every shot putter had adopted his technique.

As a student at the University of Southern California, O'Brien won the NCAA title in 1952 and 1953. He was the AAU national outdoor champion from 1951 through 1956 and in 1959 and 1960, and he won the indoor title nine straight years, from 1953 through 1961. He was also the AAU discus champion in 1955.

The 6-foot-3, 245-pound O'Brien won gold medals in his event at the 1952 and 1956 Olympics and at the 1955 and 1959 Pan-American Games. He won a silver medal in the 1960 Olympics and placed fourth in 1964.

From July 1952 to June 1956, O'Brien was the shot put winner at 116 consecutive meets. He set his first world record in 1953 with a put of 59–2¹/₄, and he improved on that 15 times during the next six years. His last world record was 63 feet, 2 inches in 1959, when he won the Sullivan Award as the nation's outstanding amateur athlete.

While others surpassed his mark, O'Brien kept improving and achieved a personal best of 64 feet, 7¹/₄ inches in 1966. He still holds the record for the combined shot put, 106 feet, 10¹/₂ inches, achieved with a right-handed put of 61 feet, ³/₄ inch and a left-handed put of 45 feet, 9¹/₂ inches.

★ National Track and Field Hall of Fame; Olympic Hall of Fame

O'Connor, Buddy (Herbert W.)

HOCKEY
b. June 21, 1916, Montreal, P.Q.

At 143 pounds, O'Connor was one of

the smallest players in the NHL during the 1940s. A clever playmaker, he joined the Montreal Canadiens in 1941, and in his second season he had four assists in one period, an NHL record which has been tied several times.

He was traded to the New York Rangers before the 1947–48 season, when he scored 60 points on 24 goals and 36 assists, finishing one point behind Elmer Lach in the NHL scoring race. He was the first player ever to win, in the same season, the Hart Trophy as the league's most valuable player and the Lady Byng Trophy for combining skillful play with gentlemanly conduct.

O'Connor retired in 1951. He scored 140 goals and had 257 assists in 509 regular season games and added 15 goals and 21 assists in 53 playoff games.

★ Hockey Hall of Fame

O'Dea, Patrick J.

FOOTBALL
b. March 17, 1872, Melbourne, Australia
d. April 4, 1962

Ranked one of the greatest kickers of all time, O'Dea was a rugby star in Australia before coming the United States in 1896 and entering the University of Wisconsin, where his brother coached track and field. He drop-kicked a 62-yard field goal and had an 87-yard punt against Northwestern in 1898.

The 6-foot, 170-pound O'Dea was also a dangerous runner; he had a 90-yard kickoff return for a touchdown in 1899 against Beloit College. He also kicked four field goals in that game.

Because of his rugby background, O'Dea was expert at kicking the ball on the run, and he was also known for his ability to curve a punt, a trick he later taught Notre Dame fullback Red Salmon. O'Dea coached Notre Dame to a 14–4–2 record from 1900 through 1901 and had a 5–3–0 record as coach at the University of Missouri in 1902.

He disappeared for more than 15 years, and it was thought that he may have joined the Australian army during World War I. Late in 1934, he was found living under the name of Charles

J. Mitchell in Westwood, California. He had assumed the new identity because he was tired of being known as a former star football player.

★ College Football Hall of Fame

O'Doul, Lefty (Francis J.)

BASEBALL
b. March 4, 1897, San Francisco, Calif.
d. Dec. 7, 1969

Originally a pitcher, O'Doul spent a long time in the minor leagues. He was with the New York Yankees briefly in 1919, 1920, and 1922, and in 1923 he appeared in 23 games, 22 of them in relief, for the Boston Red Sox. After that, he had just a 1–1 record.

Then he was moved to the outfield. He returned to the major leagues with the New York Giants in 1928, when he was 31 years old, and proved himself a tremendous hitter. Unfortunately, his career had been on hold too long. He spent only 6½ seasons in the majors as an outfielder, winning two batting titles in the process.

O'Doul hit .319 in his season with the Giants, then went to the Philadelphia Phillies in 1929. He led the league with a .398 average and 254 hits that season, hitting 32 home runs, scoring 152 runs, and driving in 122.

After batting .383 in 1930, he was traded to the Brooklyn Dodgers. He hit .336 for them in 1931 and won his second batting title with a .368 average in 1932, when he had 21 home runs and 90 RBI.

During the 1933 season, O'Doul was sent back to the Giants. He hit .306 for them, ending the season with a composite .284 average. The Giants won the pennant, and O'Doul got his only at-bat in the World Series that year, hitting a single to drive in two runs in the second game, as the Giants beat the Washington Senators in five games.

O'Doul finished his major league career by hitting .316 as a part-time player for the Giants in 1934. His career batting average was .349. He had 1,140 hits in only 970 games, including 175 doubles,

41 triples, and 113 RBI. He scored 624 runs and drove in 542.

Oerter, Alfred A., Jr.

TRACK AND FIELD
b. Aug. 19, 1936, Astoria, N.Y.

An incredible competitor, Oerter was never favored to win an Olympic gold medal in the discus, yet he did it four times, each time beating the world record holder in the event. Three times he did it with a personal best throw.

As a sophomore at the University of Kansas, Oerter had not yet won a major competition when he entered the 1956 Olympics. Fortune Gordien of the U.S., the world record holder in the discus, was favored to win, but Oerter's first throw went 184 feet, 11 inches, the best he'd ever done to that point, and Gordien couldn't beat it. In fact, Oerter had the three longest throws in the event.

Oerter finished second in the 1960 Olympic trials to Rink Babka, the world record holder, and he trailed Babka after four throws in the Olympic finals. On his fifth and final throw, he made a change in his style at the suggestion of Babka, and won the event with a distance of 194 feet, 2 inches.

On May 18, 1962, Oerter became the first to throw the discus more than 200 feet, with a world record of 200 feet, 5 inches. The record was broken shortly afterward, but Oerter regained it with a throw of 204 feet, 10½ inches on July 1. He increased it to 205 feet, 5 inches on April 27, 1963, and to 206 feet, 6 inches on April 25, 1964.

That was his last world record, as Ludvik Danek of Czechoslovakia took over before the 1964 Olympics, when Oerter turned in a remarkably courageous performance. He suffered torn cartilage in his lower ribs a week before. Given a shot of Novocain and wrapped in ice packs and bandages to prevent internal bleeding, he remarked, "If I don't do it on the first throw, I won't be able to do it all."

But he was only in third place after four throws; Danik, who had won 45 consecutive meets, was in the lead. On his fifth attempt, Oerter somehow came up with a winning throw of 201 feet, 1 inch, then doubled over with pain.

Jay Silvester of the U.S. held the world record going into the 1968 Olympics, and Oerter again had physical problems, a pulled thigh muscle and a disc problem that required him to wear a surgical collar. After a poor throw and a foul, he took off the collar and tossed it aside, then threw the discus 212 feet, 6 inches, five feet farther than he'd ever thrown it before. He became the only person to win a gold medal in the same event at four consecutive Olympics.

Oerter was the NCAA discus champion in 1957, and he tied for the title in 1958. He was the AAU national champion in 1957, 1959, 1960, 1962, 1964, and 1966. He also won a gold medal at the 1959 Pan-American Games.

★ National Track and Field Hall of Fame; Olympic Hall of Fame

O'Farrell, Bob (Robert A.)

BASEBALL
b. Oct. 19, 1896, Waukegan, Ill.
d. Feb. 20, 1988

After appearing in a total of just six games with the NL's Chicago Cubs from 1915 through 1917, O'Farrell joined the team as a backup catcher in 1918. He became the starter in 1920 and had his best offensive year in 1922, batting .324.

The Cubs traded O'Farrell to the St. Louis Cardinals during the 1925 season. An outstanding defensive catcher, he was named the league's most valuable player in 1926, when he hit .293 to help lead the Cardinals to the NL pennant. O'Farrell batted .304 in the team's seven-game victory over the New York Yankees in the World Series.

In 1927, O'Farrell became playing manager, but he was traded to the New York Giants early in the 1928 season. He returned to the Cardinals in 1933 and began the 1934 season as the playing manager of the Cincinnati Reds. The Reds released him after 91 games, and he finished the season with the Cubs. O'Farrell ended his career as a pinch hitter with the Cardinals in 1935.

In 21 seasons, O'Farrell batted .273 with 1,120 hits, including 201 doubles,

58 triples, and 51 home runs. He scored 517 runs and drove in 549.

Okoye, Christian E.

FOOTBALL
b. Aug. 16, 1961, Enugu, Nigeria

Okoye, the "Nigerian Nightmare," was named the American Football Conference's offensive player of the year by the United Press International in 1989, when he led the NFL in rushing attempts with 370 and yards gained rushing with 1,480 for a 4.0 average and 12 touchdowns.

Okoye played football for the first time at little Azusa Pacific College in California. A 6-foot-1, 260-pound running back, he was drafted by the Kansas City Chiefs in the second round of the 1987 NFL draft. He gained 660 yards on 157 carries, a 4.2 average, as a rookie.

Because of a broken thumb, he played in only nine games in 1988. After his outstanding 1989 season, he gained only 805 yards in 1990 but rushed for 1,031 in 1991. Okoye had another off season with only 448 yards and a 3.1 average in 1992, when he was used primarily as a short-yardage runner.

He retired after the 1992 season with 4,897 yards on 1,246 carries, a 3.9 average, and 40 rushing touchdowns. He also caught 42 passes for 294 yards, a 7.0 average.

Olajuwon, Hakeem A.

BASKETBALL
b. Jan. 21, 1963, Lagos, Nigeria

After graduating from Nigeria's Moslem Teachers College (actually a high school) in 1980, Olajuwon won a basketball scholarship to the University of Houston. He didn't play his freshman year but worked out with the team, learning the game's finer points, and was a consensus All-American at center in 1984, when he was named the most outstanding player in the NCAA tournament.

The 7-foot, 255-pound Olajuwon led NCAA Division I schools with a .675 field goal percentage and 13.5 rebounds and 5.6 blocked shots per game as a senior. He was chosen by the Houston

Rockets in the first round of the 1984 NBA draft.

Not a great scorer in college, where he averaged just 13.3 points a game, Olajuwon, as a professional, developed an accurate medium range jump shot to go with his power around the basket and quickly became a proficient scorer, averaging 20.6 points a game as a rookie and reaching a career high of 26.1 points in the 1992–93 season.

Olajuwon led the NBA in rebounds with 1,105 in 1988–89 and 1,149 in 1989–90 and in blocked shots with 376 in 1989–90 and 342 in 1992–93. He was named to the All-NBA first team in 1987, 1988, 1989, and 1993 and to the all-defensive first team in 1987, 1988, 1990, and 1993.

Through the 1993–94 season, Olajuwon had scored 17,899 points in 756 games, a 23.7 average, and he had collected 9,464 rebounds and 2,741 blocked shots. In 85 playoff games, he had 2,298 points, a 27.0 average, with 1,045 rebounds and 329 blocks.

Oldfield, Barney (Berna E.)

AUTO RACING
b. June 3, 1878, Wauseon, Ohio
d. Oct. 6, 1946

One of the most colorful figures in auto racing history, Oldfield boxed professionally for a time, then became a bicycle racer in 1895. The first car he ever drove was Henry Ford's new 999 in the 1902 Manufacturer's Challenge Cup race at Grosse Pointe, Michigan. Worried about the fate of his car, Ford counseled caution before the start of the race. "I'd rather be dead than broke," Oldfield supposedly replied. Driving the car as he'd learned to race bikes, by sliding through turns rather than braking for them, he won the five-mile race in 5 minutes, 28 seconds, a half-mile ahead of his nearest competitor.

In 1903, Oldfield became the first American to drive a mile in a minute. Later that year he lowered the record to 55.8, and was hired by Winton. He drove Winton's Bullet to a win over W. K. Vanderbilt, Henry Ford, and others in the world one-mile straightaway championship in Florida early in 1904 and then began barnstorming in the Peerless auto company's Green Dragon, taking on all comers.

Much of his fame was built on such barnstorming trips with a variety of cars, doing exhibitions or winning races, often fixed, on fairground tracks. He raced in the Indy 500 for the first time in 1914, finishing fifth. He was the only American driver, and his car the only American car to place in the top eight. He also finished fifth in the 1916 race.

He retired from competition in 1918, but his name lived on much longer as a synonym for daredevil speed. It also lived on for some years in an advertising slogan: "'Firestone Tires are my only life insurance,' says Barney Oldfield, world's greatest driver."

★ Indianapolis Speedway Hall of Fame

Olerud, John G.

BASEBALL
b. Aug. 5, 1968, Seattle, Wash.

The 6-foot-5, 205-pound Olerud joined the AL's Toronto Blue Jays late in the 1989 season and became a regular in 1990, when he was used mostly as a designated hitter, with some playing time at first base.

Baseball observers admired the left-handed Olerud's swing, but he didn't seem to be quite the hitter he should have been until 1993, when he became a better hitter than anyone could have predicted. Olerud was much more selective that season, collecting 114 walks compared to only 70 in 1992, and he batted nearly .400 for the first five months of the season, then cooled off and ended at .363, which was still 31 percentage points better than anyone else in the league.

Oliphant, Elmer Q.

FOOTBALL
b. July 9, 1892, Bloomfield, Ind.
d. July 3, 1975

Short but solidly built at 5-foot-7 and 174 pounds, Oliphant developed strength and toughness by working as a coal miner during his summer vacations after entering Purdue in 1910. An end as

a freshman, he was a starting halfback for his final three seasons at the school and distinguished himself as a runner and kicker.

Oliphant was named to the 1914 Helms Athletic Foundation basketball All-American team as a guard, and he also won letters in baseball and track, often competing in a track event between innings of a baseball game.

After graduating in 1914, Oliphant was appointed to the U.S. Military Academy at West Point. Eligibility rules at that time allowed him to continue in sports. He played little in his first year but had an outstanding game against Maine, running for three touchdowns, two of them on 70-yard runs, and passing for a fourth touchdown.

In 1915, Oliphant scored all of Army's points in a 10–0 win over Georgetown and a 14–0 win over Navy. He was an All-American the following season, when he scored 112 points in nine games. Because of World War I, Walter Camp didn't name an All-American team in 1917, Oliphant's final season. If he had, Oliphant undoubtedly would have made it, for he had 125 points in only eight games that season.

Oliphant also won letters in baseball, basketball, and track. As a junior, he gave up basketball for ice hockey and became the only Army athlete in history to win letters in five different sports.

In 1920 and 1921, while serving at West Point, Oliphant played some professional football with the Buffalo All-Americans, and he coached Army's track team for two seasons. After leaving the Army in 1922, he served as athletic director at Union College in Schenectady, New York, for a year before entering the insurance business.

★ College Football Hall of Fame

Oliva, Tony (Pedro)

BASEBALL
b. July 20, 1940, Pinar Del Rio, Cuba

Oliva had brief tryouts with the AL's Minnesota Twins in 1962 and 1963 and became a starting outfielder in 1964. The 6-foot-2, 190-pounder won the first of three batting titles that year with a .323 average, also leading the league with 109 runs, 217 hits, and 43 doubles.

He won a second consecutive title with a .321 average in 1965, again leading the league in hits with 185, but he batted only .192 in Minnesota's seven-game loss to the Los Angeles Dodgers in the World Series.

A right-handed thrower but a left-handed hitter, Oliva led the AL with 34 doubles in 1967, with 197 hits and 39 doubles in 1969, and with 204 hits and 36 doubles in 1970. He then won his third batting championship with a .338 average in 1971, when he was also the league's best slugger, with a .546 percentage.

He suffered a knee injury diving for a fly ball in July 1971 but continued playing despite pain. Because of extensive surgery after the season, he missed virtually all of 1972 and was never the same hitter. He played with the Twins through the 1976 season, primarily as a designated hitter, and never batted over .300 again.

In 1,676 games, Oliva had a .304 average with 1,917 hits, including 329 doubles, 48 triples, and 220 home runs. He scored 870 runs and had 947 RBI.

Olsen, Merlin J.

FOOTBALL
b. Sept. 15, 1940, Logan, Utah

An All-American tackle at Utah State in 1961, Olsen also won the Outland Trophy as the nation's outstanding collegiate lineman. He was a first-round draft choice of the NFL's Los Angeles Rams, where he became an anchor of one of the best defensive lines of the 1960s, the "Fearsome Foursome."

A Phi Beta Kappa, the 6-foot-5, 270-pound Olsen used intelligence as well as size, strength, and agility to dissect NFL offenses. Los Angeles coach George Allen once said of him, "We never had a bad game from Merlin. We always got a good game and, more often than not, a great game."

Olsen was a consensus All-Pro choice at left defensive tackle from 1966 through 1970 and in 1973, and he played in a record 14 consecutive Pro Bowls. He retired after the 1976 season and became an excellent commentator on NBC's television broadcasts of NFL football.

★ College Football Hall of Fame; Pro Football Hall of Fame

Olsen, Zoe Ann (Mrs. Jensen)

DIVING
b. Feb. 11, 1931

Olsen won her first national championships at the age of 14, in the AAU indoor 1-meter and 3-meter springboard. She was also the indoor 1-meter titlist in 1946, 1947, and 1949 and the 3-meter champion in 1948 and 1949.

In AAU outdoor meets, she won the 3-meter springboard four years in a row, from 1946 through 1949, and the 1-meter springboard in 1948 and 1949.

Olsen won a silver medal in the springboard event at the 1948 Olympics. Although she didn't win a national championship after 1949, she returned to competition to win a bronze medal in the 1952 springboard event. She was the only woman diver to win a medal in both those Olympics.

In 1949, Olsen married Jackie Jensen, a football star at the University of California who played baseball for the New York Yankees and the Boston Red Sox.

Olson, Lute (Robert Luther)

BASKETBALL
b. Sept. 22, 1934, Mayville, N.Dak.

Olson played baseball, basketball, and football at Augsburg College in Minnesota. After graduating in 1956, he coached high school basketball until 1974, when he took over at Long Beach State College and had a 24–2 record. He then went to the University of Iowa.

He was named coach of the year in 1980, when he guided Iowa to the final four in the NCAA tournament. In nine seasons there, he had a 167–91 record with six seasons of 20 or more victories. Olson moved to the University of Arizona in 1984 and quickly built a winning program. He had an 11–17 record in his first season but won four Pacific Ten championships over the next six years.

Arizona was ranked first in the nation at the end of the 1987–88 season and reached the NCAA final four.

Through the 1992–93 season, Olson had a career record of 458 wins and 179 losses for a .719 winning percentage, which ranks 30th all-time.

Omelenchuk, Jeanne

SPEED SKATING
b. March 25, 1931

From 1957 through 1965, Omelenchuk won ten U.S. and North American speed skating championships. She was the North American outdoor champion from 1957 through 1959 and in 1962 and 1963, and the U.S. outdoor titlist in 1958, 1959, 1962, and 1965. She also won the U.S. open outdoor championship in 1965.

O'Neal, Shaquille R.

BASKETBALL
b. March 6, 1972, Newark, N.J.

Quick, agile, and a great leaper, the 7-foot-1, 301-pound O'Neal was recognized as a phenomenon as a junior in high school, when he was a little, but not much, smaller. At Louisiana State University, he was an All-American in 1990 and 1991.

He led NCAA Division I teams with 14.7 rebounds a game as a sophomore and with 5.2 blocked shots per game as a junior in 1991, when he was the consensus college player of the year.

In three years as a starter at LSU, O'Neal averaged 21.6 points a game, shooting .575 from the floor. He left school after his junior year and was made the first pick in the 1992 NBA draft by the Orlando Magic.

He was named the league's rookie of the year in 1993. Through his first two seasons in the NBA, O'Neal had scored 4,270 points in 162 games, a 26.4 average, with 2,194 rebounds and 517 blocked shots.

Oosterbaan, Bennie (Benjamin G.)

BASKETBALL, FOOTBALL
b. Feb. 4, 1906, Muskegon, Mich.

A baseball, basketball, and football star in high school, Oosterbaan was named to an All-American team as a senior after his school took part in the national interscholastic basketball tournament in Chicago in 1924. That was just the beginning. At the University of Michigan, he was a three-time All-American end in football and twice an All-American forward in basketball.

With quarterback Benny Friedmann, Oosterbaan formed one of college football's first great passing combinations in 1925. Friedmann threw twelve touchdown passes that season, and Oosterbaan caught six of them. He was also a good passer. In the fashion of the day, Oosterbaan was often used on end-around plays or pulled into the backfield for a passing play. Against Ohio State in 1927, his senior season, he threw touchdown passes of 20 and 50 yards.

The 6-foot, 190-pounder had large hands that enabled him to make some spectacular catches. New York sportswriter George Trevor, who put Oosterbaan on his all-time All-American team in 1929, called him "probably the greatest of all pass receivers."

In basketball, he led the Western Conference (Big Ten) in field goals with 50 in 1926–27 and in field goals with 57 and scoring with 129 points in 1927–28. He batted .469 for the Michigan baseball team as a senior.

After graduating, Oosterbaan turned down offers to play professional football and baseball. He became an assistant football coach at Michigan instead. He was named head coach in 1948 and remained through the 1958 season, winning 63 games while losing 33 and tying 4.

★ College Football Hall of Fame

O'Rourke, Jim (James H.)

BASEBALL
b. Aug. 24, 1850, Bridgeport, Conn. d. Jan. 8, 1919

Called "Orator Jim" because of his eloquent speech, O'Rourke played every position at one time or another, but he was known as a hitter. When he was only 16, he began playing for a top semipro team, the Mansfields of Middletown, Connecticut. In 1872, the team entered the National Association, the first major professional league.

The Mansfields disbanded after that season, and O'Rourke joined the Boston Red Stockings. The National League replaced the National Association in 1875. O'Rourke remained in Boston to play for its new NL team, and he got the first hit in the history of the league.

O'Rourke led the league with 68 runs scored and 20 walks in 1877. He went to the Providence Greys in 1879, then returned to Boston the following season and led the NL in home runs with six. The Buffalo NL team signed O'Rourke as playing manager in 1881. He remained there through 1884, when he led the league with 162 hits, then joined the New York Giants.

When the Players' League was formed in 1890, O'Rourke played for its New York team, but the league lasted only one season, and he returned to the Giants. He finished his career with the Washington NL team in 1893, though he returned to catch one game for the Giants in 1904, at the age of 54.

Unlike most players of his era, O'Rourke saved his money and invested it wisely. He also received a law degree from Yale University while playing, and he practiced law after leaving baseball.

In 1,774 major league games, he had a .310 batting average with 2,304 hits, including 414 doubles, 132 triples, and 50 home runs. O'Rourke scored 1,446 runs and drove in 1,010.

★ Baseball Hall of Fame

Orr, Bobby (Robert G.)
HOCKEY
b. March 20, 1948, Parry Sound, Ont.

Boston Bruins coach Harry Sinden said of Orr, "Bobby was a star from the moment they played the National Anthem in his first NHL game." He was expected to be. Orr joined the Bruins in 1966, when he was 18, after signing a two-year contract for $75,000, an unprecedented salary for a rookie. He won the 1967 Calder Trophy as the league's outstanding first-year player.

Harry Howell won the Norris Trophy as the league's best defenseman that year, and said, "I'm glad I won it now, because it's going to belong to that Orr from now on." He was right. Orr won the Norris Trophy the next eight years.

There was never another defenseman like Orr, and probably never will be. Often playing 40 or more minutes, he could control the puck, and the game, almost at will. He is the only defenseman ever to win the Ross Trophy as the NHL's leading scorer, and he did it twice, in 1970 and 1975. He became the second player in history to score more than 100 points in a season in 1970, when he had a record 87 assists. He won the Hart Trophy as the league's most valuable player three years in a row, 1970–72, and the Conn Smythe Trophy as the most valuable player in the playoffs twice, in 1970 and 1972.

When the Bruins won the Stanley Cup in 1970, Orr scored the winning goal in overtime of the fourth and final game against the St. Louis Blues. It was his ninth goal and twentieth point of the playoffs. The Bruins won the Cup again in 1972, when Orr had 19 playoff assists to break Jean Beliveau's record.

Orr is the only player ever to receive four individual trophies in a single season. He won the Hart, Norris, Ross, and Smythe awards in 1970.

Knee injuries shortened his brilliant career. He underwent the first of several knee operations before the 1972–73 season and was often forced out of the lineup by recurring problems. The Bruins traded him to the Chicago Black Hawks in 1978, but he played only a few games in Chicago before retiring.

In 657 regular season games, Orr scored 270 goals and had 645 assists. He had 26 goals and 66 assists in 74 playoff games. His average of 1.393 points per game is fifth best in history and by far the highest for a defenseman.

★ Hockey Hall of Fame

Orton, George W.
TRACK AND FIELD
b. Jan. 10, 1873, Strathroy, Ont.
d. June 26, 1958

After graduating from the University of Toronto, where he ran track and cross-country and also played soccer, Orton entered the University of Pennsylvania in 1893 to do graduate work. He was the IC4A mile champion in 1895 and 1897, and he also established and played for Penn's first ice hockey team.

Orton won the U.S. national 1-mile championship from 1892 through 1896 and in 1900. He was the 10-mile champion in 1899 and the cross-country champion in 1897 and 1898.

Since Canada didn't have an Olympic team in 1900, Orton was invited to join the U.S. team. He won a gold medal in the 2,500-meter steeplechase and a bronze in the 400-meter hurdles as well as finishing fourth in the 4,000-meter steeplechase.

After receiving his Ph.D. from Penn in 1896, he did another year of graduate work and then became an educator. Orton was Penn's track and field coach for several years, and he served as director of Philadelphia's Municipal Stadium from 1928 to 1934.

Osborn, Harold M.

TRACK AND FIELD
b. April 13, 1899, Butler, Ill.
d. April 5, 1975

In 1924, Osborn became the only athlete to win the decathlon and a gold medal in an individual event at the same Olympics. He won the high jump with an Olympic record of 6 feet, 6 inches, and set a world decathlon record with 7,710.775 points. Earlier in the year, he had set a world high jump record of 6 feet, 8¼ inches.

Competing for the University of Illinois, Osborn tied for the NCAA and AAU outdoor high jump championships in 1922. He won the AAU outdoor title in 1925 and 1926, the indoor title four years in a row, 1923 through 1926, and he was the AAU decathlon champion in 1923, 1925, and 1926. He also won the AAU indoor 70-yard hurdles in 1925.

Osborn also competed in the standing jumps, which are no longer contested. He won the AAU indoor standing high jump from 1929 through 1931 and

was second in the standing broad jump in 1930. At the age of 37, Osborn set a world record of 5 feet, 6 inches in the standing high jump. That record has never been broken.

★ National Track & Field Hall of Fame

Osborne, Margaret (Mrs. duPont)

TENNIS
b. March 4, 1918, Joseph, Oreg.

Although best known as a great doubles player, Osborne won six singles titles in grand slam tournaments, the U.S. national championships from 1948 through 1950, Wimbledon in 1947, and the French national in 1946 and 1949.

Osborne learned to play on hard courts in California, where she developed a serve-and-volley style with an outstanding backhand smash. She and Louise Brough formed one of the best doubles teams in history, losing only eight matches from 1942 through 1957. They won the women's doubles at Wimbledon in 1946, from 1948 through 1950, and in 1954, in the U.S. nationals from 1942 through 1950 and from 1955 through 1957, and in the French national tournament in 1946, 1947, and 1949.

Osborne also teamed with Sarah Palfrey to win the U.S. women's doubles championship in 1941. Osborne won the U.S. mixed doubles with Bill Talbert from 1943 through 1946, with Ken McGregor in 1950, with Ken Rosewall in 1956, and with Neale Fraser from 1958 through 1960. Osborne and Fraser also won the Wimbledon mixed doubles championship in 1962.

★ International Tennis Hall of Fame

Osburn, Carl T.

SHOOTING
b. May 5, 1884, Jacksontown, Ohio
d. Dec. 28, 1966

From 1912 through 1924, Osburn won a total of 11 Olympic medals, including 5 golds, 4 silvers, and 2 bronzes, in target shooting.

A 1906 graduate of the U.S. Naval Academy, Osburn became a career officer, eventually rising to the rank of commander.

At the 1912 Olympics, Osburn won a

gold medal as a member of the military rifle team; silvers in the military rifle, any position, and military rifle, three position; and bronze medals as a member of the small-bore rifle, prone, team and the running deer single shot team.

The 1916 Olympics were canceled because of World War I, but Osburn came back to win four gold medals in 1920. He won individual medals in the military rifle, standing, and in the military rifle, 300- and 600-meter, prone, and he was also a member of the winning free rifle team and the military rifle 300-meter, prone, team. Osburn won a silver medal as a member of the military rifle, standing, team.

In 1924, Osburn won his twelfth medal, a silver, in the free rifle.

Osmanski, Bill (William)

FOOTBALL
b. Dec. 29, 1915, Providence, R.I.

A 5-foot-11, 195-pound fullback, Osmanski combined speed with power. Nicknamed "Bullet Bill" because he ran the sprints in track and field, he was a starter at Holy Cross College in Massachusetts from 1936 through 1938.

Osmanski was chosen in the first round of the 1939 NFL draft by the Chicago Bears. He studied dentistry at Northwestern University while playing professional football. As a rookie, Osmanski led the NFL in rushing with 699 yards on 121 carries, a 5.8 average, though he played in only seven games because of a broken leg.

In Chicago's 73–0 win over the Washington Redskins for the 1940 NFL championship, Osmanski ran 68 yards for a touchdown on the team's second play from scrimmage.

Osmanski served in the Navy during World War II and was an assistant coach with the Great Lakes Naval Training Station and Camp LeJeune teams. He returned to the Bears in 1946 and retired from playing after the 1947 season. Osmanski coached Holy Cross to a 6–14–0 record in 1948 and 1949, and then left football to practice dentistry.

During his NFL career, he gained 1,743 on 374 rushing attempts, a 4.7 average, and 20 touchdowns. Osmanski

also caught 12 passes for 170 yards, a 14.2 average, and 1 touchdown.

Ott, Melvin T.

BASEBALL
b. March 2, 1909, Gretna, La.
d. Nov. 21, 1958

Armed with a letter of recommendation from the owner of a semipro team he'd played for, Ott visited John McGraw of the New York Giants in August 1925 and asked for a tryout. He was a catcher, but when McGraw saw the 5-foot-9, 170-pounder, he asked if he'd ever played the outfield.

"Only when I was a kid," the 16-year-old Ott replied. After watching the left-handed hitter drive some batting-practice home runs into the short right field at the Polo Grounds, McGraw decided to sign him. Ott had an unusual batting style: he stood with his feet wide apart, lifted his right leg as the ball was released, then put it down quickly, after a stride of just a couple of inches, to begin his swing. McGraw was afraid a minor league manager might change his stance and ruin him as a hitter.

Ott didn't appear in any games in 1925, but he sat next to McGraw on the bench and got advice on how to hit various NL pitchers. The following season, he got into just 35 games, batting .383.

In 1928, Ott became a regular, mostly in right field but also playing second and third base at times. He led the league with 113 walks in 1929, when he batted .328 with 42 home runs and 151 RBI.

Now established as the team's starting right fielder, Ott hit 38 home runs to lead the league in 1932 and also had a league-leading 100 walks. He led in walks for a third straight year with 75 in 1933, when the Giants won the pennant.

In his first World Series game, Ott got four hits in four at-bats. He hit .389 and won the fifth and deciding game with a tenth-inning home run, as the Giants beat the Washington Senators.

Ott won his second home run title with 35 in 1934, and he also took his only RBI championship with 135 that season. He then led the NL in home runs three years in a row, with 33 in 1936, 31 in 1937, and 36 in 1938. He also led with a .588 slugging percentage in 1936, with 102 walks in 1937, and with 116 runs scored in 1938.

Named playing manager in 1942, Ott won his sixth and last home run title with 30, also leading the league in runs with 118 and in walks with 109. After slipping to .234 in 1943, he hit .288 with 26 home runs in 1944 and .308 with 21 home runs in 1945.

In 1946, he concentrated primarily on managing, appearing in only 31 games. Ott finished his playing career with just four at-bats in 1947, and he was replaced as the Giants' manager during the following season.

Ott later managed in the minor leagues and did some work as a play-by-play radio announcer, both on the "Game of the Week" broadcasts and with the Detroit Tigers.

On November 14, 1958, he and his wife were seriously injured in an auto accident. Ott died of his injuries a week later.

In 22 major league seasons, all with the Giants, Ott had 2,876 hits, including 488 doubles, 72 triples, and 511 home runs, which was the NL record when he retired. He walked 1,708 times while striking out only 896 times, and he had 1,859 runs scored and 1,860 RBI.
★ Baseball Hall of Fame

Otto, Jim (James E.)
FOOTBALL
b. Jan. 5, 1938, Wausau, Wis.

The only all-league center in the history of the American Football League, the 6-foot-2 Otto weighed only 205 pounds when he came out of the University of Miami, Florida, in 1960. He wasn't drafted by any NFL teams, so he joined the Oakland Raiders of the new AFL, went on a strength program to increase his weight by 50 pounds, and was Oakland's starting center for the next 15 seasons.

Wearing uniform number 00, Otto was an outstanding blocker who was also responsible for calling Oakland's line-blocking schemes after sizing up the defensive alignment. He was the All-AFL center from 1960 through 1969. After the league merged with the NFL in 1970 and became the American Football Conference, he was the All-AFC center from 1970 through 1972.

Otto retired after the 1974 season. In his last eight years with Oakland, he played on seven division champions and one AFL champion team.
★ Pro Football Hall of Fame

Ouimet, Francis D.
GOLF
b. May 8, 1893, Brookline, Mass.
d. Sept. 2, 1967

Ouimet's victory in the 1913 U.S. Open over two great English golfers, Harry Vardon and Ted Ray, was a great boost for American golf. It almost didn't happen, because Ouimet didn't plan to play in the tournament.

He had taken vacation time earlier in the year from his job at Wright and Ditson, a sporting goods manufacturer, to play in the U.S. Amateur, where he was eliminated in the second round. He submitted his entry for the Open because Robert Watson, president of the U.S. Golf Association, asked him to. But Ouimet had no intention of taking more time off for a tournament he wasn't likely to win.

Shortly before the Open, his supervisor saw Ouimet's name in the list of entrants and asked him about it. Ouimet said he would like to watch Vardon and Ray, but he wasn't going to compete. "As long as you're entered, you'd better plan to play," the supervisor said.

The tournament was held at The Country Club in Brookline, Massachusetts. Ouimet knew the course well. He'd grown up across the street, and he'd caddied there for years, starting when he was 11. He'd even played there a few times, in the early morning, but never an entire round because greenskeepers invariably chased him off the course.

Ouimet astounded everyone by tying Vardon and Ray after 72 holes. After 16 holes of the 18-hole playoff, he led Vardon by one shot, Ray by two. Ouimet birdied the 17th hole while Vardon took a bogey, and the young American became the first amateur ever to win the Open, finishing with a 72 to a 77 for Vardon and a 78 for Ray.

His victory was front-page news, and it did a great deal to change the public image of golf, which had previously been viewed as a sport for the very wealthy. As Herbert Warren Wind wrote, "Here was a person all of America, not just golfing America, could understand — the boy from 'the wrong side' of the street, the ex-caddie, the kind who worked during his summer vacations from high school — America's idea of the American hero."

Ouimet also won the U.S. Amateur in 1914 and 1931, the French Amateur in 1914, the Western Amateur in 1917, the Massachusetts Amateur from 1913 to 1915 and in 1919, 1922, and 1925, and the Massachusetts Open in 1932. In 1951 he became the first non-Briton ever elected captain of the Royal and Ancient Golf Club of St. Andrews.

★ PGA Hall of Fame; World Golf Hall of Fame

Owen, Benny (Benjamin G.)

FOOTBALL
b. July 24, 1875, Chicago, Ill.
d. Feb. 26, 1970

Owen was quarterback of the University of Kansas team that went undefeated in 1899 under legendary coach "Hurry Up" Yost. After coaching Washburn College in Kansas in 1900, he rejoined Yost as an assistant coach at Michigan for a year and then became head coach at Bethany College in Kansas from 1901 through 1904, compiling a 22–2–2 record.

In 1905, two years before Oklahoma became a state, Owen began coaching at the University of Oklahoma. Like Yost, he created a fast-paced offense, with the quarterback calling signals for a play while players were still lying on the ground after the previous play.

His 1911 team was the first undefeated team to play a full schedule in Oklahoma history, with a 8–0–0 record. After the 1913 season, Owen lost all of his starters, and in desperation he created what he himself called "a wide open, reckless game." Oklahoma had a 9–1–1 record, led major colleges in scoring with 435 points, and completed 25 touchdown passes.

Averaging more than 30 passes a game, the 1915 team went undefeated. Owen also produced undefeated teams in 1918 and 1920. He retired as coach after the 1926 season but remained as athletic director through 1934 and oversaw construction of a new football stadium, a fieldhouse, a golf course, tennis courts, and a baseball field.

Owen, who lost his right arm in a hunting accident, became director of intramural athletics at the school in 1935. He retired in 1938. In his 27 seasons, Owen's teams won 155 games while losing 60 and tying 19.

★ College Football Hall of Fame

Owen, Steve (Stephen J.)

FOOTBALL
b. April 21, 1898, Cleo Springs, Okla.
d. May 17, 1964

Owen loved horses as a boy in Oklahoma, and at one time he hoped to become a jockey. Instead, he grew to be a 6-foot-2, 235-pound tackle.

After playing at Phillips University in his home state, Owen joined the NFL's Kansas City Cowboys for the 1924 and 1925 seasons. He went to the New York Giants in 1926 and remained with them, as a player and coach, for 28 seasons.

Owen became player-coach of the team in 1931. He retired as a player after that season, but returned to appear in some games in 1933. The Giants lost to the Chicago Bears, 23–21, in the 1934 NFL championship game, but beat the Bears, 30–13, the following year.

That was the famous "Sneakers Game," played on an icy field at the Polo Grounds in New York. The Giants were losing, 10–3, at the half, when Owen had his players replace their football cleats with basketball shoes for better footing. The Giants scored 27 points in the fourth quarter to win.

Owen took the Giants to six more championship games, in 1936, 1938, 1939, 1941, 1944, and 1946. They won only in 1938, beating the Green Bay Packers, 23–17. In his 23 years as head coach, the Giants had 18 winning seasons.

A believer in the precept that "football is a game played down in the dirt and it always will be," Owen was especially known as a defensive strategist. His 1950 team held the powerful Cleveland Browns to just 21 points in three games, including an 8–3 loss in the division playoff. Owen devised the "umbrella defense" to stop the Cleveland passing attack. Starting with a six-man line, he had his defensive ends drop back into pass coverage. That was the origin of the 4–3–3 defense still commonly used.

After a 3–9–0 season in 1953, Owen resigned. He had an overall record of 153 wins, 108 losses, and 17 ties.

★ Pro Football Hall of Fame

Owens, Jesse (James C.)
TRACK AND FIELD
b. Sept. 12, 1913, Danville, Ala.
d. March 31, 1980

The grandson of slaves, Owens was born into a share-cropping family, and when he was seven, he was expected to pick 100 pounds of cotton a day. At nine, his family moved to Cleveland. When he entered school, a teacher asked his name, and he responded "J. C.," which is what his family called him. The teacher thought he'd said "Jesse," and that name stuck for the rest of his life.

After setting national interscholastic records in the 100- and 220-yard dashes and the long jump, Owens attended Ohio State University. Although Owens is best known for winning four gold medals at the 1936 Olympics, his most incredible performance came in the 1935 Big Ten meet, where he broke four world records and tied another in a single afternoon.

After tying the record of 9.4 seconds in the 100-yard dash, he made a single attempt at the long jump and set a new world record of 26 feet, 8¼ inches. In the 220-yard dash, he set another record of 20.3 seconds, which was also accepted as a world record for the 200-meter. Owens then rested while the 2-mile run was taking place, and ran a record 22.6 in the 220-yard low hurdles.

Owens broke or tied Olympic records nine times at the 1936 Berlin Games, often known as the "Nazi Olympics." He won gold medals in the 100-meter, the 200-meter, the long jump, and as the anchor runner on the 4 x 100-meter relay team.

After the Olympics, he revealed his secret to a British journalist: "I let my feet spend as little time on the ground as possible. From the air, fast down, and from the ground, fast up. My foot is only a fraction of the time on the track."

Owens won the male athlete of the year award from the Associated Press but was irked at not winning the Sullivan Award as the outstanding amateur athlete of the year; that went to Glenn Morris, the Olympic decathlon champion.

Shortly after the Olympics, Owens was suspended by the AAU for not competing in a Swedish meet that he'd never agreed to enter. That effectively ended his competitive career. Owens made a living for a time by going on barnstorming tours, racing against dogs, horses, and motorcycles. He worked as a paid campaigner for presidential candidate Alf Landon in 1940 and then became a playground instructor in Cleveland.

During the 1950s, Owens went into public relations and came under fire for not supporting the civil rights movement strongly enough. One black writer, William Oscar Johnson, referred to him as "a professional good example."

Owens opposed the militant black athletes who threatened to boycott the 1968 Olympics, and in 1970 he wrote a book, *Blackthink*, which criticized militancy. Two years later, however, he retracted many of his earlier views in another book, *I Have Changed*.

An incessant smoker for 35 years, he died of lung cancer at his retirement home in Tucson, Arizona.

★ National Track and Field Hall of Fame; Olympic Hall of Fame

Owens, Steve (Loren E.)

FOOTBALL
b. Dec. 9, 1947, Gore, Okla.

A power runner with a surprising turn of speed, Owens gained 3,867 yards, an NCAA record at the time, in 905 carries at the University of Oklahoma, scoring 56 rushing touchdowns. He set another record by gaining more than 100 yards in 17 consecutive games. An All-American fullback in 1969, Owens won the Heisman Trophy as the nation's outstanding college player.

Owens's brief professional career was plagued by injuries. He joined the NFL's Detroit Lions as a first-round draft choice in 1970 but missed most of the season with a separated shoulder. In 1971, Owen returned to his college form and became the first Detroit player to rush for more than 1,000 yards in a season. He gained 1,035 yards in 246 carries, a 4.2 average, and scored 8 rushing touchdowns.

However, a whole series of injuries limited his playing time from 1972 through 1974. After missing the 1975 season, Owens retired. In five NFL seasons, he gained 2,451 yards on 635 carries, a 3.9 average, and scored 20 rushing touchdowns. He caught 60 passes for 785 yards, a 13.1 average, and 4 touchdowns.

★ ★ P ★ ★

Pace, Darrell O.

ARCHERY
b. Oct. 23, 1956, Cincinnati, Ohio

Darrell Pace won four consecutive national archery championships, from 1973 through 1976. He also won the title in 1978 and 1980. At 16, he was the youngest member of the U.S. team at the world championships, where he finished 23rd. He won the world title in 1975 and 1979 and finished second to long-time rival Rick McKinney in 1977 and 1983.

After winning an Olympic gold medal in 1976, Pace was selected for the 1980 Olympic team, but the U.S. boycotted the Moscow Games that year because of the Soviet invasion of Afghanistan. In 1984, he took a 13-point lead after the first day of the four-day competition and won an easy victory.

Pace still holds the world record of 2,571 points, set in 1976, and in 1979 he established a single-round record of 1,341 out of a possible 1,440 points.

Paddock, Charlie (Charles W.)

TRACK AND FIELD
b. Aug. 11, 1900, Gainesville, Tex.
d. July 21, 1943

The title "World's Fastest Human" was coined for Paddock, who held the world records for the 100-yard and 100-meter dashes through most of the 1920s. He was a frail infant who weighed only 7½ pounds at seven months of age, and his parents moved from Texas to California in 1907 to help improve his health. As a youth, he enjoyed distance running, but he was persuaded by his father to focus on sprinting because of his great natural speed.

He first won notice as a lieutenant in the Army, when he won the 100- and 200-meter sprints at the 1919 Inter-Allied Games in Paris, setting a world record in the 200-meter. After leaving the service, he attended the University of Southern California.

Paddock's trademark was his flying finish. He would leap when about 12 feet from the finish line, arms spread wide, and break the tape with his chest while gliding through the air. That unique finish helped him win the gold medal in the 100-meter at the 1920 Olympics, when he edged Morris Kirksey by about a foot. Paddock also won the silver medal in the 200-meter in 1920 and 1924, and he was on the U.S. 400-meter relay team that won the gold medal in 1924.

On April 3, 1921, Paddock set four world records and tied a fifth. He ran the 100-meter dash in 10.4, the 200-meter in 21.6, and the 300-meter in 33.8 seconds. While running the longer metric distances, he was timed at 9.6 for 100 yards and 20.2 for 200 yards.

A journalist, Paddock was sometimes accused of professionalism for writing about track and field, and several times he was involved in controversy with the AAU. In 1923, he competed in Europe after the AAU had forbidden athletes to participate in overseas meets. Paddock declared that the AAU had no jurisdiction over him because he was competing under the auspices of the NCAA. His amateur status was suspended, but it was restored in time for him to compete in the 1924 Olympics.

He was briefly suspended again in 1928 both for writing articles about meets in which he had competed and for promoting a movie in which he had appeared as himself. Again, the suspension was lifted before the Olympics, but G. W. Wightman resigned from the American Olympic Committee as a result.

Paddock retired from competition after the 1929 season. He became a newspaper executive until 1942, when he entered the Marine Corps. He was killed in the crash of a military plane near Sitka, Alaska.

★ National Track and Field Hall of Fame; Olympic Hall of Fame

Padilla, Douglas

TRACK AND FIELD
b. Oct. 4, 1956, Oakland, Calif.

Padilla graduated in 1981 from Brigham Young University, where he had begun running the 5,000 meters with limited success. Two years later, though, he emerged as the best U.S. runner at that distance, winning four consecutive national championships from 1983 through 1986, including the 1984 Olympic trials.

He finished seventh in the Olympics but won the World Cup 5,000-meter in 1985.

Page, Alan C.

FOOTBALL
b. Aug. 7, 1945, Canton, Ohio

A defensive end in college, Page was one of four consensus All-Americans on the great Notre Dame team that was named national champion in 1966 after winning 9 games and tying 1, against second-ranked Michigan State.

Although 6-foot-4 and only 240 pounds, Page was moved to defensive tackle when he joined the NFL's Minnesota Vikings in 1967. Incredibly fast and quick off the ball, Page could not only dominate much bigger offensive lineman, he could often dominate a game.

In 1971, Page became the first defensive player ever named the NFL's player of the year by Associated Press, and he also won the United Press International award as National Football Conference player of the year. Page that season had 109 tackles, 35 assists on tackles, 10 quarterback sacks, and 3 safeties.

The intelligent and individualistic Page was suddenly released by the Vikings during the 1978 season because he had put himself on a running program that brought his weight down to 225 pounds. The Chicago Bears immediately picked him up, and he was a starter with them for four years before retiring after the 1981 season.

In his 15 professional seasons, Page started 238 games and never missed one. He recovered 24 opposition fumbles, blocked 28 kicks, had 164 sacks, and made 1,431 tackles. He was a consensus All-Pro from 1968 through 1976.

Page earned a law degree while playing pro football and became a justice of the Minnesota Supreme Court in 1992.

★ Pro Football Hall of Fame

Page, Pat (Harlan O.)

BASKETBALL
b. March 20, 1887, Chicago, Ill.
d. Nov. 23, 1965

The 5-foot-9, 160-pound Page starred in baseball, basketball, and football at the University of Chicago. Although an end, he was often used as a passer, and he once completed 21 passes in a game. A left-handed pitcher, he rejected offers from professional baseball teams to remain in school. As a sharp-shooting guard, Page led Chicago to the AAU national basketball championship· in 1907, an undefeated season in 1908–09, and three Western Conference (Big Ten) championships. He was named the Helms Athletic Foundation player of the year for his senior season, 1909–10.

In 1911, Page became the basketball coach at Chicago and also assisted football coach Amos Alonzo Stagg. He went on to Butler University in Indiana in 1921 and coached that school to the 1924 AAU national championship. After coaching at Indiana University from 1925–26 through 1929–30, he returned to Butler for three seasons. He also coached at the College of Idaho from

1937–38 through 1938–39. His overall record was 200 wins and 127 losses.
★ Basketball Hall of Fame

Paige, Satchel (LeRoy R.)
BASEBALL
b. July 7, 1906, Mobile, Ala.
d. June 8, 1982

Possibly the greatest pitcher of all time and definitely one of the most colorful, Paige got his nickname because he had a job carrying satchels at the Mobile train station when he was only seven. He spent 5½ years in the Industrial School for Negro Children after stealing some small toys when he was 12 years old.

He learned to play baseball there, and after his release he began pitching for a semipro team in 1924. Two years later, he signed with the professional Chattanooga Black Lookouts.

That was the beginning of an amazing career in which Paige won an estimated 2,000 games in 2,500 starts, with 250 shutouts and more than 40 no-hitters. He went to the Birmingham Black Barons in 1928 and to the Nashville Elite Giants in 1929, when he also began to play winter baseball in the Caribbean, pitching as many as 200 games a year.

In 1930, the Baltimore Black Sox hired him to pitch in a post-season exhibition series against a team of major leaguers led by Babe Ruth. Paige and Ruth never faced each other, but Paige struck out 22 in one of the games.

After the Elite Giants folded during the 1931 season, Paige joined the Pittsburgh Crawfords. When he didn't get the salary he wanted in 1934, he formed his own barnstorming team, the Satchel Paige All-Stars. The team's publicity poster read, "Satchel Paige, world's greatest pitcher, guaranteed to strike out the first nine men."

Paige returned to Pittsburgh in 1936, jumped to the Dominican Republic for a $30,000 offer, went back to Pittsburgh briefly, then went to the Mexican League. Strictly a fastball pitcher with exceptional control, Paige came down with a sore arm in 1938, and it seemed his career might be over.

But the Kansas Monarchs hired him, and Paige learned to throw breaking pitches. The arm finally came back into shape, and he pitched Kansas City to five pennants in nine years, often working three or four games a week. He also developed his "hesitation pitch," in which he stopped his delivery for a split-second just as he seemed about to release the ball.

In the winter of 1947, Paige pitched against the barnstorming Bob Feller All-Stars. After he struck out 16 hitters, Feller told the Cleveland Indians they should sign Paige. They did, in July 1948. At 42, he became the oldest rookie in baseball history. Paige worked in 21 games, mostly in relief, and compiled a 6–1 record with 2 shutouts, 1 save, and a 2.48 ERA.

Someone suggested he should be rookie of the year. Paige later said, "I declined the position. I wasn't sure which year the gentleman had in mind."

He was released after a bad year in 1949, when he was bothered by stomach problems, and he began barnstorming again with the Chicago American Giants. He then spent three more seasons in the majors with the St. Louis Browns, and was the AL's best relief pitcher in 1952, when he had a 12–10 record with 10 saves and a 3.07 ERA.

Released after the 1953 season, he went right back to barnstorming until 1965, when the Kansas City Athletics signed him to work in one game. The oldest player in major league history at 59, he pitched three scoreless innings against the Boston Red Sox, giving up just one hit.

After a brief stint with a minor league team in 1966, Paige retired. In 1968, the Atlanta Braves hired him as a coach so he could get the 158 days he needed to qualify for a pension.

During his brief major league career, Paige had a 28–31 record with 4 shutouts, 32 saves, and a 3.29 ERA.
★ Baseball Hall of Fame

Palfrey, Sarah H.
TENNIS
b. Sept. 18, 1912, Sharon, Mass.

Named the greatest female athlete in the history of Massachusetts in 1953, Palfrey grew up in a family that had its own private tennis court. She was the U.S. junior girls champion from 1928 through 1930.

Palfrey won the U.S. national singles title in 1941 and 1945, but she had her greatest success as a doubles player. She and Alice Marble won the Wimbledon women's doubles championship in 1938 and 1939 and were the U.S. doubles champions from 1938 through 1940.

She also won the U.S. doubles title with Betty Nuthall of England in 1930 and with Helen Hull Jacobs in 1932 and 1935. Palfrey teamed with four different partners to win four U.S. mixed doubles championships, with Fred Perry in 1932, Enrique Mayer in 1935, Donald Budge in 1937, and Jack Kramer in 1941.

★ International Tennis Hall of Fame

Palin, Septimus F.

HARNESS RACING
b. 1878, Iroquois, Ill.
d. Oct 3, 1952

Palin trained and drove harness horses at small tracks in the Midwest for years. He became suddenly famous at the age of 56 as the trainer of Greyhound, one of the greatest harness horses ever.

In 1933, owner E. J. Baker asked Palin to take over Greyhound, then a yearling. The following year, Palin drove Greyhound to a 2:04¾ in the mile, a record for two-year-old geldings. Greyhound won the 1935 Hambletonian in two heats, running a 2:02¼ and 2:02¾. Later that year, he did the mile in an even 2:00 at Springfield, Illinois, and in 1937 Greyhound broke the track record at Goshen with a time of 1:59¾. That record stood until 1966.

Before being retired in 1940, Greyhound had won 72 of 82 heats, had trotted 23 miles in times of two minutes or better, and had earned $38,952.79, which was very high for that time. His fastest time was a world record 1:55½ at Lexington in 1938.

Palin trained the first two horses to win harness horse of the year honors,

Victory Song in 1947 and Hoot Mon in 1948. Victory Song won the 1947 Kentucky Futurity with Palin driving. Hoot Mon, who won the 1947 Hambletonian, set a record for stallions by pacing a mile in 1:57⅗ at Springfield that year.

At his death in 1952, Palin held the career record for most two-minute performances with 64.

★ Hall of Fame of the Trotter

Palmer, Arnold D.

GOLF
b. Sept. 10, 1929, Latrobe, Pa.

Perhaps the most popular golfer ever, Palmer was a charismatic figure who came along just when golf was becoming a big television sport. Palmer and television suited one another perfectly.

One sportswriter said of him, "His emotions — pain, pleasure, dismay, anger, and the rest — were never hidden, and his followers could relive through him their own joys and frustrations." In his prime, he drew galleries of up to 30,000 spectators who became known collectively as "Arnie's Army."

Palmer won the U.S. Amateur Championship in 1954, shortly after graduating from Wake Forest, and he became a professional the following year, announcing, "I want to win more tournaments than anyone, ever."

He won his first major tournament, the Masters, in 1958. But he really established his reputation in 1960, when he demonstrated an amazing ability to charge from behind to win tournaments. At the Masters, he needed birdies on the last two holes to win. He got them.

In the U.S. Open, Palmer was seven strokes back going into the final round, but he shot a 65 to win. He then won the Palm Springs Open with a 65 and the Pensacola Open with a 67; he shot a 67 at the Hartford Open to get into a playoff, which he won, and finished with another 67 to take the Mobile Open.

Palmer also won the Masters in 1962 and 1964 and was the British Open champion two years in a row, 1961 and 1962, for a total of seven major championships. During most of the 1960s, Palmer, Jack Nicklaus, and Gary Player were the "Big Three" of golf, and the competition among them helped build the sport's popularity.

After 1964, Palmer never won another major championship. The distractions of business may have contributed to his decline. With the advice of manager Mark McCormack, he built a multimillion-dollar empire and spent a great deal of time flying in his private plane to attend to business affairs and make public appearances.

Nevertheless, galleries still loved him and continued to cry "Charge" when he hit a good shot, even when it was obvious that he had no chance to win. As late as 1985, Palmer was still ranked by *Sport* magazine as the highest-paid athlete in the world, because of endorsements and commercial appearances.

Palmer was the PGA tour's top money winner in 1958, 1960, 1962, and 1964, and was named player of the year in 1960 and 1962. He won the Vardon Trophy for the tour's best scoring average in 1961, 1962, 1964, and 1967. His 60 tournament victories is third best all-time.

★ World Golf Hall of Fame; PGA Hall of Fame

Palmer, Jim (James A.)

BASEBALL
b. Oct. 15, 1945, New York, N.Y.

The 6-foot-3, 196-pound Palmer, who had the looks of a matinee idol, was the AL's best pitcher during the 1970s. A 20-game winner eight times during the decade, he won three Cy Young Awards.

After appearing in just 27 games for the Baltimore Orioles in 1965, 21 of them as a reliever, Palmer joined the starting rotation in 1966 and went 15–10. He became the youngest pitcher to throw a shutout in the World Series, beating the Los Angeles Dodgers, 8–0, in Baltimore's four-game sweep.

Arm problems limited him to only nine appearances in 1967, but he came back with a 16–4 record in 1968, leading the AL in winning percentage, then won 20 or more games each of the next four seasons. He led the league with 5 shutouts and 305 innings pitched in 1970, and he won his first Cy Young Award in

1973, when he was 22–9 with 6 shutouts and a 2.40 ERA.

In 1974, arm trouble struck again, and he won only 7 games. Once more, Palmer bounced back. He led the league in victories with a 23–11 record, in shutouts with 10, and in ERA with 2.09 in 1975, winning another Cy Young, and he won his third the following season, leading in victories with a 22–13 record and in innings pitched with 315 while compiling a 2.51 ERA.

Palmer was the league leader in victories for the third year in a row with a 20–11 record in 1977, when he also led with 22 complete games and 319 innings pitched. After going 21–12 in 1976, he began to lose his mastery, although he had only one losing season in the next five, and he led the AL in winning percentage at .750 in 1982, when he went 15–5. He retired after having records of 5–4 in 1983 and 0–3 in 1984.

A right-hander, Palmer built his success on a variety of pitches, excellent control, and his ability to outsmart hitters. He had a reputation for being unwilling to pitch if he didn't feel exactly right — understandable, given his history of arm trouble — yet he pitched more than 300 innings in four different seasons, and four other times he logged 274 or more innings.

In 19 seasons, Palmer had a 268–152 record with 53 shutouts and a 2.86 ERA. He struck out 2,212 hitters while walking 1,311 in 3,948 innings.

★ Baseball Hall of Fame

Parcells, Bill (Duane C.)

FOOTBALL
b. Aug. 22, 1941, Englewood, N.J.

Parcells played football at Wichita State University, graduating in 1964, and then served as an assistant coach at several colleges until 1978, when he became head coach at the Air Force Academy. He was replaced after compiling a 3–8–0 record.

In 1980, Parcells joined the coaching staff of the NFL's New England Patriots. He went to the New York Giants as an assistant the following season and took over as head coach in 1983.

After going 3–12–1 in his first season with the Giants, Parcells guided the team to three consecutive playoff appearances and an NFL championship after the 1986 season, with a 39–20 win over the Denver Broncos in Super Bowl XXI. He was named the league's coach of the year by *The Sporting News* for that accomplishment.

The Giants slipped to 6–9–0 in 1987 but had a 10–6–0 record in 1988 without getting into the playoffs. Parcells had a 25–7–0 regular season mark over the next two years, and the Giants won their second Super Bowl victory after the 1990 season, beating the Buffalo Bills, 20–19.

Because of a heart condition, Parcells announced his retirement from coaching early in 1991 and worked as a television analyst. The condition was cleared up by angioplasty, and Parcells lost considerable weight during the next year. He seemed ready to return to coaching in 1992, interviewing for jobs with the Tampa Bay Buccaneers and the Green Bay Packers. But after having accepted the Tampa Bay job, he suddenly changed his mind.

In 1993, Parcells accepted the head coaching position with the New England Patriots. In his second season, the team went to the playoffs but lost to the Cleveland Browns in the first round.

Parent, Bernie (Bernard M.)

HOCKEY
b. April 3, 1945, Montreal, P.Q.

Growing up in Montreal, Parent idolized Canadien goalie Jacques Plante; in 1971–72, he and Plante shared goaltending duties with the Toronto Maple Leafs.

A feisty, very competitive player, Parent often battled opponents and once had a fist fight with his team's trainer, who had criticized his play during the Stanley Cup playoffs.

Parent arrived in the NHL with the Boston Bruins in 1965. After playing 51 games with them over two seasons, he went to the Philadelphia Flyers in the 1967 expansion draft, then was traded to the Maple Leafs during the 1970–71 season.

When the World Hockey Association was organized in 1972, Parent signed with the new league's Philadelphia Blazers for a reported $700,000. The Blazers moved to Vancouver after one season, and Parent refused to go with them. Instead, he stayed in Philadelphia and rejoined the Flyers. He shared the Vezina Trophy with Tony Esposito of Chicago as the NHL's outstanding goalie in 1974 and won the award outright in 1975.

He also won the Conn Smythe Trophy as the outstanding player in the Stanley Cup playoffs both years. In 1974, he held the Boston Bruins to just 3 goals in the last three games of the finals, including a 1–0 shutout in the sixth and final game. The following year, he gave up just 12 goals in six games in the final series against the Buffalo Sabres as the Flyers won their second consecutive championship.

In his 13 NHL seasons, Parent had 55 shutouts and a 2.55 goals-against average in 608 regular season games. He had 6 shutouts and a 2.43 average in 71 playoff games.

★ Hockey Hall of Fame

Parilli, Babe (Vito)

FOOTBALL
b. May 7, 1930, Rochester, Pa.

An outstanding ball handler and passer, Parilli was an All-American quarterback at the University of Kentucky in 1950 and 1951. He left the school holding NCAA career records for most touchdown passes, 50; most completions, 331; and most yards gained passing, 4,351. His 23 touchdown passes in 1950 was also a record at the time.

Parilli was named the most valuable player in the 1951 Sugar Bowl, when Kentucky ended top-ranked Oklahoma's 31-game winning streak with a 13–7 victory, and he was named the outstanding back in Kentucky's 20–7 win over Texas Christian in the 1952 Cotton Bowl.

He joined the NFL's Green Bay Packers as a first-round draft choice in 1952. Parilli spent two seasons with Green Bay, then went into military service for two years and was traded to the Cleveland Browns. After spending 1956 with the Browns, he returned to Green Bay for two more seasons.

In 1959, Parilli played for the Ottawa Roughriders of the Canadian Football League. He then joined the Oakland Raiders of the new American Football League for a season. Parilli's most productive professional seasons were spent with the New England Patriots from 1961 through 1967.

Parilli completed 153 of 337 passes for 2,345 yards and 13 touchdowns to lead the Patriots to the 1963 Eastern Division championship, but they lost 51–10 to the San Diego Chargers in the AFL title game.

He finished his playing career as Joe Namath's backup with the New York Jets in 1968. Parilli was an assistant coach with several professional teams, and he served as head coach of the World Football League's New York Stars in 1974 and the Chicago Wind in 1975.

★ College Football Hall of Fame

Parish, Robert L.

BASKETBALL
b. Aug. 30, 1953, Shreveport, La.

The 7-foot, 230-pound Parish, known as "the Chief" because of his dignified bearing, has very quietly ruled as one of the best centers in the NBA for 17 seasons and counting. After averaging 21.6 points a game during four years as a starter at Centenary College in Louisiana, he was drafted by the Golden State Warriors in the first round of the 1976 NBA draft.

After four virtually anonymous seasons with Golden State, Parish was traded to the Boston Celtics with a 1980 first-round draft choice for two of Boston's first-round picks. In his first season with the Celtics, 1980–81, they won the NBA championship. He averaged 18.9 points and more than 9 rebounds a game.

He averaged 19.0 points and more than 10 rebounds a game in 1983–84, when they won another title. Parish helped lead the Celtics to a third title in 1985–86, though his numbers declined somewhat to 16.1 points and 9.6 rebounds per game.

Remarkably durable, Parish has played in 72 or more games in each of his NBA seasons. Although he has never led the NBA in any category and has never been a first-team All-NBA selection, he has consistently posted good numbers as a scorer, rebounder, and shot blocker.

Through the 1993–94 season, Parish had played in 1,413 regular season games, scoring 22,494 points, an average of 15.9 per game, pulling down 13,973 rebounds, and blocking 2,252 shots. He also had 2,085 assists and 1,165 steals. He is second to Kareem Abdul-Jabbar in seasons played, thirteenth in scoring, ninth in field goals, and ninth in rebounds.

Parker, Ace (Clarence McK.)

FOOTBALL
b. May 17, 1912, Portsmouth, Va.

An All-American at Duke in 1936, Parker usually played tailback in the single wing but was sometimes moved to wingback so he could be used as a blocker or pass receiver. His coach, Wallace Wade, said of Parker, "He is one of the greatest players I've ever coached . . . He was a great open-field runner, a great passer, a great pass receiver, a great punter, and a great safety man."

After playing 38 games with baseball's Philadelphia Athletics in 1937, Parker joined the Brooklyn Dodgers of the NFL. As a professional, he was used primarily as a passer and kicker. He was an exceptionally accurate punter who could often put the ball out of bounds inside the opposition's 10-yard line.

Parker also played major league baseball in 1938, and he continued to play in the minor leagues until 1940, when he suffered a badly broken left ankle. He didn't expect to play much football that fall, but Dr. Mal Stevens, the Brooklyn coach, designed a special ten-pound brace for the ankle that Parker wore for the first three weeks of the season. He won the Carr Trophy as the league's player of the year.

In 1942, Parker entered the Army. He returned late in the 1945 season to play for the NFL's Boston Yanks, and he finished his career with the New York Yankees of the All-America Football Conference in 1946.

During his seven seasons as a professional, Parker completed 335 of 718 passes for 4,701 yards and 30 touchdowns. He punted 150 times for a 38.3-yard average; returned 24 punts for 238 yards, a 9.9 average; intercepted 7 passes; and kicked 25 extra points and 1 field goal. He also rushed for 14 touchdowns.
★ College Football Hall of Fame; Pro Football Hall of Fame

Parker, Dave (David G.)

BASEBALL
b. June 9, 1951, Calhoun, Miss.

During the late 1970s, Parker was establishing himself as possibly the best player in baseball. At 6-foot-5 and 230 pounds, he could hit for average and power, was an excellent defensive outfielder with a strong arm, and had enough speed to steal 20 bases. Then injuries struck.

He was a part-time player with the NL's Pittsburgh Pirates in 1973 and 1974, then became a full-time starter in 1975 and batted .308. After hitting .313 in 1976, Parker won two consecutive batting titles. In 1977, he hit .338, and he also led the league with 215 hits and 44 doubles.

Parker was rewarded with the largest salary in baseball history up to that time, $900,000 a year for five years. He responded by winning the league's most valuable player award, leading in hitting again with a .334 average, in slugging with a .585 percentage, and also hitting 30 home runs with 117 RBI.

After hitting .310 in 1979 and .295 in 1980, Parker went down with a knee problem and played a total of only 140 games in the next two seasons. He was never the same player after that, although he still had some fine years. He batted .279 with only 12 home runs in 1983 and went to the Cincinnati Reds in 1984.

A right-handed thrower but left-handed hitter, Parker batted .312 in 1985, led the league with 42 doubles and 125 RBI, and had 34 home runs. He hit 31 home runs and had 116 RBI the following season but hit only .273, and he slipped to .253 in 1987.

He joined the Oakland Athletics in 1988, when he played in only 110 games because of recurring knee problems. In 1989, he hit 22 home runs and had 97 RBI, batting .249. Parker had one last good season with the Milwaukee Brewers in 1990, when he hit .289 with 21 home runs and 92 RBI. But he was batting only .232 for the California Angels late in the 1991 season, when he was traded to the Toronto Blue Jays. He retired after that season.

In 19 major league seasons, Parker batted .290 with 2,712 hits, including 526 doubles, 75 triples, and 339 home runs. He stole 154 bases, scored 1,272 runs, and had 1,493 RBI.

Parker, Frank A.

TENNIS
b. Feb. 16, 1916, Milwaukee, Wis.

Unemotional and steady, almost plodding, Parker was ranked among the top ten U.S. tennis players for 17 consecutive years. However, he won only two national singles titles, in 1944 and 1945, and those were considered rather spurious because most of the top players were overseas during World War II. (Parker was an Army sergeant, but he served in the U.S.)

Parker was ranked eighth in the country in 1932, when he was 17. He was second behind Don Budge in 1936, behind Bobby Riggs in 1939, behind Ted Schroeder in 1942, behind Jack Kramer in 1947; and four times he was ranked third. But he reached the top spot only in those two wartime years.

In addition to his two singles titles, Parker teamed with Kramer to win the men's doubles in 1943.
★ International Tennis Hall of Fame

Parker, Jim (James T.)

FOOTBALL
b. April 3, 1934, Macon, Ga.

When Ohio State upset Michigan, 17–0, in 1955, one sportswriter summed up the game: "Ohio State's bulldozing line, led by 250-pound Jim Parker, overpowered the Wolverines on offense and overwhelmed them on defense." Parker was an All-American guard in 1956, when he won the Outland Trophy as the nation's outstanding collegiate lineman.

Parker joined the NFL's Baltimore Colts in 1957 and became a starter at offensive tackle. He was an All-Pro at the position from 1958 through 1961. Then he moved to guard and was named an All-Pro from 1962 through 1965.

Because of his great pass-blocking ability, Parker was sometimes called "Johnny Unitas's bodyguard," but he was also a strong drive blocker, and he was fast and agile enough to be a fine pulling guard on running plays. Hampered by injuries in 1967, he retired after that season. He was the first pure offensive lineman to be elected to the Hall of Fame.

★ College Football Hall of Fame; Pro Football Hall of Fame

Parseghian, Ara R.

FOOTBALL
b. May 21, 1923, Akron, Ohio

Parseghian entered Akron University in 1941 but joined the Navy after his freshman year. After he returned from the service, he enrolled at Miami University in Ohio, where he starred in three sports. A halfback, he was elected football captain for 1948, but because his original class had graduated, he was allowed to play with the Cleveland Browns of the All-America Football Conference that season.

His playing career was ended by a hip injury in 1949, and Parseghian became freshman football coach at Miami. He succeeded Woody Hayes as head football coach in 1951 and compiled a record of 39 wins, 6 losses, and 1 tie in five seasons. His 1955 team won all nine of its games, including a 6–0 upset of Indiana.

In 1956, Parseghian took over at Northwestern. Despite a lack of material compared to other Big Ten schools, he produced winning teams during the next eight years, and Northwestern beat Notre Dame four times in four tries over that period.

Notre Dame hired him away in 1964. Parseghian immediately turned a losing program into a winner. He was voted coach of the year after his first team won nine of ten games, and was named collegiate champion by the National Football Foundation.

The 1966 team was a consensus national champion despite a 10–10 tie against Michigan State in which neither team made much effort to win in the fourth quarter, for fear of making a mistake that would lose the game. Parseghian produced a third national champion in 1973, when Notre Dame beat Alabama, 24–23, in a battle of unbeaten teams in the Sugar Bowl.

An emotional, hands-on coach who often personally demonstrated blocking and tackling techniques and pass patterns, Parseghian unexpectedly resigned after the 1974 season because of the emotional strains of the job. His overall coaching record was 170 wins, 58 losses, and 6 ties, a .739 winning percentage. He has frequently done commentary on televised college games.

★ College Football Hall of Fame

Parsons, Benny

AUTO RACING
b. July 12, 1941, Detroit, Mich.

Parsons began his racing career in ARCA, a Midwestern stock car league. After winning ARCA championships in 1968 and 1969, he began running in NASCAR races. He raced well in his first several years without any major victories, placing in the top five a dozen times in 1970 and 13 times in 1971, when he had a win at South Boston, Virginia.

Although he only had one win in 1973, his 21 top ten finishes in 28 races gave him enough points for the Winston Cup championship. In 1975 he won the Daytona 500, and in 1982 he became the first driver to qualify at more than 200 mph, with a 200.176 clocking at the Winston 500 at Talladega, Alabama.

Parsons retired after the 1988 season. He had 21 victories and earnings of $3,896,539 in 526 Winston Cup races.

Pascual, Camilo A.

BASEBALL
b. Jan. 20, 1934, Havana, Cuba

At his peak during the late 1950s and

early 1960s, Pascual probably had the best curve in baseball. He combined it with a good fastball and excellent control to be a very effective pitcher, but unfortunately he played for some very bad teams in Washington and Minnesota during those years.

Pascual joined the AL's Washington Senators in 1954 and had five consecutive losing seasons before going 17–10 in 1959, when he led the league with 17 complete games and 6 shutouts. After going 12–8 in 1960, he led the AL in strikeouts three years in a row and had two 20-victory seasons during that period.

The Senators moved to Minnesota and became known as the Twins in 1961. Pascual had 221 strikeouts and a league-leading 8 shutouts that year, though he was only 15–16. He led with 206 strikeouts, 8 shutouts, and 18 complete games in 1962, when he was 20–11. He followed that with a 21–9 record and was the league leader with 202 strikeouts and 18 complete games in 1963.

Pascual's numbers began to decline in 1964, when he was 15–12, though he had four more winning seasons. Minnesota sent him back to Washington, where there was a new Senators franchise, in 1967. He was traded to the Cincinnati Reds during the 1969 season, and he finished his career as an infrequently used relief pitcher with the Los Angeles Dodgers in 1970 and the Cleveland Indians in 1971.

In 18 major league seasons, Pascual had a 174–170 record with 36 shutouts and a 3.63 ERA. He struck out 2,167 hitters and walked 1,069 in 2,930⅔ innings.

Paterno, Joseph V.

FOOTBALL
b. Dec. 21, 1926, Brooklyn, N.Y.

Paterno played quarterback for "Rip" Engle at Brown University, guiding the team to a 15–3 record over the 1948 and 1949 seasons, and he became an assistant coach to Engle at Pennsylvania State University after graduating in 1950.

When Engle retired after the 1965

season, Paterno took over as head coach. Short, slight, and bespectacled, he looks much more like a professor than a coach, and often acts more like a professor, demanding academic achievement as well as football ability from his players. More than 90 percent of his recruits graduate within five years of their entrance.

He has also put together an enviable record as a coach. Penn State was consensus national champion in 1982, 1983, 1986, and 1987; went undefeated in 1968, 1969, 1973, 1986, and 1994; and has won 16 bowl games while losing 8 and tying 1 during Paterno's tenure.

Paterno was consensus coach of the year in 1978 and 1982, the American Football Coaches Association choice in 1968, and the Football Writers Association of America choice in 1986.

Through the 1994 season, Paterno had a 269–69–3 record in his 29 years at Penn State. His victory total is fourth all-time among the NCAA Division I coaches, and his .793 winning percentage is fourteenth best.

Paterno's emphasis has generally been on a strong running game and a powerful defense. He is especially known for producing such outstanding running backs as John Cappelletti, Franco Harris, Lydell Mitchell, and Curt Warner, and such quick, intelligent linebackers as Jack Ham and Shane Conley.

Three professional teams tried but failed to lure Paterno away from Penn State. In 1969, the Pittsburgh Steelers offered him a long-term contract for $50,000 a year. The Green Bay Packers wanted to hire him as general manager and coach two years later. The most tempting offer came from the New England Patriots in 1973. Paterno agreed orally to a six-year, $1.3 million contract, but the following day he decided to turn down the job.

Patrick, Lester

HOCKEY
b. Dec. 30, 1883, Drummondville, P.Q.
d. June 1, 1960

After starring in hockey at McGill University in Montreal and in the Canadian Amateur Hockey League, Lester Patrick signed with the Renfrew Millionaires, along with his brother Frank, in 1910. There was a financial war for players going on between the Canadian Hockey Association and the National Hockey Association at the time.

When the CHA was absorbed by the NHA in 1911, Lester and Frank organized the Pacific Coast Hockey Association with financial backing from their millionaire father. The PCHA introduced blue lines and added assists to scoring figures in 1913.

The Patricks built the first two artificial ice rinks in North America, in Victoria and Vancouver, and Lester campaigned for years to have artificial ice in all major hockey cities, a goal that was finally achieved in 1926.

Lester played for various teams in the PCHA, and he was the player coach of the Victoria Cougars in 1924–25, when they won the Stanley Cup, the last team from outside the National Hockey League to do so.

Patrick became the coach of the New York Rangers in 1926 and guided the team to Stanley Cup championships in 1928 and 1933. After the heavily favored Montreal Maroons had beaten the Rangers in the first game of the 1928 finals, goalie Lorne Chabot was hit in the eye by a shot with the score tied, 1–1, in the second game. The 44-year-old Patrick took over in goal. As a defenseman during his playing days, he had often played goal when the regular goalie went to the penalty box. He shut out Montreal until the Rangers won in overtime. Chabot returned for the third game, and the Rangers went on to an upset victory in five games.

Patrick also took the titles of vice president and general manager in 1932. He retired after the 1938–39 season. In 1966, the NHL established the Lester Patrick Trophy, which is awarded for "outstanding service to hockey in the United States." The league's Patrick Division is also named for him.

★ Hockey Hall of Fame

Patterson, Floyd

BOXING
b. Jan. 4, 1935, Waco, N.C.

The youngest fighter ever to win the heavyweight championship and the first ever to regain the title, Patterson unfortunately suffered severe damage to his reputation because of his two embarrassing defeats by Sonny Liston.

Patterson grew up in Brooklyn and learned to box in a reform school for truants. He won the Olympic middleweight championship in 1952 by knocking out Vasile Tita of Romania in just 74 seconds. Cus D'Amato became Patterson's manager when he turned professional after the Olympics and taught him the unorthodox "peek-a-boo" defense, in which he held both gloves in front of his face and peered between them at his opponent.

His first professional fight was a 4th-round knockout of Eddie Godbold on September 12, 1952. He won 12 more fights before losing an unpopular 8-round decision to Joey Maxim on June 7, 1954, then won 16 in a row, including 11 consecutive knockouts.

An elimination tournament was held to choose a new heavyweight champion after Rocky Marciano retired. Patterson got into the final with a 12-round split decision over Tommy Jackson and knocked out the favorite, light heavyweight champion Archie Moore, in the 5th round on November 30, 1956, to win the title.

Patterson defended the championship four times, against unranked challengers, and then met European champion Ingemar Johansson of Sweden on June 26, 1959. Johansson knocked him out in the 3rd round. In a rematch on June 20, 1960, Patterson regained the title with a 4th-round knockout, and he knocked out Johansson again, in the 6th round, on March 13, 1961.

After another defense, Patterson seemed almost paralyzed at the sight of the glowering, brawny challenger Liston, who knocked him out in the 1st round on September 25, 1962, in Chicago. Patterson ignominiously fled from the city wearing a false moustache and dark glasses, and he went into seclusion. A rematch, in Las Vegas on July 22, 1963, had exactly the same outcome.

Patterson fought Muhammad Ali for the title on November 22, 1965, and was knocked out in the 12th round. After the World Boxing Association stripped Ali of his title, Patterson lost a decision to Jerry Quarry in a 1967 tournament. He fought Jimmy Ellis for the WBA championship on September 14, 1968, when he lost a 15-round decision.

He was inactive in 1969 but returned to the ring in September 1970. His last fight was against Ali for the North American Boxing Federation championship on September 20, 1972. Ali knocked him out in the 7th round.

Patterson won 55 bouts, 40 by knockout; lost 8, 5 by knockout; and fought 1 draw.

★ International Boxing Hall of Fame; Olympic Hall of Fame

Patton, Melvin

TRACK AND FIELD
b. Nov. 16, 1924, Los Angeles, Calif.

Patton's career as a sprinter lasted barely three years, and he never competed in an AAU national meet, but he set world records in both sprints and won two Olympic gold medals.

Running for the University of Southern California, Patton won the NCAA 100-yard dash in 1947, and he won both sprints in 1948 and 1949. He also ran on the school's 880-yard relay team that set a world record of 1:24.0 at the 1949 NCAA meet.

In the 1948 Olympics, Patton got off to a terrible start in the 100-meter dash and finished fifth. However, he came back to win the 200-meter dash, and he won a second gold medal as a member of the U.S. 4 x 100-meter relay team.

Patton twice tied the world record of 9.4 seconds for the 100-yard dash in 1947 and broke it with a 9.3 clocking at the 1948 West Coast Relays. That record was tied ten times before it was finally broken in 1961. On May 7, 1949, he ran a 20.2 in the 220-yard dash, breaking the record set by Jesse Owens in 1935. The

time was also accepted as a world record for the 200-meter.

After retiring from amateur competition in 1950, Patton ran professionally in Australia before returning to the U.S. to begin a business career.

★ National Track & Field Hall of Fame

Payton, Walter J.

FOOTBALL
b. July 25, 1954, Columbia, Miss.

Probably the greatest all-around running back in football history, Payton retired with NFL career records for most rushing yards, most passes caught by a running back, and most all-purpose yards. During his 13 seasons with the Chicago Bears, he was also the team's emergency punter, emergency place-kicker, and emergency quarterback.

A Little All-American at Jackson State in 1974, Payton was a first-round draft choice of the NFL's Chicago Bears. The solid, 5-foot-10, 203-pounder was used sparingly as a rookie and rushed for only 679 yards.

→ In 1976, Payton became a full-time starter, and he proceeded to lead the National Football Conference in rushing five years in a row, gaining 1,390 yards in 1976, 1,852 in 1977, 1,395 in 1978, 1,610 in 1978, and 1,460 in 1979.

Called "Sweetness" by his teammates because of his disposition, Payton was consensus player of the year in 1977 and *The Sporting News* National Football Conference player of the year in 1976. He won the Bert Bell Trophy as the league's most valuable player in 1985, when the Bears were NFC champions.

Many football fans were looking forward to seeing Payton score a touchdown in the Super Bowl to climax his career, but they were disappointed. The Bears beat the New England Patriots, 46–10, in Super Bowl XX, with Payton gaining only 61 yards on 22 carries. Twice Chicago was at New England's 1-yard line, but Payton wasn't given the ball either time, stirring speculation that there was a rift between him and coach Mike Ditka. Both denied it.

Payton retired after the 1987 season. He gained 16,726 yards on 3,838 carries, a 4.4 average, and scored 110 rushing touchdowns. He added 4,537 yards on 492 receptions, a 9.2 average, with 15 touchdown catches. Payton holds NFL records for most rushing touchdowns, most games rushing for 100 or more yards (77), most seasons with more than 1,000 rushing yards (10), and most rushing yards in a game (275).

★ Pro Football Hall of Fame

Peacock, Eulace
TRACK AND FIELD
b. Aug. 27, 1914, Dothan, Ala.

A great sprinter, Peacock had the misfortune to be competing at the same time as two other greats, Jesse Owens and Ralph Metcalfe. However, in 1935 Peacock beat Owens in the 100-yard or 100-meter dash three of five times. One of his victories was in the AAU national outdoor championship meet, where he also won the long jump competition over Owens.

On August 8, 1934, Peacock tied the world record of 10.3 seconds in the 100-meter dash at a meet in Oslo, Norway. That was just one stop on an extended European tour during which he competed in both sprints and the long jump and lost just twice.

Injuries prevented him from running in the 1936 Olympic trials. He tried a comeback the following year but was forced to retire because of recurring physical problems.

★ National Track & Field Hall of Fame

Pearce, Bob (Robert E.)
WRESTLING
b. Feb. 29, 1908, Wyconda, Mo.

At Oklahoma A & M University (now Oklahoma State), Pearce had a 60–4–1 record and won the 1931 NCAA wrestling championship in the 125½-pound class. He was also the AAU champion in 1930 and 1931.

Pearce won a gold medal in the bantamweight class at the 1932 Olympics. He was a professional wrestler from 1933 to 1937 and then coached wrestling at the high school and college levels.

Pearson, David G.
AUTO RACING
b. Dec. 22, 1934

After winning $13 in a 1952 hobby race, Pearson decided on a career in racing. He was very successful in NASCAR's sportsman class but couldn't get a ride in the big races. He bought his own car and tried it in 1960, but the car just wasn't up to it.

He finally got a sponsor and a good car in 1961 and won the World 600, the Firecracker 250, and the Dixie 400, becoming the first driver to win at three of NASCAR's Big Four tracks in a year. He was named rookie of the year.

After less success in 1963 and 1964, he missed the entire 1965 season because Chrysler refused to let its cars run on the NASCAR circuit, and he was driving a Dodge. But in 1966 he won 15 Grand National races to take the first of his three NASCAR championships.

His second championship came in 1968, when he had 16 wins, and he made it two in a row in 1969. Pearson concentrated on big races in 1970, making only 19 starts and winning only one. Ford, his new manufacturer, pulled out of NASCAR racing in 1971, and he went without a major victory. But in 1972 he won the Yankee 400, Motor State 500, Firecracker 400, Rebel 400, Delaware 500, and the Winston 500. The following year, he won three superspeedway races.

Pearson retired with 105 Grand National wins, second only to Richard Petty. He now manages a racing team for his son, Larry.

Peck, Bob (Robert D.)
FOOTBALL
b. May 30, 1891, Lock Haven, Pa.
d. June 19, 1932

The 5-foot-8, 179-pound Peck was fast enough to play halfback as a freshman at the University of Pittsburgh in 1913, but because of his strength he was moved to center the following year. Although he was continually matched against players who outweighed him by 20 or more pounds, Peck was named to one All-American team in 1914, and he was a consensus All-American in both 1915 and 1916. His coach, "Pop" Warner, called him the best all-around lineman he'd ever seen.

Peck captained the team in 1916. During his three years as a starter, Pittsburgh won 24 games and lost only 1. Peck also started at first base on the school's baseball team as a freshman and sophomore, and he played basketball in his freshman year.

After graduating, he became a coach at Culver Military Academy. He remained there for the rest of his life, with one year off to serve in World War I. He became the school's head football coach in 1921 and athletic director in 1930. He died of a heart attack while playing golf.
★ College Football Hall of Fame

Peckinpaugh, Roger T.

BASEBALL
b. Feb. 5, 1891, Wooster, Ohio
d. Nov. 17, 1977

A 5-foot-10½, 165-pound shortstop, Peckinpaugh was a part-time player with the AL's Cleveland Indians in 1910 and 1912 and was traded to the New York Yankees early in the 1913 season. In 1914, at the age of 23, he became the youngest manager in major league history, taking over the Yankees for the last 20 games of the season.

When the Yankees won their first pennant in 1921, Peckinpaugh batted .288 and scored 128 runs. He was traded to the Washington Senators in 1922 and played on two pennant-winning teams there, in 1924 and 1925.

He starred in Washington's seven-game World Series victory over the New York Giants in 1924, batting .417, and he was named the league's most valuable player in 1925, when he batted .294. Peckinpaugh retired after spending the 1927 season with the Chicago White Sox. He had a career average of .259, with 1,876 hits, including 256 doubles, 75 triples, and 48 home runs.

Peckinpaugh became the Cleveland manager in 1928 and was replaced during the 1933 season. He returned to manage the team again in 1941. His over-all record as a manager was 500 wins and 491 losses.

Pelé [Edson Arantes do Nascimento]
SOCCER
b. Oct. 23, 1940, Sao Paulo, Brazil

Generally considered the greatest soccer player in history, Pelé combined great speed with dazzling athletic ability that enabled him to dash past defenders and get off powerful scoring kicks, often from seemingly impossible angles.

He was probably the most famous and most popular athlete in the world before satellite communications made such stars as Michael Jordan internationally known. At 17, Pele led Brazil to the 1958 World Cup, scoring 6 of the team's 11 goals during the last three rounds.

Pele also played for World Cup champions in 1962 and 1970, when he put on a brilliant performance in the final game against Italy, making an amazing leap to head in Brazil's first goal and assisting on two others in a 4–1 win. He announced his retirement from World Cup competition after that victory, but in 1975 he accepted a three-year, $7 million contract to play for the New York Cosmos of the North American Soccer League.

His fame was so great, even among Americans who knew little or nothing about soccer, that he helped the NASL survive even after his retirement in 1977. During his 22 years as a player, he scored 1,281 goals in a sport where 30 goals in a season is a very high figure.

Pendleton, Terry L.

BASEBALL
b. July 16, 1960, Los Angeles, Calif.

The NL's most valuable player in 1991, Pendleton entered the major leagues with the St. Louis Cardinals in 1984. A switch-hitting third baseman, he was traded to the Atlanta Braves after batting only .230 in 1990.

Pendleton helped lead the Braves to two consecutive pennants, in 1991 and 1992. He led the league in hits with 187 and in batting with a .319 average in 1991, when he had 22 home runs, 94 runs scored, and 86 RBI. He had an even better overall year in 1992, hitting .311 with a league-leading 199 hits, scoring

98 runs, and driving in 105, but he finished second to San Francisco's Barry Bonds in the MVP voting.

Through 1994, Pendleton was batting .272 with 1,524 hits in 1,478 games, including 279 doubles, 37 triples, and 111 home runs. He had scored 702 runs and driven in 747.

Pennel, John

TRACK AND FIELD
b. July 24, 1940, Memphis, Tenn.
d. Sept. 26, 1992

On August 24, 1963, Pennel became the first pole vaulter to break the 17-foot barrier, with a vault of 17 feet, $^3/4$ inch. Fred Hansen and Bob Seagren both surpassed that, but Pennel improved the mark to 17-6$^3/4$ in 1966. After that was broken, he reclaimed the world record in 1969 with a vault of 17-10$^1/4$, which stood until 1973.

Pennel was considered the favorite before the 1964 Olympics, but he was in pain from a slipped disc and could vault only 15-5 to finish eleventh. In the 1968 Olympics, his vault of 17-6$^3/4$ was good only for fifth place. He retired shortly afterward.

Representing Northeast Louisiana State University, Pennel won the NAIA pole vault championship in 1962, and he was the AAU champion in 1965. He won the 1963 Sullivan Award as the outstanding amateur athlete of the year.

Pennel died of cancer.

Pennock, Herbert J.

BASEBALL
b. Feb. 10, 1894, Kennett Square, Pa.
d. Jan. 30, 1948

A 6-foot, 180-pound right-hander, Pennock began pitching for the AL's Philadelphia Athletics in 1912, at the age of 18, with no minor league experience. He appeared in only 31 games in his first two seasons, then had an 11–4 record in 1914. The Athletics sold him to the Boston Red Sox during the 1915 season. Pennock spent much of 1915 and 1916 in the minor leagues, went 5–5 for Boston in 1917, and missed all of 1918, when he was in the Navy.

In 1919, he finally became a regular starter, going 16–8. After a 16–13 record in 1920, he had two straight losing seasons and was traded to the New York Yankees. He was 29 years old and had a record of 76–72 at this point in his career.

But he blossomed with the Yankees. In his first season, 1923, he lowered his ERA to 3.13 from 4.32 the previous year and led the league with a .760 winning percentage on a 19–6 record. In a six-game World Series victory over the New York Giants, Pennock won two games.

Pennock went 21–9 in 1924, then slipped to 16–17 in 1925, when he led the league with 277 innings pitched. He helped lead the Yankees to another pennant in 1926, when he had a 23–11 record, and he won two more games in the World Series. After going 19–8 in 1927, Pennock started the third game of the World Series and retired the first 22 hitters he faced, winning 8–1.

His last good season was 1928, when he was 17–6 with a league-leading five shutouts. A sore arm kept him out of the World Series that year and troubled him for the rest of his career. Pennock remained with the Yankees through 1933 and retired after having a 2–0 record in 30 appearances with the Boston Red Sox in 1934.

Pennock later coached for the Red Sox and served as director of the team's farm system for three years before becoming general manager of the NL's Philadelphia Phillies in 1943. He died of a cerebral hemorrhage in 1948 while attending a league meeting.

Pennock relied on a screwball, curve, change-up, and excellent control, using his fastball only to keep hitters off stride. In 22 seasons, he had a 240–162 record with 35 shutouts and a 3.60 ERA. He struck out 1,227 hitters and walked only 916 in 3,571$^2/3$ innings.

★ Baseball Hall of Fame

Pennock, Stanley B.

FOOTBALL
b. June 15, 1892, Syracuse, N.Y.
d. Nov. 27, 1916

An All-American guard three years in

a row, from 1912 through 1914, Pennock was an anchor on Harvard teams that won 25 games and tied 2 without a loss. Harvard outscored its opposition 588 to 61 during that period.

The powerful Pennock was described by the Harvard *Crimson* as "the rock-ribbed Stan Pennock," and the sportswriter George Trevor in 1914 called him "a throwback to Neanderthal Man."

After graduating, Pennock went into the chemical business. He was killed in 1916 in the explosion of a plant in Newark, New Jersey.

★ College Football Hall of Fame

Penske, Roger

AUTO RACING
b. Feb. 20, 1937, Cleveland, Ohio

One of the most powerful figures in auto racing, Penske began driving sports cars shortly after graduating from Lehigh University in 1959. He won four Grand Prix races and was named driver of the year by the *New York Times* in 1962. The following year, he won the only NASCAR Grand National race he ever entered, the Riverside 250.

Penske left driving in 1965 to operate an auto dealership in Philadelphia. The following year, he founded Roger Penske Racing Enterprises, which ran cars in the Trans-American, Canadian-American Challenge Cup, Grand Prix, NASCAR, and IndyCar races.

Unhappy with USAC management, Penske teamed with another owner, U. E. "Pat" Patrick, to form Championship Auto Racing Teams (CART) in 1978. USAC and CART briefly merged into the Championship Racing League in 1980, but the partnership broke up before the year was over. CART organized an 11-race schedule in 1981 with more prize money than USAC had ever offered, and has ruled IndyCar racing ever since.

The Penske team has won the Indy 500 in 1972, 1979, 1981, 1984, 1985, 1988, 1989, 1991, and 1993. A Penske company owns the Michigan International Speedway and the Pennsylvania International Speedway and operates the Cleveland Grand Prix for Indy cars.

Penske was also instrumental in establishing the International Race of Champions.

Pep, Willie [Guglielmo Papaleo]

BOXING
b. Sept. 19, 1922, Middletown, Conn.

Nicknamed "Will o' the Wisp" because of his speed and elusiveness, Pep dropped out of high school at 16 to concentrate on boxing. He won two Connecticut state amateur championships, as a flyweight in 1938 and as a bantamweight in 1939, then became a professional.

Pep won 53 consecutive fights to gain a world featherweight championship match against Chalky Wright on November 20, 1942. He took a 15-round decision, becoming the youngest fighter to win a world title in 40 years.

He suffered his first loss in 63 fights to Sammy Angott in a nontitle bout on March 19, 1943, then went undefeated in 73 consecutive fights, which included a draw. Pep served in both the Army and the Navy during World War II and was honorably discharged in 1944.

His famous string of four matches with Sandy Saddler began on October 29, 1948, at Madison Square Garden. Pep atypically chose to brawl against Saddler and was knocked out in the 4th round. In a rematch on February 11, 1949, Pep went back to his usual elusive style and won a relatively easy decision to regain his title.

In their third fight, on September 8, 1950, Pep again boxed well although he was knocked down in the 3rd round, and it was a close match until Pep failed to come out for the 8th round because of an injured shoulder.

Saddler and Pep met for the last time on September 26, 1951. It was another brawl, both fighters fouling continually. They wrestled each other to the floor twice, taking the referee with them on one occasion. Pep couldn't come out for the 10th round because of a bad cut under an eye, allegedly caused by Saddler's thumb.

Pep kept on fighting until early 1959,

when he announced his retirement. He came back in 1965 and won nine fights but retired permanently after being knocked out by Calvin Woodward on March 16, 1966. He was later a referee, a boxing inspector, and a sports columnist.

He won an incredible 229 matches, 65 by knockout; lost 11, 6 by knockout; and fought one draw.

★ International Boxing Hall of Fame

Peppler, Mary Jo
VOLLEYBALL
b. 1944, Rockford, Ill.

The 6-foot, 155-pound Peppler was America's first world-class woman volleyball player. As a high school senior in 1962, she played for the Long Beach Shamrocks, who claimed the national championship. She then helped organize the Los Angeles Renegades, who won the 1964 title.

Peppler played on the U.S. Olympic volleyball teams in 1964 and 1968 and competed with the national team at the 1970 world championships in Bulgaria, where she was voted the best female player in the world.

After moving to Texas, Peppler organized and became player-coach of the E Pluribus Unum team of Houston, which won national championships in 1972 and 1973. However, her independent attitude wasn't appreciated by the sport's authorities, and she was told she wouldn't be allowed to try out for the 1976 Olympic team. The director of the U.S. Volleyball Association explained, "She's a gifted athlete who can't be handled."

When the International Volleyball Association was organized in 1974, Peppler played for its El Paso–Juarez team. The IVA was the first attempt to organize a professional co-ed sport, with four men and two women on each team. It folded after one season.

Peppler won $49,600 in television's "Women's Supersports" competition in 1976, finishing ahead of the basketball player Karen Logan and the diver Micki King.

Perranoski, Ronald P. [Perzanowski]
BASEBALL
b. April 1, 1936, Paterson, N.J.

The 6-foot, 192-pound Perranoski joined the NL's Los Angeles Dodgers as a left-handed relief pitcher in 1961 and had the league's best winning percentage, .842, on a 16–3 record in 1963, when he recorded 21 saves and a 1.67 ERA.

Traded to the Minnesota Twins in 1968, Perranoski led the AL with 31 saves in 1969 and 34 in 1970. He was traded to the Detroit Tigers during the 1971 season, went back to the Dodgers in 1972, and retired after appearing in eight games for the AL's California Angels in 1973.

Perranoski has been the Los Angeles pitching coach since 1981. During his 13 major league seasons, he had a 79–74 record with 179 saves and a 2.79 ERA.

Perry, Gaylord J.
BASEBALL
b. Sept. 13, 1938, Williamston, N.C.

The only pitcher ever to win Cy Young Awards in both leagues, Perry was a right-hander who was constantly accused of throwing a spitball. After retiring, he wrote a biography in which he admitted using the illegal pitch. "Without it," he said, "I'd probably been farmin' about ten years ago."

Perry had brief stints with the NL's San Francisco Giants in 1962 and 1963, then became a regular starter and had a 12–11 record in 1964. After going 8–12 in 1965, he had his first 20-victory season with a 21–8 record in 1966.

He led the league with 325⅓ innings pitched in 1969, when he was 19–14, and the following year he was the league leader in victories with a 23–13 record, in shutouts with 5, and in innings pitched with 328⅔.

After a 16–12 record in 1971, Perry was traded to the AL's Cleveland Indians. He promptly won his first Cy Young Award, leading the league in victories with a 24–16 record and in complete games with 29. He had a 1.92 ERA that season. (His brother Jim had won the award two years earlier.)

Perry was 19–19 and 21–13 over the next two years. The Indians traded him to the Texas Rangers during the 1975 season, and he went to the NL's San Diego Padres in 1978, when he won another Cy Young Award. Perry led the league in victories with a 21–6 record and in winning percentage at .778.

That was his last good season. After going 12–11 in 1979, he spent the 1980 season with Texas and the New York Yankees. He went to the Atlanta Braves in 1981 and to the Seattle Mariners in 1982. He retired after winning only 7 games while losing 14 with Seattle and the Kansas City Royals in 1983.

In 22 major league seasons, Perry had a 314–265 record with 53 shutouts and a 3.11 ERA. He struck out 3,534 hitters and walked 1,379 in 5,350⅓ innings.

★ Baseball Hall of Fame

Perry, Jim (James E.)

BASEBALL
b. Oct. 30, 1936, Williamston, N.C.

A right-handed pitcher like his younger brother Gaylord, Perry had a 12–10 record in 1959, his first season with the AL's Cleveland Indians, then had a league-leading 18 victories, .643 winning percentage, and 4 shutouts in 1960.

Arm trouble hampered him intermittently during the next several seasons. Cleveland traded him to the Minnesota Twins early in the 1963 season, and he had just 54 victories from then through 1968. However, he went 20–6 with a 2.82 ERA in 1969, then won the Cy Young Award in 1970, when he led the league in victories with a 24–12 mark.

Perry spent two more seasons with Minnesota, went to the Detroit Tigers in 1973, and returned to Cleveland in 1974. He retired after going just 4–10 with Cleveland and the Oakland Athletics in 1975.

In 17 seasons, he had a 215–174 record with 32 shutouts and a 3.45 ERA. He struck out 1,576 hitters while walking 998 in 3,285⅔ innings.

Perry, Joseph ("Joe the Jet")

FOOTBALL
b. Jan. 27, 1927, Stevens, Ark.

After scoring 22 touchdowns for Compton Junior College in 1945, Perry entered the Navy and played for the Alameda, California, Naval Station team. When he was discharged in 1948, he signed with the San Francisco 49ers of the All-America Football Conference.

As a rookie, he carried the ball only 77 times but scored 10 rushing touchdowns to lead the league. The 6-foot, 200-pounder became a starter in 1949, when he got his nickname, "Joe the Jet," after quarterback Frankie Albert said of him, "his slip-stream darn near knocks you over. He's strictly jet-propelled."

The AAFC folded after the 1949 season, and the 49ers entered the NFL. Perry led the league in rushing with 1,018 yards in 1953 and 1,049 yards in 1954 and was named to the All-Pro team both years. He also led in rushing touchdowns in 1953 with 10.

Perry went to the Baltimore Colts in 1961 and spent two seasons there. The Colts cut him after the 1962 season, when he needed to play only three more games to qualify for a pension. San Francisco brought him back in 1963 to help him qualify. He played in nine games before retiring.

In 16 professional seasons, Perry rushed 1,929 times for 9,723 yards, a 5.0 average, and 71 touchdowns. He caught 260 passes for 2,021 yards, a 7.8 average, and 12 touchdowns; and he returned 31 kickoffs for 737 yards, a 23.8 average, and 1 touchdown.

★ Pro Football Hall of Fame

Perry, Michael Dean

FOOTBALL
b. Aug. 27, 1965, Aiken, S.C.

Although he was not initially as well known as his older and bigger brother, William "the Refrigerator," Perry became recognized as one of the NFL's best defensive tackles soon after joining the Cleveland Browns as a second-round draft choice out of Clemson University in 1988.

The 6-foot-1, 285-pounder was named

the American Football Conference defensive player of the year by United Press International in 1989, when he had seven quarterback sacks and two fumble recoveries, and he made *The Sporting News* All-Pro team four years in a row, from 1989 through 1992.

Peters, Gary C.

BASEBALL
b. April 21, 1937, Grove City, Pa.

A 6-foot-2, 200-pound left-handed pitcher, Peters appeared in a total of 12 games with the AL's Chicago White Sox from 1959 through 1962. In 1963, his first full year as a starter, he was 19–8 with a league-leading 2.33 ERA.

Peters led the league in victories with a 20–8 record in 1964, when he had a 2.50 ERA. Arm troubles began to bother him in 1965, but he had the league's best ERA again in 1966, at 1.96, though his record was only 12–10 that season.

After a 16–11 mark and 2.28 ERA in 1967, Peters slumped to 4–13 in 1968 and 10–15 in 1969. He was then traded to the Boston Red Sox and had a 33–25 record with them before retiring after the 1972 season because of recurring arm problems.

In 359 games, Peters had a 124–103 mark with 23 shutouts and a 3.25 ERA. He struck out 1,420 hitters and walked 706 in 2,081 innings.

Pettit, Bob (Robert L. Jr.)

BASKETBALL
b. Dec. 12, 1932, Baton Rouge, La.

Although he averaged 27.4 points a game in his college career at Louisiana State University and was an All-American center in 1953 and 1954, there was much doubt about whether Pettit could succeed in the NBA. At 6-foot-9 and 205 pounds, he was considered too slender to be a real star.

Pettit responded by averaging 20.4 points per game and was named the league's 1954–55 rookie of the year as a forward with the Milwaukee Hawks. He used a soft, accurate jump shot to score from outside, and he used cleverness, speed, and agility to get past bigger defenders to score from close in and to outmaneuver them for rebounds.

The Hawks moved to St. Louis in 1956, and Pettit led them to their first NBA championship in 1957–58, scoring 50 points in a 110–109 victory over the Boston Celtics in the final game of the championship series.

The league's most valuable player in 1956 and 1959, Pettit led the NBA in scoring both seasons with averages of 25.7 and 29.2 points per game. He was also the league's leading rebounder in 1955–56 with 16.2 per game.

Pettit retired in 1965 after averaging more than 20 points a game in each of his 11 NBA seasons, with a high of 31.1 in 1961–62. At the time, he held NBA records for most career points with 20,880, was third in career rebounds with 12,849, and was fifth in scoring average with 26.4 per game. Pettit was named to the NBA Silver Anniversary Team in 1971.

★ Basketball Hall of Fame

Petty, Richard Lee

AUTO RACING
b. July 2, 1937, Randleman, N.C.

Stock car racing's greatest driver, Petty was born into the sport: his father, Lee, was national champion in 1954, 1958, and 1959.

In his 34-year career, Petty won a record 200 NASCAR races, 95 more than Dave Pearson, who is in second place. He's the only driver to win the Daytona 500 seven times, in 1964, 1966, 1971, 1973, 1974, 1979, and 1981, and the only one to be a seven-time NASCAR champion, in 1964, 1967, 1971, 1972, 1974, 1975, and 1979.

Petty had 356 top-five finishes in addition to his victories. He was the first stock car driver to surpass $1 million in earnings, and he ended his career with $7,755,409, which is only fourth on the all-time list because purses were smaller when he was in his prime.

Idolized by his fans and respected by other NASCAR drivers, Petty announced in October 1991 that he would finish his career with a 29-race "Richard Petty Fan Appreciation Tour" in 1992.

Wearing his trademark extra-wide sunglasses and feathered cowboy hat, Petty patiently autographed thousands of glossy photos for fans during his tour.

Fellow driver Bill Elliott said of Petty, "He's been a role model for every driver and his sponsor and NASCAR. I've always tried to work hard and be understanding of people and the fans because that's what Richard has always done."

Since retiring, Petty has concentrated on being a team owner. His son, Kyle, is one of the drivers for his team.

★ NASCAR Hall of Fame

Pfann, George R.
FOOTBALL
b. Oct. 6, 1902, Marion, Ohio

An All-American quarterback at Cornell in 1923, Pfann was short and chunky at 5-foot-9 and 172 pounds. In the single wing of his era, the quarterback was often called the blocking back, but he also had to carry the ball on plunges, and he was sometimes used as a pass receiver.

In Pfann's three years as a starter, Cornell won all 24 of its games and scored 1,051 points against 81 for its opponents. The school's most important games were against Pennsylvania. In 1921, Pfann was featured as a blocker in front of Edgar Kaw, who scored five touchdowns in a 41–0 victory. Pennsylvania was watching for Kaw in 1922, and Pfann did most of the ground gaining as Cornell won, 9–0. Kaw graduated in 1923. Pfann, captaining the team that fall, caught a 30-yard pass for one touchdown and ran five yards for the other as Cornell again beat Penn, 14–7.

George Trevor of the *New York Sun* put Pfann on the all-time All-American team he selected in 1938.

★ College Football Hall of Fame

Phillip, Andy (Andrew P.)
BASKETBALL
b. March 7, 1922, Granite City, Ill.

In the 1941–42 season, all five of the University of Illinois basketball starters were sophomores. They became known as the "Whiz Kids." Phillip was the best player of the five, a Helms Athletic Foundation All-American both as a sophomore and a junior. A 6-foot-2, 195-pound guard, he led the team to 17 victories in 18 games when the Whiz Kids were juniors, and he set Big Ten records for points with 255, field goals with 111, and points in a game with 40.

After that season, Phillip served in the Marine Corps during World War II. Ironically, he and three other former Whiz Kids returned to Illinois in 1946 as somewhat over-aged seniors. Unlike the others, Phillip became a professional star after graduating. Though not a big scorer as a pro, he was an outstanding playmaker, and his quick hands and extra-long fingers also made him a fine defender and ball stealer.

Phillip joined the Chicago Stags of the Basketball Association of America in 1947. The BAA merged with the National Basketball League to form the NBA in 1949, and the Chicago franchise folded a year later. Phillip went to the Philadelphia Warriors and led the NBA in assists in both 1950–51 and 1951–52.

Philadelphia traded him to the Ft. Wayne Pistons in 1952. Phillip finished among the top four in assists each of the next four seasons. He ended his career as a substitute with the Boston Celtics in 1956–57 and 1957–58, and the Celtics won the NBA title in his first season with them.

In 701 professional games, Phillip scored 6,384 points, an average of 9.1 a game. He was named to the Associated Press all-time All-American team in 1950.

★ Basketball Hall of Fame

Piazza, Mike (Michael J.)
BASEBALL
b. Sept. 4, 1968, Norristown, Pa.

When Piazza joined the NL's Los Angeles Dodgers near the end of the 1992 season after having been a 62nd-round choice in the 1988 free agent draft, there was considerable joking in the media about the fact that he was the godson of Dodger manager Tommy LaSorda and was with the Dodgers only because of the friendship between the two families.

He hit only .232 in 21 games that

season. However, in 1993 the 6-foot-3, 197-pound Piazza became the team's starting catcher and ended the joking by winning the league's rookie of the year award. He had a .318 average with 35 home runs and 118 RBI. Piazza was the first rookie of the year to drive in more than 100 runs, and his home run total was a record for a rookie catcher.

Pihos, Peter L.

FOOTBALL
b. Oct. 22, 1923, Orlando, Fla.

A tough, versatile player, Pihos is the only man ever to be named an All-Pro end on both offense and defense. As a sophomore at the University of Indiana in 1942, he caught a 25-yard touchdown pass to beat Minnesota, 7–0. The following season, he caught a touchdown pass against Wisconsin, then moved to fullback and ran for two touchdowns in a 34–0 victory.

Pihos entered military service in 1944 and returned to Indiana after World War II ended in 1945, playing most of the season at fullback. Granted an extra year of eligibility because of his military duty, he captained the team in 1946, then joined the Philadelphia Eagles of the NFL.

He was an All-Pro end in 1948 and 1949, when only 11 players were chosen. The Eagles won NFL championships both seasons. They went to the two-platoon system in 1952, and Pihos was named to the All-Pro defensive team. In 1953 he became an offensive specialist and was an All-Pro three more times. He led the league in receptions all three years, catching 63 for 1,049 yards and 10 touchdowns in 1953, 60 for 872 yards and 10 touchdowns in 1954, and 62 for 864 yards and 7 touchdowns in 1955.

Pihos retired after the 1955 season. In his NFL career, he caught a total of 373 passes for 5,619 yards, a 15.1 average, and 61 touchdowns.
★ Pro Football Hall of Fame

Pilgrim, Paul H.

TRACK AND FIELD
b. 1883, New York, N.Y.
d. Jan. 7, 1958

Pilgrim won a gold medal at the 1904 Olympics as a member of the winning team in the 4-mile team race, but he wasn't chosen to represent the U.S. when the "intercalated" games of 1906 were held in Athens to mark the tenth anniversary of the modern Olympics.

However, Pilgrim paid his own way to Athens and was allowed to compete. He astonished everyone by winning two gold medals. After running a 53.2 in the 400-meter run to beat the favorite, Wyndham Halswelle of Great Britain, Pilgrim came up against Halswelle and the 1,500-meter gold medalist, James Lightbody of the U.S., in the finals of the 800-meter run.

Lightbody and Pilgrim both began sprinting at the 700-meter mark to leave Halswelle behind, and Pilgrim just barely edged Lightbody in the time of 2:01.5.

In 1914, Pilgrim became manager and athletic director of the New York Athletic Club, and he held that position until his retirement in 1953.

Pilote, Pierre P.

HOCKEY
b. Dec. 11, 1931, Kenogami, P.Q.

A rough, tough defenseman, Pilote grew up in a French-speaking town and claimed that the first English words he learned were "Do you want to fight?"

After starring as an amateur with the St. Catharines TeePees, he became a professional in 1951. He had a trial with the Chicago Black Hawks in 1955–56 and joined the team as a regular the following season. He stayed with Chicago through 1967–68, then spent a final season with the Toronto Maple Leafs before retiring.

Pilote won the Norris Trophy as the NHL's best defenseman three years in a row, 1964–66, and was a first- or second-team all-star eight times. His 59 points in 1964–65 was a record for defensemen at the time.

In 890 regular season games, Pilote scored 80 goals and had 418 assists. He had 8 goals and 53 assists in 86 playoff games.
★ Hockey Hall of Fame

Pincay, Laffit, Jr.

HORSE RACING
b. Dec. 29, 1946, Panama City, Panama

The all-time money winner as a jockey with $183,815,292 through 1994, Pincay had won 8,221 races, second only to Bill Shoemaker. He was the nation's leading money winner from 1970 through 1974, in 1979, and in 1985, and he won Eclipse Awards as the top jockey of the year in 1971, 1973, 1974, 1979, and 1985.

Pincay won the Kentucky Derby aboard Swale in 1984, and he rode the Belmont Stakes winner three years in a row, Conquistador Cielo in 1982, Caveat in 1983, and Swale in 1984.

In 56 Breeders' Cup starts, Pincay has seven victories, four seconds, and nine third-place finishes for total winnings of $6,811,000. He is tied for the lead in victories and stands fourth in winnings.

His Breeders' Cup winners were juveniles Tasso in 1985, Capote in 1986, and Is it True in 1988; distaff champion Bayakoo in 1989 and 1990; juvenile filly Phone Chatter in 1993; and classic champion Skywalker in 1986.

★ National Horse Racing Hall of Fame

Pinckert, Ernie

FOOTBALL
b. May 1, 1908, Medford, Wis.

The first player from Southern California to be named an All-American twice, Pinckert was a back on the Associated Press team in both 1930 and 1931, and he was also named by Grantland Rice in 1931.

Although best known for his blocking, Pinckert was a fast, dangerous runner, and Coach Howard Jones installed a double reverse to take advantage of his speed. Pinckert had touchdown runs of 75 yards against Stanford in 1930 and 80 yards against Montana in 1931. He scored two touchdowns on the double reverse to lead Southern California to a 21–12 victory over Tulane in the 1932 Rose Bowl.

Pinckert joined the NFL's Boston Redskins in 1932 and spent nine seasons with the team, which moved to Washington in 1937. He was used mainly as a blocking back. Incomplete statistics credit him with 114 yards on 28 carries, a 4.1 average, and 21 receptions for 269 yards.

★ College Football Hall of Fame

Pinkston, Clarence E. ("Bud")

DIVING
b. Feb. 1, 1900, Wichita, Kans.
d. Nov. 18, 1961

Pinkston developed his diving skills at Stanford University before the NCAA swimming and diving championships were held. He won the AAU platform competition from 1920 through 1924 and was the 3-meter springboard champion at the 1921 indoor meet and the 1923 outdoor meet.

At the 1920 Olympics, Pinkston won a gold medal in the platform dive and a silver medal in the springboard. He won bronze medals in both events in 1924, when he met Elizabeth Becker. They were married the following year. Retired from competition, Pinkston became her coach, and she won her second gold medal in 1928.

He later served as coach and athletic director for the Detroit Athletic Club.

Pippen, Scottie

BASKETBALL
b. Sept. 25, 1965, Hamburg, Ark.

Pippen averaged 17.2 points a game at Central Arkansas University and was chosen by the Seattle SuperSonics in the first round of the 1987 NBA draft. Seattle immediately traded him to the Chicago Bulls.

The 6-foot-7, 225-pound Pippen played as a backup for two seasons, then became a starting forward who also played at guard on occasion. A good outside shot and the ability to drive to the basket made him a powerful offensive force on a team that won three straight NBA titles, from 1991 through 1993.

Pippen is also an excellent defender who was named to *The Sporting News* NBA all-defensive first team in 1992 and 1993 and to the second team in 1991. His best offensive season was 1993–94, when he averaged 22.0 points per game.

Through that season, Pippen had

scored 9,302 points in 551 regular season games, an average of 16.9 per game. He also had 3,765 rebounds, 2,862 assists, and 1,173 steals. In 110 playoff games, he scored 2,016 points, pulled down 848 rebounds, and had 210 steals.

Plank, Eddie (Edward S.)

BASEBALL
b. Aug. 31, 1875, Gettysburg, Pa.
d. Feb. 24, 1926

Plank didn't play baseball until he entered Gettysburg College when he was 21 years old. A left-handed pitcher, he joined the Philadelphia Athletics after graduating in 1901, the AL's first year as a major league, and had a 17–13 record.

He won 20 or more games each of the next four seasons and eight times in the next 14 seasons, and he had an ERA of less than 3.00 every year from 1903 until his retirement after the 1917 season.

The durable Plank led the league in games with 43 in 1903, in complete games with 35 in 1905, in winning percentage with .760 on a 19–6 record in 1906, and in shutouts with 8 in 1907 and 6 in 1911.

At a time when pitchers worked very fast, Plank was known as a frustratingly slow worker. He relied entirely on a fastball, a curve, and excellent control, often using a sidearm delivery to throw batters off stride.

Plank didn't have much luck in the World Series. He lost two games despite a 1.59 ERA in 1905, when the New York Giants beat Philadelphia in five games, and was 1–1 with a 1.86 ERA in the 1911 Series, a six-game victory over the Giants. In 1913, he allowed only two earned runs in 19 innings for a 0.95 ERA but was only 1–1 again, as the Athletics beat the Giants in five games. And he lost his only start, 1–0, in 1914, when the Athletics were swept by the Boston Braves. In Series play, he had a 2–5 record and a 1.15 ERA.

The Federal League, in its second season in 1915, lured Plank away from Philadelphia. He had a 21–11 record with St. Louis, but the league folded after that season, and he finished his career with the AL's St. Louis Browns in

1916 and 1917. He died of a stroke at the age of 50.

In 17 seasons, Plank had a 326–194 record with 69 shutouts and a 2.35 ERA. He struck out 2,246 hitters and walked only 1,072 in 4,495⅔ innings pitched. Plank gave up fewer walks than any other pitcher, with more than 4,000 innings of work.

★ Baseball Hall of Fame

Plante, Jacques (Joseph Jacques)

HOCKEY
b. Jan. 17, 1929, Shawinigan Falls, P.Q.

Montreal goaltender Gerry McNeill was having a bad time in the 1953 semifinal Stanley Cup series against Chicago. Trailing three games to two, the Canadiens called Plante up from the minors to replace McNeill. He claimed he was so nervous he could hardly tie his skates, but he gave up just one goal in two games as Montreal won the series. Plante and McNeill split the job in the final series against Boston, and the Canadiens won in five games.

The following season, McNeill was in the minor leagues, and Plante was Montreal's goalie. An excellent skater, he pioneered the technique of roaming far out of his net to get the puck and pass it to a teammate to start a rush. After his nose was broken by a shot on November 1, 1959, Plante began wearing a face mask for protection. He had previously used a mask in practice, as other goalies often did, but he was the first to wear one regularly during games.

The mask was ridiculed by some, but Plante gave up just 13 goals in the first 11 games. "I had to show good results to keep the mask," he explained. Within a few years, every goalie in the NHL was wearing a face mask patterned after Plante's.

Plante was traded to the New York Rangers in 1963. He retired after the 1964–65 season but returned to hockey with the expansion St. Louis Blues in 1967. The Blues traded him to the Toronto Maple Leafs in 1970, and he finished his NHL career with the Boston Bruins in 1972–73. He played briefly with the Edmonton Oilers of the World Hockey Association in 1974–75.

Plante won the Vezina Trophy as the NHL's best goaltender five years in a row, from 1956 through 1960 and in 1962. He and Glenn Hall shared the award with St. Louis in 1969. Plante won the Hart Trophy as the league's most valuable player in 1962; he is one of only four goalies to have won the award.

★ Hockey Hall of Fame

Player, Gary J.

GOLF
b. Nov. 1, 1935, Johannesburg, South Africa

Like Ben Hogan, Player was small for a professional golfer at 5-foot-9 and 155 pounds, and he worked very hard to achieve success. A physical fitness proponent whose ideas sometimes verged on the mystical, he worked out daily, ate raisins and sunflower seeds on the course, and wore black clothing because he believed it absorbed energy from the sun.

Soft-spoken, sincere, eternally polite, and deeply religious, Player was suspected by some of seeming too good to be true, but he converted even his critics in 1965 when he gave away his entire purse of $25,000 after winning the U.S. Open, some of it for medical research and the rest to help support junior golf.

Player finished fourth in the 1956 British Open, when he was only 20, and the following year he beat the established South African golfer Bobby Locke in a 108-hole match. He won his first major championship, the British Open, in 1959. He was also the British Open champion in 1968 and 1974.

Player won the Masters Tournament in 1961, 1974, and 1978 and the PGA championship in 1962 and 1972, giving him a total of nine major titles. He finished in the top four in the major tournaments 15 other times.

The PGA tour's leading money winner with $64,540.45 in 1961, Player spent less time on the tour than most other pros in ensuing years, preferring to stay with his wife and family on their ranch in South Africa.

He won the PGA Seniors championship in 1986, 1988, and 1990 and the U.S. Senior Open in 1987 and 1988.

★ World Golf Hall of Fame

Plumb, Mike (J. Michael)

EQUESTRIAN SPORTS
b. March 28, 1940, Islip, N.Y.

Plumb won six medals at five different Olympics, a record for an American equestrian. He was a member of the winning three-day U.S. team in 1976 and 1984 and was on silver medal teams in 1964, 1968, and 1972. He also won an individual silver medal for the 1976 three-day event.

A 1962 graduate of the University of Maryland, Plumb won an individual gold at the 1977 Pan-American Games and was a member of the gold medal team in 1973 and 1977. He won an individual silver medal and a team gold medal in the 1974 world championships.

Plunkett, Jim (James W.)

FOOTBALL
b. Dec. 5, 1947, San Jose, Calif.

Winner of the 1970 Heisman Trophy and Maxwell Award as the best college player of the year, Plunkett started at quarterback for two years at Stanford University. He completed 530 of 962 passes for 7,544 yards and 52 touchdowns, becoming the first player ever to account for more than 7,000 yards in passing and in total offense.

He joined the NFL's New England Patriots as their first-round draft choice in 1971 and was named rookie of the year after completing 156 of 328 attempts for 2,158 yards and 19 touchdowns. That was the beginning of a roller-coaster professional career.

Playing behind a shaky offensive line, the 6-foot-2, 220-pound Plunkett was frequently sacked and suffered a variety of injuries during the next four seasons. In 1976, the Patriots traded him to the San Francisco 49ers, who released him after the 1977 season.

Plunkett joined the Oakland Raiders as a backup during the 1978 season. He took over as the starter after Dan Pastorini suffered a broken leg in the fifth game in 1980, and he helped lead the Raiders to the Super Bowl title as a wild-card team. In Oakland's 27–10 win over the Philadelphia Eagles in Super Bowl XV, Plunkett completed 13 of 21 passes for 261 yards and 3 touchdowns and was named the game's most valuable player.

An injury limited his playing time in 1981. The Raiders moved to Los Angeles in 1982, when a player strike shortened the season. With Plunkett throwing well once again, the Raiders won eight of nine regular season games but lost in the second round of the playoffs.

Plunkett was replaced by Marc Wilson during the 1983 season. However, Wilson was injured, and Plunkett took over to lead Los Angeles to six victories in their last seven games. He completed 16 of 25 passes for 172 yards and one touchdown as the Raiders won Super Bowl XVIII, 38–9, over the Washington Redskins.

Plunkett missed most of the 1984 season with an injury, served as a backup in 1985 and 1986, and retired after missing all of the 1987 season with a bad shoulder. In his 17 NFL years, he completed 1,943 of 3,701 passes for 25,882 yards and 164 touchdowns. He also rushed for 1,337 yards and 14 touchdowns.

Poe, Arthur

FOOTBALL
b. March 22, 1879, Baltimore, Md.
d. April 15, 1951

One of five brothers who played football at Princeton, great-nephews of the writer Edgar Allan Poe, Arthur starred on teams that won 23 games while losing only 1 and tying 1 in 1898 and 1899. The 5-foot-7, 145-pound end ran 95 yards for a touchdown to defeat Yale, 6–0, in 1898. He also had an 80-yard touchdown against Navy and a 40-yard touchdown run against Brown.

In 1899, Poe drop-kicked the only field goal of his career from 35 yards to beat Yale, 11–10. He was named an All-American after that season, and the

Helms Athletic Foundation retroactively named him player of the year.

The other brothers were Samuel J., who played at Princeton from 1880 through 1882; Edgar Allan, 1888 through 1890; John P. Jr., 1891 through 1892; and Neilson, 1894 through 1896.

★ College Football Hall of Fame

Pollard, Fritz (Frederick D.)

FOOTBALL
b. Jan. 27, 1894, Chicago, Ill.
d. May 11, 1986

In 1921 Pollard became the first black to coach an NFL team, and the only one until Art Shell took charge of the Oakland Raiders in 1989. Five years earlier, Pollard had been the second black named to the college football All-American team.

A halfback at Brown University, the 5-foot-8, 150-pound Pollard was a fast, elusive runner who had touchdown runs of 55 and 60 yards against Yale in 1916, leading Brown to an upset 21–6 victory, Yale's only loss of the season. He also had runs of 22, 42, and 47 yards and scored two touchdowns in a 21–0 win over Harvard that season.

After serving in World War I, Pollard briefly studied dentistry before joining the Akron Indians professional football team in 1919. The team entered the American Professional Football Association (now the NFL) and became known as the Akron Pros in 1921.

Although Pollard was a star performer and co-coach of the team with Elgie Tobin, he had to cope with severe racial prejudice in Akron. He later recalled, "The fans booed and called me all kinds of names, because they had a lot of Southerners up there working. You couldn't eat in the restaurants or stay in the hotels. Hammond and Milwaukee were bad, then, too, but never as bad as Akron was."

Pollard played for the NFL's Milwaukee Badgers in 1922, then joined the Hammond, Indiana, Pros as player-coach for two seasons and part of a third. During the 1925 season, he left Hammond to play for the Providence Steamroller, then returned to Akron to finish the season. He played for Akron in 1926.

In 1927, Pollard went back to his native Chicago to organize an independent black team, the Chicago Brown Bombers, which he coached through the 1933 season. He also worked in show business as a movie producer and agent. One of his clients was Paul Robeson, the black singer and actor who had played football at Rutgers and was a teammate of Pollard's at Akron in 1920.

★ College Football Hall of Fame

Pollard, Jim (James C.)

BASKETBALL
b. July 9, 1922, Oakland, Calif.

His great leaping ability, which earned him the nickname "Kangaroo Kid," combined with intelligence and finesse, made Pollard a great basketball player. In fact, in a 1952 poll of professional players, Pollard was chosen the greatest of the period, ahead of his longtime teammate George Mikan.

The 6-foot-3, 190-pound Pollard was an All-American forward in 1942, when he starred for the Stanford team that won the NCAA championship. Pollard was the high scorer in the NCAA tournament even though he missed the final game with influenza. After serving in the Coast Guard during World War II, Pollard was an AAU All-American twice with the San Diego Dons and the Oakland Bittners.

He joined the Minneapolis Lakers of the National Basketball League in 1947. Pollard spent eight seasons with the Lakers, who moved into the NBA in 1948. They won six championships during his tenure. Although he wasn't a big scorer, his accurate corner jump shot helped take defensive pressure off Mikan, and he was also a fine rebounder and passer.

One opponent said of him, "Pollard can do more things than anyone. He is better than most big men and decidedly better than the little men . . . He is a basketball player's player all the way."

In 497 professional games, Pollard scored 6,522 points, an average of 13.1.

He also had 2,487 rebounds and 1,417 assists.

He retired in 1955 and coached La-Salle College for three years, winning 48 games while losing 28. Pollard also coached the Lakers for part of the 1959–60 season, winning only 14 of 39 games.

★ Basketball Hall of Fame

Pollard, LaTaunya

BASKETBALL
b. July 26, 1960, E. Chicago, Ind.

Pollard won the Wade Trophy as the female college player of the year in 1983 after leading the nation with 29.3 points per game. A 5-foot-9 guard at Long Beach State, she scored 907 points on 376 field goals and 155 free throws in 31 games, and she also averaged 8.9 rebounds a game. During her four years as a starter, Pollard had 2,913 points, second highest in history.

She was selected for the 1980 Olympic team that didn't play because the U.S. boycotted the Moscow Games. After graduating in 1983, Pollard played in an Italian league for one season. She damaged cartilage in her right knee during the 1984 Olympic trials and had to go undergo surgery, ending her career.

Post, Albertson Van Zo

FENCING
b. 1866, New York, N.Y.
d. Jan. 23, 1938

A strange myth grew up around Post, who won three medals in fencing at the 1904 Olympics. For years it was believed that he was a Cuban who was invited to join the U.S. Olympic team because Cuba didn't have a team.

Post actually came from a long-established New York family and was the son of a Union Army colonel who was wounded at the Battle of Antietam. A member of the New York Fencers Club, he was one of a handful of fencers to win national championships in all three major weapons. He was national foil champion in 1895, épée champion in 1896, and saber champion from 1901 through 1903.

In 1904, Post won a gold medal in the now obsolete single sticks competition at the St. Louis Olympics. He also won a silver medal in the foil and a bronze in the saber. Post competed in all three standard weapons at the 1912 Olympics but didn't reach the finals in any event.

Potter, Cindy (Cynthia; Mrs. MacIngvale)

DIVING
b. Aug 27, 1950, Houston, Tex.

Potter won a record 25 national diving championships. She was the U.S. outdoor champion in the 1-meter springboard from 1968 through 1977; in the 3-meter springboard in 1971 and 1972 and from 1975 through 1977; and in the platform dive in 1970 and 1971.

Indoors, she won 1-meter springboard titles from 1969 through 1973 and in 1976 and 1977, the 3-meter in 1969, 1970, and 1973.

Going into the 1972 Olympics, Potter was expected to win at least one medal, but she severely injured her foot during a practice session. Although able to compete, she could place only 7th in the springboard and 21st in the platform event. Potter won a bronze in the 1976 Olympic springboard competition.

Potter was also on the 1968 Olympic diving team, and she was selected again in 1980, when the U.S. boycotted the Moscow Games because of the Soviet Union's invasion of Afghanistan. In other international competition, she won a gold in the springboard and a silver in the platform at the 1970 World University Games, a bronze in the springboard at the 1975 Pan-American Games, and a silver in the springboard at the 1978 world championships.

A 1973 graduate of Indiana University, Potter later coached diving at Southern Methodist University and the University of Arizona.

Poulos, Leah

SPEED SKATING
b. Oct. 5, 1951, Berwyn, Ill.

Poulos won speed skating's world sprint championship in 1974 and took a silver medal in the 1,000-meter race at the 1976 Olympics. In September 1977, she married another U.S. Olympic speed skater, Peter Mueller, and retired from competition for two years to support him while he was in training.

Basically self-taught, Poulos once said, "I learned the basic principles by trial and error — falling down and getting up." She returned to skating in 1979, when she won her second world sprint championship, and she won two silver medals, in the 500- and 1,000-meter races, at the 1980 Olympics.

Powell, Boog (John W.)

BASEBALL
b. Aug. 17, 1941, Lakeland, Fla.

A left-handed hitter but right-handed thrower, the 6-foot-4, 240-pound Powell was named the AL's most valuable player in 1970, when he batted .297 with 35 home runs and 114 RBI to help lead the Baltimore Orioles to the pennant. He hit .294 with 2 home runs, 5 RBI, and 6 runs scored as the Orioles beat the Cincinnati Reds in a five-game World Series.

Powell was with the Orioles briefly in 1961 and became a starter in the outfield and at first base the following year. He led the league with a .606 slugging percent in 1964, when he had 39 home runs and 99 RBI.

In 1966, Powell settled in at first base and remained there for the rest of his career, although he was frequently used as the designated hitter after 1974. Though he lacked range, he was a solid defensive player who made few errors and was very adept at handling bad throws from other infielders.

Powell actually had his best season in 1969, the year before he was MVP. He batted .304 with 37 home runs and 121 RBI that year.

Baltimore traded him to Cleveland in 1975. After two seasons there, he played 50 games for the Los Angeles Dodgers in 1976, then retired. In 2,042 games, Powell hit .266 with 1,776 hits, including 270 doubles, 11 triples, and 339 home runs. He had 1,187 RBI and scored 889 runs.

Powell, John G.

TRACK AND FIELD
b. June 25, 1947, San Francisco, Calif.

At San Jose State University, Powell's best finish in the NCAA championships was a fourth place in 1969. From 1974 through 1987, though, he won the national discus championship 7 times, in 1974 and 1975 and from 1983 through 1987.

Powell set a world record with a throw of 226 feet, 8 inches at the 1975 Pan-American Games. His personal best was a 233–9 at the 1984 national championships, but that was below the world record at the time. Powell won bronze medals at the 1976 and 1980 Olympics.

Powell, Mike (Michael)

TRACK AND FIELD
b. Nov. 10, 1963, Philadelphia, Pa.

Powell was not a likely candidate to break Bob Beamon's long-standing world long jump record with a leap of over 29 feet. As a student at UCLA, his personal best was a 26–9¾ in 1985; he finished third at the national championships.

By the late 1980s, the 6-foot-3, 165-pound Powell was clearly the second-best long jumper in the world, but he continually finished behind Carl Lewis, who had been chasing Beamon's record for years. At the 1991 world championships in Tokyo, Powell stunned Lewis and the world with a jump of 29 feet, 4½ inches, bettering Beamon's 1968 mark by 2 inches. He won the Sullivan Award as the nation's outstanding amateur athlete for the accomplishment.

Powell, who finished second to Lewis to win a silver medal at the 1988 Olympics, took another silver in 1992 behind Lewis. However, he won the world championship in 1993, with Lewis out of action, beating the second place finisher by nearly a foot and a half, and he was also the national long jump champion that year.

Pownall, Harry E., Sr.

HARNESS RACING
b. Oct. 30, 1902, Brooklyn, N.Y.
d. Dec. 31, 1979

The son and grandson of harness racing drivers, Pownall began racing in 1919 and had his first winner in Goshen, New York, in July 1920. His career began to flourish when he became assistant trainer to Billy Dickerson at Arden Homestead Stable in 1937. Pownall drove Titan Hanover to the first two-minute mile ever by a two-year-old harness horse in 1944, and they won the Hambletonian the following year.

After Dickerson's death in 1948, Pownall became the stable's head trainer. He won two other triple crown races, the 1950 Kentucky Futurity with Star's Pride and the 1967 Yonkers Futurity with Pomp. Among the other horses he developed and drove were Florican, Florlis, Sharpshooter, Tassel Hanover, and Matastar, who did a 1:55⅘ at Lexington in 1962.

★ Hall of Fame of the Trotter

Poynton, Dorothy (Mrs. Hill)

DIVING
b. July 17, 1915, Salt Lake City, Utah

One of only three woman to win four Olympic medals in diving and one of only two to win diving medals at three different Olympics, Poynton was a quick learner who placed third in the national indoor 3-meter springboard and the platform event in 1927, before her twelfth birthday.

She was barely 13 when she won her first Olympic medal, a silver in the 1928 springboard dive. She won gold medals in the springboard in 1932 and 1936 and a bronze in the 1936 springboard event.

Dorothy Poynton won the national outdoor platform championship from 1933 through 1935; the indoor 1-meter springboard in 1932 and 1935; and the indoor 3-meter in 1933 and 1934. She retired from competition when she was only 21. The 5-foot-1, 112-pound Poynton later gave exhibitions and operated an aquatic club in Los Angeles.

★ International Swimming Hall of Fame

Pratt, Babe (Walter)

HOCKEY
b. Jan. 7, 1916, Stony Mountain, Man.

A 6-foot-3, 215-pound defenseman, Pratt entered the NHL with the New York Rangers in 1935–36, was traded to Toronto during the 1942–43 season, and had one season with the Bruins in 1946–47. He then played minor league hockey for several teams, retiring in 1952.

The winner of the Hart Trophy as the league's most valuable player in 1944, Pratt set a record for defensemen that season with 57 points in just 50 games; on January 8, 1944, he set a record for most assists in a game by a defenseman with 6.

The gregarious, fun-loving Pratt was banned from professional hockey for gambling early in 1946, but the ban was lifted less than three weeks later after he made a personal plea to NHL president Red Dutton.

Pratt scored 83 goals and had 209 assists in 517 regular season games. He added 12 goals and 17 assists in 64 playoff games.

★ Hockey Hall of Fame

Prefontaine, Steve R.

TRACK AND FIELD
b. Jan. 25, 1951, Coos Bay, Oreg.
d. May 30, 1975

Prefontaine discovered distance running in high school, where he ran a 4:06 mile, a 3:49.1 in the 1500-meter, an 8:46.6 in the 2-mile, a 13:43.0 in the 3-mile, and a 13:52 in the 5,000-meter run. His 2-mile time shattered the former national interscholastic record by nearly 7 seconds.

He entered the University of Oregon in 1969. Prefontaine was the first athlete ever to win the same event at the NCAA track and field championships four years in a row, taking the 3-mile/5000-meter title from 1970 through 1973. He also won the cross-country championship in 1970, 1971, and 1973, and he was the AAU national 5,000-meter champion in 1971 and 1973.

Prefontaine lacked the all-out speed needed to win races with a finishing kick, so his style was to take the lead early and wear down his competitors by setting a fast early pace. It didn't work for him in the 1972 Olympics, where he wore himself down and ran only fourth in the 5,000 meters. He finished second in the event at the 1973 world championships.

The energetic and popular Prefontaine was offered $200,000 to join the new International Track Association in 1974, but he turned it down because he wanted to run in the 1976 Olympics. Four hours after winning the 5,000-meter run at an invitational meet in Eugene, Oregon, he was killed in a one-car accident. At his death, he held American records in the 2-mile, 3,000-meter, 3-mile, and 5,000-meter runs.

★ National Track & Field Hall of Fame

Primeau, Joe (A. Joseph)

HOCKEY
b. Jan. 29, 1906, Lindsay, Ont.
d. May 15, 1989

Primeau was the center on Toronto's "Kid Line," between Harvey "Busher" Jackson and Charlie Conacher, during the late 1920s and early 1930s. In 1931–32, Jackson led the NHL in scoring, Primeau was just three points behind him, and Conacher was two points behind Primeau. He was also second in scoring in 1933–34, this time to Conacher.

After playing part of the 1928–29 season with Toronto, Primeau joined the team for good the following season. He retired as a player in 1936 and became a very successful coach. After coaching a junior amateur team to the Memorial Cup and a senior team to the Allan Cup, Primeau became the Toronto coach in 1950–51, and the Maple Leafs won the Stanley Cup. He is the only coach ever to win all three championship trophies.

Primeau scored 66 goals and had 177 assists in 310 regular season games, with 5 goals and 18 assists in 38 playoff games.

★ Hockey Hall of Fame

Prinstein, Myer

TRACK AND FIELD
b. 1880, Russia
d. March 10, 1928

Representing Syracuse University, Prinstein won the IC4A long jump championship in 1898, and shortly afterward he set a world record of 23 feet, 8⁷⁄₈ inches. At the 1899 IC4A meet he finished second to Alvin Kraenzlein, who established a new record of 24–3½ and extended that to 24–4½.

Prinstein beat Kraenzlein for the 1900 IC4A title, then regained the world record with a jump of 24–7½. He won the triple jump at the 1900 Olympics but finished second in the long jump. His jump of 23–6¼ was the best in the qualifying round on a Saturday, but the finals were scheduled for Sunday, and several U.S. athletes, among them Kraenzlein and Prinstein, agreed not to compete for religious reasons, Prinstein going along even though he was Jewish.

However, Kraenzlein did compete on Sunday and jumped 23–6½ to win the gold medal. When Prinstein learned what had happened, he punched Kraenzlein, but teammates separated them before it could turn into a real fight.

After graduating from Syracuse in 1901, Prinstein joined the Irish-American Athletic Club of New York City. In 1904, he became the only athlete ever to win the long jump and triple jump at the same Olympics, and he was also the long champion at the "intercalated" games of 1906. Prinstein was the AAU national long jump champion in 1898, 1902, and 1906.

Puckett, Kirby

BASEBALL
b. March 14, 1961, Chicago, Ill.

In ten major league seasons, Puckett has batted over .300 six times, won a batting title, and led the AL in hits four times. The solidly built 5-foot-6, 210-pounder became the Minnesota Twins' starting center fielder during the 1984 season.

After hitting .296 and .288 in his first two years, he had averages of .328, .332, .356, and .339 in 1989, when he won his batting title. He slipped to .298 in 1990, then batted .319 and .329 the next two seasons. Puckett led the league in hits with 207 in 1987, 234 in 1988, 215 in 1989, and 210 in 1992.

Also a fine defensive player, Puckett has been named to the league's All-Star team eight consecutive years, from 1986 through 1993. In 1,646 games, Puckett has a .318 batting average with 2,135 hits, including 362 doubles, 55 triples, and 174 home runs. He has 970 RBI and has scored 988 runs.

Pund, Peter (Henry R.)

FOOTBALL
b. Jan. 27, 1907, Augusta, Ga.
d. Sept. 17, 1987

Nicknamed "Peter the Great," the 6-foot-2, 200-pound Pund started at center for Georgia Tech from 1926 through 1928, and he captained the team in his senior season, when he was named an All-American. Georgia Tech won all nine of its regular season games and beat the University of California, 8–7, in the Rose Bowl.

Among the victories was a 13–0 defeat of Notre Dame. Knute Rockne wrote of Pund's performance in that game, "I counted 20 scoring plays that this man ruined . . . We were hopelessly beaten — but I had the thrill of my life to see great fighters go down in defeat before a greater fighter."

In 1969, college football's centennial year, Pund was voted the best college center of the 1920s.

★ College Football Hall of Fame

★ ★ R ★ ★

Radbourn, Charles G.

BASEBALL
b. Dec. 9, 1853, Rochester, N.Y.
d. Feb. 5, 1897

"Old Hoss" Radbourn, "the greatest of all nineteenth-century pitchers," according to his Hall of Fame plaque, entered major league baseball as an outfielder with the NL's Buffalo team in 1880 but was released after batting only .143 in six games.

He went back to the NL as a pitcher with the Providence Grays during the 1881 season and had a 25–11 record. At the time, pitchers were required to throw underhanded, and he kept on pitching that way even after the rule was changed in 1884 to allow overhanded deliveries.

As was common then, the 5-foot-9, 168-pound Radbourn often played other positions on days when he didn't pitch. Usually an outfielder on his off days, he also played every infield position at one time or another.

After going 33–20 in 1882, Radbourn led the league in victories with a 48–25 record in 1883, when he threw the ninth no-hitter in NL history, beating Cleveland, 8–0, on July 25.

Radbourn and Providence's other pitcher, Charles Sweeney, were feuding when the 1884 season opened, and Radbourn was unhappy with other teammates because of their poor fielding. He was suspended after deliberately not giving his best in a 5–2 loss on July 16.

Sweeney, now the team's only pitcher, got drunk shortly afterward and was also suspended. Radbourn rejoined the team and was given a raise. He pitched every game from July 23 to the end of the season on September 24, winning 18 in a row at one point and compiling a 60–12 record with 11 shutouts, 441 strikeouts in 678⅔ innings, and a 1.38 ERA. His 60 victories is a baseball record that will never be broken.

Radbourn never came close to that effort again. He had a 28–21 record in 1885 and went to the Boston NL team when the Providence franchise folded after that season. He won 20 or more games in four of the next five years, then went to the Boston club in the Players' League in 1890, when he was 27–12. Radbourn ended his career with the NL's Cincinnati team in 1891, when he was 11–13.

He was suffering from syphilis when he retired. Three years later, his face was disfigured, and he was partially paralyzed in a hunting accident. Radbourn became a recluse, living in the back room of a pool hall he owned in Bloomington, Illinois, for the rest of his short life.

In 11 seasons, he had a 309–195 record with 35 shutouts and a 2.67 ERA. He struck out 1,830 hitters and walked 875 in 4,535⅓ innings.

★ Baseball Hall of Fame

Rahal, Bobby (Robert W.)

AUTO RACING
b. Jan. 10, 1953, Medina, Ohio

Rahal was named the amateur driver of the year by the Sports Car Club of America in 1975, when he was a student at Denison University in Ohio. He began driving Formula and Can-Am cars after graduating and moved into Indy-Cars in 1982, when he was named CART rookie of the year.

In 1986, Rahal won six races, including the Indianapolis 500, where he set records with a 209.152 mph average for the last lap and a 170.722 mph average for the race. He became the first IndyCar driver to surpass $1 million in winnings for a season and won the CART driving championship.

He was the champion again in 1987, when he won three races and finished second in five. After only five victories in the next four years, Rahal won his third driving championship in 1992. Through the 1993 season, Rahal is the all-time leading IndyCar money winner with $13,003,241, and he is tied for tenth on the all-time list with 24 races won.

Raines, Timothy

BASEBALL
b. Sept. 16, 1959, Sanford, Fla.

After playing briefly for the NL's Montreal Expos in 1979 and 1980, the switch-hitting Raines established himself as one of the best leadoff men in baseball by batting .304, stealing a league-leading 71 bases, and scoring 61 runs in only 88 games in 1981 to be named rookie of the year.

The 5-foot-8, 178-pound Raines led the league in stolen bases the next three years in a row, with 78 in 1982, 90 in 1983, and 75 in 1984, and he also led with 133 runs scored in 1983 and 38 doubles in 1984.

His .334 average in 1986 led the league in 1986, and he was the NL's top run scorer for a second time with 123 in 1987. However, a leg injury limited him to 109 games in 1988 and reduced his speed somewhat. Although he remains a threat to steal bases, he hasn't approached his previous numbers since the injury.

Originally a second baseman, Raines has been an outfielder and occasionally the designated hitter since 1985. He became a free agent after the 1990 season

and signed with the AL's Chicago White Sox.

Through 1994, Raines had a .296 average with 2,152 hits, including 346 doubles, 105 triples, and 136 home runs. He had 764 stolen bases, 1,293 runs scored, and 742 RBI.

Ramsay, Jack (John T.)

BASKETBALL
b. Feb. 21, 1925, Philadelphia, Pa.

Ramsay entered St. Joseph's College in Philadelphia in 1942. After serving in World War II, he returned to school as a sophomore and captained the basketball team in his senior year. He then played in the Eastern Basketball League, taught school, and won a Doctor of Education degree from the University of Pennsylvania.

He returned to St. Joseph's in 1956 as basketball coach. In his 11 seasons there, the school won or shared seven Big Five championships and had seven seasons with 20 or more wins. His record was 232 victories and only 72 defeats.

In 1966, Ramsay became general manager of the NBA's Philadelphia 76ers, who won the NBA championship in 1968. Ramsay took over as coach the following season and remained until 1972, winning 174 games while losing 154. He became coach of an expansion team, the Buffalo Braves, in 1972 and got them into the playoffs three times in four seasons, compiling a 137–109 record.

The Portland Trailblazers hired Ramsay in 1976, and he guided them to an NBA championship in his first season. Led by center Bill Walton, Portland won 49 of 82 regular season games and then took 14 of 19 in the playoffs. In ten seasons, Portland won 453 games while losing 367 under Ramsay.

His last coaching stop was with the Indiana Pacers for just two years. Ramsay resigned in 1988 and became a frequent television commentator, most notably for TNT's coverage of the annual NBA draft of college players. During his professional coaching career, he had 864 wins and 783 losses. When he retired, he was second only to Red Auerbach in career victories.
★ Basketball Hall of Fame

Ramsey, Buster (Garrard)

FOOTBALL

b. March 16, 1920, Townsend, Tenn.

Ramsey played college football at William and Mary, graduating in 1943, and he was chosen by the Chicago Cardinals in the fourteenth round of the 1943 NFL draft. However, he served in the Navy during World War II and didn't join the team until 1946.

The 6-foot-1, 215-pounder starred as an offensive guard and defensive linebacker when the Cardinals won consecutive Western Division titles, in 1947 and 1948, winning the 1947 NFL championship.

He retired after the 1950 season and became a defensive coach with the Cardinals. Ramsey is credited with inventing the linebacker blitz, which he called the "red dog." He was later an assistant with the Detroit Lions and Pittsburgh Steelers.

The first head coach of the AFL's Buffalo Bills, in 1960, Ramsey had an 11–16–1 record in two seasons.

Ramsey, Frank V., Jr.

BASKETBALL

b. July 13, 1931, Corydon, Ky.

A 6-foot-3 guard at the University of Kentucky, Ramsey helped lead the school to the 1951 NCAA championship as a sophomore. Kentucky won 32 of 34 games that season and 29 of 32 in 1951–52. Because of recruiting violations, however, the school wasn't allowed to field a team the following season.

Coach Adolph Rupp kept the players together and worked them frequently in intra-squad games. The Southeastern Conference voted to give three players, Ramsey, Cliff Hagan, and Lou Tsioropoulos, an extra year of eligibility, but the NCAA wouldn't allow them to take part in post-season play. Kentucky won all 25 of its games, then sat out the NCAA tournament.

Ramsey joined the Boston Celtics of the NBA in 1954 and became the team's first "sixth man," coming off the bench to provide instant offense. With the Celtics, he frequently played small forward.

Despite his part-time role, he averaged more than 15 points a game in five of his nine professional seasons.

He missed the 1955–56 season because of military service. After he returned in the fall of 1956, the Celtics won seven NBA championships in eight seasons. Ramsey's 20-foot shot in the second overtime of the seventh and decisive game against the St. Louis Hawks won the first of those championships, in 1957.

Ramsey retired in 1964. Interestingly, the man who was nicknamed the "Kentucky Colonel" returned to basketball briefly to coach the Kentucky Colonels in the American Basketball Association in 1970–71, compiling a record of 32 wins and 35 losses.

★ Basketball Hall of Fame

Ranford, Bill (William)

HOCKEY

b. Dec. 14, 1966, Brandon, Man.

Ranford won the Conn Smythe Trophy as the outstanding player in the 1990 Stanley Cup playoffs, when he tied the NHL record for most wins by a goaltender with 16.

He entered the NHL with the Boston Bruins late in the 1985–86 season and played 41 games for Boston in 1986–87. However, he spent most of the following season in the minor leagues and was traded to the Edmonton Oilers in March 1988.

Ranford become Edmonton's full-time goaltender in 1989–90, when he had a 3.19 goals-against average during the regular season and a 2.53 average in the playoffs to help the Oilers win the Stanley Cup.

Through the 1993–94 season, Ranford had allowed 1,289 goals in 401 regular season games, a 3.21 average. He had given up 133 goals in 45 playoff games, a 2.97 average.

Rankin, Judy (Torluemke)

GOLF

b. Feb. 18, 1945, St. Louis, Mo.

Rankin won the 1959 Missouri Amateur at age 14, the youngest champion ever. The following year she was the lowest-scoring amateur in the U.S. Open, and in 1961 she won the Missouri Amateur again. Rankin joined the LPGA tour in 1962. Her first victory didn't come until 1964, when she won three tournaments.

She really came into her own in 1973, when she won the Vare Trophy for the lowest scoring average. In 1976, she won six tournaments, became the first LPGA player to win more than $100,000 in a season, won the Vare Trophy again, and was named player of the year.

Rankin repeated as Vare Trophy winner and player of the year in 1977, when she set a record by finishing in the top ten in 25 tournaments. Her last victory was in 1979, after which a back injury limited her play and playing time.

Rawls, Betsy (Elizabeth E.)

GOLF
b. May 4, 1928, Spartanburg, S.C.

Rawls didn't begin playing golf until she was 17. When she was 21, she won 1949 Texas Amateur championship, and she repeated in 1950. She joined the PGA tour in 1951, when she claimed the first of her four victories in the U.S. Women's Open; the others were in 1953, 1957, and 1960. She won the LPGA championship in 1959 and 1969.

Known as a great shot-maker and putter, Rawls won 55 tournaments, which is fourth on the all-time list behind Kathy Whitworth, Mickey Wright, and Louise Suggs.

Rawls led the tour in victories in 1952, 1957, and 1959, and was the top money winner in 1951 and 1959. She won the Vare trophy for fewest strokes per round in 1959, when she captured ten tournaments.

A Phi Beta Kappa graduate of the University of Texas with a degree in math and physics, Rawls was called the "circuit judge" because of her encyclopedic knowledge of the rules of golf. In 1970, she became the first woman ever to serve on the Rules Committee for the men's U.S. Open.

Rawls retired from the tour in 1975 and became the LPGA tournament director. In 1981 she took over as executive director of the McDonald's Championship.

★ International Women's Sports Hall of Fame; LPGA Hall of Fame

Rawls, Katherine L.

DIVING, SWIMMING
b. June 14, 1918, Nashville, Tenn.
d. April 8, 1982

Probably the most versatile swimmer and diver in history, Rawls won a total of 28 national championships in springboard diving and three swimming events between 1932 and 1938. She also won silver medals in Olympic springboard diving in 1932 and 1936 and a bronze medal as a member of the U.S. 400-meter relay team in 1936.

Rawls grew up in Florida. At 13, she placed second in the AAU national platform diving championship. She went on to win the 3-meter springboard championship from 1932 through 1934 and the 1-meter springboard in 1933 and 1934.

Her first national swimming championship came in the outdoor 220-yard breast stroke in 1931. She also won that event in 1932 and 1935. She won outdoor championships in the 440-yard freestyle in 1937 and 1938; the 880-yard freestyle in 1932, 1937, and 1938; and the 300-meter medley relay in 1934. Indoors, Rawls won the 100-yard freestyle in 1935.

Rawls's best event was the 300-meter individual medley. She won national outdoor championships at seven consecutive meets, from 1931 through 1938 (there was no competition in 1934), and she was the indoor titlist in the event six years in a row, from 1933 through 1938.

In 1937, Associated Press sportswriters voted her the athlete of the year after she became the first woman to win four national championships at one meet. Rawls repeated the feat in 1938.

She retired from competition in 1939. During World War II, Rawls (then Mrs. Theodore Thompson) was one of the first 21 women pilots selected to ferry fighting planes to combat zones for the Air Transport Command.

★ International Swimming Hall of Fame

Ray, Joie

TRACK AND FIELD
b. April 13, 1894, Kankakee, Ill.
d. May 13, 1978

America's first great miler, Ray was often called "Chesty" by sportswriters because of his competitive spirit — "chest" being used as a synonym for "heart." He was the AAU national 1-mile champion seven times, in 1915 and from 1917 through 1923, and he also won the 880-yard championship in 1919. Indoors, Ray was the national 1,000-yard champion from 1918 through 1920.

Suffering from a leg injury, Ray finished only eighth in the 1,500-meter run at the 1920 Olympics. However, he was the anchor man on an Illinois Athletic Club team that set a world record of 17:21.4 in the 4-mile relay in 1923, and in 1925 he tied the world record for the indoor mile at 4:12.0.

Ray retired soon after that but returned in 1928 to run longer distances. He won the national 10,000-meter title that year, finished second in the Boston Marathon, and ran in two Olympic events, running fifth in the marathon and fourteenth in the 10,000-meter run.

"Tex" Rickard, owner of Madison Square Garden, promoted a professional match race between Ray and Boughera El Ouafi of Algeria, the Olympic gold medalist in the marathon. Ray lost to El Ouafi in the marathon at Madison Square Garden but later beat him in a marathon at Boston Garden and in 16-mile and 20-mile races.

After retiring once again, Ray took part in many dance marathons, a craze of the late 1920s and early 1930s, and he ran a ritual mile on his birthday each year until he reached his late seventies. On his seventieth birthday, his time was 6:11.5.

★ National Track & Field Hall of Fame

Rayner, Chuck (Claude E.)

HOCKEY
b. Aug. 11, 1920, Sutherland, Sask.

Although he never won a Vezina Trophy, Rayner was an outstanding goalie, particularly strong in the playoffs, who had the misfortune to play for weak teams during most of his career.

He joined the New York Americans for 12 games in 1940/41 season and remained with them when they moved to Brooklyn the following season. After serving in the Canadian Royal Navy during World War II, he went to the New York Rangers in 1945.

Rayner won the Hart Trophy as the NHL's most valuable player in 1950, when he nearly led the Rangers to the Stanley Cup. They lost the seventh game to the Detroit Red Wings, 5–4, in the second overtime period.

Rayner retired after the 1952–53 season. He had 25 shutouts and a 3.05 goals-against average in 425 regular season games, with 1 shutout and a 2.56 average in 118 playoff games.

★ Hockey Hall of Fame

Reardon, Jeffrey J.

BASEBALL
b. Oct. 1, 1958, Pittsfield, Mass.

Reardon pitched for the University of Massachusetts before entering professional baseball in 1977. The 6-foot-1, 205-pounder was a starter in the minor leagues, but he became a relief pitcher when he joined the NL's New York Mets during the 1979 season.

A right-hander, Reardon was traded to the Montreal Expos in 1981, and he led the league with 41 saves in 1985, when he was named *The Sporting News* fireman of the year. He shared the award in 1987, after being traded to the AL's Minnesota Twins.

Reardon signed with the Boston Red Sox as a free agent in 1990 and was traded to the Atlanta Braves during the 1992 season. He joined the Cincinnati Reds as a free agent in 1993 and pitched briefly for the New York Yankees in 1994.

Through the 1994 season, Reardon had a 73–77 record with 367 saves and a 3.16 ERA. He had struck out 877 hitters and walked 358 in 1,132 innings. Reardon briefly held the major league record for most career saves but was passed by Lee Smith.

Reed, Andre D.

FOOTBALL
b. Jan. 29, 1964, Allentown, Pa.

After playing at little Kutztown State College in Pennsylvania, Reed was chosen by the Buffalo Bills in the fifth round of the 1985 NFL draft. The 6-foot-2, 190-pounder has been a consistently productive receiver for the Bills, catching 48 to 88 passes a year until being hampered by a series of injuries in 1993.

Reed was chosen to play in the Pro Bowl five years in a row, from 1988 through 1992. Not exceptionally fast, he runs excellent routes and has very good hands and is often used as a possession receiver over the middle or on the sideline.

Through the 1994 season, Reed had 624 receptions for 8,682 yards, a 13.9 average, and 60 touchdowns.

Reed, Robin L.

WRESTLING
b. Oct. 20, 1899, Pettigrew, Ark.
d. Dec. 20, 1978

While hitchhiking from his home in Oregon to New York City in 1924 to join the U.S. Olympic team, Reed stopped at Iowa State University to work out but was refused permission. He asked the coach if he could work out if he first pinned every member of the wrestling team. The coach agreed. Reed proceeded to pin every Iowa State wrestler, and he got his workout.

During practice for the Olympics in Paris, he bet he could pin Harry Steel, the U.S. heavyweight champion and eventual gold medal winner. He not only pinned Steel, but he did it five times in 15 minutes. Not surprisingly, Reed went on to win the gold medal in the featherweight class.

Undoubtedly the greatest amateur wrestler of his era, Reed never lost a match. He was the AAU 125-pound champion in 1921, the 135-pound champion in 1922 and 1924.

Reed, Willis, Jr.

BASKETBALL
b. June 25, 1942, Hico, La.

A 6-foot-10, 235-pound center, Reed starred at Grambling College. He led the team to an NAIA championship in 1961 and was named a small college All-American in 1963, after his senior year.

Only a second-round draft choice of the New York Knicks, Reed was voted the NBA rookie of the year in 1965 after averaging 19.5 points a game. He took physical beatings early in his season, as veteran players tested him, but finally Reed had enough and knocked down three opponents with a single rush toward the basket. "Everything standing up was going down," a teammate said. After that, the testing ended.

Reed combined a strong inside game with an effective short-range jump shot to score more than 20 points in five of his ten seasons with the Knicks. When the Knicks won their first NBA championship in 1970, he was named most valuable player for both the regular season and the playoffs.

His size and strength also made him an outstanding rebounder, but Reed was just as important to the team as an emotional leader. A knee injury limited him to just 11 games in 1971–72. The injury recurred in the fifth game of the 1973 championship series against the Los Angeles Lakers, and Reed missed the sixth game. However, he came limping into the seventh game, obviously in pain, and hit two shots before leaving. The emotional lift helped carry the Knicks to victory, and Reed was once again named most valuable player of the playoffs.

The bad knee never really healed, and Reed retired after the 1973–74 season. He scored 12,183 points in 650 regular season games, a 19.9 average, and had 8,414 rebounds. In 78 playoff games, he scored 1,358 points, a 17.4 average, and had 801 rebounds.

Reed returned as coach of the Knicks in 1977 but was fired after less than two seasons, winning 49 games while losing 47. As coach at Creighton University from 1981 to 1985, he had a 52–64 record. During the 1987–88 season, the New York Nets hired him and won only 7 of 28 games. He was replaced after a 26–56 record in 1989–90.

★ Basketball Hall of Fame

Reese, Pee Wee (Harold H.)

BASEBALL
b. July 23, 1919, Ekron, Ky.

The 5-foot-9, 175-pound Reese became the starting shortstop for the Brooklyn Dodgers during the 1940 season and was soon acknowledged as a team leader. He wasn't named the team's captain until 1950, but players accepted him as the unofficial captain well before that.

An excellent leadoff man, Reese lost three seasons to military service during World War II, returning to the Dodgers in 1946. He led the league with 104 walks in 1947, with 132 runs scored in 1949, and with 30 stolen bases in 1952.

Having grown up in Kentucky, Reese was uneasy when Jackie Robinson joined the Dodgers in 1947 as the major league's first black player of the twentieth century. However, he quickly recognized his new teammate's skills, and when he very conspicuously walked over to Robinson and put an arm around his shoulders before an early-season game, the gesture marked Robinson's full acceptance by the entire team.

Reese hit over .300 only once, with a .309 average in 1954, but he excelled defensively, leading NL shortstops in putouts four times. He retired after playing just 59 games for the Dodgers in 1958, their first year in Los Angeles, then spent one season with them as a coach.

In 2,166 games, Reese had 2,170 hits, including 330 doubles, 80 triples, and 126 home runs. He stole 232 bases, scored 1,338 runs, and had 885 RBI.

★ Baseball Hall of Fame

Reid, Michael B.

FOOTBALL
b. May 24, 1947, Altoona, Pa.

Originally a middle guard and linebacker at Penn State, Reid suffered a knee injury during spring practice in 1967 and missed the entire season. When he returned in 1968, he was moved to defensive tackle and became an immediate standout. A consensus All-American in 1969, Reid won the Outland Trophy as the nation's outstanding college lineman. During his two years as a starter, the team was undefeated.

The 6-foot-3, 255-pound Reid was a first-round draft choice of the NFL's Cincinnati Bengals in 1970. He was a consensus All-American Football Conference selection as defensive tackle in 1971 and 1972.

Reid retired after the 1974 season to pursue a career in music. An accomplished concert pianist, he began writing and performing country and western music in 1979 and won a Grammy Award in 1984 for his song "Stranger in My House."

★ College Football Hall of Fame

Reiser, Pete (Harold P.)

BASEBALL
b. March 17, 1919, St. Louis, Mo.
d. Oct. 25, 1981

After appearing in 58 games with the Brooklyn Dodgers in 1940, "Pistol Pete" became the team's starting center fielder in 1941 and had a sensational season. He led the NL with a .343 batting average, .558 slugging percentage, 117 runs scored, 39 doubles, and 17 triples while also playing brilliant defense.

Reiser was hitting .390 in July 1942 when he crashed into a fence while chasing a fly ball and suffered a serious concussion. Then he tried to come back before he was fully recovered. Troubled by headaches, blurred vision, and frequent dizzy spells, he ended up hitting just .310 that season and was never again the same player.

After spending three years in military service, Reiser returned to the Dodgers in 1947, when he batted .309 in 110 games. Relegated to part-time duty in 1948, he was traded to the Boston Braves the following season. He ended his playing career with the Pittsburgh Pirates in 1951 and the Cleveland Indians in 1952. He later served as a major league coach and minor league manager.

In 861 games, Reiser had a .295 average on 786 hits, including 155 doubles, 41 triples, and 58 home runs. He stole 87 bases, scored 473 runs, and had 368 RBI.

Remigino, Lindy J.

TRACK AND FIELD
b. June 3, 1931, Elmhurst, N.Y.

Remigino's victory in the 100-meter dash in 1952 was one of the greatest upsets in Olympic history. He failed to qualify for the AAU finals that year and barely scraped into the Olympic trials by finishing fifth in the NCAA championships. However, he finished second in the trials.

The Olympic final ended in a photo finish, with four runners crossing the finish line within 14 inches of each other. Remigino congratulated Herb McKenley of Jamaica, who had broken the tape. But the photos showed that Remigino's right shoulder had crossed the finish line before McKenley's chest hit the tape.

Remigino won a second gold medal as a member of the 4 x 100-meter relay team.

Running for Manhattan College, he won three IC4A championships, in the 200-meter dash in 1952 and in the 100- and 220-yard dashes in 1953.

He later became a very successful high school track coach in Hartford, Connecticut, where his teams won six outdoor and seven indoor state championships.

Renfro, Melvin L.

FOOTBALL
b. Dec. 30, 1941, Houston, Tex.

Renfro was a consensus All-American halfback at the University of Oregon as a junior in 1962, and he made *The Sporting News* All-American team in 1963. He was chosen by the Dallas Cowboys in the second round of the 1964 NFL draft.

A two-way player in college, Renfro became a defensive back with the Cowboys and also returned kicks during the early part of his career. As a rookie, he led the league with 32 punt returns, 418 yards on punt returns, 40 kickoff returns, and 1,017 yards on kickoff returns. He also intercepted seven passes and scored two touchdowns, one on an interception return and one on a punt return.

Renfro led the NFL with ten interceptions in 1969, returning them for 118 yards. An All-Pro in 1965, 1967, 1968, 1969, and 1973, he played in ten consecutive Pro Bowls, from 1964 through 1973.

He retired after the 1977 season with 52 career interceptions, three of which he ran back for touchdowns. Renfro returned 109 punts for 842 yards, a 7.7 average, and 1 touchdown, and ran back 85 kickoffs for 2,246 yards, a 26.4 average, and 2 touchdowns.

★ College Football Hall of Fame

Resta, Dario

AUTO RACING
b. 1884, Milan, Italy
d. Sept. 2, 1924

Raised in England from the age of two, Resta began racing there, setting a record of 95.7 mph in a half-mile run. He was brought to the United States by Alphonse Kaufman to drive Kaufman's Peugeot in 1915, and he promptly won the Grand Prize and the Vanderbilt Cup that year. He finished second in the Indy 500 after a long duel with Ralph DePalma that ended when one of Resta's tires blew.

In 1916 he won both the Indy 500 and the driver's championship. He raced little after that year. But in 1923 he was at Indy again, forced out of the race after 225 miles. He was killed in a crash at Brooklands in England when a tire blew and threw his car out of control.

★ Indianapolis Speedway Hall of Fame

Retton, Mary Lou

GYMNASTICS
b. Jan. 24, 1968, Fairview, W.Va.

Often described by sportswriters as a "little powerhouse," Retton brought a new dynamism into women's gymnastics, an energetic style that has become the trademark of recent American champions.

Before Retton, champion gymnasts had generally been delicate and sylphlike, graceful rather than powerful. Retton had a different body type. Though tiny by ordinary standards, at 4-foot-9 and 94 pounds, she was solid and muscular, capable of explosive movements rarely seen in women's gymnastics.

No American woman had ever won an individual Olympic medal in gymnastics until 1984. Retton won four, a gold in the all-around, a silver in the vault, and bronzes in the uneven bars and the floor exercise. She was the only woman to qualify for the finals in all four apparatus events, finishing fourth in the balance beam. Her performances came just two months after arthroscopic surgery to remove torn cartilage from her right knee.

Whie some considered Retton's medals tainted because of the Soviet boycott of the Los Angeles games, she had already demonstrated her ability to compete successfully against the best in the world. She was one of the favorites in the 1983 world championships but missed the competition because of a wrist injury. However, earlier that year she won the all-around American Cup competition, and in December she became the first American woman to win the Chunichi Cup.

Retton was named Associated Press Woman Athlete of the Year in 1984. She retired from amateur competition soon after her Olympic triumphs to do television commentary and commercials.

Retzlaff, Pete (Palmer E.)

FOOTBALL
b. Aug. 21, 1932, Ellendale, N.Dak.

A running back at South Dakota State College from 1950 to 1952, Retzlaff went to the Detroit Lions' training camp as a 22nd-round draft choice in 1953 and was cut before the season began.

After serving in the Army for two years, he rejoined the Lions in 1956 and was sold to the Philadelphia Eagles, where he spent two seasons as a backup running back. Moved to wide receiver in 1958, the 6–1, 211-pound Retzlaff tied for the league lead in receptions, catching 56 passes for 766 yards and 2 touchdowns.

A starter on the Eagles' 1960 championship team, Retzlaff moved to tight end in 1963. A strong blocker and sure-handed receiver, he won the 1965 Bert Bell Trophy as the NFL's player of the year. He caught 66 passes that season for 1,190 yards and 10 touchdowns.

Retzlaff retired after the 1966 season. In his 11 years as a professional, he caught 452 passes for 7,412 yards, a 16.4 average, and 47 touchdowns.

Reynolds, Bob (Robert O.)

FOOTBALL
b. March 30, 1914, Morris, Okla.
d. Feb. 8, 1994

Called "Horse" by his teammates at Stanford, the 6-foot-4, 225-pound Reynolds was an All-American tackle in 1934. A devastating blocker, he was also a defensive stalwart because of his surprising speed. Halfback Bobby Grayson said of Reynolds, "When he was paving the way, he banged the defenders down as though they were wooden Indians . . . On defense, he was almost unstoppable."

During his three seasons as a starter, 1933 through 1935, Stanford gave up only 99 points in 31 games, winning 23, losing 5, and tying 3.

Reynolds played in the NFL with the Detroit Lions in 1937 and 1938. He later became the president of the American League's Los Angeles Angels and vice president of the NFL's Los Angeles Rams.

★ College Football Hall of Fame

Reynolds, Butch (Henry)

TRACK AND FIELD
b. June 8, 1964, Akron, Ohio

As a junior at Ohio State in 1987, Reynolds won the 400-meter run at the NCAA and TAC championships and was third in the world championships. On August 16, 1988, Reynolds ran a world record 43.29 seconds at a meet in Zurich, Switzerland.

The International Amateur Athletic Federation (IAAF) suspended Reynolds indefinitely after he allegedly tested positive for steroid use in 1990. Reynolds brought suit, and in 1992 the U.S. Supreme Court ordered the U.S. Olympic Committee to allow him to run in the Olympic trials at New Orleans.

The IAAF threatened to suspend any other runners who competed against Reynolds, and the 400-meter heats were postponed for four days until the IAAF backed down. Reynolds ran three strong heats but was exhausted by the time he reached the finals, where he finished fifth.

Reynolds also won a separate civil suit against the IAAF for $27.3 million in damages, awarded in the fall of 1992. In an unprecedented move, a federal court seized $700,000 that a sponsor owed the IAAF and put it in escrow for Reynolds, pending appeals.

At the 1993 world championships, Reynolds finished second to teammate Michael Johnson in the 400-meter, but he ran on the winning 4 x 400-meter relay team that set a world record of 2:54.29. IAAF president Primo Nebiolo not only gave Reynolds his gold medal, he kissed both of his cheeks. "I was speechless and very touched," Reynolds said afterward.

Rice, Glen A.

BASKETBALL
b. May 25, 1967, Flint, Mich.

A 6-foot-8, 220-pounder who can shoot from outside, Rice was named most valuable player in the 1989 NCAA tournament, when he scored 184 points in six games to lead the University of Michigan to the national championship.

He averaged 18.2 points per game in his four-year college career and 25.6 per game as a senior. The Miami Heat chose Rice in the first round of the 1989 NBA draft.

Rice was named to the NBA all-rookie second team after averaging 13.6 points a game in 1989–90. His best professional season so far was 1991–92, when he averaged 22.3 points.

Through the 1993–94 season, Rice had scored 7,417 points in 396 regular season games, an average of 18.7, and he had made 523 of 1,381 three-point shots, a .379 percentage. He added 122 points in eight playoff games, a 15.3 average.

Rice, Greg (J. Gregory)

TRACK AND FIELD
b. Jan. 3, 1916, Missoula, Mont.

Running for Notre Dame University, Rice won the NCAA 2-mile championship in 1937 and 1939. Undefeated in 65 consecutive races from late 1939 until June 1943, Rice was the AAU outdoor 5,000-meter champion five years in a row, from 1938 through 1942, and he won the indoor championship four years in a row, from 1940 through 1943. He was also the AAU cross-country champion in 1941.

Rice won the Sullivan Award as the nation's outstanding amateur athlete in 1940, when he was undefeated through the U.S. season and on a European tour. He ran a world record 8:51.1 for the 2-mile in 1941.

★ National Track & Field Hall of Fame

Rice, Jerry L.

FOOTBALL
b. Oct. 13, 1962, Starkville, Miss.

A consensus small college All-American wide receiver at Mississippi Valley State in 1983 and 1984, Rice was chosen by the San Francisco 49ers in the first round of the 1985 NFL draft.

As a rookie in 1985, Rice had trouble holding onto the ball, catching just 49 passes, but he overcame that problem in 1986 and became generally recognized as the best wide receiver in football. Some had already considered him the best ever. The 6-foot-2, 200-pounder is very strong, and he's an excellent runner after catching the ball.

Rice led the league with 1,570 yards and 15 touchdowns on 86 catches in 1986, averaging 18.3 per reception, and in 1987 he set a record by catching 22 touchdown passes in only 12 games. He had 65 receptions for 1,078 yards, a 16.6 average, and was a consensus choice as the NFL player of the year.

Although he slipped somewhat to 64 receptions in 16 games the following season, Rice gained 1,306 yards, a 20.4 average, scoring nine touchdowns. He led the league in touchdown receptions the next three years, with 17 in 1989, 13 in 1990, and 14 in 1992; he was the leader in yardage with 1,483 in 1989 and 1,502 in 1990; and he also led in receptions with an even 100 in 1990.

Rice played for two Super Bowl champions and was named most valuable player of Super Bowl XXIII, after the 1988 season, when he caught 11 passes for 215 yards and a touchdown in San Francisco's 20–16 win over the Cincinnati Bengals.

Through 1994, Rice had 820 receptions for 13,189 yards, a 16.1 average, and a career record 129 touchdowns. He had also rushed 70 times for 442 yards, a 6.3 average, and 7 touchdowns.

Rice, Jim (James E.)

BASEBALL
b. March 8, 1953, Anderson, S.C.

A very strong right-handed hitter, the 6-foot-2, 205-pound Rice joined the AL's Boston Red Sox late in the 1974 season. The following year, he and teammate Fred Lynn staged a season-long battle for rookie of the year and most valuable player honors. Rice batted .309 with 22 home runs and 102 RBI, but Lynn won both awards.

After hitting a league-leading 39 home runs in 1977, Rice had his best season in 1978, when he won the MVP award, leading the league with 213 runs scored, 15 triples, 46 home runs, 139 RBI, and a .600 slugging percentage. He batted .315 that year.

Rice hit 39 home runs with 130 RBI and a .325 average in 1979, then was troubled by injuries for several seasons. He returned to health in 1983, batting .305 with a league-leading 39 home runs and 126 RBI. That was the last year in which he hit over .300. He retired after batting jut .234 in 56 games in 1989.

In 16 seasons, all with Boston, Rice batted .295 with 2,452 hits, including 373 doubles, 79 triples, and 382 home runs. He drove in 1,451 runs and scored 1,249.

Rice, Sam (Edgar C.)

BASEBALL
b. Feb. 20, 1890, Morocco, Ind.
d. Oct. 13, 1974

Rice entered the major leagues as a hard-throwing right-handed pitcher with the Washington Senators at the end of the 1915 season, and he was in the starting rotation the following year. He was originally called "Ed," but one day a sportswriter forgot his name and called him "Sam." For some reason the new name stuck for the rest of his career.

He wasn't particularly successful as a pitcher, but his left-handed hitting was impressive, and he was moved to the outfield for the second half of the season. In 1917, his first full year as an outfielder, he batted .302.

Rice spent most of 1918 in the Army, appearing in just seven games, but he returned to the Senators to bat .321 in 1919, .338 in 1920, and .330 in 1921. He led the league with 63 stolen bases in 1920, winning another nickname, "Man o' War," after the famous race horse.

He slipped to .295 in 1922 but batted .316 and led the league with 18 triples the following season, and he had a league-leading 216 hits in 1924, when he batted .334. Despite career highs of 227 hits and a .350 average in 1925, Rice failed to lead the league in either category, but his 216 hits was tops in 1926, and he set an AL record with 182 singles.

In 1927, at the age of 37, Rice seemed to be in decline when he batted only .297. However, he had averages of .328, .323, .349, .310, and .323 during the next five seasons, and as a part-time player in 1933, he batted .294. He finished his career with the Cleveland Indians in 1934.

The Washington Senators won only three pennants in their history, and Rice was on all three of the teams. He batted only .207 when the Senators beat the New York Giants in seven games in 1924, but he had a .364 average in 1925, collecting 12 hits, a World Series record for 39 years. The Senators lost in seven games to the Pittsburgh Pirates.

Rice was involved in one of the most controversial plays in baseball history during that Series. The Senators were winning, 3–1, in the eighth inning of the third game when Earl Smith of Pittsburgh hit a long drive to center field. Rice raced back, leaped, and fell into the stands. He was out of sight for nearly 15 seconds before finally emerging with the ball. The umpires ruled it a catch, and the Senators won the game.

For the rest of his life, Rice was asked about the play. His answer was always, "The umpire said I caught it." He gave the Baseball Hall of Fame a sealed letter, opened after his death, that stated that he had made the catch and that "At no time did I lose possession of the ball."

Rice had a career .322 average with 2,987 hits, with 498 doubles, 184 triples, and 34 home runs. He stole 351 bases, scored 1,514 runs, and had 1,078 RBI.

★ Baseball Hall of Fame

Richard, Rocket (Joseph Henri Maurice)

HOCKEY
b. Aug. 4, 1921, Montreal, P.Q.

Hall of Fame goalie Glenn Hall once said about Richard, "What I remember most about the Rocket were his eyes. When he came flying toward you with the puck on his stick, his eyes were all lit up, flashing and gleaming like a pinball machine. It was terrifying."

Richard was a fast, flashy skater who could shoot with either hand. At 6 feet tall and 190 pounds, he was also surprisingly strong, capable of fighting off defensemen to get position for his shot.

Though he showed his ability to score in amateur and junior hockey, there were doubts about whether he could become a true NHL star because he seemed to be injury-prone. Soon after joining the Montreal Canadiens for the 1942–43 season, he was sidelined with a broken ankle.

But in 1943–44 Richard avoided injury and scored 50 goals in a 50-game season. Other players later scored 50 or more goals, but they played in longer seasons. Only Wayne Gretzky has surpassed Richard by averaging more than a goal per game.

Richard's temper was as fiery as his play. Late in the 1954–55 season, he struck a linesman and was suspended for the duration of the season and the playoffs by NHL President Clarence Campbell. Campbell's presence at a Stanley Cup game in Montreal that spring ignited a riot that resulted in more than $100,000 damage to the city's main shopping area, near the Montreal Forum.

Richard played for eight Stanley Cup champions and was named All-Star right wing eight times. He won the 1947 Hart Trophy as the league's most valuable player. In 18 seasons, all with Montreal, he scored 544 goals and had 421 assists in 978 regular season games. He added 82 goals and 44 assists in 133 playoff games. Eighteen of his playoff goals were game winners, an NHL record. A slashed Achilles tendon ended his career in 1960.

★ Hockey Hall of Fame

Richards, Bob (Robert E.)

TRACK AND FIELD
b. Feb. 20, 1926, Champaign, Ill.

The successor to Cornelius Warmerdam, Richards dominated the pole vault for a decade. Warmerdam was the only man to vault over 15 feet until Richards did it in 1947. When Richards retired in 1957, he had 126 vaults of 15 feet or better.

At the University of Illinois, Richards's best placing in the NCAA championships was a six-way tie for first in 1947. The following year, he took control of the event by winning the first of nine AAU outdoor titles and the first of eight indoor championships.

After winning a bronze medal at the 1948 Olympics, Richards won gold medals in 1952 and 1956. He is the only man to win two golds and a total of three medals in the pole vault. He was also the gold medalist at the Pan-American Games in 1951 and 1955.

Richards won the AAU decathlon championship in 1951, 1954, and 1956 and was the all-around champion in 1953. He qualified for the 1956 Olympic decathlon but was bothered by a vaulting injury and finished twelfth.

Ordained a minister in 1948, Richards was called the "Vaulting Vicar" by sportswriters. After retiring from competition in 1957, he appeared in Wheaties advertising and commercials for 15 years and did occasional radio and television commentary.

★ National Track and Field Hall of Fame; Olympic Hall of Fame

Richards, Vincent

TENNIS
b. March 20, 1903, New York, N.Y.
d. Sept. 20, 1959

The only singles championships Richards ever won as an amateur were the 1924 Olympic gold medal and the U.S. indoor titles in 1919, 1923, and 1924, but his great volleying ability made him a master doubles player.

In 1918, when he was only 15, Richards teamed with Bill Tilden to win the U.S. national doubles championship. They were also champions in 1921 and 1922. With R. Norris Williams, Richards won the 1925 and 1926 men's doubles titles, and he won national mixed doubles championships with Marion Zinderstein in 1919 and with Helen Wills in 1924. His only Wimbledon title came in the 1924 men's doubles with Francis T. Hunter.

A trained journalist, Richards often covered the tournaments in which he played. The U.S. Lawn Tennis Association banned that practice in 1926, and Richards joined C. C. Pyle's initial professional tour in September of that year. He was a cofounder of the Professional Lawn Tennis Association in 1927. Richards won the PLTA's national singles championship in 1927, 1928, 1930, and 1933, and he won professional doubles titles from 1929 through 1933 and in 1937, 1938, and 1945.

After retiring from competition, Richards joined the Dunlop Tire and Rubber Company as general manager of the sporting goods division. He died of a heart attack.

★ International Tennis Hall of Fame

Richter, Leslie A.

FOOTBALL
b. Oct. 26, 1930, Fresno, Calif.

As a freshman at the University of California, Richter was a fullback and linebacker. He started, primarily at line-backer, in 1949, his junior year. During his last two seasons, he played guard and linebacker, did the team's place-kicking, and was a consensus All-American both years. Richter was co-captain of the football team, captain of the rugby team, and class valedictorian as a senior.

After graduating in 1952, he served in the Army for two years. A first-round draft choice of the NFL's Dallas Texans, Richter was traded to the Los Angeles Rams for 11 players, the largest deal ever made for a single player.

Richter played both offensive guard and linebacker for the Rams in 1954 and also kicked extra points and field goals. A fine all-around athlete, the 6-foot-3, 238-pounder became a defensive specialist in 1956. As a linebacker and middle guard, he was the team's defensive captain for the next six years.

When starting center Art Hunter was injured in 1962, Richter took over that position. He retired after the 1962 season. During his nine years with the Rams, Richter intercepted 16 passes and scored 193 points on one touchdown, 106 extra points, and 29 field goals.

★ College Football Hall of Fame

Rickard, Tex (George L.)

BOXING
b. Jan. 2, 1870, Sherman, Tex.
d. June 5, 1929

Rickard led a full life before he became famous as a boxing promoter. Orphaned at ten, he worked as a cowboy and town marshal, then went to the Klondike during the gold rush of 1897 and found gold at the famous Bonanza mine. While in the Klondike, he met Jack Kearns, who later became Jack Dempsey's manager, a young engineer named Herbert Hoover, and the writers Jack London and Robert Service.

With $60,000, he opened a saloon-gambling casino but was wiped out by lucky miners. After cutting wood for several months, Rickard went to Nome, Alaska, opened another saloon, and reportedly made $500,000, most of which he lost on gold claims that didn't pan out.

Rickard then went to Goldfield, Nevada, where he opened a hotel with a gambling hall and a saloon. To promote the town and the hotel, he put up $34,000 for a lightweight championship fight between Joe Gans and Battling Nelson on September 3, 1906, guaranteeing $23,000 to Nelson and $11,000 to Gans, an unusual practice at the time — most promoters simply offered fighters a cut of the gate receipts.

His next major promotion was a match between black heavyweight champion Jack Johnson and former champion Jim Jeffries on July 4, 1910, in Reno. He guaranteed the fighters $101,000 plus two-thirds of the movie rights, and still made a profit.

Rickard's most lucrative promotions involved Jack Dempsey, beginning with Dempsey's victory over champion Jess Willard on July 4, 1919, in Toledo, Ohio. The specially built 80,000-seat stadium included a special "Jenny Wren" section for women spectators.

In 1920, Rickard signed a ten-year lease for Madison Square Garden. He promoted six-day bicycle races, wrestling matches, and some boxing matches there, but he used outdoor arenas for major fights. The five Dempsey title fights promoted by Rickard during the next seven years grossed about $8 million.

Backed by several millionaire investors, Rickard built a new Madison Square Garden in 1925, and he established a new National Hockey League team, the New York Americans, to play there. Little more than three years after the garden opened, Rickard died of a ruptured appendix.

Rickard set the pattern for all major championship matches. Besides the guaranteed purses and the ballyhoo for which he was famous, he established the policy of having all seats reserved, with an army of ushers to enforce the policy. This enabled him to charge very high prices for ringside seats, which not only brought in more money but also helped make boxing popular as a form of conspicuous consumption for the elite, including socialites, financiers, and stars of Broadway and Hollywood.

★ International Boxing Hall of Fame

Rickenbacker, Eddie (Edward)

AUTO RACING

b. Oct. 8, 1890, Columbus, Ohio
d. July 23, 1973

He achieved his greatest fame as the Ace of Aces during World War I, shooting down 26 German planes in seven months. But he was an outstanding racer before that. As a salesman for the Columbus Buggy Company, he began racing in 1910 to publicize the cars he sold. He won nine of ten races in a two-day meet in Omaha, and suddenly he was an auto racer instead of a salesman.

Rickenbacker finished eleventh in the first Indy 500 in 1911 and was in fourth place the following year when a burned bearing forced him out. After winning $10,000 in a 100-mile race in 1913, Rickenbacker formed his own four-car racing team. The team won 7 of 13 major races in 1916.

His last race was in 1917; then he went into the service and became an ace fighter pilot. After the war, he formed the Rickenbacker Motor Company; it went bankrupt in 1927. Rickenbacker then raised $700,000 to buy the Indianapolis Speedway, and he turned it into a modern track.

★ Indianapolis Speedway Hall of Fame

Rickey, Branch (Wesley Branch)

BASEBALL

b. Dec. 20, 1881, Lucasville, Ohio
d. Dec. 9, 1965

Rickey played in only 120 major league games, mostly as a catcher. He batted only .239 and once set a dubious record by allowing 13 opponents to steal bases in a game. But he was probably the most important executive in the game's history.

After graduating from Ohio Wesleyan College in 1904, Rickey played minor league baseball. He appeared in 66 games with the St. Louis Browns in 1905 and 1906 and in 52 games with the AL's New York Highlanders (now the Yankees) in 1907, then studied law at Ohio State University and the University of Michigan, where he coached the baseball team in 1910 and 1911.

Rickey briefly practiced law before

returning to Michigan as baseball coach again in 1912, and the following year he was hired to help run the Browns while still coaching at Michigan. He introduced the concept of the "Ladies' Day" with the Browns in 1913.

Late that season, he became the team's manager and held that job through 1915, when he was named business manager. In 1917, Rickey moved across town to the NL's Cardinals, where he built attendance with "Ladies' Days" and "Knothole Gangs," allowing youngsters to get in free.

He took over as field manager in 1919 and introduced several new ideas, including classroom instruction, sliding pits, and batting cages. Rickey also began to organize baseball's first farm system by buying minor league teams where young players could be trained.

Rickey wasn't particularly successful as a manager and returned to the front office during the 1925 season. But with players constantly moving up from the farm system, the Cardinals won nine pennants from 1925 through 1946.

In 1943, Rickey became president and general manager of the Brooklyn Dodgers. Again he built an NL dynasty by putting together a farm system. An important difference was that beginning with the signing of Jackie Robinson in 1946, there were black players in that system.

The Dodgers won six pennants from 1947 through 1956. During that period, they had four rookies of the year, four most valuable players, and one Cy Young Award winner, all of them black.

Rickey joined Walter O'Malley and John L. Smith in purchasing the Dodgers in 1946. He sold his stock for $1 million in 1951 and became chairman of the board of the Pittsburgh Pirates. He left that position in 1959 to organize the Continental League.

The threat of a third major league forced both existing leagues to expand into new territories to preempt the Continental League's plans. Many observers thought that was Rickey's goal in the first place.

In 1963, Rickey briefly rejoined the Cardinals as a special adviser, retiring in October 1964. A little more than a year later, he suffered a heart attack while giving an acceptance speech after his induction into the Missouri Sports Hall of Fame. He died a month afterward.

An enigmatic figure, Rickey was a deeply religious man who wouldn't play or manage on Sunday, yet he initiated Sunday doubleheaders to attract more fans. Nicknamed the "Mahatma" for his supposed inscrutability, he believed in integrating the major leagues, but he also had an ulterior motive, since he knew the Dodgers could become a better team by adding black players.
★ Baseball Hall of Fame

Riedel, Ernest
CANOEING
b. June 13, 1901

Riedel won a bronze medal in the 10,000-meter kayak singles event at the 1936 Olympics. The 1940 and 1944 Olympic Games were canceled because of World War II, which probably deprived him of more medals since he was at his peak during that period.

Riedel was the national kayak champion in 1930, 1931, 1932, 1935, 1937, 1938, 1940, 1941, 1946, 1947, and 1948. (There was no competition from 1942 to 1945.) He also won the canoeing championship in 1938. Competing for the Pendleton Canoe Club of Yonkers, Riedel was a member of the national two-man championship kayak team in 1930, 1938, 1941, 1946, and 1947; a member of the four-man canoe champion team in 1930, 1931, 1935, and 1937; and a member of the four-man kayak champion team in 1930, 1931, 1937, 1941, and from 1947 through 1949.

At the age of 47, he competed in the 1948 Olympics but failed to qualify for the finals.

Rigby, Bob (Paul)
SOCCER
b. July 3, 1951, Ridley Park, Pa.

An All-American soccer goalie at East Stroudsburg State College in 1971 and 1972, Rigby joined the Philadelphia Atoms of the North American Soccer

League as a first-round draft choice in 1973. He was named the league's goalie of the year after giving up just 0.62 goals per game to lead the Atoms to a championship.

Rigby, who played for the 1972 U.S. Olympic team and the U.S. national team in 1973 and 1974, remained with Philadelphia through the 1975 season, then joined the New York Cosmos. After one year in New York, he was traded to the Los Angeles Aztecs in 1977, the Philadelphia Fury in 1979, Montreal in 1981, and the San Jose Golden Bay Club in 1973, where he finished his professional career.

After retiring from soccer, Rigby became a gymnastics instructor.

Rigby, Cathy

GYMNASTICS
b. Dec. 12, 1952, Los Alamitos, Calif.

A premature baby, Rigby was born with collapsed lungs, and she suffered a whole series of illnesses during her first five years. When she was eight, she began trampolining at a youth club and amazed her teacher by doing a back flip at her first class.

Rigby joined the Southern California Acrobatic Team in 1963 and dedicated the next ten years of her life to gymnastics. Only 4-foot-10 and 89 pounds, the pixie-like blonde helped attract public interest in gymnastics with her charm and skill, thanks to television. She was the high scorer on the 1968 Olympic team that finished sixth; she was sixteenth in the all-around competition that year.

In 1970, she won a silver medal in the balance beam at the world championships, the highest placing ever for an American woman. The event was televised on *Wide World of Sports,* giving Rigby and gymnastics exposure to a major television audience.

Rigby broke a toe during the 1972 Olympic trials, but she was given a place on the the team anyway. She was again the high scorer, finishing tenth in the all-around, and she led the team to

fourth place, then the best showing ever by a U.S. women's team.

She retired after the Olympics and began a career in show business, starring in a production of *Peter Pan* staged by NBC Entertainment. Rigby has also directed gymnastic camps, appeared in television commercials, and worked as a television commentator.

Riggin, Aileen M.

DIVING, SWIMMING
b. May 2, 1906, Newport, R.I.

The first person ever to win Olympic medals in both swimming and diving, the 4-foot-8, 70-pound Riggin was naturally nicknamed "Tiny." At 14, she won a gold medal in 1920 in the first women's Olympic springboard event ever held. Four years later, she won a silver medal in the springboard and a bronze in the 100-meter backstroke.

Riggin was the national outdoor 3-meter springboard champion from 1923 through 1925. She won the indoor 1-meter title in 1923. As a member of the Women's Swimming Association of New York, she swam on teams that won the national outdoor 880-meter freestyle relay in 1923 and 1924 and the indoor 400-yard relay in 1922, 1923, and 1925.

The first slow-motion and underwater coaching films ever made, in 1922, starred Riggin. She became a professional in 1926. She gave exhibitions, performed at the Hippodrome in New York, wrote articles, appeared in two Hollywood musicals, and helped organize Billy Rose's first Aquacade in 1937.
★ International Women's Sports Hall of Fame

Riggins, John

FOOTBALL
b. Aug. 4, 1949, Centralia, Kans.

The 6-foot-2, 230-pound Riggins, a 100-yard dash champion while in high school, was a three-year starter as a running back at the University of Kansas. He gained 1,131 yards in 1970, his senior year, and 2,706 for his career, breaking Gale Sayers's former school records.

Riggins joined the NFL's New York Jets as their first-round draft choice in

1971. He spent five seasons with the Jets, earning $75,000 in his final year, then signed a four-year, $1.5 million contract with the Washington Redskins as a free agent in 1976.

He was used mostly in short-yardage situations in his first season with Washington, and he missed much of the 1977 season with a knee injury. But he gained more than 1,000 yards each of the next two seasons.

Riggins held out for more money and missed the entire 1980 season. He returned to the Redskin training camp with a new contract in 1981, announcing, "I'm bored, I'm broke, and I'm back." He was limited to just 714 yards that season, but he scored 13 touchdowns.

After gaining 553 yards in the strike-shortened 1982 season, Riggins was named most valuable player in Super Bowl XVII. He rushed for 166 yards in 38 attempts, a 4.4 average, and had a 43-yard touchdown run in Washington's 27–17 victory over the Miami Dolphins. Riggins won the Bert Bell Trophy as the league's player of the year in 1983, when he gained 1,347 yards on 375 carries, a 3.6 average, and scored a record 24 touchdowns.

Despite a bad back, Riggins gained 1,239 yards in 1984, and he rushed for more than 100 yards in three of the first four games in 1985 before being replaced by George Rogers. Riggins retired after that season.

A unique aspect of Riggins's career was that he gained more yardage after he turned 30 than he did during his twenties. In his 14 NFL seasons, he rushed 2,916 times for 11,352 yards, a 3.9 average, and 104 touchdowns. He caught 250 passes for 2,090 yards, an 8.4 average, and 12 touchdowns.

★ Pro Football Hall of Fame

Riggs, Bobby (Robert L.)

TENNIS
b. Feb. 25, 1918, Los Angles, Calif.

The ultimate gamesman, Riggs is now best known for his "Battle of the Sexes" matches against Margaret Court and Billie Jean King, but he was a very fine player in his prime.

The only year he played at Wimbledon, 1939, Riggs won the singles, men's doubles (with Elwood T. Cooke), and mixed doubles (with Alice Marble). Riggs was also the U.S. national singles champion in 1939. After losing in the finals to Don McNeil in 1940, Riggs won the singles title again in 1941. He and Marble were the mixed doubles champions in 1940.

Riggs joined the professional tour in 1942, then entered military service. After World War II ended, he toured with Don Budge, winning 23 of their 44 matches in 1946, and he repeated as professional champion in 1947.

In 1948, Riggs and Jack Kramer reorganized the men's professional tour. Kramer overwhelmed Riggs that year, winning 69 of 89 matches, but Riggs came back to win his third professional championship in 1949 before retiring from serious competition.

The 5-foot-8 Riggs was a very canny player who used accuracy and a variety of spin and chop shots to overcome his lack of power, although he did rush the net at times as a surprise tactic.

Riggs came out of retirement in 1973 and challenged Margaret Court to demonstrate that a 55-year-old man could beat a woman in her prime. He temporarily proved his point by beating her in two sets on Mother's Day. However, he lost three straight sets to Billie Jean King in September at the Houston Astrodome before 30,472 spectators, the largest crowd ever for a tennis match. Millions more watched on prime-time television.

In a less publicized match, Riggs and Vitas Gerulaitis were badly beaten by Martina Navratilova and Pam Shriver in August 1985.

★ International Tennis Hall of Fame

Riley, Jack (John P.)

HOCKEY
b. June 15, 1920, Boston, Mass.

After playing hockey at Dartmouth College, Riley was on the 1948 U.S. Olympic team and the 1949 national team. He became head coach at the U.S. Military Academy in 1950.

Riley was best known as coach of the 1960 U.S. Olympic team that won a surprising gold medal by beating Czechoslovakia, 9–4, after trailing 4–3 at the end of two periods.

He coached at Army through the 1985–86 season, when he was succeeded by his son, Rob. Riley had a record of 542–319–20 in his 36 seasons.

★ U.S. Hockey Hall of Fame

Riley, Patrick J.

BASKETBALL
b. March 20, 1945, Schenectady, N.Y.

Riley, though only 6-foot-4, was one of the tallest players on the Kentucky team known as "Rupp's Runts" that won 27 of 29 games in 1965–66. Coached by Adolph Rupp, the team lost to Texas Western in the NCAA championship game. In his senior year, 1966–67, Riley captained Kentucky. He scored 1,464 points in his career, averaging 18.3 a game.

A first-round draft pick of the NBA's San Diego Rockets, Riley never became an NBA star. He played three seasons for the Rockets, four for the Los Angeles Lakers, and one for the Phoenix Suns before retiring in 1976. He scored 2,906 points in 528 regular season games, a 7.4 average, and also had 913 assists and 855 rebounds.

After working as an announcer and then an assistant coach for the Lakers, Riley became head coach in 1981. In his first seven seasons, Los Angeles went to the NBA finals five times and won four championships. In 1986, they became the first team since the 1968–69 Boston Celtics to win two NBA titles in a row.

Riley left the Lakers after the 1989–90 season to return to broadcasting, but he took over the New York Knicks in 1991. Through the 1993–94 season, Riley had a 701–272 regular season record for a .720 winning percentage, and he was 131–70 in the playoffs.

Rimington, Dave B.

FOOTBALL
b. May 22, 1960, Omaha, Nebr.

The only two-time winner of the Outland Trophy as the nation's best collegiate lineman, Rimington also won the Vince Lombardi Award as the outstanding lineman in 1982, his senior year at the University of Nebraska. An ardent weightlifter, he was voted Nebraska's lifter of the year in 1980 and 1981. Rimington was both a consensus All-American and an Academic All-American in 1981 and 1982.

The 6-foot-3, 288-pound Rimington joined the Cincinnati Bengals as a first-round draft choice in 1983. After missing much of his rookie season with a foot injury, he became a starter in 1984. Recurring problems with the foot forced his early retirement after the 1990 season.

Ringo, Jim (James S.)

FOOTBALL
b. Nov. 21, 1931, Orange, N.J.

A seventh-round draft choice out of Syracuse University, Ringo weighed only 211 pounds when he arrived at the Green Bay Packer training camp in 1953. After seeing how big the other linemen were, he left camp.

His wife and father talked him into going back. Ringo eventually got up to 235 pounds and set a record by starting 182 consecutive games at center, 126 with the Packers and 56 more with the Philadelphia Eagles.

During bouts with mononucleosis and a staph infection, Ringo stayed in the hospital from Monday through Friday, worked out with the team on Saturday, and played on Sunday.

He was the All-Pro center in 1957 and from 1959 through 1963. The Packers traded him to the Philadelphia Eagles after the 1963 season, and he spent four years in Philadelphia before retiring.

★ Pro Football Hall of Fame

Ripken, Calvin E., Jr.

BASEBALL
b. Aug. 24, 1960, Havre de Grace, Md.

At the end of the 1994 season, Ripken had played in 1,982 consecutive games, closing in on Lou Gehrig's major league record of 2,130, which was once thought insurmountable.

The 6-foot-4, 220-pound Ripken joined the AL's Baltimore Orioles as a third baseman and shortstop late in the 1981 season and was named *The Sporting News* rookie of the year in 1982. The following season, he was the league's most valuable player, hitting .318 and leading the league with 121 runs scored, 211 hits, and 47 doubles. He also had 27 home runs and 102 RBI.

A full-time shortstop since 1983, Ripken was named MVP again in 1991, when he had a .323 average with 34 home runs and 114 RBI. Though he has never been fast, Ripken is an excellent defensive shortstop because of his sure hands and knowledge of how to play hitters.

He holds major league records for shortstops with highest fielding percentage, .996; fewest errors, 3; most consecutive errorless games, 95; and most consecutive chances accepted without an error, 431. All were set in 1990.

Ripken's father, Cal Sr., managed the Orioles from 1987 to 1988 and was a coach with the team from 1976 through 1986 and from 1989 to the present. His brother, Billy, was Baltimore's second baseman from 1987 through 1992, and then was traded to the Texas Rangers.

Through the 1994 season, Ripken had a .277 batting average with 2,227 hits with 414 doubles, 40 triples, and 310 home runs. He had 1,179 RBI and 1,201 runs scored.

Ris, Wally (Walter S.)
SWIMMING
b. Jan. 4, 1924

Ris was trailing with only 10 meters to go in the 1948 Olympic 100-meter freestyle swim when he put on a spectacular surge to win the gold medal. He won a second gold medal on the 4 x 100-meter relay team.

During World War II, Ris swam on the Great Lakes Naval Training Station 4 x 100-yard relay team that set a world record of 3:29.1. After the war, he went to the University of Iowa and won the NCAA 100-yard freestyle in 1947 and 1948.

Ris was the AAU outdoor 100-meter freestyle champion in 1947. He won the indoor 100-yard title five years in a row, 1945–49, and was the indoor 220-yard champion in 1946.

★ International Swimming Hall of Fame

Rison, Andre P.
FOOTBALL
b. March 18, 1957, Flint, Mich.

Rison was chosen by the Indianapolis Colts in the first round of the 1989 NFL draft after playing at Michigan State. He caught 52 passes for 820 yards and 4 touchdowns as a rookie and was then traded to the Atlanta Falcons.

In four seasons with Atlanta, Rison has caught 81 or more passes each year, with a high of 93 in 1992, when he gained 1,119 yards and scored 11 touchdowns on receptions. Rison was named to *The Sporting News* all-pro team in 1990 and has played in four straight Pro Bowls.

Through 1993, Rison had caught 394 passes for 5,365 yards, a 13.6 average, and 37 touchdowns.

Ritcher, Jim (James A.)
FOOTBALL
b. May 21, 1958, Berea, Ohio

A defensive end in high school, Ritcher was moved to center when he entered North Carolina State in 1976, and in 1979 he became the first center to win the Outland Trophy as the nation's outstanding college lineman. The 6-foot-3, 245-pounder was named to some All-American teams in 1978 and was a consensus All-American as a senior.

A first-round draft choice of the NFL's Buffalo Bills in 1980, Ritcher was a backup center as a rookie. The Bills moved him to guard in his second season. After serving as a backup at both guard spots for two years, Ritcher became the team's starting left guard in 1983. He played in the Pro Bowl after the 1991 and 1992 seasons.

Ritter, Louise

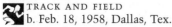

TRACK AND FIELD
b. Feb. 18, 1958, Dallas, Tex.

As a student at Texas Women's College, Ritter won three consecutive AIAW high jump championships, from 1977 through 1979. She left school for a year to concentrate on preparing for the 1980 Olympics and finished first in the trials, but the U.S. boycotted the Moscow Games that year.

In 1981, Ritter won her fourth AIAW title. After missing the better part of two years with various injuries, she set an American record of 6 feet, 7 inches in September 1983, and she won the Olympic trials again in 1984, but she was injured and could finish only eighth at the Olympic Games.

Ritter finally won a gold medal in her third attempt, at the 1988 Olympics, with an Olympic record jump of 6-8, tying her own American record, which she had set at the trials.

The TAC national champion in 1978, 1982, 1985, and 1986, Ritter also won a gold at the 1979 Pan-American Games.

Rixey, Eppa

BASEBALL
b. May 3, 1891, Culpeper, Va.
d. Feb. 28, 1963

When he retired after the 1933 season, Rixey had won more games than any other left-handed pitcher in history. But he was virtually forgotten until 1959, when his record was broken by Warren Spahn. Spahn's accomplishment revived memories of Rixey, who was inducted into the Hall of Fame four years later.

The 6-foot-5, 210-pound Rixey entered the major leagues with the NL's Philadelphia Phillies in 1912. He had just one good season in eight years with Philadelphia, compiling a 22–10 record in 1916, and he was traded to the Cincinnati Reds in 1920.

Rixey led the league in victories with a 25–13 record and in innings pitched with 313⅓ in 1922. After a 20–15 record in 1923, he had a league-leading four shutouts the following season, though he was only 15–14.

His last 20-win season was 1925, when he was 21–11, but Rixey had three more winning years, going 14–8 in 1926, 12–10 in 1927, and 19–18 in 1928. After a 10–13 record in 1928, he was used less frequently, and he appeared in only 16 games in 1933, when he was 6–3. He retired after that season.

Despite his size, Rixey didn't have a good fastball, and he liked to outsmart hitters. He once said he couldn't understand why hitters always looked for the fastball when they were ahead on the count, and were always surprised when they got a different pitch — as they usually did from him.

In 21 seasons, Rixey had a 266–251 record with mediocre teams, recording 37 shutouts and a 3.15 ERA. He struck out 1,350 hitters and walked 2,082 in 4,494½ innings.

★ Baseball Hall of Fame

Rizzuto, Phillip F.

BASEBALL
b. Sept. 25, 1918, New York, N.Y.

Nicknamed "the Scooter" for his speed and defensive range, the 5-foot-6, 160-pound Rizzuto was the AL's most valuable player in 1950, when he batted .324, scored 125 runs, had an even 200 hits, and led league shortstops in fielding percentage for the second year in a row.

Rizzuto joined the Yankees in 1941, when he hit .307. After batting .284 the following season, he spent three years in military service, returning to baseball in 1946.

A five-time All-Star, Rizzuto retired after the 1956 season and became a broadcaster for the Yankees on both radio and television. In 1,661 games, he batted .273 on 1,588 hits, including 239 doubles, 62 triples, and 38 home runs. Rizzuto stole 149 bases, scored 877 runs, and had 563 RBI.

★ Baseball Hall of Fame

Roberts, Fireball (Glenn)

AUTO RACING
b. Jan. 20, 1931, Apopka, Fla.
d. July 1, 1964

Roberts got his nickname as a hard-throwing baseball pitcher. At 17, he drove in the first NASCAR race at Daytona Beach, crashing on the ninth lap. He didn't win a major race until 1957, when he was first in the Rebel 300 at Darlington. He won the Southern 500 at the same track in 1958, repeated in the Rebel 300 in 1959, and won the Southern 500 again in 1963.

His other major victories included the Daytona 500 and the Firecracker 250 in 1959, the Dixie 400 in 1960, and the Firecracker 400 in 1963. He died of burns suffered in a crash at Darlington.
★ NASCAR Hall of Fame

Roberts, Gordy (Gordon)

HOCKEY
b. Oct. 2, 1957, Detroit, Mich.

Named for Detroit Red Wing star Gordie Howe, Roberts was virtually brought up to be a hockey player, along with his three older brothers. He dropped out of high school to play for the Detroit Junior Red Wings in 1973, and two years later he joined the New England Whalers of the World Hockey Association.

The 6-foot-1, 195-pounder was the top scorer among WHA defensemen with 61 points in 1977–78 and 57 points in 1978–79. The team moved into the NHL after the WHA folded in 1979 and became known as the Hartford Whalers. Hartford traded him to the Minnesota North Stars during the 1980–81 season.

A strong skater and excellent puck handler, Roberts is also frequently penalized for his aggressive defensive play. He was traded to the Philadelphia Flyers and then to the St. Louis Blues during the 1987–88 season. The Blues sent him to the minor leagues for three games in 1990–91, called him back briefly, and traded him to the Pittsburgh Penguins, where he played for Stanley Cup champions in 1991 and 1992. Roberts signed with the Boston Bruins as a free agent in 1992.

Roberts, Robin E.

BASEBALL
b. Sept. 30, 1926, Springfield, Ill.

After serving in the Army Air Corps immediately after graduating from high school in 1944, Roberts went to Mich-

igan State University on a basketball scholarship. Roberts also pitched well enough for the school's baseball team to get a $25,000 bonus for signing with the NL's Philadelphia Phillies in 1948.

The 6-foot, 190-pound right-hander played briefly in the minor leagues before joining the Phillies in June, compiling a 7–9 record and a 3.19 ERA. After going 15–15 in 1949, Roberts won 20 or more games each of the next six seasons.

He was the pitching leader of the "Whiz Kids" team that won the NL pennant in 1950, when Roberts was 20–11 with a league-leading five shutouts. Because he'd worked in three of the last five games of the season, Roberts didn't start until the second game of the World Series, and he lost, 2–1, in 10 innings. It was the only World Series he ever appeared in.

Roberts led the league in innings pitched with 315 in 1951, when he was 21–15. He then topped the NL in victories for four years in a row, with records of 28–7 in 1952, 23–16 in 1953, 23–15 in 1954, and 23–14 in 1955.

He was also the NL leader in complete games with 30 in 1952, 33 in 1953, 29 in 1954, 26 in 1955, and 22 in 1956; in innings pitched with 330 in 1952, 346$\frac{2}{3}$ in 1953, 336$\frac{2}{3}$ in 1954, and 305 in 1955; and in strikeouts with 198 in 1953 and 185 in 1954.

Roberts was named the NL player of the year by *The Sporting News* in 1952 and 1955, and he was chosen for the All-Star team seven years in a row, from 1950 through 1956.

All those innings pitched caught up to him in 1957, when he had a 10–22 record. He continued to work a lot during the next three seasons, going 17–14, 15–17, and 12–16, but he was traded to the New York Yankees after a 1–10 record in 1961.

The Yankees released Roberts during spring training in 1962, and he joined the Baltimore Orioles. He was 42–36 with them before returning to the NL with the Houston Astros during the 1965 season. He retired after pitching for Houston and the Chicago Cubs in 1966.

In 19 major league seasons, Roberts

had a 286–245 record, with 45 shutouts and a 3.41 ERA. He struck out 2,357 hitters and walked 902 in 4,688⅔ innings.

★ Baseball Hall of Fame

Robertson, Oscar P.

BASKETBALL
b. Nov. 24, 1938, Charlotte, Tenn.

Boston Celtics coach Red Auerbach summed up Robertson: "He's so great he scares me. He can beat you all by himself and usually does." And "Phog" Allen, a college coach for 46 years, said, "Oscar Robertson is the greatest player of all time for a fellow his size."

His size was 6-foot-5 and he weighed 220 pounds in his prime, yet he was a guard. After leading Crispus Attucks High School in Indianapolis to 45 straight wins and two state championships, Robertson entered the University of Cincinnati in 1956. He became the first sophomore to lead the nation in scoring and the first player to be the scoring leader three times.

An All-American in 1958, 1959, and 1960, Robertson averaged 33.8 points and 15.2 rebounds a game during his college career. He scored 56 points in a 1958 game to set a Madison Square Garden record and 62 in a 1960 game to set an NCAA record. After his senior year, he starred for the gold medal U.S. Olympic team and then joined the Cincinnati Royals.

His impact was immediate. The Royals improved from 14 victories to 33, and their home attendance more than tripled, from 58,244 to 207,020. Robertson led the NBA in assists, finished third in scoring, and was named the rookie of the year.

A "triple double" — having double figures in points, rebounds, and assists in a game — is considered a major accomplishment. Robertson *averaged* a triple double for the entire 1961–62 season, when he scored 2,432 points, had 899 assists, and pulled down 985 rebounds in 79 games. No other player has ever done that.

Robertson spent ten seasons with Cincinnati and averaged more than 30 points a game in six of them. He was a first-team All-Star each of his first nine seasons, and he was named the league's most valuable player for the 1963–64 season.

In 1970, he was traded to the Milwaukee Bucks, where Lew Alcindor (later Kareem Abdul-Jabbar) was entering his second season. With Robertson both scoring and feeding Alcindor, the Bucks won the NBA championship in only their third season of existence.

Robertson retired in 1974. In 1,040 regular season games, he scored 26,710 points, a 25.7 average, and had 9,887 assists and 7,804 rebounds. He scored 1,910 points in 86 playoff games, a 22.2 average, and also had 769 assists and 578 rebounds. In 1980, he was named to the NBA's 35th anniversary team.

★ Basketball Hall of Fame

Robinson, Betty (Elizabeth)

TRACK AND FIELD
b. Aug. 23, 1911, Riverdale, Ill.

When Robinson ran a 100-yard time trial for the first time, her high school track coach didn't believe the stopwatch. It said she had tied the world record.

The stopwatch was probably right. In only her second race, in the spring of 1928, Robinson did tie the world record for 100 meters, 12.0 seconds. Her third race was in the U.S. Olympic trials, where she finished second. And she won the Olympic gold medal in the 100 meters shortly before her seventeenth birthday. Robinson was the first woman to win a gold medal in track. She also ran on the 4 x 100-meter relay team that won a silver medal.

Robinson was the AAU outdoor 50-yard and 100-yard dash champion in 1929, setting a world record of 5.8 seconds for 50 yards. She ran a world record time of 11.0 seconds in the 100-yard dash in a 1928 Chicago meet, and in 1931 she set world records of 6.9 seconds for 60 yards and 7.9 seconds for 70 yards.

Robinson was almost killed in a 1931 plane crash. She suffered a severely broken leg, a crushed arm, and a serious concussion that put her in a coma for nearly two months. It was two years before she could even walk normally, but she returned to competition. Forced to use a standing start because of her injuries, she nevertheless made the U.S. Olympic team in 1936 and won her second gold medal by running a leg in the 4 x 100-meter relay event.

★ National Track & Field Hall of Fame

Robinson, Brooks C.

BASEBALL
b. May 18, 1937, Little Rock, Ark.

Known as "Hoover" or the "Human Vacuum Cleaner" because of his astounding defensive abilities at third base, Robinson could also drive in runs when they were needed.

He was with the AL's Baltimore Orioles briefly in 1955 and 1956, became a part-time player in 1957, and alternated between second base and third base in 1958. Robinson missed much of the 1959 season with a knee injury and finally settled in as a full-time starter at third base in 1960, when he hit .294.

That was the first of 15 consecutive years in which he appeared in an All-Star game and the first of 11 seasons in which Robinson led the league's third basemen in fielding percentage.

Robinson had his finest offensive season in 1964, when he was named the AL's most valuable player. He batted .317 that year with 28 home runs and a league-leading 118 RBI.

It was in the 1970 World Series, though, that Robinson really became a legend. He robbed Cincinnati of at least four hits and five runs, hit a game-winning home run, and batted .429 with six RBI and four runs scored, as Baltimore beat the Reds in five games.

In 1976, Robinson became a part-time player, batting only .211 in 71 games. He retired after the 1977 season with 16 Gold Glove awards, a record for non-pitchers. He also holds major league records for third basemen in assists, putouts, total chances accepted, double plays, and fielding percentage.

Robinson had 2,848 hits in 2,896 games, with 482 doubles, 68 triples, and 268 home runs. He drove in 1,357 runs and scored 1,232.

★ Baseball Hall of Fame

Robinson, David M.

BASKETBALL
b. Aug. 6, 1965, Key West, Fla.

When he entered the U.S. Naval Academy in 1984, Robinson was 6-foot-4. He grew to 7-foot-1 by the time he graduated, and was a consensus All-American center and college player of the year in 1987 after averaging 28.2 points a game. During his four years as a starter, he averaged 21.0 points and nearly 10 rebounds per game.

Robinson was chosen by the San Antonio Spurs in the first round of the NBA draft, although he faced four years in the Navy after graduating. There were reports that Robinson would be excused from service because of his height, which exceeded the Navy's maximum. He did serve but was released after only two years.

Reporting to the Spurs for the 1989–90 season, the 235-pound Robinson averaged 24.3 points a game and was named the league's rookie of the year. He was chosen All-NBA each of the next two years.

Very quick and strong, Robinson is an excellent shot blocker who was named to the NBA's all-defensive first team in 1991 and 1992, and he has a good outside shot in addition to being overpowering around the basket.

Through the 1993–94 season, Robinson had scored 9,971 points in 394 regular season games, an average of 25.3. He also had 4,686 rebounds, 1,473 blocked shots, 1,235 assists, and 689 steals. In 28 playoff games, he had scored 657 points for an average of 23.5, with 340 rebounds and 101 blocked shots.

Robinson, Eddie (Edward G.)

FOOTBALL
b. Feb. 13, 1919, Jackson, La.

A four-year starter at quarterback for Leland College in Louisiana, Robinson doubled as an assistant coach in 1939 and 1940, his junior and senior years. After graduating in 1941, he became head basketball and football coach at Louisiana Negro Normal and Industrial Institute, now known as Grambling College.

Robinson made Grambling the best known of the predominantly black football colleges and went on to become the winningest coach in college history. He had a perfect 8–0–0 record in his second season at Grambling, and he later produced two other undefeated teams.

The school dropped football in 1943 and 1944 because of World War II, and Robinson coached Grambling High School during these years. He returned to the college when the football program resumed in 1945.

In 52 years, Robinson has had 48 winning seasons, including 17 in a row. He recorded his 324th win on October 5, 1985, a 27–7 victory over Prairie View A & M, to break "Bear" Bryant's record of 323 victories. Through the 1994 season, Robinson had a 388–130–15 record.

Although quiet and soft-spoken, Robinson is an excellent recruiter who sells prospects on the merits of Grambling's academic program as well as the success of its football program. More than 200 of his players have performed in the NFL, including Pro Football Hall of Fame members Willie Brown, Buck Buchanan, and Willie Davis, along with Doug Williams, the first black to quarterback a winning Super Bowl team, with the Washington Redskins after the 1987 season.

★ College Football Hall of Fame

Robinson, Frank

BASEBALL
b. Aug. 31, 1935, Beaumont, Tex.

Robinson joined the NL's Cincinnati Reds in 1956, hit 38 home runs and led the league in runs scored with 122, and was named the league's rookie of the year.

He led the NL in slugging with a .595 percentage in 1960 and with a .611 percentage in 1961, when he batted .323 with 37 home runs and 124 RBI to win the most valuable player award. However, he hit only .200 in Cincinnati's

five-game loss to the New York Yankees in the World Series.

Robinson had an even better year in 1962, batting .342 with 39 home runs and 136 RBI and leading the league with a .624 slugging percentage, 134 runs scored, and 51 doubles. His production dropped somewhat, in part because of injuries, during the next three seasons, and an arrest for carrying a concealed weapon got him in trouble with Cincinnati management.

The Reds traded him to the Baltimore Orioles in 1966, and he responded with the best season of his career. Robinson won the triple crown with a .316 average, 49 home runs, and 122 RBI, also leading the AL with 122 runs scored and a .637 slugging percentage.

Robinson was named most valuable player for that performance, becoming the only man ever to win the MVP award in both leagues. He was also named male athlete of the year by the Associated Press.

He batted .311 in 1967 and had 30 home runs and 94 RBI in just 129 games because of injuries. The following year he played in only 130 games, hitting 15 home runs with 52 RBI. He came back to bat .308 and .306 the next two years, but he was traded to the NL's Dodgers after hitting only .281 in 1971.

The Dodgers sent him to the California Angels in 1973, and he spent most of the rest of his career as a designated hitter with California and the Cleveland Indians. Robinson was named playing manager of the Indians in 1975, the first black manager in major league history.

He retired as a player after the 1976 season and was fired as manager in 1977. Robinson also managed the San Francisco Giants from 1981 through 1984 and Baltimore from 1988 into the 1991 season.

In 21 seasons, Robinson batted .294 with 2,943 hits, including 526 doubles, 72 triples, and 586 home runs, fourth all-time. He stole 204 bases, scored 1,829 runs, and had 1,812 RBI.

★ Baseball Hall of Fame

Robinson, Jackie (Jack R.)

BASEBALL
b. Jan. 31, 1919, near Cairo, Ga.
d. Oct. 24, 1972

Deserted by his father when he was less than a year old, Robinson and his mother moved to Pasadena, California, where she worked as a maid. Robinson grew up in a poor neighborhood where many boys were likely to become juvenile delinquents and then criminals. But a man named Carl Anderson established organized sports in the neighborhood; Robinson and many other boys had their attention and energy diverted into a new field.

Robinson went to Pasadena Junior College and then won a scholarship to UCLA, where he lettered in baseball, basketball, football, and track. He left school in 1941, shortly before he would have received his degree, to work for the National Youth Administration as an assistant athletic director.

Drafted into the Army during World War II, Robinson became a lieutenant and was discharged late in 1944, when he became basketball coach at Samuel Houston College in Texas. Then he joined the Kansas City Monarchs of the Negro American League in 1945.

Branch Rickey, the president of the Brooklyn Dodgers, was looking for a black player to integrate major league baseball, and Robinson was one of his prospects. They had a long meeting on August 28, 1945, at which Rickey warned Robinson that he would be subjected to vicious racial epithets and probably some foul play on the field, and that he would have to hold himself back from retaliating.

Robinson accepted the role with some reluctance and signed with the Dodgers. He spent the 1946 season with their Montreal farm club in the International League and moved into the major leagues in 1947, the first black player since 1888.

Although he'd been a shortstop with Kansas City and a second baseman with Montreal, Robinson played first base that season, batted .297, led the league in stolen bases with 29, and was named the NL rookie of the year.

In 1948, he moved back to second base and hit 296. Then he had his best season, leading the league with a .342 average and 37 stolen bases, scoring 122 runs and driving in 124 to win the most valuable player award.

Robinson hit over .300 each of the next five seasons, playing all infield positions and the outfield at various times. After he hit .256 in 1955 and .275 in 1956, he was traded to the New York Giants. Rather than report to the Giants, Robinson announced his retirement.

He later worked in public relations for a restaurant chain, became active in the civil rights movement, worked for New York Governor Nelson Rockefeller, wrote for newspapers, and did television commentary.

Suffering from diabetes, Robinson had a heart attack in 1968. He appeared at the opening game of the 1972 World Series, marking the 25th anniversary of major league baseball's integration, and died of another heart attack a few weeks afterward.

In his 10 seasons, Robinson batted .311 with 1,518 hits, including 273 doubles, 54 triples, and 137 home runs. He stole 197 bases, scored 947 runs, and had 734 RBI.

★ Baseball Hall of Fame

Robinson, John A.

FOOTBALL
b. July 25, 1935, Chicago, Ill.

An end at the University of Oregon, Robinson served in the Army after graduating in 1958 and then became an assistant coach at his alma mater. He then spent three seasons as an assistant at the University of Southern California and one season on the staff of the NFL's Oakland Raiders.

In 1976, Robinson was named head coach at Southern California. He had a 67–14–0 record in seven seasons there and guided the school to victories in the Rose Bowl in 1976, 1978, and 1979, and in the Bluebonnet Bowl in 1977.

Robinson went to the NFL's Los Angeles Rams as head coach in 1983 and was named the league's coach of the year after taking the Rams to the playoffs in his first season. As he had in the college ranks, Robinson emphasized the running attack and defense to win games.

The Rams made the playoffs six times in his nine seasons, but Robinson was replaced after the team went only 3–13 in 1991.

Robinson, Sugar Ray [Walker Smith, Jr.]

BOXING
b. May 3, 1920, Detroit, Mich.
d. April 12, 1989

Walker Smith, Jr., began boxing in Harlem shortly after he moved with his mother to New York City at the age of 12. When he was 15, he wanted to enter a tournament but was told he needed an AAU membership card, which he couldn't get until he was 16. He borrowed a card from a friend, Ray Robinson, and became the 1940 Golden Gloves lightweight champion under that name.

His trainer, George Gainford, told a writer, "He's a sweet fighter, sweet as sugar," and from that point on he was known as "Sugar Ray." After winning all 89 of his amateur fights, Robinson became a professional on October 4, 1940, with a 2nd-round knockout of Joe Etchevarria.

Robinson won 40 consecutive professional bouts before losing a 10-round decision to Jake LaMotta in 1943. He didn't suffer another loss for more than eight years.

Welterweight champions Freddy Cochrane and Marty Servo refused to fight Robinson. The New York State Athletic Commission took Servo's title and announced that the winner of the Robinson-Tommy Bell fight on December 20, 1946, would be the new champion. Robinson won a 15-round decision. In his first defense, he knocked out Jimmy Doyle, who died after the fight, and Robinson donated most of his winnings to the Doyle family.

After five defenses, Robinson met LaMotta for the world middleweight championship on February 14, 1951. In a fight called the "St. Valentine's Day massacre" because of the punishment LaMotta took, Robinson won on a 13th-round knockout.

Robinson lost the title when Randy Turpin of England took a 15-round decision on July 10, 1951, but he regained it by knocking out Turpin in the 10th round on September 12.

On June 25, 1952, Robinson tried for the world light heavyweight title against Joey Maxim, and he might well have won if it hadn't been for 115-degree heat at ringside in Chicago. He was well ahead on points in the thirteenth round when he took a wild swing, missed, fell to the canvas, and could no longer continue because of heat prostration.

Robinson retired for more than a year after that fight, but he returned in 1954, and on December 9, 1955, he won the middleweight title once again. Gene Fullmer took the championship with a 15-round decision on January 2, 1957; Robinson regained it with a 5th-round knockout on May 1; Carmen Basilio won it with a 15-round decision on September 23, 1957; and Robinson regained it with a 15-round decision on March 25, 1958, becoming the only fighter ever to win a championship five times.

After losing the championship to Paul Pender on a 15-round decision on January 22, 1960, Robinson failed in his attempt to win it for the sixth time when Pender won another 15-round decision in a rematch. Robinson also had two shots at the National Boxing Association title against Gene Fullmer, but the first fight was a draw, and Fullmer won a decision in the second.

Robinson continued boxing through 1965, then retired at the age of 44. He won 174 bouts, 109 by knockout; lost 19, 1 by knockout; and fought 6 draws and 2 no-contests. Wildly popular in Europe as well as the United States, Robinson won a great deal of money fighting and spent it lavishly on pink Cadillacs and a remarkable entourage that at times included a golf instructor, barber, voice teacher, drama coach, masseur, trainers, secretary, and a dwarf mascot.
★ International Boxing Hall of Fame

Robinson, Wilbert

BASEBALL
b. June 29, 1864, Hudson, Mass.
d. Aug. 8, 1934

Robinson's 50-year career in professional baseball began in 1885, when he joined a team in the minor New England League as a catcher. The following season he went to the Philadelphia Athletics of the American Association, then a major league.

Although he didn't hit well during his early years in the majors, Robinson was respected for his defensive skills and knowledge of the game. During the 1890 season, he was traded to the Baltimore Orioles, who moved into the NL in 1892, after the American Association folded.

His hitting improved dramatically when Ned Hanlon took over as manager in 1893. Robinson's average went from .267 to .334 in 1893 and then to .353 in 1894. He slipped to .262 in 1895 but batted .347 and .315 in the next two years.

The Orioles were the best team of the 1890s, and Robinson was their captain. He and John McGraw, the team's third baseman, became good friends and opened a restaurant, The Diamond, in Baltimore.

The Baltimore franchise folded after the 1899 season. Robinson and McGraw were sold to the St. Louis NL team in 1900, but they jumped to a Baltimore team in the new AL in 1901, with McGraw as manager and Robinson as a back-up catcher. McGraw left the team to become manager of the New York Giants during the 1902 season, taking most of Baltimore's best players, and Robinson took over as manager. That was his last year as a player.

The new Baltimore franchise did no better than the old one, and it moved to New York in 1903, eventually becoming the Yankees. Robinson managed and coached for a minor league Baltimore team at times, but mainly focused on running the restaurant until 1911, when McGraw hired him to work with the Giants' pitchers.

The old friends began to argue violently in 1913 and became enemies. Robinson left the Giants to become manager of the Brooklyn Dodgers in 1914. Combative and profane on the field, genial and jovial off the field, he was immediately adored in Brooklyn as "Uncle Robbie," and the team was called the Robins during his tenure.

Brooklyn won pennants in 1916 and 1920, losing both World Series. During the 1920s, though, they became known as the "Daffiness Boys" because of the number of characters on the team, and Robinson was an appropriate leader for them. He once announced he was setting up a "Bonehead Club" with a fine for any player who made a stupid play. Then he gave the wrong lineup card to the umpires, fined himself, and became the club's first member.

In 1925, Robinson became president of the team for a short time, but he left that job to become manager again before the season was over. He resigned after the 1931 season, and in 1933 he bought a minor league team in Atlanta. He served as manager for one year, then resigned that job to become president of the team. He died less than a year later.
★ Baseball Hall of Fame

Robustelli, Andy (Andrew)

FOOTBALL
b. Dec. 6, 1925, Stamford, Conn.

A two-way end at little Arnold College, Robustelli was chosen by the Los Angeles Rams in the nineteenth round of the 1951 NFL player draft and was considered a long shot to make the team.

The Rams were impressed with his determination and toughness as a defensive end, though, and he not only made the team, he was an All-Pro in 1953 and 1955.

The 6-foot, 230-pounder was traded to the New York Giants in 1956. He spent nine seasons with the Giants, playing for six conference champions and one NFL championship team. Robustelli won the Maxwell Club's Bert Bell Award as the league's player of the year in 1962.

With the Giants, Robustelli was an All-Pro from 1956 through 1960. He retired after the 1964 season.
★ Pro Football Hall of Fame

Rockne, Knute K.

FOOTBALL
b. March 4, 1888, Voss, Norway
d. March 31, 1931

Rockne's family came to the U.S. when he was five years old, and they settled in Chicago. After graduating from high school, he went to work for several years and then entered Notre Dame in 1910, "a lone Norse Protestant on the Irish Catholic campus," as he once put it.

Although only 5-foot-8 and 145 pounds, he became a starting end on the football team and was a third-team All-American as a senior in 1913, mainly because he was the chief receiver when Notre Dame used the pass as a major offensive weapon to upset Army, 35–13.

Rockne became a chemistry instructor and assistant football coach after graduating. When head coach and athletic director Jess Harper left to enter military service in 1918, Rockne replaced him.

Notre Dame had a 3–1–2 record in his first season, then went undefeated for two years. From 1921 through 1923, Rockne's teams were 27–3–1. Led by the famous Four Horsemen in the backfield and the lesser-known Seven Mules in the line, the 1924 team won all nine of its regular season games and beat Stanford, 27–10, in the Rose Bowl.

During the next three seasons, the Fighting Irish lost 4 of 29 games, tying 2. Rockne had his worst year in 1928, when it took a 12–6 victory over Army to salvage a 5–4–0 season. The Army game lives on in football mythology. With the team trailing, 6–0, at the half, Rockne told his players that George Gipp, dying of pneumonia in 1920, had said, "Rock, someday when the going is real tough, ask the boys to go out and beat Army for me."

After that revelation, the inspired Notre Dame "won one for the Gipper." Although Gipp's deathbed request has been dismissed as a fairy tale, Rockne always insisted it was true.

Rockne's last two teams were undefeated, going 9–0–0 in 1929 and the 10–0–0 in 1930. He was one of six passengers flying from Kansas City to Los Angeles on March 31, 1931, when the plane crashed in Kansas, killing everyone aboard.

When a train brought his casket back to South Bend for burial, an estimated 10,000 people jammed into a Chicago station to see it.

One of the most famous people in the country at his death, Rockne had many money-making sidelines. He gave motivational talks to Studebaker salesmen, appeared in movie short subjects, and wrote magazine articles and books. Shortly before he died, Rockne had had offers of $75,000 from the Hearst newspapers to write a column and $50,000 from RKO Pictures to play a football coach in a movie musical.

Rockne was well known for his ability to motivate players. He once said, "A team in an ordinary frame of mind will do only ordinary things. In the proper emotional state, a team will do extraordinary things. To reach this state, a team must have a motive that has an extraordinary appeal to them."

That well-deserved reputation has obscured his skill as a football strategist. He inherited the Notre Dame shift from Jess Harper, but he turned it into a versatile offense. His use of deception, line spacing, and split ends anticipated many of the ideas behind the T formation.

When Rockne died, 23 of his former players were college head coaches, and many more were assistants. Among his most successful pupils were Eddie Anderson, Jim Crowley, Frank Leahy, Buck Shaw, and Frank Thomas.

★ College Football Hall of Fame

Rodgers, Bill (William H.)

TRACK AND FIELD
b. Dec. 23, 1947, Hartford, Conn.

Although Rodgers did some distance running at Wesleyan University in Connecticut, he gave it up during his senior year. Watching Frank Shorter win the 1972 Olympic marathon reawakened his interest, and within a few years he was the best marathoner in the world.

After finishing third in the 1975 international cross-country championship, the best placing ever for a male

American runner, Rodgers won the Boston Marathon in a U.S. record 2:09.55.

Given a good chance to win a medal in the 1976 Olympics, he ran poorly because of cramps, but he won the New York City Marathon that year. It was the first of four consecutive victories in that event, and he won the Boston Marathon three years in a row, from 1978 through 1980.

After the U.S. boycotted the 1980 Moscow Olympics because of the Soviet invasion of Afghanistan, Rodgers cut back on his schedule but continued to run occasionally during the next decade. The owner of a small chain of stores that sell running apparel and equipment, Rodgers once admitted that he was earning more than $100,000 a year from the sport while still considered an amateur.

Rodgers, Guy W., Jr.
BASKETBALL
b. Sept. 1, 1935, Philadelphia, Pa.

The 6-foot, 185-pound Rodgers was one of the finest ball handlers in basketball history. At Temple University, he averaged 19.6 points per game in three seasons as a starter and set a school record with 15 assists in a game.

A consensus All-American guard in 1958, Rodgers was a territorial pick of the Philadelphia Warriors in the NBA draft. The team moved to San Francisco before the 1962–63 season, when Rodgers led the league with 825 assists.

He was sent to the Chicago Bulls for two players, a draft choice, and cash in 1966. He was the NBA assist leader with 908 in 1966–67, his only full season with Chicago. The Bulls traded him to the Cincinnati Royals for a player, two draft choices, and cash during the 1968–69 season.

Rodgers was chosen by the Milwaukee Bucks in the 1969 expansion draft, and he retired after one season with them. He scored 10,415 points in 892 regular season NBA games, an 11.7 average, and had 6,917 assists, which was third all-time when he retired. Rodgers added 508 points and 286 assists in 47 playoff games.

Rodgers, Johnny (John)
FOOTBALL
b. July 5, 1951, Omaha, Nebr.

Winner of the 1972 Heisman Trophy as the nation's best college player, the 5-foot-9, 165-pound Rodgers was a threat to score any time he touched the ball. His greatest performance came in Nebraska's 40–6 victory over Notre Dame in the 1973 Orange Bowl, when Rodgers ran for three touchdowns, caught a 50-yard touchdown pass, and threw a 54-yard touchdown before being removed with 21 minutes still to play.

In three seasons as a starter, Rodgers rushed 152 times for 836 yards, a 5.5 average; caught 154 passes for 2,779 yards, an 18.0 average; returned punts for 1,651 yards and kickoffs for 892 yards; scored 50 touchdowns, including 9 on kick returns; and accounted for 6,210 all-purpose yards. Nebraska won national titles in 1970 and 1971 and had a 31-game winning streak during Rodgers's career.

Rodgers was drafted by the NFL's San Diego Chargers in 1973, but they refused to meet his contract demands because of his size, and he signed with the Montreal Alouettes of the Canadian Football League. He was the CFL rookie of the year. Rodgers remained with the Alouettes through the 1976 season and then joined the Chargers.

His NFL playing time was limited by injuries, and he retired after just two seasons. With the Chargers, he gained 49 yards on 4 rushes, a 12.3 average; caught 17 passes for 234 yards, a 13.8 average; returned 26 punts for 246 yards, a 9.5 average; and ran back 15 kickoffs for 353 yards, a 23.5 average.

Rodrigues, Chi Chi (Juan)
GOLF
b. Oct. 23, 1935, Bayamon, P.R.

Rodrigues is the only Hall of Fame golfer who never won a major championship. In fact, during his 25 years on the PGA tour, he won only eight tournaments and just over $1 million — about $40,000 a year. Then he joined the PGA Senior tour in 1985 and won more than 20 tournaments and $4 million in less than eight years.

Always popular with galleries, the slender, 5-foot-7 Rodrigues could drive tremendous distances. At one time, he sold for two dollars a leaflet describing the secret of his power.

But Hall of Fame voters didn't elect him for his popularity or driving ability. He was chosen primarily for the vast amount of charitable work he has done for children, in his native Puerto Rico and in Florida.

Rodriguez grew up in poverty. "In my day," he once said, "you drank milk with a fork because you didn't want that glass of milk to run out." As soon as he began making money on the PGA tour in the early 1960s, he established his own pro-am tournament to raise money for a children's hospital in Puerto Rico. Later he established the Chi Chi Rodriguez Youth Foundation, which has raised more than $1 million to help young people in Florida. And, when he retires from golf, he has said he plans to "go back to Puerto Rico and teach poor kids how not to be poor."

★ World Golf Hall of Fame

Rogers, George W., Jr.

FOOTBALL
b. Dec. 8, 1958, Duluth, Ga.

During his four years as a running back at the University of South Carolina, Rogers gained 5,204 rushing yards. He rushed for 1,894 yards in 1980, his senior year, when he was a consensus All-American and winner of the Heisman Trophy as the nation's best college football player.

The 6-foot-2, 224-pound Rogers joined the NFL's New Orleans Saints in 1981 with a five-year contract reportedly worth $1 million. He was named rookie of the year after leading the league with 1,674 yards in 378 attempts, a 4.4 average, and scoring 13 rushing touchdowns.

Rogers entered a drug rehabilitation program early in 1982 but came back to gain 535 yards in nine games during the season, which was shortened by a player strike. He gained 1,144 yards in 1983 and 914 yards in 1984, and was then traded to the Washington Redskins.

As the single running back in Washington's one-back offense, Rogers had two more seasons with more than 1,000 yards, and he led the NFL with 18 touchdowns in 1986. A toe injury cut his playing time in 1987, and he retired after that season.

In his eight NFL seasons, Rogers gained 7,176 yards on 1,692 attempts, a 4.2 average, and scored 54 rushing touchdowns. He also caught 55 passes for 366 yards, a 6.7 average.

Romig, Joseph H.

FOOTBALL
b. April 11, 1941, Salt Lake City, Utah

A high school wrestling champion, the 5-foot-10, 200-pound Romig was an All-American guard at the University of Colorado in 1960 and 1961. Fast and very strong, Romig was an outstanding middle linebacker on defense and a bulldozing blocker as a pulling guard.

An outstanding student, Romig had a 3.87 grade point average at Colorado and was also a first-team Academic All-American twice. He passed up professional football to pursue a career in astrophysics.

★ College Football Hall of Fame

Roosma, John S.

BASKETBALL
b. Sept. 3, 1900, Passaic, N.J.
d. Nov. 13, 1983

Roosma was probably the best player on the Passaic, New Jersey, High School "Wonder Teams" that won 159 consecutive games. A 6-foot-1 forward, he played in 41 of them and was the top scorer in three state championship tournaments, two of which were won by Passaic.

At the U.S. Military Academy from 1921 to 1924, Roosma won ten letters in four sports and scored 1,126 points in 74 basketball games, an average of 15.2 per game — a very high figure at a time when the winning team usually scored fewer than 40 points. Army won 70 games and lost only 3 while he was playing.

After graduating, Roosma became a career officer, serving 30 years and retiring as a colonel. During his Army career, he played for a number of service teams and also officiated college games.

★ Basketball Hall of Fame

Roper, Bill (William W.)

FOOTBALL
b. Aug. 22, 1880, Philadelphia, Pa.
d. Dec. 10, 1933

An emotional coach who believed that motivation was more important than strategy for a winning football team, Roper played end at Princeton. His fumble recovery with seconds to play set up the winning field goal in the 10–6 victory over Yale in 1899, his freshman year.

Roper graduated in 1903 and coached Virginia Military Institute to a 5–5–1 record in 1903 and 1904. He returned to Princeton to coach from 1906 through 1908, compiling a 21–4–4 record, coached Missouri to a 7–0–1 record in 1909, then came back to Princeton for two more seasons, winning 15 games while losing 1 and tying 2.

After earning a law degree, Roper coached Swarthmore in 1915 and 1916. He then went into the service during World War I and settled down as Princeton's coach for 12 more seasons, from 1919 through 1930.

His 1922 squad became known as the "Team of Destiny." Expected to lose just about every week, they won all eight games. The biggest victory was a 21–18 upset of the University of Chicago, who led, 18–7, going into the fourth quarter.

Roper left coaching after the 1930 season because of poor health. His overall record at Princeton was 89–28–6.

★ College Football Hall of Fame

Rose, Mauri

AUTO RACING
b. 1906, Columbus, Ohio
d. Jan. 1, 1981

The first driver to win the Indy 500 three times, Rose began racing on dirt tracks in 1927. The first of his ten Indy starts was in 1933, when his car failed after 125 miles. He finished second in 1934 and fourth in 1936, when he won the national driving championship.

Rose's first Indy victory came in 1941. It wasn't unusual then for a driver to start the race in one car and finish in another if the first car broke down. Rose's car was out of the race after the 60th lap. His team's second car was called in at the 180-mile mark, and Rose replaced Floyd Davis, who was in fourteenth place. Rose took the lead at 425 miles and never gave it up.

He won again in 1947 and 1948. In 1949 he was in second place with eight laps to go when his car broke down. He was running third in 1950 when his car's exhaust pipe caught fire in the pits. The fire was extinguished, but he'd lost precious time, and the race was shortened by rain before he had a chance to challenge the leaders. Rose retired after the 1951 Indy 500, in which his car failed to finish because of a collapsed wheel.

An engineer, Rose invented a device allowing amputees to drive an automobile. He said he was prouder of that accomplishment than of his racing record.

★ Indianapolis Speedway Hall of Fame

Rose, Peter E.

BASEBALL
b. April 14, 1942, Cincinnati, Ohio

Once described by a sportswriter as "the least-gifted great player," Rose was self-made, parlaying, through sheer hard work and hustle, a small amount of talent into a 24-year major league career and records for most career games and most career hits. Within three years of his retirement, he went from self-made to self-destroyed, his Hall of Fame dreams devastated by gambling and a criminal sentence for tax evasion.

When he joined the NL's Cincinnati Reds for spring training in 1963, Rose was nicknamed "Charlie Hustle" because he ran to first base even on a walk. A second baseman then, he batted .273 and scored 101 runs to win the rookie of the year award.

In 1965, Rose led the league with 209 hits, batted .312, and scored 117 runs to make the first of 17 All-Star teams. It was also the first of 15 seasons in which he hit over .300.

Rose won consecutive batting titles in 1968, when he hit .335 and also had a league-leading 210 hits, and in 1969, with a .348 average and a league-leading 120 runs scored. He was named the NL's most valuable player in 1973, when he won his third and last batting championship with a .338 average, again leading the league with 230 hits, his career high.

From 1974 through 1976, Rose led the NL in doubles and runs scored each year. He was the leader in hits once again with 215 in 1976, and he led in doubles once more with 51 in 1978.

A free agent, Rose signed with the Philadelphia Phillies in 1979 .He had moved to the outfield in 1967, then had played third base most of the time since 1975. With Philadelphia, he was a first baseman.

Rose led the league with 42 doubles in 1980 and 140 hits in the strike-shortened 1981 season, when he batted .325. However, his average dropped to .271 in 1982 and .245 in 1983, and he went to the Montreal Expos the following year. Late in the season, the Expos sent him back to Cincinnati, where he became the team's manager.

He retired as a player after the 1986 season but continued managing until the gambling scandal broke in 1989. It began with reports that Rose had lost heavily on horse and dog races, and then there were charges that he had also bet on baseball games.

Rose denied the charges steadfastly, but was banned from the sport by Commissioner A. Bartlett Giamatti on August 24, 1989. As a result of the gambling probe, Rose pleaded guilty to income tax evasion in April 1990 and was sentenced to five months in a federal prison.

The Baseball Hall of Fame board of directors in 1991 ruled that anyone banned from baseball would be ineligible for Hall of Fame membership. Although Rose's name wasn't mentioned, it was obvious that the ruling was aimed at him.

In 3,562 games, Rose had 4,256 hits, breaking Ty Cobb's record of 4,189, which had once seemed insurmountable. He had 746 doubles, 135 triples, 160 home runs, 198 stolen bases, 2,165 runs scored, 1,314 RBI, and a .303 batting average.

Rose, Ralph W.

TRACK AND FIELD
b. March 17, 1884, Healdsburg, Calif.
d. Oct. 16, 1913

Rose was the only man ever to win national championships in the shot put, discus, and javelin, and the first to put the shot more than 50 feet.

He won a total of six medals at three Olympic Games but was perhaps best known as the man who refused to dip the American flag to King Edward VII of Great Britain during the opening ceremonies of the 1908 London Games. "This flag dips to no earthly king," Rose said afterward.

The 6-foot-6, 235-pound Rose was the Olympic shot put champion in 1904 and 1908. He won a third gold medal in 1912 in the two-hand shot put. He won silver medals in the 1904 discus throw and 1912 shot put and a bronze in the 1904 hammer throw.

He was the AAU champion in the shot put from 1907 through 1910, in the discus in 1905 and 1909, and in the javelin in 1909. His put of 51 feet even at the 1909 meet was a world record that stood for more than 16 years. Earlier in 1909 he had a shot put of 51-4 and a hammer throw of 178-5, both beyond the existing world records, but the marks weren't recognized.

Rose died of typhoid fever at the age of 29.

★ National Track & Field Hall of Fame

Rosen, Albert L. ("Flip")

BASEBALL
b. Feb. 29, 1924, Spartanburg, S.C.

Rosen spent two years in college, two more in the Navy during World War II, and two final years in college, then made a belated start in professional baseball in 1947. He was with the AL's Cleveland Indians for brief periods in 1947, 1948, and 1949 before becoming the team's starting third baseman in 1950.

A right-hander, the 5-10½, 180-pound Rosen led the league with 37 home runs that year, batting .287 with 116 RBI and 100 runs scored.

After leading the league with 105 RBI in 1952, when he batted .302, Rosen had his finest season in 1953. He won the AL's most valuable player award and nearly had the triple crown as well, with a league-leading 43 home runs, 145 RBI, 115 runs scored, and .613 slugging percentage. He hit .336 to finish just behind batting champion Mickey Vernon, who had a .337 average.

Rosen suffered a broken finger in 1954 and had several other nagging injuries that forced him to retire after the 1956 season. In 1,044 games, Rosen batted .285 with 1,063 hits, including 165 doubles, 20 triples, and 192 home runs. He drove in 717 runs and scored 603.

Rosenbloom, Max ("Slapsie Maxie")

BOXING
b. Sept. 6, 1904, Leonard's Bridge, Conn.
d. March 6, 1976

Although not highly regarded as a fighter by most sportswriters and boxing aficionados, Rosenbloom had a long career and was so well liked by the average fan that he was successful in show business long after he left the ring.

Rosenbloom grew up in a tough neighborhood in New York City and spent some time in a reformatory as a young teenager. He became a professional fighter in 1923 and didn't suffer his first loss until August 22, 1925, when Jimmy Slattery beat him on a 6-round decision.

The 5-foot-11 Rosenbloom had a very long reach and developed the technique of staying out of reach of his opponents and slapping them with relatively harmless blows, which earned him his nickname. The technique also won him a lot of decisions going into his bout with Slattery for the New York light heavyweight championship on June 25, 1930. Rosenbloom took the title in 15 rounds.

He was recognized as world champion after decisioning Lou Scozza in 15 rounds on July 14, 1932. Rosenbloom held the title until Bob Olin won a questionable 15-round decision on November 16, 1934. After that, Rosenbloom did

much of his fighting on the West Coast, where he owned two restaurants.

His last bout was a 3rd-round knockout of Al Ettore on June 26, 1939, in Hollywood. Rosenbloom later appeared in a number of movies, did a nightclub act with another former fighter, Max Baer, and performed on stage in *Guys and Dolls.*

He won 210 of his 280 professional fights, only 18 by knockout. Rosenbloom lost 35, 2 by knockout, and also fought 23 draws, 19 no-decisions, and 2 no-contests.
★ International Boxing Hall of Fame

Ross, Arthur H.

HOCKEY
b. Jan. 13, 1886, Naughton, Ont.
d. Aug. 5, 1964

A defenseman, Ross played professional hockey with teams in Brandon, Manitoba; Kenora, Ontario; and Ottawa for 14 seasons before the NHL was organized in 1917. He scored one goal in three games with the NHL's Montreal Wanderers in that first NHL season.

When the Boston Bruins entered the league in 1924, Ross became the team's first coach and general manager. He resigned the coaching position after the 1927–28 season but had three more stints on Boston's bench, from 1929–30 through 1933–34, from 1936–37 through 1938–39, and from 1941–42 through 1944–45.

Under his guidance, the Bruins won Stanley Cups in 1929, 1939, and 1941. He remained as the team's general manager until his retirement in 1954. In 1947 Ross, who is credited with inventing the puck and the types of nets still used in hockey, gave the NHL the trophy named for him, which is presented annually to the league's top scorer.
★ Hockey Hall of Fame

Ross, Barney [Barnet David Rasofsky]

BOXING
b. Dec. 23, 1909, New York, N.Y.
d. Jan. 17, 1967

Ross's family moved to Chicago to operate a grocery store before he was two years old. He dropped out of school after his father was murdered in a 1924 hold-up and began boxing as an amateur under an assumed name to prevent his mother from finding out.

He won the 1929 Western Golden Gloves featherweight championship and then became a professional. Ross won 48 of his first 50 professional fights and had 1 draw in that string. He beat Tony Canzoneri for the world lightweight and junior welterweight championships with a 10-round decision on June 23, 1933.

Later that year, he gave up the lightweight crown because he could no longer make the weight limit, but continued to hold the junior welterweight title. On May 28, 1934, Ross won the world welterweight championship with a 15-round decision over Jimmy McLarnin, but McLarnin won it back in a rematch on September 17.

Ross regained the welterweight championship with another decision over McLarnin on May 28, 1935. He then surrendered the junior welterweight title. After two defenses, he lost the welterweight championship to Henry Armstrong on a 15-round decision on May 31, 1938, and retired from the ring.

During World War II, Ross served in the Marines, was wounded at Guadalcanal, and received the Silver Star for bravery. Because of his wound, he became addicted to morphine. The 1947 John Garfield movie *Body and Soul* was a fictitious version of Ross's life, and the 1957 film *Monkey on My Back* told the story of his addiction and recovery.

Ross had 81 professional bouts, and he won 73 of them, 22 by knockout. He lost 4 decisions and also fought 3 draws and 1 no-decision.

★ International Boxing Hall of Fame

Ross, Norman DeM.

■ SWIMMING
b. May 2, 1896, Portland, Oreg.
d. June 19, 1953

Ross won three gold medals at the 1920 Olympics, in the 400- and 1,500-meter freestyle swims and as a member of the 4 x 200-meter relay team. He was the AAU national outdoor champion in the 440-yard in 1917 and in the 440-yard

and 1-mile in 1920. Indoors, he won the 100-yard title in 1921 and the 220-yard title in 1917, 1918, and 1921.

A Stanford graduate, Ross served in World War I and received a law degree from Northwestern University. He was the country's first classical music disc jockey with a radio station in Chicago, where he was known as "Uncle Normie." During World War II, he was an aide to General Jimmy Doolittle.

Rote, Kyle (William Kyle Sr.)

FOOTBALL
b. Oct. 27, 1928, San Antonio, Tex.

A high school teammate of Doak Walker, Rote played behind Walker at Southern Methodist University in 1948 and 1949. When Walker was forced to miss the game against Notre Dame because of an injury, Rote replaced him as tailback in SMU's single wing and turned in a great triple-threat performance despite a 27–20 loss. He rushed for 115 yards, scored all three touchdowns, passed for 146 yards, and punted for a 48-yard average.

After Walker graduated, Rote became a starter in 1950 and was a consensus All-American. He joined the NFL's New York Giants in 1951 as a running back and occasionally as a flanker. When the Giants began using the three-end formation in 1953, Rote was moved to split end.

In 11 seasons with the Giants, he caught 300 passes for 4,797 yards and 48 touchdowns. He also rushed 231 times for 871 yards, a 3.8 average, and 4 touchdowns.

Rote retired after the 1951 season and became a sportscaster, serving for several years as an analyst on NBC television coverage of college and professional football. His son, Kyle Rote, Jr., was a professional soccer player.

★ College Football Hall of Fame

Rote, Kyle, Jr.

SOCCER
b. Dec. 25, 1950, Dallas, Tex.

After attending Oklahoma State University on a football scholarship, Rote transferred to the University of the

South in Tennessee, where he starred in soccer. A first-round draft choice of the North American Soccer League's Dallas Tornado in 1973, he led the league with 30 points on 10 goals and 10 assists and was named rookie of the year.

Rote was traded to the Houston Hurricane in 1978 and retired with 42 career goals after one season there. He worked in sports broadcasting until 1983, when he returned to soccer as player-coach of the Memphis Americans of the Major Indoor Soccer League. The team moved to Las Vegas for the following season, and Rote chose not to go.

Roth, Mark S.

BOWLING
b. April 10, 1951, Brooklyn, N.Y.

A four-time bowler of the year, from 1977 through 1979 and in 1984, Roth joined the PBA tour in 1970 but didn't win a tournament until 1975. From that point on, he was one of the PBA's most consistent bowlers.

Roth led the PBA in average from 1976 through 1979 and in 1981 and 1988, and he was the tour's leading money winner from 1977 through 1979 and in 1984, when he won the PBA Open. He tied a record by winning three straight tournaments in 1977 and set a record by winning eight in 1978. Although he failed to win a tournament in 1986, Roth still had enough high finishes to win $86,000.

His 33 tournament victories is second to Earl Anthony's 41, and, through 1993, Roth had won $1,417,487, to rank third all-time.
★ PBA Hall of Fame

Roush, Edd J.

BASEBALL
b. May 8, 1893, Oakland City, Ind.
d. March 21, 1988

Roush played briefly for the AL's Chicago White Sox in 1913 and then joined the Indianapolis team in the new Federal League in 1914. After batting .325, he went to the league's Newark franchise when the Indianapolis team folded.

The Federal League lasted just one more season, and the New York Giants bought Roush for $7,500. He hit only .188 in 39 games with New York before being traded to the Cincinnati Reds, where he became the team's starting center fielder.

A left-hander, the 5-foot-11, 170-pound Roush led the NL in hitting with a .341 average in 1917, his first full year with Cincinnati. He had the league's top slugging percentage, .455, in 1918, and led in batting average again in 1919, when he hit .321. Roush batted only .214 but scored six runs and had seven RBI when the Reds beat the Chicago White Sox five games to three in the World Series that went down in history as the "Black Sox" series.

Roush batted over .300 for each of the next eight seasons, leading the league with 41 doubles in 1923 and 21 triples in 1924. He was one of the few players of his time who ever held out for more money. Roush did it almost every year, in part because he hated spring training, but in 1922 he waited until August to sign a new contract and played in only 49 games that year.

In January 1927, Roush was traded back to the Giants. He held out once more until he received a three-year contract for $70,000. After hitting .304 in his first season, Roush played in only 46 games in 1928 because of illness, and he left the team in another contract dispute after batting .324 in 1929.

Roush sat out the entire 1930 season and returned to Cincinnati in 1931. He hit .271 in one season there before retiring.

In 1,967 major league games, Roush batted .323 with 2,376 hits, including 339 doubles, 182 triples, and 68 home runs. He stole 268 bases, scored 1,099 runs, and had 981 RBI.
★ Baseball Hall of Fame

Roy, Patrick

HOCKEY
b. Oct. 5, 1965, Quebec, P.Q.

The winner of the NHL's Vezina Trophy as the league's best goaltender in 1989, 1990, and 1992, Roy played in just one game with the Montreal Canadiens in 1984–85 and became one of the team's goalies the following season, sharing duties with Brian Hayward.

Roy won the Conn Smythe Trophy as the most valuable player in the 1986 Stanley Cup playoffs, when he had a 15–5 record with a 1.92 goals-against average. He led the NHL with a 2.47 average in 1988–89 and a 2.36 average in 1991–92.

After losing their first 1993 playoff game in overtime, the Canadiens won ten consecutive overtime games, with Roy recording more than 90 shutout minutes under the pressure of "sudden death." He was the easy winner of the Conn Smythe Trophy as Montreal won its 24th Stanley Cup.

Asked about the Montreal mystique, Quebec coach Pierre Page replied, "How do you spell mystique? It's spelled R-O-Y."

Through the 1993–94 season, Roy had given up 1,287 goals in 486 regular season games, a 2.75 average, with 27 shutouts. He had a 2.46 goals-against average in 114 playoff games, with 5 shutouts.

Royal, Darrell K.
FOOTBALL
b. July 6, 1924, Hollis, Okla.

Royal served in World War II after graduating from high school and then entered the University of Oklahoma, where he became the starting quarterback in 1948 after playing halfback for his first two years. An expert at running the split-T option play, Royal was also an accurate passer, a good punter, and a skilled defensive back who intercepted 17 passes during his career.

As head coach of the Canadian Football League's Edmonton Eskimos in 1953, he had a 17–5–0 record. Royal then took over at Mississippi State, winning 12 games while losing 8 in 1954 and 1955.

He had a 5–5–0 record at the University of Washington in 1956 and then became head coach at the University of Texas. In 20 seasons there, he won 167 games, lost 47, and tied 5. Under Royal, Texas won national championships in 1963 and 1969. The team was ranked

first in the nation after the 1970 regular season but fell to third after losing, 24–11, to Notre Dame in the Cotton Bowl.

In 1968, Royal became the first college coach to use the wishbone T, which had been invented at a Texas high school. Many other colleges soon followed his lead.

Royal retired from coaching after the 1976 season and served as athletic director until 1979. During his college coaching career, he had a 184–60–5 record. He ranks 21st in victories, and his .749 winning percentage is 29th best in NCAA Division I football.

★ College Football Hall of Fame

Rozier, Mike
FOOTBALL
b. March 1, 1961, Camden, N.J.

The 5-foot-10, 210-pound Rozier was a sprinter as well as a running back at the University of Nebraska. He won the 1983 Heisman Trophy as the nation's best college player after leading NCAA Division I rushers with 2,148 yards on 275 attempts and setting records with 7.81 yards per attempt and 29 rushing touchdowns.

The Pittsburgh Maulers of the U.S. Football League in 1984 signed Rozier to a three-year contract worth more than $1 million a year. However, the team folded after just one season, and Rozier went to the Jacksonville Bulls in 1985.

After the USFL season ended in July, Rozier joined the NFL's Houston Oilers. A chronic foot injury forced his retirement after the 1988 season. In his NFL career, Rozier rushed for 3,083 yards on 812 carries, a 3.8 average, and scored 22 rushing touchdowns. He also caught 71 passes for 568 yards, an 8,0 average, and 1 touchdown.

Rubin, Barbara Jo
HORSE RACING
b. Nov. 21, 1949, Highland, Ill.

The first U.S. woman jockey to win a flat race against male riders, Rubin took up horseback riding as exercise after being afflicted with polio when she was six years old.

She briefly attended Broward Junior

College in Florida but left in 1968 to pursue a career in thoroughbred racing. After working as an exercise rider, pony rider, and hot walker, she became an apprentice jockey in 1969.

Rubin won her first race in the Bahamas in January. On February 22, 1969, she won aboard Cohesion at Charles Town, West Virginia. Later that year, she became the first woman to ride in New York and New Jersey. Rubin was forced to retire in 1970 because of torn knee cartilage. She raced 89 times, won 22, and was in the money in 20 other races.

Rudolph, Wilma G.

TRACK AND FIELD
b. June 23, 1940, St. Bethlehem, Tenn.
d. Nov. 12, 1994

The 20th of 22 children, Rudolph weighed only 4½ pounds at birth, and she suffered a variety of illnesses, including polio, as a child. She began to walk at eight with the aid of a leg brace. The brace was replaced by corrective shoes when she was eleven.

Rudolph soon began taking off the shoes to play basketball barefoot with some of her older siblings. In high school, she starred in basketball and track. After a year of competition, she qualified, at the age of 16, for the 1956 Olympic team, and won a bronze medal for running in the 4 x 100-meter relay.

Nicknamed "Skeeter" by her high school basketball coach, Rudolph went to Tennessee State College, where she became known for sleeping a lot. A teammate once said, "I guess Wilma would rather sleep than do most anything. Next to that it's reading, but mostly in bed."

Illness kept her out of the entire 1958 season, and a pulled thigh muscle hampered her for much of 1959, although she won the first of four consecutive AAU outdoor 100-meter championships that year. The 5-foot-11, 132-pound Rudolph emerged as the U.S. hero of the 1960 Olympics. She ran a world record 22.9 in the 200-meter at the Olympic trials and set a world record of 10.3 in a preliminary 100-meter heat. Rudolph won gold medals in both sprints and was also a member of the winning 4 x 100-meter relay team.

She went on a European tour in 1961 and was immensely popular with fans everywhere. The French called her "La Perle Noire" (the Black Pearl), the Italians "La Gazella Nera" (the Black Gazelle). Rudolph tied her 100-meter record at a meet in Moscow and lowered it to 11.2 seconds four days later at Stuttgart.

In addition to her four national 100-meter titles, Rudolph was the outdoor 200-meter champion in 1960, and she won the indoor 60-meter sprint three times.

The Associated Press female athlete of the year in 1960 and 1961, Rudolph won the 1961 Sullivan Award as the outstanding amateur athlete of the year. She was only the third woman to win the honor. After retiring in 1962, Rudolph established the Wilma Rudolph Foundation, which helps underprivileged children and sponsors athletic competition for youngsters.

★ International Women's Sports Hall of Fame; National Track and Field Hall of Fame; Olympic Hall of Fame

Ruffing, Red (Charles H.)

BASEBALL
b. May 3, 1904, Granville, Ill.
d. Feb. 17, 1986

Working in coal mines as a teenager, Ruffing developed his muscles and became known as a power-hitting outfielder on sandlot teams. But he lost four toes on his left foot in a mining accident in 1921 and didn't play baseball for nearly a year.

He returned to the sport as a pitcher and signed a professional contract in 1923. After one season in the minor leagues, Ruffing joined the Boston Red Sox in 1924, but he appeared in only eight games that season.

A right-hander, the 6-foot-1½, 205-pound Ruffing struggled as a starter for five seasons with poor Red Sox teams, winning only 39 games while losing 93. After he lost his first three decisions in 1930, Ruffing was traded to the New York Yankees, where he immediately became a star, going 15–5 the rest of the season.

Ruffing had relied entirely on a fastball and curve in Boston, but the Yankees taught him how to throw a change-up, and it became an important pitch for him. He was 16–14 in 1931 and 18–7 in 1932, when he led the league with 190 strikeouts.

After slipping to 9–14 in 1933, Ruffing was 19–11 and 16–11, and then won 20 games four seasons in a row, from 1936 through 1939. He led the AL in victories with a 21–7 record and in winning percentage at .750 in 1938 and was the league leader with five shutouts in 1939.

Ruffing had a 44–25 record from 1940 through 1942 and then was drafted into the Army despite his age and missing toes. He served until the middle of the 1945 season, when he rejoined the Yankees. He was 12–4 in limited action for two years and retired after going 3–5 with the Chicago White Sox in 1947. He later served as a major league scout and minor league manager, and he was the New York Mets' first pitching coach in 1962.

In 22 seasons, Ruffing had a 273–225 record with 45 shutouts and a 3.80 ERA. He struck out 1,987 hitters and walked 1,541 in 4,344 innings.

★ Baseball Hall of Fame

Ruiz, Tracie

SYNCHRONIZED SWIMMING
b. Feb. 4, 1963, Honolulu, Hawaii

When synchronized swimming became an Olympic sport in 1984, Ruiz was its first gold medalist. In fact, she was a double gold medalist, winning both the solo and, with Candy Costie, the duet competition.

Ruiz also won gold medals in both events at the Pan-American Games in 1983. She was the world solo champion in 1982, when she and Costie finished second in the duet.

At the 1988 Olympics, Ruiz won a silver medal in the solo competition.

Runnels, Pete (James E.)

BASEBALL
b. Jan. 28, 1928, Lufkin, Tex.
d. May 20, 1991

A left-handed hitter, Runnels won two batting championships with the AL's Boston Red Sox, hitting .320 in 1960 and .326 in 1962.

Runnels entered the major leagues with the Washington Senators in 1951. He batted over .300 just once with Washington, but after being traded to Boston in 1958, he learned how to slice line drives off the short left field fence in Fenway Park and hit .314 or better in each of his first five seasons.

Originally a second baseman, Runnels was used primarily at first base in Boston. He led the league in fielding percentage at that position in 1960 and 1961. He went to the Houston Astros in the 1963 expansion draft and retired after the 1964 season. Runnels later became a coach with the Red Sox, and he managed the team briefly in 1966.

In 1,799 major league games, Runnels had a .291 average on 1,854 hits, including 282 doubles, 64 triples, and 49 home runs. He scored 876 runs and drove in 630.

Runyan, Paul

GOLF
b. July 12, 1908, Hot Springs, Ark.

Runyan's golfing style was defined by his victory in the 1938 PGA championship. In the 36-hole final, Sam Snead outdrove him by as much as 50 yards on some holes, but Runyan's great iron shots and fine putting brought him an easy win, 8 and 7.

He played in some tournaments in 1931 and 1932, then joined the PGA tour full-time in 1933. Runyan won a total of seven tournaments in two years and was the tour's top money winner in 1934. He beat Craig Wood 1-up in the 1934 PGA championship.

For the rest of his career, Runyan was eclipsed by such great players as Snead, Byron Nelson, and Ben Hogan. However, he was greatly respected as a teacher, and many professional golfers came to him for help when their games were going badly.

Runyan won the PGA Senior championship in 1961 and 1962.

★ PGA Hall of Fame; World Golf Hall of Fame

Rupp, Adolph F.

BASKETBALL
b. Sept. 2, 1901, Halstead, Kans.
d. Dec. 10, 1977

Rupp played basketball for the great "Phog" Allen at the University of Kansas, and he eventually broke Allen's record for most college coaching victories. After graduating in 1923, he coached high school basketball for seven years and then took over at the University of Kentucky in 1930.

Stern and often outspoken, Rupp once said, "I know I have plenty of enemies, but I'd rather be the most hated winning coach in the country than the most popular losing one." He became known as the "Baron of the Bluegrass" at Kentucky, where he developed one of the most successful basketball programs in history.

Using the fast break and a tenacious man-to-man defense, Kentucky teams won 874 games and lost only 190 during his 41-year tenure. His .822 winning percentage is third all-time. Rupp won 27 Southeastern Conference championships and four NCAA tournaments, in 1948, 1949, 1951, and 1958.

When the college basketball point-shaving scandal broke in 1950, Rupp snarled, "Gamblers couldn't get at our players with a ten-foot pole." However, five of his players were eventually implicated, and Kentucky was put on probation for the 1952–53 season. The school dropped basketball entirely, but Rupp held practices throughout the season, and Kentucky won all 25 of its games in 1953–54, led by Cliff Hagan, Frank Ramsay, and Lou Tsioropoulos.

The three were ruled ineligible for postseason play because they had completed their degree requirements the previous year, so Kentucky didn't compete in the 1954 NCAA tournament.

Rupp was forced to retire after the 1971–72 season because of his age. He commented, "If they don't let me coach, they might as well take me to the Lexington Cemetery." However, he became an executive with the Memphis Tams and the Kentucky Colonels in the American Basketball Association before his death.

Named the college coach of the year by United Press International in 1959, Rupp was a consensus choice for the honor in 1966. He was voted coach of the century by the Columbus, Ohio, Touchdown Club in 1967.

★ Basketball Hall of Fame

Rusie, Amos W.

BASEBALL
b. May 30, 1871, Mooresville, Ind.
d. Dec. 6, 1942

Known as the "Hoosier Thunderbolt" because of his fastball, Rusie was one of the greatest pitchers of the late nineteenth century. He joined the NL's Indianapolis team during the 1889 season and had a 12–10 record.

The franchise folded after that season, and the 6-foot-1, 200-pound right-hander went to the New York Giants. He had a 29–34 record in 1890, when he led the league with 341 strikeouts, and he was the strikeout leader again with 337 in 1891, when he was 33–20 with a league-leading 6 shutouts.

After going 31–31 in 1892, Rusie led the NL with 56 games, 50 complete games, 4 shutouts, 482 innings pitched, and 208 strikeouts in 1893. He had a 33–21 record that year, and he was the league leader in victories with a 36–13 mark in 1894, when he also had a league-leading 195 strikeouts.

Rusie led the league in strikeouts for the fifth and last time with 201 in 1895. After his 23–23 record that season, the Giants took $200 out of his pay for allegedly breaking training rules. Rusie said he wouldn't rejoin the team until the money was paid back to him. He took the issue to court and sat out the entire 1896 season.

Because he was a very popular player, other NL teams chipped in $5,000 to make up for the cut and the season he'd missed. Rusie dropped his lawsuit and returned to the Giants in 1897, when he had a 28–10 record, lifting the team from seventh to third place.

He had a 20–11 record in 1898, and the Giants wanted to cut his salary from $3,000 to $2,000. Again Rusie balked and went into retirement. He returned to the major leagues briefly with the Cincinnati Reds in 1901 but retired for good after appearing in only three games.

In only ten seasons, Rusie had a 245–174 record with 30 shutouts and a 3.07 ERA. He struck out 1,934 hitters and walked 1,704 in 3,769⅔ innings.
★ Baseball Hall of Fame

Russell, Bill (William F.)

BASKETBALL
b. Feb. 12, 1934, Monroe, La.

Russell's intimidating defense and great rebounding skills transformed basketball. After college coaches saw him in action at the 1955 NCAA tournament, they adopted "Russell's Rules," widening the free throw lane to 12 feet and making it illegal for a player to touch the ball on its downward arc to the basket.

"Doggie" Julian, the Dartmouth College coach and a member of the Rules Committee, said afterward, "We weren't planning to make any changes. But after some of the coaches saw Russell's performance, they got scared." Russell's own coach, Phil Woolpert of the University of San Francisco, predicted that the new rules would actually help Russell, explaining, "He's so much the fastest of the big men that now he'll just leave them further behind."

As a skinny, awkward 6-foot-2, 128-pounder, Russell couldn't even make his Oakland, California, high school basketball team in his sophomore year and was only a third-string player as a junior. His coordination improved, he grew to 6-foot-7, and he became a starter as a senior, but he graduated in the middle of the year.

Russell enrolled at USF in 1952. As a 6-foot-9 sophomore, he became the team's starting center, and he led the school to 55 consecutive victories and two NCAA championships during the 1954–55 and 1955–56 seasons.

Because the 1956 Olympics were held in Melbourne, Australia, they didn't take place until November. Russell postponed his professional career to play for the gold medal Olympic team. Meanwhile, the NBA's Boston Celtics had traded two established players, Ed Macauley and Cliff Hagan, for the St. Louis Hawks' first-round draft choice in order to get Russell.

He joined the Celtics in the middle of the 1956–57 season and helped lead them to their first championship. By then 6-foot-10 and 220 pounds, Russell made the team's fast break work by getting rebounds and making great outlet passes. His shot-blocking skill allowed the Celtics to use a new kind of defense, playing tough on the corners and wings to funnel the offensive players into the middle, where they would have to face Russell.

During his first ten seasons with Boston, the Celtics won nine championships, losing only in 1958, when Russell missed the last three games of the final series against St. Louis. He became the team's player-coach in 1966, the first black coach in NBA history, and took the Celtics to two more championships, in 1968 and 1969, then retired.

Russell was named the league's most valuable player in 1958, 1961, 1962, 1963, and 1965, and he led the NBA in rebounds per game with averages of 19.6 in 1956–57, 22.7 in 1957–58, 23.0 in 1958–59, 24.7 in 1963–64, and 24.1 in 1964–65. The Professional Basketball Writers' Association of America in 1980 voted him the greatest player in league history.

In 1973, Russell returned to coaching with the Seattle SuperSonics and resigned after four losing seasons. He became coach of the Sacramento Kings in 1987 but was replaced before the end of the season and became a vice president of the team.

During his 13 seasons as a player, Russell scored 14,522 points in 963 regular season games, a 15.1 average, and had 21,620 rebounds. He added 2,673 points in 165 playoff games, a 16.2 average. He holds the career record for playoff rebounds with 4,104, and he pulled down a playoff record 40 rebounds in games against St. Louis in 1960 and against the Los Angeles in 1962. As a coach, Russell had a 341–290 regular season record and was 34–27 in the playoffs.

★ Basketball Hall of Fame

Russell, Cazzie L.

BASKETBALL
b. June 7, 1944, Chicago, Ill.

A 6-foot-5 guard, Russell averaged 24.8 points per game in his sophomore year, 25.7 as a junior, and 30.8 as a senior to lead the University of Michigan to a 65–17 record during his career. He was named an All-American in 1965 and 1966 and was a consensus choice as the 1966 college player of the year.

The first draft choice of the NBA's New York Knicks, Russell signed a three-year contract for a reported $200,000. Used as a forward and guard, he averaged only 11.3 points a game in 1966–67. Russell increased his scoring to 16.9 in 1967–68 and 18.3 in 1968–69 but slipped to 11.5 in 1969–70.

A broken ankle sidelined him for 25 games in 1970–71, when he averaged only 9.2 points, and the Knicks traded him to the Golden State Warriors. He had his best career season with the Warriors in 1971–72, scoring 6,277 points in 423 games, an average of 21.4 per game.

Russell played for the Los Angeles Lakers from 1974–75 through 1976–77 and finished his career with the Chicago Bulls in 1977–78. In 817 regular season NBA games, Russell scored 12,377 points, an average of 15.1 per game. He added 852 points in 72 playoff games.

Russell, Honey (John D.)

BASKETBALL
b. May 3, 1903, Brooklyn, N.Y.
d. Nov. 15, 1973

Russell began playing professional basketball with the Brooklyn Visitations when he was 16. Virtually all the team's players were Jewish, and they had to cope with bigotry as well as opposing teams when they were away from home.

He once said of that period, "The Jew baiters got there early — they'd have stones inside the snowballs and it was hell getting inside the hall, much less playing the game."

When the American Basketball League was formed in 1925, Russell joined the Cleveland Rosenblums and helped lead the team to the ABL championship. He later played for the Brooklyn–New York Jewels, the Rochester Centrals, and the Chicago Bruins.

A four-time ABL all-star, the 6-foot-1, 175-pound Russell was generally considered the best defensive player of his era, but he could also score. He once held the professional record of 22 points in a game at a time when entire teams often scored fewer points.

Russell became coach at his alma mater, Seton Hall University, in 1936, and he coached the team to 43 straight victories from 1938 into 1941, a record at the time. He played and coached professional basketball during World War II, when Seton Hall dropped the sport, and in 1946 he became the first coach of the Boston Celtics, compiling a 42–66 record in two seasons.

In 1949, Russell returned to Seton Hall. He retired after the 1959–60 season with an overall record of 294 wins and 129 losses. Through much of his coaching career, Russell also served as a scout for major league baseball and professional football teams.

★ Basketball Hall of Fame

Ruth, Babe (George H.)

BASEBALL
b. Feb. 6, 1895, Baltimore, Md.
d. Aug. 16, 1948

Ruth was a uniquely American hero, the subject of many tall tales, most of them true. The sportswriter Paul Gallico called him "a swashbuckler built on gigantic and heroic lines," and Heywood Broun punned, "The Ruth is mighty and shall prevail."

He first learned to play baseball at St. Mary's Industrial School, where his parents placed him when he was eight years old. Ruth showed such promise as a left-handed pitcher that Jack Dunn, owner of the minor league Baltimore Orioles, signed him to a contract and became his legal guardian in 1914.

His first professional appearance came in an intra-squad game, when he hit the first of many gigantic home runs. A Baltimore sportswriter described it: "The next batter made a hit that will live in the memory of all who saw it. That clouter was George Ruth, the southpaw from St. Mary's school. The ball carried so far to right field that he walked around the bases." In fact, Ruth crossed the plate before the right fielder even picked the ball up.

Dunn was forced to break up the team and sell off his players before the season ended. The AL's Boston Red Sox paid between $20,000 and $25,000 for Ruth. The 6-foot-2, 215-pound youngster appeared in five games with the team after spending most of the season with a farm club, and he became a starting pitcher in 1915.

After an 18–8 record as a rookie, Ruth was 23–12 with a league-leading nine shutouts and 1.75 ERA in 1916, and he led the AL with 35 complete games in 1917, when he was 24–13. By 1918, he was also playing the outfield and first base. His pitching record was only 13–7 that year, but he led the league with 11 home runs in only 95 games and batted .300.

Ruth pitched in the World Series in 1916 and 1918, establishing a record of 29²/₃ consecutive scoreless innings. Ironically, the record was broken by Whitey Ford of the Yankees in 1961, the same year that Roger Maris of the Yankees hit 61 home runs to break Ruth's season record.

Used primarily as an outfielder in 1919, Ruth hit .322 and led the league with 29 home runs, 114 RBI, 103 runs scored, and a .657 slugging percentage. As a pitcher, he had a 9–5 record and a 2.97 ERA.

The financially troubled Red Sox sold Ruth to the Yankees in 1920 for $100,000 and a $300,000 loan. In New York, Ruth became a full-time right fielder and a slugger whose likes had never been seen before.

He batted .376 with a league-leading 158 runs, 54 home runs, 137 RBI, 148 walks, and an incredible .847 slugging percentage in 1920. The following year he led the league in all five categories again with 177 runs, 59 home runs, 171 RBI, 144 walks, and an .846 slugging percentage. Those are the two highest slugging percentages in baseball history.

Illness limited him to 110 games in 1922, but he came back to put up more awesome numbers in 1923, batting .393 with a league-leading 151 runs, 41 home runs, 131 RBI, 170 walks, and a .764 slugging percentage. He was named the AL's most valuable player that season.

Ruth won his only batting title with a .378 average in 1924, when he also led the league with 143 runs, 46 home runs, 142 walks, and a .739 slugging percentage. In 1925, he suffered "the bellyache heard around the world," reportedly because he consumed enormous amounts of hot dogs and soda. Actually, he underwent a secret operation to remove an intestinal abscess, played in only 98 games, and batted .290.

For the next six seasons, Ruth was the league's home run champion, hitting 47 in 1926, 60 in 1927, 54 in 1928, 46 in 1929, 49 in 1930, and 46 in 1931. He was also the leader in runs with 139 in 1926, 158 in 1927, and 163 in 1928; in RBI with 146 in 1926 and 142 in 1928; in walks with 144 in 1926, 138 in 1927, 135 in 1928, 136 in 1930, 128 in 1931, 130 in 1932, and 114 in 1933; and in slugging percentage with .737 in 1926, .772 in 1927, .709 in 1928, 697 in 1929, .732 in 1930, and .700 in 1930.

Ruth slipped to a .288 average and just 22 home runs in 1934, and a dispute broke out after the season because he wanted to manage the team. The Yankees instead offered him a minor league managing job, but he turned that down and was released to the Boston Braves. He hit three home runs for the Braves on May 25, 1935, and retired shortly afterward.

An celebrity around the world, Ruth toured Europe and Japan after spending one season as a coach with the Dodgers. He then settled down to retirement in a

New York apartment and played himself in *Pride of the Yankees,* a 1942 movie biography of Lou Gehrig.

Stricken with throat cancer, Ruth was honored for a last time at Yankee Stadium on June 13, 1948. He died less than two months later.

There can never be another legend of Ruth's caliber, not only because he was a unique human being but because sportswriters no longer handle athletes as gently as they did in the 1920s and 1930s. He was known as a drinker and womanizer, but the press never revealed those facts. When he suffered his 1925 "bellyache," most sportswriters believed he had a sexually transmitted disease, but that was never printed. Nor was the fact that he and his wife had adopted his illegitimate child by another woman.

A boy who never really grew up, Ruth was often ill at ease in adult social settings, but he genuinely loved children and spent a lot of time signing autographs and visiting children's wards in hospitals.

In his 22 major league seasons, Ruth batted .342 on 2,873 hits, including 506 doubles, 136 triples, and 714 home runs. He walked 2,056 times, struck out 2,213 times, scored 2,174 runs, and had 2,213 RBI.

The Yankees played in seven World Series during his 15 years with the team. Ruth hit .326 in 41 World Series games, with 5 doubles, 2 triples, 15 home runs, 37 runs scored, and 33 RBI.

★ Baseball Hall of Fame

Rutherford, Johnny

AUTO RACING
b. March 12, 1938, Ft. Worth, Tex.

Persistence made Rutherford one of the most successful auto racers ever — three-time winner of the Indy 500, third in career earnings with nearly $4 million, fifth in IndyCar victories with 27.

He began racing jalopies in 1959, moved into USAC in 1962, and won the 1965 sprint championship. He had a car for the 1966 Indy 500, but he broke both arms in an April crash and missed the rest of the season. In 1968, he suffered serious burns in a Phoenix crash.

In 1973, at age 35, he joined Team McLaren and won the pole position at Indy with a record speed of 198.413 mph. He finished ninth in the race.

Rutherford won his first Indy 500 in his tenth attempt, in 1974, and he also won the Pocono 500, becoming the fist driver to win two 500-mile races in the same season. Two years later, he won at Indy again.

His best season was 1980. He won the Indy 500 for the third time, had four other victories, finished in the top five 10 times in 12 starts, and won his only IndyCar championship.

In 1986, Rutherford became the oldest driver ever to win a 500-mile race, the Michigan 500.

★ Indianapolis Speedway Hall of Fame

Ryan, Elizabeth ("Bunny")

TENNIS
b. Feb. 5, 1891, Anaheim, Calif.
d. July 6, 1979

Ryan won 19 Wimbledon championships, a record for 45 years. She once said she didn't want to live to see her record broken. Later she said that if it had to be broken, she wanted Billie Jean King to do it "because Billie Jean's got guts."

Both wishes came true. Ryan died the day before King won her twentieth Wimbledon title to break the record.

Ryan wasn't as well known as other tennis players of her era because she never won a major singles championship. But she was one of the greatest doubles players in history.

She and Suzanne Lenglen teamed to win the women's doubles at Wimbledon from 1919 through 1923 and in 1925. Ryan also won the title with five other partners in 1914, 1924, 1926, 1927, 1930, 1933, and 1934. She won mixed doubles championships with five different partners in 1919, 1921, 1923, 1927, 1928, 1930, and 1932.

Ryan won the U.S. women's doubles in 1926 and the mixed doubles in 1933, and she won the French women's doubles championship in 1930 and from 1932 through 1934.

★ International Tennis Hall of Fame

Ryan, Nolan (Lynn Nolan Jr.)

BASEBALL
b. Jan 31, 1947, Refugio, Tex.

Control problems, especially in the early part of his career, and the fact that he played primarily with mediocre teams kept Ryan from having a great won-lost record. But he was still occasionally throwing fastballs at 96 miles an hour in the 1993 season, his last, when he was 46 years old, and he threw a record seven no-hitters, shattering Sandy Koufax's record of four.

Ryan joined the NL's New York Mets late in the 1966 season, spent 1967 in the minor leagues, and returned to the Mets in 1968. Used only sporadically in New York, he was traded to the AL's California Angels in 1971.

The 6-foot-2, 200-pound right-hander became a star in California, combining a fastball often clocked at more than 100 miles an hour with a big, breaking curve. He was 19–6 in his first season, leading the league with nine shutouts and 329 strikeouts in only 284 innings.

He had his only 20-victory seasons in 1973 and 1974, with records of 21–16 and 22–16. Ryan led the AL in strikeouts both years with 383 in 326 innings and 367 in a league-leading 332 innings.

After being limited to 28 starts with a sore arm in 1975, Ryan led the league in strikeouts four years in a row, notching 327 in 1976, 341 in 1977, 260 in 1978, and 223 in 1979, when he also had five shutouts to lead the AL. During that period, though, he averaged more than four walks per game, and his record was only 62–61.

Ryan was traded to the NL's Houston Astros in 1980. He had an 11–10 record in his first season with Houston and was 11–5 in 1981, when his 1.69 ERA led the league. He was the ERA leader again in 1987 at 2.76 but had only an 8–16 record to show for it. He led the league in strikeouts with 270 that year and again with 228 in 1988.

Ryan then signed with the Texas Rangers of the AL as a free agent. He led that league with 301 strikeouts in 1989 and 232 in 1990. A variety of injuries began to bother him in 1991, and he retired after the 1993 season with a record of just 22–20 over his last three years.

In his 23 major league seasons, Ryan had a 324–292 record, an average of about 13½ wins and 12½ losses a year, with 61 shutouts and a 3.19 ERA. He struck out 5,712 hitters and walked 2,795 in 5,386 innings.

Ryan, Tommy [Joseph Youngs]

BOXING
b. March 31, 1870, Redwood, N.Y.
d. Aug. 3, 1948

Ryan had his first professional fight in 1887, and he was undefeated in 31 matches when he faced Mysterious Billy Smith for the world welterweight championship on July 26, 1894, in Minneapolis. Ryan won the title with a 20-round decision.

He claimed the middleweight title when Bob Fitzsimmons vacated it in 1895, but his claim wasn't generally recognized until his 10-round decision over George Green on February 25, 1898, in San Francisco. He then relinquished his welterweight championship to fight as a middleweight.

Ryan retained the title even during a two-year retirement in 1905 and 1906. He returned to the ring for two fights in 1907. His final appearance was an exhibition against Battling Nelson on August 4, 1907.

A clever fighter with a very good left jab, Ryan was often called on as an instructor. He won 85 matches, 68 by knockout; lost 3, 1 by knockout and 1 on a foul; and fought 5 draws, 9 no-decisions, and 6 no-contests.

★ International Boxing Hall of Fame

Ryon, Luann

ARCHERY
b. Jan. 13, 1953, Long Beach, Calif.

Luann Ryon entered the 1976 Olympic Games after shooting a personal-best 2,457 at the Olympic trials. Competing in her first international tournament, she coolly surpassed that with a 2,499 to win the gold medal.

She also won her second international tournament, the 1977 world championship, shooting a 2,515 to set a women's world record. Ryon was the U.S. national champion in 1976 and 1977.

Rypien, Mark R.

FOOTBALL
b. Oct. 2, 1962, Alta.

After graduating from Washington State University in 1986, Rypien was chosen by the Washington Redskins in the sixth round of the NFL draft. He missed all of the 1987 season with a knee injury and was active for just one game in 1988 but didn't play.

The 6-foot-4, 235-pound Rypien became the team's starter during the 1989 season and was named to the Pro Bowl the following year, when he passed for 3,768 yards and 22 touchdowns against only 13 interceptions.

Another knee injury kept him out of action for nearly two months in 1990, but Rypien returned to have his finest year in 1991. He completed 249 of 421 passes for 3,564 yards and 28 touchdowns, throwing just 11 interceptions, and was named NFC player of the year by United Press International. Rypien was also chosen most valuable player in Super Bowl XXVI, when he completed 18 of 33 passes for 292 yards and 2 touchdowns in Washington's 37–24 victory over the Buffalo Bills.

After a long contract dispute, Rypien had a poor season in 1992, throwing 17 interceptions against just 13 touchdown passes. When the Redskins plummeted to a 4–12 record in 1993, he ranked last among the conference's passers.

Through 1993, Rypien had thrown 1,244 completions in 2,207 attempts for 15,928 yards and 101 touchdowns.

Ryun, Jim (James R.)

TRACK AND FIELD
b. April 29, 1947, Wichita, Kans.

Ryun may have been the greatest runner who never won an Olympic medal. The first high school student to break four minutes for the mile, he made the 1964 U.S. Olympic team as a 17-year-old but was eliminated in the semifinals of the 1500-meter run.

As a freshman at the University of Kansas in 1965, he ran a world record 3:55.3 in the mile to beat former world record holder Peter Snell of Australia.

Ryun was the AAU outdoor mile champion from 1965 through 1967, and he won the 1967 NCAA title. He set three world records in 1966, when he won the Sullivan Award as the outstanding amateur athlete of the year. On June 10, he did 1:44.9 in the 880-yard run; on July 8, he ran the 1,500 meters in 3:33.1; and on July 17, he set a record of 3:51.3 in the mile. He lowered the mile record to 3:51.1 on June 23, 1967; that stood for more than five years.

Because of mononucleosis, Jim Ryun missed much of the 1968 season, but he qualified for the Olympic 1,500-meter run and was considered a favorite for the gold medal. Going into the Olympics, he hadn't been beaten in the 1,500 or the mile for more than three years. However, Kip Keino of Kenya set a blistering pace in the Olympic final, and Ryun, tired and tight, had no chance to catch him. Keino's 20-meter margin of victory was the largest in Olympic history.

Ryun retired in 1969 but returned in 1972 for one last attempt at the Olympics. His career came to an abrupt end when he tripped on another runner's heel and was injured during a preliminary heat.

★ National Track & Field Hall of Fame

⋆ ⋆ S ⋆ ⋆

Saari, Roy A.

SWIMMING
b. Feb. 25, 1945, Buffalo, N.Y.

The son of a swimming and water polo coach, Saari grew up in California and starred in both sports as a high school student. At the University of Southern California, he won nine NCAA individual championships, a record at the time.

His titles came in the 200-meter freestyle in 1965 and 1966, the 500-meter and 1,650-meter freestyles from 1964 through 1966, and the 200-meter individual medley in 1964. Saari also swam on two championship relay teams.

Saari won the AAU outdoor 1,500-meter freestyle in 1961 and 1963 and was the indoor champion at 440 yards in 1962, 500 yards in 1963, 1,500 meters in 1962, and 1,650 yards from 1963 through 1965.

The first swimmer to break the 17-minute barrier for 1,500 meters, Saari won gold medals in the 400-meter and 1,500-meter freestyle races at the 1963 Pan-American Games. He won a silver medal in the 400-meter individual medley and was a member of the gold medal 4 x 200-meter freestyle relay team at the 1964 Olympics.

Saberhagen, Bret W.

BASEBALL
b. April 11, 1964, Chicago Heights, Ill.

Saberhagen won the AL Cy Young Award twice, in 1985 and 1989. A right-hander with a good fastball, good slider, and excellent control, he joined the AL's Kansas City Royals in 1984, when he had a 10–11 record.

He became the ace of Kansas City's staff in 1985, going 20–6 with a 2.87 ERA and only 38 walks in 235 innings. After a poor American League championship series, he sparkled in the World Series, winning two games and giving up only one earned run in 18 innings as the Royals beat the St. Louis Cardinals in seven games.

Arm trouble bothered him for the next three years, and he had a 30–28 record over that period, but he came back strong in 1989 to lead the league with 23 victories, a .393 winning percentage, 12 complete games, 262⅓ innings pitched, and a 2.16 ERA.

The arm problem recurred in 1990, when he had a 5–9 record. After going 13–8 in 1991, he was traded to the NL's New York Mets, where he was only 10–12 over the next two seasons. However, he bounced back again with a 14-4 mark and a 2.74 ERA in 1994.

Through the 1994 season, Saberhagen had a 134-94 record, with 16 shutouts. He had struck out 1,470 and walked 388 in 2,074⅔ innings.

Sachs, Leonard

BASKETBALL
b. Aug. 7, 1897, Chicago, Ill.
d. Oct. 27, 1942

Sachs attended the American College of Physical Education and played for the Illinois Athletic Club basketball team that won 32 of 33 games and the AAU national championship in 1918.

He became the coach at Loyola College of Chicago in 1925. He is generally credited with inventing the 2–2–1 zone defense, with one player positioned in front of the basket as a "goaltender."

Loyola won 32 consecutive games under Sachs in 1928–29, and in 1939 the team reached the finals of the National Invitation Tournament but lost, 44–32, to unbeaten Long Island University.

Sachs died of a heart attack shortly before the 1942–43 season opened. In 18 seasons at Loyola, his teams won 224 games and lost 129. While coaching, Sachs also played professional football as an end from 1920 through 1926 with the NFL's Chicago Cardinals, the Milwaukee Badgers, the Hammond Pros, and the Louisville Colonels.

★ Basketball Hall of Fame

Saddler, Sandy (Joseph)

BOXING
b. Feb. 25, 1926, Boston, Mass.

Unusually tall for a featherweight at 5-foot-8½, Saddler had a 70-inch reach and a powerful punch. After winning 16 of 17 amateur bouts, he turned professional on March 7, 1944, winning an 8-round decision over Earl Roys. In his second fight, he was knocked out in the 3rd round by Jock Leslie, the only knockout he ever suffered.

After scoring 56 knockouts in 94 fights, Saddler met Willie Pep for the world featherweight championship on October 29, 1948. It was the first of four fights between the two. Pep was heavily favored, but Saddler won the title with a 4th-round knockout. In a rematch on February 11, 1949, Pep regained the title on a 15-round decision.

Saddler won the vacant junior lightweight championship by decisioning Orlando Zulueta in ten rounds on December 6, 1949, and he regained the featherweight title on September 8, 1950, when Pep failed to come out for the 8th round because of a shoulder injury.

The fourth match, on September 26, 1951, was a brutal brawl. The fighters twice wrestled each other to the floor,

once taking the referee with them. Pep was forced to retire before the 10th round with a bad cut under his eye, which he claimed had been caused by Saddler's thumb. Both were suspended for six months by the New York State Athletic Commission.

Saddler remained champion until failing vision, caused by an auto accident, forced his retirement in January 1957. He won 144 bouts, 103 by knockout; lost 16, 1 by knockout; and fought 2 draws.

★ International Boxing Hall of Fame

St. Clair, Bob (Robert B.)

FOOTBALL
b. Feb. 18, 1931, San Francisco, Calif.

St. Clair was a starting end on the University of San Francisco's undefeated 1951 team. The school dropped football after that season and St. Clair played for the University of Tulsa during his senior year.

In 1953 he joined the NFL's San Francisco 49ers, who moved him to offensive tackle. The 6-foot-9, 265-pound St. Clair was nicknamed "the Geek" by his teammates because he ate raw meat, but he was also respected for his skills and intelligence. He was the team's offensive captain from 1957 until his retirement after the 1964 season.

One of the tallest NFL players during his era, St. Clair set a league record in 1956 by blocking ten field goal attempts. He was named an All-Pro in 1955.

After retiring because of a foot injury, St. Clair became a city councilman in Daly City, California, and was later elected mayor.

★ Pro Football Hall of Fame

Sakamoto, Makoto

GYMNASTICS
b. April 8, 1947, Tokyo, Japan

Sakamoto's family came to the U.S. in 1955, and he began gymnastics two years later. An extremely versatile gymnast, Sakamoto won the national all-around championship from 1963 through 1966 and in 1968 and 1972. He was the parallel bars champion in 1963, 1965, 1966,

1967, and 1968; the still rings champion in 1965 and 1966; the horizontal bar champion in 1965, 1966, 1967, and 1968; the floor exercise champion in 1965 and 1967; the pommel horse champion in 1965 and 1966; and the vault champion in 1965 and 1968.

In 1965, Sakamoto became one of the few gymnasts ever to win the national title in every event. He also won the NCAA Division I all-around, parallel bars, and horizontal bar championships in 1968.

He retired from competition in 1972 and began a career in coaching. Among his students was 1984 Olympic pommel horse champion Peter Vidmar.

Salmon, Timothy J.

BASEBALL
b. Aug. 24, 1968, Long Beach, Calif.

A 6-foot-3, 200-pound outfielder, Salmon was chosen by the AL's California Angels in the 1989 free agent draft while a student at Grand Canyon University in Arizona. He joined the Angels for 23 games at the end of the 1992 season, batting only .177.

He became a starter in 1993 and won the league's rookie of the year award after batting .283 with 31 home runs and 95 RBI. The Angels rewarded Salmon with a multiyear, multimillion-dollar contract.

Sampras, Peter

TENNIS
b. Aug. 12, 1971, Potomac, Md.

Sampras seemingly came out of nowhere in 1990, when he became the youngest man ever to win the U.S. Open men's singles championship just 28 days after his nineteenth birthday. He wasn't even ranked in the world's top ten before his victory, but he finished the year ranked fifth.

Known for his blistering 130-mile-an-hour serve, Sampras began to stalk the world's top ranking in 1992, when he climbed to third behind Jim Courier and Stefan Edberg. He achieved it in 1993, serving 22 aces in a four-set victory over Courier in the Wimbledon singles final.

Sampras dropped to second behind Courier during the month after Wimbledon, but he regained first place with an easy 6–4, 6–4, 6–3 win over France's Cedric Pioline to win his second U.S. Open in September.

Quiet and unassuming, Sampras calmly remarked to the press after his victory, "I just play my tennis, sign my autographs, and do what I have to do."

Sampson, Ralph L., Jr.

BASKETBALL
b. July 7, 1960, Harrisonburg, Va.

The 7-foot-4, 230-pound Sampson was the third player in history to be named player of the year for three years in a row. A center at the University of Virginia, he won the award from 1981 through 1983, scoring 2,228 points and pulling down 1,511 rebounds in 132 games. He also blocked 462 shots.

Sampson was the first player chosen in the 1983 NBA draft, by the Houston Rockets. He was named rookie of the year after scoring 1,722 points, collecting 913 rebounds, and blocking 197 shots. He had a record 13 blocked shots in one game.

The Rockets drafted Hakeem Olajuwon to play center in 1984, and Sampson moved to forward, where he was a success because of a good outside shot and his quickness to the basket. As time went on, however, Sampson became unhappy with the situation, and he was traded to the Golden State Warriors during the 1986–87 season.

Chronic knee problems limited his playing time from that point on, and he was forced to retire after undergoing knee surgery in March 1988.

Sandberg, Ryne D.

BASEBALL
b. Sept. 18, 1959, Spokane, Wash.

A solid hitter with power, base-running ability, and excellent defensive skills as a second baseman, Sandberg emerged as one of baseball's best players during the 1980s. He joined the NL's Philadelphia Phillies briefly in 1981 and was traded to the Chicago Cubs before the following season.

After hitting .271 and .281 in his first two full seasons, Sandberg was named the league's most valuable player in 1984, when he hit .314 with a league-leading 114 runs scored and 19 triples. He also had 19 home runs, 84 RBI, and 32 stolen bases, and he was the league's best-fielding second baseman, with a .993 percentage.

The Cubs lost to the San Diego Padres in the NL championship series that year, but Sandberg hit .368 with 2 RBI and 3 runs scored in the five games.

Sandberg led the league in runs with 104 in 1989 and 116 in 1990, when he also hit a league-leading 40 home runs to go with a .306 average and 100 RBI. After hitting .291 in 1991 and .304 in 1992, with 26 home runs each year, Sandberg was limited to 117 games by a hand injury in 1993; he hit only 9 home runs because of continued pain in the hand.

He announced his retirement early in 1994. Sandberg had a career .290 batting average with 2,080 hits, including 340 doubles, 67 triples, and 240 home runs. He stole 323 bases, scored 1,144 runs, and drove in 881. From June 21, 1989, through May 17, 1990, he went 123 games without an error, a major league record for his position.

Sande, Earle

HORSE RACING
b. Nov. 13, 1898, Groton, S.D.
d. Aug. 20, 1968

Immortalized in a Damon Runyan verse as "that handy / Guy named Sande / Bootin' a winner in," Sande was the outstanding jockey of the 1920s. He won 27 percent of the races he entered, and was in the money more than 60 percent of the time.

The top money winner among jockeys in 1921, 1923, and 1927, Sande won 39 stakes races in 1923, a record for 30 years. Among his victories that year was the Kentucky Derby, aboard 19–1 shot Zev.

Sande spent months in the hospital with a crushed left leg after a fall at Saratoga in 1924. It was thought he might never ride again, but he won his second Kentucky Derby with Flying Ebony the following year.

His riding career again seemed to be over when he retired in 1928 because of weight problems, but he came back in 1930 after losing most of his money in the stock market crash. He won the triple crown with Gallant Fox. Sande retired again in 1931 and operated his own stable for a while, then became a trainer for other owners with moderate success.

He made a final comeback attempt in 1947, riding just one winner before retiring for good. Virtually penniless because of a series of bad investments, Sande was presented with $500 by friends to help ease his retirement.

★ National Horse Racing Hall of Fame

Sanders, Barry D.

FOOTBALL
b. July 16, 1968, Wichita, Kans.

As a junior at Oklahoma State in 1988, Sanders won the Heisman Trophy, the Maxwell Award, and the Walter Camp Award as the outstanding college player of the year. The 5-foot-8, 203-pound running back combined speed, strength, and great cutting ability to gain a record 2,628 rushing yards. He also set NCAA records with 37 rushing touchdowns and 3,249 all-purpose yards.

Sanders gained 222 yards on 29 carries and scored 5 touchdowns in Oklahoma State's 62–14 victory over Wyoming in the Holiday Bowl. That was his last college game, as he elected to enter the NFL college draft after his brilliant junior season.

The Detroit Lions made him the third overall pick in the draft, and he was the NFL's rookie of the year in 1989, when he gained 1,470 yards on 280 carries, a 5.3 average, and scored 14 touchdowns.

Sanders gained more than 1,000 yards in each of his first six professional seasons, and was named to *The Sporting News* All-Pro team from 1989 through 1991 and in 1993. Through 1994, he had gained 8,672 yards in 1,763 attempts, a 4.9 average, and scored 62 rushing touchdowns. He also caught 178 passes for 1,987 yards and 6 touchdowns.

Sanders, Deion L.

BASEBALL, FOOTBALL
b. Aug. 9, 1967, Ft. Myers, Fla.

An often controversial two-sport star, Sanders was a three-time All-American defensive back at Florida State University, from 1986 through 1988, and he also played minor league baseball during the summer of 1988. He was chosen by the Atlanta Falcons in the first round of the 1989 NFL draft.

He made an immediate impact as a cornerback and kick returner, intercepting 5 passes, returning 28 punts for 307 yards and 1 touchdown, and running back 35 kickoffs for 725 yards.

Sometimes called "Neon Deion" because of his flashy style, Sanders was released by the AL's New York Yankees after appearing in 71 games with them in 1989 and 1990, and was signed by the NL's Atlanta Braves. Playing for two teams in the same city has made it easier for him to pursue careers in both baseball and football.

As a part-time outfielder in 1991, the 6-foot-1, 195-pound Sanders batted only .191, but the following season he hit .304, led the league with 14 triples in just 97 games, and stole 28 bases. He also batted .533 and stole 5 bases in the team's seven-game World Series loss to the Toronto Blue Jays. However, many Atlanta fans and most of his teammates were displeased by the fact that he could appear in only four games because he also had a commitment to play for the Falcons.

In 1993 Sanders agreed to remain with the Braves through any post-season games. He batted .276 and stole 19 bases in 95 games that season and reported late to the Falcons after the Braves lost to the Philadelphia Phillies in the league championship series. Despite his late arrival, he led the NFC with 7 interceptions.

Sanders hinted during the 1993 football season that he might decide to concentrate entirely on football after his three-year contract with the Braves expired following the 1994 season. Although a starting defensive back with the Falcons, Sanders has also been used as a wide receiver because of his great speed and breakaway running ability.

Through the 1993 season, Sanders had returned 24 interceptions for 520 yards and 3 touchdowns. As a major league baseball player, he had 220 hits, including 29 doubles, 24 triples, and 23 home runs. He had stolen 65 bases, scored 143 runs, and collected 85 RBI.

Santiago, Benito R.

BASEBALL
b. March 9, 1965, Ponce, P.R.

Santiago joined the NL's San Diego Padres late in the 1986 season and became the team's starting catcher in 1987. He was named rookie of the year after batting .300 with 18 home runs and 79 RBI.

That was the best offensive season of his career. His batting average has ranged from .230 to .270 since then, but his exceptionally strong arm, which allows him to throw to bases while still in the crouch, has made him a standout on defense.

Criticized by some for making too many pickoff throws, Santiago has led the league's catchers in errors five times, and he was the assist leader at the position with 75 in 1988 and 100 in 1991.

Santiago missed parts of the 1990 and 1992 seasons with injuries. He signed with the Florida Marlins as a free agent in 1993. *The Sporting News* named him to the NL all-star team in 1987, 1989, and 1991.

Through 1994, Santiago had a .260 average with 958 hits, including 157 doubles, 23 triples, and 109 home runs. He had scored 396 runs and driven in 466.

Saperstein, Abe (Abraham M.)

BASKETBALL
b. July 4, 1903, London, England
d. March 15, 1966

Although he was only five feet tall, Saperstein competed in baseball, basketball, and track as a high school student but wasn't even given a tryout for the basketball team at the University of Illinois. From 1920 to 1925, he played guard for the semiprofessional Chicago Reds.

In 1926 Saperstein took over management of an all-black team that played in the Savoy Ballroom in Chicago. The team was known as the Savoy Big Five at that time. On January 7, 1927, Saperstein collected $75 for a game in Hinckley, Illinois, the team's first trip outside Chicago.

Saperstein then began aggressively looking for bookings, primarily in Illinois, Michigan, and Ohio. He billed his team first as "Saperstein's New York" and then as "Saperstein's Harlem New York." During the 1930s, they became better known as the Harlem Globetrotters, though their longest trip at the time was to Western Pennsylvania.

The Globetrotters played 150 to 175 games a year during the Depression, winning well over 90 percent of the time. Because they were often involved in one-sided contests, the players began developing the showboating routines that were to make them popular around the world.

The Globetrotters played in the first World Championship Tournament in 1939, losing to the Harlem Renaissance, 27–23, in the second round, but they won the tournament in 1940 by beating the Chicago Bruins of the National Basketball League, 31–29.

After World War II, the Globetrotters did actually trot the globe. They went on a European tour in 1951 and drew a crowd of 75,000 to Olympic Stadium in Berlin. The following year, they took a cruise around the world, playing in Asia and Africa.

Saperstein was turned down in his bid for an NBA franchise in 1961, so he formed the American Basketball League. The league folded after 18 months, and Saperstein, who was its chief financial backer, lost more than $1 million. However, the three-point shot, which originated in the ABL, was adopted by the American Basketball Association in 1967, and is now an important feature of basketball at all levels.

★ Basketball Hall of Fame

Sarazen, Gene [Eugenio Saraceni]

GOLF
b. Feb. 27, 1902, Harrison, N.Y.

A school dropout who became a caddie to help support his family, Sarazen burst onto the professional golf scene in 1922, when he shot a 68 in the final round to win the U.S. Open. Then he won the PGA championship. That set up a much-publicized 72-hole match with the great Walter Hagen, which Sarazen won. He beat Hagen again in the finals of the 1923 PGA championship.

Only 5-foot-4, Sarazen was solidly built and was a remarkably long hitter for his day. He was also a supremely confident competitor in his early years. During the mid-1920s, he went on a series of exhibition tours and seemed to lose his competitive edge for a time. From 1927 through 1932, he did win about 20 tournaments, but no major titles.

Through study of slow-motion films, Sarazen decided he was holding the club too loosely. He developed an extra-heavy club to strengthen his hands during practice, and he also cured his biggest weakness by creating, after much experimentation, the modern sand wedge.

Sarazen shot 70–69–70 in the first three rounds of the 1932 British Open to build up an unbeatable lead, and he won with a record 283. After a slow start in the U.S. Open, he played the last 28 holes in just 100 strokes to win by three shots. He was named Associated Press Athlete of the year.

He won his third PGA championship in 1933, then began exhibition tours again. He missed the first Masters Tournament in 1934 because of a South American tour, but did play it in 1935. Trailing Craig Wood by three shots with only four holes to play, Sarazen holed a wood shot from 220 yards away for a double eagle on the 15th hole, tying Wood; he won the 36-hole playoff handily. Sarazen is one of only four golfers to win all four major professional tournaments.

After World War II, Sarazen became one of television's first golf commentators. For many years, he was given the honor of being the first to tee off at the Masters.

★ PGA Hall of Fame; World Golf Hall of Fame

Saubert, Jean M.

SKIING
b. May 1, 1942, Roseburg, Oreg.

Saubert dominated U.S. women's skiing in 1963 and 1964, winning six of a possible eight national championships, along with two Olympic medals.

She was the national downhill and giant slalom champion in 1963 and 1964, and she also won the slalom and alpine combined in 1964. At the Winter Olympics that year she shared the giant slalom silver medal with Christine Goitschel, and she won a bronze in the slalom.

After graduating from Oregon State in 1964, Saubert retired from competition and did graduate work at Brigham Young University. She later became a teacher and a ski instructor.

Sauer, George H., Sr.

FOOTBALL
b. Dec. 11, 1910, Stratton, Nebr. d. Feb. 5, 1994

An All-American fullback in 1933, the 6-foot, 210-pound Sauer was named outstanding player of the East-West Shrine Game after scoring both touchdowns in the West's 12–0 victory over the East.

Sauer joined the Green Bay Packers of the NFL in 1934 and retired as a player after the Packers won the 1936 league championship. In his three seasons, he gained 656 yards in 190 attempts, a 3.5 average, and scored 6 touchdowns.

In 1938 Sauer became head coach at the University of New Hampshire. His teams there won 21 games, lost 17, and tied 1 in five seasons, including a 6–0–0 record in 1942. He served in the U.S. Navy from 1943 to 1945, then coached the University of Kansas to a 15–2–3 record in 1946 and 1947. Kansas lost to Georgia Tech, 20–14, in the 1948 Orange Bowl.

At the U.S. Naval Academy in 1948 and 1949, Sauer's teams won only 3

games while losing 13 and tying 2. He moved on to Baylor, and had a 38–19–3 record in six seasons there. His teams lost to Georgia Tech, 17–14, in the 1952 Orange Bowl and to Auburn, 33–13, in the 1955 Gator Bowl.

Sauer left coaching after the 1955 season and served as Baylor's athletic director through 1960. He became the first general manager of the New York Titans when the American Football League was established in 1961, and remained with the team after it was reorganized and renamed the Jets in 1963. As director of player personnel, he drafted and signed his son, George Sauer, Jr., who became one of Joe Namath's favorite receivers.

★ College Football Hall of Fame

Sauer, Hank (Henry J.)

BASEBALL
b. March 17, 1917, Pittsburgh, Pa.

Sauer was with the NL's Cincinnati Reds briefly in 1941 and 1942, then entered military service. He returned after World War II to play in 31 games with Cincinnati in 1945. After two more seasons in the minor leagues, Sauer became a starting outfielder with Cincinnati in 1948.

The Reds traded him to the Chicago Cubs during the 1949 season. A right-hander, the 6-foot-4, 199-pounder was named the league's most valuable player in 1952, when he batted .270 with a league-leading 37 home runs and 121 RBI.

Sauer's best season was actually 1954, when he hit .288 with 41 home runs and 103 RBI. An injury limited his playing time in 1955, and the Cubs traded him to the St. Louis Cardinals in 1956. After one season there, he went to the New York Giants. Sauer finished his career with the Giants, then in San Francisco, in 1959.

In 15 seasons, he batted .266 with 1,278 hits, including 200 doubles, 19 triples, and 288 home runs. He scored 709 runs and drove in 876.

Savard, Serge A.

HOCKEY
b. Jan. 22, 1946, Montreal, P.Q.

The first defenseman to win the Conn Smythe Trophy as the outstanding player in the Stanley Cup playoffs, Savard won the award in 1969, when he played brilliantly on defense and scored a goal and an assist in the Montreal Canadiens' four-game final victory over the St. Louis Blues. St. Louis scored only three goals in the series, and Savard was a major reason.

Injuries hampered him throughout his career, but Savard managed to play 1,040 regular season games in 17 NHL years, beginning with the 1966–67 season, when he joined the Canadiens.

After winning the Smythe Trophy, he suffered a badly broken leg during the 1969–70 season. A bone graft was required to repair the fracture, but he missed much of the 1971–72 season after the leg was broken again.

Savard returned to action in February 1972. Shortly afterward, he kicked in a window to save Coach Scotty Bowman from a fire in the St. Louis hotel where the team was staying, and missed the rest of the season because of a four-inch gash in his right ankle.

In 15 seasons with the Canadiens, Savard played on seven Stanley Cup champions. He was traded to the Winnipeg Jets in 1981 and retired after the 1982–83 season.

Savard had 439 points on 106 goals and 333 assists in 1,040 regular season games. He added 19 goals and 49 assists for 68 points in 130 playoff games.
★ Hockey Hall of Fame

Sawchuk, Terry (Terrance G.)

HOCKEY
b. Dec. 28, 1929, Winnipeg, Man.
d. May 31, 1970

When Sawchuk was ten, his older brother Mike died of a heart disease, and Sawchuk inherited his goalie pads. Eight years later he began playing professional hockey in the minor leagues. He joined the NHL's Detroit Red Wings in 1950, and in 1951 he won the Calder Trophy as the league's rookie of the year.

Sawchuk used a strange, gorilla-like crouch, explaining, "When I'm crouching low, I can keep better track of the puck through the players' legs on screen shots."

It was effective. He had a goals-against average of under 2.00 in each of his first five NHL seasons, and he was sensational in Detroit's 1952 Stanley Cup victory. Sawchuk had 4 shutouts and gave up only 5 goals as the Red Wings won all 8 of their playoff games.

Sawchuk was traded to the Boston Bruins in 1955, but Detroit re-acquired him two years later. He went to the Toronto Maple Leafs in 1964, was picked up the Los Angeles Kings in the 1967 expansion draft, returned to Detroit in 1968, and was traded to the New York Rangers in 1969.

Shortly after the end of the 1969–70 season, Sawchuk and Ranger teammate Ron Stewart had a fight at Sawchuk's home in Mineola, New York, and he died of the resulting injuries.

During his 21-year career, Sawchuk had several nervous attacks that caused brief retirements. He also missed more than his share of games with injuries, including a ruptured appendix, punctured lungs, ruptured discs, severed tendons in a hand, a broken instep, and bone chips in his elbows that required three operations.

Sawchuk won the Vezina Trophy as the league's best goaltender in 1952, 1953, and 1955 and shared the trophy with Johnny Bower in 1965. He holds records for most games by a goaltender, 971, and most shutouts, 103. He gave up 2,401 goals in regular season play for a 2.52 goals-against average. In 106 playoff games, he had 12 shutouts and gave up 267 goals for a 2.64 average.
★ Hockey Hall of Fame

Sayers, Gale E.

FOOTBALL
b. May 30, 1943, Wichita, Kans.

Possibly the greatest open-field runner in history, Sayers unfortunately played only four full seasons and parts of three others as a professional. Here is just one measure of his greatness: since the NFL began keeping track of such things in 1963, only four players have scored a touchdown rushing, a touchdown receiving, and a touchdown returning a kick in a single game. Sayers did it three times — twice in 1965 and once in 1967.

An All-American at the University of Kansas in 1963 and 1964, Sayers was the Chicago Bears' first choice in the 1965 NFL college draft. He was an immediate sensation, setting a league record with 22 touchdowns, 14 rushing, 6 on pass receptions, 1 on a punt return, and 1 on a kickoff return. He tied the NFL record with 6 touchdowns against the San Francisco 49ers that year and had 2,272 combined yards.

Sayers was named the league's rookie of the year and an All-Pro. In 1966 he led the NFL in rushing with 1,231 yards and in kickoff returns with an average of 31.2 yards per runback. He averaged an incredible 37.7 yards with 3 touchdowns on just 16 kickoff returns in 1967, when he also rushed for 880 yards.

An injury to his right knee shortened his 1968 season, but he came back to lead the league in rushing again with 1,032 yards in 1969. However, his left knee was severely damaged early in the 1970 season. After two operations, he attempted a comeback in 1971 but was forced to retire.

During his NFL career, Sayers rushed 991 times for 4,956 yards, a 5.0 average, and 39 touchdowns; caught 112 passes for 1,307 yards, an 11.7 average, and 9 touchdowns; returned 28 punts for 391 yards, a 14.0 average, and 2 touchdowns; and ran back 91 kickoffs for 2,781 yards, a 30.6 average, and 6 touchdowns.

★ College Football Hall of Fame; Pro Football Hall of Fame

Schaefer, Jacob, Sr.

BILLIARDS
b. Feb. 2, 1855, Milwaukee, Wis.
d. March 9, 1909

Nicknamed the "Wizard," Schaefer was so good at old style straight-rail billiards, in which a player was allowed to "nurse" the balls near a cushion to score repeatedly, that new games were invented, among them 14.2, 18.1, and 18.2 balkline billiards.

Schaefer's greatest display of skill came in a championship match against J. F. B. McCleery in 1890, when he had a run of 3,000 to win, 3,004–15. He retired from competition after a surprising victory over Willie Hoppe at 18.2 balkline in 1908.

His son, Jacob Jr., was an 11-time world champion and Hoppe's chief competitor during the 1920s and 1930s.

Schalk, Raymond W.

BASEBALL
b. Aug. 12, 1892, Harvel, Ill.
d. May 19, 1970

The 5-foot-9, 165-pound Schalk was a remarkably durable player. He caught 108 or more games in 12 of his first 13 full seasons in the major leagues. After joining the AL's Chicago White Sox late in the 1912 season, Schalk became the team's starter the following year.

Never much of a hitter, Schalk was remarkably adept at handling the trick pitches that most of the White Sox pitchers threw, including the spitball, emery ball, and shine ball, all legal at the time. He was the first catcher to back up first base regularly on infield grounders, he was very intelligent at calling games, and he had an exceptional throwing arm.

Schalk caught 140 games for a pennant winner in 1917 and batted a respectable .273 in Chicago's six-game World Series victory over the New York Giants. He hit .304 in the 1919 World Series against the Cincinnati Reds, but the White Sox lost the series in eight games.

It was later revealed that eight members of the team were probably involved in a fix. Schalk and other White Sox players were shocked by the allegation, but he turned down $40,000 for a magazine article to tell his version of the "Black Sox scandal." He never talked much about the sordid incident.

In 1927 Schalk became Chicago's playing manager, but he appeared in only 16 games that year. He resigned under pressure in July 1928 and got a position as a coach with the New York Giants the following year, when he played in the last five games of his career.

Schalk later worked as a scout and

minor league manager, operated a bowling alley in Chicago, and was an assistant baseball coach at Purdue University.

He had a career average of only .253, but he caught a record four no-hitters and retired with a record of 1,810 assists. Schalk led AL catchers in fielding percentage in 1915, 1916, 1920, 1921, and 1922.

★ Baseball Hall of Fame

Schayes, Dolph (Adolph)

BASKETBALL
b. May 19, 1928, New York, N.Y.

A 6-foot-9 forward, Schayes was deadly with a two-hand set shot from the corner. When his defender guarded him closely to stop that shot, Schayes would fake it and drive past him to the basket.

As a senior, he led New York University to a 22–4 record in 1948. NYU reached the finals of the National Invitation Tournament that year but lost to St. Louis University. Schayes then joined the Syracuse Nationals of the National Basketball and was named rookie of the year.

The NBL merged with the NBA in 1949, and the Nationals moved to Philadelphia in 1963 and became known as the Warriors. Schayes spent just one season in Philadelphia. When he retired after the 1963–64 season, he held NBA records for games played, 1,059; points, 19,249; and free throws, 6,979. Schayes played in a record 706 consecutive games from 1952 to 1961, and he once made 50 consecutive free throws.

A tough competitor, Schayes hated to miss a game. He suffered a broken right wrist in 1952 and continued to play while wearing a cast. "The cast made me work on my left-handed shots, which soon improved," he said. "Later, when the left wrist was cracked, my right-handed shots improved."

He coached the Philadelphia 76ers and from 1963–64 through 1965–66 and the Buffalo Braves in 1970–71. He was replaced after just one game in the 1971–72 season. The NBA coach of the year in 1966, Schayes had a 151–172 record as a coach.

In his 16 seasons as a player, Schayes scored 19,249 points in 1059 games, an average of 18.2. He was among the ten players named to the NBA's Silver Anniversary team in 1971.

★ Basketball Hall of Fame

Schemansky, Norbert

WEIGHTLIFTING
b. May 30, 1924, Detroit, Mich.

The only weightlifter ever to win four Olympic medals, Schemansky was the middle heavyweight champion in 1952. As a heavyweight, he won a silver medal in 1948 and bronze medals in 1960 and 1964. He was also the gold medalist as a heavyweight at the 1955 Pan-American Games.

Schemansky won nine AAU national championships, in the middle heavyweight division from 1951 through 1953 and as a heavyweight in 1949, 1954, 1957, 1962, 1964, and 1965. He was the world middle heavyweight champion in 1951, 1953, and 1954.

He set a world record of 362 pounds in the snatch during a 1952 competition, and in 1964 he became the first American to lift a total of 1,200 pounds.

Schembechler, Bo (Glenn E. Jr.)

FOOTBALL
b. April 1, 1929, Barberton, Ohio

Schembechler was a starter at offensive tackle for Miami University of Ohio, coached by "Woody" Hayes, in 1950. After serving as an assistant coach at several colleges, including a five-year stint with Hayes at Ohio State University, Schembechler became head coach at Miami in 1963.

His teams won 40 games, lost 17, and tied 3 in six seasons before he was hired by the University of Michigan in 1969. He was consensus coach of the year in his first season, when Michigan won 8 of 11 games and ended a 22-game Ohio State winning streak with a 24–12 upset.

Michigan won the Big Ten championship and went to the 1970 Rose Bowl, but Schembechler suffered a heart attack in Pasadena and missed the game, a

10–3 loss to the University of Southern California.

Schembechler was *The Sporting News* coach of the year in 1985, when Michigan was ranked second in the country with a 10–1–1 record, which included a 27–23 victory over Nebraska in the Fiesta Bowl.

His teams generally featured a big offensive line, a powerful running attack, and strong defense. Of the 25 All-Americans coached by Schembechler in his 22 seasons at Michigan, 9 were offensive linemen and 13 were defensive players.

Schembechler, who underwent open heart surgery in 1976, retired from coaching after the 1989 season. He had a 194–48–5 record at Michigan and was 234–65–8 overall. His 234 victories is sixth among all-time NCAA Division 1 coaches and his .775 winning percentage ranks eighteenth. Despite his great record in regular season play, Schembechler won only 5 of 17 bowl games.

Schmidt, Ernie (Ernest J.)

BASKETBALL
b. Feb. 12, 1911, Nashville, Kans.
d. Sept. 6, 1986

A four-year starter at Kansas State College in Pittsburg, Kansas (now Pittsburg State University), Schmidt won the nickname "One Grand" because he scored exactly 1,000 points during his college career. He led the All-Arkansas Valley Conference in scoring three times.

After graduating in 1929, Schmidt played AAU basketball with the Denver Piggly Wiggly and Reno Creameries teams, and he was a second-team all-AAU choice at center in 1932. He later officiated Big Eight and Missouri Valley Conference games for many years.
★ Basketball Hall of Fame

Schmidt, Joseph P.

FOOTBALL
b. Jan. 18, 1932, Pittsburgh, Pa.

A series of injuries limited Schmidt's effectiveness at the University of Pittsburgh, and he wasn't chosen until the seventh round of the 1953 NFL college draft, when the Detroit Lions selected him.

The 6-foot, 222-pound Schmidt was so impressive in training camp that the Lions traded veteran linebacker Dick Flanagan to make room for him, and Schmidt became the team's starting middle linebacker.

He starred at the position for 13 seasons. A feared blitzer in passing situations, he could also overpower blockers to make the tackle on running plays, and he was fast enough to cover tight ends and backs. Running back John Henry Johnson once complained about Schmidt, "He is *always* in the way."

An All-Pro in 1954, 1955, 1956, 1957, 1958, 1959, 1961, and 1962, Schmidt tied with Philadelphia quarterback Norm Van Brocklin for the Associated Press athlete of the year award in 1960. He retired after the 1965 season with 24 interceptions, which he returned for 294 yards and two touchdowns.

Schmidt coached the Lions to a 43–34–7 record from 1967 through 1972. His 1970 team won 10 and lost 4 games during the regular season, but was defeated by Dallas, 5–0, in the first round of the playoffs.
★ Pro Football Hall of Fame

Schmidt, Mike (Michael J.)

BASEBALL
b. Sept. 27, 1949, Dayton, Ohio

With his combination of power hitting and defensive ability, Schmidt may have been the greatest third baseman in baseball history. He won a record eight NL home run titles, three most valuable player awards, and ten Gold Gloves, second only to Brooks Robinson.

The 6-foot-2, 205-pound Schmidt joined the Philadelphia Phillies late in the 1972 season and played all four infield positions in 1973, when he was terrible offensively. He struck out 136 times in just 367 at-bats and hit only .196.

Playing winter ball in Puerto Rico after that season, Schmidt "found a swing that made things happen," as he put it. He led the league with 36 home runs and a .546 slugging percentage while hitting a respectable .282 in 1974.

Schmidt was the league leader with 38 home runs each of the next two years and he led in walks with 120 in 1979. He won his first most valuable player award in 1980, when he had a league-leading 48 home runs, 121 RBI, and .624 slugging percentage. In Philadelphia's six-game World Series victory over the Kansas City Royals, Schmidt batted .381 with 2 home runs and 7 RBI.

He repeated as MVP in the strike-shortened 1981 season, when he hit 31 home runs, scored 78 runs, had 91 RBI, and earned a .644 slugging percentage to lead the league in each category. Schmidt led in home runs again with 40 in 1983 and 36 in 1984, when he also had a league-leading 106 RBI.

In 1986 Schmidt was named MVP for the third time, again winning the home run title with 37 and also leading the league with 119 RBI and a .547 slugging percentage. After he reached 35 home runs and 113 RBI in 1987, Schmidt was limited to 108 games because of injuries. He announced his retirement during the 1989 season, when he was hitting only .203.

Schmidt had a career batting average of .267 with 2,234 hits, including 408 doubles, 59 triples, and 548 home runs. He scored 1,506 runs and had 1,595 RBI. He is seventh all-time in career home runs.

Schmidt, Milton C.

HOCKEY
b. March 5, 1918, Kitchener, Ont.

Red Storey, an NHL official who frequently saw Schmidt play, once said, "I'd take five Milt Schmidts, put my grandmother in the nets, and we'd beat any team." Art Ross, who coached him for years, said, "Schmidt was the fastest playmaker of all time. By that I mean no player ever skated at full tilt the way he did and was still able to make the play."

A center, Schmidt joined the NHL's Boston Bruins in 1936. He spent three years in the Royal Canadian Air Force in World War II, then rejoined the Bruins in 1945. A three-time first-team All-

Star, he led the league in scoring with 52 points on 20 goals and 32 assists in 1940, and he won the Hart Trophy as the league's most valuable player after the 1950–51 season.

For years, beginning in the minor leagues, Schmidt was on the "Kraut Line" with Bobby Bauer and Woody Dumart. Although Dumart was of French ancestry, the line was so named because all three players were from the Kitchener-Waterloo area in Ontario, where the population was primarily of German origin.

Because of his all-out, high-speed style of play, he was often hurt, but he never missed a game if he could possibly play. During one Stanley Cup series, his knees were so badly injured that he couldn't bend them. He lay on the trainer's table to have his legs taped from ankle to thigh, and then was lifted off the table and into his skates.

Schmidt took over as Boston's coach during the 1954–55 season and retired as a player. He coached through the 1960–61 season, returned during the 1962–63 season, and remained through 1965–66. Schmidt was the team's general manager from 1967 until his retirement in 1972.

In 778 regular season games, Schmidt scored 575 points on 229 goals and 346 assists. He had 24 goals and 25 assists for 49 points in 86 playoff games.

★ Hockey Hall of Fame

Schoendienst, Red (Albert F.)

BASEBALL
b. Feb. 2, 1923, Germantown, Ill.

An outstanding fielder at second base, Schoendienst was the ideal number two hitter. A switch-hitter who choked up on the bat, he was skilled at the hit and run from either side of the plate, and he was also an excellent bunter.

He joined the NL's St. Louis Cardinals in 1945 and batted .281 for a pennant-winning team in 1946, when he led the league's second basemen in fielding percentage for the first of six times. Schoendienst hit only .233 in the Cardinals' seven-game World Series win over the Boston Red Sox, but he scored three runs.

He led the league in doubles with 43 in 1950 and batted a career high .342 in 1953, when he hit 15 home runs and scored 107 runs. During the 1956 season, the Cardinals traded him to the New York Giants.

Meanwhile, the Milwaukee Braves had been searching in vain for a second baseman for several years. They acquired Schoendienst early in the 1957 season and won their first pennant. Schoendienst led the league with 200 hits and earned a .309 average, and he batted .278 when Milwaukee beat the New York Yankees in a seven-game series.

Milwaukee won the pennant again in 1958. Bothered by illness and injury, Schoendienst hit only .262 in 105 games that season, but he batted .300 and scored five runs in the World Series, a seven-game loss to the Yankees.

Shortly after the season ended, it was discovered that Schoendienst had tuberculosis. He spent most of 1959 in treatment, playing in only five games, and returned as a part-time player in 1960. The Braves traded him back to St. Louis in 1961. He became a coach in 1963, his last season as a player, when he had only five at-bats, all as a pinch hitter.

Schoendienst was named St. Louis manager in 1965. He guided the Cardinals to two consecutive pennants — in 1967, when they won the World Series, and in 1968. He was replaced after a fifth-place finish in 1976. After coaching for the Oakland Athletics for two years, Schoendienst returned to the Cardinals as a coach. He served as interim manager for parts of the 1980 and 1990 seasons.

In 2,216 games, Schoendienst had a .289 average on 2,449 hits, including 427 doubles, 78 triples, and 84 home runs. He scored 1,223 runs and had 773 RBI. As a manager, he had a 1,041–955 record for a .522 winning percentage.
★ Baseball Hall of Fame

Schollander, Donald A.
SWIMMING
b. April 30, 1946, Charlotte, N.C.

Schollander was the first swimmer to win four gold medals at one Olympics, but his career almost ended before it really began. He grew up in Lake Oswego, Oregon, where he was the top swimmer in his age group for two years before spending a month in bed with pneumonia when he was 11.

When he began swimming again, he could no longer win races because he had moved into a higher age group. Discouraged, he wanted to give up. But his father told him, "You can quit swimming if you want to, but it will be when you're at the top of your age group, not the bottom."

In 1962 Schollander tied the world record of 2:00.4 in winning the AAU national outdoor 200-meter freestyle. He also won that event in 1963, 1964, 1966, and 1967. Schollander was the outdoor 100-meter champion in 1964, 1966, and 1967, and he won the 400-meter freestyle in 1966. He was the indoor 200-yard champion five years in a row, 1963 through 1967, and the 500-yard champion in 1964.

Shortly after graduating from high school, Schollander won individual gold medals in the 100-meter and 400-meter freestyles at the 1964 Olympics, setting a world record of 4:12.2 in the 400-meter. He was also the anchor swimmer on the gold medal 4 x 100-meter and 4 x 200-meter freestyle relay teams. He might have won more medals but was unaccountably left off the 4 x 100-meter medley relay team, and his best event, the 200-meter freestyle, was not on the Olympic program that year.

Schollander won the 1964 Sullivan Award as the nation's outstanding athlete and was named male athlete of the year by the Associated Press. He enrolled at Yale University after the Olympics and won one NCAA championship, the 200-yard freestyle, in 1968.

After winning a gold medal in the 4 x 200-meter freestyle relay and a silver in the 200-meter freestyle at the 1968 Olympics, Schollander announced his retirement, saying, "I'm finished with water — in fact, I may not take a bath or a shower for another two years." During his career, he had set eight world records in the 400-meter freestyle and nine in the 200-meter event.

★ International Swimming Hall of Fame; Olympic Hall of Fame

Scholz, Jackson V.

TRACK AND FIELD
b. March 15, 1897, Buchanan, Mich.
d. Oct. 26, 1986

A member of three U.S. Olympic teams, in 1920, 1924, and 1928, Scholz won a gold medal in the 200-meter dash in 1924, tying the Olympic record of 21.6 seconds. He also won a gold in 1920 as a member of the world record–setting 4 x 100-meter relay team, and he won a silver in the 100-meter dash in 1924.

While a student at the University of Missouri, Scholz set world indoor records for the 70-yard dash, at 7.2 seconds, and the 75-yard dash, at 7.6 seconds, in 1920.

Scholz tied the world record of 10.5 seconds for the 100-meter dash and set a new world record of 20.9 seconds for the 200-meter dash in 1920. He tied his own 200-meter record nine years later, in his last season of competition.

A journalism major in college, Scholz wrote many young adult stories and novels about sports. He appeared as a character in the 1981 movie *Chariots of Fire*, which was loosely based on events surrounding the 1920 Olympics.

★ National Track and Field Hall of Fame

Schommer, John J.

BASKETBALL
b. Jan. 19, 1884, Chicago, Ill.
d. Jan 11, 1960

The first athlete to win 12 letters at the University of Chicago, Schommer participated in track and field and played end for football teams that won Western Conference (now Big Ten) championships in 1905, 1907, and 1908.

But basketball was his best sport. A 6-foot-1 center, he led the conference in scoring three straight seasons, from 1906–07 through 1908–09, and once scored 15 field goals in a game, an as-

tounding feat in an era when two teams combined often didn't score that many. In 1908 Schommer scored a desperation 80-foot shot with time running out to defeat the University of Pennsylvania. Chicago lost only four basketball games during his four years as a starter.

Schommer coached basketball at the University of Chicago in 1910–11 while doing graduate work. In 1912 he became a professor, coach, and athletic director at the Illinois Institute of Technology. He also served as a basketball and football official for many years, calling NFL games from 1942 through 1944.

★ Basketball Hall of Fame

Schriner, Sweeney (David)

HOCKEY
b. Nov. 30, 1911, Calgary, Alta.
d. July 6, 1990

Schriner began playing professional hockey in 1933, and he joined the NHL's New York Americans in 1934. He won the Calder Trophy as the league's outstanding rookie for the 1934–35 season.

In 1935–36 Schriner scored 45 points on 19 goals and 26 assists to win the Art Ross Trophy as the league's leading scorer, and he repeated with 21 goals and 25 assists for 46 points in 1936–37.

The Americans traded Schriner to the Toronto Maple Leafs in 1939, and he helped lead Toronto to the 1942 Stanley Cup. Schriner retired after the 1943–44 season but returned to the Maple Leafs because of the World War II manpower shortage, and he played for the 1945 Stanley Cup champions.

Schriner retired in 1946. He scored 410 points on 206 goals and 204 assists in 484 regular season games and added 18 goals and 11 assists for 29 points in 60 playoff games.

★ Hockey Hall of Fame

Schroth, Clara M.

GYMNASTICS
b. Oct. 5, 1920, Philadelphia, Pa.

During her years as a competitive gymnast, Schroth worked as a secretary and trained at night at the Philadelphia Turnverein. The top American woman gymnast of her time, she won 39 national championships in the 12-year period from 1941 through 1952.

Schroth was the national all-around champion in 1945, 1946, and from 1949 through 1952. She also won national titles in flying rings in 1946 and from 1948 through 1951; in free calisthenics (now floor exercise), 1944 through 1946, 1948, and 1950 through 1952; in parallel bars, 1946, 1949, 1950, and 1952; and in side horse, 1944, 1945 (tie), 1948, 1949, 1951, and 1952.

Schroth was a member of the 1948 U.S. Olympic team that won a bronze medal in combined exercises, and she competed on the 1952 Olympic team before retiring. Schroth was also a track and field athlete; she won the standing broad jump at the 1945 AAU indoor championship meet.

Schulte, Wildfire (Frank M.)

BASEBALL
b. Sept. 17, 1882, Cohocton, N.Y.
d. Oct. 2, 1949

A solid hitter and fine defensive center fielder, Schulte joined the NL's Chicago Cubs late in the 1904 season and became a starter in 1905. Injuries troubled him for his first several years, but he led the league with 13 triples in 1906 and with 10 home runs in 1910, when he hit .301.

Schulte was named the NL's most valuable player in 1911. He batted .300 that year and had a league-leading 21 home runs, 107 RBI, and .534 slugging percentage. His home run total was the highest in the twentieth century up to that time and the fourth highest in major league history.

He then settled back into a good but not outstanding career. The Cubs traded him to the Pittsburgh Pirates during the 1916 season, and the Pirates sent him to Philadelphia the following year. Schulte retired after spending the 1918 season with the AL's Washington Senators.

A left-handed hitter and right-handed thrower, the 5-foot-11, 170-pounder had a .270 career average with 1,766 hits, including 288 doubles, 124 triples, and 92 home runs. He stole 233 bases, scored 906 runs, and had 792 RBI.

Schultz, David L.

WRESTLING
b. June 6, 1959, Palo Alto, Calif.

The national freestyle and Greco-Roman 163-pound champion in 1977, Schultz enrolled at Oklahoma State University that fall. He transferred to UCLA the following year after his brother, Mark, entered that school as a freshman. In 1979 they both transferred to the University of Oklahoma because UCLA had dropped wrestling.

The NCAA 163-pound champion in 1982, Schultz won the world championship in 1983 and the AAU national title in 1984. He easily won a gold medal at the 1984 Olympics, taking one match by a fall and winning the other five by a combined score of 42 to 2. A day later, Mark won the 180.5-pound championship.

Schultz won a bronze medal in the 1985 world championships and silver medals in 1986 and 1987, when he won another national title and also took the gold medal in his weight class at the Pan-American Games. He retired from competition after failing to make the 1988 Olympic team.

Schulz, Germany (Adolph G.)

FOOTBALL
b. April 19, 1883, Ft. Wayne, Ind.
d. April 14, 1951

The University of Michigan played 51 games during Schulz's career. He played every minute in 50 of them. In his final game, against Pennsylvania in 1908, Schulz injured his hip, was kneed in the abdomen, and hurt his hand. Yet he kept playing until, with ten minutes left, the referee called time out and ordered him to leave the game .

The 6-foot-4, 245-pound Schulz was a pioneer of modern center play. Because he had enormous hands, he could snap the ball one-handed, and he was one of the first centers to use the spiral pass. During his first two years as a starter, there was no neutral zone between the offensive and defensive linemen. Schulz developed the technique of dropping off the line on defense and moving laterally to follow the play.

Schulz had to miss the 1906 season because he took a job to earn his tuition money. He returned in 1907 and was a consensus All-American. Walter Camp left him off the 1908 All-American team but named Schulz to his all-time team in 1910. Schulz was also listed as the center on all-time All-American teams selected by Grantland Rice in 1939, Harry Stuldreher in 1940, and Jim Thorpe in 1942.
★ College Football Hall of Fame

Schwab, Frank J. ("Dutch")
FOOTBALL
b. 1895, Madera, Pa.
d. Dec. 11, 1965
Schwab graduated from high school in 1912 and worked in coal mines until World War I, when he served as a sergeant in the Army. He played for a service team, where Coach Jock Sutherland of Lafayette College saw him. He persuaded Schwab to enroll.

The 5-foot-11, 180-pounder was an All-American guard in 1921 and 1922, and he captained the squad as a senior. Lafayette won all nine of its games in 1921 and went 7–2–0 in 1922. In Schwab's four seasons as a starter, the school had a 27–7–2 record.
★ College Football Hall of Fame

Schwartz, Marchy (Marchmont H.)
FOOTBALL
b. March 20, 1909, New Orleans, La.
Named after a thoroughbred horse, Schwartz was a two-time All-American as a triple-threat halfback at Notre Dame. After spending his freshman year at Loyola University in New Orleans, he transferred to Notre Dame in 1928 and wasn't eligible to play football that season.

The 5-foot-11, 178-pounder played frequently on the 9–0–0 team in 1929 and became a full-time starter under Knute Rockne in 1930, when he helped lead Notre Dame to a second straight perfect season. Schwartz had touchdown runs of 25, 28, 40, 54, and 60 yards in the course of the year.

Rockne died in a plane crash in the off-season and was replaced by "Hunk" Anderson in 1931. Notre Dame's undefeated streak went to 26 before a 16–14 loss to the University of Southern California. Schwartz played a brilliant game against Carnegie Tech, rushing for 188 yards on 23 attempts, including touchdown runs of 58 and 60 yards.

Schwartz served as an assistant coach at Notre Dame while studying for a law degree, then assisted Clark Shaughnessy at the University of Chicago. As head coach at Creighton University from 1935 through 1939, Schwartz had a 19–22–2 record.

He rejoined Shaughnessy as an assistant coach at Stanford in 1940 and succeeded him as head coach in 1942, when the school had a 6–4–0 record. Stanford dropped football for the duration of World War II, but Schwartz returned from 1946 through 1950. He had a 28–28–4 record in his six seasons for an overall record of 47–50–6.
★ College Football Hall of Fame

Schwartzwalder, Ben (Floyd B.)
FOOTBALL
b. June 2, 1909, Pt. Pleasant, W.Va.
d. April 28, 1993
A center at the University of West Virginia, Schwartzwalder coached high school football after graduating in 1933, then served as an Army officer during World II.

He became head coach at Muhlenberg College in 1946 and had a 25–5–0 record in three seasons, including a victory over St. Bonaventure University in the 1946 Tobacco Bowl.

Schwartzwalder went to Syracuse University in 1949 to revive a moribund program. He was soon successful, producing a 7–2–0 team in 1952 and the school's first bowl bid. However, Alabama devastated Syracuse, 61–6, in the Orange Bowl.

In 1959, the American Football Coaches Association named Schwartzwalder coach of the year for producing a national champion with 10–0–0 regular season record. That team gave Schwartzwalder his first bowl victory in four appearances, beating Texas 23–14 in the Cotton Bowl.

Schwartzwalder's successful teams always featured a strong running attack, with talented backs behind a powerful offensive line. Among the outstanding runners he produced were Jim Brown, Ernie Davis, Floyd Little, Jim Nance, and Larry Csonka.

As a product of the "Black Power" movement, Schwartzwalder was pressured in 1971 to hire a black assistant coach. When he refused, all of Syracuse's black players left spring practice, and Schwartzwalder suspended them. Partly because of that problem, he was forced out of his job after the 1973 season. In 25 seasons at Syracuse, he had a 153–93–3 record and was 178–96–3 overall.

★ College Football Hall of Fame

Score, Herbert J.

BASEBALL
b. June 7, 1933, Rosedale, N.Y.

Score arrived on the major league scene like a meteor and unfortunately disappeared almost as quickly. A 6-foot-2, 185-pound left-hander who could throw as hard as any pitcher in history, he was named the AL's rookie of the year in 1955 after compiling a 16–10 record for the Cleveland Indians and leading the league in strikeouts with 245 in only 227⅓ innings.

He led the league with 5 shutouts and 263 strikeouts in 249⅓ innings in 1956, when he had a 20–9 record and a 2.53 ERA. The Boston Red Sox offered Cleveland $1 million for Score after the season, but Cleveland turned down the bid.

Early in the 1957 season, Gil McDougald of the New York Yankees rifled a line drive that shattered bones around Score's left eye. He missed the rest of the season, and although he rejoined the Indians in 1958, he never pitched successfully again.

After he struggled to a 9–11 record with a 4.71 ERA in 1959, Score went to the Chicago White Sox. He won only 6 games while losing 12 with Chicago before retiring during the 1962 season. Since 1968, Score has been Cleveland's play-by-play radio announcer.

He had a 55–46 career record with 11 shutouts and a 3.36 ERA. Score struck out 837 hitters and walked 573 in 858⅓ innings.

Scott, Barbara Ann

FIGURE SKATING
b. May 9, 1928, Ottawa, Ont.

At the age of ten, Scott was the youngest skater ever to pass Canada's gold figures test and, at 12, she finished second in the Canadian seniors championship. She won the title in 1944–46 and 1948. In 1947 she became the first North American skater to win a world singles championship, and she repeated in 1948.

The free-skating portion of the 1948 Olympic figures competition was skated on ice that had been badly rutted by two hockey games earlier in the day. Eileen Seigh of the United States, who skated before Scott, gave her a thorough description of the ice surface which helped her turn in a nearly flawless performance to win the gold medal. She and Dick Button of the U.S., who won the men's singles, ended a long period of European supremacy in the sport.

★ Canadian Sports Hall of Fame

Scott, Mike (Michael W.)

BASEBALL
b. April 26, 1955, Santa Monica, Calif.

A right-handed pitcher, the 6-foot-3, 215-pound Scott joined the NL's New York Mets in 1979 and was traded to the Houston Astros in 1983. He was an ordinary journeyman until he learned to throw the split-fingered fastball during spring training in 1985.

That pitch, which looks like an ordinary fastball but breaks sharply down just as it reaches the plate, transformed Scott into an overpowering pitcher. He had an 18–8 record with a 3.29 ERA in 1985 and won the league's Cy Young Award in 1986. He had an 18–10 record and led the NL with 5 shutouts, 306 strikeouts in 275⅓ innings, and a 2.22 ERA.

The Astros faced the New York Mets in the 1986 league championship series.

Scott had a 2–0 record, giving up just 1 earned run and striking out 19 in 18 innings, but the Mets beat Houston in six games.

Scott went 16–13 in 1987 and 14–9 in 1988, then led the league in victories with a 20–10 record in 1989. Arm trouble began to bother him in 1990 when he was just 9–13, and he retired after losing his only two starts in 1991.

In 13 seasons, he had a 124–108 record, with 22 shutouts and a 3.54 ERA. He struck out 1,469 hitters and walked 627 in 2,068⅔ innings.

Scott, Smackover (Clyde L.)

FOOTBALL, TRACK & FIELD
b. 1926, La.

His nickname described Scott's running style, but it came from the town where he went to high school, Smackover, Arkansas. In 1944 Scott was a freshman at the U.S. Naval Academy, and after a year of service, he entered the University of Arkansas in 1946. A starter for three years, he was an All-American halfback as a senior in 1948, and he was also the first player in the school's history to be named to the All-Southwest Conference team three years in a row.

Scott joined the NFL's Philadelphia Eagles in 1949, and after being traded to the Detroit Lions during the 1952 season, he retired from football. In his four years as a professional, he carried the ball 100 times for 400 yards, scoring 2 touchdowns, and caught 19 passes for 381 yards, a 20.1 average, and 4 touchdowns.

The 6-foot, 175-pound Scott had sprinter speed. Running for Navy, he won the IC4A 120-yard hurdles in 1945, and he was the NCAA 110-meter hurdle champion in 1948. He also won a silver medal in the Olympic event that year.
★ College Football Hall of Fame

Scott, Steven M.

TRACK AND FIELD
b. May 5, 1956, Upland, Calif.

Running for the University of California at Irvine, Scott won the NCAA Division II 1,500-meter championship from 1975 through 1977. Scott reached world-class status in 1977, when he ran an indoor 3:56.5 to finish second in an international race, finishing ahead of John Walker of New Zealand. He later beat Filbert Bayi of Tanzania and Steve Ovett of Great Britain in the Jamaica invitational 1,500-meter run.

Scott was the national outdoor 1,500-meter champion from 1977 through 1979 and in 1982, 1983, and 1986. He finished first in the 1,500-meter at the 1980 Olympic trials, but the U.S. boycotted the Moscow Games that year. Scott set American records of 3:48.68 in the mile and 3:31.96 in the 1,500-meter in 1981. The following year he lowered his American record in the mile to 3:47.69, and he set an American record of 4:54.71 in the rarely run 2,000-meter.

After winning a silver medal in the 1,500-meter run at the 1983 world championships, Scott took the lead in the third lap of the race at the 1984 Olympic Games but ran out of gas and finished dead last.

His final major championship came in the 1986 national outdoor 1,500-meter run. Scott was only the second athlete in history to run the mile in less than 4 minutes more than 100 times.

Seagren, Bob (Robert L.)

TRACK AND FIELD
b. Oct. 17, 1946, Pomona, Calif.

After winning a gold medal in the Olympic pole vault in 1968, Seagren was embroiled in controversy at the 1972 Olympics: he had vaulted a world best 18–5¾ that year using a carbon pole, and the IAAF ruled shortly before the Olympics that the pole was illegal.

Seagren and other vaulters protested, and the ban was lifted four days before competition was to begin. However, the night before the qualifying round, the IAAF once again posed the ban, and "illegal" poles were confiscated. Forced to vault with an unfamiliar pole, Seagren managed to win a silver medal with a vault of 17–8½.

The 6-2, 195-pound Seagren attended the University of Southern California. He won the NCAA outdoor championship in 1967 and 1969, was the AAU outdoor champion in 1966, 1969, and 1970, and won a gold medal at the 1967 Pan-American Games.

At the 1968 Olympics, Seagren astounded everyone by passing when the bar was at 17 feet, 6¾ inches. He was unfamiliar with the metric system used in international competition, and he thought that 5.35 meters was relatively low. However, he cleared 17–8½ and won the gold medal; he had the fewest misses.

Seagren set his first world record, 17–5½, on May 14, 1966. After that mark was broken, he set another record of 17–7 on June 10, 1967. That was also broken, but Seagren reclaimed the world record with a vault of 17–9 at the 1968 Olympic trials.

A knee injury and subsequent operation sidelined him for the second half of 1970 and all of 1971. While he was out of action, new world records were set several times. On May 23, 1972, Seagren cleared a record 18–4¼, becoming the first American to vault over 18 feet.

Seagren turned professional in 1973 and won the first televised Superstars competition that year. He also won the first World Superstars competition in 1976.

★ National Track & Field Hall of Fame

Sears, Dick (Richard D.)

TENNIS
b. 1861, Boston, Mass.
d. April 8, 1943

The bespectacled Sears had an unsurpassed record in national championship play. He entered 14 tennis championship events and won 13 of them.

Sears grew up watching his older brother, Fred, and second cousin, James Dwight, play tennis on one of the first courts laid out in the U.S., on a lawn in Nahant, Massachusetts. He began playing with Dwight in his early teens.

The first U.S. national tournament was held in Newport, Rhode Island, in 1881. Sears won the singles title without losing a set. He surprised his opponents by going to the net to volley at every opportunity. He later wrote, "All I had

to do was to tap the balls, as they came over, first to one side and then the other, running my opponent all over the court."

Sears and Dwight entered the doubles but lost in an early round. However, Sears won the singles and doubles titles the next six years in a row, from 1882 through 1887. Dwight was his doubles partner each year except 1885, when Sears teamed with Joseph S. Clark to win the championship.

A neck injury forced his retirement in 1888, but he recovered sufficiently to win the first U.S. court tennis championship in 1892.

★ International Tennis Hall of Fame

Sears, Eleonora R.

TENNIS, SQUASH
b. Sept. 28, 1881, Boston, Mass.
d. March 26, 1968

In 1910 a magazine article proclaimed Sears "the best all-around athlete in American society." The daughter of a wealthy shipping and real estate tycoon, she bred, trained, and rode show horses for most of her adult life. She was also an excellent golf, tennis, and squash player; she was among the first women to race a car and fly a plane; and she was the first person to swim the 4½ miles from Bailey's Beach to First Beach in Newport, Rhode Island.

Sears once skippered a yacht that beat Alfred Vanderbilt's *Walthra*, and at one time or another she played baseball and football, skated, and raced speedboats.

On a bet, Sears in January 1912 usurped a traditional male role by driving a four-in-hand down Fifth Avenue. Later that year, she wore breeches to play for an otherwise all-male polo team, spurring a California women's club to pass a resolution: "Such unconventional trousers and clothes of the masculine sex are contrary to the hard and fast customs of our ancestors. It is immodest and wholly unbecoming a woman, having a bad effect on the sensibilities of our boys and girls."

Sears probably laughed at that. A member of the highest social set, at night she played a traditional female role, wearing elegant gowns and dancing at balls. During his visit to Boston in 1924, the Prince of Wales was so charmed by Sears that he spent most of the night as her dancing partner.

Although many of her feats were inspired by dares or bets, Sears was very serious about tennis and squash. She won the U.S. women's doubles tennis championship with Hazel Hotchkiss Wightman in 1911 and 1915 and with Molla Bjurstedt Mallory in 1916 and 1917. Sears and Willis E. Davis won the mixed doubles title in 1916, and she was twice a finalist for the national singles championship. In 1928, when she was 46, she won the national women's squash title.

In her later years, Sears became known for her long-distance walks. Her best time for an annual 47-mile walk from Providence to Boston was 9 hours, 53 minutes, and she once walked from Newport to Boston, 73 miles, in 17 hours. During a visit to France she walked 42½ miles from Fontainebleu to the Ritz Bar in Paris in 8½ hours.

★ International Tennis Hall of Fame; International Women's Sports Hall of Fame

Seau, Junior (Tiaina Jr.)

FOOTBALL
b. Jan. 19, 1969, American Samoa

One of several Samoans who became football stars during the 1980s, Seau is a fast, agile, 6-foot-3, 250-pounder who was an All-American linebacker at the University of Southern California in 1989.

He was chosen by the San Diego Chargers in the first round of the 1990 NFL draft and immediately became a starting inside linebacker. Seau was named to *The Sporting News* All-NFL team in 1992 and 1993, and he played in the Pro Bowl from 1991 through 1994.

In his first five professional seasons, Seau had intercepted 2 passes, returning them for 51 yards, and had recorded 17.5 quarterback sacks.

Seaver, Tom (Thomas E.)

BASEBALL
b. Nov. 17, 1944, Fresno, Calif.

"Tom Terrific" was the first genuine superstar for the New York Mets. The 6-foot-1, 205-pound right-handed pitcher joined the team in 1967 and had a 16–13 record with a 2.76 ERA. After a 16–12 mark and a 2.20 ERA in his second season, Seaver helped pitch the Mets to the NL pennant and World Series championship in 1969.

He led in victories and winning percentage with a 25–7 record to win his first Cy Young Award. He was also named male athlete of the year by the Associated Press. Seaver had a 1–0 record in the league championship series and was 1–1 with a 3.00 ERA when the Mets beat the Baltimore Orioles in a five-game World Series.

Seaver had a league-leading 2.82 ERA and 283 strikeouts in 1970 and led in both categories again in 1971, when he had a 1.76 ERA and 289 strikeouts. He won his second Cy Young Award in 1973, going 19–10 and leading the league with 18 complete games, 251 strikeouts, and a 2.08 ERA.

The Mets beat the Cincinnati Reds in the league championship series, Seaver winning 1 of 2 games and giving up just 3 earned runs while striking out 17 in 16⅔ innings. He was 0–1 in 2 starts, despite a 2.40 ERA, in a seven-game World Series loss to the Oakland Athletics.

After an 11–11 mark in 1974, Seaver won his third Cy Young Award in 1975. He led the league in victories with a 22–9 record and in strikeouts with 243 that season, and he was the strikeout leader again with 235 in 1976, though his record dropped to 14–11.

Seaver was outspoken in his criticism of Mets' management in 1977 and he was sent to the Cincinnati Reds during the season in a controversial trade that angered New York fans. He finished the year with a combined 21–6 record and a league-leading 7 shutouts.

He never had another 20-victory season, but he led the NL with a .727 winning percentage and 5 shutouts in 1979, when he had a 16–6 mark. In the strike-shortened 1981 season, Seaver's 14 victories against only 2 losses led the league, as did his .875 winning percentage.

Suffering from arm trouble in 1982, Seaver was only 5–13. He returned to the Mets and had a 9–14 record in 1983, then enjoyed two effective seasons with the AL's Chicago White Sox, compiling marks of 15–11 in 1984 and 16–11 in 1985. He retired after slipping to 7–13 with the White Sox and the Boston Red Sox the following year.

Seaver used powerful leg drive to throw a hard fastball and sharp-breaking slider. He followed through so strongly that his right knee often scraped the mound. Pinpoint control and the ability to outsmart hitters were just as important to his success.

In 20 seasons, Seaver had a 311–205 record with 61 shutouts and a 2.86 ERA. He struck out 3,640 hitters and walked only 1,390 in 4,782⅔ innings. On April 22, 1970, Seaver struck out ten batters in a row, a major league record, and tied a record with 19 strikeouts in 9 innings against the San Diego Padres. He ranks fourth all-time in career strikeouts and eighth in shutouts.

★ Baseball Hall of Fame

Sedran, Barney (Bernard)

BASKETBALL
b. Jan. 18, 1891, New York, N.Y.
d. Jan. 14, 1969

Only 5-foot-4 and 118 pounds, Sedran was a starting guard for three seasons at the City College of New York, leading the school in scoring each year and serving as captain during his senior season. He began a 35-year career as a professional player and coach after graduating in 1912.

An amazing outside shooter, Sedran scored 34 points for Utica in a 1913 New York State League game, hitting 17 field goals from 25 to 30 feet away with baskets that had no backboards.

In 13 years as a player, Sedran performed for 15 different teams, often playing simultaneously for two or more teams in different leagues. He led a Carbondale, Pennsylvania, team to 35 con-secutive victories in 1914–15, and also played for the Philadelphia Jaspers and New York Whirlwinds, one of the top independent teams of the early 1920s. For two seasons, Sedran was the top scorer for the Whirlwinds, where he teamed with the 5-foot-7½ Marty Friedman in the backcourt. The pair were nicknamed the "Heavenly Twins."

Sedran finished his playing career with the Cleveland Rosenblums, who won the first American Basketball League championship in 1926. He coached professional teams through 1946. Among them were Kate Smith's Celtics, the New York Gothams, the Brooklyn Jewels, and the Wilmington Bombers, who won ABL titles in 1941 and 1942.

Late in his life, Sedran reminisced about the early days of pro basketball: "Ninety percent of the fellows I played with had broken noses. A good 50 years ago, it was more like hockey than basketball. If a fellow couldn't play defense, he couldn't draw a uniform. It was rough, maybe too rough."

★ Basketball Hall of Fame

Seidler, Maren

TRACK AND FIELD
b. June 11, 1952, Brooklyn, N.Y.

Competing in the shotput for the first time in 1966, before she turned 14, Seidler set a national age group record with a distance six feet farther than any other competitor.

Seidler dominated the U.S. women's shotput for more than a decade, winning national championships in 1967, 1968, and from 1972 through 1980. In 1967, at age 15, she was the youngest athlete ever to win the national title in any track and field event.

In 1974 Seidler set her first U.S. record with a distance of 56 feet, 7 inches. She eventually extended that to 62-7¾ in 1979. The record was broken in 1987, but it remains the second best by an American woman.

Seles, Monica

TENNIS
b. Dec. 2, 1973, Novi Sad, Yugo-slavia

Seles received her early tennis instruction from her father, who taught her the unorthodox two-handed approach on both the forehand and backhand. As a young teenager, she was sent to the Bollettieri Tennis Academy in Florida.

Because Seles was such an aggressive player, the other female students refused to practice with Seles, so she was matched against boys, among them Jim Courier and Andre Agassi.

Seles turned professional in 1987. She won her first major title, the French Open singles, in 1990, and the following year she supplanted Steffi Graf as the best woman player in the world. Seles won seven of the next nine grand slam singles championships: the Australian Open from 1991 through 1993 and the French Open and U.S. Open in 1991 and 1992.

On April 30, 1993, Seles was sitting on a bench during a changeover at a tournament in Hamburg, Germany, when a fan stabbed her in the back with a nine-inch knife. The fan later told police that he wanted to disable Seles so Graf could regain the world's top ranking.

The injury was at first expected to keep Seles out of action for only four weeks, but she didn't play again that year, and there was speculation that the psychological damage might have been greater than the physical damage.

Selmon, Lee Roy

FOOTBALL
b. Oct. 20, 1954, Eufaula, Okla.

The 6-foot-3, 250-pound Selmon was a consensus All-American as a defensive tackle in 1975, when he won the Outland Trophy and Lombardi Award as the outstanding college lineman of the year. A three-year starter at the University of Oklahoma, he played for teams that won 43 games while losing only 2 and tying 1.

The first player chosen in the 1976 NFL college draft, by the Tampa Bay Buccaneers, Selmon quickly established himself as a dominant defensive player. Although listed as a defensive tackle, he often moved to end or played as a standup outside linebacker to take advantage of his great speed and agility.

A consensus All-Pro for six straight seasons from 1979 through 1984, Selmon was named defensive player of the year by the Associated Press and *The Sporting News* in 1979, and was chosen as defensive lineman of the year by the NFL Players Association in 1980 and 1981. He retired after the 1985 season.

Since retiring, Selmon has been active in volunteer work with the Special Olympics and the United Negro College Fund Sports Committee. His brothers, Dewey and Lucious, also played at Oklahoma and in the NFL.

★ College Football Hall of Fame; Pro Football Hall of Fame

Sewell, Joseph W.

BASEBALL
b. Oct. 9, 1898, Titus, Ala.
d. March 6, 1990

Sewell played baseball at the University of Alabama and entered professional ball after graduating in 1920. He spent most of the season with a minor league team in New Orleans.

The Cleveland Indians, fighting for the AL pennant, suffered a tragic loss when shortstop Ray Chapman died after being hit in the head by a pitch. They paid New Orleans $8,000 for Sewell, who hit .329 during the last 22 games. Cleveland won the pennant and the World Series.

When he first arrived in the major leagues, Manager Tris Speaker advised him, "Just try to get a piece of the ball." Sewell was better at that than anyone in baseball history.

The 5-foot-6½ 155-pounder, a left-handed hitter, choked up on a heavy 40-ounce bat and it was virtually impossible to strike him out. In 7,132 official at-bats he struck out only 114 times, a record for a player with 14 or more seasons. He also set a major league record for fewest strikeouts in a season, with 4 in 1925, when he had 608 at-bats. He tied that in 1929, when he had 578 at-bats.

Sewell batted .353 in 1923 and led the AL with 45 doubles in 1924, when he hit .316. He had averages of .336, .324, .316,

.323, and .315 during the next five seasons. He dropped to .289 in 1930 and was released by the Indians.

During his last two seasons with Cleveland, Sewell had played mostly at third base, and he remained at that position with the New York Yankees. He batted .302 in 1931, then had a .272 average and a career high 11 home runs in 1932, when the Yankees won the pennant. Sewell hit .333 in their four-game victory over the Chicago Cubs in the World Series.

He retired as a player after hitting .273 in 1933, then was a coach with the Yankees for two years. He later served as a major league scout and as baseball coach at his alma mater.

In 20 seasons, Sewell had a .312 average, with 2,226 hits, including 436 doubles, 68 triples, and 49 home runs. He scored 1,141 runs and had 1,055 RBI. From late 1922 until early 1930, he played in 1,103 consecutive games, a record at the time.

★ Baseball Hall of Fame

Shantz, Bobby (Robert C.)

BASEBALL
b. Sept. 26, 1925, Pottstown, Pa.

Shantz, a clever left-handed pitcher, won the American League's most valuable player award with the Philadelphia Athletics in 1952, when he had a 24–7 record pitching for a fourth-place team that was only 79–75. He led the league in victories and winning percentage and had a 2.48 ERA.

He joined the Athletics in 1949 and had an 18–10 record for them in 1951. A sore arm limited him to 16 games in 1953 and only 2 in 1954. After going 5–10 in 1955, Shantz became primarily a relief pitcher; he had 9 saves the following year.

Philadelphia traded him to the New York Yankees in 1957, when he had a fine season as a spot starter and occasional reliever. Shantz led the league with a 2.45 ERA and had an 11–5 record with 5 saves.

He went to the NL's Pittsburgh Pirates in 1961 and split the 1962 season between the Houston Astros and the St. Louis Cardinals. Shantz retired after a 2–5 record in 1964 with St. Louis, the Chicago Cubs, and the Philadelphia Phillies.

The 5-foot-6, 142-pound Shantz was an excellent fielder. He won Gold Gloves eight years in a row, four in the AL, from 1957 through 1960, and four in the NL, from 1961 through 1964.

In 16 seasons, Shantz had a 119–99 record with 48 saves, 15 shutouts, and a 3.38 ERA. He struck out 1,072 hitters and walked 643 in 1,935⅓ innings.

Sharman, Bill (William W.)

BASKETBALL
b. May 25, 1926, Abilene, Tex.

After serving in the Navy during World War II, Sharman enrolled at the University of Southern California in 1946 and played baseball, basketball, and tennis; he was also on the college boxing, track and field, and weightlifting teams.

Sharman was named an All-American guard in 1950 after averaging 18.6 points a game. Chosen by the Washington Capitals in the NBA draft, the 6-foot-1, 190-pound Sharman played baseball as an outfielder in the Brooklyn Dodger farm system that summer.

Sharman averaged 12.2 points a game with Washington. In 1951 the Washington franchise folded, and its players went into a special dispersal draft. Sharman was chosen by the Ft. Wayne Pistons but refused to report, and was traded to the Boston Celtics. After averaging 10.7 points a game as a backup in 1951–52, Sharman became a starter the following season.

Through 1960–61, Sharman teamed with Bob Cousy to form the best backcourt combination in the league. After Bill Russell arrived during the 1955–56 season, the Celtics got their fast break going effectively, and Sharman averaged more than 20 points a game for three seasons. An excellent shooter, he was a pioneer in pulling up to take the undefended jump shot on the fast break rather than automatically going to the basket for a layup.

Sharman was also one of the best free

throw shooters in history. He led the NBA in free throw percentage seven times and had streaks of 50 and 56 consecutive free throws. His 88.3 percent on 3,143 out of 3,557 attempts was the league record for years.

After playing for NBA championship teams in 1957, 1959, 1960, and 1961, Sharman left the Celtics to become player-coach of the Los Angeles Jets in the American Basketball League. The franchise folded after only 19 games, and Sharman took over the Cleveland Pipers, guiding them to the ABL championship.

Sharman coached California State University–Los Angeles to a 27–20 record in two seasons, then went to the NBA's San Francisco Warriors in 1966. He left San Francisco for the Los Angeles franchise in the American Basketball Association in 1968, and in 1970 he shared the ABA's coach of the year honors.

The team moved to Utah in 1971, and Sharman left after one season there to take over the NBA's Los Angeles Lakers in 1971. He guided the Lakers to a 69–13 record and the league championship in his first season, and was named the NBA's coach of the year. The Lakers won Pacific Division titles each of the next two seasons, then slipped to 5th- and 4th-place finishes, and Sharman left coaching to become the team's general manager. He later served as president of the Lakers until retiring in 1988.

Sharman scored 12,665 points in 711 regular season NBA games, an average of 17.8, and had 2,779 rebounds and 2,101 assists. He added 1,446 points, 285 rebounds, and 201 assists in 78 playoff games, averaging 18.5 points a game. As a coach, Sharman had a 43–26 record in the ABL, a 133–113 record in the ABA, and a 333–240 record in the NBA.
★ Basketball Hall of Fame

Sharpe, Sterling
FOOTBALL
b. April 6, 1965, Chicago, Ill.

An All-American at the University of South Carolina in 1967, Sharpe was chosen in the first round of the NFL's 1968 college draft by the Green Bay Packers. He was the seventh player chosen.

The 6-foot-1, 205-pound Sharpe led the NFC with 90 receptions for 1,423 yards and 1 touchdown in his second season. After catching 67 passes in 1990 and 69 in 1991, he set an NFL record with 106 catches in 1992, when he also led with 1,461 yards and 13 touchdown receptions. Sharpe broke his own record the following season, catching 112 passes for 1,274 yards and 11 touchdowns.

Although not exceptionally fast, Sharpe has great moves that make him difficult to cover, and his strength and leaping ability often allow him to take passes away from defensive backs when he is covered. Through the 1994 season, Sharpe had started 112 consecutive regular season games, despite a painful "turf toe" injury and damaged Achilles tendon in 1993.

In his seven professional seasons, Sharpe has caught 595 passes for 8,134 yards and 65 touchdowns.

Shaughnessy, Clark D.
FOOTBALL
b. March 6, 1892, St. Cloud, Minn. d. May 15, 1970

Once called "football's man in motion" by the Associated Press because he changed jobs so often, Shaughnessy played tackle, end, and fullback at the University of Minnesota for Coach Henry L. Williams, and he assisted Williams for one season after graduating in 1914.

In 1915 Shaughnessy became head coach at Tulane University in New Orleans, compiling a 57–28–7 record in 11 seasons, from 1915 through 1920 and from 1922 through 1925. His last team won nine games and tied one, but the college president rejected an invitation to the Rose Bowl. Angered, Shaughnessy moved on to nearby Loyola of the South, where his first team won all ten of its games. He remained there through 1932, compiling a 48–18–5 record.

Shaughnessy then became the University of Chicago's second football coach, replacing the legendary A. A. Stagg in

1933. He had an 18–33–4 record there before the school dropped football after the 1939 season.

More important, he also served as a consultant to the Chicago Bears, who used a primitive version of the T formation. Shaughnessy worked with George Halas of the Bears to develop the modern T, featuring a hand-to-hand snap from center to quarterback and skillful ballhandling.

Sid Luckman of Columbia University became the first modern T formation quarterback in 1939. Shaughnessy installed the system at Stanford University the following season. After Stanford finished second in the nation with a 9–0–0 record in 1940 and the Bears demolished the Washington Redskins 73–0 in the NFL championship game, many teams began adopting the formation.

After a 6–3–0 record in 1941, Shaughnessy left Stanford for the University of Maryland. He spent one season there, moving to the University of Pittsburgh in 1943, but returned to Maryland in 1946.

Shaughnessy was an assistant coach with the NFL's Washington Redskins in 1947, and he took his only professional head coaching job with the Los Angeles Rams the following year. In two seasons, his teams won 14 games, lost 7, and tied 3. The Rams won the 1949 Western Division title but lost to the Philadelphia Eagles, 14–0, in the league championship game.

In 1950 Shaughnessy returned to Chicago as a consultant to the Bears. He was actually the defensive coordinator, but he wasn't given that title. The man who had invented the modern T formation now devised sophisticated defenses to stop it. Chicago's defensive schemes under Shaughnessy emphasized having linebackers reading and reacting to offensive keys that tip off where the play is going, along with "combo" pass defenses combining man-to-man and zone principles.

Shaughnessy retired after the 1962 season but returned to coach the University of Hawaii in 1965. His overall college coaching record was 149 wins, 106 losses, and 14 ties.

★ College Football Hall of Fame

Shaw, Buck (Lawrence T.)
FOOTBALL
b. March 28, 1899, Mitchelville, Iowa
d. March 19, 1977

A tackle at the University of Notre Dame, Shaw played on Knute Rockne's first unbeaten team in 1919. After graduating in 1922, he was an assistant at North Carolina State, the University of Nevada, and Santa Clara University, where he took over as head coach in 1936.

Shaw had a 47–10–4 record in seven seasons at Santa Clara. His 1937 team was unbeaten, allowing just under 70 yards per game to opposing teams. Santa Clara won two straight Sugar Bowls over Louisiana State, 21–14 in 1937 and 6–0 in 1938.

In 1945 Shaw coached the University of California at Berkeley to a 4–5–1 record. He then took over the San Francisco 49ers in the new All-American Football Conference. The AAFC folded after the 1949 season, but the 49ers entered the NFL along with the Cleveland Browns and Baltimore Colts.

Despite a fine 71–39–4 record in eight seasons, Shaw was fired after the 49ers went 7–4–1 in 1954. He then took on the challenge of building another team from scratch at the new U.S. Air Force Academy, where he was named athletic director and head football coach in 1955. The academy fielded its first football team in 1956, and Shaw had a 9–8–2 record in two seasons there.

Shaw returned to pro football with the Philadelphia Eagles in 1958, then retired after the Eagles beat the Green Bay Packers, 17–13, for the 1960 NFL championship. Shaw had an overall 60–23–7 record as a college coach and a 90–55–2 record with pro teams.

★ College Football Hall of Fame

Shaw, Timothy A.
SWIMMING
b. Nov. 8, 1957, Long Beach, Calif.

One of the few athletes to win Olympic medals in two different sports, Shaw peaked as the world's best freestyle swimmer in 1974 and 1975. At the 1974 AAU national outdoor meet, he set world records of 1:51.6 in the 200-meter, 3:54.6 in the 400-meter, and 15:31.6 in the 1,500-meter freestyle, becoming only the second man to hold world records in those three events.

Shaw won gold medals in the 200-, 400-, and 1,500-meter freestyles, and he was a member of the gold medal 4 x 200-meter freestyle relay team at the 1975 world championships, lowering his world record to 3:53.9 in the 400-meter. He also repeated as the AAU outdoor 400-meter champion and won the indoor 200- and 500-yard titles.

The winner of the 1975 Sullivan Award as the nation's outstanding amateur athlete, Shaw entered Long Beach State University that year and won NCAA titles in the 500-yard freestyle in 1976 and 1977 and in the 1,650-yard freestyle in 1976. In 1976 he won his first two Olympic medals, both silver, in the 400-meter freestyle and as a member of the 4 x 200-meter freestyle relay team.

Shaw retired from competitive swimming after the 1977 season but later became a member of the U.S. water polo team that won the gold medal in the 1983 Pan-American Games and a silver medal at the 1984 Olympics.

Shaw, Wilbur (Warren Wilbur)
AUTO RACING
b. Oct. 13, 1902, Shelbyville, Ind.
d. Oct. 30, 1954

Shaw became famous in the Midwest by running countless dirt and board track races, winning a lot of them. After suffering a fractured skull in 1923, he began using a crash helmet. Other drivers were scornful but, after Shaw survived when he was thrown from his car and landed squarely on his head, helmets were made mandatory.

Shaw was the co-owner of his Indy 500 entry, the "Pay Car," in 1936. He placed seventh that year but won the race in 1937. Then he went to Europe to compete and discovered the Maserati.

He brought one back and won the Indy 500 twice more, in 1939 and 1940, becoming the first driver to win the race twice in a row. He was in the lead after five laps in 1941 when the wheel hub broke and he fractured three vertebrae in the crash. That and World War II ended his career as a driver.

After the war, Shaw persuaded Tony Hulman to buy the Indianapolis Speedway to keep it from being demolished for industrial development. Shaw himself became president and general manager and oversaw the track's rejuvenation. He was killed in a private plane crash.

★ Indianapolis Speedway Hall of Fame

Shea, Jack (John A.)
SPEED SKATING
b. Sept. 10, 1910, Lake Placid, N.Y.

The first American athlete to win two gold medals in a single Winter Olympics, Shea won the North American overall speed skating championship in 1929 and the U.S. national overall title in 1930.

He took leave from Dartmouth College to compete in the 1932 Winter Olympics in his hometown, where he was a hero when the games began, reciting the Olympic oath on behalf of all 306 competitors. Shea won the 500-meter race by 5 yards over Bernt Evensen of Norway. He was trailing in the 1,500-meter race when the leader, Herb Taylor of the U.S., fell, and Shea went on to win by 8 yards.

Shea competed little after his Olympic victories but became town manager of Lake Placid. He was a member of the Olympic organizing committee when the Winter Games returned to Lake Placid in 1980.

Sheehan, Patty (Patricia L.)
GOLF
b. Oct. 27, 1956, Middlebury, Vt.

The daughter of the 1956 U.S. Olympic ski coach, Sheehan was one of the top skiers in her age group when she was 13. She began playing golf when her family moved to Nevada in 1967. Sheehan won four straight Nevada amateur titles, from 1975 through 1978, and was the California amateur champion in 1978 and 1979.

Sheehan joined the LPGA tour in 1981 and was named rookie of the year. Her first victory came in the Mazda Japan Classic in 1981. She was named player of the year in 1983, when she won four tournaments, including the LPGA championship. Sheehan defended that title in 1984 and also won the 1984 Vare Trophy for fewest strokes per round.

After tying Julie Inkster in the last round of the 1991 U.S. Women's Open, Sheehan won the playoff by shooting a 72 to Inkster's 74 for her third major championship and twenty-ninth overall.

The winner of more than $200,000 for 11 consecutive years, an LPGA record, Sheehan earned more than $1 million faster than any other woman golfer. She achieved that in 1985, after playing only 115 tour events.

Sheehan has often been honored for her charitable work. She founded Tigh Sheehan, a house in northern California where education, counseling, and a home environment are provided for troubled teenage girls. ("Tigh" is Gaelic for "house.") She was one of eight athletes featured on the 1987 "Sportsman of the Year" cover by *Sports Illustrated;* all eight were honored for their contributions to society.

Sheehan won the U.S. Women's Open for a second time in 1994. Through that year, she had 33 tournament victories, tenth on the all-time list, and she was fourth all-time in winnings, with $4,442,299.

★ LPGA Hall of Fame

Sheffield, Gary A.

BASEBALL
b. Nov. 18, 1968, Tampa, Fla.

The minor league player of the year in 1988, Sheffield joined the AL's Milwaukee Brewers late that season and was labeled a can't-miss prospect. Although the 5-foot-11, 190-pound right-hander was a shortstop in the minors, Milwaukee moved him to third base in 1989.

Sheffiield spent much of that season on the disabled list, batting only .247, but hit .294 in 1990. He missed much of the 1991 season with an injury and was traded to the NL's San Diego Padres, where he fulfilled his promise in 1992, leading the league with a .330 average, hitting 33 home runs, and driving in 100 runs. He was named the league's player of the year by *The Sporting News.*

During the 1993 season, San Diego began to release high-priced players to reduce its payroll and Sheffield went to the expansion Florida Marlins. Through 1994, he has a .284 career average with 101 home runs with 384 RBI in 667 major league games.

Shell, Arthur

FOOTBALL
b. Nov. 26, 1946, Charleston, S.C.

A Little All-American as an offensive and defensive tackle at Maryland State–Eastern Shore College in 1967, Shell was a third-round choice of the Oakland Raiders in the American Football League's 1968 college draft.

He spent 16 seasons with the Raiders, in Oakland and Los Angeles, and played for two Super Bowl champions, after the 1976 and 1980 seasons. The 6-foot-5, 285-pound offensive tackle was an All-American Football Conference selection in 1974, 1975, and 1977. He appeared in eight Pro Bowls.

Shell started 142 consecutive games from the first game of his rookie year until he suffered a knee injury shortly before the 1979 season and was forced to miss five games. He retired after appearing in only eight games in 1982, then became an assistant coach with the Raiders.

After the team lost three of its first four games in 1989, Shell replaced Art Shanahan as head coach, becoming the second black coach in NFL history (the first was "Fritz" Pollard, in the early 1920s). He guided the Raiders to a 7–5 record over the rest of the season. In 1990 the team was 12–4 during the regular season; they went to the American Football Conference championship game and were overwhelmed, 51–3, by the Buffalo Bills.

Through 1994, Shell had a 53–39 record as head coach.

★ Pro Football Hall of Fame

Shelton, Everett F.

BASKETBALL
b. May 12, 1898, Cunningham, Kans.
d. April 16, 1974

Shelton served in the Marine Corps during World War I and then enrolled at Phillips College in Oklahoma, the school that produced Pro Football Hall of Famer Steve Owen. He played baseball, basketball, and football at Phillips, graduating in 1923.

After a year as a high school coach, Shelton became coach of all major sports at his alma mater. His basketball teams won 48 games and lost 29 in three seasons, and he then began coaching AAU teams, including Sterling Milk, Cripes Bakery, and the St. Joseph Boosters Club. During that period, many companies offered jobs to good players and used their AAU teams as a form of promotion, especially in the Midwest.

Shelton returned to high school coaching from 1929 to 1933, then went back to AAU basketball with the Denver Safeways, who won the AAU national championship in 1937. He left Denver in 1938 for the Antlers Hotel team.

In 1939 Shelton was hired as a baseball, basketball, and golf coach at the University of Wyoming, eventually concentrating on basketball. His 1943 team won the NCAA tournament and finished third in the AAU national tournament.

Except for the 1943–44 season, when the university dropped basketball and Shelton guided the Dow Chemical AAU team, he was at Wyoming through the 1958–59 season, compiling a 328–200 record and winning eight conference championships.

Shelton went to Sacramento State College in 1959, compiling a 188–188 record in ten seasons there. He retired from coaching in 1968. He had an overall record of 850–437, including 494–347 as a college coach.

Generally credited as an originator of the five-man weave offense, Shelton conducted basketball clinics in Europe and the Far East in the early 1950s. He was commissioner of the Far West Conference from 1969 until his death.

★ Basketball Hall of Fame

Sheppard, Melvin W.

TRACK AND FIELD
b. Sept. 5, 1883, Almonesson Lake, N.J.
d. Jan. 4, 1942

Sheppard had dreamed of becoming a New York City police officer, but was rejected because of a supposed heart problem. Within the next ten years he won five Olympic medals, including four golds, set two world records, ran on four world-record relay teams, and won five national championships in the 800-meter run.

His specialty was the 800-meter/880-yard run, where he liked to take the lead early and stay there. He won that way at the 1908 Olympics, where he also scored a surprise victory in the 1500-meter run by catching and passing world record holder Harold Wilson 15 yards from the finish. Sheppard set world records in both wins, running 1:52.8 in the 800-meter and 4:03.4 in the 1500-meter. He also ran a leg on the winning 1600-meter relay team.

At the 1912 Olympics, Sheppard finished second in the 800-meter to Ted Meredith. It was one of the closest races in history, with the first four finishers all under world record time. Sheppard was again on the 1600-meter relay team, which set a world record of 3:16.6.

Sheppard was the AAU 800-meter champion from 1906 through 1908 and in 1911 and 1912. He was a member of the national 2-mile relay team in 1910 and the 1-mile and 1600-meter relay teams in 1911. All three teams set world records.

★ National Track and Field Hall of Fame

Sherrill, Jackie W.

FOOTBALL
b. Nov. 28, 1944, Duncan, Okla.

An offensive fullback and defensive linebacker at the University of Alabama, Sherrill graduated in 1967 and served as an assistant coach at several schools before taking over as head coach at Washington State University in 1976.

He had a 3–8–0 record in just one season there before going to Pittsburgh University in 1977. Sherrill's Pittsburgh teams went 50–9–1 over five seasons, and his 1983 squad was ranked second in the nation.

In 1981 Sherrill became athletic director and head coach at Texas A & M University. The hiring brought a great deal of criticism because Sherrill's reported salary of $267,000 was higher than that of the university's president.

He brought success on the field, as Texas A & M won three straight Southwest Conference championships, from 1985 through 1987. However, the program was put on probation for a number of recruiting violations, and Sherrill was forced to resign after the 1988 season.

Sherrill spent two years away from football, then went to Mississippi State University in 1991. It was another controversial hiring. Billy Brewer, coach of archrival University of Mississippi, called Sherrill "a habitual liar," but Sherrill got revenge with a 24–9 victory in the annual confrontation and ended the season with a 7–5–0 record.

In his first five seasons at Mississippi State, Sherrill guided the school to a 33–24–0 record and three bowl appearances. His overall mark through the 1994 season is 138–69–2.

Sherring, Billy (William)

TRACK AND FIELD
b. 1887, Hamilton, Ont.
d. Sept. 6, 1964

Sherring was determined to enter the 1906 Olympics and convinced that he could win the marathon. A railway brakeman, he saved money for the trip but came up short. The Hamilton, Ontario, Athletic Club raised $75 for the cause, but that wasn't enough either. So Sherring gave the money to a bartender, who bet on a horse for him. The horse won, paid 6–1, and Sherring sailed to Athens.

The 1906 Games are known as the "intercalated" Olympics because they were held to celebrate the tenth anniversary of the first modern Olympics, and therefore fell in a non-Olympic year.

Sherring and William Frank of the U.S. ran together for the first 18 miles of the marathon. Then Sherring said, "Well, good-bye, Billy," put on a burst of speed, and took such a commanding lead that he was able to walk part of the way to the finish line. He set a world record of 2:51:23.6.

When he returned to Hamilton he was presented with $5,000, which the townspeople had raised for him.
★ Canadian Sports Hall of Fame

Shevlin, Thomas L.

FOOTBALL
b. March 1, 1883, Muskegon, Mich.
d. Dec. 29, 1915

A three-time All-American end at Yale, from 1903 through 1905, Shevlin was a cocky 6-foot, 200-pounder. He was so versatile a player that coaches didn't know where to use him in his freshman year, when he played halfback, fullback, end, and tackle.

He settled at end in 1903 but started the 1904 season at fullback. After six games, he was moved back to end and was named an All-American at that position for the second time. Shevlin stayed at end in 1905 and captained a team that won all ten of its games, outscoring the opposition 222 to 4. During his four seasons at Yale, the team won 42, lost 2, and tied 1.

In the early part of the century, players for the top Eastern college football teams were celebrated athletes, often better known than professional baseball players. Shevlin, who came from a wealthy family, dressed fashionably, drove a Mercedes, carried a gold-headed cane, and reportedly had himself paged when staying in a New York hotel so people would know who he was.

His conceit didn't make him popular. He won the 1905 football captaincy by just one vote, and the outgoing captain, James Hogan, refused to shake his hand after the result was announced.

After Yale got off to a poor start in 1915, Shevlin was asked to coach the team for its games against Princeton and Harvard. Yale upset heavily favored Princeton 13–7 but lost to Harvard in the final game of the season. Shevlin contracted a severe cold on the sidelines that turned into a fatal case of pneumonia.

★ College Football Hall of Fame

Shiley, Jean M. (Mrs. Newhouse)
TRACK AND FIELD
b. Nov. 20, 1911, Harrisburg, Pa.

A high school star in basketball, field hockey, and tennis as well as track, Shiley was a member of the U.S. Olympic team in 1928, when she was only a junior in high school. She finished fourth in the high jump.

Shiley entered Temple University in 1929 and competed for Philadelphia's Meadowbrook Club because the school didn't offer women's track. She won the AAU outdoor high jump championship from 1929 through 1931, and in 1932 she tied with Babe Didrikson. She won the indoor title from 1929 through 1932, setting a world record of 5-3$^{1}/_{8}$ in 1931.

At the 1932 Olympics Shiley and Didrikson had a long duel for the gold medal. They tied at 5-5$^{1}/_{4}$, a world record, yet both failed to clear 5–6. The bar was then set at 5-5$^{3}/_{4}$ for a jump-off. Shiley and Didrikson both cleared that height, another world record, but officials ruled that Didrikson had used an illegal technique, and Shiley won the gold.

Shiley retired from competition after graduating in 1933. After her marriage in 1945, she worked as a volunteer in a Red Cross program to teach handicapped children how to swim.

★ National Track and Field Hall of Fame

Shively, Bion
HARNESS RACING
b. 1878, Goodland, Ind.
d. Feb. 23, 1970

Shively was best known as the trainer and driver of Rodney, the harness horse of the year in 1948. A 4-year-old trotter, Rodney won every race he entered that year and lost only one heat. He began the season by setting a world record of 2:31$^{3}/_{5}$ for the 1$^{1}/_{4}$ mile in the Golden West Trot at Santa Anita, winning $50,000.

In a time trial that year, Shively drove Rodney to a record 1:58 in the mile. The horse later tied that mark twice. Rodney was retired to stud in 1949. At his death in 1963, he had sired more $100,000 trotting winners than any other horse in history.

Shoemaker, Bill (William L.)
HORSE RACING
b. Aug. 19, 1931, Fabens, Tex.

Born prematurely, weighing only one pound and 13 ounces and not breathing, Shoemaker wasn't expected to live. But his maternal grandmother, Maude Harris, wrapped the tiny baby in rags, put him in a shoebox, and placed the shoebox on an open oven door, with the heat set on low. Within a short time, the baby was warm and breathing.

"He'll live, Ruby," Maude Harris said to the mother. "He's a little fighter."

Though he weighed only 80 pounds, Shoemaker was undefeated as a wrestler in the 95- to 105-pound division in high school and he was also a successful Golden Gloves boxer before leaving school at 16 to take a job cleaning out horse stalls. He soon became an exercise boy and, in 1949, an apprentice jockey.

He was an immediate success, riding 219 winners to finish second in the nation, even though he didn't get his first victory until April. In his first full season, 1950, he tied for the lead with 388 winners, which matched Walter Miller's record, set in 1906.

Bill Shoemaker led in purses with $1,329,890 in 1951, rode a record 485 winners in 1953, and led in wins again with 380 in 1954. He was also the top money winner in both years and had a record $1,876,760 in 1954.

As he got more rides in high-purse stakes races, he rode fewer mounts and his wins declined. Nevertheless, he led in victories in 1958 and 1959 and was the top money winner seven years in a row, from 1958 through 1964.

Shoemaker won the Kentucky Derby four times, aboard Swaps in 1955, Tomy in 1958, Lucky Debonair in 1965, and Ferdinand in 1986. At 54, he was the oldest jockey ever to win the race.

He would have tied the record of five Kentucky Derby victories, but when he was leading the race with Gallant Man in 1957, he thought the one-sixteenth pole was the finish, pulled the horse up, and lost to Iron Liege. The winning jockey, Eddie Arcaro, said afterward, "He's the only one I know who could have suffered that kind of experience in a race like the Derby without going to pieces. That's why the little son of a gun is going to go on and on."

He did go on to win the Belmont that year with Gallant Man. Shoemaker also won the Belmont with Sword Dancer in 1958, Jaipur in 1962, Damascus in 1967, and Avator in 1975, and he took the Preakness with Candy Spots in 1963 and Damascus in 1967.

The record for career wins was clearly within Shoemaker's reach in 1968, but he missed most of that year and part of 1969 with a severely broken leg, and shortly after returning in 1969, he suffered a broken pelvis.

On September 7, 1970, he rode his 6,003rd winner to break Johnny Longden's record. It had taken Longden 42 years and 32,000 mounts to set the record; Shoemaker broke it in 22 years and 25,000 mounts.

Two years later, Shoemaker won his 555th stakes to break Arcaro's record, and in 1985 he became the first jockey to earn more than $100 million in his career. And he still wasn't finished. After undergoing knee surgery early in 1987, Shoemaker won the Breeders' Cup Classic aboard Ferdinand.

Shoemaker retired in February 1990 with 8,833 wins in 40,350 mounts, including 1,009 stakes victories and $123,375,524 in purses. He began training horses at his own stable in California. On April 8, 1991, his car went off the road when he was driving home from a country club. Shoemaker's neck was broken in the crash. He survived by the narrowest of margins but was paralyzed from the neck down.

After six months of rehabilitation, Shoemaker returned to training horses, equipped with a mouth-operated, motorized wheelchair.

★ National Horse Racing Hall of Fame

Sholty, George F.

HARNESS RACING
b. Nov. 2, 1932, Logansport, Ind.

A basketball and football star in high school, Sholty began training and driving harness horses after graduating and got his first victory at Frankfort, Indiana, in 1951.

In 1958 Sholty had more than 100 wins in a season, and then he averaged more than 140 wins and $750,000 in purses for the next 20 years. His finest year was 1966, when he won two of the pacing triple crown races, the Little Brown Jug and Messenger Stake, with Romeo Hanover, and won one of the trotting triple crown events, the Yonkers Futurity, with Polaris.

During nearly 40 years of driving, George Sholty won 2,846 heats and had $19,950,727 in winnings.

Shore, Eddie (Edward W.)

HOCKEY
b. Nov. 25, 1902, St. Qu-Appelle-Cupar, Sask.
d. March 16, 1985

Hammy Moore, the long-time trainer for the NHL's Boston Bruins, summed up Shore: "He was the only player I ever saw who had the whole arena standing every time he rushed down the ice. You see, when Shore carried the puck, you were always sure something would happen. He would either end up bashing somebody, get into a fight, or score a goal."

A defenseman, Shore joined the Bruins in 1929, and the team all of a sudden had fans. They came to watch Shore both for his brilliant offensive rushes and his tough, often brutal defensive style.

In 1933, Shore was checked hard into the boards by King Clancy of the Toronto Maple Leafs. After picking himself up, he skated toward Toronto's Ace Bailey from behind, evidently thinking he was the culprit. Shore charged into Bailey, flipping him into the air. Bailey landed on his head, suffered a skull fracture, and nearly died.

The NHL suspended Shore for the attack, in part to protect him from retaliation by other players or fans, but the suspension was soon lifted. Two months later, an all-star game was played to raise money for Bailey's hospital bills. Before the game, Shore and Bailey met on the ice and embraced each other.

Shore took a devil-may-care attitude about violence in hockey, even when it was directed at him. He once lay unconscious for 14 minutes after the entire Montreal Maroon team ganged up on him. He had three broken teeth, two black eyes, a broken nose, and several gashes on his face. After he regained consciousness, he shrugged and told his teammates, "This is all part of hockey," and he played in the next game.

After his retirement, he told an interviewer, "The accent is on speed now. I guess it's better for the fans, but I liked it better in the old days. Then it was pretty much a fifty-fifty proposition. You socked the other guy and other guy socked you."

Shore played with the Bruins through 1938–39, then bought a minor league team, the Springfield, Massachusetts, Indians. He retired to become Springfield's player-coach after spending the 1939–40 season with Boston and the New York Americans.

He won the Hart Trophy as the league's most valuable player in 1933, 1935, 1936, and 1938. Only Wayne Gretzky and Gordie Howe have won it more than four times. In 553 regular season games, Shore scored 284 points on 105 goals and 179 assists. He added 6 goals and 13 assists for 19 points in 55 playoff games.

★ Hockey Hall of Fame

Shorter, Frank C.

TRACK AND FIELD
b. Oct. 31, 1947, Munich, Germany

The son of an American doctor who was working in Germany, Shorter attended Yale and won the NCAA 6-mile championship in 1969. He was the AAU national 3-mile champion in 1970, the 6-mile champion in 1970 and 1971, and the cross-country champion four years in a row, from 1970 through 1973.

Shorter began running the marathon in 1971, when he won gold medals in that event and in the 10,000-meter run at the Pan-American Games.

After winning the marathon in the U.S. trials, Shorter returned to his native Munich for the 1972 Olympics. The Olympic marathon started very slowly and Shorter, who usually preferred to run from behind, decided to set a faster pace. He took the lead at the 15-meter mark and held it the rest of the way.

When Shorter entered the stadium to run the final lap, he was stunned to hear jeering and boos, although they weren't meant for him. A hoaxer had run into the stadium a few minutes earlier, pretending to be the marathon winner, and security guards were hustling him away. When the crowd realized that the real winner was on the track, the jeers turned to cheers.

Shorter finished fifth in the Olympic 10,000-meter run against what was considered the greatest field ever assembled for that event. He was given the 1972 Sullivan Award as the nation's outstanding amateur athlete. In 1976 Shorter won a silver medal in the marathon, becoming the only runner ever to win two Olympic medals in the event.

A recurring foot injury forced Shorter to retire from serious competition in 1979. He founded a company that designs and manufactures running apparel, and he has frequently been a television commentator.

★ National Track & Field Hall of Fame; Olympic Hall of Fame

Shotton, Burton E.

BASEBALL
b. Oct. 18, 1884, Brownhelm, Ohio
d. July 29, 1962

A left-handed hitter and right-handed thrower, Shotton was a competent major league outfielder for 14 seasons, leading the NL in walks with 99 in 1913 and 111 in 1916 and compiling a .270 career average.

He played for the St. Louis Cardinals when Branch Rickey was managing the team. Because of his religious beliefs Rickey refused to manage on Sunday, and he chose Shotton as the team's Sunday manager.

Shotton became a coach with the Cardinals in 1923 and took over as manager of the Philadelphia Phillies in 1928. He brought the eighth-place team up to fifth, but then the Phillies sank back into the cellar, and Shotton was fired after the 1933 season.

He returned to the Cardinal organization as a minor league manager, coach, and scout. When Stan Musial's pitching career ended because of an injured throwing shoulder, it was Shotton who recommended that he be moved into the outfield because of his swing.

In 1946 Shotton retired from baseball after having served as a coach with the Cleveland Indians for four years. But then Leo Durocher, manager of the Brooklyn Dodgers, was suspended before the 1947 season. Rickey, the Brooklyn general manager, brought Shotton out of retirement to take over, and Shotton promptly guided the Dodgers to the pennant.

Durocher returned in 1948 but left midway through the season to manage the New York Giants. Shotton again came out of retirement. The team finished fifth that year but won another pennant in 1949. Shotton retired, this time for good, after a second-place finish in 1950.

Shriver, Pamela H.

TENNIS
b. July 4, 1962, Baltimore, Md.

Recurrent tendinitis in her right shoulder kept Shriver from realizing her early potential as a singles player, but she and Martina Navratilova formed one of the greatest women's doubles combinations of all time.

In 1978 Shriver became the youngest woman ever to reach the U.S. Open singles final, where she lost to Chris Evert Lloyd. The tendinitis began to bother her early in 1979, but she recovered in 1980 and was named the comeback player of the year.

The 5-foot-11, 130-pound Shriver is a powerful player with a strong first serve who likes to come to net and volley. Her volleying ability makes her an outstanding doubles player.

She and Navratilova first teamed in 1981, and they went on to win 18 grand slam championships: Wimbledon from 1981 through 1984 and in 1986; the U.S. Open in 1983, 1984, 1986, and 1987; the French Open in 1984, 1985, and 1987; and the Australian Open from 1982 through 1985 and in 1987 and 1988. They are the only women's team ever to win four consecutive grand slam titles.

Shriver's best year as a singles player was 1987, when she won 23 of 25 matches during the summer and took the Player's Challenge tournament without losing a set. She beat Evert Lloyd for the first time in the semifinals of that tournament.

In 1990 Shriver's shoulder became extremely painful, and she was forced to retire from serious competition.

Shula, Donald F.

FOOTBALL
b. Jan. 4, 1930, Grand River, Ohio

After playing both offense and defense at John Carroll University in Ohio, Shula became a defensive back with the Cleveland Browns in 1951. He spent two seasons with the Browns, four with the Baltimore Colts, and one with the Washington Redskins before retiring as a player after the 1957 season. He had 21 career interceptions and returned them for 267 yards, a 12.7 average.

Shula served as an assistant coach at the college and professional levels for five years, and in 1963 he became pro football's youngest head coach with the NFL's Baltimore Colts. He guided the

Colts to the NFL championship in 1968, when the team won 13 of 14 regular season games. However, the New York Jets beat Baltimore 16–7 in Super Bowl III.

In seven seasons at Baltimore, Shula had a 71–23–4 record. He went to the Miami Dolphins in 1970 and produced Super Bowl champions in 1972 and 1973. His 1972 team won all 17 of its games, including the playoffs, the only time that has been accomplished.

Unlike most other successful coaches, Shula has never clung to a single strategic approach. With the Colts, he emphasized a strong defense built around lineman Bubba Smith and linebacker Mike Curtis. In his early years with the Dolphins, he built a ball-control offense around the inside running of Larry Csonka and Jim Kiick and the accurate short passing of Bob Griese. After strong-armed quarterback Dan Marino joined Miami in 1983, Shula developed a pass-oriented offense.

Through 1994, Shula had a 327-158-6 record. His 327 wins is an NFL record, and his .672 winning percentage is fourth best of all-time.

Shute, Denny (Herman Densmore)

GOLF
b. Oct. 25, 1904, Cleveland, Ohio
d. May 13, 1974

Shute was overshadowed during his career by such great players as Bobby Jones, Walter Hagen, and Gene Sarazen. But he was one of the best golfers in the world during the 1930s, winning the British Open in 1933 and the PGA championship in both 1936 and 1937, when it was a match-play tournament.

After winning the West Virginia Amateur in 1923 and 1925, Shute became a professional in 1928. He lost in the finals of the PGA championship in 1931 and finished second in the 1941 U.S. Open. Shute didn't play in many tournaments after World War II, but he did win the Ohio Open in 1950 and the Akron Open in 1956.
★ PGA Hall of Fame

Siebert, Babe (Albert C.)

HOCKEY
b. Jan. 14, 1904, Plattsville, Ont.
d. Aug. 25, 1939

Originally a left wing, Siebert moved to defense midway through his NHL career. He joined the Montreal Maroons for the 1925–26 season, when they won the Stanley Cup, and went to the New York Rangers in 1932.

The Rangers won the Stanley Cup during his first season there, and he was traded to the Boston Bruins during the 1933–34 season, then went to the Montreal Canadiens in 1936. With Montreal, he won the Hart Trophy as the league's most valuable player for the 1936–37 season.

Siebert was a first-team All-Star defenseman three consecutive years, from 1936 through 1938. He drowned in a boating accident after the 1938–39 season.

In 930 games, Siebert scored 140 goals and had 156 assists for a total of 296 points. He had 8 goals and 7 assists for 15 points in 54 playoff games.
★ Hockey Hall of Fame

Sill, Aleta (Rzpecki)

BOWLING
b. Sept. 9, 1962, Detroit, Mich.

Sill began bowling when she was five and won her first professional tournament at 19. In 1982 she won the WIBC all-events title, but she didn't consider it a good year. After she became the second youngest bowler to win the WIBC Queens tournament in 1983, when she led the LPBT in earnings with $42,525, she explained her success: "I made myself practice, which I didn't do in 1982."

In 1984 Sill was the leading money winner with $81,452, a record at the time, and she also had the top average, 210.68 pins, to win the LPBT bowler of the year award. She repeated as money winner with $52,655 and average leader with 211.10 in 1985 and was again named bowler of the year.

Sill was the money leader for a fourth straight year with $36,962 in 1986. Through the 1994 season, she was second in both tournament victories, with 21, and career winnings, with $642,536.

Sime, David W.

TRACK AND FIELD
b. July 25, 1936, Paterson, N.J.

Though Sime didn't win any major championships, he turned in some excellent times during his sprinting career. He once held or co-held world records for the 100-yard, 220-yard, and 200-meter sprints and for the 220-yard and 200-meter hurdles.

Representing Duke, Sime finished second to Bobby Morrow in the 1956 NCAA 100-meter, then pulled a muscle in the 200-meter and couldn't run in the Olympic trials.

Sime did qualify for the 1960 Olympics. Matched in the 100-meter final against Germany's Armin Hary, who was known for his explosive start, Sime got off to a poor start and was in last place halfway through the race, but he almost caught Hary by literally diving across the finish line. They were both timed at 10.2, but Hary got the gold medal, Sime the silver.

In the 4 x 100-meter relay, the U.S. was trailing Germany by three meters when Sime took the baton for the anchor leg. He made up the gap, and more, for an apparent victory, but the team was disqualified for an illegal pass.

Sime turned in all his world record times in 1956. Twice he ran 9.3 in the 100-yard dash and 20.2 in the 220-yard to tie records. He set a world record for the 200-meter and 220-yard on a straightaway with a 20.0 clocking, and he ran a record-tying 22.2 in the 200-meter/220-yard low hurdles.

★ National Track & Field Hall of Fame

Simes, Jack III

CYCLING
b. 1943, N.J.

Simes's father and grandfather were both professional bicycle racers. When he was 17, he made the 1960 Olympics as a match-race sprinter, paired with Herb Francis, the first black Olympic cyclist from the U.S.

In 1962 Simes raced extensively in Europe. He returned to the U.S. to join the 1963 Pan-American Games cycling team, then went back to Europe for more racing and placed second in the Danish Grand Prix.

Simes won national championships in the 1964 road race and the 1965 and 1967 sprint competitions. He was drafted in 1967, joined the U.S. Army cycling team, and began specializing in the 1-kilometer individual time trial. He won a silver medal in that event at the 1967 Pan-American Games.

After being eliminated in the qualifying heats at the 1968 Olympics, Simes won a silver medal at the world championships in 1969; he was the first American to medal in cycling since Jack Heid in 1951. He also won the national championship in the 10-mile event in 1969.

Simes turned professional in 1970 and raced in Europe. He had a fist fight with Peter Post of the Netherlands after the two cyclists collided in a 1971 race, and he was banned from further competition. He later became executive director of the Professional Racing Organization, which controls professional cycling in the U.S.

Simmons, Al [Aloysius H. Szymanski]

BASEBALL
b. May 22, 1903, Milwaukee, Wis.
d. May 26, 1956

A young right-handed hitter who steps toward third instead of directly toward the pitcher is always warned, "Don't put your foot in the bucket." That was Al Simmons' batting style. He was such a good hitter that no one ever tried to change him, though his style won him the nickname "Bucketfoot Al."

After he spent two years in the minor leagues, the AL's Philadelphia Athletics bought his contract for a price of somewhere between $40,000 and $70,000 in 1924. He became the team's starting left fielder, hitting .308 with 102 RBI.

Simmons led the league with 253 hits, still the record for a right-handed hitter, and a .599 slugging percentage in 1925, when he batted .387. After a .341 average in 1926, he hit .392 in 1927 but finished second in the batting race to Harry Heilmann's .398.

In 1929 Simmons won the AL's most valuable player award. He hit .365 with 34 home runs, a league-leading 157 RBI, and 114 runs scored as the Athletics won the first of three consecutive pennants. Philadelphia beat the Chicago Cubs in a five-game World Series, with Simmons batting .300 and hitting 2 home runs. He got 2 hits, including a home run, in the seventh inning of the fourth game, when the Athletics scored 10 runs to overcome an 8–0 deficit.

Simmons won consecutive batting titles with a .361 average in 1930, when he also led the league with 152 runs scored, and a .390 average in 1931. In the 1930 World Series, a six-game victory over the St. Louis Cardinals, he hit .364 with 2 home runs. He batted .333 with 2 more home runs and 8 RBI in 1931, when the Athletics lost to the Cardinals in seven games.

After he led the league with 216 hits in 1932, owner-manager Connie Mack decided he had to release some of his high-salaried players because of the Depression. Simmons and two other players were sold for $150,000 to the Chicago White Sox.

He hit .331 and .344 in his first two years in Chicago, then dropped to .267 and was sold to the Detroit Tigers. He batted .327 in one season there and went to the Washington Senators, where he hit only .279 in 1937.

Simmons rebounded with a .302 average, 21 home runs, and 95 RBI in 125 games with Washington in 1938, split the 1939 season between the Boston Braves and Cincinnati Reds, and then returned to the Athletics as a player-coach. He spent 1942 out of baseball, but in 1943 he signed with the Boston Red Sox, who were desperate for players because of the World War II manpower shortages.

In Boston, he hit only .203 in 40 games. Philadelphia then rehired him as a coach. He appeared in four games in 1944, his last season as a player, but remained as a coach through 1949. After two seasons as a coach with Cleveland,

Simmons became director of a sandlot baseball program in New York City. He died of complications from phlebitis.

During his 20 major league seasons, Simmons had a .334 average on 2,927 hits, including 539 doubles, 149 triples, and 307 home runs. He scored 1,507 runs and had 1,827 RBI.

★ Baseball Hall of Fame

Simmons, Lionel J.

BASKETBALL
b. Nov. 14, 1968, Philadelphia, Pa.

A unanimous choice as college player of the year in 1990, the 6-foot-7, 210-pound Simmons starred at LaSalle University for four seasons, averaging 24.6 points per game for his career and 26.5 as a senior. He also collected 1,429 rebounds in 1,931 games.

Simmons joined the NBA's Sacramento Kings as a first-round draft choice in 1990 and was named to the league's 1990–91 All-Rookie team after averaging 18.0 points a game.

Through the 1992–93 season, Simmons had scored 3,992 points in 226 games, a 17.2 average. He also had 1,826 rebounds.

Simpson, John F., Sr.

HARNESS RACING
b. Dec. 26, 1919, Chester, N.C.

Simpson won each of harness racing's six triple crown races at least once, and twice he won two legs of a triple crown. In 1957 he drove Torpid to victories in the Cane Pace and the Little Brown Jug, and he drove Ayres to wins in the Hambletonian Stakes and the Kentucky Futurity in 1964. Ayres set a Hambletonian record with a time of 1:56$\frac{4}{5}$.

His other wins in triple crown races were with Ford Hanover in the 1951 Kentucky Futurity, Noble Adios in the 1956 Little Brown Jug, Add Hanover in the 1956 Yonkers Trot, Hickory Smoke in the 1957 Hambletonian, Bullet Hanover in the 1960 Little Brown Jug, and Thor Hanover in the 1962 Messenger Stakes.

Simpson, whose father was also a trainer and driver, began racing in 1938. He led the nation in heats won in 1950 and was the leader in heats and money won in 1951. He retired from driving in 1965 to become president and general manager of Hanover Shoe Farm. During his driving career, he recorded 1,467 wins and had $4,771,400 in winnings.

Simpson, O. J. (Orenthal James)

FOOTBALL
b. July 9, 1947, San Francisco, Calif.

The best in a long line of University of Southern California tailbacks who gained big chunks of yardage running out of the I formation, Simpson was a consensus All-American in 1967 and 1968, and he won the 1968 Heisman Trophy as the nation's outstanding college player.

Although he played in only 19 games at USC, Simpson gained 3,124 yards and scored 33 touchdowns on 621 rushing attempts. His average of 164.4 yards per game is the second best ever at an NCAA Division I school.

A first-round draft choice of the Buffalo Bills of the American Football League, Simpson wasn't an immediate success because he was used sparingly and even had to play on special teams for his first three seasons.

When Lou Saban took over as Buffalo coach in 1972, he installed an offense built around Simpson's running ability, and the 6-foot-1, 212-pounder responded by leading the NFL with 1,251 yards. In 1973 he became the first player ever to rush for more than 2,000 yards in a season, again leading the NFL, averaging 6.0 yards a carry and scoring 12 rushing touchdowns. He was named Associated Press Athlete of the Year.

Simpson rushed for more than 1,000 yards each of the next three seasons. A knee injury limited him to just 557 yards in 1977, his last season in Buffalo. He played with the San Francisco 49ers in 1978 and 1979, totaling just over 1,000 yards for those two seasons, before retiring.

An All-Pro running back from 1972 through 1976, Simpson was named American Football Conference player of the year by United Press International in

1972, 1973, and 1975. In 11 professional seasons, he gained 11,236 yards on 2,404 attempts, a 4.7 average, and scored 61 touchdowns. He also caught 203 passes for 2,142 yards, a 10.6 average, and 14 touchdowns; and returned 33 kickoffs 990 yards, a 30.0 average, and 1 touchdown.

Fifteen years after his football career ended, Simpson leaped back into the public eye in June 1994, when he was charged with the brutal murder of his ex-wife, Nicole Brown Simpson, and her friend Ron Goldman. Coverage of the case saturated newspapers and television for months. Simpson's trial began in Los Angeles on January 23, 1995. This book went to press before a verdict had been reached.

★ College Football Hall of Fame; Pro Football Hall of Fame

Sims, Billy R.

FOOTBALL
b. Sept. 18, 1955, St. Louis, Mo.

Hampered by injuries in his freshman and sophomore years at the University of Oklahoma, Sims was the nation's top NCAA Division I runner as a junior in 1978. He gained 1,762 yards on 231 attempts, a 7.6 average, and scored 20 touchdowns and he tied a record by rushing for more than 200 yards in three consecutive games.

One of only six juniors to win the Heisman Trophy as the nation's best collegiate player, Sims was also chosen player of the year by *The Sporting News* and was a consensus All-American in 1978. He repeated as an All-American in his senior year, when he finished fourth in rushing with 1,506 yards and led in scoring with 22 touchdowns.

A first-round draft choice of the Detroit Lions, the 6-foot, 200-pound Sims gained 1,303 yards in 313 carries, a 4.2 average, and scored 16 touchdowns in 1980. He was the consensus NFL rookie of the year. Sims gained more than 1,000 yards in three of his first four seasons, but suffered a serious knee injury early in October 1984. He hoped to make a comeback, but the knee did not respond to rehabilitation, and he formally announced his retirement in 1986. In his brief NFL career, he gained 5,106 yards on 1,131 carries, a 4.5 average, scoring 42 touchdowns, and he caught 186 passes for 2,072 yards, an 11.1 average, and 5 touchdowns.

Singletary, Mike (Michael)
FOOTBALL
b. Oct. 9, 1958, Houston, Tex.

A three-year starter as a linebacker at Baylor University, Singletary was voted Southwest Conference player of the year in both 1979 and 1980 and was named to some All-American teams in his senior year.

He joined the NFL's Chicago Bears in 1980 and, as middle linebacker, soon became the leader of a powerful defense that helped take the Bears to a 15–1 record in 1985 and a 46–10 victory over the New England Patriots in Super Bowl XX.

The 5-foot-11, 230-pound Singletary had the size and speed to be a very good linebacker, but his intensity, intelligence, and inspirational leadership lifted him to greatness and made him a certainty for induction into the Pro Football Hall of Fame as soon as he becomes eligible, five years after retirement.

A consensus All-Pro from 1983 through 1986, Singletary was named National Football Conference defensive player of the year by United Press International in 1984 and 1985. He retired after the 1992 season. During his 12 seasons with the Bears, he had 44 interceptions, 12 fumble recoveries, and 19 quarterback sacks.

Sington, Frederic W.
BASEBALL, FOOTBALL
b. Feb. 24, 1910, Birmingham, Ala.

One of the biggest players of his era at 6-foot-4 and 230 pounds, Sington started at tackle for the University of Alabama from 1928 through 1930 and was an All-American as a senior, when Alabama won all nine of its regular season games and beat Washington State, 24–0, in the Rose Bowl.

A Phi Beta Kappa scholar, Sington had starred in baseball, basketball, and track as well as football in high school. Although he concentrated on football at Alabama, he entered professional baseball after graduating in 1931 and spent six seasons as a reserve outfielder in the major leagues, with the Washington Senators from 1934 through 1937 and the Brooklyn Dodgers in 1938 and 1939. He had a career batting average of .271 in 181 games.

★ College Football Hall of Fame

Sinkwich, Frank (Francis)
FOOTBALL
b. Oct. 20, 1920, McKees Rocks, Pa.

One of the greatest offensive performers of his era, Sinkwich wanted to play fullback when he arrived at the University of Georgia in 1939 because he didn't think he was a good enough passer to play tailback in the single-wing. Coach Wally Butts insisted that he could be an outstanding tailback if he worked on his passing.

Sinkwich not only became a two-time All-American, he won the Heisman Trophy and the Associated Press athlete of the year award as a senior in 1942, when he set a total offense record of 2,187 yards, 1,392 passing and 795 passing. He had led the nation in rushing with 1,103 yards in 1941.

After graduating in 1943, Sinkwich joined the NFL's Detroit Lions for two seasons, winning the Joe Carr Award as the league's most valuable player in 1944. After spending a year in military service, he returned to professional football in 1946 with the New York Yankees of the All-America Football Conference. He started the 1947 season with the Yankees, was traded to the Baltimore Colts, and retired after the season ended.

During his four seasons as a professional, Sinkwich completed 121 of 301 passes for 1,913 yards and 19 touchdowns. He carried the ball 321 times for 1,090 yards, a 3.4 average, and 7 touchdowns; kicked 24 of 30 extra point attempts and 2 of 9 field goal attempts; and punted 64 times for a 41.5-yard average.

★ College Football Hall of Fame

Sipe, Brian W.

FOOTBALL
b. Aug. 8, 1949, San Diego, Calif.

Sipe played quarterback at Grossmont Junior College and San Diego State University, where he led NCAA major colleges in 1971 by completing 17.8 passes per game. He was chosen by the Cleveland Browns in the thirteenth round of the 1972 NFL draft.

For two seasons, Sipe was a nonroster member of Cleveland's taxi squad. He became a backup to Mike Phipps in 1974 and took over the starting job in 1976. The 1980 Browns, nicknamed the "Kardiac Kids" because they won so many games in the closing minutes, won the AFC Central Division title. Sipe was named NFL player of the year by Associated Press and the Pro Football Writers Association after completing 337 of 554 passes for 4,132 yards and 30 touchdowns.

Sipe lost his starting job in 1982 and he left the Browns in 1984 to play two seasons in the U.S. Football League before retiring.

In his ten NFL seasons, the 6-foot-1, 193-pound Sipe completed 1,944 of 3,439 attempts for 23,713 yards and 154 touchdowns. He also rushed for 11 touchdowns.

Sisler, George H.

BASEBALL
b. March 24, 1893, Manchester, Ohio
d. March 26, 1973

As a left-handed pitcher in high school, Sisler signed a minor league contract that was to take effect on graduation day. However, he decided to attend the University of Michigan, where his coach was Branch Rickey. Sisler showed such promise as a college player that the NL's Pittsburgh Pirates bought his contract.

A lawyer and also a scout for the AL's St. Louis Browns, Rickey had the contract voided because Sisler had been a minor at the team and didn't have parental consent. He then signed Sisler with the Browns and became the team's manager.

Sisler went directly to the Browns in 1915 without playing any minor league ball. He had a 4–4 record with a 2.83 ERA in 15 games as a pitcher; he also played 66 games at first base and in the outfield, batting .275.

Rickey decided the 5-foot-11, 170-pound Sisler had more of a future as a hitter than as a pitcher and put him at first base in 1916. Sisler became one of the greatest of all time, batting over .300 in 13 of his 15 seasons and twice hitting over .400.

He was a very unusual kind of hitter, a free swinger with some power who could also make contact. He rarely walked or struck out. Sisler was also an excellent fielder with great range; he led AL first basemen in assists six times.

After hitting .305, .353, .341, and .352 in his first four full seasons, Sisler won a batting title with a .407 average in 1920, collecting 257 hits, still the major league record, with 49 doubles, 18 triples, and 19 home runs.

He hit a league-leading 18 triples in 1921, when he batted .371, and then had one of the greatest seasons in history in 1922. He won his second batting championship with a .420 record and also led the league with 134 runs, 246 hits, 18 triples, and 51 stolen bases to win the most valuable player award. Sisler struck out only 14 times in 586 at-bats.

Double vision caused by a severe sinus infection kept him out of action the entire 1923 season, and Sisler was never again the same hitter, although he was still very good.

He returned to St. Louis as playing manager in 1924 and batted .305 and .345 the next two years before slipping to .290 in 1926. He resigned as manager because he felt the pressure was distracting him, and he batted .327 in 1927.

The Browns sold him to the Washington Senators the following year, and he was sold again, to the NL's Boston Braves, early in the season. He batted only .245 with Washington, but .340 with Boston. Sisler ended his major league career with averages of .326 in 1929 and .309 in 1930.

After two seasons playing in the minor leagues, Sisler worked for a sporting goods company, operated softball fields, and served as commissioner of the National Baseball Congress, an organization of semipro leagues.

In 1943 he became a scout for the Brooklyn Dodgers, where Rickey was general manager. When Rickey left the Dodgers for the Pittsburgh Pirates in 1951, Sisler went with him and scouted for the Pirates until his death.

Sisler had a career average of .340, with 2,812 hits, including 425 doubles, 164 triples, and 102 home runs. He stole 375 bases, scored 1,284 runs, and had 1,175 RBI.

★ Baseball Hall of Fame

Sitko, Emil M. ("Red")

FOOTBALL
b. Sept. 7, 1923, Ft. Wayne, Ind.
d. Dec. 15, 1973

Nicknamed "Six-Yard Sitko" by sportswriters because he averaged 6.1 yards per carry during his career at Notre Dame, Sitko played for such talent-laden teams that he didn't carry the ball as often as he would have at another school.

A 1949 consensus All-American halfback, the 5-foot-8, 183-pounder gained 2,226 yards on 363 carries during his four seasons at Notre Dame, scoring 26 touchdowns.

He played for the NFL's San Francisco 49ers in 1950, the Chicago Cardinals in 1951 and 1952 before retiring with a professional record of 638 yards and 3 touchdowns on 163 carries.

★ College Football Hall of Fame

Sitzberger, Kenneth R.

DIVING
b. Feb. 13, 1945, Cedar Rapids, Iowa

Sitzberger was trailing U.S. teammate Frank Gorman after nine of the ten dives in the springboard competition at the 1964 Olympics, but Gorman performed poorly on his last dive and Sitzberger was nearly flawless, winning the gold medal.

As a student at Indiana University, Sitzberger won the AAU national indoor 1-meter and 3-meter springboard championships in 1964 and 1965. He was the NCAA champion in the 1-meter from 1965 through 1967, in the 3-meter in 1956 and 1967.

Sitzberger married Jeanne Collier, who had won a silver medal in the women's Olympic springboard in 1964.

Skladany, Joseph P.

FOOTBALL
b. May 10, 1911, Larksville, Pa.
d. Aug. 9, 1972

Best known for his defensive play, the 6-foot, 180-pound Skladany was an All-American end at Pittsburgh in 1933. Pittsburgh won 24 games, lost 3, and tied 2 during his three seasons as a starter. The 1932 team was undefeated, winning 8 games and tying 2. In an 18–13 victory over Army that season, Skladany caught two 50-yard touchdown passes.

Skladany joined the NFL's Pittsburgh Pirates (now Steelers) in 1934 and played just one professional season. He caught 10 passes for 222 yards and 2 touchdowns.

He coached Carnegie Tech to a 4–0–1 record in 1943.

★ College Football Hall of Fame

Slaughter, Enos B. ("Country")

BASEBALL
b. April 27, 1916, Roxboro, N.C.

The way Slaughter scored the winning run for the St. Louis Cardinals in the seventh game of the 1946 World Series typified his style of play. He was on first base with the Cardinals and Boston Red Sox tied 3–3 in the bottom of the eighth inning. Harry Walker singled to left field. Slaughter took off and never stopped running. Boston shortstop Johnny Pesky took the relay, held the ball for a split-second until he realized that Slaughter was headed home, and threw too late.

Solidly built at 5-foot-9 and 192 pounds, Slaughter wasn't very fast, but he ran as hard as he could all the time. He was one of the best at going from first to third on a single, and he was constantly diving for fly balls and charging hits to prevent a runner from taking an extra base.

A left-handed hitter and right-handed thrower, he joined the Cardinals in 1938. Slaughter hit .320 and led the NL in with 52 doubles in his second season. After batting .306 and .311 the next two years, he won his only batting title with a .318 average in 1942, when he also led the league with 188 hits and 17 triples.

Slaughter entered the service in 1943 and returned to the Cardinals in 1946, when he hit .300 and had a league-leading 130 RBI. He led in triples with 13 in 1949, when he hit .336. During the next four years, he hit just .300 once, and the Cardinals traded him to the New York Yankees in 1954.

Playing in just 69 games, Slaughter hit .248. The Yankees sent him to the Kansas City Athletics early in the 1955 season, and Slaughter rebounded with a .315 average. He was traded back to the Yankees for the pennant drive in 1956, when he hit .281 as a part-time player. He was platooned in the outfield and used as a pinch hitter for the next two seasons, and he finished his career with the Yankees and Milwaukee Braves in 1959.

In 19 major league seasons, Slaughter batted an even .300 with 2,383 hits, including 413 doubles, 148 triples, and 169 home runs. He scored 1,247 runs and drove 1,304.

★ Baseball Hall of Fame

Sloan, Norm L., Jr.

BASKETBALL
b. June 25, 1926, Anderson, Ind.

After serving in the Navy during World War II, Sloan played guard at North Carolina State University and also won letters in football and track. He then coached Presbyterian College in South Carolina to a 69–36 record, from 1951–52 through 1954–55.

Sloan spent a year as an assistant coach before taking over at the Citadel, where he had a 57–38 mark from 1956–57 through 1959–60.

He became head coach at his alma mater in 1960 and gradually rebuilt a winning program. His 1972–73 team won all 27 of its regular season games but couldn't compete in the NCAA tournament because it was on probation. However, Sloan's squad won the 1974 NCAA championship after losing only one regular season game. He was named coach of the year by the Associated Press and the Basketball Writers' Association of America.

In 14 seasons with the Wolfpack, Sloan had a 266–127 record and won three Atlantic Coast Conference championships. In 1980, Sloan went to the University of Florida, and under his guidance, the school made its first ever NCAA tournament appearance in 1987. Florida also made the tournament in 1988 and 1989.

Because of recruiting violations, the school was put on probation in 1992 and Sloan resigned under pressure. He had a 627–393 record for a .615 winning percentage.

Sloan, Todhunter (James F.)

HORSE RACING
b. Aug. 10, 1873, Kokomo, Ind.
d. Dec. 21, 1933

Nicknamed "Toad" when he was young, Sloan later altered that to "Tod" and persuaded people that it was short for "Todhunter." He had a powerful torso but very short legs, so Sloan rode with short stirrups and adopted a style that became known as the "monkey crouch," with his knees pulled up and his head against the horse's neck.

Many laughed at his riding posture, but it proved effective, partly because it reduced wind resistance. Sloan's success persuaded other jockeys to adopt the style. From 1896 through 1898, Sloan rode 455 winners in 1,443 races, a victory ratio of nearly 38 percent.

Sloan did a great deal of racing in England beginning in 1897, but his arrogance and flamboyant lifestyle annoyed British racing authorities, who expected jockeys to be subservient. He was told not to bother applying for a British jockey license in 1900.

He returned to the U.S. and won the Futurity and Flatbush Stakes aboard Ballyhoo Bey in 1900, his last successful year. Like many jockeys, Sloan then began having weight problems. He ran a Paris bar for a time and had unsuccessful attempts at vaudeville and the movies. A heavy drinker who affected enormous cigars, he died of cirrhosis.

★ National Horse Racing Hall of Fame

Slocum, Henry W., Jr.

TENNIS
b. May 28, 1862, Syracuse, N.Y.
d. Jan. 22, 1949

Slocum played baseball and football as well as tennis at Yale, graduating in 1883, and received a law degree from George Washington University in 1885. A strong, steady player who liked to remain at the baseline and wait for his opponent to make mistakes, Slocum won the U.S. national singles championship in 1888 and 1889. He also won the 1889 doubles title with Howard Taylor.

Because of his law career, Slocum hardly played in 1890 until it was time to defend his championship, and he lost to Oliver Campbell.

Slocum never engaged in serious competition after that, but he was secretary-treasurer of the U.S. Lawn Tennis Association in 1887, treasurer in 1888, vice president from 1889 through 1891 and in 1912 and 1913, and president from 1891 to 1893. He wrote a history, *Lawn Tennis in Our Own Country.*

★ International Tennis Hall of Fame

Smart, Wayne (Thurman Wayne)

HARNESS RACING
b. Aug. 29, 1904, Ostrander, Ohio
d. Nov. 14, 1976

"Curly," as his fellow drivers called him, was a seven-time leader in the Universal Driver Rating System, which uses a formula based on starts, wins, places, and shows. Smart ranked first among those with 300 or more starts in 1952, 1953, and 1955; among those with 200 to 299 starts from 1958 through 1960; and among those with fewer than 200 starts in 1962.

The top driver at six different tracks at various times in his career, Smart won the Little Brown Jug twice, with Ensign Hanover in 1946 and with Meadow Race

in 1952. His richest win was with Gold Worth in the $75,000 American Classic in 1958.

He won 1,873 heats and had total earnings of more than $2.5 million. In 1968 he became a track superintendent but continued to train horses and drive occasionally until his death.

Smith, Alex

GOLF
b. 1872 Carnoustie, Scotland
d. April 20, 1930

Smith was one of five golf-playing brothers who came from Scotland to the United States during the 1890s. They were already golf professionals, which meant at the time that they could make clubs and maintain courses as well as play the game.

After finishing second in the U.S. Open in 1898, 1901, and 1905, Smith won the tournament in 1906 by shooting 295. It was the first time a golfer had shot better than 300 for 72 holes.

In 1910 he finished in a three-way tie in the Open with his brother McDonald Smith and John McDermott, then won the playoff. Smith was also Western Open champion in 1903 and 1906.

A fine instructor, Smith worked with both Jerry Travers and Glenna Collet Vare, who won a total of 11 national titles. He believed in playing rapidly. His motto was, "Miss them quick."

★ PGA Hall of Fame

Smith, Bill (William Jr.)

SWIMMING
b. May 16, 1924, Honolulu, Hawaii

Stricken with typhoid fever when he was six years old, Smith began swimming in irrigation ditches on a Hawaiian sugar plantation to build up his strength. He entered Ohio State University in 1942. After military service during World War II, he returned to school in 1947.

Smith won NCAA titles in the 220-yard freestyle in 1943 and in the 220- and 440-yard events from 1947 through 1949. He was the AAU national outdoor champion in the 400-meter freestyle in 1941, the 220- and 880-yard freestyles in 1942; the 100-meter in 1946; and the

200-meter in 1946 and 1947. Indoors, he won the 100-yard freestyle in 1944 and the 220- and 440-yard freestyle in 1943, 1944, 1947, and 1948.

Smith won a gold medal in the 400-meter freestyle at the 1948 Olympics and was also a member of the gold medal 4 x 200-meter relay team. He retired from competition after the Olympics to become water safety director for the Honolulu Department of Parks and Recreation.

Smith, Bruce B.

FOOTBALL
b. June 18, 1963, Norfolk, Va.

A defensive lineman at Virginia Tech, Smith was an All-American and winner of the Outland Trophy as the nation's outstanding collegiate lineman in 1984. He was chosen by the Buffalo Bills as the first pick overall in the 1985 NFL draft.

The 6-foot-4, 273-pound Smith combines brute strength with amazing quickness to rush quarterbacks. He had 76½ sacks in his first six seasons, despite missing four games with an injury in 1987 and a four-game suspension for a substance abuse problem in 1988.

A knee injury limited him to five games in 1991, but he returned to the Bills to record 14 sacks in 15 regular season games in 1992. Named an All-Pro defensive end in 1987, 1988, 1990, 1992, and 1993, Smith had been called the dominant defensive player in football, but unfortunately his image was tarnished by his team's four consecutive Super Bowl losses, in which he did not make the big plays that he is known for during the regular season.

Smith, Bruce P.

FOOTBALL
b. Feb. 8, 1920, Faribault, Minn.
d. Aug. 28, 1967

Stanley Woodward of the *New York Times* wrote of Smith, "He is the best runner, the best passer, the best kicker. He is the type of back who can go three yards with four players hanging on to him." A triple-threat tailback at the University of Minnesota, Smith was a consensus All-American and winner of the Heisman Trophy as the nation's best collegiate player in 1941.

The 6-foot, 200-pound Smith, who ran the 100-yard dash in 10.0 seconds while in high school, was noted for his ability to come up with the big play. With Minnesota trailing the University of Michigan 6–0 in 1940, he ran 80 yards on a muddy field for a touchdown that, with the conversion, gave Minnesota a 7–6 victory and preserved an undefeated season.

Smith was slowed by a knee injury in 1941, when he captained the team to a second undefeated season. Because of the injury, he sat out the first quarter of the game against Iowa. After Minnesota failed to make a first down, Smith was sent in, and he led his team to a 34–14 win. Against Michigan, he threw a 44-yard pass to set up the winning touchdown in a 7–0 victory.

Smith played himself in an autobiographical movie, *Smith of Minnesota*, after graduating in 1942; he then entered the Navy. He was named to the all-service team twice, with the Great Lakes Naval Training Station in 1942 and St. Mary's Pre-Flight School in 1943.

In 1945 Smith joined the NFL's Green Bay Packers. He spent four seasons with Green Bay and played with the Los Angeles Rams for one season before retiring from football.

★ College Football Hall of Fame

Smith, Bubba (Charles A.)

FOOTBALL
b. Feb. 18, 1945, Orange, Tex.

One of the first genuinely dominant defensive lineman, the 6-foot-8, 280-pound Smith was amazingly agile and quick. He once said that his technique was to grab an armload of opponents, sort them out until he found the one with the ball, and then throw him to the ground.

An All-American defensive end at Michigan State in 1965 and 1966, Smith joined the Baltimore Colts as their first-round draft choice in 1967 and was a starter with Baltimore for five years. He was named to the All-National Football

Conference team three years in a row, 1969 through 1971.

After missing the entire 1972 season with a knee injury, Smith lost some of his effectiveness, although he was still a very good lineman. He played for the Oakland Raiders from 1973 through 1974 and with the Houston Oilers from 1975 through 1977.

Smith, Dean E.

BASKETBALL
b. Feb. 28, 1931, Emporia, Kans.

Smith went to the University of Kansas on an academic scholarship but played baseball and basketball as well as freshman football. He was never a starter for the basketball team, which was coached by "Phog" Allen, who had learned the game from its inventor, James Naismith.

After graduating in 1953, Smith spent four years in the Air Force, the last two as an assistant basketball coach at the U.S. Air Force Academy. He then became an assistant coach to Frank McGuire at the University of North Carolina, and in 1961 he took over as head coach when McGuire left.

Because of a point-shaving scandal the school was allowed to play only 17 games, and scholarships were limited in his first season, when his team went 8–9. During the next several years there were calls for his resignation.

But Smith's 1966–67 team went 26–6 and won the Atlantic Coast Conference tournament. Since that season, North Carolina has been in post-season play every year but 1970, winning the NCAA championship in 1982 and 1993 and going to the final four seven other times. The 1970–71 team won the National Invitation Tournament.

A meticulous planner, Smith has sometimes been criticized for a controlled style of offense that prevents talented, creative players from performing at their best. Critics point out that even Michael Jordan could average 20 points a season only once in his three-year career at North Carolina.

Smith's advocates point out that his philosophy is much the same as that used by Red Auerbach of the Boston Celtics and other successful college and professional coaches: place the team concept above the individual. As a team, North Carolina has scored well. Smith's 1992–93 championship team, for example, averaged 86.1 points a game, about 12 points more than the national average that season.

Smith developed the four-corner offense originally as a delay tactic to run time off the clock late in the game, but it was later refined to take advantage of the spread-out defense to free a player streaking toward the basket for an easy shot.

In 1967, Smith become the youngest member ever of the College Basketball Rules Committee. He coached the U.S. Olympic team that won a gold medal in 1976.

Through the 1993–94 season, Smith had an 802–230 record. His .777 winning percentage is the fifth best all-time, and he is second only to Adolph Rupp in total victories.
★ Basketball Hall of Fame

Smith, Emmitt

FOOTBALL
b. May 15, 1969, Pensacola, Fla.

When Smith held out for more money at the beginning of the 1993 season, the defending champion Dallas Cowboys lost two games in a row. Smith then returned to the lineup and the Cowboys won 12 of their next 14 regular season games, then repeated as Super Bowl winners.

As a running back at the University of Florida, the 5-foot-9, 209-pound Smith was a unanimous All-American choice in 1989, and the Cowboys selected him in the first round of the 1990 NFL draft. Though not exceptionally fast, Smith has quick moves and the power to break tackles to gain extra yardage.

He wasn't a full-time starter as a rookie, when he gained 937 yards in 241 carries, but he took over the starting job in 1991 and led the NFC with 365 rushing attempts and 1,563 yards, a 4.3 average. Smith was named an All-Pro after leading the NFL with 1,713 yards and 16 rushing touchdowns in 1992.

Even though he played in only 14 games in 1993, he again led the league with 1,486 yards rushing on just 283 attempts, a 5.3 average. After gaining 132 yards on 30 carries in a 30–13 victory over the Buffalo Bills for the NFL championship, Smith became the first player ever named Super Bowl most valuable player and regular season most valuable player in the same year.

Through 1994, Smith had rushed for 7,183 yards and 71 touchdowns on 1,630 carries. He also had 1,576 yards and 4 touchdowns as a receiver.

Smith, Horton
GOLF
b. May 22, 1908, Springfield, Mo. d. Oct. 13, 1963

Now and then an athlete suddenly arrives, apparently out of nowhere, to become a star. Smith did so late in 1928, when he joined the PGA tour and won eight tournaments in little more than a year. In 1930 he went head to head against Bobby Jones in the Savannah Open and shot a 278 to beat Jones by a stroke.

After his initial surge Smith faded until, in 1934, he won the first Masters with a birdie on the 17th hole of the final round. He won again two years later by making up three strokes on the last five holes.

Smith was one of the early leaders of the PGA, joining its tournament committee in 1932. He became president of the association in 1952, while continuing to play occasionally on the tour. His last victory was in the 1954 Michigan PGA championship.
★ PGA Hall of Fame; World Golf Hall of Fame

Smith, Jackie L.
FOOTBALL
b. Feb. 23, 1940, Columbia, Miss.

The 6-foot-4, 230-pound Smith joined the NFL's St. Louis Cardinals in 1962 as a tenth-round draft choice out of Northwestern Louisiana State College. He became the team's starting tight end in 1964.

An excellent blocker and receiver, Smith was also the St. Louis punter for three seasons, from 1964 through 1966. He was named the All-Eastern Conference tight end by *The Sporting News* in 1966 and 1968.

Smith started 121 consecutive games from his rookie year until 1971, when he suffered a knee injury. He had his finest season in 1967, when he caught 56 passes for 1,205 yards and 9 touchdowns.

He spent the 1968 season with the Dallas Cowboys before retiring. At the time, Smith was the all-time leading pass receiver among tight ends with 480 receptions for 7,918 yards and 40 touchdowns. He also rushed for 327 yards and 3 touchdowns on 38 carries and averaged 39.1 yards on 86 punts.
★ Pro Football Hall of Fame

Smith, John
WRESTLING
b. Aug. 9, 1965, Oklahoma City, Okla.

The most honored wrestler in U.S. history, Smith is one of four brothers who have been involved in wrestling. His older brother Lee Roy is wrestling coach at Arizona State University; Pat won three NCAA championships; and Mark was a state high school champion.

Competing for Oklahoma State University, the 5-foot-7 Smith won NCAA championships at 134 pounds in 1987 and 1988 and was the national champion in 1986 and from 1988 through 1991. Smith is the only U.S. wrestler ever to win six world championships, and he did so in consecutive years, from 1987 through 1992.

Smith won gold medals in the 136.5-pound class at the 1988 and 1992 Olympics. He also won gold medals at the Goodwill Games in 1986 and 1990, at the Pan-American Games in 1987 and 1991, and at the World Cup tournament in 1991.

He was named outstanding wrestler in the 1987 NCAA tournament, in the 1991 world championships, and in the 1988 and 1991 national championships. Smith is the only American to win the international wrestler of the year award, in 1991, and the only wrestler to win the Sullivan Award as the nation's outstanding amateur athlete, in 1990.

Smith, Lee A.

BASEBALL
b. Dec. 4, 1957, Jamestown, La.

A menacing figure on the mound at 6-foot-6 and 269 pounds, Smith became the major league's all-time save leader in 1993. He has had an unusually long career for a relief pitcher who throws hard. Smith entered the major leagues with the NL's Chicago Cubs during the 1980 season. He led the league with 29 saves in 1983, when he had a 1.65 ERA.

The Cubs traded Smith to the AL's Boston Red Sox in 1988, and Boston sent him to the NL's St. Louis Cardinals during the 1990 season. Smith set a league record with 47 saves in 1991 and led the NL again with 43 saves in 1992.

Shortly after he set the career save record, the Cardinals traded Smith to the AL's New York Yankees, and he went to the Baltimore Orioles in 1994. Through the 1994 season, Smith had a 68–82 record and 434 saves in 887 appearances. He had struck out 1,152 hitters while walking 427 in 1,163⅔ innings.

Smith, Margaret (Mrs. Court)

TENNIS
b. July 16, 1942, Albury, Australia

Although she never seems to be given full credit for the accomplishment, Smith won 26 major singles championships, more than any other woman in history, and is one of only three women to win all four grand slam events in a year (the others are Maureen Connolly and Steffi Graf).

A solid, hard-hitting but unspectacular player, the 5-foot-9 Smith won the Australian national title from 1960 through 1966, the French title in 1962 and 1964, the U.S. title in 1962 and 1965, and Wimbledon in 1963 and 1965. She retired from competition after marrying Barry Court in 1966 and had a child.

Court persuaded her to return to competition and became her manager in 1968. Under the name Margaret Smith Court, she won the Australian and French championship in 1969, then swept all four major titles in 1970. Her 46-game victory over Billie Jean King that year was the longest women's singles final in Wimbledon history.

After becoming pregnant late in 1971, Smith Court again left competition, returning in 1973. Traveling with an entourage that included her husband, children Danny and Marika, and a nanny, she won three of the four grand slam events, the Australian, French, and U.S. championships that year. However, her best known 1973 match was a Mother's Day defeat by 55-year-old Bobby Riggs, who lost later that year to Billie Jean King.

She retired permanently after winning the 1973 Virginia Slims Trophy and leading all women players with $180,058 in winnings.

In addition to her singles championships, Smith Court won 21 women's doubles titles and 19 mixed doubles titles in grand slam tournaments.
★ International Tennis Hall of Fame; International Women's Sports Hall of Fame

Smith, Ozzie (Osborne E.)

BASEBALL
b. Dec. 26, 1954, Mobile, Ala.

The "Wizard of Oz" is unquestionably the greatest fielding shortstop ever, combining speed, quickness, leaping ability, sure hands, and a strong throwing arm. Smith makes difficult plays look easy and nearly impossible plays look merely difficult.

The 5-foot-10, 168-pound switch-hitter arrived in the major leagues with the NL's San Diego Padres in 1978 after graduating from Cal Polytech–San Luis Obispo and spending part of a season in the minor leagues.

He was quickly recognized as an outstanding defensive player, but his hitting was weak. After a .258 start as a rookie, he batted only .211, .230, and .222 with San Diego, and he was traded to the St. Louis Cardinals in 1982 for Garry

Templeton, a good fielding shortstop who was also a very good hitter.

With the Cardinals, Smith developed into a much better offensive player, an above-average hitter with skills that win games: bunting, executing the hit and run, stealing bases, and hitting the ball to the right side to advance a runner from second to third.

Smith's best offensive season was 1987, when he batted .303, stole 43 bases, scored 104 runs, and had 75 RBI. But much of his value still rests in his fielding. Smith won 13 consecutive Gold Gloves, an NL record for any position, from 1980 through 1992, and he holds a host of records for shortstops.

Among them are: most years with 500 or more assists, 8; most years leading the league in chances accepted, 8; most assists in a season, 621 in 1980; fewest errors in 150 or more games, 8 in 1991; most years leading the NL in fielding percentage, 7; most consecutive years leading the NL in fielding percentage, 4.

Through the 1994 season, Smith had 2,365 hits in 2,447 games, including 387 doubles, 66 triples, and 26 home runs. He had stolen 569 bases, scored 1,205 runs, and driven in 764.

Smith, Tommie C.

TRACK AND FIELD
b. June 5, 1944, Clarksville, Tex.

At San Jose State University, Smith played football and basketball as well as running on the track team, but he decided to focus on track in his junior year. In a career that spanned just four years, he set a total of seven world records.

Smith won the AAU and NCAA 220-yard championships in 1967 and was AAU champion in the 200-meter event in 1968. He tied the world record of 20.0 seconds for the straightaway 200-yard and 200-meter dashes in 1965. On June 11, 1966, he ran a world record 20.0 around a turn for both distances and lowered the straightaway record to 19.5 seconds.

He also anchored the first team to break the 3-minute mark in the 4 x 400-meter relay, the U.S. team that did 2:59.6 at a 1966 international meet. In 1967 Smith set world records of 44.5 in the 400-meter and 44.8 in the 440-yard dash.

With San Jose teammate John Carlos, Smith was a member of the Olympic Project for Human Rights, which originally wanted black athletes to boycott the 1968 Olympics. The boycott didn't come off. Smith and Carlos both qualified for the final in the Olympic 200-meter and agreed to stage their own protest if they won medals.

However, Smith was a doubtful starter. He had limped off the track with a pulled groin muscle after winning his semifinal heat, and he said later, "I was eighty percent certain I was out." Wrapped in tape from his waist to the bottom of his shorts, Smith not only won the event, he set a world record of 19.83 seconds, and Carlos finished third.

When the national anthem was played at the medal ceremony, Smith and Carlos bowed their heads and raised their fists in the black power salute. They were banned from further Olympic competition and expelled from the Olympic village. In the furor, Smith's gutsy performance in his victory was overlooked.

Smith joined the Cincinnati Bengals as a backup wide receiver after graduating from San Jose State in 1969 but saw little action in his three seasons. He later became track coach and athletic director at Oberlin College in Ohio, and since 1978 he has been track and cross-country coach at Santa Monica College in California.

★ National Track & Field Hall of Fame

Smoke, Marcia I. (Jones)

CANOEING
b. July 18, 1941, Oklahoma City, Okla.

After graduating from Michigan State University in 1963, Smoke dominated U.S. women's canoeing for a decade. After winning the kayak singles championship in 1964, she finished in a tie with her sister, Sperry Jones Rademaker, in 1965. Smoke then won the title from 1966 through 1970.

In 1971 there were two races, at 500

and 5,000 meters, and Smoke won both of them. She won the 500-meter race in 1972 and 1973, and her sister won the 5,000-meter both years and in 1974.

Smoke won the bronze medal in the 500-meter at the 1964 Olympics, the highest finish ever for a U.S. woman, and she placed fourth in 1968.

Snavely, Carl G.
FOOTBALL
b. July 31, 1894, Omaha, Nebr.
d. July 12, 1975

The soft-spoken, methodical Snavely played baseball, basketball, and football at Lebanon Valley College in Pennsylvania, then began coaching high school football in 1915. At Bellefonte Academy from 1924 through 1926, his teams won 34 games and tied 1. They were beaten four times by college freshman teams.

Snavely went to Bucknell in 1927 and spent seven seasons there, compiling a 42–16–8 record. His 1931 team was undefeated, winning 6 games and tying 3. He moved into major college football with North Carolina in 1935. After winning 16 games and losing only 3, Snavely left for Cornell.

Cornell had won just 2 games in the previous two seasons, and they won only 3 in Snavely's first year. Then they began to win consistently. His 1939 team won all 8 of its games, including a major upset over Ohio State, 23–14, after trailing 14–0 in the second quarter.

In 1945 Snavely returned to North Carolina. He produced an 8–1–1 team in 1946, losing to Georgia in the Sugar Bowl, 20–10. His 1948 team was undefeated in the regular season, winning 9 and tying 1, but also lost the Sugar Bowl, 14–6, to Oklahoma.

A strong believer in the single wing, Snavely never adopted the T formation. He had three losing seasons in a row, 1950 through 1952, and then left North Carolina for Washington University in St. Louis. He retired after in 1958 season. In 32 years of coaching, he had a 180–96–16 record.
★ College Football Hall of Fame

Snead, Samuel J.
GOLF
b. May 27, 1912, Hot Springs, Va.

His smooth, graceful, natural swing made Snead a great player from tee to green. He won more tournaments than any other professional golfer in history and doubtless could have won quite a few more if he had putted well.

Snead taught himself to play while a young caddie and became a professional in 1936, when he won the West Virginia Closed Pro championship. After he won five tournaments and finished second in the U.S. Open in 1937, it seemed obvious that he'd eventually win the Open, perhaps several times.

Despite all his other victories, Snead became known for not being able to win the Open. He needed a 5 on the final hole to win in 1938, but shot an embarrassing 8 and finished third. From that time on, the Open haunted him. He and Lew Worsham tied for the lead in 1947, but Worsham won the playoff. Snead was also the runner-up in 1949 and 1953.

He won his first major tournament, the PGA championship, in 1942. Snead won the 1946 British Open, the Masters and PGA in 1949, the PGA in 1951, and the Masters in 1952 and 1954.

Snead was the tour's leading money winner in 1938, 1949, and 1950, and he won the Vare Trophy for the fewest strokes per round in 1938, 1949, 1950, and 1955. Late in his career, he developed severe putting problems and went first to a croquet-style technique and then to a strange, side-saddle stance, neither of which was particularly effective.

He still showed flashes of brilliance after he reached his fifties, winning the PGA Seniors championship in 1964, 1965, 1967, 1970, 1972, and 1973. His 81 PGA tour victories is 11 more than Jack Nicklaus, who is in second place all-time. Snead earned a total of $541,514 in official tour events.
★ PGA Hall of Fame; World Golf Hall of Fame

Snider, Duke (Edwin D.)

BASEBALL

b. Sept. 19, 1926, Los Angeles, Calif.

Everybody knew about Willie Mays of the Giants and Mickey Mantle of the Yankees during the 1950s, but Brooklyn Dodger fans knew there was a third great center fielder playing in New York. They called him the "Duke of Flatbush."

Snider was a part-time player with the Dodgers in 1947 and 1948, then became a starter in 1949. He led the NL with 199 hits in 1950, when he batted .321.

For five straight seasons, from 1953 through 1957, Snider hit 40 or more home runs with a career high of 43 in 1956, when he led the league. Snider was the league leader in runs scored with 132 in 1953, 120 in 1954, and 126 in 1955. He led in RBI with 136 in 1955 and in slugging with a .627 percentage in 1953 and a .598 percentage in 1956.

Snider played in six World Series with the Dodgers and batted .286 with 11 home runs. He hit .345 with 4 home runs in 1952, when the Dodgers lost to the Yankees in seven games, and he was the hero of their seven-game win over the Yankees in 1955, when he batted .320 with 4 home runs, 5 runs scored, and 7 RBI.

Though he didn't have the speed of Mays or Mantle, Snider was a fine defensive player because of his knowledge of how to play hitters and his quick reaction to the ball.

Snider went with the Dodgers to Los Angeles in 1958 and played with them through 1962. He finished his career with the New York Mets in 1963 and the San Francisco Giants in 1964.

In 18 seasons, Snider had a .295 average on 2,116 hits, including 358 doubles, 85 triples, and 407 home runs. He scored 1,259 runs and had 1,333 RBI.

★ Baseball Hall of Fame

Snyder, Larry (Lawrence N.)

TRACK AND FIELD

b. Aug. 9, 1896, Canton, Ohio
d. Sept. 25, 1981

The Ohio high school champion in the high jump, Snyder entered Ohio State University in 1922 after serving in World War I. He captained the track team in 1924 and 1925.

Snyder coached high school sports until 1932, when he became head track coach at his alma mater. Among the athletes he coached were Glenn Davis, Jesse Owens, and Mal Whitfield, who combined to win ten Olympic gold medals. His athletes set 14 world records in various events, and he produced 52 All-Americans.

At the 1960 Olympics, Snyder was head coach of the U.S. track team that won eight gold medals. He retired in 1965.

★ National Track & Field Hall of Fame

Sonnenberg, Gustavus A.

FOOTBALL, WRESTLING

b. March 6, 1898, Ewen, Mich.
d. Sept. 12, 1944

After winning some All-American mentions as a tackle at Dartmouth College in 1920, Sonnenberg went to Detroit University. He played in the NFL with the Columbus Tigers in 1923, the Detroit Panthers in 1925 and 1926, and the Providence Steamroller in 1927 and 1928. He also played one game for Providence in 1930.

The 5-foot-8, 190-pound Sonnenberg began wrestling professionally in 1928. He developed the tactic of the "flying tackle," in which he flew through the air and hit his opponent with his head. As a result, he was sometimes known as "Gus the Goat."

In his first big match, in May 1928, Sonnenberg beat the 270-pound Wayne "Big" Munn, a former world champion. The Boston *Evening Globe* said of the match, "It looked like a rough and tumble football game, with Munn representing a live tackling dummy. Only when he had flopped Munn to the floor with his flying tackles did Sonnenberg resort to an orthodox wrestling hold."

Sonnenberg had five matches against Ed "Strangler" Lewis and won four of them. His first victory over Lewis, before a crowd of 20,000 at Boston Garden on January 4, 1929, brought him the world heavyweight championship. However, he lost the title to Ed "Don" George on December 10, 1930, and never regained it, though he continued wrestling for nearly nine years.

After winning an estimated $1 million in the ring, Sonnenberg was barred from wrestling in Rhode Island, his home base, in 1939 because of an irregular heartbeat. While serving as a physical training instructor in the U.S. Navy during World War II, Sonnenberg developed leukemia and died in a naval hospital in Maryland.

Soutar, Judy (Cook)

BOWLING

b. June 28, 1944, Leawood, Kans.

As Judy Cook, Soutar was named the 1963 "Star of Tomorrow" by the WIBC, but tomorrow didn't come until 1973, after she'd married PBA bowler Dave Soutar.

After being runner-up in 13 consecutive tournaments in 1973, Soutar won the Pearl Cup in Japan, the Ebonite Classic, and the Cavalcade of Stars, becoming only the fourth woman bowler to win consecutive tournaments. She was the tour's leading money winner and the bowler of the year.

Soutar won the WIBC Queens Tournament in 1974, and in 1975 she was again the top money winner and the bowler of the year. A four-time *Bowler's Journal* All-American, she won the WIBC doubles in 1969 and 1970 and the all-events in 1974, when she was also on the WIBC championship team.

★ WIBC Hall of Fame

Southworth, Billy (William H.)

BASEBALL

b. March 9, 1893, Harvard, Nebr. d. Nov. 15, 1969

A left-handed hitter but right-handed thrower, Southworth was a pretty good outfielder with the Cleveland Indians, Pittsburgh Pirates, Boston Braves, New York Giants, and St. Louis Cardinals, batting .297 in 13 seasons.

But he made his mark as a manager. He managed the St. Louis Cardinals for part of the 1929 season, his last as a

player, then worked in the minor leagues until 1940, when he again took over the Cardinals. They were in seventh place when he took charge but had a 69–40 record under Southworth to finish third.

After a second-place finish in 1941, the Cardinals won three straight pennants. They beat the New York Yankees in five games in the 1942 World Series, lost to the Yankees in five games in 1943, and beat the St. Louis Browns in six games in 1944.

The Cardinals finished second again in 1945 and Southworth was hired away by the Boston Braves. He took them to the 1948 pennant behind the pitching of Warren Spahn and Johnny Sain. The Boston slogan that season was "Spahn and Sain, then pray for rain" because the pitching staff lacked depth.

The Braves slipped into fourth place in 1949 and 1950, and they were in fifth when Southworth was fired during the 1951 season. He retired from baseball with a 1,044–704 record, a .597 winning percentage.

Spahn, Warren E.

BASEBALL

b. April 23, 1921, Buffalo, N.Y.

A first baseman as a youngster, Spahn couldn't win a starting job in high school so he began pitching. He signed a professional contract with the Boston Braves organization in 1940 and spent three years in the minor leagues, although he was with the Braves briefly in 1942, then went into the Army during World War II.

He became a part-time starter and reliever with the Braves in 1947, compiling an 8–5 record, and was a full-time starter the following year, when he had a 21–10 record and led the league with a 2.33 ERA and $289\frac{2}{3}$ innings pitched.

After slipping to 15–12 in 1948, Spahn led the NL in wins with a 21–14 record, in complete games with 25, in innings with $302\frac{1}{3}$, and in strikeouts with 151 in 1949. He had a league-leading 21 victories against 17 losses in 1950, when he also led with 191 strikeouts.

Spahn led the league with 7 shutouts, 26 complete games, and 164 strikeouts in 1951, and he was the strikeout leader for the fourth consecutive year with 183 in 1952. Despite a 2.98 ERA, he had only a 14–19 record that year.

The Braves moved to Milwaukee in 1953. After going 21–12 and 17–14, Spahn won 20 or more games six years in a row. He was the NL's Cy Young Award winner in 1957, when he led with 21 victories and 18 complete games and posted a 2.69 ERA. Spahn had a 1–1 record and a 4.70 ERA in Milwaukee's seven-game World Series victory over the New York Yankees.

He also led in victories with 22 in 1958, 21 in 1959, 21 in 1960, and 21 in 1961; in winning percentage with .667 in 1958; in complete games with 23 in 1958, 21 in 1959, 18 in 1960, 21 in 1961, 22 in 1962, and 22 in 1963; in shutouts with 4 in 1959 and 4 in 1961; in innings pitched with 290 in 1958 and 292 in 1959; and in ERA with 3.01 in 1961.

Spahn pitched a no-hitter in 1960, when he was 39 years old, and pitched another in 1961. He had his last outstanding season in 1963, when he went 23–7 with a 2.60 ERA. Then he suddenly became ineffective. He was sold to the New York Mets after a 6–13 record in 1964. Spahn left the major leagues after a 7–16 record with the Mets and the San Francisco Giants in 1965.

The 6-foot, 175-pound left-hander had an unusually high leg kick that brought him forward into a long, sweeping delivery. In his early years, he had a good fastball and a fine curve, but his mastery was built on control and outsmarting hitters. When he began to lose his fastball late in his career, he developed a screwball and even threw an occasional knuckleball.

Spahn managed a minor league team from 1967 through 1971 and pitched in three games in 1967, which delayed his eligibility for the Hall of Fame. Later he became pitching coach for the Cleveland Indians for two seasons.

Spahn had a career record of 363–245, with 63 shutouts and a 3.09 ERA. He struck out 2,583 hitters and walked 1,434 in 5,243⅔ innings. He holds the record for most career victories by a left-handed pitcher.

★ Baseball Hall of Fame

Spalding, Albert G.

BASEBALL
b. Sept. 2, 1850, Byron, Ill.
d. Sept. 9, 1915

By the time he was 16, Spalding was pitching for a semipro team, the Rockford, Illinois, Forest City club. In 1867 he beat the touring Washington Nationals, led by George Wright, and was offered $40 a week to clerk in a Chicago grocery store and play for its baseball team. The store went out of business, however, and Spalding returned home and began playing for Forest City again.

The team went on an eastern tour in 1870, compiling a 13–3–1 record. The National Association, the first major league, was organized the following year and Spalding joined its Boston team, managed by Harry Wright, George's brother.

Spalding had records of 19–10, 38–8, 41–14, 52–16, and 55–5 in five seasons with Boston, leading the association in victories each year. The National League replaced the association in 1876, and Spalding joined its Chicago franchise.

He and his brother, Walter, opened a sporting goods store in Chicago that year. Spalding had a 47–12 record, leading the NL in victories, in his only full season. He retired from playing after appearing in just four games in 1877 to devote full time to the business.

The company soon became the largest of its kind. Spalding bought interests in A. J. Reach and Company, a baseball manufacturer, and Wright and Ditson, a manufacturer of tennis balls and other equipment. His company also branched out into publishing, producing the annual *Spalding Guide* and pamphlets on many sports.

In the spring of 1889, Spalding took a group of 20 major league players on a world tour, introducing baseball to New Zealand, Australia, Ceylon, Egypt, Italy, France, and England. While on the tour, Spalding opened a branch in London and arranged to import bicycles and golf clubs.

Spalding continued as an adviser to the Chicago NL team, serving as its president from 1882 to 1891. He also founded the Chicago Athletic Club, and in 1903 he helped negotiate the peace agreement between the National and American Leagues.

★ Baseball Hall of Fame

Speaker, Tristram E.

BASEBALL
b. April 4, 1888, Hubbard, Tex.
d. Dec. 8, 1958

Originally a right-hander, Speaker broke his arm in a fall from a horse as a youngster, so he learned to bat and throw left-handed. He played baseball at Ft. Worth Polytechnic Institute, where he was a pitcher until the team's right fielder was injured. Speaker volunteered to replace him and became an outfielder, a position that he played throughout his career. He was spotted by a scout during his sophomore year and left school to play professionally in 1906.

After brief stints with the AL's Boston Red Sox in 1907 and 1908, Speaker became the team's starting center fielder in 1909. He batted .309, .340, and .334 in his first three full seasons, then won the league's most valuable player award in 1912, when he led the league with 53 doubles and 10 home runs, batted .383, stole 52 bases, and scored 136 runs.

The Red Sox won the pennant that year, and Speaker batted .300 in the team's seven-game World Series victory over the New York Giants. He led the AL with 193 hits, 46 doubles, and a .503 slugging percentage in 1914, then hit .322 to help lead Boston to another pennant in 1915. He batted .294 when the Red Sox beat the Philadelphia Phillies in a five-game Series.

The following season Boston wanted to cut his salary from $18,000 to $9,000, and Speaker refused to take the cut. He was traded to the Cleveland Indians for two players and $50,000. Speaker responded by leading the league in hitting with a .386 average. He was also the league leader with 211 hits, 41 doubles, and a .502 slugging percentage.

Speaker batted over .300 in 10 of the next 11 seasons and led the league in doubles with 33 in 1918, 50 in 1920, 52 in 1921, and 59 in 1923. He took over as Cleveland's playing manager in 1919 and guided the team to a pennant and World Series victory in 1920.

Late in 1926, Speaker suddenly resigned. It was later revealed that he and Ty Cobb had been accused of fixing a 1919 game between the Indians and the Detroit Tigers. Both men were cleared by Commissioner Kenesaw Mountain Landis, and Speaker went to the Washington Senators in 1927, batting .327. He ended his playing career with the Senators in 1928.

Not only a great hitter, Speaker was one of the finest defensive outfielders in history. Because of his great speed and ability to go back on the ball, he could play a very shallow center field. Twice in 1918, he caught shallow drives and made unassisted double plays at second base. He also had a strong arm: his 35 assists in 1909 tied the AL record for outfielders and still stands.

In 22 major league seasons, Speaker batted .345 with 3,514 hits, including a record 792 doubles, 222 triples, and 117 home runs. He stole 434 bases, scored 1,882 runs, and had 1,529 RBI.

★ Baseball Hall of Fame

Spears, Doc (Clarence W.)

FOOTBALL
b. July 24, 1894, DeWitt, Ark.
d. Feb. 1, 1964

Only 5-foot-7, Spears weighed 236 pounds in his playing days at Dartmouth. He was nicknamed "Fat," but was both fast and powerful. An All-American guard in 1914 and 1915, Spears earned a medical degree after graduating from Dartmouth, but coaching became his profession for nearly 20 years.

He had a 21–9–1 record in four seasons at his alma mater, 1917 through 1920, and then went to the University of West Virginia. His 1922 team was undefeated, winning 10 games and tying 1.

Among the victories was West Virginia's first-ever win over Pittsburgh. In four seasons, Spears had a 30–6–3 record.

Spears then went to Minnesota for five seasons. Because his teams had such a reputation for bruising play, most other Western Conference (Big Ten) schools refused to schedule them. In 1925 Minnesota had only three conference games. The 1927 team was undefeated, winning 6 games and tying 2.

Because of continuing disputes with the school's president and athletic director, Spears left Minnesota for Oregon in 1930. He had a 13–4–2 in two seasons there before going to the University of Wisconsin. His first Wisconsin team went 6–1–1, but had losing records in two of the next three seasons.

Spears retired in 1935 to practice medicine, but he came out of retirement during World War II to coach the University of Maryland in 1943 and 1944. His overall coaching record was 110–57–12.
★ College Football Hall of Fame

Sperber, Paula (Mrs. Carter)
BOWLING
b. March 1, 1951, Miami, Fla.

Sperber started bowling when she was 11, and at 15 she rolled a 290 in the Algiers Junior Classic. A left-hander, the 5-foot-6, blue-eyed blonde drew much notice because of her cover girl looks when she became a professional in 1969.

She was named bowler of the year in 1971, when she won the U.S. Women's Open. Sperber won the championship for a second time in 1975 and was named to the *Bowler's Journal* All-American team three times.

Sperber is married to Don Carter, one of the greatest male bowlers in history.

Spitz, Mark A.
SWIMMING
b. Feb. 10, 1950, Modesto, Calif.

Taught by his father, whose motto was, Swimming isn't everything — winning is, Spitz established himself as one of the greatest swimmers of all time by winning seven gold medals at the 1972 Olympics, all in world record times. He had also won two gold medals, a silver, and a bronze in a "disappointing" 1968 Olympic performance.

Spitz spent his early years in Hawaii, where he learned to swim, before his family moved back to California when he was 8. He won his first major title in 1966, the AAU outdoor 100-meter butterfly. In 1967 he repeated in that event and also won the AAU outdoor and indoor 200-meter butterfly events. He took five gold medals at the Pan-American Games that year, setting two world records in the process.

In 1968 Spitz won national outdoor championships in the 100- and 200-meter freestyles and the 100-meter butterfly and was indoor titlist in the 100-yard and 200-meter butterfly events. He brashly predicted that he would win six gold medals at the Mexico City Olympics but failed to win an individual gold. He was a member of the winning 4 x 100-meter and 4 x 200-meter relay teams, and he also took a silver in the 100-meter butterfly and a bronze in the 100-meter freestyle.

Spitz entered Indiana University in January 1969. He was the NCAA champion in the 100-yard butterfly four years in a row, 1969 through 1972, and he won the 200- and 500-yard freestyles in 1969 and the 200-yard butterfly in 1971 and 1972. He was also the AAU outdoor champion in the 100-meter freestyle and 200-meter butterfly in 1971 and in the 200-meter freestyle and 100-meter butterfly in 1970 and 1971. Indoors, he won AAU titles in the 100-meter butterfly in 1970, in the 100-yard freestyle, 100-yard butterfly, and 200-meter butterfly in 1972.

The winner of the 1971 Sullivan Award as the nation's outstanding amateur athlete, Spitz was named male athlete of the year by the Associated Press after his incredible performance at the 1972 Munich Olympics.

At Munich, he set world records of 51.22 seconds in the 100-meter freestyle, 1:52.78 in the 200-meter freestyle, 54.27 seconds in the 100-meter butterfly, and 2:00.70 in the 200-meter butterfly. He swam the anchor legs on the 4 x 100-meter freestyle and the 4 x 200-meter relay teams, which set world records of 3:26.42 and 7:35.78. Spitz also swam the butterfly leg on the 4 x 100-meter medley relay team, which won in a world record time of 3:48.16.

Spitz posed for a news photograph wearing all seven medals and commented afterward, "The medals weighed a lot. They have heavy, crazy chains. Really, it was hard to stand up straight wearing them all at one time."

He retired from competition immediately after the Olympics and profited from a number of television commercials and appearances during the next couple of years.

★ Olympic Hall of Fame

Sprackling, William E.

FOOTBALL
b. Sept. 6, 1890, Cleveland, Ohio
d. March 27, 1980

"Sprack" had one of the greatest games in college football history when Brown beat Yale, 21–0, in 1909. He rushed for 36 yards on 9 carries, completed 5 of 6 passes for 180 yards and 1 touchdown, returned 13 punts for 150 yards, returned 5 kickoffs for 90 yards, and kicked 3 field goals. Three weeks later, he returned a kickoff 110 yards for a touchdown in a 21–8 upset of Carlisle before a large crowd at the Polo Grounds in New York.

At only 5-foot-9 and 145 pounds, Sprackling was the quarterback on Walter Camp's All-American team in 1910; he was on the second team in 1911 and on the third team in 1909. A fiery competitor and leader, he was probably the most accurate passer of his day. His career total of 11 touchdown passes was the Brown University record for many years.

★ College Football Hall of Fame

Sprague, Bud (Mortimer E.)

FOOTBALL
b. Sept. 8, 1904, Dallas, Tex.

Sprague played tackle for some very good University of Texas teams from 1922 through 1924, but Texas was not nationally known for its football during that period. He became much better

known when he entered the U.S. Military Academy after graduating from Texas. He was named to Walter Camp's All-American team in 1926.

As a senior in 1928, Sprague captained Army to an 8–2–0 record. During his three years as a starter at Texas, the school won 20 games, lost 5, and tied 2, while Army was 24–4–1 in his three seasons there.

Sprague was one of four brothers who captained college football teams. The others played at Southern Methodist University. Howard captained the 1932 SMU team, John was SMU captain in 1936, and Charlie captained the 1938 team.

★ College Football Hall of Fame

Spurrier, Steve (Stephen O.)

FOOTBALL
b. April 20, 1945, Miami Beach, Fla.

A quarterback at Florida University, Spurrier was a consensus All-American and winner of the Heisman Trophy as college football's outstanding player in 1966. During his three seasons as a starter, he completed 392 of 692 passes for 4,848 yards and 36 touchdowns.

The 6-foot-2, 205-pound Spurrier joined the San Francisco 49ers as a first-round draft choice in 1967. For his first five seasons, he was primarily a punter, but he took over as the team's starting quarterback when John Brodie was injured in the middle of the 1972 season and led the 49ers to five wins in six games. He became a backup again with Brodie's return in 1973.

The Tampa Bay Buccaneers selected Spurrier in the 1976 expansion draft; he was a starter there for one season before retiring as a player. In his ten NFL seasons, Spurrier completed 597 of 1,151 passes for 6,878 yards and 40 touchdowns. He also rushed for 2 touchdowns.

After serving as an assistant coach on the college level for five years, Spurrier in 1983 became head coach of the Tampa Bay Bandits in the U.S. Football League. He had a 35–19 record in three seasons before the USFL folded.

Spurrier returned to the University of Florida as head coach in 1987. Through the 1994 season, he had a 69–24–2 record.

★ College Football Hall of Fame

Stabler, Ken M.

FOOTBALL
b. Dec. 25, 1945, Foley, Ala.

After graduating from the University of Alabama, Stabler was chosen in the third round of the 1968 AFL-NFL draft by the Oakland Raiders. He spent a season on the team's taxi squad, then left football for a year.

He returned to the Raiders in 1970 and was a backup for three seasons before he finally become a starter in 1973, at the age of 27. He led the league with a 62.7 completion percentage that year.

The left-handed Stabler, nicknamed "Snake" because of his ability to elude rushers, won the Bell Trophy as the NFL's most valuable player in 1974, when he was also named player of the year by Associated Press and *The Sporting News.* He completed 178 of 310 passes for 2,469 yards and a league-leading 26 touchdowns. The Raiders went to the AFC championship game but lost to the Pittsburgh Steelers, 24–13.

Stabler was again named *The Sporting News* player of the year in 1976, when he completed 207 of 343 attempts for 3,104 yards and 24 touchdowns. This time the Raiders beat the Steelers 24–7 in the AFC championship game, and Stabler threw 12 completions in 19 attempts for 180 yards and 1 touchdown as Oakland beat the Minnesota Vikings 32–14 in Super Bowl XI.

Stabler spent three more seasons with Oakland, was with the Houston Oilers in 1980 and 1981, and finished his career with the New Orleans Saints from 1982 through 1984. In his 15 seasons, he had 2,270 completions in 3,793 attempts for 27,938 yards and 194 touchdowns.

Stacy, Hollis

GOLF
b. March 16, 1954, Savannah, Ga.

Stacy won the 1969 USGA Junior Girls Championship, the youngest winner ever at 15 years and 4 months. She also won the event in 1970 and 1971 and is one of only two golfers to win the title three years in a row.

She left Rollins College to join the LPGA tour in July 1974. Her first professional victory came in the 1977 Rail Charity Golf Classic. Stacy also won the U.S. Women's Open that year, and she repeated in 1978. With her 1984 Women's Open victory, Stacy became one of only four golfers to have won the event more than twice. She also won the 1983 Peter Jackson Classic, giving her four major titles.

From 1977 through 1985 Stacy won at least one tournament a year, and in 1985 she became the LPGA's tenth millionaire. She began cutting back on her tournament play in 1988 to devote more time to golf course design. She is also an associate golf coach at the University of Southern California.

Through 1993, Hollis Stacy had won $1,717,707, fifteenth on the all-time LPGA list.

Stagg, Amos Alonzo

BASKETBALL, FOOTBALL
b. Aug. 16, 1862, West Orange, N.J.
d. March 17, 1965

"All football comes from Stagg," Knute Rockne once said. It was not much of an exaggeration: during American football's formative years, Stagg came up with hundreds of innovations, especially on offense.

An end at Yale, Stagg was named to the first All-American team in 1889, when he was a student at the divinity school. He was also an outstanding baseball pitcher who had a 17–3 career record against archrival Harvard. Because he had difficulty speaking to an audience, he gave up his plans to become a minister, and in 1890 entered the YMCA International training school at Springfield, Massachusetts, now Springfield College.

Stagg organized and coached the school's first football team, known as "Stagg's stubby Christians." One of the players was James Naismith, who invented basketball in 1891.

When the University of Chicago was established in 1892, its president, James Rainey Harper, decided that a winning football team would help the school became famous fast, and he hired Stagg for $2,500 a year, along with life tenure. Since there were no eligibility rules at the time, Stagg actually played for the first two teams he coached.

Chicago soon became a power in the Western Conference (now Big Ten), winning seven championships between 1896 and 1913. Four of his teams were undefeated. Stagg invented the idea of shifting offensive players into a new formation and running a play before the defense could react. As early as 1890, at Springfield, he developed the wingback principle by pulling his ends into the backfield.

From early in the century until the modern T formation was created in 1940, shifts and wingback formations dominated offensive football. Among Stagg's other important contributions are the quick kick, the onside kick, the use of double flankers, the pass-run option play, and the man in motion. He was also probably the first to have the quarterback standing behind the center to take a direct snap, an essential principle of the T formation.

Stagg was also instrumental in encouraging the spread of basketball through the Midwest. In 1917 he organized the National Interscholastic Basketball Tournament, which brought together high school teams from throughout the country, helping to standardize the rather haphazard rules of the time. The tournament was an annual event through 1931, when it was ended by the Depression.

Stagg left Chicago in 1932, when he reached the university's mandatory retirement age of 70, and coached at College of the Pacific from 1933 through 1946. He was named coach of the year in 1943 when his team upset UCLA and the University of California. At 89, he became co-coach with his son at Susquehanna College, handling the offense.

Pudge Heffelfinger, a teammate of Stagg's at Yale, once said, "For all his biblical precepts, Lon was the foxiest of gridiron tacticians. He thought two plays ahead of the other fellow, like a master surveying a chessboard."

Stagg had a career record of 314–199–35.

★ Basketball Hall of Fame; College Football Hall of Fame

Staley, Dawn M.
BASKETBALL
b. May 4, 1970, Philadelphia, Pa.

The 5-foot-5 Staley was named national high school player of the year in 1988 by *USA Today*, the only player under 6 feet tall to win that honor. She became a starter at the University of Virginia as a freshman, averaging 18.5 points a game.

Staley won the Naismith Trophy as the nation's outstanding woman collegiate player in 1991 and 1992 and was the winner of the 1991 Honda Broderick Cup as the outstanding college athlete of the year.

In her four years as a starter, Staley scored 2,135 points, an average of 16.3 per game, and had an NCAA record of 454 steals. She was named the outstanding player in the 1991 NCAA tournament, when Virginia lost in the finals to Tennessee.

Stanczyk, Stanley A.
WEIGHTLIFTING
b. May 10, 1925, Armstrong, Wis.

Undefeated from 1946 until the 1952 Olympics, Stanczyk won five consecutive world championships in three different weight divisions and six straight national titles in two weight divisions.

At the 1948 Olympics, Stanczyk attempted a world record of 132.5 kilograms on his third snatch. He seemed to have succeeded, and the judges ruled it a fair lift, but Stanczyk told them his knee had scraped the floor, invalidating the attempt. Despite that, he won the light heavyweight title by 37.5 kilograms, the largest margin for any weight class in Olympic history.

Stanczyk won the U.S. middleweight championship in 1947, the light heavyweight title from 1948 through 1951 and in 1953. An injury kept him from competing in 1952. He was the world champion as a lightweight in 1946, as a middleweight in 1947, and as a light heavyweight in 1949, 1950, and 1952. There was no competition in 1948 or 1951. Stanczyk won a silver medal in the light heavyweight division at the 1952 Olympics.

After placing third in the world championships in 1953 and 1954, he retired from competition. However, Stanczyk continued bowling competitively and maintained a 190 average over a 25-year period.

Stanfel, Dick (Richard)

FOOTBALL
b. July 20, 1927, San Francisco, Calif.

An All-American guard at the University of San Francisco in 1951, the 6-foot-3, 240-pound Stanfel was chosen by the Detroit Lions in the second round of the 1952 NFL draft.

Stanfel immediately became a starter on offense, and his powerful run blocking and pass protecting helped the Lions win the 1953 NFL championship.

An All-Pro in 1953 and 1954, Stanfel was traded to the Washington Redskins in 1956. He spent three seasons with Washington, making All-Pro each year. Stanfel retired after the 1958 season and became an assistant coach at Notre Dame. He has also been an assistant with several professional teams, most recently as offensive line coach for the Chicago Bears. In 1980 Stanfel served as interim coach of the NFL's New Orleans Saints, where he had a 1–3–0 record.

Stanfield, Andy (Andrew W.)

TRACK AND FIELD
b. Dec. 29, 1927, Washington, D.C.
d. June 15, 1985

Running for Seton Hall University, Stanfield won the IC4A indoor 60-meter dash and outdoor 100-meter from 1949 through 1951. He was also the outdoor 200-meter champion in 1949 and 1951. Stanfield won both sprints at the AAU national outdoor meet in 1949 and was the IC4A indoor long jump titlist in 1951.

Because of a series of leg injuries, he began to concentrate on the 200-meter/220-yard dash late in 1951. Stanfield set a world record for both distances, around a turn, of 20.6 seconds on May 5, 1951. He tied that record at the 1952 Olympic trials.

At the Helsinki Games, Stanfield won the 200-meter, tying Jesse Owens's Olympic record of 20.7 seconds, and he also ran on the gold medal 4 x 100-meter relay team. Stanfield won the AAU 200-meter title in 1952 and 1953 and was the silver medalist in the event at the 1956 Olympics. He then retired from competition.

★ National Track & Field Hall of Fame

Stargell, Willie (Wilver D.)

BASEBALL
b. March 6, 1941, Earlsboro, Okla.

The 6-foot-2½, 225-pound Stargell joined the NL's Pittsburgh Pirates briefly in 1962 and became a starter the following season, usually in left field but sometimes at first base. A left-hander, he hit 20 or more home runs each year from 1964 through 1970.

Stargell wasn't much noticed until he led the NL with 48 home runs in 1971, when he batted .295 and had 125 RBI. The Pirates won the pennant and World Series that year, but Stargell didn't get a hit in the league championship series and batted only .208 in the World Series.

He had his best overall offensive season in 1973, when he led the league with 43 doubles, 44 home runs, 119 RBI, and a .646 slugging percentage. After he batted .301 with 25 home runs and 96 RBI in 1974, injuries began to trouble him. He played in only 63 games in 1977, and it seemed his career might be nearly over.

"Pops" had one last fine season, though. A team leader in the clubhouse as well as on the field, Stargell made the disco hit "We Are Family" the Pittsburgh theme song and batted .281 with 32 home runs and 82 RBI in just 126 games to help lead the Pirates to the 1979 Eastern Division championship.

Stargell shared the league's most valuable player award in 1979 with

Keith Hernandez and was the MVP of Pittsburgh's league championship series win over the Cincinnati Reds, hitting .455 with 2 home runs. He hit 2 home runs in the first four games of the World Series against the Baltimore Orioles. Then, with Pittsburgh trailing 1–0 in the seventh game, Stargell hit a 2-run homer, and the Pirates went on to win, 4–1. He was named World Series MVP and won the male athlete of the year award from the Associated Press.

Stargell played just 67 games in 1980, 38 in 1981, and 74 in 1982 before retiring. In 21 seasons, all with Pittsburgh, he batted .282 with 2,232 hits, including 423 doubles, 55 triples, and 475 home runs. He scored 1,195 runs and drove in 1,540.

★ Baseball Hall of Fame

Starr, Bart (Bryan Bartlett)

FOOTBALL

b. Jan. 9, 1934, Montgomery, Ala.

Starr won headlines as a freshman quarterback at the University of Alabama when he threw four touchdown passes in a 1953 Orange Bowl victory over Syracuse University. However, the arrival of the one-platoon system in his sophomore year turned Starr into a part-time player, and he was virtually forgotten as a senior in 1955, when Alabama lost all ten of its games.

The Green Bay Packers chose him in the seventeenth round of the 1956 NFL draft of college players. Starr was a backup as a rookie and shared starting time with other quarterbacks for three years before taking over the job during the 1960 season, Vince Lombardi's first year with the team.

During the next eight years, Starr guided the Packers to six division championships, five league titles, and victories in the first two Super Bowls. A superbly accurate short passer, he led the league in completion percentage in 1962, 1966, 1968, and 1969, and was the NFL passing champion in 1962, 1964, and 1966. From 1964 through 1965, he through 294 consecutive passes without an interception, a record at the time.

Because the Packers used a ball-control offense that featured running, he never threw more than 295 passes a season and didn't have the high yardage and touchdown totals of other top quarterbacks. But he may have been just as important to the team as a signal caller. Although the Packers sent plays in from the sidelines, Starr changed the play at the line of scrimmage about half the time after sizing up the defense.

In the famous "Ice Bowl" game for the 1967 NFL championship, the Dallas Cowboys were winning 17–14 with 16 seconds to play and the Packers had a third down with less than a yard to go for a touchdown. On the previous two plays, halfback Donny Anderson had slipped on the icy field when taking handoffs and had gained virtually nothing. Using Green Bay's last time-out, Starr went to the sidelines and suggested running the same play, but with him keeping the ball instead of handing it off. He scored the touchdown and the Packers won, 21–14.

Starr was named the most valuable player in the first two Super Bowls. He completed 16 of 23 passes for 250 yards and 2 touchdowns in Green Bay's 35–10 victory over Kansas City and he had 13 completions in 24 attempts for 202 yards and 1 touchdown in the 33–14 win over Oakland.

He retired after the 1971 season with 1,808 completions in 3,149 attempts for 24,718 yards and 52 touchdowns. He also rushed for 15 touchdowns. Starr coached the Packers to a 52–76–2 record from 1975 through 1983.

★ Pro Football Hall of Fame

Staubach, Roger T.

FOOTBALL

b. Feb. 5, 1942, Cincinnati, Ohio

Nicknamed "Roger the Dodger" because of his great scrambling ability, Staubach was an All-American quarterback at Navy and winner of the Heisman Trophy as the nation's best college football player in 1963, his junior year.

The Dallas Cowboys selected him in the 1965 NFL draft of college players, even though Staubach had to spend four years in the Navy after graduating. He joined the team in 1969 as the oldest rookie in the league and he didn't become the Dallas starting quarterback until during the 1971 season, when he was 29.

Staubach was the NFL passing champion that year, was named National Football Conference player of the year by *The Sporting News*, and led the Cowboys to their first Super Bowl victory, a 24–3 win over the Miami Dolphins. He completed 12 of 19 passes for 119 yards and 2 touchdowns and was named the game's most valuable player.

He missed almost all of the 1972 season with a shoulder injury. In a first-round playoff game, Staubach came in at quarterback in the fourth quarter and threw two touchdown passes in the last 70 seconds to beat the San Francisco 49ers, 30–28. However, Dallas lost to Washington in the NFL championship game.

He won his second passing championship in 1973 and won two more in his final two seasons, 1978 and 1979. Staubach also quarterbacked the Cowboys to victory in Super Bowl XII, after the 1977 season, when they beat the Denver Broncos, 27–10.

During his 11 seasons with Dallas, Staubach took the Cowboys to 23 fourth-quarter victories, including 14 in the last two minutes or in overtime. He was named an All-Pro in 1971, 1976, and 1977.

Staubach completed 1,685 of 2,958 passes for 22,700 yards and 153 touchdowns. He rushed 410 times for 2,264 yards, a 5.5 average, and 20 touchdowns.
★ College Football Hall of Fame; Pro Football Hall of Fame

Stautner, Ernie (Ernest)

FOOTBALL
b. April 20, 1925, Prinzing-bei-Cham, Bavaria

After serving in the Marines during World War II, Stautner wanted to play football for Notre Dame but was turned down for being too small. He became a four-year starting tackle at Boston College, from 1946 through 1949.

He hoped to be drafted by the NFL's New York Giants, but the Giants also felt he was too small. The Pittsburgh Steelers made him their third-round draft choice in 1950.

The 6-foot-2, 235-pound Stautner was 10 or 15 pounds lighter than most defensive tackles of his era, but he missed only six games in 14 seasons. Because of his quickness, he was often moved to defensive end to rush the quarterback in passing situations, and he was occasionally used in the offensive line.

An All-Pro in 1956, Stautner played in five Pro Bowls. He retired after the 1963 season and was the long-time defensive coordinator for the Dallas Cowboys under Tom Landry.
★ Pro Football Hall of Fame

Steers, Lester

TRACK AND FIELD
b. June 16, 1917, Eureka, Calif.

Steers was almost the first high jumper to clear 7 feet. He did it at least once in practice, and several times he appeared to have done it in competition, but each time a measurement revealed that the bar was lower in the center than at the pegs that held it.

As an eighth-grader, Steers showed such promise that he was allowed to work out with the San Francisco Olympic Club track team. In 1937 he enrolled at San Mateo Junior College. After winning the AAU indoor high jump championship in 1938 and the outdoor championships in 1939 and 1940, Steers transferred to the University of Oregon.

Steers won the NCAA high jump championship and tied for best height at the AAU outdoor meet but lost the title on misses. He set a world record of 6 feet, $10^{25}/32$ inches that year; he later raised the record to 6–11. That mark wasn't broken until 1953.

When World War II began in December 1941, Steers retired from competition and worked at an Oregon shipyard for the duration of the war.
★ National Track & Field Hall of Fame

Steffen, Wally (Walter P.)

FOOTBALL
b. Oct. 9, 1886, Chicago, Ill.
d. March 9, 1937

After playing halfback and performing in the shadow of the great Walter Eckersall as a sophomore at the University of Chicago in 1906, Steffen was moved to quarterback when Eckersall graduated in 1907. The 5-foot-10, 158-pounder was named to Walter Camp's All-American first team in his senior year after having been on the second team as a junior.

A fine all-around player, Steffen was particularly dangerous as a breakaway runner. He had touchdown runs of 100 yards against Wisconsin and 75 yards against Minnesota in 1908. Steffen was also a good passer who often used the pass-run option that coach Amos Alonzo Stagg had devised for Eckersall.

"He's shifty, an artful dodger," Stagg said of Steffen, "and a keen, accurate passer . . . He is a good punter, drop-kicker, a smart playmaker, and an inspiring team leader." Steffen scored 156 points in three seasons as a starter and Chicago had a 13–2–1 record during that time.

After assisting Stagg at Chicago for several years, Steffen became head coach at Carnegie Tech from 1914 through 1932, compiling an 88–53–9 record.
★ College Football Hall of Fame

Stein, Herbert A.

FOOTBALL
b. 1899, Pittsburgh, Pa.

Originally a fullback, Stein was moved to center early in his sophomore year at Pittsburgh. He was Walter Camp's All-American at the position in 1920 and was named to Camp's third team in 1921. Parke Davis named Stein to his all-time All-American team in 1931.

Center was a very important position under "Pop" Warner, who coached Pittsburgh while Stein was there. The center had to make a long, accurate pass to the fullback in Warner's double wing, and he was a rover on defense, depended on to get to wherever the play was going and stop it.

During his three seasons as a starter, Pitt had a 21–5–4 record. In his All-American citation, Camp wrote, "Stein was really the keystone of the Pitt line. When things were disintegrating, he kept the team together."
★ College Football Hall of Fame

Steinkraus, Bill (William C.)

EQUESTRIAN SPORTS
b. Oct. 12, 1925, Cleveland, Ohio

One of the first members of the American Pony Club as a child, Steinkraus took up show jumping in 1938 and won the Maclay Trophy for hunter seat at the 1940 National Horse Show. After serving in the Army during World War II, he graduated from Yale in 1948.

Steinkraus rode for six U.S. Olympic equestrian teams, from 1952 through 1972, and was captain of the last five. In 1968 he became the first American to win an individual equestrian gold medal, taking the jumping event. The U.S. team won the bronze medal in the event. He was also a member of the 1960 and 1972 silver medal jumping teams.

He retired from competition after the 1972 Olympics and was president of the U.S. Equestrian Team from 1973 to 1983.

Steinkuhler, Dean E.

FOOTBALL
b. Jan. 27, 1961, Syracuse, Nebr.

The 6-foot-3, 275-pound Steinkuhler, who was timed at 4.67 seconds in the 40-yard sprint, was a starting offensive guard at the University of Nebraska in 1982 and 1983. He captained the team in his senior year, when he was a consensus All-American and winner of the Outland and Lombardi awards as the nation's outstanding collegiate lineman.

Because of his speed, Steinkuhler was used as a runner on Nebraska's "fumblerooski" play, on which the quarterback would take the snap from center, put the ball on the ground, and fake handoffs to running backs. In the meantime, Steinkuhler would pick the ball off the ground and run with it. He had a 19-yard touchdown run on that play in

Nebraska's 31–30 loss to the University of Miami in the 1984 Orange Bowl.

The second player chosen in the 1984 NFL draft, by the Houston Oilers, Steinkuhler suffered a knee injury midway through his rookie season. Because of the injury he was in and out of Houston's lineup through the 1989 season, and he then retired.

Steinmetz, Christian

BASKETBALL
b. June 28, 1882, Milwaukee, Wis.
d. June 11, 1963

A 5-foot-9, 137-pound guard, Steinmetz was an incredible scorer for the University of Wisconsin early in the century. At a time when teams often scored fewer than 20 points a game, he became the first college player to score more than 1,000 points in a career.

As captain of the team during the 1904–05 season, he outscored Wisconsin's opposition single-handedly with 462 points, an average of 25.7 per game. He was aided by the rule that allowed one player to take all of his team's free throws. Steinmetz hit 238 of 317 free throw attempts that season.

But he could also score from the field. He had 50 points in one game and made 20 field goals in another, still records for the school. He set another record that still stands by sinking 26 of 30 free throws in a game.

Retroactively named the first college player of the year for 1905 by the Helms Athletic Foundation, Steinmetz graduated in just three years and went on to law school. While practicing law, he coached high school basketball for a time and also officiated games.
★ Basketball Hall of Fame

Stenerud, Jan

FOOTBALL
b. Nov. 26, 1942, Festund, Norway

The first kicking specialist inducted into the Pro Football Hall of Fame, Stenerud came to the United States on a skiing scholarship from Montana State University.

Though he never played college football, Stenerud joined the AFL's Kansas City Chiefs as a soccer-style kicker in 1967, when he led the league with 21 field goals. In 1969 he kicked 16 field goals in a row, a record at the time.

Stenerud remained with the Chiefs through the 1979 season and then joined the Green Bay Packers. He kicked 22 field goals in 24 attempts for the Packers in 1981, setting an NFL record for accuracy with 91.7 percent. Stenerud ended his career with the Minnesota Vikings in 1984 and 1985.

During his 19 professional seasons, Stenerud kicked 373 field goals in 558 attempts and converted 580 of 601 extra point attempts for a total of 1,699 points, second highest in history.
★ Pro Football Hall of Fame

Stengel, Casey (Charles D.)

BASEBALL
b. July 30, 1890, Kansas City, Mo.
d. Sept. 29, 1975

When Stengel retired from professional baseball in 1967 after nearly 60 years in the sport, he said, "I want to thank all my players for giving me the honor of being what I was." It was a typical Casey Stengel line, an appropriate way for him to bow out.

Stengel at times seemed to cultivate his image as a clown. When he became a successful manager, that image for years obscured his ability to handle a team. Then, after fans realized he'd been an outstanding manager with the Yankees, he took over the worst team in baseball.

Although he once told a Senate subcommittee, "I had many years that I was not so successful as a ballplayer, as it is a game of skill," Stengel was a pretty good player. He left Western Dental College in his native Kansas City to play in the minor leagues in 1910 and came up to the NL's Brooklyn Dodgers late in the 1912 season, getting 4 hits in 4 at-bats in his first game.

A left-handed outfielder, Stengel played for the Dodgers through 1917 and batted .346 in the 1916 World Series, when Brooklyn lost in five games to the Boston Red Sox. He joined the Pittsburgh Pirates in 1918. Dodger fans booed him when the Pirates played their first game in Brooklyn. The next day, Stengel bowed to the boos, took off his cap, and a sparrow flew out.

After serving in the Navy for most of 1918, Stengel returned to the Pirates and was traded to the Philadelphia Phillies during the 1919 season. He went to the New York Giants in 1922 and played on two pennant-winning teams in two seasons. He batted .400 in the Giants' four-game World Series victory over the Yankees in 1922. In 1923 he hit an inside-the-park home run to win the first game and won the third game with another home run, but the Giants lost to the Yankees in six games.

Stengel spent his last two seasons, 1924 and 1925, with the Boston Braves. He left the major leagues with a lifetime .284 average and became a minor league playing manager.

In 1934 Stengel became manager of the Dodgers, but was fired after the 1936 season. He took over the Braves in 1938 and had six second-division finishes in six seasons there. Stengel's record in the major leagues was 581–742, and his future didn't seem bright.

He was successful in the minor leagues, though, winning two pennants in five seasons, and he was named to manage the Yankees in 1949. He took over a team that looked good on paper but had finished third the year before. The team's biggest star, Joe DiMaggio, was hobbled much of the season.

Stengel installed Yogi Berra as his starting catcher and platooned extensively at six positions. Only shortstop Phil Rizzuto had more than 500 at-bats. The patchwork paid off, as the Yankees edged the Boston Red Sox to win a pennant.

In his first five seasons, New York won five world championships. They finished second in 1954, then won five more pennants and two world championships in the next seven years. Stengel was named AL manager of the year in 1949, 1953, and 1958.

The Yankees lost the 1960 World Series to the Pittsburgh Pirates in seven games. It was announced that Stengel

had resigned shortly afterward, but he told a press conference, "I was told my services would not be desired any longer with this ball club. I had not much of an argument."

He spent 1961 working as a bank executive in California and returned to baseball as manager of the expansion New York Mets in 1962. Still beloved by many New York fans, he helped attract more than one million spectators to watch a team that lost a record 120 games.

It was a frustrating job, and Stengel showed the frustration as time went on. He once asked, desperately, "Can't anybody here play this game?" And, asked about a poor performance by one of his players, he said, "He's only 19 years old, and in another year he's got a chance to be 20."

Midway through the 1967 season, Stengel broke his hip in a fall. He announced his retirement shortly afterward. His overall record as a major league was 1,905–1,842, for a winning percentage of .508.
★ Baseball Hall of Fame

Stephens, Helen
TRACK AND FIELD
b. Feb. 3, 1918, Fulton, Mo.
d. Jan. 17, 1994

The "Fulton Flash" was timed in 5.8 seconds, matching the world record, the first time she ever ran the 50-yard dash, during a high school physical education class. High school track coach Burton Moore than began to train her.

A few days after her seventeenth birthday, Stephens entered the 1935 AAU national indoor meet. Wearing a borrowed sweatshirt and track shoes, she astounded everyone but herself by beating the great Stella Walsh in the 50-meter dash, tying the world record of 6.6 seconds. She also won the shot put and the standing broad jump. The versatile Stephens won the AAU outdoor 100-meter and 200-meter dashes and the discus throw that year.

In 1935 she enrolled at William Woods College in Missouri, where she was on the basketball, bowling, fencing, and swimming teams, as well as the track and field squad. Stephens won the 50-meter dash, standing broad jump, and shot put again in the 1936 AAU indoor meet.

She qualified for the 100-meter dash, shot put, and discus throw at the 1936 Olympic trials and won the 100-meter in a world record 11.5 seconds at the Berlin Games. The record stood until 1960. In 1936 she also won a gold medal on the 4 x 100-meter relay team, and Associated Press sportswriters named her female athlete of the year for her performances.

After her 100-meter victory, Stephens was taken to meet Adolph Hitler in his box. She later recalled the meeting: "Hitler comes in and gives me the Nazi salute. I gave him a good old Missouri handshake. He shook my hand, put his arm around me, pinched me, and invited me to spend a weekend with him."

Stephens won national championships in the 50-meter and 200-meter dashes and the shot put in 1937; then she retired from amateur competition. In just 30 months, she had competed in more than one hundred races without being defeated.

Stephens, at six feet tall, turned professional and toured with Jesse Owens, running exhibition races. She also played for barnstorming professional basketball and softball teams until joining the Marine Corps during World War II.

Stephens became a special advisor to the track program at her alma mater in 1978. She returned to competition in the 1980 Senior Olympics, winning seven gold medals. In seven years of Senior Olympic competition, she remained undefeated in the sprint races.

★ International Women's Sports Hall of Fame; National Track & Field Hall of Fame

Stephens, Junior (Vernon D.)

BASEBALL
b. Oct. 23, 1920, McAlister, N.Mex.
d. Nov. 3, 1968

An unusually powerful hitter for a shortstop, the 5-foot-10, 185-pound Stephens joined the AL's St. Louis Browns at the end of the 1941 season, appearing in just three games, and took over as a starter the following year.

Stephens led the league with 109 RBI in 1944, when he batted .293 and had 20 home runs. He was the home run leader with 24 in 1945, and he also led AL shortstops with a .961 fielding percentage that year.

His home run totals dropped to 14 and 15 the next two years, and he was traded to the Boston Red Sox, where he immediately benefited from the short Fenway Park fence. Stephens hit 29 home runs and had 137 RBI in 1948. He led the league in RBI with 159 in 1949, when he hit .290 with 39 home runs, and with 144 in 1950, when he had a .295 average and 30 home runs.

After playing in just 109 games in 1951 and 92 in 1952, Stephens split the 1953 season between the Chicago White Sox and St. Louis Browns. In 1954 the Browns moved to Baltimore and became the Orioles; Stephens batted .285 with only 8 home runs in 101 games with them that season. He retired after playing in 25 games with the Orioles and White Sox in 1955.

In 15 seasons, he had a .286 average with 1,859 hits, including 307 doubles, 42 triples, and 245 home runs. He scored 1,001 runs and had 1,174 RBI.

Stephens, Woody (Woodrow C.)

HORSE RACING
b. Sept. 1, 1913, Stanton, Ky.

After nearly a decade as a jockey, Stephens encountered weight problems and began training horses at Woodford Farm in 1940. He opened a public stable four years later and went on to become one of the most successful trainers in history.

His first major winner was Blue Man in the 1952 Preakness. Stephens trained Kentucky Derby winners Cannonade in 1974 and Swale in 1984, but his most notable success has been in the Belmont Stakes. Horses trained by Stephens won that race five years in a row, from 1982 through 1986.

The winner of the Eclipse Award as trainer of the year in 1983, Stephens has trained 11 champions, including Eclipse Award winners for six consecutive years: Smart Angle in 1979, Heavenly Cause in 1980, De La Rose in 1981, Conquistador Cielo in 1982, Devil's Bag in 1983, and Swale in 1984.

★ National Horse Racing Hall of Fame

Stephenson, Jan L.

GOLF
b. Dec. 22, 1951, Sydney, Australia

When Stephenson joined the LPGA tour in 1974, some players resented the attention she got because of her blond, blue-eyed beauty, and when she posed for sexy calendar photos to promote Dunlop golf balls, the resentment grew.

Through it all she insisted that she wanted to be known "as a player, not a sweater girl," and she did prove that she could play golf. She had already won four Australian titles, including the Australian Open, as a pro, and she had three Australian junior championships to her credit.

She was named LPGA rookie of the year in 1974, but it wasn't until 1981 that she entered the top ranks. She won the Peter Jackson Classic that year and set an LPGA record of 198 for 54 holes. Stephenson missed the first seven tournaments of 1982 with a foot injury, but still had three wins, including the LPGA championship. In 1983 she claimed her third major victory, the U.S. Women's Open.

Stephenson was known as a hard worker who would spend hours on the practice tee, but her many outside activities limited her effectiveness after 1983. She was the first woman to design courses, her golf video sold more than 50,000 copies, and she did an exercise video for people with arthritis on behalf of the Arthritis Foundation.

Stewart, Bill (William J.)

HOCKEY
b. Sept. 26, 1894, Fitchburg, Mass.
d. Feb. 14, 1964

Stewart began his unusual sports career as a hockey official in 1921. He became an NHL referee in 1928 and served until 1937, when he was named coach of the Chicago Black Hawks. Although the Black Hawks had a 14–25–9 record during the regular season, they won the Stanley Cup by upsetting the Montreal Canadiens, the New York Americans, and the Toronto Maple Leafs in the playoffs.

The only American-born coach of a Stanley Cup champion team, Stewart resigned during the 1938–39 season and returned to officiating until 1941. He was also an American League baseball umpire from 1933 through 1954 and he worked in four World Series.

Stewart coached hockey at Milton, Massachusetts, Academy and the Massachusetts Institute of Technology at various times, and he was the coach of the 1957 national team that had a 23–3–1 record but didn't take part in the world championship tournament.

★ U.S. Hockey Hall of Fame

Stewart, David K.

BASEBALL
b. Feb. 19, 1957, Oakland, Calif.

Stewart was with the NL's Los Angeles Dodgers for one appearance in 1978 and had a 13–11 record with the team over the 1981 and 1982 seasons. The Dodgers traded him to the AL's Texas Rangers during the 1983 season, and Texas sent him back to the NL in a trade with the Philadelphia Phillies in 1985.

He was released by the Phillies in May 1986. At that point, Stewart had spent five full seasons and parts of two others in the major leagues and had a 30–37 record to show for it.

The Oakland Athletics then signed him, and after one start in the minor leagues Stewart re-entered the majors and earned a 9–5 record. For the next four seasons he was one of the best pitchers in baseball, in large part because he'd mastered the split-fingered fastball.

The 6-foot-2, 200-pounder had records of 20–13 in 1987, 21–12 in 1988, 21–9 in 1989, and 22–11 in 1990. He was named the right-handed pitcher on *The Sporting News* AL All-Star team in 1988, when he had a 3.23 ERA and led the league with 14 complete games and 275²/₃ innings pitched. In 1990 he was the league leader with 4 shutouts, 11 complete games, and 257 innings.

Stewart suffered arm trouble in 1991 and 1992, recording a 23–21 mark over that stretch. He signed as a free agent with the Toronto Blue Jays in 1993 and had a 12–8 record despite spending six weeks on the disabled list with recurring arm injuries.

In five league championship series, four with Oakland and one with Toronto, Stewart had an 8–0 mark with a 2.03 ERA. He was 2–0 with a 1.69 ERA in Oakland's four-game World Series victory over the San Francisco Giants in 1989.

Through 1994, Stewart had a 166–122 record with 9 shutouts and a 3.86 ERA. He had struck out 1,683 hitters while walking 995 in 2,548 innings.

Stewart, Nelson R.

HOCKEY
b. Dec. 29, 1902, Montreal, P.Q. d. Aug. 21, 1957

The first NHL player to score more than 300 career goals, "Old Poison" often seemed to be skating on cruise control, but he had the ability to put on a sudden burst of speed to flash past defensemen and score.

Stewart entered the NHL with the Montreal Maroons in 1925 and won the Hart Trophy as the league's most valuable player. He was the scoring leader with 34 goals in 36 games. (Assists weren't recorded until the 1926–27 season.) He won the Hart Trophy in 1930, when he finished sixth in scoring with 39 goals and 16 assists for 55 points in 44 games.

In 1932, Stewart was traded to the Boston Bruins. He went to the New York Americans in 1935, split the 1936–37 season between the Americans and the Bruins, and finished his career back with the Americans from 1937–38 through 1939–40.

Stewart played 651 NHL games and scored 515 points on 324 goals and 191 assists. He had 28 points on 15 goals and 13 assists in 54 playoff games.

★ Hockey Hall of Fame

Stieb, David A.

BASEBALL
b. July 22, 1957, Santa Ana, Calif.

An outfielder on the college All-American team in 1978, while playing for Southern Illinois University, Stieb signed with the AL's Toronto Blue Jays after graduating and was converted to a pitcher in the minor leagues.

The 6-foot-1, 195-pound right-hander was called up to Toronto during the 1979 season. Stieb was named *The Sporting News* AL pitcher of the year in 1982, when he led the league with 5 shutouts, 19 complete games, and 288¹/₃ innings pitched, compiling a 17–14 record with a 3.25 ERA.

He also led the league in innings pitched with 267 in 1984 and in ERA with a 2.48 mark in 1985. Never a 20-game winner, Stieb had winning records and between 11 and 18 victories in 9 of 11 seasons with Toronto through 1990.

After spending most of the 1991 and 1992 seasons on the disabled list, Stieb was signed by the AL's Chicago White Sox as a free agent in 1993. He had a 1–3 record before being released.

Through 1993, Stieb had a 175–135 record with 30 shutouts and a 3.41 ERA. He had struck out 1,642 hitters and walked 1,017 in 2,845¹/₃ innings.

Stirnweiss, Snuffy (George H.)

BASEBALL
b. Oct. 26, 1918, New York, N.Y. d. Sept. 15, 1958

The 5-foot-8¹/₂, 175-pound Stirnweiss joined the AL's New York Yankees during the 1943 season, when he was used mostly at shortstop. Moved to second base the following year, Stirnweiss had two straight outstanding seasons.

Stirnweiss led the league with 125 runs scored, 205 hits, 16 triples, and 55 stolen bases in 1944. In 1945 he was the AL's top hitter with a .309 average. He also led the league with 107 runs scored, 195 hits, 22 triples, a .476 slugging percentage, and 33 stolen bases.

Stirnweiss slipped to .251, .256, and .252 the next three years; in 1949 he appeared in just 70 games. The Yankees traded him to the St. Louis Browns during the 1950 season. He finished his career with the Cleveland Indians, playing 50 games in 1951 and only 1 game in 1952.

In ten seasons, Stirnweiss batted .268 with 989 hits, including 157 doubles, 68 triples, and 29 home runs. He stole 134 bases, scored 604 runs, and had 251 RBI.

Stives, Karen

EQUESTRIAN SPORTS
b. Nov. 3, 1950, Wellesley, Mass.

In 1984, Stives became the first U.S. woman to win an individual medal in Olympic equestrian competition, taking a silver medal on Ben Arthur in the three-day event. She was also a member of the gold medal team.

Riding last in the team competition with the U.S. holding a slight lead over Great Britain, Stives could have won an individual gold with a faultless ride. After successfully clearing the first 10 of 12 obstacles, her horse nicked the fence on the triple jump, dropping her into second place. By clearing the twelfth jump cleanly, however, she gave the U.S. team the championship.

Stockton, John H.

BASKETBALL
b. March 26, 1962, Spokane, Wash.

After averaging 20.9 points a game in his senior year at Gonzaga University, Stockton was chosen by the Utah Jazz in the first round of the 1984 NBA draft. He spent three seasons as a backup point guard.

Since taking over as the starter, Stockton has led the league in assists every season, with 1,128 in 1987–88, 1,118 in 1988–89, 1,134 in 1989–90, 1,164 in 1990–91, 1,126 in 1991–92, and 987 in 1992–93. He was also the league's leader in steals with 263 in 1988–89 and 244 in 1991–92.

The 6-foot-1, 175-pound Stockton is a skilled penetrator with a good outside shot. An unusually durable player, he missed only four games in nine seasons. His specialty is driving to the basket to draw defenders and then passing to the open man, but he also picks up many assists while running Utah's fast break.

Through the 1993–94 season, Stockton had scored 10,870 points in 816 regular season NBA games, a 13.3 average, with 9,383 assists and 2,031 steals. His average of 11.5 assists per game is a career record, and he set season records with his 1,164 assists in 1990–92 and his average of 14.5 assists per game in 1989–90. In 84 playoff games, Stockton added 1,215 points, 929 assists, and 178 steals. On May 17, 1988, he tied the NBA record for most assists in a playoff game with 24.

Stockton played for the 1992 basketball "Dream Team" that won the Olympic gold medal.

Stone, Steven M.

BASEBALL
b. July 14, 1947, Euclid, Ohio

Stone was a mediocre pitcher for three major league teams over a nine-year period, then suddenly had a great year with the Baltimore Orioles in 1980, winning the AL's Cy Young Award with a 25–7 record and leading the league in victories and winning percentage.

The following year Stone had arm trouble, turned in a 4–7 record in only 15 appearances, and was out of baseball.

Stone, a 5-foot-10, 175-pound right-hander, entered the major leagues with the NL's San Francisco Giants in 1971. He was 11–17 in two seasons with them, then had a 6–11 record with the Chicago White Sox in 1973.

He went across town to the Cubs, where he had a 23–20 record in three seasons. Stone returned to the White Sox in 1977 and had records of 15–12 and 12–12 there before going to Baltimore in 1979. In his first season with the Orioles, he was 11–7 with a 3.77 ERA. He followed that with his Cy Young Award season.

Stone, Toni [Marcenia Lyle]

BASEBALL
b. 1921, St. Paul, Minn.

Marcenia Lyle simply wanted to play baseball. As a young girl she played in a kind of early version of the Little League, which was set up by Wheaties cereal for youngsters who collected enough box tops. During her teens, she was the only girl to attend a baseball school run by former major league catcher Gabby Street, who was then managing the minor league St. Paul Saints. And she kept playing in sandlot and pickup games, against boys and men.

She went to San Francisco, took the name Toni Stone, and played center field for an American Legion team. From there she moved to one of the outstanding black barnstorming teams, the San Francisco Sea Lions. During their tour of the South she wasn't getting the pay she'd been promised, so she jumped to the New Orleans Black Pelicans — a team that the legendary Satchel Paige had played for 20 years earlier.

In 1949 she joined the New Orleans Creoles for $300 a month. At the time, there were still black major leagues; the Creoles were in the black minor leagues. Stone played second base with the Creoles for four seasons before being signed by the Indianapolis Clowns of the Negro American League in 1953.

She became the first, and is still the only, woman to play in a professional major league. The black major leagues were weakening because, after Jackie Robinson had broken the "color barrier" in 1947, the best black players were no longer available to them. Stone's signing was probably partly an effort to get some publicity. She earned $12,000 to play in about 50 games that season, and batted .243.

The following season, she went to the Kansas City Monarchs of the Negro American League. She didn't get to play very much, so she retired when the season was over. But she kept playing sandlot and pickup games until she was 60, just as she had when she was 10 years old.

Stones, Dwight E.

TRACK AND FIELD
b. Dec. 6, 1953, Los Angeles, Calif.

Stones had the second best interscholastic high jump of 7 feet, 1½ inches when he was a senior in high school. One year later he won the 1972 U.S. Olympic trials with a jump of 7–3. He matched that at the Olympics, but it was only good for a bronze medal.

After spending a year at UCLA, Stones went to Long Beach State University. He set a world record of 7–6⅝ on July 11, 1973, and improved that to 7–7 in the 1976 NCAA outdoor finals.

A favorite going into the 1976 Olympics, Stones encountered problems. He never liked rain and he criticized the new retractable-domed stadium in Montreal because the dome wouldn't close completely and the high jump area was wet. Obviously bothered by the weather and by the boos of Montreal fans, who resented his criticism, Stones cleared only 7–4 and had to settle for the silver medal.

Just four days after the Olympics, Stones set his third and last world record with a jump of 7–7¼. He continued competing until 1979, when he was suspended for taking money in the televised Superstars event. After a brief comeback in 1983, Stones retired after failing to make the 1984 Olympic team.

Stones was the AAU high jump champion in 1973, 1974, from 1976 through 1978, and in 1983. He won the NCAA indoor and outdoor titles in 1976.

Stouder, Sharon M.

SWIMMING
b. Nov. 9, 1948, Altadena, Calif.

Stouder began swimming when she was three and entered competition when she was eight. She swam on the gold medal 4 x 100-meter medley relay team at the 1963 Pan-American Games.

She had a sensational year in 1964, winning the AAU outdoor 100-meter freestyle, 100-meter butterfly, and 200-meter butterfly, as well as the indoor 100-yard freestyle championship. Stouder set a world record in the 200-meter butterfly.

At the 1964 Olympics, Stouder won three gold medals and one silver. She took the 100-meter butterfly in a world record 1:04.7 and swam on the winning 4 x 100-meter freestyle and 4 x 100-meter medley relay teams. Dawn Fraser beat her in the 100-meter freestyle, swimming a 59.5 to became the first woman to break the one-minute mark in the event. Stouder was second in 59.9 seconds.

After winning the national indoor 100-yard butterfly for a second time in 1965, Stouder was troubled by a series of injuries that forced her early retirement.

Stout, Jimmy (James)

HORSE RACING
b. May 7, 1914, Lakewood, N.J.
d. July 12, 1976

Doing much of his riding for legendary trainer "Sunny Jim" Fitzsimmons, Stout took his first triple crown victory in the 1936 Belmont aboard Granville. He had been embarrassed earlier that year when Granville threw him at the start of the Kentucky Derby.

He won the Belmont again aboard Pasteurized in 1938 and rode Johnstown to victories in the Kentucky Derby and Belmont the following year. Stout was one of three jockeys who finished in a triple dead heat in the 1944 Carter Handicap. Brownie and Wait a Bit were running neck to neck down the stretch when Stout charged between them on Bousset. Judges studied the photo finish for hours before deciding they couldn't separate the three horses.

Stout retired from riding in 1954 and became a track official. He had 2,057 winners in 13,713 races and was in the money another 3,717 times, taking purses worth more than $6 million.
★ National Horse Racing Hall of Fame

Strange, Curtis N.

GOLF
b. Jan. 30, 1955, Norfolk, Va.

The son of a golf professional who won the 1957 Eastern Amateur, Strange began playing when he was eight years old. He won the NCAA championship and the World Amateur Cup in 1974 as a student at Wake Forest University. He also won the 1975 Eastern Amateur.

Strange left school to join the PGA tour in 1976. The 5-foot-11, 170-pounder is noted for his accuracy and consistency, but a bad temper often hampered his play during his early years as a professional.

In 1985 Strange led the tour in win-

nings with $542,321 and was named player of the year by the Golf Writers Association of America. He was also the GWAA player of the year and top money winner in 1987, when he earned $925,941.

Strange won the 1988 U.S. Open and became the first PGA player to win more than $1 million in a season that year. He was named player of the year for the third time. He defended his U.S. Open title in 1989, becoming the first player to win the tournament two years in a row since Ben Hogan in 1951.

Through 1993, Strange had 17 championship victories and $6,042,581 in winnings, seventh on the all-time list.

Strawberry, Darryl E.

BASEBALL
b. March 12, 1962, Los Angeles, Calif.

Strawberry was called up from the minor leagues by the NL's New York Mets in 1983 and won the league's most valuable player award by hitting 26 home runs and collecting 74 RBI in 122 games.

A 6-foot-6, 215-pound left-hander, Strawberry demonstrated power and speed, hitting 26 or more home runs and stealing 26 or more bases each of the next five seasons. He led the league with 39 home runs and a .545 slugging percentage in 1988.

However, in 1989, back trouble forced him to miss six weeks, and it became a chronic problem for him. The Mets traded him to the Los Angeles Dodgers in 1991. He hit 28 home runs and had 99 RBI in his first season with the Dodgers but played in only 43 games in 1992 and just 32 in 1993.

Through the 1993 season, Strawberry had 1,210 hits, including 219 doubles, 34 triples, and 290 home runs. He had stolen 205 bases, scored 780 runs, and driven in 869.

Strong, Ken (Elmer Kenneth)

FOOTBALL
b. Aug. 6, 1906, West Haven, Conn.
d. Oct. 5, 1979

One of the most versatile football

players ever, Strong was an unusually big halfback for his time, at 6-foot-1 and 210 pounds. At New York University, he was used mostly as a blocker in his sophomore season, 1926. The following year, he was the team's top runner, passer, punter, and place-kicker, and he also excelled on defense.

He captained the 1928 NYU team that lost only one game. Strong led the nation in scoring with 160 points on 22 touchdowns and 28 conversions. In a 27–13 win over previously unbeaten Carnegie Tech, he scored two touchdowns, one on a 40-yard ran, and passed for two. He had three touchdowns, including a 77-yard run, and threw a touchdown pass in NYU's 27–6 victory over the University of Missouri.

After being named to most 1928 All-American teams, Strong joined the Staten Island Stapletons of the NFL in 1929. It wasn't a very good team, winning just 10 games while losing 16 and tying 8 during his four seasons, but Strong was among the league's scoring leaders each year.

The Stapletons folded after the 1932 season and Strong went to the New York Giants. He led the league in scoring in 1933 with 64 points on 6 touchdowns, 8 extra points, and 4 field goals. He was an All-Pro halfback in 1934, when the Giants won the NFL championship. In their 30–13 victory over the Chicago Bears to win the title, Strong scored two touchdowns, one of them on a 41-yard run; kicked two extra points; and had a 38-yard field goal for a total of 17 points, a playoff record at the time.

After the 1935 season, the Giants wanted to cut his pay, so he went to the New York Yanks of the new American Football League. The NFL blacklisted him for the move. The AFL folded after two seasons, and Strong didn't play in 1938. But the blacklist was lifted and he returned to the Giants in 1939, primarily as a place-kicker.

He retired in 1940. But in 1944 the Giants asked him to come back because of the World War II manpower shortage. He became football's first placekicking specialist. He did not wear shoulder pads

and usually did not take off his watch for four more seasons of pro football. He retired for good after the 1947 season as the NFL's second leading career scorer, with 496 points on 35 touchdowns, 169 extra points, and 39 field goals.

★ College Football Hall of Fame; Pro Football Hall of Fame

Stuldreher, Harry A.

FOOTBALL
b. Oct. 14, 1901, Massillon, Ohio
d. Jan. 22, 1965

As a child, Stuldreher saw Knute Rockne play professional football with the Massillon Tigers. He went on to play quarterback for Rockne at Notre Dame as one of the "Four Horsemen." He was the only one of the four named to Walter Camp's All-American team as a senior in 1924.

A 154-pound quarterback, Stuldreher was the team's signal caller, field leader, and best passer. Rockne called him "a good, fearless blocker" and praised his ability to size up a defense and call the plays that would work.

Stuldreher played one professional game in 1925 with the Providence Steamroller, a 127–0 preseason victory over the West Point Field Artillery, then joined the Waterbury, Connecticut Blues, an independent professional team that moved to Hartford later in the season. He led them to a 9–1–0 record.

In 1926 Stuldreher went to the Brooklyn Horsemen of the new American Football League, reportedly for $750 a game. The Horsemen played only four games before merging with the Brooklyn Lions of the NFL, and Stuldreher spent the rest of the season with the Lions.

Stuldreher had been coaching Villanova while playing professionally, and in 1927 he retired as a player to continue as a coach. He left Villanova in 1937 for the University of Wisconsin, where he coached through 1947. His overall record was 110 wins, 87 losses, and 15 ties.

★ College Football Hall of Fame

Stydahar, Joseph L.

FOOTBALL
b. March 17, 1912, Kaylor, Pa.

"Jumbo Joe" was 6-foot-4 and 230 pounds in his days as a professional tackle. A three-year starter at the University of West Virginia, he captained the team in 1935, his senior year. Somehow he was overlooked for All-America honors.

He joined the Chicago Bears after graduating in 1936 and immediately became a starter. Despite his size, he was unusually quick, and he could either overpower blockers or flash past them into the backfield.

Stydahar was named All-Pro left tackle for four consecutive seasons, 1937 through 1940. He played for four Western Division champions and two NFL champions, in 1940 and 1941. After the 1942 season, Stydahar served in the U.S. Navy and was named to the All-Service team in 1944, then went to sea for a year.

He returned to the Bears as a substitute tackle in 1946, when they won another NFL championship. After retiring as a player, he become the Los Angeles Rams line coach and succeeded Clark Shaughnessy as head coach in 1950. Ironically, the former tackle who was best known for his defense turned the Rams into one of the greatest passing teams ever. They lost to the Cleveland Browns, 30–28, in the 1950 NFL championship game but beat the Browns, 24–17, for the title the following year.

One of Stydahar's key moves in 1951 was to move Elroy "Crazy Legs" Hirsch from running back to flanker. The new "three-end" offense soon became standard in the NFL.

Stydahar was fired after the Rams lost their opening game in 1952. He coached the Chicago Cardinals for two seasons, 1954–55, but won only one game each year. He then left football to run his corrugated box business — appropriately named "Big Bear."
★ College Football Hall of Fame; Pro Football Hall of Fame

Suffridge, Bob (Robert L.)

FOOTBALL
b. March 17, 1916, Fountain City, Tenn.

A member of both the 1952 Associated Press all-time All-America team and the All-Quarter-of-a-Century team chosen in a poll of sportswriters in 1949, Suffridge was a three-year starter as a guard at the University of Tennessee. He was named to the UPI All-American team in 1939 and was a consensus All-American as a senior in 1940.

The 6-foot, 190-pound Suffridge was noted for his quickness and explosive charge. He excelled at blocking kicks. In the 1941 Sugar Bowl game against Boston College, Suffridge got downfield under a punt to force a fumble that set up Tennessee's first touchdown in a 19–13 loss.

He started for the Philadelphia Eagles of the NFL in 1941 and then entered the Navy. Playing for the Georgia Navy Preflight Skyscrapers, he was named to the all-service team in 1942. After World War II ended in 1945, he played one more season with the Eagles.
★ College Football Hall of Fame

Suggs, Louise (Mae Louise)

GOLF
b. Sept. 7, 1923, Atlanta, Ga.

Suggs won two professional championships, the 1946 Titleholders and the 1947 Western Open, while she was still an amateur. She also won the 1947 U.S. Amateur championship and the 1948 British Amateur before joining the LPGA tour in 1949.

Called "Miss Slugs" by comedian Bob Hope because of her long drives, Suggs was also sometimes known as the "female Ben Hogan" because of her slow, deliberate play. She won the U.S. Open in 1949 and 1952, the LPGA championship in 1957, and the Titleholders championship in 1954, 1956, and 1959, for a total of seven major titles.

In the 1949 Open, Suggs shot a 291, then a woman's scoring record for 72 holes, and she won by 14 strokes, still the record margin of victory. She shot a

288 in the 1953 Tampa Open to break her own 72-hole record.

Suggs was the LPGA's leading money winner in 1953 and 1960 and she won the Vare Trophy for the fewest strokes per round in 1957. Her 50 tournament victories is fifth on the all-time list.

★ International Women's Sports Hall of Fame; LPGA Hall of Fame; World Golf Hall of Fame

Sullivan, John L.

BOXING
b. Oct. 15, 1958, Roxbury, Mass.
d. Feb. 2, 1918

"The Boston Strong Boy" had his first recorded fight in 1878, when he knocked out Cockey Woods in the 5th round. He became a genuine contender on January 3, 1881, with a 3rd-round knockout of Canadian heavyweight champion Jack Stewart.

Irish-born Paddy Ryan was generally considered the American champion. After Sullivan knocked Ryan out in the 9th round on February 7, 1881, he was acclaimed world champion. Sullivan capitalized on his fame by touring the country, giving exhibitions, and offering $500 to any man who could last three rounds with him. No one ever did.

In many of his exhibitions, Sullivan wore gloves and demonstrated the Marquis of Queensbury rules. He won a six-round decision over Dominick McCaffrey on August 29, 1885, to claim the Marquis of Queensbury championship.

Richard Kyle Fox, publisher of the *National Police Gazette*, disliked Sullivan and boosted Jake Kilrain as a contender. Sullivan finally agreed to meet Kilrain on July 8, 1889. He was badly out of shape from lack of training and real fighting and Kilrain appeared likely to win. After vomiting in the 44th round, however, Sullivan seemed to get his second wind. He battered Kilrain until the challenger's manager threw in the sponge as a symbol of defeat after 75 rounds.

That was the last bare-knuckle championship fight. Sullivan's next defense, against Jim Corbett on September 7, 1892, was fought under the Queens-bury Rules, which called for gloves and three-minute rounds. (Under the old bare-knuckle rules, a round ended whenever a fighter went down.) Corbett knocked Sullivan out in the 21st round to win the title.

Sullivan effectively retired from boxing after that fight, though he did stage exhibitions in 1896 and 1905. He made much more money as a performer than he did as a boxer. Sullivan appeared in several plays and a movie about his life, *The Great John L. Sullivan.* Once known as a heavy drinker, he also gave temperance lectures during vaudeville tours in his later days.

He won 38 bouts, 33 by knockout; lost 1, by knockout; and fought 3 draws in addition to his many exhibitions.

★ International Boxing Hall of Fame

Sullivan, Patrick J.

FOOTBALL
b. Jan. 18, 1950, Birmingham, Ala.

In three years as starting quarterback at Auburn University, from 1969 through 1971, Sullivan guided his team to a 25–5 regular season record and victories in two of the three bowl games in which they appeared. He passed for more than 100 yards in 28 games, more than 200 yards in 18 games, and more than 300 yards in 4 games.

Sullivan led the nation in total offense with 2,856 yards in 1970, when his average of 8.58 yards per play set an NCAA Division I record. He won the Heisman Trophy as the nation's outstanding college player in 1971. During his career at Auburn, he completed 454 of 817 passes for 6,284 yards and 53 touchdowns. He also scored 18 rushing touchdowns.

Because he was only 6 feet tall, Sullivan was not considered a major NFL prospect and he wasn't chosen until the second round of the 1972 NFL draft, by the Atlanta Falcons. He played as a backup for the Falcons through the 1975 season. During his NFL career, Sullivan completed 93 of 220 pass attempts for 1,155 yards and 5 touchdowns.

Summitt, Patricia S. (Head)

BASKETBALL
b. June 14, 1952, Clarksville, Tenn.

A star at the University of Tennessee–Martin, Summit played for three U.S. teams, winning a silver medal at the 1973 World University Games, a gold at the 1975 Pan-American Games, and a silver at the 1976 Olympics.

She received her bachelor's degree in 1974 and began coaching at the University of Tennessee that fall, while also working for her master's in physical education. Summit quickly turned the school into a major power in women's basketball.

During her first eight seasons, Summitt guided Tennessee into the final four of the AIAW tournament four times, losing in the finals in 1980 and 1981. The NCAA took over the national championship tournament in 1982, and Tennessee won titles in 1987, 1989, and 1991. Summitt's team also reached the final in 1984 but lost to Southern California.

Emphasizing aggressive defense and a strong inside game complemented by outside shooting, Summitt has compiled a 530–126 record in 20 seasons at Tennessee through the 1993–94 season. She is second in victories among active coaches, and her .808 winning percentage ranks fourth.

Summitt coached the 1979 U.S. national team that won a silver medal in the Pan-American Games and a gold medal in the world championships, the 1983 team that won a silver in the world championships, and the 1984 Olympic team that was the first to win a gold medal in women's basketball.

★ International Women's Sports Hall of Fame

Sumners, Rosalyn D.

FIGURE SKATING
b. April 20, 1964, Palo Alto, Calif.

Sumners began skating in 1970 in Edmonds, Washington, where her family had moved when she was four years old. A very consistent, stylish skater, she won three consecutive U.S. singles championships, from 1982 through 1984.

She was favored to win the gold medal at the 1984 Winter Olympics, but was edged by East Germany's Katarina Witt, who also beat her in the 1984 world championships. Sumners then became a professional with Walt Disney's World on Ice, explaining, "I'm just ready for the relaxed part of skating."

Sutcliffe, Rick (Richard L.)

BASEBALL
b. June 21, 1956, Independence, Mo.

A 6-foot-7, 240-pound right-hander, Sutcliffe was with the NL's Los Angeles Dodgers for a total of just three games in 1976 and 1978. He became a starter in 1979 and was named rookie of the year by the Baseball Writers' Association of America and rookie pitcher of the year by *The Sporting News* after compiling a 17–10 record with a 3.46 ERA.

He slumped badly to 3–9 and a 5.56 ERA in 1980 and spent much of the 1981 season on the disabled list with a sore arm. The Dodgers traded him to the AL's Cleveland Indians in 1982, when he rebounded to lead the league with a 2.96 ERA.

Sutcliffe had a 4–5 record early in the 1984 season, when he was traded to the NL's Chicago Cubs. With Chicago, he won the Cy Young Award, taking 16 of 17 decisions to lead the league with a .941 winning percentage, and he had a 2.69 ERA and 3 shutouts.

Recurring arm trouble has bothered Sutcliffe ever since. He won just 13 games in 1985 and 1986, led the league in victories with an 18–10 record in 1987, then went 13–14 and 16–11. Sutcliffe spent much of the 1990 and 1991 seasons on the disabled list and on rehabilitation assignment to the minor leagues.

The AL's Baltimore Orioles signed him as a free agent in 1992, when he was 16–15. He had a 10–10 record for Baltimore in 1993.

Through the 1993 season, Sutcliffe was 165–135 for his career with 18 shutouts and a 4.02 ERA. He had struck out 1,653 hitters while walking 1,049 in 2,630 innings.

Sutherland, Jock (John B.)

FOOTBALL

b. March 21, 1889, Cooper Angus, Scotland
d. April 11, 1948

Sutherland came to the United States when he was 18 years old, worked as a police officer for a time, then enrolled at the University of Pittsburgh when he was 25. He'd never played football before, but he was a starting guard for three years under "Pop" Warner, during which the school lost only one game. The tall, solidly built Sutherland was very strong; he won the IC4A hammer throw championship in 1918.

He coached Lafayette for five seasons, from 1919 through 1923, winning 33 games, including two against Pittsburgh, while losing 8 and tying 2. In 1924 Sutherland succeeded Warner at Pittsburgh. His first team went 5–3–1, but during the next 14 years Pittsburgh never lost two games in a row or more than two in a season.

A hard taskmaster and disciplinarian, Sutherland believed in a strong running game and ball control. Other coaches often punted on third down during that era, but Sutherland never did because he didn't want to give up the ball. In recruiting, his philosophy was to find strong, mobile high school athletes, regardless of position, and to fit them in where they were needed.

Sutherland's record of 111 wins, 20 losses, and 12 ties was marred only by three straight losses in the Rose Bowl. His 1927 team was undefeated, winning 8 games and tying 1, but lost 7–6 to Penn State in the bowl. The 1929 team won all 9 of its regular season games before losing to Southern California, 47–14. And his 1932 team won 8 and tied 2 before another horrendous loss to Southern Cal, 35–0.

In 1936 Pitt had a 7–1–1 record and won a fourth Rose Bowl invitation. This time, Sutherland's team beat the University of Washington, 21–0.

Pittsburgh had another undefeated season in 1937, winning 9 while tying 1, and went 8–2–0 in 1938. But Sutherland had had a series of disagreements with the athletic director and he announced his resignation.

The NFL's Brooklyn Dodgers hired him in 1940 and Sutherland had a 15–7–0 record in two seasons there. In 1946 the hapless Pittsburgh Steelers lured him back into coaching with a $12,500 contract plus a share of profits and an option to buy stock in the team. He ran a tough training camp to condition his players and to find out how many of them could play for him.

When the season opened, 24 of the 33 Steelers were in their first year with the team. Pittsburgh was in contention with two weeks left, but lost its last two games to finish 5–5–1. In 1947 the team was 8–4–0 and tied for first place in the Eastern Division, but lost the playoff game to the Philadelphia Eagles.

Sutherland had been suffering from agonizing headaches for much of the season. In the spring of 1948 it was discovered that he had a brain tumor, and he died despite two operations.

A talk he gave to his players when he first took over the Steelers summed up his coaching philosophy: "We must strive for perfection. One mistake is enough to cost us a ballgame, and we must have a club which refuses to make that mistake."

★ College Football Hall of Fame

Sutter, Bruce (Howard Bruce)

BASEBALL

b. Jan. 8, 1953, Lancaster, Pa.

A pioneer of the split-fingered fastball, a pitch that breaks sharply down just as it reaches home plate, Sutter was one of the premier relief pitchers in baseball during the late 1970s and early 1980s.

He entered the major leagues with the NL's Chicago Cubs in 1976. From 1977 through 1985, he had 21 or more saves each year. Sutter won the league's Cy Young Award in 1979, when he had a league-leading 37 saves and a 2.22 ERA, with 110 strikeouts in 101 innings.

Sutter, who signed with the St. Louis Cardinals as a free agent in 1981, also led the league in saves with 28 in 1980, 25 in 1981, 36 in 1982, and 45 in 1984. He had a 1–0 record and 2 saves when the Cardinals beat the Milwaukee Brewers in a seven-game World Series in 1982.

In 1985 Sutter went to the Atlanta Braves. He missed much of the 1986 season and all of the 1987 season with arm problems. After recording 14 saves for Atlanta in 1988, the problems recurred and he was forced to retire.

He had a 68–71 record with an even 300 saves and a 2.83 ERA. Sutter struck out 309 hitters and walked only 77 in 1,042 1/3 innings.

Sutton, May G. (Mrs. Bundy)

TENNIS
b. Sept. 25, 1887, Plymouth, England
d. Oct 24, 1975

Sutton's father was a U.S. Navy officer who retired and moved the family to California when she was six years old. He built a tennis court on their property and four of the five Sutton girls became very good players. Early in the century, the saying in California tennis circles was, "It takes a Sutton to beat a Sutton."

Though the youngest, May emerged as the best of the four. She went East for the first time in 1904 to win the national singles championship and she teamed with Miriam Hall to win the doubles title. The following year, Sutton became the first American of either sex to win the Wimbledon championship. She won again at Wimbledon in 1907.

Sutton had speed, a strong serve and forehand, and the willingness to rush the net and volley when the opportunity arose. She was also a pioneer in sports attire, wearing shorter skirts than other women players of the time and rolling up her sleeves to gain more freedom of movement. She predicted that some day women would actually wear shorts on the tennis court.

★ International Tennis Hall of Fame

Swilling, Patrick T.

FOOTBALL
b. Oct. 25, 1964, Toccoa, Ga.

One of the new breed of speedy outside linebackers in the Lawrence Taylor mold, Swilling played at Georgia Tech and was chosen in the third round of the 1986 NFL draft by the New Orleans Saints.

The 6-foot-3, 242-pounder was named to *The Sporting News* all-NFL team in 1991 and 1992 and has played in four consecutive Pro Bowls, from 1990 through 1993. Frequently used on blitzes, Swilling led the NFL with 17 quarterback sacks in 1991.

New Orleans traded him to the Detroit Lions for two draft choices after the 1992 season. Through 1993, Swilling had recorded 76 1/2 sacks and had intercepted 3 passes, returning them for 63 yards and 1 touchdown.

Switzer, Barry

FOOTBALL
b. Oct. 5, 1937, Crossett, Ark.

A middle linebacker, Switzer captained the Arkansas football team in 1959 and served as an assistant coach at the school from 1960 through 1965. He then became an assistant at the University of Oklahoma.

When Chuck Fairbanks left to coach the NFL's New England Patriots in 1973, Switzer took over as head coach at Oklahoma. A strong proponent of the running attack out of the wishbone T formation, he consistently produced high-scoring teams. Under his guidance, Oklahoma led the nation in rushing offense in 1974, 1977, 1978, 1981, and 1986.

Switzer coached three national championship teams, in 1974, 1975, and 1985, and Oklahoma was ranked in the top 10 ten other times during his tenure. Serious problems with Switzer's program arose in the late 1980s. Under fire, he at first refused to resign, but then gave up his job after the 1988 season.

In 16 seasons, Switzer had a 157–29–4 record. He ranks fourth all-time with an .837 winning percentage. In March 1994, he was hired to coach the NFL's Dallas Cowboys. He guided them to a 12–4 regular season record, but the Cowboys lost to the San Francisco 49ers in the NFC championship game.

T

Talley, Darryl V.

FOOTBALL
b. July 10, 1960, Cleveland, Ohio

An All-American linebacker at the University of West Virginia, Talley was chosen in the second round of the 1983 NFL draft by the Buffalo Bills. Sometimes overlooked because he plays in the same defensive unit with Bruce Smith and Cornelius Bennett, Talley has developed into an outstanding outside linebacker.

At 6-foot-4 and 235 pounds, Talley is extremely quick and durable. During his 11 NFL seasons, he has missed only four games. Through 1993, he had intercepted 8 passes, returning them for 105 yards and 1 touchdown, and had recorded 36½ quarterback sacks.

Talley was named to *The Sporting News* All-NFL team in 1990, and he played in the 1990, 1991, and 1993 Pro Bowls.

Tarkanian, Jerry

BASKETBALL
b. Aug. 8, 1930, Euclid, Ohio

After graduating in 1956 from Fresno State University, where he played basketball, Tarkanian coached in high schools for five years. He then became head basketball coach at Riverside City College, where he had a 145–22 record in four years.

His 1963–64 team won all 35 of its games. At Pasadena City College from 1966–67 through 1967–68, Tarkanian compiled a 67–4 record. During his six years at those two schools, his teams won four straight California junior college championships, from 1964 through 1967.

Tarkanian took over at Long Beach State University in 1969. He spent five seasons there, winning 122 games while losing only 20. Long Beach State played in four NCAA tournaments, losing three times to UCLA teams that went on to win the national championship.

The University of Nevada–Las Vegas teams became known as the "Runnin' Rebels" after Tarkanian began coaching there in 1973. Using a full-court pressure defense to force turnovers and easy baskets and running the fast break at every opportunity, UNLV won 503 games and lost 102 during his tenure.

In 1990, UNLV won the NCAA championship by beating Duke University 103–73. The school was scheduled to go on probation the following season because of recruiting violations, but the NCAA agreed to postpone the punishment for a year so UNLV's returning seniors would have a chance to defend their championship. In exchange, Tarkanian agreed to resign after that season.

UNLV was ranked first in the nation at the end of the 1990–91 season; the team reached the final four of the 1991 tournament but lost to Duke in the semifinal round.

After a year out of basketball, Tarkanian became coach of the NBA's San Antonio Spurs for the 1992–93 season. However, he was replaced after just 20 games.

Known as "Tark the Shark," the controversial Tarkanian was often in trouble with NCAA regulators. His teams were on probation in 1972–73 and 1975–76, and the NCAA threatened to put UNLV on probation again in 1978 if the school didn't fire Tarkanian. He won a court order preventing that, but the NCAA action was upheld in 1989 after a long legal battle.

Tarkanian's winning percentage of .837 on a 625–122 record is the highest in NCAA Division I history, and he ranks third all-time with 23 seasons of 20 or more victories.

Tarkenton, Francis A.
FOOTBALL
b. Feb. 3, 1940, Richmond, Va.

Not a great pure passer, Tarkenton was a scrambling quarterback who made things happen on offense. Coming out of the University of Georgia, he joined the new Minnesota Vikings in 1961 as a backup to George Shaw. But in the Vikings' first regular season game, he relieved Shaw, threw four touchdown passes and ran for a touchdown to lead Minnesota to a 37–13 upset over the Chicago Bears.

From that point on, Tarkenton was a starter except when sidelined by injury, which wasn't often. Although some observers predicted a short career because of his scrambling style, Tarkenton never missed a game until 1976, his sixteenth season in the NFL.

Led by Tarkenton, the Vikings became respectable by their fourth season, 1964, when they won 8, lost 5, and tied 1 to tie the Green Bay Packers for second place in the Western Conference. Then they began to slip, and in 1967 Tarkenton was traded to the New York Giants.

Tarkenton continued to put up good numbers, but the Giants were mediocre in his five New York seasons. In 1972 he was traded back to Minnesota. Less of a scrambler and more of a pocket passer at this point in his career, Tarkenton led the Vikings to three Super Bowl appearances, all losses, before retiring after the 1978 season. All-Pro quarterback in 1973 and 1975, he was the consensus

player of the year in 1975 and played in nine Pro Bowls.

In 18 NFL seasons, Tarkenton completed 3,686 of 6,467 passes for 47,003 yards and 342 touchdowns. He also ran 675 times for 3,674 yards, a 5.4 average, and 32 touchdowns.

★ College Football Hall of Fame; Pro Football Hall of Fame

Tatum, Jim (James M.)
FOOTBALL
b. Aug. 22, 1913, McColl, S.C.
d. July 23, 1959

A starting tackle at the University of North Carolina for three seasons, Tatum received some All-American mentions in 1934, his senior year. After serving as an assistant coach at several colleges for six years, he coached his alma mater to a 5–2–1 record in 1942.

Tatum entered the Navy in 1943 and was an assistant to Don Faurot, the inventor of the split T formation, at the Iowa Pre-Flight School and the Jacksonville Naval Training Station. He became head coach at the University of Oklahoma in 1946, installed the split T, and had an 8–3–0 record, including a 34–13 win over North Carolina State in the Gator Bowl.

At the University of Maryland from 1947 through 1955, Tatum had a 73–15–4 record. He produced undefeated teams in 1951, 1953, and 1955, and was named coach of the year in 1953, when Maryland was consensus national champion. He coached North Carolina to a 19–17–3 record from 1956 through 1958.

The 6-foot-3 Tatum, who weighed 220 pounds during his college years and grew to 260 pounds as a coach, was affectionately known as "Big Jim." He died of a viral infection. Tatum had an overall coaching record of 100 wins, 35 losses, and 7 ties.

★ College Football Hall of Fame

Taylor, Charley (Charles R.)
FOOTBALL
b. Sept. 28, 1941, Grand Prairie, Tex.

Taylor was a running back at Arizona State University and in 1964 and 1965, his first two seasons with the Washington Redskins. He was moved to wide receiver during the 1966 season, caught 8 passes for 111 yards in his first game at that position, and went on to lead the NFL in receptions with 72.

The 6-foot-3, 210-pounder was always a threat to go a long way because of his speed and ability to run with the ball after the catch, but he was also a sure-handed possession receiver and a good downfield blocker.

Taylor led the NFL with 70 receptions in 1967, when he was named to the All-Pro team. He played in seven Pro Bowls. Injuries hampered his play in 1970 and 1971, and he missed the entire 1976 season with a shoulder injury. Taylor retired after catching only 14 passes in 1977.

In 13 seasons, all with the Redskins, Taylor caught 649 passes, a record at the time, for 9,140 yards, a 14.1 average, and 79 touchdowns. He also rushed 442 times for 1,488 yards, a 3.4 average, and 11 touchdowns.

★ Pro Football Hall of Fame

Taylor, Chris J.

WRESTLING
b. June 13, 1950, Dowagiac, Mich. d. June 30, 1979

After wrestling at Muskegon Junior College in Michigan, the 6-foot-5, 400-pound Taylor transferred to Iowa State University in 1971. In 88 college matches he never lost and had only one draw.

The NCAA super-heavyweight champion in 1972 and 1973, Taylor was on the 1972 U.S. Olympic team as a freestyle and Greco-Roman wrestler. He lost a controversial freestyle decision to Alexander Medved of the Soviet Union, a perennial world champion. The referee who awarded the decision to Medved was subsequently banned from officiating in international competition.

Taylor won a bronze medal in his freestyle class. After graduating from college he became a professional wrestler and ballooned to more than 500 pounds. In part because of his bulk, he began to suffer from phlebitis and hepatitis, and he had to retire in 1977. He died two years later.

Taylor, Fredrick R.

BASKETBALL
b. Dec. 3, 1924, Zanesville, Ohio

The 6-foot-3, 201-pound Taylor played baseball and basketball at Ohio State University, graduating in 1950. He played professional baseball for five seasons, including a brief stint as a first baseman for the AL's Washington Senators.

In 1959, he became head basketball coach at his alma mater. His 1959–60 team, led by sophomores Jerry Lucas and John Havlicek, won the NCAA tournament championship. Ohio State reached the tournament finals in 1961 and 1962, but lost to the University of Cincinnati both years.

Taylor had a 297–158 record, a .653 winning percentage, in 18 seasons at the school and was named coach of the year by the U.S. Basketball Writers Association in 1961 and 1962. He retired after the 1975–76 season.

★ Basketball Hall of Fame

Taylor, Jim (James C.)

FOOTBALL
b. Sept. 20, 1935, Baton Rouge, La.

A tough, defiant runner, Taylor was an integral part of the Green Bay Packer championship teams that won the first two Super Bowls. He joined the Packers out of Louisiana State in 1958. A year later, Vince Lombardi took over as coach and made Taylor the starting fullback.

The 6-foot, 216-pounder was a reliable short-yardage ball carrier who rarely fumbled. When tackled, he often challenged bigger defensive linemen and linebackers to hit harder. An excellent blocker, he made Green Bay's famous power sweep work as well as it did because he could take on 250-pound defensive tackles, freeing a guard to lead interference and allowing the tight end to block on a linebacker.

Taylor rushed for more than 1,000 yards five years in a row, 1960 through 1964. His finest season was 1962, when he gained 1,474 yards and scored 19 rushing touchdowns, a record until 1983. The Associated Press named him the NFL player of the year. Four times he finished second in rushing to the great Jim Brown. An All-Pro in 1961 and 1962, Taylor played in five Pro Bowls.

In 1967, Taylor left the Packers to play for the New Orleans Saints in his native Louisiana. He spent just one season with the Saints before retiring. In his ten NFL seasons, Taylor gained 8,597 yards on 1,941 attempts, a 4.4 average, and scored 83 rushing touchdowns. He also caught 225 passes for 1,756 yards, a 7.8 average, and 10 touchdowns.
★ Pro Football Hall of Fame

Taylor, Lawrence

FOOTBALL
b. Feb. 4, 1959, Williamsburg, Va.

The prototype of the modern outside linebacker because of his rare combination of size and speed, Taylor was a defensive guard at the University of North Carolina for two seasons before being moved to linebacker as a junior. He was a consensus All-American in 1980, his senior year.

The 6-foot-3, 240-pounder was a first-round draft choice of the NFL's New York Giants in 1981, when he was not only rookie of the year, but the Associated Press defensive player of the year. After winning the AP award for a second time in 1982, Taylor held out because he wanted to renegotiate his contract. He returned to the Giants with a contract extension after missing three weeks of training camp.

United Press International named him the National Football Conference defensive player of the year in 1983 and 1986. He was named player of the year by both the Associated Press and the Professional Football Writers Association of America in 1986, when he had 20½ quarterback sacks.

Often referred to simply by his initials, L.T., Taylor entered a drug rehabilitation program early in 1988 after admitting to using cocaine. A ruptured Achilles tendon in 1992 limited his mobility somewhat, but he continued to rank among the best outside linebackers

in football until retiring after the 1993 season.

Taylor played for two Super Bowl champions, after the 1986 and 1990 seasons, was named an All-Pro six times, and was selected for the Pro Bowl ten times. He returned 9 interceptions for 134 yards and 2 touchdowns, and he recorded 126½ quarterback sacks.

Taylor, Major (Marshall W.)

CYCLING
b. Nov. 26, 1878, Indianapolis, Ind.
d. July 6, 1932

The first black athlete to become internationally famous, Taylor got his nickname when he was 13. Working for a bicycle shop in Indiana, he did trick riding while wearing a uniform with large brass buttons, and so was called "Major."

Taylor rode in his first race, a 10-mile handicap, on Memorial Day of 1892. Because of his inexperience he was given a 15-minute head start on scratch racers, and he won the race. Two years later Taylor broke the track record for a mile at the Capitol City Velodrome in Indianapolis. But track officials resented having a black person hold the record and banned Taylor from racing there again.

Louis Munger, a bicycle manufacturer and former racer, hired Taylor as a company messenger and personal valet. He took Taylor along when he moved his company from Indiana to Worcester, Massachusetts, in 1895. After winning several regional races, Taylor turned professional to ride in a six-day race at Madison Square Garden in December of 1896. He won $125 for finishing eighth and was also awarded a $200 prize for winning a half-mile race before the feature.

Billy Brady, a boxing manager, then took over Taylor's career, negotiating bonuses of as much as $1,000 for setting records and augmenting his income through side bets. Taylor drew crowds of up to 30,000 spectators to the ⅓-mile Manhattan Beach track in Brooklyn. Many of them came to watch Taylor, while many others hoped to see him lose to white riders.

Early in his career, Taylor liked to stay off the lead and win with his "gunpowder" finish, but when other riders began to team up to box him in, he reversed his strategy and tried to lead all the way through a race.

At the 1899 world professional championships in Montreal, Taylor won the 1- and 2-mile races and was second in the ½-mile. He turned down a $10,000 offer to race in Europe because he had promised his mother he would never race on Sunday.

After Taylor won the U.S. professional sprint championship in 1900, he accepted an offer to go to Europe in 1901 with the promise that there would be no Sunday racing. On a 16-city tour, he won 42 races, including the $7,500 world championship in Paris. He returned to Europe the following year and won 40 races from March to June.

He was not as successful in the U.S., in large part because white racers, led by Floyd MacFarland, ganged up on him, sometimes deliberately knocking him from his bike. After winning a total of $35,000 in 1902, Taylor considered retirement. But in 1903 he was offered $5,000, all expenses paid for himself and his wife, and good prize money with no Sunday racing if he went to Australia to race.

After winning $23,000 in four months during his 1903 tour, Taylor returned to Australia in 1904. MacFarland was also racing there; he again led a group of white riders who teamed up and prevented Taylor from winning. Frustrated, Taylor announced he was taking a vacation and returned home to Massachusetts, where he suffered a nervous breakdown.

In the meantime, European promoters sued him for $10,000 for breach of contract, and he was suspended by the National Cycling Association. The suit was finally settled in 1907, when Taylor announced his retirement after a European tour. Almost destitute, he returned to Europe in 1909 but raced poorly. Taylor retired permanently after racing unsuccessfully in the U.S. in 1910.

Taylor scraped by for years by selling his autobiography, *The Fastest Bicycle Rider in the World*. In 1932 he moved to Chicago for a job. He died of a heart attack shortly afterward and was buried in Mount Glenwood Cemetery.

On May 23, 1948, a memorial service was held at the cemetery, attended by many outstanding black athletes, including Ralph Metcalfe, Duke Slater, and Buddy Young. Taylor's body was moved to the Memorial Garden of the Good Shepherd, where a bronze tablet was erected by the Schwinn bicycle manufacturing company.

The tablet carries Taylor's image and the inscription "World's champion bicycle racer — who came up the hard way — without hatred in his heart — an honest, courageous and God-fearing, clean-living gentlemanly athlete, a credit to his race who always gave out his best — gone but not forgotten."

Taylor, Otis, Jr.

FOOTBALL

b. Aug. 11, 1942, Houston, Tex.

Taylor went to Prairie View A & M College in Texas on a basketball scholarship but also played quarterback and flanker for the football team. Though he wasn't selected until the fourth round of the 1965 AFL draft, by the Kansas City Chiefs, he was considered a major prospect by professional scouts because of his size (6-foot-3, 215 pounds), speed (4.5 in the 40-yard sprint), and jumping ability.

His basketball skills helped make Taylor one of the most feared receivers in pro football. He was noted for his leaping catches and his ability to run with the ball after a reception. Taylor was often used as a runner on the end-around play.

He led the AFL with 11 touchdown receptions in 1967. After the AFL merged with the NFL, he led the league with 1,110 yards on receptions in 1971 and was named American Football Conference player of the year by United Press International.

Taylor made some big plays in important games. His acrobatic catch of a 31-yard pass set up the Chiefs' only touchdown in a 31–10 loss to the Green Bay Packers in Super Bowl I. He turned a short pass into a 61-yard gain that led to the winning touchdown in a 1969 playoff victory over the New York Jets. And in Super Bowl IV he caught a short sideline pass, broke away from a defender, and turned it into a 46-yard touchdown play that put the game out of reach as Kansas City beat the Minnesota Vikings 23–7.

He retired after the 1975 seasons with 410 receptions for 7,306 yards, a 17.8 average, and 57 touchdowns. He carried the ball 30 times for 161 yards, a 5.4 average, and 3 touchdowns.

Teague, Bertha (Frank)
BASKETBALL
b. Sept. 17, 1906, Carthage, Mo.

Although she never played basketball, Teague organized a girls' team when she was teaching elementary school. In 1927, she became a first-grade teacher and high school basketball coach at the Byng School in Ada, Oklahoma, where her husband was superintendent.

Emphasizing peak physical condition and competitive spirit, Teague had an incredible 1,157 victories against only 115 losses, a .910 winning percentage, in 43 seasons of coaching. Her teams won Oklahoma state championships in 1936, 1937, 1938, 1940, 1950, 1952, 1965, and 1969.

Teague produced five unbeaten teams and won 30 or more games in 18 different seasons. She retired after the 1969 state championship game. The first woman elected to the Oklahoma Athletic Hall of Fame, in 1971, Teague wrote a book, *Basketball for Girls.*
★ Basketball Hall of Fame

Templeton, Dink (Richard L.)
TRACK AND FIELD
b. May, 27, 1897, Helena, Mont.
d. Aug. 7, 1962

Templeton participated in two sports at the 1920 Olympics. He failed to win a medal in the long jump, finishing fourth, but he drop-kicked a 55-yard goal to win a rugby match against France that clinched the gold medal for the U.S. team.

After graduating from Stanford in 1921, he became the school's head track coach and immediately initiated daily practices, which was unheard of at that time.

In 19 years under Templeton, Stanford won 77 percent of its dual meets and took NCAA team championships in 1925, 1928, and 1934. He coached 19 individual NCAA champions.

Templeton left coaching after the 1939 season and became a sports journalist and broadcaster.
★ National Track & Field Hall of Fame

Terlazzo, Anthony
WEIGHTLIFTING
b. July 28, 1911, Sicily, Italy
d. March 26, 1966

Terlazzo's family came to the U.S. when he was nine years old. He began weightlifting to build his strength for gymnastics and started competing in the sport in 1929. He won his first national championship as a featherweight in 1932 and took a bronze medal in the division at the Olympic games.

In 1936, Terlazzo became the first American to win an Olympic gold medal in weightlifting. He set a world featherweight record of 312.5 kilograms (698 pounds) in a competition at New York City that year.

The world featherweight champion in 1937 and 1938, Terlazzo won national titles as a featherweight in 1936 and as a lightweight in 1933, 1935, and from 1937 through 1945. His total of 13 championships is the most for an American lifter.

Terry, Bill (William H.)
BASEBALL
b. Oct. 30, 1898, Atlanta, Ga.
d. Jan. 9, 1989

After spending three years as a minor league pitcher, Terry went to work for Standard Oil in Memphis and played for the company's semipro team from 1918 through 1921. The experience enabled him to become wealthy by investing in oil after he became a major leaguer.

Terry signed with the NL's New York Giants for a $5,000 bonus in 1922 and was sent to the minors so he could learn play first base. The Giants were more impressed with Terry's bat than with his arm.

The 6-foot-1, 200-pound Terry, a left-hander, was with the Giants briefly in 1923 and joined the team as a backup first baseman the following year. He took over as the starter in 1925, when he batted .319.

After dropping to .289 in 1926, Terry hit .310 or better each of the next ten seasons. He also scored more than 100 runs and had more than 100 RBI each season from 1927 through 1932.

His greatest year was 1930, when he led the league with a .401 average and 254 hits, a league record. No other NL player has hit over .400 since. He had 39 doubles, 15 triples, 23 home runs, 129 RBI, and 139 runs scored and was named most valuable player that season.

Terry had a league-leading 20 triples and 121 runs scored in 1931, when he batted .349. He was named the team's playing manager during the 1932 season and guided the Giants to the pennant and world championship in 1933.

Bad knees limited Terry to 79 games in 1936, his last season as a player. The Giants won pennants that year and in 1937 but lost both World Series.

The Giants then began to drop in the standings, and Terry resigned after a fifth-place finish in 1941. He directed the team's farm system, which he had established, for a year before retiring to private business.

In 14 major league seasons, Terry had a .341 average on 2,193 hits, including 373 doubles, 112 triples, and 154 home runs. He scored 1,120 runs and had 1,078 RBI. As a manager, Terry had an 823–661 record for a .555 winning percentage.
★ Baseball Hall of Fame

Testaverde, Vinny (Vincent F.)
FOOTBALL
b. Nov. 13, 1963, Brooklyn, N.Y.

A two-year starter at quarterback for the University of Miami, Testaverde won the Heisman Trophy, Maxwell Award, and Walter Camp Award as the outstanding player in college football in 1986. The 6-foot-5, 215-pounder set school records for passing yards with 6,650 and touchdown passes with 49.

The first player chosen in the 1987 NFL draft, Testaverde joined the Tampa Bay Buccaneers and became their starting quarterback late in his rookie year. He had some fine games with Tampa Bay, passing for 369 yards against the New Orleans Saints in 1987 to set a rookie record and for 469 yards against the Indianapolis Colts in 1988.

However, Testaverde was often booed by fans and criticized by the press for inconsistency. His 35 interceptions in 1988 set an NFL record. After the 1992 season he was granted uncondi-tional free agency, and he joined the Cleveland Browns as a backup to Bernie Kosar. He had also been Kosar's backup at Miami in 1984.

Kosar was released by the Browns during the 1993 season and Testaverde was given the starting job. He had one of his best years as a pro, finishing third in the AFC quarterback ratings.

Through 1994, Testaverde had com-pleted 1,463 of 2,767 passes for 19,192 yards and 107 touchdowns, throwing 141 interceptions. He also rushed for 905 yards in 172 attempts, a 5.3 average, and scored 5 touchdowns.

Tettleton, Mickey L.
BASEBALL
b. Sept. 16, 1960, Oklahoma City, Okla.

Tettleton played at Oklahoma State University before entering professional baseball in 1981. A left-handed hitter, he was a backup catcher with the AL's Oak-land Athletics from 1984 through 1987. Tettleton was then released by Oakland and was signed by the Baltimore Orioles in 1988.

Tettleton became Baltimore's start-ing catcher in 1989, when he hit 26 home runs and had 65 RBI in 117 games. Because of his power, the Orioles also used him at first base and in the outfield in 1990, but he hit only 15 home runs that season and was traded to the Detroit Tigers.

Tettleton was a natural for Detroit's Tiger Stadium, with its short right-field fence. He hit 31 home runs with 89 RBI in 1991, 32 with 83 RBI in 1992, and 32 with 110 RBI in 1993, when he was used mostly at first base. However, he dropped to 17 home runs and 51 RBI in the strike-shortened 1994 season. *The Sporting News* named Tettleton to its AL All-Star team in 1989, 1991, and 1992.

Tewksbury, John W. B.
TRACK AND FIELD
b. March 21, 1876, Tunkhannock, Pa.
d. April 24, 1968

Tewksbury won five medals in the second modern Olympics in 1900. He won the 200-meter dash and the 400-meter hurdles, finished second in the 60- and 100-meter dashes, and was third in the 200-meter hurdles.

His victory over French champion Henri Tauzin in the 400-meter hurdles was a major surprise, because the event was virtually unknown in the U.S. On a course where telephone poles were laid across the track as hurdles, with a water jump near the finish line, Tewksbury turned in a remarkable time of 57.6 seconds; the world record at the time was 57.2.

Running for the University of Pennsylvania, Tewksbury won the IC4A 100- and 200-meter dashes in 1898 and 1899. He received a degree in dentistry from the University of Pennsylvania. At the time of his death, he was the last known surviving athlete from the 1900 Olympics.

Theismann, Joseph R.
FOOTBALL
b. Sept. 9, 1949, New Brunswick, N.J.

His family name was originally pronounced "Thees-man," but he changed it to rhyme with "Heisman" while a quarterback at Notre Dame to aid in the school's publicity campaign to obtain the Heisman Trophy for him. The campaign featured the slogan, "Theismann

as in Heisman." Although he had a fine senior season and was named an Academic All-American in 1970, he finished second to Stanford's Jim Plunkett in the award voting.

During his college career, Theismann completed 290 of 509 passes for 4,411 yards and 31 touchdowns. He also rushed for more than 1,000 yards. The 6-foot, 160-pounder was not considered a pro quarterback prospect because of his size. He rejected a bid from the NFL's Miami Dolphins, who planned to use him as a defensive back, and signed with the Toronto Argonauts of the Canadian Football League in 1971.

Theismann completed 382 of 679 pass attempts for 6,093 yards and 40 touchdowns in his three CFL seasons. He joined the Washington Redskins of the NFL in 1974 and became the team's starting quarterback during the 1978 season.

The Redskins won National Football Conference championships in 1982 and 1983 under Theismann's guidance. He won the Bert Bell Award as the league's player of the year in 1982, and was named player of the year in 1983 by both Associated Press and the Professional Football Writers Association.

In Super Bowl XVII, after the 1982 season, Theismann completed 15 of 23 passes for 143 yards and 2 touchdowns as Washington beat the Miami Dolphins, 27–7. The Redskins lost Super Bowl XVIII, 38–9, to the Oakland Raiders.

Against the New York Giants on November 18, 1985, Theismann suffered a compound fracture of his right leg that ended his playing career. He later became a color announcer for ESPN football telecasts.

In his 12 NFL seasons, Theismann completed 2,044 of 3,602 passes for 25,206 yards and 160 touchdowns. He rushed for 1,815 yards on 355 carries, a 5.1 average, and scored 17 touchdowns.

Thomas, Debi (Debra J.)
FIGURE SKATING
b. March 25, 1967, Poughkeepsie, N.Y.

America's first black figure skating champion, Thomas finished fourth in her first major competition, the 1983 National Sports Festival. At 5-foot-6 and 116 pounds, Thomas was a very athletic skater who generated a great deal of speed.

As a pre-medical student at the University of Colorado–Boulder, Thomas won national singles championships in 1986 and 1988. She was also the world champion in 1986, when she was named amateur sportswoman of the year by the Women's Sports Foundation.

Suffering from an ankle injury, Thomas finished second in the national and world championships in 1987. At the 1988 Olympics, she and Katarina Witt engaged in the "Battle of Carmens," so called because they both did their free skating routines to Bizet's "Carmen Suite." However, Thomas had problems with her routine and finished third, with Witt taking the gold medal.

She retired after the Olympics to study medicine at Stanford University.

Thomas, Derrick V.

FOOTBALL
b. Jan. 1, 1967, Miami, Fla.

The 6-foot-3, 242-pound Thomas was an All-American at the University of Alabama in 1988, when he won the Butkus Award as the nation's outstanding collegiate linebacker. He was chosen by the Kansas City Chiefs in the first round of the 1989 NFL draft.

Thomas immediately stepped in as a starting outside linebacker and was most effective at using his great speed to blitz the passer. He led the NFL with 20 quarterback sacks in 1990 and set a record with 7 sacks on November 11.

The Chiefs came under criticism in 1993 when they began using Thomas in a down position at the line of scrimmage instead of letting him blitz from the outside. He had only 7 sacks that season.

Named to *The Sporting News* All-NFL team from 1990 through 1992, Thomas had 76 sacks in his first six seasons. He had also recovered 12 fumbles for 37 yards and 2 touchdowns.

Thomas, Frank E.

BASEBALL
b. May 27, 1968, Columbus, Ga.

Nicknamed the "Big Hurt," Thomas is a 6-foot-5, 257-pound right-hander who in 1993 became the first player since Babe Ruth to have more than 100 RBI and more than 100 walks in each of his first three full seasons. A college All-American at Auburn University in 1989, Thomas entered professional baseball that summer.

He joined the AL's Chicago White Sox during the 1990 season, batting .330 in 60 games. Used primarily as a designated hitter in 1991, when he hit .318 with 32 home runs and 109 RBI, he became the team's starting first baseman the following season. He hit .323 with 24 home runs, 115 RBI, and a league-leading 46 doubles in 1992. Thomas led the league in walks both years with 138 in 1991 and 122 in 1992.

Thomas helped keep the White Sox in the thick of the AL's Western Division race in 1993. He was named the league's most valuable player after hitting .317 with a league-leading 41 home runs and 128 RBI. He also improved his defense considerably by reporting early to spring training to get extra practice.

Through 1994, Thomas had a .321 career average with 741 hits, including 158 doubles, 8 triples, and 142 home runs. He had scored 463 runs and driven in 484.

Thomas, Frank W.

FOOTBALL
b. Nov. 15, 1898, Muncie, Ind.
d. May 10, 1954

Thomas decided he wanted to be a football coach even before he played quarterback under Knute Rockne at Notre Dame, where he was known for following Rockne around to ask questions. After graduating in 1923, he became an assistant coach at the University of Georgia.

His first head coaching job was at the University of Chattanooga in 1925. He had a 26–9–2 record in four seasons there before returning to Georgia as an assistant once more. Thomas was persuaded by the idea that the Georgia job would be a better springboard to a major college.

In 1931, Thomas succeeded Wallace Wade at the University of Alabama. He spent 15 seasons there, compiling a record of 115 wins, 24 losses, and 17 ties, and had three undefeated, untied teams, in 1934, 1937, and 1945. All three of those teams went to the Rose Bowl. Alabama beat Stanford 29–13 in the 1935 Rose Bowl, lost, 13–0, to California in 1938, and beat Southern California 34–14 in 1946.

Thomas's teams also won the 1942 Cotton Bowl, 29–21, over Texas A & M, and the 1943 Orange Bowl over Boston College, 37–21. He missed the 1943 and 1944 seasons while in military service.

High blood pressure and a heart problem forced his retirement after the 1946 season.

★ College Football Hall of Fame

Thomas, Isiah L. III

BASKETBALL
b. April 30, 1961, Chicago, Ill.

A high school All-American in Chicago, Thomas entered Indiana University in 1979. At only 19, he was chosen for the 1980 Olympic team which didn't compete because of the U.S. boycott of the Moscow Games that year.

Thomas led Indiana to the NCAA championship in 1981, when he was named the tournament's most valuable player and a consensus All-American.

The 6-foot-1, 182-pound Thomas left school after two years, partly because of frequent clashes with Indiana Coach Bobby Knight. He was chosen by the Detroit Pistons in the first round of the 1981 NBA draft, and he made the league's All-Rookie team.

A skilled dribbler, penetrator, and passer with a respectable outside shot, Thomas has consistently had high assist totals while scoring more than most "pure" point guards do. He tied for the league lead with 914 assists in 1983–84, when he averaged 21.3 points a game, and he was the NBA leader with 1,123 assists the following year, averaging 21.2 points a game.

With Thomas guiding the offense, the Pistons won NBA championships in 1989 and 1990. He was named the most valuable player in the 1990 playoffs. Ironically, Thomas had his best single playoff game in 1988, when he set records with 25 points in a quarter, 14 field goals in a half, and 6 steals for a game against the Los Angeles Lakers. However, the Pistons lost to the Lakers in the finals.

Through the 1993–94 season, Thomas had scored 18,822 points in 979 regular season games, a 19.2 average, with 9,061 assists and 1,861 steals. In 111 playoff games, he had 2,261 points, 987 assists, and 234 steals.

Thomas, John C.

TRACK AND FIELD
b. March 3, 1941, Boston, Mass.

Thomas became the darling of the track world when he became the second athlete to clear 7 feet in the indoor high jump in 1959, at the age of 18. He was upset when media and fans criticized him harshly for only winning a bronze medal at the 1960 Olympics.

"That was the first time I learned people didn't like me," he said afterward. "They only like winners. They don't give credit to a man for trying. I was called a quitter, a man with no heart. It made me sick."

As a 17-year-old high school student in 1958, Thomas cleared 6–10¾ to win the AAU indoor high jump championship. He entered Boston University that fall and jumped an even 7 feet early in 1959, then set a world record of 7–1¼ to win another AAU indoor championship.

Thomas missed most of the 1959 outdoor season because of an injury suffered when his left foot was caught in an elevator shaft. He returned to set another indoor record of 7–1½ early in 1960, raised it to 7–2 in winning a third AAU indoor title, and raised the mark once more to 7–2½.

During the 1960 season, Thomas set outdoor records of 7–1½, 7–2, 7–2½, and 7–2¾, winning the AAU and NCAA championships and the Olympic trials. At the Rome Olympic Games, he failed to clear 7–1 and finished behind Soviet jumpers Robert Shavlakadze and Valery Brumel.

In 1961 Thomas apparently set another record of 7–3⅛, but Brumel had cleared 7–4¼ earlier the same day. He won the NCAA outdoor championship that year and was the AAU indoor and outdoor titlist in 1962. At the 1964 Olympics, Thomas and Brumel both cleared 7–1¼, but Brumel won the gold medal on fewer misses. Thomas retired shortly afterward.

★ National Track & Field Hall of Fame

Thomas, Kurt

GYMNASTICS
b. March 29, 1956, Miami, Fla.

After winning the AAU junior all-around gymnastics championship in 1973, Thomas won a scholarship to Indiana State University. He won the NCAA all-around championship in 1977, when Indiana State tied with Oklahoma for the team title, and he repeated as all-around champion in 1979.

In 1978 Thomas became the first American male gymnast to win a world championship since 1932, when he won the floor exercise title. He was also the world champion in the floor exercise and the horizontal bar in 1979, when he won the Sullivan Award as the nation's outstanding amateur athlete.

Thomas was to be a member of the 1980 Olympic team, but the U.S. boycotted the Moscow Games that year; he joined the U.S. Professional Gymnastics Classic tour. He operates a gymnastics school and frequently serves as a television commentator on the sport.

Thomas, Thurman L.

FOOTBALL
b. May 16, 1966, Houston, Tex.

As a running back at Oklahoma State University, Thomas was virtually unnoticed because he was a teammate of Barry Sanders, the 1988 Heisman Trophy winner. A year ahead of Sanders, Thomas was chosen in the second round of the 1988 NFL draft by the Buffalo Bills.

The 5-foot-10, 198-pound Thomas be-came an important part of Buffalo's hurry-up offense in his second season, rushing for 1,244 yards and gaining another 669 yards on pass receptions. He gained more than 2,000 all-purpose yards in 1991 and 1992.

Unfortunately, Thomas also became one of the symbols of Buffalo's futility in the Super Bowl. After being named NFL player of the year by the Associated Press and the Professional Football Writers' Association in 1991, Thomas missed the first two plays of Super Bowl XXVI because he couldn't find his helmet and gained only 13 yards on 10 carries in a 37–24 loss to the Washington Redskins.

The following year he was held to 10 yards on 4 rushing attempts as the Bills lost to the Dallas Cowboys, 30–20. The Bills lost the Super Bowl for a fourth straight time following the 1993 season. Thomas was benched after fumbling twice in the 30–13 defeat by the Cowboys. His second fumble was returned for the tying touchdown early in the third quarter after the Bills had taken a 13–6 halftime lead.

Through the 1994 season, Thomas had gained 8,724 yards and scored 48 touchdowns on 2,018 rushing attempts, and had caught 282 passes for 3,392 yards and 18 touchdowns.

Thompson, Cat (John A.)

BASKETBALL
b. Feb. 10, 1906, St. George, Utah

Thompson got the nickname "Cat" when his coach at Montana State College, G. O. Romney, first saw him practice and exclaimed, "That isn't a human being, that's a tree cat."

A 5-foot-9 guard, Thompson was an All-American four years in a row, from 1927 through 1930. He led Montana State to two consecutive 36–2 records and the Helms national championship in 1929, when the Helms Athletic Foundation also named him player of the year.

Thompson, who once scored 56 points in a high school game, played AAU basketball for a year after graduating from college and then became a high school coach from 1931 through 1946.

His Idaho Falls teams won two consecutive Idaho state championships.

In 1956, Thompson was named to the Helms all-time All-American team.

★ Basketball Hall of Fame

. **Thompson, David O.**

BASKETBALL
b. July 13, 1954, Shelby, N.C.

The 6-foot-4, 195-pound Thompson had a 42-inch vertical leap, speed, acrobatic moves, and outside shooting ability. In his first year at North Carolina State University, he set a school triple jump record of 49 feet, 11 inches and averaged 35.6 points a game in freshman basketball.

Thompson was a three-time All-American, from 1973 through 1975. He was the Associated Press college player of the year as a junior, when he led North Carolina State to the NCAA championship, and he was a consensus choice after his senior year. During his three years as a starter, Thompson averaged 26.8 points a game.

In 1975 Thompson joined the Denver Nuggets of the ABA and was named the league's rookie of the year after averaging 26.0 points a game. Denver was one of four franchises that moved into the NBA in 1976. An All-NBA choice in 1977 and 1978, Thompson was traded to the Seattle Supersonics in 1982. A knee injury ended his career during the 1983–84 season.

Thompson scored 11,264 points in 510 professional games, an average of 22.1 per game.

Thompson, John

BASKETBALL
b. Sept. 2, 1941, Washington, D.C.

The 6-foot-10, 230-pound Thompson was a three-year starter at center for Providence College and was chosen by the Boston Celtics in the 1964 NBA draft. He spent two seasons as the backup to Bill Russell, scoring just 262 points in 74 games, and then went into high school coaching.

Thompson had a 128–22 record in seven seasons at St. Anthony's High School in his native Washington, D.C.,

and was hired in 1972 as basketball coach at Georgetown University. He rebuilt the program by recruiting black players from inner-city schools, emphasizing an aggressive man-to-man defense, and substituting frequently to wear down opponents.

In his third season, 1974–75, Georgetown reached the NCAA tournament for the first time since 1943. The Hoyas won the 1984 championship and lost in the finals twice, in 1982 and 1985. Thompson was named coach of the year by United Press International in 1987, when his team had a 26–5 record.

Sometimes criticized for overprotecting his players — the phrase often used is "Hoya Paranoia" — Thompson is a strong believer in the importance of athletic scholarships to help underprivileged young blacks receive college educations. In 1993–94, he was a leader of the Black Coaches' Association move to boycott games if the NCAA didn't allow Division I schools to add a fourteenth basketball scholarship.

Through 1993–94, Thompson had a 503–190 record at Georgetown. His .726 winning percentage is tied for twenty-third best all-time. Thompson coached the 1984 U.S. bronze medal Olympic team.

Thompson, Robbie (Robert R.)

BASEBALL
b. May 10, 1962, West Palm Beach, Fla.

The 5-foot-11, 175-pound Thompson played all three infield positions in the minor leagues before joining the NL's San Francisco Giants in 1986. Used mainly at second base, with some time at shortstop, he was named the league's rookie of the year by *The Sporting News* after hitting .271.

In 1987, Thompson become San Francisco's full-time second baseman. A sure fielder and respectable hitter with surprising power, Thompson led the league with 11 triples in 1989.

Thompson's best season to date was 1993, when he won a Gold Glove and was selected for *The Sporting News* NL All-Star team. He hit a career high .312

that season. However, he missed most of 1994 because of a shoulder injury. Through the 1994 season, Thompson had a .263 average with 1,064 hits, including 212 doubles, 38 triples, and 106 home runs. He had 100 stolen bases, 585 runs scored, and 414 RBI.

Thompson, Samuel L.

BASEBALL
b. March 5, 1860, Danville, Ind.
d. Nov. 7, 1922

In 1884, a baseball scout from a minor league team arrived in Danville in search of Cy Thompson, who had a reputation as a good hitter. Cy, 26 years old and a successful druggist, wasn't interested in professional baseball, but he recommended his younger brother, Sam.

Sam agreed to play for $2.50 a game. Less than two years later, he joined the Detroit NL team. The 6-foot-2, 207-pound Thompson, a left-handed outfielder, was one of baseball's top power hitters during his era. He led the league with 203 hits, 23 triples, 166 RBI, a .372 batting average, and a .571 slugging percentage in 1887, his second full season in the major leagues.

A sore arm limited him to 56 games in 1888, and Thompson was sold to the Philadelphia Phillies the following year. That year he led the league with 20 home runs, becoming only the fifth player in history to reach that figure.

Thompson was the league leader with 172 hits and 41 doubles in 1890 and was tops in both categories again with 222 hits and 37 doubles in 1893. He won his second home run title with 18 in 1895, when he also led the NL with 165 RBI and a .654 slugging percentage.

After batting .298 with 12 home runs and 100 RBI in 1896, Thompson developed a bad back. He appeared in only 17 games during the next two seasons and retired. When the AL's Detroit Tigers were decimated by injuries in 1906, he came out of retirement to hit .226 in eight games with them.

Though not known for his defensive ability, Thompson is credited with the idea of throwing to home plate on one bounce so the catcher would have an easier time handling the ball.

Thompson had a .331 career batting average on 1,979 hits, including 340 doubles, 160 triples, and 127 home runs. He stole 229 bases, scored 1,256 runs, and had 1,299 RBI.
★ Baseball Hall of Fame

Thompson, Tiny (Cecil)

HOCKEY
b. May 31, 1905, Sandon, B.C.
d. Feb. 9, 1981

The 5-foot-10, 180-pound Thompson hated his nickname. He got it, he once explained, because "I used to play with older fellows when I was still a schoolboy, and alongside them I guess I looked tiny."

Thompson spent 12 seasons in the NHL and won the Vezina Trophy four times, in 1930, 1933, 1936, and 1938. He played for several amateur teams, including one in Minneapolis, and when that team turned professional in 1926, so did Thompson.

He joined the Boston Bruins in 1928 and was sold to the Detroit Red Wings early in the 1938–39 season, after the Bruins called up another future Hall of Fame goaltender, Frankie Brimsek. Thompson retired after the 1939–40 season.

Thompson considered his greatest game a 1–0 loss to the Toronto Maple Leafs in the semifinals of the 1933 Stanley Cup playoffs. The game went into six overtime periods that lasted 1 hour, 44 minutes, and 46 seconds.

In 553 regular season games, Thompson had 80 shutouts and gave up 1,183 goals, an average of 2.14 per game. He had 7 shutouts in 44 playoff games, giving up 73 goals for a 1.66 average.
★ Hockey Hall of Fame

Thomson, Earl J.

TRACK AND FIELD
b. Feb. 15, 1895, Prince Albert, Sask.
d. April 19, 1971

Although his family moved to California when he was eight years old, Thomson retained his Canadian citizenship and represented Canada at the 1920 Olympics, when he won the 110-meter hurdles in a world record 14.8 seconds.

Thomson entered Dartmouth College in 1916. After spending two years in the Royal Canadian Air Force during World War I, he returned to college and graduated in 1921.

He won the NCAA 120-yard hurdles championship in 1921, the IC4A 120-yard championship in 1920 and 1921, and the IC4A 220-yard hurdles title in 1921. He was the AAU 120-yard titlist in 1918, 1921, and 1922 and the 220-yard champion in 1921. On May 29, 1920, Thomson set a world record of 14.4 in the 120-yard hurdles.

Thomson, who recovered from a nearly fatal rifle accident in 1914, was almost totally deaf. After graduating from Dartmouth, he coached track at West Virginia University, Yale, and the U.S. Naval Academy, where he spent 37 years.
★ National Track & Field Hall of Fame

Thorpe, Jim (James F.)
FOOTBALL, TRACK AND FIELD
b. May 28, 1888, near Prague, Okla.
d. March 28, 1953

Chosen as the greatest athlete of the first half-century in a 1950 Associated Press poll, Thorpe was part Sac and Fox, part Potawatomie and Kickapoo, part Irish, and part French. He was given the Indian name "Wa-Tho-Huck," meaning "Bright Path."

Thorpe first played football at the Carlisle Indian School in 1907. He left school in the spring of 1909 but returned in 1911 at the urging of Coach "Pop" Warner. Warner later wrote of Thorpe, "He had speed as well as strength. He knew how to use his strength and speed as well as any football player or track athlete I have ever known."

In 1911, Thorpe scored a touchdown and kicked four field goals, from 15, 22, 34, and 48 yards, to defeat Harvard 18–15. Harvard didn't lose again until 1915. Thorpe scored 25 touchdowns and 198 points in 1912, but he gained his greatest fame by winning both the pentathlon and the decathlon in the Olympics that year.

In January 1913 the Amateur Athletic Union discovered that Thorpe had been paid $25 a week to play minor league baseball during the summer of 1909, and he was forced to return his gold medals, along with a number of trophies he'd received.

The Canton Bulldogs paid Thorpe $250 a game in 1915, and he led them to unofficial championships in 1916, 1917, and 1919. Canton had averaged only 1,200 fans a game before he joined the team; afterward, crowds ranged from 8,000 to 10,000.

When the American Professional Football Association was organized in 1920, Thorpe was named president for the publicity value. Though past his prime, he played for the Cleveland Indians in 1921, the Oorang Indians in 1922 and 1923, the Rock Island Independents in 1924, the New York Giants in 1925, and Canton for a final season in 1926.

Thorpe also played major league baseball, mostly with the New York Giants from 1913 through 1919. An outfielder, he appeared in just 289 games and batted .252. He hit .327 in 62 games in his final season.

After his death, a campaign arose to have his amateur status restored. The International Olympic Committee acquiesced late in 1982, and on January 18, 1983, Thorpe's gold medals were formally presented to his children.
★ National Track & Field Hall of Fame; Olympic Hall of Fame; Pro Football Hall of Fame

Thurmond, Nate (Nathaniel)
BASKETBALL
b. July 25, 1941, Akron, Ohio

"Nate the Great," a 6-foot-11, 235-pound center, was an All-American at Bowling Green State University in 1963. He joined the NBA's San Francisco Warriors as a first-round draft choice; he played mostly at forward in his first season and a half because Wilt Chamberlain was the team's starting center.

Chamberlain was traded to Philadelphia in January 1965, allowing Thurmond to move back to center. Though best known for his defense, shot blocking, and rebounding, he was also an effective scorer with a good medium-range jump shot and excellent moves around the basket. He averaged more than 20 points a game for five consecutive seasons, from 1967–68 through 1971–72.

The team became known as the Golden State Warriors during the 1971–72 season. Partly because of a chronic back problem, Thurmond's scoring average dropped to 17.1 the following season, and he was traded to the Chicago Bulls. The Bulls sent him to the Cleveland Cavaliers early in the 1975–76 season, and he retired a year later.

In 964 regular season games, Thurmond scored 14,437 points, a 15.0 average, and had 14,464 rebounds. He added 966 points and 1,101 rebounds in 81 playoff games. On February 28, 1965, Thurmond set an NBA record by pulling down 18 rebounds in one quarter.
★ Basketball Hall of Fame

Tiant, Luis C.

BASEBALL
b. Nov. 23, 1940, Marianao, Cuba

During his windup, Tiant often turned his back to the hitter and seemed to be looking into center field before uncoiling and whipping the ball to the catcher. He once threw a pitch right down the middle while stepping off the rubber and staring at a runner on second. The home plate umpire was so accustomed to Tiant's strange delivery that he called the pitch a strike, then overruled himself.

Tiant joined the AL's Cleveland Indians during the 1964 season. He led the league with 5 shutouts in 1966, though his record was only 12–11, and he was the shutout leader again with 9 in 1968, when he had a 21–9 record and a league-leading 1.60 ERA.

After he struggled to a 9–20 record in 1969, Tiant's career seemed to be over because of arm trouble. He pitched only 92 innings with the Minnesota Twins in 1970 and just 72 innings with the Boston Red Sox in 1971.

However, he suddenly regained his old form and led the AL with a 1.91 ERA in 1972, when he was 15–6 with Boston. He compiled records of 20–13 in 1973 and 22–13 in 1974, when he was the league leader in shutouts for the third time with 7, then went 18–14 to help take the Red Sox to a pennant in 1975. Tiant had a 2–0 record, including a 5-hit shutout, against the Cincinnati Reds in the World Series, but the Red Sox lost in seven games.

Tiant had a 21–12 mark in 1976 and was 25–16 during the next two seasons in Boston, then went to the New York Yankees and was 13–8 in 1979. His pitching arm began to bother him again, and he retired after appearing in nine games with the Pittsburgh Pirates in 1981 and six games with the California Angels in 1982.

In 19 seasons, Tiant had a 229–172 record, with 49 shutouts and a 3.30 ERA. He struck out 2,416 hitters and walked 1,104 in 3,486⅓ innings.

Tickner, Charles

FIGURE SKATING
b. Nov. 13, 1953, Lafayette, Calif.

Tickner didn't begin skating seriously until he was 18. After a year at the University of Nevada–Las Vegas, he dropped out to concentrate on his training. Within three years, he finished third in the 1974 U.S. championships, and he was third again in 1975.

Though a very hard worker, Tickner's relative lack of experience bothered him in international competition. A poor performance in the national championships, which were also the Olympic trials, kept him off the 1976 Olympic team.

He won the U.S. championship four years in a row, from 1977 through 1980. After finishing fifth in the worlds in 1977, Tickner won the title in 1978. However, he was fourth in 1979 and, in 1980, he finished third in both the world championships and the Winter Olympics. He then became a professional with the Ice Capades.

Ticknor, Benjamin H. II

FOOTBALL
b. Jan. 8, 1909, Canton, Mass.
d. Feb. 12, 1979

"The Great Defender" saved Harvard's 10–6 victory over Yale in 1929 by tackling Albie Booth when he seemed to be on his way to the winning touchdown. An All-American center in 1929 and 1930, Ticknor was named to Christy Walsh's 25-year All-America team in 1949.

Because of his speed, the 6-foot-2, 193-pounder was a particular star as a linebacker when that position was just being created. Harvard won only 18 games during his four-year career while losing 12 and tying 3, but had four wins over Yale, allowing just one touchdown in those four games.

★ College Football Hall of Fame

Tiger, Dick [Richard Ihetu]

BOXING
b. Aug. 14, 1929, Amaigbo, Nigeria
d. Dec. 14, 1971

After a brief amateur career, Tiger began boxing professionally in his native Nigeria in 1952. He went to England late in 1955 and won the British Empire middleweight championship by knocking out Pat McAteer in the 9th round on March 27, 1958.

Tiger lost the title to Wilf Greaves in a 15-round decision on June 22, 1960, but regained it by Koing Greaves in the 9th round on November 30.

From mid-1959 on, Tiger fought almost exclusively in North America. He took a 15-round decision over Gene Fullmer on October 23, 1962, to win the WBA version of the middleweight title. When Paul Pender retired the following year, Tiger won recognition as the world champion.

Joey Giardello decisioned Tiger in 15 rounds on December 7, 1963, and Tiger reversed the decision on October 21 of the following year to win the title back. He was knocked down for the first time in his career by Emile Griffith on April 25, 1965, and Griffith took the title with a unanimous decision.

Tiger then moved up to the light heavyweight division and won that championship by beating Jose Torres in 15 rounds on December 16, 1965. After two defenses, he suffered the only knockout of his career in the 4th round of a title fight with Bob Foster on May 24, 1968.

Tiger had four more fights during the next two years. On July 19, 1971, he announced that he was retiring because he had cancer of the liver. He returned to Nigeria and died less than five months later.

★ International Boxing Hall of Fame

Tilden, Bill (William T. II)

TENNIS
b. Feb. 10, 1893, Germantown, Pa.
d. June 5, 1953

Named the greatest player of all time by an international panel of tennis writers in 1969, Tilden was something of a late bloomer. Before 1920, he was called "One Round" because he so often played sloppily and was eliminated by lesser opponents in the early rounds of major tournaments.

He and Mary K. Browne won the U.S. national mixed doubles title in 1913 and 1914, but Tilden didn't play up to his full potential until he was 27 years old. In 1920, he became the first American male to win the Wimbledon singles title and he returned from England to win the first of six consecutive U.S. singles championships.

Tilden repeated at Wimbledon in 1921. He lost to France's Rene LaCoste in the U.S. finals in 1926, but won that title again in 1929 and took his third Wimbledon singles championship in 1930. He led the U.S. to seven consecutive Davis Cup titles from 1920 through 1926, winning 17 matches and losing 5 in his 11 years of competition.

The 6-foot-2, 165-pound Tilden was known for his "cannonball" serve, but he was a solid all-around baseline player who rarely came to net despite his size. "In any match between the perfect baseline player and the perfect net rusher, I would take the baseliner every time," he once said.

Crowds in the U.S. and Europe generally liked Tilden because of his skill and showmanship, though he was sometimes jeered for playing nonchalantly, especially early in a match. Many thought that nonchalance was a deliberate effort to add drama to matches that would otherwise have been one-sided.

Will Grimsley once wrote of him, "He was more than a mere striker of the ball. He was a tactician, an artist. The racquet was like a violin in his hands."

"Big Bill" was a showman off the court, too. Born into a wealthy family, he lost much of his money backing plays in which he himself starred, included one that he authored. He also wrote a novel, several short stories, and tennis instruction books.

The stock market crash wiped out what money he had left and Tilden became a touring pro in 1931. He won the professional singles title that year and in 1935, when he was 42 years old. As a pro, he won 340 matches while losing 147.

Tilden was still playing occasional exhibitions at his death. He died of a heart attack while packing his bags in a Hollywood hotel room to travel to a Chicago tournament.

★ International Tennis Hall of Fame

Tingelhoff, Mick (Henry Michael)
FOOTBALL
b. May 22, 1940, Lexington, Nebr.

After graduating from the University of Nebraska in 1962, Tingelhoff was signed as a free agent by the NFL's Minnesota Vikings. The 6-foot-2, 235-pounder immediately became the team's starting center.

Tingelhoff was one of the few centers ever with enough speed to pull out of the line like a guard to lead a running play. Named to the All-Pro team six consecutive years, from 1964 through 1969, he set a record for an offensive lineman by starting 240 consecutive games.

Tingelhoff retired after the 1978 season.

Tinker, Joseph B.
BASEBALL
b. July 27, 1880, Muscotah, Kans.
d. July 27, 1948

The shortstop in the famous Tinker-to-Evers-to-Chance double play combination, Tinker was a fine fielder and pesky hitter with speed. He joined the NL's Chicago Cubs in 1902 as the team's starting third baseman but was moved to shortstop early in the season.

The 5-foot-9, 175-pounder wasn't impressive at first, committing 140 errors in his first two seasons, but he went on to lead NL shortstops in fielding percentage four times from 1906 through 1911.

Late in the 1905 season, Tinker and Evers had a pregame argument that flared into a fistfight at second base during the game. They didn't speak to each other for three years after that, but the Cubs won three straight pennants and world championships from 1906 through 1908. They also won the 1910 pennant but were beaten by the Philadelphia Athletics in a five-game World Series.

Tinker played with the Cubs through 1912 and was then traded to Cincinnati, where he became playing manager. Although he hit .321, the best average of his career, the team finished seventh. After a dispute with the owner, Tinker went to the Chicago team owned by Charles Weeghman in the newly formed Federal League in 1914.

The league folded in 1916. Weeghman bought the Cubs and again installed Tinker as manager. He appeared in just seven games that season, his last in the majors. He later managed in the minor leagues and scouted for the Cubs.

In 15 seasons, Tinker batted .262 with 1,687 hits, including 263 doubles, 114 triples, and 31 home runs. He stole 336 bases, scored 774 runs, and had 782 RBI.

★ Baseball Hall of Fame

Tinsley, Gus (Gaynell C.)
FOOTBALL
b. Feb. 1, 1915, Ruple, La.

Best known for his defensive skills at Louisiana State University, the 6-foot-1, 195-pound Tinsley was looked at by the professionals as a potentially great pass receiver because of his speed and ability to run with the ball after catching. Some thought he would be another Don Hutson.

An All-American in 1935 and 1936, Tinsley caught a 47-yard pass from Sammy Baugh to beat the NFL champion Green Bay Packers in the 1937 College All-Star game, then joined the Chicago Cardinals. He had two great seasons in Chicago. In his third NFL game, he caught 3 touchdown passes, the third player in league history to accomplish that, and his 675 yards on receptions that year was a record.

In 1938, Tinsley tied Hutson's record with 41 receptions. The following season, he held out for more money, didn't get it, and coached high school football. The Cardinals lured him back with a better contract in 1940, but Tinsley was rusty from the year away. He caught just 16 passes before tearing knee ligaments while making a tackle in the eighth game of the season. The injury ended his career. As a professional, he had 93 receptions for 1,356 yards, a 14.6 average, and 7 touchdowns.

★ College Football Hall of Fame

Tippett, Andre B.
FOOTBALL
b. Dec. 27, 1959, Birmingham, Ala.

An outside linebacker for the NFL's New England Patriots, Tippett was named AFC defensive player of the year by United Press International in 1985, when he helped lead the Patriots to the conference championship. He had 16½ sacks and recovered 4 fumbles that year, returning them for 32 yards and 1 touchdown.

The 6-foot-3, 241-pounder grew up in New Jersey and attended Ellsworth Community College in Iowa before going on to the University of Iowa. He was chosen by the Patriots in the second round of the 1982 NFL draft.

A backup as a rookie, he played in only nine games but became a starter in 1983. Because of his speed, Tippett was often used as a blitzer in passing situations, especially in his earlier years. He retired after the 1993 season with 100

sacks and 17 fumble recoveries in 151 NFL games.

Tisdale, Wayman L.
BASKETBALL
b. June 6, 1964, Tulsa, Okla.

An All-American in his sophomore and junior years at the University of Oklahoma, Tisdale averaged 25.6 points a game in three years as a starter and opted to enter the NBA draft in 1985, before his senior year.

He was chosen by the Indiana Pacers in the first round, but because of defensive liabilities, the 6-foot-9, 260-pound forward averaged less than 30 minutes a game in his first three professional seasons.

Traded to the Sacramento Kings during the 1988–89 season, Tisdale got more playing time, and his scoring average increased from 17.5 to 22.3 points per game in 1989–90. However, a knee injury limited him to just 33 games the following season and has hampered him ever since.

Through 1993–94, Tisdale had scored 11,210 points in 659 regular season NBA games, a 17.0 average. He added 51 points in four playoff games.

Tittle, Y. A. (Yelberton Abraham)
FOOTBALL
b. Oct. 24, 1926, Marshall, Tex.

Unnoticed by All-American team selectors while at Louisiana State University, Tittle joined the Baltimore Colts of the All-America Football Conference in 1948. He threw 30 touchdown passes in his two AAFC seasons.

The Colts joined the NFL in 1950 after the AAFC folded, but the franchise went out of business in 1951 and Tittle was acquired by the San Francisco 49ers. After sharing quarterback duties with veteran Frankie Albert in his first season, Tittle became the starter in 1952. He led the league in touchdown passes with 17 in 1955, and in completions with 176 and completion percentage with 63.1 in 1957. He was named 1957 player of the year by United Press International.

The 49ers went to the shotgun formation in 1960 and rotated three quarterbacks, who actually played as tailbacks, for much of the season. Unhappy with that situation, Tittle was traded to the New York Giants in 1961.

He found himself in another unhappy quarterback situation in New York, sharing time with 40-year-old Charlie Conerly. But Tittle took over the job late in the season and led the Giants to a division title.

The Giants also won division championships in 1962 and 1963, when Tittle had his best years, statistically. He threw for 3,224 yards and a league-leading 33 touchdowns in 1962, when he won his second UPI player of the year award. In 1963 Tittle led the league in completion percentage, 60.2, and touchdowns, 36, and was named the AP player of the year.

Tittle retired after the 1964 season. During 17 years in pro football, he completed 2,427 of 4,395 passes for 33,070 yards and 242 touchdowns. He also rushed for 1,245 yards on 372 carries, a 3.3 average, and scored 39 touchdowns.
★ Pro Football Hall of Fame

Tobian, Gary M.

DIVING
b. Aug. 14, 1935, Detroit, Mich.

Tobian won a gold medal in springboard diving at the 1960 Olympics and finished second in the Olympic platform event in 1956 and 1960.

In 1956 Tobian lost to Mexico's Joaquim Capilla 152.44 to 152.41, stirring a U S. protest against the Soviet judge, who gave Tobian an average score of 6.35, compared to an average of 7.3 from the other judges. As a result, a rule was adopted allowing judges to be ousted for incompetence.

Tobian was the national outdoor 3-meter springboard champion in 1958, the 1-meter platform from 1955 through 1960. He also won the indoor 1-meter championship in 1958 and took a gold medal in springboard diving at the 1959 Pan-American Games.

Tolan, Eddie (Thomas Edward)

TRACK AND FIELD
b. Sept. 29, 1909, Denver, Colo.
d. Jan. 30, 1967

Tolan enrolled at the University of Michigan in 1927 hoping to play football, but at 5-foot-7 and only 140 pounds, he was better suited to track. He won the AAU outdoor 100-yard dash in 1929 and 1930 and was the 220-yard champion in 1929 and 1931. He also won the NCAA 220-yard dash in 1931.

In 1929 Tolan twice tied the world record of 10.4 seconds for the 100-meter event, and he set a world record of 9.5 seconds for 100 yards.

Ralph Metcalfe beat Tolan in both sprints at the 1932 Olympic trials and was favored to win the gold medals. However, Tolan edged him in the 100-meter dash, setting a world record of 10.3 seconds, and he easily won the 200-meter even though he stumbled shortly before the finish.

The first black athlete to win two gold medals, Tolan tried to capitalize on his sudden fame by going on a vaudeville tour with the famous dancer, Bill "Bojangles" Robinson, but it was unsuccessful. He later taught physical education.
★ National Track & Field Hall of Fame

Tonnemaker, Clayton (Frank Clayton)

FOOTBALL
b. June 8, 1928, Ogilvie, Minn.

A center and linebacker at the University of Minnesota, Tonnemaker was co-captain of the team in 1949, when he was a consensus All-American.

The 6-foot-2, 240-pounder was a first-round draft choice of the Green Bay Packers and he was named to the United Press All-Pro team as a center in 1950, his rookie year. After serving in the Korean War, he returned to the Packers for the 1953 and 1954 seasons before retiring from football.
★ College Football Hall of Fame

Toomey, Bill (William A.)

TRACK AND FIELD
b. Jan. 10, 1939, Philadelphia, Pa.

Toomey won the AAU national pentathlon championship in 1960, 1961, 1963, and 1964. Since the pentathlon isn't an Olympic event, he began competing in the decathlon in 1963, but finished fourth in the 1964 Olympic trials and failed to make the team.

Despite the lasting effects of a childhood hand injury that handicapped him in some of the field events, Toomey won a record five national championships in the event, from 1965 through 1969, and he won the gold medal at the 1959 Pan-American Games. His best performance going into the 1968 Olympics was 8,224 points, which exceeded the world record but was never ratified.

At the Olympics, Toomey had the best first-day performance in history, accumulating 4,499 points. However, on the second day he missed twice at the height of 11 feet, 9¾ inches in the pole vault and faced disqualification if he missed for the third time.

Toomey recalled, "Everything was closing in on me — the people in that huge arena, the people watching on television back home, my whole life, all those years of working and waiting for this moment. If I missed, it would be like dying." He cleared the height, went on to vault a personal best 13–9½, and won the gold medal with an Olympic record of 8,193 points.

On December 11 and 12, 1969, Toomey set a world record of 8,417 points. It was the twelfth time he scored more than 8,000 points in the event. He won the Sullivan Award as the outstanding amateur athlete of the year and retired shortly afterward.

A graduate of the University of Colorado, Toomey received a master's degree in education from Stanford University. He married Mary Rand, an English long jumper who also won a gold medal in 1964. After working as a television broadcaster and marketing consultant, Toomey became track coach at the University of California–Irvine.

★ National Track & Field Hall of Fame; Olympic Hall of Fame

Torre, Joseph P.
BASEBALL
b. July 18, 1940, Brooklyn, N.Y.

Torre went 1 for 2 as a pinch hitter for the NL's Milwaukee Braves at the end of the 1960 season and became the team's starting catcher the following year. An All-Star five seasons in a row, from 1964 through 1967, Torre spent three years with the team after it moved to Atlanta in 1968 and then was traded to the St. Louis Cardinals.

The Cardinals used him mostly at first base in 1969 and then installed him at third base for the next two seasons, his best as a hitter. Torre batted .325 in 1970 and he led the NL with 230 hits, 137 RBI, and a .363 average in 1971, when he was named the league's most valuable player.

Torre went to the New York Mets in 1975 and became the team's manager during the 1977 season, his last as a player. In 1982, he became manager of the Braves. After winning a western division title and finishing second twice, he was replaced. Since 1990, he has managed the Cardinals.

In his 18 major league seasons, Torre batted .297 with 2,342 hits, including 344 doubles, 59 triples, and 252 home runs. He had 1,185 RBI and scored 996 runs.

Towns, Spec (Forrest G.)
TRACK AND FIELD
b. Feb. 6, 1914, Fitzgerald, Ga.

After graduating from high school, Towns worked as a cab driver until a sportswriter saw him high jump over a pole that was balanced on the heads of his father and uncle, both of whom were more than 6 feet tall. As a result, he won an athletic scholarship to the University of Georgia in 1933.

He played end in football and at first was a sprinter and high jumper on the track team. Then he took up the high hurdles. He won the NCAA and AAU outdoor 120-yard hurdles championships in 1936, when he set a world record of 14.1 seconds. He tied that record five times during the year, including once in a preliminary heat at the Olympics, where he won the gold medal in 14.2 seconds.

The U.S. Olympic Committee ordered athletes to compete in Europe after the Berlin Games. Towns was angered by the decree, but he consented rather than risk suspension, and he shattered the 110-meter hurdle record by running an incredible 13.7 at an Oslo meet. The time was not ratified until two years later, after the IAAF had investigated and re-investigated the conditions.

Towns repeated as NCAA 120-yard hurdle champion in 1937 and he won the AAU indoor in 1938. He then returned to the University of Georgia as head track coach, a position he held until poor health forced his retirement in 1978.

★ National Track & Field Hall of Fame

Townsend, Anne B.

FIELD HOCKEY, LACROSSE
b. March 8, 1900, Philadelphia, Penn.
d. Feb. 3, 1984

A graduate of the University of Pennsylvania, where she was captain of the basketball and field hockey teams, "Towser" Townsend was probably the greatest field hockey player in U.S. history. She was selected for the first 15 All-American teams, from 1924 through 1938, and she was named captain every year but 1933. In 1947, at the age of 47, she was once again an All-American.

Townsend made the All-American team at four different positions, center halfback, left inside forward, right halfback and right fullback. She was also named to the women's All-American lacrosse team in 1933, 1934, 1936, and 1938.

Long active in golf and swimming, she won Pennsylvania tennis and squash championships and in 1957 she teamed with Amelie Rorer to win the national squash doubles championship for senior women. Townsend coached field hockey at the high school level, umpired games, helped establish field hockey teams, and served as president of the U.S. Field Hockey Association from 1928 to 1932.

Townsend, Bertha L. (Mrs. Toulmin)

TENNIS
b. March 7, 1869, Philadelphia, Pa.
d. May 12, 1909

Townsend won the second U.S. national women's singles championship in 1888 and repeated in 1889. She lost to Ellen Roosevelt in the challenge round in 1890, when she and Nellie Hansell finished second to Ellen and Grace Roosevelt in the women's doubles.

After marrying Dr. Harry Toulmin late in 1891, Townsend briefly retired from competition, returning in 1894 to reach the national singles final for a fourth time, losing to Helena Hellwig. Townsend also competed the national women's amateur golf tournament in 1900 and 1904, losing in the first round both times.

The 5-foot-4 Townsend, who was nicknamed "Birdie," was a hard-hitting but sometimes erratic player who often suffered from her tendency to try to hit perfect shots. She didn't compete seriously from 1895 to 1906, when she again entered the national tournament, losing in the semifinals. She died of leukemia.

★ International Tennis Hall of Fame

Trabert, Tony (Marion Anthony)

TENNIS
b. Aug. 16, 1930, Cincinnati, Ohio

At the University of Cincinnati, Trabert was a starting guard on the basketball team as well as the 1951 NCAA singles tennis champion. After serving in the Navy from 1951 to 1953, he returned to college and graduated in 1954.

The 6-foot-1, 185-pounder teamed with Bill Talbert, his teacher, to win the French national doubles title in 1950. Trabert won the 1953 U.S. national singles title and the French singles in 1954.

His finest year was 1955, when he won three legs of the grand slam, the Wimbledon, French, and U.S. singles titles. He didn't compete in the fourth event, the Australian national championships. Trabert also teamed with Vic Seixas to win the U.S. men's doubles title in 1954.

Trabert and Seixas formed the 1954 U.S. Davis Cup team in 1953 and 1954, when they upset the defending champion Australian team. Trabert had two marathon matches against Lew Hoad in Davis Cup play, losing 13–11, 6-3, 2–6, 3-6, and 7–5 in 1953 and winning 6–4, 2–6, 12–10, and 6–3 in 1954. After Seixas beat Ken Rosewall in their singles match, Trabert and Seixas beat Hoad and Rex Hartwig in doubles to clinch the cup.

In 1955 Trabert turned professional and toured with Pancho Gonzales; he lost 74 of his 101 matches over the next two years. Trabert was then replaced by Rosewall and retired from serious competition. However, he remained active in the sport as instruction editor of *Tennis* magazine, a nonplaying Davis Cup captain, an executive director of the International Professional Tennis Players Association, and as a television commentator.

Trabert had an excellent backhand drive and volley, a strong serve, and an aggressive attacking style.

★ International Tennis Hall of Fame

Trafton, George
FOOTBALL
b. Dec. 6, 1896, Chicago, Ill.
d. Sept. 5, 1971

The Chicago Bears have always had a reputation for rough play, and it all started with Trafton. He played briefly at Notre Dame but was thrown off the team because he was playing semiprofessional football on the side. In 1920, he joined the new Decatur Staley team, which became the Chicago Staleys in 1921 and the Bears in 1922.

A center, Trafton played for 13 seasons and was named to unofficial All-Pro teams in 1923, 1924, and 1926. At 6-foot-2 and 235 pounds, he was fast and agile enough to play as a rover on defense.

Trafton developed a reputation for dirty play early on, especially in Rock Island. In a 1920 game, Trafton knocked Rock Island center Harry Gunderson out of a game with an 11-stitch cut over his eye, a two-stitch cut in his lip, and a broken hand. The local newspaper commented, "Flagrant is too mild a word to describe such utter lack of sportsmanship. A cave dweller could have done no better." Another time, he tackled a Rock Island back after he'd run out of bounds, knocking him into a fence and breaking his leg. Trafton had to leave in a taxi after the game, still wearing his uniform, to escape the angry crowd.

He retired after the 1932 season.

★ Pro Football Hall of Fame

Trammell, Alan
BASEBALL
b. Feb. 21, 1958, Garden Grove, Calif.

After appearing in 19 games with the AL's Detroit Tigers in 1977, Trammell took over as starting shortstop in 1978. An excellent fielder, Trammell has hit .300 or better six times.

The 6-foot, 185-pounder had his finest season in 1987, when he batted .343 with 28 home runs and 105 RBI. After missing most of the 1992 season with an injury, Trammell came back to hit .329 in 1993, when he also played third base and the outfield.

Trammell won Gold Gloves in 1980, 1981, 1983, and 1984, and was named to *The Sporting News* AL All-Star team in 1987, 1988, and 1990.

Travers, Jerry (Jerome D.)
GOLF
b. May 19, 1887, New York, N.Y.
d. March 30, 1951

Probably second only to Bobby Jones as an amateur golfer, Travers won the U.S. Amateur championship four times, in 1907, 1908, 1912, and 1913, and lost in the 1914 finals. He had a great short game and was a great putter, which helped to make up for his poor driving.

Travers's major ambition was to win the U.S. Open. He did so in 1915 with a typical performance. In the last round, he hit his first shot out of bounds on the 10th hole, topped a very short drive on the 11th, and drove over the green on the par-3 12th, but he lost just one stroke to par because of his putting ability. After the 15th hole, he used an iron off the tee and made three pars to shoot a 75 for the round and a 297 for the tournament.

Travers never played in another major tournament after winning the Open. A cotton broker from a wealthy family, he lost most of his money in the 1929 stock market crash, and he became a professional playing exhibitions in the 1930s to earn money.

★ PGA Hall of Fame; World Golf Hall of Fame

Travis, Walter J.

GOLF
b. Jan. 10, 1862, Maldon, Australia
d. July 31, 1927

Although he didn't begin playing golf until he was 35, Travis won three U.S. Amateur championships, in 1900, 1901, and 1903. A dour, taciturn man, he went to England in 1904 and became the first American golfer to win the British Amateur, largely because of his "Schenectady putter," which he had designed.

The British were alienated by his manner, and probably by seeing a foreigner win their championship. They banned the putter and accused Travis of being so surly that he was unsportsmanlike. He never returned.

Travis won the North and South Amateur, a major tournament at the time, in 1904, 1910, and 1912. At the age of 53 he won the 1915 Metropolitan Amateur championship.

After retiring from competition, Travis became a golf course architect and served as editor of *American Golfer* magazine for many years.

★ World Golf Hall of Fame; PGA Hall of Fame

Traynor, Pie (Harold J.)

BASEBALL
b. Nov. 11, 1899, Framingham, Mass.
d. March 16, 1972

Generally considered the greatest third baseman in history before Brooks Robinson came along, Traynor played sandlot ball in the Boston area as a teenager and hoped to play for the Red Sox some day. But his minor league contract was bought for $10,000 by the Pittsburgh Pirates.

He was with Pittsburgh briefly in 1920 and 1921, and he became the starting shortstop at the beginning of the 1922 season. Then Traynor was moved to third base, where he stayed for the rest of his career, though he did play shortstop occasionally.

It was almost impossible to hit a ball past Traynor down the line. He also charged bunts well and could range far to his left, allowing the shortstop to cover more ground up the middle.

Traynor led the NL with 19 triples in 1923, when he batted .338. He never led the league in another offensive category, but he hit over .300 ten times, scored more than 100 runs twice, and had more than 100 RBI in seven different seasons.

The Pirates won the pennant in 1925, with Traynor scoring 114 runs and driving in 106. He batted .346 in Pittsburgh's seven-game victory over the Washington Senators in the World Series.

Traynor hit .342 in 1927, when the Pirates won another pennant but lost the World Series to the New York Yankees in four games. His best years as a hitter were 1929, when he batted .356 with 108 RBI, and 1930, when he had a .366 average and 119 runs batted in.

During the 1934 season, Traynor was named playing manager. He batted .309 that year but played in only 119 games because his right arm was broken in a slide home late in the season, which virtually ended his playing career. He appeared in just 57 games in 1935, didn't play at all in 1936, and was in 5 games in 1937.

Traynor was replaced as manager before the end of the 1939 season. He became a Pittsburgh scout and served as the team's radio announcer from 1944 through 1966.

In 17 major league seasons, Traynor batted .320 with 2,416 hits, including 371 doubles, 164 triples, and 58 home runs. He scored 1,183 runs and had 1,273 RBI.

★ Baseball Hall of Fame

Trevino, Lee B.

GOLF
b. Dec. 1, 1939, Dallas, Tex.

Trevino was raised by his mother and

maternal grandfather in a dirt-floored shack near a fairway of a country club outside Dallas. As a boy, he made some money by retrieving balls that left the course and selling them back to members. He found a discarded club, cut the shaft down, and used it for hitting apples.

After dropping out of school at 13, Trevino worked on the course's grounds crew and practiced his game after hours. He then joined the Marines and was stationed in Japan, where he made the service's golf team. He spent most of his two-year military career playing tournaments throughout Asia.

Trevino was discharged in 1961 and he became a golf hustler in Dallas, making an average of $200 a week. His usual ploy was to use just one club for the entire course, giving his opponent a full handicap. He also worked at a pitch and putt course, where he took on all challengers, using a one-quart soda bottle wrapped with tape as his club. Trevino later claimed he never lost a match.

In 1967, Trevino joined the PGA tour and was named rookie of the year after finishing fifth in the U.S. Open. He won the tournament in 1968, shooting a 69 on the final round to beat Jack Nicklaus by 4 strokes.

The 5-foot-7, 180-pound "Super Mex" won the Vardon Trophy for the tour's lowest average strokes per round in 1970 and was the leading money winner with $157,037. But early in 1971 he was beset by personal problems: his marriage was breaking up and his mother was dying of cancer. Trevino began drinking heavily, missed some tee times, and dropped out of a couple of tournaments.

Nicklaus approached him in the locker room at Doral Country Club that spring and said, "I hope you go right on clowning and never learn how good you are, because if you do, the rest of us might just have to pack up and go home."

That remark shocked Trevino into straightening himself out. He and Nicklaus tied for the lead in the U.S. Open later that year, and Trevino won the playoff 68 to 71. He went on to win the

Canadian and British Opens and was named the PGA player of the year and the Associated Press male athlete of the year.

Trevino repeated in the 1972 British Open, chipping in for a par on the 17th hole of the final round to edge Nicklaus by a stroke. He also won the PGA championship in 1974 and 1984 for a total of six major titles.

After turning 50 in 1989, Trevino began playing on the PGA Senior tour. He was named senior player of the year in 1990, when he won the U.S. Senior Open, and in 1992, when he won the PGA Seniors Championship and the Tradition.

Trevino won 27 PGA tournaments and, through 1993, he had won 15 Senior tournaments.

★ World Golf Hall of Fame

Trippi, Charlie (Charles L.)
FOOTBALL
b. Dec. 14, 1923, Pittston, Pa.

Called a "one-man gang" because of his versatility, Trippi was a triple-threat tailback at the University of Georgia, an outstanding runner, passer, and kicker. But his coach, Wally Butts, said of him, "with all his scoring punch, which is a halfback's key to fame, his superior value was on defense."

The 6-foot, 185-pound Trippi first won fame when he replaced the injured Frank Sinkwich in the 1943 Rose Bowl. He ran for 130 yards and completed 6 passes for 96 yards in a 9–0 win over UCLA.

After military service in World War II, Trippi returned to captain the 1946 Georgia team that won all ten of its games and beat North Carolina 20–10 in the Sugar Bowl. During the regular season, Trippi gained 1,315 yards in 175 attempts and won the Maxwell Award as college football's outstanding player.

The "Scintillating Sicilian," as some sportswriters called him, signed a four-year, $100,000 contract to play for the NFL's Chicago Cardinals in 1947. It was the highest pay a professional player had received since Red Grange's post-season barnstorming tour with the Chicago Bears in 1925–26.

It proved a good investment. The Cardinals won the NFL championship by beating the Philadelphia Eagles, 28–21. Trippi scored on a 44-yard run from scrimmage and a 75-yard punt return. He rushed for 203 yards on just 14 carries in the title game.

After four years at halfback, Trippi was the Cardinals' starting quarterback in 1951 and 1952. He again played running back in 1953, then spent two seasons playing mostly at defensive back before retiring.

In nine professional seasons, Trippi gained 3,506 yards on 687 carries, a 5.1 average, and 51 rushing touchdowns. He caught 130 passes for 1,321 yards, a 10.2 average, and 11 touchdowns. He also punted 196 times for a 40.4 average; returned 63 punts for 864 yards, a 13.7 average, and 2 touchdowns; ran back 66 kickoffs for 1,457 yards, a 22.1 average; intercepted 4 passes and returned them for 93 yards, a 23.3 average, and 1 touchdown.

★ College Football Hall of Fame; Pro Football Hall of Fame

Trottier, Bryan J.

HOCKEY
b. July 17, 1956, Val Marie, Sask.

A 5-foot-11, 195-pound center, Trottier won the 1976 Calder Cup as the NHL's rookie of the year after scoring 95 points for the New York Islanders on 32 goals and 63 assists.

He led the league with 77 assists in 1977–78; the following season he had 47 goals and 87 assists for 134 points to win the Art Ross Trophy as the league's leading scorer and the Hart Trophy as its most valuable player.

Trottier helped lead the Islanders to four consecutive Stanley Cups, from 1980 through 1983. He won the Conn Smythe Trophy as the most valuable player in the 1980 playoffs, when he scored 29 points, a record at the time, on 12 goals and 17 assists.

Remarkably, Trottier scored exactly 29 points in the playoffs each of the next two years, with a record 23 assists in

1982. His record for playoff points was broken by teammate Mike Bossy, who had 35 in 1981.

The Islanders released Trottier after the 1989–90 season, and he signed with the Pittsburgh Penguins as a free agent. He played for two more Stanley Cup champions, in 1991 and 1992, before retiring to become an assistant coach with Pittsburgh.

In 1,238 regular season games, Trottier scored 1,410 points on 520 goals and 890 assists. He added 71 goals and 113 assists for a total of 184 points in 219 playoff games.

Troy, Mike (Michael F.)

SWIMMING
b. Oct. 3, 1940, Indianapolis, Ind.

Troy learned to swim in an Indianapolis park program and began competitive swimming with the Indianapolis Athletic Club and the University of Indiana.

He won the NCAA 100- and 200-yard butterfly events in 1960, when he also swam on the winning 4 x 100-yard medley relay team. Troy was the AAU outdoor 200-meter butterfly champion in 1959 and 1960. Indoors, he won the 100-yard butterfly in 1960, the 220-yard event from 1959 through 1961.

At the 1960 Olympics, Troy set a world record of 2:12.8 to win a gold medal in the 200-meter butterfly and he swam a leg on the gold medal 4 x 200-meter freestyle relay team.

After graduating from Indiana, Troy served with the Navy in Vietnam and was decorated for bravery.

Tubbs, Billy

BASKETBALL
b. March 5, 1935, St. Louis, Mo.

Tubbs played guard at Lon Morris Junior College in Texas for two years and then went to Lamar University. After graduating in 1958, he received his master's degree from Stephen F. Austin College and became a high school coach for a season.

In 1960, Tubbs returned to Lamar as an assistant basketball coach. He took over as head coach at Southwestern University in 1971, compiling a 31–24 record in three seasons before going to North Texas State as an assistant. Lamar called him once more in 1976, this time as head coach. Tubbs had a 75–46 record through 1979–80 and produced the school's first two NCAA tournament teams.

The University of Oklahoma hired Tubbs in 1980. His high-scoring, "firehouse" style of fast-break basketball soon began to draw standing-room-only crowds to the school's new 10,861-seat Lloyd Noble Center. Tubbs guided Oklahoma to five Big Eight Conference championships in a seven-year period, in 1984 and 1985 and from 1988 through 1990. The 1988 team reached the NCAA tournament finals but lost to the University of Kansas, 83–79.

Through the 1993–94 season, Tubbs had an overall record of 439–202 for a .685 winning percentage.

Tucker, Arnold (Young Arnold)

FOOTBALL
b. Jan. 5, 1924, Calhoun Falls, S.C.

An outstanding all-around football player, Tucker was the quarterback at Army while Glenn Davis and Doc Blanchard starred in the backfield, and he usually took third billing to them, especially in 1945, his first year as a starter.

In 1946, though, Tucker came in to his own, partly because Blanchard missed much of the season with an injury. Tucker's passing, breakaway running ability, and defensive skills were invaluable to Army that year.

He threw three touchdown passes to beat Duke 19–0, had kick returns of 76 and 78 yards against Cornell, and threw 2 touchdown passes in the first half of a 34–7 victory over Pennsylvania.

Against Oklahoma, he threw a touchdown pass and set up another touchdown with his passing to give Army a 14–7 lead. Tucker intercepted a pass in the end zone in the third quarter to preserve the lead. With Oklahoma threatening to tie the game again in the fourth quarter, Tucker burst through the line from his safety position to intercept a

lateral and ran 86 yards to make the final score 21–7.

In Army's scoreless tie against another unbeaten team, Notre Dame, Tucker intercepted 3 passes and had runs from scrimmage of 30 and 32 yards. He also made a touchdown-saving tackle by catching a Notre Dame runner from behind at the Army 12-yard line.

Tucker was a consensus All-American that year and won the Sullivan Award as the nation's outstanding amateur athlete. He and Blanchard are the only two football players ever to win the award.

After graduating, Tucker became a career Air Force officer and rose to the rank of lieutenant colonel before his retirement in 1974. He then spent two years as assistant athletic director at the University of Miami.

★ College Football Hall of Fame

Tunnell, Emlen

FOOTBALL
b. March 29, 1925, Bryn Mawr, Pa.
d. July 22, 1975

The first black and the first pure defensive specialist elected to the Pro Football Hall of Fame, Tunnell amassed more yardage than most offensive specialists by returning interceptions, punts, and kickoffs.

As a freshman at the University of Toledo, Tunnell broke a vertebra in his neck and was told he would never play again. Because of the injury he was rejected by both the Army and the Navy during World War II, but he spent three years in the Coast Guard and then enrolled at the University of Iowa, where he played primarily as a defensive back.

He left Iowa after the 1947 season, though he had a year of eligibility remaining, and signed as a free agent with the New York Giants. He soon became known as "Emlen the Gremlin" for his ability to come out of nowhere for an interception.

At first one of two safeties in New York's "umbrella defense," Tunnell later became the free safety in the modern 4-3-4 alignment. The 6-foot-1, 200-

pound Tunnell had great speed and great anticipation.

He played with the Giants through 1958 and then joined the Green Bay Packers in 1959. When he retired after the 1961 season, he held the NFL record with 79 interceptions. He returned them for 1,282 yards, a 16.2 average, and 4 touchdowns. Tunnell also returned 258 punts for 2,209 yards, an 8.6 average, and 5 touchdowns, and he ran back 46 kickoffs for 1,215 yards, a 26.4 average, and 1 touchdown.

★ Pro Football Hall of Fame

Tunney, Gene (James J.)

BOXING
b. May 25, 1897, New York, N.Y.
d. Nov. 7, 1978

A most unusual heavyweight champion, Tunney came from a relatively well-to-do family and was something of a scholar, though many writers suspected his scholarship was more pretense than reality.

Tunney asked for and was given a pair of boxing gloves for his tenth birthday, and he studied the sport as a teenager. He turned professional in 1915 and had 11 fights before joining the Marine Corps in 1917.

In 1919, Tunney won the American Expeditionary Forces light heavyweight championship by defeating 20 opponents in an elimination tournament, and he also beat the AEF heavyweight champion in a 4-round match.

After being discharged, Tunney recorded 16 knockouts in 22 fights to win a match against Battling Levinsky for the American light heavyweight championship. He won a 12-round decision over Levinsky on January 13, 1922, to claim the title.

Harry Greb took the championship with a 15-round decision on May 23, 1922. It was to be Tunney's only loss as a professional. He avenged it by decisioning Greb in 15 rounds on February 23, 1923, to regain the title.

In 1925, Tunney began fighting as a heavyweight. Victories over Georges Carpentier and Tommy Gibbons, both of whom had lost championship fights to

Jack Dempsey, established him as a contender and he met Dempsey on September 23, 1926. Using a retreating, counterpunching strategy against the attacking Dempsey, Tunney won a surprising 10-round decision.

Their rematch on September 22, 1927, became one of the most famous fights in history. Tunney was winning on points when Dempsey knocked him down in the 7th round. Apparently ignorant of a recent rule requiring a fighter to go to a neutral corner after a knockdown, Dempsey stood over Tunney for several seconds. The referee didn't begin his count until Dempsey finally went to a neutral corner.

Observers estimated that Tunney was down for 14 or 15 seconds before getting up and going on to win another 10-round decision. He defended his title just once, with an 11th-round knockout of Tom Heeney, and then retired from the ring.

Tunney married an heiress, became a successful businessman, and served as the Navy's director of athletics and physical fitness during World War II. As a professional boxer, he won 57 bouts, 42 by knockout; lost 1; and fought 1 draw, 17 no-decisions, and 1 no-contest.

★ International Boxing Hall of Fame

Turley, Bob (Robert L.)

BASEBALL
b. Sept. 19, 1930, Troy, Ill.

Known as "Bullet Bob" because of his blazing fastball, the 6-foot-2, 215-pound Turley won the AL's Cy Young Award with the New York Yankees in 1958. He had a 21–7 record to lead the league in victories and in winning percentage, and he also had a league-leading 19 complete games, with 6 shutouts and a 2.97 ERA.

Turley arrived in the major leagues with the St. Louis Browns in 1951, when he appeared in only one game. He spent the following season and a half in the minor leagues before rejoining the team in 1953. The team moved to Baltimore and became known as the Orioles in 1954, when Turley led the league in strikeouts with 185.

He was traded to the Yankees the following season and had a 17–13 record. After struggling with arm trouble for two years, Turley had his Cy Young season. He then went 8–11 and 9–3 before the sore arm began to plague him again. He retired after splitting the 1963 season between the California Angels and Boston Red Sox.

Turley had a career 101–85 record with 24 shutouts and a 3.64 ERA. He struck out 1,265 hitters and walked 1,068 in 1,712⅔ innings.

Turner, Bulldog (Clyde D.)

FOOTBALL
b. Nov. 10, 1919, Sweetwater, Tex.

Turner was a Little All-American center at Hardin-Simmons in 1939 and was courted by the Detroit Lions even after the Chicago Bears made him their first draft choice in 1940. The Lions were fined $5,000 for tampering, and Turner played 13 seasons with the Bears.

The 6-foot-2, 232-pound Turner was strong, cat-quick, and supremely confident. He once said he never played against an opponent he couldn't block. As a linebacker on defense, Turner could cover the field from sideline to sideline and he was exceptionally good against the pass. He led the NFL in interceptions with 8 in 1942, returning them for 96 yards and 1 touchdown. In 1947, Turner intercepted a pass from Washington's Sammy Baugh and ran 96 yards for a touchdown, carrying Baugh on his back for the last 7 yards of the run.

Turner was named an All-Pro from 1941 through 1944 and from 1946 through 1948. He retired after the 1952 season. He had 16 career interceptions and returned them for 289 yards and 2 touchdowns. Turner coached the American Football League's New York Titans (now Jets) to a 5–9–0 record in 1962.
★ Pro Football Hall of Fame

Turner, Ted (Robert Edward III)

YACHTING
b. Nov. 19, 1938, Cincinnati, Ohio

As a student at Brown University, Turner began to establish his reputation as an outstanding yachtsman by winning nine consecutive races in the col-

lege dinghy circuit. After spending six months in the Coast Guard in 1960, he joined his father's company, Turner Advertising Agency, in Macon, Georgia.

Turner won the national Y Flyer championship in 1963, the North American Flying Dutchman championship in 1965, the inaugural Southern Ocean Racing Conference championship in 1966, and the national One-Ton championship in 1974.

Nicknamed "Captain Outrageous" by the media because of his flamboyant, attention-getting behavior, Turner successfully defended the America's Cup in 1977, when his *Courageous* defeated *Australia* in four straight races.

Taking over the family company after his father committed suicide in 1963, Turner built a television empire based in large part on broadcasting sports events. WTBS (for Turner Broadcasting System) became the first superstation, available throughout the world via satellite.

Turner bought the NL's Atlanta Braves and the NBA's Atlanta Hawks in 1976 and assigned their broadcasting rights to his station. He also bought rights to the NHL's Atlanta Flames' hockey games.

The Turner empire now also includes TNT (Turner Network Television) and CNN (Cable Network News). TNT has become a major factor in sports television, broadcasting a full schedule of NBA games, Sunday night NFL games, and Olympic events during the day and early evening.

In 1986, Turner established the Goodwill Games, an international Olympic-style sports festival. The Games were held in Moscow in 1986, in Seattle in 1990, and in St. Petersburg, Russia, in 1994.

Twigg, Rebecca

CYCLING
b. March 16, 1963, Seattle, Wash.

Twigg never went to high school. Instead, she entered the University of Washington when she was 14. She also began competitive cycling that year, finishing third in the road race at the 1977 national championships.

"I like to go fast; I always have," Twigg once commented in explaining her interest in bicycle racing. She went fast enough to win the world championship in the 3-kilometer pursuit four times, in 1982, 1984, 1985, and 1987. She was the first American ever to win that title.

In 1981, Twigg won national championships in the road race, senior pursuit, and junior time trials and she won the senior pursuit and senior time trials in 1982. After it was announced that women's cycling would be on the 1984 Olympic program, she postponed her college studies in biology to become a resident at the Olympic training center in Colorado Springs.

Twigg won four 1984 national titles, in the 1-kilometer, the points race, the individual pursuit, and the match sprint. At the Los Angeles Olympics, road racing was the only women's event. Twigg appeared to have the race won, but Connie Carpenter-Phinney edged her with a lunge at the finish line. Twigg took the silver medal.

In 1985, Twigg was the national individual pursuit and points race champion. The following year, she set a world record of 30.642 seconds in the 500-meter with a flying start and won the individual pursuit and 1-kilometer titles.

The 5-foot-6, 127-pound cyclist won three gold medals at the 1987 Pan-American Games, in individual pursuit and the road race. She retired to return to college after failing to qualify for the 1988 Olympic team.

Twilley, Howard J., Jr.

FOOTBALL
b. Dec. 25, 1943, Houston, Tex.

Though undersized at 5-foot-10 and 180 pounds, Twilley had an outstanding career as a wide receiver at the University of Tulsa, catching 261 passes for 3,343 yards and 32 touchdowns, all NCAA records at the time. He led NCAA University Division receivers with 95 in 1964 and 134 in 1965 and was a consensus All-American as a senior, when he was voted college lineman of the year by United Press International sportswriters.

Twilley joined the AFL's Miami Dolphins as a twelfth-round draft choice in 1966 and became a starter in 1968. He quickly established a reputation as a sure-handed clutch receiver who ran precise routes to make up for a lack of speed. He caught a 28-yard touchdown pass from Bob Griese for Miami's first touchdown in Super Bowl VII, a 14–7 victory over the Washington Redskins.

He retired after the 1976 season with 150 career receptions for 2,228 yards, a 14.8 average, and 23 touchdowns.
★ College Football Hall of Fame

Twyman, Jack (John K.)

BASKETBALL
b. May 21, 1934, Pittsburgh, Pa.

A 6-foot-6, 210 forward, Twyman averaged 24.6 points a game in his senior year at Cincinnati and was chosen by the Rochester Royals in the second round of the NBA draft. The team moved to Cincinnati before the 1957–58 season.

When the Royals began emphasizing the fast break in 1958, Twyman blossomed as an outstanding scorer. He was an unusual forward in that he was surprisingly fast and could generally beat his defender down the floor, and he also had a guard's touch on the outside jump shot.

Twyman averaged 25.8 points a game in 1958–59 and finished second to Wilt Chamberlain with a 31.2 average the following season. He also had averages of 25.3 in 1960–61 and 22.9 in 1961–62.

After Rochester teammate Maurice Stokes was paralyzed by a head injury in 1958, Twyman became his legal guardian and raised hundreds of thousands of dollars to pay his medical bills and finance his rehabilitation. Stokes eventually regained some movement, and Twyman bought him an electric typewriter to allow him to communicate. The first words Stokes typed were, "Dear Jack, how can I ever thank you?" Stokes died of a heart attack in 1970.

Twyman had retired from basketball four years earlier. In 11 NBA seasons, he scored 15,840 points in 823 regular season games, an average of 19.2., and pulled down 5,421 rebounds. He had 621 points in 34 playoff games, an 18.3 average, with 255 rebounds.

★ Basketball Hall of Fame

Tyson, Mike (Michael G.)

BOXING
b. June 30, 1966, Brooklyn, N.Y.

Tyson learned to box as a young teenager in a New York State juvenile delinquent center. After he was released, Cus D'Amato became his trainer. Tyson won the Golden Gloves heavyweight championship in 1984 and became a professional the following year.

He won his first 19 pro fights by knockout and won the WBC heavyweight title by knocking out Trevor Berbick in the 2nd round on November 22, 1986. Tyson then disposed of two other claimants, WBA titlist Bonecrusher Smith and IBF titlist Tony Tucker, on 12-round decisions in 1987.

If there was any doubt that he was the true champion, Tyson demolished it in 1988, beating former titlist Larry Holmes on a 4th-round technical knockout and Koing another former champ, Michael Spinks, in the 1st round.

Personal problems accumulated for Tyson in 1989, however. He was involved in a bitter divorce from the model-actress Robin Givens, his wife of less than a year; he fired his manager and trainer; and he smashed his car into a tree without suffering serious injury.

On February 10, 1990, Tyson lost the championship in a major upset. He was knocked out by a virtual unknown, James "Buster" Douglas, in the 10th round of a fight in Japan. Douglas lost the title to Evander Holyfield in his first defense and Tyson was scheduled to meet Holyfield in November 1991. The fight had to be postponed because Tyson suffered a rib injury in training.

Before it could be rescheduled, Tyson was charged with raping a Black Miss America contestant in Indianapolis. He was found guilty in February 1992 and was sentenced to six years in the Indiana Youth Center. The conviction is being appealed.

Tyus, Wyomia

TRACK AND FIELD
b. Aug. 29, 1945, Griffin, Ga.

Overshadowed during much of her early career by Tennessee State University teammate Edith McGuire, Tyus rose to the occasion at the 1964 Olympics. She lowered her personal best in the 100-meter from 11.5 to 11.2 seconds in the preliminary heats, tying Wilma Rudolph's world record, then beat McGuire to win the gold medal. She was also a member of the silver medal 4 x 100-meter relay team.

The 5-foot-7, 134-pound Tyus won the AAU outdoor 100-yard championship in 1965 and 1966 and she was also the 220-yard champion in 1966. Indoors, she won the 60-meter dash three years in a row, from 1965 through 1967, setting world records of 6.8 seconds in 1965 and 6.5 seconds in 1966.

The world record in the 100-meter was lowered to 11.1 seconds in June 1965 and Tyus tied it two weeks later. She also tied the world record of 10.3 seconds for the 100-yard dash that year and she tied it twice more in 1968.

At the 1968 Olympics, Tyus again won the 100-meter, setting a world record of 11.0 seconds. She is the only sprinter to win the same dash event at two different Olympics. She also ran the anchor leg on the 4 x 100-meter relay team that won the gold medal in a world record 42.8 seconds.

Tyus gave her gold medals to Tommy Smith and John Carlos, who had been thrown off the U.S. team and expelled from the Olympic Village for giving the "Black Power" salute during the medal ceremony for the men's 200-meter dash.

She retired from competition after the Olympics, but when the professional International Track Association was formed in 1973, she joined the circuit, saying, "I never ran just to win, and I still don't. I run because I like it."

In 1983, Tyus was named the woman sprinter on an all-time team selected by veteran track and field writers.

★ International Women's Sports Hall
  of Fame; National Track & Field
  Hall of Fame; Olympic Hall of Fame

★ ★ U ★ ★

Unitas, Johnny (John C.)
FOOTBALL
b. May 7, 1933, Pittsburgh, Pa.

Virtually unknown as a quarterback at the University of Louisville, Unitas was a ninth-round draft choice of the Pittsburgh Steelers in the 1955 NFL college draft but was cut before he even threw a pass during the exhibition season.

Unitas got a job as a pile driver and was playing for the Bloomfield, New Jersey, Rams for $6 a game when a knowledgeable fan recommended him to the Baltimore Colts. They signed him as a backup to George Shaw. When Shaw suffered a broken leg in the fourth game of the 1956 season, Unitas took over and completed 55.6 percent of his passes.

Within two years, Unitas was recognized as one of the greatest quarterbacks in NFL history. In the 1958 championship game against the New York Giants, he completed seven consecutive passes to set up a game-tying field goal and then engineered the 80-yard drive that won the game, 23–17, in overtime. He played that game wearing a nine-pound protective corset of foam rubber and steel because of three broken ribs.

A great signal-caller as well as a great passer, Unitas was praised by Vince Lombardi: "He is uncanny in his abilities, under the most violent pressure, to pick out the soft spot in a defense."

Unitas won the Bert Bell Award as the league's player of the year in 1959, when the Colts once more beat the Giants to win the league championship. He was named most valuable player in both championship games. Unitas also won the Bell Trophy in 1964 and 1967.

The All-Pro quarterback in 1958, 1959, 1964, 1965, and 1967, Unitas participated in ten Pro Bowls. He led the NFL in touchdown passes four years in a row, 1957 through 1960; in passing yardage in 1957, 1959, 1960, and 1963; in completion percentage in 1967; and in completions in 1959, 1960, and 1963.

After missing most of the 1968 season with a torn muscle in his right elbow, Unitas played two more full seasons. He had arm problems in 1971 and 1972 and was then traded to the San Diego Chargers. He spent just one season there, attempting only 76 passes, before retiring.

In 18 NFL seasons, Unitas completed 2,830 of 5,186 passes for 40,239 yards and 290 touchdowns. He also rushed for 13 touchdowns.

★ Pro Football Hall of Fame

Unseld, Westley S.
BASKETBALL
b. March 14, 1946, Louisville, Ky.

A two-time All-American at the University of Louisville, in 1967 and 1968, the 6-foot-7, 245-pound Unseld played for the U.S. championship team in the 1967 Pan-American Games and World University Games. During his three-year varsity career, he scored 1,686 points, an average of 20.6 per game, and had 1,551 rebounds.

The Baltimore Bullets chose him in the first round of the 1968 NBA draft.

Unseld was the second player in history to be named rookie of the year and the league's most valuable player in the same season (Wilt Chamberlain was the first).

Although not a great scorer as a pro, Unseld transformed the Bullets into a contending team with his strong rebounding and his uncanny ability to make accurate outlet passes to start the fast break.

The franchise moved from Baltimore to Washington in 1973 and was known as the Washington Capitals for one season. The name was changed to the Washington Bullets in 1974.

Unseld helped lead his team into the playoffs 12 consecutive times, from 1969 through 1980, and was named the most valuable player of the playoffs in 1978, when the Bullets won the NBA championship.

He retired as a player after the 1980–81 season and became a vice president of the Bullets and the Capital Center, where the team plays. In January 1988 he replaced Kevin Loughery as Washington's coach. The Bullets made it to the playoffs that year but haven't since. Through the 1992–93 season, Unseld had a 178–287 record as a coach.

In his 13 seasons as a player, he scored 10,624 points in 984 regular season games, an average of 10.8 per game, and he had 13,769 rebounds. He scored 1,260 points and had 1,777 rebounds in 119 playoff games.

★ Basketball Hall of Fame

Unser, Alfred

AUTO RACING
b. May 29, 1939, Albuquerque, N.M.

It seemed that Unser's long, illustrious career was just about over in 1985, when he was the relief driver for injured Rick Mears. All he did that year was win the IndyCar point championship for the third time, becoming the oldest driver in history to win an IndyCar race or the championship. His son, Al Jr., was second in the point standings.

Two years later, Unser became the oldest driver ever to win the Indy 500. It was his fourth victory at Indy, tying the record held by A. J. Foyt and Rick Mears.

For seven years, Unser drove supermodified cars on weekends. He spent one season, 1964, in midget cars, and in 1965 he raced in 13 IndyCar events, winning the Pikes Peak hill climb. He had three second-place finishes in 1966 and was second in the 1967 Indy 500.

Unser won three races in 1968, but a motorcycle accident sidelined him for much of the 1969 season. He came back to win five of the last six races, placing second in the point standings. And he just kept right on going in 1970, winning ten of eighteen races, including the Indy 500. He topped the championship point standings, with his brother Bobby finishing second, and he also won the dirt car championship.

In 1971 Unser became the fourth driver to win the Indy 500 two years in a row. He finished second at Indy in 1972 and won the dirt track championship again in 1973. After four subpar seasons, he won the International Race of Champions series two years in a row, in 1977 and 1978, when he won his third Indy 500. He was the national champion for the second time in 1983 and for the third in 1985, when he edged his son, Al Jr., by one point.

★ Indy Hall of Fame

Unser, Alfred, Jr.

AUTO RACING
b. April 19, 1962, Albuquerque, N.M.

Unser began racing go-carts when he was nine years old and moved to sprint car racing when he was sixteen. He was named rookie of the year by the Sports Car Club of America in 1981, when he won the SuperVee championship, setting six track records in the process. He repeated as SuperVee champion in 1982.

He also made his IndyCar debut in 1982 and won his first IndyCar race in June 1984. Unser and his father dueled for the national championship through all of the 1985 season; Al Sr. won, 151 points to 150. That prompted Al Jr. to remark, "My father taught me everything I know about racing, but he hasn't taught me everything *he* knows."

In 1986 Unser won the International Race of Champions series with two victories in the four events. His father, who had won the year before, claimed one of the other victories and finished fourth.

Al Jr. won the 1990 national driving championship and was the winner of the 1992 Indy 500.

Unser, Bobby (Robert W.)

AUTO RACING
b. Feb. 20, 1934, Albuquerque, N.M.

Unser's father and two uncles were racers. Uncle Lou won the Pike's Peak hill climb eight times, the last in 1953, when he was fifty-seven. Bobby also won it eight times, including six in a row, from 1958 through 1963.

He had a long apprenticeship, mostly in midgets and sprint cars. His first Indy car victory came in 1967. The following year he won the Indy 500 and was the national champion with a record 4,326 points, just 7 points ahead of Mario Andretti.

Unser also won the Indy 500 in 1975 and 1981 and he was the national driving champion for a second time in 1974. He ranks fourth all-time with 35 Indy Car victories, 4 behind his brother Al.

Upshaw, Gene (Eugene)

FOOTBALL
b. Aug. 15, 1945, Robstown, Tex.

Upshaw didn't play football until his senior year in high school and he was a walk-on at Texas A & I College, where he eventually got a football scholarship. The 6-foot-5, 255-pound Upshaw was chosen by the Oakland Raiders in the first round of the American Football League's 1967 draft.

He was an immediate starter with Oakland and he became offensive captain in 1969. His size and power made him ideal to block the big defensive tackles he faced, and his speed made him a terror to linebackers and defensive backs when he pulled out to lead the Raiders' power sweep.

Upshaw played with the Raiders for 15 years, retiring after the 1981 season. During that period, the Raiders played 308 regular season and post-season games, and Upshaw started 307 of them. He played in six Pro Bowls, ten AFL or AFC championship games, and three Super Bowls.

★ Pro Football Hall of Fame

★ ★ V ★ ★

Valenzuela, Fernando

BASEBALL
b. Nov. 1, 1960, Navoja, Mexico

After pitching 17⅔ innings for the Los Angeles Dodgers in 1980, Valenzuela became the first pitcher to win the NL's Cy Young and rookie of the year awards in the same season in 1981. He had a 13–7 record and led the league with 8 shutouts and 180 strikeouts in 192⅓ innings. (The 1981 season was shortened to 110 games because of a player strike.)

The chunky 6-foot, 195-pound left-hander combined a sharp breaking screwball with a good fastball and excellent control to become the ace of the Dodger staff during the next five seasons. He led the NL with 21 victories and 20 complete games in 1986, and was the leader in complete games again with 12 in 1987.

The heavy workload began to take its toll in 1988, however, when he came down with a sore arm. He struggled the next two seasons and was released by the Dodgers in 1991. The California Angels picked him up, but he was cut again after losing his only two starts.

In 1993 the Baltimore Orioles lost two pitchers to injury early in the season and signed Valenzuela. He had a couple of good outings for Baltimore but finished the season with an 8–10 record and a 4.94 ERA.

Through 1993, Valenzuela's career record is 149–128, with 29 shutouts. He has struck out 1,842 hitters and walked 1,016 in 2,434 innings.

Van Bebber, Jack F.

WRESTLING
b. July 27, 1907, Noble County, Okla.

At Oklahoma A & M (now Oklahoma State) University, Van Bebber was undefeated in three varsity seasons. He won NCAA championships in the 155-pound class in 1929 and in the 165-pound class in 1930 and 1931. Van Bebber was the AAU national champion at 163 pounds in 1930 and 1932, and at 165 pounds in 1931.

His only loss as an amateur came in an early match of the round-robin competition at the 1932 Olympic trials, but he won a spot on the team and took the gold medal in the 158.5-pound class by beating Finland's Eino Leino.

Van Bebber was a professional wrestler for two years after graduating in 1933 and retired from the sport in 1935.

Van Berg, Jack (John C.)

HORSE RACING
b. July 7, 1936, Columbus, Nebr.

The son of Marion Van Berg, a very successful thoroughbred owner and trainer, Van Berg began his own training career when he was 17 by buying horses at claiming races. He entered stakes racing in the late 1960s and led the nation in winners saddled in 1968, 1969, 1970, 1972, 1974, 1976, 1983, and 1984.

Van Berg won the Eclipse Award as trainer of the year in 1984, when his Gate Dancer won the Preakness Stakes. His most successful horse was Alysheba, the 3-year-old Eclipse winner in 1987.

Alysheba won the Kentucky Derby, Preakness, and Super Derby and earned more than $2 million that year.

★ National Horse Racing Hall of Fame

Van Brocklin, Norman

FOOTBALL

b. March 15, 1926, Eagle Butte, S.D. d. May 2, 1983

Nicknamed "Stormin' Norman" because of his fiery temperament, Van Brocklin was one of football's finest passers. He led the University of Oregon to a 9–1 record during the 1948 season, but the team lost 21–13 to Southern Methodist University in the Cotton Bowl. In three years as a starter, Van Brocklin completed 144 of 316 pass attempts for 1,949 yards and 16 touchdowns.

Van Brocklin was a first-round draft choice of the Los Angeles Rams in 1949, and he spent most of the season backing up Bob Waterfield, a fellow Hall of Famer. He started the last game of the season and threw four touchdown passes in a victory over the Washington Redskins.

In 1950 Van Brocklin and Waterfield alternated at quarterback, which made neither of them happy. Van Brocklin was the NFL's passing champion that season, completing 127 of 233 attempts for 2,061 yards and 18 touchdowns. When the Rams won the 1951 championship, Waterfield was the passing champion, but it was Van Brocklin's 73-yard touchdown pass to Tom Fears that beat the Cleveland Browns, 24–17, in the title game. He also set an NFL record by passing for 554 yards against the New York Yanks that season.

Van Brocklin won passing titles again in 1952 and 1954. But in 1956 he became a backup to Billy Wade — Waterfield had retired after the 1952 season — and it seemed as if his career might be almost over.

In 1958 Van Brocklin was given a new start, when the Rams traded him to the Philadelphia Eagles. Two years later he led the Eagles to the NFL championship, throwing for 2,471 yards and 24 touchdowns, and was a consensus player of the year choice. In his last game, the 1960 NFL Pro Bowl, he threw three touchdown passes.

During his 12 NFL seasons, Van Brocklin completed 1,553 of 2,895 passes, a percentage of 53.6, for 23,611 yards and 173 touchdowns. He also punted 523 times for a 42.9 average and rushed for 11 touchdowns.

Van Brocklin became the first coach of the Minnesota Vikings in 1961 and guided the Vikings to a second-place division finish in 1964, but he was replaced by Bud Grant after a 4–9–1 record in 1966. He took over as coach of the Atlanta Falcons during the 1968 season and was fired after the Falcons won just two of their first eight games in 1974. His overall record was 66–100–7.

★ Pro Football Hall of Fame

Van Buren, Steve W.

FOOTBALL

b. Dec. 20, 1920, La Ceiba, Honduras

A tough, bruising runner with speed, Van Buren also excelled as a linebacker in the NFL's one-platoon era. He grew up in Louisiana and played football at Louisiana State University. In his senior year, 1943, he led the nation in scoring with 110 points on 16 touchdowns and 14 conversions and was second in rushing with 847 yards in 150 attempts.

He joined the Philadelphia Eagles in 1944 and immediately became an All-Pro halfback. In 1945 he led the NFL in rushing with 832 yards on 143 carries, a 5.8 average; in touchdowns, with 18; and in scoring, with 110 points. Single-handedly he outscored both the Pittsburgh Steelers and the Chicago Cardinals.

Injuries slowed Van Buren somewhat in 1946, but he led the league in rushing and was an All-Pro the next three seasons. His 1,146 yards in 1949 was a record at the time.

The Eagles beat the Chicago Cardinals, 7–0, for the NFL championship in 1948, when Van Buren scored the only touchdown on a short run after setting it up with a 26-yard run. They repeated in 1949, beating the Los Angeles Rams 14–0. Van Buren gained 196 yards in 31 carries in that game.

A recurrent foot injury limited his playing time in 1950 and 1951. He retired after suffering a knee injury during Philadelphia's 1952 training camp.

In eight seasons, Van Buren gained 5,860 yards on 1,320 attempts, an average of 4.4 yards, and scored 69 rushing touchdowns. He returned 77 kickoffs for 2,030 yards, a 26.4 average, and 3 touchdowns. He also scored 3 touchdowns on pass receptions and 2 on punt returns, and had 2 conversions for a total of 464 points.

★ Pro Football Hall of Fame

Vance, Dazzy (Clarence A.)

BASEBALL
b. March 4, 1891, Orient, Iowa
d. Feb. 16, 1961

Vance signed his first professional baseball contract with a minor league team in 1912. He was called up to the NL's Pittsburgh Pirates in 1915, but he walked five hitters in three innings and was sent back to the minors. Late that season, the AL's New York Yankees bought his contract, and he had an 0–3 record with them.

During much of this time, Vance had a sore arm that kept him from throwing his fastball as hard as he could. He kept pitching in the minor leagues, working on his control and a curve ball, and he was purchased by the Brooklyn Dodgers after the 1921 season ended.

The 6-foot-2, 200-pound right-hander joined the Dodgers in 1922, at the age of 31, and led the NL in strikeouts for seven consecutive seasons. He was also the league leader in shutouts with 5 in 1922, 4 in 1925, 4 in 1928, and 4 in 1930; in ERA with 2.16 in 1924, 2.09 in 1928, and 2.61 in 1930; in complete games with 30 in 1924 and 25 in 1927; and in victories with 28 in 1924 and 22 in 1925.

His best season was 1924, when he had a 28–6 record and his highest career strikeout total, 262 in 308⅔ innings. The Dodgers came closer to winning a pennant that year than at any other time in Vance's career, finishing just 1½ games out.

The Dodgers were known as the "Daffiness Boys" during the 1920s. When they managed to have three runners on third in a 1926 game, Vance was the first runner there, and, as he pointed out to a rather confused umpire, he was the only player entitled to possession of the base.

Vance was traded to the St. Louis Cardinals in 1933. He went to Cincinnati in 1934 but was waived back to St. Louis before the season ended. He finished his major league career with the Dodgers in 1935, when he had a 3–2 record and 2 saves as a relief pitcher.

He had a career 197–140 record with 29 shutouts and a 3.24 ERA. Vance struck out 2,045 hitters and walked 840 in 2,967 innings.

Baseball Hall gof Fame

Vanderbilt, Harold S.

YACHTING
b. July 6, 1884, Oakdale, N.Y
d. July 4, 1970

Vanderbilt, who began sailing his own 14-foot sloop when he was 12 years old, is one of only two men to skipper three America's Cup defenders, *Enterprise* in 1930, *Rainbow* in 1934, and *Ranger* in 1937. He was a member of the syndicates that built the first two ships and he alone paid for building *Ranger.*

In 1910, Vanderbilt won his first major competition, the Bermuda race. He also won the Astor Cup for schooners in 1921, 1922, and 1925 and for sloops in 1927 and from 1934 through 1937.

Vanderbilt wrote an extensive revision of yachting rules that was adopted throughout the world after World War II, and he was a member of the syndicate that built the 1967 America's Cup defender, *Intrepid.*

Vander Meer, John S.

BASEBALL
b. Nov. 2, 1914, Prospect Park, N.J.

Like many young pitchers with good fastballs, Vander Meer was wild and erratic. He had enough promise to spend 13 seasons in the major leagues, winning more than 100 games and losing more than 100. He never had a 20-victory season.

But in 1938, pitching for the NL's Cincinnati Reds, Vander Meer set a record that will never be broken. He pitched no-hitters in two consecutive starts. The first came on June 11 against the Boston Braves. He walked three and won, 3–0.

Four days later, he faced the Dodgers in the first night game ever played at Ebbets Field in Brooklyn. After retiring the first hitter in the 9th inning, Vander Meer walked three in a row to load the bases. The next batter hit a grounder that resulted in a force play at home plate and Leo Durocher then popped out to end the game.

Vander Meer joined the Reds in the 1937 season. He led the NL in strikeouts three seasons in a row with 202 in 1941, 186 in 1942, and 174 in 1943. After spending two years in military service during World War II, he returned to the Reds in 1946 and had a respectable 17–14 record in 1948.

He went 8–14 during the next two years and retired after losing his only start with the AL's Cleveland Indians in 1951. His career record was 119–121 with 29 shutouts and a 3.44 ERA. Vander Meer struck out 1,294 and walked 1,132 hitters in 2,104 innings.

Vandivier, Fuzzy (Robert P.)

BASKETBALL
b. Dec. 26, 1903, Franklin, Ind.
d. July 30, 1983

Vandivier is probably the most unusual member of the Basketball Hall of Fame in that he essentially played for the same team for seven years, and that was the extent of his career. He never played professional or even semipro basketball.

In 1918, Vandivier was a freshman starter for the Franklin, Indiana, High School team that lost in the final game of the state championship tournament. The team won the championship the next three years, 1920 through 1922, and Vandivier was named an All-State player each season. Franklin High had an 89–8 record during that period.

The "Wonder Five" players moved on to Franklin College without even leaving home for the 1922–23 season. The team won 52 games and lost only 5 in

three years while playing major colleges such as Indiana University, Marquette, Purdue, Notre Dame, and the University of Wisconsin.

A back injury ended Vandivier's career during his senior year in college. He went on to coach at Franklin High from 1926 through 1944 and he served as the school's athletic director through 1962.
★ Basketball Hall of Fame

Van Slyke, Andy (Andrew J.)

BASEBALL
b. Dec. 21, 1960, Utica, N.Y.

A right-handed thrower but left-handed hitter, Van Slyke was drafted out of high school by the NL's St. Louis Cardinals in 1979 but didn't begin playing professional baseball until 1980.

He joined the Cardinals during the 1983 season and was traded to the Pittsburgh Pirates in 1987. Van Slyke had played first base, third base, and the outfield previously, but the Pirates made him their starting center fielder because of his speed.

Van Slyke led the league with 15 triples in 1988, when he batted .288 with 25 home runs and 100 RBI to win *The Sporting News* NL player of the year award. He batted .324 in 1992, leading the league with 45 doubles and 199 hits.

The 6-foot-2, 198-pound Van Slyke, who is very popular with the media and fans because of his quick wit, was troubled by back problems in 1993 and 1994. A Golden Glove winner from 1988 through 1992, he was named to the NL All-Star team in 1988 and 1992.

Through 1994, Van Slyke had a .276 average with 1,500 hits, including 284 doubles, 89 triples, and 156 home runs. He had stolen 238 bases, scored 803 runs, and driven in 768.

Van Wie, Virginia P.

GOLF
b. Feb. 9, 1909, Chicago, Ill.

A long, straight hitter with a beautifully smooth swing, Van Wie was one of the finest women amateur golfers of the 1930s. She won the U.S. Women's Amateur title three consecutive years, 1932 through 1934, after having finished second in 1928, 1930, and 1931.

The Western Junior champion in 1925, Van Wie also won Curtis Cup matches against Diana Fishwick in 1932 and Joyce Wethered in 1934. She was the South Atlantic Amateur champion in 1928, 1939, 1930, and 1934.

Van Wie retired from competition after 1934 to enter business. She later became a successful golf instructor.

Vare, Glenna (Collett)

GOLF
b. June 20, 1903, New Haven, Conn.
d. Feb. 10, 1989

Sometimes called the "Bobby Jones" of women's golf, Vare drew this compliment from Jones: "Her accuracy with the spoon and brassie is to me the most important part of her well-rounded game. It is, of course, her way of absorbing, to a great extent, the disadvantage of length, which some women suffer against the best males, but she does it with little disadvantage to be noticed."

Despite Jones's reference to her lack of length, Vare had a fluid swing that produced long, straight drives as well as accurate iron shots. She won the U.S. Women's Amateur a record six times, in 1922 and 1925, from 1928 through 1930, and in 1935. Vare also won the Canadian women's amateur in 1923 and 1924 and was a finalist in the British women's amateur in 1929 and 1930.

During 1933 and 1934, she was out of competition raising two young children. When she returned to win her sixth amateur championship in 1935, Vare drew galleries that would have been enormous for men's professional golf at the time. Despite rain and cold on the last day of the tournament, a crowd of 15,000 watched her beat 17-year-old Patty Berg, 3 and 2.

That was her last major tournament, but Vare continued to play recreationally for the rest of her life. She won the Rhode Island women's amateur championship in 1959, at the age of 56, and when she was 85 Vare was still shooting in the high 80s.

The Vare Trophy, awarded since 1952

to the professional woman golfer with the lowest average strokes per round, is named for her.

★ International Women's Sports Hall of Fame; World Golf Hall of Fame

Varipapa, Andy (Andrew)

BOWLING
b. 1894, Italy
d. Aug. 25, 1984

Varipapa's family came to the U.S. when he was 10 years old. He boxed professionally and played semipro baseball before becoming a full-time bowler when he was 33.

The 5-foot-9, 180-pound Varipapa was best known as a trick shot artist who put on exhibitions across the country. He made strikes blindfolded, with either hand, and with his back to the pins. In his most celebrated trick, he knocked down 14 pins on three different alleys with a single shot.

A colorful showman who kept up a constant line of patter while he performed, Varipapa was called the "Talking Machine" by one writer. He commented, "They think it's colorful, so I brag, put body English on the ball, and jump in the air when I make a big strike. But believe me when I say I'd like to cut it out."

Varipapa proved that he was also an excellent tournament bowler by winning the All-Star match-game championship in 1946, when he was 53. In 1947 he became the first bowler to win the event two years in a row.

★ ABC Hall of Fame

Vaughan, Arky (Joseph F.)

BASEBALL
b. March 9, 1912, Clifty, Ark.
d. Aug. 30, 1952

Vaughan's career batting average is second only to Honus Wagner's among shortstops, and he was also a fine fielder who led the NL in assists and putouts three times.

Nicknamed for his native Arkansas, Vaughan joined the Pittsburgh Pirates in 1932, when he hit .318. The following year he led the league with 19 triples, and he was the league leader with 94 walks in 1934, when he made the All-Star team for the first of nine consecutive times.

Vaughan had his best season in 1935, when he hit .385 to lead the league, an average has not been surpassed by an NL player since. He also led the league with 97 walks and a .607 slugging percentage.

In 1936, Vaughan was tops in the league with 122 runs scored and 118 walks, and he hit a league-leading 17 triples in 1937, even though an injury limited him to 126 games that season. He led the league in triples again with 15 in 1940.

After he hit .316 in just 106 games in 1941, Vaughan was traded to the Brooklyn Dodgers. He slipped to .277 in 1943 but batted .305 and led the league with 112 runs scored in 1943. He then spent three seasons in military service.

Vaughan returned to the Dodgers as a part-time player in 1947, when he batted .325 and played on a pennant-winning team for the only time. In three pinch-hitting appearances during Brooklyn's seven-game loss to the New York Yankees, he had a double and a walk. Vaughan retired after hitting .244 in 1948. He drowned in a boating accident two years later.

In 1,817 games, Vaughan had 2,103 hits, including 356 doubles, 128 triples, and 96 home runs. He stole 118 bases, scored 1,173 runs, and had 926 RBI.
★ Baseball Hall of Fame

Vaught, John H.

FOOTBALL
b. May 6, 1909, Olney, Tex.

Known as "Harpo" during his college years because of his curly hair, Vaught was an All-American guard at Texas Christian University in 1932, when he captained the football team. He also played basketball and was his class valedictorian.

Vaught coached high school football and was an assistant college coach until entering the Navy during World War II. He became an assistant coach at the University of Mississippi in 1946 and succeeded Howard Drew as head coach in 1947.

"Ole Miss" had won only two of nine games the previous year, but Vaught guided the team to a 9–2 record in his first season, including a 43–13 win over Tennessee.

With "Chuckin' Charley" Conerly at quarterback, his early teams featured passing. He later went to the split T formation and a strong running game. His 1960 and 1961 teams were both ranked second in national polls and Mississippi finished in the top ten eight other times during Vaught's tenure.

A heart condition forced his retirement after the 1970 season, but he returned as head coach for part of the 1973 season after Billy Kinard was fired. Vaught's overall record was 190–61–12.
★ College Football Hall of Fame

Verdeur, Joseph T.

SWIMMING
b. March 7, 1926, Philadelphia, Pa.

Solidly built and ruggedly handsome, Verdeur hoped to parlay a successful swimming career into a chance to play Tarzan in the movies. He won a gold medal in the 200-meter breaststroke at the 1948 Olympics, but he never played Tarzan.

Verdeur was a pioneer of the butterfly stroke when it was considered a variant of the breaststroke and before it became a separate event internationally. He won AAU national outdoor championships in the 200-yard breaststroke in 1943, in the 200-meter event in 1944 and from 1946 through 1949, and the 300-meter individual medley in 1944 and from 1947 through 1949.

Indoors, he was the 200-yard breaststroke champion in 1944 and from 1946 through 1948 and the 300-yard individual medley titlist from 1946 through 1950.

Swimming for LaSalle University, Verdeur won NCAA championships in the 200-yard butterfly in 1947 and 1948 and in the 150-yard individual medley in 1949 and 1950.

Versalles, Zoilo C.

BASEBALL
b. Dec. 18, 1939, Veldado, Cuba

A steady but unspectacular short-stop, Versalles was named the AL's most valuable player in 1965, when he led the league with 45 doubles, 12 triples, and 126 runs scored to help the Minnesota Twins win their first pennant. He batted .286, scoring 3 runs and driving in 4 in their seven-game World Series loss to the Los Angeles Dodgers.

Versalles played briefly with the Washington Senators in 1959 and 1960. The team moved to Minnesota in 1961, when he became the starting shortstop. The 5-foot-10, 150-pound Versalles hit .280 that year, the highest average of his career.

He led the league in triples with 13 in 1963 and 10 in 1964, as well as in his MVP season. After his average dropped to .249 in 1966 and .200 in 1967, he went to the Los Angeles Dodgers for one year and played for the Cleveland Indians and the new Washington Senator franchise in 1969. He then spent a year in the minor leagues before finishing his career with the Atlanta Braves in 1971.

In 1,400 major league games, Versalles batted .242 with 1,246 hits, including 230 doubles, 63 triples, and 95 home runs. He scored 650 runs and had 471 RBI.

Vessels, Billy D.

FOOTBALL
b. March 22, 1931, Cleveland, Okla.

Winner of the Heisman and Maxwell trophies as college football's outstanding player in 1953, the 6-foot, 190-pound Vessels was a fast, elusive, halfback at the University of Oklahoma. One of the school's assistant coaches later said of Vessels, "He was outstanding in all phases of the game, the type of player coaches dream of having on their squad someday."

Vessels was academically ineligible as a freshman, but he became a starter as a sophomore. After missing most of his junior year with a broken leg, he gained 1,072 rushing yards and scored 18 touchdowns as a senior.

He turned down an offer from the NFL's Baltimore Colts to play for the Ed-monton Eskimos of the Canadian Football League in 1953, when he was named the league's outstanding player. He suffered a serious knee injury in 1954 while playing for the Fort Sill, Oklahoma, Army Base team. Vessels joined the Colts after his discharge in 1956, but the injury limited his effectiveness, and he retired after that season. During his brief NFL career he gained 215 yards on 44 carries, a 4.9 average, and scored 2 rushing touchdowns; he caught 11 passes for 177 yards, a 16.1 average, and 1 touchdown.
★ College Football Hall of Fame

Vezina, Georges

HOCKEY
b. Jan. 1887, Chicoutimi, P.Q.
d. March 26, 1926

Nicknamed the "Chicoutimi Cucumber" because of his coolness, Vezina was playing for an amateur team when he shut out the Montreal Canadiens in an exhibition game early in 1910. That fall he became Montreal's starting goalie.

The Canadiens entered the National Hockey League when it was organized for the 1917–18 season. Official statistics weren't kept until then but Vezina was already recognized as one of the very best goaltenders in hockey.

He was also one of the most durable, starting 328 consecutive regular season games and 39 playoff games, despite the fact that he was suffering from tuberculosis during his last three seasons.

A few days after his nose was broken by a shot that also cut his head, Vezina turned in one of his greatest performances in the 1922–23 season, stopping 79 of 80 shots in a victory over the Toronto Maple Leafs. In 1923–24 he had 3 shutouts and allowed just 48 goals in 24 games. He gave up only 6 goals in six playoff games to lead Montreal to its first Stanley Cup championship since the formation of the NHL.

In the first game of the 1925–26 season, Vezina shut out Pittsburgh for one period. Early in the second period, he collapsed to the ice with severe chest pains. He was carried off the ice and taken to hospital. Vezina died of tuberculosis less than four months later.

During his nine seasons in the NHL, Vezina gave up 633 goals and had 13 shutouts in 191 regular season games. He gave up 74 goals and had 4 shutouts in 26 playoff games.

The Canadiens presented the Vezina Trophy to the NHL in 1926 as an annual award for the league's best goaltender.
★ Hockey Hall of Fame

Vidmar, Peter

GYMNASTICS
b. June 30, 1961, Los Angeles, Calif.

Vidmar began taking gymnastics lessons from Makato Sakamoto in 1972 and entered UCLA in 1979. He was the NCAA Division I all-around champion in 1982 and 1983. Vidmar also won the horizontal bar title in 1982 and tied for the parallel bars championship in 1981.

He was the AAU all-around champion in 1982 and 1984, and in 1984 he won the floor exercise and tied for the horizontal bar and parallel bars titles.

The captain of the gold medal 1984 Olympic gymnastics team, Vidmar tied with Li Ning of China for gold in the pommel horse and won a silver medal in the all-around. He led most of the way in the all-around, but finished .025 behind Koji Gushiken of Japan. Vidmar had 118.675 points, the highest total ever for an American male gymnast.

He retired from competition after the Olympics. He often serves as a television commentator on the sport, and he has made fitness training videotapes.
★ Olympic Hall of Fame

Vinci, Charles T. Jr.

WEIGHTLIFTING
b. Feb. 28, 1933, Cleveland, Ohio

Vinci faced disqualification for being overweight when competing in the 123-pound class at the 1956 Olympics. After more than an hour of exercise and running, he was still several ounces too heavy 15 minutes before the competition. A very bad haircut got him down to the limit.

Despite all the effort he'd put into losing weight, Vinci won the gold medal

with a world record of 342.5 kilograms. At the 1960 Olympics, he tied the new world record of 345.0 kilograms to win a second gold medal.

Vinci was the U.S. bantamweight champion from 1954 through 1956 and from 1958 through 1961, and he won gold medals in his class at the Pan-American Games in 1955 and 1959.

In 1955, Vinci set records for his weight class in the three power lifts with a bench press of 235 pounds, a dead lift of 600 pounds, and a 2-hand curl of 155 pounds.

Vines, Ellsworth (Henry Ellsworth Jr.)

TENNIS
b. Sept. 28, 1911, Los Angeles, Calif.
d. March 17, 1994

At 6-foot-2 and 143 pounds, Vines didn't look strong, but he was a remarkably hard hitter because of the leverage he gained from his long arms. One of several top players developed on hard public courts in California during the 1920s and 1930s, Vines spent a year at the University of Southern California on a basketball scholarship but left to concentrate on tennis.

Vines surprised observers by winning the 1931 U.S. singles championship. The four-member Davis Cup team had recently returned after losing to Great Britain, and one of the four was naturally expected to be the champion, but Vines beat George M. Lott Jr. in the final.

The following year he won the Wimbledon singles as well as the U.S. title. He had a poor year in 1933, amid speculation that he would turn professional in 1934. However, he did sign to tour against Bill Tilden, who had dominated the pro tour for the previous three years, and he beat Tilden in 47 of 73 matches.

The professional circuit fell into some disarray in 1935 and split apart in 1936, with Tilden operating one tour and his former partner, William O'Brien, leading the other. O'Brien prevailed in 1937 by signing England's Fred Perry, generally considered the best amateur in the world. But Vines beat him in 32 of 61 matches that year and 49 of 84 in 1938.

Vines retired from competitive tennis after losing 21 of 39 professional matches to Don Budge in 1939. A fine amateur golfer, he became a professional in 1942 .and won five tournaments in 1944 and 1945. He later became a teaching pro at La Quinta Country Club in Palm Springs, California.

★ International Tennis Hall of Fame

Vinson, Maribel [Mrs. Owen]

FIGURE SKATING
b. Oct. 12, 1911, Winchester, Mass. d. Feb. 15, 1961

A very daring skater for her time, Vinson dominated U.S. women's figure skating for nearly a decade. She won the national women's championship six years in a row, from 1928 to 1933. After graduating from Radcliffe College in 1933, she trained in Europe and didn't compete in the 1934 national championships, but she then won three more in a row, from 1935 through 1937.

Vinson teamed with Thornton L. Coolidge to win the national pairs title in 1928 and 1929, and with George E. B. Hill to win the pairs championship in 1933 and from 1935 through 1937. She also won the North American singles title in 1937 and teamed with Hill to win the North American pairs championship in 1935.

After turning professional in 1937, Vinson toured with her own ice show. She later became a coach. Her most successful pupil was Tenley Albright. Vinson also coached her own daughters, Maribel and Laurence Owen. In 1961, Laurence won the U.S. and North American singles titles and Maribel finished second in the North American pairs championship, with Dudley Richards.

She and her daughters were among 18 members of the U.S. skating team who were killed when a plane carrying them to the 1961 world championships crashed near Brussels, Belgium.

★ U.S. Figure Skating Association Hall of Fame

Viola, Frank J., Jr.

BASEBALL
b. April 19, 1960, Hempstead, N.Y.

Nicknamed "Sweet Music," a pun on his last name, Viola won the AL's Cy Young Award in 1988, when he had a 24–7 record with the Minnesota Twins to lead the league in victories and winning percentage. He had 2 shutouts and a 2.64 ERA that year.

Viola joined the Twins during the 1982 season. He had records of 18–12 in 1984, 18–14 in 1985, 16–13 in 1986, and 17–10 in 1987, leading up to his Cy Young year. A 6-foot-1, 225-pound left-hander, Viola relies on a good curve and change-up, a sneaky fastball, and excellent control.

The Twins traded him to the NL's New York Mets for five players during the 1989 season, when he had a combined 13–17 record. He led the NL with 35 starts and 249²/₃ innings pitched in 1990, when he was 20–12 with a 2.67 ERA. After going 13–15 in 1991, he signed as a free agent with the Boston Red Sox, where he was 25–21 over the next three years.

Through the 1994 season, Viola had a 175–146 record with 16 shutouts. He had struck out 1,821 hitters and walked 840 in 2,791²/₃ innings.

von Saltza, Chris (Susan Christina)

SWIMMING
b. Jan. 3, 1944, San Francisco, Calif.

Still listed as "Baroness von Saltza" in the *Who's Who of Swedish Nobility*, von Saltza is the granddaughter of Count Philip, who emigrated to the U.S. around the turn of the century.

In a competitive career that began when she was 11 and lasted just six years, von Saltza led a resurgence in American women's swimming in the 1960s. She was the first international champion produced by the AAU's age-group swimming program that was designed to create just such a resurgence.

Von Saltza won her first national title in the indoor 250-yard freestyle in 1957. The following year she won the outdoor 100-meter freestyle and indoor championships in the 100-yard and 250-yard events. After winning the 110-yard and 440-yard outdoor freestyle championships in 1959, von Saltza won five gold medals in Pan-American Games. She had individual victories in the 100-, 200, and 400-meter freestyle races and was a member of the 4 x 100-meter freestyle and medley relay teams.

In the 1960 Olympic trials, von Saltza set a world record of 4:44.5 in the 400-meter freestyle, becoming the first American woman to swim the event in less than five minutes. At the Rome Olympics, she was the leader of the "Water Babies," a team of 14 swimmers and 3 divers who ranged in age from 13 to 18. They turned in the best performance by a women's Olympic team since 1932. Von Saltza won three gold medals, in the 400-meter freestyle and as the anchor swimmer on the 4 x 100-meter freestyle and medley relay teams. She also won a silver medal in the 100-meter event.

Von Saltza ended her competitive career with championships in the indoor 100-yard free, 250-yard, and 500-yard freestyles and the 200-yard backstroke in 1961. She enrolled at Stanford University that fall but took a leave of absence during the 1963-64 year to teach competitive swimming throughout Asia as a representative of the State Department.

Vuckovich, Peter D.

BASEBALL
b. Oct. 27, 1952, Johnstown, Pa.

A 6-foot-4, 220-pound right-hander, Vuckovich joined the AL's Chicago White Sox during the 1975 season and went to the Toronto Blue Jays in 1977, then to the St. Louis Cardinals in 1978. He had a 39–31 record in three seasons there.

With the Milwaukee Brewers in the strike-shortened 1981 season, Vuckovich had a 14–4 record to lead the AL in victories and winning percentage. He won the Cy Young Award in 1982, when he again led with a .750 winning percentage on an 18–6 record.

Vuckovich was 0–1 when the Brewers won the 1984 American League Championship Series in five games over the California Angels and he was also 0–1

in their seven-game World Series loss to the St. Louis Cardinals.

He developed arm trouble in 1983, missed the entire 1984 season, and retired after going only 8–12 in 1985 and 1986. In 11 major league seasons, he had a 93–69 record with 8 shutouts and a 3.66 ERA. He struck out 882 hitters and walked 545 in 1,455⅓ innings.

Vukovich, Bill [William Vucerivoch]

AUTO RACING
b. Dec. 13, 1918, Fresno, Calif.
d. May 30, 1955

Paradoxically, Vukovich was known as the "Mad Russian" and the "Silent Serb." The first nickname was for his driving style, the second for his personal style. He began racing by chasing jackrabbits across fields with a Model T. As a teenager during the Depression, he found out it was possible to earn as much as $15 a week by racing on tracks.

He became known as a terror in midget cars. After being catapulted through a fence headfirst in three consecutive races, he said, "I"m going to quit. It's costing too much for crash helmets." But he kept on, winning the West Coast midget car championship in 1946 and 1947, the national championship in 1950.

Vukovich didn't seem interested in racing anything beyond midgets until he got a ride as a substitute driver in the 1950 Indy without qualifying. He ran there again without finishing in 1951, then was chosen to succeed Mauri Rose as the driver of Howard Keck's Indy car. Vukovich led the 1952 race after 192 of its 200 laps when the car failed.

In scorching heat, Vukovich led for 195 laps and won the race in 1953. He was one of only five drivers to complete the race without any relief. And he seemed not to notice the weather. After taking off his helmet in the victory circle, he commented, "You know, there aren't as many fans in the bleachers this year."

Indy was his race. It paid so much for so little work, in his eyes. He had won $7,500 without even winning in 1952, $35,800 for his victory in 1953. Vukovich didn't bother to travel the USAC Championship Trail with the other drivers, just waited for the Indy 500 to come around. He won easily in 1954, earning $29,000, bought two gas stations, and worked regular hours at one of them.

In 1955, he was leading the race once more after 55 laps when three cars crashed in front of him. Vukovich's car went over the wheel of one of them and crashed upside down in flames, killing him.

★ Indianapolis Speedway Hall of Fame

★ ★ W ★ ★

Wachter, Edward A. F.

BASKETBALL
b. June 30, 1883, Troy, N.Y.
d. March 12, 1966

Some sources say Wachter was 6-foot-6, but most agree he was 6-foot-1, which was big enough to make him the best center in the game's history, according to a poll taken in 1928. He was also very big in the sport's history.

Wachter learned to play basketball in his early teens at the YMCA in Troy, New York. By 1900, when he was 17, he was playing professionally with the Ware, Massachusetts, team in the Western Massachusetts Basketball League. In 1903, the Haverhill team acquired him for $100, probably the first player sale in the sport's history.

In what was billed as a world championship series in Kansas City, Wachter and his older brother, Lou, led the Schenectady Company E team to three straight wins over the Blue Diamonds of the Kansas City Athletic Club in 1905. That later became the Gloversville, New York, Company G team, referred to in the press as the "fast soldier" team. Gloversville beat the Buffalo Germans in a doubleheader in 1908 shortly before the Germans began a 111-game winning streak.

Ed and Lou, along with Bill Hardman and Jimmy Williamson, left that team in 1909 to form the Troy Trojans in the new Hudson River League. Coached by Ed, the Trojans won both championships before the league folded. They then moved into the New York State League

and won two more championships. When that league also folded, in 1914, the Trojans went on Midwestern tour, winning 29 straight games in 49 days, then won 9 in a row against teams in New York and Massachusetts.

Wachter's career as a player spanned a quarter-century and more than 3,000 games. He played for 12 championship teams in various leagues and coached most of them.

Generally credited with inventing the bounce pass and the fast break, Wachter emphasized team play and crisp passing as a professional player and coach and, later, as coach at Albany State, Rensselaer Polytechnic, Williams, Harvard, and Lafayette.

★ Basketball Hall of Fame

Waddell, Rube (George E.)

BASEBALL
b. Oct. 13, 1876, Bradford, Pa.
d. April 1, 1914

Left-handed pitchers are generally expected to be eccentric, and they can blame Waddell, a great pitcher who was one of baseball's first great flakes. When he joined his first major league team, Louisville of the American Association in 1897, he arrived at two o'clock in the morning and woke the manager, Fred Clarke, to let him know he was there.

After appearing in two games, Waddell was fined by Clarke for heavy drinking and he left the team. He rejoined Louisville late in the 1899 season, when he had a 7–2 record. The team moved to Pittsburgh in 1900. Fined several times for failing to show up for games, Waddell again walked out. He had only an 8–13 record that season despite a league-leading 2.37 ERA.

He was persuaded to return to Pittsburgh in 1901 but was traded early in the season to the Chicago Cubs and had a combined record of 14–16. Waddell began the 1902 season in the Pacific Coast League. The AL's Philadelphia Athletics then signed him and he had a 24–7 record with, leading the league with 210 strikeouts, even though he appeared in only 33 games.

Waddell was a great fan favorite in Philadelphia and manager Connie Mack was willing to put up with some of his strange exploits as long as he won games and drew fans. Among other things, Waddell loved fire engines and sometimes left the park at the sound of a siren. He wrestled alligators professionally, once starred in a play, and often won raises by threatening to quit baseball for vaudeville.

From 1903 through 1907, Waddell was the AL's strikeout leader, setting a record of 349 strikeouts in 1904 that wasn't broken until 1965. He also led the AL in victories with a 27–10 record and in ERA with a 1.48 mark in 1905.

After going 34–30 in 1906 and 1907, Waddell was sold to the NL's St. Louis Browns in 1908. He had a 19–14 record in his first season there, then slipped to 11–14 in 1909 and he was released during the 1910 season, when he was used primarily in relief.

Waddell continued to play in the minor leagues for three years. Early in 1912, he stood in water up to his shoulders helping to put sacks of sand in levees to protect the town of Hickman, KY, from a flood. He caught a bad cold that eventually turned into tuberculosis. After the 1913 season, he entered a sanatorium in Texas and he died there.

In 13 seasons, Waddell had a 193–143 record with 50 shutouts and a 2.16 ERA. He struck out 2,316 hitters and walked 803 in 2,961 1/3 innings.
★ Baseball Hall of Fame

Wade, Margaret (Lily Margaret)
BASKETBALL
b. Dec. 31, 1912, McCool, Miss.

Wade played basketball for three seasons at Delta State Teachers College in Mississippi. She was captain of the team in her sophomore and junior years, but the school then dropped the sport.

After graduating in 1933, Wade played semipro basketball for two years and then became a high school coach. In 19 seasons, her teams won 453 games, lost 89, and tied 6. Wade returned to her alma mater in 1959 as director of women's physical education.

In 1973, she re-established women's basketball as a sport at Delta State and became coach. Wade's teams won three consecutive AIAW championships, from 1975 through 1977, at one point winning 51 consecutive games. Her 1974–75 team was undefeated in 28 games. She retired after the 1978–79 season with a 157–23 record.
★ International Women's Sports Hall of Fame; Basketball Hall of Fame

Wade, Wallace (William Wallace)
FOOTBALL
b. June 15, 1892, Trenton, Tenn.
d. Oct. 7, 1986

Wade played for the Brown University team that went to the 1916 Rose Bowl, losing 14–0 to Washington State. He served as an assistant coach at Vanderbilt in 1921 and 1922, then interviewed for the head coaching job at the University of Kentucky. After waiting a long time for the selection committee to make a decision, he stormed into the room to announce that he didn't want the job and that, wherever he coached, his team would never lose to Kentucky. It was an accurate prophecy.

Ironically, the committee had decided to hire Wade, but he went to Alabama instead. In his third season, 1925, the school won all 9 of its games, outscoring the opposition 277 to 7, and went to the Rose Bowl. After trailing 12–0 at the half, Alabama scored 20 points in seven minutes and went on to beat the heavily favored University of Washington, 20–19.

Alabama went undefeated again in 1926 and tied Stanford, 7–7, in the Rose Bowl. During the next three seasons, however, Wade's teams won "only" 17 games while losing 10 and tying 1, and alumni began criticizing him. With one year remaining on his Alabama contract, he signed an agreement to begin coaching at Duke in 1931.

Wade's 1930 team was probably the best he had at Alabama, winning all nine games and beating Washington State, 24–0, in the Rose Bowl. His record in eight seasons was 61–13–3.

It took a little time to build a program at Duke. The school went 5–3–2 in 1931 and 7–3–0 in 1932 but, during the next nine seasons, Duke won 73 games while losing only 11 and tying 1. The 1938 and 1941 teams were both undefeated during the regular season and both went to the Rose Bowl, losing 7–3 to Southern California and 20–16 to Oregon State.

In 1942, Wade received a commission in the Army. He was involved in the D-Day landing at Normandy and the Battle of the Bulge, winning a Bronze Star. He returned to Duke in 1946 and had four winning teams in five seasons before retiring. His record in 16 seasons at Duke was 110–36–7 and he had an overall record of 171 wins, 49 losses, and 10 ties at the two schools.

Wade became commissioner of the Southern Conference after he left coaching. He held that position until January 1960.

★ College Football Hall of Fame

Wagner, Honus (John P.)

BASEBALL
b. Feb. 24, 1874, Mansfield, Pa.
d. Dec. 6, 1955

During his long major league career, Wagner played every position and led the NL in every offensive category except home runs at one time or another. Though considered by many the greatest shortstop in history, Wagner didn't even begin playing that position until his fifth season in the major leagues and didn't become a regular there for two more years.

The 5-foot-11, 200-pound Wagner joined the Louisville NL team as an outfielder during the 1897 season. The franchise folded and most of its best players, including Wagner, went to Pittsburgh in 1900. Wagner led the NL that season with a .381 batting average, .573 slugging percentage, 45 doubles, and 22 triples, leading the Pirates to their first pennant.

He was the league leader with 126 RBI and 49 stolen bases in 1901. The following season, Wagner had a league-leading 105 runs, 30 doubles, 91 RBI, .463 slugging percentage, and 42 stolen bases, and he led with 19 triples and a .355 batting average in 1903, when the Pirates won the pennant. He hit only .222 in the team's eight-game World Series loss to the Boston Red Sox.

Wagner won his third batting title with a .349 average in 1904, when he also led the league with 44 doubles, 53 stolen bases, and a .520 slugging percentage. After hitting .363 in 1905 without winning the title, he was the NL's top hitter the next four seasons in a row with averages of .339, .350, .354, and .339.

He was also the league leader in runs with 103 in 1906; in hits with 201 in 1908; in doubles with 38 in 1906, 38 in 1907, 39 in 1908, and 39 in 1909; in triples with 19 in 1908; in RBI with 109 in 1908 and 100 in 1909; in slugging with .513 in 1907, .542 in 1908, and .489 in 1909; and in stolen bases with 61 in 1907 and 53 in 1908.

The Pirates met the Detroit Tigers in the 1909 World Series, where Wagner and young Ty Cobb were the headliners. The fiery Cobb threatened to spike Wagner the first time he had a chance to steal second base. On Cobb's first attempt, the usually mild-mannered Wagner split his lip open with a hard tag. Cobb batted .231 and stole only two bases, and the Pirates won the championship in seven games with Wagner batting .333 and stealing six.

Wagner led the league with 178 hits in 1910, won his eighth and last batting title with a .334 average in 1911, and was the league leader with 102 RBI in 1912. Arthritis in his legs slowed him severely beginning in 1913, when he batted .300 in only 114 games.

He hit .252 in 194, .274 in 1915, and .287 in 1916. His last season as a player was 1917, when batted .265 in 74 games and also managed the Pirates briefly. After retiring, he coached baseball and basketball at Carnegie Tech for a time. He returned to the Pirates as a coach from 1933 through 1953.

Unusually big for a shortstop, Wagner had great range, a strong throwing arm, and enormous hands. When he fielded a grounder, he often came up with chunks of dirt and pebbles that went flying toward the first baseman with the ball.

In his 21 major league seasons, Wagner had a .327 average with 3,415 hits, including 640 doubles, 252 triples, and 101 home runs. He stole 722 bases, scored 1,736 runs, and had 1,732 RBI.
★ Baseball Hall of Fame

Wagner, Lisa (Rathgeber)

BOWLING
b. May 19, 1961, Hillsboro, Ill.

The LPBT rookie of the year in 1980, Wagner was the tour's bowler of the year in 1983, when she became the first woman to surpass $100,000 in winnings for a season. Her total of $105,500 was nearly $25,000 more than the former record. Wagner was the tour's highest scorer with a 208.50 average and she had a remarkable .6351 winning percentage in match play.

She was also named bowler of the year in 1986 and in 1988, when she had the high average of 213.02. Wagner won her only major tournament, the Women's Open, in 1988. She led the tour for a third time with an average of 211.87.

After going more than two years without a victory, she claimed her 27th tournament win in 1992. "This was a huge win for me," she said afterward. "I've bowled so badly over the last two years." In 1993, Wagner became the first woman to pass the $500,000 mark in career winnings.

Wainwright, Helen E.

SWIMMING
b. March 15, 1906

One of only three athletes to have won Olympic medals in both swimming and diving, Wainwright won a silver medal in the springboard diving event in 1920 and a bronze in the 400-meter freestyle swimming event in 1924.

Wainwright won national outdoor titles in the 100-yard, 880-yard, and 1-mile freestyles in 1922, and she was the 440-yard freestyle champion in 1924. Indoors, she won the 100-yard event in 1923 and 1924, the 220-yard event in 1922 and 1925. As a diver, Wainwright was the national indoor 1-meter champion in 1925.

She became a professional in 1926 and went on tour, performing in a portable tank in theaters. Later, she swam with several water shows. Wainwright married a career Army officer, and during World War II she donated all her medals and trophies to the war effort so they could be melted down for their metal.
★ International Swimming Hall of Fame

Walcott, Jersey Joe [Arnold R. Cream]

BOXING
b. Jan 31, 1914, Merchantville, N.J.
d. Feb. 27, 1994

Sheer persistence finally brought Walcott the heavyweight championship at the age of 37. He was the oldest fighter ever to win the title.

Walcott began boxing professionally when he was 16 but had only three fights in his first five years, and he retired in 1942 without attracting much attention. However, in 1944 a Camden promoter lured him out of retirement by giving him an advance of $500 and the promise of at least six fights during the next two years.

After Walcott beat Joey Maxim twice in 1947, he was matched against Joe Louis in the first heavyweight championship fight to be televised. Walcott put on a fine exhibition of boxing and knocked Louis down twice, but the defending champions won an unpopular split decision. In a rematch on June 25, 1948, Louis knocked Walcott out in the 11th round.

Louis retired shortly afterward. Walcott and Ezzard Charles were selected to fight for the vacant title on June 22, 1949. Charles won a 15-round decision, making Walcott the first fighter ever to lose three consecutive championship fights. Charles defended his title several times, then outpointed Walcott again on March 7, 1951.

In his fifth attempt, on July 18, 1951, Walcott won the championship by knocking Charles out in the 7th round. He fought a series of exhibitions early in 1952, then won a 15-round decision over Charles in his first defense. He lost the title on September 23, 1952, when Rocky Marciano knocked him out in the 13th round. Walcott retired after a 1st-round knockout by Marciano the following year.

He later became a referee, the head of the New Jersey State Athletic Commission, a parole officer, and the sheriff of Camden County, New Jersey. During his professional boxing career, Walcott won 50 bouts, 30 by knockout; lost 17, 6 by knockout; and fought 1 draw.
★ International Boxing Hall of Fame

Walcott, Joe
BOXING
b. April 7, 1872, Barbados, W.I.
d. October, 1935

The "Barbados Demon" was only 5-foot-2 but weighed a solid 142 pounds in his prime. He worked his way to Boston as a cabin boy in 1887 and began boxing and wrestling as an amateur. In his first professional fight, he knocked out Tom Powers in the 2nd round on Feb. 29, 1890.

Like other black fighters of his era, Walcott had difficulty getting good matches, so he frequently toured with carnivals, taking on all comers. On April 24, 1898, he fought Billy Smith for the world welterweight championship, but Smith retained the title in a 25-round draw and won a decision in a 20-round rematch on December 6 of that year.

Walcott won the title on December 18, 1901, by knocking out Jim Ferns in the 5th round at Ft. Erie, Ontario. He was champion until April 30, 1904, when he lost on a foul in the 20th round to the Dixie Kid in San Francisco. After they fought a draw later in the year, the Dixie Kid outgrew the division and vacated the title. Walcott was generally recognized as champion until he lost a 15-round decision to Honey Mellody on October 16, 1906. He retired in 1911.

In 150 official bouts, Walcott had 81 victories, 34 by knockout. He lost 24, 4 by knockout, and he also fought 30 draws and 15 no-decisions. He was killed in an auto accident.
★ International Boxing Hall of Fame

Waldorf, Pappy (Lynn O.)
FOOTBALL
b. Oct. 3, 1902, Clifton Springs, N.Y.
d. Aug. 15, 1981

Waldorf was named to Walter Camp's All-American second team as a tackle at Syracuse University in 1924, his third year as a starter. The 5-foot-11, 210-pounder also rowed crew.

After graduating in 1925, Waldorf coached high school football for a year and then went to Oklahoma City University, where he had a 13–5–1 record in two seasons. He was an assistant at the University of Kansas in 1928 before taking over at Oklahoma A & M (now Oklahoma State).

In five seasons, the Aggies had a 34–10–1 record under Waldorf and won two Missouri Valley Conference championships. In 1934, Waldorf coached Kansas State University to a 7–2–1 record and its first Big Six Conference title.

Waldorf became head coach at Northwestern University in 1935. The only private school in the Western Conference (now Big Ten), Northwestern had never enjoyed much success. Waldorf won the American Football Coaches Association's first coach of the year award in 1935. The following season, he guided Northwestern to a 7–1–0 record and its first undisputed conference championship.

After compiling a 49–45–7 record in 12 seasons at Northwestern, Waldorf in 1947 went to the University of California, which had suffered four consecutive losing seasons. From 1947 through 1950, his teams won 38 regular season games, lost 1, and tied 1. They tied for the Pacific Coast Conference title in 1948 and won it outright the next two years.

Waldorf left coaching in 1957 to become player personnel director for the NFL's San Francisco 49ers. He retired in 1972. His overall coaching record was 174 wins, 100 losses, and 22 ties.

★ College Football Hall of Fame

Walker, Doak (Ewell Doak Jr.)

FOOTBALL
b. Jan. 1, 1927, Dallas, Tex.

A great fan favorite at Southern Methodist University, Walker was a 5-foot-11, 170-pound single-wing tailback named a consensus All-American three years in a row, from 1947 through 1949. He won the 1948 Heisman Trophy as college football's outstanding player.

The "Doaker" was so popular that a double deck was added to the Cotton Bowl, SMU's home field, to accommodate all the fans who wanted to watch him play. His coach, Matty Bell, said of him, "Some called it luck, others called it destiny, but Doak had a natural knack for pulling off great deeds."

He joined the NFL's Detroit Lions in 1950 amid doubts about his size, but promptly led the league in scoring with 128 points and was named both rookie of the year and an All-Pro at halfback. A remarkably versatile player, he scored 534 points in just about every possible way during his six-year NFL career, during which the Lions won two NFL championships.

Although the Lions offered him a big contract in 1956, Walker decided to retire because of several business interests in his native Texas, where he could make more money than he could playing football.

Walker rushed 309 times for 1,520 yards, a 4.9 average, and 12 touchdowns; caught 152 passes for 2,539 yards, a 16.7 average, and 21 touchdowns; punted 50

times for a 39.1 average; returned 18 punts for 284 yards, a 15.8 average, and 1 touchdown; and ran back 38 kickoffs for 968 yards, a 35.5 average. He kicked 183 extra points and 49 field goals, threw 2 touchdown passes, and returned 2 interceptions for 60 yards.

★ College Football Hall of Fame; Pro Football Hall of Fame

Walker, Herschel J.

FOOTBALL
b. March 3, 1962, Wrightsville, Ga.

Walker was already a famous running back while still in high school, where he rushed for 6,137 yards and 86 touchdowns during his career. He also played basketball and won state championships in the shotput and both sprint events.

In 1980, Walker entered the University of Georgia and set an NCAA record for a freshman by gaining 1,616 yards. A consensus All-American, he finished third in Heisman Trophy voting, the highest placing ever for a freshman. He finished second as a sophomore and won the trophy in his junior year. He was a consensus All-American both years, becoming the first player since 1900 to make All-American in his first three college years.

Walker was also a track All-American twice, in the 4 x 100-meter relay as a freshman and in the 60-meter dash as a sophomore. Even though he passed up his senior year to play professional football, Walker ranked third all-time in career rushing with 5,259 yards.

In 1983 Walker joined the New Jersey Generals of the new U.S. Football League. He led the USFL in rushing with 1,812 yards and in rushing touchdowns with 17. Walker was named the league's player of the year in 1985, when he gained 2,411 yards in 438 carries and scored 22 touchdowns. During his 3 seasons in the USFL, he gained 5,562 yards on 1,143 attempts, a 4.9 average, and 54 touchdowns, and caught 130 passes for 1,484 yards, an 11.4 average, and 7 touchdowns.

The Dallas Cowboys made Walker the highest-paid running back in NFL history in 1986, signing him to a five-year contract reportedly worth $5 million. He showed flashes of brilliance with Dallas, but he played for mediocre teams that often had to rely heavily on the pass after falling behind early.

During the 1989 season, the Cowboys sent Walker to the Minnesota Vikings as part of a deal involving six players and twelve draft choices. Minnesota general manager Mike Lynn told the press that the trade for Walker would bring the Vikings a Super Bowl championship. But the 6-foot-2, 220-pound Walker, whose forte is using his size and strength to break through the line and then using his speed to run past linebackers and backs, didn't fit well in the Minnesota offense, which featured delayed running plays and finesse blocking.

The Vikings released him after the 1991 season and he was picked up by the Philadelphia Eagles. Through 1994, Walker had gained 7,996 yards on 1,907 carries, a 4.2 average, and had 59 rushing touchdowns. He caught 335 passes for 3,277 yards, a 9.8 average, and 13 touchdowns. Walker also returned 68 kickoffs for 1,561 yards, a 23.0 average, and 1 touchdown.

Walker, Mickey (Edward P.)

BOXING
b. July 13, 1901, Elizabeth, N.J.
d. April 28, 1961

The 5-foot-7, 145-pound Walker was rejected by the Army during World War I because of his size, and he went to work in a shipyard. After a brawl with a fellow worker who was a professional boxer, Walker decided to take up the sport in 1919.

Nicknamed the "Toy Bulldog" because of his tenacious fighting style, Walker fought in every division from welterweight to heavyweight. He fought Jack Britton for the world welterweight title on July 18, 1921, but Britton retained his championship with a 12-round draw. Walker won the title by decisioning Britton in 15 rounds on November 1, 1922.

After defending the championship six times, Walker faced Mike McTigue

for the light heavyweight championship on January 7, 1925. The result was a 12-round no-decision. Less than six months later, he lost a 15-round decision to Harry Greb in a middleweight championship fight.

Walker lost his welterweight title in a 10-round decision to Pete Latzo on May 20, 1926, then won the middleweight championship in a controversial 10-round decision over Tiger Flowers on December 3.

In 1931, Walker relinquished the title because he could no longer make the weight and he began fighting as a light heavyweight, often against heavyweight opponents. His last championship fight was against Maxie Rosenbloom for the light heavyweight title on November 3, 1933. Rosenbloom won a 15-round decision.

Walker retired in 1936 but returned for one fight in 1939. In retirement he owned several taverns, worked as a sportswriter and radio broadcaster, and appeared in Broadway plays. A student of architecture as a youth, he also took up art and had several highly praised exhibits.

In 163 professional bouts, Walker had 94 victories, 61 by knockout; he lost 19, 5 by knockout; and he fought 4 draws, 45 no-decisions, and 1 no-contest.
★ International Boxing Hall of Fame

Wallace, Bobby (Roderick J.)

BASEBALL
b. Nov. 4, 1873, Pittsburgh, Pa.
d. Nov. 3, 1960

Lifting grain sacks in a relative's feed store as a teenager helped Wallace build very strong arms and shoulders, and he starred as a pitcher in amateur and semi-pro baseball. Only 5-foot-8, he weighed a solid 170 pounds when he joined the NL's Cleveland team late in the 1894 season.

He didn't have much success as a pitcher, and in 1897 he was stationed at third base. He batted .335, scoring 99 runs and driving in 112. In 1899 Frank Robison, who owned the Cleveland team, bought the St. Louis NL team and moved most of his best players, Wallace among them, to St. Louis.

Wallace was also moved to shortstop in 1899, the position he remained at for the rest of his career. His range and strong throwing arm were perfect for shortstop, and Wallace was probably the first to use the bare-handed pickup and underhand throw to first on a slow ground ball.

The St. Louis Browns of the AL made an unprecedented offer to Wallace in 1902: a $6,500 bonus, a five-year contract for $6,250 a year, and a clause that he couldn't be traded without his consent. Wallace, who was earning the NL maximum of $2,400 a year, took it.

Sometimes compared to the great Honus Wagner, Wallace never had anything like Wagner's offensive numbers. He batted over .300 twice. But he remained with St. Louis as a starting shortstop through 1912. In 1913 a broken hand limited him to 55 games, and he suffered serious burns in an accident the following year.

Wallace retired early in the 1915 season and became an umpire. He returned to appear in 14 games with the Browns in 1916 and he ended his playing career with just 38 games back with the St. Louis Cardinals in 1917 and 1918.

After managing in the minor leagues, Wallace became a major league coach and scout for the Chicago Cubs and Cincinnati Reds. In his 25 major league seasons, Wallace had 2,309 hits, including 391 doubles, 143 triples, and 34 home runs. He stole 201 bases, scored 1,057 runs, and had 1,121 RBI.

★ Baseball Hall of Fame

Walls, Everson C.

FOOTBALL
b. Dec. 28, 1959, Dallas, Tex.

Walls wasn't drafted by any NFL team after graduating from Grambling State University in 1981, so he signed as a free agent with his hometown Dallas Cowboys and was a surprise starter at defensive back.

The 6-foot-1, 195-pounder led the league with 11 interceptions as a rookie, returning them for 133 yards, and he tied for the league lead with 7 interceptions in 1982, even though he played in only 9 games because of an injury.

Walls led in interceptions for a third time with 9 in 1985, but he was relegated to a backup role in 1988. Unhappy with that, he became a free agent and joined the New York Giants as a starter in 1990.

After the Giants released him during the 1992 season, Walls joined the Cleveland Browns but was released again in October 1993. He then retired. In his 13 NFL seasons, he intercepted 57 passes and returned them for 504 yards, an 8.8 average, and 1 touchdown.

Walsh, Bill (William E.)

FOOTBALL
b. Nov. 30, 1931, Los Angeles, Calif.

After playing quarterback at San Mateo Junior College and end at San Jose State, graduating in 1954, Bill Walsh coached high school football and was an assistant coach at both the college and professional levels.

He became head coach at Stanford University in 1977 and had a record of 17–7–0 in two seasons there, including two bowl victories. Walsh then took over the San Francisco 49ers of the NFL in 1979.

Using ideas he had developed while with the Cincinnati Bengals and the San Diego Chargers, Walsh installed an offense featuring ball control through short passes, many of them to a back or a tight end.

The 49ers won the NFC championship in 1981 and beat the Cincinnati Bengals, 26–21, in Super Bowl XVI. In 1984 they won 18 games, the most in NFL history, while losing only 1. San Francisco defeated the Miami Dolphins, 38–16, in Super Bowl XIX, rolling up 537 yards and 31 first downs in the process.

Walsh won a third Super Bowl, a 20–16 victory over Cincinnati after the 1988 season, and retired briefly to become a television commentator. His record was 102–59–1. He returned to Stanford

as head coach in 1990 and had a 35–13–0 record there through the 1993 season.
★ Pro Football Hall of Fame

Walsh, Edward A.

BASEBALL
b. May 14, 1881, Plains, Pa.
d. May 26, 1959

"Big Ed" was a 6-foot-1, 193-pound, right-handed pitcher and he had a good fastball. But it was the spitball that enabled him to win 168 games for the Chicago White Sox during the seven-year period from 1906 through 1912.

Walsh joined the White Sox in 1904 and won just 14 games while losing 6 in his first two seasons. He added the spitball to his repertoire in 1906, when he led the league with 10 shutouts and had a 17–13 record.

Although they hit only .230 with six home runs, Chicago's "Hitless Wonders" won the 1906 pennant and beat the Chicago Cubs in the World Series, with Walsh winning two games.

During the next two years, Walsh carried an amazing workload for the White Sox. He had a 24–18 record and 4 saves in 1907, when he led the AL with 56 appearances, 37 complete games, 422⅓ innings pitched, and a 1.60 ERA.

In 1908 he was the league leader in victories and winning percentage with a 40–15 record, in appearances with 66, in complete games with 42, in shutouts with 11, in saves with 6, in innings pitched with 464, and in strikeouts with 269. Walsh and Jack Chesbro are the only pitchers to have won 40 or more games during the twentieth century.

Walsh slowed down somewhat in 1909, when he had a 15–11 record, but he still led the league with 8 shutouts. He went 18–20 in 1910 despite a league-leading 1.27 ERA, and he also led the league with 45 appearances and 5 saves.

He became a workhorse again the next two years. Walsh led the AL with 56 appearances, 4 saves, 368⅔ innings, and 255 strikeouts in 1911, and with 62 appearances, 10 saves, and 393 innings pitched in 1912.

In 1913 Walsh's arm wore out. He appeared in only 29 games for the White Sox from 1913 through 1916, and he finished his career with an 0–1 record for the Boston Braves in 1917. He later managed in the minor leagues, occasionally pitching, worked briefly as an umpire, and coached for the White Sox. Walsh also coached the Notre Dame University baseball team in 1926.

In 14 major league seasons, Walsh had a 195–126 record with 57 shutouts and a 1.82 ERA. He struck out 1,736 hitters and walked 617 in 2,964⅓ innings.
★ Baseball Hall of Fame

Walsh, Stella [Stanislawa Walasiewic]

TRACK AND FIELD
b. April 3, 1911, Rypin, Poland
d. Dec. 4, 1980

The "Polish Flyer" had one of the longest careers in track and field history. She won her first AAU national championship in 1930, her 25th and last in 1951.

Her family moved to the United States when she was 2 years old. Walsh applied for American citizenship early in 1932 but then decided to represent her native Poland at the Olympics that year. She tied the world record of 11.9 seconds in the 100-meter dash and finished ninth in the discus.

Walsh also competed for Poland at the 1936 Olympics, where she finished second in the 100-meter to Helen Stephens of the United States. She became a U.S. citizen in 1947.

She first came to notice in 1930, when she became the first woman to run the 100-yard dash in under 11 seconds, running a 10.8. She was the AAU outdoor 100-yard dash, 220-yard dash and long jump champion that year.

Walsh set world records of 24.3 seconds for the 220-yard dash in 1935 and 19-9¾ for the long jump in 1938. She won AAU outdoor championships in the 100-yard dash in 1943, 1944, and 1948; the 220-yard dash in 1931, 1939, 1940, and from 1942 through 1948; and in the long jump from 1939 through 1946, in 1948, and in 1951. Indoors, she was the 220-yard dash champion in 1931, 1934, 1945, and 1946.

After the 1936 Olympics Walsh ran extensively in Europe, so she didn't take part in AAU championship meets in 1933, 1937, or 1938.

Walsh supervised women's recreation programs for the Cleveland Recreation Department for several years. While shopping in a Cleveland store, she was killed by gunfire during a robbery attempt. An autopsy, required because of her tragic death, disclosed that Walsh had male sex organs, confirming the suspicions of many of her opponents and sportswriters.

★ National Track & Field Hall of Fame

Walters, Bucky (William H.)

BASEBALL
b. April 19, 1909, Philadelphia, Pa.
d. April 20, 1991

Walters was a third baseman when he joined the NL's Boston Braves late in the 1931 season. Only a part-time player, he went to the Boston Red Sox in 1933 and to the Philadelphia Phillies during the 1934 season.

Because of his strong arm, the Phillies made a pitcher of him. With a poor team, Walters was 30–45 from 1935 through 1937, and the Phillies sold him to the Cincinnati Reds for $50,000 during the 1938 season.

Walters was named the NL's most valuable player in 1939, his first full season with Cincinnati. He led the league in victories with a 27–11 record, in complete games with 31, in innings with 319, in strikeouts with 137, and in ERA with 2.29. The Reds won the pennant but Walters was 0–2 in a four-game loss to the New York Yankees in the World Series.

In 1940, the Reds won another pennant and Walters had another outstanding season. He was the league leader in victories with a 22–10 record, in complete games with 29, in innings pitched with 305, and in ERA with 2.48. Walters also won two games when Cincinnati beat the Detroit Tigers in a seven-game World Series.

After winning 49 games while losing 44 during the next three seasons, Walters led the league in victories once more

with a 23–8 record in 1944. He remained with the Reds through 1948, spent a season in the minor leagues, and retired after appearing in one game with the Boston Braves in 1950.

In 16 seasons, Walter had a 198–160 record with 42 shutouts and a 3.30 ERA. He struck out 1,107 hitters and walked 1,121 in 3,104⅔ innings.

Walthour, Bobby (Robert Sr.)

CYCLING
b. 1878, Georgia
d. Sept. 2, 1949

The "Dixie Flyer" was one of the greatest of the early bicycle racers, first in six-day events and later in motor-paced races. The *New York Times* once said, "Bobby Walthour was to bike racing what Babe Ruth was to baseball."

He began his professional career in 1899 and won his first major victory in a six-day race at Madison Square Garden in 1901 with partner Archie McEachern of Canada. They were tied at 2,555 miles with four other teams after 142 hours, and on the final sprint lap Walthour sped away from the field to win the $4,000 prize. By 1917 Walthour had won 14 six-day races, a record at the time.

He got involved in motor-paced racing in 1903, winning the national professional championship and many other races. The following year he went to Paris on a lucrative contract and won 16 of the 17 motorpaced events he entered, including the 100-kilometer world championship race in London.

Walthour did most of his racing in Europe until the summer of 1917, when he was seriously injured after a front tire blew during a race. He was in a coma for three weeks and spent another month convalescing before returning to the United States. He agreed to enter a six-day race at Madison Square Garden in December but had to withdraw because his partner was sick.

Shortly afterward, Walthour broke his left leg when he slipped on some ice. The injury ended his racing career, but not his cycling. In 1939, when he was 60 years old, he bicycled about 800 miles from Miami to Atlanta to visit relatives.

His son, Bobby Jr., was a fine amateur cyclist who won the national track championship in 1921.

Walton, Bill (William T. Jr.)

BASKETBALL
b. Nov. 5, 1952, La Mesa, Calif.

Succeeding Lew Alcindor (known later as Kareem Abdul-Jabbar) at UCLA, Walton starred at center for teams that won 86 games while losing only 4. A winning streak that had begun with Alcindor stretched to 88 games with Walton, ending when Notre Dame beat UCLA 71–70 in January 1974.

UCLA won NCAA championships in 1972 and 1973. Walton was named the tournament's most valuable player and college basketball's player of the year both years. He also won the Sullivan Award as the nation's outstanding amateur athlete in 1973, when he scored an NCAA tournament record 44 points in UCLA's championship victory over Memphis State.

The 6-foot-11, 210-pound Walton was an All-American and consensus college player of the year for the third time in a row in 1974. During his college career, he scored 1,767 points and had 1,370 rebounds in 87 games.

He joined the Portland Trailblazers as the first choice in the 1974 NBA draft. Because of a variety of injuries, Walton had only two good professional seasons. He led the league with 14.4 rebounds and 3.25 blocked shots per game in 1976–77, when he also averaged 18.5 points. Portland won the 1977 NBA championship and Walton was named most valuable player in the finals.

In 1977–78, he averaged 18.9 points a game and was named the league's most valuable player for the regular season. Walton missed the entire 1978–79 season and signed with the San Diego Clippers as a veteran free agent. After playing in only 14 games in 1979–80, Walton missed two full seasons and most of the 1982–83 season.

The Clippers traded him to the Boston Celtics in 1985. As a backup center, he averaged 7.6 points and had 544 rebounds and 106 blocked shots in 80 games to win the league's sixth player award. The Celtics won the 1986 NBA championship.

Limited to just 10 games by a recurring foot injury in 1986–87, Walton was forced to retire. In 468 regular season NBA games, he scored 6,215 points, a 13.3 average, pulled down 4,923 rebounds and blocked 1,034 shots.

★ Basketball Hall of Fame

Waltrip, Darrell

AUTO RACING
b. Feb. 5, 1947, Owenboro, Ky.

Waltrip began Winston Cup racing in 1972 but didn't get his first victory until 1975, when he won two races. He was the Winston Cup champion in 1981, 1982, and 1985.

Among his major victories were the Winston 500 at Talladega, Alabama, in 1972 and 1982; the Coca-Cola 600 at Charlotte in 1978, 1979, 1985, 1988, and 1989; and the Southern 500 at Darlington, South Carolina, in 1992. He won the Daytona 500 in his eighteenth start in 1989.

Through 1993, Waltrip had 84 Winston Cup victories, tying him for third on the all-time list, and he was also third in career winnings with $12,396,356. Handsome, articulate, and outspoken, Waltrip has frequently appeared on television talk shows.

Waner, Lloyd J.

BASEBALL
b. March 16, 1906, Harrah, Okla.
d. July 22, 1982

The 5-foot-9, 150-pound Waner was nicknamed "Little Poison" because his older and slightly larger brother, Paul, was known as "Big Poison." The two of them combined for more than 5,500 major league hits.

Lloyd joined the NL's Pittsburgh Pirates in 1927, a year after Paul, and he led the league with 133 runs scored while batting .355. The Pirates won the pennant and Lloyd led them with a .400 average in their four-game loss to the New York Yankees in the World Series.

A right-handed thrower and left-handed hitter, Lloyd played center field and batted leadoff for most of his career. He never won a batting title, but he hit over .300 11 times, including his first six seasons with the Pirates. His career best was .362 in 1930, when he appeared in only 68 games because of illness.

Waner led the league with 20 triples in 1929 and 214 hits in 1931. The Pirates traded him to the Boston Braves early in the 1941 season; in June the Braves sent him to the Cincinnati Reds. Released by Cincinnati, he played for the Philadelphia Phillies in 1942.

After the Phillies traded him to the Brooklyn Dodgers in 1943, Lloyd announced his retirement. However, he played for the Dodgers and Pirates in 1944 and finished his playing career with the Pirates the following season. He then served as a scout for the Pirates and later for the Baltimore Orioles.

In 1,993 games, Waner batted .316 with 2,459 hits, including 281 doubles, 118 triples, and 27 home runs. He scored 1,201 runs and had 598 RBI.

★ Baseball Hall of Fame

Waner, Paul G.

BASEBALL
b. April 16, 1903, Harrah, Okla.
d. Aug. 29, 1965

The older of the Waner brothers, Paul was a left-handed pitcher at East Central State Teacher College in Ada, Oklahoma, in 1923, when the San Francisco Seals of the Pacific Coast League offered him $500 a month to play professionally. He injured his pitching arm in spring training but swung so impressively in batting practice that the Seals moved him to the outfield.

After batting .401 with 280 hits in 1974 games in 1925, Waner was purchased by the NL's Pittsburgh Pirates. He led the league with a .336 average as a rookie and also had a league-leading 22 triples.

His younger brother Lloyd joined the Pirates in 1927, when Paul won his second batting title with a .380 average, also leading the league with 237 hits, 18 triples, and 131 RBI to be named the NL's most valuable player. The Pirates lost to the New York Yankees in a four-

game World Series, but Paul batted .333 and Lloyd hit .400.

Waner batted .370 in 1928, leading the NL with 50 doubles and 142 runs scored, and he led in doubles again with 62 in 1932. After hitting .336, .368, .322, .341, and .309, he finally won a third batting championship with a .362 average in 1934, when he had a league-leading 217 hits and 122 runs scored.

His .373 average was the best in the league in 1936. After hitting .354 in 1937, he slipped to .280, then rebounded to .328 in 1939. The Pirates released him after the 1940 season, when he batted only .290.

Waner joined the Brooklyn Dodgers in 1941, but he spent most of the season with the Boston Braves. He remained with the Braves in 1942, when he collected his 3,000th major league hit against the Pirates. He was the seventh player in history to reach that total.

The Braves released him after that season. He appeared in 82 games with the Dodgers in 1943 and in 92 games with the Dodgers and New York Yankees in 1944. Waner retired after being released by the Yankees on May 3, 1945. He later wrote a booklet on hitting and served as a hitting instructor for several major league teams.

Paul was nicknamed "Big Poison," his brother "Little Poison." They supposedly got the nicknames from a Brooklyn sportswriter who actually called them "big person and little person," but the story is unsubstantiated.

In 2,549 major league games, Waner batted .333 with 3,152 hits, including 605 doubles, 191 triples, and 113 home runs. He scored 1,627 runs and had 1,309 RBI.

★ Baseball Hall of Fame

Wanzer, Bobby (Robert F.)

BASKETBALL
b. June 4, 1921, Brooklyn, N.Y.

Wanzer enrolled at Seton Hall University in 1941 but served in the Marine Corps from 1943 until 1946, when he returned to school. A 6-foot, 172-pound guard, he captained the team in 1946–47.

The Rochester Royals chose Wanzer in the 1947 National Basketball League draft. He was teamed at guard with another former Seton Hall star, Bob Davies. Davies was an outstanding ball handler, while Wanzer was known for his shooting ability.

The Royals entered the Basketball Association of America in 1948, and the BAA and NBL merged to become the NBA in 1949. Wanzer averaged 10.8 points a game in 1951–52, when Rochester finished second in the Central Division but upset the Minneapolis Lakers and New York Knickerbockers to win the NBA championship.

Wanzer led the NBA with a .904 free throw shooting percentage in 1951–52 and was named the league's most valuable player after averaging 14.6 points a game in 1952–53. He became the team's player-coach in 1955 and retired as a player in 1957 with 7,091 points in 608 games, an 11.7 average. He scored 554 points in 38 playoff games, an average of 14.6 per game. Wanzer was replaced early in the 1958–59 season after compiling a 98–136 record. He later became a high school basketball coach.

★ Basketball Hall of Fame

Ward, Duane (Roy Duane)

BASEBALL
b. May 28, 1964, Parkview, N.Mex.

The 6-foot-4, 225-pound Ward was with the NL's Atlanta Braves briefly in 1986 before being traded to the Toronto Blue Jays of the AL. He appeared in 12 games with Toronto in 1987 and then joined the team permanently in 1988 as a set-up relief pitcher and occasional closer.

The right-handed Ward, who throws an overpowering fastball, led the league in games with 81 in 1991, when he had 23 saves. He became the closer in 1993 and was the league leader with 45 saves in 71 appearances.

Ward had a 3–0 record with 2 saves and a 1.13 ERA in World Series competition, helping the Blue Jays win consecutive world championships in 1992 and 1993.

Through 1993, he had a 35–36 record with 121 saves and 3.19 ERA. Ward had

struck out 676 hitters while walking 281 in 664 innings.

Ward, Holcombe

TENNIS
b. Nov. 23, 1878, New York, N.Y.
d. Jan 23, 1967

A classmate at Harvard of Dwight F. Davis, donor of the Davis Cup, Ward was a member of the U.S. team that won the first challenge from the British in 1900. He was also on the Davis Cup team in 1902, 1905, and 1906.

Only 5-foot-9 and 133 pounds, Ward is credited with developing the "American twist" service, which bounces very high because of topspin and may break either to the right or the left. He was also an outstanding volleyer.

Ward won the U.S. singles championship in 1904, but he was at his best in doubles play. He and Davis won three straight national doubles titles, from 1899 through 1901, and he teamed with Beals Wright to win three more, from 1904 through 1906. He retired from competition after the 1906 tournament.

A long-time official of the U.S. Lawn Tennis Association, Ward served as its president from 1937 to 1947.

★ International Tennis Hall of Fame

Ward, Monte (John Montgomery)

BASEBALL
b. March 3, 1860, Bellefonte, Pa.
d. March 4, 1925

One of the most versatile players in history, Ward was also an intelligent and articulate leader of the first player revolt, and he became a successful lawyer after leaving baseball.

Ward joined the NL's Providence Grays as a pitcher in 1878, when he had a 22–13 record. He led the league in victories with a 47–19 record and in strikeouts with 239 in 1879. On June 17, 1880, he pitched the second perfect game in major league history. It was one of his league-leading 8 shutouts.

After going 18–18 and 19–12 the next two seasons, Ward was traded to the New York Giants. He had a 16–13 record for the team in 1883, but his arm went bad early in the 1884 season. Unable to pitch, Ward simply moved to shortstop. He led the league with 111 stolen bases in 1887, when he batted .338.

While playing, Ward received a law degree from Columbia University in 1885, and he was also elected president of the Brotherhood of Professional Baseball Players that year. After the 1889 season, he captained one of the teams of major league players that went on a world tour. The teams returned in early November, and Ward announced the establishment of the Players' League shortly afterward.

The new league was designed as a co-operative, with players and backers sharing equally in profits. As player-manager of the Brooklyn Wonders, Ward batted .337 in 1890, but the league folded after that year and he returned to the NL as player-manager with Brooklyn. He led the league with 88 stolen bases in 1892, then went back to the Giants in an odd transaction: Brooklyn was given a percentage of New York's gate receipts in exchange for his contract.

After two seasons as a playing manager with New York, Ward retired from baseball to practice law. He later became part owner of the Boston Braves for a short time, and he also served as chairman of baseball's rules committee.

In seven seasons as a pitcher, Ward had a 164–102 record with 24 shutouts and a 2.10 ERA. He batted .275 with 2,105 hits, including 231 doubles, 96 triples, and 26 home runs. He also stole 540 bases, scored 1,408 runs, and had 867 RBI.

★ Baseball Hall of Fame

Ward, Rodger

AUTO RACING
b. Jan. 10, 1921, Beloit, Kans.

A fighter pilot during World War II, Ward also had a part-time job as a mechanic for midget racecars. He raced one night when a driver didn't show up and took up the sport after being discharged in 1946.

After nearly five years on the California midget car circuit, Ward won the American Automobile Association stock car championship in 1951, when

he also entered his first Indy 500. He didn't finish the race that year, nor in any of the next four years. Some blamed him for the accident that killed Bill Vukovich in the 1955 Indy.

Ward later said the experience made him a true professional. He gave up smoking and drinking and began to concentrate completely on racing. After finishing eighth at Indy in 1956, he won his first major race, the Milwaukee 100, in 1957, and he had two other victories in 11 IndyCar starts. He finished fifth in the national point standings in 1958.

His best year was 1959, when he finally won at Indianapolis and had three other wins to claim the driving championship. He finished second at Indy in 1960 after a long duel with Jim Rathmann, and he was third in 1961. He won again in 1962, when he also won his second national championship.

Ward was fourth at Indianapolis in 1963 and second in 1964, his only top-ten finish that year. Rear-engined cars were beginning to take over and Ward did not like racing them. His last race was the 1966 Indy 500, in which he finished fifteenth.

★ Indianapolis Speedway Hall of Fame

Ware, Andre

FOOTBALL
b. July 31, 1968, Galveston, Tex.

A quarterback in the "run and shoot" offense at Houston University, Ware won the 1989 Heisman Trophy after completing 365 of 578 passes for 4,699 yards and 46 touchdowns. He set NCAA records with 340 yards of total offense in one quarter and 510 yards in one half against Southern Methodist University.

Ware completed 660 passes in 1,074 attempts for 8,202 yards and 75 touchdowns in his three years at Houston. He joined the NFL's Detroit Lions as a first-round draft choice in 1990. Frequently injured, the 6-foot-2, 205-pound Ware was an occasional starter with Detroit before being traded to the Minnesota Vikings early in 1994.

Through 1993, he had completed 83 of 161 passes for 1,112 yards and 5 touchdowns.

Warfield, Paul D.

FOOTBALL
b. Nov. 28, 1942, Warren, Ohio

A running back at Ohio State University, Warfield was moved to wide receiver when he joined the Cleveland Browns in 1964. Since he spent his entire professional career with ball-control teams that emphasized the run, Warfield never had more than 52 catches a season.

However, he averaged more than 20 yards a reception during his career and scored a touchdown on every fifth catch. His constant big play threat helped open up the running game and the short passes for the Browns and for the Miami Dolphins.

Warfield was traded to the Dolphins in 1970 and spent five productive seasons there. He led the NFL with 11 touchdown receptions in 1971, when he caught only 43 passes, and he averaged 20.9 yards per catch in 1972, when the Dolphins went undefeated in 17 games, including the Super Bowl.

With Miami teammates Larry Csonka and Jim Kiick, Warfield jumped to the Memphis Southmen of the World Football League in 1975. After that league folded, he returned to the Browns for two more seasons before retiring.

Warfield was an All-Pro in 1964, 1968, 1969, 1971, and 1972, and he played in eight Pro Bowls. In his 13 years in the NFL, Warfield caught 427 passes for 8,565 yards, a 20.1 average, and 85 touchdowns. He also rushed 22 times for 204 yards, a 9.3 average.
★ Pro Football Hall of Fame

Warmerdam, Cornelius ("Dutch")

TRACK AND FIELD
b. June 22, 1915, Long Beach, Calif.

When Warmerdam retired in 1947, he had pole vaulted 15 feet or more 43 times. His 15-foot record was surpassed in 1947, when the superior aluminum pole replaced the bamboo pole that Warmerdam used.

Something of a late bloomer, Warmerdam never won an NCAA championship while competing for Fresno State College. His best vault as a collegian was 14 feet, 1⅞ inches. After graduating in 1938, he represented the San Francisco Olympic Club.

A serious student of technique, Warmerdam vaulted exactly 15 feet on April 13, 1940, breaking the former world record of 14 feet, 11 inches. He eventually extended the outdoor record to 15 feet, 7¾ inches in 1942 and the indoor record to 15 feet, 8½ inches in 1943.

The winner of the 1942 Sullivan Award as the outstanding amateur athlete of the year, Warmerdam tied for the AAU outdoor championship in 1937 and won it in 1938 and from 1940 through 1944. He was national indoor champion in 1939 and 1943.

The 1940 and 1944 Olympics were canceled because of World War II, depriving Warmerdam of two almost certain gold medals, since he consistently outvaulted other competitors by a foot or more during those years.

He retired from competition in 1947. The winning vault at the 1948 Olympics was only 14 feet, 1¼ inches, more than a foot and a half below Warmerdam's record.

Warmerdam coached track at Stanford University in 1946 and 1947, then returned to his alma mater to coach basketball and track until his retirement in 1980.
★ National Track & Field Hall of Fame

Warner, Bill (William J.)

FOOTBALL
b. 1880, Springville, N.Y.
d. Feb. 12, 1944

The younger brother of "Pop" Warner, Bill was an All-American guard at Cornell in 1901 and was named to Walter Camp's second team in 1902, his senior season. He captained the team to a 19–4–0 record during those two years.

Warner coached his alma mater in 1903, winning 6 games, losing 3, and tying 1. He had a 4–3–1 record at North Carolina in 1905, an 8–3–3 record at Colgate from 1906 through 1907, and a 7–3–0 record at the University of Oregon from 1910 through 1911.
★ College Football Hall of Fame

Warner, Bonnie

LUGE
b. April 7, 1962, Mount Baldy, Calif.

Warner became fascinated by luge racing when she watched the competition at the 1980 Winter Olympics in Lake Placid, New York. She stayed there after the Olympics were over to learn the sport, then went to West Germany to train.

The U.S. women's champion in 1983, 1984, 1987, 1988, and 1990, Warner won all 12 heats in the 1984 U.S. Olympic trials and was in sixth place after the second of her four runs at the Sarajevo Games. However, she hit a wall on her third run and dropped to fifteenth place in the final standings.

At Stanford University, Warner was the goalie of the field hockey team. She continued to play field hockey after graduating because she believed the two sports complement each other.

Warner, Pop (Glenn S.)

FOOTBALL
b. April 5, 1871, near Springville, N.Y.
d. Sept. 7, 1954

As a coach, Warner was an innovator second only to Amos Alonzo Stagg, and he was probably more influential over the long run than Stagg. He created the single and double wing formations that were used by most college and professional teams for more than 20 years, and he also developed equipment that soon became standard in football.

An avid baseball player in his teens, Warner didn't play football until he was admitted to Cornell University in 1892 as a 21-year-old freshman. His younger classmates began calling him "Pop," and the nickname stuck for the rest of his life.

Warner started at guard for three seasons, receiving a law degree in 1895, when he became the coach at two colleges. He did the preseason coaching at Iowa State, but when the season began, Bert German took over. Warner went to the University of Georgia, where his teams won seven games and lost four

during two seasons. He returned to Cornell as head coach in 1897 and had a 15–5–1 record through 1898.

The superintendent of the Carlisle School for Indians in Pennsylvania told Walter Camp that he wanted to hire the best young coach in the country. Camp recommended Warner, who was signed for $1,200 a year. His first stint at Carlisle lasted five seasons and resulted in a 33–18–3 record. In 1904, Warner went back to Cornell for three seasons, winning 23 games, losing 10, and tying 2.

During his second stay at Carlisle, from 1907 through 1914, Warner developed the wingback systems of attack. The exact seasons have never been pinpointed. Interestingly, the two formations were based on entirely different philosophies. The single wing emphasized power, with pulling guards and double-team blocking at the point of attack. The double wing emphasized deception, with a wide variety of reverses, double reverses, fake reverses, and pass-run options.

Carlisle is inevitably associated with the great Jim Thorpe, who played for Warner in 1908, 1911, and 1912, but Warner had outstanding teams without Thorpe. Carlisle won 10 of 11 games in 1907 and had an 11–2–1 record in 1913. But, in 1914, a congressional investigation of the school recommended de-emphasis of football. Warner had his first losing season.

He moved on to Pittsburgh in 1915 and had his finest seasons there, winning his first 31 games until a loss to a Naval Reserve team in 1918. Stanford beckoned in 1922. Warner still had two years on his Pittsburgh contract, so he sent assistants Andy Kerr and "Tiny" Thornhill to install the double wing. In 1924 Warner took over, with Kerr and Thornhill remaining as assistants.

He took three teams to the Rose Bowl in nine seasons at Stanford. The 1924 team won 7 games and tied 1 but lost to Notre Dame, 27–10; the 1926 team won all ten of its regular season games and tied Alabama, 7–7; and the 1927 team went 7–2–1, then beat Pittsburgh, 7–6.

However, alumni complained because of five straight losses to the University of Southern California, and in 1932 Warner abruptly resigned and went to Temple. He finished his career there after the 1938 season. His overall coaching record was 313 wins, 106 losses, and 32 ties.

Warner is generally credited with originating the blocking dummy, molded fiber pads, and uniform numbers. His Stanford team in 1924 was the first to wear a distinctive color, when Warner outfitted his players in red pants.
★ College Football Hall of Fame

Waterfield, Bob (Robert S.)

FOOTBALL
b. July 26, 1920, Elmira, N.Y.
d. March 25, 1983

Waterfield played tailback in the single wing at UCLA from 1940 through 1942, then entered the Army for two years and returned to UCLA as a senior for the 1944 season.

He became a quarterback with the NFL's Cleveland Rams in 1945 and was the first rookie ever to win the Joe F. Carr Award as the league's most valuable player. He threw 14 touchdown passes in only 171 attempts, and his touchdown passes of 37 and 53 yards led the Rams to a 15–14 championship victory over the Washington Redskins.

The Rams moved to Los Angeles in 1946, and Waterfield was given a raise from $7,500 to $20,000. However, in 1949 he began sharing the quarterback job with Norm Van Brocklin. He retired after the 1952 season, in part because of his unhappiness with the situation.

He completed 814 of 1,617 passes, 50.3 percent, for 11,849 yards and 98 touchdowns. A fine all-around player, Waterfield was also a defensive safety during his first five seasons with the Rams and he returned 20 interceptions for 228 yards, an 11.4 average. He punted 315 times for a 42.4 average and kicked 315 extra points and 60 field goals.
★ Pro Football Hall of Fame

Watson, Tom (Thomas S.)

 GOLF
b. Sept. 4, 1949, Kansas City, Mo.

Born into a well-to-do family, Watson began golfing when he was 7, and he shot a 67 at 13. He played basketball and football as well as golf in high school but concentrated on golf at Stanford University.

Watson joined the PGA tour after graduating in 1971. He had little success at first because of his wildness off the tee. Early in 1974, Byron Nelson helped him straighten out his drives. That year Watson won his first tournament, the Western Open, and had $135,474 in winnings. He led the U.S. Open after three rounds but shot a 79 on the last day.

In 1975 Watson tied a U.S. Open record by shooting 135 over the first two rounds to lead the tournament, but he blew up to 78 and 77 on the final two rounds and finished ninth, leading some observers to question his nerve. He answered them by winning the British Open three weeks later.

That victory put his career on track; Watson dominated the tour for the next decade. In 1977 he outdueled Jack Nicklaus to win the Masters and the British Open, where he shot 130 over the last two rounds. He was named the tour's player of the year four years in a row, from 1977 through 1980. His 1980 earnings of $530,000 was a record at the time.

Watson won a second Masters in 1981 and was the British Open champion three more times, in 1980, 1982, and 1983. The U.S. Open eluded him until 1982, when he won in spectacular fashion. Tied for the lead after 16 holes on the final round, Watson hit his tee shot into deep grass on the par-3 17th. Told by his caddie to get it close, Watson responded, "I'm not going to get it close; I'm going to make it." He chipped in for a birdie, then sank a long birdie putt on the 18th hole to win by two shots.

The golfer of the year in 1982 and 1984, Watson is tied for eleventh with 32 tour victories. He ranks second all-time in winnings with $6,028,927.
★ World Golf Hall of Fame

Watts, Stanley H.

BASKETBALL
b. Aug. 30, 1911, Murray, Utah

Watts played basketball at Weber State College and then transferred to Brigham Young University for his last two years. After graduating, he coached at several Utah high schools before taking over at Brigham Young in 1950.

Under Watts the team toured Latin America and the Orient, playing exhibition games and conducting clinics to promote basketball.

Brigham Young won or shared eight conference titles during his 23 seasons of coaching and won the National Invitation Tournament championship in 1951 and 1967. Watts is one of only seven coaches to win 100 or more games in his first five seasons. He retired from coaching with a 431–260 record to become the school's athletic director after the 1971–72 season.

★ Basketball Hall of Fame

Weatherall, Jim (James P.)

FOOTBALL
b. Oct. 26, 1929, Cushing, Okla.
d. Aug. 2, 1992

The 6-foot-4, 245-pound Weatherall was an All-American tackle at Oklahoma in 1950 and 1951; he won the 1951 Outland Trophy as the nation's outstanding collegiate lineman. He captained the team and was its place-kicker during his senior season. During his three years as a starter, Oklahoma won 28 regular season games and lost only 2.

After two years in the Marine Corps, Weatherall played for the Edmonton Eskimos of the Canadian Football League in 1954. He was a defensive lineman with the Philadelphia Eagles from 1955 through 1957. In 1958 he retired rather than report to the Washington Redskins after the Eagles traded him. His rights were then traded to the Detroit Lions, where he played for part of the 1959 season and all of the 1960 season before retiring permanently.

★ College Football Hall of Fame

Weatherly, Joseph

AUTO RACING
b. May 29, 1922, Oak Grove, Va.
d. Jan. 20, 1964

After serving in North Africa during World War II, Weatherly began motorcycle racing. He won American Motorcycle Association national championships in the 100-mile road race in 1948 and 1949 and in the ten-mile dirt track race in 1950, then switched to stock car racing.

In 1952 Weatherly won an incredible 49 races in 83 starts, and the following year he had 52 victories, winning the NASCAR modified national championship. He moved into Grand National racing in 1955 without much success at first, but finally got a major victory at Darlington's Rebel 300 in 1960.

Weatherly won the Grand National championship in 1962 and 1963. He had a career total of 24 GN wins. He was killed in a crash at Riverside International Raceway in California. The Joe Weatherly Museum at Darlington International Raceway is named for him.

★ NASCAR Hall of Fame

Weatherspoon, Teresa G.

BASKETBALL
b. Dec. 8, 1965, Jasper, Tex.

Weatherspoon was an All-American guard at Louisiana Tech in 1987 and 1988 and she won the 1988 Wade Trophy as the nation's outstanding woman college basketball player. She was named to the all-final four team at the NCAA tournament in her junior and senior years. Louisiana Tech went to the final game both years, losing in 1987 and winning in 1988.

The 5-foot-8 Weatherspoon was an outstanding ball-handler, passer, and defensive player. During her four years as a starter, she had 958 assists and 411 steals in 131 games. She also scored 1,087 points, an average of 8.3 per game.

Weatherspoon ranks sixth all-time among NCAA Division I players in assists. She played for the U.S. team that won a gold medal at the 1988 Olympics and she was also a member of national teams at the 1986 Goodwill Games and world championships, the 1987 World University Games, and the 1992 Olympics.

Weaver, Earl S.

BASEBALL
b. Aug. 14, 1930, St. Louis, Mo.

Weaver never made it to the major leagues as a player, and he spent eight years managing in the minors, where his teams finished first or second seven times, before taking over the AL's Baltimore Orioles midway through the 1968 season.

Baltimore won three pennants and a World Series, in 1970, during his first three full seasons. After slipping to third place in 1972, the team won two more East Division titles in 1973 and 1974 but lost to the Oakland Athletics in the American League Championship Series both years.

The Orioles then finished second three years in a row, dropped into fourth place in 1978, and won the pennant in 1979. Baltimore led the Pittsburgh Pirates three games to one in the World Series that year, only to lose three games in a row.

Worn out by the tensions of the job, Weaver retired temporarily after the 1982 season. He returned to the Orioles early in the 1985 season, when they finished fourth, and he retired permanently after Baltimore finished seventh in 1986.

Feisty and combative, Weaver was ejected 91 times and suspended four times for his outbursts against umpires. He was known as a master motivator of players, but he was also one of the first managers to make extensive use of computerized statistics to aid him in his decisions.

Weaaver's autobiography is entitled *It's What You Learn after You Know It All That Counts.* He had a record of 1,480 wins and 1,060 losses. His .583 winning percentage is eighth best in history.

Weber, Dick (Richard A.)

BOWLING
b. Dec. 23, 1929, Indianapolis, Ind.

Chosen in a 1970 poll of writers as the second best bowler of all time, trailing only Don Carter, Weber dominated the PBA tour during the 1960s. He was named bowler of the year three times in that decade, in 1961, 1963, and 1965.

The son of a bowling center manager, Weber started bowling when he was 10. By 1955, he had established such a reputation as a league bowler that he joined the great Anheuser-Busch team led by Carter. That team won national championships in 1956, 1959, and 1962.

A charter member of the PBA when it was organized in 1958, Weber won the BPAA All-Star (now the U.S. Open) in 1962, 1963, 1965, and 1966, and he led the tour in earnings in 1959, 1961, 1963, and 1965. He bowled three perfect 300 games in one tournament, the 1965 Houston Open.

Weber suffered a mild stroke while bowling on the PBA seniors tour in October 1991. Two months later, he teamed with Justin Hromek to win the Senior/Touring Pro Doubles tournament, becoming the only bowler ever to win a title in five different decades.
★ ABC Hall of Fame; PBA Hall of Fame

Weber, Peter

BOWLING
b. Aug. 21, 1962, Florissant, Mo.

The son of Dick Weber, Pete is one of only three male bowlers to win each of the triple crown tournaments. He was the PBA tour's money leader with $175,491 in 1987, when he won the Firestone Tournament of Champions.

He won his second major, the PBA Open, in 1988. Weber was given a six-month suspension in September of that year for detrimental conduct that allegedly involved drug and alcohol abuse. The suspension was lifted five weeks early, on January 30, 1989.

Weber won the PBA National championship that year and also led the tour with an average of 215.53 pins. He was the PBA Open champion for a second time in 1991. Through 1994, Weber ranked second in career winnings with $1,682,608.

Webster, Bob (Robert D.)

DIVING
b. Oct. 25, 1938, Berkeley, Calif.

Great performances under pressure won two gold medals for Webster in the springboard diving event in the 1960 Olympics: he was third with three dives remaining, and he was nearly perfect on those three dives. His 1964 victory was even more dramatic because he was in sixth place with three dives to go and again was virtually flawless in the clutch.

Webster attended Santa Clara, California, Junior College and then transferred to the University of Michigan. He won the national platform championship in 1962 and 1965 and the indoor 1-meter springboard title in 1962. Webster was the first American to win the platform diving championship at the Pan-American Games, in 1963.

After retiring from competition, Webster coached at the University of Minnesota, Princeton, and Alabama. He was the coach of the U.S. diving team at the 1971 Pan-American Games.
★ International Swimming Hall of Fame

Webster, George D.

FOOTBALL
b. Nov. 25, 1945, Anderson, S.C.

An All-American defensive back at Michigan State in 1965 and 1966, Webster played the so-called "rover" position, usually lining up against the strong side of the offense.

The 6-foot-4, 225-pound Webster joined the AFL's Houston Oilers in 1967 and was moved to outside linebacker because of his size and tackling ability. He was voted the league's rookie of the year.

An All-AFL selection in his first three years, Webster suffered a knee injury in 1970 and missed a number of games before the Oilers traded him to the Pittsburgh Steelers in 1972. He finished his career with the New England Patriots from 1974 through 1976.

Webster was named to the all-time All-AFL team selected in 1970, when the league merged with the NFL. In his ten professional seasons, he intercepted 5 passes.
★ College Football Hall of Fame

Weekes, Harold H.

FOOTBALL
b. April 2, 1880, Oyster Bay, N.Y.
d. July 26, 1950

Weekes became a starting halfback against Yale during his freshman year, and a 45-yard touchdown run gave Columbia a 5–0 victory. As a sophomore in 1900, he ran 55 yards for a touchdown against Yale, but this time Columbia lost, 12–5.

Solidly built at 5-foot-10½ and 178 pounds, Weekes had great speed. His finest game was probably Columbia's 10–0 victory over Pennsylvania in 1901. Weekes gained 230 yards and scored both Columbia touchdowns, on runs of 18 and 75 yards. He was named an All-American that year.

As a senior in 1902, Weekes captained the team. He scored six touchdowns against Fordham and had a 107-yard kickoff return against Hamilton, but he was injured against Princeton. Although he played the rest of the season, he was below par. Nevertheless, he was named to Casper Whitney's second-string All-American team.

Weekes graduated in 1903 and coached the University of Kansas for one season, winning six games and losing three.
★ College Football Hall of Fame

Wehrli, Roger R.

FOOTBALL
b. Nov. 26, 1947, New Point, Mo.

A defensive back at the University of Missouri, Wehrli led the nation in punt returns in 1968 by running back 41 kicks for 478 yards, an 11.7 average, and he was a consensus All-American at safety.

Wehrli was chosen in the first round of the 1969 NFL draft by the St. Louis Cardinals, and he became a starter immediately. The 6-foot-1, 195-pounder was a hard hitter with great speed, as effective against the run as against the pass.

Named to *The Sporting News* All-

NFC team in 1970 and 1971 and from 1974 through 1976, Wehrli was selected for the Pro Bowl seven times. He retired after the 1979 season.

Wehrli intercepted 40 passes and returned them for 309 yards, a 7.7 average, and 2 touchdowns. He also ran back 42 punts for 310 yards, a 7.4 average, and had 19 fumble recoveries.

Weiland, Cooney (Ralph)

HOCKEY
b. Nov. 5, 1904, Seaforth, Ont.
d. July 6, 1985

After three years in minor league hockey, Weiland joined the NHL's Boston Bruins in 1928 and scored 43 goals in 44 games in 1929–30. He was traded to the Ottawa Senators in 1932 and to the Detroit Red Wings during the 1933–34 season. Weiland then returned to Bruins in 1935.

He retired as a player to become Boston's coach in 1939, and he guided the Bruins to the 1941 Stanley Cup. One of his key moves that season was trading Hall of Fame goaltender Tiny Thompson to make room for rookie Frank Brimsek, who recorded six shutouts in his first eight games.

Weiland coached hockey at Harvard University from 1951 until his retirement in 1971. In his 11 NHL seasons, he had 333 regular season points on 173 goals and 160 assists, and he added 12 goals and 10 assists in 45 playoff games. As a coach at Harvard, he had a 315–174–17 record for a .639 winning percentage.
★ Hockey Hall of Fame

Weinmeister, Arnie (Arnold)

FOOTBALL
b. March 23, 1923, Rhein, Sask.

Weinmeister played two-way tackle at the University of Washington and then joined the New York Yankees of the All-America Football Conference in 1948. Because of his remarkable speed, coach Ray Flaherty thought of converting the 6-foot-4, 235-pound Weinmeister to fullback, but used him at defensive tackle instead.

After being named to the All-AAFC team in 1949, the last year of the league's existence, Weinmeister went to the New York Giants in the NFL. He was an All-Pro in each of his four seasons with the Giants.

Tom Landry, a teammate and later the long-time coach of the Dallas Cowboys, said of Weinmeister, "He could operate all over the field because he was probably the fastest lineman in the league. He could also outrun most backs." In fact, the Giant coaching staff liked to haze rookie running backs by matching them in sprints against the bigger Weinmeister, who always won.

The British Columbia Lions of the Canadian Football League offered Weinmeister a $15,000 contract in 1954, against the Giants' bid of $12,000, so Weinmeister returned to his native Canada. He retired after the 1955 season.
★ Pro Football Hall of Fame

Weir, Edward

FOOTBALL
b. March 14, 1903, Superior, Nebr.

Knute Rockne called Weir "the best tackle I have ever seen." An All-American at the University of Nebraska in 1924 and 1925, Weir captained the team both of those years. The 6-foot-1 Weir weighed only 190 pounds but was surprisingly strong and very fast. He was the state pentathlon champion in high school, and he ran hurdles on the Nebraska track team.

Also a punter and place-kicker, Weir played for the NFL's Frankford Yellowjackets from 1926 through 1928. He later became an assistant football coach and head track coach at his alma mater.
★ College Football Hall of Fame

Weissmuller, Johnny (Peter John)

SWIMMING
b. June 2, 1904, Windber, Pa.
d. Jan. 20, 1984

Weak and fragile as a boy, Weissmuller was put on a high-nutrition diet to build his body, and he took up swimming on the advice of a doctor. At 15, he joined the Illinois Athletic Club.

After watching Weissmuller work out, the coach Bill Bachrach told him,

"Swear that you'll work a year with me without question and I'll take you on. You won't swim against anybody. You'll just be a slave and you'll hate my guts, but in the end you just might break every record there is."

Weissmuller, who had grown to 6-foot-3 and 195 pounds, trained for more than a year before his first serious competition, the 1921 AAU outdoor championship meet, where he won the 220-yard freestyle event.

He set world records in the 300-meter freestyle and 150-yard backstroke in 1922. Weissmuller won national titles that year in the outdoor 100-, 220-, and 440-yard freestyle swims and in the indoor 100- and 220-yard events. He won the same championships in 1923, when he also set a world record in the 150-yard backstroke, breaking the old mark by 6.8 seconds.

At the 1924 Olympics, Weissmuller won gold medals in the 100- and 400-meter freestyles, setting a world record of 5:04.2 in the 400 and an Olympic record of 59.0 in the 100. He was also a member of the 4 x 200-meter freestyle relay team that won a gold medal with a world record 9:53.4, and he played for the U.S. water polo team that won a bronze medal.

Weissmuller won 15 more national championships during the next three years. He took his fourth and fifth gold medals at the 1928 Olympics, repeating in the 400-meter freestyle and on the 4 x 200-meter relay team.

The first to swim 100 meters in less than a minute, on July 9, 1922, Weissmuller in 1924 lowered his own world record in that event from 58.6 seconds to 57.4 seconds, a time that wasn't surpassed for ten years. His record of 51.0 seconds in the 100-yard freestyle, set in 1927, stood until 1944.

A very popular athlete, Weissmuller often entertained spectators with comedy diving between swimming events. He became a professional after the 1928 Olympics, swimming exhibitions across the country, and in 1932 he starred in the first of 12 Tarzan movies. About that role, he later said, "It was up my alley.

There was swimming in it, and I didn't have much to say." Weissmuller also appeared in a number of other feature movies and in the 1956 *Jungle Jim* television series.

★ Olympic Hall of Fame

Welch, Bob (Robert L.)

BASEBALL
b. Nov. 3, 1956, Detroit, Mich.

A right-handed pitcher, Welch joined the NL's Los Angeles Dodgers midway through the 1978 season. He pitched well but not spectacularly for ten years with the Dodgers. His best season with them was 1982, when he was 16–11.

Welch went to the AL's Oakland Athletics as a free agent in 1988. After going 17–9 and 17–8 in his first two seasons there, he won the Cy Young Award in 1990. He had a 27–6 record to lead the league in victories and winning percentage. He slipped to 12–13 in 1991, then won 11 of 18 decisions in 1992, but missed a good part of the season with arm trouble. Welch was released by Oakland after winning only 12 games over the next two years.

Welch, Mickey (Michael F.)

BASEBALL
b. July 4, 1859, Brooklyn, N.Y.
d. July 30, 1941

Only 5-foot-7 and 140 pounds, Welch began pitching at a time when the rubber was only 45 feet from home plate and the ball had to be thrown underhand. As in softball, most pitchers of the era relied on speed to get hitters out, but Welch primarily used a curve and a screwball. In fact, he may have been the inventor of the screwball, which breaks in the opposite direction of a curve.

Welch entered the major leagues with the NL's Troy Haymakers in 1880 and had a 34–30 record. He was 21–18 in 1881, when the pitching distance was moved back to 50 feet, and he had a 14–16 record in 1882, despite 5 shutouts. The franchise then moved to New York City, and the team became known as the Maroons.

After going 25–23 and 39–21 in his first two seasons in New York, Welch had his best year in 1885, when he was 44–11 to lead the league with an .800 winning percentage. He had 55 complete games in 55 starts, with 7 shutouts and an ERA of 1.66.

His team was now called the Giants and Welch won the nickname "Smiling Mickey" because of a cartoon that appeared in the *New York Journal* caricaturing his lopsided grin. The affable Welch ascribed his success as a pitcher to his fondness for beer.

Welch was 33–22 in 1886 and won 22 or more games each of the next three season. He began to decline in 1890, when he was only 17–14, pitching fewer than 300 innings for the first time since 1882. He started just 15 games in 1891. After appearing in one game with the Giants in 1892, Welch spent the rest of the season in the minor leagues and then retired. He later worked for the Giants as a ticket taker at the Polo Grounds.

In 13 major league seasons, Welch had a 307–210 record with 41 shutouts and a 2.71 ERA. He struck out 1,850 hitters and walked 1,297 in 4,802 innings.
★ Baseball Hall of Fame

Wells, Wayne A.
WRESTLING
b. Sept. 29, 1946, Abilene, Tex.

As a 152-pound wrestler at the University of Oklahoma, Wells had a 69–4 record from 1966 to 1968, when he won the NCAA championship. He placed fourth at the 1968 Olympics.

Wells won the world championships in 1970, as a law school student, and he was the AAU national champion at 163 pounds in 1970 and 1972. He was the gold medalist in the class at the 1971 Pan-American Games and the 1972 Olympics. After receiving his law degree, he served as a volunteer assistant wrestling coach at his alma mater.

Werner, Bud (Wallace)
SKIING
b. Feb. 26, 1936, Steamboat Springs, Colo.
d. April 12, 1964

A last-minute replacement on the U.S. national ski team in 1954 as a 17-year-old high school student, Werner became the first American to win the prestigious Holmenkollen downhill race in Norway. The following year, he won the Stowe, Vermont, international downhill by a record margin of $5\frac{1}{2}$ seconds.

Werner won the national downhill championship in 1957 and in 1959 he swept all four men's titles, the downhill, slalom, giant slalom, and alpine combined. He was also the giant slalom and alpine combined champion in 1963.

An all-out skier who often took a line precariously close to trees and spectators, Werner was given a strong chance to medal at the 1956 Winter Olympics, but he crashed in all three races.

Before the 1960 winter games, retired champion Toni Sailer of Austria told the press, "There is only one racer in the world capable of duplicating my three gold medals at Cortina, and that is Bud Werner."

However, Werner broke a leg in training and missed the Olympics. He said later it was the best thing that had ever happened to him because "It sent me back to college to get an education. Had I won at Squaw Valley, I probably would have been a big-headed ski bum the rest of my life."

Werner competed in the 1964 Winter Olympics without medaling. Shortly afterward, he was leading in the national downhill race after one run but crashed on his second run. He then went to Switzerland to take part in a ski fashion movie being filmed by a West German company near St. Moritz. He and 16 other skiers were killed by an avalanche during the filming.

West, Belford (David Belford)
FOOTBALL
b. May 7, 1896, Hamilton, N.Y.
d. Sept. 11, 1973

West was a starting halfback for Colgate as a freshman but was moved to tackle in his sophomore year. He was named an All-American at that position as a junior, in 1916. He enlisted in the Army during World War I, then returned to Colgate to captain the team in 1919, when he was again an All-American.

He also did most of the team's punting and drop-kicking. Under the rules of his time, if a forward pass went out of bounds the opposition was given the ball at that spot. West was such an accurate passer that he was often delegated to throw the ball out of bounds near the other team's goal line instead of punting.

At Colgate, West also starred in baseball and basketball. He played professional football with the Canton Bulldogs in 1921.

★ College Football Hall of Fame

West, Jerry (Jerome A.)

BASKETBALL
b. May 28, 1938, Cabin Creek, W.Va.

An All-American forward at the University of West Virginia in 1959 and 1960, West was named most outstanding player in the 1959 NCAA tournament, when his team lost, 71–70, to the University of California in the championship final. West averaged 29.3 points as a senior and 24.8 in his three years as a starter. He started for the 1960 gold medal Olympic team.

The 6-foot-3, 185-pounder was the second player chosen in the 1960 NBA draft, by the Los Angeles Lakers, who moved him to guard. Originally called "Zeke from Cabin Creek" by his teammates because of his homespun background, he soon became known as "Mr. Clutch" because of his ability to come up with big plays.

West's college coach, Fred Schaus, summed him up: "If you sat down to build a six-foot-three-inch basketball player, you would come up with a Jerry West. He is the man that has everything — a fine shooting touch, speed, quickness, all the physical assets, including a tremendous dedication to the game."

West got off to a rather slow start as a rookie, averaging only 17.6 points a game, but he averaged 30.8 points in 1961–62 and was named to the All-NBA for the first of ten times. Almost impossible to guard effectively because of his accurate jump shot and ability to drive

to the basket, West averaged more than 25 points a game in each of the next 11 seasons and was over 30 points three or more times.

He led the NBA in scoring with a 31.2 point average in 1969–70 and in assists with an average of 9.7 per game in 1971–72, when the Lakers won the league championship. West was named most valuable player of the championship finals that season.

Named to the NBA's All-Defensive team four years in a row, from 1970 through 1973, West was frequently hurt because of his all-out, aggressive style of play. He retired after appearing in only 31 games in 1973–74 because of injuries.

West coached the Lakers to a 145–101 record from 1976–77 through 1978–79 and then became the team's general manager. The Lakers have won five NBA championships during his tenure.

In 14 NBA seasons, West scored 25,192 points in 932 regular season games, an average of 27.0, and had 6,238 assists. He averaged 29.1 points per game in his playoff career, with 4,457 points and 970 assists in 153 games.

★ Basketball Hall of Fame

Westphal, Paul D.

BASKETBALL
b. Nov. 30, 1950, Torrance, Calif.

A 6-foot-4, 195-pound guard, Westphal averaged 16.4 points a game in four years at the University of Southern California and was chosen in the first round of the 1972 NBA draft by the Boston Celtics.

Never a starter with Boston, Westphal was traded to the Phoenix Suns in 1975. He averaged more than 20 points a game for the next five seasons and was named to the All-NBA team in 1977, 1979, and 1980.

After the 1979–80 season, the Suns traded him to the Seattle Supersonics. Westphal missed much of the next season with an injury and signed with the New York Knicks as a free agent in March 1992. The Knicks waived him in 1983. Westphal spent his final season as a player with Phoenix in 1983–94.

Always respected for his court sense

and knowledge of the sport, Westphal coached Southwestern Baptist Bible College to a 21–9 record in 1985–86 and was 63–18 in two seasons at Grand Canyon College before returning to Phoenix as an assistant coach.

Taking over as head coach of the team in 1992, Westphal had a 118–46 regular season record in his first two years with Phoenix and was 19–15 in the playoffs.

As an NBA player, Westphal scored 12,809 points in 823 regular season games, an average of 15.6 points per game. He had 1,337 points in 107 playoff games.

Wharton, Buck (Charles)

FOOTBALL
b. 1865, Magnolia, Del.
d. Nov. 15, 1949

In an era when players who weighed more than 200 pounds were rare, Wharton was a titan at 6-foot-1 and 235 pounds. An All-American guard in 1895 and 1896, Wharton was captain of the 1896 University of Pennsylvania team that won 14 of 15 games. During his four seasons, the school won 52 games while losing only 4.

Wharton received a medical degree in 1899 and served for a number of years as an assistant professor of physical education at his alma mater. He and Walter Camp devised the U.S. Navy's physical training program during World War I.
★ College Football Hall of Fame

Wheat, Zack (Zachariah D.)

BASEBALL
b. May 23, 1888, Hamilton, Mo.
d. March 11, 1972

Wheat began playing semipro baseball in 1906, mainly to help support his widowed mother, and he entered the minor leagues the following season. The NL's Brooklyn Superbas (later the Dodgers) bought his contract late in the 1909 season.

A left-handed hitter and right-handed thrower, Zack Wheat became Brooklyn's starting left fielder in 1910 and held the job for 17 seasons. A 5-foot-10, 170-pound line-drive hitter, he was also a good defensive player with a strong, accurate arm.

Wheat batted .305 in 1912, the first of 13 seasons in which he hit better than .300. He led the league's outfielders in putouts in 1914 and was the slugging leader with a .461 percentage in 1916, when Brooklyn won its first pennant, but he hit only .211 in a five-game World Series loss to the Boston Red Sox.

He won the batting title with a .335 average in 1918. After slipping to .297 in 1919, he hit .328 the following season, when Brooklyn won another pennant, and he batted .333 in the team's seven-game defeat by Cleveland in the World Series.

During the next five seasons, Wheat hit .320, .335, .375, .375, and .359 without winning another batting championship. He was released after hitting .290 in 1926, and he finished his major league career with a .324 average in 88 games with the AL's Philadelphia Athletics in 1927.

Wheat then spent one season in the minor leagues before retiring. He had a career .317 average with 2,884 hits, including 476 doubles, 172 triples, and 132 home runs. He stole 205 bases, scored 1,289 runs, and 1,248 RBI.
★ Baseball Hall of Fame

Whitaker, Louis R., Jr.

BASEBALL
b. May 12, 1957, Brooklyn, N.Y.

A left-handed hitter, Whitaker played 11 games with the AL's Detroit Tigers in 1977 and became the starting second baseman the following season.

Whitaker is a solid, dependable, all-around player who can steal bases, hit with some power, and turn the double play with the best of them. He was named the league's rookie of the year in 1978, when he hit .285.

His best overall offensive year was 1982, when he hit .320 with 12 home runs and 72 RBI. Whitaker has hit 20 or more home runs four times, led the league's second basemen in fielding percentage twice, won three Gold Glove Awards, and been named to *The Sporting News* AL All-Star team twice.

Through 1994, Whitaker had a .276 average with 2,296 hits, including 406 doubles, 65 triples, and 225 home runs. He had stolen 139 bases, scored 1,350 runs, and driven in 1,040.

White, Albert C.
DIVING
b. May 14, 1895, Oakland, Calif.
d. July 8, 1982

A fine athlete, White played on an armed forces basketball team that toured Europe shortly after World War I ended. He then entered Stanford and competed on the gymnastics team that won the Pacific Coast Conference championship in 1921.

But diving was his forte. White won Olympic gold medals in both the springboard and platform events in 1924. He won ten national championships, the outdoor 3-meter springboard in 1922 and 1924; the indoor 1-meter from 1924 through 1926; and the indoor 3-meter from 1922 through 1926.

White served as an Army officer during World War II. An engineer, he was the Pacific Coast diving commissioner for the AAU for many years.

White, Benjamin F.
HARNESS RACING
b. 1873 near Whitevale, Ont.
d. May 20, 1958

White was the only harness driver to win the Kentucky Futurity seven times and one of three to win the Hambletonian four times. He began racing at fairgrounds tracks when he was 15 and made it a career at 21, when he went to work for the legendary "Pop" Geers at Village Farm in upstate New York.

Then White became the trainer for W. N. Reynolds in Kentucky and became a fixture there. He won his first Kentucky Futurity with Volga in 1916. His other victories came in 1922, 1924, 1925, 1933, 1936, and 1937. White drove Hambletonian winners in 1933, 1936, 1942, and 1943.

★ Hall of Fame of the Trotter

White, Charles R.
FOOTBALL
b. Jan. 22, 1958, Los Angeles, Calif.

The California high school athlete of the year in both football and track, White entered the University of Southern California in 1976 and became the starting tailback during his freshman year.

In 1979, his senior season, he had a spectacular performance in a nationally televised 42–33 victory over Notre Dame, gaining 261 yards on 44 carries. He rushed for 247 yards on 39 carries and scored the winning touchdown when USC beat Ohio State, 17–16, in the Rose Bowl.

A consensus All-American, White won the 1979 Heisman and Walter Camp trophies as the nation's best collegiate player. During his career at USC, he gained 5,598 yards on 1,023 attempts, a 5.5 average, and scored 49 rushing touchdowns.

White joined the NFL's Cleveland Browns as a first-round draft choice after a long holdout in 1980, but he had a troubled professional career. He admitted to cocaine use in 1982 and entered a drug rehabilitation program. A broken ankle put him on the sidelines for the entire 1983 season, and he missed much of the following season with a knee injury.

The Browns released him early in 1985 and he joined the Los Angeles Rams. White retired after the 1988 season. During his nine years in the NFL, he rushed for 3,075 yards on 780 carries, a 3.9 average, and scored 23 rushing touchdowns. He also caught 114 passes for 860 yards, a 7.5 average, and 1 touchdown.

White, Nera D.
BASKETBALL, SOFTBALL
b. Nov. 15, 1935, Macon County, Tenn.

While a student at George Peabody Col-lege in Tennessee, which didn't have a women's basketball team, White joined the Nashville Basketball Club in 1954. The 6-foot, 157-pounder was an AAU All-American 15 times in a row, from 1955 through 1969, and she played for ten AAU national champions.

White was named most valuable player in the national tournament nine times. She starred for the U.S. team that won the 1957 world championship, when she was named the best woman player in the world. The Nashville team broke up after the 1968–69 season, ending her basketball career.

In 1959 and 1965, White was named an All-American fast-pitch softball player, and she was a slow-pitch All-American in 1980. She was once timed at a women's record ten seconds circling the bases.

★ Basketball Hall of Fame

White, Randy L.
FOOTBALL
b. Jan. 15, 1953, Wilmington, Del.

An All-American defensive end at Maryland, the 6-foot-4, 245-pound White won the Outland Trophy and Lombardi Award in 1974 as the nation's outstanding college lineman. He joined the NFL's Dallas Cowboys in 1975 as their first-round draft choice.

After spending his rookie season as a part-time defensive end and outside linebacker, White was moved to tackle in Dallas's flex defense in 1976. Though he seemed undersized for the position, he used his remarkable speed and quickness to become one of the league's best inside pass rushers.

Nicknamed "Manster" (half man, half monster) by his teammates, White was named NFC defensive player of the year by United Press International in 1978, when he had 16 quarterback sacks, and he shared most valuable player honors with Harvey Martin in Super Bowl XII.

The flex defense had White playing somewhat off the line of scrimmage, between the offensive center and a guard, enabling him to read the play and then use his speed to react to the ball. White was named to most All-Pro teams five years in a row, from 1978 through 1982. Injuries began to slow him in 1986, and he retired after the 1988 season.

White, Reggie (Reginald H.)
FOOTBALL
b. Dec. 19, 1961, Chattanooga, Tenn.

Named to most 1983 All-American teams as a defensive end at the University of Tennessee, White became the NFL's all-time leader in quarterback sacks in 1993. He began his professional career with the Memphis Showboats in the U.S. Football League in 1985.

White joined the NFL's Philadelphia Eagles in 1985 and recorded 13 sacks in as many games. At 6-foot-5 and 285 pounds, White combines strength with great quickness. He can rush the passer by pushing his blocker into the offensive backfield or by spinning around him and using his speed.

The league's sack leader with 21 in 1987 and 18 in 1988, White intercepted a pass and returned it 33 yards in 1990. He has also returned 3 fumble recoveries for a total of 127 yards and touchdowns.

White became a free agent after the 1992 season and signed a four-year, $17 million contract with the Green Bay Packers, the highest salary ever paid to a defensive player. He recorded two sacks in a 17–3 victory over the Chicago Bears on October 31, 1993, to reach a record total of 130½, passing Lawrence Taylor.

White, Whizzer (Byron R.)
FOOTBALL
b. June 8, 1917, Ft. Collins, Colo.

A fast, elusive runner, White first attracted attention in his junior year at the University of Colorado, when he had kickoff returns of 90 and 102 yards and led the Mountain States Conference in scoring. In 1937, his senior year, White was the nation's leading scorer with 122 points. He gained 1,121 yards in 181 attempts, an average of 6.2 per carry, and he had both the longest punt return of the year, 97 yards, and the longest punt, 84 yards.

Colorado won all eight regular season games and played Rice in the 1938 Cotton Bowl. White returned an interception 50 yards for a touchdown, threw a touchdown pass, and kicked both extra points to give his team an early 14–0 lead. However, Rice came on to win the game, 28–14.

A consensus All-American halfback, White was also an All-Conference guard in basketball, a three-year starter on the baseball team, and an excellent student. He won a Rhodes Scholarship to attend Oxford University but postponed it for a semester to play for the Pittsburgh Pirates (now the Steelers) for $15,000, by far the highest salary in professional football at the time.

Pittsburgh had a poor team, but White led the NFL in rushing in 1938 with 567 yards. He then began his studies at Oxford but had to return to the United States when Great Britain entered World War II. White received a degree from Yale University Law School, where he was first in his class.

He played for the Detroit Lions in the NFL for two seasons, leading the league in rushing again in 1940, when he was named to the All-Pro team. After the 1941 season, White became an intelligence officer in the U.S. Navy and won two Bronze Stars. He also befriended another young naval officer, John F. Kennedy.

In 1960, White headed the national Citizens for Kennedy organization. President Kennedy appointed him to the U.S. Supreme Court on March 31, 1962.
★ College Football Hall of Fame

White, Willye B. ("Red")

TRACK AND FIELD
b. Jan. 1, 1939, Money, Miss.

White dominated the U.S. outdoor high jump competition for a decade, from 1960 through 1970, winning nine championships during that period, and she is the only American woman ever to compete in five Olympics. She won only one medal in her specialty, a silver in 1956, when she was still a high school student, but she won a gold medal as a member of the 4 x 100-meter relay team in 1964.

One of the many Tennessee State Tiger Belles who starred in track, White was the national outdoor high jump champion from 1960 through 1962, 1964 through 1966, and 1968 through 1970. She was the indoor champion in 1962

and 1968, and she also won the indoor 50-meter three times.

After her silver medal in 1956, White finished 16th in 1960, 12th in 1964, and 11th in both 1968 and 1972. She won gold medals in the long jump and the 4 x 100-meter relay at the 1963 Pan-American Games and was third in the long jump in 1959 and 1967.

White set a number of American long jump records, with a best of 21 feet, 6 inches, in 1964. She retired after the 1972 Olympics and studied nursing.
★ International Women's Sports Hall of Fame; National Track & Field Hall of Fame

Whitfield, Malvin G.

TRACK AND FIELD
b. Oct. 11, 1924, Bay City, Tex.

The first black to win the Sullivan Award as the nation's best amateur athlete, in 1954, Whitfield was the world's premier 880-yard/800-meter runner in the late 1940s and early 1950s. From June 1948 to the end of the 1954 track season, he won 66 of 69 races at those distances.

Called "Marvelous Mal" by sportswriters, Whitfield won gold medals in the 800 meter run at the 1948 and 1952 Olympics, running a 1:49.2 both times. He was a member of the winning 4 x 400-meter relay team in 1948, when he also won a bronze in the 400-meter event. In 1952, he ran on the 4 x 400-meter relay team that won a silver medal.

Whitfield joined the U.S. Air Force after graduating from high school in 1943 and served until 1952, flying bomber missions in both World War II and the Korean War. As an air force sergeant, he attended Ohio State University, winning the NCAA 800-meter run in 1948 and 1949. He was the AAU outdoor 880-yard champion from 1949 through 1951 and in 1953 and 1954, and he won the indoor 1,000-yard championship in 1954. He also won the outdoor 440-yard title in 1952 and was the Pan-American Games champion at 800 meters in 1951.

Whitfield set a world record of 1:49.2 in the 880-yard run in 1950, and he lowered that to 1:48.6 in 1953. After becoming a miler with little success in 1955, Whitfield ran a 1:49.3 in the 800-meter at the 1956 Olympic trials, just .1 second slower than his 1952 gold medal time, but he finished fifth and retired from competition shortly afterward.

Whitfield graduated from Los Angeles State College in 1956 and then became a youth officer for the U.S. Information Agency in Kenya. In that position, he conducted sports clinics throughout Africa. He later became a recreation director in Kenya and ran a training camp in Ethiopia, helping to produce many international stars.
★ National Track & Field Hall of Fame; Olympic Hall of Fame

Whitman, Malcolm D.
TENNIS
b. March 5, 1877, Andover, Mass. d. Dec. 28, 1932

The developer of the reverse twist service, which breaks toward a right-hander's backhand rather than the forehand, the 6-foot-3 Whitman was an excellent volleyer at net and also had solid ground strokes from the baseline.

As a student at Harvard, Whitman won the intercollegiate singles championship in 1896 and was the national champion three years in a row, from 1898 through 1900. He played on the first Davis Cup team in 1900, winning his only match to help the U.S. defeat the British.

Whitman retired from competition in 1901 but returned to join the Davis Cup team in 1902, winning two singles matches. He reached the finals of the 1902 national singles but lost to Englishman Reggie Doherty.
★ International Tennis Hall of Fame

Whitmire, Donald B.
FOOTBALL
b. July 1, 1922, Giles County, Tenn.

Winner of the Knute Rockne Trophy as the nation's best collegiate lineman in 1944, the 6-foot, 200-pound Whitmire split his college career between the University of Alabama and Navy. He played at Alabama in 1941 and 1942, then won

an appointment to the U.S. Naval Academy, where he was an All-American tackle in 1943 and 1944.

Alabama won 15 regular season games and lost 5 while Whitmire was a starter. The school beat Texas A & M, 29–21, in the 1942 Cotton Bowl and defeated Boston College, 37–21, in the 1943 Orange Bowl. Whitmire was named to both all-time bowl teams.

He received his commission as an ensign in 1946 and retired from the Navy in 1977 with the rank of rear admiral.
★ College Football Hall of Fame

Whiton, Swede (Herman F.)
YACHTING
b. April 6, 1904, Cleveland, Ohio d. Sept. 6, 1967

Whiton began sailing in 1920 as a student at St. Paul's School in Concord, New Hampshire. After graduating from Princeton University and doing graduate work at Harvard and Columbia, he was a member of the first U.S. Olympic yachting team in 1928. Skippering a boat named *Frieda* after his mother, Countess Frieda Frasch of Sweden, he finished sixth in a field of 13.

In 1948, Whiton won a gold medal as skipper of the Olympic 6-meter champion *Llanoria*, and he repeated in 1952 with an entirely different crew. His wife, Emelyn, filled in as a crew member in one of the 1952 races when one of the regular members became ill.

The president of an oil company, Whiton encouraged young people to take up sailing and helped instruct them. He once bought eight boats and donated them to a summer youth sailing program.

Whittingham, Charlie (Charles)
HORSE RACING
b. April 13, 1913, San Diego, Calif.

Whittingham didn't begin training on his own until he was over 40 and didn't become recognized as a truly outstanding trainer until he was nearly 60, but he has been recognized as one of the very best for more than 20 years.

Nicknamed the "Bald Eagle" because he lost his hair to a tropical disease during World War II, Whittingham originally wanted to be a jockey, but he outgrew that idea and began training horses with little success in the 1930s.

In 1939 he became an assistant trainer for Horatio Luro, and except for three years in the Marine Corps, he held that position until 1955, when he started his own public stable. He soon developed a reputation for producing upsets.

Whittingham led all trainers in winnings from 1970 through 1973 and in 1975, 1981, and 1982. He won his first Eclipse Award as trainer of the year in 1971 after winning a record 14 stakes races at Santa Anita and training two 1971 Eclipse winners — horse of the year Ack Ack and three-year-old filly champion Turkish Trousers. He also won Eclipse awards in 1982 and 1989.

Whittingham's only triple crown winner was Ferdinand, in the 1986 Kentucky Derby. Ferdinand finished second in the Preakness and third in the Belmont before winning the Hollywood Gold Cup and Breeders' Cup Classic in 1987 to win an Eclipse Award.

★ National Horse Racing Hall of Fame

Whitworth, Kathy (Kathrynne A.)
GOLF
b. Sept. 27, 1939, Monahans, Tex.

A natural athlete who excelled in several sports as a youngster, Whitworth was frustrated by golf when she first tried it at 15. She later said, "Most sports had come naturally to me, but this one — gosh, it just bugged me. At first I didn't catch on to it at all." But eventually she caught on well enough to win 88 tournaments, a record for any professional golfer, male or female.

After winning the New Mexico Amateur in 1957 and 1958, Whitworth turned professional and dominated the LPGA tour in the late 1960s and early 1970s. She was the tour's leading money winner from 1965 through 1968 and from 1970 through 1973, player of the year from 1966 through 1969 and 1971 through 1973, and winner of the Vare Trophy for lowest strokes per round average from 1965 through 1967 and 1969 through 1972.

Whitworth became the first woman golfer to exceed $1 million in career earnings with a third-place finish at the 1981 U.S. Women's Open. She tied Sam Snead's record of 84 professional victories in dramatic fashion, sinking a 40-foot putt on the final hole to win the 1983 Open, and she broke the record by winning the Rochester International in 1984. Her final victory came in the 1985 United Virginia Bank Classic.

Among her 88 wins were six victories in major tournaments: the LPGA championship in 1967, 1971, and 1973, the Titleholders championship in 1965 and 1966, and the Western Open, then considered a major event, in 1967.

The Associated Press female athlete of the year in 1965 and 1966, Whitworth was named the golfer of the decade 1968–1977 by *Golf* magazine during the celebration of the sport's centennial in 1988.

★ International Women's Sports Hall of Fame; LPGA Hall of Fame; World Golf Hall of Fame

Wicks, Sidney
BASKETBALL
b. Sept. 19, 1949, Los Angeles, Calif.

After averaging 26.0 points per game at Santa Monica City College, Wicks entered UCLA in 1968. Called by UCLA coach John Wooden the fastest and quickest big man he'd ever coached, the 6-foot-8, 235-pound Wicks was a backup in his first year and became a starting forward in the 1969–70 season.

Wicks was named the most valuable player in the 1970 NCAA tournament, when he scored 17 points and had 18 rebounds in UCLA's championship victory against the University of Jacksonville. He averaged 21.3 points a game as a senior, when he was named college player of the year by *The Sporting News* and the U.S. Basketball Writers' Association.

A first-round draft choice of the NBA's Portland Trail Blazers, Wicks became the eighth player in league history to score more than 2,000 points in his first season, averaging 24.5 points per game to win the league's rookie of the year award.

That was his best season as a professional. After four more seasons with Portland Wicks went to the Boston Celtics in 1976, and he finished his career with the San Diego Clippers from 1978–79 through 1980–81. Wicks scored 12,803 points in 760 regular season games, a 16.8 average, and had 6,620 rebounds. In nine playoff games he scored 118 points, a 13.1 average, and collected 17 rebounds.

Widseth, Edwin C.

FOOTBALL
b. Jan. 5, 1910, Gonvick, Minn.

Widseth starred at tackle for University of Minnesota teams that won 23 games and lost only 1 from 1934 through 1936. An All-American in 1935 and 1936, he was named most valuable player on the 1936 team that won seven of eight games.

The 6-foot-2, 220-pound Widseth played for the NFL's New York Giants from 1937 through 1940. He was named to the 1938 All-Pro team.
★ College Football Hall of Fame

Wigger, Lones W., Jr.

SHOOTING
b. Aug. 25, 1935, Great Falls, Mont.

A career officer in the U.S. Army, Wigger won Olympic gold medals in the small-bore rifle, three-position event in 1964 and the free rifle, three-position event in 1972. He also won a silver medal in 1964 in the small-bore, prone position.

In winning his 1964 gold medal, Wigger set a world record of 1,164 points. He and Laszlo Hammerl of Hungary both had world record scores in the prone position competition that year, but Hammerl won the gold medal on a tiebreaker because he had the best score on his last ten shots.

Wigger was the U.S. men's overall small-bore rifle champion in 1963, 1965, and 1966. He won a total of 58 national championships in various categories and

held or co-held 13 individual world records at one time or another.

Wilber, Doreen V. H.

ARCHERY
b. Jan. 8, 1930, Rutland, Iowa

Wilber won the gold medal in women's archery at the 1972 Olympics, shooting a world record score of 2,424. She didn't take up the sport seriously until she was in her early thirties, but she competed in eight national championship tournaments between 1965 and 1975, winning in 1969, 1971, 1973, and 1974, and finishing second twice.

She also won the national field archery championship in 1967, the only time she competed, and she was runner-up in the world championship tournament in 1969 and 1971.

Wildung, Dick (Richard K.)

FOOTBALL
b. Aug. 16, 1921, St. Paul, Minn.

A tackle, the 6-foot, 215-pound Wildung was noted for his speed, which often enabled him to get downfield to block ahead of the runner after having made his initial block at the line of scrimmage. That's exactly what he did against the University of Michigan in 1940, his sophomore year, enabling Bruce Smith to run 80 yards for the touchdown that won the game, 7–6.

A two-time All-American, in 1941 and 1942, Wildung captained the team as a senior. After playing for the College All-Star team that beat the NFL champion Washington Redskins in 1943, Wildung served in World War II as a PT boat skipper. He was a starting tackle for the Green Bay Packers from 1946 through 1951. After a year of retirement, he returned for one more season in 1953.
★ College Football Hall of Fame

Wilhelm, Hoyt (James Hoyt)

BASEBALL
b. July 26, 1923, Huntersville, N.C.

Wilhelm didn't get to the major leagues until he was 28 years old, yet he spent 21 seasons in the majors as an outstanding relief pitcher who relied almost entirely on the knuckleball. He was the first reliever elected to the Hall of Fame.

Joining the NL's New York Giants in 1952, he had a 15–3 record with 11 saves, leading the league with an .833 winning percentage, 71 appearances, and a 2.43 ERA. He led with 69 appearances in 1953, when he had only a 7–8 record with 15 saves.

In 1954 Wilhelm went 12–14 with seven saves and a 2.10 ERA. The Giants won the pennant and Wilhelm didn't give up a run in two appearances in the World Series, picking up a save as New York beat the Cleveland Indians in four games.

After going 8–10 with only 8 saves the next two years, Wilhelm was traded to the St. Louis Cardinals in 1957; they sent him to the AL's Cleveland Indians near the end of the season. He made his first major league start with the Indians in 1958 before being traded to the Baltimore Orioles.

Wilhelm started 27 games for Baltimore in 1959, when he had a 15–11 record with 3 shutouts and a league-leading 2.19 ERA. He was the first pitcher ever to lead both leagues in earned run average.

The Orioles moved him back to the bullpen in 1961. He had a 9–7 record with 18 saves that year and was 7–10 with 15 saves and a 1.94 ERA in 1962. Baltimore traded him to the Chicago White Sox the following season. From 1964 through 1968 Wilhelm's ERA was under 2.00 each year, and he totaled 77 saves.

Although he spent another four seasons in the major leagues, Wilhelm was inconsistent and never lasted long with one team. He was with the California Angels and Atlanta Braves in 1969 and the Braves and Chicago Cubs in 1970. In 1971 he was with the Braves again and the Los Angeles Dodgers, when he appeared in only 21 games. He retired after the 1972 season.

Wilhelm had a 142–122 record with 227 saves and a 2.52 ERA.

★ Baseball Hall of Fame

Wilkens, Lenny (Leonard R.)

BASKETBALL
b. Oct. 28, 1937, Brooklyn, N.Y.

As a 6-foot-1, 180-pound guard, Wilkens starred at Providence College and was named most valuable player of the National Invitation Tournament in 1960, when he was also chosen for several All-American teams. He averaged 14.9 points a game during his three years as a starter.

A first-round draft choice of the NBA's St. Louis Hawks, Wilkens averaged 11.7 points as a backup in his rookie season and missed most of his second season with an injury. His scoring totals increased consistently until he averaged exactly 20.0 points a game in 1967–68.

The Hawks then traded him to the Seattle Supersonics, where he became player-coach in 1969. He resigned as coach after the 1971–72 season and was traded to the Cleveland Cavaliers. He went to the Portland Trail Blazers as player-coach in 1974–75, his last season as a player.

Wilkens left Portland to become coach and director of player personnel with Seattle in 1977. He guided the Supersonics to the 1979 NBA championship.

He left coaching and became vice president and general manager of the Seattle franchise in 1985–86, then took over as coach of the Cavaliers for the 1986–87 season. He turned Cleveland into a contender but was generally unsuccessful in the playoffs. The Hawks, who had moved from St. Louis to Atlanta, hired Wilkens as head coach in 1993.

As a player, Wilkens scored 17,772 points in 1,077 regular season games, a 16.5 average, and 7,211 assists, which was 4th all-time when he retired. He had 1,031 points, a 16.1 average, and 372 assists in 64 playoff games. As a coach, he was 926–774 in regular season play after the 1993–94 season and had a 60–61 record in the playoffs.

★ Basketball Hall of Fame

Wilkins, Dominique (Jacques Dominique)

BASKETBALL
b. Jan. 12, 1960, Sorbonne, France

The son of an American soldier stationed in France, Wilkins grew up in Washington, D.C., and entered the University of Georgia in 1979. After averaging 21.6 points per game in three seasons as a starter, he chose to leave school before his senior year to enter the 1982 NBA draft.

The Utah Jazz chose him in the first round, as the third pick overall, and promptly sent him to the Atlanta Hawks for two players and a reported $1 million in cash. The 6-foot-8, 215-pound forward averaged 17.5 points and was named to the league's All-Rookie team.

A great leaper with speed, Wilkins quickly became known for his ability to soar to the basket and slam dunk the ball. With experience, he also developed an accurate jump shot that helped make him one of the NBA's top scorers. He led the league with 30.3 points per game in 1985–86.

Through the 1993–94 season, Wilkins had scored 24,019 points in 907 regular season games, a 26.5 average, and he had 6,295 rebounds. In 51 playoff games, he has scored 1,345 points for a 26.4 average, with 332 rebounds.

Wilkins, Mac (Maurice)

TRACK AND FIELD
b. Oct. 15, 1950, Eugene, Oreg.

After suffering an elbow injury as a sophomore at the University of Oregon, the 6-foot-4, 260-pound Wilkins switched from the javelin to the discus. His teammates nicknamed him "Multiple Mac" because he also competed in the shotput and the hammer throw.

Wilkins won the 1973 NCAA discus championship and was the national champion six times, in 1973 and from 1976 through 1980. He set his first world record in April 1976, and a week later he set new records on three consecutive throws.

After setting an Olympic record of 224 feet in the qualifying round of the 1976 Olympics, Wilkins had a throw of 221–5 in the finals to win the gold medal. He qualified for the 1980 Olympic team that didn't compete because of the U.S. boycott of the Moscow Games that year.

Wilkins retired from competition in 1981 but resumed the sport and won a silver medal in 1984 before retiring permanently.

★ National Track & Field Hall of Fame

Wilkinson, Bud (Charles)

FOOTBALL
b. April 23, 1915, Minneapolis, Minn.
d. Feb. 9, 1994

A guard at the University of Minnesota as a sophomore and junior, Wilkinson was moved to single-wing quarterback in 1936, when he captained the team. He was also captain of the school's hockey team in his senior season.

Wilkinson served as an assistant football coach at Syracuse University before entering the U.S. Navy in 1941. He learned the principles of the split T formation while assisting its inventor, Don Faurot, with the Iowa Pre-Flight School football team; he then served in the Pacific.

In 1946 he assisted Jim Tatum, another split T proponent, at the University of Oklahoma, and he became head coach the following season after Tatum went to the University of Maryland. Wilkinson refined the formation, introducing the "run to daylight" idea that was later made famous by Vince Lombardi and the Green Bay Packers.

As Wilkinson explained it in a 1952 article, "When we run a handoff, for example, the ball carrier has the option, when he gets the ball, of hitting anywhere from between the guards to outside of the defensive tackle."

In 17 seasons at Oklahoma, Wilkinson produced three national champions, 1950, 1955, and 1956, and four unbeaten teams, in 1949, 1950, 1955, and 1956. He was named coach of the year in 1949. Oklahoma won 31 games in a row from 1948 to 1950 and a record 47 in a row from 1953 to 1957. His overall college record was 145 wins, 29 losses, and 4 ties. Wilkinson's .826 winning percentage is eighth best all-time.

Wilkinson retired after the 1963 season and became director of the presidential physical fitness program. In 1978 he came out of retirement to coach the NFL's St. Louis Cardinals to an 11–21–0 record over two seasons.

★ College Football Hall of Fame

Williams, Billy L.

BASEBALL
b. June 15, 1938, Whistler, Ala.

A left-handed hitting, right-handed throwing outfielder, the 6-foot-1, 175-pound Williams had a virtually perfect swing and surprising power for someone with his slender frame. He was a remarkably consistent hitter from 1961 through 1974, batting between .276 and .333 each season in that stretch.

After playing with the NL's Chicago Cubs briefly in 1959 and 1960, Williams became a starter in 1961, when he batted .278 with 25 home runs to win the league's rookie of the year award. The following year he hit .298 with 22 home runs and 91 RBI and played in the first of his six All-Star games.

Williams led the NL with 205 hits and 137 runs scored in 1970, when he batted .322 with 42 home runs and 129 RBI. He won his only batting title with a .333 average in 1972. He also led the league in slugging with a .606 percentage and had 37 home runs with 122 RBI. Three more home runs and three more RBI would have brought him the triple crown.

From September 22, 1963, until September 3, 1970, Williams played in 1,117 consecutive games, an NL record at the time. He went to the AL's Oakland Athletics in 1975 and was used mostly as a designated hitter, batting .244. He retired after hitting only .211 with Oakland in 1976.

In 18 major league seasons, Williams had a .290 average on 2,711 hits, including 434 doubles, 88 triples, and 426 home runs. He scored 1,410 runs and had 1,475 RBI.

★ Baseball Hall of Fame

Williams, Cy (Fred)

BASEBALL
b. Dec. 21, 1887, Wadena, Ind.
d. April 23, 1974

Williams' career as a power hitter spanned the dead-ball and live-ball eras. A left-handed outfielder, he joined the NL's Chicago Cubs in 1912 but didn't become a starter until 1915, when he batted .257 with 13 home runs. He won the first of his four home run titles with 12 in 1916.

The Cubs traded him to the Philadelphia Phillies in 1918. In 1920, Williams batted .325 and was again the NL home run leader with 15. It was the first of six seasons in which he hit over .300.

With the livelier ball in use, Williams had a league-leading 41 home runs in 1923, when he batted .293 with 114 RBI. His fourth home run title came in 1927, when he hit 30. Williams became a part-time player in 1928 and retired after appearing in only 21 games in 1930.

In 19 seasons, he had a .292 average with 1,982 hits, including 306 doubles, 74 triples, and 251 home runs. He scored 1,024 runs and had 1,005 RBI.

Williams, Dick (Richard H.)

BASEBALL
b. May 7, 1929, St. Louis, Mo.

A journeyman infielder-outfielder, Williams spent 13 seasons in the major leagues, from 1951 through 1954 and 1956 through 1964, with five different teams. He had a career average of .260.

After managing in the minor leagues for two seasons, Williams took over the Boston Red Sox in 1967 and guided them to the AL pennant that year. The Red Sox lost a seven-game World Series to the St. Louis Cardinals.

The team slipped to fourth in 1968 and Williams was fired late in the 1969 season, with the Red Sox in third place. He took over the Oakland Athletics in 1971 and led them to three pennants in his first three seasons, winning the World Series in 1972 and 1973.

A no-nonsense disciplinarian, Williams was exasperated by the meddling of Oakland owner Charles O. Finley, and he left in 1974 to become manager of the

California Angels. After three seasons there he took over the NL's young Montreal Expos in 1977 and managed them to second-place division finishes in 1979 and 1980.

Williams was fired by the Expos late in the 1981 season and went to the NL's San Diego Padres the following year. The Padres won the 1984 pennant but lost the World Series to the Detroit Tigers in five games. Fired after a third-place finish in 1985, Williams took over the AL's Seattle Mariners the following season. He retired after being replaced in 1988.

In 21 seasons as a manager, Williams had a 1,571–1,451 record for a .520 winning percentage.

Williams, Henry L.

FOOTBALL
b. June 26, 1869, Hartford, Conn.
d. June 14, 1931

One of college football's early innovators, Williams played halfback at Yale and was also a track star. He won the IC4A 110-yard high hurdles in 1890 and 1891 and the 220-yard low hurdles in 1891.

After graduating he taught at a preparatory school near the U.S. Military Academy, which asked him to coach football during the 1891 season. Williams diagrammed plays and sent them with instructions on how to practice during the week, and on Saturday mornings he went to West Point to polish the team's performance.

Army went 4–1–1 that season and beat Navy for the first time, 32–16. Williams began studying medicine at the University of Pennsylvania in 1892 and coached high school football and track at Penn Charter School. He became an instructor in gynecology at the University of Pennsylvania until 1900, when he went to the University of Minnesota as head football coach.

Williams practiced medicine throughout his career at Minnesota. He produced undefeated teams in 1900, 1903, 1904, 1911, and 1915, and Minnesota won or shared eight Western Conference (now Big Ten) titles during his 22 years.

He was a leading proponent of legalizing the forward pass, which came about during a major rules revision in 1906. That season, Williams developed the Minnesota shift, which bewildered defenses. His tackles would line up behind the guards and shift into the line at the last moment, just before the play was run. Both tackles might go left or right to form an unbalanced line, or they might move into their usual positions to form a balanced line. Since there was no requirement for a one-second stop, as there is now, Minnesota could often attack before the defense had a chance to adjust.

Williams retired after the 1921 season with a record at Minnesota of 136 wins, 33 losses, and 11 ties. His career winning percentage of .786 is thirteenth best all-time.
★ College Football Hall of Fame

Williams, Ike (Isiah)

BOXING
b. Aug, 2, 1923, Brunswick, Ga.
d. Sept. 5, 1994

A sprinter and baseball star in high school, Williams took up boxing when he was 15 and became a professional fighter at 17. The 5-foot-6, 130-pound Williams, who had a surprisingly powerful punch, won the National Boxing Association's lightweight championship by knocking out Juan Zurita in the 2nd round on April 18, 1945.

He won the world title with a 6th-round knockout of Bob Montgomery on August 4, 1947. Williams was named fighter of the year in 1948, when he defended his title three times in less than five months. He held the championship until May 25, 1951, when James Carter knocked him out in the 9th round.

Williams retired in 1955 after knocking out Beau Jack in the 9th round. He won 124 bouts, 60 by knockout; lost 24, 6 by knockout; and fought 5 draws.
★ International Boxing Hall of Fame

Williams, John C.

ARCHERY
b. Sept. 12, 1953, Erie, Pa.

In the first round of the men's archery

competition at the 1972 Olympics, Williams set a new world record even though he completely missed the target with one of his shots. He went on to win the gold medal with a score of 2,528, the highest ever recorded for a double FITA round at the time.

Williams was a private in the U.S. Army during the Olympics and when he won the national and world championships in 1971 and 1972. He turned professional in 1972.

While attending California State University–San Bernardino, he won the Professional Archery Association titles in 1975 and 1976. After graduating, Williams became product manager for the archery division of Yamaha International.

Williams, Matthew D.

BASEBALL
b. Nov. 28, 1965, Bishop, Calif.

While playing shortstop for the University of Nevada–Las Vegas, Williams was an All-American in 1986. He then signed with the NL's San Francisco Giants. After spending parts of the 1987, 1988, and 1989 seasons with San Francisco, he took over as the starting third baseman in 1990.

Williams hit 33 home runs that year and led the league with 122 RBI. He had 34 home runs and 98 RBI in 1991, then slipped to a .227 average and 20 home runs the following season.

The 6-foot-2, 218-pounder bounced back with a .294 average, 38 home runs, and 110 RBI in 1993. A Gold Glove winner in 1990 and 1993, he was named to *The Sporting News* NL All-Star team those years.

Williams had 43 home runs and a chance at breaking Roger Maris's record of 61 when the 1994 season was ended by the players' strike. Through that season, Williams had a .253 average with 875 hits, including 146 doubles, 23 triples, and 202 home runs. He had scored 472 runs and driven in 582.

Williams, Percy

TRACK AND FIELD
b. May 19, 1908, Vancouver, B.C.

Because of rheumatic fever when he was 15 years old, Williams was told to avoid vigorous exercise. Five years later, he worked his way across Canada on a railroad dining car to take part in the 1928 Canadian Olympic trials in Toronto. He won both sprints.

The frail, 126-pound Williams won gold medals in the 100- and 200-meter dashes. His first victory was such an upset that the medal presentation was delayed while the Dutch organizers searched for a Canadian flag. Williams is still the only runner from outside the U.S. to win both Olympic sprint championships.

When he returned to Canada his mother met him for the return train trip to Vancouver, and he was presented with gifts at several stops along the way, including a silver tea service, a gold watch, a silver cup, and a bronze statue. Thousands of fans met him in Vancouver, where Williams was given a sports car and $14,500 for his college education.

Williams won the 100-yard dash at the first British Empire Games, and in 1930 he set a world record of 10.3 seconds in the 100-meter dash.
★ Canadian Sports Hall of Fame

Williams, R. Norris II

TENNIS
b. Jan. 19, 1891, Geneva, Switzerland
d. June 3, 1968

Born to a well-to-do American family, Williams received his early education in Switzerland and learned to play tennis there from a Swiss teaching professional. He and his father were returning to the U.S. aboard the *Titanic* in 1912 when the ship struck an iceberg and sank. Williams was rescued after spending more than an hour in the frigid water, but his father drowned.

A hard hitter and a risk-taker, Williams won two U.S. national singles titles, upsetting the defending champion both times. He beat Maurice McLoughlin in the 1914 title match and William Johnston in the 1916 finals.

As a student at Harvard, Williams won the intercollegiate singles championship in 1913 and 1915, and he teamed with Richard Harte to win the doubles title in 1914 and 1915. Williams also won the Wimbledon doubles with Charles S. Garland in 1920 and the U.S. national doubles with Vincent Richards in 1925 and 1926.

★ International Tennis Hall of Fame

Williams, Ted (Theodore S.)

BASEBALL
b. Aug. 30, 1918, San Diego, Calif.

Proud and cocky to the point of arrogance, Williams went to the Boston Red Sox training camp in 1938. But the team already had three outfielders who were good hitters and Williams was sent down to the minors. One of them said, sardonically, "So long, buster." Williams responded, "I'll be back, and someday I'll be earning more dough than the three of you combined."

He was back in 1939, when he batted .327 with 31 home runs and a league-leading .145 RBI. A left-handed hitter and right-handed thrower, Williams played right field that season. In 1940 he became the starting left fielder and remained at that position for the rest of his career.

The 6-foot-3 Williams weighed about 185 pounds as a rookie and was nicknamed the "Splendid Splinter." He bulked up to 205 pounds in his prime and weighed about 220 toward the end of his career, when the nickname had obviously lost its relevance.

After batting .344 and leading the league with 134 runs scored in 1940, Williams had a sensational season in 1941. He was batting exactly .400 going into the last day of the season and his manager, Joe Cronin, asked if he wanted to sit out to protect his average. Instead, Williams chose to play, got six hits in eight at-bats in a doubleheader, and finished at .406 with a league-leading 135 runs, 37 home runs, 145 walks, and .735 slugging percentage.

No player has hit over .400 since. Williams came as close as anyone with a .388 mark in 1957, when he was nearing 40. Although he had great vision, fast reflexes, and a fine natural swing, Wil-

liams owed much of his success to his scientific approach to hitting. His philosophy, later spelled out in an instructional book, was simply to wait for a pitch in a small area, where it could be hit hard.

Williams won the triple crown with a .356 average, 36 home runs, and 137 RBI in 1942, when he also led the league with 141 runs scored, 145 walks, and a .648 slugging percentage. He spent the next three seasons as a Marine Corps pilot.

He returned to action in 1946 as if he'd never been away, winning the AL's most valuable player award. He batted .342 with 38 home runs and 123 RBI, leading the league with 142 runs scored, 156 walks, and a .667 slugging percentage. The Red Sox won the pennant that year but lost to the St. Louis Cardinals in a seven-game World Series in which Williams hit only .200.

Williams won his second triple crown with a .343 average, 32 home runs, and 114 RBI in 1947. He won his fourth batting title in five years with a .369 mark in 1948. And in 1949 he won his second most valuable player award, when he batted .343 with a league-leading 43 home runs, 195 RBI, 39 doubles, 150 runs scored, and a .650 slugging percentage.

In the 1950 All-Star game Williams broke his left elbow crashing into the fence in an attempt to make a catch, and he played in only 89 games that season. After batting .318 in 1951, he was called back by the Marine Corps because of the Korean War, and he missed most of the next two seasons.

He rejoined the Red Sox late in 1953 and won another batting title with a .345 average in 1954. Williams won two more batting championships, with a .388 average in 1957, when he was named the Associated Press male athlete of the year, and a .328 average in 1958, when he became the oldest player ever to lead a league in hitting.

Williams had a love-hate relationship with Boston fans and an adversarial relationship with most of its sportswriters. He felt that he should have won most valuable player awards in 1941 and 1942. After being booed because he committed an error in his second game with the team, Williams vowed he would never tip his cap to the fans, no matter how much they cheered him. True to his vow, he refused to tip his cap to a standing ovation after hitting a home run in his last at-bat in 1960.

He remained away from baseball, pursuing his hobby of fishing and doing promotional work for Sears Roebuck until 1969, when he became manager of the Washington Senators. He guided the team to a surprising fourth-place finish and was named manager of the year. The team moved to Texas in 1972, and Williams retired permanently after that season.

In 2,292 games, all with the Red Sox, Williams had a .344 average with 2,654 hits, including 525 doubles, 71 triples, and 521 home runs. He scored 1,798 runs, drove in 1,839, and walked 2,019 times against only 709 strikeouts.

★ Baseball Hall of Fame

Willis, Bill (William K.)

FOOTBALL
b. Oct. 5, 1921, Columbus, Ohio

Center "Bulldog" Turner of the Chicago Bears said he thought he could block anyone until he played against Willis. "He was skinny and he didn't look like he should be playing guard," Turner said, "but he would jump right over you."

Willis played guard at Ohio State from 1942 through 1944, then spent a year in service. He joined the Cleveland Browns of the new All-America Football Conference in 1946 after asking coach Paul Brown for a tryout. Brown, who had coached Willis at Ohio State in 1942, invited him to camp primarily to room with fullback Marion Motley, the only other black player in the AAFC.

At 6-foot-4 and only 210 pounds, Willis was much smaller than other guards in professional football, but he was lightning quick. Nicknamed "the Cat," Willis was often suspected of being offside, but study of game films by Brown and league officials showed that he was just exceptionally fast to react to the ball.

Willis was a guard on the All-AAFC team from 1946 through 1948. The league folded in 1950 and the Browns joined the NFL, where he was an All-Pro from 1950 through 1953. He retired after the 1953 season.

★ College Football Hall of Fame; Pro Football Hall of Fame

Wills, Harry

BOXING
b. May 15, 1889, New Orleans, La.
d. Dec. 21, 1958

One of the greatest heavyweights of his era, Wills never got a championship fight because he was black and was forced to do most of his boxing against other black fighters. Many of his bouts weren't even recorded. For example, he had 15 recorded fights against Sam Langford, but the *Ring Record Book* says the two had seven other fights on unknown dates.

Wills began fighting professionally in 1910. He won a 15-round decision over Langford on November 5, 1919, in what was generally considered a black heavyweight championship bout. Wills lost the unofficial title to Bill Tate on a 1st-round foul on January 1, 1922, and he failed to regain the title in a 10-round draw just five days later.

In 1926, the New York State Athletic Commission refused to issue a license to heavyweight champion Jack Dempsey for his title defense against Gene Tunney because Dempsey refused to fight Wills. A contract for a Dempsey-Wills fight had actually been signed, and Wills received a $50,000 advance, but Dempsey instead fought Tunney in Philadelphia.

Nicknamed the "Black Panther," the powerful, 6-foot-4, 220-pound Wills suffered a setback when he lost to Jack Sharkey on October 12, 1926, because of a foul in the 13th round. He lost three of his last four fights, two by knockout, before retiring to go into the real estate business in 1932.

Wills won 62 recorded bouts, 45 by knockout; lost 8, 4 by knockout; and fought 2 draws, 27 no-decisions, and 3 no-contests.

★ International Boxing Hall of Fame

Wills, Helen (Mrs. Moody)

TENNIS
b. Oct. 6, 1905, Centerville, Calif.

The daughter of a tennis-playing doctor, Wills beat her father for the first time on her fourteenth birthday and was rewarded with a tennis club membership. She patterned her game after William Johnston's and became the first truly powerful woman player, specializing in a forehand drive.

Because of her impassiveness, Wills was nicknamed "Little Miss Poker Face," and some sportswriters and fans thought she didn't enjoy playing. But she explained, "When I play, I become entirely absorbed in the game. I love the feel of hitting the ball hard, the pleasure of a rally . . . Anyone who really loves the game can hardly be blamed for becoming completely absorbed by it while in the fun of play."

Wills reached the finals of the U.S. singles in 1922 at age 16, losing to Molla Mallory. She won the first of her seven national singles titles in 1923. The others came in 1924, 1925, 1927, 1928, 1929, and 1931. She won eight singles championships at Wimbledon, from 1927 through 1930 and in 1932, 1933, 1935, and 1938.

Her four French titles, from 1928 through 1930 and in 1932, gave her a total of 19 grand slam singles championships, second on the all-time list to Margaret Smith Court's 26. Wills never played in the fourth grand slam tournament, the Australian, which Court won 11 times.

Because she won so often, two of her defeats are among her most famous matches. In February 1926 she faced the French champion, Suzanne Lenglen, at the Carlton Tennis Club in Cannes. Scalpers were collecting as much as $50 per ticket, and carpenters were still working on additional seats when the match began. Lenglen won in straight sets, with the second set going to 8–6.

After her marriage in 1930, Wills — now known as Helen Wills Moody — skipped the national tournament. She won it in 1931 and didn't enter again in 1932, when Helen Hull Jacobs was the champion.

They faced each other in the 1933 finals. Jacobs won the first set 8–6, lost the second 6–3, and took a 3–0 lead in the third. Moody abruptly left the court at that point, saying she had a painful leg injury. However, after her default she was planning to play in a scheduled doubles match until friends talked her out of it, leading some to believe she'd faked the injury to avoid actual defeat.

After more than a year without serious competition, Moody entered the 1935 Wimbledon tournament and met Jacobs in the finals. After they split the first two sets, Jacobs took a 5–2 lead in the third, but Moody won five straight games to take the set and match. In 1938 Moody again beat Jacobs to win the singles championship at Wimbledon, her last major tournament.

A Phi Beta Kappa graduate of Stanford, Wills was an art major who wrote and illustrated an autobiography, *Tennis*, in 1928. She once said that her Phi Beta Kappa key meant more to her than all of her tennis trophies.
★ International Tennis Hall of Fame

Wills, Maury (Maurice M.)

BASEBALL
b. Oct. 2, 1932, Washington, D.C.

The switch-hitting Wills, a shortstop for most of his major league career, led the NL in stolen bases six years in a row, from 1960 through 1965. He had a high of 104 in 1962, when he also led the league with ten triples, and was named the league's most valuable player and the Associated Press male athlete of the year.

The 5-foot-11, 170-pound Wills joined the Los Angeles Dodgers during the 1959 season and became a full-time starter in 1960. He played for three pennant winners from 1963 through 1966 and starred in a seven-game World Series victory over the Minnesota Twins in 1965, batting .367 with 3 doubles, 3 stolen bases, 3 runs scored, and 3 RBI.

Wills was traded to the Pittsburgh Pirates in 1967. He began 1969 with the Montreal Expos but returned to the Dodgers during that season and retired after appearing in only 71 games in 1972.

In 1980 Wills became the manager of the AL's Seattle Mariners; he was fired before finishing the 1981 season. He was the third black manager in major league history.

Wills had a career .281 average on 2,134 hits, including 177 doubles, 71 triples, and 20 home runs. He stole 586 bases, scored 1,067 runs, and had 458 RBI.

Wilson, George ("Wildcat")

FOOTBALL
b. 1904
d. Dec. 27, 1963

Wilson was the "other halfback" with Red Grange on the 1925 All-American team. While he wasn't in Grange's class as a runner, he may well have been a better all-around football player. During his three years as a starter at the University of Washington from 1923 through 1925, the school won 28 regular season games while losing 2 and tying 2.

Washington tied Navy, 14–14, in the 1924 Rose Bowl, with Wilson scoring a touchdown. In the 1926 Rose Bowl, Alabama beat Washington, 20–19, on two touchdowns that came after Wilson left the game with a broken rib.

As tailback in the short punt formation, Wilson was often given the option to run, pass, or kick, depending on how the defense reacted.

When Grange toured with the Chicago Bears early in 1926, Wilson played against him with a Pacific Coast all-star team. Grange said afterward that nobody had ever tackled him as hard as Wilson did. That fall, Wilson played for a team nicknamed for him, the Los Angeles Wildcats, in the first American Football League.

The AFL folded after one season, and Wilson spent three years with the Providence Steamroller in the NFL. He later became a professional wrestler and toured Australia with Gus Sonnenberg.
★ College Football Hall of Fame

Wilson, Hack (Lewis R.)

BASEBALL
b. April 26, 1900, Elwood City, Pa.
d. Nov. 23, 1948

Because of his great strength, the 5-foot-6, 190-pound Wilson was nicknamed for George Hackenschmidt, a famous Russian weightlifter and wrestler in the early part of the century. He was with the NL's New York Giants for three games in 1923 and became a starting outfielder the following year.

A right-hander, Wilson was traded to the Chicago Cubs in 1926, when he led the league with 21 home runs, 69 walks, and a .539 slugging percentage. He was also the home run leader the next two seasons, with 30 in 1927 and 31 in 1928, and he had a league-leading 159 RBI in 1929.

The Cubs won the 1929 pennant and Wilson batted .471 in the World Series, but Chicago lost to the Philadelphia Athletics in five games. Wilson had a bad day in the fourth game of the Series. The Cubs were leading 8–0 going into the seventh inning, when Philadelphia cut the lead to 8–4. With two men on, Mule Haas hit a fly ball to center field and Wilson lost it in the sun, resulting in an inside-the-park home run. He later lost another fly ball in the sun and the Athletics won the game, 10–8.

Wilson had one of the greatest seasons in baseball history in 1930. He batted .356 with 56 home runs, an NL record, got 190 RBI, a major league record, and also led the league with 105 walks and a .723 slugging percentage.

After he slipped to .261 in only 112 games in 1931, the Cubs traded Wilson to the Brooklyn Dodgers. He came back somewhat with a .297 average and 23 home runs in 1932, then dropped back down to .267, and he ended his career with the Dodgers and Philadelphia Phillies in 1934.

In 1,348 games, Wilson had 1,461 hits, including 266 doubles, 67 triples, and 244 home runs. He scored 884 runs and had 1,062 RBI.
★ Baseball Hall of Fame

Wilson, Larry (Lawrence F.)

FOOTBALL
b. March 24, 1938, Rugby, Idaho

A two-way player as a halfback at the University of Utah, Wilson was tried at running back and cornerback with the NFL's St. Louis Cardinals in 1960 before being moved to free safety.

He made football history on September 17, 1961, against the New York Giants at Yankee Stadium when he ran the first safety blitz and tackled Charlie Conerly for an 11-yard loss. He blitzed several times that afternoon and had a second sack. Other teams soon began using the safety blitz.

The 6-foot, 190-pound Wilson was known as one of the league's toughest players. An excellent pass defender, he was also a fierce tackler who was more than willing to take on bigger running backs and receivers.

Wilson was named to the All-Pro team in 1963 and from 1966 through 1968. He led the league in interceptions with ten in 1966. Wilson retired after the 1972 season. In his 13 years, all with the Cardinals, he had 52 interceptions and ran them back for 800 yards, a 15.4 average, and 5 touchdowns.

★ Pro Football Hall of Fame

Wilson, Willie J.

BASEBALL
b. July 9, 1955, Montgomery, Ala.

A right-handed throwing switch-hitter, Wilson had two brief stints with the AL's Kansas City Royals in 1976 and 1977 before becoming the team's starting center fielder in 1978.

Wilson hit only .217 in his first full season but batted .303 or better the next four years, leading the league with a .332 average in 1982. He was the league leader in triples with 15 in 1980, 15 in 1982, 21 in 1985, 15 in 1987, and 11 in 1988. He also led the league with 83 stolen bases in 1979.

With his great speed, Wilson was an outstanding leadoff man even though he was a free swinger who earned few walks. He led the AL in times at bat with 705, runs scored with 133, and hits with 230 in 1980, when he also had more than 100 hits right-handed and left-handed to tie a major league record.

Wilson signed with the Oakland Athletics as a free agent after the 1990 sea-

son. He became a free agent again in 1993 and joined the NL's Chicago Cubs.

Through 1994, Wilson had a .286 average with 2,207 hits, including 281 doubles, 147 triples, and 41 home runs. He had stolen 669 bases, scored 1,169 runs, and driven in 585.

Wilt, Frederick L.

TRACK AND FIELD
b. Dec. 14, 1920, Pendleton, Ind.
d. Sept. 5, 1994

Running for Indiana University, Wilt won NCAA 2-mile and cross-country championships in 1941. After graduating in 1943, he joined the U.S. Navy, studied law at the University of Tennessee, and became an FBI agent in 1947.

Wilt won the AAU outdoor 5,000-meter championship from 1949 through 1951 and the 10,000-meter title in 1949. He was the indoor 1-mile champion in 1951, and he won the national cross-country championship in 1949, 1952, and 1953.

The winner of the 1950 Sullivan Award as the outstanding amateur athlete of the year, Wilt set a world indoor record of 8:50.7 in the 2-mile run in 1953. He retired in 1956.

★ National Track & Field Hall of Fame

Winfield, Dave (David M.)

BASEBALL
b. Oct. 3, 1951, St. Paul, Minn.

One of the finest all-around athletes ever to play in the major leagues, the 6-foot-6, 245-pound Winfield was an All-American outfielder at the University of Minnesota in 1973. After graduating he was drafted by the NFL's Minnesota Vikings, the ABA's Utah Stars, and the NBA's Atlanta Hawks, but he elected to sign with the NL's San Diego Padres.

Winfield joined the Padres in 1973 without ever playing in the minor leagues. His best season with them was 1979, when he batted .308 with 34 home runs and a league-leading 118 RBI. He became a free agent after the 1980 season and signed a multiyear, multimillion-dollar contract with the AL's New York Yankees.

After missing much of the 1981 season with an injury, Winfield had some productive years for the Yankees, but his performance was often overshadowed by an ongoing feud with owner George Steinbrenner. He batted .322 with 25 home runs and 107 RBI in 1988, then missed the entire 1989 season with a knee injury.

Winfield was traded to the California Angels during the 1990 season. He went to the Toronto Blue Jays as a free agent in 1992, helping guide Toronto to their first World Series win, and to the Minnesota Twins in 1993. Through the 1994 season he had 3,088 hits, including 535 doubles, 88 triples, and 463 home runs, with 1,658 runs scored and 1,829 RBI.

Wisniewski, Stephen A.

FOOTBALL
b. April 7, 1967, Rutland, Vt.

Wisniewski was a two-time All-American guard at Penn State, in 1987 and 1988, and was chosen by the Dallas Cowboys in the second round of the 1989 NFL draft. The Cowboys immediately traded him to the Oakland Raiders.

The 6-foot-4, 290-pounder was a backup as a rookie but moved into the starting lineup in 1990 and was an instant success. Wisniewski was named to *The Sporting News* All-NFL team from 1990 through 1993 and was also selected for the Pro Bowl all four years.

Wistert, Moose (Alvin L.)

FOOTBALL
b. June 26, 1916, Chicago, Ill.

Although the second of the three Wistert brothers in age, Alvin Wistert was the third to become an All-American tackle at Michigan. The 6-foot-3, 225-pounder dropped out of high school to work and served with the Marine Corps during World War II before entering Boston University as a 30-year-old freshman in 1946.

The following season he transferred to Michigan, where he was a UPI All-American in 1948 and 1949. The team won all ten of its regular season games in 1947 and beat the University of Southern California, 49–0, in the Rose Bowl. Wistert was named to the all-time

Rose Bowl team in a 1971 survey of sportswriters.
★ College Football Hall of Fame

Wistert, Ox (Albert A.)

FOOTBALL
b. Dec. 28, 1920, Chicago, Ill.

Wistert was named the most valuable player on the University of Michigan team that won 7 games and lost 3 in 1942, his senior season. He started at tackle for three years, during which Michigan had a 21–5–1 record.

An All-American in 1942, Wistert was co-captain of the college all-star team that beat the Washington Redskins 27–7 in 1943. He then joined the NFL's Philadelphia Eagles. An All-Pro tackle five years in a row, from 1944 through 1948, Wistert was the captain of the 1948 and 1949 teams that won NFL championships. He retired after the 1950 season.

Wistert was the second of three brothers to be All-Americans at Michigan.
★ College Football Hall of Fame

Wistert, Whitey (Francis M.)

FOOTBALL
b. Feb. 20, 1912, Chicago, Ill.
d. April, 1985

Wistert established a family tradition at the University of Michigan when he was named an All-American tackle in 1933. His two younger brothers, Albert and Alvin, were also All-American tackles at the school.

He never played serious football until he entered college, but he became a three-year starter at Michigan. During those three years, the team won 23 games, lost only 1, and tied 2. Grantland Rice, in selecting Wistert for his All-American team, wrote, "He was keen, quick, and accurate in diagnosing plays. He was a sure tackler, and it was next to impossible to fool him on trick maneuvers."

Wistert won three letters in baseball and was named most valuable player in the Western Conference (Big Ten) in 1934. After graduating, he played minor league baseball for several years.
★ College Football Hall of Fame

Wittenberg, Henry

WRESTLING

b. Sept. 18, 1918, New York, N.Y.

During his 12-year amateur wrestling career, Wittenberg won more than 400 matches and lost only 4. He won championships all seven times he entered the AAU tournament.

He began serious competitive wrestling as a student at City College of New York, where he lost only two matches, in the semifinals of the 1938 NCAA championships and the finals of the 1939 tournament. After graduating from CCNY, he represented the New York West Side YMCA.

Wittenberg was the AAU middleweight champion in 1940 and 1941. He entered the U.S. Navy in 1942 and missed the AAU championship that year and in 1945 and 1946 but was national light heavyweight champion in 1943, 1944, 1947, and 1948. He then retired for three years but returned to win another light heavyweight title in 1952.

Wittenberg won the gold medal as a light heavyweight in the 1948 Olympics and took a silver medal in the division in 1952. He coached the U.S. Olympic Greco-Roman wrestling team in 1968 and was CCNY wrestling coach from 1968 until retiring in 1978.

Wohlhuter, Rick (Richard C.)

TRACK AND FIELD

b. Dec. 23, 1948, Geneva, Ill.

Wohlhuter received the Sullivan Award as the nation's outstanding amateur athlete in 1974, when he set world records of 1:44.1 in the half mile and 2:13.9 for the 1,000-meter run. He also won the AAU national 800-meter run in an American record of 1:43.9.

As a student at Notre Dame, Wohlhuter was troubled by a variety of injuries, but he won the NCAA indoor 600-yard run as a junior in 1970 and was the outdoor 880-yard champion in 1971.

On May 12, 1972, Wohlhuter ran a 1:44.8 anchor leg when the University of Chicago Track Club set a world record of 7:10.4 for the 2-mile relay. Fifteen days later, he set a world record of 1:44.6

for the 800-meter run; his previous best had been 1:49.0.

Wohlhuter finished second in the 800-meter at the 1972 Olympic trials but fell during a heat and failed to qualify for the Olympic finals. In 1976 he won a bronze medal in the 800-meter but finished a disappointing sixth in the 1,500-meter.

He was the national 800-meter champion in 1973 and 1974 and he won the national indoor 1,000-yard title from 1974 through 1976. Wohlhuter retired in 1977.

★ National Track & Field Hall of Fame

Wojciechowicz, Alexander F.

FOOTBALL

b. Aug. 12, 1915, South River, N.J.
d. July 13, 1992

A center, the 6-foot, 235-pound Wojciechowicz anchored Fordham University's famous line, the "Seven Blocks of Granite," in 1936 and 1937. He was a consensus All-American both seasons. The team gave up only 90 points in 25 games during his three seasons as a starter. Fast and agile despite his size, Wojciechowicz won a 1936 game against Georgia by taking a lateral after a completed pass and running 45 yards for a touchdown.

He joined the NFL's Detroit Lions in 1938 and immediately became a starter, playing center on offense and linebacker on defense. Often assigned to cover the opposition's best pass receiver, Wojciechowicz intercepted seven passes in 1944, a Detroit record at the time.

The Lions released him during the 1946 season and he was picked up by the Philadelphia Eagles. Used primarily on defense, he played for championship teams in 1948 and 1949. Wojciechowicz retired after the 1950 season with 16 interceptions, which he returned for 142 yards.

★ College Football Hall of Fame; Pro Football Hall of Fame

Wood, Barry (William Barry Jr.)

FOOTBALL

b. May 4, 1910, Milton, Mass.
d. March 9, 1971

Wood was the star signal-caller, passer, and kicker on Harvard teams that beat Yale twice, 10–6 in 1929 and 13–0 in 1930. However, Yale won 3–0 in 1931, Wood's senior season. The 6-foot-1, 173-pound quarterback first won public notice as a sophomore in 1929 when he threw a 50-yard touchdown pass and kicked the extra point to tie Army, 20–20, in the closing minutes.

Named an All-American in 1931 by Grantland Rice and the Associated Press, Wood also won letters in tennis, baseball, and hockey. He was a member of the 1932 Davis Cup tennis team.

★ College Football Hall of Fame

Wood, Craig R.

GOLF
b. Nov. 18, 1901, Lake Placid, N.Y.
d. May 8, 1968

A long hitter, Wood was often referred to as the "bridesmaid" because of his second-place finishes in major tournaments. He became a professional in 1925, when he won the Kentucky Open, and he won the Kentucky PGA title the following year.

Wood was the runner-up in the 1933 British Open and in the Masters and PGA championship in 1934. He finished the 1935 Masters as a leader but placed second again after Gene Sarazen scored a double eagle on the 15th hole of the final round. In 1939, Wood birdied the final hole of the U.S. Open to tie Byron Nelson and Denny Shute. Nelson and wood both shot rounds of 68 in the first playoff, eliminating Shute, and Nelson beat Wood, 70–73, in the second playoff.

He finally won a major tournament, the Masters, in 1941 at the age of 39. Because of a back problem, he wore a restrictive corset in the U.S. Open later that year and wanted to withdraw after taking a 7 on the 1st hole. He was persuaded to continue, and he shot a 284 to win by 3 strokes.

Wood retired from serious competition in 1945 and ran an auto dealership for nearly 20 years before returning to golf as a teaching pro.

★ PGA Hall of Fame

Wood, Timothy L.

FIGURE SKATING
b. June 21, 1948, Highland Park, Mich.

A brilliant free skater, Wood sometimes had trouble with the compulsory figures, which counted for a much bigger portion of the score in his era than they do now.

He was a freshman at John Carroll University in Ohio when he won the first of three straight national singles championships in 1968. He won a silver medal in the Winter Olympics, finishing just behind surprise winner Wolfgang Schwarz of Austria. Wood was third in the world championships that year.

Wood won the world championship in 1969 and 1970. In 1969, he received three perfect scores of 6.0 and eight scores of 5.9 on his free skating program. The following year, he had two perfect scores for technical merit, one for artistic expression, and a total of 13 scores of 5.9.

He joined the Ice Capades after his second world title.

Wood, Willie (William V.)

FOOTBALL
b. Dec. 23, 1936, Washington, D.C.

At 5-foot-10 and 185 pounds, Wood was not drafted out of the University of Southern California in 1960, so he wrote letters to every NFL team asking for a tryout. Only the Green Bay Packers responded. Wood caught the eye of coach Vince Lombardi by chinning himself on the goalpost crossbar, ten feet above the ground, after an early workout.

Wood stuck with the team and became the starting free safety in 1961, when he intercepted 5 passes, returning 2 of them for touchdowns. He led the league with 9 interceptions in 1962.

In Super Bowl I, Wood had a key interception. The Packers were winning 14–10 in the third quarter when he picked off a Len Dawson pass and returned it to the Kansas City Chiefs' five-yard line, setting up a touchdown that gave Green Bay control of the game. They went on to win 35–10.

Wood retired after playing as a backup in 1971. He became head coach of the Philadelphia Bell of the World Football League in 1975. The league folded after that season. Wood then went to the Montreal Alouettes of the Canadian Football League as an assistant coach and was named head coach in 1980. He was replaced during the 1981 season.

In his 12 NFL seasons, all with the Packers, Wood had 48 interceptions and returned four of them for touchdowns. He returned 187 punts for 1,391 yards, a 7.4 average, and 2 touchdowns.

★ Pro Football Hall of Fame

Woodard, Lynette
BASKETBALL
b. Aug. 12, 1959, Wichita, Kans.

College basketball's all-time leading woman scorer with 3,649 points, Woodard was a four-time All-American at the University of Kansas, from 1978 through 1981, and she won the Wade Trophy and Broderick Award in 1981 as the outstanding player of the year.

Woodard led the nation in rebounding as a freshman in 1977–78 and in steals during her last three years, from 1978–79 through 1980–81. She played for U.S. national teams that won gold medals in the 1979 World University Games, the 1983 Pan-American Games, and the 1984 Olympics. She was also named to the 1980 Olympic team that didn't play because of the U.S. boycott of the Moscow Games.

After graduating from Kansas in 1981, Woodard played in Italy for a year, leading the league in scoring, and served as a volunteer assistant coach while working for her master's degree. She later played for the Columbus, Ohio, team in the short-lived Women's American Basketball Association. In 1985 she became the first woman to play for the Harlem Globetrotters.

Wooden, John R.
BASKETBALL
b. Oct. 14, 1910, Martinsville, Ind.

As a 5-foot-10, 183-pound guard at Purdue University, Wooden was a three-time All-American, from 1930 through 1932, and was retroactively named the 1932 player of the year by the Helms Athletic Foundation. He was nicknamed the "India Rubber Man" because his drives to the basket "often sent him bouncing off the fieldhouse floor or flying into the seventh row of the Purdue band," as *Time* magazine put it.

After graduating in 1932, Wooden became a high school coach while also playing semipro and professional basketball for Kautsky's Athletic Club and the Hammond Ciesars in the National Basketball League.

Wooden had a 218–42 record in high school before entering military service in 1943. He moved into college coaching with Indiana State after being discharged in 1946. His first team had an 18–7 record and was invited to the NAIA tournament, but Wooden turned it down because Indiana State had a black player and the NAIA had an all-white policy at the time.

Indiana State was 29–7 in 1947–48; this time Wooden accepted the NAIA invitation because blacks were allowed to play. His team lost to the University of Louisville in the championship game.

UCLA, which had never had much of a basketball program, hired Wooden in the fall of 1948. He announced to his players, "The fast break is my system. We'll win fifty percent of our games by outrunning the other team in the last five minutes." To that end, he stressed conditioning as well as fundamentals in his practices.

Wooden's 22–7 record in his first season was the best in UCLA history, and he turned out winners for the rest of his career. His glory years began in 1964, when he won his first NCAA championship with a team that averaged only 6-foot-5 in height but won 30 consecutive games.

UCLA won the NCAA title again in 1965 and then, after missing a year, won seven consecutive championships from 1967 through 1973. The first three of those teams were led by Lew Alcindor, later known as Kareem Abdul-Jabbar. With Alcindor gone, UCLA was ranked second in the country after the 1969–1970 regular season but won a fourth straight title behind Curtis Rowe and Sidney Wicks.

Rowe and Wicks spearheaded the 1971 championship, and then Bill Walton arrived at UCLA to become college basketball's dominating player for two more championship years. UCLA lost in the 1974 semifinals but won a tenth title in 1975, after which Wooden retired.

The only coach to win more than four NCAA championships, Wooden built his success not only on the fast break but on the 2–2–1 full-court zone press, which put constant pressure on opponents, forcing turnovers and quick baskets.

His UCLA teams set records that will probably never be broken, including their seven consecutive national championships, an 88-game winning streak, 38 consecutive victories in NCAA tournament play, and four seasons in which they won all 30 of their games. Wooden's overall college record of 664 wins and 162 losses places him seventh all-time in victories and fourth all-time with an .804 winning percentage.

Wooden is the only person named to the Basketball Hall of Fame as both a player and a coach. A deacon in the First Christian Church who doesn't smoke, drink, or use profanity, he projected an image that was a little too good for some critics.

A rival coach, Digger Phelps, once said of him, "He rides officials and players more than any other coach I've seen. That's so bush-league for a man of his stature, yet no referee has the nerve to reprimand him."

★ Basketball Hall of Fame

Woodruff, George W.

FOOTBALL
b. Feb. 22, 1864, Dimock, Pa.
d. March 23, 1934

Perhaps the most inventive coach during football's primitive years, Woodruff was a starting guard at Yale for four years, from 1885 through 1888. He also lettered in track and crew and was a Phi Beta Kappa student.

Woodruff was hired by the University of Pennsylvania as one of the first paid football coaches in 1892. Although he became known for his offensive innovations, his first major contribution to football was on defense. Teams at that time usually played their defensive ends near the sidelines to keep a runner from breaking loose. But Woodruff moved his ends in to within a couple of yards of the tackles and had them charge into the offensive backfield, attempting to disrupt the play before it could get going, while his defensive backs protected the outside.

In that era, a punt was a free kick that could be recovered and advanced by the kicking team. Woodruff took advantage of the rule by using a quick kick by his quarterback, sending his other backs downfield to get the ball.

His greatest innovations were the guards back formation and flying interference. Again, the rules of the day made the innovations possible. There was no requirement that seven offensive players be on the line of scrimmage, and there was no rule against offensive players being in motion when the ball was snapped.

In the guards back formation, both guards would move into the backfield in tandem beside the quarterback, and they were usually used as blockers ahead of the runner. Devised in 1894, the formation was so powerful that it was copied by most other teams and was predominant in football until about 1900.

Woodruff also probably introduced the idea of having most of his offensive players move toward the point of attack when the ball was snapped, although Amos Alonzo Stagg disputed the claim. In any event, the mass momentum plays caused by flying interference created so many injuries that major rule changes went into effect in 1906, among them the legalization of the forward pass.

Despite a record of 134 wins, 15 losses, and 2 ties in ten seasons, Woodruff was fired after the 1901 season because he had lost three straight games to Harvard. He had an 8–6 record at the University of Illinois in 1903 and was 10–4 at the Carlisle Indian School in 1905.

Woodruff practiced law throughout

his coaching career. He served as acting U.S. Secretary of the Interior in 1907 and was Pennsylvania's attorney general from 1923 to 1927.

★ College Football Hall of Fame

Woodruff, Hiram W.

HARNESS RACING
b. Feb. 22, 1817, Birmingham, N.J.
d. March 15, 1867

Woodruff came from one of the pioneer families of harness racing. His father was superintendent of the Harlem Track, the first oval harness course in the country, and his uncle ran the first major harness track in Philadelphia.

Called the "Napoleon of the Trotting Turf" by the sporting press, Woodruff began racing when trotting horses were still raced under saddle. He became famous in 1838 with the great Dutchman, who trotted three miles under harness in 7:41, shattering the old record of 8:07.

Thousands of spectators gathered at the Beacon Course in Hoboken, New Jersey, in 1839 to watch Woodruff drive Dutchman to another record of 7:32½, which stood for 33 years.

An owner, breeder, and trainer as well as a driver, his last great horse was Dexter. When Dexter was a yearling, Woodruff said, "Here is the horse that will make the best trotter we have ever seen, the king of the world." Woodruff died after Dexter had won 49 of his first 53 races.

Woodruff, John Y.

TRACK AND FIELD
b. July 5, 1915, Connellsville, Pa.

Nicknamed "Long John" because of his stride, the 6-foot-3 Woodruff was the first black American runner to succeed at distances beyond the sprints. He dominated the 800-meter/880-yard run for four years. After a loss in July 1936, he won every race he entered until his retirement in 1940, when he was only 25.

Woodruff won a track scholarship to the University of Pittsburgh in 1935. Because he was one of 12 children in a very poor family, people in his hometown donated money to buy him clothes for college.

He ran the anchor legs on teams that set world records in the 2-mile and 3,200-meter relays in 1936, but his first major individual victory came in the Olympics that year. The inexperienced Woodruff was so thoroughly boxed in early in the race that he had to slow almost to a stop to get clear of other runners. Then he surged into the lead but lost it and became boxed in again. Running wide around a pack of competitors coming into the homestretch, Woodruff took the lead once more and held it, winning the gold medal in 1:52.9.

Woodruff won the IC4A 440-yard and 880-yard runs from 1937 through 1939, and he was also the NCAA 880-yard champion in those years. He entered the AAU national meet only once, winning the 880-yard run in 1937.

Woodruff ran a world record of 1:47.8 in the 800-yard run, but it was later discovered that the track was five feet short and the record was disallowed. In 1940 he set a world indoor record of 1:47.6.

After graduating from Pittsburgh in 1939, Woodruff earned a master's degree at New York University. He retired from running after the 1940 Olympic games were canceled because of World War II and became a career Army officer, retiring in 1958 with the rank of lieutenant colonel.

★ National Track & Field Hall of Fame

Woodson, Roderick K.

FOOTBALL
b. March 10, 1965, Ft. Wayne, Ind.

An excellent high hurdler as well as a football player at Purdue University, Woodson was named the kick returner on *The Sporting News* 1986 All-American team and was selected for several other All-American teams as a defensive back.

Chosen by the Pittsburgh Steelers in the first round of the 1987 NFL draft, Woodson held out for a bigger contract until midseason and was used mainly as a kick returner when he finally reported.

In 1988 he became a starter at cornerback. The 6-foot, 200-pound Woodson quickly demonstrated outstanding ability in man-to-man coverage. He has not had high interception totals because teams are reluctant to throw into his area.

Woodson led the league in 1989 with 27.3 yards per kickoff return, running back 36 kicks for 982 yards and 1 touchdown.

He became a free agent in 1991 but was re-signed by the Steelers during training camp. His new salary was reportedly the highest ever paid to a defensive back.

Through 1994, Woodson had intercepted 42 passes and returned them for 658 yards and 3 touchdowns; had run back 218 punts for 2,043 yards, a 9.5 average, and 2 touchdowns; and had returned 205 kickoffs for 4,529 yards, a 22.1 average, and 2 touchdowns.

Woodson, Warren V.

FOOTBALL
b. Feb. 24, 1903, Ft. Worth, Tex.

Woodson played basketball, football, and tennis at Baylor University, graduating in 1924, and spent two years completing graduate work at Springfield College in Massachusetts. After compiling a 40–13–6 record as football coach at Texarkana Junior College from 1927 through 1934, he took over at Arkansas State Teachers' College.

In six seasons there, Woodson had a 40–8–3 record; then he coached at Hardin-Simmons College in Texas in 1941 and 1942. After three years of military service, Woodson returned to Hardin-Simmons in 1946 and remained there through 1951. Hardin-Simmons had undefeated teams in 1942 and 1946, winning 58 games while losing 24 and tying 6 under his guidance.

Woodson became football coach at the University of Arizona in 1952, compiling a 26–22–2 record in five seasons before going to New Mexico State University in 1957. He retired after the 1962 season with a 63–36–3 record. However, he returned to coaching at Trinity College in Texas in 1972 and had a 16–5–0 mark there. Woodson retired perma-

nently after coaching New Mexico Highlands to a 4–4–0 record in 1974.

A strong believer in the running attack, Woodson coached seven players who led the nation in rushing. He had an overall 207–99–14 record for a .669 winning percentage. Woodson ranks ninth all-time in victories.

Woolpert, Philip

BASKETBALL
b. Dec. 19, 1915, Los Angeles, Calif.

Woolpert played basketball at Loyola University in Los Angeles, graduating in 1938, and later served as freshman coach at his alma mater. He became head coach at the University of San Francisco in 1950.

After three losing seasons, Woolpert had a 14–7 record in 1954. He then produced two NCAA championship teams led by Bill Russell and K. C. Jones. USF won 60 consecutive games from 1954–55 into the 1956–57 season.

A believer in defense, Woolpert was a critic of the fast break. "It just isn't good basketball," he once said. "I wouldn't know how to go about coaching it." After Russell and Jones graduated in 1956, Woolpert had records of 21–7 and 25–2 over the next two seasons.

He left USF to become athletic director at the University of San Diego in 1959. In just nine years as a head coach, he had a 153–78 record.
★ Basketball Hall of Fame

Worsley, Gump (Lorne)

HOCKEY
b. May 14, 1929, Montreal, P.Q.

A great goaltender, Worsley had a strange NHL career with three teams. He joined the league's New York Rangers in 1952 but spent most of the season with Vancouver in the Western Hockey League, where he was named most valuable player.

In 1953–54, he became the Rangers' chief goaltender. Playing for poor clubs in New York, Worsley was once asked what team in the NHL gave him the most trouble and he responded, "The New York Rangers."

The Rangers traded Worsley to the Montreal Canadiens in 1963 but, at 34, he spent most of the year with a Quebec minor league team. He was called back up to Montreal in 1964 and shared two Vezina Trophies there, with Charlie Hodge in 1966 and Rogatien Vachon in 1968.

Worsley hated flying. When the Canadiens were traveling to a game in Los Angeles in November 1968, they had a bumpy flight from Montreal to Chicago, and Worsley refused to get on the flight to Los Angeles. He took a train to Montreal and was given a month off. After announcing his retirement on New Year's Eve, he eventually rejoined the team.

The Canadiens wanted to send him to the minor leagues once more in early 1970 because he was out of shape, but he refused to go and was traded to the Minnesota North Stars. Worsley retired permanently in January 1973.

In 21 NHL seasons and 860 regular season games, Worsley had 43 shutouts and a 2.91 goals against average. He had 5 shutouts and a 2.82 average in 70 playoff games.

Hockey Hall of Fame

Worthy, James A.

BASKETBALL
b. Feb. 27, 1961, Gastonia, N.C.

After leading the University of North Carolina to the NCAA basketball championship as a junior in 1982, when he was named the tournament's outstanding player, Worthy chose to enter the NBA draft and was chosen by the Los Angeles Lakers in the first round.

Because of his speed, Worthy is an excellent wing man on the fast break and uses quick, gliding moves to get to the basket despite his 6-foot-9, 225-pound size. He made the NBA All-Rookie team in 1982–83, averaging 13.4 points a game as a part-time player, and became a starting forward in 1984–85. Worthy has averaged more than 19 points per game in seven of his 11 seasons with the Lakers. An injury limited him to 54 games in 1991–92, and he be-

came a part-time player again the following season.

Through the 1993–94 season, Worthy had scored 16,320 points in 926 regular season games, a 17.6 average. He also had 4,708 rebounds. In 143 playoff games, he scored 3,022 points, a 21.1 average, and had 747 rebounds. Worthy was named most valuable of the NBA championship finals in 1988, when he averaged 21.1 points per game in the playoffs.

Wottle, David J.

TRACK AND FIELD
b. Aug. 7, 1950, Canton, Ohio

Easily identifiable by the golf cap he always wore when running, Wottle aspired to be a miler but was better at the half-mile/800-meter run. As a student at Bowling Green State University in Ohio, he won the U.S. Track and Field Federation mile in 1970.

Injuries kept him out of action for most of 1971, but in 1972 he won NCAA championships in the outdoor 1,500-meter run and the indoor 880-yard run. Wottle also won the AAU outdoor 800-meter run and tied the world record of 1:44.3 at the Olympic trials, where he qualified for both the 800- and 1,500-meter events.

He viewed the shorter race as little more than a tune-up for the 1,500-meter, and he was running last in the Olympic finals with just 200 meters to go. He put on a burst of speed to move into second place, and when leader Yevgeny Arzhanov stumbled while approaching the finish line, Wottle passed him to win the gold medal in 1:45.9.

Because of his surprise, Wottle forgot to take off his golf cap during the medal ceremony. Asked afterward if he wore it as some kind of protest, he burst into tears and apologized to the American people. A day later he was eliminated in the semifinals of the 1,500-meter run.

In 1973 Wottle won the NCAA 1-mile run both indoors and outdoors. After a brief professional running career, he became track coach at Bethany College in West Virginia.

Wrenn, Robert D.

TENNIS
b. Sept. 20, 1872, Highland Park, N.J.
d. Nov. 12, 1925

Wrenn won the first national inter-scholastic tennis championship in 1891 before entering Harvard, where he was a quarterback on the football team, a second baseman on the baseball team, and the cover point on the hockey team in the days of seven-man hockey.

A left-hander, Wrenn won the inter-collegiate doubles title with Fred H. Hovey in 1891 and with F. D. Winslow in 1892. He was the U.S. national singles champion in 1893, 1894, 1896, and 1897, and he teamed with Malcolm Chace to win the doubles championship in 1895.

From 1912 through 1915, Wrenn was president of the U.S. Lawn Tennis Association.

★ International Tennis Hall of Fame

Wright, Beals C.

TENNIS
b. Dec. 19, 1879, Boston, Mass.
d. Aug. 23, 1961

The nephew of Harry Wright, organizer of the first all-professional baseball team, and son of George Wright, an early baseball player and cofounder of the Wright and Ditson Sporting Goods company, Wright won a gold medal in the tennis singles at the 1904 Olympics and teamed with E. W. Leonard to win the doubles title.

Wright was the U.S. national singles champion in 1905. He and Holcombe Ward won three consecutive doubles titles from 1904 through 1906.

★ International Tennis Hall of Fame

Wright, George

BASEBALL
b. Jan. 28, 1847, Yonkers, N.Y.
d. Aug. 21, 1937

The son of an English cricket player who came to the U.S. in 1836, Wright began playing baseball in 1864 with the New York Gothams. He joined the Washington Nationals, one of the best teams of the era, in 1867. Though billed as an amateur team, the Nationals were probably at least semi-professional, but in that era few players wanted to admit they received money for a sport.

George's brother, Harry, who was 12 years older, in 1869 organized the first admittedly all-professional team, the Cincinnati Red Stockings. George was paid $1,800 to play shortstop.

The Red Stockings won all 57 of their games throughout the Midwest and the East in 1869. They stretched their winning streak to 130 games in 1870, finally losing to the Brooklyn Atlantics on June 14. The team broke up and Harry organized a Boston team to play in the new National Association, the first major league, in 1871.

George batted .412, .341, .388, .339, and .333 in the five years of the association's existence, leading Boston to the last four pennants. After the association was replaced by the NL, the Boston team entered the new league, with Harry as manager and George at shortstop.

In 1879, George went to the Providence Grays as playing manager. He spent one season there, then returned to Boston to help manage the Wright and Ditson Sporting Goods company, which he had cofounded in 1872. Originally a retail store for "cigars and base balls," the firm had become a manufacturer of equipment for several sports.

George did play a game for the Boston team in 1880, and he appeared in seven games the following year. When Harry took over as manager at Providence in 1882, George joined him for 46 games but batted only .162 and retired.

George did not end his involvement with baseball, however. He backed the Boston team in the short-lived Union Association in 1884 and became the umpire on the world tour organized by Albert G. Spalding in 1888. Wright also served on the committee that helped plan the Baseball Hall of Fame in Cooperstown.

★ Baseball Hall of Fame

Wright, Harry (William Henry)

BASEBALL

b. Jan. 10, 1835, Sheffield, England
d. Oct. 3, 1895

Wright's family moved to the U.S. when he was a year old, but he grew up playing cricket because his father was a cricketer. In 1858 he began to play the outfield for the Knickerbocker Base Ball Club.

Cricket and baseball were rivals for popularity until some years after the Civil War, and in 1865 Wright took a job as a cricket instructor in Cincinnati. He organized the Cincinnati Red Stockings, an amateur baseball club, the following year.

By 1869 Wright was concentrating on baseball. He turned the Red Stockings into the first true professional team, signing the best players he could find, including his younger brother, George, who played shortstop. The Red Stockings toured the Midwest and East, winning 130 consecutive games in 1869 and 1870.

When the National Association of Professional Base Ball Players, the first major league, was organized in 1871, Harry became manager of the Boston team, with George again at shortstop. The team finished third in the league's first season, then won four straight championships.

Wright played fairly regularly from 1871 through 1874 but appeared in only one game in 1875. The National Association folded after that season and Wright helped organize the NL, becoming manager of the new league's Boston franchise. Boston won pennants in 1877 and 1878.

In 1882 both Wrights went to the Providence Grays, Harry as manager and George, as usual, to play shortstop. Harry resigned in 1884 to take over the Philadelphia NL team. He managed there until 1894, when he became the league's chief of umpires, serving in that job until his death shortly after the 1895 season.

★ Baseball Hall of Fame

Wright, Mickey (Mary K.)

GOLF

b. Feb. 14, 1935, San Diego, Calif.

Wright began playing golf when she was 11 years old, was shooting in the 80s at 13, and won the southern California girls' championship at 14. In 1954 she won the world amateur title and was the low amateur at the U.S. Women's Open.

Babe Didrikson Zaharias, who won the Open that year, saw Wright practicing and said to her husband, "I didn't think anyone but the Babe could hit 'em like that. If I'm around five years from now, I'll have my hands full."

In 1955, Wright left Stanford University to join the LPGA tour. She won 79 tournaments from 1959 through 1968, including all three majors, the Women's Open, the LPGA championship, and the Titleholders championship, in 1961.

Wright won the Open in 1958, 1959, and 1964 and the LPGA in 1958, 1960, and 1964. She is the only woman to win both events in two different years, and she shares a record of four Open victories with Betsy Rawls. From 1960 through 1964, Wright won the Vare Trophy for the lowest strokes per round average. She was the tour's leading money winner four years in a row, 1961 through 1964.

During the 1963 season, Wright won 13 of 32 tournaments, a record, and had $31,269 in winnings. Today the same events would be worth more than $700,000. She was named female athlete of the year by the Associated Press that year and again in 1964, and *Golf* magazine chose her as woman golfer of the decade 1958–1967.

The 5-foot-9, 145-pound Wright, whose swing was often described as "perfect," left the tour in 1969 because of foot problems and an adverse reaction to sunlight. She resumed her studies at Southern Methodist University.

Wright was considered the LPGA's answer to Arnold Palmer because she drew large galleries and a large television audience at a time when golf was becoming a popular television sport. As Judy Rankin put it, "Mickey got the outside world to take a second hard look at women golfers, and when they looked they saw the rest of us."

★ International Women's Sports Hall of Fame; LPGA Hall of Fame; World Golf Hall of Fame

Wrightson, Bernie (Bernard C.)

DIVING
b. June 25, 1944, Phoenix, Ariz.

Wrightson was third in the 1968 Olympic springboard diving competition with only three dives remaining, but he performed spectacularly on three difficult dives to win the gold medal.

As a student at Arizona State University, Wrightson won the NCAA springboard championship. He tied Gary Tobian's record of seven AAU national outdoor championships, winning the 1-meter springboard from 1964 through 1966, the 3-meter springboard in 1964, 1965, and 1968, and the platform event in 1965. He was the indoor 3-meter springboard champion in 1966.

Wykoff, Frank C.

TRACK AND FIELD
b. Oct. 29, 1909, Des Moines, Iowa
d. Jan. 1, 1980

Shortly after graduating from Glendale, California, High School, Wykoff won the AAU national 100-meter championship in 1928, qualifying for the Olympic team. He finished fourth in the event at the Olympics, but won a gold medal as a member of the 4 x 100-meter relay team.

After a year at Glendale Junior College, Wykoff entered the University of Southern California in 1929. On May 10, 1930, he became the first man to run the 100-yard dash in 9.4 seconds, winning the NCAA championship. He also won the NCAA title in 1931, the IC4A 100-yard championship from 1930 through 1932, and the AAU national title in 1931. Wykoff ran the anchor leg on the USC 440-yard relay team that set a world record of 40.8 seconds in 1931.

Despite a serious back injury, Wykoff qualified for the 1932 Olympic relay team by finishing fourth in the 100-meter trials; he won his second gold medal as a member of that team. He competed

only sporadically for the next two years and temporarily retired in 1935. However, he returned in 1936 and once again won a gold medal in the Olympic relay, anchoring the U.S. team to a world record 39.8 seconds. That record stood until 1956.

★ National Track & Field Hall of Fame; Olympic Hall of Fame

Wynn, Early ("Gus")

BASEBALL
b. Jan. 6, 1920, Hartford, Ala.

After recovering from a broken leg suffered in a high school football game, Wynn decided to play baseball instead. He did so well that he was offered a contract for $100 a month to pitch in the Washington Senators' minor league system, and he left school after his junior year.

Wynn was with the Senators briefly in 1939 and 1941 and became a regular starter in 1942. He had an 18–12 record in 1943 but slipped to 8–17 in 1944 before entering the Army in September. When he returned to the Senators during the 1946 season he was 8–5, and he had a 17–15 record in 1947.

After winning 8 and losing 19 in 1948, Wynn was traded to the Cleveland Indians. Originally a fastball and knuckleball pitcher, he now added a curve to his repertoire and began to accumulate victories. After an 11–7 record in 1949, he was 18–8 in 1950, leading the league with a 3.20 ERA. He went 20–13 and 23–12 the next two seasons.

Wynn led the AL in victories with a 23–11 record in 1954, when the Indians won the pennant. He lost his only start in Cleveland's four-game World Series defeat by the New York Giants. After going 17–11, 20–9, and 14–17 in the his last three years with Cleveland, Wynn was traded to the Chicago White Sox.

The Chicago manager was Al Lopez, who had managed the Indians to their pennant. Lopez liked Wynn because of his toughness and determination. After a 14–16 record in 1958, Wynn took the Cy Young Award in 1959, when he led the league in victories with a 22–10 record. He went 1–1 in a six-game World Series loss to the Los Angeles Dodgers.

That was his last really good season, but Wynn held on in an attempt to reach 300 victories. After 13–12 and 8–2 records over the next two years, he struggled to a 7–15 mark in 1962 and was released. In June 1963, the Indians re-signed him. He lost his first two decisions but finally won his 300th game on July 12. It was his last victory.

The 6-foot, 235-pound Wynn could be an intimidating pitcher, not just because of his size but because of his willingness to throw at or near hitters. He once said he would throw at his grandmother to back her off the plate if she could hit a curve.

In 23 seasons, Wynn was 300–244 with 49 shutouts and a 3.54 ERA. He struck out 2,334 hitters and walked 1,775 in 4,564 innings.

★ Baseball Hall of Fame

Yamaguchi, Kristi T.

FIGURE SKATING
b. July 12, 1971, Hayward, Calif.

Yamaguchi fell in love with figure skating in 1976, when she watched on television as Dorothy Hamill won the gold medal in women's singles.

For years, she skated pairs as well as singles and won titles in both at the 1988 world junior championships. But in 1990 she decided that double practice sessions were preventing her from reaching her full potential, and she began to concentrate on singles skating.

After finishing second in the national championships and fourth in the worlds in 1990, Yamaguchi finished second to Jill Trenary in the 1991 nationals but won the world title. She followed that with a rare triple in 1992, when she won the national, world, and Olympic championships.

The 5-foot, 90-pound Yamaguchi is an unusual combination of grace and athleticism. Her free skating program was very difficult, incorporating as many as seven triple jumps, yet her elegant style made it seem virtually effortless.

Although she hinted that she might be back for the 1994 Winter Olympics, Yamaguchi turned professional instead. She has said she much prefers the pleasure of skating to entertain fans to the pressures of competitive skating.

Yarborough, Cale (William Caleb)

AUTO RACING
b. March 27, 1939, Timmonsville, S.C.

Yarborough spent most of his early career eking out a living in sportsman racing in South Carolina. After working as a carpenter with the Holman-Moody racing operation for a time, he got a chance to race in 1965. He won only once but finished in the top ten 34 times and earned $25,140 in purses.

He won his first major race at Atlanta in 1967 and later that year won the Firecracker 400 at the finish line. In sixteen super-speedway races, he was in the top five seven times.

In 1968, Yarborough won a record six super-speedway events, two of them — the Daytona 500 and the Southern 500 — by one second. In the early 1970s, Yarborough did some flirting with USAC racing, but he returned to NASCAR full-time late in 1972.

Yarborough was the national driving champion three consecutive years, 1976 through 1978, the only NASCAR driver ever to do so. He won the Daytona 500 in 1977, 1983, and 1984. He's the only driver to win four times at Daytona; Richard Petty did it seven times.

Though known as a daring and hard-charging driver, Yarborough set an unusual record by starting and finishing every Winston Cup Race in 1977. He won the International Race of Champions in 1984.

After 1980, Yarborough began to cut down on his schedule, entering only sixteen events a year. He became a team owner in 1986 and retired from driving in 1989.

An all-around athlete, Yarborough

briefly attended Clemson University on a football scholarship and later played professional football. Twice he was the South Carolina Golden Gloves welterweight champion.

Yary, Ron (Anthony Ronald)
FOOTBALL
b. Aug. 16, 1946, Chicago, Ill.

The 6-foot-6, 255-pound Yary was a two-time All-American tackle at the University of Southern California and he won the 1967 Outland Award and Knute Rockne Memorial Trophy as the nation's outstanding collegiate lineman. He was the premier blocker in a line that cleared the way for O. J. Simpson.

Yary joined the NFL's Minnesota Vikings as the first player chosen in the 1968 draft. Primarily a run blocker in college, Yary became an outstanding pass blocker in a Minnesota offense that reversed traditional philosophy by using the pass to set up the run.

An All-Pro from 1971 through 1977, Yary played in seven Pro Bowls and four Super Bowls. He was with the Vikings through 1981 and played for the Los Angeles Rams in 1982 before retiring.
★ College Football Hall of Fame

Yastrzemski, Carl M.
BASEBALL
b. Aug. 22, 1939, Southampton, N.Y.

When Yastrzemski joined the AL's Boston Red Sox in 1961, he was heralded as the successor to Ted Williams, not an easy role to fill. Yastrzemski didn't fill it — no one could have — but he developed into a different kind of great player who was elected to the Hall of Fame in his first year of eligibility.

The 5-foot-11, 182-pounder was, like Williams, a left-handed hitting and right-handed throwing outfielder. He had his first outstanding season in 1963, when he led the league with 183 hits, 40 doubles, 95 walks, and a .321 batting average.

After leading in doubles again with 45 in 1965 and 39 in 1966, Yastrzemski had his greatest season in 1967. He won the triple crown with a .326 average, 44

home runs, and 121 RBI, also leading the league with 112 runs, 189 hits, and a .622 slugging percentage.

He also made some outstanding defensive plays to help the Red Sox win the 1967 pennant and he batted .400 with 3 home runs, 5 RBI, and 4 runs scored in their seven-game World Series loss to the St. Louis Cardinals. "Yaz," as Boston fans knew him, was named the league's most valuable player and the Associated Press male athlete of the year.

Yastrzemski won just one more batting title, with a .301 average in 1968, and he was the league leader in runs with 125 in 1970 and 93 in 1974, but he performed consistently well until injuries began to slow him in 1980. He retired after hitting .266 in 119 games in 1983.

An excellent defensive outfielder with a strong, accurate arm, Yastrzemski was a master at playing the short left field wall in Boston's Fenway Park. He set a record by leading AL outfielders in assists seven times. When he retired, he was second all-time in games played and seventh in career hits.

In his 23 seasons, all with the Red Sox, Yastrzemski had 3,419 hits, with 646 doubles, 59 triples, and 452 home runs. He scored 1,816 runs and drove in 1,844.
★ Baseball Hall of Fame

York, Janice Lee [Mrs. Romary]
FENCING
b. Aug. 6, 1928, Calif.

York was a member of six Olympic teams, from 1948 through 1968. She reached the finals of the fencing tournament in 1952 and 1956, finishing fourth both times, and in 1968 she became the first woman to carry the American flag at the opening ceremonies.

She was the national women's foil champion in 1950, 1951, 1956, 1957, 1960, 1961, 1964, 1965, 1966, and 1968.

York, Rudy (Preston Rudolph)
BASEBALL
b. Aug. 17, 1913, Ragland, Ala.
d. Feb. 5, 1970

A strong right-handed hitter, the 6-

foot-1, 209-pound York was with the AL's Detroit Tigers briefly in 1934 but didn't join the team permanently until 1937, when he hit 35 home runs with 103 RBI in only 104 games.

Originally a catcher, York was moved to first base in 1940. He batted .316 with 33 home runs and 134 RBI that year to help lead the Tigers to a pennant. In 1943, York led the AL with 34 home runs, 118 RBI, and a .527 slugging percentage.

His production began to decline in 1944 and he was traded to the Boston Red Sox in 1946. The Red Sox traded him to the Chicago White Sox during the 1947 season, and he ended his career with the Philadelphia Athletics in 1948.

In 1,603 games, York batted .275 with 1,621 hits, including 291 doubles, 52 triples, and 277 home runs. He scored 876 runs and had 1,152 RBI.

Yorzyk, Bill (William A.)

SWIMMING
b. May 29, 1933, Northampton, Mass.

When the butterfly stroke was added to the Olympic swimming program in 1956, Yorzyk became the first champion, winning the 200-meter event in a world record 2:19.3. Yorzyk won the AAU national outdoor 200-meter butterfly from 1955 through 1958 and was the indoor 220-yard champion in 1958.

After graduating from Springfield, Massachusetts, College in 1956, Yorzyk went to medical school at the University of Toronto, where he won the Bickler Prize as the top student athlete in 1958 and 1959. He became an anesthesiologist, served as an officer in the U.S. Air Force medical corps, and was an associate physician to the 1964 Olympic team.

Yost, Hurry Up (Fielding H.)

FOOTBALL
b. April 30, 1871, Fairview, W.Va.
d. Aug. 20, 1946

Yost is known for "point-a-minute" teams at the University of Michigan, but he was a very successful coach even before arriving at Michigan in 1901.

He played tackle at Ohio Northern and the University of West Virginia from 1893 through 1896. There were virtually no eligibility rules in those days, and when Lafayette had an important game coming up against the University of Pennsylvania in 1896, Yost enrolled at the school, played that one game, and then returned to West Virginia.

In 1897 he coached Ohio Wesleyan to a 7–1–1 record, including a victory over Ohio State and a tie with Michigan. He went on to Nebraska in 1898, Kansas in 1899, and Stanford in 1900. His Kansas team won all ten of its games. When he became head coach at Michigan, he had a 31–7–2 record in four seasons at four schools.

He brought with him a halfback named Willie Heston, who had played at San Jose, California, Teachers. Heston enrolled in law school at Michigan and starred on Yost's first four teams, which won 62 games and tied 1 without a loss. The streak continued for 12 games in 1905, ending with a 2–0 loss to the University of Chicago. During those five seasons, Michigan outscored its opposition 2,821 to 56.

Yost wasn't known as a strategic innovator, but his players were exceptionally well trained and conditioned. He got his nickname, "Hurry Up," because that was his frequent exhortation. After a play, his teams were taught to line up and run another play as quickly as possible, often before the defense could get prepared.

After that remarkable beginning, Yost continued to produce winning teams, but his record wasn't quite as spectacular. He had his only losing season in 1919, a 3–4–0 record, but his 1923 team won all eight of its games. Yost temporarily retired from coaching in 1924, remaining as athletic director, but he returned for two more seasons, 1925 and 1926, producing 7–1–0 records both years. He then left coaching for good but remained as athletic director until his retirement in 1941.

Yost did more than coach winning football teams. As athletic director, he oversaw construction of the fieldhouse now named for him, the Indoor Sports Building, the Women's Athletic Building, an ice rink, and a golf course.

★ College Football Hall of Fame

Young, Buddy (Claude H.)

FOOTBALL
b. Jan. 5, 1926, Chicago, Ill.
d. Sept. 4, 1983

Only 5-foot-4 but a solid 175 pounds, Young starred in football and track at the University of Illinois. He won the NCAA 100- and 200-yard sprint championships in 1944. After spending a year in the merchant marine, he returned to school in 1946 and was named most valuable player in Illinois's 45–14 victory over UCLA in the 1947 Rose Bowl.

Young joined the New York Yankees of the All-America Football Conference in 1947. The AAFC folded in 1950, and the team, renamed the Yanks, moved into the NFL. The franchise moved from New York to Dallas in 1953 and became the Baltimore Colts in 1953.

He retired as a player after the 1955 season and scouted for Baltimore until 1964, when he became the league's director of player relations. He was killed in an auto accident.

Young led the AAFC with a 19.0-yard punt return average in 1949, and was the NFL leader in punt return yardage with 231 yards in 1951 and in kickoff return yardage with 643 in 1952. In his nine professional seasons, Young rushed for 2,727 yards in 597 carries, a 4.6 average, and 197 touchdowns, and caught 179 passes for 2,711 yards, a 15.1 average, and 21 touchdowns. He returned 67 punts for 698 yards, a 10.4 average, and 2 touchdowns, and ran back 125 kickoffs for 3,465 yards and 4 touchdowns. His career average of 27.7 yards per kickoff return is an NFL record.

Young, Cy (Denton T.)

BASEBALL
b. March 29, 1867, Gilmore, Ohio
d. Nov. 5, 1955

A simple way to express Young's greatness as a pitcher is this: he had 511 career victories, 95 more than Walter Johnson, who is in second place, and 138 more than Grover Cleveland Alexander and Christy Mathewson, who are tied for third. Another way to express it is that he averaged more than 23 victories a season for 22 seasons.

A 6-foot-2, 210-pound right-hander, Young had an explosive fastball, a pretty good curve, and excellent control. His nickname "Cy" was short for "Cyclone." One story, perhaps apocryphal, is that he once warmed up before a minor league game by throwing at a wooden fence and afterward someone remarked, "It looks like a cyclone hit that fence."

Young entered professional baseball in 1890, and the NL's Cleveland Spiders bought his contract for $250 late in the season. He pitched a three-hitter in his first start and had a 9–7 record. In 1891, he was 27–22, the first of 14 consecutive seasons and 16 overall in which he won 20 or more games; he won 30 or more five times.

The first of his great seasons was 1892, when he had a 36–12 record to lead the league with a .750 winning percentage, and he was also the leader with 9 shutouts and a 1.93 ERA. After going 34–16 and 26–21 over the next two seasons, Young led the NL in victories with a 35–10 record and in shutouts with 4 in 1895.

He was the league leader with 5 shutouts and 140 strikeouts in 1896, when he was 28–15. Young had records of 21–19 and 25–13 over the next two seasons. The Cleveland owner, Andrew Robison, also owned the St. Louis team, which had much better attendance, so he abandoned the Spiders in 1899, moving most of the best players to St. Louis.

In two seasons there, Young won 45 games while losing 35. Then he joined the Boston team in the new AL for $3,000 a season. At 34, he showed no signs of slowing down. Young led the AL in victories for its first three years with records of 33–10 in 1901, 32–11 in 1902, and 28–9 in 1903, when he was also the league leader with 7 shutouts. He won two games in Boston's victory over the Pittsburgh Pirates in the first World Series in 1903.

He threw 10 shutouts to lead the league in 1904, when he had a 26–16 record, but then began to falter. Young had two consecutive losing seasons, going 18–19 in 1905 and 13–21 in 1906. He bounced back with records of 21–15 in 1907 and 21–11 in 1908, when he pitched his third no-hitter.

Boston honored him near the end of the 1908 season with a "Cy Young Day," at which he was presented with nearly $7,500, contributed not only by fans but also by opposing players and even umpires. The team then sold him to Cleveland for $12,500.

After a 19–15 record with Cleveland in 1909, Young was only 7–10 the following year. He retired after a combined 7–9 record with Cleveland and the Boston NL team in 1911. Shortly after his death in 1955, the Cy Young Award was established to honor the outstanding pitcher of the year.

In 906 major league games, Young was 511–316, with 75 shutouts and a 2.63 ERA. He completed 749 of 815 starts and struck out 2,800 hitters while walking 1,219 in 7,354$\frac{2}{3}$ innings.

★ Baseball Hall of Fame

Young, George L.

TRACK AND FIELD
b. July 24, 1937, Roswell, N.Mex.

Young was the first runner ever to compete in four Olympics. He won a bronze medal in the 3,000-meter steeplechase in 1968, when he was also sixteenth in the marathon. He was eliminated in the preliminary heats of the steeplechase in 1960 and the 5,000-meter run in 1972, and he finished fifth in the 1968 steeplechase event.

Young won the AAU national 3,000-meter steeplechase in 1962, 1965, and 1968, the 3-mile run in 1966. He was also the national marathon champion in 1968.

★ National Track & Field Hall of Fame

Young, Sheila G. [Mrs. Ochowicz]

CYCLING, SPEED SKATING
b. Oct. 14, 1950, Detroit, Mich.

Young's father, who was a perennial Michigan state cycling champion, trained Sheila in both cycling and speed skating during her early years. She fell and broke an arm in her first important race in 1965, and speed skating became her primary sport for several years.

She burst into prominence in 1970, winning the U.S. and North American outdoor championships. The following year she again won the U.S. outdoor skating title and was national cycling sprint champion.

After narrowly missing a bronze medal in the 1972 Olympics, Young scored a rare double in 1973 by winning world sprint championships in both speed skating and cycling. Her cycling victory came despite a severe head gash, suffered during a fall, that had to be closed with clamps. Young won both world sprint championships again in 1976.

Also in 1976, Young became the first U.S. athlete to win three gold medals at a single Winter Olympics. She took a gold in the 500-meter, a bronze in the 1,000-meter, and a silver in the 1,500-meter. In March of that year, she lowered her world record for the 500-meter from 40.91 to 40.68 seconds.

Young married cyclist Jim Ochowicz in 1976 and retired to have her first child, Kate. She returned to competition in 1981, winning the national and world cycling sprint championships. After finishing second in the world championships in 1982, she retired permanently and gave birth to a second daughter, Eli. Young has served on the U.S. Cycling Federation board of directors and on the executive board of the U.S. Olympic Committee.

★ International Women's Sports Hall of Fame

Young, Steve (John Steven)

FOOTBALL
b. Oct. 11, 1961, Salt Lake City, Utah

Young entered Brigham Young University, founded and named for his great-great-great-grandfather, in 1980 and became the school's starting quarterback as a junior in 1982. A left-hander, the

6-foot-2, 205-pound Young led NCAA Division I quarterbacks with an average of 395.1 yards in total offense per game in 1983.

A consensus All-American, Young joined the Los Angeles Express of the new U.S. Football League in 1984. He completed 179 of 310 passes for 2,361 yards and 10 touchdowns. The franchise folded during the 1985 season and Young joined the NFL's Tampa Bay Buccaneers, immediately taking over as the team's starter.

Tampa Bay traded him in 1987 to the San Francisco 49ers, where he served as backup to Joe Montana until 1991, when Montana missed the entire season with an injury. Young also missed much of the season, playing in only 11 games. But he was named the NFL's player of the year in 1992 and 1994, and he emerged from Montana's long shadow by guiding San Francisco to victory in Super Bowl XXIX after the 1994 season.

In ten NFL seasons, Young has completed 1,534 of 2,416 passes for 19,775 yards and 139 touchdowns. Exceptionally fast and agile for a quarterback, he has rushed for 2,676 yards on 431 carries, scoring 20 touchdowns.

Young, Waddy (Walter R.)

FOOTBALL
b. Sept. 4, 1916, Ponca City, Okla. d. Jan. 9, 1945

The first player from the University of Oklahoma to be named an All-American, Young was a consensus choice at end in 1938. The 6-foot-3, 205-pound Young played for the NFL's Brooklyn Dodgers in 1939 and 1940 before entering military service. He was killed when his B-29 bomber crashed during the first bombing raid on Tokyo.

In his two professional seasons, Young caught 15 passes for 185 yards, a 12.3 average.
★ College Football Hall of Fame

Youngs, Ross M.

BASEBALL
b. April 10, 1897, Shiner, Tex. d. Oct. 22, 1927

Youngs attended West Texas Military Academy, where he starred in football and track. Baseball was his first love, however, and he joined a minor league team late in the 1914 season as a switch-hitting infielder. But, while he showed he could hit, he had problems in the field.

The New York Giants bought his contract for $2,000 near the end of the 1916 season and left him in the minor leagues so he could learn to play the outfield. He was with the Giants briefly in 1917 and joined the team as its starting right fielder the following year, when manager John McGraw told him to concentrate on batting left-handed.

The 5-foot-8, 162-pound Youngs hit .302 that season, and he led the league with 31 doubles in 1919, when he batted .311 and led NL outfielders with 23 assists. He had averages of .351 in 1920 and .327 in 1921, when the Giants won the first of four consecutive pennants.

Youngs batted .331 in 1922, .336 in 1923, and .356 in 1924, the year he was implicated in a bribery scandal. Jimmy O'Connell of the Giants was accused of offering a bribe to a Philadelphia player, and Youngs was allegedly one of three others who had heard the conversation. O'Connell was banned from organized baseball, but Young and his other teammates were cleared by Commissioner Kenesaw Mountain Landis.

In 1925 Youngs hit only .264, and McGraw was among those who thought he might be ill. After Youngs reported for spring training in 1926, he was diagnosed with Bright's disease, a kidney disorder. McGraw hired a male nurse to accompany him on the team's road trips.

Youngs played only 95 games in 1926, but he batted .306 and taught young Mel Ott, a converted catcher, how to play the outfield. He was forced to leave the team before the season ended and spent more than a year confined to bed in his native Texas before his death.

In his ten major league seasons, Youngs batted .322 with 1,491 hits, including 236 doubles, 93 triples, and 42 home runs. He stole 153 bases, scored 812 runs, and had 592 RBI.
★ Baseball Hall of Fame

Yount, Robin R.

BASEBALL
b. Sept. 16, 1955, Danville, Ill.

Signed right out of high school by the AL's Milwaukee Brewers in 1973, Yount became the team's starting shortstop the following season. At 18, he was the youngest regular player in the major leagues since 1906.

Highly respected for eight seasons as a slick fielder with a strong arm and a pretty good bat, Yount emerged as a major star in 1982, when he hit .339 and led the league with 210 hits, 46 doubles, and a .578 slugging percentage to win the AL's most valuable player award.

Yount batted .308 in 1983, when he had a league-leading ten triples and made the All-Star team for the third time. Because of a shoulder problem that prevented him from making the frequent long throws required of a shortstop, he was moved to center field in 1985.

Occasionally used as a designated hitter and at first base, Yount won his second most valuable player award in 1989, when he had a .318 average with 101 runs scored, 21 home runs, and 103 RBI. In 1992, he became the fifteenth player to collect more than 3,000 career hits.

Yount announced his retirement after the 1993 season. In his career, he had 3,142 hits, including 583 doubles, 126 triples, and 251 home runs. He stole 271 bases, scored 1,632 runs, and had 1,406 RBI.

★ ★ Z ★ ★

Zaharias, Babe [Mildred E. Didrikson]
GOLF, TRACK AND FIELD
b. June 26, 1914, Port Arthur,
Tex.
d. Sept. 27, 1956

Two sportswriters who saw all of the great athletes of the 1920s and 1930s saved their highest accolades for Babe Didrikson Zaharias.

Paul Gallico wrote, "She was probably the most talented athlete, male or female, ever developed in our country. In all my years at the sports desk I never encountered any man who could play as many different games as well as the Babe."

And Grantland Rice wrote of her, "She is beyond all belief until you see her perform. Then you finally understand that you are looking at the most flawless section of muscle harmony, of complete mental and physical coordination, that the world of sport has ever seen."

The daughter of Norwegian immigrants, Zaharias as a youngster worked out on gymnastic apparatus that her father built in the backyard and lifted weights improvised from a broom handle and flatirons. (Her family name was spelled "Didriksen," but she changed the spelling as an adult.)

As a young teenager playing softball with boys, she earned the nickname "Babe" because of her prodigious home runs. At 16, she began working as a typist for the Employers Casualty Insurance Company of Dallas, and she led the company basketball team to the 1931 AAU national championship. She was named female athlete of the year by the Associated Press.

Zaharias achieved national and international fame as a track athlete in 1932. Shortly after her eighteenth birthday, she won the shotput, baseball throw, long jump, 80-meter hurdles, and javelin at the AAU national championships and tied Jean Shiley for the high jump title. With 30 points, she won the team championship for Employers Casualty, finishing 8 points ahead of the University of Illinois, which had 22 athletes entered in various events. She set world records in the hurdles and javelin, and she and Shiley shared the world record in the high jump.

When she arrived in Los Angeles for the 1932 Olympics, she brashly announced, "I am out to beat everybody in sight, and that's just what I'm going to do." She won the javelin event with an Olympic record 133–4 on her first throw, even though the implement slipped out of her hand when she released it, and she ran a world record 11.7 in the 80-meter hurdles.

Zaharias and Shiley again tied in the high jump, at a world record 5–5¼ and both cleared 5–5¾ in a jumpoff, but Zaharias was disqualified because her head went over the bar before her body, which was illegal at the time, so she settled for the silver medal.

Before the year ended, she was suspended from AAU competition for allowing her photo to appear in an automobile advertisement. For several years, she barnstormed with her own basketball team, toured with the House of David baseball team, played exhibition billiards matches, and golfed as an amateur, winning the 1935 Texas Women's Championship.

She lost her amateur status as a golfer and went on an exhibition tour with Gene Sarazen, in part to publicize Babe Didrikson golf clubs. In 1938, she married professional wrestler George Zaharias.

Reinstated as an amateur in 1943, Zaharias won 40 tournaments in less than four years. From 1946 into 1947, she won 17 in a row, including the 1946 U.S. Amateur and the 1947 British Amateur. She then became a founding member of the Ladies' Professional Golf Association.

Zaharias and Patty Berg were the first stars of the LPGA tour. Zaharias won the U.S. Women's Open in 1948 and 1950. She had a colostomy because of cancer in 1953 but came back to win the Open again in 1954, when she was also the Vare Trophy winner with the lowest stroke per round average among tour players.

After the Women's Open victory, she said, "This should show people not to be afraid of cancer. I'll go on golfing for years." However, the cancer recurred the following year and took her life in 1956.

The Associated Press woman athlete of the year six times in three different decades, Zaharias in 1950 was voted the outstanding female athlete of the first half-century by AP sportswriters.

★ International Women's Sports Hall of Fame; LPGA Hall of Fame; National Track and Field Hall of Fame; Olympic Hall of Fame; World Golf Hall of Fame

Zahn, Wayne
BOWLING
b. Jan. 20, 1941, Milwaukee, Wis.

A phenomenal young bowler, Zahn finished ninth in the BPAA All-Star tournament when he was 19 and was named bowler of the year in 1966, when he was only 25. He led the PBA in average pinfall that year with 208.63 and again in 1967 with 212.14, a record at the time.

Zahn won the PBA National and the Firestone Tournament of Champions in 1966, won the National for a second time in 1968, and won the National Pro-Am in 1970. He essentially retired from the tour after the 1975–76 season to operate a bowling center in Arizona. He was the youngest bowler ever elected to the ABC Hall of Fame.

★ ABC Hall of Fame; PBA Hall of Fame

Zale, Tony [Anthony F. Zaleski]
BOXING
b. May 29, 1913, Gary, Ind.

Nicknamed the "Man of Steel" partly for his physique but also because he worked in steel mills as a youth, Zale won 87 of 95 amateur fights, 50 of them by knockout, before becoming a professional in 1934.

Zale had a somewhat inconsistent record until 1939, when he won seven consecutive fights, six by knockout. After four more victories in 1940, Zale met Al Hostak for the National Boxing Association middleweight championship on July 19. He won the title with a knockout in the 13th round.

On November 28, 1941, Zale won the vacant world middleweight championship by decisioning Georgie Abrams in 15 rounds. He served in the Navy from 1943 until 1945, then resumed fighting with six straight knockouts in 1946.

His famous series of three fights with Rocky Graziano began with a title defense on September 27. Both fighters survived early knockdowns. In the 6th round, Zale was on the verge of defeat when he suddenly threw a devastating body punch and then knocked Graziano out with a left hook.

In a rematch on July 16, 1947, the outcome was reversed. Zale pummeled Graziano for four rounds, but Graziano took over in the 5th and the referee stopped the bout in the 6th, giving Graziano the title. They met for the third time on June 10, 1948. This time, Zale took command throughout and knocked

Graziano out in the 3rd round to reclaim the title.

He had just one more fight, losing his championship to Marcel Cerdan of France on September 21, 1948, when Cerdan scored a 12th-round knockout. Zale won 70 bouts, 46 by knockout; lost 18, 4 by knockout; and fought 2 draws.
★ International Boxing Hall of Fame

Zayak, Elaine

FIGURE SKATING
b. April 12, 1965, Paramus, N.J.

Perhaps the most athletic female figure skater ever, Zayak was too exuberant a skater for the authorities that rule the sport. She won the U.S. national championship and finished second in the world championships in 1981, before her sixteenth birthday.

Although she finished third in the national competition in 1982, Zayak won the world title with an exciting exhibition of free skating that included seven triple jumps. The international governing body then adopted the "Zayak rule," limiting female competitors to three triple jumps in a performance.

In 1983 she finished second in the national championships but couldn't complete her performance in the world championships because of a stress fracture in her right ankle. After finishing third in the national and world championships and eleventh in the Olympics in 1984, Zayak left amateur skating to join the Ice Capades.

Zimmerman, Heinie (Henry)

BASEBALL
b. Feb. 9, 1887, New York, N.Y.
d. March 14, 1969

Zimmerman joined the NL's Chicago Cubs near the end of the 1907 season and was a part-time player until 1911, when he played three infield positions and batted .307. Playing mostly at third base in 1912, Zimmerman had his finest season with a .372 average, 207 hits, 41 doubles, 14 home runs, and a .571 slugging percentage.

He never came close to those numbers again. During the 1916 season, the Cubs traded him to the New York Gi-ants. He led the league in RBI with 83 that season and 102 in 1917. Late in the 1919 season, rumors circulated that Zimmerman and first baseman Hal Chase were involved in fixing games. They were both immediately removed from the lineup by manager John McGraw, and neither of them ever played major league baseball again.

No criminal charges were brought, but at a hearing into the "Black Sox Scandal" in 1920, there was testimony that Chase and Zimmerman had offered a teammate $500 to throw a 1919 game against the St. Louis Cardinals.

Zimmerman, Zimmy (August A.)

CYCLING
b. 1869, Camden, N.J.
d. Oct. 20, 1936

Zimmerman was a high jumper in high school and he took up cycling on a high-wheeled bike when he was 17. In 1891, he began racing on a modern "safety" bicycle and won the League of American Wheelmen $\frac{1}{2}$-mile race, setting a world record of 29.5 seconds over the last $\frac{1}{4}$ mile.

At the Diamond Jubilee in Springfield, Massachusetts, in 1892, Zimmerman won the 1-mile race. The prize was a buckboard with two horses and harness, valued at $1,000. He was then invited to race in the British national championships in July and he won all four races, at distances of 1, 5, 25, and 50 miles.

When "Zimmy" returned home, he was welcomed as a hero and in demand as a racer. Although he raced as an amateur, Zimmerman was allowed to accept valuable prizes under the loose standards of the era. According to the *New York Times*, among his winnings in 1892 were "29 bicycles, several horses and carriages, half a dozen pianos, a house and a lot, household furniture of all descriptions, and enough silver plates, medals, and jewelry to stock a jewelry store."

Zimmerman returned to England in 1893 but wasn't allowed to race because he was considered a professional there, especially since he had been featured in advertisements for Raleigh bicycles. However, he did race in Ireland and France before sailing back to the U.S. for the first world championship meet at the Columbian Exposition in Chicago. He easily won both races, at 1 and 10 miles.

By 1894, professional bike racing was a major sport. Zimmerman signed a contract with Raleigh to ride the company's bikes and went on a 25-race European tour. He had a bad crossing and started slowly, but he won the biggest race of all, a 1,000-meter event in Paris. Later he won a handicap race in which he gave 25 of the world's best racers a head start and passed them all. A crowd of 20,000 French spectators gave him a standing ovation when he crossed the finish line.

Zimmerman set out for Australia late in 1894. By then, he was worn out by his hectic schedule of traveling and racing, and he wasn't in top form, although he won some races. He left Australia in 1895 and went back to Europe. It was obvious that he was already past his prime at 26, but he was still wildly popular.

"Le grand Zim," as French fans called him, was invited back to Europe for exhibitions during the next ten years. He retired in 1905 to run a hotel he'd purchased in New Jersey.

Zimmerman was probably the best-known athlete of the 1890s and he was one of the first to capitalize on his fame with commercial promotions. Zimmy shoes, clothing, and bicycle toe clips were wildly popular, Toulouse-Lautrec did a lithograph of him with his bicycle, and one newspaper proclaimed, "Mr. A. A. Zimmerman stands alone as the greatest racer the world has produced . . . the champion of the world in competitive contests where brain, brawn, and muscle necessarily combine for supremacy."

Zivic, Fritzie

BOXING
b. May 8, 1913, Pittsburgh, Pa.

Zivic had a long career before he ever got a title shot. He began boxing professionally in 1931. A quick, clever fighter, the 5-foot-9 Zivic lacked a powerful punch but often knocked out opponents through a sheer accumulation of blows.

On October 4, 1940, Zivic won a surprising 15-round decision over Henry Armstrong to win the world welterweight championship. In a rematch on January 17, 1941, he knocked Armstrong out in the 12th round. It was only the second time Armstrong had been knocked out in well over 100 fights.

Freddie "Red" Cochrane took the title with a 15-round decision over Zivic on July 29, 1941. Zivic remained a very active fighter during the next five years, but never got another championship fight. He had just five bouts from 1947 until he announced his retirement early in 1949.

Zivic won 155 of his 230 professional fights, 80 by knockout. He lost 65, 4 by knockout, and also fought 10 draws.
★ International Boxing Hall of Fame

Zmeskal, Kim

GYMNASTICS
b. Feb. 6, 1976, Houston, Tex.

The first U.S. gymnast to win the all-around in the world championships, Zmeskal began working with Bela Karolyi, the former Rumanian national coach, when she was six years old. She entered her first major competition, the American Classic, in 1988.

Zmeskal emerged as one of the country's top women gymnasts in 1989, when she won the all-around, balance beam, and floor exercise in the American Classic. She also scored her first perfect 10.0 in the floor exercise while winning the all-around in the Arthur Gander Memorial meet in Switzerland that year.

In 1990, Zmeskal won the first of three consecutive U.S. all-around championships, and she had two perfect scores, in the vault and floor exercise, in winning the all-around championship at the U.S. Challenge meet.

In addition to the all-around title, Zmeskal tied for first in the floor exercise and finished second in the balance beam in the 1991 national championships. She won the all-around and floor exercise, tied for first in the balance beam, and finished second in the vault and uneven bars in 1992.

The world all-around champion in 1991, Zmeskal was the only athlete to win two gold medals, in the balance beam and floor exercise, at the 1992 world championships. Considered a strong contender for an all-around medal at the 1992 Olympics, Zmeskal had a problem on the first apparatus, the balance beam, and never recovered, finishing tenth. She missed most of the 1993 season with an injury.

The 4-foot-7, 80-pound high school student is known for a determination and competitive spirit that belie her pixielike appearance. She was named sportswoman of the year by the U.S. Olympic Committee in 1991 and has twice been a finalist for the Sullivan Award.

Zuppke, Bob (Robert C.)

FOOTBALL
b. July 12, 1879, Berlin, Germany
d. Dec. 22, 1957

In his 29 seasons as head coach at the University of Illinois, Zuppke often had inferior squads compared to the best teams in the Western Conference (now Big Ten), but he won more games than he should have because of his inventive mind.

Small, colorful, and witty, Zuppke was the unlikeliest of football coaches. His family moved from Germany to the United States when he was a year old, settling in Milwaukee, Wisconsin. He dropped out of high school when he was 13, worked as a sign painter's apprentice, went back to school, and finally graduated from the University of Wisconsin when he was 25. He was a little-used reserve quarterback.

Zuppke spent eight years coaching high school football before going to Illinois in 1913. Among his innovations were the huddle, introduced in 1919; the flea flicker, on which a receiver laterals to a teammate immediately after catching the ball; the screen pass; the use of guards pulling back to protect the passer; and the use of guards dropping back for pass defense.

In his first eight seasons, Zuppke won five Western Conference titles and tied for two others. From 1923 through 1925, he coached the legendary Red Grange, who led Illinois to an 8–0–0 season in 1923 and a 19–4–1 record over three seasons. Zuppke also had undefeated teams in 1914, 1915, and 1927.

Despite the great teams he produced, Zuppke was perhaps more noted for his major upsets. Two of them came against Ohio State, a 9–7 win in 1919 on a last-minute field goal and a 7–0 victory in 1921, Ohio State's only loss of the season. In 1916, Illinois was depleted by injuries and facing an undefeated Minnesota team at Minneapolis. Using a newly devised spread formation, Illinois scored two early touchdowns and held on to win, 14–9. Minnesota outscored its other six opponents 339 to 14 that season.

During the 1930s, material became even thinner at Illinois, and Zuppke suffered through several poor seasons. He retired after the 1941 season with a record of 131 wins, 81 losses, and 12 ties. His 29 seasons at one school is second only to A. A. Stagg's record of 41 seasons at the University of Chicago.

Zuppke's wit can be illustrated by only a couple of his many aphorisms: "Football is not a contact sport. Dancing is a contact sport. Football is a collision sport"; and "My definition of an All-American is a player who has weak opposition and a poet in the press box."

★ College Football Hall of Fame

BIBLIOGRAPHY
INDEX BY SPORT

———————

Bibliography

For a work such as this, a writer obviously has to call on a wide variety of resources, including newspaper indexes and microfilm, periodicals such as *The Sporting News* and *Sports Illustrated*, various volumes of *Current Biography*, the InfoTrak electronic databases, and book-length biographies of some of the subjects. Only the most frequently consulted sources are listed here.

Allis, Peter. *The Who's Who of Golf.* Englewood Cliffs, N.J.: Prentice-Hall, 1983.

American Athletics Annual 1993. Indianapolis: The Athletics Congress of the United States, 1993.

Appel, Martin, and Burt Goldblatt. *Baseball's Best: The Hall of Fame Gallery.* New York: McGraw-Hill, 1977.

Baker, L. H. *Football: Facts and Figures.* New York: Farrar and Rinehart, 1945.

Barron, Bill, *et al. The Official NFL Encyclopedia of Football.* New York: National Football League Properties, 1982.

Bateman, Hal. *United States Track and Field Olympians 1896–1980.* Indianapolis: The Athletics Congress of the United States, 1984.

Biracree, Tom, and Wendy Insinger. *The Complete Book of Thoroughbred Horse Racing.* Garden City, N.Y.: Doubleday, 1982.

Brown, Gene. *The Complete Book of Basketball.* New York: Arno Press, 1980.

Burrill, Bob. *Who's Who in Boxing.* New Rochelle, N.Y.: Arlington House, 1973.

CART 1993 Media Guide. Bloomfield

Hills, Mich.: Championship Auto Racing Teams, Inc., 1993.

Claassen, Harold, and Steve Boda, eds. *Ronald Encyclopedia of Football.* New York: Ronald Press, 1960.

Cohane, Tim. *Great College Football Coaches of the Twenties and Thirties.* New Rochelle, N.Y.: Arlington House, 1973.

Collins, Bud, and Zander Hollander. *Bud Collins' Modern Encyclopedia of Tennis.* Garden City, N.Y.: Doubleday, 1980.

Cummings, Parke. *American Tennis: Story of a Game.* Boston: Little, Brown, 1957.

Cutter, Robert, and Bob Fendell. *The Encyclopedia of Auto Racing Greats.* Englewood Cliffs, N.J.: Prentice-Hall, 1973.

Daley, Arthur, and John Kieran. *The Story of the Olympic Games.* New York: Lippincott, 1969.

Danzig, Allison. *The History of American Football: Its Great Teams, Players, and Coaches.* Englewood Cliffs, N.J.: Prentice-Hall, 1956.

Diamond, Dan. *NHL Hockey: The official Book of the Game.* New York: Mallard Press, 1990.

Diamond, Dan. *The Official National Hockey League 75th Anniversary*

Commemorative Book. Toronto: McClelland & Stewart, 1991.

Encyclopedia of Sailing. New York: Harper and Row, 1973.

Fischler, Shirley, and Stan Fischler, *Hockey Encyclopedia: The Complete Record of Professional Ice Hockey.* New York: Crowell, 1983.

Fleischer, Nat, and Sam Andre. *A Pictorial History of Boxing.* Secaucus, N.J.: Citadel Press, 1975.

Goldman, Herbert G., ed. *The Ring 1985 Record Book and Boxing Encyclopedia.* New York: The Ring Publishing Corp., 1985.

Grimsley, Will. *Golf: Its History, People and Events.* Englewood Cliffs, N.J.: Prentice-Hall, 1966.

Grimsley, Will. *Tennis: Its History, People, and Events.* Englewood Cliffs, N.J.: Prentice-Hall, 1971.

Hanley, Reid M. *Who's Who in Track and Field.* New Rochelle, N.Y.: Arlington House, 1971.

Hickok, Ralph. *The New Encyclopedia of Sports.* New York: McGraw-Hill, 1977.

Hickok, Ralph. *Who Was Who in American Sports.* New York: Hawthorn Books, 1971.

Hollander, Phyllis. *100 Greatest Women in Sports.* New York: Grosset and Dunlap, 1976.

Hollander, Zander, and Alex Sachare, eds. *The Official NBA Basketball Encyclopedia.* New York: Villard Books, 1989.

Hollander, Zander. *Great American Athletes of the Twentieth Century.* New York: Random House, 1966.

Hollander, Zander. *The American Encyclopedia of Soccer.* New York: Everett House, 1980.

Isascs, Neil D. *All the Moves: A History of College Basketball.* New York: Harper and Row, 1984.

Jares, Joe. *Basketball: The American Game.* Chicago: Follett Publishing Company, 1971.

Kariher, Harry C. *Who's Who in Hockey.* New Rochelle, N.Y.: Arlington House, 1973.

King, Billie Jean, with Cynthia Starr.

We HAVE Come a Long Way. New York: McGraw-Hill, 1988.

The Lincoln Library of Sports Champions (16 volumes). Columbus, Ohio: Frontier Press, 1993.

Mallon, Bill, and Ian Buchanan. *Quest for Gold: The Encyclopedia of American Olympians.* New York: Leisure Press, 1984.

Markel, Robert. *For the Record: Women in Sport.* New York: World Almanac Publications, 1985.

McCallum, John D. *The Encyclopedia of World Boxing Champions Since 1882.* Radnor, Pa.: Chilton Book Co., 1975.

Mendell, Ronald L., and Timothy B. Phares. *Who's Who in Football.* New Rochelle, N.Y.: Arlington House, 1974.

Mendell, Ronald, *Who's Who in Basketball.* New Rochelle, N.Y.: Arlington House, 1973.

Menke, Frank. *The Encyclopedia of Sports.* New York: A. S. Barnes, 1979.

Meserole, Mike, ed. *The 1994 Information Please Sports Almanac.* Boston: Houghton Mifflin, 1993.

Mokray, William G., ed. *The Ronald Encyclopedia of Basketball.* New York: Ronald Press, 1963.

Neft, David S., Richard M. Cohen, and Jordan A. Deutsch. *The Sports Encyclopedia: Pro Football, the Early Years, 1895–1959.* Ridgefield, Conn.: Sports Products, Inc., 1978

Neft, David S., Richard M. Cohen, and Jordan A. Deutsch. *The Sports Encyclopedia: Pro Football, the Modern Era, 1960 to Present.* New York: Simon and Schuster, 1989.

Nelson, Cordner. *Track and Field: The Great Ones.* London: Pelham Books, 1970.

1992–93 National Collegiate Championships. Overland Park, Kans.: National Collegiate Athletic Association, 1993.

1993 Directory and Record Book. Lake Success, N.Y.: Thoroughbred Racing Associations, Inc.

1993 LPGA Player Guide. Daytona

Beach, Fla.: Ladies' Professional Golfers Association, 1993.

Official 1993 NCAA Basketball. Overland Park, Kans.: National Collegiate Athletic Association, 1993.

Official 1993 NCAA Football. Overland Park, Kans.: National Collegiate Athletic Association, 1993.

Official 1993 PGA Tour Book. Ponta Vedra, Fla.: Professional Golfers' Association, 1993.

Official NFL Record and Fact Book. New York: National Football League Properties, 1993.

150 Years of Baseball. Lincolnwood, Ill.: Beekman House, 1989

Padwe, Sandy. Basketball's Hall of Fame. Englewood Cliffs, N.J.: Prentice-Hall, 1970.

Peterson, Robert P. *Only the Ball Was White.* Englewood Cliffs, N.J.: Prentice-Hall, 1970.

Peterson, Robert W. *Cages to Jump Shots: Pro Basketball's Early Years.* New York: Oxford University Press, 1990.

Pines, Philip. *The Complete Book of Harness Racing.* New York: Grosset and Dunlap, 1982.

Porter, David L., ed. *Biographical Dictionary of American Sports: Football.* Westport, Conn.: Greenwood Press, 1987.

Porter, David L., ed. *Biographical Dictionary of American Sports: Outdoor Sports.* Westport, Conn.: Greenwood Press, 1988.

Porter, David L., ed. *Biographical Dictionary of American Sports: Basketball and Other Indoor Sports.* Westport, Conn.: Greenwood Press, 1989.

Porter, David L., ed. *Biographical Dictionary of American Sports: 1989–1992 Supplement for Baseball, Football, Basketball, and Other Sports.* Westport, Conn.: Greenwood Press, 1992.

Robertson, William H. P. *The History of Thoroughbred Racing in America.* Englewood Cliffs, N.J.: Prentice-Hall, 1964.

Ross, John M., ed. *Golf Magazine's Encyclopedia of Golf.* New York: Harper and Row, 1979.

Scharff, Robert, ed. *Ski Magazine's Encyclopedia of Skiing.* New York: Harper and Row, 1970.

Smith, Don R. *Pro Football Hall of Fame All-Time Greats.* New York: Gallery Books, 1988.

Smith, Robert M. *Pro Football: The History of the Game and the Great Players.* Garden City, N.Y.: Doubleday, 1963.

The Sporting News Complete Hockey Book. St. Louis, MO: The Sporting News Publishing Co., 1993.

The Sporting News NBA Register. St. Louis, MO: The Sporting News Publishing Co., 1993.

The Sporting News Official Baseball Register. St. Louis, MO: The Sporting News Publishing Co., 1994.

The Sporting News Pro Football Register. St. Louis: The Sporting News Publishing Co., 1993.

The Sports Illustrated 1994 Sports Almanac. New York: Little Brown and Company, 1993.

Thorn, John, and Pete Palmer, eds. *Total Baseball: The Ultimate Encyclopedia of Baseball.* New York: HarperCollins, 1993.

Treat, Roger, ed. *The Encyclopedia of Football,* revised by Pete Palmer. Garden City, N.Y.: Doubleday, 1979.

Wallechinsky, David. *The Complete Book of the Olympics.* New York: Viking, 1988.

Watman, Mel. *Encyclopedia of Track and Field Athletics.* New York: St. Martin's Press, 1981.

Weyand, Alexander M. *Football Immortals.* New York: Macmillan, 1962.

Who's Who in American Sports. Washington, D.C.: American Biographical Society, 1928.

Wind, Herbert Warren. *Encyclopedia of Golf.* New York: Viking, 1975.

Woolum, Janet. *Outstanding Women Athletes: Who They Are and How They Influenced Sports in America.* Phoenix: Oryx Press, 1992.

Index by Sport

Alston, Walter E. (Smokey), 15
Anderson, Sparky (George L.), 21
Anson, Cap (Adrian C.), 22
Aparicio, Luis E., Jr., 23
Appling, Luke (Lucius B. Jr.), 24
Ashburn, Richie (Don Richie), 29
Averill, Earl (Howard Earl), 34
Baker, Frank (John Franklin), 38
Bancroft, David E., 40
Banks, Ernie (Ernest), 41
Barrow, Edward G., 44
Bauer, Hank (Henry A.), 47
Baylor, Don E., 50
Beckley, Jacob P., 53
Bedrosian, Stephen W., 55
Bell, Cool Papa (James T.), 57
Bell, George A. M., 57
Bench, Johnny L., 59
Bender, Chief (Charles A.), 60
Berra, Yogi (Lawrence P.), 65
Bezdek, Hugo F., 67
Blue, Vida R., 78
Blyleven, Bert (Rik Aalbert), 78
Boddicker, Mike (Michael J.), 79
Boggs, Wade A., 79
Bonds, Barry L., 81
Bonds, Bobby L., 81
Bottomley, Jim (James L.), 84
Boudreau, Louis, Jr., 85
Boyer, Kenton L., 88
Bresnahan, Roger P., 92
Brett, George H., 92
Brock, Louis C., 94
Brouthers, Dan (Dennis J.), 97
Brown, Three-Finger (Mordecai P. C.), 101
Bruton, Billy (William H.), 104
Burkett, Jesse C., 109
Burns, George H., 109
Burroughs, Jeffrey A., 110
Butler, Brett M., 111
Camilli, Dolph (Adolph L.), 115
Campanella, Roy, 116
Canseco, Jose, Jr., 119
Carew, Rodney C., 121
Carey, Max [Maximilian Carnarius], 122
Carlton, Steven N., 123
Carrigan, Bill (William J.), 126
Carter, Joe (Joseph C.), 127
Cartwright, Alexander J., 127
Case, George W., 128
Cavaretta, Philip J., 131
Cepeda, Orlando M., 132

Chance, Dean (Wilmer Dean), 135
Chance, Frank L., 135
Chandler, Spud (Spurgeon F.), 136
Chapman, Ben (William Benjamin), 137
Charleston, Oscar McC., 138
Chesbro, Jack (John D.), 139
Clark, Will (William N.), 143
Clarke, Fred C., 144
Clarkson, John G., 145
Clemens, Roger (William Roger), 146
Clemente, Roberto W., 146
Cobb, Tyrus R., 147
Cochrane, Mickey (Gordon S.), 149
Coleman, Vincent M., 151
Collins, Eddie (Edward T.), 151
Collins, Jimmy (James J.), 152
Combs, Earle B., 153
Comiskey, Charles A., 153
Cone, David B., 155
Connor, Roger, 158
Cooper, Morton C., 161
Coveleski, Stanley A. [Stanislaus Kowalewski], 166
Cravath, Gavvy (Clifford C.), 169
Crawford, Samuel E., 169
Cronin, Joseph E., 171
Cuellar, Mike (Miguel A.), 173
Cummings, Candy (William A.), 174
Cuyler, Kiki (Hazen S.), 177
Dandridge, Raymond (Hooks), 180
Daubert, Jake (Jacob E.), 182
Davis, Harry H., 186
Davis, Mark W., 187
Davis, Tommy (Herman Thomas), 187
Dawson, Andre N. (Hawk), 188
Dean, Dizzy (Jay H.), 190
Dedeaux, Rod (Raoul M.), 192
Delahanty, Edward J., 194
Denny, John A., 197
Dickey, Bill (William M.), 202
Dihigo, Martin, 203
DiMaggio, Joseph P. [Giuseppe Paolo DiMaggio], 204
Dinneen, Bill (William H.), 205
Doby, Larry (Lawrence E.), 207
Doerr, Bobby (Robert P.), 208
Doyle, Larry (Lawrence J.), 212
Drabek, Douglas D., 212
Drysdale, Donald S., 215
Duffy, Hugh, 216
Durocher, Leo E., 218
Dykstra, Lenny (Leonard K.), 220
Eckersley, Dennis L., 223
Elliott, Bob (Robert I.), 226

Billiards

Bobsledding

Bowling

Boxing

Canoeing

Court Tennis

Cycling

Diving

Golf